The Regulation of Toxic Substances and Hazardous Wastes

John S. Applegate

Professor of Law
Indiana University School of Law – Bloomington

Jan G. Laitos

John A. Carver, Jr., Professor of Law
Director, Natural Resources and Environmental Law Program
University of Denver College of Law

Celia Campbell-Mohn

Professor of Law
Vermont Law School

New York, New York
Foundation Press
2000

COPYRIGHT © 2000 By FOUNDATION PRESS

        11 Penn Plaza, Tenth Floor
        New York, NY 10001
        Phone Toll Free 1–877–888–1330
        Fax (212) 760–8705
        fdpress.com

ISBN 1–56662–758–3

TEXT IS PRINTED ON 10% POST
CONSUMER RECYCLED PAPER

To my mother and in memory of my father
J.S.A.

This is for Mary and Guido
J.G.L.

To my husband, daughter, and parents
C.C.-M.

*

PREFACE

Not long ago, environmental law was not even a law school course. In the early 1970s, pioneering casebooks established the practice of treating the subject in a single course that covered in greater or lesser detail the many facets of the law of environmental protection – from wilderness preservation and forest conservation, to air and water pollution, to disposal of solid waste. As it became increasingly obvious in the 1980s that no one can do justice to the richness and variety of environmental law in a single course, many law schools developed specialized courses in addition to the basic survey. These focused on air or water pollution, resource management, wilderness and species protection, toxic torts, hazardous wastes, and recently, international environmental law.

A single casebook, of course, can no more do justice to these many areas of environmental law than a single course can. Therefore, this casebook seeks to do justice to just one area, toxic substances and hazardous wastes. To accomplish this goal, we have tried to be comprehensive, in that all significant aspects of the subject are fully covered. Instructors will be able to use all or part of it, depending on interest and available time. It is intended to be useful as a first course in environmental law or for advanced, more specialized study. Students should be able to use the book as a learning tool and as a jumping off point for further investigation. While there is much diversity in this area of environmental law, it is bound together by the common problem of managing a certain set of chemical dangers. In writing this book, we have sought to emphasize, therefore, both the common problems and the multiplicity of regulatory responses to toxics.

The casebook takes a very direct approach to the material. It begins with a review of the foundations – scientific, political, economic, and legal – on which the law of toxic substances and hazardous wastes has been built. It then proceeds statute by statute, stressing the major "life cycle" statutes that students will most often see in practice, but also covering a variety of other statutes that present different approaches to toxics regulation. While we recognize the interactions and overlap among the several statutes, we are also firmly committed to the view that each statute has its own internal structure and integrity which are essential to a solid understanding of the subject. There are many cross-cutting issues, of course, but we have chosen not to organize the presentation around them; rather, we encourage the reader to compare and contrast the different regulatory approaches to analogous issues. Finally, the casebook explores major new directions in toxics regulation – primarily alternatives to traditional "end-of-pipe" standard setting – which, we believe, will become more important with each passing year.

We have sought to produce a casebook that is useful for a number of different kinds of course. We have also tried to move beyond the traditional format based on cases and notes, so that we could accommodate the extreme variety of materials that environmental lawyers must be able to understand and use. The book reflects this approach in a number of ways. First, like most casebooks, the text contains both primary substantive materials and materials that comment or expand on the primary materials. The primary materials consist of excerpts of law review articles, scientific and medical studies, magazine and newspaper articles, books, and the like; cases; and text written by the authors. As described below, it seemed to us that some subjects were better handled by direct exposition than by derivation from other sources. Likewise, the form of the commentary on the primary materials includes traditional notes and questions, long and short problems, boxed summary materials, and case studies. It is our hope that this presentation will both improve comprehension of often complex material and provide the basis for lively classroom discussion. The questions we ask are not intended to be rhetorical; an effective class (and effective class preparation) can be based on them.

Second, recognizing that RCRA and CERCLA are likely to be the heart of many courses using this book, we have striven for accessibility in those and related chapters. They present the legal and regulatory structures tersely, and largely in our own words. The student is invited to engage with the material through the examples and problems provided, instead of the usual case analysis. In addition, the RCRA and CERCLA chapters are followed by chapters (on siting hazardous waste facilities and on federal facilities, respectively) which act primarily as extended case studies of RCRA and CERCLA, though they treat subjects which are important in their own right.

Third, since the regulation of toxics in the health and pollution control statutes, FIFRA, and TSCA is more likely to be fully covered only in an advanced course, these chapters provide more commentary and perspective. They invite greater attention to general issues of regulatory policy – regulatory strategies, if you will – than a basic presentation of the material would require. In addition, the presentation style in these chapters is more traditional, consisting primarily of excerpted material. Here and throughout, the notes identify key issues in the main readings, place them in the context of other materials in the book, and present discussable problems related to them.

Fourth, we have structured the chapters in such a way that some parts can be passed over without losing the coherence of the whole. In the Pollution Control chapter, for instance, the instructor who wishes to spend much less time on it could eliminate the case studies and secondary sources to achieve wide coverage, or eliminate all but the Clean Water Act and Clean Air Act to achieve depth, or skip just the Atomic Energy Act and the Safe Drinking Water Act to present a mix of regulatory approaches. The chapters that are most likely to be used for both introductory and advanced courses, such as the toxicology and economics chapters, can be split: the first halves provide detailed conceptual background material, while the second halves focus on the analytical techniques that are of immediate relevance to existing practice and proposed legislation. Alternatively, an instructor can move pretty quickly through the first halves as a text, while the second halves rely more on primary sources.

To make effective use of the text, instructors and students will need a current book of environmental statutes, such as West's *Selected Environmental Law Statutes*. The text often requires students to read the statute itself, and to answer questions about it, unaided by detailed summaries or explanations. We believe that this is an essential skill for environmental lawyers. For the same reason, we usually refer to statutes by their statutory section number rather than the U.S. Code section number. Most courts follow this convention, and it better expresses the relationship among parts of a statute. Since West's statutory compilation conveniently references both sets of numbers, students should experience little difficulty with this arrangement, once it has been brought to their attention.

*

Acknowledgments

We owe a large debt of gratitude to many people and institutions who have helped us in many ways, and without whom this book could not have been written. They are: Fred Aman, Jodi Arndt, Albert Bright, Hermine Cohen, David Erlewine, Steve Errick. Alan Garber, Veronica Hites, Pam Homan, Connie Miller, Matthew Mortier, Amanda Prebble, Cathy Roberts-Suskin, Stephen P. Samuels, Alex Sponseller, Joe Tomain, Christopher Thompson, and Carson Tucker.

We also wish to acknowledge with gratitude the financial support of the University of Cincinnati College of Law, the Indiana University School of Law - Bloomington, the Rocky Mountain Mineral Law Foundation, the John A. Carver, Jr., Chair within the University of Denver College of Law (held by Jan Laitos), and Vermont Law School.

Last but not least, each of us would like to thank our families – Amy, Jesse, Jamey, and Gillian; Mary and Guido; Fred and Emma – for their patience and support along the sometimes arduous trail toward completion of this project. They are the true foundation on which this book was built.

*

Editing Conventions

In editing the excerpts that are reprinted in this book, we have followed several general editing practices. We have tried to retain the substance and style of the original works, while presenting only that which is needed to convey the relevant point. To the extent that our editing has distorted or weakened the original work, we apologize in advance the affected authors.

Specifically, we have eliminated without indication most footnotes – both substantive and citation – and most textual citation material (except for direct quotations). In some cases, we have reformatted citations to conform to the book's style or for brevity. Our additions to quoted materials are indicated by brackets in text and by "- EDS." in footnotes. Footnotes in quoted excerpts are renumbered to conform to the numbering in the chapter of this text. The form of headings in quoted excerpts has been standardized in some cases, and occasionally deleted where the organization was otherwise clear. Our deletions are indicated by starred ellipses (* * *); deletions in the original are indicated with periods (. . .).

ACKNOWLEDGMENTS

The authors gratefully acknowledge permission to reprint all or portions of the following copyrighted works:

Chapter 1
National Wildlife Federation
> Mark Van Putten, President, National Wildlife Federation, Letter to members dated Feb. 2, 1999.

Sierra Club Books
> From Hazardous Waste in America by Dr. Samuel S. Epstein, Lester O. Brown & Carl Pope, Copyright © 1982, 1983 by Epstein, Brown, and Pope. Reprinted with permission of Sierra Club Books.

University of Pittsburgh Press
> "Three Decades of Environmental Politics: The Historical context" is from EXPLORATIONS IN ENVIRONMENTAL HISTORY: ESSAYS BY SAMUEL P. HAYS, © 1998 by University of Pittsburgh Press. Reprinted by permission of the University of Pittsburgh Press.

West Publishing Company
> Campbell-Mohn, Breen, Futrell et al. eds., Sustainable Environmental Law (West. 1993) ch. 3 and conclusion.

Amherst Scientific Publishers
> The Precautionary Preference: An American Perspective on the Precautionary Principle by John S. Applegate Human and Environmental Risk Assessment, vol. 6, no. 3, published June 2000. © copyright Amherst Scientific Publishers.

Chapter 2
Cambridge University Press
> Joseph V. Rodricks, Calculated Risks: Understanding the Toxicity and Human Health Risks of Chemicals in Our Environment, pp. 62-63, 148-50, 166-60 (Cambridge U. Press 1992).

National Public Radio, All Things Considered
> © Copyright NPR® 1999. The news series by NPR's Richard Harris was originally broadcast on NPR's "All Things Considered®" on February 1, 1995, and is used with permission of National Public Radio, Ind. Any unauthorized duplication is strictly prohibited."

New England Journal of Medicine
> Robert A. Rinsky, et al, Benzene and Leukemia: An Epidemiologic Risk Assessment, 316 New England Journal of Medicine 1044-50 (Apr. 23, 1987).

Tulane Environmental Law Journal
> Junius C. McElveen, Jr., Risk Assessment in the Federal Government: Trying to Understand the Process, 5 Tulane Environmental Law Journal 45, 67-72 (1991).

Columbia Journal of Environmental Law

    Adam M. Finkel, Is Risk Assessment Really too Conservative?
Revising the Revisionists, 14 Colum. J. Envtl. L. 427, 441-47 (1989).

Science

    Paul A. Slovic, Risk Perception, 236 Science 280, 280-85 (1987).

University of Pennsylvania Law Review

    Clayton P. Gillette & James E. Krier, Risks, Courts and Agencies,
138 U. Pa. L. Rev. 1027, 1075-85 (1990).

Yale Journal on Regulation

    Howard Latin, Good Science, Bad Regulation, and Toxic Risk
Assessment, 5 Yale J. on Regulation 89, 92-134 (1988). © Copyright
1989 by the YALE JOURNAL ON REGULATION, P.O. Box 208215, New
Haven, CT 06520-8215. Reprinted from Vol. 5:89 by permission. All
rights reserved.

Chapter 3

New York Times

    William K. Stevens, Congress Asks, Is Nature Worth More than a
Shopping Mall?, New York Times, Apr. 25, 1995 at 138.

Science

    Alan J. Krupnick and Paul R. Proney, Controlling Urban Air
Pollution: A Benefit-Cost Assessment, 252 Science 522 (1991).

Universal Press Syndicate

    Cartoon by Ruben Bolling in 1992. Syndicated by Quaternary
Features, PO Box 72, New York, New York 10021. Bolling now is
under the Universal Press Syndicate name. Email
addressTomdbug@aol.com. The cartoon name is "Takes of Market-
Driven Crimes—Marin Ryder is awakened by the sounds of a
burglary."

University of Michigan Law Review

    Mary L. Lyndon, Information Economics and Chemical Toxicity:
Designing Law to Produce and Use Data, 87 Mich. L. Rev. 1795,
1810-17 (1989).

Harvard University Press

    Stephen Breyer, Breaking the Vicious Circle: Toward effective Risk
Regulation, 11-23, 33-43 (1993).

Harvard Law Review

    Colin S. Diver, Policymaking Paradigms in Administrative Law, 95
Harv. L. Rev. 393, 396-401, 428-33 (1981).

Science

    Lester B. Lave, et al., Environmental Implications of Electric Cars,
268 Science 993, 993-95 (1995).

Harvard University Press

    John D. Graham & Jonathan Baert Wiener, Confronting Risk
Tradeoffs, in Risk versus Risk: Tradeoffs in Protecting Health and the
Environment 10-17, 20-23 (John D. Graham & Jonathan Baert
Wiener, eds. 1995).

Northern Kentucky Law Review
> John S. Applegate, Comparative Risk Assessment and Environmental Priorities projects: A Forum, Not a Formula, 25 N. Ky. L. Rev. 71 (1997).

Arizona Law Review
> Mark Sagoff, At the Shrine of Our Lady of Fatima or Why Political Questions are Not All Economic, 23 Arizona L. Rev. 1283, 1283-96 (1981).

Chapter 4

American Automobile Association
> Map of Memphis, Tennessee.

Chapter 5

Random House
> A CIVIL ACTION by Jonathan Harr. Copyright © 1995 by Jonathan Harr. Reprinted by permission of Random House, Inc.

The Atlantic Monthly
> Gary Taubes, Fields of Fear 94-95 (The Atlantic Monthly, Nov. 1994).

New York Times
> Susan Sachs, Public Clamor Puts Focus on "Clusters" in Cancer Research, New York Times, Sept. 21, 1998 at A1.
>
> Kevin Sack, Louisiana Town Goes to Trial Over Waste Pit, New York Times, July 13, 1998 at A10.
>
> John Broder, Stares of Lawyerly Disbelief at a Hugh Civil Award, New York Times, Sept. 10, 1997, p. C1.

Chapter 6

Harvard University Press
> Dade W. Moeller, Environmental Health, chart on p. 257 of background radiation and chart on p. 252 of dose-response models for quantifying effects of ionizing radiation. (rev. ed. 1997).

Yale Journal on Regulation
> FDA's Implementation of The Delaney Clause: Repudiation of Congressional Choice or Reasoned Adaptation to Scientific Progress? Richard A. Merrill 5 Yale J. on Reg. 1, 12-21 (1988). © Copyright 1988 by the Yale Journal on Regulation, P.O. Box 208215, New Haven, CT 06520-8215. Reprinted from Vol. 5:1 by permission. All rights reserved.

Robert Del Tredici
> Photo of Magnification 500 times of particle of plutonium in lung tissue, Lawrence Radiation Laboratory, Berkeley California, September 20, 1982. © Robert Del Tredici.

Georgetown Law Journal
> Elinor P. Schroeder & Sidney A. Shapiro, Responses to Occupational Disease: The role of Markets, Regulation, and Information, 72 Geo. L. J. 1231, 1239-44 (1984).

MIT Press
   John M. Mendeloff, The Dilemma of Toxic substance Regulation,
   MIT Press 1988, pp. 4-12.
Duke Law Journal
   Sidney A. Shapiro & Thomas O. McGarity, Not So Paradoxical: The
   Rationale for Technology-Based Regulation, 1991 Duke L.J. 729,
   731-739.
Harvard University Press
   Susan W. Putnam & Jonathan Baert Wiener, Seeking Safe Drinking
   Water in Risk versus Risk: Tradeoffs in Protecting Health and the
   Environment (John d. Graham & Jonathan Baert Wiener eds) 141-48
   (1995).
Environment Reporter-Bureau of National Affairs
   Water Pollution: Technology Options Could Reduce Dioxin, Furans
   from Pulp, Paper Mills, 27 Envt. Rep. (BNA) 610 (1996). Reprinted
   with permission from Environment Reporter, Vol. 27, No9. 12, p. 610
   (July 19, 1996). Copyright 1996 by the Bureau of National Affairs,
   Inc. (800-372-1033) http://www.bna.com.
Environmental Law Reporter-Environmental Law Institute
   Oliver A. Houck, The Regulation of Toxic Pollutants Under the Clean
   Water Act, 21 Envtl. L. Rep. 40528 (1991).
Sidney A. Shapiro & Robert L. Glicksman
   Risk Regulation at Risk: Restoring a Pragmatic Approach, ch. 1
   (unpublished manuscript).
Duke Law Journal
   John D. Graham, The Failure of Agency-forcing: The Regulation Of
   Airborne Carcinogens Under Section 112 of the Clean Air Act, 1885
   Duke L.J. 100.

Chapter 7

Corbis/Bettmann-UPI
   Photo of DDT being sprayed on beach, reprinted in National
   Geographic Magazine, p. 132, Feb. 1996. Corbis/Bettmann-UPI ©
   1945.
Environmental Law Reporter-Environmental Law Institute
   Linda J. Fisher et al, A Practitioner's Guide to the Federal Insecticide,
   Fungicide and Rodenticide Act: Part I, 24 Envtl. L. Rept (ELI) 10449,
   10451-52 (1994).
Houghton Mifflin
   Rachel Carson, Silent Spring, (Houghton Mifflin, 1962) pp. 15-18,
   20-23, 105-09.
UCLA Journal of Environmental Law and Policy
   James A. Colopy, Poisoning the Developing World: The Exploration
   of Unregistered and Severely Restricted Pesticides from the United
   States, 13 UCLA J. Envtl. L. & Policy 167 (1994/5).

Yale Journal on Regulation

Lessons from Federal Pesticide Regulation on the Paradigms and Politics of Environmental Law Reform, Donald T. Hornstein 10 Yale J. on Reg. 369, 433-38 (1993). © Copyright 1993 by the YALE JOURNAL ON REGULATION, P.O. Box 208215, New Haven, CT 06520-8215. Reprinted from Vol. 10:369 by permission. All rights reserved.

Chapter 9

Tribune Media Services

Cartoon in EPA Journal, January/February 1990 "It isn't nice to foul Mother Nature, is it?"

Clay Bennett

Cartoon from EPA Journal, July/August 1991, "In the disposal of toxic waste, this method is still the cheapest...and the simplest way to get rid of the problem" Clay Bennett cartoon.

New York State Department of Health

New York State Department of Health, Diagram of Love Canal Emergency Declaration Area: Proposed Habitability Criteria (Albany NY: NY DOH, December 1986) appendix 6, p. 12.

Seattle Times

Duff Wilson, Fear in the Fields: How Hazardous Wastes Become Fertilizer, © Seattle Times, editorial pages of March 22, 1997.

Environmental Law Reporter-Environmental Law Institute

Jeffrey M. Gaba, The Mixture and Derived-From Rules under RCRA: Once a Hazardous Waste Always a Hazardous Waste?, 21 ELR 10033 (1991) Copyright © 1991 Environmental Law Institute®. reprinted with permission from ELR® – The Environmental Law Reporter®. All rights reserved.

Bureau of National Affairs

3 Figures. Figure of the definition of a (1) solid waste and (2) hazardous waste and (3) regulations for hazardous waste not covered in diagram 1 from 40 CFR part 260, Appendix I, Environment Reporter # 0013-9211/97. Reprinted with permission from Environment Reporter, Vol. 40 CFR part 260, Appendix I. Copyright 1997 by the Bureau of National Affairs, Inc. (800-372-1033) http://www.bna.com.

Chapter 10

Environmental Law

Michael B. Gerrard, Territoriality, Risk Perception, and Counterproductive Legal Structures: The Case of Waste Facility Siting, 27 Envtl. L. 1017 (1997).

Unpublished Monograph

John Martin Gillroy, Public Choice, Assurance, and Environmental Risk (1993).

Vermont Chapter of the Sierra Club
Cartoon from Vermont Chapter of the Sierra Club Newsletter, September 1999, "Your job, Figford, is to accent the positive economic effect our client's product (nuclear waste) will bring to the target community."

Chapter 11

The Denver Post
Steve Lipsher, Spirit of Cooperation Sought at Clean-Up Site, The Denver Post, March 30, 1998. Steve Lipsher, Mine Cleanup Proves Dirty Job, The Denver Post, Feb. 27, 1999.

The New York Times
Jim Robbins, Butte Breaks New Ground to Mop Up a World-Class Mess, New York Times, July 21, 1998.

Photo of Bridal Veil waterfall
Photo by Greg Lief (photos@gregleif.com, http://www.greglief.com).

Chapter 12

Indiana Law Journal
John S. Applegate, Beyond the Usual Suspects: The Use of Citizens Advisory Boards in Environmental Decisionmaking, 73 Ind. L. J. 903, 906-26 (1998).

Environmental Law
Frank B. Cross, The Public Role in Risk Control, 24 Envtl. L. 887 (1994).

Environmental Law Reporter-Environmental Law Institute
John S. Applegate & Stephen Dycus, Institute Controls or Emperor's Clothes? Long-Term Stewardship of the Nuclear Weapons Complexes, 28 Envtl. L. Rep. (ELI) 10631 (1998).

Chapter 13

ABA Journal
Steven Keeva, Pursuing the Right to Breathe Easy, ABA Journal, Feb. 1999, at 48-49.

American University Law Review
Alice Kaswan, Environmental Justice: Bridging the Gap Between Environmental Laws and "Justice", 47 Am. U. L. Rev. 221, 230-39 (1977).

Environmental Law Reporter-Environmental Law Institute
Jeffrey B. Gracer, Taking Environmental Justice Claims Seriously, 28 Environmental Law Reporter (ELI) 10373 (July 1998).

Chapter 14

Safety Data for Hydrogen Cyanide from http://physchem. ox.ac.uk/MSDS/H/hydrogen_cyanide.html.

Harvard Environmental law Review
Robert Abrams & Douglas H. Ward, Prospects for Safer Communities: Emergency Response, Community Right To Know, and Prevention of Chemical Accidents, 14 Harv. Envtl. L. Rev. 135, 154-63 (1990).

The Wall Street Journal

> Scott McMurray, Cleaning-Up: Chemical Firms Find That It Pays to Reduce Pollution at Source by Altering Processes to Yield Less Waste, They Make Production More Efficient, Wall Street Journal, June 11, 1991 at A1.

Columbia Journal of Environmental Law

> Stephen M. Johnson, From Reaction to Proaction: The 1990 Pollution Prevention Act, 17 Colum. J. Envtl. L. 153, 171-73, 179-203 (1992).

Georgia Law Review

> The Unfinished Business of Pollution Prevention, Kenneth Geiser, 29 Ga. L. Rev. 473, 477-79, 488-91 (1995). This article was originally published at 29 Ga. L. Rev. 473 (1995).

GLOSSARY OF ACRONYMS

ADR	alternative dispute resolution
AEA	Atomic Energy Act
AEC	Atomic Energy Commission
ALARA	as low as is reasonably achievable
ALJ	Administrative Law Judge
AOC	administrative order on consent
APA	Administrative Procedure Act
ARAR	applicable or relevant and appropriate requirement
ATSDR	Agency for Toxic Substances and Disease Registry
BAT	best available technology
BDAT	best demonstrated available technology
CAA	Clean Air Act
CAB	citizens advisory board
CAMU	corrective action management unit
CBA	cost-benefit analysis
CDC	Centers for Disease Control
CEG	conditionally exempt generator
CEQ	Council on Environmental Quality
CERCLA	Comprehensive Environmental Response, Compensation, and Liability Act
CERCLIS	Comprehensive Environmental Response, Compensation, and Liability Information System
CFC	chlorofluorocarbon
CGL	comprehensive general liability
CNS	central nervous system
CPSC	Consumer Product Safety Commission
CRA	comparative risk assessment
CV	contingent valuation
CWA	Clean Water Act
DBP	disinfection byproducts
dl	deciliter
DOE	Department of Energy
DOD	Department of Defense
DOI	Department of the Interior
DOJ	Department of Justice
DOT	Department of Transportation
EDB	ethylene dibromide
EDF	Environmental Defense Fund
EHS	extremely hazardous substance

EMF	electromagnetic fields
EMR	electromagnetic radiation
EPA	Environmental Protection Agency
EPCRA	Emergency Planning and Community Right-to-Know Act
ETS	emergency temporary standard
FDA	Food and Drug Administration
FDF	fundamentally different factors
FEMP	Fernald Environmental Management Project
FFA	federal facilities agreements
FFCA	Federal Facility Compliance Act
FFDCA	Federal Food, Drug, and Cosmetic Act (also FD&C Act)
FIFRA	Federal Insecticide, Fungicide, and Rodenticide Act
FQPA	Food Quality Protection Act
FWPCA	Federal Water Pollution Control Act (Clean Water Act)
GAO	General Accounting Office
GATT	General Agreement on Tariffs and Trade
GCP	Generic Cancer Policy
HAP	hazardous air pollutant
HRS	Hazard Ranking System
HWIR	Hazardous Waste Identification Rule
HWSA	Hazardous and Solid Waste Amendments of 1984
HWTC	Hazardous Waste Treatment Council
IAG	interagency agreement
IARC	International Agency for Research on Cancer
ICRP	International Commission on Radiological Protection
ICS	individual control strategy
IPM	integrated pest management
ITC	Interagency Testing Committee
LD50	lethal dose - 50% (measure of acute toxicity)
LDR	land disposal restriction
LEPC	local emergency planning commission
LOAEL	lowest observed adverse effects level
LQG	large quantity generator
LULU	locally undesirable land use
MACT	maximum achievable control technology
MCL	maximum contaminant level

MCLG	maximum contaminant level goal
MEI	maximally exposed individual
μg	microgram
mg	milligram
MOA	memorandum of agreement
mrem	millirem
MSDS	material safety data sheet
MTD	maximum tolerated dose
NAAQS	national ambient air quality standard
NAS	National Academy of Sciences
NBAR	nonbinding preliminary allocation of responsibility
NCI	National Cancer Institute
NCP	National Contingency Plan
NEPA	National Environmental Policy Act
NESHAP	national emission standard for hazardous air pollutants
NIMBY	not in my back yard
NOAEL	no observed adverse effects level
NPDES	National Pollutant Discharge Elimination System
NPL	National Priorities List
NRC	Nuclear Regulatory Commission
NRD	natural resource damages
NRDC	Natural Resources Defense Council
NSPS	new source performance standard
O/E	observed/expected
OIRA	Office of Information and Regulatory Affairs
OMB	Office of Management and Budget
OSC	on-scene coordinator
OSHA	Occupational Safety and Health Administration
OSHAct	Occupational Safety and Health Act
OTA	Office of Technology Assessment
OU	operable unit
PA/SI	preliminary assessment/site investigation
PCB	polychlorinated biphenyl
PEL	permissible exposure limit
PIC	prior informed consent
PMN	pre-manufacture notification
POTW	publicly owned treatment works
PP	proposed plan
PPA	Pollution Prevention Act
ppb	parts per billion
ppm	parts per million
ppq	parts per quadrillion

PRP	potentially responsible party
PTSD	post-traumatic stress disorder
PVC	polyvinyl chloride
QRA	quantitative risk assessment
RCRA	Resource Conservation and Recovery Act
RD/RA	remedial design/remedial action
RF	radio frequency
RFA	RCRA facility assessment
RfD	reference dose
RI/FS	remedial investigation/feasibility study
RME	reasonable maximum exposure
ROD	record of decision
RPM	remedial project manager
RQ	reportable quantity
SARA	Superfund Amendments and Reauthorization Act
SDWA	Safe Drinking Water Act
SERC	state emergency response commission
SQG	small quantity generator
SSAB	site-specific advisory board
SWMU	solid waste management unit
TBC	to be considered
TCE	tricholorethylene
TCLP	toxicity characteristic leaching procedure
TLV	threshold limit value
TMDL	total maximum daily load
TPQ	threshold planning quantity
TRI	Toxic Release Inventory
TRU	transuranic
TSCA	Toxic Substances Control Act
TSDF	treatment, storage, and disposal facility
UCATA	Uniform Contribution Among Tortfeasors Act
UCC	Uniform Commercial Code
UCFA	Uniform Comparative Fault Act
UMTRCA	Uranium Mill Tailings Radiation Control Act
UNEP	United Nations Environment Programme
USDA	U.S. Department of Agriculture
USGS	United States Geological Survey
UST	underground storage tank
VOC	volatile organic compound

SUMMARY OF CONTENTS

TABLE OF CONTENTS

TABLE OF PRINCIPAL CASES

THE REGULATION OF TOXIC SUBSTANCES AND HAZARDOUS WASTES

PART 1:

FOUNDATIONS

Chapter 1

Introduction: The History and Politics of Toxics Regulation

In 1962, Rachel Carson alerted the nation to the dangers of toxic chemicals in a powerful book called Silent Spring. One chapter of the book, provocatively entitled "Beyond the Dreams of the Borgias," opens thus:

> The contamination of our world is not alone a matter of mass spraying [of pesticides]. Indeed, for most of us this is of less importance than the innumerable small-scale exposures to which we are subjected day by day, year after year. Like the constant dripping of water that in turn wears away the hardest stone, this birth-to-death contact with dangerous chemicals may in the end prove disastrous. Each of these recurrent exposures, no matter how slight, contributes to the progressive buildup of chemicals in our bodies and so to cumulative poisoning. Probably no person is immune to contact with this spreading contamination unless he lives in the most isolated situation imaginable. Lulled by the soft sell and the hidden persuader, the average citizen is seldom aware of the deadly materials with which he is surrounding himself; indeed he may not realize he is using them at all.[1]

The danger remains with us today. In 1999, Mark Van Pulten, President of the National Wildlife Federation (NWF), wrote the following to NWF members:[2]

Dear Friend:

---

[1] RACHEL CARSON, SILENT SPRING 173-74 (1962).

[2] Mark Van Pulten, President, National Wildlife Federation, To members dated Feb. 2, 1999, reprinted with permission.

Every year over one billion pounds of toxic chemicals are released into the environment in the U.S. The most dangerous chemicals are persistent, bioaccumulative, toxic (PBT) chemicals like mercury and dioxins. These chemicals can persist for many years or decades, building to higher and higher concentrations as they are passed up the food chain, where they can poison wildlife, aquatic life, and people.
The threats from these chemicals are very real:

- Mercury can cause long-term damage to the nervous systems of fetuses and young children. Forty states have issued fish consumption advisories due to mercury-contaminated fish. Mercury contamination is deadly to loons-studies have linked mercury poisoning to a massive die-off of approximately 7500 loons in the Gulf of Mexico in 1983. The risks to people also are severe-according to the EPA, up to 166,000 pregnant women are exposed to harmful levels of mercury in a given year.

- Dioxins are extremely potent birth defect-causing chemicals produced by incineration of PVC plastics, and in certain manufacturing processes. Research has shown that extremely low concentrations-60 parts per trillion in tissue-can kill 50 percent of young lake trout.

These chemicals are so toxic and persist for so long that simply reducing their release into the environment will never be enough. The release of these chemicals must be completely eliminated. That is why NWF and our allies fought for and won zero discharge and virtual elimination policies adopted by the United States and Canada that are designed to eventually eliminate these chemicals from the environment.

But now the policies of zero discharge and virtual elimination are in danger.

The U.S. EPA has published its long-awaited "Multimedia Strategy for Persistent, Bioaccumulative, and Toxic (PBT) Pollutants." The strategy takes incrementally in the right direction by focusing on all pollutant sources-air, water, and land; and it is an important step in integrating EPA programs that have been fragmented and ineffective. As an effort to implement zero discharge and virtual elimination, it is worse than timid; it is actually a retreat.

The EPA strategy abandons the goal of eliminating persistent toxic substances in the Great Lakes and other watersheds, and fails to propose the most effective policy tools-bans and phase-outs of chemicals-needed to achieve that goal. It does so even though the EPA is bound by both the Clean Water Act and the

Great Lakes Water Quality Agreement with Canada to work toward zero discharge and virtual elimination goals.
We need your help.

The EPA is accepting public comments on its proposed strategy until February 16. Please write to EPA Administrator Carol Browner before Feb. 16 to urge her to develop and implement a strong PBT strategy that actually moves us toward these goals. Ask her to amend the proposed strategy in these ways:

- The PBT strategy should include a zero discharge goal that ends the release of PBTs. The current EPA proposal will continue to allow significant releases.
- The PBT strategy should use bans, phase-outs, and sunsetting of PBTs. The current EPA proposal relies on the existing permit system (which may reduce, but will not eliminate, PBTs).
- The PBT strategy should require full enforcement and implementation of existing programs. The EPA proposal relies on inadequate programs and voluntary measures that will not get us there.* * *

In May of 2000, the federal EPA released the first national accounting of toxic chemical emissions. The report showed a tripling of toxic chemical releases since 1988, primarily by electric power plants, the mining industry, and chemical wholesalers. A total of 7.3 billion pounds of toxic chemicals were reportedly released in 1998.

Are we adrift in a sea of toxic chemicals, or is this just "chemophobia," a largely irrational fear of certain kinds of chemicals, especially those that may cause cancer? What are the real risks associated with toxic substances and hazardous wastes, how are they measured and how does the law address these risks? Are bans and phase-outs the most effective and efficient tools for managing toxic and hazardous substances, or should we adopt more fine-tuned legal controls?

This casebook addresses these questions and more. In the initial chapters we study the science of toxic substances and the methods for assessing them. We consider the economic implications of treating toxic and hazardous substances, the role of the judiciary in reviewing the regulatory activities of the Environmental Protection Agency (EPA) and other federal agencies and traditional civil remedies for injuries caused by toxic substances. Building on this foundation, we then proceed, statute by statute, to analyze the federal regulatory structures that govern toxic substances and hazardous wastes. This part of the book begins with portions of federal pollution-control statutes that regulate toxics and then turns to statutes that regulate the life cycle of toxics, from manufacture and use to disposal and clean-up. Finally, we address several new trends in toxics regulation which may-and probably should in the future-become integral parts of this subject.

It is impossible to convey succinctly the breadth of the subject of toxic substance and hazardous waste regulation, or to describe all the concerns that inspired the regulatory regime (really, many regimes) that this book documents. The following excerpts in this chapter, however, provide an excellent overview. The purpose is to first provide an introduction to the subject matter, second provide a historical background, and finally to point to where it is headed in the future. The first, from *Hazardous Waste in America*, outlines the area as it stood in 1982, shortly after America's basic regulatory structures were put in place.[3] The second, from *Three Decades of Environmental Politics: The Historical Context in Government and Environmental Politics,* offers a historical account of toxics regulation and explains the political and social background of this branch of the environmental movement.[4] Finally, the authors of *Sustainable Environmental Law* survey the statutory tools for implementing environmental objectives.[5]

HAZARDOUS WASTE IN AMERICA

Samuel S. Epstein *et al.*
pp. 6-7, 14-26 (1982)[6]

Background

The Environmental Protection Agency (EPA) is the U.S. government agency charged with regulating the disposal of hazardous wastes. The EPA uses a complicated and convoluted definition of this term for legal

---

[3] SAMUEL S. EPSTEIN, LESTER O. BROWN & CARL POPE, HAZARDOUS WASTE IN AMERICA 6-7, 14-26 (1982).

[4] SAMUEL P. HAYS, THREE DECADES OF ENVIRONMENTAL POLITICS: THE HISTORICAL CONTEXT IN GOVERNMENT AND ENVIRONMENTAL POLITICS 21-37 (Michael Lacey ed) (1991).

[5] CELIA CAMPBELL-MOHN, ET AL., SUSTAINABLE ENVIRONMENTAL LAW 171-90 (1993).

[6] From Hazardous Waste in America by Dr. Samuel S. Epstein, Lester O. Brown & Carl Pope, Copyright © 1982, 1983 by Epstein, Brown, and Pope. Reprinted with permission of Sierra Club Books.

purposes. But for practical purposes, the hazardous waste problem is easy to explain.

Every process for producing useful things-food, clothing, equipment, drugs, and housing-also produces materials that are not generally regarded as useful. Either they are by-products of the production process, or they are raw materials that have served their purpose. Most of these wastes are harmless-rice straw, for example, while sometimes difficult for a farmer to remove from his fields, is hardly dangerous. But a small percentage of all these wastes are dangerous. The manufactured product itself may be dangerous-unused pesticides left over after spraying a field, for example, are chemically as harmful as those sprayed on the field, but likely are more concentrated. Or the wastes may be dangerous by-products of manufacturing a non-toxic product, such as cyanide wastes from the refining of gold.

Since hazardous wastes are not useful to the industry producing them, they have typically been disposed of in the easiest and cheapest way. A major problem now is how to ensure that those who generate such hazardous wastes do not simply dump them, but handle them without creating public health or environmental problems. In some cases, wastes are generated and dumped in large quantities by major industrial producers (producer wastes); in others, it is the consumers of a product who, having used it, get rid of it (consumer wastes). Producer wastes are typically more concentrated than consumer wastes, but their total volume may be smaller. No one really knows, for it is impossible to keep track of the wastes discarded by the ultimate consumers. At the end of World War II, the United States produced only 1 billion pounds of hazard (producer) wastes per year. The production of such waste has since increased at a rate of about 10 percent per year. The EPA now [1979] estimates that around 80 billion pounds of hazardous waste material are generated annually-about 350 pounds of hazardous waste for every inhabitant of the United States. The EPA further estimates that only 10 percent of this waste is properly disposed of.[7]

* * *

Major Chemical Categories

From a practical standpoint, it is conventional to classify hazardous wastes in the following major categories: radioactives; flammables; heavy metals; asbestos; acids and bases; and synthetic organic chemicals.

Radioactives

Those elements that are intrinsically unstable and that give off energy or charged particles as they decay into other forms are termed

---

[7] The 90% that does not go to an on-site facility or secure landfill is improperly handled in unlined lagoons or ponds, nonsecure landfills, or by ocean dumping, use of sewer systems, deep-well injection, or ordinary incinerators.

"radioactives" and are collectively know as "radionuclides." Because the energy or small particles that are being emitted by these materials have the potential to damage living tissue, radionuclides are highly hazardous. Among their other effects, they can cause immediate death, burns or injury, and even in small quantities lead to birth defects, cancer, and other chronic disease.

Radionuclides are among the more recent additions to the arsenal of industry. Certain radioactive minerals, principally uranium, thorium, and radium, occur in significant quantities in nature. In the latter part of the nineteenth century, scientists, led by Pierre and Marie Curie, investigated the properties of these minerals and learned how to separate them from their natural ores. Initially, radioactive materials were just curiosities. Radium, important though it was in helping physicists to understand the composition of matter, was an industrially insignificant element until well after World War I, and many of its early uses constituted dangerous quackery based on the notion that radiation had "magical" curing properties.

In the 1930's however, as an outgrowth of experiments in the nature of matter and of efforts to test Einstein's relativity theory, which proposed that matter could be converted to energy, physicists mastered the fission process, in which neutrons emitted from uranium were used to split other atoms, producing new radioactive elements and radioactive isotopes of known elements. Because each of these elements or isotopes has its own special properties, science rapidly developed a variety of uses for many, as radiation sources for x-rays of material welds, as medicinal tracers within the body, in nuclear power plants, as a heat source to power steam-driven turbines. By the 1960s, radioactive materials were being used in a wide diversity of industrial settings, although by far the largest source of man-made radioactive materials remained the nuclear weapons industry and nuclear power plants.

* * *

Because of this diversity of characteristics, it is difficult to generalize about the forms in which radioactive waste materials may pose a threat. In general, the faster the rate of decay and the shorter the half-life, the more intense the radiation. Similarly, while alpha emitters do not travel far, because their energy is rapidly absorbed by other atoms they encounter, they do tremendous damage at close range by giving up this energy. Thus, plutonium 239, an alpha emitter with a very long half-life, is of enormous concern because it can become lodged inside the body, in the lungs, if it breaks down into particles. Strontium 90, a beta emitter, poses a threat because it tends to accumulate in the bones in place of chemically similar calcium.

Flammables

Flammables are a miscellaneous category of chemicals whose danger derives mainly from their tendency to react strongly with other materials-in this case the oxygen in the atmosphere-giving off massive quantities of heat in the process. The most important flammables are petroleum or natural gas by-products. There are also such relatively exotic flammables as pure elemental sodium. But, like acids and bases, their very reactivity makes their hazard short-lived as, once released into the environment, they immediately come into contact with atmospheric oxygen and heat or sparks.

Heavy Metals

Just as mining was the first significant source of hazardous wastes, heavy metals were for many centuries the major component of hazardous wastes. These metals-among the most important being lead, arsenic, zinc, cadmium, copper, and mercury-were among the first raw materials ever used for technological purposes. They are often found in close conjunction with each other in nature, are relatively easy to separate from their natural ores through smelting, and are relatively easy to shape and mold, either alone or alloyed with other metals.[8]

As science and technology advanced, an ever-greater variety of uses were found for heavy metals, which were mined and processed in greater and greater quantities. For instance, lead, originally prized for its malleability and resistance to corrosion, was later used in a wide range of products and processes: in bullets for its density; in storage batteries, because of the relative ease with which it both yields up and accepts electrons; as a soldering agent to seal tin cans, because of its low melting point and ability to adhere to other metals; as a gasoline additive, to prevent irregular explosion under pressure (knocking); as a base for paints, because of its resistance to weathering; and, finally, in the nuclear industry, because its great mass enable[s] it to absorb neutrons and block radiation.

In older cities, lead can be found in tap water as it leaches from old pipes. It may also be found in old interior and even new exterior paints, or coming out of the tailpipes of automobiles from leaded gasoline, thus contaminating the streets and playgrounds of the neighborhoods.

* * *

Overall rates of utilization of most heavy metals have increased dramatically over the past century and continue to do so. For instance, worldwide production of mercury has more than doubled since World War II, and worldwide production of lead is doubling every twenty years.

* * *

Heavy metals pose a variety of health hazards. Lead, in even very small quantities, is a neurotoxin, causing learning disabilities in children, particularly in major urban ghettos, where exposures to lead are high. Lead also produces other chronic toxic effects involving a wide range of organs. Mercury is an even more powerful neurotoxin and has been

---

[8] With the revolution in miniature electronics, the use of heavy metals in batteries has become a serious problem.–EDS.

implicated in mental illness among nineteenth-century hatters, who used it to treat furs; among families in the American Southwest who accidentally ingested mercury-treated seed; and in Japan, where the population of Minamata Bay and local fishermen were afflicted by a progressive neurological disease due to high levels of mercury that had accumulated in the fish they ate. Cadmium is implicated in high blood pressure and heart disease and is carcinogenic, being implicated in lung and prostate cancer.

As wastes, heavy metals pose particular problems. Their toxicity is a function of the structure of their atoms. As elements, they are toxic. By contrast, many other materials are only toxic in particular molecular or chemical forms. These molecular forms, unlike the atomic structure of lead, are continually changing under the impact of chemical reactions. But lead-and this is the case with all heavy metals-will always remain lead regardless of what other materials it reacts with, or how it is heated or put under pressure. Neither heat nor biological processes can change it into anything else. It may temporarily take a molecular form in which it is not readily available for assimilation into living organisms, and so for a time it may be neutralized. But it will always retain the potential to be converted into a toxic form.

Asbestos

Of ancient origin and uses, asbestos is the generic name for a group of minerals composed of calcium or magnesium silicates formed into long, threadlike fibers. These fibers can be woven or spun into cloth and shaped into materials by mixing with cement or other substances. They possess the special qualities of very high resistance to heat and electricity. This combination results in a wide range of uses, including insulation of electrical wiring, hot pipes and furnaces; firemen's suits and theater curtains; and automobile brake linings.

The effects of heavy metals generally depend upon their chemical reactivity; however, it is the fibrous nature of asbestos and its resistance to biological degradation and chemical change that make it so dangerous. Because of its tiny fibers and fibrils, it easily penetrates the exposed surfaces of the lungs; there it provides a continuous irritation and cellular response, which result either in a progressive lung disease known as asbestosis or in a variety of cancers of the lung and other sites, when blood and lymph streams carry the fibers through the body.

Acids and Bases

Acids and bases are not in themselves necessarily hazardous-many common components of the body are slightly acidic or basic, as are foods. Materials that are very acidic or basic are extremely chemically reactive and corrosive. However, their hazards are likely to be relatively short-lived. Once released into the environment, acids begin to encounter bases and vice versa.

* * *

Synthetic Organic Chemicals

While heavy metals, asbestos, acids, and bases have been used for hundreds of years, synthetic organic chemicals are a relatively new category of industrial products. In the nineteenth century, limited quantities of organic chemicals, principally dyes, were developed from coal tar and wood alcohol. The more recent use of petroleum as a basic feedstock has, however, enabled synthesis of organic chemicals in relatively limitless quantities and has thus revolutionized the entire chemical industry.

The basic units of synthetic organic chemicals are hydrocarbons-materials formed through chemical reactions under heat and pressure from the remains of plants and animals and preserved in the form of fossil fuels-coal, natural gas, or petroleum. In coal and petroleum, long chains of carbon and hydrogen are strung together in large, complex molecules. The molecule of natural gas-methane, CH_4-is itself a simple, short chain, but can be easily combined into very large, long molecular chains.

* * *

United States production of synthetic organic chemicals took off sharply after World War II and increased progressively ever since. The total United States production of synthetic organic chemicals increased from about 1 billion pounds in 1940, to 30 billion in 1950, to 300 billion pounds in 1976. Growth rates of 15 percent or more are not uncommon for organic chemical industries at a time when the rest of the economy is advancing by only 4 or 5 percent per year.

* * *

Three major uses of hydrocarbons should be clearly distinguished. First, some are used as *end products* in themselves. These include lightweight hydrocarbon fractions, containing relatively small molecules, such as ethylene, toluene, benzene and styrene, some of which are important industrial solvents. Second, some are used as *intermediates,* such as ethylene and styrene, which can be linked together (polymerized) to form long-chain plastics, such as polyethylene and polystyrene, for use in insulation foam, furniture, and packaging materials. And finally, some are used for the *synthesis of novel molecules* by chemical splicing or molecular engineering, designed to meet specific industrial needs.

Such novel chemicals, with entirely new properties, have never before existed and no natural system has ever been previously exposed to them. Examples of such splicing include a wide range of *halogenated hydrocarbons,* in which atoms of chlorine, bromine, or iodine are added to basic hydrocarbon chains, producing such relatively simple new chemicals as trichloroethylene (TCE) and perchloroethylene (PCE) used as industrial solvents or degreasing agents, or more complex organic chemicals, such as the pesticides DDT, mirex, and chlordane, which after World War II were widely used against agricultural pests and insect-borne disease, such as malaria, filariasis, yellow fever, and dengue fever. By tacking chlorine onto particular hydrocarbons known as phenols, chemists produced polychlorinated biphenyls (PCBs), chemicals whose greatest value was their ability to resist breakdown from heat and electrical charges when used as insulating fluids in transformers and other electrical machinery. By adding larger numbers of chlorine atoms, chemists produced pentachlorophenol (PCP), a wood preservative used to resist termites. By using bromine instead of chlorine, an effective fire retardant-polybrominated biphenyls (PBBs)-was produced. By adding halogens, simple precursors of new plastics, such as vinyl chloride (VC), were synthesized; the VC was subsequently polymerized to form polyvinyl chloride (PVC) for use in records, plastic pipe, and a wide range of other products.

By splicing or dividing complex hydrocarbon chains in different places and in different ways, it is possible to reproduce synthetic versions of natural chemicals-as drug companies do in synthesizing hormones or some drugs. But it is also possible to split and divide the hydrocarbon chains in fossil fuels in ways that produce substances that do not naturally occur in living organisms-but which in important ways may mimic them.

The halogenated hydrocarbons are a particularly important class and exemplify many of the problems of the new petrochemical era. Their most common characteristic is an ability to suppress or alter various chemical reactions involving naturally occurring organic processes.

An additional important characteristic of the more complex halogenated organics is their resistance to degradation by natural biological reactions.

* * *

Thus, useful as they are, synthetic organic chemicals are hazardous. For example, benzene induces aplastic anemia and leukemia; VC is a highly potent carcinogen; the entire class of chlorinated hydrocarbon pesticides-DDT, dieldrin, endrin, chlordane-produces adverse reproductive effects in birds and is also carcinogenic, as demonstrated in test animals; PCBs are carcinogenic and impair fertility; and dioxin (TCDD), a contaminant of phenoxy herbicides such as 2,4,5-T, is the most toxic known chemical, inducing cancer and birth defects in experimental animals in parts-per-trillion concentrations.

Indeed, "a disproportionately large number of recognized carcinogens fall into just three families of widely used petrochemicals: aromatic amines, in the form of dyes and synthetic intermediates, particularly epoxy compounds and hydrazines; chlorinated olefins, as monomers and pesticides; and alkyl halides, as solvents and degreasing agents."[9]

—

---

[9] Internal citation omitted.

With this background in the subject matter of toxics and hazardous waste, the following excerpt provides the historical background necessary to introduce toxics and hazardous waste law. Samuel Hays describes the socio-political movement that gave rise to our present environmental laws.

THREE DECADES OF ENVIRONMENTAL POLITICS: THE HISTORICAL CONTEXT

Samuel P. Hays
in **Government and Environmental Politics (Michael J. Lacy, ed.)**
pp. 21-37 (1991)[10]

From Conservation to Environment

The new interest in environmental objectives grew out of the vast social and economic changes that took place in the United States after World War II. Although some beginnings could be seen in earlier years, in the rising interest in outdoor recreation in the 1930s, for example, or in the few cases of concern for urban air and water pollution in the late nineteenth century, these trends are little more than precedents. It was the advanced consumer economy that came into existence following World War II that gave rise to a wide range of new public needs and wants. Incomes and standards of living rose; values changed amid rising levels of education; demands persisted that government supplement the private market to advance the aims of the expanding and changing middle class.

* * *

It is customary for historians to link the environmental movement with the earlier conservation movement, yet they were quite dissimilar. While the conservation movement was concerned with efficiency in the use and development of material resources, the environmental movement was concerned with amenities and quality of life. The first was part of the history of production; the second, of the history of consumption. The conservation movement arose not from public demand but from the strivings of professionals, scientists, and administrators to turn the wasteful use of resources into more efficient production. Efforts by these leaders to fashion a sustained political base in the form of organized activity failed miserably; for example, they continually rejected the policy initiatives of the most extensive conservation public of the time-the women's clubs. The environmental movement, on the other hand, arose from the wider public to set new goals and demands about which the nation's administrative, technical, and professional leadership was usually skeptical. Environmental impulses, fueled from the public at large, constantly pressed the nation's leaders to go further than they felt desirable. Many of these reluctant participants in environmental affairs were, in fact, direct professional and institutional descendants of the early conservation leaders.

* * *

---

[10] "Three Decades of Environmental Politics: The Historical context" is from EXPLORATIONS IN ENVIRONMENTAL HISTORY: ESSAYS BY SAMUEL P. HAYS, © 1998 by University of Pittsburgh Press. Reprinted by permission of the University of Pittsburgh Press.

The new interest in pollution also served to distinguish environment from conservation. While the public interest in natural environments rested on aesthetic objectives, the concern for pollution had its roots in new attitudes toward the biological environment and human health. The emerging interest in biology and the environment was expressed in terms of "ecology," the functioning of biological systems and how pollution interfered with it.

* * *

Ideas about environmental threats to health, conversely, arose from new health aspirations that came after the control of infectious disease and were expressed in words such as "preventative medicine" and "wellness." Increasingly, control of air and water pollution came to be thought of as an aspect of advance in human health protection.

In both these expressions of concern about pollution, one could detect a sense of heightened goals and aspirations associated with a desire for a higher standard of living and "quality of life." While one could easily focus on the crisis aspect of pollution problems (and this usually was the tone of media coverage), on a more fundamental level the notion of pollution as a problem arose far more from new attitudes that valued both smoothly functioning ecosystems and higher levels of human health.

* * *

The Environmental Impulses

The environmental impulses that stemmed from these changes in values can be sorted out into different strands, each of which arose at a different point in time to take its place alongside those that had evolved earlier. The first to appear, dominating the years from 1958 to 1965, was the drive to manage resources as natural environments for human enjoyment.

* * *

Between 1965 and 1972, air and water pollution came to exercise a formative influence in environmental affairs alongside the search for natural environments. The legislative landmarks were the Clean Air Acts of 1963, 1967, and 1970, the Clean Water Acts of 1965, 1970, and 1972 and the new pesticide law of 1972. All this activity has a twist, distinctive for the times, which emphasized ecological change and which later events tended to obscure. The concern for ecology or the "integrity of biological systems" seemed to structure ideas about pollution in this first stage of public policy toward it. The concern for ecology was closely related to the earlier concern for the aesthetic natural environment out of which it evolved. The new concern for pollution was not primarily focused on human health. Instead, it emphasized the role of pollution in the functioning of ecological systems, a degraded ecology as an undesirable human context, and a concern for the protection of natural ecological processes. One heard of an overload of carrying capacity, the way in which animal populations outran food supplies, biological simplification under stress, disturbances in aquatic ecosystems under acidification, and reduced forest growth due to air pollution.

* * *

By the 1970s much of this emphasis on pollution matters had changed to focus more exclusively on human health, but between 1965 and 1972, ecology provided a transitional context of the new interest in pollution.

* * *

New Environmental Impulses

During the 1970s, three new environmental impulses emerged to take their place alongside previous ones. One of these, emphasizing resources shortages and the "limits to growth," seemed to arouse little public interest. * * *

Far more extensive in terms of popular involvement was a second new twist to environmental affairs in the 1970s, the practice and ideology of personal and community autonomy and decentralization.

* * *

Although both the limits-to-growth impulse and the personal-and-community-autonomy impulse, each in its own way, constituted new elements in environmental affairs in the 1970s, both were overshadowed in policy debate and action by new concerns for human health. These reflected a persistent transformation in human attitudes marked by the triumph over infectious disease and by the emergence of new health concerns, . . . embracing concepts such as physical fitness and optimum health. Most people were no longer worried about imminent death or uncontrolled infectious diseases. Major chemical threat episodes, such as the Donora smog, kepone in the James River and [PCBs] in Michigan and Love Canal, all dramatized the concern. Underlying it was a change in attitudes and values. Increasingly Americans expressed their interest in health in terms of a capacity to engage in daily affairs at an optimum level of physical and mental health. They began to change their personal habits of eating, smoking, drinking, and exercise. They came to look on chemical agents in the environment as having an adverse effect on their aspirations.

This new interest in human health seemed to be at variance with the dominant trends and capabilities of American science and medicine. Leaders in those fields tended to identify advances in health in terms of mortality. Periodic reports from the Surgeon General marked progress with data about reduced death rates in various age categories. Medical practitioners, moreover, tended to be concerned more with curing sickness than preventing it, and hence Americans experienced a limited ability by physicians to cope with knotty problems of optimum health. While preventive medicine had made impressive accomplishments in vaccination against infectious diseases, it now seemed to be less interested in the limitations on optimum health that might come from environmental causes. Pollution issues seemed to be wrapped up in these contradictory tendencies-the high level of aspiration by the public for greater wellness on the one hand, and the relatively limited capacity of science and medicine to respond on the other. Hence, a major aspect of the public's concern for chemical pollution was either to take matters into their own hands and avoid contaminants by means of new personal lifestyles, or to demand public action to prevent exposure. In such affairs the medical profession often followed rather than led public attitudes.

The range of health effects at issue seemed to expand steadily. Most attention was given to cancer, but soon a wider range emerged: genetic and reproductive disorders, fetal and infant malformations, neurological deficits and modified enzyme systems, lowered immunity and premature aging. Interest in chemical pollution as a possible cause of such health effects seemed to widen. Attempts to prevent exposure to carcinogens led to many battles over specific chemicals and to unsuccessful efforts to establish generic cancer regulation, first by the EPA in its formulation of "cancer principles" in the mid-1970s, and then by the Occupational Safety and Health Administration (OSHA) in its abortive "generic cancer" policy a few years later.[11] Cancer took up most of the debate, but expanding scientific knowledge tended to expand the range of concerns that were being taken more seriously with each passing year.

* * *

Occupational health provided an especially sharp focus for these concerns. In earlier years, occupational hazards had been thought of primarily in terms of physical injury, but after World War II, occupational illness received increasing attention. The use of antibiotics made other problems such as cancer and reproductive defects more visible.

* * *

Here was the crux of the political interplay: the public was demanding that frontiers of knowledge and action with respect to health be expanded more rapidly than was possible, given the limited capabilities of science and medicine. Public controversy revealed how little was known about the presence of chemicals of potential harm, either in the environment or in humans. On a wide range of subjects, public demand for knowledge and action outran capability.

The historic change that all this implied for health science and medicine was the task of retooling from concern with acute effects of high-level exposures to the more subtle chronic effects of persistent low-level ones. Scientific method and analysis appropriate for the first were found to be far less able to identify the second. Thus, epidemiological studies that traditionally relied on the 5 percent confidence level used by biostatisticians might not be appropriate for smaller effects, because these were almost invariably, by their very size, beyond such limits. Such was the relationship found between lead and child behavior. Environmental

---

[11] The fate of OSHA's Generic Cancer Policy is discussed in detail in Chapter 6, *infra.*— EDS.

demands had contributed in no small part to the extension of chemical measurement capabilities from parts per million to parts per trillion in concentration. But the cost of such measurement made it all but impossible to chart the presence of chemicals, such as dioxin, in more than a few cases. A new test for blood lead developed in the late 1970s greatly lowered the cost of surveillance, but for most of the new health effects, diagnostic cost greatly limited the public demand for knowledge. The public desire to know was thwarted by the increasing "real cost" of knowing.

Underlying the new concern for chemical harm was the public perception of a chemical world out of control. In a series of episodes, from the early experience with atomic testing and pesticides to later cases of toxic chemicals in air and water and on land, the public gradually formulated fairly clear notions about the chemical universe: chemicals were persistent, not biodegradable, lasting in the environment for long periods of time; they were ubiquitous, transported through air and water to places far distant from their source; they "biomagnified" in the food chain so as to become more highly concentrated in the higher orders of mammals; and they were mysterious in that they could suddenly appear in ways not previously known or suspected. Chemicals dispersed into the environment affected biological life, and humans in particular, in such a way that their effects could be even partially controlled only with the greatest difficulty. The nuclear episode at Three Mile Island conveyed the image of a technology that was out of control; the sudden realization that hazardous waste had been permitted to pervade the environment and now seemed impossible to contain reinforced that perception. How could an individual person bring under control a potential harm which the nation's prevailing institutions could not?

* * *

NOTES

1. According to Hays, what are the major eras of environmental regulation and what are the key features of each? How will the concerns that Hays identifies be reflected in environmental law? What will be the objectives of environmental regulation? Given the gap between the public demand for protection and scientific knowledge, what difficulties would you expect to encounter in regulating toxics?

2. Congress responded to the historical and political developments Hays describes-and the underlying toxicological and economic conditions-through a complex array of statutes. One purpose of this casebook is to introduce you to these statutes. You will notice that the universe of toxic substances and hazardous wastes can be divided in numerous ways. The Epstein excerpt divides it by type of hazard, though in other parts of the book he and others divide by source, health effect, and other categories. The relevant statutes do the same, creating overlaps

and gaps, and sometimes attacking the problem in a relatively ineffective way. How would you categorize the toxics universe for regulatory purposes?

The problems of categorizing toxic wastes and hazardous substances illustrate a broader point about toxics regulation. It is a young area of the law and we are still trying to figure out the best way to regulate these materials. Thus, mere knowledge of the black letter law is insufficient training for lawyers in this field. You will also need to understand how the laws function, because they are constantly changing and because they are an overlay on a vast socio-political and historical framework. A major challenge throughout this casebook is not only to understand the toxic and hazardous substances laws, but also to analyze and critique them as legal tools and expressions of policy. The first steps are to analyze what legal tools each of the environmental statutes is using, how these tools are implemented, where else they might be applied, and how effective they are when applied.

—

Now that you have been introduced to the subject matter and history of toxics and hazardous waste law, it is time to consider how to regulate them. The following excerpt will help you begin to understand and evaluate this area of environmental law.

SUSTAINABLE ENVIRONMENTAL LAW

Celia Campbell-Mohn *et al.*
§4.2, pp. 171-90 (1993)[12]

There are [many] types of legal tools that environmental statutes use to implement the objectives [of environmental law]. Each of these strategies or tools has attributes and detriments that make it effective in some circumstances and not in others. As Edmund Muskie surmised in drafting the [Clean Air Act], Yankee ingenuity requires a combination of the best tools for the job at hand.

* * *

Command-and-Control Standards

The most ubiquitous tool to achieve environmental objectives is command-and-control standards. Command-and-control standards are regulations issued by the government to prescribe the level of pollutant that a facility may emit. There are two types of command-and-control regulations. Performance-based standards set ambient quality levels. Regulators then extrapolate the quantity of a pollutant that a facility may

---

[12] Reprinted from Sustainable Environmental Law, Campbell-Mohn, Breen, Futrell et al. Eds., (1993) with permission of the West Group.

emit from the ambient standard. Technology-based standards control discharges based on technological feasibility.

Command-and-control regulations are the nuts and bolts of environmental tools. Virtually every environmental statute relies partially on command-and-control regulation.

* * *

Some form of command-and-control regulation is unavoidable except within a purely free market system. Because a pure free market system cannot account for generations beyond several decades, all of the objectives of environmental law cannot presently be achieved without some command-and-control overlay within other tools.

The effectiveness of the command-and-control scheme varies. Command-and-control standards are clear and easy to enforce. They provide a "level playing field" for those engaging in potentially polluting activities. Command-and-control regulations are sometimes enforced through licenses and permits.

* * *

The primary detriment of centralized command-and-control standards is that they are inflexible regarding fluctuations in natural systems and the economy. Setting national standards may lead to inflexibility at the bioregional level. For example, command-and-control regulations cannot account for the varying abilities of natural systems to respond to pollutants. They also cannot account for fluctuations within natural systems that increase or decrease the carrying capacity at different times in the natural cycle.

Present command-and-control regulations are often pollutant specific, not accounting for synergistic impacts among various pollutants. Also, in many cases, command-and-control regulations must rely on scientific evidence where values are unquantifiable. For example, basing regulations on risk assessment requires quantitative valuation of ethical judgments, such as the value of human life.

Finally, command-and-control regulation creates inefficiency by applying uniform reductions where costs of compliance vary. Present command-and-control regimes tend to disadvantage new sources to the economic advantage of existing sources.

* * *

Research and Development

The second most pervasive tool in environmental statutes is technology forcing [that is, forcing the creation and adoption of new, cleaner technologies]. Technology forcing is a form of research and development.

Technology forcing is as pervasive as command-and-control performance-based standards. Therefore, it is one of the major tools shaping environmental law.

Because technological controls are based on economic feasibility rather than on carrying capacities, there is little connection between the quantity of regulation and environmental quality. Technology forcing is inherently dependent on the regulators' political will to "force" economic hardship due to the balance it requires between mandating technological advances and considering economic feasibility. In some ways, this serves to freeze the technology at a given level rather than induce industry to search for more efficient and effective controls.

Technology forcing is one way to balance the desire to improve environmental quality and to preserve the functioning of natural systems for both present and future generations with an economic system based on growth and rooted in the tradition of externalizing the cost of pollution emissions. It mandates environmental improvement at the rate that is economically feasible.

* * *

Social Funds

An alternative to requiring users of the commons to absorb [the environmental costs of their activities] is to spread costs though society using a directed fund replenished through taxes. The rationale for a pure social fund system is that the producers provide social goods, such as employment, and therefore society at large, rather than the direct consumers of the good, should absorb some of the cost of production.

Social funds pay for the cleanup of oil and hazardous waste. The best known social fund is Superfund, which was established under the Comprehensive Environmental Response, Compensation, and Liability Act of 1980 (CERCLA). It is used to clean up hazardous waste sites where the responsible party cannot be held liable. The Oil Pollution Act of 1990 also establishes a social fund to clean up oil spills where the responsible party is unavailable or to front the money where determination of liability will be time-consuming.

The environmental funds generally accrue from a tax on the activity.

* * *

Social funds distribute the costs of an activity either to society or across the producers of the particular activity. They generally cover accidents or the mishandling of dangerous elements, because accidents are a normal part of any activity. The advantage of using social funds is that the government assumes immediate responsibility for mitigating impacts from accidents or negligent conduct. Where time is crucial, social funds can provide immediate relief, postponing questions of liability until after the hazard is abated.

* * *

Civil Penalties

Civil penalties are a standard enforcement mechanism that include fines, treble damages, punitive damages, and other penalties not related to compensation for actual damage. Civil penalties are enforceable by administrative agencies, the courts, and, in many cases, citizen groups.

Civil penalty provisions are in almost every environmental statute. For example, [The Resource Conservation and Recovery Act (RCRA)] provides for penalties of up to $25,000 for each violation of the act. Each day of noncompliance is counted as a separate violation for purposes of the penalty.

* * *

In most civil penalty provisions, Congress provides that the Administrator must consider the nature, extent, and gravity of the violation, the violator's ability to pay, the effect on the violator's ability to continue to do business, any history of prior violations, and the degree of culpability. EPA has issued a series of policy statements delineating how it implements these provisions.

If the theory behind civil penalties is deterrence, civil penalties should be higher than the cost of restoring the natural system or fixing the damage. Civil penalties are effective only when they are stringent enough to change behavior rather than simply being incorporated as a cost of doing business.

Rather than flat ceilings on civil penalties, no matter what the nature of the harm, value to society, or significance of the natural system, a formula based on the percentage of corporate earnings deemed necessary to deter behavior considering mitigating factors may make this tool more effective and more likely to achieve environmental objectives.

* * *

Liability

The purpose of legal liability is to compensate entities for damage and, in some cases, to restore them or to make them whole. Liability can be imposed either through statute or common law. Liability can also be imposed for economic harm and natural resource damage.

The two main sources of statutory liability are CERCLA and the 1990 Oil Pollution Act.

The primary use of common-law liability in environmental law is in actions for toxic torts. Toxic torts are actions brought under common-law tort principles by individuals for compensation for bodily injury incurred because they were involuntarily exposed to chemicals. Causation is difficult to prove because the burden of scientific uncertainty is on the plaintiff.

* * *

The laws providing for natural resource damages allow the government to sue for monetary compensation for harm to the environment. "The money is then used to restore the environment to its original condition, or where that is not possible, [to] make up for the harm by improving the environment elsewhere in the same general vicinity."[13]

---

[13] Barry Breen, *Citizen Suits for Natural Resource Damages: Closing a Gap in Federal Environmental Law*, 24 WAKE FOREST L. REV. 851, 853 (1989).

Liability is an underutilized tool to implement environmental objectives in federal environmental law. This may be due in part to the fact that liability is a jurisprudential tool rather than an executive tool. There are two ways in which liability is underused. First, liability exists in few environmental laws. Second, those laws limit who can bring causes of action.

* * *

This limited application of liability may be based in part on a desire to limit the role of the judiciary because the judicial branch is countermajoritarian. Also, the courts may become clogged with litigation, thereby diminishing their ability to hear cases in a timely and judicious manner, undermining the deference upon which they rely for power and diluting the rule of law.

On the other hand, one of the traditional functions of the judicial system is to balance harms among individuals based on precedent and existing and enduring community values. This judicial task can arise either through common law or through statutory causes of action. For example, common-law actions, such as public nuisance, require courts to balance community objectives against individual rights. Assigning liability is a traditional legal function.

* * *

Liability is a tool to address causes, not just symptoms. If traditional notions of causation are extended to include the risk imposed on the community and unknowing individuals from resource depletion, including, for example, loss of species diversity, soil depletion, and atmospheric destruction, the effectiveness of environmental law at meeting the objectives would greatly increase.

* * *

Planning

Planning is the establishment of goals, policies, and procedures to achieve objectives. One of the purposes of planning is to assure opportunity for public participation in resource decisionmaking.

* * *

Planning, like liability, is constrained by preconceived notions of its limits. The capacity of planning as a tool to achieve environmental objectives has yet to be explored.

Resources are extracted from natural systems, manufactured, used as products or released as externalities, and then disposed of in the environment. To date, most planning has been applied to resource extraction on public lands, with some planning for control of externalities. Planning to maximize environmental objectives needs to consider each step of this process, not just the beginning and the end. Resource to recovery planning, which considers the carrying capacity of specific natural systems in terms of extraction as well as assimilation, is necessary to achieve at least the sustainability and perhaps the intergenerational equity objectives.

* * *

Economic Incentives

Unlike liability and planning, economic incentives are becoming a powerful tool, since they are beginning to be enacted into law. There are basically three paradigms within which economic incentives work: (1) a totally free market system, where there are no limits on use of common resources, only charges for use; (2) a cost-benefit system, where the common resources can be utilized only if the costs outweigh the benefits; and (3) a user-charge system, where effluent fees and marketable rights function within a regulatory overlay. Within these three paradigms, economic incentives include taxes, subsidies, marketable rights, effluent fees, emissions trading, pollution insurance, waste deposit and refund programs, and compensatory mitigation banking. Direct congressional appropriations are also a form of economic incentive [as are taxes directed at activities due to their environmental effects].

* * *

Economic incentives provide a mechanism to spur innovation, reduce litigation, reduce administrative costs, provide flexibility, and increase efficiency. Their various manifestations, such as taxes, subsidies, marketable rights, effluent fees, and emissions trading, not only make environmental law more efficient but also promote innovation.

Even the most ardent proponents of economic incentives, however, agree that they are not a panacea and must be used in the context of a command-and-control overlay that sets minimum standards that are implemented through economic mechanisms. An entirely free market system would not maximize environmental objectives because environmental externalities exemplify market failure. In addition, although market incentives maximize efficiency, they do not move toward achievement of all the objectives, such as intergenerational equity or biocentrism.

* * *

Criminal Sanctions

Legal tools evolve to reflect present community values and knowledge. Criminal sanctions are an example of this evolution. The traditional element of *mens rea* . . . is no longer necessary to sustain a criminal conviction for environmental damage; knowing and willful conduct is sufficient. Courts also impute liability from the acts of employees of the corporation, even if the corporation took reasonable steps to prevent the conduct.

* * *

Criminal sanction is the hammer among environmental tools. Since the Department of Justice formed its Environmental Crimes Section in 1982, it has imposed fines of more than $26 million in 430 pleas and convictions. Criminal sanctions for violations of environmental statutes are plentiful.

* * *

Criminal sanctions are effective at maximizing environmental objectives through deterrence. There is no other tool that so explicitly balances achieving community environmental values and preserving individual liberty. The evolution and use of criminal sanctions indicate that achieving environmental objectives is a high social priority. It is curious that other tools, such as liability and planning, which affect liberty less directly than criminal sanctions, are not utilized as fully.

* * *

Information Dissemination

Rather than relying on deterrence like most of the tools, information dissemination relies on both consumer preferences and corporate managers' aversion to shame. It is a subtle but powerful tool to achieve environmental objectives.

The most effective use of information as a tool to achieve environmental objectives is EPA's toxics release inventory (TRI). Title III of the Superfund Amendments and Reauthorization Act of 1986 requires EPA to develop TRI to encourage corporations to voluntarily reduce their toxic emissions.

* * *

Another aspect of information dissemination is public education. Education can include seals of approval and awards. Voluntary certificates of competence and mandatory training are also important types of information and education.

Information dissemination simultaneously maximizes both individual liberty and community environmental objectives. By relying on public opinion and consumer preference to choose environmentally superior products, information dissemination maximizes environmental goals by relying on individual choice. The primary disadvantage of information dissemination, and the reason it is not a panacea, is that present community values do not always reflect enduring choices. Information dissemination also has costs. Importantly, information dissemination alone is probably insufficient to achieve objectives, such as sustainability or intergenerational equity.

* * *

Property Rights

A property right grants the owner legal control of a resource, including the right to exclude others. The bundle of rights that adhere to a property owner change over time, sometimes honoring community values and sometimes honoring individual autonomy. A delicate balancing of common laws, such as takings, nuisance, and the public trust, constantly refines and redefines the elements of property ownership. Earl Murphy observes:

> The determination of what constitutes property is not a closed subject. Relationships and objects in nature continue to pass in and out of the definition of what constitutes property. Similarly the questions of who owns how much title in whatever is redefined as property, and what the titleholder may do in relation to that property, remain open for expansion and direction.[14]

* * *

There are two categories of tools that can be used to limit private property uses. First, land-use planning-through land banking, easements, zoning, planned unit developments, land trusts, and transferable development rights-can limit the uses of private property. Second, common-law remedies for environmental harm-including adverse possession, private nuisance, waste, public and private easements, restrictive covenants, eminent domain, community property, and the public trust doctrine-can limit the uses of private property or the alienation of public property.

States also enforce communal environmental choices through property rights. For example, the New Jersey Environmental Cleanup Responsibility Act requires facilities to submit either a negative declaration or a cleanup plan before closing, selling, or transferring operations. Such state laws inject community environmental choices into the bundle of rights inherent in property ownership-in this case, the right to transfer the property.

* * *

As the definition of the bundle of rights evolves over time, it comes to reflect increased understanding of the importance of preserving natural systems. For example, in early wetlands cases some courts recognize that destruction of wetlands is not a right inherent in the ownership of private property. More recent cases, however, reflect a counterrevolution back to emphasis on private property rights.

* * *

As courts continue to expand and contract private property rights to reflect communal knowledge and understanding, the bundle of rights inherent in private property ownership may some day no longer include the right to irreparably impair natural systems. This evolution of the definition of property rights would be based on the theory that the public owns an interest in the perpetuation of the functioning of natural systems that transcend the property. Property rights are thus one of the most powerful tools in environmental law.

* * *

---

[14] EARL MURPHY, NATURE, BUREAUCRACY, AND THE RULES OF PROPERTY 234 (1977).

Contracts

[Contracts are] the least used tool of environmental law. There are several creative ways that private parties can enter voluntary agreements that seek to achieve environmental objectives. These include "friendly neighbor contracts" and land trust conservation easements. In friendly neighbor contracts, citizen groups agree not to oppose permit applications by corporations if the corporations meet prescribed environmental standards. Some environmental groups are working on publishing standards for such contracts. If friendly neighbor contracts persist, the potential exists to create a shadow government through private actions.

* * *

Contracts . . . allow for individual liberty while providing an inducement to private parties to promote communal choices. Like market incentives, they could be a carrot. It is surprising that they are not more fully utilized in environmental law. Also, like market incentives, they alone cannot achieve all the environmental objectives. For example, it may be impossible to achieve sustainability or intergenerational equity by relying solely on contracts.

* * *

———

Chapter 2 will introduce you to the concepts of risk and uncertainty. Much of the difficulty in regulating toxic substances and hazardous wastes stems from both long latency periods and the probabilistic nature of exposure. The following excerpt introduces the concept of precautionary principle, which underlies regulation in this field.

THE PRECAUTIONARY PREFERENCE: AN AMERICAN PERSPECTIVE ON THE PRECAUTIONARY PRINCIPLE

John S. Applegate
6:2 Human & Ecological Risk Assessment ___ (2000)

I. Introduction

The precautionary principle has by now attained the status of a fixture in international environmental lawmaking. Precautionary (or at least preventive) measures have been authorized by international legal instruments since the 1960s, and numerous important global and regional agreements adopt the precautionary principle as a fundamental basis for environmental regulation (Sands, 1994). Nevertheless, the precautionary principle is new to United States environmental law and environmental policy discussions. Statutes, regulations, and court cases do not mention it by name, and one searches nearly in vain for references to it in environmental law news services before 1997. Even then, the items overwhelmingly concern international or foreign, rather than domestic, environmental law. Despite its non-appearance, the precautionary principle addresses several fundamental issues in American environmental regulation. It espouses a goal of preventing rather than reacting to environmental harm and it raises issues of risk, scientific uncertainty, and cost that are very familiar to Americans.

* * *

II. The Meaning of the Precautionary Principle

Despite its wide acceptance as a foundation of international environmental law, the precise meaning of the precautionary principle remains surprisingly elusive. It has been defined variously over the last two or three decades in international legal instruments and by commentators, and the overall concept admits of varying degrees of environmental protection. Instead of relying on a single definition, therefore, we will work with precautionary elements.

* * *

Elements of the Precautionary Principle

Even if a single definition of the precautionary principle cannot be established, it is possible to derive a set of four interrelated functional elements from the various statements of the principle. The elements have been characterized in a number of ways (Hickey & Walker, 1995; Stewart, 2000; O'Riordan & Cameron, 1994b), but for present purposes it is helpful to isolate four: a *trigger* for regulatory attention; the *timing* of regulatory action in relation to the acquisition and definiteness of the supporting information; the nature of the regulatory *response*; and a suite of regulatory strategies that are often said to flow from the principle. The contents of the elements are set out in Table 1.

Table 1. Elements of the Precautionary Principle	
Trigger	Potential serious or irreversible environmental harm
Timing	Anticipatory action, before causation can be scientifically established
Response	· Total avoidance · Measures to minimize or mitigate harm · Cost-effective regulatory measures · Study alternative with an eye to prevention
Regulatory Strategies	· Bans and phase-outs · Environmental effects assessment · Pollution prevention · Reversed burden of proof · Polluter pays · Generic regulation and regulation of surrogates

Since all regulatory schemes must address these aspects of regulation in one way or another, the elements will help to translate from general statements of the international precautionary principle to specific provisions of American environmental law.

1. Trigger

The application of the precautionary principle is triggered by the identification of a potentially serious or irreversible environmental harm that might be averted by regulating a particular activity or chemical substance. The target of regulation can range from construction activities with large-scale effects on ecosystems, to air or water pollution, to the use of chemicals in pesticides or the manufacture of products that may increase cancer risks to individuals who come into contact with them. The precautionary principle *per se* gives little guidance on the quantum of proof required for a potential harm to be identified or what is serious enough to warrant application of the principle. Some advocates of the precautionary principle would require that the harms be both serious and irreversible, on the theory that taking regulatory action in advance of proof of causation (the next element) is only necessary if the harms are irreversible (Sands, 1994; Attfield, 1994). Others (including UNCED, 1992) would appear to limit the operation of the precautionary principle to situations in which the consequences of an action or substance are so great as to be beyond our capacity to predict with accuracy (Barton, 1998; Weintraub, 1992). Still others would require that there be technological options actually available to minimize the harms or to capture valuable benefits of the new technology (Ashford, 1999; Fullem, 1995). However, virtually all formulations of the principle are general and in the disjunctive, so the scope of concern is quite broad.

2. Timing

Timing refers to the relationship between taking regulatory action and the degree of scientific knowledge concerning the environmental effect of concern. The typical American practice is to take regulatory action only *after* the relevant authority establishes at the very least a cause-and-effect relationship between the harm and the targeted activity. The central feature of the precautionary principle, by contrast, is to encourage regulatory action *before* the causal relationship between the activity and harm has been fully proven (Geiser, 1999; Jordan & O'Riordan, 1999). Like U.S. regulation, its goal is to prevent, not cure (Pearce, 1994). Nevertheless, the precautionary principle differs, as Tait as observed, from even preventive regulation under the U.S. paradigm, because such preventive regulation requires a demonstration of the likely cause-and-effect relationship before preventive action can take place (Tait & Levidow, 19). The precautionary principle, instead, is the lineal descendant of the German *Vorsorgeprinzip*, and the translated ideas of "foresee and forestall" carry a crucial temporal element (Raffensperger & Tickner, 1999b; Boehmer-Christiansen, 1994).

The term that best describes this timing is *anticipatory* (Bodansky, 1991; Raffensperger & Tickner, 1999b; Jordan & O'Riordan, 1999), and the activity or chemical of concern is placed in abeyance pending the development of better data. The precautionary principle does not itself clarify *how* anticipatory the action may be or how much uncertainty may remain about the causal relationship. At some point, surely, one would regard the connection as purely speculative and thus beneath the regulatory horizon. Above that point, a range of options is possible, and the reference to absence of "full scientific certainty" may suggest a relatively substantial threshold for taking action.

3. Response

The greatest variation in versions of the precautionary principle appears in the appropriate regulatory response to an identified hazard. The strongest version of the precautionary principle (adopted by its most enthusiastic advocates and strongest critics, alike) anticipates a decision to abjure entirely the identified action or chemical. Clearly, this would avoid the harm of concern, though it might create or perpetuate others. Less draconian responses are also available, which would provide lead time (phase-outs) or require action to minimize or mitigate the identified harm. Other formulations require "commensurate" (Climate Change Convention, 1992; Montreal Protocol, 1987), "proportionate" (Jordan & O'Riordan, 1999), the "least hazardous alternative" (Lundmark, 1998), or, of course, "cost-effective" measures. The minimalist version of the precautionary principle is that potential hazards be studied and alternatives be developed with an eye toward finding ways to prevent the harm altogether (NUUK Declaration, 1993), an approach that has been described (not disparagingly) as erecting a "speed bump" in technology development (Tickner, 1999). The range from bans and phase-outs to studies of alternatives is enormous and must be accounted for in any overall evaluation of the precautionary principle.

4. Regulatory Strategies

The foregoing elements of the precautionary principle can be expressed in a number of specific legal requirements. These constitute an element of the precautionary principle in the sense that they are the regulatory strategies that implement the principle, and they are frequently described as part of, or at least the natural consequence of, the precautionary principle (Tickner 1999). Indeed, the precautionary principle is often presented as an amalgam of differing and not necessarily very closely related strategies (O'Riordan & Cameron, 1994b).

Bans and phase-outs. Especially with respect to chemical hazards, the regulatory strategy most often associated with the precautionary principle is the complete ban or the phase-out of a substance. Greenpeace, for example, advocates a global ban on chlorine, viewing it as the *radix malorum* of the environment, implicated in many of the most serious and persistent contaminants to which humans and ecosystems are exposed (PCBs, dioxins, furans, organochlorine pesticides, etc.):

> Chemical policies should be based on the precautionary principle: when there is reason to believe a substance or class of substances may cause harm to health or the environment, it should not be used or produced. . . .
>
> With a single programme — a chlorine phase-out — much of the world's most severe toxic pollution could be stopped. . . .

(Greenpeace, 1999)

Bans avoid entirely the harm of concern, and so phasing out chemicals and activities of concern (or not allowing them in the first place) is frequently advocated as a way to implement the precautionary principle (Fuierer, 1995; Montague, 1999; Tickner, 1999; Wahlstrom, 1999).

Environmental effects assessment. The precautionary principle places certain actions and chemicals "on hold" while their environmental effects are investigated. Advocates of the precautionary principle see the gathering of evidence concerning environmental effects to be an essential part of the implementing the precautionary principle (Tickner, 1999). Some make analysis of alternatives — essentially a structured information-gathering process — the centerpiece of the principle (O'Brien, 1999).

Pollution prevention. Pollution prevention is a strategy that nearly everyone agrees is a good way to implement the precautionary principle and a good idea in general. Prevented pollution does not enter the environment and do harm, and the up-front expenditures are often cheaper than later remediation. The precautionary principle and pollution prevention share the temporal characteristic of anticipatory action. The new Canadian Environmental Protection Act, is intended to "move away from treating symptoms to treating the causes of pollution, and to become proactive instead of reactive by invoking the precautionary principle" (BNA, 1997). For this reason, too, several treaties adopt pollution prevention in the same breath as the precautionary principle.

Reversed burden of proof. The temporal and information-gathering aspects of the precautionary principle imply the existence of a period between the first suggestions that a problem exists (the "trigger") and the later development of more definitive evidence. The key to the precautionary principle ("timing") is that during this interim period no action is taken. Put another way, the status quo for the precautionary principle is no-action or no-chemical; whereas, industrialized economies often regard the development and the deployment of new technologies as the status quo. The person seeking to change the status quo typically has the burden of justification. Therefore, if the status quo is no-action, then the developer must justify itself; if it is development, then the proponents of restriction must justify themselves. The interim "holding period" in the precautionary principle gives developers a strong incentive to develop the requisite information to justify the action or chemical. Formal allocation of the burden of proving safety is sometimes regarded as a corollary of the precautionary principle (Baender, 1991; Cranor, 1999; Raffensperger & Tickner, 1999b; Jordan & O'Riordan, 1999; Ozonoff, 1999), and sometimes as an integral part of it (Tickner & Raffensperger, 1999b (app. A); Wahlstrom, 1999; O'Riordan & Cameron, 1994b).

Polluter pays. It is a curiosity of modern environmental discourse that two-p concepts, *e.g.*, precautionary principle, public participation, pollution prevention, and polluter pays, proliferate. The polluter pays principle has its origins in the economics of externalities — that is, efficiency will be improved and resources optimally distributed if actors internalize all of the costs (including environmental harm) of their activities — and so is conceptually distinct from the precautionary principle. However, polluter pays is frequently portrayed as a kind of twin of the precautionary principle, as in the European Union's constitutional arrangements (EU Treaty, 1993; Lundmark, 1998). This is presumably because a polluter-pays regime addresses harms that the precautionary structures are unable to avoid, and because it establishes an incentive to take precautionary action to avoid liability (Tickner, 1999).

Generic and surrogate regulation. Finally, the precautionary principle favors generic regulation of classes of activities or chemicals, instead of a chemical-by-chemical approach. Alternatively, certain single characteristics of a chemical or activity could trigger regulatory action, which avoids the need to study its entire risk profile. In the abstract, the precautionary principle is no more "generic" than any other approach; however, regulatory strategies that facilitate regulation on a broad front with a minimum of up-front information clearly advance the precautionary goal. For example, environmental justice advocates have argued that the disparate impact of chemicals should be measured by exposure alone:

> To do so institutionalizes the precautionary principle that when the effects of exposures are unknown, particularly their chronic, multiple and synergistic effect, we must behave as if we valued human life and health above short-term profit-taking by the permitted polluting activity. (BNA, 1998)

International action is urged for persistent organic pollutants under the rubric of the precautionary principle, because it would prevent additional harm from chemicals whose effects, once released into the environment, are particularly difficult to mitigate (Hague Recommendation, 1989; Durnil, 1999; Tickner, 1999; O'Riordan & Cameron, 1994b).

All of the foregoing strategies have in common the goal of taking regulatory action in advance of harm occurring, despite incomplete knowledge regarding the nature and extent of the harm in specific cases. They deploy information generating techniques, restrictions, anticipatory timing, incentives, and generic regulation to permit further investigation and regulatory action when a potential harm appears. Each of these specific strategies can be found in American environmental law, though, like the other elements of the precautionary principle, usually in a highly qualified form.

III. The Precautionary Principle in Legislative Aspiration

The elements of the precautionary principle may be readily discerned in a wide range of provisions of United States environmental law (Bodansky, 1994). No existing statutes explicitly draws on the precautionary principle, to say nothing of being modeled on it. Rather, they share important elements or characteristics. The focus on serious and irreversible harms, a willingness to regulate under conditions of uncertainty, and the mandate to take action in advance of harm occurring, are all firmly embedded in U.S. regulatory structures. Precaution is clearly one of the principal goals of Congress in drafting and of the Environmental Protection Agency (EPA) in administering environmental legislation. It is reflected, operationally, in six kinds of provisions: planning and alternatives analysis, special regulatory treatment of certain categories of harm, the transition from tort to risk-based regulation, the adoption of margins of safety in standard-setting, the policy of erring on the side of safety in risk management, and the shifting the burden of proof from the public to polluters.

* * *

Margins of Safety

Early environmental legislation frequently instructed EPA to control pollution to levels that provided a "margin of safety" for human health and the environment (CAA; CWA). Borrowed from engineering, margins of safety are designed to account for errors in calculation and unexpected events. It is a precautionary measure in that restrictions are imposed (or, more precisely, a greater level of restriction is imposed) despite the absence of evidence that injuries will occur. For risk regulation, however, the margin of safety idea is generally conceded to be a malapropism — an effort to fit a response to mechanical accidents to probabilistic phenomena — so EPA and the courts have interpreted margin of safety language to permit regulators leeway in a number of distinct ways.

The use of margins of safety that is most true to its engineering origins is a kind of generalized caution or keeping one's distance. Reviewing EPA's regulation of PCBs under the Clean Water Act, the D.C. Circuit said:

> [T]he public and the environment were not to be exposed to anything resembling the maximum risk. Not only was EPA to provide a "margin of safety," but the margin was to be greater than "normal" or "adequate": the margin was to be "ample." "Ample" is defined as "abundant; plentiful; more than adequate."

> Clearly Congress intended that in dealing with toxic pollutants that pose a threat to human health, margins of safety should be generous to ensure protection of human health and aquatic ecosystems to the greatest extent possible. (EDF v. EPA, 1978)

Likewise, the "adequate margin of safety" language in the Clean Air Act was held to permit EPA to make multiple conservative assumptions and to use high-end values at several points in its analysis of the health effects of lead (Lead Industries Association v. EPA, 1979). Later cases have viewed margin of safety language as a general authorization for EPA to use its discretion to reduce exposure levels below the level that the existing data would otherwise seem to indicate (NRDC v. EPA, 1987; EDF v. EPA, 1978; American Trucking Association v. EPA, 1999).

In its regulation of polychlorinated biphenyls (PCBs) under the Clean Water Act, EPA used margins of safety to justify a categorical approach to that family of chemicals. It extrapolated from high-chlorinated PCBs, about which the agency had considerable toxicity data, to low-chlorinated PCBs, about which it had little. It is, of course, entirely possible that variations of the same chemical structure can have different toxic effects (the isomers of dioxin are a case in point); nevertheless, the potential danger persuaded the reviewing court that the Clean Water Act permitted EPA to take action (EDF v. EPA, 1978). This is exactly the structure of the precautionary principle: where initial, but not conclusive evidence, suggests a danger, preventive action can be taken in advance of obtaining more definitive data.

EPA and Congress have also used the margin of safety idea to permit regulatory action where sizable and fundamental uncertainties surrounding the toxicology of cancer and similar diseases precludes a conclusive demonstration of the very existence of a risk. This interpretation of margin of safety is most distant from the engineering analogy, but it is very close to the precautionary principle. "Margin of safety" in section 307(a) of the Clean Water Act permitted EPA to set a low standard for toxic water pollutants even though the evidence of carcinogenicity was too weak to make a specific finding on that point (Hercules, Inc. v. EPA, 1978). An even more striking use of margins of safety was described in the *Vinyl Chloride* case:

> The [Clean Air Act] nowhere defines "ample margin of safety." The Senate Report, however, in discussing a similar requirement in the context of setting ambient air standards under section 109 of the Act, explained the purpose of the "margin of safety" standard as one of affording "a *reasonable* degree of protection ... against hazards which research has not yet identified." (emphasis added). . . . Furthermore, in a discussion of the use of identical language in the [Clean Water Act], this court has recognized that, in discharging the responsibility to assure "an ample margin of safety," the Administrator faces "a difficult task, indeed, a

veritable paradox--calling as it does for knowledge of that which is unknown--[but] ... the term 'margin of safety' is Congress's directive that means be found to carry out the task and to reconcile the paradox." *Environmental Defense Fund v. EPA*, 598 F.2d 62, 81 (D.C. Cir.1978) [the PCBs case, *supra*]. . . . (NRDC v. EPA, 1987)

The phrase "hazards which research has not yet identified" perfectly describes the kind of anticipatory regulation that is at the heart of the precautionary principle.

Erring on the Side of Safety in Risk Management

The fundamental scientific problem in *Reserve Mining*, discussed above, was that toxicological theory and the extrapolation of some animal tests suggested that ingested asbestos could cause cancer, but that there was no direct evidence that it did. Indeed, the only direct studies seemed to show that there was no effect. The court of appeals, however, mindful of the serious dangers of *inhaled* asbestos, did not find this state of the evidence inconsistent with a phase-out of Reserve's tailings:

> The district court decided, and we agree, that the study cannot be deemed conclusive in exonerating the ingestion of fibers in Lake Superior water as a hazard. . . . Thus, while this study crucially bears on the determination of whether it is necessary to close Reserve down immediately, the negative results do not dispose of the broader issue of whether the ingestion of fibers poses *some danger* to public health justifying abatement on less immediate terms. (Reserve Mining Co. v. EPA, 1975)

The court, in other words, was concerned that reports showing no effect were expressing a false negative. In his seminal work on the regulation of toxic substances, Talbot Page explained that protective legislation is naturally more concerned about false negatives than false positives, and so it will tend to distrust negative (no-effect) results and embrace positive ones (Page, 1978). Advocates of the precautionary principle, likewise, emphasize the importance of not relying on negative evidence when the underlying science is complex and uncertain and there is some reason to believe that harm may be caused (Barrett & Raffensperger, 1999).

Regulation in the face of negative evidence is one instance of erring on the side of safety. Another is the use of conservative default values and assumptions in quantitative risk assessment. To account for uncertainty, the standard operating procedure in risk assessment is to adopt values that, if erroneous, would probably over- rather than understate the risk. These uncertainties can occur in each of the four steps of quantitative risk assessment (National Research Council, 1983). In the hazard identification phase — the determination whether a substance is or is not a carcinogen — the default position is that evidence of a carcinogenic effect is favored over evidence showing none. (This is the false negatives issue again.) For dose-response — that is, toxic potency — it is typical in the absence of strong evidence to the contrary to assume that a carcinogen has no "threshold" concentration below which it poses no risk of causing cancer. Risk assessors also assume that one can extrapolate the results of high-dose animal testing to low-dose human exposure, high-quality human data being a rarity. For exposure assessment, the typical unknowns are not so much uncertainty as variability. The standard practice is to choose values that lie at the high end of the spectrum of, for example, exposure or metabolism. It is common for risk assessments to rely upon a hypothetical "maximally exposed individual," whose characteristics are designed to assure that almost no one in the real world would be more exposed. Finally, because uncertainty frequently exists in several areas, conservative assumptions regarding the multiple steps of risk assessment are often combined, resulting in an "upper bound" or "worst case" risk estimate.

In *Lead Industries Association v. EPA*, the court explained the rationale for this approach, which EPA had used in assessing airborne lead:

> For example, the House Report accompanying the Amendments states that one of its purposes is "[t]o emphasize the preventive or *precautionary nature* of the [Clean Air Act], *i.e.*, to assure that regulatory action can effectively prevent harm before it occurs; to emphasize the predominant value of protection of public health[.]" The Administrator notes that protecting the public from harmful effects requires decisions about exactly what these harms are, a task Congress left to his judgment. He notes that the task of making these decisions is complicated by the absence of any clear thresholds above which there are adverse effects and below which there are none. Rather, as scientific knowledge expands and analytical techniques are improved, new information is uncovered which indicates that pollution levels that were once considered harmless are not in fact harmless. Congress, the Administrator argues, was conscious of this problem, and left these decisions to his judgment partly for this reason. In such situations the perspective that is brought to bear on the problem plays a crucial role in determining what decisions are made. Because it realized this, Congress, the Administrator maintains, directed him to *err on the side of caution* in making these judgments. (Lead Industries Association v. EPA, 1979 (emphasis added))

Responding to uncertainty is a core function of the precautionary principle. As the court's statement suggests, the use of conservative values and assumptions in risk assessment is a precautionary response to scientific uncertainty.

Shifting Burdens from the Public to the Polluter

The last category is something of a potpourri of procedural and substantive provisions that require the environmental risk-creator to justify commencing or continuing its actions. In some instances this takes the form of shifting the technical burden of proof; in others it is a matter of incentives to provide information or minimize environmental harm.

The ordinary allocation of the burden of proof in American regulatory law is, as the Supreme Court has been at pains to emphasize (Industrial Union Department, AFL-CIO v. American Petroleum Institute, 1980), on the proponent of the regulation (APA). Since restrictions on activities and chemicals are proposed by a regulatory agency, either before or after an activity has begun or a chemical is being used, the burden of proof ordinarily lies with the agency. A licensing system, however, requires the proponent of an activity or product to demonstrate the safety of a product or activity *in advance*. It places the applicant in the position of proposing to do or use something and hence relocates the burden of proof to the would-be actor.[15] Licensing is rare in American environmental law, but it is the distinguishing feature of regulation of pesticides under the Federal Insecticide, Fungicide, and Rodenticide Act (FIFRA). In upholding EPA's regulation of the pesticides heptachlor and chlordane, the D.C. Circuit stated, "This court has repeatedly held that the 1964 amendments to FIFRA were specifically intended to shift the burden of proof from [EPA] to the registrant (EDF v. EPA, 1976). The purpose of the shift was two-fold: to place on hold pesticides whose safety was doubted by EPA, and to create an incentive for the producers and users of pesticides to provide good safety data.

In the 1970s, the D.C. Circuit made particularly aggressive use of the FIFRA burden of proof. For existing pesticides, the usual process (called a cancellation proceeding) for imposing restrictions requires EPA to make an initial determination that a particular pesticide is not reasonably safe for a particular use. This determination triggers a hearing on the relative risks and benefits of the pesticide. The court ruled that during the period between the finding of a potential hazard and the hearing, EPA had the burden of justifying a decision *not* to restrict (suspend the registration of) the pesticide.

> Once risk is shown, the responsibility to demonstrate that the benefits outweigh the risks is upon the proponents of continued registration. Conversely, the statute places a "heavy burden" of explanation on an Administrator who decides to permit the

---

[15]This is to be distinguished from permit systems under, for example, the air and water statutes. While the applicant for a permit may have the burden of demonstrating ability to comply with existing rules and regulations, the agency was the proponent of the rules and regulations themselves. Since scientific complexity and uncertainty are far more pronounced at the rulemaking stage, a permit system does not effectively shift the burden of proof.

continued use of a chemical known to produce cancer in experimental animals. (EDF v. EPA, 1976)

This exactly parallels the timing feature of the precautionary principle. Restrictive action is taken *during* the interim period between initial information indicating a potential hazard and the development of definitive information.

California's Proposition 65 takes the same approach to all chemicals "known by the state of California to cause cancer." It forbids discharges into drinking water sources and requires that warnings be provided *unless* the regulated entity "clearly shows by scientifically valid testing according to generally accepted principles" that "the exposure poses no significant risk" (Proposition 65). Thus, an initial finding of carcinogenicity places the burden of proving reasonable safety on the industry. Moreover, it imposes a moratorium on use or releases during the interim period between identification of the hazard and resolution of the safety *vel non* of the chemical. It thus gives the industry not only the burden of proof, but also an incentive to develop toxicity information (Roe & Pease, 1998).

Congress has declined to adopt such a sweeping reversal of the usual burden of proof in most environmental regulation. However, at the height of its frustration with the Reagan-Gorsuch EPA in 1984, it passed the Hazardous and Solid Waste Amendments (HWSA) to the Resource Conservation and Recovery Act (RCRA). RCRA is the main federal statute dealing with the land disposal of solid and hazardous waste. HWSA directed EPA to regulate specified wastes by specified dates. Determined that the HSWA deadlines would not go the way of previous ones, Congress established a set of "hammers" to force agency action. If EPA failed to establish the required waste disposal standards by the stated dates, then far more stringent standards (for instance, an outright ban on land disposal) would automatically be applied (RCRA). Like Proposition 65, this gave the regulated industry an incentive to develop information to speed rather than delay the promulgation of waste disposal rules; if adequate data are not produced, strict protective action is taken.

IV. Precaution in Legislation: Compromise and Competition

* * *

Explicit Legislative Compromise: Unreasonable Risk

The four major statutes whose principal concerns are toxic substances and hazardous wastes — the Federal Insecticide, Fungicide, and Rodenticide Act (FIFRA), the Toxic Substances Control Act (TSCA), the Resource Conservation and Recovery Amendments (RCRA) to the Solid Waste Disposal Act, and the Comprehensive Environmental Response, Compensation, and Liability Act (CERCLA, or Superfund) — all deploy a similar substantive standard for regulatory action, which can generically be called the "unreasonable risk" standard (Applegate, 1991). It is anything but blindly precautionary. The unreasonable risk standard exhibits four essential characteristics: regulation of risk of harm instead of actually realized harm; a quantitatively undefined regulatory goal of a greater-than-zero risk; facilitation and incorporation of cost-risk-benefit balancing; and implementation of this balancing through ad hoc or case-by-case determinations. The first of these is precautionary in nature, but (as the reader has no doubt come to expect) the remaining three characteristics substantially compromise the preventive effect. The unreasonable risk standard neither expects the complete avoidance of harm, nor does it limit the consideration of technology, feasibility, cost, and pretty much any other relevant information. Unreasonable risk does not require that a regulation be cost-*justified*, that is, that its calculated benefits outweigh its calculated costs, but it certainly invites this comparison and decisions based thereon. Tickner describes unreasonable risk this way:

> Current decision-making approaches ask questions such as: "How safe is safe"; "What level of risk is acceptable"; and "How much contamination can a human (usually a healthy adult male) or ecosystem assimilate without showing any obvious adverse effects?" The Precautionary Principle asks a different set of questions such as "How much contamination can be avoided while still maintaining necessary values?"; "What are the alternatives to this activity that achieve a desired goal (a service, product, etc.)?"; and "Do we need this activity in the first place?" (Tickner, 1999)

EPA has expressed a distinct preference for the unreasonable risk kind of standard, because it permits the agency to consider health and environmental effects together with cost, technological feasibility, and other relevant factors, in an "integrated" fashion. EPA's CERCLA regulations (the National Contingency Plan), for example, require EPA to consider nine criteria in selecting clean-up remedies (NCP). The basic requirements are a mix of unreasonable risk[16] and standards drawn from other statutes. Only two of the nine (long-term effectiveness and permanence, and preference for treatment) drive toward strictly precautionary remedies, in the sense that they would entirely forstall the risks from the site from recurring. But these criteria are balanced against others, and the others include cost, short-term risks, and technical and administrative implementability, all of which may cut against fully preventive remedies. This is not necessarily a bad thing, of course. Short-term risks, for example, may be so high that the most preventive remedy is unjustified (Applegate & Wesloh, 1998). But it should be quite apparent that the precautionary approach is significantly moderated by the

---

[16]"Protective of human health and the environment" becomes a risk range from 1/10,000 to 1/1,000,000 (NCP).

unconstrained balancing of factors in CERCLA and in the unreasonable risk standard generally.

* * *

V. Conclusion

The precautionary principle — or, more properly, elements of the precautionary principle — is firmly entrenched in American environmental law, but it appears in a diluted or compromised form. It is probably not even accurate to say that the precautionary principle *per se* is at work in U.S. environmental law. It does not represent the terms in which the law was developed, and it is at most one of several policies that environmental law pursues. Precaution, in U.S. law, is a preference, and not a principle.

In the final analysis, the most important contribution of the new emphasis on the precautionary principle may be to remind us of the original reasons for moving from a tort-based system for environmental harm to a regulatory system: inadequate information and the desire to prevent rather than merely compensate injury. In this sense, the precautionary principle is at the heart of American environmental law. However, the difficulty of the task of preventing injury under conditions of uncertainty (if only to avoid trivial problems and perverse solutions), and the countervailing demands of development and economic efficiency, render American law more ambivalent, more complex, and more subject to contending forces than adherence to a principle would suggest. All in all, it may be most accurate to say that U.S. environmental law reflects the *debate* over the uncertainty, timing, response, and regulatory strategy elements of the precautionary principle, rather than any firm adoption or rejection of the principle itself.

—

The nature of the problem, the objectives of regulation, and the tools for regulating toxic substances and hazardous wastes are the principal ingredients of the regulatory system we will now explore. In seeking to control these ingredients, the law must take account of the physical facts of toxic substances and their effect on humans and the environment; the economic and social system that generates, uses and disposes of them; the political response to the benefits and dangers of toxics; and the components of the legal system itself that facilitate and in some ways limit the management of toxic substances. Each element presents unknowns, choices, and contradictions. In short, the regulation of toxic substances and hazardous wastes is a work in progress. It changes as scientific knowledge changes, as social concerns and political goals change and as we find better ways to achieve those goals. This casebook aims to provide you with the tools you will need to work effectively with the existing law of toxic substances and-perhaps more importantly-to shape what it will become.

Chapter 2

Toxicology and Risk Assessment

The environmental law of toxic substances and hazardous wastes can be thought of as a branch of public health law. Its principal concern, from this point of view, is the protection of humans from various threats to their health, specifically from toxic materials in the ambient environment. Toxic substances have effects on the natural environment, too, and, thanks to *Silent Spring*, these effects may be said to have initiated the present level of concern over toxics. Nevertheless, human health has become the primary measure of environmental hazard and of the regulatory response. In fact, as we will see, toxics regulation focuses to a remarkable (and probably unjustifiable) extent on one particular effect-cancer-in one particular species-humans.

We will explore some of the consequences of this way of thinking in later chapters, but one important consequence is that environmental regulation must be based on the identification of substances that affect human health, the specific adverse effects that they cause, and the quantities in which they have such effects. This describes, in a nutshell, the science of toxicology, and toxicology and toxicologists play a central role in the regulation of toxic substances and hazardous wastes.

The translation of toxicology into measure that can in turn become the basis for regulatory action is the province of an analytical technique known as quantitative risk assessment. Risk assessment combines toxicity information (the identification of hazards and their potency) with exposure data, and it characterizes the targets of the hazard and the severity of the hazard. It is important from the outset to recognize some of the fundamental assumptions inherent in this procedure.

- First, it assumes that environmental health hazards can adequately be characterized as "risks," specifically risks to human health. Implicit in this assumption is the view that some degree of risk is unavoidable and/or acceptable. Since locating that point of acceptability is the object of the regulatory schemes we will study, the reliance on risk is of fundamental importance.
- Second, it assumes that these risks are capable, at least in principle, of being quantified, that is, being expressed in numerical terms. Given the many uncertainties in the toxicology of environmental contaminants, this poses a serious practical difficulty for environmental regulation.
- Third, the idea of quantitative risk assessment as an outgrowth of toxicology assumes that the assessment of environmental hazards is conceptually distinguishable from the way that they are regulated. This basic distinction, between the description of the problem and the response to the problem, is embodied in the formal division between risk *assessment* and risk *management*. The distinction has been the subject of much debate, however, for reasons that we will explore. We will examine this the distinction in terms of the proper role of risk assessment in environmental decisionmaking.

For environmental lawyers, the last is the key issue. Throughout this chapter (and, indeed, this book) we must consider how and to what extent scientific and technical information should determine environmental law and policy.

A. The Science of Toxic Substances

"All substances are poisons; there is none which is not a poison. The right dose differentiates a poison and a remedy," observed the sixteenth-century Swiss physician Paracelsus, and so was born the science of toxicology. Toxicology is the study of the adverse effects of external substances (of whatever origin) on humans and other living things. Paracelsus' dictum-often abbreviated as "the dose makes the poison"-points up the central problem of studying poisons: they have different effects, including beneficial effects, in different amounts and in different species. Discovering or predicting the effects of a substance on people or animals is an exceptionally complex enterprise, often fraught with uncertainties. Small wonder, then, that the law of toxic substances and hazardous wastes is complicated and often conceptually difficult. It reflects the uncertainty in our understanding of the nature and severity of toxic effects, which in turn results from an incomplete understanding of the mechanism of toxic injury.

Toxicologists distinguish among three types of harmful effects of chemicals: acute (or fast), chronic (slow), and carcinogenic (cancer-causing). The same chemical can have all three effects, depending, as Paracelsus said, on the dose. At relatively high doses, arsenic has its famous lethal effect; at lower doses (*i.e.*, not immediately fatal doses) it affects eyesight, the peripheral nervous system, and the vascular system; and at lower doses still, where the exposure is not even noticed, it can cause cancer. Really potent toxics have effects at much lower doses than slightly toxic or effectively nontoxic substances.[1] In fact, the lethal, chronic, and carcinogenic differences among chemicals can vary by orders of magnitude.[2] Alpha radiation is twenty times more biologically potent than x-radiation; the "tetra" isomer of the dioxin molecule is many times more potent than the "hexa" isomer.[3]

1. Fast and Slow Poisons

The acute effects of a chemical substance are the ones we most commonly associate with poisons.[4] Because they appear quickly after exposure, it is usually easy to identify both the causative substance and the physical effect-illness, death, or other dysfunction (in the case of alcohol, intoxication means drunkenness). Most toxicological studies of acute effects concentrate on the potency of the substance in question. This is typically measured as the single dose level that is lethal to 50 percent of the animals being tested (LD50). The lower the dose, the higher the potency of the chemical.

Acute toxicity is important in itself for many chemicals. While environmental law (as opposed to, say, occupational health or consumer protection law) tends to concentrate on other effects, EPA has begun an extensive program under the Clean Air Act for setting acute levels of exposure to toxic air pollutants.[5] Significantly, even though LD50 data are

---

[1] Since the dose makes the poison, even extremely benign substances (say, table sugar) could in theory be administered in lethal doses to humans. It is very unlikely to happen; however, lethal doses of sugar have been administered to rats.

[2] An order of magnitude means a multiple of ten. It represents a proportionally large difference, but not necessarily an absolutely large one. One order of magnitude separates both 0.01 and 0.001 grams and 1,000,000 and 100,000 grams, yet the former difference is 9 milligrams and the latter is 900 kilograms.

[3] Excellent introductions to toxicology for the non-specialist include DADE W. MOELLER, ENVIRONMENTAL Health (rev. ed. 1997); JOSEPH V. RODRICKS, CALCULATED RISKS: UNDERSTANDING THE TOXICITY AND HUMAN HEALTH RISKS OF CHEMICALS IN OUR ENVIRONMENT (1992); and BERNARD D. GOLDSTEIN & MARY SUE HENIFIN, REFERENCE GUIDE TO TOXICOLOGY, IN FEDERAL JUDICIAL CENTER, REFERENCE MANUAL ON SCIENTIFIC EVIDENCE (1994). JOHN HARTE *ET AL.*, TOXICS A TO Z: A GUIDE TO EVERYDAY POLLUTION HAZARDS (1991), is a handy introduction to toxicological concepts and a dictionary of the health effects of specific substances and activities.

[4] The discussion of acute toxicity is based on Rodricks, *supra*, at 62-63. Rodricks' chapter on acute toxicity is an excellent source of further information on this topic.

[5] 42 U.S.C. § 7412 (r). In this context (as with acute toxicity generally) note that death is not the only acute effect of concern. EPA has identified three levels of non-lethal acute effects-irritation and detection of the presence of the chemical ("notable discomfort"); "irreversible or other serious, long-lasting effects or impaired ability to escape"; and "life-threatening effects or death"-within exposure periods of 30 minutes, 1 hour, 4 hours, and 8 hours. Brief, low concentration exposures to chlorine, for example, can produce the symptoms of an asthma attack. EPA, National Advisory Committee for Acute Exposure Guideline Levels for Hazardous Substances, 62 Fed. Reg. 58840, 58841, 58843-44 (1997). More familiar are the

relatively easy to obtain and the most commonly available chemical toxicity data, EPA expects that it will take ten years to identify acute toxicity levels of hazardous air pollutants. What does that suggest about the availability of toxicity data for other effects?

Acute toxicity is more important for our purposes for two reasons. First, it introduces us to the idea of risk. The LD50 test does not require that all of the tested animals die, only half of them. Thus, at the LD50 dose, any individual animal is exposed to a 50 percent *risk* of death, not a certainty. Given individual variation, this is the most that we can accurately say about acute toxicity, and the same will be true of carcinogenesis. Second, the non-lethal effects on test animals provide important clues to longer-term effects. They may also suggest synergistic or antagonistic effects between different chemicals. All of this information will be of great value as we turn to the less obvious effects of toxic substances.

The technical difference between acute and chronic toxicity is the duration of exposure before effects are noted. In practical terms, there are also differences in type of effect. Thus, acute toxicity is usually associated with frank illness (including, but not limited to, death), whereas chronic toxicity alters some aspect of an organism's metabolism or bodily system, which may go unnoticed because it falls short of frank illness. Such effects are of obvious regulatory interest, however, because they may be precursors or early warning signs of the serious illnesses and effects with which we are concerned. The following case discusses the chronic effects of lead. Pay particular attention to the many steps required to move from toxicologic information to regulatory response.

LEAD INDUSTRIES ASSOCIATION, INC. V. EPA

647 F.2d 1130 (D.C. Cir. 1979), *cert. denied*, 449 U.S. 1042 (1980)

J. SKELLY WRIGHT, Chief Judge:

* * *

I. BACKGROUND

Man's ability to alter his environment to achieve perceived goals has undoubtedly made an enormous contribution to his economic and social well-being. This undertaking is not, however, without attendant costs. One of these costs is the toll that these alterations may exact on the environment itself and, in turn, the dangers that this may pose for the public health and welfare. Unfortunately, man's ability to alter the environment often far outstrips his ability to foresee with any degree of certainty what untoward effects these changes may bring. The issues presented by these cases illustrate this sad fact.

---

so-called Draize tests that the Food and Drug Administration requires to be conducted on animals to measure the skin and eye irritation effects of drugs and cosmetics.

Lead's environmental significance is a consequence of both its abundance and its utility. The relative abundance of lead in the earth's crust makes it unique among the toxic heavy metals. And centuries of mining and smelting, and the use of lead in a variety of human activities, have increased the natural background concentration of lead in the environment. But it is only since the industrial age and the use of lead as a gasoline additive that lead has become pervasive. Today lead is ubiquitous. It is found in almost every medium with which we come into contact food, water, air, soil, dust, and paint, each of which represents a potential pathway for human lead exposure through ingestion or inhalation. The widespread presence of this toxic metal in the environment poses a significant health risk. Lead is a poison which has no known beneficial function in the body, but when present in the body in sufficient concentrations lead attacks the blood, kidneys, and central nervous and other systems and can cause anemia, kidney damage, severe brain damage, and death.

* * *

III. THE LEAD STANDARDS RULEMAKING PROCEEDINGS

As required by statute, EPA's first step toward promulgating air quality standards for lead was to prepare a criteria document. * * *

The Criteria Document identified a variety of effects of lead exposure on the blood-forming system. We will discuss only the effects that played an important role in the Administrator's analysis. Anemia, which can be caused by lead-induced deformation and destruction of erythrocytes (red blood cells) and decreased hemoglobin synthesis,[6] is often the earliest clinical manifestation of lead intoxication. Symptoms of anemia include pallor of the skin, shortness of breath, palpitations of the heart, and fatigability. The Criteria Document concluded, after a review of various studies, that in "children, a threshold level for anemia is about 40 μg Pb/dl, whereas the corresponding value for adults is about 50 μg Pb/dl." (The concentration of lead in the blood is measured in micrograms of lead per deciliter of blood μg Pb/dl.)

The Criteria Document also examined other more subtle effects on the blood-forming system, associated with lower levels of lead exposure. The most pertinent of these "subclinical"[7] effects for purposes of these cases is lead-related elevation of erythrocyte protoporphyrin (EP elevation). According to the Criteria Document, this phenomenon must, for a number of

---

[6] Hemoglobin is the protein which transports life-sustaining oxygen from the respiratory system to all cells in the body. It consists of a combination of heme and globin, and lead interferes with hemoglobin synthesis by inhibiting synthesis of the globin moiety and affecting several steps in synthesis of the heme molecule.

[7] According to the Criteria Document, "subclinical" effects "are disruptions in function, which may be demonstrated by special testing but not by the classic techniques of physical examination; using the term 'subclinical' in no way implies that those effects are without consequences to human health." Stedman's Medical Dictionary defines "subclinical" as "(d)enoting a period prior to the appearance of manifest symptoms in the evolution of a disease."

reasons, be regarded as an indication of an impairment of human health. First, EP elevation indicates an impairment in the functioning of the mitochondria, the subcellular units which play a crucial role in the production of energy in the body, and in cellular respiration. Second, it indicates that lead exposure has begun to affect one of the basic biological functions of the body production of heme within the red blood cells. Heme is critical to transporting oxygen to every cell in the body. Third, EP elevation may indicate that any reserve capacity there may be in the heme synthesis system has been reduced. Finally, the Criteria Document noted that lead's interference with the process of heme synthesis in the blood may suggest that lead interferes with production of heme proteins in other organ systems, particularly the renal and neurological systems. The Criteria Document reported that the threshold for EP elevation in children and women is at blood lead levels of 15-20 μg Pb/dl, and 25-30 μg Pb/dl in adult males. While suggesting that some of the initial hematological effects of lead exposure may constitute relatively mild effects at low blood lead levels, the Criteria Document concluded that "they nevertheless signal the onset of steadily intensifying adverse effects as blood lead elevations increase. Eventually, (these) * * * effects reach such magnitude that they are of clear cut medical significance as indicators of undue lead exposure." The Criteria Document did not identify a particular blood lead level at which regulatory response was appropriate, but it did note with approval the 1975 guidelines issued by the Center For Disease Control, which use elevated EP at blood lead levels of 30 μg Pb/dl as the cut-off point in screening children for lead poisoning.

The Criteria Document also examined the effects of lead exposure on the central nervous system. Among the most deleterious effects of lead poisoning are those associated with severe central nervous system damage at high exposure levels. The Criteria Document noted that neurological and behavioral deficits have long been known to be among the more serious effects of lead exposure, but it pointed out that there is disagreement about whether these effects are reversible, and about what exposure levels are necessary to produce specific deleterious effects. Much of the impetus for the debate on these questions has been provided by the continual emergence of new information suggesting that lead exposure levels previously thought to be harmless actually cause significant neurological damage. The more severe neurological effects of high level lead exposure are the clinical syndrome of lead encephalopathy. Early symptoms include dullness, restlessness, irritability, headaches, muscular tremor, hallucinations, and loss of memory. These symptoms rapidly progress (sometimes within 48 hours) to delirium, mania, convulsions, paralysis, coma, and death. The Criteria Document expressed particular concern that the onset of these serious symptoms can be quite abrupt, even in the absence of prior overt or clinical symptoms of disease. After a review of various studies, the Criteria Document concluded that the blood lead threshold for these neurological effects of high level exposure is 80-100 μg Pg/dl in children, and 100-200 μg Pb/dl in adults.

The Criteria Document also went on to consider the evidence on whether lower level lead exposures can affect the central nervous system, particularly in children. It acknowledged that the issue is unsettled and somewhat controversial, but it was able to conclude, after a careful review of various studies on the subject,[8] that "a rather consistent pattern of impaired neural and cognitive functions appears to be associated with blood lead levels below those producing the overt symptomatology of lead encephalopathy." The Criteria Document reported that "(t)he blood lead levels at which neurobehavioral deficits occur in otherwise asymptomatic children appear to start at a range of 50 to 60 μg/dl, although some evidence tentatively suggests that such effects may occur at slightly lower levels for some children."

In addition to examining the health effects of lead exposure, the Criteria Document also discussed other issues critical to the task of setting air quality standards for lead. One of these issues is the relationship between air lead exposure and blood lead levels a relationship commonly referred to as the air lead/blood lead ratio. The Criteria Document acknowledged that derivation of a functional relationship between air lead exposure and blood lead levels is made difficult by the fact that the relationship is not a linear one; rather, the ratio tends to increase as air lead levels are reduced. The Document was nevertheless able to conclude, after a detailed examination of the relevant studies, that air lead/blood lead ratios fall within a range of 1:1 to 1:2 (μg Pb/m^3 air): (μg Pb/dl blood) at the levels of lead exposure generally encountered by the population, *i.e.*, blood lead levels increase by between 1 and 2 μg Pb/dl of blood for every 1 μg Pb/m^3 of air. (Air lead content is measured in micrograms of lead per cubic meter of air μg Pb/m^3.) The Criteria Document reported that the studies indicate that the ratio for children is at the upper end of this range or even slightly above it.

Finally, the Criteria Document also examined the distribution of blood lead levels throughout the population, concluding that there is a significant variability in individual blood lead responses to any particular level of air lead exposure. It further found that this variability is consistent and predictable, and that the application of established statistical techniques to the distribution of individual blood lead levels would make it possible to predict what proportion of the population would be above or below any particular blood lead level at a given level of air lead exposure. The Criteria Document looked into the question whether any sub-groups within the population are particularly vulnerable to the effects of lead exposure. It concluded that preschool-age children and pregnant women are particularly sensitive to lead exposure, the latter mainly because of the risk to the unborn child.

---

[8] Some of these studies suggested that low level lead exposure may cause central nervous system deficits, resulting in impaired concept formation and altered behavioral profiles, may interfere with the normal intellectual development of lead-exposed children, and may cause subtle neurological damage.

B. The Proposed Standards

* * * In the preamble to the proposed standards the Administrator explained the analysis EPA had employed in setting the standards.

The Administrator first pointed out that a number of factors complicate the task of setting air quality standards which will protect the population from the adverse health effects of lead exposure. First, some sub-groups within the population have a greater potential for, or are more susceptible to the effects of, lead exposure. Second, there are a variety of adverse health effects associated with various levels of lead exposure. Third, the variability of individual responses to lead exposure, even within particular sub-groups of the population, would produce a range of blood lead levels at any given air lead level. Fourth, airborne lead is only one of a number of sources of lead exposure and the relative contribution from each source is difficult to quantify. Finally, the relationship between air lead exposure and blood lead levels is a complex one.

In response to the first problem the Administrator began by noting that protection of the most sensitive groups within the population had to be a major consideration in determining the level at which the air quality standards should be set. And he determined that children between the ages of 1 and 5 years are most sensitive to the effects of lead exposure both because the hematologic and neurologic effects associated with lead exposure occur in children at lower threshold levels than in adults, and because the habit of placing hands and other objects in the mouth subjects them to a greater risk of exposure. Next, the Administrator examined the various health effects of lead exposure and proposed that EP elevation should be considered the first adverse health effect of lead exposure because it indicates an impairment of cellular functions, and should be the pivotal health effect on which the lead standards are based. Accordingly, he proposed that the air lead standards be designed to prevent the occurrence of EP elevation in children. In order to accomplish this, and to address the problem of variable responses to lead exposure, the Administrator selected 15 μg Pb/dl, the lowest reported threshold blood lead level for EP elevation in children, as the target mean population blood lead level.[9] He reasoned that setting the target mean population blood lead level at the lowest reported threshold blood lead level for EP elevation would ensure that most of the target population would be kept below blood lead levels at which adverse health effects occur. The Administrator also discussed the alternative approaches of basing the standard on more severe effects such as anemia, or attempting to decide the actual level

---

[9] The target mean population blood lead level is the blood lead level that will ensure that the great majority of the target population is protected from the adverse health effects of lead. Given the variability in individual blood lead responses to lead exposure, a population with a mean blood lead level of 15 μg Pb/dl will have individuals with blood lead levels higher and lower than 15 μg Pb/dl, but since 15 μg Pb/dl is the lowest blood lead level at which EP elevation has been detected, most children will be kept below blood lead levels at which adverse health effects occur.

of EP elevation which represents an adverse effect on health, and then making an adjustment to allow a margin of safety. He specifically invited comments on these alternative approaches. Finally, the Administrator outlined another approach to calculating the target mean population blood lead level involving the use of statistical techniques discussed in the Criteria Document.[10]

Having selected a target mean population blood lead level, the Administrator's next step was to allow for the multiplicity of sources of lead exposure. He thus had to estimate the amount of blood lead that should be attributed to non-air sources. The Administrator admitted that any amount he selected could be no more than a theoretical national average, and on the basis of the evidence available he proposed that the lead standards should be based on the general assumption that 12 μg Pb/dl of blood lead should be attributed to non-air sources. Given the target mean population blood lead level of 15 – μg Pb/dl and the assumed contribution from non-air sources of 12 μg Pb/dl, the maximum allowable contribution from ambient air is 3 μg Pb/dl. The final step in his analysis was to determine what air lead level would prevent the ambient air contribution to blood lead levels from exceeding 3 μg Pb/dl. This step required determining the relationship between air lead exposure and blood lead levels, *i.e.*, the air lead/blood lead ratio. On the basis of the information in the Criteria Document, the Administrator selected a ratio of 1:2 as appropriate for calculating the effect of air lead exposure on blood lead levels in children.

Thereafter, calculation of the air quality standard was a mathematical exercise * * *.

V. STATUTORY AUTHORITY

* * *

[The argument of the Lead Industries Association (LIA)] appears to touch on two issues. The first concerns the type of health effects on which the Administrator may base air quality standards, *i.e.*, the point at which the Administrator's regulatory authority may be exercised. This issue, as LIA suggests, does concern the limits that the Act, and its legislative history, may place on the Administrator's authority. The second issue appears to be more in the nature of an evidentiary question: whether or not the evidence in the record substantiates the Administrator's claim that the health effects on which the standards were based do in fact satisfy the requirements of the Act. Although these two issues are closely related, they are conceptually distinct, and they are best examined separately.

---

[10] This alternative approach would use lognormal statistical procedures to determine what mean population blood lead levels would keep a specified percentage of the population below a blood lead level chosen to represent the safe blood lead level for the average individual. The Administrator pointed out that he had misgivings about this approach because it might overestimate the degree to which the mean population level should be below the threshold blood lead level, particularly since 15 μg Pb/dl is the lowest reported threshold blood level for EP elevation.

Section 109(b) [of the Clean Air Act, 42 U.S.C. § 7409,] does not specify precisely what Congress had in mind when it directed the Administrator to prescribe air quality standards that are "requisite to protect the public health." The legislative history of the Act does, however, provide some guidance. The Senate Report explains that the goal of the air quality standards must be to ensure that the public is protected from "adverse health effects." And the report is particularly careful to note that especially sensitive persons such as asthmatics and emphysematics are included within the group that must be protected. It is on the interpretation of the phrase "adverse health effects" that the disagreement between LIA and EPA about the limits of the Administrator's statutory authority appears to be based. LIA argues that the legislative history of the Act indicates that Congress only intended to protect the public against effects which are known to be *clearly harmful* to health, maintaining that this limitation on the Administrator's statutory authority is necessary to ensure that the standards are not set at a level which is more stringent than Congress contemplated. The Administrator, on the other hand, agrees that primary air quality standards must be based on protecting the public from "adverse health effects," but argues that the meaning LIA assigns to that phrase is too limited. In particular, the Administrator contends that LIA's interpretation is inconsistent with the precautionary nature of the statute, and will frustrate Congress' intent in requiring promulgation of air quality standards.

The Administrator begins by pointing out that the Act's stated goal is "to protect and enhance the quality of the Nation's air resources so as to promote the public health and welfare and the productive capacity of its population[.]" Section 101(b)(1), 42 U.S.C. § 7401(b)(1). This goal was reaffirmed in the 1977 Amendments. For example, the House Report accompanying the Amendments states that one of its purposes is "[t]o emphasize the preventive or precautionary nature of the act, *i.e.*, to assure that regulatory action can effectively prevent harm before it occurs; to emphasize the predominant value of protection of public health[.]" The Administrator notes that protecting the public from harmful effects requires decisions about exactly what these harms are, a task Congress left to his judgment. He notes that the task of making these decisions is complicated by the absence of any clear thresholds above which there are adverse effects and below which there are none. Rather, as scientific knowledge expands and analytical techniques are improved, new information is uncovered which indicates that pollution levels that were once considered harmless are not in fact harmless. Congress, the Administrator argues, was conscious of this problem, and left these decisions to his judgment partly for this reason. In such situations the perspective that is brought to bear on the problem plays a crucial role in determining what decisions are made. Because it realized this, Congress, the Administrator maintains, directed him to err on the side of caution in making these judgments. First, Congress made it abundantly clear that considerations of economic or technological feasibility are to be subordinated to the goal of protecting the public health by prohibiting any consideration of such factors. Second, it specified that the air quality standards must also protect individuals who are particularly sensitive to the effects of pollution. Third, it required that the standards be set at a level at which there is "an absence of adverse effect" on these sensitive individuals. Finally, it specifically directed the Administrator to allow an adequate margin of safety in setting primary air quality standards in order to provide some protection against effects that research has not yet uncovered. The Administrator contends that these indicia of congressional intent, the precautionary nature of the statutory mandate to protect the public health, the broad discretion Congress gave him to decide what effects to protect against, and the uncertainty that must be part of any attempt to determine the health effects of air pollution, are all extremely difficult to reconcile with LIA's suggestion that he can only set standards which are designed to protect against effects which are *known to be clearly harmful to health*.

We agree that LIA's interpretation of the statute is at odds with Congress' directives to the Administrator. * * * It may be that it reflects LIA's view that the Administrator must show that there is a "medical consensus that [the effects on which the standards were based] are harmful * * *." If so, LIA is seriously mistaken. This court has previously noted that some uncertainty about the health effects of air pollution is inevitable. And we pointed out that "[a]waiting certainty will often allow for only reactive, not preventive regulat[ory action]." *Ethyl Corp. v. EPA, supra*, 541 F.2d [1, 25 (D.C. Cir.), *cert. denied*, 426 U.S. 941 (1976)]. Congress apparently shares this view; it specifically directed the Administrator to allow an adequate margin of safety to protect against effects which have not yet been uncovered by research and effects whose medical significance is a matter of disagreement. This court has previously acknowledged the role of the margin of safety requirement. In *Environmental Defense Fund v. EPA*, 598 F.2d 62, 81 (D.C.Cir.1978), we pointed out that "[i]f administrative responsibility to protect against unknown dangers presents a difficult task, indeed, a veritable paradox calling as it does for knowledge of that which is unknown then, the term 'margin of safety' is Congress's directive that means be found to carry out the task and to reconcile the paradox." Moreover, it is significant that Congress has recently acknowledged that more often than not the "margins of safety" that are incorporated into air quality standards turn out to be very modest or nonexistent, as new information reveals adverse health effects at pollution levels once thought to be harmless. Congress' directive to the Administrator to allow an "adequate margin of safety" alone plainly refutes any suggestion that the Administrator is only authorized to set primary air quality standards which are designed to protect against health effects that are known to be clearly harmful.

Furthermore, we agree with the Administrator that requiring EPA to wait until it can conclusively demonstrate that a particular effect is adverse to health before it acts is inconsistent with both the Act's precautionary and preventive orientation and the nature of the Administrator's statutory responsibilities. Congress provided that the Administrator is to use his judgment in setting air quality standards precisely to permit him to act in the face of uncertainty. And as we read the statutory provisions and the legislative history, Congress directed the Administrator to err on the side of caution in making the necessary decisions. We see no reason why this court should put a gloss on Congress' scheme by requiring the Administrator to show that there is a medical consensus that the effects on which the lead standards were based are *"clearly harmful to health."* All that is required by the statutory scheme is evidence in the record which substantiates his conclusions about the health effects on which the standards were based. Accordingly, we reject LIA's claim that the Administrator exceeded his statutory authority and turn to LIA's challenge to the evidentiary basis for the Administrator's decisions.

VI. HEALTH BASIS FOR THE LEAD STANDARDS

LIA does not question a number of the steps in the Administrator's analysis. It does not disagree with his selection of children between the ages of one and five years as the target population, or the decision to set a standard that would keep 99.5 percent of the children below the maximum safe individual blood lead level. In addition, LIA does not challenge the Administrator's suggestion that the standards should be based on an assumption that non-air sources contribute 12 μg Pb/dl to blood lead levels. LIA does, however, challenge other key elements in the Administrator's analysis.

A. Maximum Safe Individual Blood Lead Level

LIA attacks the Administrator's determination that 30 μg Pb/dl should be considered the maximum safe individual blood lead level for children, maintaining that there is no evidence in the record indicating that children suffer any health effects that can be considered adverse at this blood lead level. * * *

* * *

LIA's challenge to the Administrator's findings concerning the health significance of EP elevation also stresses that this phenomenon is only a "subclinical" effect. But the clinical/subclinical distinction has little to do with the question whether a particular effect is properly viewed as adverse to health. Rather, the distinction pertains to the means through which the particular effect may be detected: observation or physical examination in the case of clinical effects, and laboratory tests in the case of subclinical effects. Thus describing a particular effect as a "subclinical" effect in no way implies that it is improper to consider it adverse to health. While EP elevation may not be readily identifiable as a sign of disease, the Administrator properly concluded that it indicates a lead-related interference with basic biological functions. * * *

* * *

To be sure, the Administrator's conclusions were not unchallenged; both LIA and the Administrator are able to point to an impressive array of experts supporting each of their respective positions. However, disagreement among the experts is inevitable when the issues involved are at the "very frontiers of scientific knowledge," and such disagreement does not preclude us from finding that the Administrator's decisions are adequately supported by the evidence in the record. It may be that LIA expects this court to conclude that LIA's experts are right, and the experts whose testimony supports the Administrator are wrong. If so, LIA has seriously misconceived our role as a reviewing court. It is not our function to resolve disagreement among the experts or to judge the merits of competing expert views. Our task is the limited one of ascertaining that the choices made by the Administrator were reasonable and supported by the record. That the evidence in the record may also support other conclusions, even those that are inconsistent with the Administrator's, does not prevent us from concluding that his decisions were rational and supported by the record.

Having determined that we must uphold the Administrator's decisions concerning the health effects that are the basis for the lead standards, we turn to petitioners' other challenges to the Administrator's analysis.

B. Margin of Safety

Both LIA and St. Joe argue that the Administrator erred by including multiple allowances for margins of safety in his calculation of the lead standards. Petitioners note that the statute directs the Administrator to allow an "adequate margin of safety" in setting primary air quality standards, and they maintain that as a matter of statutory construction the Administrator may not interpret "margin" of safety to mean "margins" of safety. In petitioners' view, the Administrator in fact did just this insofar as he made allowances for margins of safety at several points in his analysis. They argue that margin of safety allowances were reflected in the choice of the maximum safe individual blood lead level for children, in the decision to place 99.5 percent of the target population group below that blood lead level, in the selection of an air lead/blood lead ratio at 1:2, and in the Administrator's estimate of the contribution to blood lead levels that should be attributed to non-air sources. The net result of these multiple allowances for margins of safety, petitioners contend, was a standard far more stringent than is necessary to protect the public health. * * *

EPA responds by maintaining that allowances for a margin of safety were made only at two points in its analysis: in the selection of a maximum safe individual blood lead level of 30 μg Pb/dl and in the decision to set a standard designed to keep 99.5 percent of the target population below that blood lead level. It argues that the statutory requirement of a margin of safety does not mandate adoption of the method suggested by St. Joe. Rather, EPA suggests, it indicates the precautionary orientation the Administrator is to bring to bear on the task of setting air quality standards. How conservative he must be in making particular judgments must, the Agency maintains, depend on such factors as the amount of uncertainty involved, the size of the population affected, and the severity of the effect. EPA argues that petitioners' claims about multiple allowances for margins of safety indicate that they have failed to recognize the difference between providing for a margin of safety and making a scientific judgment in the face of conflicting evidence.

We agree with the Administrator that nothing in the statutory scheme or the legislative history requires him to adopt the margin of safety approach suggested by St. Joe. Adding the margin of safety at the end of the analysis is one approach, but it is not the only possible method. Indeed, the Administrator considered this approach but decided against it because of complications raised by the multiple sources of lead exposure. The choice between these possible approaches is a policy choice of the type that Congress specifically left to the Administrator's judgment. This court must allow him the discretion to determine which approach will best fulfill the goals of the Act. As we pointed out in *Hercules Inc. v. EPA,* 598 F.2d [91, 108 (D.C. Cir. 1978)], "Decision between the alternatives is a quintessential policy judgment within the discretion of EPA. We cannot accept [the] notion that the administrator of the agency created to protect the environment lack[s] even the capability to exercise the discretion with which he was entrusted by Congress." (Emphasis in original.) Where, as here, the Administrator has provided an explanation of why he chose one method rather than another, and this explanation and his choice are not irrational, we must accept his decision. *See Industrial Union Dep't, AFL-CIO v. Hodgson,* 499 F.2d [467, 475-76 (D.C. Cir. (1974)].

We also agree with the Administrator's suggestion that petitioners have ignored the distinction between scientific judgments based on the available evidence and allowances for margins of safety. In every instance in which the Administrator's judgment on a particular issue differed from petitioners' they attributed his decision to an allowance for a margin of safety. To be sure, there is no bright line that divides these two types of decisions, but they are nonetheless conceptually distinct. In any event, whatever the nature of the decision, the real test, as petitioners recognize, is whether the decision is reasonable when examined in light of the evidence in the record. * * *

* * *

[The court affirmed EPA's lead standard.]

NOTES

1. What are the chronic effects of concern in the *Lead Industries* case? Why are they controversial?

2. Describe the analytical steps from health to emission limitations, and the science and policy issues that each step raises. What are the required items of information? What are the policy choices that the agency makes at each step? What is the basis for its choices-science, policy, or a combination of the two?

3. What is the statutory language that EPA is applying? Does the court agree with the agency position on the meaning of the statute?

How do the agency and court deploy the statutory language to account for uncertainty? How does the interpretation of the statute allow for considering subclinical effects? Where else is this precautionary approach relied on?

4. *Margin of safety.* The court relies heavily on the idea of a "margin of safety" to justify support of the agency. One issue the court discusses is whether single or multiple margins of safety is appropriate. How does the court resolve the question? Do you find it convincing?

How else do EPA and the court rely on a margin of safety?

**PROBLEM
TOXIC EFFECTS IN CHILDREN**

You probably noticed that EPA chose to study lead levels in children and that the Lead Industries Association did not challenge that choice (even though it challenged just about everything else that EPA did). Why?

> A fundamental maxim of pediatric medicine is that children are not "little adults." Profound differences exist between children and adults. Infants and children are growing and developing. Their metabolic rates are more rapid than those of adults. There are differences in their ability to activate, detoxify, and excrete xenobiotic compounds. All these differences can affect the toxicity of pesticides in infants and children, and for these reasons the toxicity of pesticides is frequently different in children and adults. * * *
>
> * * *
>
> * * * Differences in size, immaturity of biochemical and physiological functions in major body systems, and variation in body composition (water, fat, protein, and mineral content) all can influence the extent of toxicity. Because newborns are the group most different anatomically and physiologically from adults, they may exhibit the pronounced quantitative differences in sensitivity to pesticides. *The committee found that quantitative differences in toxicity between children and adults are usually less than a factor of approximately 10-fold.*

NATIONAL RESEARCH COUNCIL, PESTICIDES IN THE DIETS OF INFANTS AND CHILDREN 3-4 (1998) (emphasis in original). Another detailed study of children and pesticides can be found in JOHN WARGO, OUR CHILDREN'S TOXIC LEGACY: HOW SCIENCE AND LAW FAIL TO PROTECT US FROM PESTICIDES 172-234 (2d ed. 1998). Wargo warns in particular that "many forms of averaging have been used by [EPA to describe risks], each of which effectively lowered estimates of risk. Averaging together food consumption and detected residue statistics trivializes most risks. Further these averages cast public attention away from minorities [*i.e.,* including children] bearing risks." *Id.* at 219-20.

How should regulations react to the differences between adults and children? Did EPA average in the *Lead Industries'* case? Should it make a difference that, as some have argued, children greatly benefit from toxic chemicals (pesticides) that provide an abundant and varied food supply, that cancer remains a much rarer event among children than adults, and that children's health overall is improving?[11]

2. Cancer

The generic term "cancer" covers over one hundred diseases of different organs and systems of the human body, which have in common certain features. The principal distinguishing characteristic is the abnormal, apparently unconstrained proliferation of cells-"mitosis run amuck," in the words of one writer[12]-which invade neighboring tissues or, in the case of metastases, invade tissues in a wholly separate part of the body.

The 30 trillion cells of the normal, healthy body live in a complex, interdependent condominium, regulating one another's proliferation. Indeed, normal cells reproduce only when instructed to do so by other cells in their vicinity. Such unceasing collaboration ensures that each tissue maintains a size and architecture appropriate to the body's needs.

Cancer cells, in stark contrast, violate this scheme; they become deaf to the usual controls on proliferation and follow their own internal agenda for reproduction. They also possess an even more insidious property-the ability to migrate from the site where they began, invading nearby tissues and forming masses at distant sites in the body. Tumors composed of such malignant cells become more and more aggressive over time, and they become lethal when they disrupt the tissues and organs needed for the survival of the organism as a whole.

Robert A. Weinberg, *How Cancer Arises*, SCIENTIFIC AMERICAN 62, 62 (Sept. 1996). Cancerous cells can be found in discrete tumors or in systems like the blood. In either case, the result is that both the cancerous structure and its neighbors can no longer function properly; if unchecked, this leads to death.

While much is now known about how cancers develop, much less is known about the causes of the initial dysfunction in the genetic material that controls cell behavior.[13] Most cancers have no determinable cause in the sense of a discrete external event that gave rise to it. Indeed, while cancer has been

---

[11] *See* Stephen Huebuer & Kenneth Chitton, *Children's Crusade*, 15:2 ISSUES IN SCIENCE & TECH. 35 (Winter 1998/99)(arguing that children are not a major cancer worry).

[12] SANDRA STEINGRABER, LIVING DOWNSTREAM: AN ECOLOGIST LOOKS AT CANCER AND THE ENVIRONMENT 241 (1997). This book is an excellent introduction to and exploration of the scientific and human dimensions of cancer.

[13] *See* Webster V. Cavenee & Raymond L. White, *The Genetic Basis of Cancer,* SCIENTIFIC AMERICAN 72 (March 1995).

known from the earliest times, it was only in 1775 that the idea of chemical induction of cancer was suggested by British physician Percival Potts, who noticed the association between soot and the high rates of scrotal cancer among London chimney sweeps. (The carcinogenicity of specific chemical constituents of soot were confirmed early in this century.) The chemical induction of cancer has become the standard by which appropriate regulation of toxic substances is measured, because cancer is both a dread disease and an extremely sensitive marker for harmful effects.

CALCULATED RISKS: UNDERSTANDING THE TOXICITY AND HUMAN HEALTH RISKS OF CHEMICALS IN OUR ENVIRONMENT

Joseph V. Rodricks
pp. 148-50, 156-57, 166-70 (1992)

As a matter of exposition it is probably easiest to begin with a description of what are currently considered to be the major events in the development of malignancies from normal cells. The picture presented captures the process in only a very broad way, and dozens of intricacies will be omitted. This is justified on two grounds. First, scientific consensus on the model might be said to exist only at the broad level; scientists are still struggling to understand and agree on details. ***

It has seemed pretty clear for several decades, from both studies in humans and in experimental settings, that carcinogenesis is a *multi-stage* process. At the broadest level, the process can be thought of as one in which a normal cell is first converted to a permanently deranged cell, which is called a neoplastic cell, and a second sequence in which the neoplastic cell develops into a tumor, a neoplasm, that the pathologist can observe: neoplastic conversion and neoplastic development.

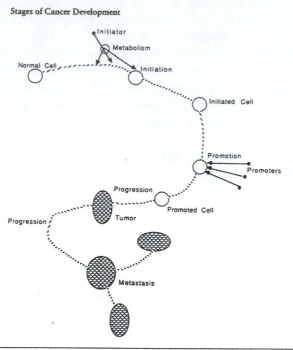

Figure 2.1–Stages of Cancer Development[14]

How does the neoplastic cell come about? It seems pretty clear that the *initiating event* is brought about when the chemical carcinogen, which is in many, if not most, cases a metabolite and not the administered chemical, reaches a cell's nucleus and chemically reacts with DNA, the genetic material. This reaction constitutes DNA damage, an unwelcome event because this magnificent molecule controls the life of the cell and the integrity of its reproduction. Fortunately, cells have a tremendous capacity to repair DNA damage; these repair mechanisms have been at work probably since life began to evolve, because most types of cells have always been assaulted by DNA-damaging radiation and chemicals from many natural sources. If some of the damage is not repaired, and this happens because repair is not 100% efficient, and the cell undergoes replication when the damage is present, then the damage is passed on to the new cells, and can become permanent–a *mutation* has occurred. * * *

Experts refer to all cells that have been so altered in their genetic features as *initiated* cells. The initiated cells might be fully neoplastic, in which case their proliferation takes place in a wild, uncontrolled fashion, or more commonly, they are only partially neoplastic. In the latter case the abnormal cells may still be under some control, and held in check by the actions of certain biological factors inherent to the organism in which the neoplastic

---

[14] Source: FRANK B. CROSS, ENVIRONMENTALLY INDUCED CANCER AND THE LAW: RISKS, REGULATION, AND VICTIM COMPENSATION 8 (1989).

conversion is occurring (the host). But some proliferation of these abnormal cells may also occur, brought about perhaps by continued chemical assault. Cell killing by chemically-induced toxicity may cause tissues to produce more cells at faster rates, *i.e.*, to *proliferate*, and during this proliferation phase the abnormal cells can be further converted to fully neoplastic cells because of "genetic errors" that also proliferate–rapidly proliferating cells are at increased risk of this type of error.

Neoplastic cells may remain unobtrusive, under the regulatory control of various host factors. But when these controls, which may involve some intricate molecular communications between cells, break down, the abnormal cells can begin to grow and develop. The process is enhanced by chemicals called *promoters*, about which more later. After this *progression* to full-fledged malignancies takes place, usually by way of what pathologists refer to as the "benign" state. Promotion and progression are thus the two processes involved in creating a cancer out of a neoplastic cell. * * *

* * *

Some important conclusions emerge even from this rudimentary profile of mechanisms. Metabolism is as significant in carcinogenesis as it is in the production of other forms of toxicity, so a thorough evaluation of risk would require knowledge of species' differences in metabolism, and the influence of the size of the dose on metabolic behavior.

Initiating events involve gene damage and this may result in the fixation in the cell's genetic material of a permanent abnormality. This feature of carcinogenesis perhaps makes it different in kind from most other forms of toxicity. Here the chemical insult occurs and the damage it produces remains in cells even if exposure to the insulting chemical ceases! If doses of the genotoxic agent keep piling up, so do the numbers of those permanent changes. This rather frightening picture is made less so when we recall that cells have a tremendous capacity to repair DNA damage before it becomes fixed, so that not every damaging event, in fact perhaps only a tiny fraction of them, actually translates to a mutation, and only a small fraction of mutations will likely occur at sites that are critical for the development of cancer.

One implication of this view of initiation–and an exceedingly important one–is expressed in the "no-threshold" hypothesis for carcinogens. Any amount of a DNA damaging chemical that reaches its target (the DNA) can increase the probability of converting a cell to a neoplastic state.

This does not mean that every such event will cause a neoplastic conversion, but only that the probability, or risk, of that occurrence becomes greater than zero as soon as the effective target-site concentration of the gene-damaging chemical is reached, and that the risk increases with increasing target-site concentration.

Various mathematical models have been developed to explore the implications for dose-response relations of what is known about carcinogenicity mechanisms. Under some sets of assumptions consistent with these mechanisms, the risk of neoplastic transformation at low doses is directly proportional to the target site dose. This is the so-called straight-line, or linear, model of dose-response; a picture of it is presented in the next chapter.

Actually, the notion that human cancers might result from exceedingly small doses arose first in connection with radiation-induced malignancies. In the 1950s E.B. Lewis of the California Institute of Technology proposed, based on studies of leukemia rates among Japanese atomic bomb survivors and cancer rates among radiologists, that cancer risks might exist at all doses greater than zero, and that a linear dose-response relation is to be expected.

A linear, no-threshold model might be appropriate to describe the dose-response relation for a genotoxic carcinogen, but it is less clear that it is suitable for promoters that act through non-genotoxic mechanisms. Some experts contend that sustained, high level dosing is needed to promote carcinogenesis–the dose needs to be sufficiently large to induce a persistent state of cell proliferation or a breakdown in cell-to-cell communication. Until a *threshold dose* for these toxic effects is exceeded, these experts suggest, significant enhancement of the carcinogenic process is unexpected. * * *

* * * But under the "no-threshold hypothesis" risks continue to exist at all doses, even if they can not be detected in animal experiments, and disappear completely only when the dose goes to zero.

* * *

Suffice it to say that no clear scientific consensus exists on the subject of thresholds, and may never, because identifying experimental means to resolve the debate is extraordinarily difficult. * * *

—

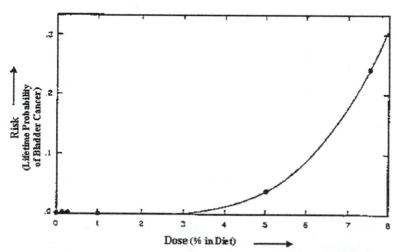

Figure 2. Dose-response curve for saccharin-induced bladder tumors in rats. Dose is expressed as per cent saccharin in the animals' diets. Response (risk) is the fraction of animals in each dosed group developing bladder tumors over their lifetimes–also called the lifetime probability of bladder cancer. Data were reported by Taylor and co-workers, Toxicology and Applied Pharmacology, Vol.29, page 154 (1974).

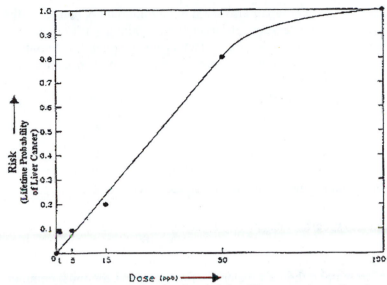

Figure 3. Dose-response curve for aflatoxin-induced liver tumors in rats. Dose is expressed as parts-per-billion (micrograms per kilogram) aflatoxin in the animals' diets. Response (risk) is the fraction of animals in each dose group developing liver tumors over their lifetimes–also called the lifetime probability of liver cancer. Data were reported by G.N. Wogan and associates in 1974 in Food and Cosmetics Toxicology, Vol. 12, pages 681-5

Figures 2.2 & 2.3–Threshold & Non-Threshold Carcinogens[15]

NOTES

1. This account of the mechanism of cancer is broadly accepted, and it underlies EPA's view of carcinogenesis. *See* EPA, Proposed Guidelines for Carcinogen Risk Assessment, 61 Fed. Reg. 17960, 18004-06 (1996). What are the basic features of the cancer mechanism? Why are they important for managing carcinogens?

2. *Thresholds*. What is meant by a "threshold" for carcinogenesis? Why is the nonexistence of a threshold assumed for carcinogens? Why is it sometimes called a "one-hit" theory? Note that there is evidence pro and con. How should EPA choose between them?

3. *Cancer and age*. Although cancer is associated in most of our minds with untimely death, as a public health phenomenon it is primarily a disease of old age. Under the molecular theory of cancer advanced above, this can be explained as the natural result of the accumulation of insults to the cells' genetic material–the more insults, the greater the probability of an effect.

> [A] variety of factors appear to play a role in the greater incidence of tumors in the elderly. The latency period between exposure to a carcinogenic agent and the development of cancer, for example, is often between twenty and forty years. Reduced efficiency and

---

[15] JOSEPH V. RODRICKS, CALCULATED RISKS: UNDERSTANDING THE TOXICITY AND HUMAN HEALTH RISKS OF CHEMICALS IN OUR ENVIRONMENT, (Cambridge U. Press 1992).

accuracy of DNA repair also seem to be important. Changes in the rate of cell proliferation in target tissues, along with changes in hormones and in other growth factors that regulate proliferation, together may also contribute to the increased incidence of cancer among the elderly.

WARGO, *supra*, at 173-74.

—

Carcinogens share other characteristics, as well, that are not directly related to the threshold question, though they are related to the mechanism. Some of the more important ones are summarized below:

Nontraceability. * * * A few relatively unusual cancers are linked to specific substances. Mesothelioma, for example, is uniquely caused by asbestos, a fact that has simplified a number of actual cases. [Thus mesothelioma is called a *signature* effect of asbestos.] Unfortunately, the vast majority of cancers, and the most common cancers, may be caused by scores of different chemicals. When these cancers develop, it becomes virtually impossible to say with confidence which substance "caused" the cancer. It is even more difficult to determine that a certain substance played a given role at a specific stage of cancer development. Causes of cancer leave no "marker" in the body identifying the nature of their lethal role.
* * *

Latency. If cancer happened as suddenly as the Bhopal deaths from methyl isocyanate, it would be much easier to find the cause of certain cancers. Cancer, however, typically takes decades to develop from initiation to metastasis. Determining the source of any specific cancer therefore requires a historical search into exposures long past.
* * *

Apparent Randomness. Science has revealed certain factors that contribute to cancer, ranging from environmental pollutants to genetic susceptibility. Yet it appears that none of these factors is certain to cause cancer, and it is very unusual that any factor even appears to make cancer more probable than not. Rather, exposure to current environmental cancer-inducing factors typically may create a 1 in 10,000 (1×10^{-4}) risk of cancer or less. Thus only about 1 out of 10,000 similarly situated persons will get cancer because of a given exposure. The very expression of this risk, in terms of odds, implies the seeming randomness of the cancer risk.

This is not to suggest that those individuals who actually contract cancer are simply unlucky. Cancer may one day prove to be entirely deterministic, with our present probabilities explained by the numerous biological interactions of the cancer development process or defined genetic characteristics of the cancer victim. Scientific knowledge, however, is decades away from establishing cancer causation with such deterministic precision. For now and the foreseeable future, the law must respond to a disease that strikes individuals with apparent randomness.

FRANK B. CROSS, ENVIRONMENTALLY INDUCED CANCER AND THE LAW: RISKS, REGULATION, AND VICTIM COMPENSATION 12-14 (1989).

The non-signature, latency, randomness, and relative rarity characteristics combine with the mechanism of carcinogenesis to require a new approach to regulation. In moving from acute to chronic to cancer concerns, we have moved from organism-level, to cell-level, to molecule-level effects. A cellular theory of carcinogenesis implies that the occurrence of cancer is a matter of probability, not certainty. When considering acute and chronic toxic effects, we commonly treat the relationships between the external agent of the effect and the appearance of the effect as mechanistic (or deterministic), that is, given a particular exposure to a particular person, we can be quite certain of its effect in him or her.[16] Chemically induced cancer at low doses, on the other hand, is probabilistic (or stochastic); we cannot know in advance whatever specific individual will get cancer, only that there is a certain probability of that occurring.

> Deterministic effects are those for which the severity of the effect varies with the dose, and for which a threshold may therefore occur. Stochastic effects are those for which the probability that an effect will occur, rather than the severity of the effect, is regarded as a function of the dose, without threshold.

MOELLER, ENVIRONMENTAL HEALTH, *supra*, at 248.

Perhaps the single most important consequence of a probabilistic mechanism of chemical carcinogenesis was described by former Deputy Administrator of EPA Al Alm: "Many EPA professionals no longer used bi-modal terms such as safe or unsafe, but rather began to think and talk in probabilistic terms." Al Alm, *Why We Didn't Use "Risk" Before*, 17 EPA J. 13 (Mar.-Apr. 1991). As a result cancer danger is expressed in terms of risk and regulation is based on risk; complete safety-zero risk-is not regarded as a realistic goal; therefore, the regulatory system must find a way to set the "acceptable" level of risk. These issues characterize toxics regulation, and, as we shall see, the pose its fundamental challenge.

At a more practical level, probabilistic cancer effects are far more difficult to identify and measure than acute and chronic effects. This has tremendous consequences for the regulatory system, because it both increases the cost of obtaining the relevant toxicology information and reduces the certainty of the information obtained. The following description of toxicology testing methods illustrates the problem.

---

[16] Technically, however, as we saw above, we measure even acute toxicity probabilistically, that is, as a risk, using the LD50 metric.

RISK ANALYSIS: A GUIDE TO PRINCIPLES AND METHODS FOR ANALYZING HEALTH AND ENVIRONMENTAL RISKS

John J. Cohrssen & Vincent T. Covello
pp. 27-36, 39-54 (Council on Environmental Quality, 1989)

Epidemiological Studies

Epidemiological studies are concerned with the patterns of disease in human populations and the factors that influence these patterns. In general, scientists view well-conducted epidemiological studies as the most valuable information from which to draw inferences about human health risks. For example, a study of chemical carcinogens conducted by the Office of Science and Technology Policy came to the conclusion that "a positive finding in a well-conducted epidemiological study can be viewed as strong evidence that a chemical poses a carcinogenic risk to humans."

Unlike the other analytical approaches described in this section, epidemiological methods can be used to study the direct effects of hazardous substances on human beings. * * * Epidemiological studies also help identify actual hazards to human health without prior knowledge of disease causation and can complement and validate information about hazards generated by animal laboratory studies.

Compared to other techniques used in risk analysis, epidemiology is relatively well suited to situations where exposure to the risk agent is high (such as cigarette smoking), where adverse health effects are unusual (such as rare forms of cancer), where the symptoms of exposure to the risk agent are known, where the link between the causal risk agent and adverse effects in the affected population is direct and clear, where the risk agent is present in the bodies of the affected population, and where high levels of the risk agent are present in the environment (*e.g.*, in the soil or drinking water). However, many of the environmental health risk agents currently subject to regulatory and societal concern do not fall into these categories. As a result, epidemiological studies used in risk analysis have important limitations that constrain their usefulness. These limitations arise not from epidemiology *per se*, but rather from the nature of the specific risk analysis needs to which epidemiology is sometimes applied. For example, one limitation of epidemiological studies is that they can be conducted only for hazards to which people already have been exposed. They are generally not useful for predicting effects of new substances or technologies.

A second limitation is the lack of experimental controls. For obvious moral, ethical, and practical reasons, researchers can neither control nor account completely for the behavior of study subjects that may affect their health and therefore influence the study results.

A third limitation is that epidemiological studies may fail to account for the effects of multiple sources of exposure. If both exposed and unexposed groups in a study (for example, in a study of a chemical in the water supply) are exposed to a risk agent from another unidentified source or medium (such as air), the study results may not show an association although one is actually present.

A final limitation of epidemiological studies is that they have poor sensitivity and are generally unable to detect small increases in risk unless very large populations are studied. At low exposure levels, adverse effects may be very difficult to detect. For example, to identify any change in the number of genetic defects that could be caused by one additional X-ray (a 3-millirem dose) per person per year, a study would need to observe a population of 700 million people for three generations. Even then, a positive result would not prove 100 percent certainty of harm, and a negative effect would not prove certainty of zero risk.

* * *

In Vivo *Animal Bioassays*

For most hazards, adequate epidemiological or human clinical data are not available. Many risk analyses prepared for regulatory risk decisions rely on information from laboratory studies on live animals. Pathogenic studies of microorganisms are most often conducted in guinea pigs, mice, and some primates. Studies of chemical carcinogenicity are most often conducted in rats and/or mice.

* * *

Subchronic Exposure Tests

Properly conducted subchronic tests for chemicals involve repeated exposure of two species of test animals for 5 to 90 days by exposure routes corresponding to expected human exposures. Often, more than one exposure route is tested. At least three dose levels are used to help define the dose-response relationship and to identify the no observed adverse effects level (NOAEL) and the lowest observed adverse effects level (LOAEL). Subchronic tests also are used to determine the maximum tolerated dose (MTD), the largest dose a test animal can receive for most of its lifetime without demonstrating adverse effects other than carcinogenicity.

Subchronic tests provide useful information about the dose-response relationship of a test substance, and they also help to identify pharmacokinetic and metabolic reactions and define appropriate dose levels for chronic toxicity tests.

Long-Term Chronic Exposure Tests

In studies of chronic effects of chemicals, test animals receive daily doses of the test agent for approximately two years. Well-conducted experiments have at least three dose levels: the maximum tolerated dose (MTD), a fraction of the MTD, and unexposed control. * * *

Because of the need to detect small effects, and because the doses in chronic studies are lower than in acute or subchronic studies, a larger number of test animals-usually about 50 of each sex for each dose level-must be used to detect statistically significant effects. Thus, two major drawbacks if chronic animal bioassays are the time needed to conduct and analyze them (two to three years) and their large cost in terms of animals required (several hundred, depending upon the number of species, the number of each sex, and the doses tested).

* * *

As predictors of acute and chronic adverse effects in other species, and in humans particularly, *in vivo* animal bioassays are limited and controversial. For example, long-term animal bioassays may not be completely reliable predictors of carcinogenicity in humans. * * *

There are several reasons for the difficulties in estimating human responses on the basis of *in vivo* animal bioassay results. Physiology and metabolic pathways that affect the response to a chemical differ considerably among species. For tests of chemicals or radiation, another limitation is the large differences between the doses used (per kilogram of body weight) in the bioassays and the doses to which humans are typically exposed. Doses used in bioassays are necessarily relatively high so as to increase the sensitivity of the experiments, whereas human exposures tend to be much lower (and, as discussed subsequently, actual doses to human tissues may be lower still). Thus, extrapolation from higher test doses to lower environmental concentrations creates large uncertainties in the validity of such bioassays as a means of identifying potential chemical or radioactive hazards.

Despite these shortcomings, animal bioassays are widely viewed as the best available analogy for identifying adverse human health effects in the absence of good human epidemiological data. In addition, tests on animals are still widely used in estimating ecological effects.

Short-Term In Vitro *Cell and Tissue Culture Tests*

In the past decade, there has been explosive growth in the quantity, variety, and quality of laboratory tests using *in vitro* cell and tissue cultures to study the effects of risk agents on biological organisms. The low cost and relative speed with which cell and tissue tests can be conducted have earned them an important role in screening potentially hazardous substances and in providing additional sources of evidence for carcinogenicity.

* * *

The predictive value of *in vitro* genetic toxicity tests for carcinogenicity *in vivo* is controversial. Most of the debate has centered around the predictive value of the Ames test which, is the most widely used mutagenicity assay. Researchers investigating the relationship between carcinogenicity and mutagenicity in the Ames test have reported correlations exceeding 90 percent. More recent evidence, which includes testing of a larger number of non-carcinogens, indicates the correlation is not as great as originally suggested. * * *

In general, the accuracy of *in vitro* tests for carcinogenicity is compromised by (1) the lack of direct correspondence between the mechanisms of genetic toxicity used in the assays and current understanding of carcinogenesis; (2) the difficulty of extrapolating from simple cellular systems to complex, higher organisms; (3) the use of different protocols and different interpretive rules by different laboratories; (4) metabolic activation systems that differ from *in vivo* activation systems; (5) the limited number of risk agents tested (except for the Ames test), making validation difficult; and (6) the limited number of non-carcinogens tested.

* * *

Structure-Activity Relationship Analysis

The simplest and most frequently employed first step in any analysis of a potentially hazardous risk agent or new technology is to compare it with similar agents or technologies for which the presence or absence of hazard is known. EPA's Office of Toxic Substances, for example, relies heavily on a technique known as structure-activity relationship (SAR) analysis for analyzing hazards associated with most of the new chemicals for which it received premanufacture notices. EPA evaluates this information to determine whether more data (for example, from *in vitro* or *in vivo* tests) may be required.

SAR analysis involves comparing the molecular structure and chemical and physical properties of a chemical having unknown hazards with the molecular structures and physiochemical properties of other, similar chemicals having known toxic or carcinogenic effects. Knowledge of the relationship between a particular structural feature or physiochemical property and the physiological or molecular mechanisms by which the feature or property induces adverse effects strengthens the usefulness of SAR analysis.

* * *

Frequently, as in the examples cited above, SAR analysis (or its biological analogue) is the only readily available source of information about the hazards of new technological developments. The predictive value of such data, however, is uncertain. Seemingly insignificant differences in chemical structures or physiochemical properties (or species classification) may obscure significant differences in hazardous characteristics. For example, the chemical 2-acetylaminofluorene is a well-documented carcinogen, whereas its close chemical relative, 4-acetylaminofluorene is not carcinogenic.

NOTES

1. Why is it important to the regulatory system-legislators, regulators, affected parties-to understand how toxicity is tested?

2. Why can't scientists make direct, real-time observations? What are the strengths and weaknesses of the available tests? If you represent a party challenging a regulatory action based on a long-term animal bioassay, for example, what lines of inquiry might you use to challenge the validity of the study?

3. *Confounding factors.* Epidemiology is really a subject in itself that cannot be done justice here, but it is often critical to establishing a causal link between a substance and disease in every type of toxics regulation. As the reading suggests, the inference of causation must be undertaken cautiously.

Even when an association exists, researchers must determine whether the exposure causes the disease or whether the exposure and disease are caused by some other confounding factor. A confounding factor is both a risk factor for the disease and associated with the exposure of interest. For example, researchers may conduct a study that finds individuals with gray hair have a higher rate of death than those with hair of another color. Instead of hair color having an impact on death, the results might be explained by the confounding factor of age. * * * When researchers find an association between an agent and a disease, it is critical to determine whether the association is causal or the result of confounding.

* * *

Confounding factors that are known in advance can be controlled during the study design and through study group selection. Unanticipated confounding factors that can be identified can sometimes be controlled during data analysis if data are gathered about them. There is always a risk, however, that an undiscovered confounding factor is responsible for a study's findings.

Linda A. Bailey *et al.*, Reference Guide on Epidemiology *in* FEDERAL JUDICIAL CENTER, REFERENCE MANUAL ON SCIENTIFIC EVIDENCE 158 -64 (1994).

4. *Costs.* The costs of toxicology studies are substantial. The standard two-year rodent study for carcinogenicity costs up to $ 4 million and takes at least five years to complete. How is this relevant to the regulatory system?

5. *The data gap.* The limitations on testing data were analyzed by the National Academy of Sciences in 1984. It concluded that for "the great majority of [toxic] substances, data considered to be essential for conducting a health-hazard assessment are lacking." * * * "The information available * * * is scanty, and the resources * * * do not suffice to test all chemicals for every possible health effect."[17] The Academy's conclusions are summarized in Figure 2.4.

---

[17] NATIONAL ACADEMY OF SCIENCES, TOXICITY TESTING: STRATEGIES TO DETERMINE NEEDS AND PRIORITIES 205-208 (1984).

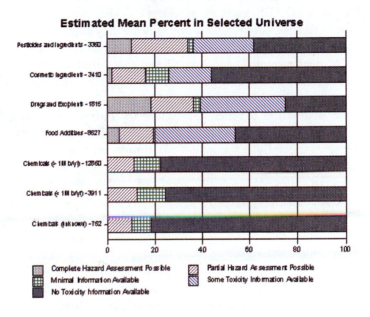

Figure 2.4–The Data Gap

In a later study of carcinogens in the human diet, the NAS concluded:

Numerous and extensive gaps in the current knowledge base were apparent as the committee endeavored to examine the risk of human cancer from naturally occurring versus synthetic compnents of the diet. These gaps are so large-and resources are so limited-that careful prioritization of further research efforts is essential. The following recommendations emphasize the need for expanded epidemiologic studies, more human exposure data, improved and enhanced testing methods, more detailed data on dietary components, and further mechanistic studies, if these gaps are to be filled. These research endeavors may prove inadequate, however, when the complexity and variability of diets and food composition, as well as human behavior, are considered.

NATIONAL RESEARCH COUNCIL, CARCINOGENS AND ANTICARCINOGENS IN THE HUMAN DIET 11-12 (1996). Another recent survey of chemicals found "sufficient information for safety assessment" for 7% of TRI chemicals released to air, 34% of chemicals released to water, and 3% of all high-volume chemicals. David Roe & William S. Pease, *Toxic Ignorance,* THE ENVTL. FORUM (ENVTL. L. INST.) 26-27 (May/June 1998). These conclusions remain largely accurate and apply to virtually all areas of toxic risk regulation.[18]

---

[18]See, e.g., CARL F. CRANOR, REGULATING TOXIC SUBSTANCES: A PHILOSOPHY OF SCIENCE AND THE LAW 4 (1993) (summarizing studies by the Office of Technology Assessment in 1982 and 1987); NATIONAL RESEARCH COUNCIL, SCIENCE AND JUDGMENT IN RISK ASSESSMENT 144-

6. *NOAEL and LOAEL.* The results of a well-designed bioassay will always include a LOAEL, and may include a NOAEL, for each effect studied. What is the difference between them and why are they important? The finding of a NOAEL may indicate a threshold, *but not necessarily*-why?

7. *False positives and negatives.* Given their limitations, animal tests raise a serious risk of error in their conclusions. The error can go in two directions: a false positive or a false negative.

The distinction between the failure to find an effect and the conclusion that there is no effect is not trivial. This distinction is so important, especially in the area of environmental risk management, that its blurring can be given the name *fallacy of false negative.* The fallacy is to believe that a decision procedure designed to limit false positives necessarily yields *any* conclusion about the nonexistence of an effect when there is a negative finding. * * *

This does not mean that decision makers can never draw negative conclusions from negative findings. However, in order to do so the structure of the problem must be investigated directly. The less uncertain the structure (*i.e.*, the more information available), the more likely it is that a negative finding will lead to a valid conclusion.

* * * But in environmental risk, with long latencies and diffusion of effects, effects are well hidden. For these risks, * * * careful investigation is required to support a negative conclusion drawn from a negative finding. In one model of carcinogens in drinking water, where the chance of a false positive was held to 5 percent, the chance of a substantial effect going undetected was still 40 percent.

The attuned reader will find the fallacy of the false negative ubiquitous in legal, regulatory, and statistical reasoning. When the press reports that saccharin has been in use for 70 years without a single human cancer death proven as a result of its use, the suggested inference is that this is evidence of saccharin's non-carcinogenicity to humans. Before drawing this inference, regulatory institutions and other decision makers should investigate the likelihood of detecting saccharin carcinogenity even if, for example, it should contribute 700 to 1,000 extra cancer deaths a year. This type of question is rarely posed or investigated in statistical and other studies of environmental risks. Without its investigation, negative findings are largely devoid

---

59 (1994) (not enough for 189 hazardous air pollutants); OFFICE OF TECHNOLOGY ASSESSMENT, COMPLEX CLEANUP: THE ENVIRONMENTAL LEGACY OF NUCLEAR WEAPONS PRODUCTION 62-64 (1991); JOHN WARGO, OUR CHILDREN'S TOXIC LEGACY 270-76 (2d ed. 1998); Wendy Wagner, *Choosing Ignorance in the Manufacturing of Toxic Products*, 82 CORNELL. L. REV. 733 (1997); John S. Applegate, *The Perils of Unreasonable Risk: Information, Regulatory Policy, and Toxic Substances Control*, 91 COLUM. L. REV. 261, 284-98 (1991); John Chelen, *Erasing the Data Deficit*, 15 THE ENVTL. FORUM (ENVTL. L. INST.) 35 (Jan./Feb. 1998); Mary L. Lyndon, *Information Economics and Chemical Toxicity: Designing Laws to Produce and Use Data*, 87 MICH. L. REV. 1795, 1796-99 (1989).

of meaning, especially for environmental risks where the probabilities of false negatives are likely to be substantial. For a meaningful interpretation of a negative finding, there must first be an explicit investigation of the power of the statistical or other decision procedure to detect hidden effects.

Talbot Page, *A Generic View of Toxic Chemicals and Similar Risks*, 7 ECOLOGY L.Q. 207, 231-33 (1978). Why does the problem of the false negative arise under the testing regimens described above? Should toxic risk differ from other aspects of the law (say, criminal or tort law) in its management of these potentials for error?

8. *Noncarcinogens: reference dose and hazard index.* For noncarcinogens, EPA uses reference dose (RfD) to measure toxicity.

> The RfD is an estimate, with an uncertainty spanning perhaps an order of magnitude, of a daily exposure to the human population (including sensitive subgroups) that is likely to be without an appreciable risk of deleterious health effects during a lifetime. The RfD is derived from a [NOAEL or LOAEL] that has been identified from a subchronic or chronic scientific study of humans or animals. The NOAEL or LOAEL is then divided by the uncertainty factor to derive the RfD.
>
> The use of an uncertainty factor is important in the derivation of the RfD. EPA has established certain guidelines (shown below) to determine which uncertainty factor should be used:
>
> > 10-Valid experimental results for appropriate duration. Human exposure.
> >
> > 100-Human data not available. Extrapolation from animal studies of less than chronic exposure.
> >
> > 1-10-Additional safety factor for use of a LOAEL instead of a NOAEL.
> >
> > Other-Other uncertainty factors are used according to scientific judgment when justified.
>
> In general, an uncertainty factor is calculated to consider intra- and interspecies variations, limited or incomplete data, use of subchronic studies, significance of the adverse effect, and the pharmacokinetic factors.

EPA, National Primary Drinking Water Regulations, 56 Fed. Reg. 3526, 3532 (1991). (Note the use of margins of safety in this analysis.) To ascertain risk levels for noncarcinogens, the dose (exposure) estimate is divided by the RfD to obtain the *hazard index.* If the hazard index is less than 1, the chemical exposure is unlikely to lead to adverse health effects; if greater than 1, some remedial action is indicated.

MECHANISTIC v. STATISTICAL PROOF

Note that there is a disjunction between the tests for cancer that rely on statistical association and the studies of the mechanism of cancer that try to pinpoint physical changes. Clearly, statistical studies would be immensely strengthened by mechanistic data, and scientists debate how to match the two kinds of data. Some indication of the difficulty of obtaining mechanistic data is found in the fact that the mechanism connecting smoking to lung cancer was discovered only recently.

A team of researchers says it has found a direct scientific link between smoking and lung cancer, a discovery that adds yet another piece to the already substantial evidence that tobacco-smoking is a cause of cancer.

The findings, published today in the journal Science, report the first evidence from the cell biology level linking smoking to lung cancer. The scientists say a chemical found in cigarette smoke has been found to cause genetic damage in lung cells that is identical to the damage observed in many malignant tumors of the lung.

The findings reported today establish the long-missing link, in the opinion of experts in the field of cancer genetics, and may also play a role in pending litigation about smoking illnesses and passive smoking.

While many scientists have long been convinced by statistical studies and animal experiments that tobacco causes cancer, a statistical association was not in itself absolute proof. This shortfall has allowed defenders of smoking to deny that cigarettes cause cancer, and scientists have not known the exact mechanism of causation that would put the matter beyond doubt.

David Stout, *Direct Link Found Between Smoking and Lung Cancer*, NEW YORK TIMES, Oct. 18, 1996, p. A1.

We all tend to associate cancer with untimely death, and many of us have known people whose lives were tragically cut short by this disease. Nevertheless, in the population as a whole, cancer is a common occurrence.

Epidemiologists project that * * * 40 percent of Americans will eventually be stricken with the disease, and more than one in five will die of it * * *. [However,] the horrendous casualties from lung cancer obscure the general headway that has been made. Put aside lung cancer (a largely preventable disease), and the death rate from all other types has declined by 3.4 percent since 1973–by 13.3 percent in people younger than 65.

John Rennie & Ricki Rusting, *Making Headway Against Cancer,* SCIENTIFIC AMERICAN 57, 59 (Sept. 1996). A more pessimistic view is taken by

Steingraber, who notes that the incidence of all types of cancer rose 49.3% from 1950-1991, and 35% if lung cancer is excluded. She and others believe that the leading suspect for this increase in cancer is the huge increase in the production of synthetic chemicals since World War II. Steingraber, *supra*, at 40-43.

These overall statistics do not, however, answer the question, of the over 500,000 cancer deaths that occur each year in the United States, how many were caused by environmental pollution? Efforts to find answers are hampered by the same uncertainties that make individual causation difficult to determine. Nevertheless, some general conclusions are possible. According to a recent overview of cancer causes, over half of the cancer deaths in the United States are caused by smoking and a high-fat/low-fiber diet; each represents about 30 percent of cancer deaths. Other identifiable external causes are small by comparison. Alcoholic beverages, a sedentary lifestyle, radiation (most of which is naturally occurring, like sunlight), occupational exposures to chemicals, and viruses and infection, each contribute between 2 and 5 percent. Environmental contamination from all sources is estimated by epidemiologists to cause about 2 percent of cancer deaths. Dimitrios Trichopoulos *et al.*, *What Causes Cancer?*, SCIENTIFIC AMERICAN 81-87 (Sept. 1996). Others have suggested that most human exposure to carcinogens comes from nature:

> About 99.99 percent of all pesticides in the human diet are natural pesticides from plants. All plants produce toxins to protect themselves against fungi, insects, and animal predators such as humans. Tens of thousands of these natural pesticides have been discovered, and every species of plant contains its own set of different toxins, usually a few dozen. When plants are stressed or damaged (when attacked by pests), they greatly increase their output of natural pesticides, occasionally to levels that are acutely toxic to humans.
>
> We estimate that a typical American eats about 1,500 mg per day of natural pesticides, which is 10,000 times more than the average daily consumption of synthetic pesticide residues. The concentration of natural pesticides is usually measured in parts per million (ppm) rather than parts per billion (ppb), which is the usual concentration of synthetic pesticide residues or of water pollutants. We also estimate that a person ingests annually about 5,000 to 10,000 different natural pesticides and their breakdown products.
>
> * * *
>
> Surprisingly few of these thousands of plant toxins in our diet have been involved in animal cancer tests, but of those tested in at least one species of animal, about half (27/52) are carcinogenic.
>
> * * *
>
> Cooked food is a major dietary source of substances that cause cancer in rodents. The average person consumes about 2,000 mg per

day of burned material, which contains many substances that are rodent carcinogens and many other substances that have not yet been tested. Roasted coffee, for example, contains about 1,000 chemicals. Only 26 have been tested, and of these 19 cause cancer in rodents. The 10 mg of known natural rodent carcinogens in a cup of coffee would be equivalent in amount ingested to a year's worth of synthetic pesticide residues (assuming half of the untested synthetic residue weight turns out to be carcinogenic in rodents). The other chemicals, about a thousand, remain to be tested.

Bruce N. Ames & Lois Swirsky Gold, *Environmental Pollution and Cancer: Some Misconceptions* in PHANTOM RISK: SCIENTIFIC INFERENCE AND THE LAW (Kenneth R. Foster *et al.*, eds.), pp. 154-75 (1993).

How does this context affect your view of cancer and chemicals? An environmental policy analyst has made the point that "environmental programs can reduce the cancer rate only marginally, because cancers caused by the external environmental contamination (other than radiation) amount to 2 to 3 percent of all cancers caused." DANIEL J. FIORINO, MAKING ENVIRONMENTAL POLICY 128-29 (1995). *See also* Cranor, *supra*, at 4 (attributing somewhat higher contributions of pollution to cancer). Does the fact that there are already many carcinogens out there logically force the conclusion that new ones are of little concern? Or does it suggest that we should act aggressively to control those causes over which we have some influence?

3. Case Study: Non-Cancer, Low-Dose Toxic Effects

Just as chemicals are not the only environmental causes of cancer, cancer is not the only disease that shares the characteristics of being latent, non-threshold, irreversible, dreaded, and so on. Just as it took years to prove that chemicals could cause cancer, it will take a great deal of time and experimentation to demonstrate that chemicals cause (if they do) other non-obvious, long-term effects. Some of these potential effects are discussed in the next reading.

ENVIRONMENTAL HEALTH

Dade W. Moeller
pp. 24-25 (rev. ed. 1997)

Reproductive toxicity. Toxic effects on reproduction may occur anywhere within a continuum of events ranging from germ cell formation and sexual functioning in the parents through sexual maturation in the offspring. The relationship between exposure and reproductive dysfunction is highly complex because exposure of the mother, father, or both may influence reproductive outcome. In addition, critical exposures may include maternal exposures long before or immediately prior to conception as well as exposure of the mother and fetus during gestation.

Developmental toxicity (teratogenesis). The type of illness involving the formation of congenital defects has been known for decades and is an important cause of morbidity and mortality among newborns. Developmental effects encompass embryo and fetal death, growth retardation, and malformations, all of which can be highly sensitive to chemical exposures. For some years no connection was suspected between such effects and chemicals; toxicologists had a tendency to assume that the natural protective mechanisms of the body, such as detoxication, elimination, and the placental barrier, were sufficient to shield the embryo from maternal exposure to harmful chemicals. These concepts changed dramatically after the clinical use of thalidomide, a sedative first employed in Germany in the late 1950s to relieve morning sickness in pregnant women.

Neurotoxicity. Although fewer than 10 percent of the approximately 70,000 chemicals in use have been tested, almost 1,000 have been identified as known neurotoxicants in humans and other animals. The multitude of impacts on humans range from cognitive, sensory, and motor impairments to immune system deficits. For this reason classification of chemical neurotoxic action is constantly evolving, and the application of data from studies in animals to estimation of the risks of neurologic disease in humans is very complicated. Often there are major differences between the degree of neurotoxic response observed in animals and that found in humans.

Immunotoxicology. Various toxic substances are known to suppress the immune function, leading to reduced host resistance to bacterial and viral infections, and to parasitic infestation, as well as to reduced control of neoplasms. The importance of these effects is well illustrated by the concern about AIDS, in which the infected person often dies owing to inability to resist an organism that would not be a problem in a healthy individual. Certain toxic agents can also provoke exaggerated immune reactions leading to local or systemic reactions.

In recent years some scientists have postulated that certain people have "multiple chemical sensitivity," which can lead to a type of "chemical AIDS." The supposition is that exposures to trace concentrations of multiple chemicals present in the environment may impair the body's immune system.

NOTES

1. EPA takes these effects seriously. Noncancer effects were studied in the recent reassessment of dioxin (TCDD), which was intended to be a state-of-the-art assessment of one of the most troublesome environmental contaminants. The study concluded that "altered development may be among the most sensitive TCDD end points in laboratory animal systems although the likelihood and level of response in humans are much less clear." Related reproductive effects were found in laboratory animals. Likewise, the immune system "is a target for toxicity of TCDD and structurally related compounds,"

including PCBs. "It is well recognized that suppressed immunological function can result in increased incidence and severity of infectious diseases as well as some types of cancer." EPA, Dioxin Reassessment (External Review Draft, Aug. 1994), ch. 9, pp. 9-44, 48, 81.

2. Several of the above effects are not fatal, and even cancer is not necessarily a fatal disease. (In public health terminology, they represent morbidity rather than mortality effects.) Environmental regulation, however, most often concerns itself with death as the relevant outcome. How should environmental regulation respond to non-fatal outcomes?

3. Endocrine disrupters, that is, synthetic chemicals that mimic existing hormones, are a recent and controversial subject of toxicologic concern. They have received widespread attention as the result of the publication of THEO COLBORN *ET AL*., OUR STOLEN FUTURE: ARE WE THREATENING OUR FERTILITY, INTELLIGENCE AND SURVIVAL? (1996), which asserted that growing pollution burdens are disrupting hormonal balances, causing infertility, reducing sperm counts, and causing neurological disorders worldwide. The issue is being actively studied by EPA and the National Institute of Environmental Health and Safety. While this effect is new, it presents several problems with which you should now be familiar. The following discussion, from the radio news program *All Things Considered*, illustrates many of the sources of uncertainty and the scientific and policy implications of uncertainty for "cutting-edge" science.

PESTICIDES MAY POSE HAZARDS TO WILDLIFE

National Public Radio, *All Things Considered* (Feb. 1, 1995)[19]

LINDA WERTHEIMER, Host: Three decades ago a book changed the way people looked at the world. The book was *Silent Spring*. In it, Rachel Carson drew the world's attention to the fact that some pesticides were killing wildlife and posing a cancer threat to people. That book and the movement it spawned ultimately led the government to ban DDT and related chemicals. Today, there is a growing concern that wildlife and people could be harmed by chemicals that don't kill outright, but which disrupt the delicate balance of hormones needed for healthy growth and development.

RICHARD HARRIS, Reporter: * * * As you fly into this city [Orlando] in central Florida you may notice that one of the many lakes in the area looks dramatically different. It's not blue like the rest, but pea soup green. This is Lake Apopka, the fourth largest lake in Florida and the most polluted one in the state. Another tale of serendipity is unfolding here.

---

[19] © Copyright NPR® 1999. The news series by NPR's Richard Harris was originally broadcast on NPR's "All Things Considered®" on February 1, 1995, and is used with permission of National Public Radio, Ind. Any unauthorized duplication is strictly prohibited."

We head out into the lake and biologist Lou Guilette explains this story involves the American alligator.

LOU GUILETTE, Biologist: Back in these little openings behind the reeds that we are seeing here, a lot of times we'll actually see an animal or two hanging out, especially in the evening or at night you see lots of juveniles spread out into those little areas. In fact, you just heard a splash there in the background and that was an alligator, right back there in the corner.

RICHARD HARRIS: Here's where the serendipity comes in. Back in the late 1970's alligators were so abundant on Lake Apopka the state sent a biologist out to see whether some could be hunted for their hides without harming the population in the lake.

LOU GUILETTE: What he found was one of the densest populations of alligators in the State of Florida. But about 1981, 1982, 1983, the population began to crash. As a matter of fact, in a period of three years between '81 and '83 the population crashed by 90 percent.

RICHARD HARRIS: Guilette, a zoologist at the University of Florida, joined a team of scientists to investigate this mysterious decline.

LOU GUILETTE: The only thing we could come up with when we looked at all of the various factors that there seemed to be a very strong relationship time wise, between the spill that took place on the southwest part of the lake and the decline of the alligators.

RICHARD HARRIS: The spill in 1980 was from a now defunct pesticide factory. Huge quantities of sulfuric acid spilled into the lake burning the marsh as it went. And along with that acid came the pesticides dicofol and DDT. Biologists watched with horror as alligator carcasses floated by belly up. The damage wasn't just to the adults. In the worst year, 80 percent of the alligators eggs also failed to hatch and many that did hatch were deformed. So, Guilette became suspicious that this was more than a case of simple poisoning.

At a community college 80 miles northwest of Lake Apopka, a few dozen baby alligators roam around in a pen. These foot-long youngsters hatched from eggs taken from Lake Apopka and a clean lake nearby.

LOU GUILETTE: OK, what we need to do is to grab probably about 10 to 15 of the biggest hatchlings that are in here. OK?

RICHARD HARRIS: Lou Guilette and his colleagues think these gators may hold the key to understanding what happened at Lake Apopka.

LOU GUILETTE: The primary reason we're actually raising these animals out here is that we have noted over the last two or three years that most of the animals on Lake Apopka appear to have abnormal sexual development.

RICHARD HARRIS: Not only are their genitals mixed up like the gulls that were injected with DDT, but their hormones are all out of whack. Young males have too little of the male hormone testosterone and too much of the female hormone estrogen. Guilette suspects that hormone disruption is also responsible for the most highly publicized problems with the Lake Apopka alligators.

LOU GUILETTE: We are very intrigued with the fact that these animals all have very, very small penises compared to what is supposed to be normal.

RICHARD HARRIS: Today, Guilette and a graduate student are checking up on their needle-toothed troop of young alligators.

STUDENT: One fifty six point five.

RICHARD HARRIS: First they are weighed, then Guilette takes a blood sample from the nape of their necks. They aren't too thrilled about that.

LOU GUILETTE: That's OK, baby.

RICHARD HARRIS: Guilette gently withdraws the needle from one protesting alligator.

LOU GUILETTE: There you go, and I have urine running down my leg.

STUDENT: Alligator urine.

LOU GUILETTE: Alligator urine, that's right. Let's clarify that! It's big. It was scared.

RICHARD HARRIS: Guilette has a lot of work to do before he can prove that the malformed reproductive organs, the hormone imbalances and the small penises are due to the chemical spill. Most important, he hasn't completed the studies to show whether chemicals injected into alligator eggs will damage the embryos by disrupting their hormone or endocrine systems. But Guilette says he has already seen enough.

LOU GUILETTE: I believe that Lake Apopka is a very, very good example of how a wildlife species can be affected by a contaminant as an endocrine disrupter.

RICHARD HARRIS: The big question in his mind is whether this problem is peculiar to highly contaminated places like Lake Apopka or whether it's a widespread threat to wildlife and possibly people as well. The person who has made this question the focus of her career for the past several years is Theo Colborn at the World Wildlife Fund. She says it may be tempting to conclude that this lake is just a fluke.

THEO COLBORN, World Wildlife Fund: But if you start looking at the scientific literature not only from around the United States but around the world, you begin to see similar patterns in other wildlife populations.

RICHARD HARRIS: Colborn says, for example, birds and fish in the Great Lakes arc clearly suffering from hormonal problems.

THEO COLBORN: You can hardly find a fish in the Great Lakes that doesn't have an enlarged thyroid. We've been tinkering with a system that we don't know enough about and so we've created problems that we never anticipated and didn't think were there.

RICHARD HARRIS: But while the activist part of Theo Colborn is convinced there is a problem we need to address now, the scientist in her readily admits serious weaknesses in the evidence.

THEO COLBORN: It's definitely hypothetical because where there is no way you're going to be able to link any effect with a specific chemical, especially if it was the result of maternal exposure in an individual that actually survived and made it through birth and is running around today. So, it's going to be hypothetical, it's going to be hypothetical forever.

RICHARD HARRIS: If this is always going to be hypothetical because it's so hard to get to the bottom of it, that creates very difficult problems for policy makers, because the world is full of an infinite number of hypothetical threats. How do you deal with this?

THEO COLBORN: Well, there comes a time when we can't count on the scientists. There have to be people out there who suddenly say there is a moral issue here, there is an ethical issue here. It goes beyond all of the science, it goes beyond economics and risk benefit, it reaches the point where someone says, you know, it's time we do something about this.

RICHARD HARRIS: And Colborn has taken on that crusade. Supporters call her the "Rachel Carson of the 1990's." She's asking society to reconsider its use of chemicals.

THEO COLBORN: Individuals should really be encouraging organic farming, family farming, so that the person who is using chemicals realizes he doesn't need to use chemicals. A lot of little things—individuals can form community groups and say we will no longer tolerate these kinds of chemicals in our neighborhood, in our homes, we're not going to use this particular product near my child, I don't want the schools using certain products in the schools, let's go back and scrub with Ivory soap or something like that. The point is, it means going back. It means looking at things a little differently.

RICHARD HARRIS: But some of Theo Colborn's colleagues are quite uncomfortable with the ground she has staked out. As a scientist at the University of California, Robert Rusbro was pivotal in the effort to ban DDT 20 years ago. Today, he says practically every example of hormone disruption in the wild involved sites that were extremely heavily contaminated with DDT or PCBs, chemicals that have both been banned in this country for decades. What we are seeing now, Rusbro argues, is the fading tail end of an old problem.

ROBERT RUSBRO, Scientist: During the DDT era, the cormorants of the Great Lakes were essentially wiped out, there were just a few pairs left. But over the past decade the populations have been expanding rapidly. So, 10 years ago there were no cormorants that had birth defects, and the ones that do have birth defects are in a bay that is very contaminated with PCBs. Now, granted, that is a very undesirable situation, but it's certainly better than no cormorants at all.

RICHARD HARRIS: The same goes for the bald eagle, now recovering strongly after a disastrous brush with DDT. And the western gulls in California that caused concern initially, also returned to normal long ago.

ROBERT RUSBRO: We're seeing a continually improving situation instead of something that might suggest worse things to come.

RICHARD HARRIS: In fact, Rusbro is quite concerned about Theo Colborn's crusade on this issue. He notes that a widely publicized theory two years ago linking breast cancer to DDT exposure is faltering. He says there is a very real chance Theo Colborn's hypothesis will falter, too, and he says that could harm the credibility of environmental research in general.

ROBERT RUSBRO: And credibility is so important and I just hate to see it squandered away with things that will eventually be shown not to merit the consideration they're getting.

RICHARD HARRIS: Rusbro's concern is shared by many scientists looking into the question of hormone disrupters. Even Franklin Percival who collaborates with Lou Guilette at Lake Apopka, is reluctant to draw the same bold conclusions about the alligators.

FRANKLIN PERCIVAL, Scientist: We have some fairly damning information that something is awry, badly awry, in Lake Apopka, but I don't think we have the information yet to say exactly what the problem is. It would probably be a good bet that it's contaminants, but you can lose that bet.

RICHARD HARRIS: Lou Guilette acknowledges these doubts.

LOU GUILETTE: Yes, science must define in more detail the complete borders of this problem. How extensive is the problem? How much does this problem contribute to wildlife declines or human health declines that we see? I do not believe that it's the time for us to sit back and collect more data and more data and wait to make policy decisions. I think there is enough data right now to certainly move policy-wise against a number of chemicals.

RICHARD HARRIS: In fact, federal scientists are developing tests to identify chemicals that could disrupt hormones. Right now, scientists don't know what chemicals could be worrisome or at what doses. So, no one can say whether controlling these compounds would be a simple task or a huge challenge to the way we use chemicals today. The higher the stakes, the more proof regulators are likely to require before they conclude that hormone disrupters could represent the next *Silent Spring*.

NOTES

1. Are you persuaded that the Lake Apopka alligators have been poisoned? Even if they have been, what uncertainties remain concerning endocrine disruption generally? What science and policy issues does remaining uncertainty raise? Should EPA take action against dicofol on the basis of Guilette's finding?

2. *Human fertility.* Hormone disruption is not limited to animals. A number of scientists have noted a world-wide decline in male fertility, *i.e.*, low sperm counts, and some have attributed this to exposure to synthetic estrogens or estrogen-like chemicals. It is notable, for example, that lower sperm counts are associated with urban living, where exposure to environmental hormone disrupters are presumably the highest. The evidence for this phenomenon is reviewed in Lawrence Wright, *Silent Sperm*, 71 THE NEW YORKER 42 (Jan. 15, 1996). More recent studies have found that sperm counts among men living in U.S. cities are holding steady, and, the *New York Times* reported, "men in New York City, for unknown reasons, consistently

have the highest sperm counts of all." Gina Kolata, *Are U.S. Men Less Fertile? Latest Research Says No*, NEW YORK TIMES (nat'l ed.), p. A3 (Apr. 29, 1996).

3. *Burden of proof.* More generally, should we rethink the general presumption that a chemical may be produced until it is proven hazardous? One review of Colborn's book was critical of her sometimes cavalier approach to the rigors of scientific proof, but nevertheless compared it to *Silent Spring*:

> The urgency of the present authors' message is strongly reminiscent of that of Rachel Carson in *Silent Spring*, a comparison the authors encourage. The critical response to *Our Stolen Future* is also strongly reminiscent of the response to Carson's book. In both cases, some segments of the scientific community have come out swinging. For instance, in 1962, a review of *Silent Spring* in *Chemical and Engineering News* stated, "In view of the mature, responsible attention which this whole subject receives from able qualified scientific groups * * * (whom Miss Carson chooses to ignore); in view of her scientific qualification in contrast to those of our distinguished scientific leaders and statesmen, this book should be ignored." In 1996, a discussion of *Our Stolen Future* in the *Washington Post* quoted John Giesy, past president of the Society of Environmental Toxicology and Chemistry as saying, "Frankly, Colburn [sic] doesn't know very much. She reads the entire literature and picks and chooses things that support her preconceived views." It also quotes Larry Lipshultz, professor of urology at Baylor College of Medicine: "Something is missing in *Our Stolen Future* and that's called science."

> Perhaps the critical reaction to *Silent Spring* has lessons for our own times. As its reviewer in the *New York Times* stated, "despite the drawbacks of 'Silent Spring'-and to some extent because of them–it is an important book. 'Uncle Tom's Cabin' would never have stirred a nation had it been measured and 'fair'." The *Christian Science Monitor* noted, "Miss Carson has undeniably sketched a one-sided picture. But her distortion is akin to that of the painter who exaggerates to focus attention on essentials. It is not the half-truth of the propagandist." Even after Carson "stirred a nation," the regulatory community took 10 years to respond to a growing threat. From a distance of more than 30 years we know that Carson's anxiety about DDT and chlordane was not misplaced. Do we have the luxury of waiting another 30 years to determine if Colborn and her colleagues are overstating their case against PCBs and other so-called endocrine disrupters?

Anne N. Hirschfield, *et al.*, *Book Review-Problems Beyond Pesticides*, 272 SCIENCE 1444 (1996).

4. The Food Quality Protection Act of 1996, which establishes new risk-based standards for pesticide residues in foods, includes provisions for endocrine testing and screening for endocrine effects. 21 U.S.C. § 346a(p). As part of this effort, EPA sponsored a study of endocrine disrupters by the National Academy of Sciences. Its report, *Hormonally Active Agents in the Environment* (1999), was claimed as a victory by both sides. Those who believe that some chemicals cause endocrine disruption were heartened by the fact that the NAS did not dismiss the idea but called for additional research. Those who believe that endocrine disruption is a myth pointed to the NAS conclusion that endocrine effects are far from proven.[20]

How should EPA respond to this equivocal evidence? If endocrine disruption is real, it could be catastrophic, so preemptive action may be warranted. But if there is no effect at low doses, or the effect is very weak, regulation could impose unjustified costs and hardships on the makers and users of the suspect chemicals. This is a recurrent problem in EPA's regulation of toxic substances, and it derives directly from their toxicological properties.

B. Quantitative Risk Assessment

The nature of toxic substances seems to demand that we characterize their effects and regulate them in terms of the probabilistic concept of risk. Since probabilities are mathematical constructs, it seems also to follow that risks are quantifiable. Quantitative risk assessment is the procedure for numerically describing environmental risks. It has become the analytical tool of choice for characterizing existing conditions, for defining environmentally satisfactory conditions, and for analyzing the means of moving from the existing to the satisfactory condition.

1. The Red Book Framework for Risk Assessment

A 1983 publication of the National Academy of Sciences (NAS), *Risk Assessment in the Federal Government: Managing the Process,* familiarly known as the Red Book, set out the form of risk assessment that has come to dominate environmental regulation. In its present form, quantitative risk assessment is profoundly influenced by the problem of non-threshold carcinogens, and this in turn affects the ways in which we regulate such substances. The NAS and others have refined this model on a number of occasions since then; however, the basic framework has remained intact. Explication and criticism of various aspects of the Red Book formulation fill libraries, so we will focus on just a few issues here. We begin with the Academy's own statement of its framework.

---

[20] For a particularly vociferous example of this point of view, *see* Gregg Easterbrook, *Science Fiction*, The New Republic (Aug. 30, 1999).

RISK ASSESSMENT IN THE FEDERAL GOVERNMENT: MANAGING THE PROCESS

National Research Council[21]
pp. 18-28 (1983)

RISK ASSESSMENT AND RISK MANAGEMENT

We use *risk assessment* to mean the characterization of the potential adverse health effects of human exposures to environmental hazards. Risk assessments include several elements: description of the potential adverse health effects based on an evaluation of results of epidemiologic, clinical, toxicologic, and environmental research; extrapolation from those results to predict the type and estimate the extent of health effects in humans under given conditions of exposure; judgments as to the number and characteristics of persons exposed at various intensities and durations; and summary judgments on the existence and overall magnitude of the public-health problem. Risk assessment also includes characterization of the uncertainties inherent in the process of inferring risk.

The term *risk assessment* is often given narrower and broader meanings than we have adopted here. For some observers, the term is synonymous with *quantitative risk assessment* and emphasizes reliance on numerical results. Our broader definition includes quantification, but also includes qualitative expressions of risk. Quantitative estimates of risk are not always feasible, and they may be eschewed by agencies for policy reasons. Broader uses of the term than ours also embrace analysis of perceived risks, comparisons of risks associated with different regulatory strategies, and occasionally analysis of the economic and social implications of regulatory decisions-functions that we assign to risk management.

The Committee uses the term *risk management* to describe the process of evaluating alternative regulatory actions and selecting among them. Risk management, which is carried out by regulatory agencies under various legislative mandates, is an agency decision-making process that entails consideration of political, social, economic, and engineering information with risk-related information to develop, analyze, and compare regulatory options and to select the appropriate regulatory response to a potential chronic health hazard. The selection process necessarily requires the use of value judgments on such issues as the acceptability of risk and the reasonableness of the costs of control.

STEPS IN RISK ASSESSMENT

Risk assessment can be divided into four major steps: hazard identification, dose-response assessment, exposure assessment, and risk characterization. A risk assessment might stop with the first step, hazard identification, if no adverse effect is found or if an agency elects to take

---

[21] The operating arm of the National Academy of Sciences is the National Research Council (NRC); consequently, the author of Academy reports is the Council.

regulatory action without further analysis, for reasons of policy or statutory mandate.

Of the four steps, *hazard identification* is the most easily recognized in the actions of regulatory agencies. It is defined here as the process of determining whether exposure to an agent can cause an increase in the incidence of a health condition (cancer, birth defect, etc.). It involves characterizing the nature and strength of the evidence of causation. Although the question of whether a substance causes cancer or other adverse health effects is theoretically a yes-no question, there are few chemicals on which the human data are definitive. * * *

Dose-response assessment is the process of characterizing the relation between the dose of an agent administered or received and the incidence of an adverse health effect in exposed populations and estimating the incidence of the effect as a function of human exposure to the agent. It takes account of intensity of exposure, age pattern of exposure, and possibly other variables that might affect response, such as sex, lifestyle, and other modifying factors. A dose-response assessment usually requires extrapolation from high to low dose and extrapolation from animals to humans. A dose-response assessment should describe and justify the methods of extrapolation used to predict incidence and should characterize the statistical and biologic uncertainties in these methods.

Exposure assessment is the process of measuring or estimating the intensity, frequency, and duration of human exposures to an agent currently present in the environment or of estimating hypothetical exposures that might arise from the release of new chemicals into the environment. In its most complete form, it describes the magnitude, duration, schedule, and route of exposure; the size, nature, and classes of the human populations exposed; and the uncertainties in all estimates. Exposure assessment is often used to identify feasible prospective control options and to predict the effects of available control technologies on exposure.

Risk characterization is the process of estimating the incidence of a health effect under the various conditions of human exposure described in exposure assessment. It is performed by combining the exposure and dose-response assessments. The summary effects of the uncertainties in the preceding steps are described in this step.

The relations among the four steps of risk assessment and between risk assessment and risk management are depicted in [Figure 2.5]. The type of research information needed for each step is also illustrated.

—

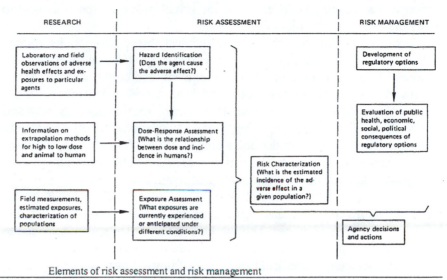

Elements of risk assessment and risk management

Figure 2.5–The Red Book Model

NOTES

1. *Assessment and management.* How are risk assessment and risk management different in theory? Do you see any difficulties in putting the distinction into practice?

2. *The risk formula.* The basic formula for quantitative risk assessment is: adverse effect × likelihood of occurrence = toxicity; toxicity × amount of exposure = risk. To what extent is the Red Book framework necessarily quantitative? What would qualitative risk assessment look like?

3. *Bibliography.* Many, many works are readily available that describe quantitative risk assessment. Authoritative descriptions of the current state of the art include: National Research Council, *Science and Judgment in Risk Assessment* (1994); National Research Council, *Understanding Risk: Informing Decisions in a Democratic Society* (1996); Presidential/ Congressional Commission on Risk Assessment and Management, *Risk Assessment and Risk Management in Regulatory Decision-Making* (1997). EPA has recently issued an updated proposal for comprehensive guidance on risk assessment, EPA, Proposed Guidelines for Carcinogen Risk Assessment, 61 Fed. Reg. 17960 (1996).

a. Hazard Identification

Hazard identification is the first step in the Red Book's risk assessment process. It answers the general causation question, Does Chemical X cause Effect Y? This is a threshold issue: without the causal finding, performing the remainder of the risk assessment would be pointless. Perhaps the best way to illustrate hazard identification, and to distinguish it from the related dose-response assessment, is to examine an actual study of the relationship between benzene and leukemia.[22]

Toxicology studies of various kinds (clinical observations, epidemiology, and animal bioassays) over several decades had suggested a causal association between benzene, a common industrial solvent, and certain cancers of the blood and lymphatic systems, notably leukemia. To clarify this relationship, a group of scientists at the National Institute for Occupational Safety and Health (NIOSH), the research wing of the Occupational Safety and Health Administration (OSHA), undertook a retrospective epidemiological study of workers exposed to benzene. Their study was based on the recorded causes of death of workers at three Ohio plants that manufactured rubber film. The manufacturing process involved dissolving natural rubber in benzene, spreading it on a conveyor, and then evaporating and recovering the benzene, leaving a thin film of rubber. The workers at these plants were exposed to significant amounts of benzene (though usually within applicable legal limits), and their exposures had been closely followed by their employers for compliance purposes. As a result, these workers presented an unusually good opportunity to study the toxic effects of benzene on a human population.

In their initial pass through the data, Robert A. Rinsky and his colleagues compared the expected number and cause of deaths in the population as a whole, based on standard mortality patterns, with the number and cause of deaths in the worker population that was studied. Their results are summarized below:

Table 1. Observed and Expected Deaths from All Causes, All Malignant Neoplasms, and Lymphatic and Hematopoietic Cancers in Rubber Workers Exposed to Benzene[23]		
CAUSE OF DEATH	NO. OF DEATHS	
	OBSERVED	EXPECTED
All causes	330	331.6
All malignant neoplasms	69	66.8
Lymphatic & hematopoietic cancers	15	6.6
Leukemia	9	2.7
Multiple myeloma	4	1.0

---

[22] Robert A. Rinsky *et al.*, *Benzene and Leukemia: An Epidemiologic Risk Assessment*, 316 NEW ENGLAND JOURNAL OF MEDICINE 1044 (1987).

The Rinsky study is a very important part of the regulation of toxic substances, because the data reported in it were part of the basis for the OSHA regulations that were overturned in the landmark Supreme Court case on toxics regulation, Industrial Union Department, AFL-CIO v. American Petroleum Institute, 448 U.S. 607 (1980) (it is reprinted in Chapter 4, *infra*), also known as the *Benzene* case.

[23] Adapted from Rinsky *et al.*, *supra*, at 1046 (table 1).

The researchers found a statistically significant increase in deaths from all lymphatic and blood system cancers, especially leukemia and multiple myeloma. There was no similar increase in mortality from all causes of death combined or from all cancers combined. OSHA regarded these findings as a strong demonstration of a causal link between benzene and leukemia. Can you see why?

The International Agency for Research on Cancer (IARC) has developed a set of qualitative criteria for describing the strength of the evidence for the carcinogenicity of a substance in humans. They are: (1) sufficient, which requires a causal connection for humans, and two species or two studies in animals; (2) limited, that is, a credible association for humans, and one study in animals; (3) inadequate; and (4) evidence for *lack* of carcinogenicity, which requires multiple, consistent negative results, *e.g.*, multiple studies in two or more animal species. These judgments are often translated into the following, somewhat different categorization:

Group 1–carcinogenic in humans

Group 2A–probably carcinogenic

Group 2B–possible carcinogenic

Group 3–not classifiable

Group 4–probably not carcinogenic under the tested conditions of exposure.

(Query: Why is Group 4 stated differently from the others?) Benzene is regarded as a Group 1 carcinogen. Why?

EPA recently updated its research on benzene and concluded that no change in the current classification is warranted. Benzene remains a "known human carcinogen," placing it in a very exclusive club. While its actual mechanism of action remains unknown, EPA concluded that there is no basis for abandoning the assumption of no threshold. *See* EPA, Carcinogenic Effects of Benzene: An Update (April 1998) http://www.epa.gov/ncea/benzene.htm.

The data in Table 1 (together with the other studies of benzene) fulfil the hazard identification function for a risk assessment of benzene. But notice what is left out of the analysis. The table classifies deaths only by disease, so there is no indication of the effects of benzene at different doses, nor is there any accounting for the latency period between exposure and health effect. Therefore, while the data in Table 1 identify a hazard, they do not establish the potency of the chemical at different levels of exposure. The latter, of course, is the province of dose-response assessment.

To fill this gap, Rinsky and his collaborators reanalyzed their data in a second study. The results are summarized below:

Table 2. Observed and Expected Deaths from Leukemia in 1165 White Men with at Least One Day of Exposure to Benzene from January 1, 1940, through December 31, 1965, According to Cumulative Exposure and Years of Latency[24]

LATENCY (YR)	EXPOSURE (PPM-YR)				
	0.001-40	40-200	200-400	>400	TOTAL*
	observed/expected deaths				
<5	2/0.10	0/0.02	—	—	2/0.12
5-10	0/0.16	0/0.05	0/0.01	—	0/0.22
10-15	0/0.22	1/0.07	1/0.02	0/0.00	2/0.31
15-20	0/0.27	1/0.09	1/0.03**	2/0.01	3/0.39
20-25	0/0.32	0/0.10	0/0.03	1/0.01	1/0.46
25-30	0/0.37	0/0.12	0/0.04	0/0.01	0/0.54
>30	0/0.40	0/0.16	1/0.04	0/0.01	1/0.62
Total*	2/1.83	2/0.62	2/0.17	3/0.04	9/2.66

* The numbers of expected deaths has been rounded.

**Probably should read 0/0.03.–EDS.

The NIOSH researchers concluded that the data in Table 2 show "a marked, progressive increase [in leukemia] with increasing cumulative exposure to benzene." (Latency, however, demonstrated no particular pattern.) Compare Table 1 and Table 2. How are they different? How much data went into each? What does Table 2 show that Table 1 does not?

Why is the additional information in Table 2 useful to regulators? That is, why not base regulatory action against benzene on the results in Table 1 alone?

The NIOSH investigators went on to extrapolate a dose-response curve applicable to the low exposures (1-10 ppm) anticipated by OSHA's regulation. They calculated that leukemia risk would be dramatically reduced by lowering exposures to 1 ppm, and that at 0.1 ppm the risk would be indistinguishable from background rates of leukemia. We now turn to the issues raised by dose-response assessment.

b. Dose-Response

As the Rinsky study demonstrates, the complexity of the dose-response assessment is much greater than the initial hazard identification. The level of uncertainty is much greater, as well. "The uncertainties inherent in risk assessment can be grouped in two general categories: missing or ambiguous information on a particular substance and gaps in current scientific theory. When scientific uncertainty is encountered in the risk assessment process, inferential bridges are needed to allow the process to continue." Red Book,

---

[24] Adapted from Rinsky *et al.*, *supra*, at 1046 (table 2).

supra, at 28. These "inferential bridges" are usually called "default assumptions."

The two most important areas of dose-response assessment in which default assumptions are required to bridge gaps in knowledge or information are (1) the application of animal test results to human beings, and (2) effects at very low levels of exposure, because (1) for obvious reasons, direct experimentation on humans (other than epidemiology, which has limitations we have seen) is impossible, and (2) scientists need to use high doses to stimulate observable effects in the laboratory. The following excerpt from EPA's most recent risk assessment guidelines addresses the proper use of these default assumptions.

PROPOSED GUIDELINES FOR CARCINOGEN RISK ASSESSMENT

Environmental Protection Agency
61 Fed. Reg. 17960, 17964-70 (1996)

1.3. Use of Default Assumptions

* * *

In the 1983 report, NAS defined the use of "inference options" (default options) as a means to bridge inherent uncertainties in risk assessment. These options exist when the assessment encounters either "missing or ambiguous information on a particular substance" or "gaps in current scientific theory." Since there is no instance in which a set of data on an agent or exposure is complete, all risk assessments must use general knowledge and policy guidance to bridge data gaps.

* * *

[One difficulty is deciding when to replace the (usually conservative[25]) default assumptions with experimental findings.] Judgments about plausibility and persuasiveness of [alternative] analyses vary according to the scientific nature of the default. An analysis of data may replace a default or modify it.
* * *

* * *

The 1994 NRC report [*Science and Judgment, supra*] notes that "[a]s scientific knowledge increases, the science policy choices made by the Agency and Congress should have less impact on regulatory decision making. Better data and increased understanding of biological mechanisms should enable risk assessments that are less dependent on conservative default assumptions and more accurate as predictions of human risk." Undoubtedly, this is the trend as scientific understanding increases. However, some gaps in knowledge and data will doubtless continue to be encountered in assessment of even data-rich cases, and it will remain necessary for risk assessments to continue using defaults within the framework set forth here.

---

[25] "Conservative," in this context, means precautionary, that is, erring (if at all) on the side of safety. It has nothing to do with political conservatism.

1.3.2. Major Defaults

* * *

1.3.2.2. Is the Presence or Absence of Effects Observed in an Animal Population Predictive of Effects in Exposed Humans? The default assumption is that positive effects in animal cancer studies indicate that the agent under study can have carcinogenic potential in humans. Thus, if no adequate human data are present, positive effects in animal cancer studies are a basis for assessing the carcinogenic hazard to humans. This assumption is a public health conservative policy, and it is both appropriate and necessary given that we do not test for carcinogenicity in humans. The assumption is supported by the fact that nearly all of the agents known to cause cancer in humans are carcinogenic in animals in tests with adequate protocols. Moreover, almost one-third of human carcinogens were identified subsequent to animal testing. Further support is provided by research on the molecular biology of cancer processes, which has shown that the mechanisms of control of cell growth and differentiation are remarkably homologous among species and highly conserved in evolution. Nevertheless, the same research tools that have enabled recognition of the nature and commonality of cancer processes at the molecular level also have the power to reveal differences and instances in which animal responses are not relevant to humans. Under these guidelines, available mode of action information is studied for its implications in both hazard and dose response assessment and its effect on default assumptions.

* * *

1.3.2.4. How Do Toxicokinetic Processes Relate Across Species? A major issue is how to estimate human equivalent doses in extrapolating from animal studies. As a default for oral exposure, a human equivalent dose is estimated from data on another species by an adjustment of animal oral dose by a scaling factor of body weight to the 0.75 power. [The principal alternative, body surface area, was rejected as the standard default.]

* * *

1.3.2.5. What Is the Correlation of the Observed Dose Response Relationship to the Relationship at Lower Doses? The overriding preferred approach is to use a biologically based or case-specific model for both the observed range and extrapolation below that range when there are sufficient data. While biologically based models are still under development, it is likely that they will be used more frequently in the future. The default procedure for the observed range of data, when the preferred approach cannot be used, is to use a curve-fitting model.

In the absence of data supporting a biologically based or case-specific model for extrapolation outside of the observed range, the choice of approach is based on the view of mode of action of the agent arrived at in the hazard assessment. A linear default approach is used when the mode of action information is supportive of linearity or, alternatively, is insufficient to support a nonlinear mode of action. The linear approach is used when a view of the mode of action indicates a linear response, for example, when a conclusion is made that an agent directly causes alterations in DNA, a kind of interaction that not only theoretically requires one reaction, but also is likely to be additive to ongoing, spontaneous gene mutation.

* * *

The linear default is thought to generally produce an upper bound on potential risk at low doses, *e.g.*, a 1/100,000 to 1/1,000,000 risk; the straight line approach gives numerical results about the same as a linearized multistage procedure. This upper bound is thought to cover the range of human variability although, in some cases, it may not completely do so. The EPA considers the linear default to be inherently conservative of public health.

—

The EPA guidance makes clear that the choice of default assumptions is a matter of both science and policy. This has become a point of controversy in toxics regulation, because there are some who advocate a "pure" science-based approach to risk assessment and risk regulation. As Professor Wagner's article makes clear, however, this aspiration, while superficially appealing, is neither descriptive of current risk assessment practices nor a realistic (or even meaningful) goal.[26]

THE SCIENCE CHARADE IN TOXIC RISK REGULATION

Wendy E. Wagner
95 COLUM. L. REV. 1613, 1618-26 (1995)

A. The Mixture of Science and Policy

Science-based regulations are typically based on a vague statutory mandate that requires the agency to set standards or take action at the point at which a chemical substance "presents or will present an unreasonable risk of injury to health or the environment." The initial step of translating "unreasonable risk" into a quantitative goal is often resolved with a single, express policy choice, such as a risk averse goal that no more than one in one million persons be adversely affected. The second and final step-determining the concentration at which any particular toxic substance actually poses a predetermined quantitative heath risk-requires a more extended inquiry and presents several significant challenges. These difficulties and their implications for policymaking are considered below.

1. Limits of Science.-First, and despite appearances to the contrary, contemporary science is incapable of completely resolving the level at which a chemical will pose some specified, quantitative risk to humans. In assessing the health risks of formaldehyde, for example, scientific experimentation can establish the effects of high doses of formaldehyde on the total number of

---

[26] We pursue this issue in more detail in section B(3) of this chapter, *infra*.

nasal tumors in laboratory mice, but quantification of the effects of low doses on humans currently lies beyond the reach of science.

Nuclear physicist Alvin Weinberg first identified these gaps in knowledge as "trans-science"-"questions which can be asked of science and yet *which cannot be answered by science.*"[27] In contrast to the uncertainty that is characteristic of all of science, in which "the answer" is accompanied by some level of unpreventable statistical noise or uncertainty, trans-scientific questions are uncertain because scientists cannot even perform the experiments to test the hypotheses. This can be due to a variety of technological, informational, and ethical constraints on experimentation. For example, ethical mores prohibit direct testing on humans, leaving investigators to extrapolate the effects of a toxic substance on humans from studies conducted on animals. Even when some segment of the human population has been exposed to a toxic substance, isolating that substance's impact may be statistically impossible because of the many other factors that adversely affect human health.

Since trans-scientific issues arise from a variety of practical and theoretical limitations on scientific experimentation, the ability of science to quantify adverse health effects of low levels of toxins can be quite limited. To reach a final quantitative standard, policy considerations must fill in the gaps that science cannot inform. This combination of science and policy necessary to the resolution of issues concerning toxics regulation has led to the classification of these issues as "science-policy" problems.

2. The Fragmented Contributions of Science.-A second problem arising in the attempt to quantify health risks is that those insights which science is able to provide are fragmented and occur sporadically throughout the larger investigation. The search for a "safe" concentration of a chemical, which poses only minimal risks to human health, immediately breaks down into a sequence of smaller sub-questions that often alternate between questions that can be resolved with science and others that cannot.

* * *

This mix of science and policy can be illustrated by depicting a few hypothetical stages in an agency's effort to determine the maximum concentration of a carcinogen, such as formaldehyde, acceptable in public drinking water. Typically, the best information available on carcinogenicity consists of laboratory studies in which animals have been exposed to high concentrations of the specified chemical. One of the first trans-scientific questions that arises is whether to count all tumors found in test animals after exposure or only those tumors that prove to be malignant. Although the decision will dramatically affect quantification of the hazard posed by the chemical, guidance provided by science in selecting among the options is

---

[27] Alvin M. Weinberg, *Science and Trans-Science*, 10 MINERVA 209, 209 (1972). As Dr. Weinberg points out, it is not that scientists have not tried to answer trans-scientific questions, or even that they have not been given the funds to answer these questions, it is simply that science can only go so far in answering them.

limited. Once this trans-scientific question has been resolved with a nonscientific determination, the statistical results will provide valuable quantitative information on the effects of high levels of the substance on animals. Extrapolating these results to potential effects of low levels of the substance on humans then presents the next two trans-scientific junctures, which are often collapsed into one. First, an extrapolatory model must be selected that will predict low-dose effects on animals based solely on high-dose data. Although there are several scientifically plausible extrapolatory models, the choice of one model over another cannot be resolved by science and thus must be determined by policy factors. This policy choice will have significant implications for the level ultimately chosen as adequate to protect public health. Second, since the similarities between animals and humans with regard to their sensitivity to carcinogens are largely unknown and incapable of being studied directly, a policy choice must again be made. For example, in many standard-setting efforts decision makers adopt the risk averse assumption that humans are one hundred times more sensitive to the adverse effects of a carcinogen than test animals. After these trans-scientific junctures have been bridged with policy choices, further resolution of the inquiry then turns back to science for estimates of the average daily adult intake of water and scientifically plausible models for absorption of the carcinogen in an adult. The absorption model ultimately selected will again be based on policy considerations.

Since dozens of such issues arise in determining the concentration at which a chemical causes adverse health effects, the number of scientific and trans-scientific subquestions that must be addressed in the course of a single standard-setting project is substantial, and the cumulative effect of these subquestions can have profound policy implications.* * *

NOTES

1. Why are default values necessary and important for dose-response analysis? What is the justification for adopting conservative values?

2. *Types of uncertainty.* Two types of uncertainty give rise to the need to use default assumptions:

Information uncertainty and *knowledge uncertainty* * * *. [I]nformation uncertainty arises when relevant data is not collected, although it could be or when existing information is not made available to the decisionmaker who needs it. Knowledge uncertainty, in comparison, stems from a lack of adequate scientific understanding, or from situations where the collection of necessary information is infeasible.

There is no clear demarcation between information uncertainty and knowledge uncertainty; the marginal point at which information becomes so difficult or expensive to collect that it is effectively unobtainable will often be indistinct. Nevertheless, the dichotomy is significant from a legal perspective because the consequences of allocating the burdens of production and proof may vary greatly depending on the nature of the uncertainty presented. Information uncertainty can be eliminated if the value of the missing data makes collection worthwhile. A doctrine designating one party responsible for resolution of information uncertainty presents that party with a realistic choice: either provide the information or surrender the point. Which alternative is selected depends on how the designated party perceives the relative costs and benefits of production. The picture is quite different when knowledge uncertainty is involved. Research may be directed toward a critical problem, but there is rarely any assurance that the desired knowledge can be acquired, especially within the time frame associated with a specific legal controversy. Thus, a rule assigning legal responsibility for knowledge uncertainty also determines the eventual result in most cases: whoever bears that burden generally loses.

Howard A. Latin, *The "Significance" of Toxic Health Risks: An Essay on Legal Decisionmaking Under Uncertainty*, 10 ECOLOGY L.Q. 339, 356-57 (1982).[28] Where do the low-dose and animal-to-human assumptions fit into these categories? What difference does it make in risk assessment?

3. The resolution of these uncertainties involves both science and "trans-science," as Wagner points out.[29] How are the two different? How are they reflected in EPA's default assumptions?

What difference does it make whether an assumption is science or trans-science, toxicology or policy? For one thing, it turns out that different people will make different judgments. While it may come as no surprise that scientists employed by industry have different views of, say, the propriety of

---

[28] A similar division was advanced by other scholars:

    1. Available and definite

    2. Available and indefinite

    3. Unavailable but theoretically obtainable

        A. Practically obtainable without significant commitment of resources

        B. Practically obtainable with significant commitment of resources

        C. Practically unobtainable

            (1) Necessary resource commitment too great

            (2) Necessary time too long

    4. Unavailable and theoretically unobtainable

Marcia R. Gelpe & A. Dan Tarlock, *The Uses of Scientific Information in Environmental Decisionmaking*, 48 S. CAL. L. REV. 371, 394-95 (1974). A more complex categorization is developed in Vern R. Walker, *The Siren Song of Science: Toward a Taxonomy of Scientific Uncertainty for Decisionmakers*, 23 CONN. L. REV. 567 (1991).

[29] *See also* Thomas O. McGarity, *Substantive and Procedural Discretion in Administrative Resolution of Science Policy Questions: Regulating Carcinogens in EPA and OSHA*, 67 GEO. L.J. 729 (1979).

using animal models than government scientists, this is surely what we think of as a political difference, rather than pure "science."[30]

4. *Low-dose linearity.* One of the most contentious areas for default assumptions is the extrapolation from high to low doses. The following description of the risks of trichloroethylene (TCE), a common drinking water pollutant, goes a long way toward explaining why:

> The bioassay data are fit to four analytical models: logit, multistage, probit, and Weibull. These four models are chosen somewhat arbitrarily and are representative of models currently in use. It is well-known that other models could be used to fit the same data. There are no biologically based criteria for choosing one model over another. The models are in the form of analytical expressions that can be used to fit the high-dose data mathematically.

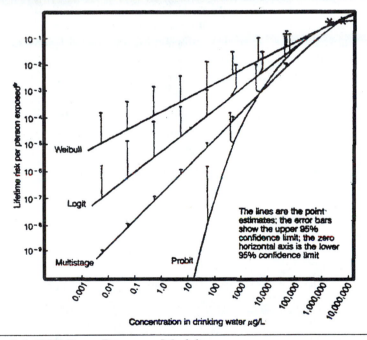

Figure 2.6–TCE Dose-Response Models

* * *

Although the dose-response curves projected by each model * * * start at the same points, they diverge significantly at lower dose levels. At a concentration of 50 μg/L TCE in drinking water, the Weibull model provides a risk estimate approximating 1×10^{-2}, whereas the probit model provides an estimate of 10^{-10}. These estimates provide a range of uncertainty equivalent to not knowing

---

[30] *See* Frances M. Lynn, *OSHA's Carcinogens Standard: Round One on Risk Assessment Models and Assumptions,* in THE SOCIAL AND CULTURAL CONSTRUCTION OF RISK (Branden B. Johnson & Vincent T. Covello, eds. 1987) at 345, 352-55.

whether one has enough money to buy a cup of coffee or pay off the national debt.

Cothern *et al., Estimating Risk to Human Health*, 20 ENVTL. SCI. & TECH. 111, 114-15 (1986). What are we to make of a range of uncertainty that spans cups of coffee and the national debt? Can the range be narrowed? How?

Why does EPA still use the linear, non-threshold model, even though it is not demonstrably correct?

5. *Susceptible individuals and groups.* As we saw with lead's effects on children, not all individuals react the same way to toxic chemicals.

> Genetic, nutritional, metabolic, and other differences make some segments of a population more susceptible than others to the effects of a given exposure to a given chemical; however, current regulatory approaches for reducing risks associated with chemical exposures generally do not include information on differences in individual susceptibility or encourage gathering evidence to identify them. In the absence of specific information about differences in susceptibility, risk assessments rely on assumptions and safety factors that are presumed to be protective of sensitive individuals.

* * *

	Factor Affecting Response to Exposure
Asthmatics	Increased airway responsiveness to allergens, respiratory irritants, and infectious agents
Fetuses	Sensitivity of developing organs to toxicants that cause birth defects
Infants and young children	Sensitivity of developing brain to neurotoxic agents such as lead
Socio-economic groups	Underlying nutritional deficits and poor access to health care
Elderly	Diminished detoxification and elimination mechanisms in kidney and liver

2 Presidential/Congressional Commission, *supra*, at 71-72.[31] Should environmental standards be set on the basis of the characteristics of susceptible individuals and groups? Can one draw an analogy to the so-called eggshell skull victim?[32]

6. A list of all of the points of uncertainty throughout the risk assessment process would be quite long. The more important uncertainties includes:

---

[31] *See also* Robert R. Kuehn, *The Environmental Justice Implications of Quantitative Risk Assessment*, 1996 U. ILL. L. REV. 103, 121-26 (arguing that minority communities are often more susceptible to environmental contamination than averaged data suggests).

[32] *See* Alfred C. Aman, Jr., *The Earth as Eggshell Victim: A Global Perspective on Domestic Regulation*, 102 YALE L.J. 2107, (1993) (citing Vosburg v. Putney, 50 N.W. 403 (Wis. 1891)).

- Classifying which animal carcinogens are human carcinogens
- Chemical to chemical
- Use of most sensitive sex/strain/tumor site in typical rodent studies vs. average sensitivity in a species
- Credit negative findings
- Use of human data vs. most sensitive animal sex/species/strain/tumor site.
- Individual human susceptibility
- Count benign tumors or not
- Use of linear vs. nonlinear extrapolation models; thresholds
- Use of contrary human data, mechanistic information
- Use of upper 95% confidence limits vs. plausible upper bounds vs. maximum likelihood estimates
- Use of different interspecies scaling factors: surface area (body weight) vs. body weight vs. body weight
- High to low dose; maximum tolerated dose
- Use of pharmacokinetic information in risk assessment: dose of substance at exchange boundary vs. dose at target organ
- Risks estimated for total population vs. target population
- Use of different *de minimis* risk thresholds to trigger regulatory action
- Adding vs. not adding theoretical risks for different substances
- The effects of mixtures of chemicals
- Expected vs. maximum exposures
- Consideration of potential synergisms or antagonisms with other carcinogens or promoters.

Adapted from CARL F. CRANOR, REGULATING TOXIC SUBSTANCES: A PHILOSOPHY OF SCIENCE AND THE LAW 221 (1993). A similar list can be found in the Red Book, *supra*, at 29-33. Professor Cranor notes that the choice of assumptions can make quantitative differences in outcome that cover several orders of magnitude.

c. Exposure Assessment

Exposure assessment follows the chemical of concern from its external source to its target cells in the body. As you can imagine, this is a complex process, involving many stages. These can be divided into three main phases: movement of the chemical outside the receptor organism, movement across the barriers (*e.g.,* skin) between the environment and the organism's body, and movement inside the organism's body. The initial parts of a molecule's journey (why a molecule?) are called "pathways," that is, the paths from source to human or ecological receptor. This phase is also known as "environmental fate and transport." It is pictured in Figure 2.7.

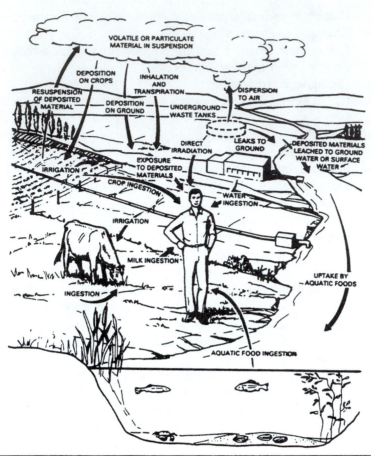

Figure 2.7–Exposure pathways[33]

The next stage is called "routes of exposure," which in animals are ingestion, inhalation, and dermal absorption. The final phase is pharmacokinetic, that is, the way that an organism handles an external substance from intake to output. The following excerpt summarizes the exposure information that must be supplied by observation or assumption to be able to perform a risk assessment.

RISK ASSESSMENT IN THE FEDERAL GOVERNMENT: TRYING TO UNDERSTAND THE PROCESS

Junius C. McElveen, Jr.
5 TUL. ENVTL. L.J. 45, 67-72 (1991)

The major exposure pathways for hazardous substances are inhalation, ingestion, and dermal contact. Thus, most risk assessments first look at the potential contamination of air, water, food, and soil or dust. Obviously, once the sources of potential exposure have been identified, a second question

---

[33] Source: Pacific Northwest Laboratory.

must be answered: What percentage of the substance is apt to get into the body and cause problems? The first of these questions is generally addressed by performing a contaminant release analysis, which examines the various ways that contaminants can be released from their sources into the air, water, food, or soil. The second question is answered by performance of a two-step evaluation: (1) a contaminant fate analysis is performed, which considers questions of transport, transformation, and ultimate fate of the contaminants; and (2) identification and characterization of potentially exposed populations is performed.

Air

a. Contaminant Release

Obviously, since very few sites have air sampling locations built in, either sampling must be done or assumptions have to be made. In addition, when assessing potential future contamination, researchers must replace measurements of actual concentrations with models of possible results. Although these models may use some measurements, they also rely on several assumptions. Thus, for example, the potential for air contamination depends mainly on the emissions of fugitive soils or dusts and the volatilization of contaminants. Emissions of soils depend on wind speed, the roughness and cloddiness of the surface, the moisture content of the surface soil, the kind and amount of surface vegetative cover, the amount of soil surface, and the lay of the land. To the extent measurements of each of these parameters does not occur, assumptions must be made about them. * * * Releases of volatiles depends on chemical properties, the depth and type of soil cover, and the amount of exposed area.

b. Contaminant Fate

The dose of a substance people actually receive depends on the substance, how much is absorbed, and the extent of their potential exposure. Potential exposure depends on the dispersion patterns of airborne materials and the concentration of contaminants in the airborne mixture. The concentration depends, in part, on whether materials are transferred out of air or are transformed. Transformation may occur, due to photolysis (breakdown because of reactions with solar energy) and oxidation (breakdown because of reactions with oxidants, like ozone, in the atmosphere). Computer models are available to analyze the atmospheric fate of many substances.

c. Populations

Risk assessors are also interested in the size and characteristics of the population potentially affected. The risk presented by a substance at a site is diminished if very few people are potentially exposed. Therefore, population data must be gathered. Assumptions must also be made about inhalation rates, contaminant concentrations, and the length of time exposure continues.

Water

Evaluation of potential exposure to contaminants that may be waterborne generally considers two types of potential contamination: groundwater and surface water. Similar types of inquiries that are made about air are also made regarding water. The questions "what likelihood is there that substances will get into the water?" and "what likelihood is there that substances will get into the body?" are significant. That likelihood is determined by measurements, where possible, and by assumptions, where measurements are not possible.

a. Contaminant Releases

i. Surface Water

Some of the factors that are considered in attempting to determine if a substance can get into surface water include: The potential for soil to erode, the leachability of the material through the soil, and the speed with which that movement occurs. Those determinations are, in turn, dependent on a variety of factors having to do with the permeability of the soil and the extent to which the hazardous substance can bind to materials moving through that soil.

* * *

ii. Groundwater

For groundwater, factors affecting contaminant release include rainfall, percolation rate of the soil, the solubility of the chemicals being studied, and the area being evaluated.

b. Contaminant Fate

i. Surface Water

The fate of contaminants in surface water depends on several factors. The first factor to be considered is the type of water body, since flowing water bodies, such as rivers and streams, are viewed much differently than nonmoving water bodies, such as lakes and estuaries. Second, the fate of contaminants depends on dilution potential. That potential, in turn, is dependent on mixing zone characteristics, the nature and extent of decay and removal processes, stream flow, and contaminant release.

ii. Groundwater

The fate of contaminants in groundwater also depends on a number of factors. The first step in groundwater contamination modeling is to determine the nature, depth, extent, direction, and velocity of flow of aquifers in the area of the contaminants. This is not easy, and well logs, characterizations by the U.S. Geologic Survey, and other sources of information need to be consulted.

Next, the direction and velocity of contaminant migration need to be determined, along with the contaminant concentration and volume. It should be recalled that groundwater contamination results when solid contaminants are liquified or leached by rain or other precipitation. The liquid contaminants then percolate into an aquifer, contaminating the groundwater. The viscosity and density of liquid contaminants affect the rate of migration. Finally, the migration rate is affected by the permeability of the soil through which the contaminant must move to reach the aquifer. In addition, as has been noted for other contaminants, transformation and retardation can occur, which affect migration rate by either preventing the substances from reaching the aquifer or postponing that arrival for a very long time.

c. Populations

i. Surface Water

The potentially exposed populations include all those who are served by a water supply that draws water from a contaminated water source, and those who may be exposed through potential ingestion or dermal contact. Those who may be exposed (through ingestion or dermally) in recreational activities, such as swimming or fishing, must also be considered.

ii. Groundwater

As in the case of surface water, if contaminated groundwater is a supply of drinking water, the population using that supply is potentially exposed. To the extent that occurs, all populations identified as potentially exposed to surface or drinking water contamination should be included in the population analysis.

Soil/Dust

Soil and dust are rarely ingested deliberately. They are ingested inadvertently, however, particularly by children who are at play, crawl around, or put their toys in their mouths. Therefore, the presence of hazardous substances in soil and dust is one which must be addressed in risk assessments. Here, issues include the measurement of contaminant levels to determine how substances might be transported to the soil or dust. * * *

On the issue of the dose which actually reaches target organs, the questions include: How much soil or dust is actually ingested, how much of the contaminant in the soil or dust gets out of its matrix in the digestive tract, and how much crosses the gut barrier. In addition, the size of the exposed populations and the amount of time they are exposed to the contaminant need to be considered.

Food

There are a number of ways that risk assessors assume hazardous substances can get into food. In looking at this issue, foods are generally divided into leaf crops (lettuce), root crops (potatoes), fruit crops (tomatoes), and animal life (fish, poultry, or livestock).

First, the substances may be deposited on the surface of the food. This can be accomplished by air deposition, for leaf or fruit crops, or by soil deposition, for a root crop. Second, contamination might be absorbed by the food item. One such example of absorption is the buildup of the pesticide DDT (a water-unsoluble solid, used as an insecticide) in fish and other marine organisms. Harm, such as the potential danger to birds and other wildlife from eating contaminated fish, small animals, grasses, leaves or fruit, is often considered in this portion of the risk assessment as well.

NOTES

1. Can you identify all of the points at which measurements or assumptions are necessary in exposure assessment? It might help to draft a schematic of the exposure process.

2. *Chemical properties.* The physical properties of chemicals are important to exposure analysis in several ways. For example, solubility in water is crucial to understanding the movement of a toxic substance through the environment. Even weight is important-heavier elements travel less far, so soil contamination near an air emission source is likely to be highly concentrated close to the source and limited at a distance.

Another property, emphasized at the beginning of the environmental movement by Rachel Carson in her study of DDT in *Silent Spring,* is bioaccumulation.

> The terms bioaccumulation, bioconcentration, and biomagnification all denote processes that concentrate a chemical substance in living tissues. Bioconcentration is the process by which a toxic substance enters an aquatic organism through the gills or epithelial tissues and is concentrated in the body. Bioaccumulation is the process by which a toxic substance is taken up by an organism not only from water, but also from food, and is the broader term. Frequently, "bioconcentration" and "bioaccumulation" are used as if they were synonyms. Biomagnification denotes the process by which a compound concentrates as it moves up the food chain. This article will use bioaccumulation in a broad sense to include the buildup of a substance in exposed organisms from all three processes. We distinguish among the terms only when necessary to ensure scientific accuracy.

Richard L. Williamson *et al.*, Gathering Danger: The Urgent Need to Regulate Toxic Substances That Can Bioaccumulate, 20 ECOLOGY L.Q. 605, 607-09 (1993).[34]

The other side of the coin is bioavailability. To the extent that a substance to which the body is exposed does not present itself in a way that is not bioavailable-is not taken up-then the exposure is less. For example, metals that are bound to other soil components are less likely to be leached out, or taken up by plants, or released in the body, and so exposure and/or dose is lower.[35]

3. The third phase of exposure analysis can be encapsulated in the warning that exposure does not equal dose. Depending on the route of

---

[34] *See also* LUTHER J. CARTER, NUCLEAR IMPERATIVES AND PUBLIC TRUST: DEALING WITH RADIOACTIVE WASTE 52 (1987) (reporting that oysters downstream of DOE's Hanford nuclear plant concentrated "radioactive zinc . . . at 200,000 times its concentration in the seawater, although even in the oysters it was present at only 40 to 50 trillionths of a curie per gram").

[35] *See* Elizabeth Anderson, *Scientific Developments in Risk Assessment: Legal Implications*, 14 COLUM. J. ENVTL. L. 411, 418-21 (1989).

exposure, a chemical will meet different fates in the body and will have different effects. For example, a recent NAS study of radon in drinking water determined that radon that is ingested is of little health concern, but that when it is inhaled it is a serious problem: 20 out of 13,000 stomach cancers yearly can be attributed to radon, while 19,860 out of 160,000 lung cancers have some involvement with radon.[36]

4. *Variability.* The TCE risk assessment discussed above found, in addition to the large differences in calculated toxicity, substantial variation among exposure scenarios *within a single household*. Even using consistent average assumptions, exposure of the adult male was a third of that of a formula-fed infant. The authors explained:

> The level of exposure to any pollutant present in drinking water is the result of many personal daily choices and several factors over which we have very little direct control. Where we live, what we eat and drink, and how old we are all have a profound influence on the magnitude of exposure. Also, the physical and chemical characteristics of the pollutant govern the amount that stays in the water and that which is transported into indoor air.
>
> * * *
>
> Adults in tropical areas may consume twice as much liquid as the average, as may athletically inclined adults when engaged in strenuous physical activity. Persons who are ill also may consume much more water than the average. Social behavior ritualized around the drinking of tea or coffee may lead to increased water consumption, although boiled water may contain smaller amounts of contaminants. A recent Canadian study shows that children under 5 years old, 10% of the children 6-17 years old, and 2% of the adult population consume more than 0.03 [liters per day] of drinking water for every kilogram of body weight.

Cothern *et al.*, *supra*, at 113-14.

Risk assessors have traditionally handled variability of exposure by using the "maximally exposed individual" (MEI) to make their calculations, a this hypothetical construct assumes extreme and often outlandish behaviors (farming in the nude, clinging to a factory fence for seventy years, playing in a highway median strip) that are deliberately chosen to assure that actual exposures would be lower. Recent attempts to refine these assumptions include the use of high-end exposure estimates (HEEEs) which are based on the most exposed *actual* individuals and which take account of the size of the population exposed.

5. *Highly exposed populations and environmental justice.* Some minority populations are exposed to higher than usual levels of single or multiple toxic substances, due to cultural practices, location of residence, occupational

---

[36] Warren E. Levy, *Radon More Dangerous in Air than in Water*, NEW YORK TIMES, Sept. 16, 1998.

exposures, dietary habits, and other behavior patterns. Should exposure assumptions be refined even further by using the most exposed *typical* individual (in case the most exposed actual individual is idiosyncratic)? The most likely exposure scenario? The average or median level of exposure?

Population	Examples of factors that affect exposure
Industrial and agricultural workers	Greater exposure to job-related hazardous chemicals through breathing and skin contact; more lung exposure associated with physically demanding work
Subsistence and sport fishers	Higher fish consumption, consumption of unusual parts of fish
Infants and children	Higher consumption of fruit, vegetables, and fruit juices, higher inhalation rates
Low-income and minority-group communities	Greater exposure to lead from lead paint in houses and soils; greater exposure to second hand cigarette smoke; inequitable distribution of risk-generating activities

2 Presidential/Congressional Commission, *supra*, at 75-76.[37] Are lifestyle differences relevant to risk assessment? Should they be?

6. Exposure assessment clearly requires the exercise of judgment by risk assessors, as dose-response assessment did. What kind of uncertainty is present in exposure assessment–information, knowledge, or both?

d. Risk Characterization

Risk characterization is technically simple: toxicity × exposure. But the uncertainty and variability discussed above complicate matters considerably. A multiplication formula is simple if the values are certain and fixed, but what should be done with uncertain numbers and ranges of values? The following excerpts describe three different but related aspects of risk characterization: its content, alternative expressions of risk, and the uses of risk characterization.

PROPOSED GUIDELINES FOR CARCINOGEN RISK ASSESSMENT

Environmental Protection Agency
61 Fed. Reg. 17960, 17999-18000 (1996)

The values supported by a risk characterization throughout the process are transparency in environmental decisionmaking, clarity in communication,

---

[37] With respect to children, *see also* NATIONAL RESEARCH COUNCIL, PESTICIDES IN THE DIETS OF INFANTS AND CHILDREN 3-4 (1998) ("Differences in exposure were generally a more important source of differences in risk than were age-related differences in toxicologic vulnerability.")

consistency in core assumptions and science policies from case to case, and reasonableness. While it is appropriate to err on the side of protection of health and the environment in the face of scientific uncertainty, common sense and reasonable application of assumptions and policies are essential to avoid unrealistic estimates of risk. Both integrative analyses and the Risk Characterization Summary present an integrated and balanced picture of the analysis of the hazard, dose response, and exposure. The risk analyst should provide summaries of the evidence and results and describe the quality of available data and the degree of confidence to be placed in the risk estimates. Important features include the constraints of available data and the state of knowledge, significant scientific issues, and significant science and science policy choices that were made when alternative interpretations of data existed. Choices made about using default assumptions or data in the assessment are explicitly discussed in the course of analysis, and if a choice is a significant issue, it is highlighted in the summary.

Specific guidance on hazard, dose response, and exposure characterization appears in previous sections. Overall, the risk characterization routinely includes the following, capturing the important items covered in hazard, dose response, and exposure characterization.

- Primary conclusions about hazard, dose response, and exposure, including equally plausible alternatives,
- Nature of key supporting information and analytic methods,
- Risk estimates and their attendant uncertainties, including key uses of default assumptions when data are missing or uncertain,
- Statement of the extent of extrapolation of risk estimates from observed data to exposure levels of interest (*i.e.*, margin of exposure) and its implications for certainty or uncertainty in quantifying risk,
- Significant strengths and limitations of the data and analyses, including any major peer reviewers' issues,
- Appropriate comparison with similar EPA risk analyses or common risks with which people may be familiar, and
- Comparison with assessment of the same problem by another organization.

RISK ASSESSMENT AND RISK MANAGEMENT IN REGULATORY DECISION-MAKING

The Presidential/Congressional Commission on Risk Assessment and Risk Management
vol. 2, pp. 85-88 (Final Report 1997)

Risk characterization is the primary vehicle for communicating health risk assessment findings. * * *

Risk assessment is an uncertain process that requires both scientific data and science-based judgment. Risk assessments are conducted to estimate risks below the range of observable events in people or in studies of laboratory animals. For example, 10-100 percent of laboratory animals exposed to a relatively high dose of a carcinogen throughout their lives might develop cancers, but regulatory agencies are expected to protect populations from exposure to doses of chemicals that might pose a risk of up to one in a million, not one in 10. The impact of a one-in-a-million cancer risk on a population cannot be detected or measured, because one-fourth of that population is already expected to die of cancer, even in the absence of a particular chemical exposure. As a result, estimates of small risks are speculative; they cannot be verified. Expressing a small risk solely in numerical terms, especially in single numbers, is misleading and falsely conveys accuracy.

* * *

Often, qualitative information is more useful and understandable than quantitative estimates of risk. Qualitative assessments include a careful description of the nature of the potential health effects of concern, who might experience the effects under different exposure conditions, the strength and consistency of the evidence that supports an agency's classification of a chemical or other exposure as a health hazard, and any means to prevent or reverse the effects of exposure. Qualitative information should also include the range of informed views about a risk and its nature, likelihood, and strength of the supporting evidence. For example, if an agency considers a substance likely to be a human carcinogen on the basis of studies of laboratory animals, but there is some evidence that the classification is flawed, both views should be presented. A discussion of that uncertainty would note the several types of evidence that support the substance's classification as a likely human carcinogen and also the contradictory evidence. Based on this type of discussion, the risk manager might conclude that because the weight of the scientific evidence supports the substance's classification, the best option is to regulate it as a carcinogen in the interest of protecting public health (*i.e.*, invoking the precautionary principle). Alternatively, the risk manager might conclude that the evidence is so uncertain that it is best to focus on conducting additional research or to maintain the status quo. * * *

While quantitative uncertainty characterizations are not always effective risk communication tools, we believe that using distributions to reflect the variability in a population's exposure characteristics can be useful. Considering exposure variabilities will also help clarify whose risks are being considered and the relationship between individual and population risk estimates. All stakeholders can easily comprehend that not all members of a population are exposed to identical doses of contaminants, and that different activities are associated with different exposures. For example, information on reference standards could be compared to a distribution of a population's exposures like that in Figure [2.8] derived using Monte Carlo techniques and exposure data from a hazardous waste site.

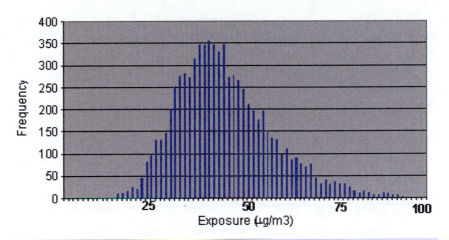

Figure 2.8–Monte Carlo Distribution

In this example, if the concentration of a chemical associated with a 10^5 cancer risk were 80 milligrams per cubic meter of air, the risk manager and other decision-makers would recognize that most of the population is exposed to less than that concentration. The participants might decide that there is little cause for concern or might attempt to identify the characteristics of the segment of the population in the upper end of the distribution and consider risk reduction options directed at that segment. If the concentration of concern were 20 milligrams per cubic meter of air, participants would see that most of the population is exposed to higher concentrations, and would want to implement more extensive risk management measures directed at the entire population. The participants might also be interested in comparisons of exposures to contaminant concentrations associated with 10^{-4} or 10^{-6} cancer risks.

UNDERSTANDING RISK: INFORMING DECISIONS IN A DEMOCRATIC SOCIETY
National Research Council
pp. 2-4 (1996)

The view of risk characterization as a translation or summary is seriously deficient. What is needed for successful characterization of risk must be considered at the very beginning of the process of developing decision-relevant understanding. Risk characterization should not be an activity added at the end of risk analysis; rather, its needs should largely determine the scope and nature of risk analysis.

* * *

A risk characterization must address what the interested and affected parties believe to be at risk in the particular situation, and it must incorporate their perspectives and specialized knowledge. * * *

Adequate risk analysis and characterization thus depend on incorporating the perspectives and knowledge of the interested and affected parties from the earliest phases of the effort to understand the risks. The challenges of asking the right questions, making the appropriate assumptions, and finding the right ways to summarize information can be met by designing processes that pay appropriate attention to each of these judgments, inform them with the best available knowledge and the perspectives of the spectrum of decision participants, and make the choices through a process that those parties trust.

Risk characterization is the outcome of an *analytic-deliberative process*. Its success depends critically on systematic analysis that is appropriate to the problem, responds to the needs of the interested and affected parties, and treats uncertainties of importance to the decision problem in a comprehensible way. Success also depends on deliberations that formulate the decision problem, guide analysis to improve decision participants' understanding, seek the meaning of analytic findings and uncertainties, and improve the ability of interested and affected parties to participate effectively in the risk decision process. The process must have an appropriately diverse participation or representation of the spectrum of interested and affected parties, of decision makers, and of specialists in risk analysis, at each step.

Analysis and deliberation can be thought of as two complementary approaches to gaining knowledge about the world, forming understandings on the basis of knowledge, and reaching agreement among people. *Analysis* uses rigorous, replicable methods, evaluated under the agreed protocols of an expert community-such as those of disciplines in the natural, social, or decision sciences, as well as mathematics, logic, and law-to arrive at answers to factual questions. *Deliberation* is any formal or informal process for communication and collective consideration of issues. Participants in deliberation discuss, ponder, exchange observations and views, reflect upon information and judgments concerning matters of mutual interest, and attempt to persuade each other. Government agencies should start from the presumption that both analysis and deliberation will be needed at each step leading to a risk characterization.

Deliberation is important at each step of the process that informs risk decisions, such as deciding which harms to analyze and how to describe scientific uncertainty and disagreement. Appropriately structured deliberation contributes to sound analysis by adding knowledge and perspectives that improve understanding and contributes to the acceptability of risk characterization by addressing potentially sensitive procedural concerns.

Deliberation needs to be broader and more extensive for some decisions and at some steps than other. It should have, in addition to the involvement of appropriate policy makers and scientific and technical specialists, sufficiently diverse participation from across the spectrum of interested and affected parties to ensure that the important, decision-relevant knowledge enters the process, that the important perspectives are considered, and that the parties' legitimate concerns about the inclusiveness and openness of the process are addressed.

NOTES

1. What are the purposes of risk characterization, according to the above descriptions? Who uses risk assessments? How do the purposes and audience(s) affect its content?

2. Should risk be characterized as individual risk (*e.g.*, 1×10^{-4}) or population risk (*i.e.*, expected number of deaths over a given period of time)? Why does EPA-and Congress, when it has been this specific-use individual risk measures?

3. *Monte Carlo*. The idea of presenting risk distributions is relatively new. The most common technique, referred to by the Presidential/Congressional Commission, is Monte Carlo analysis, in which known distributions are randomly combined to come up with a final distribution that is more statistically valid, *i.e.*, more likely to reflect reality.[38] Why are distributions better than point estimates? Better than high-low-average? Why has risk assessment previously used point estimates? Are distributions a real improvement?

4. *Why quantify?* In a recent statement on environmental justice remedies, the U.S. Conference of Mayors demanded that EPA develop methods for assessing risk "that are precise, based on sound, peer-reviewed science, and provide a high degree of certainty in decision-making outcomes." 66 U.S.L.W. 2799, 2800 (June 30, 1998). Similarly, the Fifth Circuit has asserted: "To make precise estimates, precise data are required." *Gulf South Insulation v. CPSC*, 701 F2d 1137, 1146 (5th Cir. 1983). In light of what you have read so far, do you think it very likely that EPA can produce such a thing? Why not? (In fact, isn't "precise estimates" almost an oxymoron?) Should we abandon quantitative risk assessment in favor of qua*l*itative risk assessment?

5. *Risk assessment and democracy*. What does "transparency" mean in the EPA guidance? Why is it important? Why does the National Academy emphasize "deliberation?" Does the emphasis on deliberation encroach on risk *management*?

6. *Multiple conservatism*. A frequent criticism of risk assessment is the practice of compounding of conservative assumptions. Critics argue that multiple conservatism results in "worst case scenarios" rather than risk assessments. Defenders of the practice point out that, since the true values are either unknown, unknowable, or variable (that is why assumptions are being used in the first place), we cannot be certain that the "worst case" is not in

---

[38] For a very helpful discussion of the Monte Carlo technique, *see* Susan R. Poulter, *Monte Carlo Simulations in Risk Assessment-Science, Policy, and Legal Issues*, 9 RISK: HEALTH, SAFETY & ENVT. 7 (1998).

fact the actual case.[39] Should EPA rethink its practice of using multiple conservative assumptions? If so, which assumptions should be revised? Is it feasible, for example, to replace assumptions with a single uncertainty factor?

As we saw above, the use of multiple conservative assumptions was upheld in *Lead Industries Association*. Should courts rethink their deference to EPA's judgment on this point?

2. Risk Management

Risk assessment can be used to make three kinds of determinations: the extent of existing risks, acceptable target (or residual) risk levels, and priorities. These determinations are risk *management* activities, and we now consider the role of risk assessment in reaching these decisions. We must also consider the non-numerical aspects of risk that go into public risk decisions-which are inevitably political (in the broad sense of the term) decisions-and the role that non-risk factors play in such decisions. It is impossible to understand the debates over risk assessment without understanding the uses to which risk assessment is put.

RISK ASSESSMENT AND RISK MANAGEMENT IN REGULATORY DECISION-MAKING

The Presidential/Congressional Commission on Risk Assessment and Risk Management
vol. 1, pp. 1-46 (Final Report 1997)

Risk management is the process of identifying, evaluating, selecting, and implementing actions to reduce risk to human health and to ecosystems. The goal of risk management is scientifically sound, cost-effective, integrated actions that reduce or prevent risks while taking into account social, cultural, ethical, political, and legal considerations.

Our definition of risk management is broader than the traditional definition, which is restricted to the process of evaluating alternative regulatory actions and selecting among them.* * *

* * *

Creative, integrated strategies that address multiple environmental media and multiple sources of risk are needed if we are to sustain and strengthen the environmental improvements and risk reduction our nation has attained over the last 25 years. To help meet these needs, the Commission has developed a systematic, comprehensive Risk Management Framework.

---

[39] *See, e.g.*, Adam M. Finkel, *Is Risk Assessment Really Too Conservative? Revising the Revisionists*, 14 COLUM. J. ENVTL. L. 427 (1989).

Figure 2.9–Risk Management Framework

* * *

Every stage of the Framework relies on three key principles:

Broader contexts. Instead of evaluating single risks associated with single chemicals in single environmental media, the Framework puts health and environmental media problems in their larger, real-world contexts. Evaluating problems in context involves evaluating different sources of a particular chemical or chemical exposure, considering other chemicals that could affect a particular risk or pose additional risks, assessing other similar risks, and evaluating the extent to which different exposures contribute to a particular health effect of concern. The goal of considering problems in their context is to clarify the impact that individual risk management actions are likely to have on public health or the environment and to help direct actions and resources where they will do the most good.

Stakeholder participation. Involvement of stakeholders-parties who are concerned about or affected by the risk management problem-is critical to making and successfully implementing sound, cost-effective, informed risk management decisions. For this reason, the Framework encourages stakeholder involvement to the extent appropriate and feasible during all stages of the risk management process. * * *

Iteration. Valuable information or perspective may emerge during any stage of the risk management process. This framework is designed so that parts of it may be repeated, giving risk managers and stakeholders the flexibility to revisit early stages of the process when new findings made during later stages shed sufficiently important light on earlier deliberations and decisions.

NOTES

1. What is the role of quantitative risk assessment in the Commission's "Framework"? How does it differ from the Red Book model set out earlier in the chapter? Does risk play a larger or smaller role? Is there a clear demarcation between assessment and management? Should there be one?

2. The National Academy of Sciences has more recently taken a similar view of risk management in terms of the need to communicate effectively with and involve the public in risk decisions. On the role of risk assessment, NAS concluded: "Risk assessment is a set of tools, not an end in itself. The limited resources available should be spent to generate information that helps risk managers to choose the best possible course of action among the available options." NATIONAL RESEARCH COUNCIL, SCIENCE AND JUDGMENT IN RISK ASSESSMENT 15 (1994).

—

Congress sets regulatory standards for toxics in a variety ways, using different verbal formulations and specifying the consideration of different criteria. We will explore the full range of these differences in later chapters of this book. Focusing on the risk element of these standards, however, one finds that the level of existing risk that triggers regulatory action (the "predicate") and the level of residual risk (the "target") that meets Congressional goals differ from statute to statute.

For the purposes of either a predicate or a target, the possible regulatory risk levels form a spectrum from zero to 100 per cent risk, that is, from absolute safety to actual harm. In view of the impracticality of either extreme, the task is to find an appropriate middle level of risk. The essential goal is to encourage EPA to concentrate on real risks, those of sufficient seriousness to justify the expenditure of significant social resources.

The nonzero levels range as follows, very roughly from most to least protective of human health:

- A *de minimis risk* standard excludes from regulatory action only trivial risks;
- An *unreasonable risk* standard is higher than a de minimis standard and recognizes a compromise between safety and cost;
- A *near-unreasonable risk* standard is described by its authors, Cross, Lave, and Byrd, as "discernible risk." It denotes a risk large enough that actual harm could in theory be detected in a population of the size actually exposed to the chemical;
- A *lowest-feasible* standard sets the permissible level of risk based on the technological capacity of the relevant industry to reduce exposure. It is usually but not necessarily less stringent than the above risk-based standards;
- A *cost-effectiveness* standard considers cost to the extent of choice among alternative methods for achieving a fixed level of safety;

- A *cost-benefit justification* standard requires that the benefits of the controls outweigh their costs. Followed literally, it would tolerate very risky levels of a very useful chemical.

These levels vary in stringency, precision, and information demands. The consideration of many factors makes for flexibility and more precise action, but also requires greater regulatory resources.

John S. Applegate, *Worst Things First: Risk, Information, and Regulatory Structure in Toxic Substances Control*, 9 YALE J. ON REG. 277, 305-09 (1992).

The application of these risk levels and non-risk criteria to specific situations is the main job of risk management. From this perspective, the role of risk assessment is to measure the effectiveness or the benefits (in terms of reduced risk) of proposed regulatory measures.

Industry and its allies in the regulatory reform movement, who are most concerned about costs of regulation, contend that rational decisionmaking requires cost-benefit or cost-effectiveness analyses of all carcinogen regulations. Quantitative risk assessment is essential to such analyses. It allows cancer deaths to be translated into monetary terms.

James P. Leape, *Note, Quantitative Risk Assessment in Regulation of Environmental Carcinogens*, 4 HARV. ENVTL. L. REV. 86, 87 (1980).[40]

---

[40] *See also* Roy E. Albert, *Carcinogen Risk Assessment in the U.S. Environmental Protection Agency*, 24 CRITICAL REVIEWS IN TOXICOLOGY 75, 84 (1994) ("It will be remembered that carcinogen risk assessment was created to support the development of exposure standards based on balancing risks and benefits.").

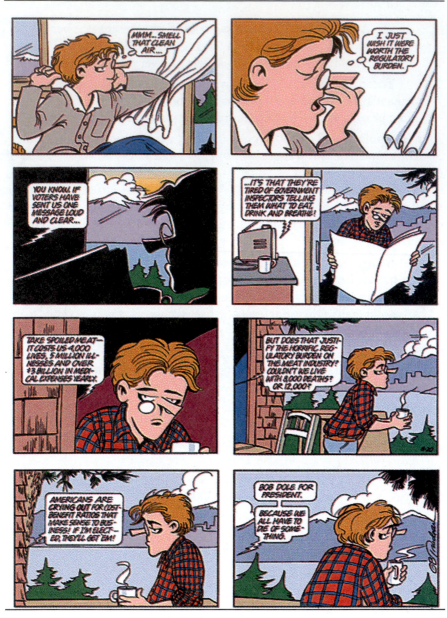

Figure 2.10[41]

While the strictly numerical use of risk assessment as an element in a risk-cost-benefit formula is a logical consequence of quantifying risk, it has been challenged on the ground that the numerical expression is an incomplete account of environmental risk. Risk assessment purports to be a technical, scientific procedure. Yet one reason for involving the public is that, even putting aside the non-scientific management function, the public views risk

---

[41] © Copyright G.B. Trudeau, Universal Press Syndicate (1995).

itself differently from technical experts. The following two articles document the phenomenon and offer some suggestions for addressing it.

RISK PERCEPTION

Paul A. Slovic
236 Science 280, 280-85 (1987)

Whereas technologically sophisticated analysts employ risk assessment to evaluate hazards, the majority of citizens rely on intuitive risk judgments, typically called "risk perceptions." For these people, experience with hazards tends to come from the news media, which rather thoroughly document mishaps and threats occurring throughout the world. The dominant perception for most Americans (and one that contrasts sharply with the views of professional risk assessors) is that they face more risk today than in the past and that future risks will be even greater than today's. Similar views appear to be held by citizens of many other industrialized nations. These perceptions and the opposition to technology that accompanies them have puzzled and frustrated industrialists and regulators and have led numerous observers to argue that the American public's apparent pursuit of a "zero-risk society" threatens the nation's political and economic stability. Wildavsky commented as follows on this state of affairs.

> How extraordinary! The richest, longest lived, best protected, most resourceful civilization, with the highest degree of insight into its own technology, is on its way to becoming the most frightened.
>
> Is it our environment or ourselves that have changed? Would people like us have had this sort of concern in the past? Today, there are risks from numerous small dams far exceeding those from nuclear reactors. Why is the one feared and not the other? Is it just that we are used to the old or are some of us looking differently at essentially the same sorts of experience?

During the past decade, a small number of researchers has been attempting to answer such questions by examining the opinions that people express when they are asked, in a variety of ways, to evaluate hazardous activities, substances, and technologies. This research has attempted to develop techniques for assessing the complex and subtle opinions that people have about risk. With these techniques, researchers have sought to discover what people mean when they say that something is (or is not) "risky," and to determine what factors underlie those perceptions. The basic assumption underlying these efforts is that those who promote and regulate health and safety need to understand the ways in which people think about and respond to risk.

* * *

[Studies of risk perception have consistently shown significant differences between expert and lay perceptions of risk. Nuclear power, for example, is regarded as relatively non-risky by experts and relatively dangerous by lay persons. Contrariwise, non-nuclear electric power and x-rays are regarded as quite risky by experts and not very risky by lay persons. However, on many others (motor vehicles, smoking, and alcohol are high; vaccinations, power mowers, and food coloring are low) there is general agreement.]

These studies have shown that perceived risk is quantifiable and predictable. Psychometric techniques seem well suited for identifying similarities and differences among groups with regard to risk perceptions and attitudes. They have also shown that the concept "risk" means different things to different people. When experts judge risk, their responses correlate highly with technical estimates of annual fatalities. Lay people can assess annual fatalities if they are asked to (and produce estimates somewhat like the technical estimates). However, their judgments of "risk" are related more to other hazard characteristics (for example, catastrophic potential, threat to future generations) and, as a result, tend to differ from their own (and experts') estimates of annual fatalities.

Another consistent result from psychometric studies of expressed preferences is that people tend to view current risk levels as unacceptably high for most activities. The gap between perceived and desired risk levels suggests that people are not satisfied with the way that market and other regulatory mechanisms have balanced risks and benefits. Across the domain of hazards, there seems to be little systematic relationship between perceptions of current risks and benefits. However, studies of expressed preferences do seem to support Starr's argument that people are willing to tolerate higher risks from activities seen as highly beneficial. But, whereas Starr concluded that voluntariness of exposure was the key mediator of risk acceptance, expressed preference studies have shown that other (perceived) characteristics such as familiarity, control, catastrophic potential, equity, and level of knowledge also seem to influence the relation between perceived risk, perceived benefit, and risk acceptance.

* * *

Factor-Analytic Representations

Many of the qualitative risk characteristics are correlated with each other, across a wide range of hazards. For example, hazards judged to be "voluntary" tend also to be judged as "controllable", hazards whose adverse effects are delayed tend to be seen as posing risks that are not well known, and so on. Investigation of these relations by means of factor analysis has shown that the broader domain of characteristics can be condensed to a small set of higher order characteristics or factors.

The factor space presented in Fig. [2.10] has been replicated across groups of lay people and experts judging large and diverse sets of hazards. Factor 1, labeled "dread risk," is defined at its high (right-hand) end by perceived lack of control, dread, catastrophic potential, fatal consequences, and the inequitable distribution of risks and benefits. Nuclear weapons and nuclear power score highest on the characteristics that make up this factor.

Factor 2, labeled "unknown risk," is defined at its high end by hazards judged to be unobservable, unknown, new, and delayed in their manifestation of harm. Chemical technologies score particularly high on this factor.

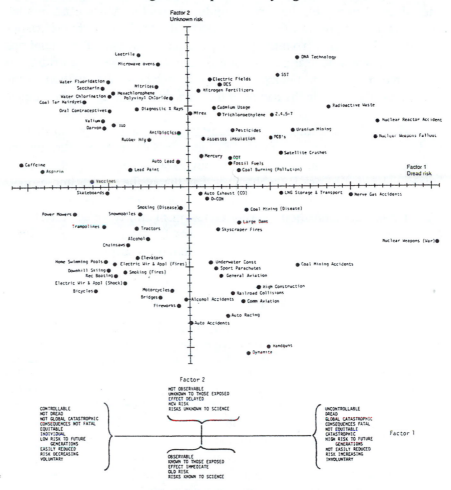

Figure 2.11 – Factors in Risk Perception

* * *

Placing Risks in Perspective

A consequence of the public's concerns and its opposition to risky technologies has been an increase in attempts to inform and educate people about risk. Risk perception research has a number of implications for such educational efforts.

One frequently advocated approach to broadening people's perspectives is to present quantitative risk estimates for a variety of hazards, expressed in some unidimensional index of death or disability, such as risk per hour of exposure, annual probability of death, or reduction in life expectancy. Even though such comparisons have no logically necessary implications for acceptability of risk, one might still hope that they would help improve people's intuitions about the magnitude of risks. Risk perception research suggests, however, that these sorts of comparisons may not be very satisfactory even for this purpose. People's perceptions and attitudes are determined not only by the sort of unidimensional statistics used in such tables but also by the variety of quantitative and qualitative characteristics reflected in Fig. [2.10]. To many people, statements such as, "the annual risk from living near a nuclear power plant is equivalent to the risk of riding an extra three miles in an automobile," give inadequate consideration to the important differences in the nature of the risks from these two technologies.

* * *

Perhaps the most important message from this research is that there is wisdom as well as error in public attitudes and perceptions. Lay people sometimes lack certain information about hazards. However, their basic conceptualization of risk is much richer than that of the experts and reflects legitimate concerns that are typically omitted from expert risk assessments. As a result, risk communication and risk management efforts are destined to fail unless they are structured as a two-way process. Each side, expert and public, has something valid to contribute. Each side must respect the insights and intelligence of the other.

RISK, COURTS, AND AGENCIES

Clayton P. Gillette & James E. Krier
138 U. PA. L. REV. 1027, 1075-85 (1990)

How might we resolve this difference in outlook, and the conflicting risk assessments that result? The easy way would be to reject one of the opposing views as senseless or irrational. The expert perspective hardly deserves this treatment, as intuition alone makes obvious: surely risk and its minimization have *something* to do with actual human loss, measured in death and illness. The sense of body counting is thus apparent. Some experts, though, are unwilling to concede that more than bodies count, and that the lay view, too, makes sense; they are generous only in their scorn. They take the easy way and dismiss "the public's understanding" as "insane" at worst, "irrational" at best. Their contempt, however, is utterly unwarranted.

* * *

Return, then, to the public's rich image of risk, and reflect for a moment on its many dimensions. People have a lower tolerance for involuntary than for voluntary exposure. Even on its surface, the concern here is easily understood, and closely related to the dimensions of uncontrollability and uncertainty. Voluntary exposure pre-supposes knowledge. Knowledge coupled with freedom of action facilitates individual choice and efforts to control events bearing on the choice. To be forced to face a risk, on the other hand, or to be ignorant of it, or to sense that no one is really in command of it, leaves one's well-being in the hands of others, or of no one. Either alternative is obviously inferior, under most circumstances, to being in charge.

Upon deeper examination, this sense of voluntariness might trivialize the true concern. Suppose my situation (say I am an unskilled worker) "forces" me to "choose" a risky occupation, in exchange for some wage premium. Is my exposure to the risk "voluntary"? Suppose, more generally, that I rightly see life as full of difficult choices. Is it sensible to say that, given my power to choose-given that any choice is "voluntary"-I should accept without complaint whatever consequences follow? The answer might be yes if the world were organized in a way consistent with ideal values and principles, but it is not. Behind the notion of voluntariness, then, there may lurk more fundamental concerns about autonomy and equality and power among individuals in the society, for it is the pre-existence of these that lets free choice be morally interesting. People perhaps are saying that more risks seem consistent with such ideals and others not, and registering the view by showing a greater acceptance of risks that they regard as "voluntary" in fundamentally important ways, as opposed to "chosen" in some narrower sense.

The foregoing account enlightens us about other popular dimensions of risk, such as the enhanced dislike of delayed (latent) effects, and of irreversible ones. Latency frustrates knowledge, and irreversibility frustrates control. They make it more difficult for us to govern our own circumstances-and also to govern our governors. How do we hold accountable officials whose mistakes or misdeeds manifest themselves only decades after a term of office? And how do we correct for what they have done, if what they have done is uncorrectable? Latency and irreversibility practically deny us the fruits of trial-and-error, perhaps the best means yet devised by which to resolve uncertainty.

What of the special dislike of manmade as opposed to natural hazards? Once again, a story grows out of what has been said thus far: Humans might treat each other with motives that Nature could never have, and this matters. Mark Sagoff develops this theme in the course of considering why the government should regulate artificial risks more strictly than natural ones, even if they are "no more dangerous" (obviously, in the sense of body counting). First, people are responsible for artificial risks, but not for natural ones, and the government's job is to regulate what people do. Second, only manmade risks can, in any meaningful sense, threaten autonomy, an additional reason to be especially wary of them. Third, the harms we suffer because of the acts of others carry special injury; we mourn the deaths from a natural flood but reset, deeply, the ones from a broken dam. We "are concerned not simply with safety but with responsibility and guilt as well."

These same concerns arise in the case of those manmade risks we and others classify as "public": risks generated by highly centralized high technologies. The is especially so because public risks entail so much uncertainty (given their complexity), imply such considerable power, and are capable of such calamitous effects. The last consideration, in particular, implicates the public's aversion to the possibility of disastrous consequences and brings us to the cluster of factors that enter into what is termed "dread." Dread correlates significantly with some aspects of risk that we have already discussed, such as involuntariness and uncontrollability, but also with such others as inequitable distributions, threats to future generations, and catastrophic potential–each of which speaks almost for itself.

The idea of inequitable distributions, for example, reflects the view that just as a right thinking society should concern itself with the distribution of wealth, so too should it do so with the distribution of risk. For example, risks that might result in death or disease are often considered worth taking because they confer significant benefits not otherwise available. This risk burden may be regarded as equitably distributed only if it is borne by those who simultaneously enjoy the benefits. Burdens imposed on others, or diverted to future generations, generate worries about exploitation. Alternatively, risks concentrated in time and space might be regarded as inequitable or otherwise unacceptable because concentration can result in losses that are avoided by broader distributions. This suggests, then, a link between inequitable distributions and catastrophic potential. Concentrated risks can threaten whole communities, and the loss of a community (think of Love Canal, of Chernobyl) is the loss of a valued thing distinct and apart from the disaggregated bodies of a community's citizens.

* * *

Whatever its motivations, the experts' approach to risk is obviously not senseless. Yet neither is the public's approach. This is why we said in the introduction to this section that the problem comes down to one of competing rationalities. Admit this, and it unarguably follows that the choice of approach is an ethical and political one that technical experts have neither the knowledge nor the authority to dictate, because the issue transcends technocratic expertise. Were we to defer to agencies simply on the basis of their technical proficiency, the ethical-political question would be begged entirely. Agencies could be expected to resort to methods the use of which denies the very values at stake (it is, after all, the claim of methodological proficiency that grounds the argument for deference in the first place). And, to return to the idea with which we began this section, methodological proclivities would bias agency risk processing in the direction of too much public risk-as viewed from the public's perspective.

NOTES

1. *A richer conception of risk.* Can you enumerate the qualities of risk that differentiate the expert and lay perspectives? Are some more important than others?

2. What do Gillette & Krier add to Slovic's point? Is the *quantification* of risk to blame? What other non-risk factors should be considered?

3. *Adolescent smoking.* The current rise in adolescent smoking clearly defies logic, but it also seems to defy risk perception predictions, inasmuch as the dangers of smoking are widely understood. Slovic has suggested that this

trend may be explained by adolescents' failure to perceive the nature and severity of the experience of cancer. Paul Slovic, *Do Adolescent Smokers Know the Risk?* 47 DUKE L.J. 1133 (1998). If true, does this support or undermine Slovic and Gillette & Krier's arguments that public risk perception should be accorded weight in regulatory decisions?

4. *The vicious circle.* Justice Stephen Breyer, in a popular book written before his appointment to the Supreme Court, decried Congress's and regulators' responsiveness to risk public perception. A representative excerpt can be found in Chapter 3(B)(2)(d). What is Breyer's response to Slovic and Gillette & Krier?

5. If expert and lay definitions of risk differ so dramatically, how are legislators, agencies, and courts to make risk decisions? Should EPA be permitted (encouraged?) to rely upon public opinion? Are Gillette & Krier advocating a smaller role for agencies in risk regulation and a larger role for non-expert role bodies like courts? How do you think that the regulatory system should be constructed, with respect to substantive standards, burdens of proof, and evidentiary requirements? The next reading offers one suggestion.

UNDERSTANDING RISK: INFORMING DECISIONS IN A DEMOCRATIC SOCIETY

National Research Council
pp. 79-82 (1996)

Broadly based deliberation can be used to frame a problem so that knowledge generated about it will be relevant to the needs and understandings of the various parties to a decision. Such deliberation may improve the quality of a solution or increase the likelihood of finding novel solutions by redefining problems. For example, the South Florida ecosystem management project used broadly based deliberation to arrive at its formulation of the problem as a choice among development plans. The participants believed that this formulation would encourage analyses that would address issues of concern to all who would be affected by development in the region.

Broadening the base for deliberation can improve the knowledge base for decisions. For example, nonscientists may have critical information-such as knowledge of local conditions-that can be used to check the reasonableness of assumptions incorporated into technical analysis. Appropriate environmental monitoring may also depend on knowledge of local conditions. Broadly based deliberation can also help ensure that analysis addresses the problems that concern the interested and affected parties. The goal is to avoid studies that require many years and dollars, yet fail to advance risk characterization.

* * *

Deliberation can clarify the nature and extent of agreements and disagreements among participants. For instance, in situations in which uncertainties are large or data are incomplete, deliberation among scientists, public officials, and interested and affected parties can help clarify the extent to which disagreements are rooted in differences in how people or groups see the problem, how they interpret existing data, or in their values. This clarification can inform decisions about whether further analysis might help resolve the disagreements.

Deliberation can also promote mutual exchange of information and increase understanding among interested and affected parties. For example, in the South Florida case, natural and social scientists and agency personnel carefully considered issues in ecosystem management that might concern the various interested and affected parties in order to develop an analysis that might facilitate dialogue among the parties. Similarly, the Hanford Future Site Uses Working Group spent considerable time defining the common base of information that all participants wanted to consider in developing land use options. This process gave agency personnel, as well as other interested and affected parties, a richer perspective on the problems at the Hanford site and the nature of the parties' concerns. Analytic techniques such as multi-attribute utility analysis may also be used to increase mutual understanding by clarifying which values the various participants consider important.

Deliberation also has the potential to yield more widely accepted choices, both about risk characterization and about policy. For example, dispute about an exposure assessment is less likely when the assumptions built into it have been agreed to in advance by the interested and affected parties. Similarly, deliberation may arrive at more acceptable ways to provide information. During the aftermath of the 1979 nuclear power accident at Three Mile Island, neighboring residents were highly critical and suspicious of General Public Utilities, the company that owned the plant, and of the Nuclear Regulatory Commission (NRC). When the operator proposed venting the krypton gas that had accumulated in the containment dome as a first step in gaining access to the reactor vessel, public opposition was strong. Reassurances that the risk was "minor" were not convincing. Different actors used forms of deliberation in their efforts to address the issue. Pennsylvania Governor Thornburgh conferred with two environmental organizations that represented opposition viewpoints. When they were satisfied that they understood the risks and that the risks were acceptable, the governor approved venting the krypton. The NRC held public hearings. A local mayor proposed providing nearby neighborhoods with radiation monitoring equipment and involving a team of local citizens in the design and operation of a radiation monitoring plan that it was hoped would help residents understand the risks.

Broadly based deliberation can also increase acceptance of the substantive decisions that follow risk characterization. For example, numerous case studies support the claim that disputes about siting municipal and hazardous waste disposal facilities are lessened when the interested and affected parties are made part of the decision-making team. As already noted, such participatory deliberation builds acceptability of decisions in part by fulfilling democratic norms. People are more willing to accept the results of processes they perceive as fair, balanced, and reasonable and that allow them an adequate opportunity to have a fair say. Thus, mutual agreement on the selection of technical consultants is more likely to lead to acceptable analyses and, in some cases, has also reduced the number of "dueling experts."

NOTES

1. How, according to the National Academy, does public participation improve the risk assessment process? Can you think of other reasons? Are there parts of the risk assessment and management process that the public should be more or less involved with? Excluded from?

2. Who are "the stakeholders"? How should "deliberation" among them be organized? Will this work for national, as opposed to local, problems? We will return to the question of public participation in risk-based decisionmaking in Chapter 12(B) (Federal Facilities), *infra.*[42]

3. Perspective: "Good Science," Science Policy, and Information

Uncertainty is a defining feature of toxics regulation. We have encountered the problem of lack of information in at least two contexts in this chapter: the sheer amount of information needed to assess toxic substances fully, and the types of uncertainty that remain. For risk managers, uncertainty poses the practical problem of whether to go forward on the basis of what is known, to delay action until more is known, or to take interim action pending further study. This is a question that the law influences strongly. In an area marked by pervasive uncertainty, the greater the proof required for action, the less action can be taken. We will return to this problem again and again in this book.

In the following readings, Professor Latin describes the consequences of demanding elaborate scientific proof ("good science"), and Professor Wagner documents the misuse of scientific proof in toxics decisionmaking.

---

[42] For further discussion of public involvement in risk assessment, *see* Presidential/Congressional Commission on Risk Assessment and Management, *supra*, at 15-18; John S. Applegate, *Comparative Risk Assessment and Environmental Priorities Projects: A Forum, Not a Formula*, 25 N. KY. L. REV. 71 (1998); John S. Applegate, *A Beginning and Not an End in Itself: The Role of Risk Assessment in Environmental Decisionmaking*, 63 U. CIN. L. REV. 1643 (1995).

GOOD SCIENCE, BAD REGULATION, AND TOXIC RISK ASSESSMENT

Howard Latin
5 YALE J. ON REG. 89, 92-134 (1988)[43]

There is an inherent tension between the disciplinary norms of good science and good regulation. Unlike in pure scientific research, where the proper response to uncertainty is reservation of judgment pending the development of adequate data and testable hypotheses, the risk-assessment process cannot be suspended without significant social consequences. A finding that a vital issue is currently indeterminate would be entirely consistent with the practice of good science, but "no decision" on a possible toxic hazard inescapably is a decision that promotes interests which benefit from the regulatory status quo. Risk assessment is not driven by the pursuit of knowledge for its own sake, the explicit goal of science, but by the need to decide whether potentially severe health hazards should be allowed to continue or whether high control costs should be imposed with potentially severe economic consequences. Thus, scientists in regulatory proceedings are expected to produce 'answers' in a timely manner even if their predictions are highly speculative. Any reluctance to relax the standards of proof and certainty generally required of valid science may introduce a bias in favor of regulatory inaction.

Science aims at the dispassionate pursuit of truth. In contrast, scientists in risk-assessment proceedings frequently represent industries, labor unions, consumers, environmentalists, or agency bureaucracies with great interests at stake. These affiliations may often explicitly or unintentionally color interpretations of available evidence. Scientists seldom base conclusions on data and experiments that cannot be reproduced, but information in regulatory hearings is routinely submitted by affected parties and frequently cannot be replicated or effectively challenged by other participants. Scientists tend to design research studies in light of which data are available and which experiments may be feasible, whereas the critical questions in risk-assessment proceedings are usually determined by statutory or judicial requirements that need not be responsive to the state of scientific knowledge. Budgetary and time limitations often influence the scientific research agenda, but no good scientist would feel that definitive answers must be produced irrespective of resource constraints. The opposite predisposition may be appropriate for good regulators. These comments are not intended to call into question the competence or ethics of all scientists who participate in risk assessments. Rather, the point is that the risk-assessment process is fundamentally shaped by the requirements, constraints, and adversarial climate of regulation, not by the disciplinary norms of science.

---

[43] © Copyright 1989 by the YALE JOURNAL ON REGULATION, P.O. Box 208215, New Haven, CT 06520-8215. Reprinted from Vol. 5:89 by permission. All rights reserved.

The illusion that risk assessment is a purely scientific activity reduces the visibility and political accountability of policy judgments that often guide regulatory decisions on toxic hazards. A comparison of conflicting risk-assessment principles adopted by agencies under different administrations shows that regulators frequently do consider policy criteria when they select specific risk estimates. Federal agencies have recently employed controversial risk-assessment assumptions to justify inaction on some hazardous substances. Regulators have also attempted to make determinations based on "good science" without considering the implications of this approach for decisionmaking costs, regulatory delays, and opportunities for obstructive or strategic behavior by affected parties. Risk assessors often respond to scientific uncertainties by adopting conservative safety-oriented positions on some important issues while they use best-current-scientific-guess, middle-of-the-range, methodological-convenience, or least-cost treatments on other material issues. EPA and other agencies have never explained the scientific or policy rationales underlying these inconsistent treatments of uncertainty, and risk managers may not recognize that substantial inconsistency exists. In light of these diverse risk-assessment practices, I contend that regulatory policy judgments as well as scientific judgments must be applied coherently, explained forthrightly, and tested actively through public debate.

* * *

III. Ramifications of EPA's Emphasis on "Good Science"

The risk-assessment practices described above indicate that EPA's attempt in its carcinogen guidelines and benzene proceedings to base risk estimates on "the most scientifically appropriate interpretation" entails several controversial social ramifications:

A. Trade-offs Between the Pursuit of "Good Science" and Effective Protection Under Uncertainty

Although current guidelines embody some conservative risk-assessment principles, the individualized "weight of evidence" approach[44] coupled with agency attempts to tailor all analyses in light of changing scientific knowledge will often reduce the degree of protection previously afforded * * *. Few if any of the revised treatments in the guidelines have achieved general scientific acceptance, and EPA does not contend that most uncertainties can be resolved with reasonable scientific assurance. Given the imperfect state of the risk-assessment art, regulators must decide how much potential but uncertain public protection should be traded for some potential but uncertain improvement in the accuracy of scientific judgments that EPA clearly recognizes are far from reliable. The present guidelines assume that every tentative step, however provisional, in the direction of "good science" is warranted regardless of its possible effect on the scope of protection. The

---

[44] EPA used a "weight of evidence" approach to replace the need for assumptions on several points in the risk assessment.-EDS.

wisdom of this presumption is surely a public policy issue rather than a purely scientific question.

The new guidelines reflect a relative shift in EPA's emphasis on two recurring questions in toxic substances regulation: Is there sufficient reliable evidence that a chemical produces "toxic" effects at high or unknown past exposure levels, and is there enough evidence to derive reliable quantitative risk-assessments at specific exposure levels. If the Agency delays regulation until the "weight of evidence" enables predictions about specific dose-response relationships, as the guidelines presume, then EPA may allow years of continued exposures to a known toxic substance because the precise level of toxicity cannot be reliably estimated. The Agency decision to wait until regulators can meet the particularized evidentiary requirements of the guidelines is equally a decision to stress scientific validity rather than safety after an indeterminate toxic hazard has been qualitatively identified. This preference is neither inevitable nor consistent with past practices.

* * *

B. Effects on Agency Behavior

The pursuit of "good science" based on individualized circumstances is likely to increase the decisionmaking costs and time requirements associated with the risk-assessment process.[45] * * * The carcinogen guidelines, however, never address EPA budgetary restrictions or the time-lag, with accompanying irreversible health effects, that may occur while regulators wait for sufficient data to make reliable scientific judgments.

A more subtle ramification is that the guidelines invite Agency officials to evaluate their own performance, and that of their subordinates, in terms of scientific competency rather than regulatory competency. If the primary decisional criteria is whether regulators select the "most scientifically appropriate interpretation to assess risk," officials may be reluctant to choose speculative treatments that increase public safety under conditions of uncertainty but cannot be identified as the most plausible scientific theories among a constellation of competing hypotheses. Moreover, the majority of interveners in regulatory proceedings are sponsored by affected industries or trade associations, which means the scientific performance of agency officials will regularly be monitored and challenged by industry scientists who advocate less conservative risk assessment practices. Agency bureaucrats, like other people, are sensitive to criticism and may deliberately or subconsciously seek to placate persistent critics.

---

[45] In a later article, Latin argues that it makes more sense to rely on inefficient regulatory systems that require less information to develop and implement, than it does to adopt theoretically "fine-tuned" regulations which require large amounts of information. *See* Howard Latin, *Ideal Versus Real Regulatory Efficiency: Implementation of Uniform Standards and "Fine-Tuning" Regulatory Reforms*, 37 STAN. L. REV. 1267 (1985).-EDS.

C. Increased Opportunities for Obstructive Behavior by Affected Parties

Even if Agency risk assessors are assumed to be motivated solely by a desire to conduct the best possible scientific analyses based on the available evidence, a comparable assumption cannot be applied to the goals of interveners who espouse conflicting private interests. The primary incentive of industry representatives is to minimize regulatory costs, not to promote good science. The primary interest of environmentalist interveners is to minimize health and ecological risks irrespective of regulatory costs, not to promote good science. The "weight of evidence" approach embodied in the carcinogen guidelines allows parties in each proceeding to make any conceivable scientific argument-and some inconceivable ones if past practices are any guide-that may affect agency decisionmaking directly through the force of debatable scientific arguments or indirectly through increased delays and costs.

D. Increased Opportunities for Abuse of Discretion by Agency Decisionmakers

Emphasis on individualized "weight of evidence" judgments may enable regulators to make ideologically motivated decisions under the guise that they represent "good science." * * *

* * *

E. Susceptibility to Intrusive Judicial Review

Agency contentions that toxic controls are grounded on "good science" may increase the vulnerability of regulations to hostile judicial review. The CPSC, for example, tried to regulate urea-formaldehyde foam insulation on the basis of one experiment in which more than 40% of the animals contracted cancer within 24 months. This finding showed an unusually high degree of carcinogenic potency in comparison with the animal data on other toxics in widespread use. In *Gulf South Insulation v. Consumer Product Safety Commission*, the Court of Appeals for the Fifth Circuit overturned the formaldehyde regulation because the judicial panel decided "it is not good science to rely on a single experiment, particularly one involving only 240 subjects, to make precise estimates of cancer risk * * *. *To make precise estimates, precise data are required.*"[46] The opinion provided no intimation of how much precision is required for risk estimates nor how much "precise data" are necessary to constitute substantial evidence in support of regulatory judgments. The Fifth Circuit judges, however, apparently were prepared to make this decision themselves rather than to defer to Agency determinations.

* * *

Unrealistic judicial requirements for comprehensive agency assessments of all potentially relevant factors and for a high degree of scientific precision have substantially emasculated environmental control programs in the past

---

[46] 701 F.2d 1137, 1146-47 (5th Cir. 1983)(emphasis added). The case is discussed further in Chapter 4(C), *infra.*-EDS.

decade. Yet, EPA's current "good science" orientation exacerbates this problem. Regulated industries and other interveners invariably can challenge the scientific bases of carcinogen risk assessments because uncertainty is pervasive and agency officials must adopt many debatable procedures in response to resource constraints and limited data. If regulators explicitly rely on quasi-legislative policy choices under conditions of scientific uncertainty, rather than pretending that their risk-assessment decisions are predicated on reliable scientific judgments, appellate courts might be less prone to accept arguments that agency analyses are irrational or flawed from a scientific perspective. There is no perfect way for administrators to protect their decisions against unsympathetic appellate review, but the current agency emphasis on "good science" invites judicial criticism of toxic risk assessments on grounds where the assessments are sure to be especially vulnerable.

THE SCIENCE CHARADE IN TOXIC RISK REGULATION

Wendy E. Wagner
95 COLUM. L. REV. 1613, 1628-60 (1995)

In a perfect world, scientists and policy specialists would strive to separate trans-scientific[47] issues from issues that can be resolved with scientific experimentation. Policy choices would be made at each trans-scientific juncture, the basis for each choice would be explained, and the public would find the agency's policy decisions clear and accessible.

Not surprisingly, in the real world a completely different picture emerges. Agency scientists and bureaucrats engage in a "science charade" by failing first to identify the major interstices left by science in the standard-setting process and second to reveal the policy choices they made to fill each trans-scientific gap. Toxics standards promulgated under science-based mandates are covered-from the preamble to the regulatory impact analysis-with scientific explanations, judgments, and citations. Major policy decisions that undergird a quantitative toxic risk standard are at best acknowledged as "agency judgments" or "health policies," terms that receive no elaboration in the often hundreds of pages of agency explanations given for a proposed or final toxic standard and appear in a context that gives readers the impression they are based on science. Although this science charade appears to pervade virtually every toxics rule promulgated since the late 1970s, whether the agency engaged in the charade deliberately or inadvertently appears to vary from standard to standard.

* * *

[Wagner goes on to provide examples of the "intentional charade" and the "premeditated charade," in the latter of which scientific information is developed *post hoc* to justify a policy decision. She goes on to consider the political, legal, and bureaucratic incentives for engaging in the charade.]

---

[47] Wagner defined "trans-scientific" in an earlier part of the article. *See* Chapter 2(B)(1)(b), *supra.*-EDS.

One of the best examples of this scientific dueling is the Natural Resources Defense Council's (NRDC's) attempt to ban Alar, a growth regulator used widely on apples,[48] and the scientific counterattacks mounted by both industry and the EPA. Although "[a] good scientist [could] argue the [Alar] case either way," both NRDC and the industry neglected to disclose that their points of difference with EPA were over risk assessment policy assumptions that could not be grounded in science[49] and instead, apparently for strategic reasons, presented the controversy as one over science. NRDC staff cited the quantitative results of their statistics with misleading precision, reporting in their widely disseminated study that Alar causes an "estimated 240 cancer cases per 1,000,000 population among children who are average consumers of Alar-treated food, and a whopping 910 per 1,000,000 * * * for heavy consumers, " and charging in a subsequent interview on 60 Minutes that "Alar is 'a cancer-causing agent that is used on food' and 'the EPA knows [it] will cause cancer in thousands of children over their lifetime.'" NRDC also orchestrated a direct attack on EPA's science, alleging that EPA had relied on outdated consumption data and had drastically underestimated the consumption of certain foods by preschoolers, but NRDC failed to indicate the tremendous scientific uncertainty regarding its own risk assessment estimates. The response by industry was equally deceptive in its characterization of the Alar debate as one concerning "good science." Although EPA did not resort to direct, counter-science attacks, its initial

---

[48] Alar, which is the trade name for the chemical daminozide, was introduced in the United States in the 1960s and used by apple growers to keep ripening apples on the trees and red during post-harvest storage. Alar was considered a pesticide and was registered by EPA under the Federal Insecticide, Fungicide, and Rodenticide Act in 1963. Concern over the carcinogenicity of daminozide and its byproduct, 1,1-(unsymmetrical) dimethylhydrazine (UMDH), began in the early 1970s. In 1985, following a series of reviews and meetings, EPA published a notice of intent to cancel registrations permitting the use of daminozide on foods. EPA's Scientific Advisory Panel concluded that EPA's information was inadequate for a cancellation and EPA postponed cancellation pending the development of better data. In 1989, based on the results of studies conducted between 1985 and 1989, EPA again published a notice of intent to cancel daminozide, but EPA extended the use for an additional 18 months pending the cancellation proceedings.

A leading national environmental organization, the NRDC, was unsatisfied with EPA's delay and launched a major media campaign against Alar. With the help of a public relations firm, NRDC targeted a number of powerful media sources, which included airing a story on the 60 Minutes television program, arranging a news conference with Meryl Streep to announce the formation of NRDC's "Mothers and Others for Pesticide Limits" campaign, and releasing a publication, Intolerable Risk: Pesticides in Our Children's Food.

[49] *See* Leslie Roberts, *Alar: The Numbers Game-The Dispute over Cancer Danger from Alar Highlights Just How Uncertain Risk Assessment Is*, 243 Science 1430, 1430 (1989) ("What's lost in all the charges and counter-charges [on Alar] is a sense of just how squishy the numbers are, on either side. Risk estimates . . . really represent a best guess, built on myriad assumptions, some of which are invariably value laden.").

The major divergence between the risk assessment used by NRDC and that used by EPA stemmed from equally valid, but different selections of potency factors (the number of cancers likely to arise from a given dose) and differences in the estimated exposure (how many apples children eat).

reaction to NRDC's campaign did not assist in dispelling the characterization of the debate as one exclusively over science. A confused public panicked and boycotted Alar-tainted apples as a result of NRDC's powerful science-based campaign. Only a few months later, Uniroyal, the manufacturer of Alar, voluntarily withdrew the product from the market, despite growing scientific consensus both within the U.S. and abroad that Alar was not a potent carcinogen.

NOTES

1. In view of the negative consequences of pursuing "good science" instead of "good regulation," why would a regulatory agency like EPA pursue good science at all? Are you persuaded that Latin has correctly identified the consequences of relying on "good science"? Or is Latin's dichotomy between good science and good regulation a false one (as many EPA officials would certainly argue)?

2. How is the "science charade" a response to uncertainty? Do Latin's and Wagner's arguments complement each other? Are there common solutions to the problems they identify?

3. Is a more individualized determination of proof requirements preferable? The Presidential/Congressional Commission has recommended that formal "value-of-information" analyses should be undertaken to determine whether to go forward now or to await additional information, and to identify the necessary information.

> Risk management is complicated by uncertainty and by the issue of how much information is enough to justify regulatory action. Risk managers face a dilemma: is it better to make a regulatory decision now based on an inherently uncertain risk assessment, or is it preferable to collect additional information first and then decide? Value-of-information techniques provide an analytic framework for resolving this dilemma and for preventing the regulatory paralysis associated with unbounded data gathering and analysis.

* * *

> When the effects of pollution may be persistent, irreversible, or catastrophic, risk managers should be reluctant about committing to strategies that require long-term data collection prior to undertaking protective actions. On the other hand, the costs of action could be reduced considerably if the risk manager can phase in new regulatory requirements gradually rather than imposing them immediately. Even if information about risk is fairly precise, there may be considerable uncertainty about the cost and effectiveness of various control strategies. Under these conditions, additional data collection about cost or effectiveness would make more sense than development of more precise risk estimates. As soon as a risk-related problem is identified, however, social impacts can begin, especially at the

community level. For example, decreased property values and fear of disease may occur regardless of the availability of information or uncertainty about the magnitude of the risk. Efforts to obtain additional information must be balanced against a community's desire to address the risk promptly.

2 Presidential/Congressional Commission, *supra*, at 91-92. Is this responsive to the data problem indicated above? Is it responsive to Wagner's and Latin's criticisms of the current regulatory system?

4. *Risk reform.* Nearly all of the issues that we have covered in this chapter coalesce in several proposals in recent Congresses to reform environmental, health, and safety regulation by requiring the performance of risk assessments more frequently and expanding their influence on regulatory decisions. As an exercise, find S. 981, 105TH CONG., 1ST SESS. (1997) (as amended). What are the key provisions? Can you find evidence of compromise in it?[50]

---

[50] For critiques of the more aggressive risk reform legislation, *see* Celia Campbell-Mohn & John S. Applegate, *Learning from NEPA: Some Guidelines for Responsible Risk Legislation*, 23 HARV. ENVTL. L. REV.93 (1999); John S. Applegate, *A Beginning and Not an End in Itself: The Proper Role of Risk in Environmental Decisionmaking*, 63 U. CIN. L. REV. 1643 (1995); Thomas O. McGarity & Sidney A. Shapiro, *OSHA's Critics And Regulatory Reform*, 31 WAKE FOREST L. REV. 587, 612-22 (1996).

Chapter 3

Economics and Regulatory Analysis

Economics is a social science that has a unique perspective on, and its own terminology for, the relationship between people and resources. To an economist, people are consumers who wish to maximize their individual welfare. These consumers seek selfish satisfaction, well-being, and an ultimate goal called "utility." Environmental problems are thus also economic problems. Environmental insults impose costs on individuals and the economy, and they are expensive to control and clean up. A society of consumers allocates resources so as to increase aggregate welfare, often through a market governed by resource supply and consumer demand. Unfortunately, this scenario rarely operates smoothly, in part because relevant information is limited, in part because there is a scarcity of resources available to satisfy all human preferences, in part because many activities that increase one person's welfare decrease another's, and in part because one often requires another's cooperation to maximize welfare. These problems go by names such as "collective goods" or "negative externalities." For example, a hazardous waste dumped into the ocean is difficult to restrict because it is impossible to exclude dumpers from a collective good like the sea. Likewise, a toxic substance emitted into the atmosphere from a smokestack becomes a cost borne by individuals downwind of the stack, which is often "external" to the owner of the smokestack producing the emissions.

An entire chapter has been devoted to the economic basis of regulation because economic concepts permeate the various legal approaches that are discussed in this book. Economics plays an important role in the decisional calculus used to guide policy. Government has many tools available to it when confronted with a dysfunctional market. When government policymakers are choosing among options, economic analysis is a useful guide. This chapter explains how an economic approach looks at the creation of toxic substances and hazardous wastes and undergirds any regulatory basis for their control and removal.

A. Introduction: Economic Criteria for Evaluating Success of Regulatory Responses to Environmental Problems

In order to determine the success or failure of any given regulatory action (as well as any non-regulatory, purely private action), economic analysis does not merely ask if the problem that was the object of the action remains or has been abated. Instead, economists take into account the fact that society is comprised of many persons, where each has a selfish desire to be individually satisfied. One person's set of preferences may be quite different from another's; individuals might also be more or less willing to pay for the production of any given resource. When economists judge the success or failure of a regulatory effort, they ask two questions: (1) Have limited resources available been allocated so as to maximize each separate individual's welfare? (2) Does the regulation maximize the well-being of the sum total of all the individuals in the society (*i.e.*, has collective or aggregate welfare been maximized)? When both individual and collective welfare is increased, then the regulation is said to meet the economic success criterion of efficiency.

Achieving efficiency is difficult. The sum of individual benefits associated with a regulatory action affecting a resource allocation must always be reduced by the sum of individual costs that are inevitably produced. These costs include the direct costs of achieving a particular resource allocation, the costs of foregoing other available allocations (opportunity costs), and the costs of bringing about an allocation, which are not reflected in its price (social costs). If the total of these costs exceeds the social benefits, then the regulatory response has then failed to meet the efficiency criterion.

An equally powerful reality that prevents the achievement of economic efficiency is the fact that a regulatory action cannot allocate resources so that every individual preference is maximized. Because resources are not infinite, individuals often must choose between competing preferences. This is true for each person and for the aggregate of persons living in a society. Neither can have it all. For example, assume that as a collective matter, society wishes to produce a chemical that has many desirable qualities. Assume also that production of the chemical always has one highly undesirable result–a byproduct of the production process is a toxic substance whose release contaminates rivers and streams. The society wishes to have the maximum amount of the desirable chemical, *and* it wishes to have the maximum number of clean water bodies. However, it becomes quickly apparent that the greater the production of the chemical, the more rivers and streams are polluted. The only way to have the greatest number of clean water bodies is to halt the production of the valuable chemical. The relationship between the amount of chemical produced and clean rivers and streams is illustrated in Figure 3.1.

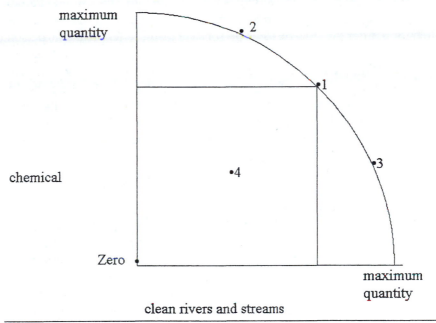

Figure 3.1–Production Possibility Frontier

The curve in Figure 3.1 is known to economists as the production possibility frontier, and it demonstrates an important fact about regulatory actions which seek to bring about an allocation among resources. In our example there are two resources, the chemical and clean waters. Any regulation wishing to work a proper allocation of these two resources must confront the fact that as more chemical is produced, the quantity of clean water decreases. Conversely, as the amount of available clean water increases, the quantity of the useful chemical decreases. This society can never have a situation where *both* chemical production and clean water is maximized. The best a regulatory allocation can accomplish is some tradeoff between chemical and unpolluted waters.

What is the correct tradeoff? If every individual in this two-resource society has an identical desire, and if this desire is to have an equal proportion of chemical and clean waters, a regulatory authority charged with reflecting this collective preference would select point 1 in Figure 3.1. Point 1 is the only point on the curve where society can produce an equal amount of chemical and clean waters. However, such unanimity of choice does not exist in most societies. It is far more likely that some individuals will prefer more chemical and less clean waters (point 2), and some will want the opposite allocation (point 3). Given the inevitable divergence of desires among individuals about the allocation between the chemical and clean waters, how can the regulatory authority pick a point on the curve that will maximize the preferences of all individuals in this society?

The most widely accepted efficiency criterion for assessing whether an action maximizes individual welfare is the one developed by Vilfredo Pareto (1848-1923). According to Pareto, a change in the allocation of resources is called for if, after the change, some persons are made better off and no person is made worse off. Such a change is said to meet the criterion of "Pareto-superiority." If the initial allocation between chemical and clean waters is at point 4 in Figure 3.1, *within* the production possibility frontier, then a reallocation to point 1 would be a Pareto-superior move. This reallocation would yield more chemical and more clean water. Both chemical and clean water lovers are made better off, and neither is made worse off. Indeed, a move from point 4 to any point along the curve is Pareto-superior. For example, a reallocation for point 4 to point 2 would increase the quantity of chemical produced, but would not decrease the amount of clean water. No one is made worse off.

Once this society decides to make a Pareto-superior move to the production possibility frontier curve, then the question that arises is this: *where* on the curve is the optimal point that satisfies the efficiency criterion? The Pareto efficiency criterion can tell us when a reallocation is necessary (*e.g.*, when the initial allocation is at point 4 in Figure 3.1), and it can tell us when the reallocation has resulted in a economically efficient status which has maximized both individual and collective welfare (when Pareto-optimality is attained). But it cannot, in a society where there are varying preferences among individuals, help us to decide *which* among many reallocations will produce Pareto-optimality. Nor does the Pareto criterion judge or rank among preferences. It may be that by some objective, long-term measure, more clean water is better for a society than more chemicals. This value judgment is irrelevant to the Pareto efficiency criterion. If an individual's preference for more chemicals at the expense of cleaner waters is short-sighted (or even stupid), the fact that the preference may be foolish does not play a role in ascertaining where along the curve there is Pareto-optimality.[1]

The Pareto efficiency criterion is in one other important way a limited standard for assessing the ultimate success of an action that produces a

---

[1] The Pareto efficiency criterion also assumes (wrongly) that those who prefer one allocation (*e.g.*, more chemicals) are no more fervent in their preference than those who prefer the contrary allocation (*e.g.*, more waters).

reallocation of resources.[2] Any reallocation will affect some individuals differently than others, and this means that different points along the curve will have different distributional consequences. For example, in Figure 3.1, reallocation from point 3 to point 2 will cause an increase in chemical production, and benefit not only those who prefer more chemicals, but also those who are involved in the production of the chemicals (*e.g.*, the owners of the raw materials, the labor pool that is employed by the manufacturer). Conversely, individuals who live downstream of the chemical producer will experience more polluted streams and less clean waters. The economist using Pareto efficiency criterion is not concerned with the fact that one group benefits and the other suffers from the reallocation. The economist looks at the reallocation simply as reflecting a preference for one resource (the chemical) over another (clean water). Various non-economic disciplines, such as law and politics, must be employed to determine whether such distributional effects are fair.[3] As Guido Calabresi explained in his landmark economic study of tort law:

> Just as economic theory cannot decide for us whether we want to save the life of a trapped miner, so it cannot tell us how far we want to go to save lives and reduce accident costs. Economic theory can suggest one approach–the market–for making the decision. But decisions balancing lives against money or convenience cannot be purely monetary ones, so the market method is never the only one used.
>
> * * *
>
> In other words, although the market can help us to decide how far we wish to go to avoid accidents, it cannot solve the whole problem for us. And when we overrule the market and ban an accident-causing activity that can pay its way or subsidize an activity that cannot, we are not violating absolute laws. We are making the same type of choice between accidents and accident-causing activities that the market makes, but we are choosing, for perfectly valid reasons, to make it in a different way. We are preferring a collective approach or method . * * *

GUIDO CALABRESI, THE COSTS OF ACCIDENTS: A LEGAL AND ECONOMIC ANALYSIS 170-71 (1970).

---

[2] An alternative to the Pareto efficiency criterion, the Kaldor-Hicks criterion, holds that a reallocation is proper when at least one individual is made better off, and when those who benefit by the change can (though they need not) compensate those made worse off. *See also* Waldron, *Criticizing Economic Analysis of Law*, 99 YALE L.J. 1441 (1990).

[3] *See generally* J. RAWLS, A THEORY OF JUSTICE (1971); R. NOZICK, ANARCHY, STATE, AND UTOPIA (1974).

B. The Choice of Means: Market or Government?

Despite its limitations, economists generally agree that the Pareto criterion is the most useful way of judging whether economic efficiency has been achieved. However, since the Pareto criterion does not tell us how to allocate resources so as to achieve optimality, the next logical task is to select a system for allocation that will at least have the highest probability of attaining optimality. There are two basic ways by which decisions can be made to allocate resources: the market system and government.

In a market system, there is an initial allocation of resources to individuals, and thereafter each individual can bargain with others to alter this allocation. Market prices reflect both the cost of the resource, as well as its desirability relative to competing resources. Purchasers buy at the prices they deem acceptable for the nature of the product, thus signaling to producers what product should be on the market at what prices. Government's role is minimal, other than protecting ownership rights in a resource, and providing a mechanism for enforcing completed bargains. On the other hand, in a system where government makes all resource allocative decisions, such as in the old Soviet Union, the distribution and movement of resources among individuals is done centrally. Instead of individuals making their own decisions about resources in light of their own preferences, this job is performed by a government agency. The agency has to guess about—or dictate—the preferences of market actors, and choose among various governmental tools as means of satisfying these preferences.

We shall see a broad progression from reliance on market mechanisms to cope with toxic substances and hazardous wastes to increasingly sophisticated forms of governmental intervention. For toxic substances and hazardous wastes, government intervention falls into three broad phases, as dissatisfaction with the prevailing method of addressing these environmental problems provided a justification for adoption of the next. This country turned first to the common law system of after-the-fact compensation, especially tort law and property law, to correct market imperfections that resulted in harm to the environment. When privately-initiated litigation remedies proved too limited and fragmented (discussed more fully in Chapter 5 (Toxic Torts), *infra*), the United States next tried a more centralized, government response. This collective action adopted a regulatory model, which relied on the passage of environmental statutes, whose commands were carried out by administrative agencies. When these traditional regulatory methods appeared (to some) to be excessively cumbersome and expensive, policymakers responded by requiring agencies to subject their actions to cost-benefit analysis.

The Evolution of Government responses to the Problem of Toxic Substances and Hazardous Wastes

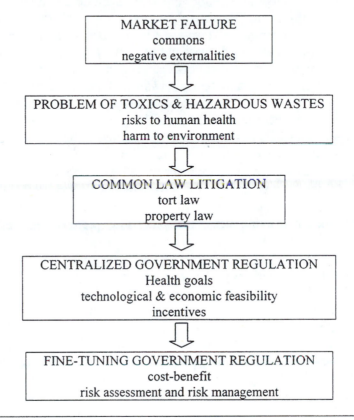

Figure 3.2–Evolution of government responses.

1. The Market

"The market" is the generic name given to the social system of bargains in which individual actors buy and sell goods and services, signaling their willingness to enter into transactions through price mechanisms. It is an extremely decentralized system designed to permit individuals to express their preferences to the full extent that their resources permit.

a. How Markets Work

If a society chooses to rely on a market system as the primary allocative mechanism, economists predict that, if certain unrealistic conditions are met, the behavior of individuals singly and collectively will be optimized in terms of efficiency, and a Pareto-optimal allocation of that society's resources will be achieved. This kind of market may be called a perfectly functioning market, because only the operation of a perfect market can bring about Pareto-optimality. Virtually all markets are imperfect. Nevertheless, it is helpful to see how a perfect market works, because it will help us to understand markets that do exist. Also, toxic pollution, the subject of this book, is caused in large part by the imperfections inherent in real markets. Since these environmental harms are the product of an imperfect market, a non-market (*i.e.*, governmental) response can be structured so as to correct the market breakdowns that originally spawned the harms.

A perfect market system does not depend upon government intervention, other than the creation of a system of laws which permits and protects the ownership of private property and which enforces private agreements which reallocate resources between individuals and groups of individual (firms). The primary decisionmakers in a market are the suppliers of resources (who sell), and the individuals that demand the resources (who purchase).[4] According to an assumption called rational choice theory, all these individuals will make choices in order to maximize their own welfare, not the welfare of others (in other words, individuals will be selfish, not altruistic). It is the extremely decentralized, selfish expression of many individual preferences for particular components of the economic world that comprises the market.

A market has four central features. First, it relies on *prices*. A price is the economic value associated with a given resource. It is typically a number that reflects the various costs of getting the resource to market, plus some profit for the individual who sells it. Prices serve two important functions: they allocate a limited supply of a resource, and they discourage wasteful use of resources. The former function becomes evident when one considers what happens when an item in commerce becomes scarce; its market price will rise. The higher price helps ensure that whenever and wherever supply is limited, there will be a powerful incentive to produce more of these items and distribute them to where there is a shortage. The latter function is a reflection of what occurs when prices are too high–there will be fewer individuals demanding the high priced product. This prospect serves to encourage producers to eliminate wasteful and expensive practices, and to become more efficient, so as to lure more customers through a lower price.

Second, the market operates pursuant to the law of *demand*. This law describes the way humans normally behave–if someone wants or needs something, that person will be less willing to pay for another unit of that item if the price rises. If a graph plots price on the vertical axis and quantity demanded on the horizontal axis, the demand curve is downward sloping. For example, if water could be purchased for $25/gallon and then rose to $50/gallon, the law of demand says that less water will be purchased. The inverse relationship between price and demand does not hold true when another unit is different than the original unit, and if the consumer values the next, different unit more than the original. If water contaminated with toxics can be purchased for $25/gallon, but non-toxic water can be purchased for

---

[4] The word "resources" encompasses natural resources, finished goods, commodities, labor, capital, and services.

$100/gallon, the same amount of water might be purchased despite its higher price, if consumers were willing to pay for poison-free water.[5]

Third, while consumer-purchaser behavior in the market constitutes the law of demand, producer behavior creates the corollary law of *supply*. This law holds that as prices increase, producers will place more of their product on the market. The classic supply curve (with price on the vertical axis and quantity produced on the horizontal axis) is upward sloping. The exact market supply curve for any given product represents the amount of a product that can be supplied in light of all the costs of production. The price for a product will be set at the equilibrium point, where supply equals demand. If supply exceeds demand, there is disequilibrium and producers will reduce the price. If demand exceeds supply, producers well raise the price. The perfect market is thereby self-regulating.

Finally, in a perfect market there is *perfect competition*. If a supplier's product is not wanted (*i.e.*, there is no demand), or if the product is too costly (*i.e.*, there is too much waste in the production process), then producers of a competing product, or producers of the same product at a lower price, will replace the original supplies. This phenomenon, reflecting the economic self-interest of producers, helps to ensure that useless, expensive, or inefficient goods are eventually driven from the market. This state of perfect competition can occur only if all resources are capable of exchange and reallocation among market participants, and if all purchasers and suppliers have complete information about each other. Perfect competition also requires that there be no transaction or external costs, and no external benefits. Transaction costs are the costs of coordination and of obtaining information necessary to engage in a market transaction. External costs are costs which are not borne by producers when creating the product, and which therefore are not reflected in the product's price. External benefits mean that individuals external to the purchase of the product also benefit from the purchase.

b. Why Markets Fail

Unfortunately, the perfect market exists only in economists' dreams. Real markets have several defects that contribute to the creation of significant social harms, including environmental harms. These deficiencies are so fundamental to a market system, and the negative consequence so grave, that some non-market (*i.e.*, government) response is usually in order. A classic market system finds itself unable to cope with two interrelated realities contributing to the problem of environmental contamination: the "commons" and "negative externalities."

---

[5] Sometimes a product is so necessary to individuals that even a steep rise in price will not slacken demand. For example, for automobile owners who have no access to mass transit systems, gasoline is such a "necessary" product. When demand does not fall despite a rise in price, the demand is said to be "inelastic."

i. The Commons

The problem of the commons ultimately stems from the operation of the proposition we have seen before, that rational human beings act in their own self-interest. When individuals own property, they will seek to maximize their interest in that property. Similarly, when property is not capable of ownership, individuals wishing to maximize their welfare will try to take advantage of this free resource and will not pay for its use. This will eventually result in over-use and degradation of the resource.

Some resources are not readily subject to private ownership. These include the atmosphere, bodies of water like lakes and oceans, and much of the earth under the surface. Economists call such resources the commons, collective goods, or public goods. Commons do not have owners with well defined property rights. There is no one owner exercising exclusive control over the resource, which means that owners cannot identify other owners, and there can be no exchanges or transactions between owners. More importantly, the most critical characteristic of private property, the right to exclude others, is absent.

When individuals cannot be excluded, the self-correcting nature of the market system fails. The collective good is either not supplied at all, or if it is supplied, it is over-used. This is true for two reasons. First, when a resource is a collective or public good, individuals will want to take advantage of what is, in effect, a free commodity. Since everyone wants to maximize individual welfare, no one is willing to pay the price that will cover the costs of utilizing the collective good. Second, it is rational for each individual to assume that others will pay the price for use of the resource, and, because individuals cannot be excluded from it, the individuals will have free use of the resource. Of course, since every individual user of the resource reasons the same way, ultimately no one will pay for the resource. The inevitable result will be the overuse of the resources.[6] For example, if a firm can dispose of hazardous wastes without cost by dumping them into an adjacent lake, it has no incentive to spend enormous amounts of money on treatment. Sooner or later, however, the lake's water quality will be degraded.

To extend the analogy, if the firm voluntarily chooses to treat the wastes, and if the lake is not owned by anyone, the benefits associated with treated wastes would be enjoyed by all lake users. The firm has thereby created a positive collective good–a lake uncontaminated with a hazardous waste. However, since individuals cannot be excluded for the lake, the firm cannot charge lake users a price that will cover the costs of treating the wastes. Moreover, no individual lake user will pay the costs of treatment, because lake users will realize that they can still use the lake without payment, as a result of the lake's nonexcludability characteristic. They will prefer to be *free riders*, and hope others will pay for the waste treatment. Nor is it likely that

---

[6] The classic statement of this principle is Garrett Hardin, *The Tragedy of the Commons*, 162 SCIENCE 1243 (1968).

lake users will band together and pay the firm to treat its wastes, because it may be costly to organize (transaction costs) and because they cannot coerce all affected users to join. For this reason, too, there is little chance that this firm, in an unregulated market, will choose to treat the wastes before dumping them into the lake. The lake will become contaminated with hazardous wastes.

ii. Negative Externalities

The converse of a collective good is a negative externality (sometimes known as a social cost). Both collective goods and negative externalities are the result of private decisions that affect not just the producer and purchaser, but also third parties not directly involved in the exchange. A collective good often acts as a receptacle for negative externalities, which cause harm. A negative externality is usually defined as the cost of a market activity that is excluded from the decisionmaking process of the producer of the cost, because someone other than the producer will ultimately have to pay for or absorb the cost. Since such costs are not internalized by the producer, which creates them, the producer will set the price of the product too low. This too-low price will give purchasers an incorrect market signal, and, as a result, both supply and demand for the product will be too high.

Consider the case of a firm that produces a toxic substance as a necessary part of that firm's production process. Properly accounted for, the injuries to individuals that result from exposure to the toxic substance are costs of the production process. But they are external to the producer because the market does not compel the price of the product to reflect them. These negative external costs are borne not by the purchaser of the product, but by unfortunate individuals who are outside the producer-purchaser transaction.

On its own, the market provides no mechanism for such costs to be internalized. The market ensures that the producer bears only the cost of land, labor, raw resources, and capital. The price of the eventual product will reflect just these costs and not the environmental costs of the production process. The purchasers of the product will make decisions based on a price that does not include environmental costs. This price will be lower than it would have been had the environmental costs been internalized. Purchasers will therefore not reduce their demand for the product. Because the firm, which causes a negative externality, pays no part of the social cost, there is no incentive for the producer-firm to eliminate the toxic substance associated with the production process.

iii. Transaction Costs

Transaction costs are the expenses, monetary and otherwise, of completing the exchanges upon which a market system depends. In one sense, they are not a market *failure*, because they are inevitable in exchange-based systems. Even the simplest bargain requires the expenditure of time for communication between the parties to the exchange. When the terms of the bargain become lengthy and complex, the parties need a central place to meet (like a stock exchange), or the form of communication is sophisticated (a computer, say), transaction costs can be quite significant.

Transaction costs are not limited to the bargaining process itself, however. "In general, transaction costs include the costs of identifying the parties with whom one has to bargain, the costs of getting together with them, the costs of the bargaining process itself, and the costs of enforcing any bargain reached."[7] Indeed, in the context of environmental regulation—and especially toxic regulation—these other costs dwarf those of the actual bargaining. For example, suppose that the people exposed to the toxic emissions of a factory wished to bargain with the factory for a reduced level of emissions. Given the low doses, long latency periods, and relative rarity of carcinogenic effects, it will require a huge expenditure of resources just to identify the affected individuals. To name just two issues, toxicological research will be needed to establish the existence and severity of the effects, and atmospheric science will be needed to determine the chemical's environmental fate and transport. Moreover, once the relevant population has been identified, substantial resources will need to be expended to communicate and negotiate with such a large group. Finally, the parties must establish a way to monitor and if necessary compel compliance with the bargain agreed to. This, too, could well require sophisticated equipment and a large investment of time and effort.

In the environmental setting, the difficulty and expense of simply gathering all of the affected parties usually makes bargaining a practical impossibility. The added expenses of identification, negotiation, and enforcement, leave the traditional bargaining model viable only in rare circumstances. Therefore, in this sense at least, transaction costs cause the market to fail to resolve a particular set of conflicts over resources. Conversely, perfecting such a market requires finding ways to reduce transaction costs dramatically.

iv. Information

We saw in Chapter 2 that there is a substantial deficit of information about the toxicity of the chemicals to which we are exposed in the environment. This is a challenge for risk assessment, which depends on the availability of such information, and it is also a market failure. Without complete information, markets cannot function properly, because information is needed for accurate prices. From your reading of Chapter 2, do you think that prices for goods or activities that use toxic substances are likely to be accurate? Why or why not?[8]

---

[7] A. MITCHELL POLINSKY, AN INTRODUCTION TO LAW AND ECONOMICS 12 (1983).

[8] *See* Howard A. Latin, *Environmental Deregulation and Consumer Decisionmaking Under Uncertainty*, 6 HARV. ENVTL. L. REV. 187, 205-17 (1982) (giving reasons that they will be inaccurate).

If lack of information is a problem, why doesn't the market supply it? In an ordinary market, in which uncertainty is clearly undesirable, one would expect incentives to exist to generate missing information. For example, in the market for petroleum, producers do not know with certainty where oil may be found under the earth. Nevertheless, they expend huge sums of money (as does the government, but that is another story) on geological research and observations to locate likely spots for drilling. Given the massive uncertainty surrounding toxicity, this has clearly not happened with chemicals. The following excerpt seeks to explain why not.

INFORMATION ECONOMICS AND CHEMICAL TOXICITY: DESIGNING LAWS TO PRODUCE AND USE DATA

Mary L. Lyndon
87 MICH. L. REV. 1795, 1810-17 (1989)

The market for chemicals will not produce and distribute data on toxicity and exposure unless an incentive structure is developed and maintained. Several factors work to prevent the current system from providing such incentives.

The dearth of toxicity data is in part due to the 'public good' nature of the information. The virtues of flexibility and ease of transfer that characterize public goods becomes liabilities in commerce, because public goods cannot easily be held for exclusive use. If only one person 'buys' the information, others may still benefit; the costs of producing the data cannot be recouped by multiple individual sales. Because public goods are difficult to own and to control, the market produces them at lower levels than may be desirable.

Information is an especially problematic public good, because purchasers do not know its value until it has been acquired. Research is affected by this dynamic. It is also a risky investment because one cannot know ahead of time whether the effort will yield anything of value. In spite of these handicaps, research and development are traditionally a major area of investment. Private research has been supported by legal protections, such as copyright and patent law.

Cost-reducing inventions are one kind of information likely to be produced privately. But toxicological data has a less ready marketability than many cost-saving inventions. It has value only to those who bear the costs that it reduces. Since even the individual victims of chemical-related disease can rarely identify its specific cause, little demand has developed for assurance of safe or low-risk chemical products.

A further disincentive to private research is the fact that the information produced is often inexact. Toxicologists currently have three basic tools with which to gather data: laboratory cell analyses, bioassays, and epidemiology. Each has strengths and weaknesses that support different levels of confidence in their results.

* * *

Epidemiological studies and bioassays are both costly. Moreover, the cost of an individual bioassay has risen dramatically during the past decade. Firms will be reluctant to make substantial investments in research that produces uncertain health data, instead of new products.

Of course, the price of toxicological knowledge cannot be understood as a simple function of the expense of conducting individual studies. Toxicological research as a social enterprise has produced a substantial amount of health information in a relatively short span of time, and as the field matures, it is developing new methodologies. A developed and accessible database on chemical characteristics is itself a powerful research tool. Also, as toxicology identifies sources of disease, it fills out the cost-benefit equation: it identifies the externalities of chemical toxicity. In addition, it may allow for continued use of a chemical by making possible preventive medicine and by reducing the cost to society of using the chemical. Unfortunately, these benefits may not be recovered by individual firms, or their impact may not be easily identifiable as the results of one company's research. Thus, firms are unlikely to undertake costly testing, because the benefits are public and cumulative and not reflected in the corporate balance sheet. Toxicological data collection is beyond the reach of the individual and is a problematic investment for firms.

Another important influence on data production is the simple fact that toxicity and exposure are negative features of chemical products. As long as no way exists for buyers to identify the toxic effects of specific chemicals, there is no commercial incentive for chemical producers to identify and publicize them. Sellers will not willingly reveal negative characteristics of their products. Comprehensive and accessible toxicity rating systems would support affirmative advertising, but without a developed information context, there is no incentive to study a chemical: the long-term health effects remain invisible for one's own products and for those of one's competitors.

A series of market dysfunctions arises from these factors. The invisibility of chemical toxicity has destructive effects on the market for chemicals. If product quality cannot be gauged by consumers, the overall quality of products in the market will be affected. Buyers' inability to screen products removes any incentive for manufacturers to differentiate between toxic and nontoxic products and to screen before production. The result is a higher overall level of toxicity in products than would result if toxicity were a visible characteristic. Chemical products with lower toxicity will be penalized by the presence in the market of some unknown number of toxics.

Indeed, as long as the information market remains undeveloped, ignorance of toxicity may be an advantage to a product. New or unstudied chemicals will do better in relation to chemicals that have been shown to have some indication of toxicity. Ignorance will tend to prevail.

NOTES

1. Similar incentives and disincentives apply to consumer products that have or may have toxic properties. *See* Wendy E. Wagner, *Choosing Ignorance in the Manufacture of Toxic Products*, 82 CORNELL L. REV. 773, 793-96 (1997); Mary L. Lyndon, *Tort Law and Technology*, 12 YALE J. REG. 137 (1995).

2. Responses to market failures can be seen as occurring in three stages: first, market mechanisms step in (for example, the price of oil reflects increased investment in oil exploration); second, private law remedies increase the incentive to discover more information; third, the government intervenes to produce information. Can you think of examples of each. In what sense is tort law market-correcting? What reasons do the excerpts give for the failure of market correction? Can you think of others? Why does private law fail to generate toxicology information?

3. What kinds of governmental intervention are justified by the scarcity of information?

c. How To Correct Market Failures

i. The Coase Theorem

In his landmark article, *The Problem of Social Cost,* Nobel laureate Ronald Coase argued that the problem of market actors taking advantage of collective goods or producing negative externalities is really "a problem of a reciprocal nature."[9] In his article he demonstrated that the goal of efficiency would be achieved regardless of whether producers have the legal right to generate negative externalities into a commons, or the victims of these externalities have the right to not be subject to the externalities. This efficient outcome would always be achieved if both producers and victims could freely bargain among themselves.

---

[9] R. H. Coase, *The Problem of Social Cost,* 3 J.L. & ECON. 1, 2 (1960): "The question is commonly thought of as one in which A inflicts harm on B and what has to be decided is: how should we restrain A? But this is wrong. . . . To avoid harm to B would inflict harm on A. The real question is: Should A be allowed to harm B or should B be allowed to harm A?"

Figure 3.3–Ronald H. Coase[10]

Assume that a firm discharges a toxic substance into the environment (the commons), where it threatens to injure a person who is not a customer of the firm (making the toxic substance a negative externality). If the producer is assigned the right to generate the negative externality, and if the victim considers it important to avoid exposure to the toxic substance, the victim will purchase the "right to pollute" from the producer. This will eliminate the negative externality (though it may create free riders). If the victim is assigned the right to be free of the toxic substance, then the producer will have to take steps to avoid either its creation or its discharge into the environment-or to purchase the right to pollute from the victim. This, too, eliminates the undesirable externality, but it will redistribute the cost of eliminating it. The Coase Theorem shows that in a perfect market an efficient result will be achieved either way, regardless of which party is initially assigned a legal right.

Of course, as a practical matter, victims and producers of externalities cannot bargain with each other to arrive at the economically efficient outcome. First, the Coase Theorem works only if bargaining is costless, but bargaining always entails transaction costs. These costs are typically too high to permit implementation of the Coase Theorem, and they are particularly steep when there are many victims. There will be costs associated with identifying victims, negotiating an agreement with the producer of the externality, and enforcing any exchange of rights. Also, when there are multiple victims, each will be tempted to be a free rider on other victims' payments. Free ridership discourages victim participation in an agreement,

---

[10] Photo courtesy of R.H. Coase.

because any given victim cannot usually be excluded from the benefits that would follow if all other victims negotiate an agreement to pay the producer to stop the externality. And if the victims tried to circumvent the free rider problem by requiring unanimous participation by all victims, one victim could either hold out long enough to force the others to act without that victim, or extort high compensation from the others as the price for unanimity.

Apart from the unrealistic assumption of zero transaction costs, the Coase Theorem does not work very well because it requires precisely-defined property rights as a pre-condition to trading. If commons are present, or uncertainty prevails, which is often the case when environmental problems are involved, property rights are poorly defined and ownership is fuzzy. When neither producer nor victim has an identifiable resource for which a price can be negotiated, and about which an allocation can be achieved, bargaining cannot occur.

The final practical problem with the Coase Theorem is that it only is concerned with the economic goal of efficiency. Efficiency is attained irrespective of the initial assignment of rights because of bargaining. However, efficiency is not necessarily sensitive to the distributional consequences of the bargain[11] For example, assume that it is efficient to continue the externality, but the right to be free of the externality is given to the victim. If a producer of externalities can compensate victims for the right to continue the creation of the externality, that wealth transfer may bring about several unfortunate consequences. The "winners" in the transaction (the compensated victims) may already be wealthy, and thereby be less worthy to receive wealth (the rich get richer). Also, if the externalities are toxic in nature, and if they continue for a lengthy time, even though the victims might be compensated in the short term, they could be killed by the externalities in the long term. Alternatively, if pollution rights are assigned to the polluter, the victims may not have the resources to purchase the pollution rights.

ii. Government as a Market-Corrective Mechanism

Reliance on the market produces problems associated with collective goods and negative externalities. Since private bargaining cannot correct for these defects, a society must necessarily rely on some kind of government intervention. If this intervention seeks only to address market imperfections that produce collective goods and negative externalities, then some government intervention is necessary to overcome market distortions. The government may act to exclude nonpaying consumers from the commons, or

---

[11] Another important flaw in the Coase Theorem is that is assumes that a victim's willingness to pay for the elimination of a negative externality is identical to the victim's willingness to receive compensation from the externality-producer wishing to continue the externality. In the area of environmental harms, there may be a significant divergence between the willingness to pay to preserve a natural resource, and the willingness to be compensated to give it up. *See* Cass R. Sunstein, *Endogenous Preferences, Environmental Law*, 22 J. LEGAL STUDIES 217 (1993).

to internalize costs otherwise borne by those outside the producer-purchaser transaction, or both.[12]

In the case of commons, the government would have to create private legal rights in collective goods, so that the individuals or firms that produced them would be able to charge a price for their use. If a resource is not assigned a price for its use or enjoyment, then there is no incentive for it to be supplied, because the resource-producer receives no benefit. Moreover, the absence of price means that users will succumb to the free rider principle, and overuse the resource. On the other hand, if government intervention allows the otherwise collective good to command a price, then there is both an incentive for a supplier to produce it and a disincentive for consumers to be free riders. Unfortunately, the physical realities of most environmental commons (*e.g.,* air, water bodies) make it extremely difficult for the government to create private legal rights in them. Moreover, even if there were property rights in such commons, the owner of the right could neither easily exclude persons, nor charge others for their use.

For negative externalities, such as the harm caused by toxic substances discharged into the environment, the government can act to internalize them so that the producer of the externality has to pay for them. Government action can internalize externalities either by placing a tax on their production, or by ensuring that payment of external costs is paid for by those responsible for producing them.[13] If the creator of the problem must pay for the negative externality, then the costs associated with the externality are not a cost borne by innocent third parties, but rather costs of production. As such, this cost will be reflected in the price of the good that is the end result of a process that produces the harm. Since the price will rise after the cost has been internalized, the demand for the good will fall and the producer will supply less of the good whose process of creation otherwise causes a harm. Alternatively, the producer will find ways to produce the good with fewer externalities. In either case, the harm will diminish.

2. Government Action

a. Goals

An imperfect market allocates resources poorly (in economic terms, inefficiently), and so government must step in and try to allocate resources directly. Economists typically assume that when markets cannot bring about

---

[12] For a good overview of the failure of the market paradigm and rise of regulation, *see also* Thomas O. McGarity, *Media-Quality, Technology, and Cost-Benefit Balancing Strategies for Health and Environmental Regulation*, 46(3) L. & CONTEMP. PROBS. 159 (Summer 1983).
[13] Government rules can bring about such payment either by imposing fines or financial civil penalties on externality producers, or by making them liable for any harm caused to others. *See generally* FRED ANDERSON, *ET AL.*, ENVIRONMENTAL IMPROVEMENT THROUGH ECONOMIC INCENTIVES (1982).

efficiency, government action should seek to bring about this same goal. In other words, a society forced to rely on government intervention should choose legal rules that will maximize the chances of economic efficiency. Nonetheless, it should be remembered that efficiency may not be a helpful standard with respect to environmental matters. The efficiency criterion only focuses on immediate, short-term human preferences for benefits quantifiable in dollar terms, and measured by willingness to pay in order to receive those benefits. It also does not account for the distributional consequences of a market allocation. When government intervenes, therefore, efficiency is only one of a number of goals that it may pursue.

The full costs of toxic substances and hazardous wastes are often realized only in the long term. Often the costs of an assault on the environment are borne principally not by an individual or a group of individuals, but by an ecosystem (*e.g.*, a tropical rain forest) or a natural resource (*e.g.*, the atmosphere's ozone layer). In such cases the human harm is discernible only collectively or several generations later. Conversely, because the benefits of cleanup may not be enjoyed for decades, the value of cost-internalization is heavily discounted. Also, neither environmental costs nor benefits are easily economically quantified. When attempts at measurement are made, it is usually impossible to include in the calculus the ethical or political preference for a clean, natural earth free of toxic substances and hazardous wastes.[14]

b. How Government Intervention Works

As we have seen, even a purely market-based system requires that government play some minimal role to protect property and enforce contracts. When the level of government intervention must escalate to address market limitations, each legal response is designed to alter the behavior of market actors. Underlying these governmental responses is rational choice theory, which assumes that individuals seek to maximize their own welfare and avoid incurring costs. Thus, each type of government intervention is intended to provide incentives or disincentives to rational individuals, who will then predictably choose a course of action which will result in less environmental contamination by toxic substances and hazardous wastes.[15]

---

[14] For ethical theories of environmental protection, *see, e.g.,* ALDO LEOPOLD, A SAND COUNTY ALMANAC (1968); CHRISTOPHER STONE, EARTH AND OTHER ETHICS (1987).

[15] Professor Weiner describes a "toolbox" of three kinds of instruments that government regulators can select from or combine to address environmental problems:

> 1. Conduct instruments: regulations specifying the sources' technology of production (command-and-control regulations, design standards, technology-based standards, traditional negligence rules);
> 2. Price instruments: regulations forcing sources to pay the social cost of the entitlement to generate external harm (liability rules, taxes, abatement subsidies); or
> 3. Quantity instruments: regulations allocating entitlements to generate to be free from external harm (property rules, performance standards, tradable allowances).

Jonathan Baert Wiener, *Global Environmental Regulation: Instrument Choice in Legal Context*, 108 YALE L.J. 677, 705 (1999).

i. Addressing Problems Caused by the Commons and Negative Externalities

The government has many ways of addressing difficulties posed by the commons or collective goods. One is to divide collective goods into individual parcels and rely on the common law of property to create private ownership interests. Once persons have a property right in a commons, then use of the commons could require the consent of and payment to the owner. The common law of property is unable to parcel out definable interests in the atmosphere, however, and it can only in some limited contexts create ownership interests in water and underground resources.[16]

Government can also impose financial penalties or fines on those who produce negative externalities. Economic charges have the effect of internalizing the externality by forcing the producers to bear all the costs (including the social costs) of their activities. Government can provide this financial disincentive directly to producers of externalities by imposing on them a fee which varies by quantity of the externality that is generated. Government can also proceed indirectly by assigning to those injured by the externality a common law tort right to be free of it. When liability rules permit victims to sue externality-producers, the defendants in this action will, in theory, either be deterred from continuing their production of social costs, or be forced to compensate the victims for damages incurred.[17]

ii. Command and Control Regulation

The government may adopt a purely regulatory approach which "commands" firms to stop the production of a negative externality. This command typically takes the form of a standard which must be obeyed by the externality-producer. An ambient or media-quality standard determines the amount of a toxic substance or hazardous waste that can be present anywhere in the relevant environment. A performance standard prescribes the pollution-control results that must be achieved by an individual firm. Both an ambient and performance standards rely on the market-based decision of individual firms to determine exactly how to be in compliance with the applicable standard.[18]

---

[16] Western water law gives individuals a usufructary right to use (but not possess) water. Under most common law property systems, if a subsurface estate is not separate from the surface estate, the owner of a surface parcel often also owns the earth under the surface.

[17] *See* Calabresi and Melamed, *Property Rules, Liability Rules, and Inalienability: One View of the Cathedral,* 85 HARV. L. REV. 1089 (1972). Common law court actions have two defects: (1) a lawsuit brought by one person on behalf of all victims creates a collective good and free rider problem, and (2) litigation pursued by an individual for the sole benefit of the individual may not require the externality-producer to compensate for all the social costs it generates.

[18] Another more coercive type of standard, a specification standard, seeks to reduce externalities by requiring firms to install a particular device, or implement a certain production process.

One of the great difficulties associated with setting either type of standard is knowing the proper amount or quantity of an externality that is acceptable. Standard setting is particularly troublesome with respect to toxic substances and hazardous wastes. What is the level of a toxic substance that can safely be discharged into the environment? How much of a hazardous waste can be dumped at a site, and what quantity may remain after clean up? These are questions usually answered in part by cost-benefit analysis. If the goal of regulation is to approximate the result that bargaining in the market would have achieved, the government can apply a cost-benefit test to its regulation:

> The amount of money that the neighbors are willing to pay to the manufacturer to reduce the environmental damage depends on the value of undamaged lands to them. This is the "benefit" in a cost-benefit test. The manufacturer's willingness to reduce the environmental damage is a function of the cost to it of reducing the damage. This is the "cost" in a cost-benefit test. The manufacturer will reduce the environmental damage up to the point where the cost of any further reduction exceeds the amount of money that the neighbors are willing to pay. The government can replicate this result by requiring a reduction in environmental damage up to the point where the costs and benefits of such an action are equated.

SIDNEY A. SHAPIO & ROBERT L. GLICKSMAN, RISK REGULATION AT RISK (forthcoming). We will discuss cost-benefit analysis later in the chapter.

There is a common view among economists, legal scholars, and policy analysts that command-and-control (*i.e.,* non-market-based) regulation is *necessarily* inefficient because it offers regulated firms relatively little flexibility in setting levels of environmental protection and deter-mining means of compliance. Professors Cole and Grossman, however, contend that there are situations, particularly when a regulatory regime is first imposed, in which an inflexible system is most efficient. When the marginal costs of pollution control are low, the transaction costs of shifting regulatory regimes are high, and information costs are high, a market-based system will perform worse than command-and-control. Daniel H. Cole & Peter Z. Grossman, *When Is Command-and-Control Efficient? Institutions, Technology, and the Comparative Efficiency of Alternative Regulatory Regimes for Environmental Protection,* 1999 WIS. L. REV 887.

iii. Market Creation

If the government wishes to adopt a least-cost externality control program when there are multiple externality producers, it can create a market which fixes a limit on the quantity of externality that is allowable. In such a market further government intervention is unnecessary, as producers will bargain among themselves to reduce the level of externality to the pre-set limit. Producers, not the government, will set the price that will determine whether a trade among externality-producers will occur.

For example, assume that the government wishes to reduce the amount of a hazardous waste which has been dumped into the environment. Assume also that several firms have been responsible for disposing of this hazardous waste, and for creating attendant negative externalities. To reduce the amount of this waste in the environment, the government could establish a total annual ceiling for its release[19] and require that any source have a marketable permit to discharge the waste. If a firm is able to reduce its waste discharge relatively inexpensively, and if this reduction results in a quantity of waste that is beneath the ceiling level, the firm can sell its discharge permit to firms whose waste levels exceed the ceiling, but which are not economically able to reduce the amount of their waste. The two firms will negotiate the price of the discharge allowance. The government has thereby created a market system that lowers hazardous waste levels by permitting regulated firms to trade waste discharge allowances.

There are three theoretical advantages to government mimicking the market. First, the only government action needed is to set the ceiling on the externalities and ensure that it is not exceeded. Second, since the cost of government intervention is relatively low, total social costs will be less than if every firm had to comply with detailed command and control regulations. Third, the market will ensure that the least-cost strategy will be adopted by the two classes of externality-producers: (1) those for whom externality reduction is less expensive, and (2) those for whom it is less expensive to bear the cost of being able to produce the externality. The former will sell allowances, and the latter will purchase them.

---

[19] The ceiling may be set by reference to economic efficiency, human and environmental health, technological capacity, or a combination of considerations.

Figure 3.4

c. The Forms of Government Intervention

Governmental intervention in the marketplace can take many forms. The strengths and weaknesses of each is what this book is all about—each statute that we study adopts one or more forms of intervention. Since the book explores more than a dozen statutes, some of which deploy several separate regulatory techniques, it may be helpful to set out, in summary form, a smaller number of types of regulatory interventions that will recur throughout the book.

Health-based goals. The regulatory strategy of much environmental legislation is to identify chemicals and wastes that may be harmful and then to set standards limiting the quantity of these pollutants based solely or primarily on protecting human health and the environment. For such statutes, the costs of achieving the standard, as well as the technological feasibility of attaining the standards, are secondary or irrelevant considerations. If achievement of the prescribed levels of pollution is impossible (without forgoing the polluting activity altogether) or simply too expensive, so be it. Health-based standards are intended to be "technology forcing," that is, to create an incentive for affected industries to develop technologies that can achieve very low levels of pollution. Examples of successful technology forcing include automobiles that can run on unleaded gasoline, catalytic converters, and substitutes for ozone-depleting chlorofluorocarbons.

Technological feasibility. Unlike health-based standards, feasibility standards require that health be protected only to the extent that it is possible to do so, now or in the foreseeable future. A feasibility-limited approach thus assumes the continued presence in the environment of toxic substances and hazardous wastes that may be quite harmful, because it is not feasible to abate them to a more safe level. When a standard is technology-based, the permissible level of a toxic substance or hazardous waste in the environment is that level which is achievable in light of scientific, chemical, and engineering technology.[20] When establishing this standard, the decisionmaking agency must determine whether the appropriate control level is that achieved with technology by the most advanced plants in the industry, plants that are representative of the industry, or older, economically marginal plants.[21] On the whole, the availability of technology diminishes as the degree of pollution control increases.

---

[20] An achievable standard is often one which is technologically possible, given the costs of developing, purchasing, and servicing the technology. *See, e.g.,* Rybachek v. EPA, 904 F.2d 1276 (9th Cir. 1990); National Lime Ass'n. v. EPA, 627 F.2d 416 (D.C. Cir. 1980). Conversely, a statute can require that a technology-based standard be determined irrespective of costs. *See, e.g.,* United States v. Akzo Coatings of America, Inc., 949 F.2d 1409 (6th Cir. 1991). When consideration of costs in determining a technology-based standard is appropriate, this does not necessarily require the standard-setter to engage in a sophisticated cost-benefit analysis. *See* Weyerhaeuser Co. v. Costle, 590 F.2d 1011 (D.C. Cir. 1978).

[21] *See, e.g.,* Reynolds Metal Co. v. EPA, 766 F.2d 519 (4th Cir. 1985).

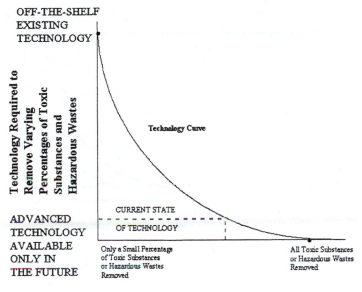

Amount of Removal

Figure 3.5–Technology Curve

Cost-benefit balancing. To some degree, the availability of a technology is a function of cost. Engineering capacity may exist in theory, but it would be absurdly expensive to implement. In this sense, feasibility-based standards take cost into account only at the point at which it becomes prohibitive. Other regulatory techniques take cost into account from the outset of the analysis. Under a variety of formulas, which we will discuss under cost-benefit analysis, cost-benefit balancing allows industry to argue that the costs that a regulatory standard would impose are out of proportion to their benefits in risk reduction. In evaluating the cost of a particular intervention, one often looks not at the total cost of the action but rather at the marginal or incremental cost. The idea of marginal cost is central to economic analysis of regulation, and it is a straightforward concept. One divides each part of that action and looks at only the cost of the last part, *i.e.*, the increment or margin.[22] (This is exactly how the graduated federal income tax works: there is a higher tax rate for additional increments of income. Thus, the last dollars you earn are taxed at a higher rate than the first.) As this graph of estimated air pollution control costs in Los Angeles illustrates, the result is that the cumulative costs of pollution control remain flat for quite a long time, after which they rise sharply.

---

[22] For a general treatment of these issues, *see* TOM TIETENBERG, ENVIRONMENTAL AND NATURAL RESOURCE ECONOMICS 324-52 (4th ed. 1996).

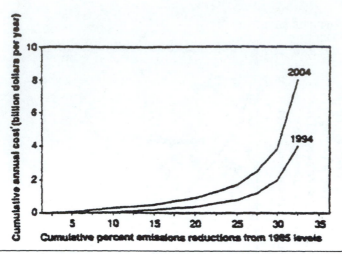

Figure 3.6–Cumulative Cost Curve (Reflecting Rising Marginal Costs)[23]

Under cost-benefit balancing, this pattern would have a profound effect on the stringency of government regulation. The point at which the costs begin to accelerate rapidly is often called the "knee of the curve," and one definition of economic feasibility would be that point, on the theory that reductions beyond that point are no longer cost-effective.

Incentives. Standards based upon health-based goals, technological feasibility, and economic balancing are sometimes known as command-and-control regulations because they establish a level of control and then command that it be met within a particular time period. The type regulation most favored by economists is a financial charge ("pollution tax") imposed on the discharge or production of toxics and hazardous wastes. This creates an economic disincentive to engage in practices that have a negative social cost where that cost is not borne by the entity causing the cost; however, the decision on precisely how much pollution to emit is left to the individual firm, based on the financial consequences of increased taxation. Another alternative to command-and-control standards is an approach designed to mimic the market by establishing an overall allowable level of an environmental contaminant, allocating to individual market actors permits rights, making these rights transferable (for a price set by market forces), and thus letting the market actors decide how to achieve the pre-set level. Such a program of transferable pollution permits creates a system of property rights. It should bring about the desired level of pollution reduction at the least cost, because the transferable permits will establish a price for specific quantities of pollution within the relevant market.

Information production. To the extent that the market imperfection at issue is uncertainty or lack of information, regulation can also be designed to

---

[23] Alan J. Krupnick & Paul R. Portney, *Controlling Urban Air Pollution: A Benefit-Cost Assessment,* 252 SCIENCE 522, 523 (1991).

collect and generate information, either through direct command or by creating incentives. Toxics statutes have components that collect and compile existing data, require record keeping and reporting by firms, and permit monitoring and inspections by the government, authorize original research by the government itself, condition certain activities on the obtaining of a license that requires the firm to provide certain information, and require regulated entities to undertake their own testing of chemicals or activities. Of these, techniques that in effect place the burden of proving safety on the private firm can have a dramatic effect on the scope and content of regulation under conditions of uncertainty.

d. The Costs of Government Intervention

Despite the many tools at its disposal, government is rarely able to bring about Pareto-optimal conditions or to eliminate problems associated with the commons and negative externalities. There is a tension between reliance on market mechanisms and reliance on government intervention as competing means of maximizing aggregate social welfare by producing the optimal allocation of resources. One consequence of this market-government competition is that a decision to intervene with government is often merely a prelude to a future decision to turn to the market as a better resource allocative medium; conversely, since the market has serious down-sides, policymakers eventually must choose government intervention as an alternative. There is thus a circular regulatory life cycle that begins with the market as the preferred resource allocative mechanism, then seeks government assistance when the market fails, and returns to the market when government regulation itself fails. This life cycle has six identifiable stages.

Life Cycle of Government Regulation

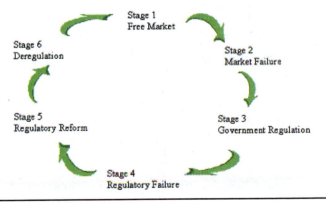

Figure 3.7–Regulatory Life Cycle

In Stage 1, the free market, there is little government intervention. This stage is premised on the superiority of market forces, generally reinforced by the common law. The market failures that arise during Stage 2, such as the twin problems of the commons and externalities, justify the government intervention that occurs in Stage 3. Inadequate or inefficient government action creates regulatory failure, or Stage 4. Regulatory failure often results when the government intervention is perceived to be unsuccessful in addressing the market failure that was the original catalyst for the intervention. It may also occur when the cost of government actions are thought to exceed the benefits. There are two reactions to regulatory failure. In the last two stages of the regulatory life cycle, government can attempt to correct the failure through regulatory reform, which typically entails experimentation with different regulatory tools (Stage 5). Or, government can extract itself from the market altogether by deregulation (Stage 6). If government intervention is terminated, resources are allocated again by the market, which is a return to Stage 1.

The history of toxic substances and hazardous wastes closely tracks the regulatory life cycle. Before there were environmental laws, market forces governed the production of toxic substances and the disposal of hazardous wastes (Stage 1). When the market proved unable either to regulate their discharge into the commons, or to internalize the resulting social costs, (Stage 2) extensive government intervention occurred (Stage 3). Many of the statutes reviewed in this book were enacted to address the market's failure to deal with the environmental problems of toxics and hazardous wastes. By the end of the 20th Century, however, serious questions were being raised about the extent and cost of all this environmental regulation, as well as its redistributive effects (Stage 4). Lawmakers have in two ways decided to revise traditional regulatory approaches to toxic and hazardous waste contaminants. First, regulatory reform (Stage 5) has been instituted by the requirement that risk assessment and cost-benefit analysis become a pre-condition to regulation. Second, a form of deregulation (Stage 6) has manifested itself in the creation of markets which fix a cap on the amount of toxic substance or hazardous waste allowable within that market. Traditional market forces, not government intervention, will ensure a reduction of these pollutants by permitting generators of these pollutants to trade allowances to pollute (up to the cap) among themselves.

The cyclical shifts between market and government reflect the imperfections of the market and of governmental intervention to correct the market. They share one fundamental imperfection, that is, the problem of uncertainty and scarce information. Three other imperfections are specific to governmental intervention.

i. The Direct Costs of Using Government

The great advantage of markets for setting prices and allocating goods is their decentralization of decisionmaking, because centralized government action entails enormous information, administrative, and decisionmaking costs. Information must be gathered and organized; decisionmaking bodies (agencies, regulators, courts) must be created and staffed; decisions must be made about the type of government intervention that is appropriate and the allocation of resources that seems closest to being optimal. For example, with toxic substances and hazardous wastes, accurate and reliable acquisition of scientific information about the nature and effect of these contaminants requires years of expensive laboratory and field testing. Large bureaucracies must be created to carry out or control the tests. Armies of policymakers must then assimilate the data collected to determine a hierarchy of targets and to develop a system (or a standard), which efficiently limits the discharge, disposal, or cleanup of the toxic material or hazardous waste. A powerful enforcement mechanism must also be established so that market participants are sanctioned for failure to comply with applicable government regulations.

Another cost associated with government intervention is the cost of governmental coordination. This cost has both a vertical and horizontal component. Vertical coordination is needed between the different levels of government (e.g., federal, state, local) that may respond to externalities. This coordination entails political considerations (is a government response to the dumping of hazardous wastes a local, state, or federal matter?), and constitutional law limitations (if the response is at a state or local level, is there federal preemption or is the non-federal response a violation of the dormant commerce clause?).[24] Horizontal coordination is necessary when the object of governmental intervention is a negative externality that respects no political borders. Such is the case with toxic substances that may be discharged into air or flowing water courses; toxics may also be the result of manufacturing a product which is widely purchased in the national market place. If the externality problem is neither produced nor experienced just within the boundaries of one political jurisdiction, any government attempt at addressing the problem must in some fashion include the governing bodies of all the other affected jurisdictions.[25] Horizontal coordination is also required

---

[24] Recent Supreme Court cases addressing federal issues involving toxic substances and hazardous wastes include: Gade v. National Solid Waste Management Ass'n, 505 U.S. 88 (1992)(preemption); Exxon Corp. v. Hunt, 475 U.S. 355 (1986) (preemption); C & A Carbone, Inc. v. Town of Clarkstown, 511 U.S. 383 (1994)(dormant commerce clause); Chemical Waste Management, Inc. v. Hunt, 504 U.S. 334 (1992) (dormant commerce clause).

[25] One approach to the problem of overlapping political jurisdictions is "ecosystem management." Several federal agencies, particularly the U.S. Forest Service, have attempted to incorporate this new policy into the management of public lands. The tenets of ecosystem management are (1) a large target area; (2) managed over a long period of time; (3) along natural rather than jurisdictional boundaries; (4) where an interdisciplinary approach among all sciences; and (5) coordination and cooperation between federal agencies, states, and private landowners, (6) achieves the goal of resource diversity and sustainability. See M. HUNTER, WILDLIFE, FORESTS, AND FORESTING: PRINCIPLES OF MANAGING FORESTS FOR BIOLOGICAL DIVERSITY (1990). None of the federal environmental regulatory programs—the Clean Air Act, Clean Water Act, RCRA, or CERCLA—are written to incorporate ecosystem principles. There has been little success when litigation has been pursued which argues that the language of various public land statutes mandates ecosystem management. See Kirchbaum v. Kelly, 844 F. Supp. 1107, 1114 (W.D. Va. 1994); Sierra Club v. Robertson, 845 F. Supp. 485, 502 (S.D.Ohio 1994).

when numerous statutes regulate the same activities or substances, an all to frequent occurrence in environmental regulation.[26]

ii. Political Self-Interest

When government intervention is implemented through legislative action, the statutory product does not necessarily further the general public interest,[27] because the political process of enacting legislation creates pressures that too often force legislators to act at odds with the public good. Political scientists and economists who have studied the legislative process have developed an explanation for the recurring divergence between the needs of the public and the realities of legislative decisionmaking; this model of the dynamics of the political process is known as Public Choice Theory.

One branch of the Public Choice, Decision Theory, posits that it is impossible to create a process of representative, collective decisionmaking that represents the majority will all the time.[28] The observable preference of any given legislator will vary with the options presented to the legislature that are subject to a vote, which in turn will affect the preference of the majority of legislators on any given matter. Because legislative majorities shift depending upon the option being voted on, the voting process under majority rule relies more on the order in which issues are placed before legislators, and less on whether the vote is consistent with the public interest. One consequence of this phenomenon is that voting outcomes are often by those who control the voting agenda of the legislature.[29]

The other branch of Public Choice, Motivation Theory, holds that legislative voters act to advance their own self interest, primarily the desire to be reelected. In order to be reelected, legislators desire more money contributed to their campaigns and less money contributed to their opponents' campaigns. This allocation of money enhances the reelection chances of the

---

It has been suggested that the Toxic Substances Control Act perform this integrating function. *See* Lakshman D. Guruswamy, *Integrating Thoughtways: Re-Opening of the Environmental Mind*, 1989 WIS. L. REV. 463; Chapter 8 (TSCA), *infra*.

[26] *See* John C. Dernbach, *The Unfocused Regulation of Toxic and Hazardous Pollutants*, 21 HARV. ENVTL. L. REV. 1 (1997)(discussing the overlapping regulation of particular chemicals).

[27] The public interest is furthered when legislation successfully balances two principles— economic efficiency (greatest good for the greatest number) and protection of individual rights. *See* D. LYONS, ETHICS AND THE RULE OF LAW 156-7 (1984); R. SOLOMON, A PASSION FOR JUSTICE: EMOTIONS AND THE ORIGINS OF THE SOCIAL CONTRACT 95-7 (1991).

[28] KENNETH ARROW, SOCIAL CHOICE AND INDIVIDUAL VALUES (2D ED. 1963).

[29] The agenda setting process in legislatures is controlled by a small group within legislative committees. These legislators may manipulate the itinerary to serve their own interests, at a cost to the public interest. *See* Elhauge, *Does Interest Group Theory Justify More Intrusive Judicial Review?*, 101 YALE L.J. 31, 103-105 (1991); Riker & Weingast, *Constitutional Regulation of Legislative Choice: The Political Consequences of Judicial Deference to the Legislatures*, 74 VA. L. REV. 373, 385-93 (1988); Blydenburgh, *The Closed Rule and the Paradox of Voting*, 33 J. POL. 57 (1971); J. BUCHANAN AND G. TULLOCK, THE CALCULUS OF CONSENT (1962).

incumbent and diminishes the chances of the challenger. Large groups with diffuse interests (*e.g.*, the general public) are usually unwilling or unable to spend time and money to further the reelection chances of a legislator. By contrast, small, focused, special interest groups have the money, time, willingness, and expertise necessary to play an important role in a legislator's campaign for reelection. The prudent legislator wishing to further that legislator's own interests is thus more than happy to vote so as to further the interests of lobbyists. The interests of the public, to the extent they diverge from a focus group's interests, are ranked lower as a voting preference.[30]

iii. Unsuccessful Responses to Risk

Public Choice suggests that legislators and regulators may be insufficiently responsive to the public good for reasons of self-interest. Alternatively, government may be *too responsive* to public wishes by failing to interpose its technical expertise between popular opinion and regulatory action. We saw in Chapter 2 that a salient feature of toxics regulation is its focus on risk instead of actual harm. There is great scientific uncertainty about which substances may be harmful, the nature and gravity of the harm when (and if) it is experienced, and the quantity of the substance in the environment that must be present to produce the harm. There may be a tendency, suggested by the materials on risk perception, to overstate the seriousness of such risks in comparison to the benefits of the activity and/or the costs of remediation. This, at least, is the position taken by Judge (now Justice) Stephen Breyer.

BREAKING THE VICIOUS CIRCLE: TOWARD EFFECTIVE RISK REGULATION

Stephen Breyer
pp. 11-23, 33-43 (1993)

Three serious problems currently plague efforts to regulate small, but significant, risks to our health. I call these problems tunnel vision (or "the last 10 percent"), random agenda selection, and inconsistency. Scientific,

---

[30] See D. FARBER AND P. FRICKEY, LAW AND PUBLIC CHOICE (1991); Rubin, Beyond Public Choice: Comprehensive Rationality in the Writing and Reading of Statutes, 66 N. Y. U. L. REV. 296 (1993); Macey, Promoting Public-Regarding Legislation Through Statutory Interpretation: An Interest Group Model, 86 COLUM. L. REV. 223 (1986). The first months of the Republican majority in the House of Representatives provided many examples of this phenomenon in action. *See* Engelberg, 100 Days of Dreams Come True For Lobbyists,, N.Y. TIMES, April 14, 1995, at A8; Engelberg, Business Leaves the Lobby and Sits at Congress's Table, N.Y. TIMES, March 31, 1995, at A1; Cushman, Lobbyists Helped the G.O.P. in Revising Clean Water Act, N.Y. TIMES, March 22, 1995, at A1 (commenting on proposed revisions to the Clean Water Act, drafted largely by "narrow interests," such as the Chemical Manufacturers Association, which would define factories as being in "statistical compliance" with their pollution discharge permits, as long as pollution levels were not exceeded with "unusual frequency").

technical, and legal articles in this area confirm that these problems are significant. * * *

Problem One: Tunnel Vision, or "The Last 10 Percent"

Tunnel vision, a classic administrative disease, arises when an agency so organizes or subdivides its tasks that each employee's individual conscientious performance effectively carries single-minded pursuit of a single goal too far, to the point where it brings about more harm than good. In the regulation of health risks, a more appropriate label is "the last 10 percent," or "going the last mile." The regulating agency considers a substance that poses serious risks, at least through long exposure to high doses. It then promulgates standards so stringent–insisting, for example, upon rigidly strict site cleanup requirements–that the regulatory action ultimately imposes high costs without achieving significant additional safety benefits. A former EPA administrator put the problem succinctly when he noted that about 95 percent of the toxic material could be removed from waste sites in a few months, but years are spent trying to remove the last little bit.

Problem Two: Random Agenda Selection

The literature also suggests a serious problem with the creation of regulatory agendas and with the establishment of rational priorities among the items that are included in those agendas. * * *

Some critics point out that, of the more than sixty thousand chemical substances potentially subject to regulation, only a few thousand have undergone more than crude toxicity testing. The General Accounting Office, for example, after a recent examination of EPA's testing agenda, under the 1976 Toxic Substances Control Act, found that the relevant EPA Committee had recommended only 386 substances for testing as of 1990. The GAO wrote that the testing program "has made little progress," that EPA "has received complete test data for only six chemicals," that the untested chemicals, in all likelihood, include harmful chemicals, and that the agency has no particular strategy for determining which of these many chemicals are likely to need testing and which are not. * * *

Problem Three: Inconsistency

The regulation of small risks can produce inconsistent results, for it can cause more harm to health than it prevents. Sometimes risk estimates leave out important countervailing lethal effects, such as the effect of floating asbestos fibers on passers by or on asbestos-removal workers (who, in fact, do not wear completely protective clothing). Sometimes the regulator does not, or cannot easily, take account of offsetting consumer behavior, as, for example, when a farmer, deprived of his small-cancer-risk artificial pesticide, grows a new, hardier crop variety that contains more "natural pesticides" which may be equally or more carcinogenic.

* * *

In considering the causes of the regulatory problems identified [above], I wish to consider how public perceptions, Congressional actions and reactions, and technical regulatory methods reinforce each other. They tend to create a vicious circle, diminishing public truth in regulatory institutions and thereby inhibiting more rational regulation. * * *

Public Perceptions

Study after study shows that the public's evaluation of risk problems differs radically from any consensus of experts in the field. Risks associated with toxic waste dumps and nuclear power appear near the bottom of most expert lists; they appear near the top of the public's list of concerns, which more directly influence regulatory agendas. * * *

There is a far simpler explanation for the public's aversion to toxic waste dumps than an enormous desire for supersafety, or a strong aversion to the tiniest risk of harm—namely, the public does not believe that the risks are tiny. The public's "nonexpert" reactions reflect not different values but different understandings about the underlying risk-related facts. * * *

People react more strongly, and give greater importance, to events that stand out from the background. Unusual events are striking. We more likely notice the (low-risk) nuclear waste disposal truck driving past the school than the (much higher-risk) gasoline delivery trucks on their way to local service stations. Journalists, whose job is to write interesting stories, know this psychological fact well.

Congressional Action and Reaction

A second element of the circle consists of Congressional reaction to perceived risk and to regulatory problems, which takes the form of detailed statutory instructions. * * *

Regardless, Congress is not institutionally well suited to write detailed regulatory instructions that will work effectively. For one thing, legislation originates in different subcommittees, including several with overlapping jurisdiction, each of which must compete for political time and attention. Each subcommittee may consider the particular problems that it has studied as the most important, deserving a place at the head of the regulatory queue, whether or not dispassionate observers would reach the same conclusion. Finally, Congress is highly responsive to public opinion, as it ought to be. This means, however, that if the public finds it difficult to order risk priorities, Congress is also likely to find it difficult to write an effective agency agenda for addressing risk. The second element of the vicious circle is connected to the first.

Uncertainties in the Technical Regulatory Process

The circle's third element consists of the uncertainties embedded in the regulatory process, and the assumptions the regulators must make in order to arrive at recommendations for actions despite those uncertainties. Predicting risk is a scientifically related enterprise, but it does not involve scientists doing what they do best, namely developing theories about how x responds to y, other things being equal. Rather, it asks for predictions of events in a world where the "other things" include many potentially relevant, rapidly changing circumstances, requiring the expertise of many different disciplines to reach a conclusion. A waste site evaluation, for example, may require knowledge of toxicology, epidemiology, meteorology, hydrology, engineering, public health, transportation, and civil defense, disciplines with different histories, different methods of proceeding, and different basic assumptions. Moreover, where prediction involves a weak relationship, such as that between a small doses of a substance and a later cancer death, as well as long lead times, such as exposure for twenty years or more, it is difficult or impossible for predictors to obtain empirical feedback, which is necessary (for them as for all of us) to confirm or correct their theories.

—

Justice Breyer offers a number of reasons for the high social costs (in the sense of inefficiency) of the regulation of toxics, and he suggests that a more thorough and more clear-headed analysis of costs and benefits would result in more efficient-and more generally sensible-regulation. This point of view is shared by many lawyers, economists, and policymakers. It is also shared by Congress and regulatory agencies, which mandate and use varying amounts of risk, cost, and benefit analysis to develop regulatory programs and set standards. We now turn to these techniques, which are designed to improve the efficiency and effectiveness, and reduce the social costs, of regulation

C. Regulatory Analysis: "Fine-Tuning" Government Regulation

The use of centralized government regulation to address the problem of toxic substances and hazardous wastes has not been without controversy. Producers of toxic substances and activities which dump hazardous wastes have complained that the gains to the environment have not been worth the considerable private costs associated with discharge abatement, manufacturing process changes, and waste clean-up. Legislators have wondered whether the public costs of regulation and the private costs of compliance regulation are justified in light of the uncertainty surrounding the possible harmful effects of toxics and hazardous wastes. Questions about the net benefits gained from controlling substances and wastes that may or may not produce harm have caused lawmakers and courts to require agencies to fine-tune their regulatory actions pursuant to cost-benefit and risk assessment strategies. We have already examined, in Chapter 2, risk assessment as a method for determining the need for and the appropriate stringency of regulatory action. We now turn to two other analytical techniques, both of which incorporate risk information: comparative risk analysis and cost-benefit analysis.

1. The Culture of Analysis

Regulator agencies rely on various analytical techniques to help them to identify problems requiring resolution, to set priorities among those problems, to select remedies, to determine the extent of the remedy, and to justify their decisions to reviewing courts. A rigorous analytical approach is a cultural artifact of the rise of a science-based regulatory agency, but it also provides several concrete benefits to the regulatory process.[31] As Professor McGarity has observed:

> Rational analysis is essential to the integrity of the rulemaking process under the Administrative Procedure Act. Unless an agency can demonstrate both that a rule is rational related to goals that Congress intended for the agency to consider and that it has support in the data, assumptions, and reasoning in the rulemaking record, a reviewing court is likely to find that the agency has been arbitrary and capricious in promulgating the rule.

THOMAS O. MCGARITY, REINVENTING RATIONALITY: THE ROLE OF REGULATORY ANALYSIS IN THE FEDERAL BUREAUCRACY 112-23 (1991). He goes on to enumerate several other virtues of analysis: asking the right questions, identification of options, gathering and analyzing information, justification by explicit reference to articulated policies, explicit identification of information gaps and assumptions, identifying research needs, making "correct" decisions, facilitating policy management by differentiating factual basis and policy judgment, informing Congress and the public, and avoiding unjustifiably burdensome regulation.

The model of analysis to which McGarity refers is implicitly comprehensive, in the sense that it aspires to examine all aspects of a problem and to reach a resolution that is the "best" accommodation of the relevant data, needs, and goals. This is not, however, the only way to reach a rational decision. In a pathbreaking article, political scientist Charles E. Lindblom demonstrated that a process with more modest aims–which he called "incrementalism"–could be more effective for particular types of decisions. *The Science of "Muddling Through,"* 19 PUBLIC ADMIN. REV. 79 (1959). Professor Colin Diver applied this analysis to regulatory agencies.

POLICYMAKING PARADIGMS IN ADMINISTRATIVE LAW

Colin S. Diver
95 HARV. L. REV. 393, 396-401, 428-33 (1981)

I. TWO MODELS OF THE POLICYMAKING PROCESS

† † †

---

[31] For an interesting and useful discussion of the cultural issues, *see* SHEILA JASANOFF, THE FIFTH BRANCH: SCIENCE ADVISORS AS POLICYMAKERS (1990).

A. Comprehensive Rationality

Comprehensive rationality entails four steps. First, the decisionmaker must specify the goal he seeks to attain. Second, he must identify all possible methods of reaching his objective. Third, he must evaluate how effective each method will be in achieving the goal. Finally, he must select the alternative that will make the greatest progress toward the desired outcome.

Only a superhuman decisionmaker could faithfully adhere to the ideal of comprehensive rationality. He would have to be able to identify goals unambiguously, which would sometimes require reconciliation of numerous competing objectives. He would need a Jovian imagination to conceive of every possible means to attain his goals. Finally, he would have to anticipate the precise consequences of adopting each alternative and to invent a metric that permits comparison among them.

* * *

B. Incrementalism

An alternative model of how policy should be made is "incrementalism." This model has three characteristic features. First, policymaking is piecemeal and tightly restricted in scope. Policymakers consider only a handful of alternatives, which differ only slightly from each other and from the status quo. For each alternative, moreover, analysts consider only a limited range of future consequences. They routinely exclude remote or uncertain consequences, even though those consequences might prove momentous. Second, the process is dynamic and remedial. Policymaking becomes a series of small adjustments and avowedly temporary "fixes." Errors are corrected and problems are solved; lofty visions of some preferred social state play no part. Finally, incrementalism is decentralized. Policy is made by many actors at many levels of government and indeed in the society at large. In such a system, policy is a sequence of reactions as much to changes in the positions of other participants as to changes in the outside world.

* * *

C. Comparing the Two Models

Comprehensive rationality emphasizes static choice. It seeks the best of all options available at a given moment. The prospect of change does not inhibit analysis but rather becomes a factor in the analysis. Comprehensive rationality does not, of course, deny that policies will need to be modified over time. But it is a system of comparative statics, not continuous motion: a series of vivid tableaux, each as complete as circumstances will permit. The synoptic thinker conceives of the world as a closed system in which the causal interrelationships of all elements can, in principle, be specified. Once goals are adopted, the system dictates the solution.

Incrementalism, by contrast, involves a continuous sequence of small adjustments. Its practitioners do not expect to achieve permanent solutions but only to react continually to new circumstances. The policy framework is an incomplete system that describes only the most immediate connections among a handful of variables. Policies are made by adapting to exogenous changes, not by restructuring entire systems.

Reducing the two models to a set of rules for policymaking reveals the contrast between them. The synoptic model demands that values be clearly and authoritatively articulated before any individual policy decisions are made. Issues should be addressed in order of their importance to attaining the specified values. The process for making policy decisions must be open-minded and expansive; it must encourage thorough collection of evidence, probing analysis, and explicit choice by specified criteria. Questions must all be resolved at once and not permitted to drag on into the future.

The incrementalist paradigm requires a different blueprint. Its focus on short-term remedies demands that policy once made be easy to adjust, that interests once neglected be able to make themselves heard later on. Goals must remain fluid to accommodate divergent interests and changing facts. And power to make policy must be fragmented, not concentrated in a single pair of hands.

* * *

V. STRIKING THE PROPER BALANCE
* * *

The singular advantage of incrementalism is its ability to accommodate uncertainty and diversity. Where comprehensive rationality tortures fundamental value conflicts into an uncomfortable and often illusory truce, incrementalism creates a quasi-market for their serial reconciliation. While non-incrementalist policies are doomed to rigidity by the very political overselling needed to launch them, the modesty of incremental undertakings enables them more readily to adapt to novel circumstances. Where the synoptic method erects a flimsy bulwark of false certainty against the tide of technical and social change, incrementalism deals only with the present, leaving tomorrow to tomorrow.

Yet the incremental method is not wholly preferable to comprehensive rationality even when uncertainty and conflict prevail. As doubt and strife intensify, incrementalism increasingly taxes the resources of the decisionmaker. To accommodate diverse preferences while adjusting to changing circumstances demands more and more organizational slack. Resources husbanded by avoiding *ex ante* policy specification can be consumed in spades by a process of *ex post* policy elaboration. Even more important, incrementalism can succeed only as long as its remedial apparatus functions smoothly. Here, Lindblom's market analogy is particularly apt. Like the economist's ideal marketplace that it mirrors, incrementalism is itself subject to the problem of "externalities." A policy decision made in response to a highly focused grievance can easily impinge on persons not directly involved. Followers of Lindblom, of course, recognize this danger. But, they would reply, the flip side of selectivity is accessibility. By reducing the expense of making individual decisions, exclusivity encourages later proceedings to correct any untoward results.

Yet the spillover costs of incremental decisionmaking may go uncorrected for at least two reasons: the irreversibility of the external harm, and the political and economic impotence of an affected interest. The remedial character of incrementalism is nullified if the interests harmed at one stage lack the resources to seek later relief or can do so only after relief has become impossible.

These considerations suggest the following principles to guide architects of administrative policymaking. The synoptic paradigm should be the preferred way to make policy in relatively stable environments. Given contemporary ferment in regulatory and social policy, examples are somewhat difficult to find. * * * As recent environmental regulation attests, dogmatic insistence on analytic rigor during the infancy of a regulatory scheme is a recipe for incoherence. * * *

Even in unstable environments, comprehensive rationality should be favored when either of two additional conditions exists. The first is when small errors in policy can cause irreversible or even catastrophic harm. Some current examples are the regulation of nuclear power plant safety and the nuclear fuel cycle, and the regulation of carcinogenic substances in food, consumer products, the environment, and the workplace. Protection of endangered species has similarly high stakes, if not the same intensity of public concern. It is more difficult to classify regulation of conventional nontoxic air and water pollutants. At some point, an incremental increase in pollution may cause a transformation in the ecological balance. Normally, however, adverse environmental outcomes are sufficiently detectable and reversible to be amenable to incrementalist repair.

Synoptic treatment is also appropriate in those policy regimes involving egregious–and irremediable–misallocations of political power among persons most intimately affected. This factor is prominent in such administrative programs as regulation of immigration and naturalization, public assistance, housing and nutritional services for the poor, antidiscrimination regulation, and programs for Native Americans. Because the intended beneficiaries of these programs have little access to political power, legal advice, and self-help, they are often unable to participate in any agency proceeding. Therefore only the synoptic model, in which the decisionmaker *must* consider all interests–including those not immediately before him–can give adequate protection to these beneficiaries.

This leaves a large reservoir of public issues better suited to the incrementalist model. These government functions must live with acute technical uncertainty or heightened value conflict, but without the risk of irreversible catastrophe or irremediable inequalities. One can draw likely candidates from numerous fields of regulation: nonnuclear energy production and use, broadcasting, collective bargaining, anticompetitive and deceptive business practices, and most safety hazards (but not necessarily health hazards) in consumer products, workplaces, and transportation. Many of these areas, such as energy and safety regulation, involve a high degree of technological uncertainty. Others, like collective bargaining and workplace accident prevention, involve sharply focused conflict not easily amenable to generic resolution.

NOTES

1. Describe a synoptic *versus* an incremental approach to toxics regulation. Why does Diver recommend a synoptic or comprehensive approach?

Are there any reasons to prefer an incremental approach? Consider the following:

> There are reasons, then, to avoid a participatory, incremental, trial-and-error method of muddling in favor of holistic, systematic, "synoptic" methods of expert comprehensive analysis (perfectly represented by quantitative risk assessment). These are said to be preferable when "small errors in policy can cause irreversible or even catastrophic harm." Unfortunately, however, the synoptic methodology is itself troublesome, on a number of grounds. First is the widely accepted opinion that it depends on "firmness of data and consensus on goals"-things hard to come by in the case of public risks. Second is the problem of latency, which might well affect even the incentives of expert analysts. Consider, for example, the mundane point that weather forecasters are regarded by careful students of such matters as being among the very best and most reliable of prognosticators. There are, no doubt, technical and technological reasons for this, such as regular advances in meteorology and the development of orbiting satellites, but there is also the intriguing fact that weather prediction is performed in such an elegant system of almost instantaneous meaningful feedback. Bad weather-folk simply don't survive. In the case of bad public risk assessors, though, latency frustrates the forces of natural selection that might otherwise help eliminate poor assessors and managers. By the time their errors are discovered, they are likely to be out of office, perhaps even deceased, making it difficult (or impossible) to hold them accountable. The absence of long-term accountability could result in shirking, laxity, and an unwarranted focus on the short term. Third is the apparent fact that synoptic decision making can itself lead to calamity, suggesting perhaps that the sheer intractability of public risk makes muddling through the lesser of two evils. Robert Dahl seems to reach this conclusion. He argues against expertise despite the dangers of bad guesses by ordinary people, comforting himself with the notion that "the opportunity to make mistakes is the opportunity to learn." In the same vein, Ida Hoos, a staunch critic of systems methodology, reckons that "[m]uddling through is probably safer in the long run than the wrong cure."

Clayton P. Gillette & James E. Krier, *Risk, Courts, and Agencies*, 138 U. PA. L. REV. 1027,1107-09 (1990). Are you persuaded that an incremental approach would be better?

2. Incrementalism is not without critics, both as a normative theory of administrative behavior and as a description of the ways decisions are in fact made.

> Decisions by consent among partisans without a society wide regulatory center and guiding institutions should not be viewed as the preferred approach to decisionmaking. In the first place, decisions so reached would, of necessity, reflect the interests of the most powerful, since partisans invariably differ in their respective power positions; * * *.

> Secondly, incrementalism would tend to neglect *basic* society innovations, as it focuses on the short run and seeks no more than limited variations from past policies. * * *

> * * * While incremental decisions greatly outnumber fundamental ones, the latter's significance for society decisionmaking is not commensurate with their number. * * * [I]t is often the fundamental decisions which set the context for the numerous incremental ones. * * * [M]ost incremental decisions specify or anticipate fundamental decisions * * *.

Amitai Etzioni, *Mixed-Scanning: A "Third" Approach to Decisionmaking*, 46 PUBLIC ADMIN. REV. 385, 387-88 (1967).

Incrementalism also favors the status quo. It is "an ideological reinforcement of the pro-inertia and anti-innovation forces prevalent in all human organizations"; whereas the "rational-comprehensive model has at least the advantage of stimulating administrators to get a little outside their regular routine." Yehezkel Dror, *Muddling Through–"Science" or Inertia?*, 24 PUBLIC ADMIN. REV. 153, 155 (1964). The modern jargon for Dror's point is "thinking outside the box."

Others have noted that an incremental decisionmaking system reinforces the tendency, all too common in busy senior administrators' working lives, to focus on the urgent, short-term issues at the expense of the *important*, long-term ones. "In time, the official can lose track of priorities. And this is where a conscientious official could be lulled into complacency by Lindblom's theory of incrementalism." Bruce Adams, *The Limitations of Muddling Through: Does Anyone in Washington Really Think Anymore?*, 39 PUBLIC ADMIN. REV. 545, 547 (1979). Justice Breyer describes a related symptom as "tunnel vision," in which "an agency so organizes or subdivides its tasks [- a deliberate and appropriate incrementalist strategy for simplification -] that each employee's individual conscientious performance effectively carriers single-minded pursuit of a single goal too far." BREYER, BREAKING THE VICIOUS CIRCLE, *supra*, at 11.

3. Other scholars have advocated a "third way" between the synoptic and incremental.

A mixed-scanning strategy would include elements of both approaches by employing two cameras: a broad-angle camera that would cover all parts of the sky but not in great detail, and a second one which would zero in on those areas revealed by the first camera to require a more in-depth examination. While mixed-scanning might miss areas in which only a detailed camera could reveal trouble, it is less likely than incrementalism to miss obvious trouble spots in unfamiliar areas.

Etzioni, *supra*, at 389-90. Lindblom himself later adopted a mixed approach, which he called "probing" to describe simplifying strategies for policy-making where knowledge is either too great or too uncertain to yield definitive answers. CHARLES E. LINDBLOM, INQUIRY AND CHANGE: THE TROUBLED ATTEMPT TO UNDERSTAND AND SHAPE SOCIETY (1990). Professor Hornstein advocated this approach for pesticide regulation:

* * *

Identifying the reasonably proximate causes of environmental problems (the qualifier "reasonably proximate" is important), will in many instances require far less information than developing full-fledged dose-response relationships to pinpoint environmental effects. Once some degree of scientific screening separates out real from truly nonexistent problems, cause-oriented reform is more likely than effects-based regulation to identify and address human activity that can cause multiple environmental problems. Perhaps most importantly, the focus of cause-oriented reform should be on incentives most likely to ameliorate environmentally harmful activity without greatly reducing the benefits of such activity. Because incentive structures can be difficult to design, cause-oriented reform may in many instances need to proceed experimentally. To that extent, it envisions a far more dynamic and incremental regulatory process than the static calibrations of comprehensive rationality and risk-oriented reform. Yet such a dynamic approach to regulation not only promises to avoid large miscalculations by government but also promises to develop incentives for cost-effective innovation among private market participants.

Donald T. Hornstein, *Lessons from Federal Pesticide Regulation on the Paradigms and Politics of Environmental Law Reform*, 10 YALE J. ON REG. 369, 380-88 (1993).[32]

4. Diver's comments on antidiscrimination programs raise an issue that we will return to periodically throughout the book and concentrate on in Chapter 13 (Environmental Justice). Environmental justice advocates assert that environmental risk is unevenly distributed throughout the United States, and that it disproportionately affects poor people and racial and ethnic

---

[32] *See also* Richard N.L. Andrews, *Long-Range Planning in Environmental and Regulatory Agencies*, 20 ECOLOGY L.Q. 515 (1993)(advocating a mixed approach for strategic planning).

minorities. One reason for this is said to be the underrepresentation of such persons in the halls of governmental and nongovernmental power. How would a synoptic approach to toxics regulation address this problem? Would it be effective?

2. Comparative Risk Analysis

Quantitative risk assessment, as we have seen, is the basis for assessing the dangers of a particular place or activity, and for deciding how and how aggressively to regulate an activity or location. Risk assessment can also be used to *compare* different activities for various reasons. One reason may be simply to place it in perspective, as we did in the discussion of "Cancer in Context" in Chapter 2. More pointedly, we may want to know whether the problem is serious–something we should worry about and even regulate–or insignificant–not worth the commitment regulatory resources. Such characterizations are a form of comparison that is very common in making acceptability and similar determinations along the risk continuum.

Some have argued that such comparisons should be the explicit basis for regulation. That is, we should not regulate relatively trivial problems, we should defer regulations of relatively less serious problems, and we should not take regulatory action when it would do more harm than good. Comparative risk assessment (sometimes known by its acronym, CRA) is therefore advocated as a way to determine where to invest regulatory resources, the appropriate degree of stringency (by reference to other risky behaviors, other chemicals, etc.), and whether the regulatory remedy is riskier than the original problem. The last use-in essence, asking whether the cure is worse than the disease-presents the most compelling case for CRA.[33]

The following article describes the surprising results of the application of CRA to an air pollution reduction program. It is followed by an excerpt that describes the general problem of tradeoffs between different risks.

ENVIRONMENTAL IMPLICATIONS OF ELECTRIC CARS

Lester B. Lave *et al.*
268 SCIENCE 993, 993-95 (1995)

California and the Northeast states have passed laws requiring that 2% of model year 1998 cars must be "zero emissions" vehicles-that is, electric cars. Required sales of electric cars are to increase after 1998. Electric vehicle technology has the advantage that it produces no air pollution at the point of use, so that if the electricity is generated in a distant place, electric cars are a

---

[33] *See* Frank B. Cross, *When Environmental Regulations Kill: The Role of Health/Health Analysis*, 22 ECOLOGY L.Q. 729 (1995). Edward W. Warren & Gary E. Marchant, *"More Good than Harm": A First Principle for Environmental Agencies and Reviewing Courts*, 20 ECOLOGY L.Q. 379 (1993) (advocating judicial authority to impose a "more good than harm" standard on agency action, based on the court's own determination of good and harm).

means of switching the location of environmental discharges. A large crowded city such as Los Angeles or New York has large amounts of discharges, even if care is taken to protect the environment, because the millions of gasoline-powered vehicles in such cities emit large quantities of carbon monoxide, nitrogen oxides, and volatile organic compounds. Electric vehicle technology can move emissions to less crowded and less polluted locations. Centralized electric generation plants may also be able to achieve fewer emissions per vehicle mile than do internal combustion engines in vehicles.

The environmental effects of internal combustion engines are well known. Pollution controls have lowered emissions from a controlled car by 98% as compared with those from an uncontrolled car. For electric vehicles, generating electricity for recharging batteries can cause considerable environmental harm. Analyses have been done on the environmental effects of gasoline as compared with those of electricity generation. In response to the electric vehicle mandate, automakers have proposed ultra low emissions vehicles.

We focus on the environmental consequences of producing and reprocessing large quantities of batteries to power electric cars. For vehicles that are to be mass produced in late 1997, lead-acid batteries are likely to be the only practical technology. Smelting and recycling the lead for these batteries will result in substantial releases of lead to the environment. Lead is a neurotoxin, causing reduced cognitive function and behavioral problems, even at low levels in the blood. Environmental discharges of lead are a major concern. For example, eliminating tetraethyl lead (TEL) from U.S. gasoline greatly reduced blood-lead levels in children.

Alternative battery technologies that are currently available include nickel-cadmium and nickel metal hydride batteries, which are much more expensive than lead-acid batteries. In addition, nickel and cadmium are highly toxic to humans and the environment. Technologies such as sodium-sulfur and lithium-polymer batteries are unlikely to be commercially available for years.

Characteristics of Electric Vehicles and Batteries

A gasoline engine supplied with a 40-liter tank (less than 11 gallons) giving 15 km/liter (about 35 miles per gallon) allows a range of 600 km (about 375 miles). A kilogram of gasoline is equivalent to 13,000 watt-hours (Wh); in contrast, a typical lead-acid battery contains only 38 Wh per kilogram. Even adding in the engine, transmission, and so forth, a gasoline-powered car has more than seven times the range of an equivalent electric car using current technology.

The large weight of batteries needed to supply energy means that an electric car will be heavier, will cruise at lower speeds, and will have much less range than an equivalent gasoline vehicle. The focus of electric vehicle design is thus an extremely light-weight vehicle that is capable of carrying the batteries.

* * *

Using 4% losses from virgin production, 2% losses from recycling and reprocessing, and 1% losses from battery manufacturing, we calculated the amount of lead discharged into the environment for the two vehicle scenarios[* * *.] The lead discharge ranges from 1340 mg of lead per kilometer (for the existing technology battery that has the lowest energy density and shortest lifetime distance and uses virgin lead) to about 117 mg of lead per kilometer (for a goal technology battery that has high energy density and long lifetime driving distance and uses scrap lead). If a large number of electric cars are produced, the demand for lead for batteries will surge, requiring that more lead be mined.

In 1972, leaded gasoline sold in the United States contained 2.1 g of lead per gallon. A vehicle of comparable size and weight to those of an electric car, the Geo Metro, gets about 19 km/liter (45 mpg). Using leaded gasoline, this vehicle would emit 22 mg of lead per kilometer (or 35 mg per mile), with 25% of the lead retained in the engine and exhaust of the car. Thus, an electric car using batteries with newly mined lead releases 60 times the peak fraction released by combustion of leaded gasoline. If use of recycled lead and technology goal batteries is assumed, the lead releases are only five times the TEL emissions per kilometer.

The comparison is not as bad as these ratios suggest. Lead from gasoline went into the air in population centers, the route most likely to expose humans. Most of the lead discharged from lead smelting and reprocessing would go to land discharges where it is less available. However, according to 1992 TRI figures, 17% of the total lead and 11% of the lead compounds released to the environment from on-site lead processing facilities is emitted into the air. Lead in solid waste would slowly leach into the environment, exposing humans. Secondary lead smelters are located around the United States, with major facilities in the Northeast and California. Eventually, even some lead discharged in rural areas would find its way into water and windblown dust, exposing people in major cities. Recovery of lead discharged into the environment can be extremely expensive.

Conclusions and Policy Implications

Electric cars have been criticized for their cost and poor performance as compared with current cars. The more fundamental problem is that these vehicles do not deliver the promised environmental benefits. A 1998 model electric car is estimated to release 60 times more lead per kilometer of use relative to a comparable car burning leaded gasoline. The United States banned TEL in large part for health reasons. Electric vehicles would introduce lead releases to reduce urban ozone, a lesser problem. These lead discharges would damage ecology as well as human health. Even with incremental improvements in lead-acid battery technology and tighter controls on smelters and lead reprocessors, producing and recycling these batteries would discharge large quantities of lead into the environment.

Electric vehicles will not be in the public interest until they pose no greater threat to public health and the environment than do alternative technologies, such as vehicles using low-emissions gasoline. Nickel-cadmium and nickel metal hydride batteries are much more expensive and highly toxic; they do not appear to offer environmental advantages. Sodium-sulfur and lithium-polymer technologies may eventually be attractive.

CONFRONTING RISK TRADEOFFS

in Risk versus Risk: Tradeoffs in Protecting Health and the Environment
John D. Graham & Jonathan Baert Wiener
10-17, 20-23 (1995)

Experience with Risk Tradeoffs

Historical experience offers ample reason to suspect that risk tradeoffs are ubiquitous. The following examples provide some evidence of diversity of risk tradeoffs in the national campaign to reduce risk. In each case, it is important to keep in mind that recognizing that a risk tradeoff is occurring simply shows the existence of the phenomenon; without further analysis one cannot say that the countervailing risks necessarily outweigh the reduction in the target risk.

* * *

- The major policies adopted to control pollution in the United States have been aimed at one target environmental medium (air, water, or land) at a time, with the result that pollution has too often been merely shifted from one medium to another instead of reduced overall. For example, the 1977 Clean Air Act requirement that all coal burning power plants install scrubbers to remove sulfur dioxide from their smokestacks has generated tons of sulfur sludge that must be disposed of elsewhere, and has ironically also increased emissions of other pollutants such as the greenhouse gas carbon dioxide because scrubbers reduce energy efficiency, thus requiring extra fuel to be consumed to produce the same amount of electricity.

* * *

- The ban on the fungicide EDB removed its cancer risk, but in turn may have left on grains and nuts a fungus that promotes aflatoxins more carcinogenic than the fungicide.

* * *

- Cyclamates, used as artificial sweeteners, were banned on the ground that they were carcinogenic. This invited consumers to turn to the artificial sweetener saccharin, which was itself later banned for the same reason (but Congress suspended the ban). Meanwhile, prohibiting artificial sweeteners to reduce cancer risk may increase consumption of sugar, with attendant risks of weight gain in some consumers and particular risks for diabetics.

* * *

- The ban on ocean dumping of industrial wastes may have encouraged disposal or incineration of such wastes on land, closer to human populations and fragile freshwater ecosystems.
- Policies to stop chlorination of drinking water, in order to reduce the risk of cancer associated with chlorine, may increase more immediate risks from water borne microbial diseases that the chlorine was meant to kill. For example, the largest outbreak of cholera in recent history, which killed nearly 7,000 people and afflicted over 800,000, was apparently unleashed in 1991 in part as a result of Peru's decision to cease chlorinating its drinking water, spurred by U.S. risk assessments classifying chlorination as carcinogenic.

* * *

- Removing asbestos from buildings to protect residents may increase the risk of asbestos exposure to removal workers.
- Cleanup of hazardous waste sites can reduce risks of chemical contamination of soil and groundwater, but the cleanup activity also creates increased risks of accidental fatalities, especially in construction and transportation jobs. For a hypothetical typical site, the accident fatality risk from cleanup appears to be several times larger than the health risk from not cleaning up. Still, the accident risk may be viewed as voluntarily undertaken (and may be compensated by market wage premiums) while the chemical risk may be viewed as more involuntarily incurred; relative risks may vary by site and by type of cleanup; and the cleanup may also provide ecological benefits.

* * *

Urging that decisionmakers employ RTA [*i.e.*, risk tradeoff analysis] nonetheless obliges us to articulate some way to judge which countervailing risks are worthy of concern: how many ripples in the pool should analysts investigate? This question asks about the value of more information (to better decisions) and the cost (including delay of decisions) of obtaining that information. The answer, unsurprisingly, is that it depends-on the importance of the countervailing risk and hence the value of amassing information about it, compared to the cost of gathering that information. As we hope the case studies demonstrate, not all countervailing risks are of equal seriousness, and efforts to remedy target risks should not always be held up while countervailing risks are being addressed. There will be situations in which the costs of learning more about countervailing risks do not justify the resulting gains in overall risk reduction. But there will also be cases where the costs of obtaining additional information are well worth it, rewarded by the reduction in countervailing risks. And the use of RTA may help identify opportunities to reduce both target and countervailing risks-a net gain for society.

* * *

Recognizing Risk Tradeoffs

Like all complex phenomena, risk tradeoffs are difficult to describe coherently and comprehensively. In order to articulate more systematically the kinds of tradeoffs that may occur in response to an intervention, we present in Table [3.1] a conceptual matrix that has been helpful to us in describing the phenomenon.

This typology defines risk tradeoffs along two dimensions. One dimension considers whether the adverse outcome resulting from the countervailing risk is the same as or different from the adverse outcome resulting from the target risk. The other dimension considers whether the population bearing the countervailing risk is the same as or different from the population bearing the target risk. The magnitudes of the risks are not addressed by this typological matrix, but are addressed below in terms of the factors to be weighed in RTA.

	Compared to the Target Risk, the Countervailing Risk is:	
Compared to the Target Risk, the Countervailing Risk affects:	SAME TYPE	DIFFERENT TYPE
SAME POPULATION	Risk Offset	Risk Substitution
DIFFERENT POPULATION	Risk Transfer	Risk Transformation

Table 3.1–Typology of Risk Tradeoffs

* * *

We define a "target risk" as the risk that is the primary focus of risk-reduction efforts. For example, the "target risk" in hypertension control is usually the chance of a heart attack or stroke due to elevated blood pressure. The "target population" is the group of individuals who are intended to benefit from reduction in the target risk. In contrast to the target risk, we define a "countervailing risk" as the chance of an adverse outcome that results from an activity whose ostensible purpose is to reduce the target risk. Perhaps the classic illustrations of countervailing risks are the side effects of a medication, or the risk of death from anesthesia during surgery. Note that the target risk in one context could be a countervailing risk in another context; for example, elevated cancer incidence is a target risk of policy to control toxic chemicals, but a countervailing risk of estrogen treatment to reduce osteoporosis after menopause.

NOTES

1. Graham & Wiener implicitly justify CRA in utilitarian or efficiency terms. Moral arguments for CRA also exist:

> The most frequently advanced justification for comparative risk analysis is economic, as some members of Congress now urge. We currently spend such huge sums on reducing risks that we cannot afford to do so inefficiently. But there are strong moral grounds for

comparative risk analysis. We owe it to ourselves to confront our choices honestly.

It is just this moral dimension that accounts, paradoxically, for a final source of resistance to use of comparative risk analysis. There is something in all of us, in our desire to preserve social comity, that resists comparative risk analysis. Comparative risk analysis rubs our noses in the choices we must make to solve one problem while neglecting another, or to protect one group while turning away from helping another.

Comparative risk analysis asks us to make explicit our implicit choices. We do not want to hear that scarcity is not just an economic law but is part of the human condition, that it can be avoided for some but not for all.

Comparative risk analysis thus belongs with other unpleasant tasks, such as deciding whether to have surgery or writing a will. When forced to gaze on our choices, we want to avert our eyes, to avoid facing the moral consequences of the implicit and explicit decisions made. For certain choices-what Guido Calabresi and Phillip Bobbitt aptly called "tragic choices"-strong feelings may be mobilized: choices involving lifesaving technologies; life-taking activities such as military service; and perhaps even choices to regulate to protect life, health, or the environment. Yet we have a moral obligation to confront the fact that our implicit choices to protect or leave unprotected, to spend or not to spend, and to allocate scarce resources to less productive uses have consequences just as explicit choices do. Comparative risk analysis, by definition, calls on us to face up to the moral implications of these choices.

Frederick R. Anderson, *CRA and Its Stakeholders: Advice to the Executive Office in* COMPARING ENVIRONMENTAL RISKS: TOOLS FOR SETTING GOVERNMENTAL PRIORITIES 78 (Clarence J. Davies, ed. 1996).

2. Lave *et al.* present a choice between electric and gasoline cars, but a third alternative may exist, cars operating with liquified natural gas. Natural gas is abundant (but hard to transport) and it burns very cleanly. If you were the U.S. motor vehicle czar, would CRA help you to decide which technology to pursue? What questions would it leave unanswered?

3. *Risk ladder*. What does a risk-based comparison look like? Perhaps the best known was used in (though not authored by) Justice Breyer in his book on toxic risk regulation. It assigns specific numerical value to a wide variety of activities and places them on a vertical scale. *See* BREYER, *supra*, at 4-5. How might regulators (and the public) use the risk ladder? Based on your understanding of risk assessment, do you see any weaknesses in such a risk ladder?

4. *RTA*. How does Graham & Weiner's typology of risk comparisons help to evaluate risks and their alternatives? Does it expose any weaknesses in CRA?

What is the "national campaign to reduce risk" to which Graham & Weiner refer? Is that a fair description of the environmental movement? If not, why not?

COMPARATIVE RISK ASSESSMENT AND ENVIRONMENTAL PRIORITIES PROJECTS: A FORUM, NOT A FORMULA

John S. Applegate
25 N. KY. L. REV. 71, 75-91 (1997)

A. From Risk to Priorities

[The article begins by tracing the use of QRA in environmental decisionmaking, a story with which you are already familiar from Chapter 2.]

[Once] risk became established as the principal measure of EPA's activities, * * * [it] took on a life of its own, and it came to be perceived as the *raison d'etre* for the agency. By the end of William Ruckelshaus' second stint as Administrator of EPA, risk reduction defined EPA's mission. If risk reduction in the various media for which EPA is responsible (air, water, solid waste, industrial chemicals, etc.) is the goal, then the logic of making risk comparisons across EPA's programs is well nigh irresistible. EPA wanted to know if it was applying the same standards to air, water, and radiation, for example. EPA also wanted to know whether it was targeting the most serious threats and whether its efforts in various programs were equally effective in reducing risk. Given the chronic and substantial gap between EPA's actual resources and the number of environmental threats that EPA might usefully address, these questions are not just interesting, they are essential to responsible management. The acceptance of the basic risk metric, in other words, opened up whole new vistas of useful analysis within and across EPA's many programmatic areas, and it was not long before EPA vigorously pursued these possibilities.[34]

* * *

* * * Outside EPA, comparative risk assessment attracted a great deal of academic, policy, and Congressional interest as well. It is as a result of EPA's sponsorship that state and local environmental priorities projects were begun and sustained. * * *

B. The Comparative Risk Debate

Commentators have distinguished two versions of comparative risk assessment. The "hard" version emphasizes quantitative comparisons of risk, ideally resulting in a unified ranking of risks from highest to lowest. This usually includes a large element of technical or expert assessment of risk, and it requires a very substantial amount of information to be successful. The "soft" version is less quantitative, and its environmental data and results are

---

[34] The two most important EPA studies were EPA, Unfinished Business: A Comparative Assessment of Environmental Problems (1987), and EPA Science Advisory Board, Reducing Risk: Setting Priorities and Strategies for Environmental Protection (1990).–EDS.

more narrative (*i.e.*, conveyed in words and descriptions rather than in numbers). In practice, most priorities projects * * * chose the soft approach for two reasons. First, they did not have nearly enough firm data available to make credible quantitative evaluations of risks across all of the programmatic areas or environmental media that were being compared. Second, narrative description avoided the problem of comparing unlike problems, such as drinking water and workplace safety, or radon and hazardous waste sites.

The logic of comparative risk and quantitative risk assessment, however, treats soft comparisons as a second-best to quantitative comparison. If one is serious about determining which problems are worst and which solutions are most cost-effective, the thinking goes, one should attempt to understand exactly how the hazards and remedial programs rank. Given limited resources and a goal of risk reduction, such an analysis would reveal definitively how best to allocate the resources. Hence, the existence of a hard version exerts a constant pressure to make more definitive quantitative comparisons across greater numbers of activities. Ironically, though, it is in the hard, quantitative version of risk comparison that the weaknesses of the technique are most apparent and most serious. Despite the apparently ineluctable logic of setting environmental priorities and of utilizing comparative risk to set them, comparative risk has substantial and fundamental limitations which are suggested by many projects' choice of a soft version of comparative risk.

At the most practical level, the problem is information. The data to support credible quantitative descriptions of a broad range of environmental problems simply does not exist. This "data gap" could be remedied to some extent by massive spending on data generation and gathering, though this begs the question whether comparative risk is where that money should be spent. However, that spending would still leave a substantial area of uncertainty that results from our incomplete scientific understanding of the effects of pollutants in the environment. Filling these gaps and uncertainties with assumptions and default values is antithetical to the kind of rigorous quantitative conclusions to which the hard version of comparative risk aspires. Moreover, the existing information is not uniformly distributed or available to all. Many commentators have noted that industry holds much of the relevant data, especially on its processes and the hazards of its activities and products. This is to be expected, of course, but environmentalists are justifiably concerned that priority setting based on selectively revealed information will be not only inaccurate, but skewed.

Risk itself has a distinct technical and political "allure" to beleaguered regulators and industries. It offers an apparently scientific justification for regulatory action (or inaction) that considers other dangers and, through cost-benefit analysis, the benefits of a particular activity. The choice of quantified risk as the measure of environmental danger is itself a policy choice and a value judgment. To some degree, risk is problematic because it has its own potential for inaccuracy–where information is scarce and judgment must fill the gaps, misperception or biased perception undermine claims to objectivity.

More important, quantification distracts attention from the underlying value choices, and it obscures fundamental changes that might avoid the trade-offs altogether. Also, by focusing on adjusting risk consequences, we may be discouraged from examining underlying causes.

Fundamentally, risk is a grossly incomplete way of looking at environmental problems. * * *

[T]here are many kinds of risks, and they affect many different groups of people and the environment in different ways. * * *

The foregoing is often referred to as the "apples and oranges" problem with comparing risks. As Adam Finkel has pointed out, however, there is no difficulty in comparing apples and oranges, as long as the criteria for comparison are clearly understood and are material to the decision to be made. The problem is that risk per se does not constitute an all-inclusive basis for comparison among environmental problems. Yet such comparisons are at the heart of the comparative risk assessment enterprise, which, by its own terms, treats all human health risks as interchangeable with each other and with effects on the natural environment and social welfare. General comparisons cannot be avoided in environmental priorities projects because they are the purpose of the projects, but precise risk rankings that emerge from environmental priorities projects should be viewed with skepticism and used with caution.

C. More Modest Claims for Risk Comparison

Even if one could find or generate adequate data to give comparative risk assessment some semblance of precision, there are too many non-numerical considerations, such as public values, risk distribution, differing characteristics of different risks, and the like, to permit a fair analysis of environmental problems in quantitative terms. Does this mean that comparing environmental hazards and setting priorities is impossible or pointless? No—it means that the claims for comparative risk and environmental priority setting need to be more modest ("softer") than its strongest proponents allow, and, interestingly, closer to the actual practice of comparative risk projects.

* * *

* * * First, a priorities project should beware of, which is not to say that it should completely abjure, specific risk rankings and comparisons across risk endpoints. The hard version that relies on quantified risk clearly asks too much of extant risk data and of technical rationality. It is simply misleading to suggest that the data are available that would support a precisely calibrated hierarchy of environmental problems or actions. * * *

Second, a broader conception of the basis of priority setting means that the relevant considerations cannot be limited to items that are quantifiable, even in theory. Values and policy choices are not only an inescapable part of environmental decisionmaking, they may in fact dominate it. To turn the process into a technocratic exercise misses the ethical basis of environmental regulation, and it certainly undercuts the political viability of the results. * * *

Third, the priority setting process must involve and be understandable to the people who are affected by the problems being ranked. Except perhaps as an internal analytical exercise, environmental priority setting cannot be a technical project run exclusively by environmental policy experts. * * *

NOTES

1. What are the internal limitations of risk comparison, that is, the difficulties of using risk as the metric for environmental protection? For an excellent critique of comparative risk assessment along these lines, *see* Donald T. Hornstein, *Reclaiming Environmental Law: A Normative Critique of Comparative Risk Analysis*, 92 COLUM. L. REV. 562 (1992).

2. Graham & Wiener find risk trade-offs among a wide variety of types of harm. Why do they find this helpful?

On the other hand, these kinds of comparisons may encourage the comparison of totally unlike risks, the "apples and oranges" problem. What are the dimensions along which risks differ?

3. *Lessons from the LSAT.* Applegate has also suggested that the use of risk assessment to compare and evaluate environmental and safety hazards might be analogized to the use of the LSAT to compare and evaluate applicants for admission to law school.

> To anyone involved in higher education, many of the concerns about quantitative risk assessment and comparative risk assessment have a familiar ring. The Law School Admissions Test (LSAT), Scholastic Aptitude Test (SAT), and other standardized tests similarly seek to establish a metric–a "common yardstick," as one College Board publication puts it–against which applicants can be evaluated and compared. Many regard such quantification with suspicion, and not without some justification: quantifying a nonnumerical quality like "aptitude" is an oversimplification that excludes other aspects of the individual. Moreover, numbers have a persuasive power, perceived precision, and resultant authority that can obscure underlying uncertainty or variation. On the other hand, quantification survives and even thrives. The LSAT can be used both as an "indicator of certain mental abilities related to academic performance in law school" and as a tool for comparing and ranking students. Especially in combination with the undergraduate grade point average, the LSAT correlates with success in the first year of law school. While this is not the only endpoint one might choose, it is at least relevant to admissions decisions. The standardized test is an efficient and readily understandable means of expressing certain ideas or concepts. More importantly, it provides a uniform standard for the core task of selecting among highly diverse individuals, which itself provides a kind of equity. I do not want to overstate the analogy to risk assessment or to comment on the underlying question of the

validity of standardized testing. Nevertheless, some familiar principles for the proper management of LSAT scores might tell us something about the proper use of risk assessment.

John S. Applegate, *A Beginning and Not an End in Itself: The Role of Risk Assessment in Environmental Decisionmaking*, 63 U. CIN. L. REV. 1643, 1667-72 (1995). Is this a useful analogy? What does it tell us about the strengths and limitations of comparative risk assessment?

4. *Zero-sum game.* Is it implicit in risk comparison that we are operating in a "zero-sum game" in which attention to one area means lack of attention to another, or stringency against one hazard means laxity toward another? Graham & Wiener certainly take that general position (though recognizing exceptions). A more absolute argument may be found in W. KIP VISCUSI, FATAL TRADEOFFS: PUBLIC AND PRIVATE RESPONSIBILITIES FOR RISK (1992), and GUIDO CALABRESI & PHILIP BOBBIT, TRAGIC CHOICES (1978). Donald Hornstein argues that this approach systematically ignores more fundamental solutions that reduce risk overall. Donald T. Hornstein, *Lessons from Federal Pesticide Regulation on the Paradigms and Politics of Environmental Law Reform*, 10 YALE J. ON REG. 369 (1993).

3. Cost-Benefit Analysis

Cost benefit analysis, like comparative risk assessment, takes several forms, but all share the basic characteristic of comparing the improvement brought about by a particular regulatory action-its benefits, often in the form of risk reduction-against its disadvantages-its cost. Also like CRA, cost-benefit analysis can be used to decide whether to regulate and how to regulate.

a. The Case for Cost-Benefit Analysis

The fundamental justification for cost-benefit analysis is economic efficiency: we should not spend more to improve something than the cost harm it causes, and when we do regulate, it should be in the way that garners the most benefits with the least cost. This, too, is directly analogous to comparative risk assessment. The argument for efficiency is not limited to economics. There are also moral arguments for least-cost regulation, as the following suggests:

> Why is it that the environmental legislation of the early 1970s effectively proscribed considering costs in setting most standards, yet economic impacts are now at the center of virtually every environmental legislative and regulatory debate? Answering this question forces one to step back and review briefly the environmental progress that the United States has made during the past 27 years. In traveling around the country today, one can certainly find environmental problems in some localized areas, but rivers are no longer bursting into flames, nor are cities so polluted that midday

occasionally resembles nightfall. Back in 1970, our environmental problems were big, obvious, and serious. Today, however, air quality is dramatically better. Now the most polluted day in Los Angeles is better than an average or even a good day 27 years ago in most of the country's industrial cities. Water quality has improved in many places as well, though much less dramatically.

In solving many of the worst problems, we have in effect picked the "low-hanging fruit" of easy control options. Effecting further improvements in environmental quality is vastly more expensive today than it was in 1970, and that is one reason for our current preoccupation with the economics of the environment. By way of illustration, it can now cost as much as $50,000 to prevent the discharge of a single ton of volatile organic compounds in Los Angeles, whereas decades ago one could do so for as little as 50 cents. In this case, at least, the cost of pollution control has grown by as much as five orders of magnitude.

We have also witnessed a significant change in public perceptions of the benefits of pollution control. In the 1970s, environmental problems were regarded-rightly, in many instances-as posing serious and immediate risks to public health. Now many people-and not merely those in the regulated business community-feel that the problems with which the United States is dealing are probably far less serious. * * * Many in Congress, academia, the media, and the world at large are increasingly of the view that the nation needs to do a better job of balancing the good that we get from a cleaner environment with the added costs that we incur.

* * *

In one sense, in fact, it may be immoral *not* to take costs into account in setting environmental standards. Resources are limited in any society, even one as wealthy as the United States. As a consequence, no society can do everything that its citizens might like. On the contrary, every society has to set priorities Oust as individuals do), choosing which things to do and which not to do. Failure to consider costs makes it impossible to get the most from the available resources and ultimately means saving fewer lives, preventing fewer illnesses, and protecting fewer species or areas than one otherwise could. Arguably, this comes far closer to acting immorally than does generating pollution by burning fossil fuels or converting materials from one form to another.

To act morally, therefore, we simply must set priorities and weigh both the costs and the benefits of particular environmental and natural resource regulations. That is, we have to ask how much it will cost to attain a certain improvement in environmental quality and whether that is the best way to spend the money. It may well be, for instance, that by spending the same money in some other way we can effect a more substantial improvement in environmental quality or augmentation of our natural resources.

Paul R. Portney, *Counting the Cost: The Growing Role of Economics in Environmental Decisionmaking, 40:2* ENVIRONMENT *14, 36-37* (Mar. 1998). Portney gives a good account of the rationales for cost-benefit analysis, but note that he makes several assertions and assumptions that are debatable. For example, is it true that the "world at large" has begun to question the cost of environmental regulation? Is it consistent with the view expressed by others that the public unreasonably wants absolute safety? Which is true? What other assumptions underlie Portney's arguments?

CONGRESS ASKS, IS NATURE WORTH MORE THAN A SHOPPING MALL?

William K. Stevens
N.Y. Times, April 25, 1995, at B8

But cost-benefit analysis is problematic

Increasingly over the last few years, Federal regulators have been criticized on the ground that they spent billions of dollars to attack environmental and health threats without adequately considering whether the benefits justified the costs.

In cleaning up toxic waste, for example, is it really worth the expense to make the site as spotless as a kitchen? Might some of the money be better spent on another problem?

The main problem, say many experts in cost-benefit analysis and the assessment of risk, is that these analytical tools are too inexact, too prone to large margins of error, too dependent on assumptions and too riddled with value judgements–necessarily so–to be employed [in legislation].

How much, for instance, is an endangered ecosystem worth compared with the commercial or industrial development that could replace it? Many experts say that scientists and economists do not yet know nearly enough to answer the question quantitatively; that in the end, the attempt would often boil down to a subjective reckoning . * * *

Dr. Nicholas A. Ashford of the Massachusetts Institute of Technology, an expert in cost-benefit analysis, says that the technique "is not ready for prime time and I doubt that it will ever be." * * *

Generally speaking, environmental benefits are harder to measure than costs, but even costs estimates are "ballpark at best," seven experts said in [a] letter to the Senate. History has shown, said Dr Ashford, that costs usually have been overestimated and benefits under-estimated.

It is especially difficult to measure the value of natural ecosystems. While scientists know in a broad sense that nature has enormous value–not least, it supports human life–economists and scientists have often been frustrated in trying to attach dollars to specific slices of nature or natural functions.

These experts have tried to calculate how much people would pay for the use and enjoyment of nature. And it may, for instance, be possible to gauge in narrow terms the relative economic value of clear-cut logging versus recreational use of a forest. But how much are undiscovered medicinal plants worth? Or an individual species or ecosystem with no obvious special utility that is on the brink of extinction? The answers are elusive, perhaps unobtainable.

To some scientists, the exercise is pointless, or worse, because it devalues nature. They point out that while insurance companies may be able to put a dollar value on a human life, moral arguments place

human life beyond economics. What is true   should be true of a wild species.
of an individual human, some say, is or

Cost-benefit analysis is one important way to test whether a government policy is successful. As its name implies, a cost-benefit analysis calculates values for all of the favorable impacts (benefits) and unfavorable impacts (costs) of a policy, in order to select the policy that produces the highest overall net benefit (total benefits less total costs). A simplified version of a cost-benefit analysis can be demonstrated by considering the society represented in Figure 3.1 at the beginning of this chapter. The market participants in this society wish to enjoy both clean waters and a chemical whose manufacture causes a toxic substance to be released into adjacent waters. The release degrades the waters. If this society wishes to control the release of the toxic substance by requiring the chemical company to install technology which cleans the effluent stream, it may be worthwhile to perform a cost-benefit analysis on different control levels in order to determine which one yields the highest net benefit.

Table 3.2 summarizes the primary categories of costs and benefits that would be relevant to policymakers charged with subjecting a regulatory option to a complete cost-benefit analysis.[35]

---

[35] A cost-effectiveness analysis is different from a cost-benefit analysis. The former considers which policy option accomplishes its purpose at the lowest cost; the latter compares costs and benefits of alternative policies and selects the one with the highest net benefits.

COSTS OF POLICIES	BENEFITS OF POLICIES
1. Opportunity Costs (the value of opportunities lost—measured by wiliness to pay for them—by a policy; this may include the cost of doing without the substance or activity affected by the policy)	**1. Human Lives Saved** (economic value of a human life multiplied by the number of lives lost by for the policy)
2. Compliance Costs (the cost—typically borne by regulated entities—of technology and process changes needed to achieve the policy)	**2. Human Health Protected** (medial expenses avoided as a result of the policy)
3. Social Resource Cost (the policy's effect on the markets for goods and services—often manifested by changed prices, and different levels of supply and demand)	**3. Third Party Benefits** (indirect benefits to people who would be willing to pay for a cleaner environment, even through such third parties may never, or only in the distant future, experience the policy)[36]

Table 3.2–Elements of costs and benefits

Cost-benefit analysis also assumes, as it must, that one can predict with some degree of certainty the costs and benefits that will be caused by a policy, and that one can calculate an economic value for each relevant cost and benefit. Is this possible? How can one quantify, for example, the opportunity cost for either an activity or a substance, when it is impossible to know for certain the social value that is foregone when each is replaced by a more environmentally-friendly alternative? Or, how can one quantify the value of nature in an unpolluted state?

In addition, there can be great uncertainty about the extent to which toxics pose health and environmental risks. Policymakers must balance the benefits of risk reduction against the costs of policies designed to reduce risk. The risk reduction side of this balance is particularly tricky, because of (1) uncertainty about the health and environmental effects of toxics and hazardous wastes, and (2) difficulties inherent in placing a value on health and environmental risks. Consequently, quantitative risk assessment becomes the basis of the benefits side of cost-benefit analysis. This is a major reason for the importance of quantifying risk.

---

[36] Different methods may be used to calculate how much such third parties would pay for policies that do not directly affect them. *Contingent valuation method* uses surveys to measure how much potential users of an area might pay to enhance its environmental quality sufficiently to justify a visit there. *Option Value* determines how much individuals are willing to pay to ensure future availability of a resource. *Existence value* seeks to calculate either the value that people place in an environmental improvement for its own sake, or the value that some people place on the fact that other people at another time may enjoy the improvement. *See, e.g.* Binger, Copple, and Hoffman, *The Use of Contingent Valuation Methodology in Natural Resource Damage Assessments: Legal Fact and Economic Fiction*, 89 NW. U. L. REV. 1029 (1995).

b. Models of Cost-Benefit Analysis

To agree that cost should play some role in environmental decisionmaking—or as Professor Sunstein puts it, "No sensible regulatory program . . . can be indifferent to cost"[37]—is not to determine how large that role should be. Even where cost is not considered irrelevant, cost might be merely a reported fact, or it might be one of many items for consideration, or a prime consideration, or dispositive. Several years ago, William Rodgers memorably described four models of cost-benefit analysis.

A. The Heretical Model: Cost-Oblivious

* * *

In adopting these provisions, Congress may rely upon a number of assumptions. Three examples are illustrative. First, Congress may perform an intuitive cost-benefit analysis, estimating that the benefits of minimum health standards outweigh the costs of attaining them. Agency consideration of benefits and costs is preempted by Congress's political assessment of the balance. Second, Congress may forbid the agency from considering costs (even though benefits may not outweigh costs in all cases) because the transaction costs of performing a formal analysis in each case would exceed the benefits of the resulting distinctions. This argument essentially holds that benefits generally outweigh costs, and it would be "inefficient" to study all cases in order to find the few instances where this is not so.

Third, Congress may adopt minimum standards without regard for even an intuitive cost-benefit analysis, because of a moral judgment that efficiency considerations are inappropriate in some areas of regulation. This decision reflects the value judgment that, at least where some health hazards are concerned, the public has a right to a minimal level of protection regardless of what a cost-benefit analysis suggests. * * *

* * *

B. The Nominal Convert: Cost-Effective

A congressional determination that the benefits of a goal are worth its costs does not mean that cost-benefit analysis has no role to play. Congress may mandate a formal analysis to determine the most efficient means for attaining that goal. The use of cost-benefit techniques in this role is the cost-effective model. * * *

* * *

C. The Practicing Parishioner: Cost-Sensitive

The cost-sensitive model requires that costs be considered by the agency but stops short of mandating a formal cost-benefit analysis. The legislative directive is a broad delegation of authority to the

---

[37] CASS R. SUNSTEIN, AFTER THE RIGHTS REVOLUTION: RECONCEIVING THE REGULATORY STATE 90 (1990)

agency to determine what is "feasible," "economically practicable," or "the best practicable." The cost-sensitive approach is, along with cost-effectiveness, the dominant congressional model for the use of cost-benefit analysis; it makes costs pertinent in vague and varying ways to numerous energy, health, and environmental decisions.

The cost-sensitive model enables, and often requires, the agency to consider a range of factors of congressional interest other than economic efficiency. * * *

* * *

Congress has many concerns on its collective mind, and directives that agency regulation be sensitive to costs facilitate consideration of goals other than pure efficiency. At the same time, however, the broad delegations characteristic of such statutes give too little guidance to the agencies, leading to charges of runaway regulation and calls for regulatory reform. * * *

* * *

D. The High Priest: Strict Cost-Benefit Analysis

The model imposing upon agencies the most stringent obligations to consider costs and benefits is the requirement of a formal cost-benefit analysis. While intuition suggests that a legislative model embracing a strict cost-benefit formula might contain an enforceable substantive efficiency standard, the observable consequences are procedural in nature-requiring better definition, quantification, and a sharper description of alternatives. The most striking feature of cost-benefit analysis is that it stands out as a technical solution looking for a problem it can solve. It is impossible to discover a single example of decisionmaking being reduced to simple computation by a preordained form: if that is the classic case, it does not exist.

William H. Rodgers, Jr., *Benefits, Costs, and Risks: Oversight of Health and Environmental Decisionmaking*, 4 HARV. ENVTL. L. REV. 191, 201-14 (1980).

Within a month of his inauguration, President Reagan issued Executive Order No. 12291. It was the cornerstone of his announced policy of regulatory relief for American businesses and industry. In addition to imposing cost-benefit analysis on regulatory agencies, it further centralized review of regulation in the Office of Management and Budget.

EXECUTIVE ORDER NO. 12291

46 Fed. Reg. 13193 (1981)

Sec. 2. *General Requirements.* In promulgating new regulations, reviewing existing regulations, and developing legislative proposals concerning regulation, all agencies, to the extent permitted by law, shall adhere to the following requirements:

(a) Administrative decisions shall be based on adequate information concerning the need for and consequences of proposed government action;

(b) Regulatory action shall not be undertaken unless the potential benefits to society for the regulation outweigh the potential costs to society;

(c) Regulatory objectives shall be chosen to maximize the net benefits to society;

(d) Among alternative approaches to any given regulatory objective, the alternative involving the least net cost to society shall be chosen; and

(e) Agencies shall set regulatory priorities with the aim of maximizing the aggregate net benefits to society, taking into account the condition of the particular industries affected by regulations, the condition of the national economy, and other regulatory actions contemplated for the future.

Sec. 3. Regulatory Impact Analysis and Review.

(a) In order to implement Section 2 of this Order, each agency shall, in connection with every major rule [*i.e.*, a rule that has an annual effect of $ 100 million on the economy or is likely to cause another type of substantial economic dislocation], prepare, and to the extent permitted by law consider, a Regulatory Impact Analysis. * * *

* * *

(d) To permit each proposed major rule to be analyzed in light of the requirements stated in Section 2 of this Order, each preliminary and final Regulatory Impact Analysis shall contain the following information:

(1) A description of the potential benefits of the rule, including any beneficial effects that cannot be quantified in monetary terms, and the identification of those likely to receive the benefits;

(2) A description of the potential costs of the rule, including any adverse effects that cannot be quantified in monetary terms, and the identification of those likely to bear the costs;

(3) A determination of the potential net benefits of the rule, including an evaluation of effects that cannot be quantified in monetary terms;

(4) A description of alternative approaches that could substantially achieve the same regulatory goal at lower cost, together with an analysis of this potential benefit and costs and a brief explanation of the legal reasons why such alternatives, if proposed, could not be adopted; and

(5) Unless covered by the description required under paragraph (4) of this subsection, an explanation of any legal reasons why the rule cannot be based on the requirements set forth in Section 2 of this Order.

* * *

Sec. 9. *Judicial Review.* This Order is intended only to improve the internal management of the Federal government, and is not intended to create any right or benefit, substantive or procedural, enforceable at law by a party against the United States, its agencies, its officers or any person. The determinations made by agencies under Section 4 of this Order, and any Regulatory Impact Analyses for any rule, shall be made part of the whole record of agency action in connection with the rule.

NOTES

1. What is the cost-benefit standard that Executive Order No. 12291 advocates? Where does it fit into Rodgers' scale? To what extent are agencies required to meet it? (Examine §§ 3(a) and 9 carefully.) Could the President require that agencies only promulgate regulations whose benefits exceed their costs?

2. *The market.* Cost-benefit analysis can be viewed as a kind of surrogate for the market in circumstances where the market is unlikely to function efficiently.

> We all know that a government agency charged with the responsibility of defending the nation or constructing highways or promoting trade will invariably wish to spend "too much" on its goals. An agency succeeds by accomplishing the goals Congress set for it as thoroughly as possible–not by balancing its goals against other, equally worthy goals. This fact of agency life provides the justification for a countervailing administrative constraint in the form of a central budget office. Without some countervailing restraint, EPA and OSHA would 'spend'–through regulations that spend society's resources but do not appear in the federal government's fiscal budget–"too much" on pollution control and workplace safety. This tendency is reinforced by the "public" participation in the rulemaking process, which as a practical matter is limited to those organized groups with the largest and most immediate stakes in the results. Although presidents and legislatures are themselves vulnerable to pressure from politically influential groups, the rulemaking process–operating in relative obscurity from public view but lavishly attended by interest groups–is even more vulnerable. A substantial number of agency rules could not survive public scrutiny and gain two legislative majorities and the signature of the president.

Christopher C. DeMuth & Douglas H. Ginsburg, *White House Review of Agency Rulemaking*, 99 HARV. L. REV. 1075, 1081 (1986). DeMuth and Ginsburg remind us that cost-benefit analysis has a political as well as an economic role: it can be used as a bulwark against the demands of environmental groups. Is that consistent with the statutory commands to EPA and OSHA?

3. In addition to Professor Rodgers' category, we have seen two other risk-cost-benefit scales in the book. One, in Chapter 2(B)(2)(a), compared risk levels; the other, in Chapter 3(B)(2)(c), compared regulatory strategies.

Role of Risk	Type of Regulation	Role of Cost
De minimis risk	Health-based	Cost-oblivious
Unreasonable risk	Technological feasibility	Cost-effective
Discernible risk	Cost-benefit comparison	Cost-sensitive
Lowest feasible risk	Incentives	Cost-justified
Most cost-effective risk	Information Production	
Benefits outweigh costs		

Table 3.3–Risk-Cost-Benefit Scales

How are these spectra of risk and cost related to each other? Can they be reconciled as a single spectrum of regulatory stringency, or are there too many variables? Would it be better if they were reconcilable?

c. Difficulties of Implementation

In the following excerpt, Krupnick and Portney report their study of the costs and benefits of pollution control measures to reduce levels of ground-level (as opposed to stratospheric) ozone (O_3) in areas that have not attained the Clean Air Act's national ambient air quality standards (NAAQS). The first part of the article describes a cost-benefit analysis of reducing emissions of volatile organic compounds (VOCs) in urban nonattainment areas across the nation. The second applies a similar methodology to the Los Angeles area, where nonattainment is severe and so the costs of control could be expected to be relatively low (because the marginal cost of control rises sharply) and the benefits relatively high.

It is more important to focus on the authors' methods and the way that they handled gaps in information, than on their actual results. In this connection, you should read the letters in response to the article. In considering these materials, remember that ozone is more prevalent and its effects better understood than most toxic pollutants, so this example probably understates the difficulties of implementing cost-benefit analysis for toxics.

The Los Angeles study is followed by an article by the philosopher Mark Sagoff, who argues that cost-benefit analysis, even if it could be technically perfected, answers the wrong questions about environmental protection.

CONTROLLING URBAN AIR POLLUTION: A BENEFIT-COST ASSESSMENT

Alan J. Krupnick & Paul R. Portney
252 SCIENCE 522, 522-27 (1991)

Environmental regulation is important to our health and well-being and also is quite expensive. For these reasons, we must look carefully at our environmental laws and regulations to see what they will accomplish and at what cost.

* * *

Reducing Ozone in Urban Areas

To evaluate the benefits and costs of reducing ambient O_3 concentrations, one must first estimate the VOC reductions expected in various areas and the O_3 improvements that they imply. Then the costs of the measures to be used to obtain the VOC reductions and the benefits associated with the O_3 improvements can be estimated.

In 1989, the Office of Technology Assessment (OTA) released a major study of air quality problems in the United States. The study estimated the changes in emissions of VOCs and, subsequently, reductions in O_3 design values that would result in the years 1994 and 2004 from the application of all currently available VOC control technologies in nonattainment areas and some added control in clean areas. No transportation control plans or additional controls on nitrogen oxides (NO_x) were included.

As estimated by OTA, by the year 2004 these control measures would reduce total annual emissions of VOCs in nonattainment areas from about 11 million to about 7 million tons, representing a 35% reduction. Depending on the particular urban area in question, the annual VOC reduction would vary from 20 to 50%. Our benefit and cost estimates pertain to this predicted change in air quality.

* * *

Costs. According to OTA, the annualized cost associated with this ambitious set of measures would be $6.6 billion to $10.0 billion in the nonattainment areas alone, or about $1800 to $2700 per ton of VOC reduced there. Adding in the costs that would be borne in attainment areas raises the estimated total to $8.8 billion to $12.8 billion per year.

Of all the control measures examined, reducing the volatility of gasoline accounts for the greatest emission reduction (about 14%) and would also be the most cost-effective control technology because this reduction would cost between $120 and $740 annually per ton of VOC reduced. At the other extreme, OTA found that using methanol (an 85% blend) to power fleet vehicles would be an expensive measure: $8,700 to $51,000 per ton of VOC reduction. A ranking of individual approaches by cost effectiveness shows that marginal costs increase sharply for obtaining any more than a 30% reduction in VOC emissions.

Benefits. How does one ascertain the amount individuals would be willing to pay for the air quality improvements that OTA projects? We concentrate on acute health benefits because protecting health is the primary justification for setting air quality standards under the Clean Air Act and because only acute health effects have been linked convincingly to O_3 concentrations. Other benefits could accrue in the form of reduced damage to exposed materials, crops, and other vegetation and possibly reductions in the prevalence of chronic illness.

To determine the acute health benefits associated with the estimated 35% reduction in VOC emissions in nonattainment areas, we used a county-level model developed for this purpose. The model predicts reduced baseline O_3

concentrations in each area for each day of the O_3 season on the basis of the percentage reductions in O_3 design values obtained from OTA. These air quality changes must then be mapped into improved human health. To do so, we combined area-specific data on air quality improvements and population with dose-response functions based on epidemiologic and clinical (controlled laboratory) studies relating ambient O_3 concentrations to various symptoms and other adverse human health effects. Thus, for example, the predicted air quality improvement in a particular urban area in the year 2004 can be translated into fewer asthma attacks, reduced incidence of coughing and chest discomfort, reduced number of days of restricted activity, and the like on the basis of predicted population of that area in that year. * * *

* * *

We estimated the reduced incidence of the quantifiable adverse health effects in the year 2004 accompanying a 35% reduction in emissions of VOCs for an estimated 129 million people living in the 94 metropolitan areas (322 counties) predicted to be in nonattainment in 2004. For each metropolitan area, we made separate calculations on the basis of the predicted change in air quality there and then aggregated these estimates to obtain the national estimates.

From the epidemiologic studies, we found that the average asthmatic will experience about 0.2 fewer days per year on which he or she has an asthma attack and that the average nonasthmatic will experience about 0.1 fewer minor restricted activity days per year because of reduced VOC emissions and subsequently improved air quality. In addition, nonasthmatics will experience other minor health benefits as well in the form of reduced number of symptom days.

To convert these predicted changes in physical health into economic benefits, it is necessary to ascertain individuals' willingness to pay for a reduced incidence of illness and adverse symptoms. To do so, we drew on a number of studies designed to uncover these values, primarily through questioning of both healthy and infirm respondents with supplemental data on the out-of-pocket medical costs and lost income that may be associated with illness or symptomatic effects. These studies have found an average value of $25 for each asthma attack prevented, $20 for a reduction of one restricted activity day (on which an individual is neither bedridden nor forced to miss work but must alter his or her usual pattern in some way), and $5 for one fewer day of occasional coughing. When reduced incidence is combined with these values, the predicted aggregate dollar benefits across the United States from these improvements in individuals' acute health status amount to $250 million per year.

By using clinical rather than epidemiologic [*i.e.*, mechanistic instead of statistical] studies to estimate health benefits, we arrive at a somewhat larger value for acute health benefits. For example, we predict that the number of coughing spells of 2 hours' duration would be reduced by as much as 2.5 episodes per person per year. Also, fewer episodes of shortness of breath and pain on deep inspiration are predicted to occur. Both are important consequences of air pollution control. We estimate that the annual monetary benefits associated with these improvements in health would be on the order of $800 million annually.

Comparison. To summarize, according to OTA, the costs associated with a 35% reduction in nationwide emissions of VOCs in nonattainment areas will be at least $8.8 billion annually by the year 2004 and could be as much as $12 billion. Yet the acute health improvements that we predict to result from these changes are valued at no more than $1 billion annually and could be as little as $250 million. The high estimate relies on the most generous of the four clinical studies that the EPA sanctioned in its staff paper on the health effects associated with O_3 and other photochemical oxidants. We also assumed that exercise rates would be high in the exposed population (which increases health benefits), and we included benefits even for those engaged in light or moderate exercise. Subject to the caveats discussed below, total health benefits are still relatively small.

In contrast to, say the removal of lead from gasoline, for which estimated benefits are well in excess of costs, the benefit-cost comparison for national O_3 control is unfavorable. The reasons for this are, in part, the relatively small improvements in ambient O_3 levels that the controls effect (which in turn imply fairly small benefits) as well as the high costs of control.

The Los Angeles Plan

What about air pollution control efforts in Los Angeles, the nation's most notably polluted metropolis? * * *

* * *

On the basis of this approach, we estimate that reduced O_3 concentrations will effect an annual reduction of 22 million person-days on which adverse respiratory or other symptoms will be experienced by South Coast residents. In dollar terms, these benefits amount to about $300 million annually. According to the South Coast officials, reduced ambient particulate concentrations will result in $700 million annually in reduced morbidity; reduced particulate loadings will provide $700 million annually in reduced materials damage, and another $130 million in materials damage will be saved as a result of reductions in ambient SO_2. We take these at face value.

In all, annual benefits to human health are predicted to be $3 billion ($2 billion in premature mortality, $0.3 billion in O_3 related morbidity, and $0.7 billion for particulate-related morbidity). If one includes the South Coast's estimates of materials damage, total annual benefits rise to about $4 billion. This is far short of the $13 billion per year that the plan may cost.

Caveats and Uncertainties

To this point, we have presented benefits and costs as point estimates, but there are clearly great uncertainties in making such estimates. It is essential to understand them and to bear them in mind in interpreting the findings above.

With respect to our national comparison, OTA's estimate of control costs has a number of limitations. For instance, OTA did not estimate the cost of the mandatory introduction of alternative motor vehicle fuels (methanol, ethanol, or reformulated gasoline) such as is called for in the new Clean Air Act amendments. This will add approximately $3 billion to annual costs. Also, OTA did not anticipate the second round of vehicle emissions reductions that will almost surely be required under the amendments; this will add another $5 billion annually. Finally, no attempt was made to estimate nonpecuniary costs. For instance, OTA estimates that an enhanced motor vehicle inspection and maintenance program will cost about $50 per vehicle annually, including fees, administrative costs, and repair costs. The opportunity cost of people's time is ignored, however, even though the time spent can be significant. If this time were properly priced, it could add up to $7 per vehicle.

There is also great uncertainty about the costs of the South Coast plan. Marginal costs generally begin to rise sharply at higher levels of control, and VOCs have been controlled longer and more stringently in Southern California than in any other part of the country. For this reason, the controls envisioned in the South Coast plan could prove to be more expensive than anticipated. Also, we have little experience in the United States with stringent transportation control measures. If they are implemented and prove to be quite inconvenient to those affected, costs could be higher than those projected here. It is impossible to provide anything approaching statistical confidence intervals for either the national or the South Coast plan.

There are several respects in which costs could be much lower than those forecast here for both national and Los Angeles area air pollution control. For example, the cost of vehicle emissions controls are based on modest extensions of proven control technology (the catalytic converter). If, however, the electrically heated catalyst can be perfected and produced relatively inexpensively, control costs may be overstated here. Similarly, breakthroughs in reformulated gasoline or other alternative motor vehicle fuels could bring costs down considerably. Likewise, if the pace of technologic innovation accelerates sharply for VOC control from stationary sources, the same conclusion would apply. Finally (and particularly in Los Angeles), if driving restrictions eventually are imposed, and if commuters easily adapt to them, O_3 control costs may be lower than projected here.

Perhaps it is not surprising that uncertainties are greater concerning the benefit estimates presented here. These uncertainties arise from several sources, primarily the prediction of physical effects and the attribution of dollar values to them. For instance, if we had used the analysis of Whittemore and Korn instead of that of Holguin *et al.* to predict changes in asthma attacks, estimated benefits to asthmatics would be less than half those included above.

The largest such uncertainty concerns the link between particulate matter at current ambient concentrations and premature mortality. The statistical associations that epidemiologists and others have found between city mortality rates and annual particulate levels do not offer convincing evidence of the existence and magnitude of such effects; for instance, these effects become insignificant with minor changes in sample composition and model specification, and even the best of these studies uses a poor proxy (sulfates) for the particles now thought to be the causal agents (acid aerosols). Because the total number of deaths from lung disease in the South Coast is 4000 annually, attributing a reduction of 2000 premature deaths to the South Coast's plan seems likely to be optimistic.

In monetizing the reduced frequency of respiratory symptoms or disease, a range of values could have been used. In the literature, the range cited for an asthma attack is $10 to $40; for a restricted-activity day, the corresponding range is $10 to $30; for a symptom day, it is $3 to $10.

The choice among epidemiologic and clinical studies, and among values to assign to physical effects, can have an important effect on estimated benefits. If we had used only upper bound estimates to predict each type of acute health effect from O_3 and, correspondingly, to attribute dollar values to reduced incidence of each, acute health benefits nationwide of a 35% VOC reduction would be $2 billion annually, and acute health benefits in the South Coast (of meeting only the O_3 standard) would be $2.4 billion per year. If we had used lower bound estimates, on the other hand, benefits would be 3% of our upper bound estimate.

There is another important caveat to be attached to the benefit estimates presented above, one that can only impart a downward bias to them. Specifically, we excluded certain types of benefits for which it was impossible to predict physical effects or to make reasonable dollar attributions. For instance, some animal toxicologic studies suggest that prolonged exposure to O_3 can permanently reduce the elasticity of the lung and, hence, initiate chronic respiratory illness. Although there is no convincing epidemiologic evidence for this potential effect in humans to date, such a finding would affect any benefit-cost analysis of efforts to control ground-level O_3 either nationally or locally. Similarly, we excluded in our estimates of national as well as South Coast benefits any improvements in forests or agricultural output in rural regions that might result from VOC control in urban areas because of the difficulty of translating emission reductions in urban areas into reduced ambient concentrations in agricultural regions. Also omitted are possible reductions in damage to rubber and other products exposed to O_3. Nevertheless, including such agricultural benefits would be unlikely to add more than $1 billion to the national total predicted here; South Coast benefits would increase minimally. Finally, the totals omit a dollar attribution for the improved visibility that should result from reduced ambient sulfate concentrations.

It is important to find ways to predict the physical likelihood of the exclusions identified here and to ascertain individuals' willingness to pay for any such improvements. These omitted categories would have to have large benefits associated with them, however, to tip the apparently unfavorable balance between benefits and costs for either the national or the regional air pollution control plans that we have examined.

Conclusions and Policy Implications

It is unpleasant to have to weigh in such a calculating manner the pros and cons of further air pollution control efforts. We would all prefer limitless resources so that every pollution control measure physically possible could be pursued. Because resources are scarce, however, the real cost of air pollution control is represented by the government programs or private expenditures that we forego by putting our resources into reducing VOC emissions. In the health area alone, $10 billion invested in smoking cessation programs, radon control, better prenatal and neonatal health care, or similar measures might contribute much more to public health and well-being.

Although we have discussed both national and regional air pollution control plans in all-or-nothing terms, neither plan is indivisible. Because the benefits and costs of air pollution control are sure to vary considerably among metropolitan areas, it may make economic sense to control a great deal in some places but little in others. Further controls will almost inevitably be justified in the Los Angeles area, where despite concerned efforts over the last 30 years air pollution is quite clearly unacceptable and adverse health effects are the most significant. On the basis of cost estimates made by the South Coast authorities in the Los Angeles area, particularly attractive VOC control possibilities include reformulating coatings used in the manufacture of wood furniture, modifying aircraft engines, and substituting less volatile cleaning solvents. By the same token, one must be especially careful in evaluating the benefits of mandatory van-pooling and other transportation control measures that have possibly large nonpecuniary costs. Even if such efforts temporarily relieve freeway congestion, new drivers may appear in the commuting brigade and wipe out apparent pollution reductions. The important point to emphasize is that all control measures must be viewed with an eye toward the good that they are likely to do and the costs that they are likely to impose.

Next, although smog is the pollution problem with which Los Angeles is most often associated, a substantial share of the benefits of further air pollution control there appears to arise from reduced particulate concentrations, according to the [California air pollution authority]. Controlling VOCs will have no direct effect on these particulates and will be quite expensive. It may make sense for authorities there to reorient their control plan toward particulate control to maximize health benefits per dollar of pollution control.

Finally, implicit in our discussion is discomfort with the premises on which our national air quality standards are now based. If, as seems likely, there are no pollution concentrations at which safety can be assured, the real question in ambient standard setting is the amount of risk that we are willing to accept. This decision must be informed by economics. Although such economic considerations should never be allowed to dominate air pollution control decisions, it is inappropriate and unwise to exclude them.

LETTERS TO THE EDITOR

253 SCIENCE 606-09 (1991)

Alan D. Krupnick and Paul R. Portney write that pollution control costs in Los Angeles are likely to exceed benefits. This hardly qualifies as news, as some experts maintain that costs may be overstated initially and benefits are usually understated because we know (or think we know) how to calculate only a few of them. Their main message should have been the sorry state of affairs of our knowledge of the types of effects that drive these kinds of benefit calculations.

Krupnick and Portney do not consider effects on mortality resulting from pollutants other than sulfate aerosols, effects on hospital usage, or effects on the underlying morbidity of the population. Mortality effects dominate their calculation, even though they use a value of life far less than others have recently used and much less than the geometric mean of their own range. Increasing the value of lives prematurely lost might have balanced the control costs but would also demand that this element be examined much more closely. For example, age at death and degree of prematurity clearly merit consideration.

* * *

Fredrick W. Lipfert & Samuel C. Morris
Dept. of Applied Science
Brookhaven National Laboratory

As the project director of the Office of Technology Assessment's (OTA's) study of urban ozone, cited extensively in Krupnick and Portney's article, I would like to offer a different perspective on the issue. * * *

Ironically, Krupnick and Portney's over-reliance on the strengths of their analysis-the quantification of benefits and costs-leads to the article's major weakness. Decision-makers need to consider both what we *know well* and can quantify and what we *understand only poorly* when they are weighing the benefits and costs of achieving the ozone standard. The unknowns, on both sides of the equation, are considerable.

* * *

Krupnick and Portney draw their bottom lines from the "known" portions of the benefit-cost comparison, that is, the costs for the two-thirds of the emissions reductions needed to reach the standard in all areas and the benefits from the selected acute health effects for which data allow such an estimate. To be fair, they do briefly mention that potential chronic health effects are not included in their estimate, but the unfamiliar reader is given no clue about the intense concern and debate over such a possibility.

Krupnick and Portney appear to lament the fact that benefit-cost assessment does not have a more prominent role in clear air decisionmaking. Their benefit assessment was, in fact, part of the debate over the reauthorization of the Clean Air Act, but Congress reached a different conclusion.

* * *

Thus the 42 members of the House Energy and Commerce Committee substituted their own judgments about the value of avoiding acute respiratory symptoms for those obtained from the economics literature. Moreover, they made judgments about the value of avoiding potential, but unproved, chronic health risks. I find this quite reasonable. The four valuation studies used by Krupnick and Portney used mail or telephone surveys of between 40 and 400 adults each, asking participants how much they would be willing to pay to avoid specific respiratory symptoms. The results of these studies provide useful information to Congress, but do we really want these studies to supersede the judgment of our elected representatives? In the end, it is the responsibility of the Congress to be the arbiter of our nation's collective values and to make the tough, yet necessary, judgment calls when our scientific and technical "crystal ball" is cloudy.

Robert M. Friedman
Office of Technology Assessment

Krupnick and Portney miss the mark in estimating the costs and benefits of cleaning up the air in the South Coast Air Basin, which includes the Los Angeles metropolitan area.

On the cost issue, the authors rely on old estimates made before the region's 20-year clean air plan was adopted in 1989. Experience in implementing the plan has since shown that the cost estimates for many of the measures were high. As the measures have been implemented, costs have fallen by almost half, largely because of rapid advances in technology, such as new and cleaner paints and materials that have eliminated the need for expensive retrofit controls. Many measures will actually save money by conserving on energy and materials.

A comprehensive cost estimate by our staff for the 1991 update of the South Coast Air Quality Management District's clean air plan estimates total costs at $6.11 billion a year, not counting $2.19 billion a year in transportation infrastructure investments. While trains, car pool lanes, and other transit facilities will improve air quality, their primary benefit will be in managing the growing traffic gridlock that is eating away at the region's economic productivity and making life miserable for many residents.

On the benefits side, the authors concentrate on only the acute health benefits of controlling ozone, basing their conclusions on a clinical study in which the response of individuals to various levels of ozone was measured in a controlled laboratory setting. To examine the benefits of reducing particulates, the authors use sulfate as an indicator.

There are serious flaws with this approach. First, people do not live in laboratories, so any estimate of benefits based on a clinical test underestimates the degree of health effects from pollution. In reality, people in the South Coast Air Basin are exposed to a broad mix of pollutants, including raw hydrocarbons, acidic particles, polycyclic organic matter, nitrogen dioxide, heavy metals, carbon monoxide, and ozone. Many of these compounds are carcinogenic, such as benzene. * * *

Our estimate of the health benefits of meeting the ozone standard and fine particulate standard alone is $9.4 billion a year. Additional benefits would accrue by meeting the standards for nitrogen dioxide and carbon monoxide. Because controlling emissions from the automobile and other combustion sources can reduce each of these pollutants, as well as toxic substances such as benzene, we expect that the benefits could easily double. Moreover, a recent study by Detels *et al.* shows that exposure to the mix of pollutants prevalent in the South Coast Air Basin causes permanent loss of lung function.

What is most bothersome about the author's argument is its stark avoidance of moral principle. I do not suspect that the authors, for instance, would tolerate anyone dumping even the most minute quantity of poison into their drinking water or food. In essence, though, that is what is happening each day in the air. And despite what the economic studies say, I defy the authors to look an asthmatic straight in the eye and tell them that their last life-threatening asthma attack could be valued at $25.

James M. Lents
Executive Officer
South Coast Air Quality Management District

I am intrigued by the fact that the "questioning of both healthy and infirm respondents with supplemental data on the out-of-pocket medical costs and lost income" caused by air pollution led Krupnick and Portney to assign "an average value of $25 for each asthma attack prevented" and, for nonasthmatics, "$20 for a reduction of one restricted activity day (in which an individual is neither bedridden nor forced to miss work but must alter his or her pattern in some way)."

It is understandable that economists will welcome some method-indeed, almost any method-of quantifying noneconomic goods so that they can be factored into their equations, but noneconomists may be excused for looking askance at an evaluation process that essentially equates prevention of a serious and at times life-threatening disease with allowing a jogger to carry out his daily run in comfort.

Bernard Miller
Department of Chemistry
University of Massachusetts

The thoughtful article by Krupnick and Portney about air pollution benefits and costs seems to ignore some obvious problems, but its conclusion is sweeping: "the costs of proposed new controls are found to exceed the benefits, perhaps by a considerable margin." The study examines ozone, volatile organic compounds (VOC), and coughs. This is troubling for several reasons. First, a general view of the current major air pollution problems would rank forest health, visibility, agricultural damage, and lake acidification as greater problems than coughing. This is because U.S. successes in air pollution control have eliminated an acute health threat in much of the country. Second, ozone arises from the interaction of VOC and nitrogen oxides in sunlight. Focusing only on volatile organic compounds misleads the reader. Third, VOC and nitrogen oxides originate in the same fossil fuel combustion activities that release carbon dioxide and other pollutants. Ozone prevention policies that also reduce fossil fuel energy use are reducing the rate of accumulation of greenhouse gases.

Overall, I think the authors' conclusion is not justified by their analysis.

Duane Chapman
Department of Agricultural Economics
and Program of Global Warming
Institute for Social and Economic Research
Cornell University

Response [by Krupnick & Portney]: Although Lipfert and Morris take us to task about a number of points, we are in perfect agreement with what we take to be their basic point: that the epidemiology of urban air pollution is still in a confused state because of, among other things, the difficulty of isolating pollutant-specific health effects when urban air contains a heterogeneous soup of harmful substances.

* * *

Friedman also observes that Congress conducted its own implicit benefit-cost analysis in voting on the urban air quality provision in the 1990 amendments to the Clean Air Act. Bully! That's exactly how such decisions ought to be made. But if an overworked Congress is capable of making qualitative benefit-cost comparisons of air pollution measures, surely the administrator of the Environmental Protection Agency (EPA) is also. Why not allow him or her to make explicit yet qualitative trade-offs between economic, environmental, and other considerations when setting National Ambient Air Quality Standards, emission standards for hazardous air pollutants, and so on? Because these standards drive air pollution control in the United States today, the same kind of balancing Friedman attributes to Congress could enable EPA to set more sensible national environmental goals.

* * *

Lents appears to miss a subtle point with regard to the consequences of the South Coast plan-costs are not merely out-of-pocket expenditures. Consumer convenience carries with it a very real economic value. For example, mandatory car-pooling would reduce out-of-pocket commuting costs for gasoline and for other expenses that are shared. But there is a reason besides cheap gas and subsidized parking why freeways in Los Angeles and other urban areas are choked with single-passenger cars: people place a high value on being able to go to work when they want, come home when they want, and go to business appointments during the day at their own convenience. Giving this up would be a "cost" that would have to be reckoned into the evaluation of any regulatory program affecting consumer-commuters.

Lents comments that clinical studies always underestimate health effects in the field. In fact, the reverse is quite possible. Individuals engaged in normal day-to-day activities often can take steps to avoid actions that place them at risk from pollution. Subjects in clinical studies generally do not have this option. For instance, individuals in clinical studies are sometimes required to exercise moderately (or even heavily) while being exposed to varying concentrations of ozone or other pollutants. In everyday settings, however, many of these individuals would avoid or postpone such exercise on account of high pollution levels.

* * *

Lents also references the work of Detels *et al.* to suggest that the mix of air pollutants found in Los Angeles may be related to permanent loss in lung function. *If* this finding is substantiated, and *if* this loss in lung function is significant enough to affect the way people live or the time at which they die, all bets are off on our estimates of the benefits of the South Coast plan. We make this clear in our article.

Lents raises "moral principles" toward the end of his letter. We leave it to readers to decide this question: at a time when so many households in Los Angeles and in the nation suffer from hunger, crime, poor health, homelessness, addiction, illiteracy, and other problems, can it *really* be wrong to ask whether the best use of society's next million, billion, or ten billion dollars lies in reducing urban ozone concentrations? That seems to us to be exactly the kind of question that we, and Lents, should be asking all the time.

Miller objects to the dollar values assigned to the improvements in human health (fewer asthma attacks) that would accompany reduced ambient ozone concentrations. Few economists are content with the valuation of reduced morbidity or premature mortality, including the empirical implementation of theoretical measures believed to be correct. We can only reemphasize the point we made in our article-that values like $25 per avoided asthma attack come from questionnaires administered to ordinary citizens, *including asthmatics*, and that these values represent average responses after mitigation measures are taken. We have no doubt that more careful extensive questioning in the future would lead to revisions in the value of avoiding acute illness and also to an improved understanding of the value of preventing chronic illness. For now, however, we can only make use of the best results available and indicate, as we did quite carefully, that uncertainties are great. Readers uncomfortable with our approach should remember that values are assigned implicitly whenever policy decisions are made; difficult as it may be, we prefer to see such assignments made explicitly and in the open.

AT THE SHRINE OF OUR LADY OF FATIMA *OR* WHY POLITICAL QUESTIONS ARE NOT ALL ECONOMIC

Mark Sagoff
23 ARIZ. L. REV. 1283, 1283-96 (1981)

Lewiston, New York, a well-to-do community near Buffalo, is the site of the Lake Ontario Ordnance Works, where years ago the federal government disposed of the residues of the Manhattan Project. These radioactive wastes are buried but are not forgotten by the residents who say that when the wind is southerly, radon gas blows through the town. Several parents at a recent Lewiston conference I attended described their terror on learning that cases of leukemia had been found among area children. They feared for their own lives as well. On the other side of the table, officials from New York State and from local corporations replied that these fears were ungrounded. People who smoke, they said, take greater risks than people who live close to waste disposal sites. One speaker talked in terms of "rational methodologies of decisionmaking." This aggravated the parents' rage and frustration.

The speaker suggested that the townspeople, were they to make their decision in a free market and if they knew the scientific facts, would choose to live near the hazardous waste facility. He told me later they were irrational-"neurotic"-because they refused to recognize or to act upon their own interests. The residents of Lewiston were unimpressed with his analysis of their "willingness to pay" to avoid this risk or that. They did not see what risk-benefit analysis had to do with the issues they raised.

If you take the Military Highway (as I did) from Buffalo to Lewiston, you will pass through a formidable wasteland.[38] Landfills stretch in all directions and enormous trucks—tiny in that landscape—incessantly deposit sludge which great bulldozers then push into the ground. These machines are the only signs of life, for in the miasma than hangs in the air, no birds, not even scavengers, are seen. Along colossal power lines which crisscross this dismal land, the dynamos at Niagara send electric power south, where factories have fled, leaving their remains to decay. To drive along this road is to feel, oddly, the mystery and awe one experiences in the presence of so much power and decadence.

* * *

At the Shrine of Our Lady of Fatima, on a plateau north of the Military Highway, a larger than life sculpture of Mary looks into the chemical air. The original of this shrine stands in central Portugal where in May, 1917, three children said they saw a Lady, brighter than the sun, raised on a cloud in an evergreen tree. Five months later, on a wet and chilly October day, the Lady

---

[38] You will also pass within a few blocks of Love Canal.–EDS.

again appeared, this time before a large crowd. Some who were skeptical did not see the miracle. Others in the crowd reported, however, that "the sun appeared and seemed to tremble, rotate violently and fall, dancing over the heads of the throng . * * *"

The Shrine was empty when I visited it. The cult of Our Lady of Fatima, I imagine, has only a few devotees. The cult of Pareto Optimality, however, has many. Where some people see only environmental devastation, its devotees perceive efficiency, utility, and the maximization of wealth. They see the satisfaction of wants. They envision the good life. As I looked over the smudged and ruined terrain I tried to share that vision. I hoped that Our Lady of Fatima, worker of miracles, might serve, at least for the moment, as the Patroness of cost-benefit analysis. I thought of all the wants and needs that are satisfied in a landscape of honeymoon cottages, commercial strips, and dumps for hazardous waste. I saw the miracle of efficiency. The prospect, however, looked only darker in that light.

Political and Economic Decisionmaking

This essay concerns the economic decisions we make about the environment. It also concerns our political decisions about the environment. Some people have suggested that ideally these should be the same, that all environmental problems are problems in distribution. According to this view, there is an environmental problem only when some resource is not allocated in equitable and efficient ways.

This approach to environmental policy is pitched entirely at the level of the consumer. It is his or her values that count, and the measure of these values is the individual's willingness to pay. The problem of justice or fairness in society becomes, then, the problem of distributing goods and services so that more people get more of what they want to buy: a condo on the beach, a snowmobile for the mountains, a tank full of gas, a day of labor. The only values we have, according to this view, are those that a market can price.

How much do you value open space, a stand of trees, an "unspoiled" landscape? Fifty dollars? A hundred? A thousand? This is one way to measure value. You could compare the amount consumers would pay for a townhouse or coal or a landfill to the amount they would pay to preserve an area in its "natural" state. If users would pay more for the land with the house, the coal mine, or the landfill, than without—less construction and other costs of development—then the efficient thing to do is to improve the land and thus increase its value. That is why we have so many tract developments, pizza stands, and gas stations. How much did you spend last year to preserve open space? How much for pizza and gas? "In principle, the ultimate measure of environmental quality," as one basic text assures us, "is the value people place on these * * * services or their *willingness to pay*.

Willingness to pay: what is wrong with that? The rub is this: not all of us think of ourselves simply as *consumers*. Many of us regard ourselves *as citizens* as well. We act as consumers to get what we want *for ourselves*. We act as citizens to achieve what we think is right or best *for the community*. The question arises, then, whether what we want for ourselves individually as consumers is consistent with the goals we would set for ourselves collectively as citizens. Would I vote for the sort of things I shop for? Are my preferences as a consumer consistent with my judgments as a citizen?

They are not. I am schizophrenic. Last year, I fixed a couple of tickets and was happy to do so since I saved fifty dollars. Yet, at election time, I helped to vote the corrupt judge out of office. I speed on the highway; yet I want the police to enforce laws against speeding. I used to buy mixers in returnable bottles-but who can bother to return them? I buy only disposables now, but to soothe my conscience, I urge my state senator to outlaw one-way containers. I love my car, I hate the bus. Yet I vote for candidates who promise to tax gasoline to pay for public transportation. And of course, I applaud the Endangered Species Act, although I have no earthly use for the Colorado squawfish or the Indiana bat. I support almost any political cause that I think will defeat my consumer interests. This is because I have contempt for-although I act upon-those interests. I have an "Ecology Now" sticker on a car that leaks oil everywhere it's parked.

The distinction between consumer and citizen preferences has long vexed the theory of public finance. Should the public economy serve the same goals as the household economy? May it serve, instead, goals emerging from our association as citizens? The question asks if we may collectively strive for and achieve only those items we individually compete for and consume. Should we aspire, instead, to public goals we may legislate as a nation?

The problem, insofar as it concerns public finance, is stated as follows by R.A. Musgrave, who reports a conversation he had with Gerhard Colm:

> He [Colm] holds that the individual voter dealing with political issues has a frame of reference quite distinct from that which underlies his allocation of income as a consumer. In the latter situation the voter acts as a private individual determined by self-interest and deals with his personal wants; in the former, he acts as a political being guided by his image of a good society. The two, Colm holds, are different things.

* * *

Liberty: Ancient and Modern

When efficiency is the criterion of public safety and health, one tends to conceive of social relations on the model of a market, ignoring competing visions of what we as a society should be like. Yet it is obvious that there are competing conceptions of what we should be as a society. There are some who believe on principle that worker safety and environmental quality ought to be protected only insofar as the benefits of protection balance the costs. On the other hand, people argue-also on principle-that neither worker safety nor environmental quality should be treated merely as a commodity to be traded at the margin for other commodities, but rather each should be valued for its own sake. The conflict between these two principles is logical or moral, to be resolved by argument or debate. The question whether cost-benefit analysis should play a decisive role in policy-making is not to be decided by cost-benefit analysis. A contradiction between principles-between contending visions of the good society-cannot be settled by asking how much partisans are willing to pay for their beliefs.

The role of the *legislator*, the political role, may be more important to the individual than the role of *consumer*. The person, in other words, is not to be treated merely as a bundle of preferences to be juggled in cost-benefit analyses. The individual is to be respected as an advocate of ideas which are to be judged according to the reasons for them. If health and environmental statutes reflect a vision of society as something other than a market by requiring protections beyond what are efficient, then this may express not legislative ineptitude but legislative responsiveness to public values. To deny this vision because it is economically inefficient is simply to replace it with another vision. It is to insist that the ideas of the citizen be sacrificed to the psychology of the consumer.

* * *

Nowhere are the rights of the moderns, particularly the rights of privacy and property, less helpful than in the area of the natural environment. Here the values we wish to protect-cultural, historical, aesthetic, and moral-are public values. They depend not so much upon what each person wants individually as upon what he or she thinks is right for the community. We refuse to regard worker health and safety as commodities; we regulate hazards as a matter of right. Likewise, we refuse to treat environmental resources simply as public goods in the economist's sense. Instead, we prevent significant deterioration of air quality not only as a matter of individual self-interest but also as a matter of collective self-respect. How shall we balance efficiency against moral, cultural, and aesthetic values in policy for the workplace and the environment? No better way has been devised to do this than by legislative debate ending in a vote. This is very different from a cost-benefit analysis terminating in a bottom line.

Values are Not Subjective

It is the characteristic of cost-benefit analysis that it treats all value judgments other than those made on its behalf as nothing but statements of preference, attitude, or emotion, insofar as they are value judgments. The cost-benefit analyst regards as true the judgment that we should maximize efficiency or wealth. The analyst believes that this view can be backed by reasons, but does not regard it as a preference or want for which he or she must be willing to pay. The cost-benefit analyst tends to treat all other normative views and recommendations as if they were nothing but subjective reports of mental states. The analyst supposes in all such cases that "this is right" and "this is what we ought to do" are equivalent to "I want this" and "this is what I prefer." Value judgments are beyond criticism if, indeed, they are nothing but expressions of personal preference; they are incorrigible since every person is in the best position to know what he or she wants. All valuation, according to this approach, happens *in foro interno*; debate *in foro publico* has no point. With this approach, the reasons that people give for their views do not count; what does count is how much they are willing to pay to satisfy their wants. Those who are willing to pay the most, for all intents and purposes, have the right view; theirs is the more informed opinion, the better aesthetic judgment, and the deeper moral insight. * * *

* * *

A market or quasi-market approach to arithmetic, for example, is plainly inadequate. No matter how much people are willing to pay, three will never be the square root of six. Similarly, segregation is a national curse and the fact that we are willing to pay for it does not make it better, but only us worse. The case for abortion must stand on the merits; it cannot be priced at the margin. Our failures to make the right decisions in these matters are failures in arithmetic, failures in wisdom, failures in taste, failures in morality-but not market failures. There are no relevant markets which have failed.

What separates these questions from those for which markets are appropriate is that they involve matters of knowledge, wisdom, morality, and taste that admit of better or worse, right or wrong, true or false, and not mere economic optimality. Surely environmental questions-the protection of wilderness, habitats, water, land, and air as well as policy toward environmental safety and health-involve moral and aesthetic principles and not just economic ones. This is consistent, of course, with cost-effectiveness and with a sensible recognition of economic constraints.

NOTES

1. *Difficulties of implementation.* What limitations do Krupnick and Portney acknowledge in their study of air pollution control? Which do their critics add? Do some of the implementation problems raise more fundamental questions about the use of cost-benefit analysis at all?

In their conclusion, Krupnick and Portney state, "Further controls will almost inevitably be justified in the Los Angeles area, where * * * air pollution is quite clearly unacceptable and adverse health effects are the most significant." Doesn't this contradict the results of their study? What is the basis for finding Los Angeles air unacceptably dirty if the costs of cleaning it outweigh the benefits?

2. *Monetizing.* Perhaps the most obvious, and certainly one of the most troubling, difficulties of cost-benefit analysis is assigning monetary values to costs and benefits that are not otherwise thought of or treated as market commodities. Krupnick and Portney spend a lot of time on this problem with respect to asthma attacks. How did they resolve the difficulty?

Other difficulties abound in assigning a monetary value to non-monetary things. As Krupnick and Portney acknowledge, their technique of inferring the value of being free of asthma attacks is indirect, requiring numerous inferences and assumptions. Why not simply ask people how much they would demand to have an asthma attack inflicted on them? Or should we ask them how much they would be willing to pay to avoid one? What is the difference between using the "selling" price for an asthma attack and the "buying" price? Will the wealthy and the poor systematically give different answers to such questions, and if so, does that undermine the validity of the technique?

3. *Discount rate.* Another serious difficulty is the discount rate to be applied to costs and benefits. Under basic economic theory, the present value of future income or expense must be discounted by presumed inflation, rates of return, and other factors to reflect the basic idea that money now is worth more to a person than future money. It follows that costs and benefits that will appear in or continue into the future must be discounted to their present values. The choice of discount rate has an enormous impact on any calculation that includes value that continues well into the future, and there is no "correct" discount rate. Different people adopt different rates, largely on the basis of political and social views, because technical economic arguments can support a large range of rates.

Professor Driesen has argued that cost-benefit analysis "exacerbates tendencies to focus myopically on short-term costs to regulated companies, even when imposition of costs upon them may economically benefit their workers and/or competitors in the short-term and society in the long-term." David M. Driesen, *The Societal Cost of Environmental Regulation: Beyond Administrative Cost-Benefit Analysis*, 24 ECOLOGY L.Q. 545, 550 (1997).[39] Why do you suppose that would be the case? Is there a general tendency for costs to be felt in the (undiscounted) present and benefits in the (discounted) future?

4. *Cost.* Even putting aside discount rate problems, estimating the costs of a regulatory intervention is, in fact, not much more exact than estimating risk. The standard criticism of environmental, health, and safety regulation is that it requires enormous expenditures of social resources in relation to small gains. Further, those expenditures are extremely inconsistent in terms of cost-per-life-saved from one agency (and even one regulation) to the next. The empirical basis for these claims is a table developed by a economist at the Office of Management and Budget in the 1980s, and the table has been cited in practically any study that you can name of the costs of regulation. Recently, however, this table has been subjected to careful scrutiny which has found that it is filled with unproven assumptions, unenacted regulations, and selective use of relevant data.[40]

---

[39] Professors Lisa Heinzerling and Richard Revesz have recently published detailed critiques of standard discounting practices. *See* Lisa Heinzerling, *Environmental Law and the Present Future*, 87 GEO. L.J. 2025 (1999); Lisa Heinzerling, *Discounting Life*, 108 YALE L.J. 1911 (1999); and Richard L. Revesz, *Environmental Regulation, Cost Benefit Analysis, and the Discounting of Human Lives*, 99 COLUM. L. REV. 941 (1999).

[40] *See* Winston Harrington *et al.*, *On the Accuracy of Regulatory Cost Estimates (Resources for the Future Discussion Paper* 99-18, Jan. 1999) (finding that *ex ante* estimates of total direct costs usually exceeded actual costs); Lisa Heinzerling, *Regulatory Costs of Mythic Proportions*, 107 YALE L.J. 1981 (1998) (exhaustive analysis of OMB table); Michael B.

What was the source of Krupnick and Portney's cost estimates for the regulations that they considered? What are the weaknesses in those estimates? We are justifiably reluctant to credit individuals' own statements about their willingness to pay for or sell a health impact—is the method for obtaining cost estimates any different?

5. Much of the foregoing might be described as operational critiques, in that they address flaws in implementing cost-benefit analysis but do not necessarily question the whole enterprise. Mark Sagoff questions the whole enterprise. What are his criticisms of cost-benefit analysis? Do the operational critiques support his arguments?

Like Krupnick and Portney, however, Sagoff throws in a comment that seems at odds with the gist of his article. He says, "This is consistent, of course, with cost-effectiveness and with a sensible recognition of economic constraints." What then is the proper role of cost-benefit analysis, in Sagoff's view? Another way of thinking about this question is to ask whether cost-benefit analysis is inevitably tied to an economic understanding of efficiency.

6. Professor McGarity suggests that it is important to ask *who* is supporting increased use of cost-benefit analysis, and then *why*? He pointedly observes:

> Professor Sunstein observes that the "current system of public regulation is extraordinarily inefficient." By paying greater attention to the costs and benefits of regulations, agencies could make vast sums of otherwise wasted money available for desirable social ends. Society would therefore be better off if Congress subjected regulatory programs to an over-arching cost-benefit decision criterion. In the same vein, Justice Breyer suggests that the moneys spent cleaning up hazardous waste sites should be directed toward "vaccinations, . . . prenatal care, or mammograms," or perhaps offering counseling to those who are genetically predisposed to carcinogenic risks. * * *
>
> This suggestion, that a vast potential exists for bettering society only if current programs are administered more efficiently, casts cost-benefit advocates in the role of altruistic defenders of the poor and the powerless, and a few, like Professor Sunstein, may aptly fit that description. But in the real political world the strongest advocates of cost-benefit analysis are large corporations, trade associations and associated think tanks, not exactly entities cut in the mold of Mother Teresa. Regulatees like to see governmental intervention measured by a cost-benefit test not to make more resources available to the poor, but to make more resources available to themselves. Even under the highly contestable assumption that a cost-benefit decision criterion would eliminate waste, no vehicle exists for channeling the

---

Gerrard, *Demons and Angels in Hazardous Waste Regulation: Are Justice, Efficiency, and Democracy Reconcilable?*, 92 NW. U.L. REV. 706, 727-28 (1998) (book review) (briefer treatment, urging caution in use of table).

savings to the most deserving social programs. The savings will invariably go to the regulatees, who may or may not spend them on activities that benefit society. Absent some governmental vehicle for directing how regulated entities spend the resources saved by less stringent regulation, they will devote resources to things that make their shareholders happy.

Thomas O. McGarity, *A Cost-Benefit State*, 50 ADMIN. L. REV. 7, 33-35 (1998). McGarity goes on to list several ways in which the increased use of cost-benefit analysis consistently favors the regulated entities and not the beneficiaries of regulation: slowing down the regulatory process, recasting protective legislation as efficiency legislation, devaluing non-monetizable ("soft") considerations, and promoting the influence of technical experts. Is McGarity right? Does the Los Angeles Basin cost-benefit study bear him out? What are the long-term consequences of a greater reliance on cost-benefit analysis on the regulatory system?

7. *The costs and benefits of cost-benefit.* Excellent summaries of the virtues and vices of risk assessment, comparative risk analysis, and cost-benefit analysis can be found in McGarity, *supra, at* 32-74; Thomas O. McGarity & Sidney A. Shapiro, *OSHA's Critics and Regulatory Reform*, 31 WAKE FOREST L. REV. 587, 622-32 (1996), and Richard H. Pildes & Cass R. Sunstein, *Reinventing the Regulatory State*, 62 U. CHI. L. REV. 1, 46-52 (1995).

d. "Soft" Cost-Benefit Analysis

It should be apparent by now that the utility and appropriateness of cost-benefit analysis is not a yes-no question. As Krupnick, Portney, Sagoff, and their interlocutors all recognized in the previous section, economic analysis has its uses. They also recognized, to a greater or lesser degree, its limitations. To the extent–and it is a very large extent–that costs and benefits are part of the regulation of toxic substances, it is critically important to understand how the costs and benefits are calculated and to understand the legal standard that is being applied. Of course, these are related questions, and the following excerpt illustrates this relationship. Executive Order No. 12866, issued by President Clinton, replaced President Reagan's No. 12291 (excerpted above). As you read it, look for its handling of both the calculation and standards issues-and for other forms of regulatory analysis that we have studied. You will also notice that the order addresses agencies' choice of regulatory strategies, which we discussed at the beginning of this chapter.

EXECUTIVE ORDER NO. 12866

58 Fed. Reg. 51735 (1993)

Section 1. Statement of Regulatory Philosophy and Principles.

(a) *The Regulatory Philosophy.* Federal agencies should promulgate only such regulations as are required by law, are necessary to interpret the law, or are made necessary by compelling public need, such as material failures of private markets to protect or improve the health and safety of the public, the environment, or the well-being of the American people. In deciding whether and how to regulate, agencies should assess all costs and benefits of available regulatory alternatives, including the alternative of not regulating. Costs and benefits shall be understood to include both quantifiable measures (to the fullest extent that these can be usefully estimated) and qualitative measures of costs and benefits that are difficult to quantify, but nevertheless essential to consider. Further, in choosing among alternative regulatory approaches, agencies should select those approaches that maximize net benefits (including potential economic, environmental, public health and safety, and other advantages; distributive impacts; and equity), unless a statute requires another regulatory approach.

(b) *The Principles of Regulation.* To ensure that the agencies' regulatory programs are consistent with the philosophy set forth above, agencies should adhere to the following principles, to the extent permitted by law and where applicable:

(1) Each agency shall identify the problem that it intends to address (including, where applicable, the failures of private markets or public institutions that warrant new agency action) as well as assess the significance of that problem.

(2) Each agency shall examine whether existing regulations (or other law) have created, or contributed to, the problem that a new regulation is intended to correct and whether those regulations (or other law) should be modified to achieve the intended goal of regulation more effectively.

(3) Each agency shall identify and assess available alternatives to direct regulation, including providing economic incentives to encourage the desired behavior, such as user fees or marketable permits, or providing information upon which choices can be made by the public.

(4) In setting regulatory priorities, each agency shall consider, to the extent reasonable, the degree and nature of the risks posed by various substances or activities within its jurisdiction.

(5) When an agency determines that a regulation is the best available method of achieving the regulatory objective, it shall design its regulations in the most cost-effective manner to achieve the regulatory objective. In doing so, each agency shall consider incentives for innovation, consistency, predictability, the costs of enforcement and compliance (to the government, regulated entities, and the public), flexibility, distributive impacts, and equity.

(6) Each agency shall assess both the costs and the benefits of the intended regulation and, recognizing that some costs and benefits are difficult to quantify, propose or adopt a regulation only upon a reasoned determination that the benefits of the intended regulation justify its costs.

(7) Each agency shall base its decisions on the best reasonably obtainable scientific, technical, economic, and other information concerning the need for, and consequences of, the intended regulation.

(8) Each agency shall identify and assess alternative forms of regulation and shall, to the extent feasible, specify performance objectives, rather than specifying the behavior or manner of compliance that regulated entities must adopt.

* * *

Sec. 6. Centralized Review of Regulations. The guidelines set forth below shall apply to all regulatory actions, for both new and existing regulations, by agencies other than those agencies specifically exempted by the Administrator of OIRA [*i.e.*, the Office of Information and Regulatory Analysis, the regulatory review section of OMB]:

(a) *Agency Responsibilities.* (1) Each agency shall (consistent with its own rules, regulations, or procedures) provide the public with meaningful participation in the regulatory process. In particular, before issuing a notice of proposed rulemaking, each agency should, where appropriate, seek the involvement of those who are intended to benefit from and those expected to be burdened by any regulation (including, specifically, State, local, and tribal officials). In addition, each agency should afford the public a meaningful opportunity to comment on any proposed regulation, which in most cases should include a comment period of not less than 60 days. Each agency also is directed to explore and, where appropriate, use consensual mechanisms for developing regulations, including negotiated rulemaking.

* * *

(3) * * * (c) For those matters identified as, or determined by the Administrator of OIRA to be, a significant regulatory action within the scope of section 3(f)(1), the agency shall also provide to OIRA the following additional information developed as part of the agency's decisionmaking process (unless prohibited by law):

(i) An assessment, including the underlying analysis, of benefits anticipated from the regulatory action (such as, but not limited to, the promotion of the efficient functioning of the economy and private markets, the enhancement of health and safety, the protection of the natural environment, and the elimination or reduction of discrimination or bias) together with, to the extent feasible, a quantification of those benefits;

(ii) An assessment, including the underlying analysis, of costs anticipated from the regulatory action (such as, but not limited to, the direct cost both to the government in administering the regulation and to businesses and others in complying with the regulation, and any adverse effects on the efficient functioning of the economy, private markets (including productivity, employment, and competitiveness), health, safety, and the natural environment), together with, to the extent feasible, a quantification of those costs; and

(iii) An assessment, including the underlying analysis, of costs and benefits of potentially effective and reasonably feasible alternatives to the planned regulation, identified by the agencies or the public (including improving the current regulation and reasonably viable nonregulatory actions), and an explanation why the planned regulatory action is preferable to the identified potential alternatives.

* * *

Sec. 11. Revocations. Executive Orders Nos. 12291 and 12498; all amendments to those Executive orders; all guidelines issued under those orders; and any exemptions from those orders heretofore granted for any category of rule are revoked.

NOTES

1. *Kinder, gentler cost-benefit analysis.* In what ways is Executive Order No. 12866 simply a softer version of No. 12291? In what ways does No. 12866 differ substantially from No. 12291? Does No. 12866 successfully address the theoretical difficulties with cost-benefit analysis? What about the practical difficulties?

2. There have been other efforts to establish guidelines for cost-benefit analysis. The same Presidential/Congressional Commission that issued recommendations on risk assessment also addressed the uses and limitations of economic analysis. Among its recommendations -

The tools of economic analysis should be recognized as legitimate and useful ways to obtain information for the Risk Management Framework and for regulatory decisions that will affect health, safety, and the environment, but not as the sole or overriding determinant of those regulatory decisions. Information about costs and benefits that are intangible and that cannot be assigned monetary values should be addressed and considered explicitly.

Economic analysis should present information, where practicable, that can be used to provide a firmer basis for evaluating any inequitable distributions of costs and benefits.

The primary sources of uncertainty associated with the results of economic analysis should be identified, characterized, stated explicitly, and communicated clearly. The results of economic analyses should not be expressed as though they are precise measures of actual economic costs and benefits.

To achieve more nearly consistent benefit valuation among regulatory agencies, the value of mortality risks should be stated explicitly and valued with best estimates or ranges of estimates and with consistent use of procedures and basic assumptions.

Development of federal guidelines for benefit valuation involving stakeholder input should be considered.

Risk assessors and economists who must rely on the results of risk assessments to estimate benefits should collaborate more to reduce the inconsistencies between scientific and economic approaches to characterizing risks and risk reduction alternatives. Risk assessors and economists should expand their methods to reduce mismatches.

2 Presidential/Congressional Commission, *supra*, at 93-101. A somewhat more technocratic list of principles, adopted by some of the nation's leading environmental economists (including Paul Portney), can be found at Kenneth J. Arrow *et al.*, *Is There a Role for Benefit-Cost Analysis in Environmental, Health, and Safety Regulation?*, 272 SCIENCE 221 (1996) (answering "yes"). For a technical defense of a similar role for cost-benefit analysis, *see* Matthew D. Adler and Eric A. Posner, *Rethinking Cost-Benefit Analysis,* 109 YALE L.J. 165 (1999).

3. Both President Clinton and the risk commission advocate the consideration of a wide range non-monetary factors in cost-benefit analysis. However, by adding so many additional factors do we rob cost-benefit analysis of its analytical power to tell us in dollar terms what we have bought and for how much? Indeed, doesn't the analysis become tautologous—by adding extra benefit value to account for our desire to take a particular regulatory action, are we doing any more than restating our conclusion that we prefer taking this action to other actions? Would it be better just to leave CBA in its fairly "pure" form, but recognize that it is only one factor in environmental decisions?

PROBLEM
PROPOSED REGULATORY REFORM LEGISLATION

As part of its 1994 "Contract with America," House Republicans proposed a Job Creation and Wage Enhancement Act that would fundamentally change the rules by which regulatory agencies (in particular, environmental, safety, and health agencies) made decisions. H.R. 9, 104TH CONG., 1ST SESS. (1995). The regulatory reform part of the legislation eventually passed the House as H.R. 1022, 104TH CONG., 1ST SESS. (1995). Similar bills were introduced in the Senate, but the Senate Republican leadership was unable to muster the votes needed to cut off debate. As a result, broad regulatory reform was never enacted, though bits and pieces of it were.

First, locate the text of H.R. 1022. Second, identify the key provisions—why were they proposed? Third, imagine yourself a lobbyist for a "beneficiary" of environmental, health, or safety legislation (say, an environmental or union group). What provisions cause you most concern, and why? Are there modifications you can make in the text to make the statute acceptable, or must you simply oppose the whole effort? Fourth, as a beneficiary lobbyist, how do you respond to the argument that H.R. 1022 merely codifies Executive Order No. 12866?[41]

---

[41] For a critical review of regulatory reform legislation, *see* Celia Campbell-Mohn & John S. Applegate, *Learning from NEPA: Guidelines for Responsible Risk Legislation*, 23 HARV. ENVTL. L. REV. 93 (1999).

Chapter 4

The Judicial Role in Toxics Regulation

In our tripartite system of government, all three branches have opportunities to exercise legal control over environmental regulation and the agencies that do the regulating. Congress exercises legal control by writing the substantive requirements and prescribing the procedures that the agencies must follow. Less obviously, Congress uses its appropriations and oversight functions to influence the agency on both general policy and particular issues.[1] The executive branch exercises legal control through the regulations it promulgates to fill gaps in the legislation and through the positions it takes in particular cases. The President also exercises control through review of agency regulations by the Office of Information and Regulatory Affairs (OIRA) within the Office of Management and Budget (OMB), pursuant to Executive Order No. 12866 (1993). OIRA reviews regulations for political and managerial consistency, as well as for conformity with Administration policy on risk, cost, and benefits.[2]

---

[1] For excellent discussions of the extra-legal methods of congressional influence, *see* Richard Lazarus, *The Tragedy of Distrust in the Implementation of Federal Environmental Law*, 54 L. & CONTEMP. PROBS. 311, 336-40 (Autumn 1991), and PETER L. STRAUSS, AN INTRODUCTION TO ADMINISTRATIVE JUSTICE IN THE UNITED STATES 56-60 (1989).

[2] President Clinton's Executive Order No. 12866 is built on the foundations of President Reagan's Executive Orders No. 12291 (1981) and No. 12,498 (1985). Risk assessment and cost-benefit analysis are discussed in detail in chapters 2 and 3, *supra*. For the pros and cons of OIRA review, *see generally* Chris DeMuth & Douglas Ginsburg, 99 HARV. L. REV. 1075 (1986); Alan B. Morrison, *OMB Interference with Agency Rulemaking: The Wrong Way to Write a Regulation*, 99 HARV. L. REV. 1059 (1986); Cass Sunstein, *Cost-Benefit Analysis and the Separation of Powers*, 23 ARIZ. L. REV. 1267 (1981).

OMB's interference in EPA's efforts to regulate asbestos provides an instructive example of both executive control through OIRA and congressional control through oversight. OMB had persuaded EPA to delay its proposed asbestos regulations by transferring the matter to OMB. A thorough congressional investigation into OMB's actions resulted in EPA reconsidering the transfer and issuing the regulations. *See* EPA'S ASBESTOS REGULATIONS: HEARING BEFORE THE SUBCOMM. ON OVERSIGHT AND INVESTIGATIONS OF THE HOUSE ENERGY AND COMMERCE COMM., 99TH CONG., 1ST SESS. (1985); EPA'S ASBESTOS REGULATIONS: REPORT ON A CASE STUDY ON OMB'S INTERFERENCE IN AGENCY RULEMAKING (Comm. Print 1985).

At least in theory, the courts have only a limited, reactive role. They are empowered to review agency actions for conformity with statutory substance and procedure, and for minimal rationality. It is often claimed that over eighty percent of EPA's regulations are subjected to judicial challenge. While a recent study has demonstrated that the number is closer to 35%,[3] it undoubtedly *seems* like 80% to many observers, not least the agency itself, because litigation has an impact out of all proportion to its frequency. In addition, special and often elaborate provisions for judicial review are an element of virtually all major environmental legislation. As a result, an agency like EPA must assume that its handiwork will be revisited in a judicial tribunal. Since the agency is extremely anxious to avoid reversal, it adopts additional procedures and develops an exceptionally thorough record to justify its better decision. This development has been criticized as "ossification" of a flexible regulatory process.[4]

The judicial role goes deeper, however, and has in reality become an integral part of the regulatory system. There has been a lively debate over the last two decades as to whether the judicial role facilitates or hinders effective regulation. In this chapter, we examine this debate. As you read the chapter, ask yourself, first, how judicial review affects the regulation of toxic substances and hazardous wastes, and second, whether such review plays a positive role, both on the whole and in specific instances. The chapter addresses these questions in three contexts:

- a landmark environmental law case, the licensing of the Vermont Yankee Nuclear Power Station. This case illustrates the forms that administrative action can take, the substantive significance of the choice of procedures, and the courts' role in monitoring agency procedure;
- an exposition of the standard methodology for substantive judicial review, focusing on two environmental law cases that have profoundly shaped modern judicial review; and
- a case study of judicial review of (mainly) asbestos regulation, which illustrates the varying degrees of deference that courts give to an agency's substantive judgments.

---

[3] Cary Coglianese, *Assessing Consensus: The Promise and Performance of Negotiated Rulemaking,* 46 Duke L. J. 1255, 1296-1301 (1997).

[4] The term "ossification" was coined by Donald Elliott, a former general counsel of EPA. It struck a chord and is discussed in Thomas O. McGarity, *Some Thoughts on Deossifying the Rulemaking Process*, 41 DUKE L.J. 1385 (1992); Richard J. Pierce, Jr., *Seven Ways to Deossify Rulemaking*, 47 AD. L. REV. 59 (1995); Robert Glicksman & Christopher H. Schroeder, *EPA and the Courts: Twenty Years of Law and Politics*, 54 L. & CONTEMP. PROBS. 249 (1991); *but see* Patricia M. Wald, *Regulation at Risk: Are Courts Part of the Solution or Most of the Problem?*, 67 S. CAL. L. REV. 621 (1994) (disagreeing that judicial review is a major reason for ossification).

Taken together, these materials will give you the basic framework and vocabulary you need to understand the exercise of judicial control over agency decisions.

A. Forms of Agency Action: The Vermont Yankee Litigation

The Administrative Procedure Act (APA), 5 U.S.C. §§ 551-559, 701-706, creates the basic template of procedures by which federal agencies act. While individual statutes often add to, amend, or even replace the procedures in the APA, they seldom depart far from its basic categories. The APA operates on a four-part structure, the two axes of which are rulemaking *versus* adjudication, and formal *versus* informal proceedings. Though not defined as such in the APA itself (*see* 5 U.S.C. § 551(4),(6)), adjudication generally involves individualized, case-by-case determinations that resemble judicial decisionmaking. Rulemaking typically consists of general, prospective, legislation-like pronouncements. Formal proceedings are trial-like and involve distinct adversarial parties, a neutral presiding official, witnesses, cross-examination, and a closed record upon which the decision must be based. Informal proceedings require only notice, an opportunity to comment in writing on a proposal, and a "concise general statement of [] basis and purpose" accompanying the final action. Importantly, informal action does not require that a defined administrative record be created to support the agency's decision or that the decision be based exclusively on the material in whatever record the agency does create. These variables yield the following matrix:

	Rulemaking	Adjudication	Record	Scope of Review
Formal	§§ 553 + 556, 557	§§ 554 + 556,557	closed	"substantial evidence" § 706(2)(E)
Informal	§ 553 (notice-and-comment)	——[5]	open	"arbitrary and capricious" § 706(2)(A)

In practice, the influence of the judicial and legislative models of agency action, and some facilitating case law,[6] has resulted in a bipolar system in

---

[5] The procedural requirements for informal adjudication are set by the underlying substantive statute (*e.g.*, the Social Security Act) and regulations, or, at a minimum, the Due Process Clause of the Constitution.

[6] *U.S. v. Florida East Coast Ry.*, 410 U.S. 224 (1973), made it very difficult to demand that the agency use formal trial-like procedures in promulgating rules, by requiring that the precise triggering language in the APA be used in the underlying statute. Appellate courts have also read broadly agencies' authority to use rulemaking instead of adjudication. *See* American

which the agency uses either quasi-legislative informal rulemaking or quasi-judicial formal adjudication to carry out its mandates. This choice, moreover, is largely within the discretion of the agency.[7] The legislation-like informal rulemaking has come to dominate the formation of environmental policy, though informal adjudication abounds for individualized determinations like permits.

The saga of the Vermont Yankee Nuclear Power Station illustrates the nature of the APA's procedural options and the significance of the choice among them. The Nuclear Regulatory Commission (NRC) is charged with licensing nuclear power plants. Safety is at the heart of NRC's evaluation, and in the 1970s one of the great unresolved problems of nuclear power was the safe permanent disposal of used (or "spent") fuel. Spent fuel is highly radioactive and will remain so for a very long time.[8] Disposal of spent fuel, therefore, is a safety issue in every licensing proceeding for every plant. However, the problem does not differ from plant to plant, as spent fuel does not vary greatly and each plant makes only a marginal contribution to the total storage problem. Licensing proceedings are formal adjudications. However, in licensing the Vermont Yankee plant, NRC addressed the health risk of waste disposal in a separate, informal rulemaking. Environmental groups challenged this procedure in the D.C. Circuit. The court of appeals agreed that it was inadequate, but the Supreme Court reversed in a sharply worded opinion. Subsequently, the Court ruled on the substantive merits of NRC's position. Portions of the three cases are set out below.

NATURAL RESOURCES DEFENSE COUNCIL V. NUCLEAR REGULATORY COMMISSION

547 F.2d 633 (D.C. Cir. 1976), rev'd, 435 U.S. 519 (1978)

BAZELON, Chief Judge.

* * *

Hosp. Ass'n v. NLRB, 899 F.2d 651 (7th Cir. 1990), aff'd, 499 U.S. 606 (1991) (holding that "in each case" language in underlying statute did not preclude use of general rules).

[7] See NLRB v. Bell Aerospace Co., 416 U.S. 267 (1974).

[8] The appellate court noted:

> We were informed at argument that the Vermont Yankee plant will produce approximately 160 pounds of plutonium wastes annually during its 40-year life span. Plutonium is generally accepted as among the most toxic substances known; inhalation of a single microscopic particle is thought to be sufficient to cause cancer. Moreover, with a half-life of 25,000 years, plutonium must be isolated from the environment for 250,000 years before it becomes harmless. Operation of the facility in question will also produce substantial quantities of other "high-level" radioactive wastes in the form of strontium-90 and cesium-137 which, with their shorter, 30-year half-lives, must be isolated from the environment for "only" 600 to 1000 years.

NRDC v. NRC, 547 F.2d 633 (D.C. Cir. 1976). The problem of long-lived radioactive wastes is taken up again in Chapter 13(C) (Federal Facilities), infra.

Appeal number 74-1385 involves a proceeding to license a specific nuclear reactor (the Vermont Yankee Nuclear Power Station located near Vernon, Vermont). * * * The Appeal Board held that Licensing Boards * * * need not consider the "operations of the reprocessing plants or the disposal of wastes" in individual licensing proceedings.

Appeal number 74-1586 involves a rulemaking proceeding which the Commission instituted shortly thereafter with specific reference to the *Vermont Yankee* decision. The purpose of the rulemaking was to reconsider whether environmental effects of all stages of the uranium fuel cycle should be included in the cost-benefit analysis for licensing individual reactors. The Commission concluded the environmental effects of the fuel cycle, including waste disposal, were "relatively insignificant," but that it was preferable to take them into account. Therefore, a rule was promulgated requiring a series of specified numerical values (set out as Table S-3 accompanying the rule) be factored into the cost-benefit analysis for an individual reactor. These values are intended to represent the incremental contribution of an additional reactor to the environmental effect of the fuel cycle [, which NRC deemed to be minimal]. The rule further provides that in addition to Table S-3, "No further discussion of such environmental effects shall be required." * * *

The primary argument advanced by the public interest interveners is that the decision to preclude "discovery or cross-examination" denied them a meaningful opportunity to participate in the proceedings as guaranteed by due process. They do not question the Commission's authority to proceed by informal rulemaking, as opposed to adjudication. They rely instead on the line of cases indicating that in particular circumstances procedures in excess of the bare minima prescribed by the Administrative Procedure Act, 5 U.S.C. § 553, may be required.* * *

In order to determine whether an agency has lived up to [its responsibility to take "a good, hard look at the major questions before it"], a reviewing court must examine the record in detail to determine that a real give and take was fostered on the key issues. This does not give the court a license to judge for itself how much weight should be given particular pieces of scientific or technical data, a task for which it is singularly ill-suited. It does require, however, that the court examine the record so that it may satisfy itself that the decision was based "on a consideration of the relevant factors." Where only one side of a controversial issue is developed in any detail, the agency may abuse its discretion by deciding the issues on an inadequate record.

* * *

The only discussion of high-level waste disposal techniques was supplied by a 20-page statement by Dr. Frank K. Pittman, Director of the AEC's Division of Waste Management and Transportation. This statement, delivered during the oral hearings, was then incorporated, often verbatim, into the revised version of the Environmental Survey published after the comment period. Dr. Pittman began his statement by acknowledging that he was "broadly involved" with the subject of high-level waste management since he heads the division of the AEC charged with "responsibility for the development, construction and operation of facilities for ultimate management of commercial high-level waste."

Dr. Pittman proceeded to describe for the first time in public the "design concepts" for a federal surface repository for retrievable storage of high-level waste. This is essentially a warehouse in which sealed canisters containing cylinders of solidified nuclear wastes can be stored in water-filled basins recessed into the ground on a temporary basis (up to 100 years), until such time as a permanent waste disposal scheme is devised, when they can be removed. While the "intended life" of the facility is only 100 years, some high-level wastes must be isolated for up to 250,000 years. Therefore, the Environmental Survey states, without further explanation, that in the future a "permanent" Federal repository for "geologic storage of high-level wastes" will be established and that the "Federal government will have the obligation to maintain control over the site in perpetuity."

Until recently the AEC planned to dispose of wastes by burying them deep inside abandoned salt mines. These plans were postponed indefinitely after a series of technical difficulties, including the discovery the salt mines might be susceptible to underground flooding.

* * *

Dr. Pittman's description of the new plan—now also postponed indefinitely—to build a surface storage facility can only fairly be described as vague, but glowing. * * * [The court went on to criticize several other aspects of Dr. Pittman's analysis along similar lines.]

In substantial part, the materials uncritically relied on by the Commission in promulgating this rule consist of extremely vague assurances by agency personnel that problems as yet unsolved will be solved. That is an insufficient record to sustain a rule limiting consideration of the environmental effects of nuclear waste disposal to the numerical values in Table S-3. To the extent that uncertainties necessarily underlie predictions of this importance on the frontiers of science and technology, there is a concomitant necessity to confront and explore fully the depth and consequences of such uncertainties. Not only were the generalities relied on in this case not subject to rigorous probing in any form but when apparently substantial criticisms were brought to the Commission's attention, it simply ignored them, or brushed them aside without answer. Without a thorough exploration of the problems involved in waste disposal, including past mistakes, and a forthright assessment of the uncertainties and differences in expert opinion, this type of agency action cannot pass muster as reasoned decisionmaking.

Many procedural devices for creating a genuine dialogue on these issues were available to the agency including informal conferences between interveners and staff, document discovery, interrogatories, technical advisory committees comprised of outside experts with differing perspectives, limited cross-examination, funding independent research by interveners, detailed annotation of technical reports, surveys of existing literature, memoranda explaining methodology. We do not presume to intrude on the agency's province by dictating to it which, if any, of these devices it must adopt to flesh out the record. * * * Whatever techniques the Commission adopts, before it promulgates a rule limiting further consideration of waste disposal and reprocessing issues, it must in one way or another generate a record in which the factual issues are fully developed.

VERMONT YANKEE NUCLEAR POWER CORP. v. NATURAL RESOURCES DEFENSE COUNCIL

435 U.S. 519 (1978)

Mr. Justice REHNQUIST delivered the opinion of the Court.

* * *

[T]his much is absolutely clear. Absent constitutional constraints or extremely compelling circumstances the "administrative agencies 'should be free to fashion their own rules of procedure and to pursue methods of inquiry capable of permitting them to discharge their multitudinous duties.'" * * *

There are compelling reasons for construing [the APA] in this manner. In the first place, if courts continually review agency proceedings to determine whether the agency employed procedures which were, in the court's opinion, perfectly tailored to reach what the court perceives to be the "best" or "correct" result, judicial review would be totally unpredictable. And the agencies, operating under this vague injunction to employ the "best" procedures and facing the threat of reversal if they did not, would undoubtedly adopt full adjudicatory procedures in every instance. Not only would this totally disrupt the statutory scheme, through which Congress enacted "a formula upon which opposing social and political forces have come to rest," but all the inherent advantages of informal rulemaking would be totally lost.

Secondly, it is obvious that the court in these cases reviewed the agency's choice of procedures on the basis of the record actually produced at the hearing, and not on the basis of the information available to the agency when it made the decision to structure the proceedings in a certain way. This sort of Monday morning quarterbacking not only encourages but almost compels the agency to conduct all rulemaking proceedings with the full panoply of procedural devices normally associated only with adjudicatory hearings.

Finally, and perhaps most importantly, this sort of review fundamentally misconceives the nature of the standard for judicial review of an agency rule. The court below uncritically assumed that additional procedures will automatically result in a more adequate record because it will give interested parties more of an opportunity to participate in and contribute to the proceedings. * * * If the agency is compelled to support the rule which it ultimately adopts with the type of record produced only after a full adjudicatory hearing, it simply will have no choice but to conduct a full adjudicatory hearing prior to promulgating every rule [which will] seriously interfere with that process prescribed by Congress.

—

Once the procedural question was resolved, the focus of the *Vermont Yankee* proceedings again turned to the merits of the fuel cycle issue. Like the great majority of cases in this book, the judgments that NRC had to make were not simple facts subject to traditional judicial testing under a "more likely than not" or a credibility test. Rather, like risk assessment, they are exercises of judgment or discretion by an expert agency to which Congress has delegated the decision. Such decisions are usually reviewed under the "arbitrary and capricious" standard.

BALTIMORE GAS & ELECTRIC CO. v. NATURAL RESOURCES DEFENSE COUNCIL, INC.

462 U.S. 87 (1983)

Justice O'CONNOR delivered the opinion of the Court.

* * *

In 1979, following further hearings, the Commission adopted the "final" Table S-3 rule. Like the amended interim rule, the final rule expressly stated that Table S-3 should be supplemented in individual proceedings by evidence about the health, socioeconomic, and cumulative aspects of fuel cycle activities. The Commission also continued to adhere to the zero-release assumption that the solidified waste would not escape and harm the environment once the repository was sealed. It acknowledged that this assumption was uncertain because of the remote possibility that water might enter the repository, dissolve the radioactive materials, and transport them to the biosphere. Nevertheless, the Commission predicted that a bedded-salt repository would maintain its integrity, and found the evidence "tentative but favorable" that an appropriate site would be found. The Commission ultimately determined that any undue optimism in the assumption of appropriate selection and perfect performance of the repository is offset by the cautious assumption, reflected in other parts of the Table, that all radioactive gases in the spent fuel would escape during the initial 6 to 20 year period that the repository remained open, and thus did not significantly reduce the overall conservatism of the S-3 Table.

The Commission rejected the option of expressing the uncertainties in Table S-3 or permitting licensing boards, in performing the NEPA analysis for individual nuclear plants, to consider those uncertainties. It saw no advantage in reassessing the significance of the uncertainties in individual licensing proceedings * * *.

* * *

* * * Here, the agency has chosen to evaluate generically the environmental impact of the fuel cycle and inform individual licensing boards, through the Table S-3 rule, of its evaluation. The generic method chosen by the agency is clearly an appropriate method of conducting the hard look required by NEPA. The environmental effects of much of the fuel cycle are not plant specific, for any plant, regardless of its particular attributes, will create additional wastes that must be stored in a common long-term repository. Administrative efficiency and consistency of decision are both furthered by a generic determination of these effects without needless repetition of the litigation in individual proceedings, which are subject to review by the Commission in any event.

* * *

[A] reviewing court must remember that the Commission is making predictions, within its area of special expertise, at the frontiers of science. When examining this kind of scientific determination, as opposed to simple findings of fact, a reviewing court must generally be at its most deferential.

* * *

In sum, we think that the zero-release assumption—a policy judgment concerning one line in a conservative Table designed for the limited purpose of individual licensing decisions—is within the bounds of reasoned decisionmaking. It is not our task to determine what decision we, as Commissioners, would have reached. Our only task is to determine whether the Commission has considered the relevant factors and articulated a rational connection between the facts found and the choice made. Under this standard, we think the Commission's zero-release assumption, within the context of Table S-3 as a whole, was not arbitrary and capricious.

NOTES

1. Why did the agency choose to proceed the way it did? What was the substantive impact of the choice of procedure? Conversely, why was NRDC dissatisfied with the procedure? What would have been the value to NRDC of additional procedures?

2. *Procedural review.* The *Vermont Yankee* litigation was part of a larger strategy by environmental and anti-nuclear activists to exploit what they viewed as the Achilles' heel of nuclear power, the disposal of highly radioactive spent fuel. Clearly, NRC believed that a disposal solution would be found. In hindsight, however, NRC's critics seem to have been correct— the disposal problem has proven intractable. Twenty years after the *Vermont Yankee* litigation, NRC's original disposal plans have been abandoned in favor of storage in Yucca Mountain, Nevada, and actual use of that facility will not begin for years, if ever. In the meantime, spent nuclear fuel is stored in "temporary" facilities at power plants.[9]

---

[9] For further discussion of the impasse over spent fuel disposal, *see* DOUG EASTERLING & HOWARD KUNREUTHER, THE DILEMMA OF SITING A HIGH-LEVEL NUCLEAR WASTE REPOSITORY (1995); K.S. SHRADER-FRECHETTE, BURYING UNCERTAINTY: RISK AND THE CASE AGAINST GEOLOGICAL DISPOSAL OF NUCLEAR WASTE (1993); JAMES FLYNN *ET AL.*, ONE HUNDRED CENTURIES OF SOLITUDE: REDIRECTING AMERICA'S HIGH-LEVEL NUCLEAR WASTE POLICY

Since NRC did not have a very good answer to the waste disposal question, why did NRDC pursue a procedural remedy in the first place? The Supreme Court suggested that the procedural issue was not even a close case. Were substantive grounds for review unavailable or less effective? Why?

3. The harshness of the Supreme Court's tone in *Vermont Yankee* is often attributed to an effort to stem what it saw as a rising tide of "hybrid rulemaking," that is, judicial direction to agencies to adopt formal procedures in informal rulemaking.

While *Vermont Yankee* effectively brought judicial development of hybrid procedures to a halt, it could not (of course) affect Congressional innovation. Even before the *Vermont Yankee* decision, Congress began to provide explicitly for rulemaking procedures, usually borrowed from formal proceedings, beyond the APA's notice-and-comment minimum. Many of these hybrid statutes are represented in this book. Read, for example, section 307(d) of the Clean Air Act, 42 U.S.C. § 7607(d), and sections 4(b)(5) and 19 of TSCA, 15 U.S.C. §§ 2603(b)(5), 2618. What additional procedures do they require? Why were they added? What effect are they likely to have on agency decisionmaking.[10] Remember that the procedural provisions of the underlying substantive statute always trumps the APA, which acts as something of default procedure.

(1995); NATIONAL RESEARCH COUNCIL, TECHNICAL BASES FOR YUCCA MOUNTAIN STANDARDS (1995); NATIONAL RESEARCH COUNCIL, RETHINKING HIGH-LEVEL RADIOACTIVE WASTE DISPOSAL: A POSITION STATEMENT OF THE BOARD ON RADIOACTIVE WASTE MANAGEMENT (1990).

[10] For an example of the effect on TSCA rulemaking, *see* Corrosion Proof Fittings v. EPA, 947 F.2d 1201, 1211-13 (5th Cir. 1991), parts of which are reprinted below in Chapter 8 (TSCA).

Professors McCubbins, Noll, and Weingast have described in detail the ways in which the structuring of judicial review in a statute is a product political trade-offs among affected parties. Matthew D. McCubbins *et al., Structure and Process, Politics, and Policy: Administrative Arrangements and the Political Control of Agencies*, 75 VA. L. REV. 431 (1989).

> ### PROBLEM
>
> Why do we have judicial review in the first place? What does it add to the regulatory process? "Two broad sets of criteria bear on any evaluation of judicial review: (1) rule of law values of accuracy, consistency with statutory command, predictability, and rational basis; and (2) substantive goals such as efficiency, protection of environmental quality, or income redistribution." Robert Glicksman & Christopher H. Schroeder, *EPA and the Courts: Twenty Years of Law and Politics*, 54 L. & CONTEMP. PROBS. 249, 299 (Autumn 1991). How do these criteria apply to judicial review of the Vermont Yankee licensing decision? Using that decision as a model, what would you say are the costs and benefits of judicial review?
>
> At the end of this chapter, we encourage you to revisit the reasons for judicial review. Do you still feel that it is a good idea? Are there limitations that you would impose? Should it be expanded?

B. The Methodology of Judicial Review

The APA authorizes judicial review by broadly granting a right of review "to any adversely affected person." 5 U.S.C. § 702. With one important exception (CERCLA remedy selection), this is uniformly confirmed and even expanded in the statutes that we will study. The APA also sets out six specific grounds for judicial review. 5 U.S.C. § 706(2)(A)-(F). In all cases, the reviewing court can overturn an action that is

- unconstitutional
- contrary to statute
- procedurally flawed, or
- "arbitrary, capricious, an abuse of discretion, or otherwise not in accordance with law."

Formal actions are reviewable, in addition, under the stricter "substantial evidence" standard. In rare cases, *de novo* review is required, but usually on the record developed by the agency itself.

This section describes the way that courts go about their business of reviewing agency decisions. We first examine the standard of review of decisions that are based primarily on an agency's factual or policy judgments. We then turn to agencies' interpretation of the statute under which it is operating.

CITIZENS TO PRESERVE OVERTON PARK V. VOLPE

401 U.S. 402 (1971)

Opinion of the Court by Mr. Justice MARSHALL, announced by Mr. Justice STEWART.

The growing public concern about the quality of our natural environment has prompted Congress in recent years to enact legislation designed to curb the accelerating destruction of our country's natural beauty. We are concerned in this case with § 4(f) of the Department of Transportation Act of 1966, as amended, and § 18(a) of the Federal-Aid Highway Act of 1968. These statutes prohibit the Secretary of Transportation from authorizing the use of federal funds to finance the construction of highways through public parks if a "feasible and prudent" alternative route exists. If no such route is available, the statutes allow him to approve construction through parks only if there has been "all possible planning to minimize harm" to the park.

Petitioners, private citizens as well as local and national conservation organizations, contend that the Secretary has violated these statutes by authorizing the expenditure of federal funds for the construction of a six-lane interstate highway through a public park in Memphis, Tennessee. * * *

Overton Park is a 342-acre city park located near the center of Memphis. The park contains a zoo, a nine-hole municipal golf course, an outdoor theater,[11] nature trails, a bridle path, an art academy, picnic areas, and 170 acres of forest. The proposed highway, which is to be a six lane, high-speed, expressway, will sever the zoo from the rest of the park. Although the roadway will be depressed below ground level except where it crosses a small creek, 26 acres of the park will be destroyed. The highway is to be a segment of Interstate Highway I-40, part of the National System of Interstate and Defense Highways. I-40 will provide Memphis with a major east-west expressway which will allow easier access to downtown Memphis from the residential areas on the eastern edge of the city.

---

[11] It is reported that Elvis Presley auditioned his trademark hips on July 30, 1954, at the Overton Park band shell. *See* VINCE STATEN, UNAUTHORIZED AMERICA: A TRAVEL GUIDE TO THE PLACES THE CHAMBER OF COMMERCE WON'T TELL YOU ABOUT 58 (1990)—EDS.

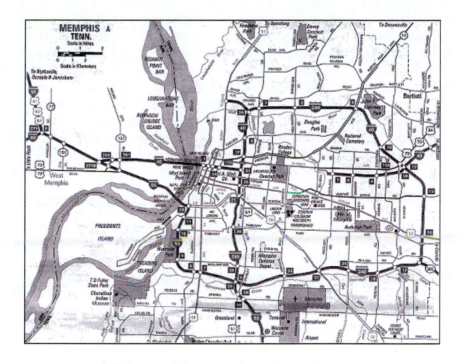

Figure 4.1–Map of Memphis, Tennessee[12]

Although the route through the park was approved by the Bureau of Public Roads in 1956 and by the Federal Highway Administrator in 1966, the enactment of § 4(f) of the Department of Transportation Act prevented distribution of federal funds for the section of the highway designated to go through Overton Park[13] until the Secretary of Transportation determined whether the requirements of § 4(f) had been met. * * * Final approval for the project–the route as well as the design–was not announced until November 1969, after Congress had reiterated in § 138 of the Federal-Aid Highway Act that highway construction through public parks was to be restricted. Neither announcement approving the route and design of I-40 was accompanied by a statement of the Secretary's factual findings. He did not indicate why he believed there were no feasible and prudent alternative routes or why design changes could not be made to reduce the harm to the park.

* * *

A threshold question–whether petitioners are entitled to any judicial review–is easily answered. Section 701 of the Administrative Procedure Act, 5 U.S.C. § 701, provides that the action of "each authority of the Government of the United States," which includes the Department of Transportation, is subject to judicial review except where there is a statutory prohibition on

---

[12]Source: American Automobile Assoc.

[13] The highway map of Memphis shows the otherwise inexplicable gap in I-40 where the Overton Park segment would have gone.–EDS.

review or where "agency action is committed to agency discretion by law." In this case, there is no indication that Congress sought to prohibit judicial review and there is most certainly no "showing of 'clear and convincing evidence' of a . . . legislative intent" to restrict access to judicial review. *Abbott Laboratories v. Gardner*, 387 U.S. 136, 141.

Similarly, the Secretary's decision here does not fall within the exception for action "committed to agency discretion." This is a very narrow exception. The legislative history of the Administrative Procedure Act indicates that it is applicable in those rare instances where "statutes are drawn in such broad terms that in a given case there is no law to apply." S.REP. NO. 752, 79TH CONG., 1ST SESS., 26 (1945).

Section 4(f) of the Department of Transportation Act and § 138 of the Federal-Aid Highway Act are clear and specific directives. Both the Department of Transportation Act and the Federal-Aid to Highway Act provide that the Secretary "shall not approve any program or project" that requires the use of any public parkland "unless (1) there is no feasible and prudent alternative to the use of such land, and (2) such program includes all possible planning to minimize harm to such park . . . ." This language is a plain and explicit bar to the use of federal funds for construction of highways through parks—only the most unusual situations are exempted.

Despite the clarity of the statutory language, respondents argue that the Secretary has wide discretion. They recognize that the requirement that there be no "feasible" alternative route admits of little administrative discretion. For this exemption to apply the Secretary must find that as a matter of sound engineering it would not be feasible to build the highway along any other route. Respondents argue, however, that the requirement that there be no other "prudent" route requires the Secretary to engage in a wide-ranging balancing of competing interests. They contend that the Secretary should weigh the detriment resulting from the destruction of parkland against the cost of other routes, safety considerations, and other factors, and determine on the basis of the importance that he attaches to these other factors whether, on balance, alternative feasible routes would be "prudent."

But no such wide-ranging endeavor was intended. It is obvious that in most cases considerations of cost, directness of route, and community disruption will indicate that parkland should be used for highway construction whenever possible. Although it may be necessary to transfer funds from one jurisdiction to another, there will always be a smaller outlay required from the public purse when parkland is used since the public already owns the land and there will be no need to pay for right-of-way. And since people do not live or work in parks, if a highway is built on parkland no one will have to leave his home or give up his business. Such factors are common to substantially all highway construction. Thus, if Congress intended these factors to be on an equal footing with preservation of parkland there would have been no need for the statutes.

Congress clearly did not intend that cost and disruption of the community were to be ignored by the Secretary. But the very existence of the statutes indicates that protection of parkland was to be given paramount importance. The few green havens that are public parks were not to be lost unless there were truly unusual factors present in a particular case or the cost or community disruption resulting from alternative routes reached extraordinary magnitudes. If the statutes are to have any meaning, the Secretary cannot approve the destruction of parkland unless he finds that alternative routes present unique problems.

Plainly, there is "law to apply" and thus the exemption for action "committed to agency discretion" is inapplicable. But the existence of judicial review is only the start: the standard for review must also be determined. For that we must look to § 706 of the Administrative Procedure Act, which provides that a "reviewing court shall . . . hold unlawful and set aside agency action, findings, and conclusions found" not to meet six separate standards. In all cases agency action must be set aside if the action was "arbitrary and capricious, an abuse of discretion, or otherwise not in accordance with law" or if the action failed to meet statutory, procedural, or constitutional requirements. 5 U.S.C. §§ 706(2)(A),(B),(C),(D). In certain narrow, specifically limited situations, the agency action is to be set aside if the action was not supported by "substantial evidence." And in other equally narrow circumstances the reviewing court is to engage in a *de novo* review of the action and set it aside if it was "unwarranted by the facts." 5 U.S.C. §§ 706(2)(E),(F).

Petitioners argue that the Secretary's approval of the construction of I-40 through Overton Park is subject to one or the other of these latter two standards of limited applicability. First, they contend that the "substantial evidence" standard of § 706(2)(E) must be applied. In the alternative, they claim that § 706(2)(F) applies and that there must be a *de novo* review to determine if the Secretary's action was "unwarranted by the facts." Neither of these standards is, however, applicable.

Review under the substantial-evidence test is authorized only when the agency action is taken pursuant to a rulemaking provision of the Administrative Procedure Act itself, 5 U.S.C. § 553, or when the agency action is based on a public adjudicatory hearing. *See* 5 U.S.C. §§ 556, 557. The Secretary's decision to allow the expenditure of federal funds to build I-40 through Overton Park was plainly not an exercise of a rulemaking function. And the only hearing that is required by either the Administrative Procedure Act or the statutes regulating the distribution of federal funds for highway construction is a public hearing conducted by local officials for the purpose of informing the community about the proposed project and eliciting community views on the design and route. 23 U.S.C. § 128. The hearing is nonadjudicatory, quasi-legislative in nature. It is not designed to produce a record that is to be the basis of agency action—the basic requirement for substantial-evidence review.

Petitioners' alternative argument also fails. *De novo* review of whether the Secretary's decision was "unwarranted by the facts" is authorized by § 706(2)(F) in only two circumstances. First, such *de novo* review is authorized when the action is adjudicatory in nature and the agency fact-finding procedures are inadequate. And, there may be independent judicial fact-finding when issues that were not before the agency are raised in a proceeding to enforce nonadjudicatory agency action. Neither situation exists here.

Even though there is no *de novo* review in this case and the Secretary's approval of the route of I-40 does not have ultimately to meet the substantial-evidence test, the generally applicable standards of § 706 require the reviewing court to engage in a substantial inquiry. Certainly, the Secretary's decision is entitled to a presumption of regularity. But that presumption is not to shield his action from a thorough, probing, in-depth review.

The court is first required to decide whether the Secretary acted within the scope of his authority. This determination naturally begins with a delineation of the scope of the Secretary's authority and discretion. As has been shown, Congress has specified only a small range of choices that the Secretary can make. Also involved in this initial inquiry is a determination of whether on the facts the Secretary's decision can reasonably be said to be within that range. The reviewing court must consider whether the Secretary properly construed his authority to approve the use of parkland as limited to situations where there are no feasible alternative routes or where feasible alternative routes involve uniquely difficult problems. And the reviewing court must be able to find that the Secretary could have reasonably believed that in this case there are no feasible alternatives or that alternatives do involve unique problems.

Scrutiny of the facts does not end, however, with the determination that the Secretary has acted within the scope of his statutory authority. Section 706(2)(A) requires a finding that the actual choice made was not "arbitrary and capricious, an abuse of discretion, or otherwise not in accordance with law." To make this finding the court must consider whether the decision was based on a consideration of the relevant factors and whether there has been a clear error of judgment. Although this inquiry into the facts is to be searching and careful, the ultimate standard of review is a narrow one. The court is not empowered to substitute its judgment for that of the agency.

The final inquiry is whether the Secretary's action followed the necessary procedural requirements. Here the only procedural error alleged is the failure of the Secretary to make formal findings and state his reason for allowing the highway to be built through the park.

Undoubtedly, review of the Secretary's action is hampered by his failure to make such findings, but the absence of formal findings does not necessarily require that the case be remanded to the Secretary. Neither the Department of Transportation Act nor the Federal-Aid Highway Act requires such formal findings. Moreover, the Administrative Procedure Act requirements that there be formal findings in certain rulemaking and adjudicatory proceedings do not apply to the Secretary's action here. And, although formal findings may be required in some cases in the absence of statutory directives when the nature of the agency action is ambiguous, those situations are rare. Plainly, there is no ambiguity here; the Secretary has approved the construction of I-40 through Overton Park and has approved a specific design for the project.

* * *

* * * Moreover, there is an administrative record that allows the full, prompt review of the Secretary's action that is sought without additional delay which would result from having a remand to the Secretary.

That administrative record is not, however, before us. The lower courts based their review on the litigation affidavits that were presented. These affidavits were merely 'post hoc' rationalizations, which have traditionally been found to be an inadequate basis for review. And they clearly do not constitute the "whole record" compiled by the agency: the basis for review required by § 706 of the Administrative Procedure Act.

Thus it is necessary to remand this case to the District Court for plenary review of the Secretary's decision. That review is to be based on the full administrative record that was before the Secretary at the time he made his decision. But since the bare record may not disclose the factors that were considered or the Secretary's construction of the evidence it may be necessary for the District Court to require some explanation in order to determine if the Secretary acted within the scope of his authority and if the Secretary's action was justifiable under the applicable standard.

* * *

* * * It may be that the Secretary can prepare formal findings including the information required by DOT Order 5610.1 that will provide an adequate explanation for his action. Such an explanation will, to some extent, be a "post hoc rationalization" and thus must be viewed critically. If the District Court decides that additional explanation is necessary, that court should consider which method will prove the most expeditious so that full review may be had as soon as possible.

Reversed and remanded.

NOTES

1. *Overton Park* is the classic description of "arbitrary and capricious" review. Beyond that, it establishes a framework for all aspects of judicial review. What are the analytical steps that the Court follows?

2. *The record on review.* What evidence was before the Court concerning the Secretary's reasoning? The Court clearly believes that more is available—what materials might it have in mind?

What type of administrative action was before the Court in *Overton Park*? How do the Court's instructions to the district court and agency compare with the requirements of the APA?[14] Does *Vermont Yankee* overrule this aspect of *Overton Park*?

3. You will recall from civil procedure that courts review lower tribunals' determinations on questions of law and fact quite differently. Traditionally, a lower court's determinations of fact are given considerable deference (they are overturned only if "clearly erroneous"), while questions of law are decided by the appellate court *de novo*. Much the same arrangement operates in judicial review of agency action. Formal factual determinations are to be upheld if supported by "substantial evidence," *see, e.g., Universal Camera Corp. v. N.L.R.B.*, 340 U.S. 474 (1951), whereas questions of law are for the court. *E.g., N.L.R.B. v. Hearst Publications, Inc.*, 322 U.S. 111 (1944). How should the Secretary's decision to approve the Overton Park segment of I-40 be characterized? Is it a factual determination? Is it a question of law? Or is it some *tertium quid*—exercise of discretion? If so, how does exercise of discretion differ from law and fact? How does the *Overton Park* analysis handle an agency's judgment on the merits?

4. To learn more about the political and legal setting of *Overton Park*, you should read Professor Strauss' fascinating study of the background of the case. *See* Peter L. Strauss, *Revisiting Overton Park: Political and Judicial Controls Over Administrative Actions Affecting the Community*, 39 UCLA L. REV. 1251 (1992).

—

In addition to the mechanical elements of the *Overton Park* method for reviewing discretion, there is the more subtle, less objective question of rigor. Consider the tone or "mood" of the review in *Baltimore Gas* and *Overton Park*: the Court is quite uncritical of the agency's reasoning in the former, and demanding in its review in the latter. In fact, Justice Marshall's description of arbitrary and capricious standard of review in *Overton Park* lends itself not only to the *Baltimore Gas* approach, but also to a far more rigorous mode of judicial review. This came to be known as "hard look" review from Judge Harold Leventhal's idea that the courts must assure themselves that the agency has taken a "hard look" at the facts and alternatives in reaching its conclusion.[15] We saw this approach echoed in the original *Vermont Yankee* opinion.

The nature, feasibility, and propriety of in-depth scrutiny by the courts was most famously debated in the several opinions in *Ethyl Corp. v. EPA*, 541 F.2d 1 (D.C. Cir.), *cert. denied*, 426 U.S. 941 (1976), in which EPA's rule phasing out lead in gasoline was challenged. The court's majority stated:

> There is no inconsistency between the deferential standard of review and the requirement that the reviewing court involve itself in

---

[14] See William F. Pedersen, Jr., *Formal Records and Informal Rulemaking*, 85 YALE L.J. 38, 60 (1975).

[15] Harold Leventhal, *Environmental Decisionmaking and the Role of the Courts*, 122 U. PA. L. REV. 509, 511 (1974).

even the most complex evidentiary matters; rather, the two indicia of arbitrary and capricious review stand in careful balance. The close scrutiny of the evidence is intended to educate the court. It must understand enough about the problem confronting the agency to comprehend the meaning of the evidence relied upon and the evidence discarded; the questions addressed by the agency and those bypassed; the choices open to the agency and those made. The more technical the case, the more intensive must be the court's effort to understand the evidence, for without an appropriate understanding of the case before it the court cannot properly perform its appellate function. But that function must be performed with conscientious awareness of its limited nature. The enforced education into the intricacies of the problem before the agency is not designed to enable the court to become a superagency that can supplant the agency's expert decision-maker. To the contrary, the court must give due deference to the agency's ability to rely on its own developed expertise. The immersion in the evidence is designed solely to enable the court to determine whether the agency decision was rational and based on consideration of the relevant factors. It is settled that we must affirm decisions with which we disagree so long as this test is met.

Ethyl, 541 F.2d at 36.[16]

The Supreme Court's acceptance of hard look review remained unclear for a long time. In *Motor Vehicle Manufacturers Association v. State Farm Mutual Automobile Insurance Co.*, 463 U.S. 29 (1983), however, the Court gave tacit approval to hard look review by itself undertaking a highly critical review of NHTSA's on-again, off-again passive restraint rules for cars. Delays and reversals of position had characterized the regulatory process throughout, and the deregulatory Reagan administration, egged on by a financially strapped auto industry, proposed simply to rescind existing passive restraint requirements. The Court reversed, unanimously on two of the three issues presented. The Court examined in detail the evidence presented to the agency and the factors it considered. Note in particular how the court utilizes both the "relevant factors" and "error of judgment" prongs of *Overton Park*:

> [T]he agency has relied on factors which Congress has not intended it to consider, entirely failed to consider an important aspect

---

[16] Judges Leventhal and David Bazelon wrote concurring opinions which are worth reading in their entirety. Bazelon argued that generalist courts should limit their review to procedural questions upon which they could claim some expertise. (This approach was rendered considerably less viable by *Vermont Yankee*, of course.) Judge Leventhal expanded on the majority's view, declaring, "The substantive review of administrative action is modest, but it cannot be carried out in a vacuum of understanding. Better no judicial review at all than a charade that gives the imprimatur without the substance of judicial confirmation that the agency is not acting unreasonably." *See also* International Harvester Co. v. Ruckelshaus, 478 F.2d 615 (D.C. Cir. 1973).

of the problem, offered an explanation for its decision that runs counter to the evidence before the agency, or is so implausible that it could not be ascribed to a difference in view or the product of agency expertise. * * *

* * *

The automobile industry has opted for the passive belt over the airbag, but surely it is not enough that the regulated industry has eschewed a given device. For nearly a decade, the automobile industry waged the regulatory equivalent of war against the airbag and lost—the inflatable restraint was proven sufficiently effective. Now the automobile industry has decided to employ a seatbelt system which will not meet the safety objectives of Standard 208. This hardly constitutes cause to revoke the standard itself. Indeed, the Motor Vehicle Safety Act was necessary because the industry was not sufficiently responsive to safety concerns. The Act intended that safety standards not depend on current technology and could be "technology-forcing" in the sense of inducing the development of superior safety design. If, under the statute, the agency should not defer to the industry's failure to develop safer cars, which it surely should not do, a fortiori it may not revoke a safety standard which can be satisfied by current technology simply because the industry has opted for an ineffective seatbelt design.

463 U.S. at 43, 49. This approach would clearly take a dim view of NRC's reliance on Dr. Pittman's conclusory testimony in *Vermont Yankee*.[17] And yet *State Farm* and *Baltimore Gas* were decided in the same year! What does that tell you about the use of hard look review?

Sometimes courts have said that hard look review is triggered by certain "danger signs." These include sudden changes or complete reversals of existing policy,[18] lack of consistency,[19] failure to consider significant alternatives,[20] or the use of improper methodology, or failure to conduct necessary tests.[21] Several of these criticisms can be found in *State Farm*, and they may go some way toward explaining the Supreme Court's apparent embrace of hard look in that case.

It was noted above that, despite *Vermont Yankee*, much hybrid rulemaking is practiced because Congress requires it by statute. Statutory hybridization often includes, in addition to extra procedural steps, the requirement that informal rulemaking be reviewed on a "substantial evidence" basis. Substantial evidence was originally designed for the review of formal

---

[17] In fact, NRC questioned Pittman in detail about his testimony, but the D.C. Circuit apparently did not regard this fact as altering the summary character of the evidence.

[18] Greater Boston Television Corp. v. FTC, 444 F.2d 841 (D.C. Cir. 1973).

[19] Catholic Medical Center v. NLRB, 589 F.2d 1166 (2d Cir. 1978).

[20] National Citizens Committee for Broadcasting v. FCC, 567 F.2d 1095 (D.C. Cir. 1977).

[21] South Terminal Corp. v. EPA, 504 F.2d 2401 (2d Cir. 1974); U.S. v. Nova Scotia Food Products Corp., 568 F.2d 2401 (2d Cir. 1977).

agency action on the basis of a closed record. A closed record and weighing of the evidence seems natural for traditional factual questions (*e.g.,* how many snail darters live below the Tellico Dam?), but not for the uncertainty, prediction, and policy (*e.g.*, whether lead "endangers" human health) that is typically the basis of informal rulemaking.

Originally, the use of substantial evidence was simply a legislative compromise between formal and informal proceedings, intended mainly to gain support for substantively wide-ranging social legislation.[22] However, it also signaled a congressional desire for a more critical standard of judicial review. The precise difference in degree of scrutiny between the substantial evidence and arbitrary and capricious standards may be nonexistent, as Justice Scalia has argued.[23] Nevertheless, substantial evidence retains a "vague reputation as the more demanding" standard[24]—in Frankfurter's words, a more critical "mood"[25]—and courts consistently treat it as such. Justice Marshall observed in his dissent in *Industrial Union Dep't, AFL-CIO v. American Petroleum Institute*:

> This standard represents a legislative judgment that regulatory action should be subject to review more stringent than the traditional "arbitrary and capricious" standard for informal rulemaking. We have observed that the arbitrary and capricious standard itself contemplates a searching [review]. * * * Careful performance of this task is especially important when Congress has imposed the comparatively more rigorous "substantial evidence" requirement. * * *

448 U.S. 607, 705 (1980). In TSCA, for example, the legislative history is clear that this is what Congress intended[26] and reviewing courts have obliged with stringent review of TSCA regulations.[27]

---

[22] *See* Industrial Union Dep't, AFL-CIO v. Hodgson, 499 F.2d 467, 473-76 (D.C. Cir. 1974); Associated Industries v. Dep't of Labor, 487 F.2d 342 (2d Cir. 1973) (Friendly, J.); Amoco Oil Co. v. EPA, 501 F.2d 722, 742 (D.C. Cir. 1974).

[23] Scalia and Goodman have argued persuasively that there ought to be no difference in degree of scrutiny and that the main difference between them should be reliance on an exclusive record. Antonin Scalia & Frank Goodman, *Procedural Aspects of the Consumer Product Safety* Act, 20 UCLA L. REV. 899, 933-36 (1973); *see also* Assoc. of Data Processing Serv. Organizations v. Board of Governors of the Federal Reserve System, 745 F.2d 677, 683-86 (D.C. Cir. 1984) (*per* Scalia, J.); Note, *Convergence of the Substantial Evidence and Arbitrary and Capricious Standards of Review During Informal Rulemaking*, 54 GEO. WASH. L. REV. 541 (1986).

[24] Scalia & Goodman, *supra*, at 934.

[25] Universal Camera Corp. v. NLRB, 240 U.S. 474, 487 (1951).

[26] H.R. REP. NO. 1341, 94th CONG. 2D SESS. 56 ("searching review").

[27] *See* Shell Chemical Co. v. EPA, 826 F.2d 295, 297-98 (5th Cir. 1987); Ausimont U.S.A., Inc. v. EPA, 838 F.2d 93, 96 (3d Cir. 1988); Chemical Mfrs. Ass'n v. EPA, 859 F.2d 977, 991 (D.C. Cir. 1988); Corrosion Proof Fittings v. EPA, 947 F.2d 1201, 1213-14 (5th Cir. 1991).

"Substantial" does not mean conclusive, however. "A reasonable person could draw from this evidence the conclusion that exposure to EtO presents a risk of cancer. Thus, the

---

PROBLEM

In 1989, OSHA issued its "lockout/tagout" safety standard, which required that machines under repair be locked or, if locking was infeasible, tagged, to prevent the nearly 150 deaths per year that are caused by workers inadvertently starting machines while others are repairing them. The cost of such precautions is relatively small—extremely small when one considers the benefits in lives saved and lost work time avoided. Nevertheless, in 1991 the D.C. Circuit remanded the lockout/tagout standard because it had failed to perform a required cost-benefit analysis. *International Union, UAW v. OSHA*, 938 F.2d 1310 (D.C. Cir. 1991). In the course of the discussion, the panel complained that the existing cost-benefit analysis was inadequate because it had not broken down costs and benefits on an industry-by-industry basis. Given the possibility that the costs and benefits differed significantly among industries, the court said, it could not evaluate whether the cost-benefit standard had been met on the basis of aggregated data. *Id.* at 1322-24. Is this an appropriate exercise of hard look review? Why or why not? Even if you do not like the result, how is it different from other instances of hard look review? Isn't it merely "judicial confirmation that the agency is not acting unreasonably," as Judge Leventhal said?

CHEVRON, U.S.A., INC., v. NATURAL RESOURCES DEFENSE COUNCIL

467 U.S. 837 (1984)

Justice STEVENS delivered the opinion of the Court.

In the Clean Air Act Amendments of 1977, Congress enacted certain requirements applicable to States that had not achieved the national air quality standards established by the Environmental Protection Agency (EPA) pursuant to earlier legislation. The amended Clean Air Act required these "nonattainment" States to establish a permit program regulating "new or modified major stationary sources" of air pollution. Generally, a permit may not be issued for a new or modified major stationary source unless several stringent conditions are met. The EPA regulation promulgated to implement this permit requirement allows a State to adopt a plantwide definition of the term "stationary source."[28] Under this definition, an existing plant that

---

substantial evidence test is met[, e]ven if a reasonable person could also draw the opposite conclusion. . . . ." Public Citizen Health Research Group v. Tyson, 796 F.2d 1479, 1489 (D.C. Cir. 1986).

[28] "(i) "Stationary source" means any buildings, structures, facility, or installation which emits or may emit any air pollutant subject to regulation under the Act." (ii) "Building, structure, facility, or installation" means all of the pollutant-emitting activities which belong to the same industrial grouping, are located on one or more contiguous or adjacent properties, and are

contains several pollution-emitting devices may install or modify one piece of equipment without meeting the permit conditions if the alteration will not increase the total emissions from the plant. The question presented by these cases is whether EPA's decision to allow States to treat all of the pollution-emitting devices within the same industrial grouping as though they were encased within a single "bubble" is based on a reasonable construction of the statutory term "stationary source."

* * *

II

When a court reviews an agency's construction of the statute which it administers, it is confronted with two questions. First, always, is the question whether Congress has directly spoken to the precise question at issue. If the intent of Congress is clear, that is the end of the matter; for the court, as well as the agency, must give effect to the unambiguously expressed intent of Congress.[29] If, however, the court determines Congress has not directly addressed the precise question at issue, the court does not simply impose its own construction on the statute, as would be necessary in the absence of an administrative interpretation. Rather, if the statute is silent or ambiguous with respect to the specific issue, the question for the court is whether the agency's answer is based on a permissible construction of the statute.[30]

"The power of an administrative agency to administer a congressionally created . . . program necessarily requires the formulation of policy and the making of rules to fill any gap left, implicitly or explicitly, by Congress." *Morton v. Ruiz*, 415 U.S. 199, 231 (1974). If Congress has explicitly left a gap for the agency to fill, there is an express delegation of authority to the agency to elucidate a specific provision of the statute by regulation. Such legislative regulations are given controlling weight unless they are arbitrary and capricious, or manifestly contrary to the statute. Sometimes the legislative delegation to an agency on a particular question is implicit rather than explicit. In such a case, a court may not substitute its own construction of a statutory provision for a reasonable interpretation made by the administrator of an agency.

* * *

In light of these well-settled principles it is clear that the Court of Appeals misconceived the nature of its role in reviewing the regulations at issue. Once it determined, after its own examination of the legislation, that Congress did

---

under the control of the same person (or persons under common control) except the activities of any vessel" 40 CFR §§ 51.18(j)(l)(i) and (ii) (1983).

[29] The judiciary is the final authority on issues of statutory construction and must reject administrative constructions which are contrary to clear congressional intent. If a court, employing traditional tools of statutory construction, ascertains that Congress had an intention on the precise question at issue, that intention is the law and must be given effect.

[30] The court need not conclude that the agency construction was the only one it permissibly could have adopted to uphold the construction, or even the reading the court would have reached if the question initially had arisen in a judicial proceeding.

not actually have an intent regarding the applicability of the bubble concept to the permit program, the question before it was not whether in its view the concept is "inappropriate" in the general context of a program designed to improve air quality, but whether the Administrator's view that it is appropriate in the context of this particular program is a reasonable one. Based on the examination of the legislation and its history which follows, we agree with the Court of Appeals that Congress did not have a specific intention on the applicability of the bubble concept in these cases, and conclude that the EPA's use of that concept here is a reasonable policy choice for the agency to make.

* * *

Statutory Language

* * *

We are not persuaded that parsing of general terms in the text of the statute will reveal an actual intent of Congress. We know full well that this language is not dispositive; the terms are overlapping and the language is not precisely directed to the question of the applicability of a given term in the context of a larger operation. To the extent any congressional "intent" can be discerned from this language, it would appear that the listing of overlapping, illustrative terms was intended to enlarge, rather than to confine, the scope of the agency's power to regulate particular sources in order to effectuate the policies of the Act.

Legislative History

In addition, respondents argue that the legislative history and policies of the Act foreclose the plantwide definition, and that the EPA's interpretation is not entitled to deference because it represents a sharp break with prior interpretations of the Act.

Based on our examination of the legislative history, we agree with the Court of Appeals that it is unilluminating. * * *

* * *

Policy

The arguments over policy that are advanced in the parties' briefs create the impression that respondents are now waging in a judicial forum a specific policy battle which they ultimately lost in the agency and in the 32 jurisdictions opting for the "bubble concept," but one which was never waged in the Congress. Such policy arguments are more properly addressed to legislators or administrators, not to judges.

In these cases, the Administrator's interpretation represents a reasonable accommodation of manifestly competing interests and is entitled to deference: the regulatory scheme is technical and complex, the agency considered the matter in a detailed and reasoned fashion, and the decision involves reconciling conflicting policies. Congress intended to accommodate both interests, but did not do so itself on the level of specificity presented by these cases. Perhaps that body consciously desired the Administrator to strike the balance at this level, thinking that those with great expertise and charged with responsibility for administering the provision would be in a better position to do so; perhaps it simply did not consider the question at this level; and perhaps Congress was unable to forge a coalition on either side of the question, and those on each side decided to take their chances with the scheme devised by the agency. For judicial purposes, it matters not which of these things occurred.

Judges are not experts in the field, and are not part of either political branch of the Government. Courts must, in some cases, reconcile competing political interests, but not on the basis of the judges' personal policy preferences. In contrast, an agency to which Congress has delegated policy-making responsibilities may, within the limits of that delegation, properly rely upon the incumbent administration's views of wise policy to inform its judgments. While agencies are not directly accountable to the people, the Chief Executive is, and it is entirely appropriate for this political branch of the Government to make such policy choices—resolving the competing interests which Congress itself either inadvertently did not resolve, or intentionally left to be resolved by the agency charged with the administration of the statute in light of everyday realities.

When a challenge to an agency construction of a statutory provision, fairly conceptualized, really centers on the wisdom of the agency's policy, rather than whether it is a reasonable choice within a gap left open by Congress, the challenge must fail. In such a case, federal judges—who have no constituency—have a duty to respect legitimate policy choices made by those who do. The responsibilities for assessing the wisdom of such policy choices and resolving the struggle between competing views of the public interest are not judicial ones: "Our Constitution vests such responsibilities in the political branches." *TVA v. Hill*, 437 U.S. 153, 195 (1978).

We hold that the EPA's definition of the term "source" is a permissible construction of the statute which seeks to accommodate progress in reducing air pollution with economic growth. "The Regulations which the Administrator has adopted provide what the agency could allowably view as . . . [an] effective reconciliation of these twofold ends . . . ."

The judgment of the Court of Appeals is reversed.

NOTES

1. *The Chevron two-step.* What, precisely, is the question posed to the Court in *Chevron*? Would you characterize it as factual, legal, or exercise of discretion? Where does the question fit into the *Overton Park* framework?

How does *Chevron* instruct courts to analyze the "bubble" question? What evidence should the court use to resolve the first part of the analysis? The second?

2. Statutory questions would seem to present little question of deferring to agency judgment; after all, no less an authority than Chief Justice Marshall declared that it is "emphatically the province and duty of the judicial

department to say what the law is." *Marbury v. Madison*, 1 Cranch 137 (1803). Is the *Chevron* approach an abdication of judicial responsibility? How does the Court justify its approach?

3. *Chevron's impact.* The *Chevron* analysis has proven difficult to follow. Cases are legion in which the litigants dispute, and the reviewing court splits on, the identity of the "precise question," whether there is ambiguity in the statute, whether legislative history may be used to clarify ambiguity, and whether the agency's interpretation is "reasonable" or whether a "plausible" interpretation is good enough.[31] Nevertheless, the *Chevron* case and its progeny have profoundly altered the role of the courts in reviewing agency action. The net effect has been to broaden substantially the area in which the agency can exercise its discretion, and to transfer power from the courts and Congress to the executive branch (how?).[32] For reviews of *Chevron's* impact, *see* Theodore L. Garrett, *Judicial Review after* Chevron*: The Courts Reassert Their Role*, 10 NAT. RESOURCES & ENVT. 59 (Fall 1995); Mark Seidenfeld, *A Syncopated* Chevron*: Emphasizing Reasoned Decisionmaking in Reviewing Agency Interpretation of Statutes*, 73 TEX. L. REV. 83 (1994). Deference to agency judgment is usually thought to be "good" for environmentalist positions, but this assumption is challenged in Richard J. Lazarus & Claudia M. Newman, *City of Chicago v. Environmental Defense Fund: Searching for Plain Meaning in Unambiguous Ambiguity*, 4 N.Y.U. ENVTL. L.J. 1 (1995). They argue that the sweeping language of many environmental statutes is more environment-friendly than agency interpretations.

C. Asbestos: A Case Study of Judicial Deference to Administrative Judgment

The ambivalence that characterized *Overton Park's* description of the arbitrary and capricious scope of review ("searching and careful" yet "narrow") persists. Reviewing courts have precedents available to them for either extremely deferential or extremely searching review. As we saw, the Supreme Court employed "hard look" review in *State Farm* in the same year that nuclear waste disposal received a "soft glance" in *Baltimore Gas*. In some cases, the underlying statute will suggest a "mood," but the application of the scope of review remains a case-by-case matter, largely beyond general prescription.

---

[31] *Compare, e.g.,* Rust v. Sullivan, 500 U.S. 173 (1991) (upholding interpretation of abortion funding statute), *with* Aramco v. EEOC, 449 U.S. 244 (1991) (reversing agency interpretation of Civil Rights Act). *See* Donald W. Stever *et al.*, *The Supreme Court, EPA, and Chevron: The Uncertain Status of Deference to Agency Interpretation of Statutes*, 25 E.L.R. 10127 (1995) (concluding that the degree of deference to agency judgment is largely settled, but that the decision when to invoke *Chevron* is not).

[32] *See* Glicksman & Schroeder, *supra*

The degree of judicial scrutiny that an agency can expect profoundly affects its willingness to act and, of course, its success. This case study examines three principal decisions reflecting three judicial approaches to agency decisions based on uncertain science:

> They are confrontation, avoidance, and deference. We use the term *confrontation* nonpejoratively to refer to situations in which the courts * * * face scientific questions directly and purport to resolve them on their merits. * * * *Avoidance* is usually assumed either by reformulating a dispute so that a scientifically uncertain question is no longer posed or by resolving the dispute on some other ground. The third stance is *deference* to another authoritative decisionmaker, such as a regulatory agency.

Kenneth S. Abraham & Richard A. Merrill, *Scientific Uncertainty and the Courts*, ISSUES IN SCI. & TECH. 93, 94 (Winter 1986). In comparing the three decisions, note that they differ both in the asserted legal grounds for review and in the degree to which the respective courts are critical of the agency's reasoning. To aid in comparison, most of the materials involve the regulation of asbestos, a known human carcinogen.[33] (The subject of the remaining materials, benzene, is also a known carcinogen.) To the extent, therefore, that asbestos regulations can be successfully challenged in court, toxics whose properties are less well understood will be all the more vulnerable to judicial rejection.

The landmark *Reserve Mining* case was the first major judicial encounter with the problem of toxic risk. Moreover, the case marks the point at which the pollution paradigm of environmental law (dumping asbestos-bearing mining waste into Lake Superior) merged into the toxics paradigm (asbestos as a threat to human health). On the night of May 20, 1973, an EPA toxicologist dreamt that asbestos fibers from Reserve Mining's tailings would find their way into the drinking water of Duluth, Minnesota, which used Lake Superior for this purpose. THOMAS F. BASTOW, "THIS VAST POLLUTION": *UNITED STATES OF AMERICA v. RESERVE MINING CO.* 96-100 (1986). As the following case relates, the dream was true.

RESERVE MINING CO. v. EPA

514 F.2d 492 (8th Cir. 1975) (*en banc*)

BRIGHT, Circuit Judge.

The United States, the States of Michigan, Wisconsin, and Minnesota, and several environmental groups seek an injunction ordering Reserve Mining Company to cease discharging wastes from its iron ore processing plant in Silver Bay, Minnesota, into the ambient air of Silver Bay and the

---

[33] Not surprisingly, virtually all of the agencies and statutes that we will study have regulated it. *See* Corrosion Proof Fittings v. EPA, 947 F.2d 1201, 1201 n.1 (5th Cir. 1991).

waters of Lake Superior. [The plaintiffs alleged violations of, *inter alia*, the pre-1972 Federal Water Pollution Control Act (FWPCA).] * * *

* * *

In 1947, Reserve Mining Company (Reserve), then contemplating a venture in which it would mine low-grade iron ore ("taconite") present in Minnesota's Mesabi Iron Range and process the ore into iron-rich pellets at facilities bordering on Lake Superior, received a permit from the State of Minnesota to discharge the wastes (called "tailings") from its processing operations into the lake.

Reserve commenced the processing of taconite ore in Silver Bay, Minnesota, in 1955, and that operation continues today. Taconite mined near Babbitt, Minnesota, is shipped by rail some 47 miles to the Silver Bay "beneficiating" plant where it is concentrated into pellets containing some 65 percent iron ore. The process involves crushing the taconite into fine granules, separating out the metallic iron with huge magnets, and flushing the residual tailings into Lake Superior. The tailings enter the lake as a slurry of approximately 1.5 percent solids. The slurry acts as a heavy density current bearing the bulk of the suspended particles to the lake bottom. In this manner, approximately 67,000 tons of tailings are discharged daily.[34]

* * *

Until June 8, 1973, the case was essentially a water pollution abatement case, but on that date the focus of the controversy shifted to the public health impact of the tailings discharge and Reserve's emissions into the ambient air. [The plaintiffs alleged that the material discharged by Reserve was identical or substantially identical to amosite asbestos. Reserve disputed this characterization of the tailings, but the district court and court of appeals found (a) that tailings fibers were found in Duluth drinking water and (b) that they could be characterized as asbestos.] * * *

* * *

On April 20, 1974, the district court entered an order closing Reserve's Silver Bay facility. [Reserve sought and obtained as stay from the Eighth Circuit, pending a decision from the full court.] * * *

* * *

The claim that Reserve's discharge of tailings into Lake Superior causes a hazard to public health raises many of the same uncertainties present with respect to the discharge into air. Thus, the previous discussion of fiber identity and fiber size is also applicable to the water discharge. In two respects, however, the discharge into water raises added uncertainties: first, whether the ingestion of fibers, as compared with their inhalation, poses any danger whatsoever; and second, should ingestion pose a danger, whether the exposure resulting from Reserve's discharge may be said to present a legally cognizable risk to health.

---

[34] The Silver Bay processing operation employs about 3,000 workers and is central to the economic livelihood of Silver Bay and surrounding communities.

1. *Ingestion of Fibers as a Danger to Health.*

All epidemiological studies which associate asbestos fibers with harm to health are based upon inhalation of these fibers by humans. Thus, although medical opinion agrees that fibers entering the respiratory tract can interact with body tissues and produce disease, it is unknown whether the same can be said of fibers entering the digestive tract. If asbestos fibers do not interact with digestive tissue, they are presumably eliminated as waste without harmful effect upon the body.

The evidence bearing upon possible harm from ingestion of fibers falls into three areas: first, the court-sponsored tissue study, designed to measure whether asbestos fibers are present in the tissues of long-time Duluth residents; second, animal experiments designed to measure whether, as a biological phenomenon, fibers can penetrate the gastrointestinal mucosa and thus interact with body tissues; third, the increased incidence of gastrointestinal cancer among workers occupationally exposed to asbestos, and the hypothesis that this increase may be due to the ingestion of fibers initially inhaled.

a. *The Tissue Study.*

Recognizing the complete lack of any direct evidence (epidemiological or otherwise) on the issue of whether the ingestion of fibers poses a risk, the trial court directed that a tissue study be conducted to determine whether the tissues of long-time Duluth residents contain any residue of asbestos-like fibers.

The study sought to analyze by electron microscope the tissues of recently deceased Duluth residents who had ingested Duluth water for at least 15 years; that is, approximately since the beginning of Reserve's operations. As a "control" check on results, tissue samples were obtained from the deceased residents of Houston, Texas, where the water is free of asbestos fibers. Although this study was necessarily expedited, plaintiffs' principal medical witness, Dr. Selikoff, testified to the sound design of the study and expressed his belief that it would yield significant information.

One of the court-appointed experts, Dr. Frederick Pooley, in explaining the results of the study, stated that he found that the tissues of the Duluth residents were virtually free of any fibers which could be attributed to the Reserve discharge. * * *

As we noted in the stay opinion, the parties dispute the significance to be attributed to the results of this study. Dr. Selikoff, prior to the conclusion of the study, expressed this view:

> Now, our feeling was that no matter what air samples show or water samples show or anything else, unless it is found that asbestos is in the tissues of people who have drunk this water * * * if we do not find it in the tissues in appreciable quantities, then I would risk a professional opinion that there is no danger, at least up to this point, to the population no matter what our samples show or water samples.

After negative results had been actually obtained, however, plaintiffs argued, and the district court agreed, that because the specimens of tissue represented only a microscopically minute body area, the actual presence of fibers may have been overlooked.

* * *

The district court decided, and we agree, that the study cannot be deemed conclusive in exonerating the ingestion of fibers in Lake Superior water as a hazard. The negative results must, however, be given some weight in assessing the probabilities of harm from Reserve's discharge into water. The results also weigh heavily in indicating that no emergency or imminent hazard to health exists. Thus, while this study crucially bears on the determination of whether it is necessary to close Reserve down immediately, the negative results do not dispose of the broader issue of whether the ingestion of fibers poses some danger to public health justifying abatement on less immediate terms.

b. Animal Studies and Penetration of the Gastrointestinal Mucosa.

At a somewhat more theoretical level, the determination of whether ingested fibers can penetrate the gastrointestinal mucosa bears on the issue of harm through ingestion. If penetration is biologically impossible, then presumably the interaction of the fibers with body tissues will not occur.

This medical issue has been investigated through experiments with animals which, unfortunately, have produced conflicting results. * * *

On this conflicting scientific evidence, Dr. Brown[35] testified that the [conflicting] studies provide some support for the hypothesis that asbestos fibers can penetrate the gastrointestinal mucosa[36]

c. Excess Gastrointestinal Cancer Among the Occupationally Exposed

The affirmative evidence supporting the proposition that the ingestion of fibers poses a danger to health focuses on the increased rate of gastrointestinal cancer among workers occupationally exposed to asbestos dust. Plaintiffs' experts attribute this excess incidence of gastrointestinal cancer to a theory that the asbestos workers first inhaled the asbestos dust and thereafter coughed up and swallowed the asbestos particles.

The attribution of health harm from ingestion rests upon a theoretical basis. As Dr. Selikoff explained, there are several possible explanations for the increased evidence of gastrointestinal cancer, some of which do not involve ingestion. Moreover, as noted previously, the excess rates of gastrointestinal cancer are generally "modest," and substantially lower than the excess rates of mesothelioma and lung cancer associated with inhalation

---

[35] Dr. Arnold Brown, a distinguished physician, served as both a technical advisor and impartial witness for the district court.–EDS.

[36] We note from the record that while attempts to induce tumors in experimental animals through the inhalation of fibers have succeeded, attempts to induce tumors by ingestion have generally failed. * * *

of asbestos dust. Also, the experts advised that an analysis of a small exposed population may produce statistically "unstable" results.

The existence of an excess rate of gastrointestinal cancer among asbestos workers is a matter of concern. The theory that excess cancers may be attributed to the ingestion of asbestos fibers rests on a tenable medical hypothesis. Indeed, Dr. Selikoff testified that ingestion is the "probable" route accounting for the excess in gastrointestinal cancer. The occupational studies support the proposition that the ingestion of asbestos fibers can result in harm to health.

2. Level of Exposure Via Ingestion.

The second primary uncertainty with respect to ingestion involves the attempt to assess whether the level of exposure from drinking water is hazardous. Of course, this inquiry is handicapped by the great variation in fiber counts, and Dr. Brown's admonition that only a qualitative, and not a quantitative, statement can be made about the presence of fibers.

In spite of these difficulties, the district court found that the level of exposure resulting from the drinking of Duluth water was "comparable" to that found to cause gastrointestinal cancer in asbestos workers. The court drew this finding from an elaborate calculation by Dr. Nicholson in which he attempted to make a statistical comparison between the fibers probably ingested by an asbestos worker subject to an excess risk of gastrointestinal cancer with the probable number of amphibole fibers ingested by a Duluth resident over a period of 18 years. * * * Reserve witness Dr. Gross performed a calculation similar to Dr. Nicholson's, but using somewhat different assumptions, and concluded that Duluth water would have to contain several hundred million fibers/liter and be ingested for 60 years before an exposure comparable with occupational levels would be reached.

The comparison has other weaknesses, for without regard to the comparability of the gross exposure levels, the dynamics of the exposure process are markedly different. The vagaries attendant to the use of assumptions rather than facts result in comparisons which are of dubious accuracy. Thus, Dr. Brown testified that, if Nicholson's calculations were correct, he would conclude only that the risk was non-negligible.

The Nicholson comparison, although evidentially weak, must be considered with other evidence. The record does show that the ingestion of asbestos fibers poses some risk to health, but to an undetermined degree. Given these circumstances, Dr. Brown testified that the possibility of a future excess incidence of cancer attributable to the discharge cannot be ignored:

* * *

After some degree of exposure to the literature and to the testimony given in this trial I would say that the scientific evidence that I have seen is not complete in terms of allowing me to draw a conclusion one way or another concerning the problem of a public health hazard in the water in Lake Superior.

* * *

As a medical person, sir, I think that I have to err, if err I do, on the side of what is best for the greatest number. And having concluded or having come to the conclusions that I have given you, the carcinogenicity of asbestos, I can come to no conclusion, sir, other than that the fibers should not be present in the drinking water of the people of the North Shore.

C. Conclusion.

The preceding extensive discussion of the evidence demonstrates that the medical and scientific conclusions here in dispute clearly lie "on the frontiers of scientific knowledge." *Industrial Union Department, AFL-CIO v. Hodgson*, 499 F.2d 467, 474 (1974). The trial court, not having any proof of actual harm, was faced with a consideration of (1) the probabilities of any health harm and (2) the consequences, if any, should the harm actually occur.

* * *

In assessing probabilities in this case, it cannot be said that the probability of harm is more likely than not. Moreover, the level of probability does not readily convert into a prediction of consequences. On this record it cannot be forecast that the rates of cancer will increase from drinking Lake Superior water or breathing Silver Bay air. The best that can be said is that the existence of this asbestos contaminant in air and water gives rise to a reasonable medical concern for the public health. The public's exposure to asbestos fibers in air and water creates some health risk. Such a contaminant should be removed.

As we demonstrate in the following sections of the opinion, the existence of this risk to the public justifies an injunction decree requiring abatement of the health hazard on reasonable terms as a precautionary and preventive measure to protect the public health.

IV. FEDERAL WATER POLLUTION CONTROL ACT

The district court found that Reserve's discharge into Lake Superior violated §§ 1160(c)(5) and (g)(1) of the Federal Water Pollution Control Act (FWPCA). These two provisions authorize an action by the United States to secure abatement of water discharges in interstate waters where the discharges violate state water quality standards and "endanger * * * the health or welfare of persons." § 1160(g)(1).

* * *

In this review, we must determine whether "endangering" within the meaning of the FWPCA encompasses the potential of harm to public health in the degree shown here. * * * The term "endangering," as used by Congress in § 1160(g)(1), connotes a lesser risk of harm than the phrase "imminent and substantial endangerment to the health of persons" as used by Congress in the 1972 amendments to the FWPCA. 33 U.S.C. § 1364.

In the context of this environmental legislation, we believe that Congress used the term "endangering" in a precautionary or preventive sense, and, therefore, evidence of potential harm as well as actual harm comes within the purview of that term. We are fortified in this view by the flexible provisions for injunctive relief which permit a court "to enter such judgment and orders enforcing such judgment as the public interest and the equities of the case may require." 33 U.S.C. § 1160(c)(5).

* * *

The record shows that Reserve is discharging a substance into Lake Superior waters which under an acceptable but unproved medical theory may be considered as carcinogenic. As previously discussed, this discharge gives rise to a reasonable medical concern over the public health. We sustain the district court's determination that Reserve's discharge into Lake Superior constitutes pollution of waters "endangering the health or welfare of persons" within the terms of §§ 1160(c)(5) and (g)(1) of the Federal Water Pollution Control Act and is subject to abatement.

* * *

VII. REMEDY

* * *

* * * In the absence of proof of a reasonable risk of imminent or actual harm, a legal standard requiring immediate cessation of industrial operations will cause unnecessary economic loss, including unemployment, and, in a case such as this, jeopardize a continuing domestic source of critical metals without conferring adequate countervailing benefits.

We believe that on this record the district court abused its discretion by immediately closing this major industrial plant. * * *

Reserve shall be given a reasonable time to stop discharging its wastes into Lake Superior. * * * Assuming agreement and designation of an appropriate land disposal site, Reserve is entitled to a reasonable turn-around time to construct the necessary facilities and accomplish a changeover in the means of disposing of its taconite wastes.

* * *

NOTES

1. *The scientific problem.* What was EPA's theory of the mechanism of harm? What evidence did EPA assemble in support of its request for an injunction? What gaps remained in its evidence? Why weren't the gaps fatal to EPA's case?

2. *Scientific uncertainty.* The effect of asbestos in drinking water remains uncertain. Is it ever likely to be resolved? Which of the two types of scientific uncertainty, information uncertainty and knowledge uncertainty (described in Chapter 2, *supra)*, is at work in *Reserve Mining*? If the uncertainty is resolvable, what is the justification for the court's permitting regulation to go forward? If not, what is the justification for, in effect, placing the burden of proof on Reserve?

3. *Science and procedural setting.* You have no doubt noticed that the procedural setting of *Reserve Mining* is not quite the same as ordinary review of agency decisionmaking. How is it different? What effect would you expect it to have on the level of judicial scrutiny of agency action? Note the district

court's use of specially appointed experts and specially ordered studies. Is this an appropriate judicial role? Where does EPA's expertise fit in?

4. *Science and judicial review.* The Eighth Circuit justified its position in part on the basis of *Hodgson*, a case reviewing OSHA's first major asbestos regulations. Despite a "substantial evidence" standard of review, the D.C. Circuit adopted a deferential tone:

> From extensive and often conflicting evidence, the Secretary in this case made numerous factual determinations. With respect to some of those questions, the evidence was such that the task consisted primarily of evaluating the data and drawing conclusions from it. The court can review that data in the record and determine whether it reflects substantial support for the Secretary's findings. But some of the questions involved in the promulgation of these standards are on the frontiers of scientific knowledge, and consequently as to them insufficient data is presently available to make a fully informed factual determination. Decision making must in that circumstance depend to a greater extent upon policy judgments and less upon purely factual analysis. Thus, in addition to currently unresolved factual issues, the formulation of standards involves choices that by their nature require basic policy determinations rather than resolution of factual controversies. Judicial review of inherently legislative decisions of this sort is obviously an undertaking of different dimensions.

> For example, in this case the evidence indicated that reliable data is not currently available with respect to the precisely predictable health effects of various levels of exposure to asbestos dust; nevertheless, the Secretary was obligated to establish some specific level as the maximum permissible exposure. After considering all the conflicting evidence, the Secretary explained his decision to adopt, over strong employer objection, a relatively low limit in terms of the severe health consequences which could result from over-exposure. Inasmuch as the protection of the health of employees is the overriding concern of OSHA, this choice is doubtless sound, but it rests in the final analysis on an essentially legislative policy judgment, rather than a factual determination, concerning the relative risks of underprotection as compared to overprotection.

Industrial Union Dep't, AFL-CIO v. Hodgson, 499 F.2d 467, 474-75 (D.C. Cir. 1974). Should it make a difference that *Hodgson* was reviewing a rulemaking and *Reserve Mining* was an injunctive action? What are the "policy judgments" in EPA's position in *Reserve Mining*?

5. *Science and statutory standard.* The degree of judicial deference depends on a number of factors, one of which is the substantive standard (*versus* scope of review) set out in the statute. What is the test for adequate safety in *Reserve Mining*? How did it affect the outcome?

6. The *Reserve Mining* approach was followed and elaborated upon in *Ethyl Corp. v. EPA*,[37] discussed above, which affirmed EPA's lead phase-out rule for gasoline:

> * * * The court thus allowed regulation of the effluent on only a "reasonable" or "potential" showing of danger, hardly the "probable" finding urged by Ethyl as the proper reading of the "endanger" language in Section 211 [of the Clean Air Act, 42 U.S.C. § 7545]. The reason this relatively slight showing of probability of risk justified regulation is clear: the harm to be avoided, cancer, was particularly great. * * *

> * * * Where a statute is precautionary in nature, the evidence difficult to come by, uncertain, or conflicting because it is on the frontiers of scientific knowledge, the regulations designed to protect the public health, and the decision that of an expert administrator, we will not demand rigorous step-by-step proof of cause and effect. Such proof may be impossible to obtain if the precautionary purpose of the statute is to be served. Of course, we are not suggesting that the Administrator has the power to act on hunches or wild guesses. * * * However, we do hold that in such cases the Administrator may assess risks. He must take account of available facts, of course, but his inquiry does not end there. The Administrator may apply his expertise to draw conclusions from suspected, but not completely substantiated, relationships between facts, from trends among facts, from theoretical projections from imperfect data, from probative preliminary data not yet certifiable as "fact," and the like. We believe that a conclusion so drawn a risk assessment may, if rational, form the basis for health-related regulations under the "will endanger" language of Section 211.

541 F.2d 1, 19-20 (D.C. Cir. 1976) (*en banc*), *cert. denied*, 426 U.S. 941 (1976). Why does it follow from the "endanger" standard that EPA "may assess risks"? Does the court mean quantitative risk assessment? What would be the alternative?

7. *The role of cost.* The "endanger" standard is vague on the role of cost in the agency's or court's deliberations. How did *Reserve* handle the cost issue? How should cost be handled where equitable flexibility is unavailable?

8. Should the protectiveness of *Reserve Mining* be taken a step further? In *Certified Color Mnfrs. Ass'n v. Mathews*, 543 F.2d 284, 297-98 (D.C. Cir. 1976), the court upheld FDA's suspension of Red Dye No. 2 on the basis of a single study that was by no means conclusive of carcinogenicity:

> Courts have traditionally recognized a special judicial interest in protecting the public health, particularly where "the matter is as sensitive and fright laden as cancer." Where the harm envisaged is

---

[37] Actually, *Reserve Mining* itself relied on the panel opinion in *Ethyl*, which was superseded by the *en banc* opinion, which in turn relied on *Reserve Mining*.

cancer, courts have recognized the need for action based upon lower standards of proof than otherwise applicable.

This sounds almost like the level of protection that Chief Justice Stone suggested was due constitutional rights in his famous *Carolene Products* footnote. *U.S. v. Carolene Products Co.*, 304 U.S. 144, 152-53 n.4 (1938). Others have made similar suggestions. What is the basis for special judicial attention? Why cancer in particular? Is this consistent with the idea of risk assessment? Of quantitative risk assessment?

———

We now detour briefly from asbestos to benzene so that we can examine one of the Supreme Court's very few pronouncements on toxic risk. Because the Court has ventured into this area so little, at least on substantive questions, the *Benzene* case (as it is generally known) has had an extremely strong influence. You will see it or echoes of it throughout the materials in this book. No treatment of judicial review of toxics regulation would be complete without it.

INDUSTRIAL UNION DEP'T, AFL–CIO V. AMERICAN PETROLEUM INST.
(THE *BENZENE* CASE)
448 U.S. 607 (1980)

Mr. Justice STEVENS announced the judgment of the Court and delivered an opinion, in which THE CHIEF JUSTICE and Mr. Justice STEWART joined and in Parts I, II, III-A, III-B, III-C and III-E of which Mr. Justice POWELL joined.

The Occupational Safety and Health Act of 1970 (Act) was enacted for the purpose of ensuring safe and healthful working conditions for every working man and woman in the Nation. This litigation concerns a standard promulgated by the Secretary of Labor to regulate occupational exposure to benzene, a substance which has been shown to cause cancer at high exposure levels. The principal question is whether such a showing is a sufficient basis for a standard that places the most stringent limitation on exposure to benzene that is technologically and economically possible.

The Act delegates broad authority to the Secretary to promulgate different kinds of standards. The basic definition of an "occupational safety and health standard" is found in § 3(8), which provides:

> The term 'occupational safety and health standard' means a standard which requires conditions, or the adoption or use of one or more practices, means, methods, operations, or processes, reasonably necessary or appropriate to provide safe or healthful employment and places of employment. 29 U.S.C. § 652(8).

Where toxic materials or harmful physical agents are concerned, a standard must also comply with 6(b)(5), which provides:

> The Secretary, in promulgating standards dealing with toxic materials or harmful physical agents under this subsection, shall set the standard which most adequately assures, to the extent feasible, on the basis of the best available evidence, that no employee will suffer material impairment of health or functional capacity even if such employee has regular exposure to the hazard dealt with by such standard for the period of his working life. Development of standards under this subsection shall be based upon research, demonstrations, experiments, and such other information as may be appropriate. In addition to the attainment of the highest degree of health and safety protection for the employee, other considerations shall be the latest available scientific data in the field, the feasibility of the standards, and experience gained under this and other health and safety laws. 29 U.S.C. § 655(b)(5).

Wherever the toxic material to be regulated is a carcinogen, the Secretary has taken the position that no safe exposure level can be determined and that § 6(b)(5) requires him to set an exposure limit at the lowest technologically feasible level that will not impair the viability of the industries regulated. In this case, after having determined that there is a causal connection between benzene and leukemia (a cancer of the white blood cells), the Secretary set an exposure limit on airborne concentrations of benzene of one part benzene per million parts of air (1 ppm), regulated dermal and eye contact with solutions containing benzene, and imposed complex monitoring and medical testing requirements on employers whose workplaces contain 0.5 ppm or more of benzene. 29 CFR §§ 1910.1028(c), (e) (1979).

* * *

I

Benzene is a familiar and important commodity. It is a colorless, aromatic liquid that evaporates rapidly under ordinary atmospheric conditions. Approximately 11 billion pounds of benzene were produced in the United States in 1976. Ninety-four percent of that total was produced by the petroleum and petrochemical industries, with the remainder produced by the steel industry as a byproduct of coking operations. Benzene is used in manufacturing a variety of products including motor fuels (which may contain as much as 2% benzene), solvents, detergents, pesticides, and other organic chemicals.

The entire population of the United States is exposed to small quantities of benzene, ranging from a few parts per billion to 0.5 ppm, in the ambient air. Over one million workers are subject to additional low-level exposures as a consequence of their employment. The majority of these employees work in gasoline service stations, benzene production (petroleum refineries and coking operations), chemical processing, benzene transportation, rubber manufacturing, and laboratory operations.

Benzene is a toxic substance. Although it could conceivably cause harm to a person who swallowed or touched it, the principal risk of harm comes from inhalation of benzene vapors. When these vapors are inhaled, the benzene diffuses through the lungs and is quickly absorbed into the blood. Exposure to high concentrations produces an almost immediate effect on the central nervous system. * * *

Industrial health experts have long been aware that exposure to benzene may lead to various types of nonmalignant diseases [, including serious and potentially fatal blood disorders].

* * *

As early as 1928, some health experts theorized that there might also be a connection between benzene in the workplace and leukemia. In the late 1960's and early 1970's a number of epidemiological studies were published indicating that workers exposed to high concentrations of benzene were subject to significantly increased risk of leukemia. [In 1976, the National Institute for Occupational Safety and Health (NIOSH), OSHA's research arm, reported its believe that recent] studies provided "conclusive" proof of a causal connection between benzene and leukemia.[38] * * *

* * *

In its published statement giving notice of the proposed permanent standard, OSHA did not ask for comments as to whether or not benzene presented a significant health risk at exposures of 10 ppm or less. Rather, it asked for comments as to whether 1 ppm was the minimum feasible exposure limit. As OSHA's Deputy Director of Health Standards, Grover Wrenn, testified at the hearing, this formulation of the issue to be considered by the Agency was consistent with OSHA's general policy with respect to carcinogens. Whenever a carcinogen is involved, OSHA will presume [in accordance with its Generic Cancer Policy] that no safe level of exposure exists in the absence of clear proof establishing such a level and will accordingly set the exposure limit at the lowest level feasible. The proposed 1 ppm exposure limit in this case thus was established not on the basis of a proven hazard at 10 ppm, but rather on the basis of "OSHA's best judgement at the time of the proposal of the feasibility of compliance with the proposed standard by the [a]ffected industries." Given OSHA's cancer policy, it was in fact irrelevant whether there was any evidence at all of a leukemia risk at 10 ppm. The important point was that there was no evidence that there was not some risk, however small, at that level. The fact that OSHA did not ask for comments on whether there was a safe level of exposure for benzene was indicative of its further view that a demonstration of such absolute safety simply could not be made.

* * *

_____

[38] These included the studies that are reported in the Rinsky article in Chapter 2, *supra*.—EDS.

As presently formulated, the benzene standard is an expensive way of providing some additional protection for a relatively small number of employees. [The standard did not cover gas station employees, who were numerically the largest group of exposed workers.] According to OSHA's figures, * * * [o]ver two-thirds of [exposed] workers (24,450) are employed in the rubber-manufacturing industry. Compliance costs in that industry are estimated to be rather low, with no capital costs and initial operating expenses estimated at only $34 million ($1,390 per employee); recurring annual costs would also be rather low, totaling less than $1 million. By contrast, the segment of the petroleum refining industry that produces benzene would be required to incur $24 million in capital costs and $600,000 in first-year operating expenses to provide additional protection for 300 workers ($82,000 per employee), while the petrochemical industry would be required to incur $20.9 million in capital costs and $1 million in initial operating expenses for the benefit of 552 employees ($39,675 per employee).

Although OSHA did not quantify the benefits to each category of worker in terms of decreased exposure to benzene, it appears from the economic impact study done at OSHA's direction that those benefits may be relatively small. * * *

II

* * *

Any discussion of the 1 ppm exposure limit must, of course, begin with the Agency's rationale for imposing that limit. The written explanation of the standard fills 184 pages of the printed appendix. Much of it is devoted to a discussion of the voluminous evidence of the adverse effects of exposure to benzene at levels of concentration well above 10 ppm. This discussion demonstrates that there is ample justification for regulating occupational exposure to benzene and that the prior limit of 10 ppm, with a ceiling of 25 ppm (or a peak of 50 ppm) was reasonable. It does not, however, provide direct support for the Agency's conclusion that the limit should be reduced from 10 ppm to 1 ppm.

The evidence in the administrative record of [nonmalignant] adverse effects of benzene exposure at 10 ppm is sketchy at best. [The Court then undertook a lengthy and highly critical analysis of the evidence for risk of blood disease at levels at and above 10 ppm.] * * *

* * *

With respect to leukemia, evidence of an increased risk (*i.e.*, a risk greater than that borne by the general population) due to benzene exposures at or below 10 ppm was even sketchier. Once OSHA acknowledged that the NIOSH study it had relied upon in promulgating the emergency standard did not support its earlier view that benzene had been shown to cause leukemia at concentrations below 25 ppm, there was only one study that provided any evidence of such an increased risk. That study, conducted by the Dow Chemical Co., uncovered three leukemia deaths, versus 0.2 expected deaths, out of a population of 594 workers; it appeared that the three workers had never been exposed to more than 2 to 9 ppm of benzene. The authors of the study, however, concluded that it could not be viewed as proof of a relationship between low-level benzene exposure and leukemia because all three workers had probably been occupationally exposed to a number of other potentially carcinogenic chemicals at other points in their careers and because no leukemia deaths had been uncovered among workers who had been exposed to much higher levels of benzene. In its explanation of the permanent standard, OSHA stated that the possibility that these three leukemias had been caused by benzene exposure could not be ruled out and that the study, although not evidence of an increased risk of leukemia at 10 ppm, was therefore "consistent with the findings of many studies that there is an excess leukemia risk among benzene exposed employees." The Agency made no finding that the Dow study, any other empirical evidence, or any opinion testimony demonstrated that exposure to benzene at or below the 10 ppm level had ever in fact caused leukemia. [T]he Court of Appeals noted that OSHA was "unable to point to any empirical evidence documenting a leukemia risk at 10 ppm . * * *"

In the end OSHA's rationale for lowering the permissible exposure limit to 1 ppm was based, not on any finding that leukemia has ever [in fact] been caused by exposure to 10 ppm of benzene and that it will *not* be caused by exposure to 1 ppm, but rather on a series of assumptions indicating that some leukemias might result from exposure to 10 ppm and that the number of cases might be reduced by reducing the exposure level to 1 ppm. In reaching that result, the Agency first unequivocally concluded that benzene is a human carcinogen. Second, it concluded that industry had failed to prove that there is a safe threshold level of exposure to benzene below which no excess leukemia cases would occur. In reaching this conclusion OSHA rejected industry contentions that certain epidemiological studies indicating no excess risk of leukemia among workers exposed at levels below 10 ppm were sufficient to establish that the threshold level of safe exposure was at or above 10 ppm. It also rejected an industry witness' testimony that a dose-response curve could be constructed on the basis of the reported epidemiological studies and that this curve indicated that reducing the permissible exposure limit from 10 to 1 ppm would prevent at most one leukemia and one other cancer death every six years.

Third, the Agency applied its standard policy with respect to carcinogens, concluding that, in the absence of definitive proof of a safe level, it must be

---

[39] In his dissenting opinion, Mr. Justice MARSHALL states that the Agency did not rely "blindly on some Draconian carcinogen 'policy'" in setting a permissible exposure limit for benzene. He points to the large number of witnesses the Agency heard and the voluminous record it compiled as evidence that it relied instead on the particular facts concerning benzene. With all due respect, we disagree with Mr. Justice MARSHALL's interpretation of the Agency's rationale for its decision. After hearing the evidence, the Agency relied on the same policy view it had stated at the outset, namely, that, in the absence of clear evidence to the contrary, it must be assumed that no safe level exists for exposure to a carcinogen. The

assumed that any level above zero presents *some* increased risk of cancer. As the federal parties point out in their brief, there are a number of scientists and public health specialists who subscribe to this view, theorizing that a susceptible person may contract cancer from the absorption of even one molecule of a carcinogen like benzene.

Fourth, the Agency reiterated its view of the Act, stating that it was required by § 6(b)(5) to set the standard either at the level that has been demonstrated to be safe or at the lowest level feasible, whichever is higher. If no safe level is established, as in this case, the Secretary's interpretation of the statute automatically leads to the selection of an exposure limit that is the lowest feasible. Because of benzene's importance to the economy, no one has ever suggested that it would be feasible to eliminate its use entirely, or to try to limit exposures to the small amounts that are omnipresent. Rather, the Agency selected 1 ppm as a workable exposure level, and then determined that compliance with that level was technologically feasible and that "the economic impact of * * * [compliance] will not be such as to threaten the financial welfare of the affected firms or the general economy." It therefore held that 1 ppm was the minimum feasible exposure level within the meaning of § 6(b)(5) of the Act.

* * *

It is noteworthy that at no point in its lengthy explanation did the Agency quote or even cite § 3(8) of the Act. It made no finding that any of the provisions of the new standard were "reasonably necessary or appropriate to provide safe or healthful employment and places of employment." Nor did it allude to the possibility that any such finding might have been appropriate.

III

Our resolution of the issues in these cases turns, to a large extent, on the meaning of and the relationship between § 3(8), which defines a health and safety standard as a standard that is "reasonably necessary and appropriate to provide safe or healthful employment," and § 6(b)(5), which directs the Secretary in promulgating a health and safety standard for toxic materials to "set the standard which most adequately assures, to the extent feasible, on the basis of the best available evidence, that no employee will suffer material impairment of health or functional capacity. . . ."

* * *

Agency also reached the entirely predictable conclusion that industry had not carried its conceadedly impossible burden, of proving that a safe level of exposure exists for benzene. As the Agency made clear later in its proposed generic cancer policy, it felt compelled to allow industry witnesses to go over the same ground in each regulation dealing with a carcinogen, despite its policy view. The generic policy, which has not yet gone into effect, was specifically designed to eliminate this duplication of effort in each case by foreclosing industry from arguing that there is a safe level for the particular carcinogen being regulated.

A

Under the Government's view, § 3(8), if it has any substantive content at all, merely requires OSHA to issue standards that are reasonably calculated to produce a safer or more healthy work environment. Apart from this minimal requirement of rationality, the Government argues that § 3(8) imposes no limits on the Agency's power, and thus would not prevent it from requiring employers to do whatever would be "reasonably necessary" to eliminate all risks of any harm from their workplaces. With respect to toxic substances and harmful physical agents, the Government takes an even more extreme position. Relying on § 6(b)(5)'s direction to set a standard "which most adequately assures * * * that no employee will suffer material impairment of health or functional capacity," the Government contends that the Secretary is required to impose standards that either guarantee workplaces that are free from any risk of material health impairment, however small, or that come as close as possible to doing so without ruining entire industries.

If the purpose of the statute were to eliminate completely and with absolute certainty any risk of serious harm, we would agree that it would be proper for the Secretary to interpret §§ 3(8) and 6(b)(5) in this fashion. But we think it is clear that the statute was not designed to require employers to provide absolutely risk-free workplaces whenever it is technologically feasible to do so, so long as the cost is not great enough to destroy an entire industry. Rather, both the language and structure of the Act, as well as its legislative history, indicate that it was intended to require the elimination, as far as feasible, of significant risks of harm.

B

By empowering the Secretary to promulgate standards that are "reasonably necessary or appropriate to provide safe or healthful employment and places of employment," the Act implies that, before promulgating any standard, the Secretary must make a finding that the workplaces in question are not safe. But "safe" is not the equivalent of "risk-free." There are many activities that we engage in every day—such as driving a car or even breathing city air—that entail some risk of accident or material health impairment; nevertheless, few people would consider these activities "unsafe." Similarly, a workplace can hardly be considered "unsafe" unless it threatens the workers with a significant risk of harm.

Therefore, before he can promulgate *any* permanent health or safety standard, the Secretary is required to make a threshold finding that a place of employment is unsafe—in the sense that significant risks are present and can be eliminated or lessened by a change in practices. This requirement applies to permanent standards promulgated pursuant to § 6(b)(5), as well as to other types of permanent standards. For there is no reason why § 3(8)'s definition of a standard should not be deemed incorporated by reference into § 6(b)(5). The standards promulgated pursuant to § 6(b)(5) are just one species of the genus of standards governed by the basic requirement. That section repeatedly uses the term "standard" without suggesting any exception from, or qualification of, the general definition; on the contrary, its directs the Secretary to select "*the* standard"—that is to say, one of various possible alternatives that satisfy the basic definition in § 3(8)—that is most protective. Moreover, requiring the Secretary to make a threshold finding of significant risk is consistent with the scope of the regulatory power granted to him by § 6(b)(5), which empowers the Secretary to promulgate standards, not for chemicals and physical agents generally, but for "*toxic* materials" and "*harmful* physical agents."[40]

* * *

In the absence of a clear mandate in the Act, it is unreasonable to assume that Congress intended to give the Secretary the unprecedented power over American industry that would result from the Government's view of §§ 3(8) and 6(b)(5), coupled with OSHA's cancer policy. Expert testimony that a substance is probably a human carcinogen—either because it has caused cancer in animals or because individuals have contracted cancer following extremely high exposures—would justify the conclusion that the substance poses some risk of serious harm no matter how minute the exposure and no matter how many experts testified that they regarded the risk as insignificant. That conclusion would in turn justify pervasive regulation limited only by the constraint of feasibility. In light of the fact that there are literally thousands of substances used in the workplace that have been identified as carcinogens or suspect carcinogens, the Government's theory would give OSHA power to impose enormous costs that might produce little, if any, discernible benefit.

If the Government was correct in arguing that neither § 3(8) nor § 6(b)(5) requires that the risk from a toxic substance be quantified sufficiently to enable the Secretary to characterize it as significant in an understandable way, the statute would make such a "sweeping delegation of legislative power" that it might be unconstitutional under the Court's reasoning in *A.L.A. Schechter*

---

[40] The rest of § 6(b)(5), while requiring the Secretary to promulgate the standard that "most adequately assures . . . that no employee will suffer material impairment of health or functional capacity," also contains phrases implying that the Secretary should consider differences in degrees of significance rather than simply a total elimination of all risks. Thus, the standard to be selected is one that "most adequately assures, to the extent feasible, on the basis of the best available evidence," that no such harm will result. The Secretary is also directed to take into account "research, demonstrations, experiments, and such other information as may be appropriate" and to consider "[i]n addition to the attainment of the highest degree of health and safety protection for the employee . . . the latest available scientific data in the field, the feasibility of the standards, and experience gained under this and other health and safety laws."

Mr. Justice MARSHALL states that our view of § 3(8) would make the first sentence in § 6(b)(5) superfluous. We disagree. The first sentence of § 6(b)(5) requires the Secretary to select a highly protective standard once he has determined that a standard should be promulgated. The threshold finding that there is a need for such a standard in the sense that there is a significant risk in the workplace is not unlike the threshold finding that a chemical is toxic or a physical agent is harmful. Once the Secretary has made the requisite threshold finding, § 6(b)(5) directs him to choose the most protective standard that still meets the definition of a standard under § 3(8), consistent with feasibility.

Poultry Corp. v. United States, 295 U.S. 495, 539 [(1935)], and *Panama Refining Co. v. Ryan*, 293 U.S. 388 [(1935)]. A construction of the statute that avoids this kind of open-ended grant should certainly be favored.

C

The legislative history also supports the conclusion that Congress was concerned, not with absolute safety, but with the elimination of significant harm. The examples of industrial hazards referred to in the Committee hearings and debates all involved situations in which the risk was unquestionably significant [, for example, byssinosis ("brown lung," caused by cotton dust) and asbestosis]. * * *

Moreover, Congress specifically amended § 6(b)(5) to make it perfectly clear that it does not require the Secretary to promulgate standards that would assure an absolutely risk-free workplace. * * *

* * *

D

Given the conclusion that the Act empowers the Secretary to promulgate health and safety standards only where a significant risk of harm exists, the critical issue becomes how to define and allocate the burden of proving the significance of the risk in a case such as this, where scientific knowledge is imperfect and the precise quantification of risks is therefore impossible. The Agency's position is that there is substantial evidence in the record to support its conclusion that there is no absolutely safe level for a carcinogen and that, therefore, the burden is properly on industry to prove, apparently beyond a shadow of a doubt, that there is a safe level for benzene exposure. The Agency argues that, because of the uncertainties in this area, any other approach would render it helpless, forcing it to wait for the leukemia deaths that it believes are likely to occur before taking any regulatory action.

We disagree. As we read the statute, the burden was on the Agency to show, on the basis of substantial evidence, that it is at least more likely than not that long-term exposure to 10 ppm of benzene presents a significant risk of material health impairment. Ordinarily, it is the proponent of a rule or order who has the burden of proof in administrative proceedings. *See* 5 U.S.C. § 556(d). In some cases involving toxic substances, Congress has shifted the burden of proving that a particular substance is safe onto the party opposing the proposed rule[41] The fact that Congress did not follow this course in enacting the Occupational Safety and Health Act indicates that it intended the

---

[41] *See* Environmental Defense Fund, Inc. v. EPA, 548 F.2d 998, 1004, 1012-1018 (1977), *cert. denied*, 431 U.S. 925, where the court rejected the argument that the EPA has the burden of proving that a pesticide is unsafe in order to suspend its registration under the Federal Insecticide, Fungicide, and Rodenticide Act. The court noted that Congress had deliberately shifted the ordinary burden of proof under the Administrative Procedure Act, requiring manufacturers to establish the continued safety of their products.

Agency to bear the normal burden of establishing the need for a proposed standard.

In this case OSHA did not even attempt to carry its burden of proof. The closest it came to making a finding that benzene presented a significant risk of harm in the workplace was its statement that the benefits to be derived from lowering the permissible exposure level from 10 to 1 ppm were "likely" to be "appreciable." The Court of Appeals held that this finding was not supported by substantial evidence. Of greater importance, even if it were supported by substantial evidence, such a finding would not be sufficient to satisfy the Agency's obligations under the Act.

* * *

Contrary to the Government's contentions, imposing a burden on the Agency of demonstrating a significant risk of harm will not strip it of its ability to regulate carcinogens, nor will it require the Agency to wait for deaths to occur before taking any action. First, the requirement that a "significant" risk be identified is not a mathematical straitjacket. It is the Agency's responsibility to determine, in the first instance, what it considers to be a "significant" risk. Some risks are plainly acceptable and others are plainly unacceptable. If, for example, the odds are one in a billion that a person will die from cancer by taking a drink of chlorinated water, the risk clearly could not be considered significant. On the other hand, if the odds are one in a thousand that regular inhalation of gasoline vapors that are 2% benzene will be fatal, a reasonable person might well consider the risk significant and take appropriate steps to decrease or eliminate it. Although the Agency has no duty to calculate the exact probability of harm, it does have an obligation to find that a significant risk is present before it can characterize a place of employment as "unsafe."[42]

Second, OSHA is not required to support its finding that a significant risk exists with anything approaching scientific certainty. Although the Agency's findings must be supported by substantial evidence, 29 U.S.C. § 655(f), § 6(b)(5) specifically allows the Secretary to regulate on the basis of the "best available evidence." As several Courts of Appeals have held, this provision requires a reviewing court to give OSHA some leeway where its findings must be made on the frontiers of scientific knowledge. *See Industrial Union Dept., AFL-CIO v. Hodgson*, * * *. Thus, so long as they are supported by a body of reputable scientific thought, the Agency is free to use conservative

---

[42] In his dissenting opinion, Mr. Justice MARSHALL states: "[W]hen the question involves determination of the acceptable level of risk, the ultimate decision must necessarily be based on considerations of policy as well as empirically verifiable facts. Factual determinations can at most define the risk in some statistical way; the judgment whether that risk is tolerable cannot be based solely on a resolution of the facts." We agree. Thus, while the Agency must support its finding that a certain level of risk exists by substantial evidence, we recognize that its determination that a particular level of risk is "significant" will be based largely on policy considerations. At this point we have no need to reach the issue of what level of scrutiny a reviewing court should apply to the latter type of determination.

assumptions in interpreting the data with respect to carcinogens, risking error on the side of overprotection rather than underprotection.

Finally, the record in this case and OSHA's own rulings on other carcinogens indicate that there are a number of ways in which the Agency can make a rational judgment about the relative significance of the risks associated with exposure to a particular carcinogen.

It should also be noted that, in setting a permissible exposure level in reliance on less-than-perfect methods, OSHA would have the benefit of a backstop in the form of monitoring and medical testing. Thus, if OSHA properly determined that the permissible exposure limit should be set at 5 ppm, it could still require monitoring and medical testing for employees exposed to lower levels. By doing so, it could keep a constant check on the validity of the assumptions made in developing the permissible exposure limit, giving it a sound evidentiary basis for decreasing the limit if it was initially set too high. Moreover, in this way it could ensure that workers who were unusually susceptible to benzene could be removed from exposure before they had suffered any permanent damage.

E

Because our review of these cases has involved a more detailed examination of the record than is customary, it must be emphasized that we have neither made any factual determinations of our own, nor have we rejected any factual findings made by the Secretary. We express no opinion on what factual findings this record might support, either on the basis of empirical evidence or on the basis of expert testimony; nor do we express any opinion on the more difficult question of what factual determinations would warrant a conclusion that significant risks are present which make promulgation of a new standard reasonably necessary or appropriate. The standard must, of course, be supported by the findings actually made by the Secretary, not merely by findings that we believe he might have made.

In this case the record makes it perfectly clear that the Secretary relied squarely on a special policy for carcinogens that imposed the burden on industry of proving the existence of a safe level of exposure, thereby avoiding the Secretary's threshold responsibility of establishing the need for more stringent standards. In so interpreting his statutory authority, the Secretary exceeded his power.

* * *

Mr. Chief Justice BURGER, concurring.

---

[43] * * * In this case the Agency did not have the benefit of animal studies, because scientists have been unable as yet to induce leukemia in experimental animals as a result of benzene exposure. It did, however, have a fair amount of epidemiological evidence, including both positive and negative studies. Although the Agency stated that this evidence was insufficient to construct a precise correlation between exposure levels and cancer risks, it would at least be helpful in determining whether it is more likely than not that there is a significant risk at 10 ppm.

* * *

* * * When discharging his duties under the statute, the Secretary is well admonished to remember that a heavy responsibility burdens his authority. Inherent in this statutory scheme is authority to refrain from regulation of insignificant or *de minimis* risks. *See Alabama Power Co. v. Costle*, 636 F.2d 323, 360-361 (1979) (opinion of Leventhal, J.) [(interpreting the Clean Air Act)]. When the administrative record reveals only scant or minimal risk of material health impairment, responsible administration calls for avoidance of extravagant, comprehensive regulation. Perfect safety is a chimera; regulation must not strangle human activity in the search for the impossible.

Mr. Justice POWELL, concurring in part and concurring in the judgment.

I join Parts I, II, III-A III-B, III-C, and III-E of the plurality opinion. * * *

* * * I conclude that the statute also requires the agency to determine that the economic effects of its standard bear a reasonable relationship to the expected benefits[, as the Fifth Circuit did.[44]] An occupational health standard is neither "reasonably necessary" nor "feasible," as required by statute, if it calls for expenditures wholly disproportionate to the expected health and safety benefits.

OSHA contends that § 6(b)(5) not only permits but actually requires it to promulgate standards that reduce health risks without regard to economic effects, unless those effects would cause widespread dislocation throughout an entire industry. Under the threshold test adopted by the plurality today, this authority will exist only with respect to "significant" risks. But the plurality does not reject OSHA's claim that it must reduce such risks without considering economic consequences less serious than massive dislocation. In my view, that claim is untenable.

* * *

* * * OSHA's interpretation of § 6(b)(5) would force it to regulate in a manner inconsistent with the important health and safety purposes of the legislation we construe today. Thousands of toxic substances present risks that fairly could be characterized as "significant." Even if OSHA succeeded in selecting the gravest risks for earliest regulation, a standard-setting process that ignored economic considerations would result in a serious misallocation of resources and a lower effective level of safety than could be achieved under standards set with reference to the comparative benefits available at a lower cost. I would not attribute such an irrational intention to Congress.

* * *

Mr. Justice REHNQUIST, concurring in the judgment.

* * *

---

[44] The Fifth Circuit stated: "Although the agency does not have to conduct an elaborate cost-benefit analysis, it does have to determine whether the benefits expected from the standard bear a reasonable relationship to the costs imposed by the standard. The only way to tell whether the relationship between the benefits and costs of the benzene standard is reasonable is to estimate the extent of the expected benefits and costs." American Petroleum Inst. v. OSHA, 581 F.2d 493, 503 (5th Cir. 1978).—EDS.

[Justice Rehnquist invoked the constitutional nondelegation doctrine which requires Congress to provide an "intelligible standard" for agencies to follow when it delegates decisionmaking power to them. Justice Rehnquist argued that Congress had not done so in § 6(b)(5).]

In considering these alternative interpretations, my colleagues manifest a good deal of uncertainty, and ultimately divide over whether the Secretary produced sufficient evidence that the proposed standard for benzene will result in any appreciable benefits at all. This uncertainty, I would suggest, is eminently justified, since I believe that this litigation presents the Court with what has to be one of the most difficult issues that could confront a decisionmaker: whether the statistical possibility of future deaths should ever be disregarded in light of the economic costs of preventing those deaths. I would also suggest that the widely varying positions advanced in the briefs of the parties and in the opinions of Mr. Justice STEVENS, THE CHIEF JUSTICE, Mr. Justice POWELL, and Mr. Justice MARSHALL demonstrate, perhaps better than any other fact, that Congress, the governmental body best suited and most obligated to make the choice confronting us in this litigation, has improperly delegated that choice to the Secretary of Labor and, derivatively, to this Court.

* * *

* * * Read literally, the relevant portion of § 6(b)(5) is completely precatory, admonishing the Secretary to adopt the most protective standard if he can, but excusing him from that duty if he cannot. In the case of a hazardous substance for which a "safe" level is either unknown or impractical, the language of § 6(b)(5) gives the Secretary absolutely no indication where on the continuum of relative safety he should draw his line. Especially in light of the importance of the interests at stake, I have no doubt that the provision at issue, standing alone, would violate the doctrine against uncanalized delegations of legislative power. [He found no other indications in the statutory language or legislative history, nor was delegation unavoidable.]

* * *

If we are ever to reshoulder the burden of ensuring that Congress itself make the critical policy decisions, these are surely the cases in which to do it. It is difficult to imagine a more obvious example of Congress simply avoiding a choice which was both fundamental for purposes of the statute and yet politically so divisive that the necessary decision or compromise was difficult, if not impossible, to hammer out in the legislative forge. Far from detracting from the substantive authority of Congress, a declaration that the first sentence of § 6(b)(5) of the Occupational Safety and Health Act constitutes an invalid delegation to the Secretary of Labor would preserve the authority of Congress. If Congress wishes to legislate in an area which it has not previously sought to enter, it will in today's political world undoubtedly run into opposition no matter how the legislation is formulated. But that is the very essence of legislative authority under our system. It is the hard choices, and not the filling in of the blanks, which must be made by the elected representatives of the people. When fundamental policy decisions underlying important legislation about to be enacted are to be made, the buck stops with Congress and the President insofar as he exercises his constitutional role in the legislative process.

* * *

Mr. Justice MARSHALL, with whom Mr. Justice BRENNAN, Mr. Justice WHITE, and Mr. Justice BLACKMUN join, dissenting.

* * *

* * * The plurality ignores the plain meaning of the Occupational Safety and Health Act of 1970 in order to bring the authority of the Secretary of Labor in line with the plurality's own views of proper regulatory policy. The unfortunate consequence is that the Federal Government's efforts to protect American workers from cancer and other crippling diseases may be substantially impaired.

* * *

Unlike the plurality, I do not purport to know whether the actions taken by Congress and its delegates to ensure occupational safety represent sound or unsound regulatory policy. The critical problem in cases like the ones at bar is scientific uncertainty. While science has determined that exposure to benzene at levels above 1 ppm creates a definite risk of health impairment, the magnitude of the risk cannot be quantified at the present time. The risk at issue has hardly been shown to be insignificant; indeed, future research may reveal that the risk is in fact considerable. But the existing evidence may frequently be inadequate to enable the Secretary to make the threshold finding of "significance" that the Court requires today. If so, the consequence of the plurality's approach would be to subject American workers to a continuing risk of cancer and other fatal diseases, and to render the Federal Government powerless to take protective action on their behalf. Such an approach would place the burden of medical uncertainty squarely on the shoulders of the American worker, the intended beneficiary of the Occupational Safety and Health Act. It is fortunate indeed that at least a majority of the Justices reject the view that the Secretary is prevented from taking regulatory action when the magnitude of a health risk cannot be quantified on the basis of current techniques.

* * *

II

The plurality's discussion of the record in this case is both extraordinarily arrogant and extraordinarily unfair. It is arrogant because the plurality presumes to make its own factual findings with respect to a variety of disputed issues relating to carcinogen regulation. It should not be necessary to remind the Members of this Court that they were not appointed to undertake independent review of adequately supported scientific findings made by a technically expert agency. And the plurality's discussion is unfair because its characterization of the Secretary's report bears practically no resemblance to what the Secretary actually did in this case. Contrary to the plurality's suggestion, the Secretary did not rely blindly on some Draconian carcinogen "policy." If he had, it would have been sufficient for him to have observed that benzene is a carcinogen, a proposition that respondents do not dispute. Instead, the Secretary gathered over 50 volumes of exhibits and testimony and offered a detailed and evenhanded discussion of the relationship between exposure to benzene at all recorded exposure levels and chromosomal damage, aplastic anemia, and leukemia. In that discussion he evaluated, and took seriously, respondents' evidence of a safe exposure level.

* * *

III

A

* * *

The decision to take action in conditions of uncertainty bears little resemblance to the sort of empirically verifiable factual conclusions to which the substantial evidence test is normally applied. Such decisions were not intended to be unreviewable; they too must be scrutinized to ensure that the Secretary has acted reasonably and within the boundaries set by Congress. But a reviewing court must be mindful of the limited nature of its role. *See Vermont Yankee Nuclear Power Corp. v. NRDC*, 435 U.S. 519 (1978). It must recognize that the ultimate decision cannot be based solely on determinations of fact, and that those factual conclusions that have been reached are ones which the courts are ill-equipped to resolve on their own.

Under [the appropriately deferential] standard of review, the decision to reduce the permissible exposure level to 1 ppm was well within the Secretary's authority. * * *

* * *

B

The plurality avoids this conclusion through reasoning that may charitably be described as obscure. According to the plurality, the definition of occupational safety and health standards as those "reasonably necessary or appropriate to provide safe or healthful * * * working conditions" requires the Secretary to show that it is "more likely than not" that the risk he seeks to regulate is a "significant" one. The plurality does not show how this requirement can be plausibly derived from the "reasonably necessary or appropriate" clause. Indeed, the plurality's reasoning is refuted by the Act's language, structure, and legislative history, and it is foreclosed by every applicable guide to statutory construction. In short, the plurality's standard is a fabrication bearing no connection with the acts or intentions of Congress.

* * *

C

The plurality is obviously more interested in the consequences of its decision than in discerning the intention of Congress. But since the language and legislative history of the Act are plain, there is no need for conjecture about the effects of today's decision. "It is not for us to speculate, much less act, on whether Congress would have altered its stance had the specific events of this case been anticipated." *TVA v. Hill*, 437 U.S. [153, 185 (1978)]. I do not pretend to know whether the test the plurality erects today is, as a matter of policy, preferable to that created by Congress and its delegates: the area is too fraught with scientific uncertainty, and too dependent on considerations of policy, for a court to be able to determine whether it is desirable to require identification of a "significant" risk before allowing an administrative agency to take regulatory action. But in light of the tenor of the plurality opinion, it is necessary to point out that the question is not one-sided, and that Congress' decision to authorize the Secretary to promulgate the regulation at issue here was a reasonable one. In this case the Secretary found that exposure to benzene at levels above 1 ppm posed a definite albeit unquantifiable risk of chromosomal damage, nonmalignant blood disorders, and leukemia. The existing evidence was sufficient to justify the conclusion that such a risk was presented, but it did not permit even rough quantification of that risk. Discounting for the various scientific uncertainties, the Secretary gave "careful consideration to the question of whether the[ ] substantial costs" of the standard "are justified in light of the hazards of exposure to benzene," and concluded that "these costs are necessary in order to effectuate the statutory purpose * * * and to adequately protect employees from the hazards of exposure to benzene."

* * *

In these circumstances it seems clear that the Secretary found a risk that is "significant" in the sense that the word is normally used. There was some direct evidence of chromosomal damage, nonmalignant blood disorders, and leukemia at exposures at or near 10 ppm and below. In addition, expert after expert testified that the recorded effects of benzene exposure at higher levels justified an inference that an exposure level above 1 ppm was dangerous. The plurality's extraordinarily searching scrutiny of this factual record reveals no basis for a conclusion that quantification is, on the basis of "the best available evidence," possible at the present time. If the Secretary decided to wait until definitive information was available, American workers would be subjected for the indefinite future to a possibly substantial risk of benzene-induced leukemia and other illnesses. It is unsurprising, at least to me, that he concluded that the statute authorized him to take regulatory action now.

Under these circumstances, the plurality's requirement of identification of a "significant" risk will have one of two consequences. If the plurality means to require the Secretary realistically to "quantify" the risk in order to satisfy a court that it is "significant," the record shows that the plurality means to require him to do the impossible. But the regulatory inaction has very significant costs of its own. The adoption of such a test would subject American workers to a continuing risk of cancer and other serious diseases; it would disable the Secretary from regulating a wide variety of carcinogens for which quantification simply cannot be undertaken at the present time.

There are encouraging signs that today's decision does not extend that far. My Brother POWELL concludes that the Secretary is not prevented from taking regulatory action "when reasonable quantification cannot be accomplished by any known methods." The plurality also indicates that it would not prohibit the Secretary from promulgating safety standards when quantification of the benefits is impossible. * * *

* * * [T]he record amply demonstrates that in light of existing scientific knowledge, no purpose would be served by requiring the Secretary to take steps to quantify the risk of exposure to benzene at low levels. Any such quantification would be based not on scientific "knowledge" as that term is normally understood, but on considerations of policy. For carcinogens like benzene, the assumptions on which a dose-response curve must be based are necessarily arbitrary. To require a quantitative showing of a "significant" risk, therefore, would either paralyze the Secretary into inaction or force him to deceive the public by acting on the basis of assumptions that must be considered too speculative to support any realistic assessment of the relevant risk. *See* McGarity, *Substantive and Procedural Discretion in Administrative Resolution of Science Policy Questions: Regulating Carcinogens in EPA and OSHA*, 67 GEO.L.J. 729, 806 (1979). It is encouraging that the Court appears willing not to require quantification when it is not fairly possible.

* * *

NOTES

1. What is the Court's holding—on what grounds did the plurality overturn the benzene standard? Did the justices find that OSHA lacked evidence of carcinogenicity? Why is burden of proof such a critical issue here?

The plurality opinion also includes some important dicta, including comments on the acceptable levels of risk and quantification of risk estimates. What guidance does the plurality give for subsequent cases?

2. *Costs and benefits.* The plurality states early in the opinion that OSHA's regulation "is an expensive way of providing some additional protection for a relatively small number of employees." How is this relevant to judicial review? Why does the plurality say it?[45]

What were the options open to the Court in dealing with regulation it deemed unwise? Clearly, it could not simply overturn the regulation because it disagreed (why not?). What is Justice Powell's solution? Why doesn't the

---

[45] *See* Richard E. Levy & Robert L. Glicksman, *Judicial Activism and Restraint in the Supreme Court's Environmental Law Decisions*, 42 VAND. L. REV. 343 (1989).

plurality adopt it? What does Chief Justice Burger suggest in his concurrence?

3. *The nondelegation doctrine.* Where does Justice Rehnquist place the blame? Accepting the view that the OSHAct represents a kind of congressional failure, why did Congress draft the legislation that way to begin with? Would the dissenters' position be a better solution to the delegation problem?[46]

4. *Asbestos.* The plurality suggested that asbestos was different from benzene and that the regulation of asbestos is more easily justified. How are they different? How does the Court know this? Is the reasoning of *Reserve Mining* consistent with *Benzene*?

5. Would the plurality's position still be tenable if *Benzene* had been decided after *Chevron*?

ASBESTOS INFORMATION ASS'N/NORTH AMERICA V. OSHA

727 F.2d 415 (5th Cir. 1984)

E. GRADY JOLLY, Circuit Judge:

The Asbestos Information Association (AIA), an organization of American and Canadian manufacturers of asbestos products, asks this court to determine whether the Occupational Safety and Health Administration (OSHA) properly by-passed normal notice-and-comment rulemaking procedures in favor of creating an Emergency Temporary Standard (ETS)[47] lowering workers' permissible exposure level (PEL) to ambient asbestos fibers from 2.0 fibers per cubic centimeter (f/cc)[, the standard imposed by the rulemaking that was upheld in *Hodgson*,] to 0.5 f/cc. We hold that OSHA did not invoke its ETS powers properly.

* * *

No new data or discovery leads OSHA to invoke its extraordinary ETS powers and lower the asbestos PEL. Rather, OSHA bases its conclusion that a grave danger exists on quantitative risk assessments, which are mathematical extrapolations, of the likelihood of contracting an asbestos-related disease at various levels of exposure to asbestos particles. The risk assessment, which OSHA completed in July of 1983, and a meeting a few months earlier between the Assistant Secretary of Labor and a recognized expert in the

---

[46] After the *Benzene* decision, the nondelegation doctrine quickly returned to near-oblivion and remained there until a very recent decision of the D.C. Circuit. In *American Trucking Ass'n v. EPA*, 175 F.3d 1027 (D.C. Cir. 1999), a panel of the court ruled that EPA's air quality standards for ozone and particulate matter were fatally flawed because the Clean Air Act provided insufficient guidance to the agency in setting appropriate levels. The court remanded the regulations to EPA to remedy the problem, a resolution which seems to violate the elementary principle of the nondelegation doctrine that the failure is in *Congress* not giving give sufficient direction, not in the agency failing to follow the Congressional directive.

[47] The legal standard for issuing emergency temporary standards may be found at 29 U.S.C. § 655(c).–EDS.

asbestos epidemiology field, heightened OSHA's awareness of the asbestos situation and precipitated the ETS.

OSHA calculated the likelihood of developing lung cancer, mesothelioma, and gastrointestinal cancer due to contact with ambient asbestos fibers at different exposure levels. By applying its calculations to an estimated working population exposed to asbestos, OSHA claims that 210 lives eventually can be saved from cancer by lowering the PEL to 0.5 f/cc for six months.[48] These figures include deaths that will occur at OSHA's estimated current actual exposure levels and include employees working in environments where the density of ambient asbestos particles is 20 f/cc, ten times the current PEL. Even if, however, OSHA removes from the computation those employees who do not enjoy the benefit of the current 2.0 f/cc PEL because it is not enforced in their work place, and counts only those employees who are exposed to ambient asbestos between the levels of 2.0 f/cc and 0.5 f/cc, OSHA estimates it can save 80 lives by lowering the PEL for six months.

OSHA calculated the number of lives saved by first deriving a mortality rate, which is the number of excess deaths because of exposure to ambient asbestos particles at different levels.[49] It

then multiplied the number of workers currently exposed at those levels by the mortality rate. Finally, to obtain a projected number of lives saved, it subtracted the number of deaths that it estimates will continue to occur even at the new PEL from the number of deaths likely to occur at the higher levels of exposure, which resulted in 210 deaths for six months exposure.

* * *

The type of administrative proceeding giving rise to the regulation, and the form of the record it produces, inevitably influences judicial review. A record like the one before us cannot be reviewed as a record in which adversary proceedings have narrowly focused the facts and issues in dispute. While we do not question risk assessment as a valid means of satisfying the substantial-evidence requirement, OSHA's reliance on several studies to compute a mathematical quantitative risk assessment, and its reliance on [reports by private firms commissioned by OSHA], makes the evidence supporting OSHA's action elusive indeed.

---

[48] Six months is the period during which the *emergency* standard would be in place, before a permanent standard takes effect—EDS.

[49] Because of the latency period for most asbestos-related cancers, OSHA had no observations for asbestos-related deaths under the current 2 f/cc PEL. OSHA calculated a mortality rate for the 2 f/cc PEL by estimating the cumulative number of particles to which a worker will be exposed over varying lengths of time at 2.0 f/cc, and then applying the mortality rate to higher exposures over a shorter period of time. For example, a worker exposed to 0.2 f/cc for ten years would be as likely to develop cancer as a worker exposed to 0.4 f/cc for five years. The validity of this calculation depends on the assumption accepted by most, but not all, researchers that the likelihood of developing asbestos-related cancer varies directly with the number of fibers inhaled, and is not independently affected by intensity or duration of exposure.

* * * [T]he nature of the evidence in this case requires that we inquire into whether OSHA "carried out [its] essentially legislative task in a manner reasonable under the state of the record before [it]." In making this inquiry, we must, of course, defer to OSHA's fact-finding expertise. The extent to which the supporting evidence has survived public and scientific scrutiny, however, will affect the weight given to it by an inexpert judiciary[50]

* * *

The ETS statute requires that the Secretary issue an ETS only after he finds substantial evidence indicating both that a "grave danger" exists and that an emergency standard is "necessary" to protect workers from such danger. Thus, the gravity and necessity requirements lie at the center of proper invocation of the ETS powers. No one doubts that asbestos is a gravely dangerous product. The gravity we are concerned with, however, is not of the product itself, but of six months exposure to it at 0.5 f/cc, as compared with six months exposure at 2.0 f/cc. Our inquiry, then, is a narrow one, and requires us to evaluate both the nature of the consequences of exposure, and also the number of workers likely to suffer those consequences.

* * *

* * * OSHA has made the *number* of deaths avoided—at least 80—the basis for its rulemaking. Yet it is apparent from an examination of the record that the actual number of lives saved is uncertain, and is likely to be substantially less than 80. Both the gravity of the risk as defined by OSHA and the necessity of an ETS to protect against it are therefore questionable.

Additionally, although risk assessment analysis is an extremely useful tool, especially when used to project lifetime consequences of exposure, the results of its application to a small slice of time are speculative because the underlying data-base projects only long-term risks. Epidemiologists generally study only the consequences of long-term exposure to asbestos. Indeed, OSHA concedes some unreliability and uncertainty to be inherent in risk assessment generally. Applying the risk assessment process to a period of six months, one-ninetieth of OSHA's estimated working lifetime, only magnifies those inherent uncertainties.

By holding as we do in this case, however, we do not intimate at all that risk-assessment analysis is inappropriate evidence on which to base any standard, temporary or permanent. We say no more than that evidence based on risk-assessment analysis is precisely the type of data that may be more uncritically accepted after public scrutiny, through notice-and-comment rulemaking, especially when the conclusions it suggests are controversial or subject to different interpretations.

* * *

---

[50] When new data or, as in this case, new mathematical extrapolations, provide the basis for the new rule, independent peer reviews may be extraordinarily helpful to the court. Precisely because the data has not been scrutinized, however, the court has particular interest in having access to both favorable and unfavorable peer reviews.

NOTES

1. What are the grounds for the court's rejection of the new PEL of 0.5 f/cc? Are they evidentiary or statutory? Given the lack of dispute that asbestos is (to quote the court) "gravely dangerous," and that attainment of 0.5 f/cc is feasible (probably by using respirators), how is it that the standard is overturned?[51]

2. The court in *Asbestos Information* also complained of the lack of peer review of the studies that OSHA relied upon. What does this mean? Is the implicit requirement that OSHA arrange for such reviews consistent with *Vermont Yankee*? Is it consistent with an emergency procedure to control exposure to asbestos? Or is it simply reaping what *Benzene* sowed?

3. In *Chlorine Chemistry Council v. EPA*, 206 F.3d 1286 (D.C. Cir. 2000), the court remanded a Safe Drinking Water Act standard on the ground that it was not based on "the best available peer-reviewed science," as required by the statute. *See* 42 U.S.C. § 300g-1(b)(3)(A). The agency had adopted a goal for chloroform based on its usual assumption that it is a non-threshold carcinogen, despite its previously stated view that there exists compelling evidence that chloroform in fact has a threshold. EPA adopted its usual assumption because it was facing a legislative deadline and did not want to depart from its usual policy without further study. The court held that this course of action violated the "best available" evidence standard in the statute. Is this an avoidance or a confrontation case, that is, is the basis of the court's decision statutory interpretation or a finding that the court has acted irrationally?

4. *Hazard identification*. Contrast the D.C. Circuit's approach to the evidence on which OSHA based its ETS for ethylene oxide (EtO):

> Taking the epidemiological and experimental studies together, OSHA found that EtO causes cancer in laboratory animals and poses a significant cancer risk for humans. While each study individually may not be a model of textbook scientific inquiry, the cumulative evidence is compelling. * * * While some of OSHA's evidence suffers from shortcomings, such incomplete proof is inevitable when the Agency regulates on the frontiers of scientific knowledge." A reasonable person could draw from this evidence the conclusion that exposure to EtO presents a risk of cancer. Thus, the substantial evidence test is met[, e]ven if a reasonable person could also draw the opposite conclusion.

Public Citizen Health Research Group v. Tyson, 796 F.2d 1479, 1489, 1495 (D.C. Cir. 1986). Using the analogy of risk assessment, this might be called the "hazard identification" approach, whereas both *Benzene* and *Asbestos Information* emphasized dose-response data. What is the effect of

---

[51] OSHA's asbestos regulations fared better in *Building & Construction Trades Dep't, AFL-CIO v. Brock*, 838 F.2d 1258 (D.C. Cir. 1988), which upheld most of OSHA's new permanent PEL of 0.2 f/cc.

concentrating on the dose-response phase of the risk assessment process? How would you characterize *Reserve Mining* in this respect?

—

Asbestos Information built on a tradition of sorts in the Fifth Circuit of extremely critical review of federal health and safety regulations. *Asbestos Information* followed the appellate decision in *Benzene* (which the Supreme Court affirmed, on different grounds), and it was in turn followed by a case that is the epitome of the "confrontation" approach to judicial review, *Gulf South Insulation v. Consumer Product Safety Comm'n*, 701 F.2d 1137 (5th Cir. 1983).[52] *Gulf South* invalidated CPSC's regulation of urea formaldehyde foam insulation (UFFI):

> While the Commission correctly notes that the epidemiologic evidence is not conclusive, its exclusive reliance on the Chemical Institute study in its Global 79 risk assessment is equally unsupportable. In the study 240 rats were exposed to an average of 14.3 ppm formaldehyde for six hours a day, five days a week. After 24 months 103 of the rats developed nasal carcinomas. This was the only empirical datum with respect to formaldehyde carcinogenicity that was incorporated into the Global 79 model. But in a study as small as this one the margin of error is inherently large. For example, had 20 fewer rats, or 20 more, developed carcinomas, the risk predicted by Global 79 would be altered drastically.
>
> The element of doubt present here is similar to that with respect to formaldehyde levels [to which homeowners would be exposed]. The Federal Panel's findings that the Chemical Institute study was valid and that formaldehyde should be presumed to pose a cancer risk to man do not authenticate the use of the study's results, and only those results, to predict exactly the cancer risk UFFI poses to man. As Dr. Higginson aptly stated, it is not good science to rely on a single experiment, particularly one involving only 240 subjects, to make precise estimates of cancer risk.
>
> This problem is exacerbated by concerns about the Chemical Institute study raised by the industry. Although the average level of formaldehyde exposure in the experiment was 14.3 ppm, the rats in fact were exposed regularly to much higher doses. Measurements of between 17 and 20 ppm were not uncommon. The highest recorded level was a near-lethal 32.4 ppm. We do not have to agree with the industry that this disparity renders the study invalid for all purposes to conclude that the Commission could not properly use the study as it did. To make precise estimates, precise data are required.

* * *

---

[52] The tradition continued in *Corrosion Proof Fittings v. EPA*, 947 F.2d 1201 (5th Cir. 1991), which we will study in detail in Chapter 8 (TSCA), *infra*, in which the court read TSCA to require disaggregation of marginal *costs* of regulatory options.

The industry attacks the Commission's cancer findings on several on the grounds. Most of them relate to assumptions made by the commission in its risk assessment. Although several of these contentions present substantial questions,[53] we do not address them. The predictions made by the risk assessment model are no better than the data base. We have concluded that this base was inadequate. The Commission improperly relied on in-home data gathered largely from complaint homes. It failed to conduct a controlled study of randomly selected residences. The result is that the Commission's finding that UFFI poses an unreasonable risk of cancer is not supported by substantial evidence on the record as a whole.

701 F.2d at 1146-47. *Gulf South* is perhaps best known for its assertion that the agency, in the court's judgment, had not used "good science" in determining the risks of UFFI. *Asbestos Information* makes similar assertions. It is debatable, at best, whether federal judges are equipped to make such judgments, and even if they are, whether that is their proper role.

The *Gulf South* court also asked for "precise estimates" and "precise data," a preference also shared by *Asbestos Information*. CPSC and OSHA clearly followed *Benzene*'s lead by quantifying the risk, but to no avail. This suggests that agencies facing hostile courts are presented with a Hobson's choice in toxics regulation: either they acknowledge the inherent uncertainties in the data and risk reversal for failure to make "precise estimates," or they attempt precise estimates and risk reversal for the inherent uncertainties in the data.

Professor Wagner has suggested that a better approach to reviewing risk assessments would be to follow the approach of the majority in the *Ethyl* case, discussed above.

Wright's reasoning in his majority opinion suggests a three-step approach to addressing socio-scientific disputes, an approach that appears undiscovered and yet clearly surpasses the reasoning adopted in other, more famous opinions that address socio-scientific issues. In the first step, Judge Wright asks whether the administrator's task of promulgating a standard for lead in gasoline could be resolved completely by existing science. After discussing the numerous reasons why scientific experimentation alone was unable to determine certain facets of the larger inquiry concerning a "safe" level of lead in gasoline, Wright concludes that, given the

---

[53] At least two of the assumptions are of questionable validity. The Commission assumed that at identical exposure levels the effective dose for rats is the same as that for humans. The industry points out that the effective dose for mice is much less than that for rats and argues that it is far more sensible to assume that rats equal mice than that rats equal humans.

Probably the most controversial assumption incorporated into Global 79 is that the risk of cancer from formaldehyde is linear at low dose—in other words that there is no threshold below which formaldehyde poses no risk of cancer. As the Commission acknowledges, this assumption leads inescapably to the conclusion that ambient air is carcinogenic, albeit to a lesser extent that UFFI.

precautionary nature of the statute, the administrator is not only authorized but arguably obliged to develop a standard in the face of scientific uncertainty. Although this first step seems wholly unremarkable, it is surprisingly the step at which many highly respected judges, Justice Stevens and Judge Wilkey among them, have stumbled. In fact, courts that demand that agency protective regulations be supported by definitive and comprehensive scientific experiments appear to be one of the major causes of the paralysis that slows the promulgation of regulations for a large category of agency rulemakings.

After determining that the agency's assignment involves more than just the exercise of scientific expertise, Wright proceeds to examine whether the agency has accurately separated those questions that have been resolved by scientific experimentation from those that have not. This second step is even more unprecedented in the judicial review of socio-scientific problems. Most judges who have successfully employed the first step do not even pretend to separate facts the agency treats as truths from those requiring an exercise of policy judgment; instead, they defer to the agency's result without analysis. While this undiscerning review prevents rules from being unnecessarily remanded because a judge misunderstands the underlying socio-science or expert disputes, it may have the adverse effect of causing agencies to overstate the complexity and scientific esoterica of rulemakings in order to make it more difficult for the courts to understand and thus scrutinize their actions.

In the third step, Wright grants the EPA wide bounds of substantive discretion and examines the agency's record only to ensure that (1) the agency arrived at a regulatory decision that is supported by, or at least logically related to, the undisputed scientific facts, and (2) the resulting policy judgments made to fill the gaps in scientific knowledge fall within the bounds of discretion provided by Congress in the authorizing statute. This "logical linkage" step of judicial review removes the judge from substantively interfering in areas in which the agency is both an expert in science and policy, but retains the court as a critical check in ensuring agency rules serve the public interest in an analytically rigorous way. Both accomplishments have been areas of past judicial failure.

Wendy E. Wagner, Ethyl: *Bridging the Science-Law Divide*, 74 TEX. L. REV. 1291, 1293-95 (1996). The beauty of the *Ethyl* approach is that it frankly recognizes both the limitations of existing data and the difficulties of obtaining better information. This frees the court from pursuing chimerical certainty and precision, and enables it to concentrate on the real issue, which is the faithful application of statutory policies designed to protect human health and the environment. From what you have learned about risk assessment, is Wagner right?

Chapter 5

Toxic Torts

Although much of the law of hazardous waste and toxic substances revolves around statutes that are implemented and enforced by administrative agencies, private parties may seek relief from exposure to environmental poisons by resorting to common law and statutory tort doctrine. The body of law that has emerged as a result of private litigation against polluters is often called "toxic torts." This chapter explores the characteristics of a toxic tort and the unique problems that arise when private parties rely on courts, not agencies, to redress toxic harms.[1]

A toxic torts case presents difficult problems of proof at nearly every stage of the proceedings. The chapter is organized around the legal issues and litigation-related matters that are inevitably confronted by plaintiffs and defendants engaged in a toxic tort lawsuit. These include: (1) the nature of the harm that triggers the lawsuit and for which relief is sought; (2) causation, that is, tracing the plaintiffs harm to a substance or activity under the control of the defendant; (3) legal theories of recovery, such as nuisance, trespass, negligence, and strict liability; (4) case management techniques, like consolidating suits and class actions; (5) defenses, e.g., assumption of risk, contributory negligence; and (6) the interpretation of defendant's liability insurance agreements. The first five of these issues are, in effect, hurdles that a plaintiff must overcome in order to find the defendant liable. Insurance is usually a topic of primary interest to defendants, who seek to construe their liability policies as broadly as possible to cover the activity that is the subject of the plaintiffs lawsuit.

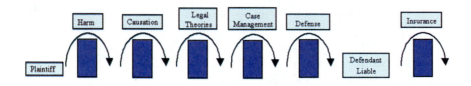

Figure 5.1–Proof Issues

A. Special Characteristics Of A Toxic Tort Case

Because toxic tort cases generally involve a claim of injury based on the actual or threatened release of and exposure to some type of toxic substance, a plaintiff bringing suit will encounter certain problems of proof at trial. The most common problem involves causation, and the majority of this subchapter is devoted to issues surrounding proof of causation. Other problems of proof at trial discussed below are: identifying the proper defendant; mustering reliable scientific and expert testimony; dealing with latent illness; and managing "mass"toxic torts.

---

[1]Two law school books that address the topic of toxic torts are GERALD W. BOSTON AND M. STUART MADDEN, LAW OF ENVIRONMENTAL AND TOXIC TORTS (1994); JEAN M. EGGEN, TOXIC TORTS IN A NUTSHELL (1995).

1. Proof of Causation

Because toxic tort cases generally involve a claim of injury based on the actual or threatened release of and exposure to some type of toxic substance, a plaintiff bringing suit will encounter certain problems of proof at trial. Perhaps the most difficult problem a plaintiff will face in a toxic tort case is establishing a causal link between a toxic substance and the plaintiff's injury, as well as the specific connection between the defendant, the targeted toxic substance, and the plaintiff. Sometimes causation difficulties are compounded when the plaintiff can identify a geographic source of the harm (*e.g.*, a local waste disposal site), but cannot determine who, among several entities that contributed to the site, is responsible for the specific harm suffered.

The centerpiece of a toxic tort case is the plaintiff's effort to draw a factual connection between some injury suffered by the plaintiff, and an activity, product, or substance traceable to some defendant. When the agent of harm is an allegedly toxic substance or hazardous activity, plaintiffs confront several complicating realities. If the injury is an illness or birth defect, the medical and scientific community may not be able to pinpoint the precise cause. This is particularly true when the injury is cancer, where hard clinical evidence linking chemical substances to that disease is often lacking. Sometimes, the plaintiff's disease appears throughout the general population and is not limited to persons who have been exposed to a substance that may be traced to a defendant. The plaintiff will have difficulty establishing that the disease is attributable only to the defendant, since others not exposed to the defendant's product or activity also have the disease. Proof of causation may also be thwarted by a long latency period between the time when the plaintiff encounters a potentially dangerous substance and the time when the injury first manifests itself. Other intervening events or actions may by then have caused or contributed to the harm.

Such difficulties have meant that a plaintiff in a toxic tort case must be prepared, as a practical matter, to face three different types of causation issues.[2] The chart in Figure 5.2 shows how causation is proved. First, the plaintiff must be able to rule out other factors that may have produced the injury and that are not connected to the defendant. For example, should the injury be cancer, it is possible that the disease has been caused by a plaintiff's smoking or exposure to second-hand smoke; genetic predisposition to cancer based on family history; exposure to chemicals other than the ones

---

[2] Two types of causation are legally required, of course. *Cause-in-fact* or but-for causation entails presentation of evidence establishing the chain of specific factual events leading up to harm. *Proximate cause* involves the closeness of the relationship between the defendant's product or activity and the harm. The plaintiff must present evidence demonstrating that this relationship is not so remote or attenuated as to make the harm unforeseeable by the defendant. But-for causation is typically the issue in toxic torts, and that is the type discussed here.

manufactured or discarded by the defendant; or earlier illness, not caused by the defendant, that made the plaintiff more susceptible to the cancer.

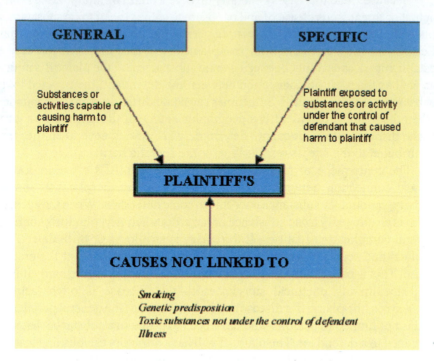

Figure 5.2–Causation Chart

Second, the plaintiff must establish *general* causation. This kind of causation requires proof that the particular substance be *capable* of causing the specific injury suffered by the plaintiff. *See Koehn v. Ayers,* 26 F. Supp. 2d 953, 955 (S.D. Tex. 1998); *Allen v. Pennsylvania Eng'g Corp.,* 102 F.3d 194, 199 (5th Cir. 1996) (scientific knowledge of the harmful level of exposure to a chemical is a fact necessary to sustain the plaintiffis burden in a toxic tort case). Put another way, the plaintiff must offer evidence that there is at least a *risk* that her particular injury is attributable to the toxic substance to which the plaintiff was exposed. See Margaret Berger, *Eliminating General Causation: Notes Toward a New Theory of Justice and Toxic Torts,* 97 COLUMBIA L. REV. 2117 (1997). Sometimes the fact of government regulation of the substance might affect the question of causation. See Richard J. Pierce, Jr., *Causation in Government Regulation and Toxic Torts,* 76 WASH. U. L.Q. 1307 (1998).

Third, specific causation must be proved. Specific causation establishes that *this* defendant's product or activity caused *this* plaintiff's injury.[3] In the ordinary torts case (say, an automobile accident) general and specific causation are, for all practical purposes, indistinguishable. However, where causation must be demonstrated by statistical rather than mechanistic evidence (you will recall this distinction from Chapter 2), the difference between them becomes pronounced, as the following two cases demonstrate.

FEREBEE V. CHEVRON CHEMICAL CO.

736 F.2d 1529 (D.C. Cir. 1984), *cert. denied*, 469 U.S. 1062 (1984)

MIKVA, Circuit Judge:

This is an appeal by Chevron Chemical Company from a judgment rendered against it after a jury trial in a suit brought by the minor children and the estate of Richard Ferebee. Ferebee, an agricultural worker at the Beltsville Agricultural Research Center (BARC), an installation of the United States Department of Agriculture located in Beltsville, Maryland, allegedly contracted pulmonary fibrosis as a result of long-term skin exposure to dilute solutions of paraquat, a herbicide distributed in the United States solely by Chevron. When Ferebee died before trial, his estate continued with a survival action and a wrongful death count was added on behalf of his minor children. After a first trial ended in a mistrial, a second jury returned a verdict on the wrongful death count for $60,000 against Chevron. That verdict was based on the theory that Chevron's failure to label paraquat in a manner which adequately warned that long-term skin exposure to paraquat could cause serious lung disease made Chevron strictly liable for Ferebee's injuries.

After unsuccessfully moving for a directed verdict and a judgment notwithstanding the verdict, Chevron now asks this court to overturn the jury's verdict. * * *

Background

Paraquat is an important agricultural herbicide that has been sold in the United States since 1966. Paraquat is known to be toxic and to cause acute injury if directly absorbed into the body. For this reason, the sale and labeling of paraquat has been extensively regulated since 1966 by the federal government, first by the Department of Agriculture and currently by the Environmental Protection Agency (EPA).

At trial, the jury was presented with a complicated set of facts. In 1967 Richard Ferebee began work as an agricultural worker at BARC. His job frequently required him to spray various chemicals, including insecticides and

---

[3] *See, e.g.*, Sterling v. Velsicol Chemical Corp., 647 F.Supp. 303 (W.D. Tenn. 1986), *aff'd in part and rev'd in part*, 855 F.2d 1188 (6th Cir. 1988).

herbicides, on greenhouse plants and, in the summer, on plants outside in the fields. Mr. Ferebee began spraying paraquat in the summer of 1977. He ordinarily sprayed six or seven times a month for between one and three hours. He used the product regularly during the outdoor growing seasons of 1977, 1978, and 1979.

When Mr. Ferebee sprayed paraquat in the fields, he frequently got the dilute spray on his skin, typically when he used his hands to shield plants while he sprayed weeds growing around them. In addition, in a videotape deposition taken before his death, Mr. Ferebee described two incidents of more extensive exposure to paraquat. The first occurred soon after he began spraying the compound. On that day, Ferebee spent several hours walking behind a tractor that was spraying paraquat. His head and bare arms became drenched with spray. At the end of the day, he began to feel dizzy and exhausted. When he went home, he was too tired to wash or change his clothes and fell asleep instantly. The dizziness and other symptoms did not persist, however, and he later returned to work.

Mr. Ferebee's second major exposure to paraquat also occurred during the 1977 growing season. On that occasion, he was spraying paraquat with a hand-held sprayer for some time when he noticed that the sprayer was defective and had leaked paraquat solution all over his pants. He stopped spraying and cleaned up as much as possible, but was not able to change his clothes until he went home.

Even before 1977, Mr. Ferebee was not a picture of perfect health. He was overweight, suffered from high blood pressure, and had a life-long sinus problem. Nonetheless, in late 1977, according to Mr. Ferebee's testimony, he began to notice a marked change in his physical condition, most notably increasing shortness of breath. Over the next several years, Mr. Ferebee's condition progressively deteriorated. In November of 1979 he checked into Capital Hill Hospital, where Dr. Muhammad Yusuf, a pulmonary specialist, diagnosed Ferebee's disease as pulmonary fibrosis. Dr. Yusuf referred Mr. Ferebee to the National Institutes of Health, where he was treated during 1981 and 1982 by Dr. Ronald G. Crystal, Chief of the Pulmonary Branch of the Heart, Lung, and Blood Institute. After several consultations and tests, both Drs. Yusuf and Crystal concluded that Ferebee's pulmonary fibrosis was caused by paraquat poisoning. Mr. Ferebee's lung condition continued to degenerate, and on March 18, 1982, he died.

In the legal action prosecuted by Ferebee's estate and minor children, appellees presented both of Mr. Ferebee's treating physicians as expert witnesses. Both Dr. Yusuf and Dr. Crystal testified that, in their opinion, paraquat had caused Mr. Ferebee's pulmonary fibrosis. To support this view, they relied not only upon their own observation of Mr. Ferebee and the medical tests performed on him, but also upon medical studies which, they asserted, suggested that dermal absorption of paraquat can lead to chronic lung abnormalities of the sort characterized as pulmonary fibrosis. Appellees then argued to the jury that Chevron had not adequately labeled paraquat to warn against the possibility that chronic skin exposure could lead to lung disease and death and that this failure was a proximate cause of Mr. Ferebee's illness and death. Chevron appeals the jury's verdict which was necessarily based on acceptance of this theory.

* * *

Causation

Chevron first argues that the jury was obligated to reject appellee's theory that long-term exposure to paraquat caused Ferebee's illness and death. Chevron acknowledges that paraquat is known to be toxic, but argues that it is only acutely toxic—that is, that any injuries resulting from exposure to paraquat occur within a very short time of exposure, such as days or weeks, and that when exposure ceases, so too does the injury. In this case, Ferebee did not experience any of the symptoms of pulmonary fibrosis until late 1978, at which point it had been ten months since he last sprayed paraquat, and his chronic inflammatory lung disease continued to worsen long after his final use of paraquat in August of 1979. Plaintiffs' theory of recovery was thus that paraquat, when absorbed through the skin, can attack the lungs in such a way as to cause chronic and self-perpetuating inflammation. Chevron argues that there has never been any evidence nor any suggestion that paraquat can cause chronic injury of this sort and that, in any event, Ferebee could not have been exposed to enough paraquat to injure him in this fashion.

The short answer to Chevron's argument is that two expert witnesses refuted it and that the jury was entitled to believe those experts. Both Drs. Crystal and Yusuf, who are eminent specialists in pulmonary medicine and who were Ferebee's treating physicians, testified that paraquat poisoning was the cause of Ferebee's illness and death. Both admitted that cases like Ferebee's were rare, but Dr. Crystal identified three other cases he felt were similar to that of Mr. Ferebee. Chevron argues that these cases can be distinguished from Mr. Ferebee's, but it is not our role to decide the merits of Chevron's attempted distinctions; Dr. Crystal thought the cases were similar, and the jury was entitled to believe him. Chevron of course introduced its own experts who were of the view that Ferebee's illness was not caused by paraquat, but the testimony of those witnesses, who did not treat Mr. Ferebee or examine him, can hardly be deemed so substantial that the jury had no choice but to accept it. The experts on both sides relied on essentially the same diagnostic methodology; they differed solely on the conclusions they drew from test results and other information. The case was thus a classic battle of the experts, a battle in which the jury must decide the victor.

Chevron seeks to avoid this conclusion by asserting that expert *opinion* testimony must be generally accepted in the scientific community before it can be introduced as evidence and that the views of Drs. Crystal and Yusuf, while not rejected by the medical community, are sufficiently novel *at this point* as to be inadmissible. * * * Thus, a cause-effect relationship need not be clearly established by animal or epidemiological studies before a doctor can testify that, in his opinion, such a relationship exists. As long as the basic methodology employed to reach such a conclusion is sound, such as use of tissue samples, standard tests, and patient examination, products liability law does not preclude recovery until a "statistically significant" number of people have been injured or until science has had the time and resources to complete sophisticated laboratory studies of the chemical. In a courtroom, the test for allowing a plaintiff to recover in a tort suit of this type is not scientific certainty but legal sufficiency; if reasonable jurors *could* conclude from the expert testimony that paraquat more likely than not caused Ferebee's injury, the fact that another jury might reach the opposite conclusion or that science would require more evidence before conclusively considering the causation question resolved is irrelevant. That Ferebee's case may have been the first of its exact type, or that his doctors may have been the first alert enough to recognize such a case, does not mean that the testimony of those doctors, who are concededly well qualified in their fields, should not have been admitted.

Finally, Chevron argues that its expert, Dr. Fisher, proved that it was physically impossible for Ferebee to have been exposed to enough paraquat to cause him any injury. Dr. Fisher's testimony, however, went only to the amount of paraquat necessary to cause the short-term illnesses that have long been recognized to follow from paraquat exposure. Accepting Dr. Fisher's testimony as true, as plaintiffs did not at trial, it still would not necessarily follow that the same amount is needed to trigger a chronic case like that which Ferebee allegedly contracted. The jury could therefore have concluded that Ferebee had been exposed to sufficient amounts of paraquat to cause the chronic disease from which he suffered—even if that exposure was not substantial enough to produce acute symptoms. The dose-response relationship at low levels of exposure for admittedly toxic chemicals like paraquat is one of the most sharply contested questions currently being debated in the medical community; surely it would be rash for a court to declare as a matter of law that, below a certain threshold level of exposure, dermal absorption of paraquat has no detrimental effect. We therefore conclude that there was sufficient evidence of causation to justify submission of that issue to the jury.

* * *

* * * Accordingly, we affirm the decision of the district court and allow the jury's verdict to stand.

IN RE "AGENT ORANGE" PRODUCT LIABILITY LITIGATION

611 F. Supp. 1223 (E.D.N.Y. 1985)

WEINSTEIN, Chief Judge.

Defendants, seven chemical companies, have moved to dismiss or in the alternative for summary judgment. Plaintiffs are Vietnam veterans and members of their families who have opted out of the class previously certified by the court pursuant to Rule 23(b)(3) of the Federal Rules of Civil Procedure.[4] Q that as a result of the veterans' exposure to Agent Orange, a herbicide manufactured by the defendants, they suffer from various health problems. * * *

The most serious deficiency in plaintiffs' case is their failure to present credible evidence of a causal link between exposure to Agent Orange and the various diseases from which they are allegedly suffering. Various other reasons why the motion for summary judgment must be granted are set forth below.

* * *

In support of their contention that Agent Orange did not cause the various ailments that allegedly afflict the veteran plaintiffs, defendants rest upon a number of epidemiological studies. As this court has indicated in extensive and repeated recorded colloquy with counsel and in prior opinions, all reliable studies of the effect of Agent Orange on members of the class so far published provide no support for plaintiffs' claims of causation.

Epidemiological studies rely on "statistical methods to detect abnormally high incidences of disease in a study population and to associate these incidences with unusual exposures to suspect environmental factors." Dore, *A Commentary on the Use of Epidemiological Evidence in Demonstrating Cause-in-Fact*, 7 HARV.ENVTL.L.REV. 429, 431 (1983). In their study of diseases in human populations, epidemiologists use data from surveys, death certificates, and medical and clinical observations.

A number of sound epidemiological studies have been conducted on the health effects of exposure to Agent Orange. These are the only useful studies having any bearing on causation.

All the other data supplied by the parties rests on surmise and inapposite extrapolations from animal studies and industrial accidents. It is hypothesized that, predicated on this experience, adverse effects of Agent Orange on plaintiffs might at some time in the future be shown to some degree of probability.

The available relevant studies have addressed the direct effects of exposure on servicepeople and the indirect effects of exposure on spouses and children of servicepeople.[5] No acceptable study to date of Vietnam veterans and their families concludes that there is a causal connection between exposure to Agent Orange and the serious adverse health effects claimed by plaintiffs. Chloracne and porhyria cutanea tarda are the only two diseases that

---

[4] The court had previously approved a settlement between the defendants and the opt-in plaintiffs in an opinion reported at 597 F. Supp. 740 (E.D.N.Y. 1984)—EDS.

[5] The studies examined miscarriages and birth defects in children of Agent Orange-exposed servicepeople, and Vietnam veterans' general health, as compared to the general population—EDS.

have been recognized by Congress as having some possible connection to Agent Orange exposure, but no proof has been shown of any relationship of these diseases to these plaintiffs. [The court then reviewed the available studies in detail.]

* * *

Plaintiffs cite a number of studies conducted on animals and industrial workers as evidence of a causal link between exposure to TCDD and the development of various hepatotoxic, hematotoxic, genotoxic, and enzymatic responses. None of these studies do more than show that there may be a causal connection between dioxin and disease. None show such a connection between plaintiffs and Agent Orange.

Plaintiffs also rely on several depositions and affidavits by experts. As indicated below, to the extent that these experts rely on available epidemiological studies, the studies supply no basis for an inference of causation. There is simply no other reliable data on which an expert can furnish reliable testimony. Thus, no expert tendered by plaintiffs would be permitted to testify under Rules 702 and 703 of the Federal Rules of Evidence.

Even most of plaintiffs' experts express doubt about causation, except for some ill-defined possible "association" as compared with associations with any specific other products or natural carcinogens; none supports the conclusion that present evidence permits a scientifically acceptable conclusion that Agent Orange did cause a specific plaintiff's specific disease.

It is significant that like Doctors Singer and Epstein, whose affidavits are described in detail below, the various experts referred to in the preceding paragraph apparently had no physical contact with individual plaintiffs. For example, Dr. Silbergeld, whose opinion is relied upon heavily in plaintiffs' briefs, states:

In preparing this affidavit, I have not seen any material related to the plaintiffs in this litigation, no medical records or other descriptions of the medical status of these persons.

Plaintiffs offer the opinion of two experts who conclude that in the cases of the specific opt-out plaintiffs before the court, exposure to Agent Orange caused adverse health effects. One is Dr. Singer's submission. The other is Dr. Epstein's.

Plaintiffs submitted two affidavits on causation by Dr. Barry M. Singer. Their wording is virtually identical. Dr. Singer's affidavits were accompanied by 282 "affidavits" by individual veteran plaintiffs. The latter are form statements, signed by either the plaintiff or his attorney, or both. * * *

The forms typically allege that the plaintiff "saw spraying of Agent Orange, entered defoliated areas and consumed local food and water." The forms then describe the plaintiff's diagnosed medical problems and refer to an attached "checklist" for a description of alleged Agent Orange related symptoms.

The checklists allow the individual to identify any or all of a number of symptoms that they attribute to their exposure to Agent Orange in Vietnam. In addition to general symptoms such as fatigue, space is provided in which to indicate specific skin, skeletal-muscular, gastro-intestinal, visual and behavioral disorders, as well as to identify any tumors as malignant or nonmalignant. Finally, the checklist asks for information about the individual's offspring. A perusal of the checklists reveals that plaintiffs believe they suffer most frequently from "behavioral" disorders: memory loss, increased irritability, anger and anxiety, insomnia, confusion, depression, and tremors.

The final part of the form affidavits describes the individual's medical history, and asks for a description of tobacco, alcohol, and drug use. This portion also alleges no exposure to any toxic chemical besides Agent Orange.

Dr. Singer, who is board certified in internal medicine, hematology, and oncology, reaches a number of conclusions based on his review of the numerous form affidavits with their attached checklists. He bases his opinion on his medical background, a review of the literature on the biomedical effects of Agent Orange, and an examination of the individual affidavits. He apparently did not examine any medical records or any plaintiffs. In discussing his conclusions, the numbers from his two separate affidavits will be combined.

Dr. Singer notes at the outset that 2,4-D, 2,4,5-T, and 2,3,7,8-tetrachlorodibenzo-p-dioxin ("dioxin") "are potent and toxic agents *capable of inducing* a wide variety of adverse effects both in animals and in man." Dr. Singer then analyzes the various ailments suffered by the individual affiants.

Fifty-four plaintiffs, Dr. Singer reports, suffer from some form of hepatic (liver) abnormality, either abnormal liver function tests, hepatitis, cirrhosis of the liver, or pericentral steatosis. He notes that liver disorders have been reported to develop in humans after industrial exposure and accidents, and in dogs, rats, mice, and primates after subacute and chronic exposure. For example, "[i]n both mice and rats, small doses of TCDD predictably produce an increase in liver weight."

Dr. Singer also asserts that 2,4,5-T "produces liver enzyme abnormalities * * * liver swelling and centrilobular necrosis" (death of a central liver lobule, or functional unit of the liver), and that one plaintiff suffered from a bile duct microadenoma (small, usually benign tumor in the passage between the liver and gall bladder) and from fatty metamorphosis of the liver. He concludes that "these compounds are *capable of producing* marked alteration in hepatic architecture and function" and that the liver abnormalities plaintiffs allege are "*consistent with* " the known effects of polychlorinated herbicides. (Emphasis supplied.) Although Dr. Singer does not reveal the studies that he relies upon to reach this conclusion, it is clear he is not referring to studies that analyze the effects of Agent Orange on exposed veterans. In any event, the liver disorders Dr. Singer finds in the animal and industrial studies differ substantially from those plaintiffs report they suffered. [The court found a similar pattern with respect to the other effects that Dr. Singer examined.]

* * *

As a review of Dr. Singer's affidavit reveals, he attributes some 37 separate diseases, disorders, and symptoms—including baldness and diarrhea—to exposure to Agent Orange. He mentions only two doubtful examples of chloracne and none of porphyria cutanea tarda, the two afflictions Congress considered worthy of a statutory presumption of service connection, although not without reservations.

Stripped of its verbiage, Dr. Singer summarizes his overall conclusion by stating that if the affiants are telling the truth and if there is no cause for their complaints other than Agent Orange, then Agent Orange must have caused their problems. Dr. Singer states:

> Assuming the truth of the affidavits submitted, and absent any evidence of pre-existing, intervening, or superseding causes for the symptoms and diseases complained of in these affidavits, it is my opinion to a reasonable degree of medical probability (that is, more likely than not) that the medical difficulties described by the affiants were proximately caused by exposure to Agent Orange.

Put differently, Dr. Singer's analysis amounts to this: the affiants complain of various medical problems; animals and workers exposed to extensive dosages of CDD have suffered from related difficulties; therefore, assuming nothing else caused the affiants' afflictions, Agent Orange caused them. One need hardly be a doctor of medicine to make the statement that if X is a possible cause of Y, and if there is no other possible cause of Y, X must have caused Y. Dr. Singer's formulation avoids the problem before us: which of myriad possible causes of Y created a particular veteran's problems. To take just one of the diseases reported by plaintiffs in an undifferentiated form, and relied upon by Dr. Singer, hepatitis: this is a disease common in the civilian population and there is not the slightest evidence that its incidence is greater among those exposed to Agent Orange than those not exposed. It may well be that hepatitis among Vietnam veterans is greater than among those who did not serve there because of greater incidence of this problem in Vietnam resulting from drug abuse and generally unsanitary conditions. There is no showing that among Vietnam veterans the incidence of hepatitis is greater in those exposed to Agent Orange.

* * * His analysis, in addition to being speculative, is so guarded as to be worthless.

* * *

IV. LAW

* * *

C. Law of Causation

* * *

As Professor Rosenberg has summarized existing law, courts are divided between "strong" and "weak" versions of the preponderance rule. Rosenberg, *The Causal Connection in Mass Exposure Cases: A "Public Law" Vision of the Tort System*, 97 HARV.L.REV. 851, 857 (1984). Under the "strong" version, plaintiff must offer both epidemiologic evidence that the probability of causation exceeds fifty percent in the exposed population and "particularistic" proof that the conduct complained of caused him harm individually. [The "weak" version would permit a verdict for all plaintiffs solely on statistical evidence relating to the groups, that is, whether it was more than 50% likely that the substance caused the effect in the group.]

Miller v. National Cabinet Co., 168 N.E.2d 811 (N.Y. 1960), is illustrative. There, the New York Court of Appeals held that plaintiff failed to establish a causal connection between exposure to benzene contained in varnish removers and development of leukemia. Plaintiff's expert lacked any statistical studies and merely concluded that it was "possible" benzene could cause leukemia—refusing to say whether it had in fact caused plaintiff's death. The Court of Appeals concluded that the expert's uncertainty coupled with the lack of statistical evidence precluded the establishment of causation and dismissed the claim.

Plaintiffs rely on *Ferebee v. Chevron Chemical Co.*, [*supra*], for the proposition that courts do not require epidemiological and particularistic evidence to establish causation in fact. *Ferebee* involved the death of an agricultural worker who died of pulmonary fibrosis, allegedly as a result of long-term exposure to paraquat. Plaintiff's treating physicians, eminent specialists in pulmonary medicine, testified that paraquat poisoning caused his death. Defendants argued that the views of plaintiff's experts were not yet accepted by the medical community and as such were inadmissible.

The Court of Appeals in *Ferebee* found this argument—essentially based on Federal Rule of Evidence 702—unpersuasive. The question is not whether the opinion itself is accepted in the relevant community, but instead whether the technique is. Inference from examination and testing, the court found, is clearly an accepted methodology. Thus, the *Ferebee* court concluded:

> [a]s long as the basic methodology employed to reach such a conclusion is sound, such as use of tissue samples, standard tests, and patient examination, products liability law does not preclude recovery until a 'statistically significant' number of people have been injured or until science has had the time and resources to complete sophisticated laboratory studies of the chemical.

This conclusion with respect to Mr. Ferebee's claims is fully consistent with dismissal of the instant plaintiffs' claims. *Agent Orange* presents an entirely different set of problems. *Ferebee* did not require epidemiologic studies because, unlike the instant case or *Miller*, plaintiff presented technically competent, probative evidence by his treating physicians that the chemical in question in fact led to his death. Moreover, while the *Ferebee* court did not require epidemiologic studies, presumably it would have considered such studies relevant had they existed. In the *Agent Orange* case, no competent particularistic evidence has been presented and the relevant epidemiologic evidence is negative. Finally, in *Ferebee*, plaintiff established long-term, intensive exposure to paraquat. The veterans' exposure to Agent Orange, even were we to grant full force to their inadequate affidavits, was much more attenuated.

In sum, the court does not read *Ferebee* as espousing a more relaxed version of the preponderance standard for establishing causation-in-fact. In *Ferebee*, plaintiff's experts were relatively certain of the cause of his disease and no epidemiological proof was necessary. *Ferebee* is thus consistent with the established rule that a plaintiff must offer evidence that causation was more than 50 percent probable.

* * *

D. Other Grounds

1. Lack of Proof of Who Was Harmed and Who Caused Harm

Having voluntarily given up the advantages of the class action, each plaintiff is in the position of being unable to prove either (1) that his disease is due to Agent Orange, or (2) that any particular defendant produced the Agent Orange to which he may have been exposed. No case has ever permitted recovery in such a situation. There is no possible theory of law on which these individual opt-out plaintiffs can recover.

* * *

NOTES

1. What does *Agent Orange* require plaintiffs to prove in terms of causation? How did the opt-out plaintiffs fail in this?

2. Did Mr. Ferebee meet the *Agent Orange* test? Was he required to?

3. The "strong" causation requirement is elaborated in one of the Bendectin cases, which involved the claim that an anti-morning-sickness drug caused birth defects. In *Richardson v. Richardson-Merrell*, 649 F. Supp. 799 (D.D.C. 1986), *aff'd*, 857 F.2d 823 (D.C. Cir. 1988), the court explained that the plaintiff needed to show *both* that Bendectin could cause the injuries complained of in *any*one, and that it caused them in the plaintiff *herself*. Richardson failed on both counts, the latter in large part because the vast majority of birth defects are of unknown origin, and there is no way to identify the precise cause in a particular case.

The California Supreme Court has adopted a test for causation that requires only that the plaintiff allege that the defendant's product was a "substantial factor" in bringing about the plaintiff's harm. Specifically, a plaintiff must identify each product allegedly causing the injury, and then allege:

> (1) exposure to each of the toxic materials claimed to have caused a specific illness;

(2) as a result of the exposure, the toxins entered the plaintiff's body;

(3) illness, and that each toxic that entered plaintiff's body was a substantial factor in bringing about the illness;

(4) each toxin absorbed was manufactured or supplied by a named defendant.

Bockrath v. Aldrich Chemical Co., 980 P.2d 398 (Cal. 1999). How is this test different from the "strong" causation requirement?

4. How did Judge Weinstein justify approving the multi-million-dollar settlement with the opt-in plaintiffs and also dismissing the claims of the opt-outs for lack of evidence? Were the two groups factually different? Or can *Agent Orange* be seen as addressing a difficult institutional question in mass tort compensation? What can be said for the *Agent Orange* resolution?

5. A distinct issue from the elements of causation is the quality of evidence that supports that evidence. The United States Supreme Court addressed that question in the *Daubert* case, discussed below.

—

A close look at three particularly troublesome issue areas will illustrate the problems inherent in proving causation. First, we will look at contaminated well issues, and the causation problems that arose in a widely-publicized case in Woburn, Massachusetts, where contamination of water supplies probably resulted in the deaths of several children. Jonathan Harr's 1996 bestseller, A CIVIL ACTION, chronicled how the children's parents and their lawyer tried to use common law tort and the judicial system to hold the corporations that allegedly contaminated the town's well water with toxic substances accountable for the children's injuries. Next, we will look into power lines and other sources of electromagnetic radiation alleged to pose hazards to human health, and nearby property owners' fears that the lines' electromagnetic fields would cause them future physical harm. Finally, we will explore a "sick school" situation that has not yet resulted in litigation, but may, depending upon the resolution of causation issues. In the sick school case, teachers and schoolchildren are suffering both actual and potential injuries allegedly caused by pesticides applied to farmland adjacent to their elementary school.

As you read the following excerpts, consider the critical role played by causation. Ask whether specific or general causation are at issue, and note situations where causes other than the defendant's conduct may be responsible for the private party's harm.

a. Contaminated Water Wells

In early 1972, citizens in the town of Woburn, Massachusetts, were alarmed because several children began getting seriously ill. As these children started to die of leukemia throughout the 1970s, the families of Woburn searched for answers. Who, or what, was responsible for this seemingly high incidence of cancer among their children? What did the children all share in common? They all drank from the same water supply, which the town furnished its residents from a series of wells.

Jonathan Harr describes how the situation unfolded:

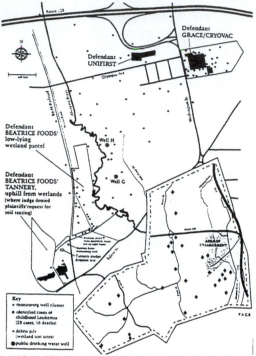

Large Map: adapted from exhibit at trial, *Anderson, et al. v. WR Grace Co., Beatrice Foods, Unifirst Co., et al.*, showing location of Public Wells G and H, the three main defendants, the Beatrice wetland parcel that was a major source of contamination, and the Aberjona River, a creek wending through the middle of the area Inset Overview Map: shows the area served by wells G and H, and the 28 identified childhood leukemia cases (16 fatal) that occurred there between the time the wells were opened and the time of the trial.

Figure 5.3–Woburn Massachusetts[6]

The Woburn police were summoned in the spring of 1979 to investigate the appearance of 184 barrels of industrial waste on a plot of vacant land in northeast Woburn. The person responsible for dumping the barrels in Woburn, the so-called midnight dumper, was never caught, and the barrels were taken away before their contents could cause any harm. The whole event would have been inconsequential had it not been for the vigilance of the state environmental inspector who handled the case. He thought it prudent to test samples of water from Wells G and H, which lay just a half mile to the south.

---

[6] Source: Z. PLATER, R. ABRAMS, W. GOLDFARB, AND R. GRAHAM, ENVIRONMENTAL LAW AND POLICY: NATURE, LAW, AND SOCIETY (2d ed. 1998) at 235.

The results of those tests reached the desk of Gerald McCall, acting director for the northeast region of the state environmental department, on Tuesday afternoon, May 22. McCall took one look at the analysis and quickly telephoned the Woburn city engineer. He told the engineer to shut down Wells G and H immediately. Both of the wells were "heavily contaminated" with trichloroethylene, commonly known as TCE, an industrial solvent used to dissolve grease and oil. The lab found 267 parts per billion of TCE in Well G and 183 in Well H. The wells also contained lesser amounts of four other contaminants, among them tetrachloroethylene, known as perc, another industrial solvent. The Environmental Protection Agency listed both solvents as "probable" carcinogens.

* * *

Reverend Young unfolded the map with the leukemia cases and showed it to Mulligan [the plaintiffs' original lawyer] * * *. "The odds of a cluster like this occurring by chance," the minister told Mulligan, "are on the order of a hundred to one."

Mulligan seemed impressed. Twelve children with leukemia—eight of them within a half-mile radius, six of them living almost next door to each other—and contaminated drinking water. It was, in legal terms, as Mulligan later said, "almost *res ipsa loquitur*"—the thing speaks for itself. There was, however, Mulligan pointed out, one significant problem: Who was to blame for the TCE in the wells? Reverend Young replied that the Environmental Protection Agency had just begun an investigation. Once the agency completed its report, they'd know the source.

* * *

The agency had narrowed its focus to a single square mile of the Aberjona River valley, some 450 acres surrounding Wells G and H. Contractors for the EPA had drilled test wells along the periphery of that square mile. On the northeast side, chemical analysis of the groundwater revealed high concentrations of TCE migrating through the soil in a featherlike plume toward Wells G and H. Even higher concentrations of TCE were found in groundwater to the west of the two wells, under fifteen acres of wooded, undeveloped land alongside the Aberjona River. The EPA listed the names of several industries situated around the perimeter of the square mile, but it did not identify which of those were responsible for the contamination.

* * *

The EPA report was highly technical, filled with maps of bedrock and groundwater contours, well logs, and scientific jargon. To decipher it, [the lawyer's assistant] hired a Princeton University professor, an expert in groundwater contamination and hazardous wastes. The professor [said] that the underground plume of TCE coming from the northeast appeared to originate at a manufacturing plant owned by W. R. Grace, the multinational chemical company.

The other source of contamination, to the west of Wells G and H, came from the fifteen acres of wooded land that was owned by the John J. Riley Tannery. And the tannery, it turned out, was itself owned by the giant Chicago conglomerate Beatrice Foods, producer of dozens of consumer goods, from Samsonite luggage to Playtex bras, Peter Pan peanut butter and Tropicana orange juice.

Both companies ranked high in the Fortune 500. In the lexicon of personal injury lawyers, they had "deep pockets," and this fact had weight for [the Plaintiffs' lawyer]. Personal injury law is not a charitable enterprise. To a lawyer working on a contingency fee and paying the expenses of a case himself, it is crucial that the defendant either have assets, preferably a lot of them, or a big insurance policy. [H]aving Grace and Beatrice as defendants in the case was like learning that a woman his mother kept trying to set him up with had a huge trust fund.

* * *

The first stage of the trial, the judge announced to the lawyers, would deal with the question of whether Beatrice and Grace were responsible for contaminating the city wells. The "waterworks" phase of the case, the judge called it. "Unless you get the product being dumped on the property and getting into the water, there's no case. There's no point in going any further."

If, however, the jury *did* find Beatrice and Grace liable, continued the judge, the second stage of the trial would address the medical question—had the chemicals in fact made the surviving family members sick and killed the children? "If the jury decides that favorably," continued the judge, "then you have to ask, 'How much is that worth? How much compensation do you give somebody for the loss of a child?'" The judge paused, and then he said in a low voice, "What a question!"[7]

---

[7] JONATHAN HARR, A CIVIL ACTION, 36, 46, 78-9, 289-7 (1996)

b. Toxic Power Lines

Figure 5.4

FIELDS OF FEAR

Gary Taubes
The Atlantic Monthly, Nov. 1994, pp. 94-95

The proposition that electromagnetic fields may be hazardous to your health began with Nancy Wertheimer, a Harvard-educated experimental psychologist who now works with the Department of Preventive Medicine at the University of Colorado. In the spring of 1974 and for much of the next two years, Wertheimer drove the streets of greater Denver searching for possible causative agents of childhood cancer.

What Wertheimer found was that the homes of children who developed cancer were, with suspicious regularity, located near high-current electric power lines. Wertheimer spent two more years with Ed Leeper, a friend with an education in physics, analyzing her data and checking her methods. "We stayed as quiet as we could," she told me recently. "We didn't want people getting anxious."

Their research was published in the March, 1979, issue of the American Journal of Epidemiology, under the title "Electrical Wiring Configurations and Childhood Cancer." Wertheimer and Leeper wrote,

Electrical power came into use many years before environmental-impact studies were common, and today our domestic power lines are taken for granted and generally assumed to be harmless. However, this assumption has never been adequately tested. Low-level harmful effects could be missed, yet they might be important for the population as a whole, since electric lines are so ubiquitous.

The scientific community paid little attention to Wertheimer's research until a decade later, when the *New Yorker* writer

Paul Brodeur immortalized Wertheimer in a three-part "Annals of Radiation" series in June of 1989. A year later Brodeur's articles appeared in a book titled, with little ambiguity, *Currents of Death: Power Lines, Computer Terminals, and the Attempt to Cover Up Their Threat to Your Health*. Brodeur and *The New Yorker* returned to the subject in 1990 and 1992, in articles that were republished last year in a book titled *The Great Power-Line Cover-up: How the Utilities and the Government Are Trying to Hide the Cancer Hazard Posed by Electromagnetic Fields*.

Unlike Wertheimer's research, Brodeur's annals had almost immediate impact. In the years since the first series appeared, half a dozen government agencies have entered the business of assessing the health hazards of electromagnetic fields (known as EMF)–in particular, the magnetic fields emitted by both high-voltage power lines and "feeder" power lines, which go from house to house; appliances; home wiring; computer terminals; and anything else that plugs into a wall socket or carries electricity into a home or across the countryside. Congress has mandated that the Department of Energy organize a $65 million five-year research program, and the National Cancer Institute is conducting a $5 million five-year study to assess whether exposure to EMF can cause or promote childhood leukemia, the most common form of childhood cancer. The motivation for the NCI study, says Martha Linet, an NCI epidemiologist, is less any evidence than the fact that "the public is very concerned and we, of course, are concerned as well."

The cost to society of public anxiety about EMF now exceeds $1 billion annually, according to a July, 1992, article in the journal *Science*, written by H. Keith Florig, of Resources for the Future, an environmental-research institute in Washington, D.C. Florig's estimate takes into account everything from the decrease in prices of real estate near high-voltage lines to the cancellation of or moratoria on new power-transmission projects to the cost of active efforts to reduce EMF exposure.

THE GREAT POWER-LINE COVER-UP

Paul Brodeur
pp. 111-12 (1993)

The EPA Report–a three-hundred-and-sixty-seven-page document entitled "Evaluation of the Potential Carcinogenicity of Electromagnetic Fields"–had come to light in March of 1990, when someone in the Agency had sent a draft version of it to Louis Slesin, the editor and publisher of *Microwave News*, a pioneering and influential newsletter that had been covering developments in the research into the hazards of exposure to radiation from power lines and other sources since the early 1980s.

* * *

[T]he summary and conclusions section of the report contained a persuasive indictment of power-line magnetic field as a cancer-producing agent. Its authors stated that five of six case-control studies published in the peer-reviewed medical literature showed that children living in homes near power lines giving off strong magnetic fields were developing cancer more readily than children who did not live near power lines. This association was statistically significant in three of the studies; and in two studies in which magnetic-field measurements had been made children exposed to fields of between two and three milligauss or above were experiencing a significantly increased risk of developing cancer.

—

Soon after these sensational (and frightening) reports began to be publicized, some homeowners in San Clemente, California filed a tort action against San Diego Gas and Electric Company. The complaint alleged that the power lines under the control of the company were in "close proximity to" the plaintiffs' property, and have emitted "high and unreasonably dangerous levels of electromagnetic radiation upon plaintiffs' property."[8] As a result, the plaintiffs asserted a cause of action for private nuisance based on their fear that the [electromagnetic] fields would cause them physical harm. When the case finally reached the California Supreme Court, a central issue involved causation. The Court said the threshold question to be decided was "whether power line electric and magnetic fields pose a danger to health. * * *"[9] This question was answered in part by a 1989 background paper prepared for the Congressional Office of Technology Assessment by the Department of Engineering and Public Policy of Carnegie Mellon University. The Court used the paper to help resolve both the causation issue, and the issue of whether the plaintiffs had stated a legal claim upon which relief could be granted.

SAN DIEGO GAS & ELECTRIC CO. v. SUPERIOR COURT

920 P.2d 669, 676-77 (Cal. 1996)

Because * * * electric and magnetic fields are non-ionizing and cannot cause significant tissue heating, it was long believed they could not have any effect on human health. Beginning in the mid-1970's, however, laboratory studies on cell cultures showed that these fields can affect certain activities of certain types of cells. Although the results were suggestive, several serious problems remained. [At this point the Court relies on the Office of Technology Assessment paper]. First, there was no known mechanism to explain how these extremely weak fields could disturb the much stronger fields arising naturally from human cell activity. Second, disturbances at the cellular level do not necessarily extrapolate to adverse effects on the organism as a whole: the organism can tolerate some disturbances and compensate for others. Biological effects, in short, are not always harmful. Third, the dose-response relationship was unknown. With most environmental hazards, *e.g.*, toxic chemicals, the higher the dose, the greater the response or effect. But this did not appear to be true of electric and magnetic fields: a number of the laboratory studies observed biological effects only in narrow ranges of field strength, frequency, or length of exposure; above and below those ranges there were no effects. Contrary to expectation, therefore, in such cases weaker fields would not necessarily be "safer" than stronger fields.

---

[8] San Diego Gas & Elec. Co. v. Superior Court, 920 P.2d 669, 678-79 (Cal. 1996).
[9] *Id.* at 677.

[The Court then turned to the question of whether a fear of future harm will support a cause of action for private nuisance.] [I]n order to award * * * damages on a nuisance theory the trier of fact would be required to find that reasonable persons, viewing the matter objectively (1) would experience a substantial fear that the fields cause physical harm and (2) would deem the invasion so serious that it outweighs the social utility of [the company's] conduct. Such findings, however, would be inconsistent with the * * * reports of advisory groups and experts * * * that the available evidence does not support a reasonable belief that * * * electric and magnetic fields [from power lines] present a substantial risk of physical harm, and that unless and until the evidence supports such a belief regulated utilities need take no action to reduce field levels from existing power lines.

—

The Court's reluctance to find a causal connection between power lines and cancer was further supported by subsequent research.[10]

BIG STUDY SEES NO EVIDENCE POWER LINES CAUSE LEUKEMIA

Gina Kolata
New York Times, July 3, 1997, p. A1

For the last 18 years, the debate over whether power lines cause cancer has been passionate and sometimes furious. Even when the National Academy of Sciences last November found no evidence of risk, it suggested further research on childhood leukemia. Now a large, meticulously designed study has found no evidence that electric power lines cause leukemia in children, researchers said yesterday.

The new study was a collaboration between scientists at the National Cancer Institute and childhood leukemia specialists from the nation's leading medical centers. It

---

[10] For further information on EMF, *see* Patsy W. Thomley, *EMF at Home: The National Research Council Report on the Health Effects of Electric and Magnetic Fields*, 12 J. LAND USE AND ENVTL. L. 309 (1998); Michael C. Anibougu, *The Future of Electromagnetic Field Litigation*, 15 PACE ENVTL. L. REV. 523 (1998). In a 1999 report to Congress, the National Institute for Environmental Health Sciences said that, while there have been some statistical associations between EMF and childhood leukemia, "virtually al the laboratory evidence in animals and humans . . . fails to support a causal relationship" between EMF and cancer.

involved 636 children with acute lymphoblastic leukemia, the most common childhood cancer, and 620 healthy children who were matched to the cancer patients by race, age and residential neighborhood.

Scientists assessed the children's exposure to magnetic fields that power lines produce, measuring the fields in the children's residences, past and present, and where the mothers lived when they were pregnant. They directly measured the fields in the children's' yards, schools and day care centers and even had the children walk around with measurement devices. Investigators doing the measurements did not know which children had had cancer.

Then the researchers asked, Did the children who developed leukemia have a higher exposure to magnetic fields?

The answer, published in today's issue of The New England Journal of Medicine, is "no," with one caveat: Those children whose exposure was above 0.300 microteslas had a slightly higher risk of leukemia. But, the researchers cautioned, there were very few children with these high exposures—just 45 out of the 638 children with cancer. And yet at the very highest exposures, the risk went back to almost normal. What this meant to the researchers was that there was no trackable relationship between level of exposure and level of risk, what is normally called a dose-response curve.

c. The Sick School

LETHAL PESTICIDE NEAR SCHOOL DIVIDES COMMUNITY

Richard Cole
The Denver Post, Dec. 13, 1997, p. 25A

Just over the fence from Amesti Elementary School on California's Central Coast, strawberries and raspberries thrive on some of the world's most fertile farmland.

But when ominous warning signs go up, and plastic tarpaulins cover the rich earth, the children at Amesti don't chase errant soccer balls onto that field.

Fall is the season for methyl bromide, a highly effective but controversial pesticide- and the latest battleground between chemical-dependant agriculture and urban sprawl.

Fall is also the season, say many of Amesti's teachers and parents, for a rash of strange ailments that have plagued the school for years.

"They are hard to pinpoint because they are flu-like symptoms, or they are headaches, or they are nosebleeds, or things that could be anything," says second-grade teacher Corinne Walcott. "When there are methyl bromide applications, children and teachers have experienced things like numbness in their faces for as long as several weeks."

For years, teachers considered the illnesses isolated problems, a normal part of the school experience.

Then they looked at the symptoms of methyl bromide poisoning. Alarm bells rang.

Blurred vision. Weakness. Dizziness. Nosebleeds. Headaches. And in more severe cases, pneumonia, paralysis, heart problems, fetal damage and ultimately death.

"My portable (classroom) is right by these raspberry fields," says second-grade teacher Karen Kite. "The wind comes directly from the field right into my windows. Some day I would like to have a choice to start a family, but these things are reproductive poisons."

When the school year started–along with the pesticide applications–the teachers decided they'd had enough. They talked to equally alarmed parents.

* * *

On Sept. 27, grower Will Garrouette began injecting methyl bromide into the field next to Amesti.

And on Sept. 27, about 270 of the school's 650 students stayed home. In subsequent applications, the number of absences dropped to around 100.

* * *

The boycott angered school officials. They lost tens of thousands of dollars in state reimbursement because of the absences.

They felt that teachers were fanning unfounded hysteria in children and parents.

"It's what it does to the kids," says Terry McHenry, assistant superintendent of the Pajaro Valley Unified School District. "They're scaring kids about being outside. They're scaring them about coming to school."

* * *

What testing has been done shows no exposure above Californiaís maximum level of 210 parts per billion, officials say.

A test of Amesti teachers after an Oct. 18 spraying found normal levels of methyl bromide in their bloodstream, say Santa Cruz County health officials.

Led by Gov. Pete Wilson, the state has continually fought efforts to ban or further restrict methyl bromide. The governor has said a ban could cost the state 10,000 jobs and nearly $350 million in crop losses.

But the pesticide can be lethal if misused. At least 15 deaths have been attributed to methyl bromide since 1982, all involving fumigated buildings. The state finally banned such use.

The United Farm Workers union has conducted a battle against the pesticide, which it fears is poisoning workers sent into the fields.

Figure 5.5–Proposed Antenna Tower on Lookout Mountain, Colorado

PROBLEM

Consider whether there is sufficient evidence in the following situation to show a causal connection between adverse health effects (brain and central nervous system tumors) and broadcast towers:

At the edge of Denver, Colorado, there is a foothill called Lookout Mountain. The pinnacle of Lookout Mountain contains the tall needles of broadcasting antennas, clustered together in an "antenna farm." Here is the most concentrated cluster of television and FM towers in the nation. For the thousands of residents of Lookout Mountain, and for residents of the nearby Genesee community, the electro-magnetic radiation (EMR) coming from the towers is a potential health problem. Those residents who are in the direct line of sight of the towers are experiencing a hundred, or in some cases, a thousand times more EMR than the average American citizen.

A coalition of television stations wants to build the tallest tower of all, over 850 feet high. The stations would send out new, powerful signals from the tower, to provide state-of-the-art digitalized high definition television to viewers in and around Denver. The amount of radiated power from the antennas on the new tower could double the intensity being broadcast from the existing antenna farm. The television broadcasters believe that they have no choice. They are facing a congressionally mandated deadline of November 1999 to begin broadcasting digital television signals.

A coalition of homeowners' associations and neighborhoods in the vicinity of the existing antenna farm (CARE—Canyon Area Residents for the Environment) is opposing construction of the new tower. CARE is concerned that there may be health effects—especially brain cancers and leukemias—that may be caused by long-term exposure to excessive amounts of radiated power. The entity representing the television stations, the Lake Cedar Group, claims there are no health effects from the existing towers, and there would be no health effects from the proposed tower. Moreover, the Lake Cedar Group maintains that the tower site would be in compliance with federal standards, which permits 200 microwatts per square centimeter.

A recent Press Release from CARE states:

For Immediate Release

COLORADO DEPARTMENT OF HEALTH TO REVEAL RESULTS OF BRAIN CANCERS AUDIT IN THE VICINITY OF THE LOOKOUT MT. ANTENNA FARMS AT PUBLIC COMMUNITY MEETING
✝ ✝ ✝

A Delaware Limited Liability Company, Lake Cedar Group, is proposing to * * * erect a broadcast tower on Lookout Mt. that would double the amount and geographic area of radiation in this community.

- At Ralston Elementary School, for example, approx. 3.2 miles from the proposed tower, the radiation would increase from about 0.5 to about 7.48 microwatts per centimeter squared. The expected amounts of radiation at Ralston would be higher than the average amount now at residences near the existing towers and higher than the level recorded in the US Embassy in Moscow, when the Soviets were eavesdropping with microwave radiation. Adverse health consequences to Embassy staff were recorded.

- CARE requested this cancer study because Lookout Mt. is the most intense and complex electromagnetic radiation environment in a residential area in the country and because of the following reported research:

- A growing number of scientists believe that electromagnetic radiation causes adverse health effects ranging from loss of sleep and irritability to reduction in melatonin production and various cancers.

- An increase in the risk of brain and lymphoid cancers with exposure to RF radiation has been reported for US Air Force personnel; radio, TV and radar operators, and for Polish military personnel. Studies of humans exposed to RF radiation indicate increases in lymphoid cancer in three epidemiological studies of communities in close proximity to commercial or military radio/TV broadcast antennae in Hawaii, England and Australia.

At about the same time that CARE issued its press release, the Colorado Department of Health has issued a preliminary report on the tower issue. It states, in relevant part:

This study is a follow-up to an investigation of cancer incidence in the Lookout Mountain area that was conducted by the Colorado Department of Public Health and Environment in June 1998. The current study examines the incidence of brain and central nervous system (CNS) tumors in small subunits, called block groups, within the census tract studied in 1998. This study was prepared in response to citizen concerns about the occurrence of brain cancers in residents living near broadcast antenna towers in the Lookout Mountain area.

* * *

After review and analysis of the study results, the [study] concluded that some evidence supported and some did not support an association between radiofrequency exposure from the antennas with the occurrence of brain and central nervous system tumors.

The findings the [study] considered to be *consistent* with an association were as follows:

- Statistically elevated risk ratios occurred in block groups 2 and 3, which are the block groups closest to the antenna towers;

- All cases or their surviving family members indicated when interviewed that the residence where that person lived at the time of their diagnosis had an unobstructed view of the towers. While line of sight does not confirm or quantify exposure, studies have shown that radiofrequency readings are greatly reduced at locations where line of sight to the towers is blocked by a mountainside or even other buildings or trees;

- For all block group 2 cases, interviews indicated that all individuals had resided in the area for longer than 10 years which is generally believed to be the least amount of time necessary for adult cancer to be diagnosed or recognized clinically after an exposure of concern has occurred; and

- None of the block 2 cases had worked in an occupation associated with an increased risk of developing brain or central nervous system tumors, although questions were not included in the interview about other possible exposures inside or outside the home which might also contribute to increased rates of brain or central nervous system tumors.

The findings the [study] considered to be *inconsistent* with an association were as follows:

- The cell type of the tumors and the gender of the cases were not the same for the two block groups with a statistically significant increase in the number of observed cases; the three cases in block group 2 were diagnosed with benign meningioma and all occurred in women for the 1985-1997 time period; in block group 3, four of five cases occurred in men, all of whom were diagnosed with malignant astrocytomas or glioblastomas. Findings of epidemiologic studies such as this are generally strengthened when both genders show a similar pattern of tumor occurrence since exposure around the home would be expected to affect men and women similarly;

- The follow-up interviews conducted indicate that 2 of the 5 cases in block group 3 had lived near the Lookout Mountain antennas less than 5 years. In addition, four of the five persons diagnosed with a brain or central nervous system tumor in block group 3 also had worked in an occupation with an increased risk of developing a brain tumor; and

- There were no sudden increases seen in the occurrence of cases for any given calendar year and the pattern of case distribution over the time period studied was no different in the block groups where elevated risk ratios occurred than for other block groups farther away from the antenna towers.[11]

On the basis of the foregoing evidence, how would you advise the television stations? Keep in mind that your clients firmly believe that there is no risk and that they are under considerable pressure to erect new broadcasting capacity *somewhere*. If they proceed with their plans to build the new tower, what is the likelihood that they will be successfully sued for causing toxic injury?

2. Who Is the Proper Defendant?

Under traditional tort theory, the plaintiff must show that the defendant's product or conduct was responsible for the harm suffered by the plaintiff. In a toxic tort case, it may be impossible to identify who caused the injury. Even when the plaintiff can pinpoint a toxic substance that produced some medical ailment, it may not be possible to know who, among several manufacturers of the substance, was the one who actually made the substance that injured the plaintiff. Or, if the plaintiff has been injured from groundwater contaminated from a waste disposal site, it may be possible to identify the manufacturers of the toxic substances dumped into the site, but impossible to know which such substance, among several, caused the plaintiff's harm. When the plaintiff is unable to identify the defendant or defendants responsible for the harm suffered, the traditional rule is that the tort action must be dismissed.

However, some courts have adopted theories of liability to assist the beleaguered plaintiff. Under *market share liability*, manufacturers who produce a fungible and unidentifiable product that injures the plaintiff are held liable in proportion to their respective market shares. *See Sindell v. Abbott Laboratories*, 607 P.2d 924 (Cal. 1980); *Hymowitz v. Eli Lilly & Co.*, 539 N.E. 2d 1069 (N.Y. 1989). While market-share liability, or a variant of it, has been adopted in several jurisdictions for DES cases, courts that have addressed the issue have rejected market share theory in toxic tort cases. *City of Philadelphia v. Lead Industries Assoc., Inc.*, 994 F.2d 112 (3d Cir. 1993) (market share liability not adopted in lead-based paint litigation because of unfairness to defendants); *Goldman v. Johns-Manville Sales*

---

[11] *The Incidence Of Brain And Central Nervous System Tumors In Residents In The Vicinity Of The Lookout Mountain Antenna Farm.* Report of the Colorado Department of Public Health and Environment in Collaboration with the Department of Environmental Health, Colorado State University and Jefferson County Department of Health and Environment, February 1999.

Corp., 514 N.E. 2d 691 (Ohio 1987) (asbestos litigation involving varying asbestos contents in the products of various manufacturers).

Alternative liability holds that all tortfeasors who are unable to exculpate themselves are jointly and severally liable for the plaintiff's injury. *Summers v. Tice*, 199 P.2d 1 (Cal. 1948). The RESTATEMENT (SECOND) OF TORTS § 433B(3) adopts alternative liability:

> Where the conduct of two or more actors is tortious, and it is proved that harm has been caused to the plaintiff by only one of them, but there is uncertainty as to which one of them has caused it, the burden is upon each such actor to prove that he has not caused the harm.

The rationale behind alternative liability is that independently operating defendants may be in a better position to identify who was responsible for the plaintiff's injury. Alternative liability therefore makes no sense when manufacturers of a dangerous product are in no better position than the plaintiffs to determine the specific defendant who caused the alleged injury, *see Collins v. Eli Lilly & Co.*, 342 N.W. 2d 37 (Wis. 1984), as is frequently the case in toxic torts litigation.

Enterprise liability permits liability to attach on the basis of an entire industry's culpable conduct. Each defendant who contributes to the development of an unreasonable industry-wide safety standard (*e.g.*, one established by a trade association) may be liable if the industry standard is found deficient. *Hall v. E.I. Du Pont Nemours & Co.*, 345 F.Supp. 353 (E.D.N.Y. 1972) (blasting caps). In the rare instances where enterprise liability has been found, the following facts are present: (1) a small number of manufacturers, virtually all of whom are named defendants, produced the injury-causing product; (2) the defendants had joint knowledge of the risks inherent in the risks, and possessed a joint capacity to reduce the risks; (3) each delegated responsibility to set safety standards to a third party representative of the defendants, which failed to reduce the risk.

Courts have been reluctant to adopt these theories of liability in toxic tort cases. Why? Can you make the argument that they are particularly *appropriate* for toxic torts?

3. Evidence and Expert Testimony

If causation is to be proved, it must be by the introduction of scientific and medical evidence through expert testimony. Judicial exclusion of some of this evidence is usually fatal to the case. The traditional approach to the admissibility of such evidence was deferential. Look back at *Ferebee*: What is the standard that the D.C. Circuit applied to the admissibility of the plaintiff's evidence in that case? What were the plaintiff's experts' qualifications to opine on causation issues? What was the basis for their conclusions?[12]

However, as deference began to lose favor in public regulation, courts in civil cases became increasingly concerned that juries were being allowed to reach multi-million-dollar verdicts on the basis of highly questionable scientific evidence.[13] Whatever the merits of this claim in general, it gathered support from the Bendectin litigation. Benedectin was an anti-nausea drug prescribed to combat morning sickness. Perhaps by analogy to Thalidomide and DES, other pregnancy drugs that proved to have disastrous adverse effects, concern arose regarding the teratogenic effects of Bendectin, and parents of children with birth defects began to file suit. Whereas the evidence linking both Thalidomide and DES to subsequent harm was strong and the connection is today virtually uncontroverted, the evidence on Bendectin is far less clear. However, since the defendants were rarely in a position to offer an alternative explanation of the birth defect, the plaintiffs had notable success with juries, though almost none in keeping the verdicts after post-trial motions and appeal.[14] This seemed to point to the need for courts to step in to control juries and, in effect, to vindicate the judgment of the Food and Drug Administration that Bendectin is safe. (It remains an approved drug.) Indeed, the Fifth Circuit cited *Gulf South* in support of its view that, among other weaknesses, the plaintiffs could not rely on animal data. *Brock v. Merrill-Dow Pharmaceuticals*, 874 F.2d 307 (5th Cir. 1989), *revised*, 884 F.2d 166 (5th Cir.), *rehearing en banc denied*, 886 F.2d 1314, *cert. denied*, 494 U.S. 1046 (1990).[15]

Bendectin at last reached the Supreme Court in *Daubert v. Merrell Dow Pharmaceuticals*, 509 U.S. 579, 589-94 (1993), which set the standard for admissibility of scientific evidence in the federal courts today. Justice

---

[12] The Seventh Circuit took a similar "battle of the experts" approach in Wells v. Ortho, 788 F2d 741 (7th Cir.), *cert. denied*, 479 U.S. 950 (1986) (upholding jury verdict contrary to view of majority of medical community).

[13] Bendectin was a constant theme of the tort-reform movement of the 1980s. *See, e.g,* PETER W. HUBER, GALILEO'S REVENGE: JUNK SCIENCE IN THE COURTROOM (1991); PETER W. HUBER *ET AL.*, PHANTOM RISK: SCIENTIFIC INFERENCE AND THE LAW (1993). Apart from the outrageous anecdotes that Huber and others cite, however, the evidence of a widespread problem is extremely weak. *See* Marc Galanter, *Real World Torts: An Antidote to Anecdotes*, 55 MD.L.REV. 1093 (1996).

[14] For excellent reviews of the Bendectin litigation, *see* Michael O. Green, *Expert Witnesses and Sufficiency of Evidence in Toxic Substances Litigation: The Legacy of the Agent Orange and Bendectin Litigation*, 86 NW. U.L. REV. 643 (1992); Joseph Sanders, *From Science to Evidence: The Testimony on Causation in the Bendectin Cases*, 46 STAN. L. REV. 1 (1993).

[15] There is a split among courts in accepting animal studies to demonstrate human effects. *See* Sterling v. Velsicol Chemical Corp., 855 F.2d 1188 (6th Cir. 1988) (accepting); *but see* In re Agent Orange Litigation, 611 F. Supp. 1223, 1231 (E.D.N.Y. 1984), *aff'd*, 818 F.2d 187 (2d Cir. 1987), *cert. denied*, 487 U.S. 1234 (1988) (rejecting it).

Blackmun departed strongly from the laissez-faire "battle of the experts" approach:

> [U]nder [Rule 702] the trial judge must ensure that any and all scientific testimony or evidence admitted is not only relevant, but reliable.
>
> The * * * subject of an expert's testimony must be "scientific . . . knowledge." * * * But, in order to qualify as "scientific knowledge," an inference or assertion must be derived by the scientific method. Proposed testimony must be supported by appropriate validation—*i.e.*, "good grounds," based on what is known. In short, the requirement that an expert's testimony pertain to "scientific knowledge" establishes a standard of evidentiary reliability.

* * *

> * * * We are confident that federal judges possess the capacity to undertake this review. Many factors will bear on the inquiry, and we do not presume to set out a definitive checklist or test. But some general observations are appropriate.
>
> Ordinarily, a key question to be answered in determining whether a theory or technique is scientific knowledge that will assist the trier of fact will be whether it can be (and has been) tested. "Scientific methodology today is based on generating hypotheses and testing them to see if they can be falsified; indeed, this methodology is what distinguishes science from other fields of human inquiry." * * *
>
> Another pertinent consideration is whether the theory or technique has been subjected to peer review and publication. Publication (which is but one element of peer review) is not a *sine qua non* of admissibility; it does not necessarily correlate with reliability, * * * [b]ut submission to the scrutiny of the scientific community is a component of "good science," in part because it increases the likelihood that substantive flaws in methodology will be detected. * * *

* * *

> Finally, "general acceptance" can yet have a bearing on the inquiry. * * * Widespread acceptance can be an important factor in ruling particular evidence admissible, and "a known technique that has been able to attract only minimal support within the community," may properly be viewed with skepticism.

The *Daubert* case, in other words, interprets the Federal Rules of Evidence to impose a test of "scientific validity" for admissibility.[16] This test requires the trial judge to ensure that any scientific testimony or evidence admitted is not only relevant, but also reliable. *Daubert* also serves as the standard for many state rulings on the admissibility of scientific evidence.[17]

Consequently, before ruling on evidence, trial courts may undertake a preliminary inquiry to ascertain whether the proffered evidence or testimony meets the *Daubert* standard. A number of courts have looked favorably on medical testimony that relies heavily on a temporal relationship between an illness and a causal event. These courts do not believe that *Daubert* requires a physician to rely on definitive published studies in such a situation to establish that a chemical is the most likely cause of a plaintiff's illness. For example, if a person was doused with chemical X and immediately thereafter developed symptom Y, the need for published literature showing a correlation between the two is lessened. *Heller v. Shaw Industries, Inc.*, 167 F.3d 146, 154-155 (3d Cir. 1999). (What does this suggest about the result in *Ferebee*?) *But see Moore v. Ashland, Chemical, Inc.*, 151 F.3d 269 (5th Cir. 1998) (rejecting a pulmonary specialist's testimony linking a former truck driver's respiratory illness to on-the-job exposure to hazardous chemicals, because the testimony—based on "speculative" clinical observations rather than peer-reviewed scientific studies—fell short of the *Daubert* standard for admissible expert testimony).

The Court has reaffirmed its adherence to *Daubert* in more recent cases. In *General Electric Co. v. Joiner*, 522 U.S. 136 (1997), the Court ruled that trial courts' decisions to exclude evidence should be reviewed under the very deferential "abuse of discretion" standard. In *Kumho Tire Company, Ltd. v. Carmichael*, 526 U.S. 137 (1999), the Court warned that judges should make certain that an expert, whether basing testimony upon professional studies or personal experience, employs in the courtroom the same level of rigor required in the expert's relevant field. However, judges retain great leeway in determining whether an expert's methods are sound. In sum, courts may reject theories that they find are unreliable, not backed by hard evidence, and that may cause delay and confusion. *In re TMI*

---

[16] This test is derived by Federal Rule of Evidence 702, which governs the admissibility of expert testimony:

    If scientific, technical, or other specialized knowledge will assist the trier of fact to understand the evidence or to determine a fact in issue, a witness qualified as an expert by knowledge, skill, experience, training, or education, may testify thereto in the form of an opinion . . . .

[17] *See generally* Daniel J. Capra, *The Daubert Puzzle*, 32 GA. L. REV. 699 (1998); Anthony Z. Roisman, *The Courts, Daubert, and Environmental Torts: Gatekeepers or Auditors?*, 14 PACE ENVIR. L. REV. 545 (1997); C. Cranor, John Fischer, and David Eastmond, *Judicial Boundary Drawing and the Need for Context-Sensitive Science in Toxic Torts After Daubert*, 16 VA. ENVTL. L.J. 1 (1996).

Litigation, 193 F.3d 613 (3d Cir. 1999); *In re Paoli R.R. Yard PCB Litigation,* 113 F.3d 444 (3d Cir. 1997). Evidence of causation will be excluded when based upon subjective opinion, instead of accepted scientific methodology. *O'Connor v. Commonwealth Edison Co.,* 13 F.3d 1090 (7th Cir. 1994). Courts are also skeptical of experts proposing to testify based on opinions developed expressly for purposes of litigation, as opposed to matters growing naturally out of research. *Freeport-McMorran Resource Partners v. B-B Paint,* 56 F.Supp. 2d 823 (E.D.Mich. 1999).

PUBLIC CLAMOR PUTS FOCUS ON 'CLUSTERS' IN CANCER RESEARCH

Susan Sachs
New York Times, Sept. 21, 1998, p. A1

Linda Gillick began her quest convinced that science and a little common sense could explain why in one ordinary patch of New Jersey seashore, an unusual number of children, her son Michael among them, have similar types of cancers.

She reasoned that it must be something in the water or air, some unnoticed chemical lurking under a toxic waste dump or factory—but in any case, a specific culprit that she assumed could be located, analyzed and then eradicated.

"When you have something that is grossly abnormal, you need to find out the indicator that is different from somewhere else," said Mrs. Gillick, who organized a movement by residents that persuaded the state to make a comprehensive environmental study of her town, Toms River, and of surrounding Dover Township in Ocean County. "What do we have that's different—that's the key."

As logical as it may sound, Mrs. Gillick's assumption represents a challenge to traditional science's previous approach to cancer clusters. Many scientists say that they simply do not exist—that there is a lot of cancer everywhere and that neighborhood concentrations of the disease result from chance, not from the environment. But people who live in areas where the incidence of cancer is higher than expected have rarely been content with that rationale.

Many of these people are turning their discontent into political action. Armed with the clout that gave them an audience with President Clinton in August and a starring role in some of Senator Alfonse M. D'Amato's re-election campaign advertisements, they have caused tens of millions of dollars to be dedicated to new research into cancer clusters.

"This is pushing science to a new era—of eco-genetic epidemiology," said Ruth Allen, an environmental epidemiologist with the Federal Environmental Protection Agency. She is the agency's project leader for a $21 million study of elevated breast cancer rates on Long Island. "This is where molecular biomarkers of disease and geographical variations are examined together."

Across the country, health officials are re-examining old monitoring data, using newly refined techniques to search for chemicals that may not have been looked at in earlier air, water and soil tests in communities where cancer clusters are suspected. Ambitious studies are under way using plain gumshoe detective work combined with computer mapping that can fine-tune the picture of what is in a community's environment, identify how people might be exposed to synthetic chemicals and determine whether small amounts of such chemicals may be toxic to humans.

In addition to the investigation of certain childhood cancers in Dover Township and breast cancer on Long Island, there are statewide studies of cancer and chemical use in Connecticut and California, a Federal study of elevated breast cancer deaths in mid-Atlantic and Northeast states, and Federal studies of childhood and adult brain cancers near toxic waste sites in several states.

Cancer clusters, a shorthand phrase to describe higher-than-expected concentrations of similar cancers in one discrete area, have been in the national vocabulary for decades. They can be notoriously difficult to document with standard statistical analysis. Sometimes the data involve such small numbers of cases that epidemiologists cannot make a conclusion about whether an anomaly exists. Sometimes, according to the National Cancer Institute, scientists find "a true excess," but cannot explain it.

"There are so many types of cancer and birth defects that just by chance alone you'd expect any one of them to be high in any one little town," said Dr. Bruce N. Ames, a biochemist and molecular biologist who directs the National Institute of Environmental Health Sciences Center at the University of California at Berkeley.

In a view widely held in the scientific world, he said that the money devoted to research into environmental links to cancer is misspent and that there is "no convincing evidence" that synthetic chemicals in the atmosphere are an important cause of cancer in humans. "I'd put my money into basic research, not into chasing hypothetical risks," Dr. Ames said.

Like a growing number of lay people who have become advocates, the Gillick family was not willing to have Dover Township's record of childhood cancers written off as a statistical fluke. The township in southern New Jersey has had 90 cases over a 12-year period, compared with the 67 cases that New Jersey health officials said could be expected during that time.

"It's important to look at everything— the water, the soil, the air, all of it, and try to find an answer," said Michael Gillick, who was found to have neuroblastoma when he was 3 _ months old.

Now 19, with a shrunken body that is painfully contorted by the disease, he said he realizes that all the research may never tell him why he, or any other cancer victim, is sick. "It's too late for me," Mr. Gillick said, "I already have what I have. I accept it. It's my wish that this not happen to others."

Public clamor for answers has prodded many states, including New York and New Jersey, to process and publish cancer data faster. In April, for example, the New York State Assembly appropriated $1 million for a comprehensive statewide cancer mapping project. It was to correlate the types and locations of specific cancers—information already assembled in the state cancer registry—with data for specific neighborhoods on past and present water quality, pesticide and chemical emissions, radiation exposure, industrial pollution and local toxic waste sites.

Many states, including Hawaii, Illinois and California, have undertaken statewide cancer mapping projects. The proliferation of cancer mapping reflects a growing trend nationwide to integrate two sets of data that are widely and publicly available: one on toxic chemical releases and the other on geographical variations in the incidence of some diseases. The trend follows a decade of intense focus on cancer risk factors like diet, life style and heredity.

"Communities now are saying we don't have any of these risk factors, and still we have a problem," said Dr. Allen of the Environmental Protection Agency. "They ask commonsense questions that are at once simple and profound."

Dr. Allen said that "scientists have new tools and new hypotheses that they are testing," but that the political impetus for environmental research came after advocates of cancer-cluster]studies in places like Toms River and Long Island presented elected officials with raw data from their own homemade cancer maps. Politicians have responded.

"They now look at graphical information and say: 'Gee, in my district it's this number, and in yours it's that. What's going on?'" Dr. Allen said.

THE ROLE OF EPIDEMIOLOGY IN PROVING INDIVIDUAL CAUSATION

Reference Manual on Scientific Evidence, Federal Judicial Center, pp. 167-170 (1994)

Epidemiology is concerned with the incidence of disease in populations and does not address the question of the cause of an individual's disease. This [latter] question, sometimes referred to as specific causation, is beyond the domain of the science of epidemiology. Epidemiology has its limits at the point where an inference is made that the relationship between an agent and a disease is causal (general causation) and where the magnitude of excess risk attributed to the agent has been determined; that is, epidemiology addresses whether an agent can cause a disease, not whether an agent did cause a plaintiff's disease.

* * *

There are two legal issues that arise with regard to the role of epidemiology in proving individual causation: admissibility and sufficiency of evidence to meet the burden of production. The first issue tends to receive less attention by the courts but nevertheless deserves mention. An epidemiological study that is sufficiently rigorous to justify a conclusion that it is scientifically valid should be admissible, as it tends to make an issue in dispute more or less likely.

Far more courts have confronted the role that epidemiology plays with regard to the sufficiency of the evidence and the burden of production. The civil burden of proof is described most often as requiring the fact finder to "believe that what is sought to be proved * * * is more likely true than not true." The relative risk from an epidemiological study can be adapted to this 50% plus standard to yield a probability or likelihood that an agent caused an individual's disease. The threshold for concluding that an agent was more likely the cause of a disease than not is a relative risk greater than 2.0. Recall that a relative risk of 1.0 means that the agent has no effect on the incidence of disease. When the relative risk reaches 2.0, the agent is responsible for an equal number of cases of disease as all other background causes. Thus, a relative risk of 2.0 implies a 50% likelihood that an exposed individual's disease was caused by the agent. A relative risk greater than 2.0 would permit an inference that an individual plaintiff's disease was more likely than not caused by the implicated agent. A substantial number of courts in a variety of toxic substances cases have accepted this reasoning.

* * *

[A] few courts conclude that a plaintiff may satisfy his or her burden of production even if a relative risk less than 2.0 emerges from the epidemiological evidence. For example, genetics might be known to be responsible for 50% of the incidence of a disease. If genetics can be ruled out in an individual's case, then a relative risk greater than 1.5 might be sufficient to support an inference that the agent was more likely than not responsible for the plaintiff's disease.

NOTES

1. For another perspective on anomalies, read Atul Gawande, *The Cancer-Cluster Myth*, excerpted in Chapter 14.

2. Why do cancer clusters appear frequently in toxic tort litigation? Why are they thought to be probative of causation?

3. Are cancer clusters in effect a form of epidemiology? If so, what are their limitations as proof of causation?

4. How would epidemiological studies fare under the *Daubert* standard? Should they be admissible for limited purposes?

4. Latent Illness

The effects of exposure to a toxic substance or hazardous activity often do not manifest themselves until long after the initial exposure. The long latency period associated with toxic harms (*e.g.*, cancer, birth defects, genetic mutation) create several problems for plaintiffs whose injury may remain undetected for years, or even decades. One obvious problem involves causation. When many years (or generations) pass between an exposure and an injury, the collection of evidence and identification of responsible tortfeasors becomes difficult. *See Borel v. Fibrebound Paper Prods. Corp.*, 493 F.2d 1076 (5th Cir. 1973) (asbestos). Long latency periods also mean that plaintiffs who have been exposed to a toxic substance, but who have not yet developed any symptoms, may wish to seek recovery on the basis of increased *risk* of future illness. *See Ayers v. Township of Jackson*, 525 A.2d 287 (N.J. 1987); Note, *Latent Harms and Risk-Based Damages*, 111 HARV. L. REV. 1505 (1998).

LOUISIANA TOWN GOES TO TRIAL OVER WASTE PIT

Kevin Sack
New York Times, July 13, 1998, p. A10

GRAND BOIS, La., July 10—The people of Grand Bois say their symptoms began almost immediately that day in March 1994 when eight tractor trailers loaded with oil field sludge rumbled past their tiny Acadian community and into an adjacent waste disposal site.

"When the trucks took the curve, the smell just took over the community," said Clarice M. Friloux, a 32-year-old mother of two. "The kids were getting off the school bus with their shirts over their faces. They stayed sick with diarrhea and dizziness for several days. Our noses were burning, sore throats. You'd wake up with swollen, puffy eyes."

For 10 days the convoys continued, 81 trucks in all, bringing waste laced with substances like benzene, xylene, hydrogen sulfide and arsenic from an Exxon petroleum treatment plant in Alabama. Men sheathed in white protective suits unloaded the waste into a giant open earthen pit, just

333 feet from the tin-roofed home of Lyes L. Verdin.

Mr. Verdin is a charcoal-haired bantam of a man whose Cajun accent is as impenetrable as the humidity along Bayou LaFourche. He maintains that his 8-year-old daughter, Angel, has suffered since that day from chronic headaches, rashes and diarrhea so severe that he must keep a bucket in his family car. As shipments have continued, residents across Grand Bois have blamed ailments from dizziness to chest pains on the chemicals.

On Monday, in a courtroom in nearby Thibodaux, Mr. Verdin and his neighbors in this settlement will seek their revenge. Led by a 33-year-old New Orleans lawyer who took the case two years out of law school, the first 11 of 301 plaintiffs—virtually the entire population of Grand Bois—will present their case against Exxon and the Campbell Wells Corporation, the former owners of the disposal site.

The trial pits the grandmamas and fishermen of Grand Bois against the most powerful industry in the state, an industry that won a Congressional exemption 18 years ago to allow it to dispose of oil field waste with virtually no regulation.

The residents are seeking at least $8 million in compensatory damages and unspecified punitive damages. Separate lawsuits have been filed in state and Federal courts seeking injunctions to shut down the waste disposal site.

The trial in Thibodaux, which is expected to last at least a month, will be watched closely by the oil industry, by Federal regulators and by the state government. Publicity about the problems in Grand Bois (pronounced Gran BWAH) has become an irritant for Gov. Mike Foster, who is distrusted by the residents and who, in turn, is deeply frustrated that the community has rejected the state's offers of medical and environmental testing.

Mr. Foster said that without the benefit of comprehensive testing, he remains unconvinced that the waste site is the source of the community's health problems. That is essentially the position taken by Exxon and Campbell Wells.

"We have not discovered a problem yet," said Mr. Foster, a first-term Republican who is considered friendly to business. "I mean, we can't identify a problem." Clearly exasperated, he said he empathized with the community but added: "I'm tired of it and I want to get it resolved. It is not good for the state of Louisiana to have these kinds of allegations floating around out there."

Here along the murky bayous of southern Louisiana, there has long been an uneasy coexistence between the oil industry and the vibrant, insular culture of the Cajuns and Houma Indians. It is a place where gleaming silver petrochemical plants rise out of vast stands of sugar cane like Oz out of the poppy fields. The gentle breezes that sway beards of Spanish moss in the oaks may also carry odors of sulphur and diesel across the porches of Acadian cottages.

But rarely have the tensions been as exposed as in Grand Bois, a community of 94 houses, too small for the maps, where residents see the neighboring waste pits as a threat to a beloved way of life. Folks here inevitably describe their hamlet as a single extended family, where people trust one another enough to leave keys in their car ignitions and where special occasions are celebrated around kettles of boiling crawfish.

The people fish and crab and work in the shipyards and hospitals. Even if they wanted to move away from the 18 waste cells, which are contained by low levees, few could afford to do so without selling their homes. For the time being, that is impossible. Residents have lined the main road with homemade signs warning of toxic chemicals and depicting the Grim Reaper. The real estate market is, to say the least, depressed.

The community's emotions swing from anger to sadness and fear. "I've had my life," said Joyceline M. Dominique, a 58-year old grandmother of 12 who has filled five composition books with a chronicle of her family's ailments. "If I go, so be it. But with the children, these are the best years of their lives."

The trial is certain to become a battle of experts, thick with testimony about chemical compounds and medical histories. A central piece of evidence will be the blood and urine testing conducted by Dr. Patricia M. Williams, director of the Occupational Toxicology Outreach Program at the Louisiana state University Medical Center in Shreveport.

She found that 74 percent of the 99 women and children tested had stippled red blood cells, a deformity typically caused by heavy metal poisoning or chemical exposure.

"Normally you would find zero," Dr. Williams said. "So when you see such a spectrum with all these different children from different households, you have to say there's an outside environmental reason."

The residents' case will not be easy to prove, and not only because of the circumstantial nature of the evidence.

In 1980, when memories of the 1979 gas shortage were still stark, Congress granted petroleum exploration and production companies an exemption from the hazardous waste disposal regulations that apply to most other industries.

Those who question the exemption, including Carol M. Browner, the Administrator of the Environmental Protection Agency, call it a sweetheart deal for an industry protected by powerful politicians.

Industry spokesmen, like Mark Rubin, the senior manager for exploration and production of the American Petroleum Institute, say the exemption was granted because only small amounts of the waste produced by oil drilling are toxic and because stricter rules would cost the industry more than $1 billion a year.

The exemption left the regulation of oil field waste disposal to the states. And in Louisiana, where the petroleum industry employed 79,000 people last year, oil field waste has been defined as nonhazardous.

That leaves Gladstone Jones 3d, the confident young lawyer for the Grand Bois residents, to prove that Exxon and Campbell Wells were negligent in their handling of the waste, and to convince a jury that his negligence claim outweighs the protection afforded by the oil industry's regulatory exemption.

In the end, the ambiguous evidence and the likely long latency period led to an unclear solution. Before the case went to the jury, Campbell Wells settled out of court for perhaps as high as $10 million, and agreed to close the four sludge pits nearest to the town. The jury eventually found in favor of four plaintiffs, but ordered Exxon to pay just $35,000 in damages.

A second issue arising from latent illness involves the statute of limitations. Under traditional statute of limitations doctrine, the period of time within which the plaintiff may bring the claim runs from the time of the "accrual" of the claim. If this concept were to apply to toxic torts characterized by latent illness, the action would have accrued at the time of the last exposure. Since the illness does not, because it is latent, become evident until many years after the last exposure, most plaintiffs' claims would be time-barred. Several jurisdictions have addressed this inherent problem with latent illnesses by ruling, through judicial decision or statute, that the cause of action accrues when the plaintiff knew or should have known of the injury, and of the potential cause. Several cases have concluded that a plaintiff suffering from a latent illness does not have a duty actively to investigate possible causes of the illness in order to satisfy the "knew or should have known" test and thereby preserve the cause of action. *Evanson v. Osmore Wood Preserving Company of America*, 899 F.2d 701 (7th Cir. 1990); *Joseph v. Hess Oil*, 867 F.2d 179 (3d Cir. 1989). *See also Buttram v. Owens-Corning Fiberglas Corp.*, 941 P.2d 71, 80 (Cal. 1997) (diagnosis and discovery of actual injury should be the date on which a cause of action should be deemed to accrue).

A third legal issue associated with latent illness is whether an insurer of the plaintiff, under a comprehensive general liability policy, must indemnify the insured (usually a losing defendant in a toxic tort action) when a plaintiff is awarded compensation for an illness manifested long after exposure. This issue is answered according to what act causes the insurance policy to apply. If *exposure* to a toxic substance is that act, then the insurance policy provides coverage if the policy was in effect at the time of the plaintiff's exposure. If the *presence of the illness* is the critical act, then coverage must be supplied by the insurance carrier whose policy is applicable at the time of the discovery of the illness. *Eagle-Picher Industries, Inc. v. Liberty Mutual Insurance Co.*, 829 F.2d 227 (10th Cir. 1987). Some courts find coverage by any insurance policy in effect throughout the entire exposure-to-disease-manifestation period. The rationale here is that a toxic substance causes injury from the time of first exposure to the discovery of the illness. *Keene Corp. v. Insurance Company of North America*, 667 F.2d 1034 (D.C. Cir. 1981).

5. "Mass" Tort Litigation: Who Is a Proper Plaintiff?

Toxic tort litigation is unique because a combination of causal indeterminacy and the potential of large numbers of claimants (their numbers can be in the thousands) stretches the ability of the American judicial system to accommodate fairly the needs of multiple plaintiffs and defendants. Courts have struggled to manage problems that arise when (1) the identification of plaintiffs injured by a defendant is extremely difficult, and (2) there are large numbers of potential plaintiffs who may have been exposed to the harmful substance or activity. These issues often emerge in so-called mass tort cases, where many claimants have ingested a common substance, been exposed to a consumer product, or been poisoned by a toxic chemical.

In regard to identification of Plaintiffs, it may be impossible to know precisely who has been injured by the defendant's product or activity because of long latency periods between exposure to a toxic substance and development of disease. Some who have been in contact with the harm-producing agent, and who develop an illness, may have become sick because of some other cause, like smoking. These individuals may never know whether their illness was attributable to the toxic substance or activity at issue, or to something else. Moreover, some exposed persons may not have manifested any symptoms at the time the litigation commences. These "future" claimants certainly deserve relief, even after the lawsuit is over.

For plaintiffs who are unsure whether their illness can be traced to the defendant or to some independent factor, courts may loosen the causation requirement. Such plaintiffs may be able to shift to the defendant the burden of *disproving* causation by showing, often with statistical data, that the defendant's actions increased the risk of harm, and that the plaintiff's personal history and lifestyle were inconsistent with the illness contracted. *See Allen v. United States*, 588 F.Supp. 247 (D. Utah 1984), *rev'd on other grounds*, 816 F.2d 1417 (10th Cir. 1987). Future victims may obtain relief if defendants agree, pursuant to some broad pre-trial settlement, to provide compensation to parties who (1) were exposed in the past to the toxic product, and (2) submit claims in the future when and if the injury occurs. *See Carlough v. Amchem Products, Inc.*, 834 F. Supp. 1437 (E.D. Pa. 1993).

In regard to managing mass tort cases effectively, it is often helpful to aggregate the plaintiffs. A class action, pursuant to Rule 23 of the Federal Rules of Civil Procedure, allows a few individuals to sue as representatives of a large group of claimants. A class action permits plaintiffs who might not otherwise pursue a claim to be represented as part of the class. A class action serves the twin goals of judicial economy and protection of those who cannot afford to press individual claims separately. Courts accept class actions when the following conditions are present:

- The class is so large that joinder of all members is impractical;
- Claims of representative plaintiffs are typical of class members;
- Representatives of the class will fairly and adequately protect the interests of the class
- Common issues of law and fact predominate; and
- Class action will not be so unmanageable or confusing as to unduly prejudice defendants. *De Saro v. Industrial Excess Landfill, Inc.*, 587 N.E. 2d 454 (Ohio App. 1991); *Sterling v. Velsicol Chemical Corp.*, 855 F.2d 1188 (6th Cir. 1988).

Before a class action can commence, the class must be defined so that the court knows who the plaintiffs are and whose interests are being represented. The class must have some kind of commonality, such as exposure to a toxic substance. A good example of this kind of class can be found in the Agent Orange litigation. The judge there defined the relevant class as those members of the United States, New Zealand, and Australian armed forces who had manifested some injury after being exposed to phenoxy herbicides in Vietnam. *In re Agent Orange Product Liability Litigation*, 100 F.R.D. 718 (D.N.Y. 1983). Standing problems may preclude defining a class as persons who were exposed to a toxic substance but have not yet become symptomatic. *McElhaney v. Eli Lilly & Co.*, 93 F.R.D. 875 (D.S.D. 1982).

PROBLEM

In a mass tort case involving a toxic substance (*e.g.*, asbestos products), may the plaintiffs be required to resolve their claims through alternative dispute resolution (ADR) instead of in court? Or does the ADR process deny plaintiffs due process by depriving them of their day in court? *See, e.g., Amchem Products, Inc. v. Windsor*, 521 U.S. 591 (1997).

Another method for managing mass toxic torts is consolidation, governed by Federal Rule of Civil Procedure 42(a). Consolidation of individual actions against a defendant or group of defendants is appropriate when the plaintiffs' claims present a common question of law or fact. If the court in its discretion concludes that commonality exists, and consolidation furthers judicial economy while avoiding repetition, then the decision to consolidate may occur even without the consent of the parties. If, on the other hand, there are disparities among the various plaintiffs' claims, as well as factual differences (*e.g.*, exposure at different locations, for different times, manifesting different diseases), consolidation may be impermissible. *See, e.g., Malcom v. National Gypsum Co.*, 995 F.2d 346 (2d Cir. 1993); *In re Fibreboard Corp. v. Pittsburgh Corning Corp.*, 893 F.2d 706 (5th Cir. 1990).

B. The Plaintiff's Case

Causation is perhaps the salient feature of toxic tort litigation, but plaintiffs must also prove the other elements of a tort cause of action. A lawyer representing a plaintiff must ask: Under what legal theory should she bring suit? Should the claim be founded in common law tort or in statutory law? What kind of harm should be alleged? What kind of relief should be sought?

1. Legal Theories of Recovery

Toxic tort plaintiffs most often base their claim on one of two legal theories—trespass or nuisance. This is because in most toxic tort cases, there has been some invasion of the plaintiff's property which has in some way interfered with its use.

a. Trespass

The tort of trespass applies when some type of physical invasion interferes with another person's exclusive possession of real property. While trespass is traditionally classified as an intentional tort, the defendant need not have intended to enter onto the plaintiff's property. The tort of trespass is satisfied if the plaintiff can prove that the defendant intended the act that resulted in the trespass. In a toxic tort case, where the claim is based upon the movement of noxious liquids from one property to another, the defendant is liable for a neighbor's damage therefrom, when there is good reason to know or expect that there would be passage from defendant's to plaintiff's land. In *Scribner v. Summers*, 84 F.3d 554 (2d Cir. 1996), although the defendant did not intend waste water used in a cleaning process to enter plaintiff's land, the court determined that there had been a trespass because the defendant should have expected that barium particles would pass from its pavement into the waste water and onto plaintiff's property.

b. Nuisance

A nuisance is an interference with the use and enjoyment of a person's property. There are two types of nuisance, public and private. The RESTATEMENT (SECOND) OF TORTS §821B defines a public nuisance as an "unreasonable interference with a right common to the general public." Such public rights are usually protected by a public body, such as a health department. *State of New York v. Schenectady Chemicals, Inc.* 479 N.Y. S.2d 1010 (N.Y.A.D. 3 Dept. 1984). In toxic tort cases, private individuals are sometimes able to bring public nuisance claims, but they "must have suffered harm of a kind different from that suffered by other members of the public exercising the right common to the general public that was the subject of interference." REST. (2d) § 821C. This is referred to as the "special injury" rule, and has been applied strictly by courts. *See Briggs & Stratton Corp. v. Concrete Sales & Services*, 29 F. Supp. 2d 1372, 1376 (M.D. Ga. 1998) (release of hazardous substance was not public nuisance as it did not affect a common right of all members of the public); *Brown v. Petrolane, Inc.*, 102 Cal. App. 3d 720 (Cal. App. 1980) (court refused to allow public nuisance action brought by private citizens who were fearful of the proximity of explosive substances handled by defendant). *See also Venuto v. Owens-Corning Fiberglas Corp.*, 22 Cal. App. 3d 116 (Cal. App. 1971) (court held that individuals complaining of emissions from a plant polluting air and causing health complaints among neighboring residents could not maintain action for public nuisance because same injuries were suffered by all residents). Some courts, however, permit private parties to bring public nuisance actions when individual health problems constitute the special injury. *Anderson v. W.R. Grace & Co.*, 628 F. Supp. 1219 (Mass. 1986).[18] In certain states, polluting a body of water is a public nuisance. *State of California v. Campbell*, 138 F.3d 772, 782 (9th Cir. 1998).

A private nuisance claim does not have the special inquiry requirement. The essence of the cause of action is that the defendant's actions constituted an "unreasonable" interference with the plaintiff's use and enjoyment of the property. Diminution of market value alone, buttressed by no accompanying or personal property damage, does not constitute unreasonable interference. *National Telephone Co-op Assn. v. Exxon Corp.*, 38 F.Supp. 2d 1 (D.D.C. 1998). But a private nuisance claim is stated if the allegation is both diminution of property value *and* fear for the health of the plaintiff's

---

[18] *See* David P. Hodas, *Private Actions for Public Nuisance: Common Law Citizen Suits for Relief From Environmental Harm*, 16 ECOLOGY L. Q. 837 (1989).

children resulting from the defendant's dumping activities. *Lewis v. General Electric Co.* 37 F.Supp. 2d 55 (D.Mass. 1999).

Reasonableness is a subjective judgment that involves the weighing of several factors: the manner, the place, and the circumstances; the relative priority dates of plaintiff and defendant in location; the character of neighborhood; and nature of the alleged wrong. *Williams Pipeline Co. v. Bayer Corp.*, 964 F. Supp. 1300 (S.D. Iowa 1997). *See also Crowe v. Coleman*, 113 F.3d 156 (11th Cir. 1997) (because of proximity and the nature of the hazardous substance, one landowner was liable in private nuisance to immediately adjacent landowner in connection with seepage of gasoline from his property to the other landowner's property). RESTATEMENT (SECOND) OF TORTS 821B lists as factors in determining "unreasonableness" whether the conduct is of a "continuing" nature and whether it has produced a "permanent" or "long-lasting" effect.

The tort of trespass is often confused with the tort of nuisance. The former is based on an interference with plaintiff's interest in possession of property; the latter with the plaintiff's use and enjoyment of it. *See Rudd v. Electrolux Corp.*, 982 F. Supp. 355, 369 (M.D. N.C. 1997) (continued migration of contaminants is a nuisance, while a trespass is when a contaminant crosses onto adjoining property). In some pollution cases the courts have emphasized the physical similarities of trespass and nuisance actions and have permitted the plaintiff to proceed on both theories simultaneously or on a merged version of the two. *See Martin v. Reynolds Metals Co.* 342 P. 2d 86 (Or. 1959); *Bradley v. American Smelting and Refining Co.* 709 P. 2d 782 (Wash. 1985).

WOOD v. PICILLO

443 A.2d 1244 (R.I. 1982)

WEISBERGER, Justice.

This is an appeal from a judgment of the Superior Court entered after trial without the intervention of a jury. Finding that the defendants created a public and private nuisance in maintaining a hazardous waste dump site on their Coventry farm, the trial justice enjoined further chemical disposal operations at the defendants' property and ordered the defendants to finance cleanup and removal of the toxic wastes. The defendants now contend that the trial justice erred in finding the disposal operation to be a public and private nuisance. We strongly disagree. Accordingly, the judgment of the Superior Court is affirmed.

The testimony elicited during the extensive hearings conducted on this case revealed the following dramatic events. On September 30, 1977, an enormous explosion erupted into fifty-foot flames in a trench on defendants' Coventry property. Firefighters responded to the blaze but could not extinguish the flames. As the fire raged within the trench, additional explosions resounded. From the conflagration billowed clouds of thick black smoke that extended "as far as the eye could see on the Eastern horizon."

Not unexpectedly, the extraordinary blaze aroused the interest of various state officials. The state fire marshal declared the dump site a fire hazard and ordered defendants to cease disposal activity and to remove all flammable wastes. Personnel from the Department of Environmental Management (DEM) also investigated the dumping operation, conducting soil, water, chemical, and topographical analyses of defendants' property and adjacent areas. Despite the fire marshal's order and the ongoing official investigations, the dumping and burying of chemical wastes continued.

A general description of the Picillo property and adjacent lands is helpful in evaluating the evidence. According to the testimony of various witnesses, the Picillos owned acreage on Piggy Hill Lane in Coventry, Rhode Island. Piggy Hill Lane, which serves only the Picillos' property, is a winding dirt road running from Perry Hill Road. Near the entrance of the property defendants maintain pigs, and two houses are also located in this general area. A three-to five-acre clearing in once-wooded land lies approximately 800 feet uphill from the two homes. It is this clearing that houses the chemical dump site. About 600 feet downhill to the north-northwest of the clearing is a marshy wetland. The wetland is part of the Quinabog River Basin; the wetland waters drain in a gradual southwesterly flow into the Quinabog River, Wickford Pond, the Roaring Brook, and Arnold Pond. These fish-inhabited waters are utilized both by the general public and by a commercial cranberry grower.

The dump site proper might best be described in the succinct expression of the trial justice as "a chemical nightmare." John Quinn, Jr., chief of the DEM's solid-waste management program, visited defendants' property on October 13, 1977, and testified to what he saw. Quinn stated that at one side of the clearing lay a huge trench which he estimated to be 200 feet long, 15 to 30 feet wide, and 15 to 20 feet deep. A viscous layer of pungent, varicolored liquid covered the trench bottom to a depth of six inches at its shallowest point. Along the periphery of the pit lay more than 100 fifty-five gallon drum-type and five-gallon pail-type containers. Some of the containers were upright and sealed, some tipped, and some partially buried; some were full, some partially full, and some empty. An official from the state fire marshal's office also visited the dump site. He testified that on October 15, 1977, he observed a truck marked "Combustible" offloading barrels of chemical wastes. The truck operator knocked the barrels off the truck's tailgate directly onto the earth below, and chemicals poured freely from the damaged barrels into the trench. In 1979 state officials discovered a second dump site when "sink holes" emitting chemical odors opened in the earth at some distance from the previously described pit.

Several witnesses testified at trial to the immediate and future effects of the chemical presence. Neighbors of the Picillos reported that in the year preceding the fire, tractor-trailer traffic to and from defendants' property greatly increased. According to the testimony many of the trucks bore "Flammable" warnings and the name of a chemical company. The neighbors also testified that on several occasions during the summer of 1977 pungent odors forced them to remain inside their homes. The odors were described variously as "sickening," "heavy," "sweet," "musky," "terrible," and like "plastic burning." One neighbor testified that the odors induced in her severe nausea and headaches, while another stated that on one occasion fumes from the Picillo property caused her to cough severely and to suffer a sore throat that lasted several days.

At trial expert witnesses developed a scientific connection between the neighbors' experiences and the Picillos' operations. Laboratory analyses of samples taken from the trench, monitoring wells, and adjacent waters revealed the presence of five chemicals: toluene, xylene, chloroform, III trichloroethane, and trichloroethylene. Doctor Nelson Fausto, a professor of medical sciences in the pathology division of the Department of Biological and Medical Sciences at Brown University, described the toxic effects of the five discovered chemicals. Doctor Fausto testified that chloroform is a narcotic and an anesthetic that will induce vomiting, dizziness, and headaches in some persons exposed to it. Trichloroethane and trichloroethylene, according to Dr. Fausto, are similar to chloroform in chemical structure and in toxic effect. Toluene and xylene are also toxins, Dr. Fausto testified, that may cause irritation of the mucous membranes in the upper respiratory tract.

Doctor Fausto explained that the chemicals in question also exert chronic or long-term effects on animals and humans. According to the professor, chloroform, trichloroethane, and trichloroethylene are strong carcinogens that cause cirrhosis (cell death) of the liver and hepatoma (cancer of the liver). Doctor Fausto asserted that there is no safe level of human or animal exposure to these chemicals. Regarding toluene and xylene, Dr. Fausto testified that neither is as yet known to be carcinogenic, but both exert a toxic effect on bone marrow, causing anemia in susceptible persons. Additionally, Dr. Fausto stated, the presence of chloroform in areas where it might be heated presents further potential danger. Heated to sixty-eight degrees Fahrenheit, chloroform converts to phosgene gas, a nerve gas of the type utilized in World War I. Doctor Fausto stated that direct sunlight would provide sufficient heat to turn chloroform present in surface water into phosgene.

According to the experts, the chemicals present on defendants' property and in the marsh, left unchecked, would eventually threaten wildlife and humans well downstream from the dump site. Mr. Frank Stevenson, the principal sanitary engineer for the DEM, and Dr. William Kelly, an Associate Professor of civil and environmental engineering at the University of Rhode Island, testified as experts in soil mechanics and groundwater hydrology. The experts established that the soil at the dump site consisted of an unstratified composition of sand, gravel, and silt of varying sizes. The permeable nature of this soil would allow any liquid or chemical in or on it to percolate down to the water table and to travel with the groundwater in a northerly flow. The opinion of the experts was buttressed by the documented presence of toluene, xylene, chloroform, trichloroethane, and trichloroethylene in the northern marsh and in several monitoring wells. The only possible source of the pollutants, according to Dr. Kelly, was the Picillo dump site.

Expert testimony further revealed that the chemicals had traveled and would continue to travel from the dump site into the marsh at the rate of about one foot per day. From the marsh, predicted the experts, the chemicals would flow in a southwesterly direction into the Quinabog River and its tributaries Moosup River and Roaring Brook, and Wickford Pond. These waters are inhabited by fish and used by humans for recreational and agricultural purposes.

On these and other facts the trial justice determined the dump site to be a public and private nuisance. He found also that the current danger to the public health and safety posed by the chemical presence would worsen unless effective remedial action was quickly taken. The trial judge thus permanently enjoined disposal operations on defendants' property and ordered that all chemicals and contaminated earth be removed to a licensed disposal facility. Because defendants had in the past displayed an unwillingness or inability to remedy the danger, the Superior Court justice authorized plaintiffs to effectuate cleanup of defendants' property at defendants' expense.

The defendants contend that the evidence adduced at trial was insufficient to support a finding of public and private nuisance. The defendants point to two alleged evidentiary inadequacies: (1) that plaintiffs failed to establish any significant injury to persons or to natural wildlife and (2) that plaintiffs failed to meet their obligation to show that defendants acted negligently in disposing chemical wastes on their property. We find both assertions to be without merit.

The essential element of an actionable nuisance is that persons have suffered harm or are threatened with injuries that they ought not have to bear. Distinguished from negligence liability, liability in nuisance is predicated upon unreasonable injury rather than upon unreasonable conduct. Thus, plaintiffs may recover in nuisance despite the otherwise nontortious nature of the conduct which creates the injury.

In his brief defendant has accurately stated that the injury produced by an actionable nuisance "must be real and not fanciful or imaginary * * *." *See generally Blomen v. N. Barstow Co.*, 85 A. 924, 926 (R.I. 1913). The defendant next suggests that the injuries in the case at bar are of the insubstantial, unactionable type. It is this statement, however, rather than the purported injuries, that is fanciful. The testimony to which reference is made in this opinion clearly establishes that defendants' dumping operations have already caused substantial injury to defendants' neighbors and threaten to cause incalculable damage to the general public. The Picillos' neighbors have displayed physical symptoms of exposure to toxic chemicals and have been restricted in the reasonable use of their property. Moreover, expert testimony showed that the chemical presence on defendants' property threatens both aquatic wildlife and human beings with possible death, cancer, and liver disease. Thus, there was ample evidence at trial to support the finding of substantial injury implicit in the trial justice's finding of public and private nuisance.

The defendants' remaining contention is that Rhode Island case law requires plaintiffs to prove negligence as an element of the nuisance case and that plaintiffs failed to do so. Generally, this court has not required plaintiffs to establish negligence in nuisance actions. * * *

* * * As a matter of scientific fact the courses of subterranean waters are no longer obscure and mysterious. The testimony of the scientific experts in this case clearly illustrates the accuracy with which scientists can determine the paths of groundwater flow. Moreover, decades of unrestricted emptying of industrial effluent into the earth's atmosphere and waterways has rendered oceans, lakes, and rivers unfit for swimming and fishing, rain acidic, and air unhealthy. Concern for the preservation of an often precarious ecological balance, impelled by the spectre of "a silent spring," has today reached a zenith of intense significance. * * * We now hold that negligence is not a necessary element of a nuisance case involving contamination of public or private waters by pollutants percolating through the soil and traveling underground routes.

NOTES

1. How is nuisance different from negligence? Given the behavior of the defendants in this case, why did the plaintiffs want to avoid relying on a negligence theory? The tort of negligence is discussed below.

2. What does the advance of the science of hydrogeology (groundwater movement) have to do with the requirement *vel non* of negligence in this kind of nuisance action?

3. What kinds of harms did the plaintiffs' rely upon to support their claims? From what you know of toxic substances, is *Wood* a broadly useful case or is it limited to rather extreme facts?

c. Negligence

The basic elements of a common law negligence claim are (1) duty; (2) breach of duty; (3) actual loss or harm; and (4) causal connection between the breach of duty and the harm. As noted above, plaintiffs encounter difficulty proving the elements of a standard negligence claim because causation is sometimes impossible to establish in light of the long latency period between exposure to the toxic substance and manifestation of illness. Asserting a claim of negligence also requires the plaintiff to show that the defendant had knowledge of the dangers at the time of exposure, and further, that there was foreseeable harm to the plaintiff. For example, in *Redland Soccer Club v. Dept. of Army of U.S.*, 55 F.3d 827 (3rd Cir. 1995), plaintiffs asserted that exposure to toxic wastes deposited by the U.S. Army in a landfill that was later converted to a soccer field constituted negligence. The court stated that the plaintiffs "must establish that the Army's failure to exercise reasonable care towards them, and any breach of its duty, exposed them to an elevated risk of foreseeable harm, which resulted in injury." A plaintiff may also claim that the defendant violated a standard of care or conduct established by statute or regulation, and thus that the defendant is negligent "per se." In jurisdictions where negligence per se is recognized, the plaintiff must show that the relevant statute was enacted (1) to protect the class of persons of which the plaintiff is a member, and (2) to address the kind of harm that the plaintiff suffered. In toxic tort cases, many courts hesitate to apply a presumption of negligence, though some plaintiffs have been successful.[19]

d. Strict Liability

Under a theory of strict liability the plaintiff can recover for injury without showing fault on the part of the defendant, if she can show that the defendant is engaging in an "abnormally dangerous activity." The development of the abnormally dangerous activity doctrine began with the English case of *Rylands v. Fletcher*, L.R. 3 H.L. 330 (1868), which emphasized the inappropriateness of certain activities to their locations ("non-natural use"). The modern criteria is embodied in the RESTATEMENT OF TORTS:

> In determining whether an activity is abnormally dangerous, the following factors are to be considered:
> - existence of a high degree of risk of some harm to the person, land or chattels of others;
> - likelihood that the harm that results from it will be great;
> - inability to eliminate the risk by the exercise of reasonable care;
> - extent to which the activity is not a matter of common usage;
> - inappropriateness of the activity to the place where it is carried on and;
> - extent to which its value to the community is outweighed by its dangerous attributes.

---

[19] *See, e.g.,* Bagley v. Controlled Environment Corp., 503 A.2d 823 (N.H. 1986) (court allowed a negligence per se claim under state statute which required operators of hazardous waste facilities to obtain a permit.)

REST. (2D) TORTS § 520.

The policy behind holding a toxic tort defendant strictly liable is that, despite the social utility of the activity, the defendant is introducing an extraordinary risk of harm to the public. *See, e.g., Dept. of Environmental Protection v. Ventron Corp.*, 468 A.2d 150 (N.J. 1983) (court ruled that mercury and other toxic wastes are "abnormally dangerous" and disposal of them, past or present, is an abnormally dangerous activity); *T. & E Indus. Inc. v. Safety Light Corp.*, 587 A. 2d 1249 (N.J. 1991) (court ruled that processing, handling and disposal of radium constituted an abnormally dangerous activity, where processor's successor was strictly liable for resulting harm after radium was dumped into vacant urban lot). *But see McDonald v. Timex Corp.*, 9 F. Supp. 2d 120, 122-23 (D. Conn. 1998) (actively dumping hazardous wastes on property not necessarily an abnormally dangerous activity if the wastes are not so inherently dangerous that the risk of probable injury may be eliminated by due care).

e. Warranty

A purchaser of a product found to be harmful may wish to sue the seller if there have been any assurances made about the nature of the product. These lawsuits allege breach of warranty. The law governing claims arising from breach of warranty is found in Article Two of the Uniform Commercial Code (UCC). A warranty may be express, in which case it is subject to UCC §2-313, which provides that a seller makes an express warranty by an (1) affirmation of fact or promise made, (2) description of the goods, or (3) sample or model. A plaintiff may also assert a claim based on breach of implied warranty, as established in UCC §2-314. This provision is based on the idea that there is an implied warranty of merchantability in a contract of sale between buyer and seller.

In *Fleming Farms v. Dixie AG Supply*, Inc., 631 So.2d 922 (Ala. 1994), purchasers who bought a product to reduce the adverse effect of chemicals used on cotton brought claims for breach of express and implied warranty after the product allegedly damaged their cotton crops. The label on the product stated that it was a "safener," and would reduce damage to their cotton. The plaintiffs asserted that this declaration constituted an "affirmation of fact or promise and became part of the basis of the bargain," and was therefore an express warranty. Alternatively, plaintiffs asserted a breach of implied warranty of merchantability claim. The court rejected both arguments, primarily because a "warranty disclaimer" that had been printed in large, bold print in the center of a receipt form proved sufficient to limit defendant's liability. *See also B.C.F. Oil Refining, Inc. v. Consolidated Edison Co.*, 982 F. Supp. 302, 309 (S.D. N.Y. 1997) (oil refining company which hired carrier to transport waste oil could not reasonably have relied on carrier for information on composition of liquid waste, and thus could not maintain breach of warranty claim based on carrier's delivery of waste which contained hazardous materials).

f. Statutory Causes of Action

A plaintiff may wish to supplement common law claims with ones based in statutory law. For example, where it has been adopted by a state legislature, the Model Toxics Control Act provides that a past or present property owner is liable for the cleanup and damages to the environment caused by the release of toxic substances. *Dash Point Village Assoc. v. Exxon Corp.*, 937 P.2d 1148 (Wash. App. 1997). Like most toxics statutes, the Comprehensive Environmental Response, Compensation and Liability Act (CERCLA) contains a citizen suit provision that allows "any person" to bring an action directly against a "person * * * who is alleged to be in violation of any standard, regulation, condition, requirement, or order" pursuant to CERCLA. CERCLA §310(a)(1), 42 U.S.C. §9659(a)(1). This provision permits persons to act as private attorneys general to remedy violations of the Act.[20] Although CERCLA contains no private right of action for damages for persons who claim to have been injured by releases of hazardous wastes encompassed by the statute (the remedies available are injunctive relief and civil penalties), it does contain a savings clause that recognizes and preserves the rights of individuals to pursue their tort claims under state law. CERCLA §310(h), 42 U.S.C. §9659(h). As a result, a toxic tort defendant may find that it is both jointly and severally liable under CERCLA, and in common law. *United States v. Occidental Chemical Corp.*, 965 F. Supp. 408 (W.D. N.Y. 1997) (city liable under CERCLA and in public nuisance); *State of New York v. Shore Realty Corp.*, 759 F.2d 1032 (2d Cir. 1985) (same). CERCLA liability is the subject of Chapter 11.

When federal statutory law exists in areas traditionally addressed by private causes of action, the federal statute may preempt a cause of action based on state statutory or common law. *Compare Cipollone v. Liggett Group, Inc.*, 505 U.S. 504 (1991) (the Federal Cigarette Labeling and Advertising Act requiring warnings on cigarette packages preempted common law claims based on failure of warn); *Roberts v. Florida Power & Light Co.*, 146 F.3d 1305 (11th Cir. 1998) (federal safety regulations under

---

[20] The United States Supreme Court has limited the scope of citizen suits by requiring that the citizen plaintiff meet constitutional standing demands. Lujan v. National Wildlife Federation, 504 U.S. 555 (1992). In the case of citizen suits under the Clean Water Act, 33 U.S.C. §1251-1387, the Court has held that violations must be ongoing or repetitive for a citizens' suit to be proper. Gwaltney of Smithfield v. Chesapeake Bay Foundation, 484 U.S. 49 (1987). On the other hand, where a federal environmental statute does not explicitly provide for a citizen suit, a court may acknowledge the existence of an *implied* private right of action if there is evidence of congressional intent to allow such suits. Middlesex County Sewage Authority v. National Sea Clammers Assoc., 453 U.S. 1 (1981).

Atomic Energy Act of 1954 conclusively establish duty of care owed in liability action arising from exposure to nuclear radiation); *Papas v. Upjohn Co.*, 985 F.2d 516 (11th Cir. 1993) (labeling of pesticides pursuant to the Federal Insecticide, Fungicide, and Rodenticide Act (FIFRA) preempted state claims alleging manufacturer's failure to warn consumers of hazardous chemicals in the product); *with Wisconsin Public Intervenor v. Mortier*, 501 U.S. 597 (1991) (FIFRA did not preempt the regulation of pesticides by local governments). State statutes can also preempt common law toxic tort claims. *See San Diego Gas & Electric Co. v. Superior Court*, 920 P.2d 669 (Cal. 1996) (state Public Utilities Act preempted private nuisance action brought against utility owners of power lines). When employees bring common law causes of action against their employees because of exposure to a toxic substance in the work place, the existence of workers' compensation schemes may preclude the lawsuit. *See Picard v. Zeit Exploration Co., Inc.*, 636 So. 2d 922 (La. App. 1994) (where employee of oil storage tank repair company sued owner of oil storage tank for injuries from exposure to toxic substances in tank while cleaning it, the state workers' compensation statute precluded the employee's private common law tort claim).

2. Nature of the Harm and Remedies

In most toxic tort cases, plaintiffs believe they have suffered some physical injury resulting from exposure to toxic substances or hazardous wastes. The injury is typically some physical illness or medical condition. In other cases, there may be no immediate personal harm, but the otherwise healthy plaintiff may have an enhanced risk of disease in future due to exposure to a toxic chemical. Or the injury is not physical, but economic. When the harm alleged is anything other than simple medical injury, a toxic tort plaintiff may have to overcome certain obstacles that arise with non-physical harms.

- *Enhanced risk.* Claims based upon the risk of developing some illness in the future as a result of exposure to a toxic substance fly in the face of traditional notions of injury. A plaintiff bringing an enhanced risk action is not only basing the claim on some future event—the illness or disease for which she is at risk—but the plaintiff also cannot guarantee that the event will occur at all. Courts have offered varying resolutions to the problems inherent in enhanced risk cases. Some jurisdictions require a present physical injury so that there is some evidence of extant harm that can form the basis of a higher probability of similar future injury. *See Brafford v. Susquehanna Corp.*, 586 F. Supp. 14 (D. Colo. 1984) (present injury exists when at the time of the lawsuit damage exists to cellular and subcellular structures). The leading case for claims alleging only increased risk is *Ayers v. Township of Jackson*, 525

A.2d 287 (N.J. 1987). In *Ayers*, none of the plaintiffs were, at the time of the lawsuit, suffering any physical injuries or illnesses stemming from the defendant's contamination of their drinking water supply. Ordinarily, this would be the end of the case. However, the court agreed that increased risk alone was actionable, but required that the plaintiffs demonstrate that the actual risk be quantified. When risk cannot be quantified, such as when science cannot assess whether other factors not under control of the defendant may contribute to the likelihood of future illness, the increased risk claim will be rejected. *See also Hagerty v. L & L Marine Services, Inc.*, 700 F.2d 315 (5th Cir. 1986) (enhanced risk recognized when the toxic exposure "more probably than not" will lead to cancer).

- *Emotional distress.* Although psychological harm can be raised alongside physical harm arising from exposure to a toxic substance, some plaintiffs who have not yet developed any symptoms may seek compensation based on their present fear of future illness.[21] Several jurisdictions permit recovery for emotional distress based on a fear of future cancer, even when the plaintiff is healthy, and can prove only there has been contact with a cancer-producing agent. *Bernbach v. Timex Corp.*, 989 F. Supp. 403, 408 (D. Conn. 1996); *Herber v. Johns-Mansville Corp.*, 785 F.2d 79 (3d Cir. 1985); *Devlin v. Johns-Mansville*, 495 A.2d 495 (N.J. Super. 1985). Some courts that permit recovery for emotional distress require the plaintiff to prove more than the fact of exposure. In California, the emotional distress must be based on a knowledge, grounded in reliable medical or scientific data, that the quantitative likelihood of developing cancer is more likely than not. *Potter v. Firestone Tire and Rubber Co.*, 863 P.2d 795 (Cal. 1993). *See also* E. Jean Johnson, *Environmental Stigma Damages: Speculative Damages in Environmental Tort Cases*, 15 UCLA J. OF ENVTL. L. & POLICY 185 (1997).

- *Economic loss.* Where the nature of the plaintiff's injury is economic, unaccompanied by physical injury or injury to real property, courts have typically denied recovery under strict liability and negligence theories.[22] For example, in *Adams v. Star*

---

[21] Fear of developing leukemia from power lines was one of the allegations made in the San Diego Gas & Electric Co. case noted above. Emotional distress for witnessing a family member die of a disease caused by defendant's alleged conduct was a claim raised in the Woburn, Massachusetts case, Anderson v. W.R. Grace & Co., 628 F. Supp. 1219, 1228-1230 (D. Mass. 1986).

[22] Jurisdictions adopting RESTATEMENT (SECOND) OF TORTS §40213 may allow recovery for economic losses based on fraudulent or negligent misrepresentation. The RESTATEMENT

Enterprise, 51 F.3d 417 (4th Cir. 1995), landowners argued that a Virginia statute imposing strict liability for discharges of oil onto private lands did not require actual physical damage to property, but allowed recovery for the diminution in the value of their properties resulting from their proximity to the defendant's oil spill. The Court denied recovery, primarily because the statute permitted liability only when there was "injury to property," but this phrase did not encompass purely economic losses.

When courts permit recovery for economic injury, they focus on the relative bargaining power of the parties, and the allocation of loss to the better risk-bearer. *Mainline Tractor & Equipment Co. v. Nutrite Corp.*, 937 F. Supp. 1095 (D. Vt. 1996). Even if parties can receive relief for purely economic losses resulting from the effects of the defendant's operation of a hazardous facility, plaintiffs must introduce evidence establishing their economic losses; it is not sufficient to merely present evidence that the defendant's actions were a potential cause of injury. *In re Hanford Nuclear Reservation Litigation*, 894 F. Supp. 1436 (E.D. Wash. 1995) (although plaintiffs proved a decline in fish runs during the years a nuclear facility discharged effluent into the Columbia River, the Court will not infer economic injury from the declines, or from the fact that the plaintiffs caught less fish during this time).

The following three cases illustrate the possibilities for and the limitations of these theories of liability.

ANDERSON V. W.R. GRACE & CO.

628 F. Supp. 1219 (D. Mass. 1986)

SKINNER, District Judge.

This case arises out of the defendants' alleged contamination of the groundwater in certain areas of Woburn, Massachusetts, with chemicals, including trichloroethylene and tetrachloroethylene. Plaintiffs allege that two of Woburn's water wells, Wells G and H, drew upon the contaminated water until the wells were closed in 1979 and that exposure to this contaminated water caused them to suffer severe injuries.

Of the 33 plaintiffs in this action, five are the administrators of minors who died of leukemia allegedly caused by exposure to the chemicals. They bring suit for wrongful death and conscious pain and suffering. Sixteen of the 28 living plaintiffs are members of the decedents' immediate families. These plaintiffs seek to recover for the emotional distress caused by

---

(SECOND) OF TORTS §929 governs awards of damages for injury to property resulting from past invasions that do not amount to a total destruction of property. *See* Richard E. Spiedel, *Warranty Theory, Economic Loss, and the Privity Requirement: Once More Into the Void*, 67 B.U. L. REV. 9 (1987).

witnessing the decedents' deaths. Three of the living plaintiffs also contracted leukemia and currently are either in remission or treatment for the disease. The 25 non-leukemic plaintiffs allege that exposure to the contaminated water caused a variety of illnesses and damaged their bodily systems. All of the living plaintiffs seek to recover for their illnesses and other damage, increased risk of developing future illness, and emotional distress. Six of the plaintiff families still reside in the area above the allegedly contaminated water. These plaintiffs seek injunctive relief under a nuisance theory.

Two of the defendants, W.R. Grace & Co. and Beatrice Foods Co. (collectively "defendants"), have jointly moved for partial summary judgment on several of plaintiffs' claims. * * *

* * *

B. Claims for Emotional Distress.

Defendants move for summary judgment on plaintiffs' claims of emotional distress on the grounds that the non-leukemic plaintiffs' distress was not caused by any physical injury. They also move for summary judgment on the emotional distress claims of plaintiffs who witnessed a family member die of leukemia, arguing that Massachusetts law does not recognize such a claim. Some plaintiffs are in both of these separate categories.

1. Physical Injury.

In seeking summary judgment on the non-leukemic plaintiffs' claims for emotional distress, defendants rely on *Payton v. Abbott Labs*, 437 N.E.2d 171 (Mass 1982). In *Payton*, the Supreme Judicial Court answered a certified question as follows:

> [I]n order for . . . plaintiffs to recover for negligently inflicted emotional distress, [they] must allege and prove [they] suffered physical harm as a result of the conduct which caused the emotional distress. We answer, further, that a plaintiff's physical harm must either cause or be caused by the emotional distress alleged, and that the physical harm must be manifested by objective symptomatology and substantiated by expert medical testimony.

Defendants attack plaintiffs' claims of emotional distress at three points: they argue that plaintiffs did not suffer physical harm as a result of defendants' allegedly negligent conduct; that, if the plaintiffs did suffer any harm, it was not "manifested by objective symptomatology"; and that any manifest physical harm did not cause the claimed emotional distress.

The Third Amended Complaint alleges only that "each plaintiff has suffered a direct adverse physical affect [sic] . . ." Plaintiffs make a slightly more specific claim to physical injury in their answers to interrogatories. Each plaintiff states that exposure to contaminants in the water drawn from Wells G and H affected my body's ability to fight disease, [and] caused harm to my body's organ systems, including my respiratory, immunological, blood, central nervous, gastro-intestinal, urinary-renal systems . . .

This alleged harm is sufficient to maintain plaintiffs' claims for emotional distress under *Payton*. As used in that opinion, the term "physical harm" denotes "harm to the bodies of the plaintiffs." 437 N.E.2d at 175 n. 4. In requiring physical harm rather than mere "injury" as an element of proof in a claim for emotional distress, the court required that a plaintiff show some actual physical damage as a predicate to suit.

Defendants argue that plaintiffs' alleged harm is "subcellular" and therefore not the type of harm required to support a claim for emotional distress under *Payton*. I disagree. The Supreme Judicial Court requires that plaintiffs' physical harm be "manifested by objective symptomatology and substantiated by expert medical testimony." 437 N.E.2d at 181. In setting forth this requirement, the court did not distinguish between gross and subcellular harm.[23] Instead, the court drew a line between harm which can be proven to exist through expert medical testimony based on objective evidence and harm which is merely speculative or based solely on a plaintiff's unsupported assertions. The phrase "manifested by objective symptomatology" does not indicate that the necessary harm need be immediately apparent but that its existence must be objectively evidenced. Where, as in this case, the harm is not obvious to the layman, its existence may not be demonstrated solely by the complaints of the alleged victim; it must also be "substantiated by expert medical testimony." Upon review of the pleadings and the affidavits of plaintiffs' expert, I cannot say as a matter of law that this standard will not be met at trial.

The alleged damage to plaintiffs' bodily systems is manifested by the many ailments which plaintiffs claim to have suffered as a result of exposure to the contaminated water.[24] Dr. Levin apparently will testify to the existence of changes in plaintiffs' bodies caused by exposure to the contaminated water. He will base his testimony on objective evidence of these changes, including the maladies listed in [the margin]. In one affidavit, Dr. Levin states that "[t]he clinical manifestation of [the cellular changes] is a function of the host . . . Some individuals will manifest this damage as skin rashes and arthritis, while others will manifest the same

---

[23] This should remind you of the discussion of injury in *Lead Industries Ass'n* in Chapter 2, *supra*. Do the courts reach similar or different conclusions?—EDS.

[24] The list of ailments varies from plaintiff to plaintiff. The ailments include shortness of breath, decreased visual acuity, frequent waking, hoarseness, muscle aching, fatigue, chest pain, sore irritated dry throat, respiratory infections, stress incontinence, tingling, numbness, joint stiffness and aching, dry sensitive skin, rashes, cold sores, red burning eyes, headaches, diarrhea, vomiting, abdominal distress, post nasal discharge, nasal congestion, and nosebleeds.

damage as cancer." Dr. Levin explicitly states that the changes in plaintiffs' systems have "produced illnesses related to these systems, which are indicated [in the Answers to Interrogatories]." Although the affidavit does not specifically identify the illnesses suffered by each plaintiff as a result of the changes, nor state that plaintiffs suffered more ailments than the average person would have over the same time span, it is sufficient evidence of harm to support the existence of a factual dispute and bar summary judgment.

Under *Payton*, of course, injury is not sufficient. The harm allegedly caused by defendants' conduct must either have caused or been caused by the emotional distress. The Complaint does not state that plaintiffs' emotional distress was caused by any physical harm. Plaintiffs only allege that "[a]s a result of the knowledge that they . . . have consumed hazardous chemicals, the plaintiffs have suffered and will continue to suffer great emotional distress."

Plaintiffs provide more specific information about the source of their emotional distress in their answers to defendants' interrogatories. Each plaintiff states that "[a]s a result of the contaminated water . . . I have experienced depression and anxiousness." Plaintiffs also claim that:

> The defendants' conduct in contributing to the pollution of the groundwater serving Wells G and H and their failure to prevent, monitor, acknowledge, or correct the pollution has affected my mental and emotional state. It has caused me to suffer anxiety, depression, fear, anger, frustration, hopelessness and distress . . . .

None of these claims for emotional distress arise from physical injuries caused by defendants' conduct. Accordingly, they are not compensable under *Payton*, or under ordinary principles of recovery for mental suffering. *Barney v. Magenis*, 135 N.E. 142 (Mass. 1922) (allowing recovery for mental suffering "connected with and growing out of the physical injury").

However, certain elements of plaintiffs' emotional distress stem from the physical harm to their immune systems allegedly caused by defendants' conduct and are compensable. Plaintiffs have stated that the illnesses contributed to by exposure to the contaminated water have caused them anxiety and pain. The excerpts from plaintiffs' depositions appended to defendants' motion indicate that plaintiffs are also worried over the increased susceptibility to disease which results from the alleged harm to their immune systems and exposure to carcinogens. As these elements of emotional distress arise out of plaintiffs' injuries, plaintiffs may seek to recover for them.

Defendants contend that plaintiffs' physical harm did not "cause" plaintiffs' distress over their increased susceptibility to disease as required by *Payton*. They argue that the fear arose out of discussions between plaintiffs and their expert witness, Dr. Levin, in which the expert informed plaintiffs of their suppressed immune systems. Assuming, as I must for purposes of motion, that Dr. Levin is telling the truth, this argument is frivolous.

Plaintiffs can recover "only for that degree of emotional distress which a reasonable person, normally would have experienced under [the] circumstances." *Payton*, 437 N.E.2d at 181; *see* RESTATEMENT (SECOND) OF TORTS § 436A, comment c. The Supreme Judicial Court has explicitly stated that the reasonableness of a claim for emotional distress is to be determined by the trier of fact. Accordingly, defendants' motion for summary judgment on the non-leukemic plaintiffs' claims for emotional distress is DENIED.

2. Witnessing death of a family member.

The second issue raised by defendants' motion is whether Massachusetts recognizes a claim for emotional distress for witnessing a family member die of a disease allegedly caused by defendants' conduct. This differs from the question considered in the preceding section because the concern now is whether the plaintiffs can recover for distress caused by witnessing the injuries of others, not by their own condition. The plaintiffs do not claim any physical harm resulted from this emotional distress.

The plaintiffs proceed on alternative theories: (1) that they were in the "zone of danger", RESTATEMENT (SECOND) OF TORTS § 313(2) (1965), and (2) that they themselves were the victims of an "impact" from the same tortious conduct that caused the death of the children.

The Supreme Judicial Court has adverted to the "zone of danger" rule on a number of occasions, but in my opinion the court has never adopted that rule. The basic rule is one of the foreseeability of the emotional harm. Furthermore, in every circumstance but one, the harm for which damages may be recovered is not the emotional distress itself, but physical harm resulting from the emotional distress. In the one additional circumstance, damages may be recovered for emotional distress over injury to a child or spouse when the plaintiff suffers contemporaneous physical injury from the same tortious conduct that caused the injury to the close relative. *Cimino v. Milford Keg, Inc.*, 431 N.E.2d 920, 927 (Mass. 1982).

* * *

Accordingly, the plaintiffs would be entitled to go forward on the basis of *Cimino*, if it were not for three further prudential limitations on recovery of a bystander for emotional distress resulting from injuries to another. These are the requirements of physical proximity to the accident, temporal proximity to the negligent act, and familial proximity to the victim. The plaintiffs in this case satisfy the requirement of [physical proximity], because they were present during the illness and death of the children, and at least 16 of them apparently satisfy the requirement of [familial proximity], because they are immediate family members of the decedents, but they do not meet the test imposed by *Miles* [*v. Edward O. Tabor, M.D., Inc.*, 443 N.E. 2d 1302 (Mass. 1982)] [*i.e.,* temporal proximity].

In *Miles*, a mother developed severe symptoms of emotional distress after the death of her baby, which occurred some two months after the tortious act of the defendant. The Supreme Judicial Court denied recovery because Miles' emotional distress resulted from her child's death and not from experiencing or witnessing the effects of the defendant's negligence in the delivery room. In a footnote, the court distinguished *Cimino* because the emotional distress there was not a delayed response but occurred at the time of the defendant's negligent act. For emotional distress to be compensable under Massachusetts law, therefore, the distress must result from immediate apprehension of the defendant's negligence or its consequences. In each of the cases in which recovery for the emotional distress of a bystander has been allowed, there has been a dramatic traumatic shock causing immediate emotional distress. Such is not the case here. There is no indication in the Massachusetts cases that liability would be extended to a family member's emotional distress which built over time during the prolonged illness of a child.

Imposition of liability in that case, while logically indistinguishable from the trauma situation, would violate the Massachusetts court's demonstrated prudential inclination to keep the scope of liability within manageable bounds.

* * *

In my opinion, in the present state of the law in Massachusetts, the Supreme Judicial Court would not permit recovery for emotional distress arising from the negligently induced illness of another, and therefore the plaintiffs may not recover for such emotional distress in this case.

C. Claims for increased risk of future illness.

Plaintiffs seek to recover damages for the increased risk of serious illness they claim resulted from consumption of and exposure to contaminated water. Defendants argue that Massachusetts does not recognize a claim for increased risk of future harm, regardless of whether plaintiffs have suffered physical harm. This issue has not been directly addressed by the Massachusetts courts. It was not decided in *Payton*.

Plaintiffs view their claim as merely an element of damages, compensation for the risk of probable future consequences stemming from negligently inflicted present harm. * * *

* * *

The answer to this question depends on the connection between the illnesses plaintiffs have suffered and fear they will suffer in the future. Unfortunately, the nature of plaintiffs' claim for increased risk of future illness is unclear on two counts. Nothing in the present record indicates the magnitude of the increased risk or the diseases which plaintiffs may suffer. Paragraph 63 of the Third Amended Complaint only alleges the plaintiffs face an "increased risk of serious illness", and the affidavits of plaintiffs' expert only state that exposure to the chemicals "can induce" cancer and result in an "increased susceptibility to disease" including an "increased propensity to serious illnesses as well as cancer." Insofar as plaintiffs seek to recover for their probable future costs and suffering due to ailments of the types they already claim to have endured, they may seek damages in this action. However, plaintiffs also claim an increased risk of leukemia or other cancers. These diseases seem at least qualitatively different from the illnesses plaintiffs have actually suffered. The record is insufficient to determine whether leukemia and other cancers are part of the same disease process as the other illnesses alleged to have resulted from exposure to the contaminated water. If they are part of the same disease process, then plaintiffs may seek recovery for the future illness in this action by showing a "reasonable probability" that they will occur. If, however, they are distinct diseases, then plaintiffs must wait until the disease has manifested itself to sue.

* * *

A further reason for denying plaintiffs' damages for the increased risk of future harm in this action is the inevitable inequity which would result if recovery were allowed. "To award damages based on a mere mathematical probability would significantly undercompensate those who actually do develop cancer and would be a windfall to those who do not." *Arnett v. Dow Chemical Corp.*, No. 729586, slip op. at 15 (Cal.Super.Ct. Mar. 21, 1983). In addition, if plaintiffs could show that they were more likely than not to suffer cancer or other future illness, full recovery would be allowed for all plaintiffs, even though only some number more than half would actually develop the illness. In such a case, the defendant would overcompensate the injured class.

Accordingly, action on plaintiffs' claims for the increased risk of serious future illness, including cancer, must be delayed. If the future illnesses stem from the same disease process as the illnesses plaintiffs presently complain of, recovery must be sought in this action. If the disease processes are different, however, the cause of action for the future illness will not accrue until the illness manifests itself.

* * *

AYERS V. TOWNSHIP OF JACKSON

525 A.2d 287 (N.J. 1987)

STEIN, Justice.

* * *

Th[is] litigation involves claims for damages sustained because plaintiffs' well water was contaminated by toxic pollutants leaching into the Cohansey Aquifer from a landfill established and operated by Jackson Township. After an extensive trial, the jury found that the township had created a "nuisance" and a "dangerous condition" by virtue of its operation of the landfill, that its conduct was "palpably unreasonable,"—a prerequisite to recovery under N.J.S.A. 59:4-2—and that it was the proximate cause of the contamination of plaintiffs' water supply. * * *

* * *

I

The evidence at trial provided ample support for the jury's conclusion that the township had operated the Legler landfill in a palpably unreasonable manner, a finding that the township did not contest before the Appellate Division. Briefly summarized, the proof showed that prior to 1971 the township operated another landfill that was the subject of complaints by neighboring residents and at least one citation for violation of state regulations. When the prior landfill's capacity was exhausted, the township opened the Legler landfill in 1972. The Department of Environmental Protection (DEP) granted a conditional permit for the new landfill, excluding liquid or soluble industrial wastes and limiting the depth of waste deposits to a specific grade above the level of the groundwater. The evidence indicated that, from the inception of the landfill's operation, the township failed to monitor the quantity and types of liquid waste dumped at the landfill, and ignored its duty to control and limit the depth of the trenches in which wastes were deposited. There was substantial evidence that the township disregarded the conditions imposed by DEP, and that the township's negligent operation of the landfill resulted in chemical contamination of the groundwater in the area and the underlying aquifer.

* * *

Claims for Enhanced Risk and Medical Surveillance

No claims were asserted by plaintiffs seeking recovery for specific illnesses caused by their exposure to chemicals. Rather, they claim damages for the enhanced risk of future illness attributable to such exposure. They also seek to recover the expenses of annual medical examinations to monitor their physical health and detect symptoms of disease at the earliest possible opportunity.

Before trial, the trial court granted defendant's motion for summary judgment dismissing the enhanced risk claim. It held that plaintiffs' proofs, with the benefit of all favorable inferences, would not establish a "reasonable probability" that plaintiffs would sustain future injury as a result of chemical contamination of their water supply. * * *

* * *

1.

Our evaluation of the enhanced risk and medical surveillance claims requires that we focus on a critical issue in the management of toxic tort litigation: at what stage in the evolution of a toxic injury should tort law intercede by requiring the responsible party to pay damages?

* * *

Although state statutes of limitations are invariably identified as procedural obstacles to mass exposure litigation, the extent of the problem posed by such statutes varies widely among jurisdictions. Because of the long latency period typical of illnesses caused by chemical pollutants, victims often discover their injury and the existence of a cause of action long after the expiration of the personal-injury statute of limitations, where the limitations period is calculated from the date of the exposure. Most jurisdictions have remedied this problem by adopting a version of the "discovery rule" that tolls the statute until the injury is discovered. Few states follow New Jersey's discovery rule that tolls the statute until the victim discovers both the injury and the facts suggesting that a third party may be responsible. However, we note that CERCLA now preempts state statutes of limitation where they provide that the limitations period for personal-injury or property-damage suits prompted by exposure to hazardous substances starts on a date earlier than the "federally required commencement date." That term is defined as "the date plaintiff knew (or reasonably should have known) that the personal injury or property damages * * * were caused or contributed to by the hazardous substance * * *concerned." 42 U.S.C.A. § 9658.

The single controversy rule "requires that a party include in the action all related claims against an adversary and its failure to do so precludes the maintenance of a second action." *Aetna Ins. Co. v. Gilchrist Bros., Inc.*, 428 A.2d 1254 (N.J. 1981). The doctrine may bar recovery where, as here, suit is instituted to recover damages to compensate for the immediate consequences of toxic pollution, but the initiation of additional litigation depends upon when, if ever, physical injuries threatened by the pollution are manifested.

* * *

Accordingly, we concur with the principle advanced by the trial court and endorsed by other federal and state courts, *see Hagerty v. L & L Marine Servs., Inc.*, 788 F.2d 315, 320-21 (5th Cir.), *modified on other grounds*, 797 F.2d 256 (5th Cir.1986), that neither the statute of limitations nor the single controversy rule should bar timely causes of action in toxic-tort cases instituted after discovery of a disease or injury related to tortious conduct, although there has been prior litigation between the parties of different claims based on the same tortious conduct.

Another commonly identified obstacle to judicial resolution of mass exposure tort claims is the difficulty encountered by plaintiffs in proving negligence. Although causes of action for trespass and nuisance may be available to redress property injuries, most personal injury actions in toxic tort litigation seek recovery on the basis of the defendant's negligence. *But cf. State of New Jersey, Dep't of Envtl. Protection v. Ventron Corp.*, 468 A.2d 150 (N.J. 1983) (holding that the disposal of toxic wastes is an abnormally dangerous activity and that a landowner is strictly liable for damage to others caused by toxic wastes stored or disposed of on his property); N.J.S.A. 58:10-23.11g(c) (imposing strict liability for cleanup and removal costs on any person who has discharged a hazardous substance). It is frequently argued that a negligence standard unfairly imposes on plaintiffs the difficult burden of establishing by a cost-benefit analysis that the cost to defendant of taking precautionary measures is outweighed by the probability and gravity of harm. * * *

By far the most difficult problem for plaintiffs to overcome in toxic tort litigation is the burden of proving causation. * * *

* * *

The legal issue we must resolve, in the context of the jury's determination of defendant's liability under the Act, is whether the proof of an unquantified enhanced risk of illness or a need for medical surveillance is sufficient to justify compensation under the Tort Claims Act. In view of the acknowledged difficulties of proving causation once evidence of disease is manifest, a determination of the compensability of post-exposure, pre-symptom injuries is particularly important in assessing the ability of tort law to redress the claims of plaintiffs in toxic-tort litigation.

2.

Much of the same evidence was material to both the enhanced risk and medical surveillance claims. Dr. Dan Raviv, a geohydrologist, testified as to the movements and concentrations of the various chemical substances as they migrated from the landfill toward plaintiffs' wells. Dr. Joseph Highland, a toxicologist, applied Dr. Raviv's data and gave testimony concerning the level of exposure of various plaintiffs. Dr. Highland also compiled toxicity profiles of the chemical substances found in the wells, and testified concerning the health hazards posed by the chemicals and the exposure levels at which adverse health effects had been experimentally observed. According to Dr. Highland, four of the chemicals were known to be carcinogenic, and at least four of the chemicals were capable of adversely affecting the reproductive system or causing birth defects. Most of the chemical substances could produce adverse effects on the liver and kidney, as well as on the nervous system. For at least six of the chemicals, no data was available regarding carcinogenic potential. He also testified that the exposure to multiple chemical substances posed additional hazards to plaintiffs because of the possibility of biological interaction among the chemicals that enhanced the risk to plaintiffs.

Dr. Highland testified that the Legler area residents, because of their exposure to toxic chemicals, had an increased risk of cancer; that unborn children and infants were more susceptible to the disease because of their immature biological defense systems; and that the extent of the risk was variable with the degree of exposure to the chemicals. Dr. Highland testified that *he could not quantify the extent of the enhanced risk of cancer* because of the lack of scientific information concerning the effect of the interaction of the various chemicals to which plaintiffs were exposed. However, the jury could reasonably have inferred from his testimony that the risk, although unquantified, was medically significant.

* * *

Dr. Susan Daum, a physician affiliated with the Mount Sinai Hospital in New York and specializing in the diagnosis and treatment of diseases induced by toxic substances, testified that plaintiffs required a program of regular medical surveillance. Acknowledging her reliance on the report of Dr. Highland, Dr. Daum stated that plaintiffs' exposure to chemicals had produced "a reasonable likelihood that they have now or will develop health consequences from this exposure."

She testified that the purpose of the medical surveillance program was to permit the earliest possible diagnosis of illnesses, which could lead to improved prospects for cure, prolongation of life, relief of pain, and minimization of disability. Dr. Daum specified the series of tests and procedures that would constitute an appropriate program, described each procedure and explained its purpose, and estimated the annual cost of each test.

* * *

3.

The trial court declined to submit to the jury the issue of defendant's liability for the plaintiffs' increased risk of contracting cancer, kidney or liver damage, or other diseases associated with the chemicals that had migrated from the landfill to their wells. If the issue had not been withheld, the jury could have concluded from the evidence that most or all of the plaintiffs had a significantly but unquantifiably enhanced risk of the identified diseases, and that such enhanced risk was attributable to defendant's conduct.

* * *

Except for a handful of cases involving traumatic torts causing presently discernible injuries in addition to an enhanced risk of future injuries, courts have generally been reluctant to recognize claims for potential but unrealized injury unless the proof that the injury will occur is substantial. * * *

Among the recent toxic tort cases rejecting liability for damages based on enhanced risk is *Anderson v. W.R. Grace & Co.*, 628 F.Supp. 1219 (D.Mass.1986). That case, recently settled for an undisclosed amount, involved defendants' alleged chemical contamination of the groundwater in areas of Woburn, Massachusetts. Plaintiffs alleged that two wells supplying water to the City of Woburn drew upon the contaminated water, and that exposure to the contaminated water caused five deaths and severe personal injuries among plaintiffs. Among the claims for personal injuries dismissed before trial were plaintiff's claims for damages based on enhanced risk. Relying on the Massachusetts rule regarding prospective damages, the *Anderson* court reasoned that "recovery depends on establishing a 'reasonable probability' that the harm will occur." However, the *Anderson* court held that the plaintiffs failed to satisfy this threshold standard. They had not quantified their alleged enhanced risk: "Nothing in the present record indicates the magnitude of the increased risk or the diseases which plaintiffs may suffer." * * *

The majority of courts that have considered the enhanced risk issue have agreed with the disposition of the District Court in *Anderson*.
* * *

Other courts have acknowledged the propriety of the enhanced risk cause of action, but have emphasized the requirement that proof of future injury be reasonably certain. *See Hagerty v. L & L Marine Servs.*, 788 F.2d 315, 319 (5th Cir. 1986) ("[A] plaintiff can recover [damages for enhanced risk] only where he can show that the toxic exposure more probably than not will lead to cancer."); *Wilson v. Johns-Manville Sales Corp.*, 684 F.2d 111, 116-19 (D.C.Cir.1982) (holding that in latent disease cases statute of limitations period does not begin until disease is manifest and observing that "recovery of damages based on future consequences may be had only if such consequences are 'reasonably certain.'"); *Sterling v. Velsicol Chemical Corp.*, 647 F.Supp. [303, 321-22 (W.D. Tenn. 1986), aff'd in part, rev'd in part, 855 F. 2d 1188 (6th Cir. 1988)] (upholding cause of action for enhanced susceptibility to injury based on chemical contamination of plaintiffs' wells where "reasonable probability" standard is met); * * *.

Additionally, several courts have permitted recovery for increased risk of disease, but only where the plaintiff exhibited some present manifestation of disease. *See Jackson v. Johns-Manville Sales Corp.*, 781 F.2d 394, 412-13 (5th Cir.) (allowing recovery for increased risk of cancer where evidence indicated that due to asbestos exposure, plaintiff had greater than fifty percent chance of contracting cancer; "[o]nce the injury becomes actionable—once some effect appears—then the plaintiff is permitted to recover for all probable future manifestations as well"), *cert. denied*, 478 U.S. 1022 (1986); * * *

We observe that the overwhelming weight of the scholarship on this issue favors a right of recovery for tortious conduct that causes a significantly enhanced risk of injury. * * *

Our disposition of this difficult and important issue requires that we choose between two alternatives, each having a potential for imposing unfair and undesirable consequences on the affected interests. A holding that recognizes a cause of action for unquantified enhanced risk claims exposes the tort system, and the public it serves, to the task of litigating vast numbers of claims for compensation based on threats of injuries that may never occur. It imposes on judges and juries the burden of assessing damages for the risk of potential disease, without clear guidelines to determine what level of compensation may be appropriate. It would undoubtedly increase already escalating insurance rates. It is clear that the recognition of an "enhanced risk" cause of action, particularly when the risk is unquantified, would generate substantial litigation that would be difficult to manage and resolve.

Our dissenting colleague, arguing in favor of recognizing a cause of action based on an unquantified claim of enhanced risk, points out that "courts have not allowed the difficulty of quantifying injury to prevent them from offering compensation for assault, trespass, emotional distress, invasion of privacy or damage to reputation." Although lawsuits grounded in one or more of these causes of action may involve claims for damages that are difficult to quantify, such damages are awarded on the basis of events that have occurred and can be proved at the time of trial. In contrast, the compensability of the enhanced risk claim depends upon the likelihood of an event that has not yet occurred and may never occur—the contracting of one or more diseases the risk of which has been enhanced by defendant's conduct. It is the highly contingent and speculative quality of an unquantified claim based on enhanced risk that renders it novel and difficult to manage and resolve. If such claims were to be litigated, juries would be asked to award damages for the enhanced risk of a disease that may never be contracted, without the benefit of expert testimony sufficient to establish the likelihood that the contingent event will ever occur.

On the other hand, denial of the enhanced-risk cause of action may mean that some of these plaintiffs will be unable to obtain compensation for their injury. Despite the collateral estoppel effect of the jury's finding that defendant's wrongful conduct caused the contamination of plaintiffs' wells, those who contract diseases in the future because of their exposure to chemicals in their well water may be unable to prove a causal relationship between such exposure and their disease. We have already adverted to the substantial difficulties encountered by plaintiffs in attempting to prove causation in toxic tort litigation. Dismissal of the enhanced risk claims may effectively preclude any recovery for injuries caused by exposure to chemicals in plaintiffs' wells because of the difficulty of proving that injuries manifested in the future were not the product of intervening events or causes.

It may be that this dilemma could be mitigated by a legislative remedy that eases the burden of proving causation in toxic-tort cases where there has been a statistically significant incidence of disease among the exposed population. Other proposals for legislative intervention contemplate a funded source of compensation for persons significantly endangered by exposure to toxic chemicals. We invite the legislature's attention to this perplexing and serious problem.

In deciding between recognition or nonrecognition of plaintiffs' enhanced-risk claim, * * * we decline to recognize plaintiffs' cause of action for the unquantified enhanced risk of disease, and affirm the judgment of the Appellate Division dismissing such claims. We need not and do not decide whether a claim based on enhanced risk of disease that is supported by testimony demonstrating that the onset of the disease is reasonably probable [*i.e.*, more likely than not], could be maintained under the Tort Claims Act.

4.

The claim for medical surveillance expenses stands on a different footing from the claim based on enhanced risk. It seeks to recover the cost of periodic medical examinations intended to monitor plaintiffs' health and facilitate early diagnosis and treatment of disease caused by plaintiffs' exposure to toxic chemicals. At trial, competent medical testimony was offered to prove that a program of regular medical testing and evaluation was reasonably necessary and consistent with contemporary scientific principles applied by physicians experienced in the diagnosis and treatment of chemically-induced injuries.

The Appellate Division's rejection of the medical surveillance claim is rooted in the premise that even if medical experts testify convincingly that medical surveillance is necessary, the claim for compensation for these costs must fall, as a matter of law, if the risk of injury is not quantified, or, if quantified, is not reasonably probable. This analysis assumes that the reasonableness of medical intervention, and, therefore, its compensability, depends solely on the sufficiency of proof that the occurrence of the disease is probable. We think this formulation unduly impedes the ability of courts to recognize that medical science may necessarily and properly intervene where there is a significant but unquantified risk of serious disease.

* * *

The same issue was recently considered by the Fifth Circuit in *Hagerty v. L & L Marine Servs., Inc., supra.* In *Hagerty,* the plaintiff was employed as a tankerman on a barge being loaded with chemicals at a Union Carbide plant in Puerto Rico. Because of a defect in the barge or loading equipment, or both, Hagerty was completely drenched with dripolene, a carcinogenic chemical containing benzene, toluene, and xyolene. In a later mishap he was sprayed again with the same chemical. He experienced dizziness, leg cramps, and a stinging sensation in his extremities. He consulted several doctors and, at their suggestion, obtained periodic medical and laboratory tests to ensure early detection and treatment of cancer. He sued his employer and Union Carbide Corporation seeking damages for his enhanced risk of disease, for emotional distress associated with the fear of contracting cancer, and for the cost of medical examinations to aid in detecting symptoms of disease. The district court granted summary judgment for defendants.

Although affirming the grant of summary judgment on the enhanced risk claim, the court of appeals reversed as to the claims for emotional distress and medical surveillance. The court held that these causes of action were cognizable because plaintiff's injury was "discernible on the occasion when he was drenched with the toxic chemical," and that he was therefore "entitled to recover damages for all of his past, present and probable future harm attributable to defendant's tortious conduct." Despite its dismissal of the enhanced risk claim because of the insufficiency of proof of the likelihood of disease, the court viewed the cost of medical surveillance as an appropriate item of damage:

In addition to any damages for mental distress, Hagerty correctly asserts that he is entitled to recover for the continuing expense of his periodic medical checkups. A plaintiff ordinarily may recover reasonable medical expenses, past and future, which he incurs as a result of a demonstrated injury. Moreover, under the "avoidable consequences rule," he is required to submit to treatment that is medically advisable; failure to do so may bar future recovery for a condition he could thereby have alleviated or avoided. Hagerty testified that he undergoes the checkups at the advice of his physician to ensure early detection and treatment of a possible cancerous condition. We agree that the reasonable cost of those checkups may be included in a damage award to the extent that, in the past, they were medically advisable and, in the future, will probably remain so.

* * *

Compensation for reasonable and necessary medical expenses is consistent with well-accepted legal principles. It is also consistent with the important public health interest in fostering access to medical testing for individuals whose exposure to toxic chemicals creates an enhanced risk of disease. The value of early diagnosis and treatment for cancer patients is well-documented.

Harm in the form of increased risk of future cancer attributable to delay in diagnosis and treatment has become so widely accepted by the medical community that the existence of such harm could be reasonably inferred from this professional common knowledge. A survey of the medical literature indicates that it is universally agreed within the medical community that delay in cancer diagnosis and treatment usually increases the risk of metastasis.

Although some individuals exposed to hazardous chemicals may seek regular medical surveillance whether or not the cost is reimbursed, the lack of reimbursement will undoubtedly deter others from doing so. An application of tort law that allows post-injury, pre-symptom recovery in toxic tort litigation for reasonable medical surveillance costs is manifestly consistent with the public interest in early detection and treatment of disease.

Recognition of pre-symptom claims for medical surveillance serves other important public interests. The difficulty of proving causation, where the disease is manifested years after exposure, has caused many commentators to suggest that tort law has no capacity to deter polluters, because the costs of proper disposal are often viewed by polluters as exceeding the risk of tort liability. However, permitting recovery for reasonable pre-symptom, medical-surveillance expenses subjects polluters to significant liability when proof of the causal connection between the tortious conduct and the plaintiffs' exposure to chemicals is likely to be most readily available. The availability of a substantial remedy before the consequences of the plaintiffs' exposure are manifest may also have the beneficial effect of preventing or mitigating serious future illnesses and thus reduce the overall costs to the responsible parties.

Other considerations compel recognition of a pre-symptom medical surveillance claim. It is inequitable for an individual, wrongfully exposed to dangerous toxic chemicals but unable to prove that disease is likely, to have to pay his own expenses when medical intervention is clearly reasonable and necessary. * * *

We find a helpful analogy in *Reserve Mining Co. v. EPA*, 514 F.2d 492 (8th Cir.1975),[25] where the issue was whether to grant injunctive relief compelling defendant to cease discharging wastes from its iron ore processing plant into the air of Silver Bay, Minnesota, and the waters of Lake Superior. The court concluded that "[i]n assessing probabilities in this case, it cannot be said that the probability of harm is more likely than not." Moreover, the court said, "the level of probability does not readily convert into a prediction of consequences." The best that could be said was that the existence of the contaminant in the air and water gave rise to "a reasonable medical concern for the public health." The public's exposure to the contaminant in the air and water created "some health risk." The court ruled that "the existence of this risk to the [affected] public justifies * * * requiring abatement of the health hazard on reasonable terms as a precautionary and preventive measure to protect the public health." The critical holding for our purposes is that the public health interest may justify judicial intervention even when the risk of disease is problematic.

Our conclusion regarding the compensability of medical surveillance expenses is not dissimilar to the result in the *Reserve Mining* case. The likelihood of disease is but one element in determining the reasonableness of medical intervention for the plaintiffs in this case. Other critical factors are the significance and extent of their exposure to chemicals, the toxicity of the chemicals, the seriousness of the diseases for which individuals are at risk, and the value of early diagnosis. Even if the likelihood that these plaintiffs would contract cancer were only slightly higher than the national average, medical intervention may be completely appropriate in view of the attendant circumstances. A physician treating a Legler-area child who drank contaminated well water for several years could hardly be faulted for concluding that that child should be examined annually to assure early detection of symptoms of disease.

Accordingly, we hold that the cost of medical surveillance is a compensable item of damages where the proofs demonstrate, through reliable expert testimony predicated upon the significance and extent of

---

[25] This case may be found in Chapter 4 (Judicial Role).

exposure to chemicals, the toxicity of the chemicals, the seriousness of the diseases for which individuals are at risk, the relative increase in the chance of onset of disease in those exposed, and the value of early diagnosis, that such surveillance to monitor the effect of exposure to toxic chemicals is reasonable and necessary. In our view, this holding is thoroughly consistent with our rejection of plaintiffs' claim for damages based on their enhanced risk of injury. That claim seeks damages for the impairment of plaintiffs' health, without proof of its likelihood, extent, or monetary value. In contrast, the medical surveillance claim seeks reimbursement for the specific dollar costs of periodic examinations that are medically necessary notwithstanding the fact that the extent of plaintiffs' impaired health is unquantified.

We find that the proofs in this case were sufficient to support the trial court's decision to submit the medical surveillance issue to the jury, and were sufficient to support the jury's verdict.

5.

The medical surveillance issue was tried as if it were a conventional claim for compensatory damages susceptible to a jury verdict in a lump sum. The jury was so instructed by the trial court, and neither plaintiffs' nor defendant's request to charge on this issue sought a different instruction.

* * *

In our view, the use of a court-supervised fund to administer medical-surveillance payments in mass exposure cases, particularly for claims under the Tort Claims Act, is a highly appropriate exercise of the Court's equitable powers.

STERLING v. VELSICOL CHEMICAL CORP.

855 F.2d 1188 (6th Cir. 1988)

RALPH B. GUY, Jr., Circuit Judge, on rehearing.

* * *

I. FACTS

In August, 1964, the defendant, Velsicol Chemical Corporation (Velsicol), acquired 242 acres of rural land in Hardeman County, Tennessee. The defendant used the site as a landfill for by-products from the production of chlorinated hydrocarbon pesticides at its Memphis, Tennessee, chemical manufacturing facility. Before Velsicol purchased the landfill site and commenced depositing any chemicals into the ground, it neither conducted hydrogeological studies to assess the soil composition underneath the site, the water flow direction, and the location of the local water aquifer, nor drilled a monitoring well to detect and record any ongoing contamination. From October, 1964, to June, 1973, the defendant deposited a total of 300,000 55-gallon steel drums containing ultra hazardous liquid chemical waste and hundreds of fiber board cartons containing ultra hazardous dry chemical waste in the landfill.[26]

* * *

* * * Additionally, in 1978, the state, the USGS, the EPA, and Velsicol all commenced numerous extensive ground water surveys of the site and surrounding area. The surveys collectively identified twelve to fifteen drinking water wells, which were adjacent to the site, as contaminated with high levels of chlorinated hydrocarbons. Specifically, the surveys established that six of these wells were contaminated by carbon tetrachloride in excess of 100 parts per billion and high amounts of chloroform. The users of these wells, and all wells within 1,000 acres around the landfill site, were advised to stop using them for any purpose.

In 1978, forty-two plaintiffs sued Velsicol in the Circuit Court of Hardeman County, Tennessee, on behalf of themselves and all others similarly situated for damages and injunctive relief. The complaint sought $1.5 billion in compensatory damages and $1 billion in punitive damages. * * * The class action proceeded to trial with the five representative plaintiffs proposed by the plaintiffs' counsel (Steven Sterling, Daniel Johnson, Curry Ivy, James Wilbanks, and James Maness, Jr.).

After a bench trial of the five claims, the district court found Velsicol liable to the plaintiffs on legal theories of strict liability, common law negligence, trespass, and nuisance. * * *

* * *

V. COMPENSATORY DAMAGES

Velsicol argues that, even assuming proof of a proximate causation, the district court improperly awarded the five representative plaintiffs compensatory damages for their respective injuries and disabilities. The five representative plaintiffs, their exposure to Velsicol's chemicals, and their respective injuries are as follows:

Steven Sterling: Plaintiff Sterling, who was born December 25, 1922, in Hardeman County, Tennessee, utilized a well adjacent to his residence (Sterling well) for drinking purposes until November, 1977, and for all

---

[26] The district court concluded that spent hydrocarbons buried at the landfill disposal site included not only chlorobenzene, hexachlorobutadiene, hexachloroethane, hexachloronerbornadiene, naphthalene, tetrachloroethylene, toluene, hexachlorocyclopentadiene, and benzene, but also the known carcinogens carbon tetrachloride and chloroform. The drums and cartons containing these chemicals were deposited in trenches that were 15 feet deep and 12 to 15 feet wide and covered with approximately 3 feet of soil. Velsicol took no precautions to insure the drums from bursting and, invariably, some of the drums would leak their contents into the soil. Furthermore, the trenches were neither lined nor covered with any impermeable material to prevent the chemical waste from leaking into the soil. Velsicol eventually placed a clay cap over the landfill site in 1980 only after state authorities threatened a lawsuit over the imminent danger the landfill posed to the environment.

other purposes until November, 1978. During that time, he claimed to have drunk between ten and twelve glasses of the well water each day. He observed that, beginning in 1975, the well water developed a distinct odor, a bad taste, and contained an oily substance. Sterling testified that after ingesting, and otherwise using, the well water for a prolonged period of time, he suffered from headaches, nervousness, stomach and chest pains, shortness of breath, ringing in his ears, fatigue, loss of appetite and weight, nausea, coughing, vomiting, and peripheral neuropathy. Sterling further testified that he suffered from an enlarged liver with abnormal hepatic function, and an eighty percent reduction in his kidney function. Additionally, he developed emphysema in early 1976. Sterling was a heavy smoker for over forty-five years and previously worked in a cotton mill.

[The other representative plaintiffs had comparable symptoms and medical histories.]

* * *

A. Extent of Injury and Disability

Velsicol asserts there was insufficient medical proof of the causal connection between ingestion of contaminated water and certain injuries. First, we focus upon that portion of the award attributed to the plaintiffs' actual physical injuries and then upon the portion of the award attributed to their increased susceptibility to cancer and other diseases.

1. Presently Ascertainable Injuries

* * *

Velsicol specifically avers that the plaintiffs failed to prove to a reasonable medical certainty that Wilbanks' kidney cancer, all of the plaintiffs' loss of kidney and liver functions and central nervous system injuries, and Wilbanks' and Ivy's optic atrophy and neuritis were caused by ingesting contaminated water. With respect to Wilbanks' kidney cancer, plaintiffs' testifying physician, Dr. Rhamy, stated that "based upon a reasonable medical certainty . . . its more likely [that Wilbanks' kidney cancer] was caused by the chemicals . . . ." While Dr. Rhamy conceded that "[n]o one knows what causes cancer of the kidney," his testimony that Wilbanks' environmental exposure to carbon tetrachloride was the reasonable and probable cause for his kidney cancer constitutes sufficient medical proof. The plaintiffs' testifying physicians, Drs. Balistreri, Clark, Rhamy, and Rodricks, further testified to a reasonable medical certainty that each of the plaintiff's loss of kidney and liver functions and central nervous system disorders were caused by their exposure to the contaminated water.

However, the plaintiffs failed to prove to a reasonable medical certainty that either Wilbanks' or Ivy's optic atrophy and neuritis were caused by ingesting or otherwise using the contaminated water. While plaintiffs' own expert neuroopthamologist, Dr. Drewery, stated that Ivy's eye problems and his exposure to carbon tetrachloride were causally related and that his reduction in visual acuity and visual field were compatible with toxic exposure, Dr. Drewery, based upon his own tests, concluded that Ivy did not have optic atrophy. * * *

2. Increased Risk of Cancer and Other Diseases

Plaintiffs sought to recover damages for the prospect that cancer and other diseases may materialize as a result of their exposure.[27] The district court awarded the five representative plaintiffs damages predicated upon their being at risk for, or susceptible to, future disease.

Where the basis for awarding damages is the potential risk of susceptibility to future disease, the predicted future disease must be medically reasonably certain to follow from the existing present injury. While it is unnecessary that the medical evidence conclusively establish with absolute certainty that the future disease or condition will occur, mere conjecture or even possibility does not justify the court awarding damages for a future disability which may never materialize. Tennessee law requires that the plaintiff prove there is a reasonable medical certainty that the anticipated harm will result in order to recover for a future injury. Therefore, the mere increased risk of a future disease or condition resulting from an initial injury is not compensable. While neither the Tennessee courts, nor this court, has specifically addressed damage awards for increased risk or susceptibility to cancer and kidney and liver diseases, numerous courts have denied recovery where plaintiffs alleged they might suffer from these future diseases or conditions as a result of existing injuries. [The court discussed *Ayers* and *Hagerty, supra*, in detail.] * * *

In the instant case, the district court found an increased risk for susceptibility to cancer and other diseases of only twenty-five to thirty percent. This does not constitute a reasonable medical certainty, but rather a mere possibility or speculation. Indeed, no expert witnesses ever testified during the course of trial that the five representative plaintiffs had even a probability—*i.e.*, more than a fifty percent chance—of developing cancer and kidney or liver disease as a result of their exposure to defendant's chemicals.

* * * the district court's award of compensatory damages to each of the five representative plaintiffs is remanded for recalculation to exclude that

---

[27] In awarding damages to the plaintiffs for their increased risk to cancer and other diseases, the [trial] court stated in pertinent part:

[I]t must be emphasized that the increased susceptibility to kidney and liver disease and cancer is a presently existing condition in each plaintiff who suffered exposure to the various toxins. Plaintiffs produced scientific experts who testified, that, to a reasonable degree of scientific certainty, each plaintiff now has a presently existing condition known as "enhanced or increased susceptibility" to disease. Finally, they testified that the condition resulted from consuming the Velsicol chemicals in the water.

In sum, it is generally recognized that a plaintiff is entitled to damages for an enhanced risk of injury occasioned by a defendant's wrongdoing. There is simply no element of speculation in awarding those damages between the condition and defendant's wrongdoing.

portion of the damage award attributed to increased susceptibility to cancer and other diseases.

B. Fear of Increased Risk of Cancer and Other Diseases

Velsicol next argues that the district court erroneously awarded the five representative plaintiffs compensatory damages or, in the alternative, excessive damages for fear of increased risk of contracting cancer and other diseases. Mental distress, which results from fear that an already existent injury will lead to the future onset of an as yet unrealized disease, constitutes an element of recovery only where such distress is either foreseeable or is a natural consequence of, or reasonably expected to flow from, the present injury. *See Payton v. Abbott Labs*, 437 N.E.2d 171 (Mass. 1982). However, damages for mental distress generally are not recoverable where the connection between the anxiety and the existing injury is either too remote or tenuous. While there must be a reasonable connection between the injured plaintiff's mental anguish and the prediction of a future disease, the central focus of a court's inquiry in such a case is not on the underlying odds that the future disease will in fact materialize. To this extent, mental anguish resulting from the chance that an existing injury will lead to the materialization of a future disease may be an element of recovery even though the underlying future prospect for susceptibility to a future disease is not, in and of itself, compensable inasmuch as it is not sufficiently likely to occur. In the context of certain types of injuries and exposures to certain chemicals, cancerphobia has been one basis of claims for mental anguish damages.[28]

In Tennessee, damages for fear arising from an increased risk of disease are recoverable. *Laxton v. Orkin Exterminating Co.*, 639 S.W.2d 431 (Tenn. 1982). In *Laxton*, the plaintiffs' water supply was contaminated by the carcinogens chlordane and heptachlor when defendant serviceman sprayed the exterior of plaintiffs' house for termites. The Department of Water Quality Control told plaintiffs to cease using the water for any purpose and to obtain a new water source. As a result of ingesting the contaminated water for over a period of eight months, the plaintiffs worried about their health and the health of their children. The court awarded the plaintiffs $6,000 each for their mental suffering resulting from their reasonable apprehension of the harmful effects to their own and their children's health due to consuming or otherwise using the contaminated water. The *Laxton* court noted that the period of "mental anguish" deserving compensation was confined to the time between the discovery of ingestion of toxic substances and the determination that puts to rest the fear of future injury.

In the instant case, the plaintiffs' fear clearly constitutes a present injury. Each plaintiff produced evidence that they personally suffered from

---

[28] Cancerphobia is merely a specific type of mental anguish.

a reasonable fear of contracting cancer or some other disease in the future as a result of ingesting Velsicol's chemicals. Consistent with the extensive line of authority in both Tennessee and other jurisdictions, we cannot say that the district court erred in awarding the five representative plaintiffs damages for their reasonable fear of increased risk of cancer and other diseases.

In the alternative, Velsicol asserts that the district court awarded excessive damages to the plaintiffs. The amount of the damage award in a personal injury action is for the jury or, in a non-jury case, the trial judge who heard the evidence. Absent a showing of bias, passion, or corruption, excessiveness of a verdict is left to the trial court's discretion. The appellate court will only consider whether the trial court abused that discretion by granting awards so large as to shock the judicial conscience. When considering whether an award is so excessive, this court considers other awards in other cases, as well as the nature and extent of the injuries.

* * *

C. Immune System Impairment and Learning Disorders

Velsicol argues that the district court erroneously awarded all of the plaintiffs damages for alleged impairment to their immune systems and to plaintiff Maness for his additional learning disorders due to his immune system impairment. Velsicol specifically alleges that the court improperly admitted and relied upon testimony which purported to show Velsicol's chemicals harmed plaintiffs' immune systems because the principles upon which the experts based their conclusions were not in conformity to a generally accepted explanatory theory.

[The court agreed with Velsicol on this point.]

D. Post-Traumatic Stress Disorder

Velsicol argues that the district court improperly awarded four of the five representative plaintiffs damages for post-traumatic stress disorder (PTSD). Both this court and the courts of Tennessee are familiar with, and have awarded compensatory damages for, PTSD. On appeal, Velsicol specifically argues that the plaintiffs failed to prove the requisite elements of PTSD.

* * *

Plaintiffs' drinking or otherwise using contaminated water, even over an extended period of time, does not constitute the type of recognizable stressor identified either by professional medical organizations or courts. Examples of stressors upon which courts have based awards for PTSD include rape, assault, military combat, fires, floods, earthquakes, car and airplane crashes, torture, and even internment in concentration camps, each of which are natural or man-made disasters with immediate or extended violent consequences. Whereas consumption of contaminated water may be an unnerving occurrence, it does not rise to the level of the type of psychologically traumatic event that is a universal stressor. * * * Since each plaintiff failed to satisfy all of the criteria necessary for a diagnosis of PTSD, we reverse the district court's award of damages.

E. Impaired Quality of Life

Velsicol argues that the district court erred in awarding three non-resident representative plaintiffs damages for impaired quality of life based upon a nuisance theory. Velsicol specifically alleges that plaintiffs Ivy and Maness, who were never residents of the affected area, and plaintiff Wilbanks, who relocated before state authorities counselled residents to locate an alternative water source, were not entitled to this category of damages as they had no standing to bring a nuisance action. In awarding plaintiffs damages for impaired quality of life, the district court stated in pertinent part:

> [I]t is well settled and a traditional principle of law, that damages for anxiety, discomfort and other distress are recoverable in a nuisance action. In other words, such claims are an incidental element of damages to the property damages recoverable when a nuisance is created. . . . . One of the prime reasons a nuisance is actionable is that it adversely affects the occupants' right to enjoy the property. In the case of a residence, the life of the occupants is disrupted. *In a sense, then, although a nuisance is a property action, its gravamen is the disruption of the lives and well being of the residents.* The residents may recover damages for the disruption in the quality of their lives caused by the wrongdoing of defendants. It is well-settled that disruption and inconvenience, in addition to the mental injury are compensible [sic] items in a nuisance action. Simply put, plaintiffs may testify to, and recover damages for, the disruption in their everyday lives and the inconvenience caused by their lack of a potable water supply.

647 F.Supp. at 321 (emphasis added).

While Tennessee recognizes impairment of enjoyment of life as an element of intangible damages, the court may not award this category of damages to non-residents on the theory of a nuisance action. Courts that have awarded damages on this basis have properly limited their award to residents of the area affected by the nuisance. The district court erred in awarding damages to non-resident plaintiffs on the basis of a nuisance theory. Accordingly, we reverse the district court's award of damages for impairment of quality of life to plaintiffs Ivy, Maness, and Wilbanks.

F. Lost Wages and Earning Capacity

* * *

G. Diminution of Property Value

Velsicol asserts that the district court erred in finding that the current value of one of the representative plaintiff's property was limited to its value as that of timberland. Velsicol asserts that, given the fact that the plaintiff continues living on the property and that the county tax assessor devalued the property by only twenty-eight percent, meant the property had a higher value. Velsicol further asserts that the district court's formula for calculating the diminution of property value for all property owners in the putative class was arbitrary and impermissibly speculative. We disagree with the defendant's contentions.

* * *

Under Tennessee law, the measure of damages for injury to realty is the difference in market value before and after the commission of the tort allegedly reducing the value of the realty. * * * We find that the district court properly valuated Sterling's property and, moreover, properly differentiated the value of property within the separate "zones" in recognition of the diminution of the value of property within a certain proximity to Velsicol's landfill. * * *

* * *

VII. PUNITIVE DAMAGES

Lastly, Velsicol argues that the district court erred in awarding the entire class punitive damages on the grounds of Velsicol's conduct during the course of litigation, upon the baseless conclusion it willfully and wantonly violated state law in disposing its chemicals, and before determining compensatory damages to the entire class.

In awarding punitive damages, the district court stated in pertinent part:

The Court has concluded that a single award of punitive damages is appropriate and should be awarded in this case. The Court finds this decision appropriate, because it has heard all of the evidence on all of the significant issues that can be presented for decision in this class action. The Court finds Velsicol's actions in locating, creating, maintaining and operating its chemical waste burial site constituted gross negligence and a wilful and wanton disregard for the health and well being of plaintiffs and the adjacent environment. This is particularly true when the Court considers Velsicol's superior knowledge about chemicals used in its manufacturing process.

647 F.Supp. at 307. The district court noted there were at least three possible justifications for such an award and then based the award upon a portion of the profits Velsicol earned as a result of utilizing the landfill rather than incinerating the chemicals.

In assessing its award of punitive damages, the district court stated:

[V]elsicol's actions in creating, maintaining and operating its chemical waste burial site, with superior knowledge of the highly toxic and harmful nature of the chemical contaminants it disposed of therein, and specifically its failure to immediately cease dumping said toxic chemicals after being warned by several state and federal agencies . . . constituted gross, wilful and wanton disregard for the health and well-being of the plaintiffs, and therefore is supportive of an award of punitive and exemplary damages.

The Court further concludes that Velsicol's attempt to allege that plaintiffs were guilty of assuming the risk, or were guilty of contributory negligence is without factual basis and so outrageous as to subject the defendant to punitive damages.

In addition the Court further finds that Velsicol has also attempted to shift the liability and causation for the psychological disorders suffered by the plaintiffs to the local, state and federal authorities, claiming that the defendant cooperated with them in their attempts to monitor the situation and persuade Velsicol to limit its activities. They contend that news coverage of this case specifically caused the post-traumatic stress disorder. The Court concludes that these attempts by Velsicol are also so outrageous that punitive damages should be imposed.

647 F.Supp. at 323-24.

Punitive damages are allowed under Tennessee law and are given in excess of, and in addition to, compensatory damages. They are awarded in cases involving fraud, malice, gross negligence, or oppression, or where a wrongful act is done with a bad motive or recklessly as to imply a disregard of social obligation, or where there is such willful misconduct as to raise a presumption of conscious indifference. In the state of Tennessee, punitive damages are not recoverable as a matter of right, but are within the sound discretion of the trial judge. We will not reverse an award of punitive damages without proof of an abuse of discretion. Moreover, in reviewing a trial court's justification for awarding such damages, we view the record in its entirety rather than each particular factor in isolation. The theory behind awarding punitive damages is not to compensate an injured plaintiff for personal injury but to punish a defendant and deter him from committing acts of similar nature.

* * *

There is * * * evidence supporting the district court's determination that Velsicol violated state law in establishing, utilizing, and refusing to cease disposal operations at the landfill disposal site. It was within the district court's discretion to consider defendant's disregard of state law in making its award. Lastly, the district court need not defer its award of punitive damages prior to determining compensatory damages for the entire class of 128 individuals. So long as the court determines the defendant's liability and awards representative class members compensatory damages, the district court may in its discretion award punitive damages to the class as a whole at that time. Because the district court erred in awarding punitive damages, in part, upon the positions taken by Velsicol at trial, we remand for recomputation of punitive damages.

For the foregoing reasons, we AFFIRM IN PART, REVERSE IN PART, and REMAND for recalculation of damages.

NOTES

1. *Harms and remedies*. The harms that a court is willing to redress and the remedies that it is willing to grant are two sides of the same coin. Put another way, the permissible remedies tell us what kinds of harm are cognizable in tort. List the harm/remedy pairs that were addressed in the *Anderson*, *Ayers*, and *Sterling* cases. What are the limitations placed on each harm/remedy? Are there any common themes?

2. *The "present value" of risk*. You can think of some of the remedies discussed in the cases as providing a surrogate measure of risk or as something that gives risk a present value. Which remedies fit this description? Which do not? Can you see a pattern in terms of the willingness of courts to grant such relief?

3. *Compensatory damages*. Where a plaintiff suffers a physical injury resulting from exposure to a toxic substance, a court will typically award money damages intended to compensate the plaintiff for the harm. However, the nature and extent of injury and illness to a plaintiff is often unknown at the time a suit is filed. This is particularly true in toxic tort cases, where the lengthy latency periods may result in illnesses many years after the initial exposure, sometimes long after the lawsuit is filed. A plaintiff seeking compensatory damages must, at the time of trial, prove damages for any present injury or illness, as well as any future losses likely to result either from the present injury, or from exposure to the toxic substance. This principle, known as the "single recovery rule," is intended to award damages to a plaintiff for all losses resulting from an injury at one time, to avoid further suits if the toxic substance produces more harm after the trial is over.[29]

4. *Claims for medical monitoring*. This relief seeks to reimburse for future costs associated with diagnostic tests and periodic medical examinations thought necessary because of the likelihood of disease after the termination of the lawsuit. Medical monitoring is needed only when there is an increased risk that such monitoring is reasonably anticipated to be incurred as a result of some earlier exposure to a toxic substance.[30] While most jurisdictions do not require the plaintiff to manifest any present symptoms of illness, the plaintiff must be able to prove exposure to some toxic or hazardous substance under the control of the plaintiff, making

---

[29] The types of losses that are typically associated with an injury include medical expenses, lost wages and/or earning capacity, medical complications, and pain and suffering. *See* Capelouto v. Kaiser Found. Hosp., 500 P.2d 880 (Cal. 1972) (the concept of "pain and suffering" includes recovery for physical pain, as well as fright, nervousness, grief, anxiety, worry, mortification, shock, humiliation, indignity, embarrassment, apprehension, terror or ordeal).

[30] Medical monitoring does not compensate for any damages associated with enhanced risk, as such, or for the plaintiff's emotional distress over becoming sick in the future.

medical monitoring necessary due to increased risk of future disease, where testing procedures exist that can detect the onset of disease at an early stage. *In re Paoli Yard PCB Litigation*, 916 F.2d 829 (3d Cir. 1990); *Merry v. Westinghouse Electric Corp.*, 684 F. Supp. 847 (M.D. Pa. 1988).[31] These pros and cons of medical monitoring were addressed in the *Ayers* case, *supra*. Why did the court distinguish between medical monitoring and enhanced risk claims? What must a plaintiff prove to recover medical monitoring costs? More generally, should courts address toxic injury by simply requiring defendants to purchase health insurance for successful plaintiffs?

5. *Permanent damages in lieu of injunctive relief.* Injunctive relief depends in part on the plausibility of abating the nuisance, or taking affirmative action to restore damaged property to its previous condition. Where one or both of these are improbable or impossible, courts may award permanent damages as compensation, instead of an injunction. A good example of this type of situation is found in *Boomer v. Atlantic Cement Co.*, 257 N.E. 2d 870 (1970), where plaintiff landowners sought an injunction restraining the operator of a cement plant from emitting dust and raw materials, and conducting excessive blasting which created a public nuisance. The court determined that it appeared unlikely that techniques to eliminate the nuisance would be developed within any short period of time, and chose to award permanent damages to compensate the plaintiffs for the servitude that the defendants had placed on the land. The downside of a permanent damages remedy is that the defendant is able to continue engaging in activities which harm the environment. *See* A. Mitchell Polinsky, *Resolving Nuisance Disputes: The Simple Economics of Injunctive and Damage Remedies,* 32 STAN. L. REV. 1075 (1980). The *Ayers* court, *supra*, confronted a similar issue in approving medical monitoring damages—whether to require a lump sum payment up front or to permit the court to impose an as-needed, insurance-like scheme. *Ayers* permitted the trial court to choose between them: What factors do you think should be considered in making this decision?

6. *Injunctive relief.* One element of relief demanded, but not considered by the court in *Sterling,* is an injunction. Injunctive relief can take two forms. A "prohibitory" injunction stops a defendant from engaging in a certain activity, while a "mandatory" injunction requires a defendant to take steps to remedy an existing or potential harm. Since it is an equitable remedy, courts possess a great deal of discretion in granting and shaping injunctive relief. The RESTATEMENT provides a list of factors to be considered in granting an injunction, including:

---

[31] *See* Nicholas Shannin, *Converging Theories: An Analysis of the Future of Medical Monitoring as a Remedy for the Victims of Powerline Radiation Torts*, 7 U. OF FLA. J.L. & PUB. POLICY 127 (1995).

- the nature of the interest to be protected,
- the relative adequacy to the plaintiff of injunction and of other remedies,
- any unreasonable delay by the plaintiff in bringing suit,
- any related misconduct on the part of the plaintiff,
- the relative hardship likely to result to defendant if an injunction is granted and to plaintiff if it is denied,
- the interests of third persons and of the public, and
- the practicability of framing and enforcing the order or judgment.

REST. (2D) OF TORTS § 936(1). *See also Village of Wilsonville, et al, v. SCA Services, Inc.*, 426 N.E. 2d 824 (Ill. 1981) (court balanced the relative hardship to be caused to the plaintiffs and the operator of the site before granting a permanent injunction enjoining the operation of the chemical waste disposal site that presented a public nuisance, and requiring the defendant to restore the property to its previous condition).

7. *Punitive damages*. Punitive damages differ from compensatory damages in that they are intended to punish the defendant and in so doing to deter others from engaging in similar conduct. The RESTATEMENT (SECOND) OF TORTS §908 permits punitive damages when the defendant's conduct is "outrageous," because of the "defendant's evil motive or his reckless indifference to the rights of others." Factors that are relevant in judging whether a toxic tort defendant is sufficiently "evil" to warrant punitive damages include whether the defendant intentionally violated state pollution standards, manipulated the discharges in an attempt to escape detection, disregarded neighbors' complaints, and withheld information from state health officials. *Orjias v. Louisiana-Pacific Corp.*, 31 F.3d 995 (10th Cir. 1994). If the standard for punitive damages has been met,[32] the jury sets the actual amount of the damages. The dollars awarded in a punitive damages verdict vary according to the plaintiff's litigation expenses, the degree of hazard to the public posed by the defendant's product or conduct, the financial worth of the defendant, the extent to which the defendant profited from its misconduct, and the amount deemed necessary to deter other potential defendants. *Johns-Manville Sales Corp. v. Janssens*, 463 So.2d 242 (Fla. App. 1984). As punitive damages become larger and more frequent, particularly with toxic torts, there have been calls for both legislative reform[33] and judicial review[34] of the reasonableness of enormous awards.

---

[32] In some jurisdictions, the burden of proof has been changed by statute to a "clear and convincing" standard, which is higher than the traditional tort standard of a "preponderance of the evidence." CAL. CIV. CODE §§294 (West 1970, Supp. 1995).

[33] *See, e.g.*, COLO. REV. STAT. §13-21-102(1) (1989) (limiting the amount a plaintiff can recover in punitive damages to the amount received in compensatory damages).

PROBLEM

The following excerpt describes a large punitive damages award in a toxic torts case. After reading the account of the damages awarded, ask yourself whether you think the damages assessed were excessive. If you think they were excessive, how would you recalculate?

STARES OF LAWYERLY DISBELIEF AT A HUGE CIVIL AWARD

John Broder
New York Times, Sept. 10, 1997, p. C1

Big civil-damages awards have become an increasingly common feature of the American legal landscape, but Monday's nearly $3.5 billion punitive-damages assessment in a 1987 Louisiana railway fire is being seen as a case unto itself.

The accident that spawned the huge award was little noticed outside Louisiana and did not cause widespread injury or death. Questions were raised about the long-term health effects of the chemical fire, but no definitive studies have established lasting medical damage.

The award has left legal experts shaking their heads. Advocates of tort reform say the case is a prime example of the need to limit or abolish punitive damages and to discourage the filing of class-action claims.

Many of the case's specifics remained unclear today, including the potential for latent damage to the health of thousands of residents of the neighborhood near the fire and the culpability of the companies that shared blame for the accident.

The size of the verdict may be partly explained by the residents' anger at the storage of highly flammable and toxic chemicals in rail cars in their poor, largely black neighborhood where citizens have little money or political influence. Lawyers for the residents said they were victims of "environmental racism."

Still, the $3.5 billion judgment, representing seven times the ultimate payout in 1989 from the lethal chemical explosion at Bhopal, India, stunned participants and independent analysts alike. To be sure, India originally sought $3 billion in compensation for more than 3,000 deaths.

Brent Barriere, one of a team of lawyers defending the five transportation companies in the case, called the verdict outrageous and said it was the result of a jury's riding a "runaway train."

He said that the award bore no relationship to the actual damages borne by the 8,000 people temporarily evacuated from their homes 10 years ago when a tank

---

[34] *See, e.g.*, BMW of North America, Inc. v. Gore, 517 U.S. 559 (1996) (a punitive damages award may be grossly excessive if there is great disparity in the harm suffered by the plaintiff and the punitive damages).

car containing butadiene, a volatile chemical used to make synthetic rubber, began to leak and then burst into flames in a New Orleans rail yard.

* * *

Referring to the railway companies, Wendell Gauthier, a New Orleans lawyer representing many of the class-action plaintiffs, asserted: "These scoundrels, they took the position that there's nobody back there worth caring about, they're all black, they're all poor and nobody cares about them. If it was your family out there, would you feel the verdict was outrageous?"

* * *

[I]n the Louisiana rail-car accident, the jury appears to have been motivated chiefly by urgings from plaintiff's lawyers to "send a message" to the corporate defendants, rather than by a damage analysis.

Mr. Gauthier argued in court that the companies had been "careless and indifferent" to the people living near the rail yard. He said in an interview that the residents sustained mental anguish, financial costs and physical pain as a result of the evacuation.

Kimbra Whitney, one of the jurors, told reporters on Monday that she had been persuaded by Mr. Gauthier's argument that the companies did not show adequate regard for the safety and comfort of residents.

"I felt the evidence showed they were unconcerned," she said.

But lawyers who try to defend corporations and individuals against civil-damage suits said that such juries set an impossible standard for behavior. It is not enough, they said, to follow the law and exercise reasonable care; companies must show proper "concern" for potential victims of their actions.

C. The Defendant's Response

After a plaintiff files a toxic tort case, the defendant is likely to respond in one of three ways. First, the defendant may seek to reject a specific cause of action by arguing that the plaintiff has failed to state a claim that satisfies the substantive elements of that particular tort. Second, the defendant may raise a common law affirmative defense, typically grounded in the plaintiff's misconduct. Third, statutory defenses may be asserted.

1. Failure to State a Cause of Action in Tort Law

The defendant can seek to show that the defendant's conduct does not fit the legal requirements of the tort or torts alleged by the plaintiff. For example, if a plaintiff brings a negligent trespass claim against a manufacturing plant alleging that the plant's discharge of PCBs had caused damage to the plaintiff's property, the claim will be dismissed if the plaintiff cannot prove the actual harm caused by the claimed presence of PCBs on her property. *See e.g., Mercer v. Rockwell Int'l Corp.*, 24 F. Supp. 2d 735 (W.D. Ky. 1998). Or, if the plaintiff is a purchaser of contaminated property who seeks recovery from the seller for cleanup expenses under a negligence theory, the plaintiff typically must establish that the defendant had a duty to plaintiffs to maintain the property in a safe condition. If the defendant can show that there is no such duty under the common law, then the plaintiff has failed to state a cause of action negligence against the defendant. *See, e.g., Cross Oil Co. v. Phillips Petroleum Co.*, 944 F. Supp. 787 (E.D. Moreover., 1996); *Dartron Corp. v. Uniroyal Chemical Co.*, 893 F. Supp. 730 (N.D. Ohio 1995). Or, if the plaintiff brings a toxic tort action against a tire factory alleging nuisance as a result of the factory's release of petroleum naptha into the soil near the plaintiff's property, the court will conclude that that complaint has failed to state a claim in nuisance if the plaintiff has not alleged how the naptha plume under its property interferes with the use and enjoyment of the land. *Bradley v. Armstrong Rubber Company*, 130 F.3d 168 (5th Cir. 1997).

Another way for the defendant to argue that the plaintiff has failed to state a toxic tort cause of action is to show the court that the plaintiff's remedy does not lie in tort law at all. For example, the "economic loss" doctrine holds that a party bringing a tort claim cannot recover damages if the claim arises out of a commercial transaction. *Stoughton Trailers, Inc. v. Henkel Corp.*, 965 F. Supp. 1227 (W.D. Wis. 1997). The doctrine rests upon the general distinction between contract and tort law: when contractual expectations are frustrated because of a defect in the subject matter of a contract, the remedy lies in contract; when the subject matter of a contract causes physical harm to persons or property other than the contract's subject matter, a remedy lies in tort. *Compare Northridge Co. v. W.R. Grace and Co.*, 471 N.W. 2d 179 (Wis. 1991) (court agreed plaintiff had stated claim in tort—negligence— when plaintiff's suit against the seller of an asbestos-based fireproofing material did not allege damages because of injury to the product itself, but rather the claim was that the product released toxic substances into the environment and caused damage to the building, and a health hazard to the occupants), *with Raytheon Co. v. McGraw-Edison Co.*, 979 F. Supp. 858 (E.D. Wis. 1997) (action in tort is *not* stated by purchaser of contaminated land, who in effect is asserting that the product itself—the land—is defective because it is contaminated, and therefore any damages incurred are because of injury to the product itself).[35]

2. Common Law Affirmative Defenses

The common law affirmative defenses most frequently asserted in toxic tort cases are: (1) assumption of risk; (2) contributory negligence; and (3) "coming to the nuisance." In order to raise the assumption of risk defense in a toxic torts case, the defendant must prove that the plaintiff knew that the exposure was dangerous, appreciated the nature or extent of the danger, and voluntarily exposed himself to the danger. RESTATEMENT (SECOND) OF TORTS § 840C. In *Cornell v. Exxon Corp.*, 162 A.2d 892, 558 N.Y.S. 2d 647 (1990), the defendant raised the assumption of risk defense in response to plaintiff's nuisance, trespass, and negligence claims arising from drinking

---

[35] Some jurisdictions recognize an exception to the economic loss doctrine for a select group of intentional torts, such as negligent misrepresentation and fraud in the inducement of a contract. Huron Tool and Engineering Co. v. Precision Consulting Serv., Inc., 532 N.W.2d 541 (Mich. App. 1995); HTP, Ltd. v. Lineas Aereas Costarricenses, S.A., 685 So.2d 1238 (Fla. 1996).

contaminated well water. Since the plaintiffs were advised not to drink the water, but continued using it for bathing, cooking, and cleaning purposes, the court determined there was a factual question for the jury whether the plaintiffs had knowledge of the risk and still voluntarily chose to encounter it. The *Cornell* case illustrates the difficulties facing defendants who must present evidence that the plaintiff had knowledge of the risk. Because of long latency periods with most toxic substances, the exposure to the substance could have occurred many years before the toxic tort claim is filed, making it nearly impossible for defendants to collect evidence regarding the plaintiff's knowledge dating back to the time of the exposure.

Contributory negligence is addressed in the RESTATEMENT (SECOND) OF TORTS § 840B. The availability of the defense varies according to the nature of the defendant's conduct. If the defendant's negligent conduct causes a nuisance, contributory negligence is a defense. If the defendant's conduct has produced an abnormally dangerous condition, contributory negligence is a defense only if the plaintiff has voluntarily assumed the risk of harm. If the defendant knows that its conduct is causing a nuisance and intentionally continues, then contributory negligence is not a defense.

The "coming to the nuisance" defense can be raised only when plaintiffs have acquired property after the creation of the nuisance. Most jurisdictions have rejected this defense when the plaintiff alleges a toxic tort. *See Patrick v. Sharon Steel Corp.*, 549 F. Supp. 1259 (N.D. W. Va. 1982). The RESTATEMENT (SECOND) OF TORTS § 840D characterizes coming to the nuisance not as an absolute defense, but as one factor to consider in determining whether a claim has been stated. Some early decisions still accept the defense when the plaintiffs knowingly placed themselves in harm's way, and when the coming to the nuisance defense protects reasonable expectations of existing industry. *Fischer v. Atlantic Richfield*, 774 F. Supp. 616 (W.D. Okl. 1989); *East St. Johns Shingle Co. v. City of Portland*, 246 P.2d 554 (Or. 1952).

3. Statutory Defenses

In addition to traditional common law defenses, statutes of limitations and repose can defeat a toxic tort action. Both act to prevent plaintiffs from bringing a lawsuit that is too late. Conversely, statutes waiving sovereign immunity permit plaintiffs to sue government defendants otherwise protected from such litigation.

a. Statute of Limitations

A statute of limitations defense prevents a plaintiff from commencing a claim after a certain period of time. In the case of a recurrent or continuing trespass, a statute of limitations also creates the window of time for assessing damages, that is, damages may not be collected for the period of time before the limitations period.[36]

ANDERSON V. W.R. GRACE & CO.

628 F. Supp. 1219 (D. Mass. 1986)

A. Statute of Limitations.

  1. Michael Zona.

  Defendants argue that Michael Zona's wrongful death action is barred by the statute of limitations. The Massachusetts wrongful death statute provides in pertinent part: "An action to recover damages under this section shall be commenced within three years from the date of death . . ." This wrongful death action was filed in May of 1982, more than eight years after Michael Zona died on February 23, 1974. Plaintiffs contend that the action was timely filed because the statute was tolled until May, 1979, when they discovered the alleged cause of Michael Zona's death, by the Massachusetts "discovery rule", which tolls the statute of limitations until a plaintiff knows or reasonably should know that he or she has been harmed as a result of the defendant's conduct. The Supreme Judicial Court has not decided whether the discovery rule will toll the statute of limitations contained in the Massachusetts wrongful death statute, M.G.L. c. 229, § 2.

* * *

  As noted above, the discovery rule is a method of defining when a cause of action accrues. The principle behind the discovery rule is that "a plaintiff should be put on notice before his or her claim is barred by the passage of time." Olsen, 445 N.E.2d at 611. The notice required by the rule includes knowledge of both the injury and its cause—that plaintiff "has been harmed as a result of the defendant's conduct." *Fidler v. Eastman Kodak Co.*, 714 F.2d 192, 198 (1st Cir.1983) (quoting Olsen, 445 N.E.2d at 611).

* * *

  The present state of Massachusetts law does not, therefore, foreclose the possibility that a discovery rule might be applied in starting the limitation period notwithstanding the statutory reference to the time of death. I cannot predict with any confidence what the Supreme Judicial Court would do with this issue. It is an issue well suited to certification. Since certification would not produce an answer before trial, the solution is to DENY the defendants' motion at the present time, subject to their right to renew the issue by motion

---

[36] Where pollution is recurrent, such that a new cause of action arises day by day, or injury by injury, a nuisance action can be brought for damages incurred within the applicable statute of limitations period. Nieman v. NLO, Inc., 108 F.3d 1546 (6th Cir. 1997); Brown v. County Commissioners, 622 N.E. 2d 1153 (Ohio App. 1993).

for judgment notwithstanding the verdict in the event of a verdict for the plaintiff. The issue can then be certified to the Supreme Judicial Court on a full factual record for which that court has expressed a preference over questions certified in the abstract.

2. James Anderson and Carl Robbins, III.

Defendants argue that the wrongful death claims relating to James Anderson and Carl Robbins, III, are barred by the wrongful death statute in effect in 1981, the year in which Anderson and Robbins died. In pertinent part, the statute read:

> No recovery shall be had under this section for a death which does not occur within two years after the injury which caused the death.

The crucial issue is when plaintiffs' decedents suffered "the injury which caused the death." Defendants contend that the injury which caused the deaths of Anderson and Robbins occurred no later than at the time they were diagnosed as having leukemia. If so, the wrongful death actions would be barred. Anderson was diagnosed as having leukemia during January, 1972, and died on January 18, 1981. Robbins was diagnosed in October, 1976, and died on August 8, 1981. Plaintiffs argue that the time of diagnosis is irrelevant because Anderson's and Robbins' exposure to the contaminants allegedly causing their leukemia continued until the wells were closed in May, 1979. In an affidavit, plaintiffs' expert states:

> Repeated and chronic exposure to the contaminants which occurred at least up until the wells were closed, May, 1979, for two of the children, Carl Robbins and James Anderson, after the manifestation of the lymphoreticular malignancies, aggravated and complicated the leukemic illnesses and processes, and contributed to and hastened the children's early demise.

Plaintiffs argue that this is sufficient injury to bring the claims within the statute.

The Massachusetts courts have not been faced with the need to construe the phrase "injury which caused the death" because the injuries at issue in the cases were a result of accidents of brief duration. In this action, the alleged cause of death was prolonged exposure to harmful chemicals rather than a single incident. I conclude that the "injury which caused the death" was plaintiffs' decedents' entire exposure to the contaminants up to the time the wells were closed. The affidavit of Dr. Levin establishes, for purposes of this motion, that each additional day of exposure to the contaminants contributed to the death of James Anderson in that, if Anderson had not been exposed to the chemicals after his leukemia had been diagnosed, he would have lived longer.[37] The later exposure was thus a cause of death.

* * *

The broadest interpretation of the rule, however, does not save the case of Carl Robbins, III, whose last exposure to the allegedly contaminated water was more than two years prior to his death in August of 1981. Accordingly, defendants' motion is ALLOWED with respect to the claims of Carl Robbins, III, and DENIED with respect to those of James Anderson.

———

As *Anderson* suggests, the application of a statute of limitations in a toxic tort case is complicated by the long latency periods of toxic and hazardous materials. When there is a long period of time between a plaintiff's initial exposure to the harm-producing agent and manifestation of an injury or illness, the question is: at what point does the claim accrue? The injury giving rise to the claim can be said to occur at the time of exposure or, much later, at the time an illness manifests itself.

Historically, tort actions were thought to accrue at the time of initial exposure. This meant that a plaintiff whose illness did not become known, or was not discovered, until many years after the exposure would usually find the tort claim time-barred, since the statute of limitations would have begun to run on the date of exposure. *See, e.g., Bassham v. Owens-Corning Fiber Glass Corp.,* 327 F. Supp. 1007 (D.N.M. 1971). This "exposure rule" seemed unfair for toxic substances, because it precluded claims before plaintiffs would have reason to know of harm resulting from exposure—or even, in many cases, to suspect that exposure had occurred. Both legislatures and courts responded to the unfairness inherent in the exposure rule by adopting a "discovery rule" that an action accrues when a plaintiff knew, or should have known, of an injury or illness. *See, e.g.,* N.Y. CIV. PRAC. L. & R. 214-c(2) (McKinney 1990) (statute of limitations begins to run at the time a reasonable person would have discovered the injury); *Urie v. Thompson,* 337 U.S. 163 (1949) (statute of limitations should be triggered at time of discovery of latent illness).

Three issues have arisen with respect to the discovery rule. First, how should courts decide whether a plaintiff "should have known" that an actionable tort claim has arisen? *See Kullman v. Owens-Corning Fiberglas Corp.,* 943 F.2d 613 (6th Cir. 1991) (plaintiff's action time-barred because he

---

[37] You know from Chapter 2 (Toxicology and Risk Assessment) that this is unlikely to be the case, as a matter of the science of carcinogenesis. Is it nevertheless a fair resolution of the limitations issue?—EDS.

should have known that the dust breathed in the workplace might have been responsible for his breathing problems that eventually was diagnosed as asbestosis). Second, to what extent must the plaintiff be aware not only of an illness, but also of its cause? *See Seneca Meadows Inc. v. ECI Liquidating, Inc.*, 983 F. Supp. 360, 363 (W.D. N.Y. 1997) (claim accrues when plaintiff "had actual knowledge of both the injury and its cause"); *Everson v. Osmose Wood Preserving Company of America*, 899 F.2d 701 (7th Cir. 1990) (statute of limitations began to run when the plaintiff had knowledge of a "reasonable possibility" that a workplace chemical was the cause of his symptoms). Third, should the discovery rule apply to damage to property? *See Dombrowski v. Gould Electronics, Inc.*, 954 F. Supp. 1006 (M.D. Pa. 1996) (discovery rule applies, and statute of limitations begins to run, when plaintiff-homeowners became aware of the fact that they had suffered diminution in value of their residences because of neighboring battery crushing plant); *contra, Corporation of Mercer University v. National Gypsum Co.*, 877 F.2d 35 (11th Cir. 1989) (property damage claim not subject to discovery rule).

What was the basis for distinguishing among the plaintiffs in *Anderson*? Does it seem fair to you? If not, how would you revise the discovery rule— remembering that statutes of limitation still have an important role to play in protecting defendants from stale claims?

b. Statutes of Repose

Statutes of limitations bar claims brought beyond a certain period of time after the accrual of the claim; statutes of repose bar claims brought by a plaintiff beyond a designated period of time after the happening of a certain event, such as the date of sale of a product. Where the running of a statute of limitations may depend on the plaintiff's discovery of the claim or manifestation of illness, statutes of repose bar any claim made beyond a designated amount of time after a specific event, whether or not the elements of a claim have accrued. Statutes of repose operate as an "absolute time limit beyond which liability no longer exists and is not tolled for any reason because to do so would upset the economic balance struck by the legislative body." *First United Methodist Church v. U.S. Gypsum Co.*, 882 F.2d 862, 866 (4th Cir. 1989). *See, e.g., United Proteins, Inc. v. Farmland Indus. Inc.*, 915 P.2d 80 (Kan. 1996) (plaintiff's suit in trespass and nuisance against a fertilizer manufacturing plant whose release of toxic chemicals had contaminated the aquifer beneath the plaintiff's pet food plant was barred by a statute of repose). The discovery rule, in other words, is of no help in avoiding a statute of repose.

c. Government Immunity

Generally speaking, governmental entities enjoy sovereign immunity from most kinds of lawsuits, including toxic tort actions, by private parties. The policy behind sovereign immunity is to protect government decisionmakers from involvement in private litigation so that they may function effectively without fear of liability. Governments may waive their sovereign immunity by statute. Both federal and state statutes give to private parties a limited cause of action in tort against federal and state governments, subject to a myriad of exceptions.[38]

The Federal Tort Claims Act, 28 U.S.C. §1346(b), is waiver of sovereign immunity from tort claims against the United States for injury, wrongful death, or property damage as a result of a negligent act or omission by a Government employee within the scope of employment. The Federal Tort Claims Act would otherwise give private parties a cause of action against the federal government for toxic torts, but for the sweeping "discretionary function" exception. Pursuant to this exception, the United States may not be held liable for any claim "based upon the exercise or performance or the failure to exercise or perform a discretionary function or duty * * *, whether or not the discretion involved be abused." 28 U.S.C. §2680(a).

There are usually two inquiries that address whether the discretionary function exception applies. The initial inquiry is whether the plaintiff's injury was the result of a discretionary function or duty. The United States Supreme Court in *Berkovitz v. United States*, 486 U.S. 531 (1988) established that this prong of the exception does not apply "when a federal statute, regulation, or policy specifically prescribes a course of action for an employee to follow." If this first inquiry is satisfied, then a court must determine whether the challenged conduct was of a kind that the discretionary function exception was designed to shield. Since the exception was intended to prevent lawsuits against officials making non-mandatory policy judgments, especially where those judgments are meant to further the public interest, federal officials making or implementing discretionary policy will typically be immune from a tort action. *See, e.g., Angle v. United States*, 931 F. Supp. 1386 (W.D. Mich. 1994) (exception applicable to negligence action brought on behalf of an infant child who allegedly suffered lead poisoning from lead-based paint found in military family housing, because the federal government's decision not to remediate the hazard or warn residents of it was based upon a policy judgment about the substantial commitment of resources that would have been required to alleviate the toxic risks of lead-based paint in military housing).[39]

---

[38] The extent to which the federal government may be sued for violating federal environmental statutes, such as CERCLA, RCRA, the Clean Air Act, and Clean Water Act, is discussed below in Chapter 13.

[39] State and local governments also enjoy sovereign immunity. This immunity from toxic tort claims can be waived by a state statute, which, like the Federal Torts Claims Act, often contains a variety of exceptions to liability. *See, e.g.,* Kerrey v. Scientific, Inc., 497 A.2d 1310 (N.J. Super. 1985) (New Jersey Tort Claims Act not applicable to toxic tort action brought against State for licensing landfills and failing to properly inspect them, when Act provided that no public entity may be liable for licensing or improperly supervising a landfill).

A NOTE ON INSURANCE

When toxic tort litigation ensues, regardless of whether the suit involves a toxic product, disposal of hazardous wastes, or a CERCLA action, issues regarding insurance coverage become critical to the defendant. Claims against defendants are often in the millions of dollars—not to mention the costs of the litigation itself—and in rare cases billions of dollars. Defendants facing these kinds of costs (the insured) hope that their liability insurance agreements will be construed broadly so as to cover the activities that engendered the lawsuit. Insurance companies (the insurers) seek to limit their exposure, both by arguing for a narrow interpretation of the relevant policy, and by including within insurance agreements exclusions for toxic tort claims. *See* Kenneth Abraham, *The Maze of Mega-Coverage Litigation*, 97 COLUMBIA L. REV. 2102 (1997). As a result, a great deal of toxic tort litigation revolves around the scope of the defendant's insurance, rather than the validity of the plaintiff's claims. Limits of insurance coverage often determine settlement amounts.

Insurance indemnifies insureds for both the costs of defending litigation (regardless of outcome) and of judgments, settlements, and other elements of the insured's liability. *See, e.g., Chemical Leaman Tank Lines v. Aetna Cas. and Surety Co.*, 177 F.3d 210 (2d Cir. 1999)(a duty to indemnify requires an insurer to pay on behalf of the policyholder all sums that the insurer is contractually obligated to pay as damages because of harms or losses—including costs incurred in connection with remedial investigation and feasibility study mandated under CERCLA—covered by the policy); *Aetna Cas. and Surety Co. v. Dow Chemical Co.*, 44 F. Supp. 2d 847 (E.D. Mich. 1997)(duty to defend may exist when it is ultimately determined there is no duty to indemnify under policy). The latter aspect, coverage of liability, is typically governed by a "comprehensive general liability" (CGL) policy, the terms of which are standard throughout the insurance industry. By 1966, most CGL policies used this language to establish the insuring agreement:

> [The insurer] hereby agrees to pay on behalf of the insured all sums which the insured shall be legally obligated to pay *as damages* because of *bodily injury* or *property damage* to which this insurance applies caused by an *occurrence* . * * *[40]

---

[40] Most CGL policies also contain language requiring the insurance company to defend any "suit" against the insured. The duty to defend often arises from the allegations in the complaint against the insured. Susan Randall, *Redefining the Insurer's Duty to Defend*, 2 Conn. Ins. L. J. 221,222 (1997). The legal question that has arisen is what constitutes a "suit" within this language. *Compare* Northern Security Ins. Co. v. Mitec Telecom, 38 F. Supp. 2d 345 (D.Vt. 1999) (demand letter sent to insured by counsel for homeowners notifying insured that groundwater beneath house was contaminated with TCE from insured's lot was not a

An insurance policy includes both terms of coverage and of exclusion. Around 1970, the insurance industry added a pollution exclusion to the standard CGL policy in 1970. The original pollution exclusion clause was known as the "sudden and accidental" exclusion, and it provided that the policy did not apply to bodily injury or property damage arising out of —

> the discharge, dispersal, release, or escape of * * * toxic chemicals, * * * waste materials, * * * contaminants or *pollutants* into or upon the land, the atmosphere or any water course * * *; but this exclusion does not apply if such * * * release * * * is *sudden and accidental* . * * * This insurance does not apply to property damage to property *owned or occupied* by or rented to the insured.

This exclusion—in particular the "sudden and accidental" and "property damage" phrases—engendered much litigation. *See, e.g., Lakeside Non-Ferrous Metals v. Hanover Ins. Co.*, 172 F.3d 702 (9th Cir. 1999) (trespass and nuisance claims arising out of insured's contamination of land involved "property damage" subject to pollution exclusion, and could not be recast as personal injury claim). As a result, insurers changed the language of the pollution exclusion clause in the 1980s by deleting the "sudden and accidental" exception and simplifying the conditions that would trigger the

---

"suit"), *with* Compass Ins. Co. v. City of Littleton, 984 P.2d 606 (Colo. 1999) (coercive EPA actions initiated under CERCLA were "suites."

Under pre-1996 policies the insurer agreed to pay damages because of bodily injury or property damage "caused by an accident." *See, e.g.*, St. Paul Fire v. McCormick & Baxter, 923 P.2d 1200 (Or. 1996) (an "accident" in a CGL policy is not necessarily only an unintended event that results from unintentional acts, but also an incident or occurrence that happens by chance, without design and contrary to intention and expectation).

When there are multiple CGL insurers, there are two approaches that can be used. Under the "pro rata" approach, liability for continuing injury is allocated among all triggered liability policies according to the insurer's proportion of time on risk; under "joint and several" liability approach, each insured is jointly and severally liable for continuing injury. U.S. Fidelity & Guaranty Co. v. Treadwell Corp, 58 F.Supp 2d 77 (S.D.N.Y. 1999).

exclusion's applicability. This more insurer-friendly provision is known as the "absolute" pollution exclusion, and it dominates the insurance market today. *See Gencorp, Inc. v. American Interm. Underwaters*, 178 F.3d 804 (6th Cir. 1999) (absolute pollution exclusion does not violate public policy). Although the sudden and accidental exclusion has largely been replaced by the absolute pollution exclusion, it still has relevance for toxic tort litigation because a court may decide that an older policy applies.

Based on the materials on toxic torts, what other problems would you expect to find in determining the coverage for alleged injury from toxic and hazardous materials?

PART 2:

TOXIC SUBSTANCES AND TOXIC POLLUTION

Chapter 6

Toxics Regulation in Public Health and Pollution Control Statutes

From the beginning of the Environmental Decade, and before, Congress clearly recognized the special status of toxic substances. Much regulation of toxic substances occurs, therefore, under the rubric of statutes whose main objects are public health (in the traditional sense) and pollution control. Even though toxic substances are only a small part of each statute's mandate, together they regulate many important carcinogens. In addition, these statutes represent a veritable menu of approaches to toxics regulation, some of which work poorly, some of which repair failures of prior methods, and some of which may show real promise for the future. We emphasize the comparative aspect of these statutes in this chapter, because in an ever-evolving area like environmental law there are always opportunities to learn from experience.

A. The Federal Food, Drug, and Cosmetic Act

1. The Delaney Clause

The Federal Food, Drug, and Cosmetic Act (FFDCA) invests the Secretary of Health and Human Services, who acts through the Commissioner of the Food and Drug Administration (FDA), with the responsibility for the safety of many aspects of the nation's food supply, for the approval of human and animal drugs and medical devices, and for the safety of cosmetics. The FFDCA prohibits the sale of foods and drugs that are "adulterated" or "misbranded," meaning that they are, respectively, unsafe for human consumption or labeled in a way that renders them unsafe or is otherwise deceptive.

Carcinogens are the particular subject of the Delaney Clause, named after its sponsor, Congressman James Delaney of New York. While the FFDCA can be traced to the Pure Food Act of 1906, the Delaney Clause dates from the 1958 Food Additives Amendments. It was subsequently applied to color additives in 1960.[1] Under section 408 of the FFDCA (enacted in 1954), pesticide residues on raw agricultural commodities are regulated for safety, but safety is balanced against the interest in an "adequate, wholesome, and economical food supply."[2] 21 U.S.C. § 346a. Section 409, which contains the Delaney Clause, replaces, for carcinogens, that standard with a much more stringent one:

> *(a) Unsafe food additives; exception for conformity with exemption or regulation*
>
> A food additive shall, with respect to any particular use or intended use of such additives, be deemed to be unsafe for the purposes of the application of clause (2)(c) of section 342(a) of this title [prohibiting "adulterated" food], unless—
>
> (1) it and its use or intended use conform to the terms of an exemption * * *
>
> (2) there is in effect, and it and its use or intended use are in conformity with, a regulation issued under this section prescribing the conditions under which such additive may be safely used; * * *.

---

[1] The Delaney Clause proper can be found at 21 U.S.C. § 348, and the color additives language at 21 U.S.C. § 376. Related provisions regarding animal drug residues can be found at 21 U.S.C. § 360b.

[2] The so-called Delaney Paradox, discussed below, was rectified in the Food Quality Protection Act of 1996, Pub. L. No. 104-170, 110 Stat. 1489, but the central *proviso* of the Delaney Clause was untouched. *See* James S. Turner, *Delaney Lives! Reports of Delaney's Death are Greatly Exaggerated*, 28 ENVTL. L. REP. (ENVTL. L. INST.) 10003 (1998).

(b) Petition for regulation prescribing conditions of safe use; contents; description of production methods and controls; samples; notice of regulation

(1) Any person may, with respect to any intended use of a food additive, file with the Secretary a petition proposing the issuance of a regulation prescribing the conditions under which such additive may be safely used.

* * *

(c) Approval or denial of petition; time for issuance of orders; evaluation of data; factors

* * *

(3) No such regulation shall issue if a fair evaluation of the data before the Secretary-

(A) fails to establish that the proposed use of the food additive, under the conditions of use to be specified in the regulation, will be safe: *Provided,* That no additive shall be deemed to be safe if it is found to induce cancer when ingested by man or animal, or if it is found, after tests which are appropriate for the evaluation of the safety of food additives, to induce cancer in man or animal, except that this proviso shall not apply with respect to the use of a substance as an ingredient of feed for animals which are raised for food production, if the Secretary finds (i) that, under the conditions of use and feeding specified in proposed labeling and reasonably certain to be followed in practice, such additive will not adversely affect the animals for which such feed is intended, and (ii) that no residue of the additive will be found (by methods of examination prescribed or approved by the Secretary by regulations, which regulations shall not be subject to subsections (f) and (g) of this section) in any edible portion of such animal after slaughter or in any food yielded by or derived from the living animal; or

(B) shows that the proposed use of the additive would promote deception of the consumer in violation of this chapter or would otherwise result in adulteration or in misbranding of food within the meaning of this chapter. * * *

21 U.S.C. §348.

Despite being for many years the object of a concerted and broad-based effort for reform, the key proviso of the Delaney Clause remains unchanged from 1958. The following excerpt describes some of the difficulties in implementing the Delaney Clause.[3] As you read the materials in this section,

---

[3] For excellent descriptions of the Delaney Clause's passage and implementation by FDA by its former Chief Counsel, *see* Richard A. Merrill, *Regulating Carcinogens in Food: A Legislator's Guide to the Food Safety Provisions of the Federal Food, Drug, and Cosmetic*

ask yourself (1) why there was (and remains) broad support for changing the Delaney Clause, and (2) why Congress has nevertheless been unwilling to do so, except tangentially.

FDA's IMPLEMENTATION OF THE DELANEY CLAUSE: REPUDIATION OF CONGRESSIONAL CHOICE OR REASONED ADAPTATION TO SCIENTIFIC PROGRESS?

Richard A. Merrill
5 YALE J. ON REG. 1, 12-21 (1988)[4]

The coverage of the Delaney Clause, and thus the problems encountered in administering it, are largely a function of two circumstances: (1) the number of substances that fall within the definition of 'food additive,' and (2) the number of substances within this universe that are found to 'induce cancer.' Through the 1970s, scientific advances in two arenas enlarged dramatically the universe of substances to which the Delaney Clause might apply. At the same time, a consensus began to emerge among public health experts that while a substantial portion of human cancer was linked with diet, little could be attributed to synthetic chemicals in food.

FDA officials were not oblivious to these developments. Agency spokespersons remarked on the dramatic advances in analytical chemistry which were revealing 'additives' in food whose occurrence had not previously been expected. They also recognized that more comprehensive and sensitive testing of chemicals was expanding the list of proven animal carcinogens. And they became less hesitant about pointing out that the food supply contains hundreds of trace chemicals, most present 'naturally,' that have been associated with tumor formation in experimental animals. Furthermore, Agency officials were reminded of the growing concern about the links between dietary patterns and human cancer when food producers began promoting products as high in fibre or rich in Vitamin C while invoking the findings of the National Cancer Institute. These developments eroded both of the assumptions of the framers of the Delaney Clause: few chemical 'additives' caused cancer, but those few presented a serious threat to public health.

1. Progress in Analytical Chemistry: Enlarging the Universe of 'Additives'

Regulation of chemicals used in food production and processing, such as pesticides and packaging materials, has for decades depended on the capacity of FDA inspectors to measure residues and thereby enforce health-based

---

Act, 77 MICH. L. REV. 171 (1978); Richard A. Merrill, *FDA's Implementation of the Delaney Clause: Repudiation of Congressional Choice or Reasoned Adaption to Scientific Progress?*, 5 YALE J. REG. 1 (1988).

[4] © Copyright 1988 by the YALE JOURNAL ON REGULATION, P.O. Box 208215, New Haven, CT 06520-8215. Reprinted from Vol. 5:1 by permission. All rights reserved.

limits on their occurrence. The protection afforded by such limits in turn depended on the sensitivity of the analytical methods chosen to enforce them. Improvements in analytical chemistry have had the disconcerting propensity to reveal residues where there should be none, thus requiring the Agency to set more stringent limits or explain why the residues it could now detect were safe.

* * * Until 1955, assay methods for specific pesticide residues were primitive; most were colorimetric (involving color comparisons using standard reference solutions) or nonspecific. * * * The development of thin layer and gas chromatography improved analytical sensitivities by more than one thousand times. These powerful technologies were in their infancy in 1958.

* * *

A recent example demonstrates how advances in chromatographic analysis can create a regulatory problem. P-toluidine, a contaminant in some color additives, is an animal carcinogen. Chemists had not detected P-toluidine in Green No. 6 using gravity elution chromatography, which had a limit sensitivity thought to be at least 250 ppm. In 1979, however, a scientist using high pressure liquid chromatography (HPLC) reported that there might be P-toluidine contamination in Green No. 6. The subsequent use of HPLC with ultraviolet absorption or fluorescence detectors to analyze the separated chemicals proved capable of detecting P-toluidine residues down to ten ppm. This technique confirmed in 1982 that P-toluidine was present at an average concentration of 393 ppm. The information about Green No. 6 raised suspicions concerning Green No. 5, which was derived from Green No. 6. Chemists using HPLC with fluorescence detected the presence of P-toluidine in Green No. 5 at levels of .57 to 2.54 ppm.

Just as improvements in instrumentation have allowed FDA scientists to detect more substances in food at lower concentrations, other agencies have discovered increasing numbers of previously undetected chemicals in the environment. The Environmental Protection Agency began monitoring organic chemicals in the nation's drinking water in 1973, when it reported finding 253 different chemicals. By 1979, it had identified more than 700 'foreign' chemicals in drinking water.

FDA scientist Albert Kolbye summarized the trend:

> [A]nalytical chemists can now detect a whole new galaxy of low levels of substances in food. Previously the limits of qualitative identification and quantitative measurement were in the parts per thousand range: today parts per trillion are not uncommon and in some instances routine. This represents a millionfold increase in our ability to detect 'chemicals' in food.

The universe of detectable chemicals 'added' to human food had thus grown vastly larger than the universe of additives legislators had confronted in 1958.

2. Progress in Toxicology: Enlarging the Universe of Carcinogens

Proponents of the Delaney Clause did not expect that significant numbers of food ingredients would prove to be carcinogenic. In a 1957 article advocating that carcinogenic additives be forbidden, National Cancer Institute (NCI) scientist W. C. Hueper identified only four direct food additives, eight food colors, and three classes of chemical contaminants as potential targets. Hueper stated:

> It is unlikely * * * that many of the presently used additives and contaminants of foodstuffs, especially most of those of purely inorganic nature, unless they are radioactive or belong to the group of carcinogenic metals * * * introduce any carcinogenic hazard into the general food supply. * * *

The 1960s marked not only the advent of systematic testing of chemicals for carcinogenicity, but also the rapid increase in the number of intentional food additives in use. * * *

* * * A National Academy of Sciences (NAS) committee[5] in 1984 reviewed a list of 8,627 chemicals 'regulated or classified by FDA * * * as direct food additives, indirect food additives, GRAS [*i.e.,* generally recognized as safe] substances, colors, and flavors.' It found there was 'no toxicity information available' for forty-six percent of the chemicals. Data sufficient for a complete risk evaluation were available only for five percent.

Moreover, the 8,000-plus food-use substances represented less than one-sixth of the rapidly expanding universe of chemicals to which humans are exposed. Within this larger universe, the number of chemicals identified as animal carcinogens appears to have grown more sharply: 'When the Delaney amendment was adopted approximately twenty-five years ago, chemical carcinogens were considered rare in man's environment. * * * The number of chemicals which have been shown to be carcinogenic in animals over the past decade has grown enormously and represents a wide spectrum of unrelated chemical structures.' The Task Force on Environmental Cancer placed the estimate of carcinogens at 'about 1,000 chemicals.' * * *

While the percentage of chemicals that display carcinogenicity is probably not large, increased testing has produced a steady increase in the total number of reported animal carcinogens. * * *

* * *

3. Shifting Focus from Man-Made to Natural Dietary Constituents

Both the structure and the language of the FD&C Act betray a bias in favor of home-prepared products of American agriculture and a suspicion of 'artificial' ingredients. The Food Additives Amendment embodies this prejudice, excluding from its coverage substances 'generally recognized as safe' based on their prior use in food while requiring premarket proof of safety for most chemical additives. Scientific debate during the 1950s

---

[5] This is the *Toxicity Testing* report excerpted in Chapter 2, *supra.*—EDS.

reinforced this dichotomy, focusing suspicion on a relatively small number of foreign chemicals and, if only by silence, exonerating basic constituents of the food supply.

By the 1970s, the dialogue between researchers and public health officials had changed dramatically. Sir Richard Doll and Richard Peto estimated that nearly one-third of all cancers are diet-related, but attributed no more than one percent to chemical additives in food (including pesticides). Bruce Ames continued to report the results of research identifying carcinogens naturally present in food, arguing that regulation of carcinogenic risks has been mistakenly preoccupied with man-made chemicals. In the face of this consensus, it is not surprising that FDA officials should have become uncomfortable with legal interpretations that dictated automatic banning of trace chemicals and ingredients shown to be carcinogenic in animal bioassays.
* * *

* * *

C. Administrative Escapes from the Delaney Clause

When administrators conclude that a legislative mandate no longer makes sense they can be expected to respond in one of two ways: They may circumscribe the cases to which the mandate applies, or they may attempt to reinterpret the mandate. FDA Commissioners have done both.
* * *

[Merrill goes on to describe these responses, some of which were extremely byzantine. They included distinguishing between "added" food constituents and "food additives," "carcinogens" that do not "induce cancer," migrating food packaging materials, and "constituents" of additives (the Constituents Policy).]

NOTES

1. *Parse the statute.* (a) Where is the Delaney *Clause*? What is the substantive standard that it imposes? To what does the clause apply? To what does it *not* apply?

(b) The standard seems to be absolute. Is there any room for FDA to exercise discretion not to apply it? For example, we have previously seen (in Chapter 2) that there are many areas in which the risk assessment process involves policy decisions. Could any of the following choices be used by FDA to avoid application of the Delaney Clause-

- animal *versus* human carcinogens
- possible *versus* probable *versus* known carcinogens
- potent *versus* weak carcinogens
- negligible cancer risk?

(c) Where is the burden of proof under the Delaney Clause? How can you tell? Why is the burden placed where it is?

2. Merrill asserts that the principal problem with the Delaney Clause is the erosion of the assumptions upon which it was based. What are the assumptions behind the Delaney standard? How have they eroded and what has been the effect on the clause?

To take a contrary position, haven't the developments in science that Merrill describes simply shown that the problem is even worse that Rep. Delaney imagined? Why does the expanded scope of the problem cast *doubt* on its significance?

3. *Natural and artificial*. Merrill also alludes to the finding presented in Chapter 2, *supra*, that many naturally occurring substances in food are carcinogenic. Why did this development increase FDA's discomfort with the Delaney Clause?

4. *Risk assessment at FDA*. The birth of risk assessment in the field of toxicology has been traced to FDA's need to manage residues from carcinogenic animal drugs, such as DES. Joseph V. Rodricks, *Origins of Risk Assessment in Food Safety Decision Making*, 7 J. AM. COLL. OF TOXICOLOGY 539 (1988). The Delaney Clause applies a less stringent standard to animal drugs, and FDA adopted risk assessment to make the required determination. Why had FDA not needed risk assessment for the Delaney Clause proper?

Paradoxically, the growing importance of quantitative risk assessment fueled opposition to the strict Delaney Standard. Why?

———

By the mid-1980s, FDA was fed up with the many subterfuges that it had developed for avoiding application of the Delaney Clause. It explicitly adopted a "*de minimis*" or "negligible risk" standard for certain color additives, relying heavily on the ability of quantitative risk assessment to identify risk levels, on EPA's adoption of *de minimis* risk standards for carcinogens (also based on risk assessments), and on judicial precedent that had permitted EPA, in the absence of express statutory indications to the contrary, to ignore *de minimis* risks.[6] This sparked a challenge from Ralph Nader's group, Public Citizen.

PUBLIC CITIZEN V. YOUNG

831 F.2d 1108 (D.C. Cir. 1987)

WILLIAMS, Circuit Judge:

The Color Additive Amendments of 1960 (codified at 21 U.S.C. § 376 (1982)), part of the Food, Drug and Cosmetic Act (the "Act"), establish an elaborate system for regulation of color additives in the interests of safety. A

---

[6] *See* FDA/HHS, Listing of D&C Orange No. 17 for Use in Externally Applied Drugs and Cosmetics, 51 Fed. Reg. 28331 (1986); FDA/HHS, Listing of D&C Red No. 19 for Use in Externally Applied Drugs and Cosmetics, 51 Fed. Reg. 28346 (1986).

color additive may be used only after the Food and Drug Administration ("FDA") has published a regulation listing the additive for such uses as are safe. Such listing may occur only if the color additive in question satisfies (among other things) the requirements of the applicable "Delaney Clause," one of three such clauses in the total system for regulation of color additives, food and animal food and drugs. The Clause prohibits the listing of any color additive "found . . . to induce cancer in man or animal."

In No. 86-1548, Public Citizen and certain individuals challenge the decision of the FDA to list two color additives, Orange No. 17 and Red No. 19, based on quantitative risk assessments indicating that the cancer risks presented by these dyes were trivial. This case thus requires us to determine whether the Delaney Clause for color additives is subject to an implicit "*de minimis*" exception. We conclude, with some reluctance, that the Clause lacks such an exception.

* * *

I. THE DELANEY CLAUSE AND "DE MINIMIS" EXCEPTIONS

A. Factual Background

The FDA listed Orange No. 17 and Red No. 19 for use in externally applied cosmetics on August 7, 1986. In the listing notices, it carefully explained the testing processes for both dyes and praised the processes as "current state-of-the-art toxicological testing." In both notices it specifically rejected industry arguments that the Delaney Clause did not apply because the tests were inappropriate for evaluation of the dyes. It thus concluded that the studies established that the substances caused cancer in the test animals.

* * *

* * * The scientific review panel found the lifetime cancer risks of the substances extremely small: for Orange No. 17, it calculated them as one in 19 billion at worst, and for Red No. 19 one in nine million at worst. The FDA explained that the panel had used conservative assumptions in deriving these figures, and it characterized the risks as "so trivial as to be effectively no risk." It concluded that the two dyes were safe.

The FDA candidly acknowledged that its safety findings represented a departure from past agency practice: "In the past, because the data and information show that D & C Orange No. 17 is a carcinogen when ingested by laboratory animals, FDA in all likelihood would have terminated the provisional listing and denied CTFA's petition for the externally applied uses . . . without any further discussion." It also acknowledged that "[a] strictly literal application of the Delaney Clause would prohibit FDA from finding [both dyes] safe, and therefore, prohibit FDA from permanently listing [them] . . . ." Because the risks presented by these dyes were so small, however, the agency declared that it had "inherent authority" under the *de minimis* doctrine to list them for use in spite of this language. It indicated that as a general matter any risk lower than a one-in-one-million lifetime risk would meet the requirements for a *de minimis* exception to the Delaney Clause.

Assuming that the quantitative risk assessments are accurate, as we do for these purposes, it seems altogether correct to characterize these risks as trivial. * * *

* * *

B. Plain Language and the De Minimis Doctrine

The Delaney Clause of the Color Additive Amendments provides as follows:

> a color additive . . . (ii) shall be deemed unsafe, and shall not be listed, for any use which will not result in ingestion of any part of such additive, if, after tests which are appropriate for the evaluation of the safety of additives for such use, or after other relevant exposure of man or animal to such additive, it is found by the Secretary to induce cancer in man or animal . . . .

21 U.S.C. § 376(b)(5)(B).

The natural—almost inescapable—reading of this language is that if the Secretary finds the additive to "induce" cancer in animals, he must deny listing. Here, of course, the agency made precisely the finding that Orange No. 17 and Red No. 19 "induce[ ] cancer when tested in laboratory animals." * * *

The setting of the clause supports this strict reading. Adjacent to it is a section governing safety generally and directing the FDA to consider a variety of factors, including probable exposure, cumulative effects, and detection difficulties. 21 U.S.C. § 376(b)(5)(A). The contrast in approach seems to us significant. For all safety hazards other than carcinogens, Congress made safety the issue, and authorized the agency to pursue a multifaceted inquiry in arriving at an evaluation. For carcinogens, however, it framed the issue in the simple form, "If A [finding that cancer is induced in man or animals], then B [no listing]." There is language inviting administrative discretion, but it relates only to the process leading to the finding of carcinogenicity: "appropriate" tests or "other relevant exposure," and the agency's "evaluation" of such data. Once the finding is made, the dye "shall be deemed unsafe, and shall not be listed." 21 U.S.C. § 367(b)(5)(B).

Courts (and agencies) are not, of course, helpless slaves to literalism. One escape hatch, invoked by the government and CTFA here, is the *de minimis* doctrine, shorthand for *de minimis non curat lex* ("the law does not concern itself with trifles"). The doctrine—articulated in recent times in a series of decisions by Judge Leventhal—serves a number of purposes. One is to spare agency resources for more important matters. But that is a goal of dubious relevance here. The finding of trivial risk necessarily followed not only the elaborate animal testing, but also the quantitative risk assessment process itself; indeed, application of the doctrine required additional expenditure of agency resources.

More relevant is the concept that "notwithstanding the 'plain meaning' of a statute, a court must look beyond the words to the purpose of the act where its literal terms lead to 'absurd or futile results.'" *Alabama Power Co. v. Costle*, 636 F.2d 323, 360 n. 89 (quoting *United States v. American Trucking Ass'ns*, 310 U.S. 534, 543, (1939)). Imposition of pointless burdens on regulated entities is obviously to be avoided if possible, especially as burdens on them almost invariably entail losses for their customers: here, obviously, loss of access to the colors made possible by a broad range of dyes.

We have employed the concept in construing the Clean Air Act's mandate to the Environmental Protection Agency to set standards providing "an ample margin of safety to protect the public health," 42 U.S.C. § 7412(b)(1) (1982). That does not, we said, require limits assuring a "risk-free" environment. Rather, the agency must decide "what risks are acceptable in the world in which we live" and set limits accordingly. *See Natural Resources Defense Council, Inc. v. EPA*, 824 F.2d 1146, 1164-65 (D.C.Cir.1987) (citing *Industrial Union Dep't, AFL-CIO v. American Petroleum Inst.*, 448 U.S. 607, 642, (1980). Assuming as always the validity of the risk assessments, we believe that the risks posed by the two dyes would have to be characterized as "acceptable." Accordingly, if the statute were to permit a *de minimis* exception, this would appear to be a case for its application.[7]

Moreover, failure to employ a *de minimis* doctrine may lead to regulation that not only is "absurd or futile" in some general cost-benefit sense but also is directly contrary to the primary legislative goal. In a certain sense, precisely that may be the effect here. The primary goal of the Act is human safety, but literal application of the Delaney Clause may in some instances increase risk. No one contends that the Color Additive Amendments impose a zero-risk standard for non-carcinogenic substances; if they did, the number of dyes passing muster might prove minuscule. As a result, makers of drugs and cosmetics who are barred from using a carcinogenic dye carrying a one-in-20-million lifetime risk may use instead a noncarcinogenic, but toxic, dye carrying, say, a one-in-10-million lifetime risk. The substitution appears to be a clear loss for safety.

Judge Leventhal articulated the standard for application of *de minimis* as virtually a presumption in its favor: "Unless Congress has been extraordinarily rigid, there is likely a basis for an implication of *de minimis* authority to provide [an] exemption when the burdens of regulation yield a gain of trivial or no value." But the doctrine obviously is not available to thwart a statutory command; it must be interpreted with a view to

---

[7] We do not, of course, purport to decide the appropriate dividing point between *de minimis* and other risks. FDA's proposed one-in-one-million dividing point has been used by EPA to distinguish acceptable and unacceptable risks. FDA has used the same break point to determine whether the general safety clause of the Act applies.

"implementing the legislative design." Nor is an agency to apply it on a finding merely that regulatory costs exceed regulatory benefits.

Here, we cannot find that exemption of exceedingly small (but measurable) risks tends to implement the legislative design of the color additive Delaney Clause. The language itself is rigid; the context—an alternative design admitting administrative discretion for all risks other than carcinogens—tends to confirm that rigidity. Below we consider first the legislative history; rather than offering any hint of softening, this only strengthens the inference. Second, we consider a number of factors that make Congress's apparent decision at least a comprehensible policy choice.

1. Legislative History

The Delaney Clause arose in the House bill and was, indeed, what principally distinguished the House from the Senate bill. The House included it in H.R. 7624, and the Senate accepted the language without debate, 106 CONG. REC. 15,133 (1960). The House committee gave considerable attention to the degree of discretion permitted under the provision. The discussion points powerfully against any *de minimis* exception, and is not contradicted either by consideration on the House floor or by a post-enactment colloquy in the Senate.

* * *

Taken as a whole, the remarks do not seem strong enough to undermine the inference we have drawn that the clause was to operate automatically once the FDA squeezed the scientific trigger. * * *

2. Possible Explanations for an Absolute Rule

Like all legislative history, this is hardly conclusive. But short of an explicit declaration in the statute barring use of a *de minimis* exception, this is perhaps as strong as it is likely to get. Facing the explicit claim that the Clause was "extraordinarily rigid," a claim well supported by the Clause's language in contrast with the bill's grants of discretion elsewhere, Congress persevered.

Moreover, our reading of the legislative history suggests some possible explanations for Congress's apparent rigidity. One is that Congress, and the nation in general (at least as perceived by Congress), appear to have been truly alarmed about the risks of cancer. This concern resulted in a close focus on substances increasing cancer threats and a willingness to take extreme steps to lessen even small risks. Congress hoped to reduce the incidence of cancer by banning carcinogenic dyes, and may also have hoped to lessen public fears by demonstrating strong resolve.

A second possible explanation for Congress's failure to authorize greater administrative discretion is that it perceived color additives as lacking any great value. For example, Congressman Delaney remarked, "Some food additives serve a useful purpose . . . . However, color additives provide no nutrient value. They have no value at all, except so-called eye appeal." Representative Sullivan said, "we like the bright and light [lipstick] shades but if they cannot safely be produced, then we prefer to do without these particular shades." And Representative King: "The colors which go into our foods and cosmetics are in no way essential to the public interest or the national security . . . . [C]onsumers will easily get along without [carcinogenic colors]."

It is true that the legislation as a whole implicitly recognizes that color additives are of value, since one of its purposes was to allow tolerances for certain dyes—harmful but not carcinogenic—that would have been banned under the former law. There was also testimony pointing out that in some uses color additives advance health: they can help identify medications and prevent misapplications where a patient must take several. Nevertheless, there is evidence that Congress thought the public could get along without carcinogenic colors, especially in view of the existence of safer substitutes. Thus the legislators may have estimated the costs of an overly protective rule as trivial.

So far as we can determine, no one drew the legislators' attention to the way in which the Delaney Clause, interacting with the flexible standard for determining safety of non-carcinogens, might cause manufacturers to substitute more dangerous toxic chemicals for less dangerous carcinogens. But the obviously more stringent standard for carcinogens may rest on a view that cancer deaths are in some way more to be feared than others.

Finally, as we have already noted, the House committee (or its amanuenses) considered the possibility that its no-threshold assumption might prove false and contemplated a solution: renewed consideration by Congress.

Considering these circumstances—great concern over a specific health risk, the apparently low cost of protection, and the possibility of remedying any mistakes—Congress's enactment of an absolute rule seems less surprising.

* * *

D. The Meaning of "[I]nduce Cancer"

After Public Citizen initiated [this] litigation, the FDA published a notice embellishing the preamble to its initial safety determinations. These notices effectively apply quantitative risk assessment at the stage of determining whether a substance "induce[s] cancer in man or animal." They assert that even where a substance does cause cancer in animals in the conventional sense of the term, the FDA may find that it does not "induce cancer in man or animal" within the meaning of 21 U.S.C. § 376(b)(5)(B). * * * [T]he notices argued:

> The words "induce cancer in man or animal" as used in the Delaney Clause are terms of art intended to convey a regulatory judgment that is something more than a scientific observation that an additive is carcinogenic in laboratory animals. To limit this judgment to such a simple observation would be to arbitrarily exclude from FDA's

consideration developing sophisticated testing and analytical methodologies, leaving FDA with only the most primitive techniques for its use in this important endeavor to protect public health. Certainly the language of the Delaney Clause itself cannot be read to mandate such a counterproductive limit on FDA's discharge of its responsibilities.

The notices acknowledged that the words "to induce cancer" had not been "rigorously and unambiguously" so limited in the previous notices. This is a considerable understatement. The original determinations were quite unambiguous in concluding that the colors induced cancer in animals in valid tests; the explanations went to some trouble to rebut industry arguments to the contrary. Despite these arguments, FDA concluded that the tests demonstrated that the dyes were responsible for increases in animal tumors.

The plain language of the Delaney Clause covers all animals exposed to color additives, including laboratory animals exposed to high doses. It would be surprising if it did not. High-dose exposures are standard testing procedure, today just as in 1960; such high doses are justified to offset practical limitations on such tests: compared to expected exposure of millions of humans over long periods, the time periods are short and the animals few. Many references in the legislative history reflect awareness of reliance on animal testing, and at least the more sophisticated participants must have been aware that this meant high-dose testing. A few so specified.

All this indicates to us that Congress did not intend the FDA to be able to take a finding that a substance causes only trivial risk in humans and work back from that to a finding that the substance does not "induce cancer in . . . animals." This is simply the basic question—is the operation of the clause automatic once the FDA makes a finding of carcinogenicity in animals?—in a new guise. The only new argument offered in the notices is that, without the new interpretation, only "primitive techniques" could be used. In fact, of course, the agency is clearly free to incorporate the latest breakthroughs in animal testing; indeed, here it touted the most recent animal tests as "state of the art." The limitation on techniques is only that the agency may not, once a color additive is found to induce cancer in test animals in the conventional sense of the term, undercut the statutory consequence. As we find the FDA's construction "contrary to clear congressional intent," *Chevron U.S.A. v. Natural Resources Defense Council, Inc.,* 467 U.S. 837, 843 n. 9, (1984), we need not defer to it.

* * *

In sum, we hold that the Delaney Clause of the Color Additive Amendments does not contain an implicit *de minimis* exception for carcinogenic dyes with trivial risks to humans. We based this decision on our understanding that Congress adopted an "extraordinarily rigid" position, denying the FDA authority to list a dye once it found it to "induce cancer in . . . animals" in the conventional sense of the term. We believe that, in the color additive context, Congress intended that if this rule produced unexpected or undesirable consequences, the agency should come to it for relief. That moment may well have arrived, but we cannot provide the desired escape.

NOTES

1. What, precisely, was the dispute in this case? How does the Delaney Clause issue arise?

2. What are the legal arguments for a *de minimis* stardard? Why have the courts found *de minimis* preferable as a matter of policy?

The court suggests that the Delaney ban may actually be perverse in terms of overall safety. How could that come about? Is the solution to weaken Delaney or to close its loopholes?

3. How did the *Public Citizen* court interpret Delaney? What were the grounds on which the court rejected the *de minimis* standard, despite its sharp (if implicit) criticism of zero-risk?

4. *The Delaney Paradox and the Food Quality Protection Act of 1996.* The Delaney Clause distinguishes between carcinogens and all other food hazards, and it bans the former when they are food additives. But what about pesticide residues (the reason your mother told you to wash fruits and vegetables)? Aren't they added to foods? Under the pre-1996 FFDCA, the answer was yes and no. First, the federal pesticide statute (FIFRA) permitted the use of pesticides under a risk-benefit standard. 7 U.S.C. § 136a(c)(5). Pesticide residues were permitted on raw agricultural commodities as long as they were below a "tolerance level" established through a risk-benefit calculation (unlike the Delaney Clause). Moreover, such residues could legally "flow through" to processed agricultural commodities as long as they did not concentrate in the manufacturing process. 21 U.S.C. §§ 342(a)(2)(B)-(C), 346a. This was the Delaney Paradox: some foods containing pesticide residues were subject to a *de minimis* risk standard, and some to a *zero risk* standard.[8] FDA sought to use this inconsistency in treatment to leverage reconsideration of the *Public Citizen* case, but in *Les v. Reilly*, 968 F.2d 985 (9th Cir. 1992), the Ninth Circuit refused to permit a *de minimis* standard to be applied to pesticides covered by the Delaney Clause.

Our first question must be: is this really a paradox?[9] What is wrong, if anything, with the state of affairs in which pesticides that concentrate are treated more severely than ones that do not? One commentator has argued persuasively that the Delaney Paradox is based on a huge misunderstanding of the relevant statutory provisions. The real inconsistency, he argues, is that

---

[8] *See* NATIONAL RESEARCH COUNCIL, REGULATING PESTICIDES IN FOOD: THE DELANEY PARADOX (1987); EPA, Regulation of Pesticides in Food: Addressing the Delaney Paradox Policy Statement, 53 Fed. Reg. 41104 (1988).

[9] Of course, it does not come close to meeting the dictionary definition of "paradox." The relevant provisions were carefully and explicitly harmonized by Congress. "Paradox" is used here as a generic pejorative, suggesting an irrational distinction.

carcinogenic residues are allowed *at all* despite the Delaney Clause's clear mandate concerning additives generally. *See* James S. Turner, *Delaney Lives! Reports of Delaney's Death Are Greatly Exaggerated*, 28 ENVTL. L. REP. (ENVTL. L. INST.) 10003 (1998). If Turner is right, then the second question must be: is exempting pesticide residues from Delaney "paradoxical"-or is it possible that Congress balanced the competing goals pretty well?

Be that as it may, Congress and many others (including the National Academy of Sciences) were convinced that the distinction was irrational, and, faced with a court order to begin canceling the registrations of several important pesticides that ran afoul of Delaney, Congress passed the Food Quality Protection Act of 1996. The revised statute provides a single standard for all pesticide residues, which is defined as "a reasonable certainty that no harm will result from the aggregate exposure the pesticide chemical residue, including all anticipated dietary exposures and other exposures for which there is reliable information." 21 U.S.C. § 346a(b)(2)(A)(ii). Moreover, EPA (not FDA) must explicitly consider the effects on infants and children when establishing a tolerance level. 21 U.S.C. § 346a(b)(2)(C)(i).[10] What do you make of the new "reasonable certainty" language? What about the "aggregate exposures" and the focus on infants and children? Will these ease or complicate the setting of tolerances?

2. Case Study: Saccharine

FDA's proposal to ban saccharine as a sweetener in most foods and drinks focused national attention on the potential consequences of implementing the Delaney Clause. Many saw it as the inevitable showdown between the Delaney Clause and the public appetite for numerous food additives, and they predicted that Delaney would lose. As this case study shows, things worked out differently.[11]

---

[10] The FQPA and its background are helpfully described in Dominic P. Madigan, Note, *Setting an Anti-Cancer Policy: Risk, Politics, and the Food Quality Protection Act of 1996*, 17 VA. ENVTL. L.J. 187 (1998). For the view that the FQPA still overregulates pesticide residues, *see* Frank B. Cross, *The Consequences of Consensus: Dangerous Compromises of the Food Quality Protection Act*, 75 WASH. U. L.Q. 1155 (1997).

[11] For more detailed discussions of the saccharine case, *see* KATHRYN HARRISON & GEORGE HOBERG, RISK, SCIENCE, AND POLITICS: REGULATING TOXIC SUBSTANCES IN CANADA AND THE UNITED STATES 77-98 (1994); Richard A. Merrill & Michael R. Taylor, *Saccharine: A Case Study of Government Regulation of Environmental Carcinogens*, 5 VA. J. NAT. RES. L. 1 (1985).

FDA'S IMPLEMENTATION OF THE DELANEY CLAUSE: REPUDIATION OF CONGRESSIONAL CHOICE OR REASONED ADAPTATION TO SCIENTIFIC PROGRESS?

Richard A. Merrill
5 YALE J. ON REG. 1, 29-32 (1988)

No chronicle of FDA's implementation of the Delaney Clause would be complete without examining its abortive 1977 effort to ban saccharin—the last occasion it sought to enforce the Clause. A detailed account of this episode is available elsewhere; a brief summary will reveal its key lessons.

In April, 1977, FDA proposed to withdraw approval for the use of saccharin in all foods, including artificially sweetened soft drinks, and in ingested cosmetics and drugs as well. The Agency said it would entertain new drug applications for table-top sweetening products made of saccharin, provided they were accompanied by clinical evidence that the products were effective in weight control. This announcement was based on the results of a series of animal experiments, culminating in a Canadian government study which demonstrated that saccharin induced malignant tumors in second-generation male rats. As the legal basis for its proposal, FDA invoked both the Delaney Clause and the Food Additives Amendment's 'general safety clause.'

FDA's proposal triggered protests from consumers, legislators, clinicians who treated juvenile diabetics, and manufacturers of saccharin sweetened foods. Congress acted quickly to prevent implementation of the ban, directing FDA to commission studies by NAS and amending the FD&C Act to foreclose for two years any FDA action based on the existing animal test to ban or restrict use of saccharin. The Saccharin Ban Moratorium provisions have been reenacted four times. [It is still in effect.]

Though they foresaw opposition from several quarters, FDA officials were surprised by its intensity and had not seriously explored interpretations of the statute that might have allowed them to avoid a ban of saccharin. To be sure, none of the escape routes the Agency had previously charted (or later devised) appeared plausible. Saccharin was unequivocally a 'food additive' in the Agency's view because only five years earlier it had promulgated what it termed an 'interim food additive regulation' to confirm the legality of saccharin use while further tests were underway. The Canadian study appeared to confirm that it was pure saccharin, not some contaminant, that caused tumors in male rats. The SOM [*i.e.*, sensitivity of method, or below detection limits] theory did not fit, for saccharin was ingested directly by humans. Furthermore, the estimated cancer risk attributable to saccharin consumption (roughly one in ten thousand) was measurably higher than the figure FDA had only recently embraced as the threshold of 'significance.' Even if agency officials had anticipated the possibility, the *de minimis* doctrine could not have saved saccharin.

In short, by 1977 FDA officials believed that they had exhausted every available excuse for not enforcing the Delaney Clause, including the claim that more time was needed to complete and analyze studies of saccharin's effects, a claim which had sustained the ingredient for nearly a decade. FDA's proposed ban of saccharin can therefore be viewed as the reluctant action of an agency that had already come to question the wisdom of the Delaney Clause and in other contexts had exploited legal devices to avoid it.

This interpretation of the history is consistent with, though it does not corroborate, the view voiced by groups who claimed that FDA invoked the Delaney Clause in order to bring it into ridicule and enhance the prospects for Congressional repeal. After all, they argued, FDA could have relied solely on the general safety clause to support its proposed ban; its emphasis on Delaney seemed gratuitous. In any event, the Agency's proposed ban provoked a Congressional rebuke—despite its protestations that it was merely carrying out Congress's instructions. But Congress left the Clause intact, crafting language that preserved it for all other food (and color) additives found to induce cancer, and later ignoring proposals to modernize the food safety provisions of the FD&C Act.

The repudiation of its saccharin proposal taught FDA officials that some food ingredients enjoy a distinct status. Congress's rejection of the very premises that inspired enactment of the Delaney Clause sent a clear message: some ingredients are too important to ban. A second, more important lesson was that legislative revision of the law was improbable. Congress was prepared to create exceptions to the FD&C Act's general requirements—including ingredient-specific exceptions to the Delaney Clause—but it seemed unwilling to entertain seriously any categorical revisions of this icon. Almost none of the food safety bills subsequently introduced risked frontal repeal of the anticancer language that Congress almost casually, perhaps even reluctantly, had included in 1958. The saccharin episode, therefore, probably strengthened the conviction among some FDA officials—and others outside the Agency—that if the problems presented by literal application of the Delaney Clause were to be solved, administrators would have to solve them.

NOTES

1. Why did FDA propose banning saccharine in the first place? Why did FDA invite applications for medical uses at the same time that it banned others? Is this rationale fairly limited to medical use?

2. As Merrill describes, Congress did not agree with FDA's decision to ban saccharine. Instead, it enacted the Saccharin Study and Labeling Act, Pub.L. 95-203, § 3, Nov. 23, 1977, 91 Stat. 1452 (as amended), which imposed a moratorium on FDA's authority to ban saccharine:

During the period ending May 1, 2002, the Secretary- * * *

(2) may * * * not take any other action under the Federal Food, Drug, and Cosmetic Act to prohibit or restrict the sale or distribution of

saccharin, any food permitted by such interim food additive regulation to contain saccharin, or any drug or cosmetic containing saccharin, solely on the basis of the carcinogenic or other toxic effect of saccharin as determined by any study made available to the Secretary before the date of the enactment of this Act [Nov. 23, 1977] which involved human studies or animal testing, or both.

It further provided that products containing saccharine will be considered misbranded unless its label bears the following statement:

> USE OF THIS PRODUCT MAY ABE HAZARDOUS TO YOUR HEALTH. THIS PRODUCT CONTAINS SACCHARIN WHICH HAS BEEN DETERMINED TO CAUSE CANCER IN LABORATORY ANIMALS.

21 U.S.C. §343(o)(1). The next time you see a pink package of artificial sweetener, turn it over and you will see this label. Is this an adequate or appropriate substitute for a ban?

Is it a rational risk decision to exempt saccharine from the usual rule for carcinogens? Congress in fact responded to the saccharine ban quickly and with only spotty information about its benefits. There are several non-cancer reasons that reliance on saccharine is misplaced.[12]

3. *Aflatoxin.* Some years later, FDA faced a similar problem with aflatoxin, the toxic product of a mold that unavoidably contaminates a number of food crops, including corn and peanuts. While the contamination most often occurs at levels at or below the limit of detection, aflatoxin is almost certainly a potent human carcinogen.[13] Nevertheless, FDA has consistently refused to ban food additives containing trace amounts of aflatoxin (for example, peanuts or grain that are part of another food) under the Delaney Clause.[14] Indeed, it has even refused to set an formal "tolerance level" for aflatoxin, preferring the more informal route of establishing an "action level" below which it will take no regulatory action, a strategy that the Supreme Court approved on *Chevron* grounds. *See* Young v. Community Nutrition, 476 U.S. 975 (1986). Why do you think that FDA has refused to take action against aflatoxin? Should it ban aflatoxin-containing foods under the Delaney Clause?

4. Even though Congress overruled the Delaney Clause for saccharine, abolished the Delaney Paradox in the 1996 Food Quality Protection Act, and was under considerable pressure to get rid of Delaney permanently, it has left

---

[12]*See* DENNIS REMINGTON & BARBARA HIGA, THE BITTER TRUTH ABOUT ARTIFICIAL SWEETNERS (1987)(noting that regular use of artificial sweetners increases rather than decreases the intake of other sugars).

[13]NATIONAL RESEARCH COUNCIL, CARCINOGENS AND ANTICARCINOGENS IN THE HUMAN DIET 72-74 (1996).

[14]*See* Richard A. Merrill, *Regulation of Toxic Chemicals,* 58 TEX. L. REV. 463, 477-79 (1980)(book review).

the core clause totally intact. Is there a principled reason for Congress to approach revision of the Delaney Clause on a case-by-case basis, *e.g.*, saccharine in 1977, peanut butter next, then common pesticides? Can you argue that this is, in fact, an appropriate long-term solution to the Delaney Clause?

5. If there are good reasons *not* to regulate saccharine and aflatoxin, should FDA have the discretion simply to decline to act? As Merrill & Taylor have pointed out, the FFDCA was transformed over time from a *policing* statute, in which it sought out bad actors among foods and food additives, to a *licensing* statute, which required all additives to be approved in advance.[15] Obviously, one advantage of a policing statute is the opportunity to exercise prosecutorial discretion in individual cases. What are the advantages of licensing?

6. On May 15, 2000, the National Toxicology Program announced that it is proposing to "delist" saccharine as a human carcinogen, because nearly two decades of further testing has indicated that saccharine's carcinogenic effect on rats is not applicable to humans. Does this change in saccharine's status (if approved) mean that the original decision to ban saccharine was wrong? Does it make a legal difference under the Delaney Clause?

B. The Occupational Safety and Health Act

1. The Problem of Worker Health and Safety

Much of environmental law, including toxics regulation, is devoted to the ill effects of industrial development. In this regard, we think of air and water pollution, solid and hazardous waste, and even consumer products. The other important side effect is worker safety and health:

> Many workplaces are dangerous places. The Occupational Safety and Health Administration [OSHA] estimates that each day an average of seventeen persons are killed at work and another 16,000 persons are injured. The estimated annual cost of occupational injuries and illnesses is in excess of $80 billion. * * *

> Two recent studies estimate that the number of occupational disease-related deaths ranges from 50,000 to 95,000 deaths annually. Other studies place the number of disease-related fatalities between 124,000 and 210,000 annually. To put these estimates in perspective, occupational disease accounts for a larger percentage of cancer deaths than environmental pollution and it kills more persons each year than such other preventable causes of death as motor vehicle accidents, diabetes, and homicides.

---

[15] Merril & Taylor, *supra*, at 14-15.

Sidney A. Shapiro, *Forward: Occupational Safety and Health: Policy Options and Political Reality*, 31 HOUSTON L. REV. 13, 14-16 (1994). While the general average of workplace injury rates is not far from the rate of home accidents (is this an argument for not regulating?), there is substantial variation among industries. The general average is 4 fatalities per 100,000 workers, but agriculture (26), construction (15), and transportation (12) are much higher.[16] Non-fatal injuries occur at higher rates, and it should go without saying that many non-fatal workplace injuries are extremely serious and disabling.

Enacted in 1970, the Occupational Safety and Health Act (OSH Act) established within the Department of Labor a new agency, the Occupational Safety and Health Administration (OSHA), to be responsible for promulgating and enforcing workplace safety and health standards to protect American workers. The act's substantive regulatory structure is straightforward. Section 5 establishes a general duty on the part of employers to provide safe workplaces and of employees to follow safety rules. Section 6 creates three classes of health and safety standards that OSHA may promulgate-"start-up," readily promulgated standards based on existing governmental or industry "national consensus" standards (§ 6(a)); regular health and safety standards, which may be updates or revisions of the national consensus standards (§ 6(b)); and "emergency temporary standards" for risks that need to be addressed before the rulemaking process would normally be completed (§ 6(c)). OSHA is specifically authorized to issue standards that require warnings and the provision of health and safety information to workers (§ 6(b)(7)). Section 6 also establishes special procedures for the promulgation and judicial review of standards, including adoption of the "substantial evidence" test (§ 6(f)). Inspection and enforcement powers, recordkeeping and medical monitoring, penalties for violations, and judicial and administrative review of enforcement actions are provided in the remainder of the statute.

The OSH Act also contains a special provision for "toxic materials or harmful physical agents." § 6(b)(5). While the nature, severity, and number of injuries varies widely among workplaces, the workplace has a special importance in the toxics area. The effects of many of the most notorious toxic substances came to light first in the occupational setting. Asbestos-induced illness is primarily found in workers who installed it and the data showing a link between benzene and leukemia came from rubber workers. In arguing against the introduction of a new gasoline additive, a manganese-based chemical known as MMT, two physicians analogized the dangers to human beings of the lead gasoline additives that were produced by the same company:

---

[16] Thomas O. McGarity & Sidney A. Shapiro, *OSHA's Critics and Regulatory Reform*, 31 WAKE FOREST L. REV. 587, 593 (1996).

Soon after Ethyl [Corp.] began producing [lead additives in 1922], 80 percent of the perhaps 40 chemical workers at its plant in Bayway, N.J., began hallucinating, some developed acute convulsions and five died. Others were left permanently psychotic.

A brief moratorium was imposed on production. But after a hasty study, the chemical was declared safe, plant conditions were improved and the additive was put back in gasoline. * * *

Astonishingly, it took some 60 years before scientists and regulators finally concluded, in the early 1980's, that lead from car exhausts affected children's brains. * * *

Today, as in 1922, workers have again provided the first warning of M.M.T.'s toxicity. Miners of manganese have high rates of psychosis and many suffer from a condition similar to Parkinson's disease.

Herbert J. Needleman & Philip J. Landrigan, *Toxins at the Pump*, NEW YORK TIMES, Mar. 13, 1996, op. ed. Ironically, even *cleaning up* toxic materials like asbestos or contaminants at Superfund sites presents serious risks to remediation workers.[17] In short, it is usually among workers that the exposure to toxic substances is highest and among whom one sees early and actual (as opposed to statistically predicted or estimated) effects.

Moreover, the relatively high incidence of exposure to toxic substances in the workplace has important distributional consequences. In the environmental remediation context, for example, we incur relatively high toxic risks to workers to prevent relatively low ones to the general public. This is, in effect, a *transfer* of risk from the general population to a specific subset of it. The same is true of toxic exposures generally, since a subset of the population-those who work with the hazardous materials-are subjected to most of the risk. Consequently, no survey of the law of toxic substances would be complete without examining work-related injury; indeed, a significant portion of the law has developed in this area.

RESPONSES TO OCCUPATIONAL DISEASE: THE ROLE OF MARKETS, REGULATION, AND INFORMATION

Elinor P. Schroeder & Sidney A. Shapiro
72 GEO. L.J. 1231, 1239-44 (1984)

Private markets work on the basis of self-interest. Buyers demand the goods or services they most desire and sellers obtain the greatest financial reward by providing those products. Economists regard this result as efficient because scarce resources are not utilized to provide products that are less desirable to consumers. In a truly efficient market, the cost of a product must reflect the value of all the resources that are used for its manufacture and

---

[17] These situations are described in John S. Applegate & Steven M. Wesloh, *Short Changing Short-Term Risk: A Study of CERCLA Remedy Selection*, 15 YALE J. ON REG. 269 (1998).

production. Therefore, if a manufacturing process produces toxic substances that cause illnesses, the manufacturer should pay for all of the costs associated with those illnesses.

Ordinarily, there would be no incentive for a manufacturer to pay for those external costs created by its manufacturing process. If, however, the law authorized persons harmed by toxic emissions to enjoin their production, the polluting firm would be required to purchase the "right" to continue to pollute from those adversely affected. Faced with this prospect, the manufacturer would expend resources to abate the toxic emissions up to the point at which it would be less expensive to purchase the right to pollute. By comparison, if the law authorized the manufacturer to pollute, persons damaged by the toxic emissions would band together to pay the manufacturer to control pollution. Preventive efforts would be purchased up to the point at which the reduction in emissions would no longer be worth the purchase price. Professor Coase has suggested that in a smoothly functioning market the amount spent on prevention and the level of toxic emissions would be the same under either rule. Under either legal regime, government action would be necessary only to enforce the necessary contract and property rights.

In the workplace, however, the employer would have to purchase the right to pollute under either set of rules. If workers were authorized to enjoin the production of toxic emissions, the employer would have to purchase from the employees the right to continue production. If workers could not seek an injunction, they would demand compensation in the form of wage premiums or take jobs with equal pay and less risk. If the payments made to workers under either set of rules accurately reflected the risk faced by the employees, the employer would have absorbed, or internalized, what were previously external costs.

The actual existence of wage premiums for hazardous work predicted by the economic model has been difficult to establish empirically. A few studies have found that the risk of death from workplace accidents is reflected in wage rates. One study found similar evidence for nonfatal injuries. Other economists have characterized the evidence as inconsistent support for the existence of wage premiums. Moreover, because of the lack of data on occupational disease, most studies of wage premiums have been limited to the risk of injury rather than the risk of disease. Professor Viscusi, who concluded that modest wage premiums were paid to workers, did find that there were no statistically distinguishable differences between compensation for known health and known safety risks. By comparison, Dr. Irving Selikoff, in a study of compensation for asbestos-related disease, found a "virtual absence of a significant wage premium" for asbestos insulation workers, even though the powerful construction unions and the workers themselves knew of the virulent health hazard presented by asbestos.

Researchers have offered various explanations for the apparent failure of the wage premium theory. One explanation is that wage premiums will be paid only if some workers are mobile and can easily take less risky jobs if their employers do not pay adequate premiums. With high unemployment, a change in jobs is not a realistic alternative for many people. Further, the transaction costs associated with switching jobs, such as loss of pension rights and seniority, the necessity of becoming familiar with a new employer, and the expense of moving, may be too high for many workers. These factors may explain in part the results in the Selikoff study. As a practical matter, longtime asbestos insulation workers may have been unwilling to surrender seniority and other job rights and may have been unable to acquire new job skills. In addition, the most mobile workers have traditionally been the young, who would be the most likely to underestimate or ignore the risk of contracting a work-related disease.

A second explanation is that wage premiums will be paid only if workers are well informed about the risks they face. For the many substances about which precise information is generally unavailable, the theory fails because workers do not have the information needed to bargain for wage premiums.

A third explanation is that wage structures have become fixed and resistant to change in large industries that use hierarchical wage classifications. This occurs because unions wish to avoid situations in which some workers receive disproportionately more or less than other workers because their jobs have become more or less risky. For example, between the 1963 and 1971 job classifications in the steel industry there were no changes in the hazard and surroundings ratings of more than 600 jobs, although it is likely that technological changes alone had caused at least some changes in the relative safety of the jobs.

For organized workers, collective bargaining between employer and union could be, but is not, a powerful vehicle for achieving changes in the workplace to decrease risks. Unions traditionally have not shown much interest in bargaining over health and safety issues. There was very little union political interest in health and safety before the passage of the Occupational Safety and Health Act in 1970, and occupational disease did not become a union bargaining concern until the late 1970s. Although there is some evidence that union concern with workplace dangers has increased in recent years, it is not clear that union bargaining activity has had any significant effect in promoting the health and safety of workers.

A recent analysis of 400 collective bargaining agreements revealed that eighty-two percent contained occupational safety and health provisions, but these provisions seldom provided workers with significant rights they would not have had anyway. * * *

There may be several reasons for labor's seeming failure to make health concerns a major issue in collective bargaining. First, unions generally do not possess the technical and financial resources necessary to determine hazardous exposure levels, to offer feasible alternatives to current methods of operation, and to monitor compliance with any agreement reached with an employer. Second, some unions apparently fear potential liability to their members if they assume any role in assuring workplace safety. Third, because most employers feel that safety and health concerns are intertwined with management of the production process, they may be reluctant even to discuss these issues with the union, much less to agree to change their production methods. Finally, a union will be successful in negotiating only if it is able and willing to enforce its demands with economic action. Many unions may not be strong enough to sustain a strike against the employer, particularly if the employees are relatively unskilled and therefore easily replaced. Even if the union could gain important concessions through striking, its members may not be willing to strike over a noneconomic issue which they view as less crucial than increased wages and fringe benefits.

NOTES

1. *Wage premiums.* Schroeder & Shapiro are in essence defending the need for regulation of workplace health and safety. Against what? Is there an argument that workplace regulation is not necessary at all? The market paradigm of workplace safety has been succinctly stated by W. Kip Viscusi:

> Under ideal conditions of full information and voluntary job choice, workers will demand and receive a wage premium for risky jobs. For the worker at the margin, this risk premium should just offset the worker's valuation of the job risk. If the risk premium were lower, then the marginal worker would not take the job. If it were higher, the number of applicants would increase and drive the wage premium down. Risk premiums also encourage firms to achieve a socially optimal level of workplace hazards. Employers will lower health risks whenever the cost of extra health precautions is less than the savings in reduced risk premiums that result from the extra safety measures.
>
> In an efficient market, moreover, a worker could invest his risk premiums in insurance if he wanted protection against the risk of economic losses due to occupational disease. Each worker could purchase coverage up to the point at which the benefit of additional insurance was exactly equal to its cost. Alternatively, the employer could take out insurance for the worker and decrease wages by the amount of the insurance premium. If all markets were operating efficiently, the resulting combination of risk premiums and insurance coverage would provide socially optimal levels of workplace health quality and occupational disease compensation.

W. Kip Viscusi, *Structuring an Effective Occupational Disease Policy: Victim Compensation and Risk Regulation*, 2 YALE J. ON REG. 53, 56-57 (1984). Thus, workers demand higher wages-a "wage premium"-to engage in activities that pose a greater risk to them. All other things being equal, the window washer hanging on the outside of a skyscraper would be paid more than the office worker on the other side of the window.

Of course, not everything is equal, and determining the existence *vel non* of a wage premium is devilishly difficult. Viscusi claims to have been able to detect a wage premium for hazardous work, though not for toxic risks, W. KIP VISCUSI, RISK BY CHOICE: REGULATING HEALTH AND SAFETY IN THE WORKPLACE 38-45, 96-106 (1983); however, his method of proof is necessarily indirect and has been criticized. *See, e.g.,* Thomas O. McGarity & Sidney A. Shapiro, *OSHA's Critics and Regulatory Reform*, 31 WAKE FOREST L. REV. 587, 605-07 (1996). Viscusi therefore claims that, even though the market undoubtedly has some imperfections, a distinct risk premium can be deduced from labor data:

> As my empirical results indicate, the annual compensation for all job risks averages $900 per worker. Unlike stuntmen and other workers who received clearly significant hazard premiums, a typical worker in a hazardous occupation does not receive enough additional remuneration to be obvious to the casual observer. It is also important to note, however, that the risks incurred are not very large; the probability of a fatal injury is only about 10^{-4}. To ascertain whether the amounts accepted by workers for additional risks are small enough to suggest some form of market failure, one should examine not the absolute level of risk compensation, but the implicit values of life and of injury. The empirical results indicate that the magnitudes of these values are quite impressive-in the millions for fatalities and on the order of at least $20,000 for injuries. Although there is no way to ascertain whether these values are above or below those that would prevail if workers were perfectly informed, the magnitudes are at least suggestive in that they indicate substantial wage compensation for job hazards.

> These finding do not imply that the government should not intervene. They do indicate, however, that it is doubtful that one can base the case for intervention on the absence of compensation for risks of death and injury. * * * [Indeed, if] safety standards reduce the perceived risks faced by workers, their wages will fall in a competitive market.

VISCUSI, *supra*, at 107.

2. The economic response, set out by Schroeder & Shapiro, to the wage premium argument is that there is *market failure* in the occupational setting generally; therefore, reliance on wage premiums to compensate workers is misplaced. How does the market fail in the occupational setting? How do toxic risks differ in this respect from mechanical risks like falling or electrocution?

3. *Environmental justice.* The following suggests another source of difficulty for the wage premium theory:

A distinct pattern emerged by World War II linking environmental exploitation with income, ethnicity, and race. Whites with northern European backgrounds working in management and skilled craft positions attained the greatest insulation from hazardous wastes and also received the highest wages. More recent European immigrants occupied a middling position; benefitting from upward mobility, they concentrated in semiskilled production jobs that paid moderately and involved some exposure to noxious waste emissions. Blacks and Mexicans fared the worst, earning the least and laboring under the harshest conditions.

ANDREW HURLEY, ENVIRONMENTAL INEQUITIES: CLASS, RACE, AND INDUSTRIAL POLLUTION IN GARY, INDIANA, 1945-1980 (1995).[18] One of the areas to which black and Hispanic workers were most frequently relegated, the coke plant, involved intense and sustained exposure to an extremely carcinogenic suite of off-gases (coke oven emissions) from the coking process. This suggests that, at least as a descriptive matter, there are conditions in which wage is *inversely* correlated with risk. Does this argue for governmental intervention in workplace health and safety? How would you expect Viscusi to respond to this information?

4. If the problem with workplace injuries is market failure, then presumably the solution is to repair the market, that is, to make it work as it is supposed to. What kinds of health and safety regulation would accomplish this? Is this good enough, or are there non-market or non-economic reasons to regulate workplace safety? What are they?

Viscusi argues that lack of wage premiums is no argument for regulating workplace safety. Why? Assuming that he is correct, what other arguments for such regulation exist?

5. *Assumption of risk.* You will recall that at the beginning of this section, we observed that toxic risks to workers were in a sense a transfer from the public to a particular subset of the public. Ordinarily, this might be an argument for regulation to correct the inequity, but it can be argued that, even if such a transfer of risk occurs, it is voluntarily accepted by the workers and therefore does not cry out for correction. Are workplace risks in fact voluntarily assumed? Are they voluntarily *enough* assumed to make the distribution of risk fair? Is fairness a reason to regulate workplace safety?

6. *Unions.* Quite apart from health and safety regulation, one of the ways to repair the market is to create greater equality of bargaining power between workers and employers. This is just what labor unions are supposed to do. If unions can be established (they can), and if they can bargain over health and

---

[18] *See also* George Friedman-Jiménez, *Achieving Environmental Justice: The Role of Occupational Health*, 21 FORDHAM URBAN L.J. 605 (1994). *See also* Thomas O. McGarity & Sidney A. Shapiro, *Poverty and the Politics of Occupational Safety and Health*, 1(1) KANSAS J.L. & PUBLIC POLICY 129 (Summer 1991).

safety issues (they can), why have OSHA? Why not just rely on union pressure to make the workplace safer?

Interestingly, as Schroeder & Shapiro point out, even though at least major unions have the capability of doing so, health and safety are seldom a major item in collective bargaining.[19] Ralph Nader, who was deeply involved in the passage of the OSH Act, has said that "my single memory of that struggle was that by and large, with a few exceptions, the labor unions were not where they should have been. * * * it was very hard to get the AFL-CIO very excited over it in terms of committing muscle and resources just as it was very hard to get the United Mine Workers under Tony Boyle very excited about the Coal Mine Health and Safety law that passed in 1969." Ralph Nader, *Occupational Safety and Health Act*, 31 HOUSTON L. REV. 1, 1-2 (1994). Nader attributes this phenomenon to the general problem that "we as a society do not take occupational safety and health seriously." *Id.* What are other reasons for unions' apparent lack of interest in pushing safety and health aggressively at the bargaining table? If unions don't feel strongly enough to bargain about it, why should the government regulate it?

In the excerpt above, Viscusi notes that wages should fall in a competitive market when safety standards are put into place. Is that correct, at least in theory? What is the implication of telling workers that regulation will reduce wages? Might this have something to do with labor's position on workplace safety? Note that a similar trade-off is often said to exist between job security and other forms of environmental regulation.

2. Judicial Interpretation of the Occupational Safety and Health Act

Now read the relevant provisions of the OSH Act, 29 U.S.C. §§ 652 and 655. What hazards does section 6(b)(5) cover? Why is it separate from other kinds of standards?

What is the legal standard imposed by section 6(b)(5)? What are the factors that the agency is to consider?[20] Compare it to the Delaney Clause-how is it different? Why?

We now turn to two Supreme Court decisions interpreting section 6(b)(5), the *Benzene* and *Cotton Dust* cases. In rereading *Benzene*, pay particular attention to the substantive analysis that the Court requires of OSHA. Consider also how *Benzene* and *Cotton Dust* are related, and whether they are consistent with each other.

---

[19] For a version of the union role that stresses their interest in occupational safety and health and their willingness to bargain for health and safety regulation, *see* VISCUSI, RISK BY CHOICE, *supra,* at 53-58.

[20] For an overview of the case law interpreting the various parts of § 6, *see* MARK A. ROTHSTEIN, OCCUPATIONAL SAFETY AND HEALTH §§ 68-80 (4th ed. 1998).

INDUSTRIAL UNION DEP'T, AFL-CIO V. AMERICAN PETROLEUM INST.
(THE *BENZENE* CASE)
[The text of *Benzene* can be found in Chapter 4 (Judicial Role), *supra*.]

NOTES

1. *The Generic Cancer Policy.* The plurality and dissent refer several times to OSHA's cancer policy. What was the gist of the policy? Does it strike you as out of line with your understanding of carcinogenesis? If not, what is the plurality's objection to it? At the time of the *Benzene* decision, the so-called Generic Cancer Policy (GCP) had been proposed as a rule,[21] and the *Benzene* case was its death knell.

Look back at the Rinsky studies in the risk assessment material in Chapter 2(B). It seems that OSHA *could* have developed and relied upon dose-response data if it had wanted to. Why did OSHA (and the Department of Justice, which represented OSHA) choose to rely on the GCP instead?

2. Explain the analysis that the plurality requires of OSHA. How is this derived from the relevant statutory language? Why does the GCP fail to meet this test? How does the plurality's approach differ from the concurrence and the dissent?

3. *Burden of proof.* One of the central features of the *Benzene* case is its emphasis on the allocation of the burden of proof. Who has the burden of proof, and what is the evidentiary standard that must be met? Specifically, how do the "substantial evidence," "more likely than not," and "significant risk" standards interact? Are they separate questions, and if so, does the plurality confuse them?

Why does the plurality allocate the burden as it does? Professor Latin has strongly criticized the plurality's allocation of the burden of proof, emphasizing the difficulty of meeting such a burden with respect to toxic substances. He calls the plurality's decision a "reductive treatment of uncertainty," that is, it considers only one dimension of the question. Latin urges courts to examine the relevant statutory interests, the particular factual situation, the respective abilities of the parties to resolve uncertainty, and the desirable result (*i.e.*, action or inaction) in the face of uncertainty. Howard A. Latin, *The "Significance" of Toxic Health Risks: An Essay on Legal Decisionmaking Under Uncertainty*, 10 ECOLOGY L.Q. 339 (1982). How do these factors weigh in the regulation of benzene?

4. *Quantification and risk assessment. Benzene* has generally been understood to require agencies to quantify (or attempt to quantify) the risks of the substance at issue. OSHA itself concluded that *Benzene* requires the agency to "attempt to quantify risk, if possible, and determine whether the

---

[21] *See* OSHA, Proposed Rule on the Identification, Classification, and Regulation of Toxic Substances Posing a Potential Carcinogenic Risk, 42 Fed. Reg. 54148 (1977).

risk is significant." OSHA, Occupational Exposure to Benzene, 52 Fed. Reg. 34,460, 34,461 (1987). What does the plurality *in fact* require? Is the requirement to quantify a fair implication from the opinion's language? Does Chief Justice Burger's concurrence help to clarify the matter?

5. How does cost figure into the plurality's resolution of the case? Is it part of the analysis required of OSHA? Did it motivate the plurality to find fault with OSHA's procedures?

If cost is relevant to the plurality's analysis, why didn't those justices simply adopt Justice Powell's position on the applicable legal standard?

6. On what ground does Justice Rehnquist think that the entire statute is unconstitutional? Why does section 6(b)(5) fail the constitutional non-delegation test?

Why did Congress write the law as it did? Does Justice Rehnquist describe an appropriate ideal for health and safety regulation? Should Congress have been more specific? *Could* it have been?

7. *Generic rulemaking.* When it opened for business in 1970, OSHA had its work cut out for it. Among toxic substances alone, it had hundreds of potential subjects of regulation. OSHA's progress was, in fact, quite slow. *See generally* THOMAS O. MCGARITY & SIDNEY A. SHAPIRO, WORKERS AT RISK: THE FAILED PROMISE OF THE OCCUPATIONAL SAFETY AND HEALTH ADMINISTRATION (1993). The Generic Cancer Policy addressed OSHA's difficulties in one way; a decade later, OSHA attempted another form of "generic" regulation in another effort to speed its production. In 1989, OSHA adopted a single Air Contaminants Standard that adopted PELs for 428 substances, many of which were merely adoptions of previously issued national consensus standards. OSHA was explicit in acknowledging its need to show progress: as of 1988, it had issued only 24 substance-specific health standards.

In *AFL-CIO v. OSHA*, 965 F.2d 962 (11th Cir. 1992), however, the Air Contaminants Standard was reversed and remanded. While the court found that OSHA was free to regulate more than one substance in a single rulemaking, "the PEL for each substance must be able to stand independently, *i.e.*, that each PEL must be supported by substantial evidence in the record considered as a whole and accompanied by adequate explanation." *Id.* at 972. After *Benzene*, of course, this required the predicate showing of significant risk and the determination of feasibility for each chemical. What is the legal basis for this holding? Can this case be reconciled with the Supreme Court's willingness to accept a "generic" value of zero in calculation of the risks of disposal of spent fuel in the *Vermont Yankee* litigation, discussed in Chapter 4 (Judicial Role), *supra*? What about the handling of categories for setting effluent limitations under the Clean Water Act?

How far does the individuation requirement extend? Does OSHA have to establish the "feasibility" of each chemical for each affected industry? Can it group industries (*e.g.*, mining) or must it examine subsets of industries (*e.g.*, specialty steel)? Under *Air Contaminants*, who decides? *See* Air

Contaminants, 965 F.2d at 982 & n.28 (criticizing use of economy-wide cost averages in determining economic feasibility); International Union, United Automobile, Aerospace & Agricultural Implement Workers of America, UAW, v. OSHA, 37 F.3d 665 (D.C. Cir. 1994) (accepting OSHA's explanation on remand for its decision to adopt single standard applicable to all general industry employers, rather than to disaggregate industries).

8. *Subsequent regulation of benzene.* The benzene standard was eventually re-promulgated, in essentially its original form, after seven years of steady work on the standard and more litigation. The preamble to the final PEL is in many ways the gold standard of justification of risk regulation. It explores cost issues (technological feasibility, economic feasibility, percentage of industry revenue), alternative regulatory techniques (averaging, short-and long-term exposure levels, action levels for monitoring, differentiation among industries, flexible mechanisms (engineering controls and personal protective devices), signs and labels, training, and hazard communication)-and it brings to bear an enormous range of risk data, including multiple epidemiology studies, human dose-response data, multiple animal studies, and risk assessments by outside agencies, other neutral bodies and even industry. The agency concluded that the reduction from 10 ppm to 1 ppm-

> will result in substantial reduction in the workers' risk of developing leukemia and other diseases of the blood and blood-forming organs. According to OSHA's best estimates, a working lifetime of exposure to benzene at 10 ppm would cause an excess leukemia risk of 95 leukemia deaths per 1000 exposed workers. * * * These are clearly significant risks, greatly exceeding the excess risks of occupationally related accident deaths in high and average risk industries which are 30 and 3 per 1000 workers, respectively.
>
> The new standard will create a minimum reduction in excess risk of 90 percent, a very substantial reduction based on comparing exposures at 10 ppm and 1 ppm. On the basis of the current distribution of exposures, OSHA estimates that the new standard will prevent a minimum of 326 deaths from leukemia and disease of the blood and blood-forming organs over a working lifetime of 45 years.

OSHA, Occupational Exposure to Benzene, 52 Fed. Reg. 34460, 34460-61 (1987). Does this new rationale meet the requirements of *Benzene*?

On the broader policy question, one has to ask what was gained (and who gained it) by the delay. As an observer has noted, "if OSHA's risk assessments are accurate, by delaying promulgation of the stricter PEL judicial intervention has resulted in the exposure of thousands of workers to risks that will result in scores of additional deaths." PERCIVAL *ET AL.*, ENVIRONMENTAL REGULATION: LAW, SCIENCE, AND POLICY 513 (2d ed. 1996). Is this a fair criticism of the *Benzene* case?

AMERICAN TEXTILE MNFRS. INST. V. DONOVAN
(THE *COTTON DUST* CASE)

452 U.S. 490 (1981)

Justice BRENNAN delivered the opinion of the Court.

Congress enacted the Occupational Safety and Health Act of 1970 (Act) "to assure so far as possible every working man and woman in the Nation safe and healthful working conditions ...." 29 U.S.C. §651(b). The Act authorizes the Secretary of Labor to establish, after notice and opportunity to comment, mandatory nationwide standards governing health and safety in the workplace. 29 U.S.C. §§ 655(a), (b). In 1978, the Secretary, acting through the Occupational Safety and Health Administration (OSHA), promulgated a standard limiting occupational exposure to cotton dust, an airborne particle byproduct of the preparation and manufacture of cotton products, exposure to which induces a "constellation of respiratory effects" known as "byssinosis." * * *

Petitioners in these consolidated cases, representing the interests of the cotton industry, challenged the validity of the "Cotton Dust Standard" in the Court of Appeals for the District of Columbia Circuit pursuant to § 6(f) of the Act. They contend in this Court, as they did below, that the Act requires OSHA to demonstrate that its Standard reflects a reasonable relationship between the costs and benefits associated with the Standard. Respondents, the Secretary of Labor and two labor organizations, counter that Congress balanced the costs and benefits in the Act itself, and that the Act should therefore be construed not to require OSHA to do so. They interpret the Act as mandating that OSHA enact the most protective standard possible to eliminate a significant risk of material health impairment, subject to the constraints of economic and technological feasibility. The Court of Appeals held that the Act did not require OSHA to compare costs and benefits. We granted certiorari, to resolve this important question, which was presented but not decided in last Term's *Industrial Union Dept. v. American Petroleum Institute*, and to decide other issues related to the Cotton Dust Standard.

I

Byssinosis, known in its more severe manifestations as "brown lung" disease, is a serious and potentially disabling respiratory disease primarily caused by the inhalation of cotton dust. Byssinosis is a "continuum ... disease" that has been categorized into four grades. In its least serious form, byssinosis produces both subjective symptoms, such as chest tightness, shortness of breath, coughing, and wheezing, and objective indications of loss of pulmonary functions. In its most serious form, byssinosis is a chronic and irreversible obstructive pulmonary disease, clinically similar to chronic bronchitis or emphysema, and can be severely disabling. At worst, as is true of other respiratory diseases including bronchitis, emphysema, and asthma, byssinosis can create an additional strain on cardiovascular functions and can contribute to death from heart failure. One authority has described the increasing seriousness of byssinosis as follows:

> In the first few years of exposure [to cotton dust], symptoms occur on Monday, or other days after absence from the work environment; later, symptoms occur on other days of the week; and eventually, symptoms are continuous, even in the absence of dust exposure.[22]

* * *

The Cotton Dust Standard promulgated by OSHA mandatory PEL's over an 8-hour period of 200 μg/m^3 for yarn manufacturing, 750 μg/m^3 for slashing and weaving operations, and 500 μg/m^3 for all other processes in the cotton industry. These levels represent a relaxation of the proposed PEL of 200 μg/m^3 for all segments of the cotton industry.

* * *

On the basis of the evidence in the record as a whole, the Secretary determined that exposure to cotton dust represents a "significant health hazard to employees." and that "the prevalence of byssinosis should be significantly reduced" by the adoption of the Standard's PEL's. In assessing the health risks from cotton dust and the risk reduction obtained from lowered exposure, OSHA relied particularly on data showing a strong linear relationship between the prevalence of byssinosis and the concentration of lint-free respirable cotton dust. Even at the 200 μg/m^3 PEL, OSHA found that the prevalence of at least Grade ½ byssinosis would be 13% of all employees in the yarn manufacturing sector.

In promulgating the Cotton Dust Standard, OSHA interpreted the Act to require adoption of the most stringent standard to protect against material health impairment, bounded only by technological and economic feasibility. * * * The agency expressly found the Standard to be both technologically and economically feasible based on the evidence in the record as a whole. Although recognizing that permitted levels of exposure to cotton dust would still cause some byssinosis, OSHA nevertheless rejected the union proposal for a 100 μg/m^3 PEL because it was not within the "technological capabilities of the industry." * * *

---

[22] Descriptions of the disease by individual mill workers, presented in hearings on the Cotton Dust Standard before an Administrative Law Judge, are more vivid:

> "When they started speeding the looms up the dust got finer and more and more people started leaving the mill with breathing problems. My mother had to leave the mill in the early fifties. Before she left, her breathing got so short she just couldn't hold out to work. My stepfather left the mill on account of breaching [sic] problems. He had coughing spells til he couldn't breath [sic], like a child's whooping cough. Both my sisters who work in the mill have breathing problems. My husband had to give up his job when he was only fifty-four years old because of the breathing problems."

* * *

Byssinosis is not a newly discovered disease, having been described as early as in the 1820's in England, and observed in Belgium in a study of 2,000 cotton workers in 1845.

The Court of Appeals upheld the Standard in all major respects. * * *

II

The principal question presented in these cases is whether the Occupational Safety and Health Act requires the Secretary, in promulgating a standard pursuant to § 6(b)(5) of the Act, 29 U.S.C. § 655(b)(5), to determine that the costs of the standard bear a reasonable relationship to its benefits. Relying on §§ 6(b)(5) and 3(8) of the Act, 29 U.S.C. §§ 655(b)(5) and 652(8), petitioners urge not only that OSHA must show that a standard addresses a significant risk of material health impairment, but also that OSHA must demonstrate that the reduction in risk of material health impairment is significant in light of the costs of attaining that reduction.[23] Respondents on the other hand contend that the Act requires OSHA to promulgate standards that eliminate or reduce such risks "to the extent such protection is technologically and economically feasible."[24] To resolve this debate, we must turn to the language, structure, and legislative history of the Act.

---

[23] Petitioners ATMI *et al.* express their position in several ways. They maintain that OSHA "is required to show that a reasonable relationship exists between the risk reduction benefits and the costs of its standards." Petitioners also suggest that OSHA must show that "the standard is expected to achieve a significant reduction in [the significant risk of material health impairment]" based on "an assessment of the costs of achieving it." Allowing that "[t]his does not mean that OSHA must engage in a rigidly formal cost-benefit calculation that places a dollar value on employee lives or health," petitioners describe the required exercise as follows:

> "First, OSHA must make a responsible determination of the costs and risk reduction benefits of its standard. Pursuant to the requirement of Section 6(f) of the Act, this determination must be factually supported by substantial evidence in the record. The subsequent determination whether the reduction in health risk is 'significant' (based upon the factual assessment of costs and benefits) is a judgment to be made by the agency in the first instance."

> Respondent Secretary disputes petitioners' description of the exercise, claiming that any meaningful balancing must involve "placing a [dollar] value on human life and freedom from suffering," and that there is no other way but through formal cost-benefit analysis to accomplish petitioners' desired balancing. Cost-benefit analysis contemplates "systematic enumeration of all benefits and all costs, tangible and intangible, whether readily quantifiable or difficult to measure, that will accrue to all members of society if a particular project is adopted." Whether petitioners' or respondent's characterization is correct, we will sometimes refer to petitioners' proposed exercise as "cost-benefit analysis."

[24] As described by the union respondents, the test for determining whether a standard promulgated to regulate a "toxic material or harmful physical agent" satisfies the Act has three parts:

> "First, whether the 'place of employment is unsafe—in the sense that significant risks are present and can be eliminated or lessened by a change in practices.' Second, whether of the possible available correctives the Secretary has selected 'the standard . . . that is most protective.' Third, whether that standard is 'feasible.'" We will sometimes refer to this test as "feasibility analysis."

A

* * * Although their interpretations differ, all parties agree that the phrase "to the extent feasible" contains the critical language in § 6(b)(5) for purposes of these cases.

The plain meaning of the word "feasible" supports respondents' interpretation of the statute. According to Webster's Third New International Dictionary of the English Language 831 (1976), "feasible" means "capable of being done, executed, or effected." Accord, The Oxford English Dictionary 116 (1933) ("Capable of being done, accomplished or carried out"); Funk & Wagnalls New "Standard" Dictionary of the English Language 903 (1957) ("That may be done, performed or effected"). Thus, § 6(b)(5) directs the Secretary to issue the standard that "most adequately assures . . . that no employee will suffer material impairment of health," limited only by the extent to which this is "capable of being done." In effect then, as the Court of Appeals held, Congress itself defined the basic relationship between costs and benefits, by placing the "benefit" of worker health above all other considerations save those making attainment of this "benefit" unachievable. Any standard based on a balancing of costs and benefits by the Secretary that strikes a different balance than that struck by Congress would be inconsistent with the command set forth in § 6(b)(5). Thus, cost-benefit analysis by OSHA is not required by the statute because feasibility analysis is.

When Congress has intended that an agency engage in cost-benefit analysis, it has clearly indicated such intent on the face of the statute. One early example is the Flood Control Act of 1936:

> "[T]he Federal Government should improve or participate in the improvement of navigable waters or their tributaries, including watersheds thereof, for flood-control purposes if the *benefits to whomsoever they may accrue are in excess of the estimated costs*, and if the lives and social security of people are otherwise adversely affected." [33 U.S.C. §701a (emphasis added)].

A more recent example is the Outer Continental Shelf Lands Act Amendments of 1978, providing that offshore drilling operations shall use

> "the best available and safest technologies which the Secretary determines to be economically *feasible*, wherever failure of equipment would have significant effect on safety, health, or the environment, except where the Secretary determines that the *incremental benefits are clearly insufficient to justify the incremental costs of using such technologies.*" [43 U.S.C. §1347 (emphasis added)].

These and other statutes demonstrate that Congress uses specific language when intending that an agency engage in cost-benefit analysis. *See Industrial Union Dept. v. American Petroleum Institute, supra,* at 710, n. 27

(MARSHALL, J., dissenting). Certainly in light of its ordinary meaning, the word "feasible" cannot be construed to articulate such congressional intent. We therefore reject the argument that Congress required cost-benefit analysis in § 6(b)(5).

B

Even though the plain language of § 6(b)(5) supports this construction, we must still decide whether § 3(8), the general definition of an occupational safety and health standard, either alone or in tandem with § 6(b)(5), incorporates a cost-benefit requirement for standards dealing with toxic materials or harmful physical agents. Section 3(8) of the Act, (emphasis added), provides:

> "The term 'occupational safety and health standard' means a standard which requires conditions, or the adoption or use of one or more practices, means, methods, operations, or processes, *reasonably necessary or appropriate* to provide safe or healthful employment and places of employment."

Taken alone, the phrase "reasonably necessary or appropriate" might be construed to contemplate some balancing of the costs and benefits of a standard. Petitioners urge that, so construed, § 3(8) engrafts a cost-benefit analysis requirement on the issuance of § 6(b)(5) standards, even if § 6(b)(5) itself does not authorize such analysis. We need not decide whether § 3(8), standing alone, would contemplate some form of cost-benefit analysis. For even if it does, Congress specifically chose in § 6(b)(5) to impose separate and additional requirements for issuance of a subcategory of occupational safety and health standards dealing with toxic materials and harmful physical agents: it required that those standards be issued to prevent material impairment of health *to the extent feasible*. Congress could reasonably have concluded that *health* standards should be subject to different criteria than *safety* standards because of the special problems presented in regulating them.

Agreement with petitioners' argument that § 3(8) imposes an additional and overriding requirement of cost-benefit analysis on the issuance of § 6(b)(5) standards would eviscerate the "to the extent feasible" requirement. Standards would inevitably be set at the level indicated by cost-benefit analysis, and not at the level specified by § 6(b)(5). For example, if cost-benefit analysis indicated a protective standard of 1,000 μg/m^3 PEL, while feasibility analysis indicated a 500 μg/m^3 PEL, the agency would be forced by the cost-benefit requirement to choose the less stringent point. We cannot believe that Congress intended the general terms of § 3(8) to countermand the specific feasibility requirement of § 6(b)(5). Adoption of petitioners' interpretation would effectively write § 6(b)(5) out of the Act. We decline to render Congress' decision to include a feasibility requirement nugatory, thereby offending the well-settled rule that all parts of a statute, if possible, are to be given effect. Congress did not contemplate any further balancing by the agency for toxic material and harmful physical agents standards, and we should not "'impute to Congress a purpose to paralyze with one hand what it sought to promote with the other.'"

C

The legislative history of the Act, while concededly not crystal clear, provides general support for respondents' interpretation of the Act. The congressional Reports and debates certainly confirm that Congress meant "feasible" and nothing else in using that term. Congress was concerned that the Act might be thought to require achievement of absolute safety, an impossible standard, and therefore insisted that health and safety goals be capable of economic and technological accomplishment. Perhaps most telling is the absence of any indication whatsoever that Congress intended OSHA to conduct its own cost-benefit analysis before promulgating a toxic material or harmful physical agent standard. The legislative history demonstrates conclusively that Congress was fully aware that the Act would impose real and substantial costs of compliance on industry, and believed that such costs were part of the cost of doing business. * * *

* * *

III

Section 6(f) of the Act provides that "[t]he determinations of the Secretary shall be conclusive if supported by substantial evidence in the record considered as a whole." Petitioners contend that the Secretary's determination that the Cotton Dust Standard is "economically feasible" is not supported by substantial evidence in the record considered as a whole. In particular, they claim (1) that OSHA underestimated the financial costs necessary to meet the Standard's requirements; and (2) that OSHA incorrectly found that the Standard would not threaten the economic viability of the cotton industry.

* * *

A

OSHA derived its cost estimate for industry compliance with the Cotton Dust Standard after reviewing two financial analyses, one prepared by the Research Triangle Institute (RTI), an OSHA-contracted group, the other by industry representatives Thomas). The agency carefully explored the assumptions and methodologies underlying the conclusions of each of these studies. From this exercise the agency was able to build upon conclusions from each which it found reliable and explain its process for choosing its cost estimate. * * *

* * *

B

After estimating the cost of compliance with the Cotton Dust Standard, OSHA analyzed whether it was "economically feasible" for the cotton industry to bear this cost.[25] OSHA concluded that it was, finding that "although some marginal employers may shut down rather than comply, the industry as a whole will not be threatened by the capital requirements of the regulation" [and that "compliance with the standard is well within the financial capability of the covered industries"]. In reaching this conclusion on the Standard's economic impact, OSHA made specific findings with respect to employment, energy consumption, capital financing availability, and profitability. To support its findings, the agency relied primarily on RTI's comprehensive investigation of the Standard's economic impact.

* * *

V

When Congress passed the Occupational Safety and Health Act in 1970, it chose to place pre-eminent value on assuring employees a safe and healthful working environment, limited only by the feasibility of achieving such an environment. We must measure the validity of the Secretary's actions against the requirements of that Act. For "[t]he judicial function does not extend to substantive revision of regulatory policy. That function lies elsewhere-in Congressional and Executive oversight or amendatory legislation." *Industrial Union Dept. v. American Petroleum Institute, supra*, 448 U.S., at 663 (BURGER, C. J., concurring).

---

[25] In one of their questions presented, petitioners ATMI *et al.* ask whether "the statutory requirement that compliance with an OSHA standard must be 'economically feasible' can be satisfied merely by the agency's conclusion that the standard will not put the affected industry out of business." However, in argument in their brief petitioners appear to treat this issue primarily as a substantial evidence question. They finally summarize their position as follows:

> "OSHA must present a responsible prediction, supported by substantial evidence, of what its standard will cost and what impact it will have on such factors as production, employment, competition, and prices. And the agency must explain in a cogent manner-on the basis of intelligible criteria-why it concludes that a standard having such an economic impact is 'feasible.'"

As our review of OSHA's economic feasibility determination demonstrates, OSHA presented a "responsible prediction" of what its Standard would cost and its impact on "production, employment, competition, and prices." The agency concluded that its Standard is feasible because "compliance with [it] is well within the financial capability of the covered industries." OSHA also found that the industry "will be able to meet the demands for production of cotton products." We take these findings to mean, as the Secretary suggests, that "[a]t bottom, the Secretary must [and did] determine that the industry will maintain long-term profitability and competitiveness." This interpretation by the Secretary is certainly consistent with the plain meaning of the word "feasible." *See* Industrial Union Dept. v. American Petroleum Institute, 448 U.S., at 717-718, n. 30, (MARSHALL, J., dissenting). Therefore, these cases do not present, and we do not decide, the question whether a standard that threatens the long-term profitability and competitiveness of an industry is "feasible" within the meaning of § 6(b)(5) of the Act.

Accordingly, the judgment of the Court of Appeals is affirmed * * *.

[Justice Powell did not participate in the decision; Justice Stewart dissented on the ground that OSHA had not demonstrated the feasibility of the PELs by substantial evidence; and Justice Rehnquist and Chief Justice Burger renewed Rehnquist's objection in *Benzene* that the OSHA standard violated the non-delegation doctrine.]

NOTES

1. What does *Cotton Dust* add to *Benzene*? Is the Court correct in asserting that *Benzene* left the cost-benefit question open, or has the Court changed its mind? Note, for example, the treatment of the definition-in *Cotton Dust*: in what ways is it consistent with *Benzene*? What ways is it inconsistent?

2. What does "feasible" mean? What are the elements of a feasibility determination, as described by the Court?

What is "feasibility analysis" and how is it different from "cost-benefit analysis"? What is the relationship between feasibility and cost in *Cotton Dust*?

Nominally, under *Benzene*, the same burden of proof that applied to the finding of "significant risk" applies to the finding of feasibility. This in fact requires the consideration of large amounts of economic and technical information, as part III of the opinion suggests. Latin has argued that the same reasons that suggest that the burden of proof was misplaced in *Benzene* (uncertainty in predicting effects, access to information, etc.) apply with equal force to the feasibility determination. Howard A. Latin, *The Feasibility of Occupational Health Standards: An Essay on Legal Decisionmaking Under Uncertainty*, 78 NW. U.L. REV. 583, 600-08 (1983). In *Cotton Dust*, are there any indications that the Court might have retreated from the "more likely than not" stance in *Benzene*?

3. *Technology-based regulation.* Professor McGarity has suggested that, given the law of diminishing returns, "feasibility" means looking for the "knee of the curve" in the graph of the escalating marginal costs of control: "In practice the regulatory entity examines the costs of the various available technologies, compares their efficacy, and looks for the point at which costs begin to escalate much more rapidly than efficacy." Thomas O. McGarity, *Media-Quality, Technology, and Cost-Benefit Balancing Strategies for Health and Environmental Regulation*, 46(3) L. & Contemp. Probs. 159, 205 (Summer 1983). Is this a sensible interpretation of "feasible"? Does it avoid some the complexity otherwise imposed by the *Benzene* case, or does it pose its own problems?

More generally, McGarity views technology-based standards as a good alternative to risk-cost-benefit standards. *Id.* at 203-24. What are the potential advantages of a technology-based approach?

What are the potential drawbacks? The ability to encourage new and better technologies is usually regarded as a weakness of technology-based standards, but that depends in part on how far they look into the future. The courts of appeals have split on the question of how much "technology forcing" the OSH Act does. The views range from *Texas Independent Ginners Ass'n v. Marshall*, 630 F.2d 938, 413 (5th Cir. 1980), which limited OSHA to "existing, nearly developed or available technology"; to *AFL-CIO v. Brennan*, 530 F.2d 109, 121 (3d Cir. 1975), which expanded OSHA's options to technology that "looms on today's horizon"; to *United Steelworkers v. Marshall*, 647 F.2d 1189, 1266 (D.C. Cir. 1980), *cert. denied*, 421 U.S. 913 (1981), which allowed OSHA "highly speculative projections about future technology." Which standard do you think best reflects the statutory language?

4. *"The best we can."* Less quantitatively, McGarity argues that the real meaning of feasibility and other technology-based standards is that we should do "the best we can" to reduce identified risks.

> * * * The statutory language, however, rarely prescribes a finely tuned balancing of environmental considerations against feasibility considerations for setting technology-based standards. The language, rather, is aspirational. The agency is told to require the implementation of the "best available technology economically achievable," or the "best technological system of continuous emission reduction which * * * has been adequately demonstrated," or the technology capable of producing the "lowest achievable emission rate." Economic considerations are relevant to the standard-setting process, but they are not meant to dominate it. The economic impact of achieving technology-based standards is to be considered along with a host of other factors that may legitimately affect the regulatory entity's decision. * * * Congress has, in other words, announced to the world: "If we cannot have a perfectly clean workplace and environment, then we shall do the best that we can."[26]
>
> While neither of these goals meets the policy-oriented economist's efficiency criterion, they are both rational *political* end points. Society may rationally decide to make costs a relevant consideration to a media-quality approach only at the extremes and err on the side of overprotection. Similarly, a rational society might pledge itself to do the best that it can in pursuit of safe workplaces and a healthy environment even though it recognizes that even those efforts will not make those places safe or healthy in any absolute

---

[26] Addressing the rationale for the technology-based effluent limitations of the 1972 amendments to the Clean Water Act, Senator Bayh explained: "The whole thrust of the bill is to force industry to do the best job it can do to clean up the nation's water and to keep making progress without incurring such massive costs that economic chaos would result."

sense and even though they may, in the policy-oriented economist's opinion, cost too much.

McGarity, *supra*, at 199. Does this help to understand the statute and its application to benzene and cotton dust?

5. *Personal protective devices.* Frequently, the cheapest way to handle exposure to dangerous substances is through personal protective devices, like respirators. As a matter of policy, however, OSHA prefers to use engineering or work practice controls. *See* 45 Fed. Reg. at 5222-27. The cotton dust standard allowed mills to use respirators as a transitional control strategy. Why does OSHA take this position? Is it permitted by the statute?

6. *Flexibility.* As we have seen, the common complaint about the Delaney Clause is its absolutism: once it is activated by a finding that the additive is at all carcinogenic, all use of the chemical as a food additive is banned. As a result, both the trigger for agency action (finding of carcinogenicity) and the required response (banning use as an additive) are extremely inflexible. How does the *Benzene/Cotton Dust* standard differ? Where has the Court found flexibility in section 6(b)(5)?

3. Dialogue: Regulatory Reform, *or* Is OSHA Too Strict?

The OSH Act and its implementation by OSHA were attacked by industry in the *Benzene* and *Cotton Dust* (and in countless other appellate) cases as being irrationally strict in regulating the workplace. Industry's success in litigation and the burdens thus imposed on the agency have greatly limited its activity and effectiveness. This has led some observers to ask whether the act is too stringent, and whether a less stringent statute would result in more complete (and more sensible) regulation of the workplace. As this issue is a recurring one-a particularly dramatic example is the Clean Air Act-we now pause to consider it.

Three excerpts follow. The first presents the argument that overregulation causes underregulation, the second responds to the first, and the third suggests a different strategy altogether for improving workplace safety.

THE DILEMMA OF TOXIC SUBSTANCE REGULATION

John M. Mendeloff
pp. 4-12 (1988)

A Concise Statement of the Normative Argument
* * *

The finding that overly strict [according to Mendeloff's cost-benefit analyses] health and safety standards have frequently been set does not preclude the possibility that some more moderate regulatory action is justifiable. The high costs of these standards typically resulted from exposure reductions of 90 to 99.8 percent. But because the cost per death averted is strongly affected by the degree to which exposures are reduced, reductions of 50 percent might have been easily justifiable. By the same token, the finding that past standards have been set too strictly does not preclude the possibility that additional standards are needed. In addition, of course, new hazards may be identified that have not been addressed at all.

The Reagan administration campaigned in 1980 against overregulation and made regulatory relief a major component of its initial economic package (along with budget cuts and tax cuts). It tried, with mixed success, to require agencies to use benefit-cost analyses to guide their decisions. The other leg of the regulatory relief effort was to encourage a slowdown in the generation of new regulations, reflecting a strongly held view of many of its leaders that most rules were, on net, undesirable.

The casual lumping together of the charges that regulation has been both too strict and too extensive is particularly unfortunate because it obscures some important relationships between the two issues and, in so doing, some possible remedies. It is generally agreed that, where markets "fail" (because of inadequate information or externalities), regulation of hazards can *potentially* be beneficial. Yet, if we expect that the regulatory response will be improper-that standards will not reflect the most efficient approach or will be set far too strictly-we may prefer inaction on the grounds that it is the lesser of two evils. In this manner overregulation may cause underregulation. Ironically, the costs of overregulation would include not only the excessive costs of strict regulation but also the potential benefits foregone when we decide that no standard is better than an overly strict one.

An important implication of this view is that, if standards are set more sensibly, with more attention to weighing costs and benefits, we should be willing to regulate more extensively than we would otherwise. For example, suppose that an agency, instead of issuing one new standard a year with a reduction in exposure of 95 percent, issued five new standards with reductions of 50 percent each. It is highly likely that the second approach of regulating more hazards less strictly would be more cost-effective-would lower the average cost for each fatality averted. (As noted, however, critics might still claim that even these less strict standards impose net costs and thus that more extensive regulation should be shunned.) The Reagan administration's regulatory policy comes down hard on the side of weighing costs and benefits but ignores altogether the implications for extensiveness.

The lesson of this book is that a comprehensive plan for regulatory reform of standard-setting programs should simultaneously consider the pace and extent of regulation as well as the strictness of individual standards.

* * *

One great paradox found in many standard-setting agencies is the disparity between their activist rhetoric and their cautious actions. The statutes and regulations emphasize their preventive goals; they should not wait until "the bodies are counted" before taking action. The agencies have adopted rules for interpreting evidence, especially animal bioassay data, that clearly take more pains to avoid false negatives (that is, identifying hazardous chemicals as innocuous) than false positives (identifying innocuous chemicals as hazardous). Yet, if we look at programs with highly protective mandates and potentially broad scope, such as OSHA's health program and the EPA's hazardous air pollutant program, we find that not only have they addressed a paltry number of hazards but also in almost every case they have chosen hazards from the small category for which evidence of disease in humans (as opposed to animals) is available. In these programs regulations based solely on animal evidence have not been attempted, even though they are the quintessential preventive measure.

Several factors help to explain this apparent anomaly, but I need mention only one here. The statutory requirement to set standards stringently makes it more difficult to justify them as sensible public policy. Of course, courts are not supposed to assess regulations in these terms. Yet, faced with standards that they perceive as constituting overregulation, judges sometimes reject them on procedural grounds, arguing that the agency has not amassed enough evidence to show that they are necessary or feasible. In the Supreme Court's benzene decision, for example, the plurality's concern about overregulation led it to argue that OSHA had to show that it was "more likely than not" that exposure at currently allowable limits constituted a "significant risk." Yet such a requirement could easily preclude wise preventive measures. * * *

The regulatory regime envisioned here would be more tolerant of regulations that were precautionary, that is, that accepted a higher level of false positives in order to reduce the number of false negatives. But this change would be tolerable only if the agencies did seek to balance costs and benefits, rather than always trying to achieve the "lowest feasible level" and the "best achievable control technology."

The Positive Argument

The argument that overregulation causes underregulation implies that the initial direction of any policy change-for example, toward less or greater protection-will be at least partially offset by its impact on the pace of that activity. For example, the Supreme Court's 1981 cotton dust decision forbidding the use of cost-benefit analysis in OSHA health standards was hailed as a union victory, but one effect was to strengthen the Reagan administration's resolve to avoid setting new standards. The most obvious alternative model of standard setting views strictness and extensiveness as unrelated. The implication of this alternative view would be that Reagan officials would not have issued rules at a faster pace even if they had been allowed to set less stringent standards.

What analysis underlies the argument that strictness does reduce extensiveness? * * *

* * *

1. Court appeals by industry become more likely and better funded. Of course, less strict standards increase the threat of appeals by pro-regulatory

groups. This threat is probably not fully offsetting. Defenders of strict regulation have smaller resources than industry groups. More important, their objective is to reduce delay, which will sometimes preclude challenging rules that they view as too lax.

2. Strict standards face a higher probability of failing judicial scrutiny. * * *

3. The information that an agency needs to justify a standard is more likely to be withheld by industry groups if they believe that the agency will behave unreasonably.

4. Both White House economists and political operatives are more likely to try to delay rules that they (or industry) perceive as particularly inefficient or burdensome.

5. In the larger ideological arena it also seems likely that there are long-run trade-offs between strictness and pace. Industry complaints about overregulation are less likely to elicit sympathy from the attentive public when there are only a few highly protective standards to complain about. But the political and symbolic attractions of strict regulation may wear thin when it becomes more extensive. * * *

We should also note that similar processes are at work in the area of enforcement. A stricter standard will elicit more opposition from firms in the enforcement stage. Specifically, we would expect firms to make greater efforts to avoid having noncompliance detected; and, once their noncompliance is detected, to litigate more frequently to delay or avoid compliance measures. In addition, with a stricter standard, fewer firms will voluntarily comply; at least this is true if we assume (as is usually the case) that penalties are a fixed sum, not related to the magnitude of the violation. The reason is that the stricter standard raises the costs of compliance but not the costs of noncompliance. Although these responses will probably not prevent actual exposures from decreasing when a stricter standard is adopted, the decrease will be less than a model of perfect compliance would predict. How much less is an empirical question.

Not So Paradoxical: The Rationale for Technology-Based Regulation

Sidney A. Shapiro & Thomas O. McGarity
1991 Duke L.J. 729, 731-39

Even assuming that OSHA has engaged in "overregulation," as Mendeloff defines the term,[27] it does not necessarily follow that underregulation has resulted. Sunstein argues,[28] relying again on Professor

---

[27] In the preceding passage, Shapiro & McGarity criticized the cost-benefit analyses with which Mendelhoff supported his claim of overregulation.—Eds.

[28] This article is a response to one by Professor Cass Sunstein, *Paradoxes of the Regulatory State*, 57 U. Chi. L. Rev. 407, 416 (1990), in which Sunstein adopted Mendeloff's analysis of

Mendeloff, that overregulation leads to underregulation because the "threat of draconian regulatory requirements gives industries powerful incentives to fight regulation wherever they can, and gives agencies a powerful incentive not to promulgate or enforce them." OSHA's actual experience in setting standards, however, [contradicts] the naive belief that less stringent standards will reduce industry opposition.

For example, the standard that Sunstein identifies as the most "reasonable" of all OSHA's early standards-the asbestos standard-was fiercely challenged by industry, even though the adverse effects of asbestos on workers were incontrovertible. In addition, the industry fought OSHA's attempts to amend the 1972 asbestos standard for over a decade, even though Mendeloff himself concedes that cost-benefit calculations warrant even further reductions in asbestos exposure. The suggestion that industry will be persuaded not to challenge a standard that imposes substantial costs on its members merely by the fact that the benefits to someone else will be even larger than the costs to the industry is clearly fanciful.

Moreover, the fate of OSHA's new air contaminants standard provides an even clearer contradiction of the Sunstein-Mendeloff thesis that strict regulation spurs industry opposition and agency inaction. In the new regulation, OSHA adopted less stringent standards for air contaminants by relying almost exclusively on threshold limit values (TLVs) established by the American Conference of Governmental and Industrial Hygienists (ACGIH), rather than promulgating feasibility-based standards for each of the more than 400 substances for which permissible exposure limits (PELs) already existed. This approach cannot be characterized as unduly stringent, even by Mendeloff's own cost-benefit test; he predicts that these moves to relax regulatory requirements will overcome the overregulation/underregulation problem.

However, the new standard was challenged by twenty-eight different companies and trade associations. OSHA attempted to settle the cases by compromising with the challengers. Most of the proposed concessions were made by OSHA and involved reductions in the stringency of the new PELs. Despite OSHA's willingness to make significant concessions to avoid litigation, eleven challengers insisted on going to court.

The fact that so many companies and trade associations were willing to undergo the substantial expense of a judicial challenge is understandable, given the economics of the situation. OSHA estimated that the average annual cost of complying with each of the 376 PELs in the air contaminants standard was about $2 million. Because judicial review "delay[s] the implementation of OSHA standards by an average of two years," a company or trade association could save its industry $320,000 by filing an appeal, assuming an

---

OSHA. A similar critique can be found in John P. Dwyer, *Overregulation*, 15 ECOLOGY L.Q. 719 (1988) (book review of Mendeloff).—EDS.

eight percent annual interest rate. Therefore, even if the trade association discounted the prospects of victory, it could justify an appeal to its members as long as the appeal cost less than $320,000. If the association's lawyers spent 500 hours on the appeal (which seems more than sufficient to appeal even a complicated standard), the association could afford legal fees of up to $640 an hour and still save its members money compared to the costs of immediate compliance with the OSHA standard. Investment in an appeal becomes more attractive when the trade association can purchase legal services at less than $640 an hour (a likely possibility), when the industry can place the money saved into investments that yield a higher return than eight percent, or when the standard is likely to cost the industry more than $2 million.

* * *

This experience suggests that industry will generally resist any new OSHA regulation as long as companies find it economically beneficial to invest resources in litigation over investments in safety. How cost-beneficial OSHA's standards appear to disinterested economists is irrelevant to the industry.

Ultimately, the argument that "overregulation causes underregulation" fails because of its one-sided view of the problem of industry opposition. We therefore urge that instead of concentrating on overregulation (as do Sunstein and Mendeloff) and in effect yielding to industry extortion, Congress should focus on the underregulation side-by making it easier for OSHA to regulate. This could be done by reducing the burden of proof that OSHA must present to defend strict standards.

REFORMING OSHA: SOME THOUGHTS FOR THE CURRENT LEGISLATIVE AGENDA

Thomas O. McGarity
31 HOUSTON L. REV. 99, 113-17 (1994)

Even more fundamental changes in occupational safety and health could result from changing the law to empower workers to protect themselves. Under the current statute, workers play only a very modest role in enforcing OSHA standards and the general duty clause. For example, although the OSH Act allows employees to accompany OSHA inspectors on their rounds, they rarely participate in the settlement negotiations between the employers and OSHA officials that invariably precede the final assessment of civil penalties. In the past, these informal settlement conferences, which do not always include the inspector who issued the citation, have resulted in dramatic reductions in penalties. In addition, although employers are entitled to contest OSHA citations, workers and their representatives have no right to challenge a penalty on the ground that it was not sufficiently harsh to send the appropriate message to the employer. Employees may only challenge a citation on the ground that "the period of time fixed in the citation for the abatement of the violation is unreasonable."

Employees may reasonably wonder whether OSHA and the employers are attempting to hide something by engaging in closed-door settlement negotiations, and employees may legitimately fear that the agency officials may "give away the store." On the assumption that sunlight is the best of disinfectants, Congress could amend the OSH Act to give employees and their representatives the unqualified right to observe settlement negotiations. In addition, Congress could give employees the power to persuade an administrative law judge that particular settlement terms were too lenient and provide the ability to secure an order to continue the enforcement proceedings. Given OSHA's extremely limited resources, the threat of an employee challenge is a necessary counterweight to the employer's ever present threat to litigate the assessed penalty. * * *

Congress could, however, go further and empower employees to file citizen enforcement actions against their employers, much like the citizen enforcement actions that environmental groups may file under the pollution control statutes. In an age of reduced governmental enforcement resources, one way to "reinvent government" is to deputize workers as private attorneys general to enforce OSHA standards. There is a risk, however, that employees or their representatives would abuse this power to secure other concessions in labor negotiations. This potential for abuse could be reduced to some extent by limiting worker enforcement actions to standards that OSHA had promulgated through full notice and comment procedures. This would prevent workers from seizing upon trivial consensus standards in enforcement actions to extract other concessions. If this limitation proved insufficient, Congress could address the problem directly by providing for sanctions that could be levied in the event an employee threatens a worker enforcement action for purposes unrelated to worker health and safety.

Empowering workers to take action to protect themselves presumes that they are likewise protected from retaliation by the employer. The current statute contains anti-retaliation provisions, but in the past OSHA has not been a diligent protector of employee whistle-blowers. Under Section 11(c) of the OSH Act, only OSHA may challenge adverse action taken in retaliation for the exercise of employee rights. To the extent that OSHA is not willing to take up an employee's cause, the retaliation goes unpunished.

* * *

Finally, numerous labor leaders and employers have suggested that employees be empowered to operate cooperatively with employers in labor-management safety committees, which have the power to shut down operations that pose unreasonable health and safety risks to employees. The reform legislation adopts this idea and requires employers to establish safety and health committees that would have the power to review the employer's health and safety plan, incidents resulting in accidents or illness, and injury and illness records, as well as conduct inspections in response to employee complaints. The committees could also make recommendations to the employer for health and safety improvements. Once again, however, it is important that employees serving on these committees be protected against retaliation.

NOTES

1. What is "overregulation"? What is "underregulation"? How are they measured? Why is their measurement controversial?

2. According to Mendeloff, what is the proper goal of the OSHA regulatory system? Do Shapiro & McGarity agree? How do these differences affect the respective authors' approaches to analytical tools (like cost-benefit analysis) and to the substantive legal standards that should be applied in the OSH Act?

3. According to Mendeloff, how does overregulation produce underregulation? Are these empirical assertions, or do they depend on logical extrapolation from assumptions about human and firm behavior?

Putting aside their methodological disagreements, why do Shapiro & McGarity disagree that overregulation causes underregulation?

4. *Regulatory reform.* What are the implications of Mendeloff's position for regulatory reform? How should occupational safety and health regulation be reformed?

What are the reforms that Shapiro & McGarity advocate? Are there areas of agreement with Mendeloff?

5. *Empowerment.* McGarity does not argue for replacing direct regulation of the workplace with a system of worker enforcement like the litigation system. Rather, he advocates a combined system. What are the advantages of worker enforcement? Would such a system be sufficient without direct regulation? Would a combined system be greater than the sum of its parts, that is, is there synergy between direct regulation and worker enforcement?

C. The Atomic Energy Act

Like the Delaney Clause and the OSH Act, the public health provisions of the Atomic Energy Act (AEA) are not primarily administered by EPA. They are nevertheless important parts of environmental law, because each statute controls important toxic hazards and each offers insights into EPA's regulatory activities. This section begins with a description of the special characteristics of radiation hazards (Chapter 2 dealt with chemical hazards) and then explores the "ALARA" standard that is unique to radiation protection.

1. Ionizing Radiation

The health effects of radiation have been studied in considerable detail. The effects at very low doses are not free from doubt, but the mechanism and higher-dose health effects are understood relatively well compared to chemicals. Radiation can have acute effects, including death, as was demonstrated in accidental exposures during the Manhattan Project, the atomic bombing of Hiroshima and Nagasaki, and among emergency workers responding to the Chernobyl disaster. Chronic effects-for example, cancer-are of much greater concern, however, because many human activities release low levels of radiation, including nuclear weapons testing, nuclear power generation, medical x-rays, and television viewing.

CLOSING THE CIRCLE ON THE SPLITTING OF THE ATOM

Department Of Energy
p. 39 (1995)

Before 1896, scientists believed that atoms were immutable and eternal. The discovery of radiation changed this view forever. Since its discovery, scientists have studied radiation intensely. Its potential for commercial and medical benefits, and its health risks, became quickly apparent. In comparison with many nonradioactive chemicals, radiation is easy to detect and measure, and hundreds of studies have quantified its effects on living organisms. Nonetheless, it is not possible to predict its exact effects on a specific person. There is no doubt that high levels of radiation cause serious health damage. The precise effects of low-level radiation continue to be controversial.

What is Radiation?

Radiation is energy emitted in the form of particles or waves. Radioactive materials like radium are naturally unstable and spontaneously emit radiation as they "decay" to stable forms. Although the term "radiation" includes microwaves, radiowaves, and visible light, we are referring to the high energy form called "ionizing" radiation (*i.e.,* strong enough to break apart molecules), which produces energy that can be useful, but can also damage living tissue.

Kinds of Radiation

The four major types of radiation are:

Alpha particles are heavy particles, consisting of two neutrons and two protons. Because the particles are slow moving as well as heavy, alpha radiation can be blocked by a sheet of paper. However, once an alpha emitter is in living tissue, it can cause substantial damage.

Beta particles consist of single electrons. They are moderately penetrating and can cause skin burns from external exposure, but can be blocked by a sheet of plywood.

Gamma rays are high-energy electromagnetic rays similar to X-rays. They are highly penetrating and several inches of lead or several feet of concrete are necessary to shield against gamma rays.

Neutrons are particles that can be both penetrating and very damaging to living tissue, depending on their energy and dose rate.

* * *

How Can Radiation Cause Damage?

In living organisms, the chemical changes induced by high doses of radiation can lead to serious illness or death. At lower doses, radiation can damage DNA, sometimes leading to cancer or genetic mutations. Even the "natural background" radiation level (which depends on geographic location, altitude, and other factors) imposes some risk of illness. An estimated 82 percent of the average radiation exposure received by people in the United States comes from natural sources.

Understanding Radiation Hazards

Measuring a substance's radioactivity is only the first step toward understanding its potential hazards to living organisms. Other important factors include -

Type of radioactivity. Some radiation, such as alpha particles, can cause chemical changes at short range. Other kinds, such as neutrons, can be harmful from distant external sources.

Chemical stability. Radioactive substances that can burn or otherwise react are more susceptible to being dispersed into the environment. For instance, some forms of plutonium can spontaneously ignite if exposed to air.

Biological uptake. Radioactive elements incorporated into organisms are more harmful than those that pass through quickly. Many radioactive elements are readily absorbed into bone or other tissues. Radioactive iodine is concentrated in the thyroid, while radium and strontium are deposited in bone. Insoluble particles like plutonium oxide can remain in lung tissue indefinitely.

Dose and dose rate. Dose rate is the amount of radiation received in a given time period, such as rem per day. In general, the risks of adverse health effects are higher when exposure is spread over a long period than when the same dose is received at one time.

Dose location. Some kinds of living tissue are more sensitive to radiation than others.

The combined effect of the above factors makes the risk posed by even a simple radiation exposure difficult to estimate. Real-world wastes from nuclear weapons production often contain many different radioactive constituents-along with various chemicals-introducing even more uncertainty. However, the hazards can be better defined by considering the particular types of radiation emitted by each radioactive element and by modeling likely pathways of exposure.

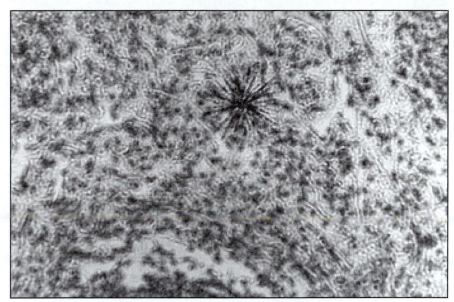

Particle of plutonium in lung tissue. The black star of this picture shows tracks made by alpha rays emitted from particle of plutonium in the lung tissue of an ape. Alpha rays do not travel far, but once inside the body they can penetrate the more than 10,000 cells within their range. *Magnification 500 times.*

Figure 6.1–Particle of Plutonium in Lung Tissue[29]

—

As the above excerpt indicates, radioactivity is the process by which an atom of one element (or isotope of an element) decays or disintegrates into a different element or isotope. Radioactive atoms are known as *radionuclides*. Radiation is the energy that released as particles or waves at the time of disintegration. Because much ionizing radiation comes from the decay of unstable atoms, each radionuclide has a defined life expectancy. This is a probabilistic phenomenon, and it is measured by the time it takes for half of the atoms in a given quantity of the material to decay. The half-life of naturally occurring uranium, for example, is 4.51 billion years, the half-life of radium is 1,620 years, and the half-life of radon is 3.82 days. Thus, if you started with 1000 atoms of radon, after 3.82 days you would have 500, after another 3.82 days 250, after another 3.82 days 125, and so on. A rule of thumb in health physics is that an element or isotope remains hazardous for ten times its half-life. Plutonium, the highly toxic man-made element that fuels nuclear weapons, has a half-life of about 24,000 years. When can we stop worrying about human exposure to existing stocks of plutonium?

Radiation is measured in terms of its *activity,* that is, the number of nuclei that disintegrate in a given period of time. These units are known as Curies (Ci, replaced by the more modern becquerels (Bq)). One gram of radium

---

[29]© Copyright Robert Del Tredici. "Particle of Plutonium in Lung Tissue" dated 1982.

emits 1 Curie; whereas 1,500,000 grams of naturally occurring uranium emit the same 1 Curie; but only 0.00000653 gram of radon emits 1 Curie. A more immediately useful measurement is a calculated figure that describes the biological effect of radiation in terms that are equivalent across types of radiation-rem, now replaced by sieverts (Sv)[30]-which takes into account the energy and intensity of the radiation in relation to x-ray or gamma radiation and the sensitivity of the target organ. Different organs have different sensitivities to radiation; reproductive organs are about twice as sensitive as the lung, for example.

Human beings are exposed to a significant amount of ionizing radiation that has nothing to do with industrial or military activity, or indeed to any human activity whatsoever. The average annual effective dose to the U.S. public from all sources is about 360 millirem (mrem) (3.6 mSv), of which 200 mrem is from radon and 100 mrem from cosmic, terrestrial, and internal sources. Its distribution among different sources is set out in the pie charts (Figure 6.3) below. By comparison, the Nuclear Regulatory Commission's annual limits (not averages) are 5000 mrem for occupational exposures and 100 mrem for the general public. 10 C.F.R. part 20. EPA seeks to achieve a 15 mrem standard for remediation sites, because that level achieves an appropriate risk level. By comparison, the exposure from a full set of dental x-rays is about 40 mrem, and nuclear power plant workers receive about 300 mrem/year.

As with chemical carcinogens, there is a lively debate about the low-dose effects of ionizing radiation. Also like chemicals, the low-dose effects of radiation on humans are difficult to study directly. While the survivors of the Hiroshima and Nagasaki bombings have been studied in great detail, their exposure was limited to a single, very large dose, which is not how most people are exposed. Studies of the victims of radiation accidents and of nuclear workers have produced conflicting data, though there is a consensus that higher rates of cancer can be found among populations with long-term exposures at many times the natural background levels. Whether or not there is a threshold below which the effects disappear also remains contested. A recent survey of the evidence concludes -

In general, mutations induced by radiation in cultured human cells follow a linear model (graph A). In contrast, cell death is related exponentially to dose (graph B). Further complicating the situation is that the shape of the curve appears to vary with the nature of the ionizing radiation* * * . for X rays and gamma rays, the data appeared to support a relationship combining the linear and quadratic models (graph C). Although newer data appear to support this conclusion with regard to leukemia, it now appears that the induction

---

[30] Technically, this is the absorbed dose (measured in rads or, now, grays (Gy)) times the appropriate weighting factor for the type of radiation. The weighting factor for gamma and x-radiation is 1; for alpha radiation, it is 20.

of solid tumors (cancers of the thyroid, breast, and bone) follows a linear model.

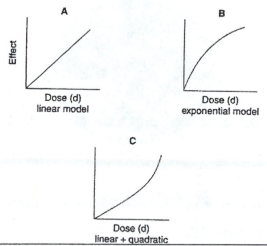

Figure 6.2–Dose-Response to Radiation

DADE A. MOELLER, ENVIRONMENTAL HEALTH 252-53 (rev. ed. 1997).

An additional, intriguing element of the puzzle is the theory of *hormesis*, that radiation in not only not linear at low doses, but that it has beneficial effects. It is known that radiation (and some chemicals) actually do excite additional DNA repair activities at very low doses, and it is theorized that this is a logical evolutionary adaption to the low levels of naturally occurring background radiation to which virtually all life forms are continually exposed. Whether this has regulatory significance is, however, debatable, since the current natural and anthropogenic background presumably already exceed the hormetic fraction of a person's dose. In that case, all exposures above background will have a linear appearance, regardless of whether radiation is linear to zero.

Radiation hazards are mostly managed through exposure control instead of toxicity reduction. Toxicity reduction can be achieved by waiting (why?), but this strategy does not work well for long-lived radionuclides. Since exposure can be limited by shielding, time, and distance (the inverse square rule that applies to light also applies to radiation), most systems for protecting human health concentrate on placing barriers between the radiation source and the environment, limiting the duration of exposure, and keeping the source and the receptors separated. We now turn to the legal standard for exposure control.

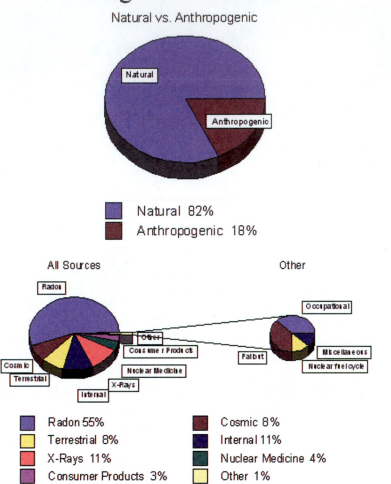

Figure 6.3–Radiation Sources[31]

2. ALARA

Originally enacted in 1946 and amended to more or less its present form in 1954, the Atomic Energy Act (AEA), 42 U.S.C. §§ 2011 et seq., has two basic purposes: to facilitate the use of atomic energy for domestic purposes and to assign to the federal government responsibility for the health and safety risks associated with the nuclear fuel cycle. These are, unfortunately, conflicting goals-on the one hand, the AEA promotes nuclear development, and on the other it imposes regulatory limitations-and the tension between them heavily influences the regulation of radiation hazards under the Act.

---

[31]Charts are based on data from MOELLER, *supra,* at 257.

To some extent, the current provisions of the AEA resolve these conflicting roles by allocating promotional and regulatory responsibilities to separate agencies.[32] The Department of Energy (DOE)(successor to the Atomic Energy Commission (AEC)) is responsible for the promotion of nuclear energy, including the production of nuclear fuel and reactor-produced isotopes, and for the development, production, and testing of nuclear weapons.

Safety regulation is spread across several agencies.[33] The Nuclear Regulatory Commission (NRC) has the primary responsibility for regulating nuclear safety, but it does not enjoy a regulatory monopoly. EPA coordinates federal regulation of radiation hazards that impact the ambient environment, such as airborne radiation releases and water-quality effects. Ordinarily, this involvement comes in the form of general guidelines, and other agencies operate within EPA's guidelines to achieve their regulatory objectives. For example, if an NRC licensee adversely affects an EPA water-quality regulation, the NRC must require its licensee to correct the infraction. Likewise, DOE must comply with the AEA and EPA requirements in its weapons production and environmental remediation activities. Congress created OSHA to assure occupational safety, and this mandate also overlaps NRC's jurisdiction. Pursuant to a memorandum of understanding between OSHA and NRC,[34] NRC retains control over almost all risks associated with radioactive material. OSHA, on the other hand, is responsible for the traditional risks found in the workplace, such as noxious gases and falling objects. OSHA's specific regulations dealing with ionizing radiation contain requirements that are identical to NRC's.

The AEA directs that NRC regulations be "in accord with the common defense and security and will provide adequate protection to the health and safety of the public." 42 U.S.C. § 2232(a). NRC follows a "cradle-to-grave" philosophy, it regulates the possession, storage, use, and manufacture nuclear materials, and the devices that contain these materials. To accomplish these objectives, NRC promulgates technical requirements for the nuclear industry generally and for different categories of nuclear facilities (*i.e.*, nuclear fuel cycle and source material facilities); in addition, it licenses facilities like hospitals and laboratories.

With the splitting of the AEC into the NRC and DOE, the conflicting roles problem (the "Promotion Paradox," as Peter Huber has described it) was presumed solved. But the NRC is not widely regarded as a pit-bull kind of

---

[32] Before 1974, the Atomic Energy Commission (AEC) performed both functions.

[33] *See generally* Peter Huber, *Electricity and the Environment: In Search of Regulatory Authority*, 100 HARV. L. REV. 1002, 1004 (1987).

[34] 53 Fed. Reg. 43950 (1988). The complexities of these arrangements are detailed in Neal Smith & Michael Baram, *The Nuclear Regulatory Commission's Regulation Of Radiation Hazards in the Workplace: Present Problems And New Approaches To Reproductive Health*, 13 ECOLOGY L.Q. 879 (1987).

regulator. For example, while EPA and OSHA are regularly chastised for their supposed police-state tactics (a claim invariably made by persons with no actual experience of police-state tactics), NRC does not have a strongly adversarial relationship with its regulated industry. Moreover, EPA recently took the dramatic step of deciding that it will not adopt NRC radiation standards for its Superfund program because EPA believes that the NRC standards are too lenient. Anti-nuclear activists like to say that NRC stands for "nobody really cares." Even discounting the industrialists' and activists' hyperbole, there is clearly a sense that NRC is a *de facto* supporter of nuclear power. Is this a bad thing? Could it realistically be otherwise? Does regulation actually promote nuclear power?

While Congress did not expressly preempt the field, courts have understood the AEA to grant the federal government exclusive authority in the field of nuclear safety.[35] There are, however, two methods by which states can attempt to regulate nuclear energy. First, the AEA was not intended to hinder the states in guarding against economic disruption due to energy costs.[36] As such, states can attempt to control the proliferation of nuclear facilities by invoking economic concerns. Second, NRC can relinquish specific regulatory authority to a state by written agreement. NRC and its Agreement States currently oversee about 22,000 licensees for the production and handling of nuclear materials.

An extremely convoluted regulatory structure governs the disposal of radioactive waste. Multiple, overlapping, and sometimes conflicting standards of different federal agencies and of the states make it difficult to determine the proper standards to apply in a given situation. Radioactive wastes fall into several legal or regulatory categories:

- spent nuclear fuel, that is, irradiated reactor fuel rods;
- high-level wastes, mainly derived from the reprocessing of fuel rods or targets to extract plutonium and other products;
- transuranic (TRU) wastes, mostly clothing and other items contaminated with plutonium;
- low-level radioactive wastes, some of which, despite the name, are as hazardous as high-level wastes (these are further divided into Class A, B, C, and Greater-than-Class-C wastes);
- mixed low-level wastes, that is, low-level radioactive wastes that are combined with chemically hazardous wastes;
- uranium mill tailings, the enormous volumes of broken rock spoil from the mining of uranium ore, which produce radon;
- uranium and thorium production byproducts, also known as 11e(2) material.

---

[35] *See, e.g.*, NRDC v. NRC, 582 F.2d 166 (2d Cir. 1978).
[36] *See* Pacific Gas and Electric Co. v. State Energy Resources Conservation and Dev. Comm'n, 461 U.S. 190 (1983).

These categories are subject to regulation by DOE (for military wastes), NRC, EPA, and the states.[37] Where there is concurrent authority, typically NRC specifies design and issues licenses for disposal facilities, EPA sets the standards for environmental protection, and DOE or a commercial entity owns and builds the physical facilities. This is a recipe for confusion, compounded by the tendency for the nuclear agencies (NRC and DOE) to focus on precautions based on particular isotopes and exposure scenarios, while EPA tends to focus on residual risk levels.[38]

The military use of nuclear materials, *i.e.*, the development, production, and testing of nuclear weapons, poses radiological risks to the health of workers and the public, to the environment, and to peace and national security.[39] The peaceful use of atomic energy also presents unavoidable risks from catastrophe (*e.g.*, a meltdown), releases into the environment, and occupational exposure. In view of the AEA's goal to promote nuclear energy, a zero-exposure regulatory standard for these risks was obviously out of the question. Instead, NRC promulgated numerical exposure values that amount to a ceiling on acceptable doses. These ceiling numbers are supposed to be relatively unimportant in practice, however, because of the overriding *ALARA* standard.

ALARA is the acronym for: "**as low as is reasonably achievable** taking into account the state of technology and the economics of improvements in relation to the benefits to the public health and safety and other societal and socioeconomic considerations and in relation to the utilization of atomic energy in the public interest." 10 C.F.R. § 20.1003. NRC has elaborated:

> The radiation exposure limits referenced in 10 CFR Part 20 are considered safe; but to ensure additional margin of safety the NRC has adopted the concept of ALARA . * * * An underlying principle

---

[37] *See* John S. Applegate & Stephen Dycus, *Institutional Controls or Emperor's Clothes? Long-Term Stewardship of the Nuclear Weapons Complex*, 28 ENVTL. L. REP. (ENVTL. L. INST.) 100631, 10635 (1998); Patrick J. Rohan, *Radioactive Waste*, *in* 4 ZONING AND LAND USE CONTROLS 25B-1 to 25B-61 (1997); Charles H. Montange, *Federal Nuclear Waste Disposal*, 27 NAT. RESOURCES J. 309 (1987); Karen Geer, Note, *Below Regulatory Concern: The Nuclear Regulatory Commission's Solution for Radioactive Waste Management*, 2 FORDHAM ENVTL. L. REP. 139 (1991).

[38] For discussion of the difficulties of harmonizing the management of toxic and radioactive materials, *see* David P. Overy & Allan C.B. Richardson, *Regulation of Radiological and Chemical Carcinogens: Current Steps Toward Risk Harmonization*, 25 ENVTL. L. REP. (ENVTL. L. INST.) 10657 (1995); Paul A. Locke *et al.*, *Chemical and Radiation Environmental Risk Management: Foundations, Common Themes, Similarities, and Differences* (Environmental Law Institute workshop discussion draft, June 1998). Conflicts arise most frequently under the Clean Air Act, which regulates emissions of radionuclides; the Safe Drinking Water Act, which establishes limitations on radioactive contamination of groundwater; RCRA, which regulates disposal of hazardous wastes; and CERCLA, which requires clean-up of sites that are radioactively contaminated.

[39] These activities produced an almost inconceivable amount of environmental contamination, described in more detail in Chapter 12 (Federal Facilities), *infra*.

of ALARA is that radiological protection should be pursued to reduce exposures to a point where any further reduction in risk would not justify the effort required to accomplish it. It must be noted that the application of the ALARA goal involves highly subjective value judgments, which may also include economic and other sociological factors.

In the matter of General Electric, 24 N.R.C. 325 (1986). ALARA, therefore, has three key elements. First radiation exposure must be limited to only those exposures that are necessary. For the general public, NRC regulations limit exposure to that which is "absolutely necessary." 10 C.F.R. § 20.1(c). Second, the NRC-established numerical values are the ceiling for occupational and public exposure. 20 C.F.R. §§ 20.1201, 20.1301. These limits are subdivided by persons exposed (workers, pregnant or minor workers, and the public) and to targets of exposure (general bodily or sensitive tissues). Workers at an NRC-licensed facility may receive up to an annual dose of 5 rem. For the general public, the facility's operator must limit the annual exposure to 0.1 rem. It is possible, however, to petition NRC for permission up to 0.5 rem annually, based on achievement of the ALARA standard. Third, the facility must strive to reduce exposure as far below the ceiling as practical. This determination is inherently subjective and involves cost-benefit analysis.[40] The precise weight to give economic and social factors is complicated by the uncertainty of nuclear risk. To balance this uncertainty, regulators assume a linear dose response, that is, health risks are assumed to increase with the amount of exposure. In light of the possible deleterious consequences when exposed to even low-levels of radiation, ALARA is intended to ascribe considerable weight to the risk side of the balance. In any event, this is an individualized determination for each facility. *See York Committee for a Safe Environment v. United States Nuclear Regulatory Comm'n*, 527 F.2d 812 (D.C.Cir. 1975).

For the general public, EPA standards for exposure outside a site's boundaries must also be met, and they are considerably lower (100 *vs.* 25 mrem/yr) than the NRC level. 40 C.F.R. § 190.10(a).[41]

ALARA has had a fairly cool reception in the courts, however. As you read the following cases, think about the strengths of the ALARA standard and about the reasons that courts have had difficulty with it.

---

[40] Neal Smith & Michael Baram, *The Nuclear Commission's Regulation of Radiation Hazards in the Workplace: Present Problems and New Approaches to Reproductive Health*, 13 Ecol. L.Q. 879 (1987).

[41] EPA's radiation standards in a number of areas are much lower than NRC's, in part because EPA's standards are driven by target risk levels between 10^{-4} and 10^{-6} and the 100 mrem/yr standard only achieves a 2×10^{-3} risk level. Background radiation at 300 mrem/yr yields a 1×10^{-2} (or 1 in 100) excess lifetime risk.

SILKWOOD V. KERR-MCGEE CORP.

485 F. Supp. 566 (W.D. Okla. 1979),
aff'd in part and rev'd in part, **667 F.2d 908 (10th Cir. 1983),**
rev'd, **464 U.S. 238 (1984)**

THEIS, Chief Judge.

This is a personal injury action for damages caused through exposure to radiation suffered by plaintiff's decedent as a consequence of plutonium escaping a nuclear fuel processing plant operated by defendants. A lengthy jury trial culminated May 18, 1979, in a jury's answers to interrogatories finding actual damages of $505,000.00 and punitive damages of $10,000,000.00. The jury's answers also indicated liability of both defendants on strict liability and also on the basis of defendants' negligence. The Court accepted the verdict and on June 21, 1979, entered judgment in accordance therewith.

This matter now comes before the Court on defendants' alternative motions for judgment notwithstanding the verdict or for a new trial. * * * For the reasons stated herein, the Court finds these motions without merit and denies defendants their requested relief.

* * *

In this case plaintiff sought to establish that culpable conduct of defendants permitted plutonium to escape from the Cimarron nuclear fuel reprocessing facility operated by defendants, and that this plutonium caused injury to Silkwood. How plutonium, once outside the plant, came into Silkwood's apartment is an issue quite distinct from how it escaped the facility.

Implicit in virtually all defendants' arguments in these motions is the suggestion that plaintiff ought not to recover unless he can demonstrate that an agent of Kerr-McGee actually deposited plutonium in Silkwood's apartment. The Court is well aware of the public speculation that has surrounded the facts of this case and the various theories of covert conspiracies advanced to explain intentional conduct that brought plutonium into Silkwood's apartment.[42] Neither public speculation nor charges of conspiracy or intentional contamination, however, formed any part of plaintiff's claim in this trial. The sole issue before this jury was whether defendants were responsible or liable for the plutonium's escape and whether Silkwood was injured as a result of that escape. * * *

* * *

Having decided that federal preemption does not bar imposition of liability under state law, the Court must address the effect of federal regulations on the judgment of defendants' conduct by the jury. [Defendants

---

[42] These speculations are presented in Mike Nichols' film *Silkwood* (1983), starring Meryl Streep, Kurt Russell, and Cher.—EDS.

argue that their compliance with federal regulations conclusively negates claims of their negligence or strict liability.] * * *

* * *

The purpose of AEC regulations, [including the ALARA principle,] and the posture of the government agency at the time of their promulgation, render it unwise to bestow upon these health and safety operational regulations an absolute deference as conduct reasonable under any circumstances. When the AEC initially undertook promulgation of health and safety regulations, the atomic industry was just beginning to develop. Thus, the AEC faced the unique problem of promulgating regulations in advance of the development of those problems it was intending to regulate. Additionally, a variety of different types of facilities existed with diverse safety and security problems, and the AEC was inexperienced in the regulation of any industrial activities. These factors made it unwise, and even impossible, for the AEC to devise a set of government rules that would cover all atomic activities.

Sound logic supports the proposition that compliance with statutory and regulatory provisions does not necessarily lead to the inference that negligent conduct is not present.

(I)n a field developing as rapidly as atomic energy, particularly as to our knowledge of the injurious effect of radiation, it would be most unfortunate if statutes, administrative regulations, or decisional rules should develop hard and fast lines as to what is or is not a reasonable standard of conduct.

STASON, ESTEP, AND PIERCE, ATOMS AND THE LAW, at 154.

This is especially true when the AEC itself acknowledges that these regulations are not static or final standards for reasonable care upon which the industry might absolutely rely without additional safety precautions. The agency itself originally recognized that atomic energy regulation would be a slow evolutionary process with an emphasis in agency regulations on encouraging private industry both to develop their own measures of self-regulation and to improve upon the standards imposed by the government. The AEC originally announced its intention to rely on certain measures of protection that it expected industry itself to put into effect, even though the Atomic Energy Act authorized the AEC to describe in detail the required measures of protection.

The AEC still acknowledges that its regulations evolve with time and are established or modified as operational experience is gained in new plants and as further information is obtained from ongoing research and development programs. A Director of Regulations of the AEC has recently cited the need for continuing development of operational procedures at nuclear facilities. Others have also noted the need for constantly improving regulations governing the handling of nuclear fuels and the AEC's own awareness of the need for better standards.

These and other reasons support the proposition that the general rule should be no different for the atomic industry. Compliance with government safety regulations should be accepted as evidence of acting reasonably, but should not be used as conclusive proof because too many variables exist in any given situation for an absolute standard to apply.

* * *

The same general rule is applicable to actions for radiation injuries where a plaintiff's exposure is within the maximum permissible exposure regulations established by the AEC. These regulations are not intended to represent levels of radiation exposure at which no injury may be inflicted. Indeed, the exposure level regulations were adopted by the AEC from standards originally promulgated by the National Council for Radiation Protection and the International Commission on Radiological Protection solely as guides for good radiation practices rather than strict levels of safety. Both the NCRP and ICRP have continuously emphasized that these recommendations were furnished as guides and both bodies cautioned against their adoption as rigid standards. Both the AEC and the Environmental Protection Agency adopt the position that these levels are not a "safe" or threshold level below which injury does not become a possibility.

Thus, the standards represent a balancing of social benefit against estimated cost, a calculated risk in an area where scientific knowledge of low level radiation exposure effects is insufficient to determine the precise risk actually involved.

> The setting of exposure standards at a given level requires the weighing of these risks and benefits to be derived therefrom. The weighing requires a value judgment as well as a measuring, and thus the standards are not scientific numbers below which no danger exists.

* * *

> There has been a history of disagreement with the established radiation protection standards on the part of some members of the scientific community. The basis for this disagreement has often been the fact that science has been unable to fully discover the biological effects and costs of ionizing radiation. * * * This ignorance makes it impossible to assess fully the risks attendant to exposure in ionizing radiation.

Crowther v. Seaborg, 312 F.Supp. 1205, 1231-32 (D.Colo.1970).

Indeed, this acknowledgment of the limitations of the regulations led to the adoption in 1970 of the concept of "as low as practicable," later changed to "as low as reasonably achievable." This additional standard imposes on licensed operators the duty to maintain the release of radioactive material to unrestricted areas as far below the regulation limits as is practicable (now reasonably achievable).

Even though the maximum permissible exposure ceiling has been frequently rendered more stringent over the years, the regulations still embrace the idea that exposures within the standards pose a potential for personal injury. "In view of our present lack of knowledge as to exactly how damaging small doses (of radiation) are likely to be over a long period of time, the Commission's exposure regulations cannot be said to fix definitively the point at which radiation becomes unacceptably dangerous." Stason, Estep, and Pierce, Atoms and the Law, *supra*, at 128.

Some writers, however, have expressed their view that more deference should be paid these exposure limit regulations. In their treatise on the subject, Professors Stason, Estep and Pierce suggest that whenever someone is exposed to radiation where the amount of radiation received, or the circumstances in which it was received, do not violate the applicable health and safety regulations, compliance should be argued to prove reasonable conduct. These authors urge that where the AEC makes a deliberate judgment on the specific issue of maximum exposure levels, a judge should hold compliance with that requirement as conclusive proof of compliance with a reasonable standard of conduct.

* * *

More recent writers have also suggested that a greater deference be given governmental exposure limits, but they acknowledge that as presently written, the regulations may not be so construed. These authors suggest possible use of the government regulations as a per se defense to a latent injury radiation claim, whereby a court would find that a plaintiff has failed to establish causation of his cancer by any exposure within the permissible governmental limits. The writers acknowledge that:

> (a)t the present time, however, the AEC has not declared the permissible dose level standards to be absolute safety limits. Nowhere in the regulations does any such language appear. The standards are considered only to be guidelines. Their use as a negligence-limiting factor, therefore, is severely limited. Employees are in no way precluded from bringing suit upon radiation exposures even well below the maximum permissible standards. * * *

These writers acknowledged that the standards represent a policy of balancing the benefits to society from the use of atomic energy and the possible harm to individuals from radiation. They continue:

> Implicit in this decision is the assumption that, although very slight, some harm may be possible to those exposed below the permissible standards. It is, therefore, difficult to argue that these should be a judicially noticeable standard which would serve as a per se defense through the refusal of courts to consider any possible causal link between radiation and injury.

Keyes and Howarth, *Approaches to Liability for Remote Causes: The Low Level Radiation Example*, 56 IOWA L. REV. 531 (1975).

* * *

Even the adoption of the Stason, Estep and Pierce suggestion would not aid the Kerr-McGee defendants here. As noted in the record, Silkwood's exposure took place at home in her apartment. Although her body burden constituted approximately one-fourth of that permitted by regulation for a radiation worker during her lifetime, it exceeded by two and a half times the exposure permitted to any other member of the public. The mere fortuity of her employment rendered the exposure within governmental guidelines. Any visitor in the apartment who received the same exposure would represent a clear violation of the exposure limit regulations.

It is also clear that the circumstances under which Silkwood received the exposure were not embraced by the government regulations. The ten-fold difference in standards for workers and non-workers obviously does not reflect a medical judgment that non-workers are more prone to the biological effects of radiation. Rather, the standards reflect the philosophy that a radiation worker tacitly assumes the very small risk attributed to receiving radiation doses not exceeding the currently acceptable permissible limits. Assuming that the worker is properly informed of the nature and magnitude of the risk, as far as known, the market price for labor needed to induce workers to accept the occupational hazard should be commensurate with the risk. The market price of labor essentially compensates the worker for taking the risk.

Silkwood, of course, did not assume in her occupation the risk of the contamination of her apartment. Nor were her employment wages designed to compensate her for any possible radiation exposure to which she might be subjected by a Kerr-McGee accident unrelated to her work at the plant. The jury in this case failed to find proof that the plutonium was carried by Silkwood from the facility. In essence, no showing was here made that Silkwood's contamination was an "occupational hazard" the risk of which an employee customarily assumes. Thus, the argument for application of the higher permissible exposure regulations for workers fails under these conditions. Even were these standards entitled to conclusive effect, in all likelihood the Court could not have so instructed the jury in the instant case.

* * *

[Defendants similarly contend in] these motions that they had no duty to contain plutonium within their facility, other than that imposed by federal law, to protect members of the public from this dangerous substance. Unless federal law imposed the obligation, and presumably unless federal law imposed liability for its breach, defendants are allegedly immune for any damages caused by the escape of plutonium.

This proposition is, of course, legally unsupportable. As noted above, these defendants had a duty under part 20 of Title 10 of the Code of Federal Regulations to maintain the release of radiation "as low as reasonably achievable." Compliance with this standard cannot be demonstrated merely through control of escaped plutonium to within any absolute amount. *See York Committee for a Safe Environment v. United States Nuclear Regulatory Comm'n*, 527 F.2d 812 (D.C.Cir. 1975). It is, therefore, not inconsistent with any Congressional design to impose liability upon defendants for actual damages for escape of plutonium caused by negligence or lack of reasonable conduct. Nor is it inconsistent to impose punitive damages for the escape of plutonium caused by grossly negligent, reckless and willful conduct. Common law duties also exist for the breach of which liability may be imposed, as discussed above.

* * *

IN RE TMI [THREE MILE ISLAND]

67 F.3d 1103 (3d Cir. 1995),
cert. denied sub nom. General Public Utilities Corp. v. Dodson 516 U.S. 1154 (1996)

SCIRICA, Circuit Judge.

In 1979, an accident occurred at a nuclear power facility near Harrisburg, Pennsylvania, releasing radiation into the atmosphere and catapulting the name, "Three Mile Island," into the national consciousness. Sixteen years later, we are called on once again to consider the Three Mile Island accident as we determine the appropriate standard of care for the operators of the facility.

I. Procedural History

The accident at the Three Mile Island ("TMI") nuclear power facility occurred on March 28, 1979. As a result, thousands of area residents and businesses filed suit against the owners and operators of the facility, alleging various injuries.[43] This case involves the consolidated claims of more than 2000 plaintiffs for personal injuries allegedly caused by exposure to radiation released during the TMI accident.

* * *

Contending they had not breached the duty of care, defendants then moved for summary judgment, which the district court denied. After holding that federal law determines the standard of care and preempts state tort law, the district court found the standard of care was set by the federal regulations: 1) prescribing the maximum permissible levels of human exposure to radiation[44] and 2) requiring radiation releases to be "as low as is reasonably achievable," which is known as the "ALARA" principle. The court held that each plaintiff must prove individual exposure to radiation in order to establish causation, but not to establish a breach of the duty of care.

---

[43] Defendants have settled non-personal injury claims brought by individuals, businesses, and non-profit organizations within a twenty-five mile radius of the TMI facility.

[44] See 10 C.F.R. §§ 20.105, 20.106 (1979). For a discussion of these regulations, see infra part III.B.1.

Upon defendants' motion, the district court certified for interlocutory appeal the [question whether] 10 C.F.R. §§ 20.105 and 20.106, and not ALARA, constitute the standard of care to be applied in these actions; * * *.

* * *

III. Statutory and Regulatory History
* * *

B. Regulations

Volume 10 of the Code of Federal Regulations (1979)[45] governs energy matters, and its first chapter regulates the Nuclear Regulatory Commission ("NRC"). Parts 20 and 50 of Chapter 1 are the relevant sections.

1. 10 C.F.R. Part 20

Part 20 of 10 C.F.R. ch. 1 outlines "Standards for Protection Against Radiation." Under the "General Provisions" of Part 20, § 20.1(c) provides a statement of the ALARA principle:

> In accordance with recommendations of the Federal Radiation Council, approved by the President, persons engaged in activities under licenses issued by the Nuclear Regulatory Commission . . . should, in addition to complying with the requirements set forth in this part, make every reasonable effort to maintain radiation exposures, and releases of radioactive materials in effluents to unrestricted areas, *as low as is reasonably achievable*. The term "as low as is reasonably achievable" means as low as is reasonably achievable taking into account the state of technology, and the economics of improvements in relation to benefits to the public health and safety, and other societal and socioeconomic considerations, and in relation to the utilization of atomic energy in the public interest.

(emphasis added).

Immediately following the "General Provisions" of Part 20 is a subpart covering "Permissible Doses, Levels, and Concentrations," which regulates exposures of radiation to persons on the property of a nuclear facility, *see* 10 C.F.R. §§ 20.101-.104,[46] as well as those off premises. The latter regulations, governing "unrestricted areas,"[47] are relevant here because plaintiffs were outside the TMI premises when the alleged radiation exposures occurred.

---

[45] In this case, the relevant federal regulations were those in place at the time of the TMI accident in 1979. Unless otherwise noted, all citations to the Code of Federal Regulations refer to the 1979 version.

[46] These regulations apply to persons in "restricted areas," which are defined as "any area access to which is controlled by the licensee for purposes of protection of individuals from exposure to radiation and radioactive materials." 10 C.F.R. § 20.3(a)(14).

[47] An "unrestricted area" is "any area access to which is not controlled by the licensee for purposes of protection of individuals from exposure to radiation and radioactive materials, and any area used for residential quarters." *Id.* § 20.1(a)(17).

Section 20.105 sets the "[p]ermissible levels of radiation in unrestricted areas," *i.e.*, outside the TMI facility's boundaries. It mandates that the NRC approve license applications if the applicant shows its plan is not likely to cause anyone to receive radiation in excess of 0.5 rem per year. § 20.105(a). In subsection (b), the regulation provides that except as authorized by the NRC, no licensee shall cause "[r]adiation levels which, if an individual were continually present in the area, could result in his receiving a dose in excess of" two millirems in any hour or 100 millirems in any week. The parties dispute whether the § 20.105 standard governing off-site exposure was violated during or after the TMI accident.

While § 20.105 defines the levels of radiation permitted in unrestricted areas, § 20.106 defines the levels of radioactivity permitted in liquid or airborne effluents released off premises. It provides that licensees "shall not possess, use, or transfer licensed material so as to release to an unrestricted area radioactive material in concentrations which exceed the limits specified in Appendix 'B', Table II of this part, except as authorized . . . ." Appendix B then lists more than 100 isotopes of almost 100 radioactive elements and provides the maximum permissible level of releases. Defendants admit that the radiation levels at the boundary of the TMI facility exceeded the § 20.106 standards after the 1979 accident.[48] Nevertheless, they claim that no plaintiff was in an area exposed to the impermissible levels.

2. 10 C.F.R. Part 50

In order to understand the ALARA concept and whether it forms part of the standard of care, it is necessary to examine Part 50 of 10 C.F.R. ch. 1, which covers the "Domestic Licensing of Production and Utilization Facilities." Section 50.34a(a) requires that applications for construction permits include certain information about equipment design:

An application for a permit to construct a nuclear power reactors [sic] shall . . . also identify the design objectives, and the means to be employed, for keeping levels of radioactive material in effluents to unrestricted areas as low as is reasonably achievable. The term "as low as is reasonably achievable" as used in this part means as low as is reasonably achievable taking into account the state of technology, and the economics of improvements in relation to benefits to the public health and safety and other societal and socioeconomic considerations, and in relation to the utilization of atomic energy in the public interest. The guides set out in Appendix I provide numerical guidance on design objectives for light-water-cooled nuclear power reactors to meet the requirements that radioactive material in effluents released to unrestricted areas be kept as low as is

---

[48] * * * Nevertheless, defendants contend "that no excess releases reached any inhabited areas, much less those inhabited by Plaintiffs. For example, Defendants' evidence indicates that the only regions where the effluents and the dose exceeded the federal levels were Three Mile Island itself, some of the Susquehanna River, and some other uninhabited islands in the river."

reasonably achievable. These numerical guides for design objectives and limiting conditions for operation are not to be construed as radiation protection standards.

* * *

IV. Duty of Care

A fundamental disagreement in this case centers on which of the federal regulations, or combination thereof, sets the applicable standard of care for nuclear power defendants. Plaintiffs contend the ALARA regulations articulate the duty owed by defendants, while defendants claim that 10 C.F.R. §§ 20.105 and 20.106 govern.

The district court held that a "tri-level scheme," combining the ALARA regulations and 10 C.F.R. § 20.106, constituted the applicable standard of care. The court found that nuclear power defendants could not be held liable for radiation emissions below the minimum levels set by Appendix I of 10 C.F.R. part 50. The court continued:

> [I]f Plaintiffs can prove that Defendants' emissions exceeded those levels set out in § 20.106, Defendants will have violated the relevant standard of care and will be held liable, provided Plaintiffs are also able to satisfy the causation and harm elements of their claims. If the evidence indicates that emissions levels fall between the two standards, Defendants may be held liable if Plaintiff can prove (along with the causation and harm prongs) that Defendants did not use their best efforts to reduce radioactive emissions.

Both plaintiffs and defendants challenge this holding and, as we have noted, the district court certified whether 10 C.F.R. §§ 20.105 and 20.106, and not ALARA, constitute the applicable standard of care.

A. Development of Radiation Protection Standards

We begin our analysis with a review of 10 C.F.R. §§ 20.105 and 20.106. In 1957, the Atomic Energy Commission ("AEC") issued regulations "to establish standards for the protection of [nuclear plant] licensees, their employees and the general public against radiation hazards." The dosage for persons in "unrestricted areas" (the public) was limited to ten percent of that permitted for persons in "restricted areas" (plant employees). The preface to the regulation explained, "It is believed that the standards incorporated in these regulations provide, in accordance with present knowledge, a very substantial margin of safety for exposed individuals. It is believed also that the standards are practical from the standpoint of licensees."

In 1960, the AEC substantially revised these regulations. Upon recommendations from the Federal Radiation Council and the National Committee on Radiation Protection, the AEC promulgated §§ 20.105 and 20.106, setting 0.5 rem as the maximum yearly radiation exposure allowed for the general public.[49] The AEC concluded the new regulations represented "an appropriate regulatory basis for protection of the health and safety of employees and the public without imposing undue burdens upon licensed users of radioactive material." The AEC stated:

> Recommended limits on exposure, based upon extensive scientific and technical investigation and upon years of experience with the practical problems of radiation protection, represent a consensus as to the measures generally desirable to provide appropriate degrees of safety in the situations to which these measures apply. While the numerical values for exposure limits established in this regulation provide a conservative standard of safety, the nature of the problem is such that lower exposure limits would be used if considered practical. At the same time, if there were sufficient reason, the use of considerably higher exposure limits in this regulation would not have been considered to result in excessive hazards.

Four years later, in 1964, the AEC amended § 20.106 (and the Appendix B levels to which § 20.106 refers) to incorporate new recommendations made by the Federal Radiation Council to the President. The new limitations were designed "to protect individuals in the general population from exposure to radiation as a result of intake of radioactivity through air and water." *Id.* These regulations remained in effect at the time of the TMI accident in 1979.

B. Development of ALARA

A decade after promulgation of §§ 20.105 and 20.106, the Atomic Energy Commission amended 10 C.F.R. parts 20 and 50 to incorporate an early version of the ALARA rule. The AEC noted that a general purpose of its regulatory policy was to ensure "radiation exposures to the public should be kept as low as practicable." The AEC then promulgated two sections in Part 50 to further this policy. First, it added § 50.34a to ensure that applicants for nuclear license permits identified "the design objectives, and the means to be employed," for keeping levels of radioactive material in effluents as low as practicable. Second, it enacted § 50.36a to require that licenses issued to nuclear operators include technical specifications to keep releases of radiation as low as practicable.

In 1975, these regulations were modified in two ways. First, the Nuclear Regulatory Commission, the statutory successor to the Atomic Energy Commission, added Appendix I to define the "as low as practicable" admonition with numerical criteria. But in doing so the agency emphasized the criteria were not to be considered "radiation protection standards."

---

[49] In 1991, the NRC issued new regulations reducing the annual permissible exposure rate for the public to 0.1 rem per individual–down from the 0.5 rem standard that had existed for more than three decades. The1991 regulations adopted recommendations made by the International Commission on Radiological Protection in 1977. Even with these reductions, the permissible exposure rate for the public in the United States remained higher than the .05 rem public exposure limit in Great Britain and the .03 rem limit in Germany.

Second, the NRC replaced the term "as low as practicable" with "as low as reasonably achievable"; the former term was deemed "less precise" and already had been replaced by the International Commission on Radiological Protection ("ICRP").

C. Case Law

In framing their arguments, both plaintiffs and defendants rely on decisional law, although we find the applicable case law inconclusive. * * * [W]e note that no court appears to have actually applied ALARA as part of the duty of care [even when the court adopted the numerical standards].

D. Duty of Care

After reviewing the regulations, the reasons behind their promulgation, and the relevant case law, we hold that §§ 20.105 and 20.106 constitute the federal standard of care. These regulations represent the considered judgment of the relevant regulatory bodies-the Federal Radiation Council, EPA, AEC, and NRC-on the appropriate levels of radiation to which the general public may be exposed. *See, e.g.*, 25 Fed.Reg. 8595, 8595 (1960) (Sections 20.105 and 20.106 "provide an appropriate regulatory basis for protection of the health and safety of employees and the public without imposing undue burdens upon licensed users of radioactive material."). In fact, the heading for this category of regulations is "Permissible Doses, Levels, and Concentrations," and the relevant regulations are phrased in terms of the maximum levels of radiation that may be released.

Although plaintiffs assert that § 20.105 applies exclusively to nuclear plant employees, we disagree. Part 20 of 10 C.F.R. ch. 1 is divided into separate sections governing permissible dose limits for individuals in "restricted areas," *see* §§ 20.101, 20.103, and "unrestricted areas," *see* §§ 20.105, 20.106. The definitions of "restricted" and "unrestricted areas" demonstrate that the C.F.R. sections governing persons in "unrestricted areas" were intended to cover persons outside a nuclear plant's boundaries, *i.e.*, the general public. The case law, while differing over the use of the ALARA standard, appears to have uniformly accepted this meaning.

Plaintiffs also contend that the Part 20 dose standards govern only during normal operating conditions, not during accidents. But neither the language of the regulations nor its history suggests this interpretation. Instead, we believe the Part 20 dose limits were intended as the maximum permitted under all conditions, accident and normal operations alike. The NRC itself has adopted this interpretation, stating it "believes that the dose limits for normal operation should remain the primary guidelines in emergencies," and we believe this agency interpretation is entitled to some deference.

For many of the same reasons that we adopt §§ 20.105 and 20.106 as the applicable standard of care, we reject the ALARA regulations as part of that standard. First, we believe the language of the ALARA regulations compels this result. Section 50.34a explicitly provides:

> The guides set out in Appendix I provide numerical guidance on design objectives for light-water-cooled nuclear power reactors to meet the requirements that radioactive material in effluents released to unrestricted areas be kept as *low as is reasonably achievable. These numerical guides for design objectives and limiting conditions for operation are not to be construed as radiation protection standards.*

(emphasis added). The regulation could not be more clear. The guidelines that satisfy ALARA "are not to be construed as radiation protection standards." In fact, § 50.36a(b) expressly permits continued operation of a nuclear plant if radiation releases rise above the Appendix I ALARA levels so long as they remain "within the limits specified in § 20.106."

Second, the regulation that incorporated the Appendix I guidelines (that contains ALARA language) explained that the "radiation protection standards" of 10 C.F.R. Part 20 continued to protect public health:

> It should be emphasized that the Appendix I guides as here adopted by the Commission are not radiation protection standards. The numerical guides of Appendix I which we announce today are a quantitative expression of the meaning of the requirement that radioactive material in effluents released to unrestricted areas . . . be kept "as low as practicable."

The Commission's radiation protection standards, which are based on recommendations of the Federal Radiation Council (FRC) as approved by the President, are contained in 10 CFR Part 20, "Standards for Protection Against Radiation," and remain unchanged by this Commission decision . . . . [T]hese FRC standards which have been previously adopted give appropriate consideration to the overall requirements of health protection and the beneficial use of radiation and atomic energy. The Commission believes that the record clearly indicates that any biological effects that might occur at the low levels of these standards have such low probability of occurrence that they would escape detection by present-day methods of observation and measurement.

Furthermore, as we have noted, the Atomic Energy Commission adopted the reasoning of the Federal Radiation Council in promulgating the ALARA regulations. The Federal Radiation Council stipulated it had intended that federal agencies would determine the reasonableness of radiation releases.

Finally, ALARA is defined as meaning "as low as is reasonably achievable taking into account the state of technology, and the economics of improvements in relation to benefits to the public health and safety, and other societal and socioeconomic considerations, and in relation to the utilization of atomic energy in the public interest." As the district court noted, if jurors make the ALARA determination, then this "results, essentially, in a negligence standard." Adopting ALARA as part of the standard of care would put juries in charge of deciding the permissible levels of radiation exposure and, more generally, the adequacy of safety procedures at nuclear plants-issues that have explicitly been reserved to the federal government in general and the NRC specifically.[50]

Adoption of a standard as vague as ALARA would give no real guidance to operators and would allow juries to fix the standard case by case and plant by plant. An operator acting in the utmost good faith and diligence could still find itself liable for failing to meet such an elusive and undeterminable standard. Our holding protects the public and provides owners and operators of nuclear power plants with a definitive standard by which their conduct will be measured.

NOTES

1. What are the strengths and weaknesses of the ALARA approach? How is it different from the typical EPA approach? Does this reflect the dual purposes of the AEA? Greater confidence in industry?

2. *Assumptions.* ALARA approach is based on three assumptions: a non-threshold dose response to radiation, intensive supervisory involvement with regulated entities, and industry consistently outperforming exposure ceilings. Neal Smith & Michael Baram, *The Nuclear Regulatory Commission's Regulation Of Radiation Hazards in the Workplace: Present Problems And New Approaches To Reproductive Health*, 13 ECOLOGY L.Q. 879 (1987). How does ALARA reflect the no-threshold assumption? How would proof of a threshold (or hormesis) change ALARA?

How does ALARA depend on NRC's enforcement capability? In fact, NRC inspectors are virtually in residence at nuclear power plants and involved in all kinds of minute details about their operation. Could this work at other agencies? For EPA, the large number of pollution sources, the uncertainties surrounding evidence of environmental violations, and the time and expense of monitoring emissions combine to create a massive enforcement task. Since EPA lacks the resources to monitor industries completely, environmental enforcement heavily depends on the cooperation of regulated industries. As a result, noncompliance remains commonplace. Consequently, EPA is exploring other avenues such as technical assistance, public education and outreach, comparative risk analysis, strategic planning, market incentives, voluntary agreements, public-private partnerships, and pollution prevention.[51]

---

[50] Defendants concede that the NRC may cite operators of nuclear plants when it believes they have not complied with ALARA. Our holding does not diminish this NRC authority.

[51] For more detailed discussion of EPA's enforcement challenges, *see* Jeffrey Rachlinski, *Perceptions of Fairness in Environmental Regulation*, in STRATEGIES FOR ENVIRONMENTAL ENFORCEMENT 340 (1995); Eileen Mullen, *Encouraging Compliance with Federal Environmental Regulations: Government Procurement Policy as a Carrot and Stick*, in STRATEGIES FOR ENVIRONMENTAL ENFORCEMENT 203 (1995); CLIFFORD S. RUSSELL, ENFORCING POLLUTION CONTROL LAWS 61, 82-85 (1996); Dana A. Rasmussen, *Enforcement*

The permissible limits of exposure have declined precipitously since dose standards were first introduced in 1925. The 1925 recommendations were 156 rem per year; by 1950 the recommendation was 50 rem per year; and the current standard is 5 rem per year, with 1-2 rem as the preferred average. Isn't this evidence that the nuclear industry does in fact seek to outperform the numerical standards and that ALARA is in fact effective at reducing exposure? How does it reflect the differences between NRC and EPA?

3. *The role of cost.* How should the cost-benefit standard be set? At the "knee of the curve"? For the purposes of *designing* a nuclear reactor, NRC has suggested an appropriate investment of $1000 per man-rem averted. 10 C.F.R. part 50, app. I, § II.D (1998).

The differing numerical standards for occupational and public risk can be attributed to an economic understanding of nuclear regulation. While it may seem counter-intuitive to allow greater exposure to those with the most prolonged and intimate exposure, the regulations take the view that the general public is the least able to avoid the risk, while occupational exposure results from the worker's voluntary choice to undertake the additional risk in exchange for a premium. How should cost figure into other elements of ALARA?

4. How were the courts in *Silkwood* and *TMI* being asked to use the ALARA standard? Why is the distinction between a federal and state standard of care so important? Why did the courts reject ALARA as a duty of care? What do their reasons say about *regulatory* use of ALARA?

The 1991 and 1994 revisions to NRC's regulations added ALARA to part 20 and dropped the distinction between the general public in restricted and unrestricted areas, respectively. *Bohrmann v. Maine Yankee Atomic Power Co.*, 926 F. Supp. 211 (D. Me. 1996), a case brought by students who were exposed to radiation while touring a nuclear power plant, followed the *TMI* holding and applied only the numerical dose limits. However, in *McCafferty v. Centerior Service Co.*, 983 F.Supp. 715, 719-20 (N.D. Ohio 1997), the court ruled that the 1991 changes fundamentally changed the applicable standard of care:

> Without the 1991 amendment, the Court would be in agreement with the [Third Circuit's] conclusion [in *TMI*]. Inclusion of the ALARA principle within Part 20's "Standards for Protection Against Radiation," however, demonstrates an intention to have the ALARA principle-*i.e.* efforts to have occupational doses and doses to the public "as low as is reasonably achievable"-act as a standard for radiation protection. It is true that an ALARA regulation remains in part 50 and, as the Third Circuit emphasized in *In re TMI*, it cautions

---

in the U.S. Environmental Protection Agency: Balancing the Carrots and Sticks, 22 ENVTL. L. 333 (1992); JOEL A. MINTZ, ENFORCEMENT AT THE EPA: HIGH STAKES AND HARD CHOICES (1995); LeRoy C. Paddock, *Environmental Enforcement at the Turn of the Century*, 21 ENVTL. L. 150 (1991).

that the guidelines in the related appendix shall not "be construed as radiation protection standards." 10 C.F.R. § 50.34(a). But the ALARA principle contained in Part 20 makes no mention of the Appendix to Part 50 and contains no such cautionary statement. Moreover, applying ALARA as a standard of care would be consistent with the settled rule that issues of nuclear safety are "reserved to the federal government in general and the NRC specifically." *In re TMI*, 67 F.3d at 1115. In this public liability action, the jury will be bound to apply ALARA, a federal regulation dealing with the issue of nuclear safety.

In short, both the ALARA regulation and the numerical occupational dose limits expressed in Part 20 (10 C.F.R. §§ 20.1101 and 20.1201, specifically) set forth the applicable standard of care in this public liability action. Accordingly, Plaintiffs' negligence and reckless and wanton misconduct claims are inappropriate for summary judgment and are matters for trial.

Does *McCafferty* take adequate account of the Third Circuit's other reasons for declining to adopt ALARA?

5. *Operations, accident, and disposal.* The *Silkwood* and *TMI* cases discuss ALARA in the context of normal operations and accidents, respectively. As *TMI* points out, accidents are not separately regulated in terms of releases, though the Price-Anderson Act limited the liability of civilian nuclear power plants for accidental releases. Disposal, the delibrate placing of radioactive material in the environment, has long been the Achilles' heel of the nuclear industry. It is regulated pursuant to the Nuclear Waste Policy Act of 1982 and the Nuclear Waste Policy Amendments of 1987, both of which seek disposal sites for low-level and high-level radioactive waste. How would the ALARA principle apply to the disposal setting?

D. The Safe Drinking Water Act

The Safe Drinking Water Act (SDWA) was originally enacted in 1974, in the midst of the intense period of environmental lawmaking in the early 1970s. It required EPA to promulgate two kinds of standards: national primary drinking water regulations, which are legally binding standards addressed to health effects, and national secondary drinking water regulations, which are not enforceable by the federal government and are addressed to welfare effects such as the appearance and odor of water.[52] The primary regulations were to be in the form of performance standards, though they

---

[52] There is a direct analogy, of course, to the primary and secondary national ambient air quality standards under the Clean Air Act, 42 U.S.C. § 7409(b), which are based on health and welfare effects, respectively.

could instead require the adoption of particular treatment standards if measurement of a particular contaminant was too difficult. The primary standards (which, have attracted the lion's share of EPA's attention) were themselves divided into two types, recommended maximum contaminant levels goals (MCLGs) and maximum contaminant levels (MCLs), a feature that has remained central to the statutory structure. Since most Americans obtain their drinking water from groundwater, which is protected only indirectly by the Clean Water Act, the 1974 SDWA also provided for regulation of underground injection wells (a method of waste disposal) and for a program of protection of drinking water (termed "sole-source") aquifers. The states were to be the main enforcers of the program, pursuant to federal standards.

EPA's progress in issuing drinking water regulations was extremely slow. By 1986, it had regulated about twenty of over two hundred contaminants of concern, so Congress amended the SDWA to impose an aggressive schedule of rulemakings, to mandate certain treatment techniques, and to address specific issues, such as a ban on lead-containing materials in plumbing. To meet these new deadlines, EPA developed a six-phase priority plan for addressing particular types of contaminants:

- volatile organic compounds;
- synthetic organic chemicals, microbials, lead, and copper;
- radionuclides;
- disinfectants and disinfection byproducts;
- inorganic chemicals and pesticides;
- miscellaneous.

However, the Reagan administration's continued hostility to the SDWA resulted in little regulatory action EPA's inaction led to a series of successful action-forcing suits by an Oregon organization called the Bull Run Coalition.

The 1996 amendments to the SDWA sought to loosen what had become the stranglehold of the 1986 schedule, so that EPA could spend more time developing a scientific basis for its regulations and could do a better job of setting priorities based on risk. The 1996 amendments coincided with the major push in the 104th Congress to reform risk assessment and to require additional risk, cost, and benefit analyses before promulgating environmental regulations. Consequently, the current statute includes a fairly detailed section on risk assessment and cost analysis. *See* 42 U.S.C. § 300g-1(b)(3).[53] The 1996 amendments also provided additional source-protection measures and additional funding for compliance by small drinking water systems.[54]

---

[53] As a review exercise, you might want to evaluate these provisions in light of the materials on risk and cost analysis in Chapters 2 and 3.

[54] For a thorough history of the Safe Drinking Water Act through the 1996 amendments, *see* William E. Cox, *Evolution of the Safe Drinking Water Act: A Search for Effective Quality Assurance Strategies and Workable Concepts of Federalism*, 21 WM. & MARY ENVTL. L. & POL'Y REV. 69 (1997), on which the foregoing account is based.

1. A Two-Tiered Standard

As noted above, the primary drinking water standards are divided into maximum contaminant levels goals (MCLGs) and maximum contaminant levels (MCLs), only the latter of which are actually enforceable. This two-part division is fundamental to the operation of the SDWA. The following case discusses the relationship between MCLGs and MCLs, and between both and the science of toxic pollutants.

NATURAL RESOURCES DEFENSE COUNCIL v. EPA

824 F.2d 1211 (D.C. Cir. 1987)

MIKVA, Circuit Judge:

Three sets of petitioners seek review of a final rule of the Environmental Protection Agency (EPA or the agency) that promulgated recommended maximum contaminant levels (recommended levels) for eight volatile organic compounds (VOCs). The rule established recommended levels of zero for five VOCs that the EPA found to be known or probable carcinogens, a recommended level above zero for one compound the agency found to be a possible carcinogen, and recommended levels above zero for two compounds the agency determined to be non-carcinogens. Several petitioners challenge the EPA's general determination to set recommended levels for known or probable carcinogens at zero. In addition, two industrial petitioners challenge the inclusion of a particular VOC in the category of known or probable carcinogens, while petitioner Natural Resources Defense Council (NRDC) contests EPA's decision to set a recommended level above zero for the compound determined to be a possible carcinogen. Finding the agency's determinations to be well within the bounds of its authority under the Safe Drinking Water Act, we affirm the rule in all respects and deny the petitions for review.

I. BACKGROUND

The Drinking Water Act provides the statutory framework for the rule under review. Congress amended the Act in June 1986, after the agency action under review, but, with one exception which we detail below, the amendments do not bear on this case, and we refer in this opinion to the provisions in the pre-1986 version of the Act on which the agency relied. The most important of these provisions for current concerns is section 300g-1. That section requires the Administrator of the EPA to regulate the level of contaminants in drinking water using a three-step process. The first step is the immediate promulgation of "interim primary drinking water regulations." In the second step, which is our focus here, the Administrator must establish recommended levels for certain contaminants. To be precise, the Administrator is required to promulgate rules establishing recommended levels "for each contaminant, which in his judgment based on the report [of an independent scientific organization], may have any adverse effect on the health of persons." If the Administrator determines that a recommended level is necessary for a particular contaminant, "such recommended maximum contaminant level shall be set at a level at which, in the Administrator's judgment based on such report, no known or anticipated adverse effects on the health of persons occur and which allows an adequate margin of safety." The recommended levels thus promulgated are non-enforceable health goals. They serve, however, as the benchmark for the third step of the regulatory process—the promulgation of maximum contaminant levels (MCLs), which are federally enforceable standards. Under the Drinking Water Act, a MCL must be set "as close to the [recommended level] as is feasible." Thus, whereas recommended levels are aspirational levels set without regard to practical impediments, MCLs are set at the lowest level feasible, taking into account considerations of cost and available technology and treatment techniques.

EPA began the process that culminated in the rule under review in March of 1982, when the agency published an advance notice of proposed rulemaking for regulation of certain VOCs that had been detected in drinking water. In the notice, the agency requested comment on whether to set recommended levels for carcinogenic VOCs at zero or at "some finite relative risk level." In June of 1984, the agency issued a proposed rulemaking, in which it announced a plan to regulate nine of the VOCs listed in the advance notice. The agency proposed recommended levels above zero for the noncarcinogenic VOCs, on the theory that an organism can tolerate and detoxify a certain threshold level of such compounds. For the carcinogenic VOCs, the agency tentatively determined to set the recommended levels at zero, reasoning that any exposure to these compounds would present a risk to human health.

The agency rulemaking here under review followed in November of 1985. The rulemaking assigned recommended levels to eight VOCs according to a three-category scheme. Category I comprised known or probable carcinogens, which the agency concluded should have recommended levels of zero. EPA determined that five of the VOCs properly belonged in this category. One of these five was trichloroethylene, or "TCE."[55] EPA acknowledged that the evidence of TCE's carcinogenicity was more equivocal than was the evidence for the other four VOCs in this category, but the agency nevertheless decided to regulate TCE as a probable carcinogen. The EPA placed one VOC, vinylidene chloride,[56] in Category II—VOCs for which there is some equivocal evidence of carcinogenicity. EPA decided not to treat vinylidene chloride as a carcinogen, and it did not set a recommended level of zero for the compound. Rather, the agency decided to establish a

---

[55] TCE was a widely used commercial degreaser. In addition to industrial uses, it was used in some cases to dissolve fatty material in drainage pipes in septic systems, a technique almost certain to bring it into contact with groundwater.—EDS.

[56] Vinylidene chloride is used in the manufacture of plastics.—EDS.

recommended level for vinylidene chloride based on the compound's risk of causing non-cancerous liver and kidney damage. In setting the actual recommended level, however, the agency factored in the equivocal evidence of vinylidene chloride's carcinogenicity. The EPA placed the remaining two VOCs in Category III—contaminants for which there is inadequate or no evidence of carcinogenicity—and assigned recommended levels above zero to these compounds.

These consolidated petitions for review followed. They raise three basic claims. The first is that the agency should not have promulgated recommended levels of zero for all VOCs it considered to be known or probable carcinogens. The second is that the EPA unreasonably characterized TCE as a probable carcinogen. The third claim, brought by NRDC, is that the EPA was required to set a recommended level of zero for vinylidene chloride in light of the agency's finding that the compound is a possible carcinogen. We examine these contentions in turn.

II. DISCUSSION

A. Recommended Levels of Zero for Known or Probable Carcinogens

Faced with the unenviable task of challenging the goal of a total absence of known or probable carcinogens in the nation's drinking water, industrial petitioners offer two arguments. The first of these is the contention by petitioners Chemical Manufacturers Association and American Petroleum Institute that the EPA's decision to set recommended levels of zero for the five Category I VOCs was based solely on a misconception that the Drinking Water Act compelled such a result. In support of this claim, petitioners cite language in the order in which the agency refers to a "mandate" from Congress. Petitioners also maintain that the agency placed undue reliance on a passage from the Drinking Water Act's legislative history that states that in cases where there is no safe threshold for a contaminant, the recommended level "should be set at the zero level." In petitioners' view, the agency considered itself bound to set a recommended level of zero for all known or probable carcinogens, overlooking the possibility that such contaminants do have a tolerably safe threshold within the meaning of the Drinking Water Act.

The record soundly contradicts petitioners' characterization of the EPA's decisionmaking. The rule under review noted that the agency had requested comments on three distinct options for setting recommended levels for carcinogens, including nonzero levels based on a calculation of the finite relative risk of each compound. The final rule itself, far from revealing an abdication of judgment, evidences a reasoned determination by EPA that known and probable carcinogens have no safe threshold. The agency wrote, for example

> EPA believes that the zero level is necessary to prevent known or
> anticipated effects from human or probable human carcinogens

including a margin of safety. No other margin of safety would be adequate since EPA does not believe a threshold for carcinogens exists.

The agency did state that "it believed a [recommended level] of zero was more consistent with the [Drinking Water Act] mandate and the legislative history." The mandate to which this passage refers, however, as the final rule later makes clear, is not a perceived congressional directive to set recommended levels for carcinogens at zero, but rather, "the direction of Congress that EPA set [recommended levels] to prevent known or anticipated effects with a margin of safety." The Drinking Water Act clearly does impose this obligation on the agency. Thus, there is no indication that the agency misconstrued or failed to meet its responsibilities under the Drinking Water Act, or that it failed to adequately consider alternatives to the approach it ultimately adopted. Rather, EPA made an expert judgment that there is no safe threshold level for known or probable carcinogens, and set recommended levels of zero for those compounds accordingly.

Petitioners' second argument is that under the Drinking Water Act, the agency is required to make a predicate finding of "significant risk" before it can regulate a VOC at all. Petitioners contend that the Drinking Water Act must be interpreted to encompass this requirement, because otherwise the statute would confer unfettered discretion to regulate on the EPA, in violation of the delegation doctrine set out by the Supreme Court * * *. In advancing this argument, petitioners rely on the Supreme Court's decision in *Industrial Union Department, AFL-CIO v. American Petroleum Institute*, popularly known as the "*Benzene*" decision. In *Benzene*, the Court construed the Occupational Safety and Health Act (OSHA) as prohibiting the Secretary of Labor from issuing standards to provide safe or healthful employment without a threshold determination "that a place of employment is unsafe—in the sense that significant risks are present and can be eliminated or lessened by changing practices." Three members of the plurality opinion suggested that one reason for favoring such a construction of OSHA was to avoid any concern of an unconstitutionally broad delegation of legislative power. Petitioners seize upon this language to claim that the EPA lacked authority to regulate the five Category I VOCs unless it first found that even negligible amounts of the compounds in drinking water presented a significant risk to human health.

The Court based its decision in *Benzene* on a close reading of the statutory language of OSHA, which we note differs significantly from the statutory scheme that we confront in this case. The OSHA language that the Supreme Court interpreted as incorporating a requirement of a finding of significant risk directed the Secretary to set standards "reasonably necessary and appropriate to provide safe or healthful employment." 29 U.S.C. § 652(8). The Drinking Water Act, by contrast, directs the Administrator to establish a recommended level for "each contaminant which, in his judgment . . . *may have any* adverse effect on the health of persons." 42 U.S.C. § 300g-

1(b)(1)(B) (emphasis added). This language is inconsistent with a requirement that the Administrator make a threshold finding of significant risk; a contaminant may have some adverse effect on the health of persons without posing a significant risk to human health.

Petitioners' reliance on *Benzene* is unwarranted not only because of the differences between the two statutory schemes. Whatever the impact of the decision on statutory schemes other than OSHA, *Benzene* applies only if Congress has not specifically set the agency's regulatory agenda. *Benzene* could not possibly apply in this case because Congress in fact has now told the EPA to regulate the VOCs that are the subject of the rule under review. The 1986 amendments to the Drinking Water Act specifically direct EPA to establish national primary drinking water regulations for 83 enumerated VOCs, including the eight compounds which the EPA regulated in this rule. Petitioners point out that the amendments also permit the EPA to substitute a specific contaminant for one of the contaminants enumerated by Congress if, in the judgment of the agency, regulation of the substitute contaminant is more likely to be protective of public health. This added measure of discretion, however, in no way alters the fact that Congress has given a preliminary directive to the EPA to regulate the VOCs at issue here. Thus, we need not determine whether the *Benzene* decision might have applied by analogy to the unamended Drinking Water Act. Congress now has issued precise marching orders instructing the EPA to regulate these VOCs, and that is all the agency needs to know. *See American Mining Congress v. Thomas*, 772 F.2d 617, 627-28 (10th Cir. 1985) (significant risk determination by EPA inappropriate and unnecessary where Congress had indicated its desire for regulation).

B. Promulgation of a Recommended Level of Zero for TCE

Petitioners Halogenated Solvent Industry Alliance and Diamond Shamrock Chemicals Company protest at length the EPA's decision to categorize TCE as a probable carcinogen, which resulted in the agency's promulgation of a recommended level of zero for TCE. Petitioners argue that the EPA miscategorized TCE because any risk presented by the compound is at most *de minimis*. TCE's carcinogenicity has been the subject of at least six scientific studies on mice, which have produced varying results. Petitioners belittle the two studies that have indicated that TCE may be a human carcinogen, while they trumpet the studies that point the other way. In brief, petitioners argue that the positive studies are unreliable because they involved suspect dosage levels, dosage methods, TCE grades, mice strains, and mice housing.

Happily, it is not for the judicial branch to undertake comparative evaluations of conflicting scientific evidence. Our review aims only to discern whether the agency's evaluation was rational. EPA provided ample explanation for its decision to classify TCE as a probable carcinogen. It received and replied to extensive comments on the issue, and it detailed its reasons for giving greater weight to the positive studies than to the negative or inconclusive studies. To summarize the EPA's reasoning, the agency was particularly impressed by finding in two different studies that TCE caused a significant increase in the incidence of liver tumors in mice. Although we gather there is some disagreement in the scientific community as to the relevance of evidence of mouse tumors, EPA's proposed guidelines for carcinogen risk-assessment reasonably take such findings as sufficient evidence of carcinogenicity in the absence of certain contraindications, none of which was present in the studies in question. Moreover, the agency identified concrete flaws in the negative studies. The agency also took note of the consensus among scientists that where cancer is concerned, positive results in one study are not necessarily negated by negative results in another. EPA, in sum, made a reasonable choice to categorize TCE as a probable carcinogen based on a rational evaluation of somewhat conflicting scientific evidence. As we previously have stated, "in an area characterized by scientific and technological uncertainty [w]here administrative judgment plays a key role, . . . this court must proceed with particular caution, avoiding all temptation to direct the agency in a choice between rational alternatives." We are satisfied that the alternative for which the agency opted was rational, and we therefore have no cause to disturb the EPA's choice.

C. Failure to Promulgate a Zero Recommended Level for Vinylidene Chloride

NRDC does not dispute EPA's finding that vinylidene chloride is a possible-rather than a known or probable-human carcinogen. NRDC instead contends that Congress intended that EPA treat possible carcinogens no differently from known or probable ones. NRDC argues that EPA's regulatory scheme in effect imposes a requirement that a compound be found to be carcinogenic by a preponderance of the evidence before the agency will establish a recommended level of zero for it. Such a threshold requirement, NRDC contends, violates EPA's obligation to resolve uncertainty on the side of protecting public health.

We agree with NRDC that a preponderance-of-the-evidence threshold test would probably be inconsistent with Congress' directions in the Drinking Water Act. If the evidence established, for example, a 40% probability that a compound was carcinogenic, the agency's decision not to regulate would be difficult to square with the Drinking Water Act's instruction to the agency to establish a recommended level for each contaminant which, in its judgment, may have any adverse effect on health. Such a decision might well constitute an abuse of the discretion the agency is granted under the Drinking Water Act. But that situation in no way describes the instant case, and certainly there is no indication in the final rule that the agency has adopted a general policy not to establish a recommended level for a VOC unless a preponderance of the evidence demonstrates that it is a carcinogen. NRDC perhaps has taken too much to heart the agency's use of the word "possible" in its categorization of different VOCs. Although that label on its face could augur a preponderance-of-the-evidence test, the agency's explication of the Category II-compounds for which there is *some equivocal evidence* of carcinogenicity—makes it clear that the EPA has no such test in mind. Nor does the EPA's treatment of vinylidene chloride suggest that the agency employed a threshold preponderance-of-the-evidence test. The EPA here reasonably concluded that the evidence of vinylidene chloride's carcinogenicity was not even close to being in equipoise. The agency pointed out that no fewer than a dozen long-term animal studies had not demonstrated that vinylidene chloride has any carcinogenic effect. Against this data EPA weighed two studies that revealed a possibility of carcinogenic or protocarcinogenic effects, and it noted that the results in both of these studies had limitations that made their applicability to humans highly questionable. The agency therefore had adequate support for its conclusion that the evidence of TCE's carcinogenicity was sparse and equivocal.

Whether the EPA, having reached such a conclusion, properly declined to set a zero recommended level for vinylidene chloride involves essentially a question of statutory interpretation. The Drinking Water Act provides that the Administrator shall establish recommended levels for each contaminant which, "in his judgment . . . may have any adverse effect on the health of persons." 42 U.S.C. § 300g-1(b)(1)(B). By its terms, the statute grants discretion to the Administrator to determine whether there is sufficient evidence to justify establishing a recommended level for a particular compound. Unless the agency must regulate as a carcinogen every VOC whose carcinogenicity it cannot conclusively disprove, an interpretation that would read the concept of administrative judgment out of the Act, the EPA has discretion not to treat a compound as a carcinogen notwithstanding some equivocal evidence to the contrary. *See Environmental Defense Fund v. EPA*, 598 F.2d 62, 88 (D.C.Cir.1978) (where evidence of a chemical's carcinogenicity is inconclusive, Administrator has discretion whether to regulate). EPA's decision not to establish a recommended level for vinylidene chloride based on the compound's carcinogenicity thus does not violate the statutory scheme of the Drinking Water Act.

Although EPA did not set a recommended level for vinylidene chloride based on the compound's carcinogenicity, the agency decided that the compound's other toxic effects did warrant the establishment of a recommended level. In then calculating the actual recommended level for vinylidene chloride, EPA divided by ten in order to take account of vinylidene chloride's possibly carcinogenic effects. NRDC argues that it was arbitrary and capricious for the agency to refuse to establish recommended level of zero based on vinylidene chloride's risk of carcinogenicity but then to take account of the very same risk in setting the recommended level for the compound. We disagree. A careful parsing of the statutory language provides ample support for EPA's action. The Drinking Water Act provides for promulgation of recommended levels in two steps. In the first, the

Administrator determines whether a contaminant may have any adverse effect on the health of persons. If a contaminant may have an adverse effect (for example, in the case of vinylidene chloride, because of its noncarcinogenic risks), the Administrator is directed to set the recommended level at a level at which "*no* known or anticipated adverse effects on the health of persons occur *and* which allows an adequate margin of safety." The statute thus leaves room for the EPA to consider in its actual setting of the recommended level risks other than those that catalyzed the preliminary decision to establish a recommended level. Here, the EPA did just that, concluding that the equivocal evidence of vinylidene chloride's carcinogenicity, although not sufficient to justify establishing a recommended level on that ground alone, was palpable enough to be accounted for at the "adequate margin of safety" stage. This is neither an unreasonable interpretation of the statute nor an unwise choice of policy.

* * *

III. CONCLUSION

The coincidental opposition to EPA's rule by public-interest forces and industrial representatives is not relevant to the reviewing process and is not a factor for our consideration, except that it reflects EPA's careful efforts to carry out its regulatory obligations. The rule under review is measured and well within the regulatory contours established by Congress under the Drinking Water Act. Accordingly, for the foregoing reasons, the petitions for review are denied and the final rule under review is affirmed.

NOTES

1. Under the current statute, what is the process for promulgating an MCL? What triggers the process? Why is it so complicated?

What is the relationship between the MCL and the maximum contaminant level goal (MCLG)? What are the applicable regulatory standards or targets of the two tiers?

2. *EPA's calculus.* EPA's own description of its method for calculating MCLGs and MCLs illustrates the complexities of managing carcinogens and of moving from toxicity data to performance standards.

- First, carcinogens are divided into three categories depending on the strength of the evidence for carcinogenicity. Category I carcinogens ("strong evidence" or IARC Groups A, B_1, B_2) automatically receive a zero MCLG; Category II ("limited evidence," IARC Group C) use either the reference dose (RfD) method plus a margin of safety, or a 10^{-4} to 10^{-6} risk range; Category III ("inadequate or no animal evidence," IARC Groups D, E) use the RfD method.

- Second, for Category II and III carcinogens, the NOAEL or LOAEL is divided by an uncertainty factor to obtain the RfD. The uncertainty factor ranges from 10 to 1000, depending on the strength of the evidence of carcinogenicity; an extra factor of 10 is added if a LOAEL is used instead of a NOAEL.

- Third, the RfD is multiplied by body weight (70 kg male) and divided by average daily water consumption to determine the drinking water equivalent level (DWEL).
- Fourth, the DWEL is multiplied by the percentage of the total daily exposure to the contaminant that is contributed by drinking water (the default value is 20%) to arrive at the MCLG.
- Fifth, for Category II carcinogens, a further margin of safety or slope factor is added.
- Sixth, the feasibility-based MCL is determined.

EPA, National Primary Drinking Water Regulations-Synthetic Organic Chemicals, 56 Fed. Reg. 3526, 3531-34, 3547 (1991). Where are the uncertainties in this calculation? How does EPA handle them? Are they adequately accounted for? What types of evidence does EPA use for each value and for uncertainties and assumptions?

3. Turning to the *NRDC* case itself, why do both parties challenge the MCLGs, since they are non-binding? One possibility, not mentioned by the court, is that Superfund clean-up standards are set by reference to the MCLGs. *See* 42 U.S.C. § 9621 (d)(2)(A). Why would Superfund legislation take this position? Does it make sense?

4. How does the court justify upholding EPA's zero MCLG policy? Is this analysis appropriate in light of *Benzene*?

5. Why are the two VOCs, vinylidene chloride and TCE, treated differently? Are different types of uncertainty involved? What was EPA's position on the merits?

6. *The 1996 Amendments*. The *NRDC* case was decided under the pre-1996 section 1412. The relevant portions of previous version, § 1412(b)(4)-(5) read as follows:

(4) Each maximum contaminant level goal established under this subsection shall be set at the level at which no known or anticipated adverse effects on health of persons occur and which allows an adequate margin of safety. Each national primary drinking water regulation for a contaminant for which a maximum contaminant level goal is established under this subsection shall specify a maximum level for such contaminant which is as close to the maximum contaminant level goal as is feasible.

(5) For the purposes of this subsection, the term "feasible" means feasible with the use of the best technology, treatment techniques and other means which the Administrator finds, after examination for efficacy under field conditions and not solely under laboratory conditions, are available (taking cost into consideration). * * *

How does this compare to the new language? How was Congress trying to change EPA's decisionmaking under the SDWA? To what extent does the new section 1412 undermine the *NRDC* case? What aspects of the case survive?

7. *Uncertainty and margins of safety.* Margins of safety and uncertainty factors figure prominently in EPA's calculations. Why did NRDC object to using a margin of safety to respond to uncertainty about carcinogenicity? Does the use of margins of safety and uncertainty factors for Category II carcinogens make sense?

Can risk assessment and management be effectively separated in this analysis? Suppose that, as the new section 1412(b)(3)(B) requires, EPA fully revealed the equivocal evidence on carcinogenicity of TCE and vinylidene chloride. Won't that simply encourage challenges to the standards and strengthen the hands of their opponents? Is that a bad thing?

2. Case Study: Disinfection Byproducts

Carcinogens are, in fact, a relatively small part of the task of the SDWA; its primary focus is conventional biological contaminants of the kind that cause outbreaks of infectious disease. These functions do not appear at first glance to conflict, but unfortunately one of the main methods for preventing the outbreak of disease is chlorination of drinking water supplies, and some of the breakdown products of chlorination have been linked to cancer. Disinfection byproducts, therefore, may pose a difficult choice between controlling different injuries. The following excerpts present two points of view on this question. In reading them, consider, first, whether a true tragic choice is presented or whether there are ways out of it. Second, consider how the values expressed by the authors of the two readings differ from each other and which values are embodied in the statute.

LIVING DOWNSTREAM: AN ECOLOGIST LOOKS AT CANCER AND THE ENVIRONMENT

Sandra Steingraber
pp. 202-04 (1997)

Chlorine gas is a noxious poison. However, the problem with chlorinated drinking water does not lie with chlorine itself. Rather, in a manner reminiscent of the way that air pollutants combine in the atmosphere to create new chemical species, the problem begins when elemental chlorine spontaneously reacts with organic contaminants already present in water. Their organochlorine offspring are known as disinfection by-products. Hundreds exist, and several are classified as probable human carcinogens. Trihalomethanes, a small subgroup of volatile disinfection by-products, are currently receiving the most scientific and regulatory attention. Chloroform is the most common one. As with any waterborne volatile compound, our route of exposure to trihalomethanes is threefold: ingestion, inhalation, and absorption. Indeed, trihalomethanes appear as one of the major chemical culprits in the bathing studies already discussed.

Volatile organic compounds in drinking water, then, can have variant life histories. Some may be escapees from landfills, waste dumps, farm fields, or industrial parks. These compounds arrive in our water supply ready-made, their chemical conformations intact. Others may be formed on-site at the waterworks. In this way, the chloroform present in finished tap water has at least two possible pedigrees: it could have leaked into the water supply as a contaminant, or it could have been created during the process of chlorination. All volatile organic compounds classified as trihalomethanes are regulated as a group, regardless of the precise genealogy or the individual components of the mixture. Their maximum-contaminant-level is 100 parts per billion. Their maximum-contaminant-level goal is zero. In the EPA's chart of drinking-water standards, along the row labeled "Total Trihalomethanes" and under the column titled "Potential Health Effects" is a single word: *cancer*.

Many studies all telescope into this one word. The early investigations were ecological in design and compared cancer rates in communities with and without chlorinated water. Conducted in Ohio, Louisiana, Wisconsin, Iowa, Norway, and Finland, these studies consistently found associations between water chlorination and cancers of the bladder and rectum. In a second wave of case-control and cohort studies, researchers then pursued the link between cancer and chlorination more intensely. These researchers interviewed individuals about the details of their tap-water habits, controlled for lifestyle confounders, used historical water records to estimate past exposures, and even gathered information about the sources of drinking water at previous residences. Carried out in Wisconsin, Illinois, Louisiana, Massachusetts, Maryland, North Carolina, Colorado, and Norway, these studies suggested an association between water chlorination and cancer, especially in regard to bladder and rectal cancers, and especially when drinking water is drawn from above-ground sources, such as rivers.

* * *

Giving people cancer in order to ensure them a water supply safe from disease-causing microbes is not necessary. Part of the solution lies in making wider use of alternative disinfection strategies. These include granular activated charcoal (which binds with contaminants and removes them) and ozonation (which bubbles ozone gas through raw water to kill microorganisms). Both techniques have been used successfully in many U.S. and European communities.

SEEKING SAFE DRINKING WATER

Susan W. Putnam & Jonathan Baert Wiener
in **Risk Versus Risk: Tradeoffs in Protecting Health and the Environment (John D. Graham & Jonathan Baert Wiener, eds.) pp. 141-48 (1995)**

How do we compare the health risks of microbial disease and chemical disinfectants? The risks of microbial and chemical hazards differ substantially with respect to their outcomes, severity, certainty, timing, and distribution among population groups.

The adverse health effects of microbial disease are uncomfortable, debilitating, and potentially fatal. The diarrheal and other disabilities can last for only a few days, or they can drag on for many months. The effects occur promptly after exposure, often in a population already in a vulnerable state due to age (children and the elderly) or disability. For the most part in the United States, however, the disease effects are nonfatal and usually reversible. The issue is primarily one of morbidity [*i.e.,* illness and disease], not mortality. (This is not true in developing countries, where diarrhea and dehydration due to poor water quality kill millions of children each year.) For example, mortality rates from enterovirus infections have been reported to range from less than 0.1 percent to 1.8 percent. Since this may only reflect hospitalized cases, the actual mortality rate for all cases may be even lower.

Chlorine risks, on the other hand, present a very different picture. Disease occurs only after long-term, cumulative exposure of often many decades. The affected population is usually middle-aged or older; rarely are children afflicted with the types of cancer thought to be associated with chlorinated water. Here, as with most suspected carcinogens, the endpoints of interest include mortality as well as morbidity.

Microbial risks can be estimated and foreseen with a high degree of certainty. Waterborne microbes can be isolated, identified, and studied to assess their risk level, and specific effects in humans can be shown to be caused by specific organisms. There is a wealth of historical data indicating the types of diseases that result from consumption of pathogen-infested water supplies. Although the dose-response relationship is not clearly defined for microbial disease, it is suspected that even a modest number of microorganisms can infect much of the population-particularly the most vulnerable groups-that drinks from the contaminated water supply. With the high prevalence of pathogens naturally occurring in water sources, the likelihood of disease resulting from untreated (or poorly treated) drinking water is high.

The certainty of cancer predictions from exposure to chlorinated drinking water, on the other hand, is much lower. With chlorine, as with many chemicals, it is more difficult to isolate the health effects and to prove a causal relationship between the chemical and human cancer. The data are far from conclusive. Risk assessments of chlorine's carcinogenic potential necessitate multiple extrapolations from animal bioassays (from high-dose experimental exposure to low-dose actual exposure, and across species from laboratory animals to humans) and various assumptions and choices made in the mathematical modeling processes. Similarly, the epidemiological data on human exposure are plagued by multiple confounding sources of cancer (such as smoking or diet), as well as by imprecise measurements of chlorine and chloroform levels, water consumption, and other elements. There are no dose-response data for humans, and the actual number of excess cancers seen in the studies is small. In addition, the data on other exposures to chlorine in drinking water, such as from swimming, showering, or washing fruits and vegetables, are very limited.

The issue remains how to weigh sensibly the target and countervailing risks. It is difficult to compare sudden, predictable episodes of diarrhea among children to latent, uncertain cases of cancer among adults. It is hard to balance an almost certain level of morbidity (and an uncertain level of mortality) in the present against a highly uncertain chance of cancer morbidity and mortality several decades in the future. Disease at hand demands action, but there is also strong support for protecting against future adverse outcomes; and the particular risk of cancer may provoke special public anxiety.

The challenge of trying to manage and reduce these diverse risks is further complicated by difficult economic, ethical, and attitudinal issues. For example, some say that a risk may be more acceptable to the public if it is naturally occurring (waterborne microorganisms) rather than technologically imposed (chemical disinfectants). But an immediate and present risk-the effects of which are readily apparent, unpleasant, and clearly consume resources in the form of medical treatment, work days lost, and so forth-may be less acceptable than the nebulous possibility of risk transpiring many decades down the road. The immediacy of disease raises the call for action-witness the recent clamor over microbial infections from fast-food hamburgers. Another factor is that some types of risk appear to be particularly dreaded, regardless of what the data show about likelihood and mortality rates. Many people in this country, for example, appear to have a deep-seated fear of cancer. Any time that the term "cancer" is even vaguely associated with a risk, no matter how uncertain the data may be, some people will demand that all possible steps be taken to eliminate that risk. The cancer risk associated with chlorine and its by-products triggers a demand from certain sectors of the population for removal of the chemical from public water supplies, even though such removal would increase the risk of immediate microbial disease.

An additional critical element in weighing these risks is the issue of who suffers each risk. Although risks in drinking water are borne by the same population in general-everyone must consume water to survive (though some can afford to purchase bottled water)-there is a difference in the subpopulations most vulnerable to each risk. Microbial disease would be injurious to many people, but especially to children, the frail elderly, and those with immune system deficiencies such as AIDS. The fatalities in the Milwaukee cryptosporidium outbreak in 1993 were concentrated among people with AIDS. Cancer from [trihalomethanes], by contrast, is principally a threat to middle-aged adults who have consumed chlorinated water over many decades. As our society ages, cancers later in life may be of greater concern to a growing share of the electorate.

Similarly, the burden of risk alleviation may not be shared equally by different subgroups of the population. Were restrictions to be placed on the amount of chlorine that could be added to water supplies, lower-income and smaller communities and households, with more limited resources, would be less able to expend the necessary funds to switch to an alternative disinfection or to purchase bottled water. These communities and households could be forced to lower the chlorine level to comply with the regulations without adequate protection against microbial disease. In addition, the solutions for the water systems of large communities may not be easily transferable to small systems. Given a choice, some communities might prefer to accept the long-term risk of chlorination rather than face the immediate risk of waterborne disease; others might decide differently.

Even in communities that could implement new alternatives to chlorine, the economic burden would not be easy to bear. Meeting federal requirements from the Safe Drinking Water Act and its amendments has been estimated to cost the nation's water suppliers more than $14 billion per year which is ultimately passed on to the consumer of taxpayer. Converting the nation from chlorination to ozonation might add another $6 billion per year. Historically, Americans have enjoyed cheaper water than in many other countries, but many families will find their water bills rising as alternatives are sought to the present treatment technology. Water is not a commodity that consumers can do without, so a rise in price would most likely cause hardship for some American families. And increased regulations and restrictions placed on chlorination systems may induce the outlays of additional funds for drinking water that would otherwise have been spent for other public health activities or household purchases.

* * *

The concern over trihalomethane levels has spurred increasing use of alternative disinfectants. For example, both the state of Kansas and the Metropolitan Water District of Southern California now use chloramination for the maintenance of a disinfection residual in their distribution systems. Ozone disinfection processes, widely used in Europe, have also been on the increase in the United States. Recent improvements in the reliability and efficiency of ozonation technology, coupled with its high efficacy against resistant protozoan cysts and viruses, have strengthened the desirability of this chlorine alternative.

New options include modifications to the chlorination process to reduce chlorine by-products. Particular attention has focused on reducing the level of organic precursors in the water to protect against trihalomethane production. Once THMs are formed, they are very difficult to remove, so the goal is to prevent their initial formation. One way to try to accomplish this is to pretreat the source water, with technologies such as granular activated carbon or other absorbents, to remove organic materials before the water enters the disinfection process. Another solution under investigation involves moving the chlorination step to a point in time after much of the organic material has been removed through the other treatment stages.

Again, however, these technological alternatives pose their own countervailing risks. For example, prechlorination of low-quality water is important to maintaining the efficacy of the other disinfection stages. This step is essential in removing algae and other growth from the treatment machinery and equipment and ensuring their optimum function and efficiency. Without this step, the effectiveness of the disinfection process in preventing microbial diseases may be severely compromised.

* * *

* * * But would these options be worse than the process they replace? None of the chemical alternatives has both the biocidal and residual properties of chlorine, nor many of its secondary benefits. Even less is known about the toxicological properties of these alternatives and their by-products than is understood for chlorine. And reducing chlorination without effective alternatives may unleash deadly microbial diseases. * * *

NOTES

1. *EPA's DBP rulemaking.* Following several years of study and debate, EPA promulgated a final rule for disinfection byproducts (DBP) in December 1998, setting new, lower standards for the permissible levels of total trihalomethanes (TTHMs), including chloroform, in drinking water. EPA, National Primary Drinking Water Regulations: Disinfectants and Disinfection Byproducts, 63 Fed. Reg. 69390 (1998). However, EPA called this a "Stage 1" rule, because the permissible residual DBP levels would not impair water suppliers' ability to disinfect water. Lower levels of DBP, which might affect disinfection, are reserved for a subsequent "Stage 2." The Stage 1/Stage 2 division has three important features for the drinking water regulation: (a) it reflects EPA's recognition that it had insufficient information to perform an adequate risk-risk analysis and its desire to move forward with some degree of regulation in the interim; (b) the division was the result of regulatory negotiation, which recommended a two-stage process due to lack of information; and (c) since the Stage 1 rule did not impair disinfection, the cost-benefit analysis was able to focus only on the benefits of reduced risk of cancer and to ignore the trade-off of cancer and microbial risks.

2. *A threshold for chloroform.* EPA's rulemaking acknowledges that a significant body of testing suggests that chloroform may have a carcinogenic threshold. However, it was unwilling to take what it regarded as a major departure from its usual MCLG policy on the basis of existing information. This question, too, was put over for Stage 2. 63 Fed. Reg. at 69401. One interesting aspect of the threshold debate is that the chloroform cancer threshold may be *higher* than the current technology-based MCL; since the current MCL permits full disinfection, the risk-risk trade-off might become moot.

The D.C. Circuit relied on the requirement in the 1996 amendments that MCLGs and MCLs be based on "the best available peer-reviewed science," 42 U.S.C. § 300g-1(b)(3)(A), to overturn the chloroform MCLG in *Chlorine Chemistry Council v. EPA*, 206 F.3d 1286 (D.C. Cir. 2000). In the DBP rule, EPA had retained its zero MCLG for chloroform, following its usual default assumption that it is a non-threshold carcinogen, despite its previously stated view that there exists compelling evidence that chloroform in fact has a threshold. EPA explained that it was facing a legislative deadline and did not want to depart from its usual policy without further study. The court held that this course of action violated the "best available" evidence standard. Is this case an isolated example of EPA engaging in bad rulemaking under a deadline, or does it bespeak the court's willingness to use the risk assessment provisions to overturn agency action that it considers unjustified?

3. *Risk-risk choices.* EPA clearly recognizes the need to undertake some risk-risk comparisons to evaluate the relative effects of microbials and of disinfection byproducts. Procedurally, how should it go about making that judgment in the Stage 2 DBP process? Is the negotiating committee a good tool for this? What substantive standard should it apply? What other data would you need? What about risk distribution and susceptible populations?

4. Congress specifically recognized the DBP problem in the 1996 amendments to the SDWA. *See* 42 U.S.C. § 300g-1(b)(2), (5), (6), (8). What guidance does Congress give to EPA? How does it compare to the guidance for contaminants generally?

Interestingly, on the question of radon in drinking water, Congress *blocked* EPA's proposed radon regulations, even though radon, unlike chlorine, has no countervailing benefits. *See* 42 U.S.C. § 300g-1(b)(13). For helpful commentary on these provisions, *see* A. Dan Tarlock, *Safe Drinking Water: A Federalism Perspective*, 21 WM. & MARY ENVTL. L. & POL'Y REV. 233, 257-59 (1997).

5. *Chlorine: radix malorum.* Many environmental activists have noted that chlorine is a building block of many of the toxic chemicals of greatest environmental concern: chloroform and other THMs, dioxins, organochlorine pesticides like DDT, vinyl chloride, chlorofluorocarbons (CFCs), polychlorinated biphenyls (PCBs), and so on. It is also highly toxic in itself. In the spirit of pollution prevention, it has been suggested that chlorine *per se* be phased out of use for any or for any but the most necessary purposes. For

discussion of proposed chlorine bans, *see* Alana M. Fuierer, Comment, *The Anti-Chlorine Campaign in the Great Lakes: Should Chlorinated Compounds Be Guilty until Proven Innocent?*, 43 BUFF. L. REV. 181 (1995); Gordon Graff, *The Chlorine Controversy*, 98(1) TECH. REV. 54 (Jan. 1995); and the Greenpeace USA website, http://www.greenpeaceusa.org/toxics/overview.htm.

E. The Clean Water Act

The Clean Water Act (CWA) is one of the two major pieces of federal pollution control legislation, the other being the Clean Air Act. The CWA is a long and complex statute, and it has spawned even longer and more complex administrative structures that directly control the behavior of regulated entities. In very general outline, the CWA, as originally enacted in 1972 and subsequently amended, requires that sources of water pollution are required to obtain discharge permits from EPA or from a state operating under an EPA-approved program. The permits require multiple stages of increasingly stringent control of pollutants. For so-called "conventional" water pollutants (sewage effluents, for example), the first stage is the level of pollution achievable by the "best practicable technology"; the next stage, to be achieved at a later date, is the level achievable by the "best available technology"(BAT); then the water quality is to be made suitable for fishing and swimming ("fishable-swimmable"); and finally discharge of pollutants is to be eliminated entirely.

Toxic water pollutants, however, are managed somewhat differently. The 1972 CWA provided for rigorous, uncompromising health-based standards.[57] The stringency of these standards, while very much intended by Congress,[58] paralyzed EPA because of the lack of needed data and the difficulty of

---

[57] The 1972 version read, in relevant part:

> (2) * * * the Administrator, * * * shall publish a proposed effluent standard (or a prohibition) for [each listed] pollutant or combination of pollutants which shall take into account the toxicity of the pollutant, its persistence, degradability, the usual or potential presence of the affected organisms in any waters, the importance of the affected organisms and the nature and extent of the effect of the toxic pollutant on such organisms, and he shall publish a notice for a public hearing on such proposed standard to be held within thirty days. As soon as possible after such hearing, but not later than six months after publication of the proposed effluent standard (or prohibition), unless the Administrator finds, on the record, that a modification of such proposed standard (or prohibition) is justified based upon a preponderance of evidence adduced at such hearings, such standard (or prohibition) shall be promulgated.
> * * *
>
> (4) Any effluent standard promulgated under this section shall be at that level which the Administrator determines provides an ample margin of safety.

[58] Other evidence of special stringency for toxics can be found in §§ 101(a)(3) and 301(*l*) of the Act.

establishing a cause-and-effect relationship between pollutants and health effects, especially under the procedural burdens that Congress also imposed.[59] Frustrated by what it regarded as EPA's dithering on toxic water pollutants, NRDC filed several lawsuits against EPA to force it to act. They were finally resolved in a consent decree (signed by District Judge Flannery, and hence known as the Flannery Decree) in which EPA agreed to regulate a specified number of toxic pollutants by dates certain.[60] This energized EPA to pursue toxic water pollutants aggressively, and it energized Congressional support for renewed attention to toxic pollutants in the 1977 Amendments to the CWA.[61]

1. Best Available Technology

The legal standard proposed by EPA, adopted in the consent decree, and later enacted in the amended section 307 was radically different from the 1972 statutory language.[62] Read the regulatory sections of the current CWA that deal most directly with toxic water pollutants: sections 301(a),(b)(2),(c),(*l*), 304(a),(b)(2),(g),(*l*), 307. What is the regulatory schedule that applies to toxic water pollutants? What is the legal standard that applies to toxic water pollutants? How does the standard differ from other pollutants?

The key term, obviously, is *best available technology economically achievable*, or BAT. What does the statute say about the meaning of BAT? In *Chemical Manufacturers Ass'n v. EPA*, 870 F.2d 177, *modified*, 885 F.2d 253 (5th Cir. 1989), an appellate court held that "Congress intended these limitations to be based on the performance of the single best-performing plant in an industrial field." It went on:

> * * * we reject the petitioners' premise that the limitations are unachievable unless all plants in the data-base have met the limitations. The legislative history of the CWA indicates that the "best available technology" refers to the single best performing plant in an industrial field. The EPA urges that because the Act and the legislative history do not provide more particular guidance, it was free to determine the "best" plant on a pollutant-by-pollutant basis. * * * The EPA's interpretation of the Act is rational and is not precluded by the legislative history.

---

[59] This is not the last time that you will see Congress exchanging substantive stringency, to please environmentalists, for procedural complexity, to please industry. This trade-off is perhaps the defining characteristic of the Toxic Substances Control Act.

[60] NRDC v. Train, 8 ERC (BNA) 2120, 2122 (D.D.C. 1976), *rev'd in part on other grounds sub nom.* NRDC v. Costle, 561 F.2d 904 (D.C. Cir. 1977).

[61] The story of the Flannery Decree is lucidly told in Rosemary O'Leary, *The Courts and the EPA: The Amazing "Flannery Decision,"* 5(1) NATURAL RESOURCES & ENVT. 18 (Summer 1990).

[62] It is worth asking whether this approach-EPA and interest groups deciding among themselves what the policy should be, and Congress tagging along afterwards to ratify their deal-is an appropriate way to make environmental policy.

* * * [Thus,] an exceedance by one of the data-base plants is irrelevant so long as another data-base plant demonstrates that the limitations are achievable.

870 F.2d at 239. What are the pros and cons of the BAT standard imposed by the 1977 Amendments to the CWA? If Congress adopted it to remedy the failure of the 1972 health-based standards, will the technology-based standard fall prey to problems of inefficiency, failing to promote pollution prevention, stifling innovation, and ignoring the health-based reasons for regulation in the first place?[63]

Central to the operation of a BAT standard is the proper categorization of industries and industrial processes. The Supreme Court addressed this question in the context of EPA's authority to permit variances (basically, time extensions) from effluent standards for toxics. EPA had permitted the variances at issue based on so-called fundamentally different factors (FDF), that is, the claim that the source of the toxic pollutant is fundamentally different from other sources of the pollutant on which the technological feasibility of the standard was based.

CHEMICAL MANUFACTURERS ASSOCIATION V. NATURAL RESOURCES DEFENSE COUNCIL

470 U.S. 116 (1985)

Justice WHITE delivered the opinion of the Court.

The Clean Water Act, the basic federal legislation dealing with water pollution, assumed its present form as the result of extensive amendments in 1972 and 1977. For direct dischargers—those who expel waste directly into navigable waters—the Act calls for a two-phase program of technology-based effluent limitations, commanding that dischargers comply with the best practicable control technology currently available (BPT) by July 1, 1977, and subsequently meet the generally more stringent effluent standard consistent with the best available technology economically achievable (BAT).

* * *

Thus, for both direct and indirect dischargers, EPA considers specific statutory factors and promulgates regulations creating categories and classes of sources and setting uniform discharge limitations for those classes and categories. Since application of the statutory factors varies on the basis of the industrial process used and a variety of other factors, EPA has faced substantial burdens in collecting information adequate to create categories and

---

[63] *See* Howard Latin, *Regulatory Failure, Administrative Incentives, and the New Clean Air Act*, 21 ENVTL. L. 1647, 1661 (1991) (summarizing others' views); Christopher H. Schroeder, *In the Regulation of Manmade Carcinogens, If Feasibility Analysis is the Answer, What is the Question?*, 88 MICH. L. REV. 1483 (1990) (reviewing FRANK B. CROSS, ENVIRONMENTALLY INDUCED CANCER AND THE LAW (1989)).

classes suitable for uniform effluent limits, a burden complicated by the time deadlines it has been under to accomplish the task. Some plants may find themselves classified within a category of sources from which they are, or claim to be, fundamentally different in terms of the statutory factors. As a result, EPA has developed its FDF variance as a mechanism for ensuring that its necessarily rough-hewn categories do not unfairly burden atypical plants.[64] Any interested party may seek an FDF variance to make effluent limitations either more or less stringent if the standards applied to a given source, because of factors fundamentally different from those considered by EPA in setting the limitation, are either too lenient or too strict.

The 1977 amendments to the Clean Water Act reflected Congress' increased concern with the dangers of toxic pollutants. The Act, as then amended, allows specific statutory modifications of effluent limitations for economic and water-quality reasons in §§ 301(c) and (g). Section 301(*l*), however, added by the 1977 amendments, provides:

> The Administrator may not modify any requirement of this section as it applies to any specific pollutant which is on the toxic pollutant list under section 307(a)(1) of this Act.

In the aftermath of the 1977 amendments, EPA continued its practice of occasionally granting FDF variances for BPT requirements. The Agency also promulgated regulations explicitly allowing FDF variances for pretreatment standards and BAT requirements. Under these regulations, EPA granted FDF variances, but infrequently.

---

[64] The challenged FDF variance regulation with respect to indirect dischargers, 40 CFR § 403.13 (1984), provides in relevant part: * * *

"(d) Factors considered fundamentally different. Factors which may be considered fundamentally different are:

"(1) The nature or quality of pollutants contained in the raw waste load of the User's process wastewater:

"(2) The volume of the User's process wastewater and effluent discharged;

"(3) Non-water quality environmental impact of control and treatment of the User's raw waste load;

"(4) Energy requirements of the application of control and treatment technology;

"(5) Age, size, land availability, and configuration as they relate to the User's equipment or facilities; processes employed; process changes; and engineering aspects of the application of control technology;

"(6) Cost of compliance with required control technology.

"(e) Factors which will not be considered fundamentally different. A variance request or portion of such a request under this section may not be granted on any of the following grounds:

"(1) The feasibility of installing the required waste treatment equipment within the time the Act allows;

"(2) The assertion that the Standards cannot be achieved with the appropriate waste treatment facilities installed, if such assertion is not based on factors listed in paragraph (d) of this section;

"(3) The User's ability to pay for the required waste treatment; or

"(4) The impact of a Discharge on the quality of the [publicly owned treatment works'] receiving waters." * * *

* * *

Neither are we convinced that FDF variances threaten to frustrate the goals and operation of the statutory scheme set up by Congress. The nature of FDF variances has been spelled out both by this Court and by the Agency itself. The regulation explains that its purpose is to remedy categories which were not accurately drawn because information was either not available to or not considered by the Administrator in setting the original categories and limitations. 40 C.F.R. § 403.13(b) (1984). An FDF variance does not excuse compliance with a correct requirement, but instead represents an acknowledgment that not all relevant factors were taken sufficiently into account in framing that requirement originally, and that those relevant factors, properly considered, would have justified—indeed, required—the creation of a subcategory for the discharger in question. As we have recognized, the FDF variance is a laudable corrective mechanism, "an acknowledgment that the uniform . . . limitation was set without reference to the full range of current practices, to which the Administrator was to refer." *EPA v. National Crushed Stone Assn.*, 449 U.S. 64, 77-78 (1980). It is, essentially, not an exception to the standard-setting process, but rather a more fine-tuned application of it.

We are not persuaded by NRDC's argument that granting FDF variances is inconsistent with the goal of uniform effluent limitations under the Act. Congress did intend uniformity among sources in the same category, demanding that "similar point sources with similar characteristics . . . meet similar effluent limitations." EPA, however, was admonished to take into account the diversity within each industry by establishing appropriate subcategories.

NRDC concedes that EPA could promulgate rules under § 307 of the Act creating a subcategory for each source which is fundamentally different from the rest of the class under the factors the EPA must consider in drawing categories. The same result is produced by the issuance of an FDF variance for the same failure properly to subdivide a broad category. Since the dispute is therefore reduced to an argument over the means used by EPA to define subcategories of indirect dischargers in order to achieve the goals of the Act, these are particularly persuasive cases for deference to the Agency's interpretation.

NRDC argues, echoing the concern of the Court of Appeals below, that allowing FDF variances will render meaningless the § 301(*l*) prohibition against modifications on the basis of economic and water-quality factors. That argument ignores the clear difference between the purpose of FDF waivers and that of §§ 301(c) and (g) modifications, a difference we explained in *National Crushed Stone*. A discharger that satisfies the requirements of § 301(c) qualifies for a variance "simply because [it] could not afford a compliance cost that is not fundamentally different from those the Administrator has already considered" in creating a category and setting an effluent limitation. A § 301(c) modification forces "a displacement of calculations already performed, not because those calculations were incomplete or had unexpected effects, but only because the costs happened to fall on one particular operator, rather than on another who might be economically better off." FDF variances are specifically unavailable for the grounds that would justify the statutory modifications. 40 C.F.R. §§ 403.13(e)(3) and (4) (1984). Both a source's inability to pay the foreseen costs, grounds for a § 301(c) modification, and the lack of a significant impact on water quality, grounds for a § 301(g) modification, are irrelevant under FDF variance procedures.

EPA and CMA point out that the availability of FDF variances makes bearable the enormous burden faced by EPA in promulgating categories of sources and setting effluent limitations. Acting under stringent timetables, EPA must collect and analyze large amounts of technical information concerning complex industrial categories. Understandably, EPA may not be apprized of and will fail to consider unique factors applicable to atypical plants during the categorical rulemaking process, and it is thus important that EPA's nationally binding categorical pretreatment standards for indirect dischargers be tempered with the flexibility that the FDF variance mechanism offers, a mechanism repugnant to neither the goals nor the operation of the Act.

NOTES

1. *Categories.* Why are categories so important in the CWA? Now take a look at § 301 of the statute. What happened to the holding of *CMA v. NRDC* when Congress reauthorized the Clean Water Act in 1987?

2. *Uniformity.* The *CMA* case highlights one of the most persistent problems with a technology-based system, the complexity of the required analysis of proper categories and subcategories of industrial processes and of the alternative technologies to the existing ones. This is particularly the case when individualized determinations must be made, as is the case for variances:

> Under the FWPCA technology-based regulatory program for industrial dischargers, the EPA must devise five separate sets of categorical standards tailored to the technological and economic characteristics of several hundred subcategories of polluting industries. * * *
>
> * * * The Supreme Court [has affirmed the need for uniformity.] Expert agencies are entitled to deference in the interpretation of their statutory mandates; Congress emphasized the need for uniformity in the treatment of comparable dischargers; Congress intended all facilities within each subcategory to achieve the performance of the best plants in that subcategory; and "[t]he petitioners' view of the Act would place an impossible [administrative] burden on EPA."[65]

---

[65] E.I. du Pont de Nemours & Co. v. Train, 430 U.S. 112 (1977).

Despite the arguments it cited in favor of uniform treatments, the Court [in *CMA*] approved the EPA's creation of an individualized "fundamentally different factors" (FDF) variance that allows a firm to demonstrate either significantly different engineering and technical constraints or significantly different compliance costs from those used to establish the categorical limits. In *EPA v. National Crushed Stone Ass'n*, the Supreme Court approved the EPA's decision to exclude consideration in FDF proceedings of each facility's financial capacity to absorb the required compliance costs. Justice White correctly reasoned that FDF variances based on claims by individual dischargers of financial incapacity would frustrate the statutory intent to upgrade the level of industrial pollution control efforts. The Supreme Court again stressed the congressional insistence on uniformity within categories of dischargers:

> [T]he approach of giving variances to pollution controls based on economic grounds has long ago shown itself to be a risky course: All too often, the variances became a tool used by powerful political interests to obtain so many exemptions for pollution control standards and timetables on the filmsiest [sic] of pretenses that they become meaningless. In short, with variances, exceptions to pollution cleanup can become the rule, meaning further tragic delay in stopping the destruction of our environment.[66]

Unfortunately, the Court failed to recognize that an individualized variance procedure for differences in technical characteristics and compliance costs presents a similar potential for abuse. The regulations at issue covered about 4,800 crushed stone and 6,000 coal facilities. Under the current FDF treatment, state or EPA regional administrators determine whether any of those dischargers should be granted particularized variances, and there is no mechanism for assuring that facilities with comparable characteristics will receive comparable emissions limits. * * *

Howard Latin, *Ideal Versus Real Regulatory Efficiency: Implementation of Uniform Standards and "Fine-Tuning" Regulatory Reforms*, 37 STAN. L. REV. 1267, 1314-16 (1985); *see also* Howard A. Latin, *The Feasibility of Occupational Health Standards: An Essay on Legal Decisionmaking Under Uncertainty,* 78 NW. U.L. REV. 583 (1983). Does this mean that the overall BAT strategy is unworkable? If so, why did EPA and Congress embrace it?

3. *Alternatives-based regulation.* While BAT, like feasibility under the OSH Act, is appropriately termed a technology-based standard, it can also be thought of as a *alternatives-based* standard, inasmuch as it requires the

---

[66] EPA v. National Crushed Stone Assn'n, 449 U.S. 64, 81 (1980).

comparison ("best") of available technologies. Oliver Houck argues that alternatives-based standards suffer from the weaknesses of not knowing where to stop looking for alternatives (different production techniques, different processes altogether, different products for achieving the same functionality?) and of being exhausting, often speculative work for agencies.[67] For a taste of the complexity of the BAT process, consider the following description of EPA's task in regulating the paper industry:

> Dioxin and furans in waste water from pulp and paper mills could be greatly reduced under two technology options included in Environmental Protection Agency guidelines, the agency said July 15 (61 FR 36835).

> EPA said dioxin and furans in waste water discharges from bleached papergrade kraft and soda mills could be cut 95 percent and 99 percent, respectively, from 1992 levels under the technology options that involve substituting chlorine dioxide for chlorine. * * *

> The first option involves completely substituting chlorine dioxide for chlorine. The second is the one taken from the Dec. 17, 1993, proposal and includes oxygen delignification or extended cooking with the substitution.

> Final effluent standards and guidelines for mills in the pulp and paper industry will be issued in phases consisting of several subcategories with the bleached papergrade kraft and soda subcategory and the papergrade sulfite subcategory coming first, the EPA notice said. It is in these two categories that EPA has acquired the new data for several technologies including "complete chlorine dioxide substitution (without oxygen delignification); oxygen delignification (OD) or extended cooking plus complete chlorine dioxide substitution; extended cooking plus OD plus complete chlorine dioxide substitution; OD plus ozone bleaching plus complete substitution with chlorine dioxide; and totally chlorine-free (TCF) processes," the notice said.

> * * *

> For the papergrade sulfite subcategory, EPA has new bleach plant data for elemental chlorine-free processes and totally chlorine-free processes, the notice said.

> Additionally, the agency said it may segment further the mills in the papergrade sulfite subcategory because comments and new data reveal that the initial technologies being considered may not be suitable for all such mills. EPA will seek further comment on this matter. The three segments being considered are pulp and paper production at:

---

[67] *See* Oliver A. Houck, *Of Bats, Birds and B-A-T: The Convergent Evolution of Environmental Law*, 63 MISS. L.J. 403, 420-31, 444-62 (1994).

- Papergrade sulfite mills using an acidic cooking liquor of calcium, magnesium, or sodium sulfite;
- Papergrade sulfite mills using an acidic cooking liquor of ammonium sulfite; and
- Specialty grade sulfite mills.

EPA said the technology basis for the products made by the first segment "is likely to be totally chlorine-free bleaching, as proposed." One option being considered is oxygen and peroxide-enhanced extraction, followed by peroxide bleaching.

For the second segment, the agency said totally chlorine-free bleaching "is not demonstrated and may not be feasible for the full range of products" from U.S. ammonium-based sulfite mills. "EPA expects to promulgate bleach plant effluent limitations for dioxin, furan, and chlorinated phenolic compounds for the ammonium-based segment," the notice said. The option being considered for this segment is substituting chlorine dioxide for chlorine, peroxide-enhanced extraction, and elimination of hypochlorite, the notice said.

For the specialty grade sulfite mills, EPA said data show "pulp and product characteristics have not been achieved using [totally chlorine-free] bleaching technologies," although the research is continuing. But the agency does not expect to issue final effluent limitation guidelines and standards for this subcategory in 1996. However, EPA said alternative bleaching processes developed as a result of the research "should contribute to substantial reductions from current operating practices in the generation and release of pollutants, including, for example, air emissions of chloroform and discharge of chlorinated organic compounds in waste waters."

* * *

In addition, the agency is considering a voluntary incentives program to reward mills that further reduce pollutant discharges by installing advanced pollution-prevention technologies.

Water Pollution: Technology Options Could Reduce Dioxin, Furans from Pulp, Paper Mills, 27 ENVT. REP. (BNA) 610 (1996).

4. *Pretreatment.* Water pollution is an even more complex problem than it may at first appear, because toxics can reach waterways through several routes. The most obvious, and the primary focus of the CWA, are point sources that discharge directly to a waterway. Another and increasingly important source is "nonpoint" pollution, that is, run-off from roads, parking lots, lawns, and farms.

The CWA addresses two additional pathways. First, toxic pollutants can be discharged to a sewer, a "publicly owned treatment works" (POTW) in the CWA lexicon. Discharge to a POTW presents several potential problems: it may interfere with the operation of the POTW (say, poisoning bacteria); it may pass through the POTW without being eliminated or detoxified; easy disposal is a disincentive to pollution prevention and byproduct reclamation; and it makes tracing the polluter very difficult. How does the CWA address this problem? *See* §§ 301(b)(1)(A)(ii), 307(b). What standards apply to "pretreatment"? What is the role of cost? Why can the discharger take account of the effects of the POTW itself? If the toxic pollutant does not actually interfere with the POTW, however, why require pretreatment?

Second, and partly due to the imperfections of the pretreatment system, toxics can be found in sewage sludge and can enter the environment when sludge is incinerated, landfilled, or used as fertilizer. The CWA addresses this pathway, as well:

> * * * In 1987, Congress enacted another amendment to the CWA, the Water Quality Act, to require the EPA to issue specific regulations for the use and disposal of sewage sludge. Under the amended Act, the EPA must identify and set numeric limits for toxic pollutants that "may be present in sewage sludge in concentrations which may adversely affect public health or the environment," and establish management practices for the use and disposal of sludge containing these toxic pollutants. 33 U.S.C. § 1345(d)(2). Its regulations are to be issued in two phases-the first round to be promulgated "on the basis of available information," the second to encompass pollutants unaddressed by the first round. * * *

Leather Industries of America v. EPA, 40 F.3d 392, 394-95 (D.C. Cir. 1994). EPA's sludge regulations were largely rejected in *Leather Industries*, and have since been repromulgated. EPA, Standards for the Use or Disposal of Sewage Sludge, 60 Fed. Reg. 54764 (1995).

2. Water Toxics in the Courts

EPA's ability to regulate toxic substances depends heavily on the leeway that the courts grant the agency in judicial review. The searching review that we have seen OSHA receive from the Supreme Court and appellate courts has nearly paralyzed that agency. Under the Clean Water Act, by contrast, EPA has been given considerable discretion. As you read the next two cases, look for the statutory basis for the courts' deference to agency judgments.

RESERVE MINING CO. V. EPA

514 F.2d 492 (8th Cir. 1975) (*en banc*)

[The text of *Reserve Mining* can be found in Chapter 4 (Judicial Role), *supra*.]

ENVIRONMENTAL DEFENSE FUND V. EPA

598 F.2d 62 (D.C. 1978)

TAMM, Circuit Judge:

We are called upon in these consolidated cases to review challenges to the Environmental Protection Agency's (EPA) first regulations prohibiting discharge into the nation's waterways of a toxic substance, polychlorinated biphenyls (PCBs), under the Federal Water Pollution Control Act Amendments. For the reasons that follow, we uphold the EPA's regulations.

I. FACTS AND PRIOR PROCEEDINGS

A. Factual Background on PCBs

PCBs are a group of related chlorinated hydrocarbon chemicals useful in several industrial processes and toxic to a wide variety of organisms, including man. The chemistry of PCBs figures prominently in this case and will be discussed below. At this point, we need note only that PCBs fall into two chemical categories: PCBs with a low chlorine content (less chlorinated PCBs) and PCBs with a high chlorine content (more chlorinated PCBs). More chlorinated PCBs have been manufactured and used since 1929. For decades, they served in a variety of industrial uses such as ink solvents, plasticizers, adhesives, and textile coatings, but their principal use was and is in electrical equipment. PCBs are nonflammable liquids that are highly resistant to electrical current. Therefore, they have been widely used to fill electrical devices such as capacitors and transformers, aiding in the storage of electrical charge without creating the fire hazard that would occur if a flammable filler were used.

Awareness of the danger from PCBs to the environment and to man was slow to develop. Although large quantities of PCBs were manufactured and leaked into the environment, the PCBs detected in the environment were long mistaken for pesticide residues, which they resemble chemically. It was not until the mid-1960's that the presence of PCBs in the environment and the harm they inflict were recognized and distinguished from the pesticide problem. As we shall discuss below, it became apparent from scientific studies that more chlorinated PCBs built up to dangerous levels in the sediments of waterways, in the water, in fish, and ultimately in humans, creating a serious risk of death for aquatic organisms and disease (particularly cancer) for man.

In 1971-72, in response to public and government pressure, PCBs manufacturers and users took initial steps to reduce the PCBs danger. Manufacture was shifted from the more chlorinated PCBs to the less chlorinated PCBs, because it was hoped that less chlorinated PCBs were less dangerous. PCBs use was limited to closed electrical equipment, where the need was greatest and the leakage was least. Some effort was made to control discharge of PCBs into waterways.

However, in 1972-74 manufacturers were curtailing their efforts to find acceptable substitutes for PCBs, and manufacture of less chlorinated PCBs continued at high volumes, *e.g.*, forty million pounds in 1974. EPA's initial effort to control discharge of PCBs into waterways, the precursor of the proceeding now on review, ended in failure in 1973-74. Discharges of PCBs into the nation's waterways continued.

Developments in the early and mid-1970's heightened the public concern about PCBs and resulted in new regulatory efforts in late 1975 and early 1976. Monitoring of residues in fish revealed that industrial discharges of PCBs were rendering fish in many waterways unhealthy for human consumption. This monitoring culminated in a state proceeding, in which New York's Department of Environmental Conservation found that discharges of PCBs by General Electric, a major manufacturer of electrical equipment containing PCBs, had rendered most upper Hudson River fish dangerous to eat. Similar situations threatened the fishing industry in the Great Lakes and elsewhere.

While the General Electric case was pending, a national conference on PCBs hazards was held in November 1975 that resulted in greater awareness of the nationwide threat posed by PCBs and contributed to the renewed EPA effort to regulate and control PCBs discharges. The EPA regulations now on review are the culmination of that effort.

Following the 1975 renewal of EPA's regulatory effort, further information accumulated with respect to the health hazards posed by PCBs. Moreover, substitutes for PCBs were developed in this country and in Japan that would serve adequately in electrical equipment without creating a fire hazard. Congress became impatient and wrote a special provision devoted solely to PCBs into the Toxic Substances Control Act of 1976, 15 U.S.C. 2605(e). Considering that there are few statutes aimed so particularly at control of an individual chemical, we construe this provision as a significant comment on the failure of existing regulatory mechanisms. Failure of existing regulatory mechanisms to control PCBs contributed materially both to passage of the preventive sections of the Toxic Substances Control Act and to strengthening, in 1977, of the toxics provision of Federal Water Pollution Control Act Amendments of 1972. * * * In sum, the history of EPA's PCBs proceedings is a history of frustration of a congressional mandate for action. Regulatory steps that Congress expected to take little more than one year took four years.

* * *

Following the failure in 1974 of its initial regulatory efforts, and consistent with the regulatory program and consent decree eventually adopted, EPA set out in 1975 to investigate PCBs more thoroughly. It commissioned a survey of the scientific literature on PCBs, and sponsored a national conference on PCBs in November 1975. It engaged Dr. Ian Nisbet, an expert in toxicity of PCBs, to prepare a Criteria Document. The Criteria Document served to collect and focus past research on more chlorinated

PCBs, but as we will discuss, it contained substantially less material on less chlorinated PCBs.

Based on these preparations, EPA proposed effluent standards for PCBs discharges on July 14, 1976. The proposed standards allowed on the average no more than one part per billion of PCBs in certain discharges by manufacturers of electrical equipment, and prohibited any PCBs in other discharges by manufacturers of electrical equipment and in all discharges by manufacturers of PCBs. The proposed regulations made no distinction between more chlorinated PCBs and less chlorinated PCBs.

* * *

Toxic substances, such as these, create a special danger in several ways. As demonstrated by a number of disasters involving widespread human poisoning or massive kills or contamination of fish, shellfish, birds, and other wildlife, many chemicals discharged into waters are lethal or injurious even in minute doses. Toxic chemicals have been identified repeatedly as a cause of cancer, through studies both of persons exposed to such chemicals on the job and elsewhere, and of animals in the laboratory and the field. Moreover, toxic substances often have characteristics besides toxicity that magnify their danger. These characteristics include (1) physical and chemical factors such as resistance to detoxification by sunlight and water, and mobility in the air and water; and (2) biological factors, such as tendencies not to be safely degraded by organisms, but rather to accumulate in organisms or to degrade into other toxic substances. Finally a most troubling characteristic of toxic substances is how little they are understood by scientists. New discoveries about their nature and effects are made constantly, but existing knowledge seems inadequate to measure their full danger.

* * *

V. EVIDENTIARY BASIS FOR REGULATION OF LESS CHLORINATED PCBs

A. Arguments of the Parties

The principal claim of industry petitioners is that EPA's regulations lack an adequate basis in the record to the extent that they cover less chlorinated PCBs because the record consists, in large part, of studies of related, but different substances (more chlorinated PCBs). In order to rule on this claim, we have no alternative except to venture into a difficult realm of chemistry and toxicology, for, however deferential may be our review, we cannot rule on an issue without a firm grasp of it.

PCBs are a group of related chemicals that have two aspects in common. First, they share a basic chemical structure known as the "biphenyl" structure, consisting of two rings of carbon atoms with hydrogen atoms attached. Second, instead of a simple biphenyl structure PCBs have one or more chlorine atoms substituting for one or more hydrogen atoms. From these two aspects comes the name "polychlorinated biphenyls." PCBs vary with respect to how much chlorine is substituted for hydrogen, ranging from one to ten chlorine atoms per molecule of PCBs.

Commercially, PCBs are manufactured and sold in the form of mixtures. Some mixtures contain predominantly PCBs with few chlorine atoms per molecule; these are termed "less chlorinated PCBs." Other PCBs mixtures contain predominantly PCBs with more chlorine atoms per molecule; these are termed "more chlorinated PCBs."

As we have discussed, more chlorinated PCBs were the main PCBs in use from 1929 until the early 1970's. In the early 1970's, under public and government pressure, PCBs manufacturers and users shifted from more chlorinated to less chlorinated PCBs. The chemical and electrical industries were able to shift relatively rapidly from use of one PCBs mixture to another. However, this shift created the "knowledge gap" that underlies the principal issue in this proceeding. As a practical matter, scientific knowledge about the effects of chemicals cannot keep up with the ability of industrial laboratories to create new ones. Most of the available scientific studies on PCBs concern more chlorinated PCBs, either because the studies were conducted over the decades when more chlorinated PCBs were the main PCBs in use, or because, even after the early 1970's, scientists continued to study the more chlorinated PCBs.

Accordingly, EPA faced a familiar choice in this proceeding. On one hand, it could regulate a substance whose properties were incompletely understood (less chlorinated PCBs) by relying, in major part, upon its knowledge about more familiar substances (more chlorinated PCBs), despite the uncertainties of extrapolation from one substance to another. On the other hand, it could delay regulation until science could more fully explore the risks of the new substance.

Industry petitioners contend that EPA lacked an adequate basis for regulation because of this incompleteness in the scientific knowledge about less chlorinated PCBs mixtures. They argue that EPA "could not have reasonably hoped to regulate Aroclors 1016 and 1242 (less chlorinated PCBs) without commissioning extensive studies on comparative mammalian toxicity. The Agency failed to commission such studies. * * * It is the failure of the Administrator to present studies relating to Aroclors 1016 and 1242 which has led to his attempt to build an elaborate evidentiary house of cards." Petitioners assert, in effect, that EPA cannot rely upon merely suggestive evidence or upon extrapolation from data concerning related substances to justify regulation of the less chlorinated PCBs. They insist that EPA must trace a line of direct causation from each substance it regulates to the danger requiring regulation.

In response, EPA disputes that it must produce such direct proof concerning the danger posed by every regulated substance. EPA notes that the statutory standard calls for setting discharge levels at the level that will provide "an ample margin of safety," and cites prior authority, particularly *Ethyl Corp. v. EPA*, 541 F.2d 1 (D.C. Cir.) (*en banc*), *cert. denied*, 426 U.S.

941 (1976), to support its position. In EPA's view, action need not be delayed while a risky situation persists that is, until the extent of the danger is fully ascertained. EPA contends that ample evidence showing the danger of more chlorinated PCBs together with scientific reasoning and evidence that less chlorinated PCBs share some dangerous qualities of more chlorinated PCBs, constitutes an adequate basis for regulation.

B. Applicable Legal Standards

Section 307(a)(2) sets forth the relevant factors for setting toxic effluent standards. It requires EPA to "take into account" six factors in proposing such standards: "the toxicity of the pollutant, its persistence, degradability, the usual or potential presence of the affected organisms in any waters, the importance of the affected organisms and the nature and extent of the effect of the toxic pollutant on such organisms."

The six factors consist of two groups. The first three factors, toxicity, persistence, and degradability, constitute a carefully drafted tripartite division of the relationship between a toxic substance and the environment. Toxicity concerns the adverse biological effects of toxic substances on life in the environment.[68] Persistence concerns the physical and chemical effects of the nonliving environment (such as sunlight and water) on toxic substances.[69] Degradability concerns the effects of the living environment on toxic substances.[70] Taken together, the three factors were intended to cover comprehensively the fate of toxic substances in the environment and their effects on living organisms.

The last three factors concern "affected organisms" : their presence (usual or potential) "in any waters," their importance, and the effect on them of the toxic substance. Inclusion of these factors requires EPA to focus on specific effects on specific important organisms as well as on the general toxicity, persistence, and degradability of the substance. On the list of "affected organisms" is, of course, man, although other organisms may certainly trigger the last three factors.

Based on these factors, section 307(a)(4) directs EPA to set discharge standards at a level providing an "ample margin of safety." The parties dispute the significance of this important subsection. EPA argues that this

---

[68] Under the rubric of toxicity, EPA takes into account lethal effects, sublethal injurious effects, carcinogenicity, mutagenicity, synergistic effects with other substances, and similar matters.

[69] Under the rubric of persistence, EPA takes into account the physical measurements of the size and history of accumulations of substances in the environment, the capacity of air and water to break down, alter, or transport substances, the tendency of substances to adhere to sediments, and similar physical and chemical matters.

[70] In the discussion of degradability, EPA takes into account the ability of organisms to metabolize or eliminate substances, the toxic intermediates produced during metabolism, bioaccumulation and biomagnification, and similar matters concerning the effects of the organisms on the substances, and the effects that the substances have on organisms, in turn, as a result of degradation, bioaccumulation and similar processes.

subsection gives it latitude to protect against risks that are incompletely understood, in essence to "err" on the side of "overprotection" with respect to known risks in order to provide safety from unknown dangers. Industry petitioners disagree.

On examination of the wording of the statute and the legislative background, we find ourselves in agreement with EPA, whose interpretation of the complex statutes it administers is, of course, entitled to some deference. Despite the problems associated with estimating the scale of incompletely understood dangers, Congress required EPA to set standards that would protect against them.

The "ample margin of safety" standard was taken originally from technical jargon for use in section 112 of the Clean Air Act Amendments of 1970, the hazardous pollutants provision. One academic commentator has traced the history of the use of this term:

> The term [margin of safety] seems to have been borrowed in the first instance from the field of engineering. It is a common engineering practice to incorporate a factor of safety into the design of a structure to "ensure that under full working loads the stress will nowhere exceed a safe working limit." The safety factor is meant to compensate for uncertainties and variabilities in design, materials workmanship, and so forth; the greater the variability, the larger the factor of safety.

> That the use of the term "margin of safety" in section 307(a) was similarly meant by Congress to take into account and compensate for uncertainties and lack of precise predictions in the area of forecasting the effects of toxic pollutants is confirmed by reference to the Clean Air Act. FWPCA section 307(a) is very similar to section 112 of the Clean Air Act. Among the similarities is the requirement in both that any standard set should provide "an ample margin of safety." * * *
>   * * *

> Congress * * * provided in section 307(a) of the FWPCA, as in section 112 of the Clean Air Act, that the "margin of safety" be "ample." This is in contrast to the requirement of section 109 of the Clean Air Act that primary air standards assure an "*adequate* margin of safety"; the requirement of the Safe Drinking Water Act that contaminant levels for public water supplies be set at a level to assure "an *adequate* margin of safety"; or the requirement of section 303(d)(1)(C) of the (1972 Act) that waste load allocations be established at simply "a margin of safety."

> "Ample" is defined as "abundant; plentiful; more than adequate." Clearly Congress intended that in dealing with toxic pollutants that pose a threat to human health, margins of safety should be generous to ensure protection of human health and aquatic ecosystems to the greatest extent possible.

Khristine L. Hall, *The Control of Toxic Pollutants Under the Federal Water Pollution Control Act Amendments of 1972*, 63 IOWA L.REV. 609, 629-30 (1978) (footnotes omitted) (emphasis in original). The foregoing analysis demonstrates that the term "margin of safety" was intended to provide protection "against hazards which research has not yet identified." Moreover, the public and the environment were not to be exposed to anything resembling the maximum risk. Not only was EPA to provide a "margin of safety," but the margin was to be greater than "normal" or "adequate" : the margin was to be "ample." If administrative responsibility to protect against unknown dangers presents a difficult task, indeed, a veritable paradox calling as it does for knowledge of that which is unknown then, the term "margin of safety" is Congress's directive that means be found to carry out the task and to reconcile the paradox. Addition of a generous measure "ample" is Congress's recognition that the EPA would need great latitude in meeting its responsibility.

* * *

D. Adequacy of the Basis for EPA Regulations

1. EPA's policy judgments concerning extrapolation

Industry petitioners contend that EPA lacked an adequate basis for the regulations under review because of the incomplete scientific knowledge about less chlorinated PCBs. In effect, they assert that EPA must demonstrate the toxicity of each chemical it seeks to regulate through studies demonstrating a clear line of causation between a particular chemical and harm to public health or the environment. We do not agree.

The principal basis for rejecting petitioners' views is the wording of the statute. As we stated, the "ample margin of safety" provision directs EPA to guard against incompletely known dangers. EPA, in its expert policy judgment, relied on its knowledge about a known substance to assess the danger of one about which less is known. Petitioners suggest no alternative approach for the agency short of waiting for conclusive proof about the danger posed by a less understood substance. However, by requiring EPA to set standards providing an "ample margin of safety," Congress authorized and, indeed, required EPA to protect against dangers before their extent is conclusively ascertained. The statute thus does not deny EPA the authority that petitioners would have us withhold. Indeed, the legislative history indicates that Congress intended EPA to take into account "the availability of data on similar substances or compounds." Moreover, the Clean Water Act of 1977 supports the notion that extrapolation from data about related substances is a valid approach. In 1977, Congress did not list individual substances, but rather listed families of substances, recognizing that similarities among substances render them susceptible to regulation by group.

Proper deference in judicial review to the scientific expertise of the Administrator also militates against precluding EPA from regulating less chlorinated PCBs on the basis of what is known about related substances. The risks posed by toxic substances, and the extent to which one substance has effects similar to those of related substances, are matters on the frontiers of scientific knowledge. *Industrial Union Dept., AFL-CIO v. Hodgson* [*supra*, Chapter 4]. EPA, not the court, has the technical expertise to decide what inferences may be drawn from the characteristics of related substances and to formulate policy with respect to what risks are acceptable.

Moreover, we are currently in a period of rapid change in assessing and regulating toxic substances. TSCA has established new regulatory mechanisms that may well lead to wholesale estimation of the risks of toxic substances. A holding from this court that only one technique of risk assessment (such as "extensive studies on comparative mammalian toxicity"), is acceptable to the detriment of others would unnecessarily inhibit EPA from evaluating new approaches and formulating appropriate policy.

Finally, in reviewing EPA's policy of regulating less chlorinated PCBs in part on the basis of what is known about more chlorinated PCBs, we must recognize considerations of administrative feasibility. The number of toxic substances subject to regulation seems very large. Regulation of so many substances could well be extremely difficult if EPA were precluded from drawing inferences from available data on well-known, related substances. Moreover, requiring proof of causation for each chemical would force EPA to expend resources in areas that are well-enough known so that inference is acceptable, when those resources could be otherwise employed in areas where knowledge is inadequate. In ruling on the type of proof and procedure required for making individual determinations, the Supreme Court has construed statutes protecting the environment and public health in light of considerations of administrative feasibility.

2. EPA's factual determination of the particular risks here

[The court approved the adequacy of EPA's evidence of toxicity (including (i) evidence bearing on aquatic organisms, (ii) evidence bearing on man, and (iii) evidence concerning the special quality of carcinogenicity), persistence, and degradability.]

* * *

NOTES

1. *Litigation and regulation.* What section of the CWA did the court rely on in *Reserve Mining*? How did the court interpret that section to apply to Reserve Mining's asbestos discharges? What are the drawbacks to that approach?[71]

---

[71] The *Reserve Mining* analysis is helpfully compared to feasibility and cost-benefit analysis in Daniel A. Farber, *Risk Regulation in Perspective: Reserve Mining Revisited*, 21 ENVTL. L. 1321 (1991).

What is the legal standard applied in the PCB case? How does it differ from the standard applied in *Reserve Mining*? Which is easier to meet? Why are two different standards available in the Clean Water Act?

2. Why are PCBs so dangerous? Why are they "toxic" (§ 502(13)), while more common forms of water pollution are not?

3. The *Hercules* case, decided at the same time as *EDF*, was similarly expansive in its reading of the 1972 version of section 307. *See Hercules, Inc. v. EPA*, 598 F.2d 91 (D.C. Cir. 1978). *Hercules* held that the exclusion of cost and feasibility from the considerations enumerated in section 307 was deliberate and that, consequently, they provided no defense to EPA's health-based standards. The court also allowed EPA several other stringent policies, such as reliance on risks to small populations and rejection of receiving water quality as a factor. Much of *Hercules*, therefore, was rendered moot (as to new regulations) by the 1977 Amendments to the CWA. *EDF* has greater long-term significance-why?

4. Is *EDF* consistent with *CMA, supra*? What role did categories have in the *EDF* case?

PROBLEM
MARGIN OF SAFETY

Since the *Reserve Mining, EDF*, and *Hercules* cases were decided, the composition of the federal courts has undergone a substantial change in personnel and in approach to environmental regulation. Nowhere is the change more apparent than the D.C. Circuit, and it is exemplified by the court's treatment of EPA's regulation of sewage sludge, required by the 1987 Amendments. Speaking to one part of the regulation (the caps on concentrations of the toxic metals chromium and selenium, set out in Table 3 of the regulations), the court's approach could not be more different from the foregoing cases:

> Petitioners argue that the 99th percentile caps are not risk-based and therefore exceed the EPA's statutory authority under the enabling legislation. The statute directing the EPA to issue the Round One pollutant limits for sewage sludge provides:
>
>> [T]he Administrator shall identify those toxic pollutants which, on the basis of available information on their toxicity, persistence, concentration, mobility, or potential for exposure, *may be present in sewage sludge in concentrations which may adversely affect public health or the environment,* and propose regulations specifying acceptable management practices for sewage sludge containing each such toxic pollutant and establishing numerical pollutant for each use identified under paragraph (1)(A).

33 U.S.C. § 1345(d)(2)(A)(i) (emphasis added). It further instructs that the management practices and numerical criteria so established "shall be *adequate* to *protect public health and the environment from any reasonably anticipated adverse effects of each pollutant.*" 33 U.S.C. § 1345(d)(2)(D) (emphasis added).

In determining whether the 99th percentile limits in Table 3 are a permissible interpretation of the statute, we turn to *Chevron* and its progeny. We must first determine whether Congress' intent is clear as to the permissibility of the agency's interpretation. If it is not, "the question for the court is whether the agency's answer is based on a permissible construction of the statute."

The EPA does not contest that its statutory authority is limited to promulgating regulations "adequate to protect public health and the environment from any reasonably anticipated adverse effects." 33 U.S.C. § 1345(d)(2)(D). As a matter of *Chevron's* first step, then, there is no dispute that the statute clearly mandates regulations based on "reasonably anticipated adverse effects," and, thus, bearing some relation to risk. The EPA argues, however, that the 99th percentile caps fulfill this mandate of adequate protection from reasonably anticipated adverse effects and bear a relation to risk because they provide "an additional safety mechanism." The EPA suggests two ways in which the 99th percentile caps function as a safety mechanism: (1) they provide a "margin-of-safety" "necessary to ensure 'adequate' protection from these pollutants"; and (2) they prevent current sewage sludge practices-found to be safe in the aggregate-from deteriorating. We conclude, however, that the EPA has failed to show that the 99th percentile caps are risk-related, and thus that they accord with the express mandate of the statute.

First, the EPA states that the 99th percentile caps are based on "a margin-of-safety analysis [that] is consistent with the legislative intent underlying section 405 of the Act." Whatever the underlying legislative intent, we do not view the 99th percentile caps as merely a "margin-of-safety" device. The fact that one cap is more restrictive than another does not automatically make it a "margin of safety." Rather, a margin of safety must be rooted in an analysis of risk. "[T]he Administrator [must] base[ ] his conclusion as to an adequate margin of safety on a reasoned analysis and *evidence of risk.*" *American Petroleum Institute v. Costle*, 665 F.2d 1176, 1187 (D.C.Cir.1981) (emphasis added), *cert. denied*, 455 U.S. 1034 (1982).

The 99th percentile caps are not related to risk. In its initial version of the regulations, the EPA proposed to cap all pollutants at the higher of the pathway-generated numbers and the *98th* percentile level. This proposal came under heavy attack from "a specially convened group of sewage sludge experts," the Land Practices Peer

Review Committee ("PRC"). The PRC, composed of "experts from EPA, academia, environmental groups, and units of state and local government agencies," concluded that the *98th* percentile approach was "arbitrary," would "either over-or under-regulate," and "ha[d] no technical merit." It pointed to the absence of any relation between the percentile numbers and risk, noting that, because the percentile concentrations are purely descriptive, they "may be insignificant from a risk standpoint" just as easily as they "may pose significant risks." We can discern no reason-and the EPA has provided none-why the 99th percentile numbers are less "arbitrary" or have more "technical merit" than the 98th percentile figures. We find no support for the 99th percentile caps as a risk-based margin of safety for chromium and selenium, the two pollutants capped by the 99th percentile in Table 3.

Leather Industries of America, Inc. v. EPA, 40 F.3d 392, 399-401 (D.C. Cir. 1994). The court was equally critical of EPA's use of conservative assumptions regarding application rates and exposure scenarios.

How does the *EDF* court use the "margin of safety" language of the CWA in *EDF*? Was it an appropriate use of the term? What else might "margin of safety" mean?

How does the *Leather Industries* interpretation of "margin of safety" differ from the *EDF* interpretation? Which best reflects Congressional intent? Which is preferable, and why?

3. Case Study: Dioxin and Water Quality Standards

The original federal water pollution legislation was based on the quality of the bodies of water it regulated. By 1972, it was clear that this approach had not succeeded in improving water quality, and so Congress shifted strategies to the technology-based system in sections 301, 304, and 307 of the CWA, on which we have focused to this point. Nevertheless, like some vestigial organ, sections 302 and 303 remain embedded in the statutory structure, retaining a role for water quality and for the states.[72] The water quality standards perform two very different functions. At one level, they act as a safety net or backstop to ensure that technology-based standards do an

---

[72] This account is largely taken from Oliver A. Houck, *The Resurrection of Water Quality Standards-Based Regulation Under the Clean Water Act*, 27 ENVTL. L. REP. (ENVTL. L. INST.) 10329 (1997); Oliver A. Houck, *TMDLs, Are We There Yet?: The Long Road Toward Water Quality-Based Regulation Under the Clean Water Act*, 27 ENVTL. L. REP. (ENVTL. L. INST.) 10391 (1997); Oliver A. Houck *TMDLs III: A New Framework for the Clean Water Act's Ambient Standards Program*, 28 ENVTL. L. REP. (ENVTL. L. INST.) 10415 (1998); and Oliver A. Houck, TMDLs IV: THE FINAL FRONTIER, 29 ENVTL. L. REP. (ENVTL. L. INST.) 10469 (1999).

adequate job of actually improving water quality. (Why is this a concern?) At another level, they provide the platform for improving water quality *beyond* the achievements of even very successful technology-based standards, as a way of redeeming the promise of fishable-swimmable waters.

Sections 302 and 303 set out a multi-step process: see if you can identify them in the statute. Note the areas in which the individual states take the lead, especially identifying appropriate uses of bodies of water, determining the total maximum daily load (TMDL) for pollutants, and developing plans for achieving water quality goals. The water-quality system was until fairly recently a dead letter. The states took little or no action on them, and EPA, preoccupied with the difficulties of promulgating its technology-based standards, did little to press the matter. However, starting with a Seventh Circuit case in 1984,[73] new life has been breathed into the standards under the threat of citizen enforcement setting "constructive" TMDLs of zero.

The 1987 Amendments to the CWA did little to change the regulation of technology-based effluent limitations for toxics, other than to mandate a new round of such standards (§ 304(m)). On the water quality side, however, it required the development of *numerical* (why "numerical"?) water quality criteria for toxics (§ 303(c)(2)(B)). And section 304(*l*)—

> provided a blueprint with a tight, five-year timetable for the accelerated cleanup of toxic hotspots. The blueprint looked familiar: states would (1) identify and list toxic polluted waters, (2) identify each point source of toxic pollutants into these waters and the loadings from each source, and (3) prepare an "individual controls strategy" (ICS) achieving toxic standards for each listed water through additional permit limitations. If the states did not execute, as in § 303(d), EPA would. This was, of course, the same water-quality-upgrade process that states were supposed to be performing under § 303(d), but that had been shelved in the face of other priorities; the hotspot ICSs were TMDLs, limited to point sources and toxins.

Houck, *TMDLs: The Resurrection, supra,* at 10341. Houck concludes that there is reason for optimism, based on broad-based support for section 304(*l*) and a flurry of initial activity by the states, that the hotspot strategy will offer an effective approach to toxics regulation. Nevertheless, it is too soon to evaluate the *quality* of the states' plans to abate toxic pollutants or to measure the aggressiveness of their enforcement. Houck also recognizes some of the pitfalls of a water-quality-based system, as the following excerpt illustrates.

---

[73] Scott v. City of Hammond, 741 F.2d 992 (7th Cir. 1984).

THE REGULATION OF TOXIC POLLUTANTS UNDER THE CLEAN WATER ACT

Oliver A. Houck
21 ENVTL. L. REP. (ENVTL. L. INST.) 10528, 10549-54 (1991)

Exceptionally low doses of 2,3,7,8-TCDD elicit a wide range of toxic responses in animals, including carcinogenicity, teratogenicity, fetotoxicity, reproductive dysfunction and immunotoxicity . * * * This compound is the most potent animal carcinogen evaluated by EPA.

EPA, The National Dioxin Study

The regulation of dioxin-and more specifically a single form of 75 different isomers of dioxin called *2,3,7,8*-tetrachlorodibenzo-*p*-dioxin (2,3,7,8-TCDD)-illustrates the complexities, uncertainties, inadequacies, and disparities that characterize the current return to regulation by water quality standards. EPA studies describe 2,3,7,8-TCDD as "by far the most potent carcinogen evaluated to date by the Agency" and "also the most potent reproductive toxin yet evaluated by EPA." Doses as low as .001 parts per trillion have produced cancer in test animals. No identifiable threshold has been found safe for aquatic life. The 2,3,7,8-TCDD compound is persistent in the environment and adheres strongly to soils and sediments; it has a "high potential for bioaccumulation." This combination of characteristics is worth a pause: dioxin is the most lethal chemical ever produced and, once released into the environment, it does not go away.

Dioxin has long been associated with the herbicide 2,4,5-T, a component of Agent Orange, but its presence in wastewater discharges was not suspected during the development of technology standards for the industrial categories identified in the *NRDC v. Train* consent decree, and as a consequence no effluent limitations were developed. In 1983, however, surveying the extent of dioxin contamination at manufacturing and waste disposal sites around the country, EPA noted high levels of the chemical in fish in the Great Lakes and in "major river systems," and "a previously unsuspected possible source of contamination," pulp and paper mills. Here began an extended series of actions and reactions based on a wildly imprecise science and a federal impulse to shift whatever regulatory burden was necessary to the states.

In February 1984, EPA promulgated water quality criteria for dioxin indicating that "for the maximum protection of human health," the ambient water concentration should be "zero," but since "zero may not be an attainable level at this time," established risk levels ranging from 0.0013 parts per quadrillion (ppq) for a risk level of 10^{-7} (one in ten million), to .13 ppq for a risk of 10^{-6} (one in 100,000). These levels were derived from assumptions about carcinogenicity, toxic thresholds, and exposure pathways now familiar to aficionados of risk assessment. No levels were set for aquatic or other life.

Nor were any overtures made to set technology standards for dioxin discharges from the pulp and paper industry.

* * *

In August 1988, with technology standards still not scheduled for formulation, EPA released an "interim strategy document" calling for "aggressive action" on dioxin. EPA's goal was said to be nothing less than "to eliminate the presence of dioxin in discharges from pulp and paper mills." EPA's goal would be achieved, somewhat less forthrightly, by obliging the states to develop water quality standards for dioxin. Having already set a water quality criteria range for dioxin several years earlier, and within that range having adopted a criterion of 0.013 ppq, EPA also announced, however, that it was "considering making the potency factor for dioxin less stringent," raising its criterion nearly 20 times to 0.2 ppq. Whatever was intended by this announcement, it was a confession that EPA had less than full confidence in its criteria levels, and an invitation for state departures. As an added inducement to state action, EPA indicated that it would set its own dioxin standards for states that failed to adopt them, and that it would employ its level of 0.013 ppq. The corollary did not need to be expressed: if they acted, the states could thumb their noses at 0.013.

In May 1990, this interim strategy became final, with additional guidance on state permitting and testing procedures. EPA thus shifted to the states the burden of dealing with the most potent toxin yet known, at levels that cannot be detected by even the most sophisticated conventional means and must instead, be "extrapolated from downstream sediments and fish fillets" (leading to controversies among scientists over whether one counts the whole fish or just the fillets), on assumptions of risk so tenuous that EPA was considering abandoning them, on water bodies that varied widely in flow and quality, on formulae for projecting water quality impacts that varied with assumptions of flow, quality, and acceptable zones of "mixing," on "acceptable" human deaths that could vary from one in ten thousand to one in ten million, and on no aquatic or other health levels at all. Adding to the mystery of it all, that same month an EPA Assistant Administrator announced that dioxin produced in paper manufacturing was not a significant health or environmental threat, but that it probably would be subject to tougher regulation anyway.

By May 1990, 21 states had adopted or proposed numerical water quality standards for dioxin. The mechanism for converting these standards to effluent limitations on an expedited basis was § 304(*l*), requiring ICSs for "hot spot" water segments. EPA had predicted that § 304(*l*) would have the largest impact on papermills, because of their association with dioxin. As it turned out, at the end of the § 304(*l*) process dioxin limits were proposed for 88 of 98 identified papermills. Impacts such as these do not go unchallenged, and the paper industry has strongly opposed any standard more stringent than 1.2 ppq as unnecessary for human health and unduly burdensome. The strength of this campaign and the flexibility offered states in standard setting has resulted in state human health standards for dioxin that range from well below to well above EPA's recommended .0013 ppq. Georgia proposed the somewhat astonishing level of 7.2 ppq. The standards of Alabama, Georgia, Maryland, and Virginia exceed those adopted in Minnesota by 10,000 times. By late March 1991, 36 states had adopted dioxin criteria, 16 of them at EPA's level, 5 below, and 14 above.

Before examining several state dioxin standards more closely, two observations from these data should not be allowed to escape. Since early in 1987, at full steam ahead, we have managed to produce standards for one chemical compound, 2,3,7,8-TCDD, for one parameter, human health. Aquatic or other environmental criteria are scarcely envisioned. Second, of the seven least protective standards adopted in 36 states, five are those of southern states. Of the seven additional states with new standards pending, the three least protective are Arizona, Mississippi, and South Carolina. Of five additional states where standards were expected, the least protective, by a factor of 100, is Texas. Levels of human health, and therefore permissible levels of discharge, are being regionalized, generally along the lines of the Civil War, with obvious implications for industrial inducement and growth. * * *

* * *

Viewing the issue more broadly, no issue more than dioxin demonstrates that the science of even the best studied toxins is inadequate to produce anything but near-arbitrary decisions on numerical, health, and environmental standards. As one dioxin researcher has concluded:

> This series of events shows many of the problems with quantitative risk assessment. There is uncertainty about even the most basic questions such as the classification of tumors in laboratory animals. A large number of assumptions are required, each of which must be independently justified. Because of the uncertainty and the number of assumptions, it may be possible, in the absence of checks and balances, to construct nearly any result.

EPA's approvals of Virginia and Maryland's standards are indeed predicated on the inadequacies of its supporting science and of the arbitrariness of its assumptions. We do not know whether we are measuring body surface or body weight; whole fish or fillets; carp or crawfish; native American seiners or beef-eating Texans; waters at mean flow, harmonic mean flow, average low flow, or historic low flow; pure waters or already-polluted waters; bioaccumulation ratios of 5,000 or 150,000; * * * and we are arriving at ambient state standards that vary up to 1,000 times.

Compounding this uncertainty is the prospect of legal challenges to whatever standards are approved. It is the states that will have to defend the standards against industry, and a process that requires them to defend standards adopted against their will is a recipe for failure. Compounding the problem further is the fact that, under a water quality-based program, even were state dioxin standards identical and all waters of the same designated "use," great variations among states and within states will be produced by the mere fact of whether the mill is located on a large or small water body, and the assumptions the state makes in calculating its water quality and flow. New plants will be driven to the weaker states and the larger bodies of water: welcome to the South. As several states have noted, southern mills will "not have to do very much" to comply with southern standards.

The case of dioxin also illustrates the exhaustion of spirit with which EPA is approaching the alternative remedy of a technology-based standard, BAT. We are into the sixth year of specific awareness that pulp and paper mills produce extraordinary levels of dioxin, and BAT has yet to be proposed. Indeed, EPA has, in practice if not by design, shifted the burden of developing BAT to the states, or at least to those states in the north and west willing to face the paper industry. EPA will use the states" case-by-case best professional judgment (BPJ) process to develop its BAT, perhaps by "late 1993."

Whether BAT will further limit dioxin discharges, or ratify the status quo, remains to be seen. What is startling, however, on review of this limited slice of the dioxin spectrum (one that does not include important developments in, for example, the Great Lakes), is how much money, time, and effort is being spent to study, justify, challenge, and otherwise prove an indicator-water quality effects-that is probably incapable of definitive proof and that is not at all what so much money, effort, and time could be best spent doing. Throughout this discussion of dioxin, we have assumed its production as a consequence of producing bleached paper. Chlorine bleach and wood pulp make dioxin. Already, leading members of the paper industry, while fighting a rear-guard action against strict standards, are converting to bleaching by chlorine dioxide and by hydrogen peroxide, processes far less polluting. If we expand the focus of what we are examining to include the whole process-whitened paper, not necessarily by chlorine-we arrive at improved results. Nowhere in this process, however, do we ask the obvious question: why do we need so many bleached milk cartons, tissues, and the rest of an itinerary that other nations, equally modernized, may apparently do without?

Unfortunately, rather than address the obvious, we are about to engage in yet another expenditure of money, effort, and time reexamining the risks of dioxin. On April 10, 1991, EPA announced a new review, with an explanation from the Administrator that "some factors may decrease the level of concern" and "others may result in estimates of increased risk." Anyone expecting more definitive results to emerge from this review has more boundless faith in science than Dr. Faust. The industry is poised, with its experts, to show the current standards "too stringent." Environmental organizations are readying themselves to prove the standards "too weak." In all likelihood, neither will emerge content, or convinced. For certain, neither will be proven wrong. We continue to pursue a will-o-the-wisp.

On the other hand, the saga of dioxin offers at least a glimpse of a silver lining. The near-routine predictions of layoffs, plant closings, and economic ruin notwithstanding, when the paper industry has had, at last, to convert to a less polluting process, it has done so. At bottom, the struggle is not over the ability not to pollute, but over lead time and competitiveness. Any solution to toxic pollution will have to accommodate these legitimate industry needs. A solution, on the other hand, that fosters differing state standards and differing state applications of these standards breeds uncertainty, contention, unfairness, and endless opposition.

NOTES

1. How were uncertainties in risk assessment exploited by EPA, the states, and industry? Is this a particular problem in regulating dioxin, or is it more general?

2. Why is there any role for the states at all in setting dioxin standards?

3. Houck has unkind words for both BAT and water quality standards. Why? We encountered technology-based standards before, under the OSH Act, and noted that they have several strengths and several weaknesses. What are the strengths and weaknesses of the BAT approach to water pollution?

Water quality standards, of course, were designed to overcome some the limitations of a technology-based approach. Why were they ineffective with respect to dioxin?

4. *Lead time.* Houck suggests that the real problem to be addressed is "lead time and competitiveness"? What does he mean? What sort of standard does that suggest? How would it be translated into legally binding requirements?

Arguably, one benefit of only specifying performance is that it would allow the best technology to emerge through more traditional processes of market-driven innovation. There is no reason, in this view, not to be strict-indeed, strictness encourages innovation because lax regulations can be handled incrementally-but being strict does not require setting specific technologies. Michael E. Porter & Claas van der Linde, *Green and Competitive: Ending the Stalemate,* 73(5) HARV. BUS. REV. 120 (Sept.-Oct. 1995). *See also* Richard B. Stewart, *Regulation, Innovation, and Administrative Law: A Conceptual Framework*, 69 CALIF. L. REV. 1256 (1981) (emphasizing the effectiveness of incentives rather than threats (carrots rather than sticks) in encouraging innovation).

5. *Technology-based regulations for paper mills.* Should the lead-time approach be applied to phasing out chlorine, as was discussed in connection with the Safe Drinking Water Act? In 1998, EPA issued its long-awaited effluent limitations for pulp and paper mills. (They were issued as a "cluster" with Clean Air Act regulations for the same industries.) It required the replacement of elemental chlorine processes with chlorine dioxide, though it

stopped short of insisting on a totally chlorine-free process (EPA had considered both options). 63 Fed. Reg. 18504 (1998).

A few months later it was reported that a chlorine dioxide process was already used in 54% of worldwide pulp production, while totally chlorine-free processes were used in only about 6% (60 plants, mostly outside the U.S.) of the world market. *Water Pollution: Elemental Chlorine-Free Bleaching Leads World Market in Pulp Production*, 29 ENVT. REP. (BNA) 1361 (1998). In view of these facts, is the chlorine dioxide process BAT? Is the totally chlorine-free process BAT? Do these developments support or undermine a lead-time approach?

6. Nonpoint sources have become the major remaining source of water pollution in the United States-in part due to the success in controlling point sources-and they include many toxic constituents, fertilizers, pesticides, used motor oil, and other substances. Congress has taken what can only be called baby steps in the area of nonpoint discharges. The new section 309 appears at first glance to be based on the 307(*l*) template, but it imposes no schedules, provides no substantive standards, and authorizes no federal intervention if the states fail to take action. How should Congress direct EPA to address nonpoint source pollution? What are the difficulties that Congress might expect to encounter?

F. The Clean Air Act

The Clean Air Act (CAA) took its present form at the beginning of the Environmental Decade. As with the Clean Water Act, the existing state-based regulatory system had been unsuccessful in addressing the severe pollution problems that Congress perceived, and so the 1970 "amendments" in effect created a new legal structure for dealing with air pollution. The 1970 CAA received major overhauls in 1977 and again in 1990.[74] The latter amendments, which focused heavily on hazardous air pollutants, make the CAA a particularly interesting study in the regulation of toxics, because they incorporate many of the crucial developments of the 1980s in the assessment and management of toxic substances.

1. Before 1990

The 1970 Clean Air Act divided the nation into many air quality control regions, established federal standards for the ambient concentrations of conventional pollutants[75] in such regions (the national ambient air quality standards, or NAAQS), and required the states to set source-by-source emissions limitations in state implementation plans (SIPs) to meet the

---

[74] For a useful overview of the development of the Clean Air Act, *see* Arnold W. Reitze, Jr., *The Legislative History of U.S. Air Pollution Control,* 34 HOUSTON L. REV. 679 (1999).

[75] The six "criteria" pollutants are ground-level ozone, hydrocarbons (carbon monoxide, carbon dioxide), particulate matter, sulfur dioxide, nitrogen oxides (NO_x), and lead.

NAAQS.[76] The 1977 Amendments to the CAA focused primarily on adjustments to the system of NAAQS and SIPs, responding both to unanticipated technical problems (for example, prevention of significant deterioration of air quality where it exceeded the NAAQS) and to severe delays in attaining the NAAQS levels in many areas.

Congress created a very different regulatory regime for new sources of conventional pollutants and for toxic air pollutants. The new source performance standards (NSPS) and national emission standards for hazardous air pollutants (NESHAPs),[77] respectively, establish national emissions limitations that apply to all regions. The NESHAPs, codified in section 112, exemplified the by now familiar "margin of safety" approach to toxic substances:

(a) Definitions. For the purposes of this section -

(1) The term "hazardous air pollutant" means an air pollutant to which no ambient air quality standard is applicable and which in the judgment of the Administrator causes, or contributes to, air pollution which may reasonably be anticipated to result in an increase in mortality or an increase in serious irreversible, or incapacitating reversible, illness.

* * *

(b) List of hazardous air pollutants; emission standards; pollution control techniques

(1)(A) The Administrator shall, within 90 days after December 31, 1970, publish (and shall from time to time thereafter revise) a list which includes each hazardous air pollutant for which he intends to establish an emission standard under this section.

(B) Within 180 days after the inclusion of any air pollutant in such list, the Administrator shall publish proposed regulations establishing emission standards for such pollutant together with a notice of a public hearing within thirty days. Not later than 180 days after such publication, the Administrator shall prescribe an emission standard for such pollutant, unless he finds, on the basis of information presented at such hearings, that such pollutant clearly is

---

[76] Motor vehicles are a (and in many urban areas, *the*) major source of air pollution, including air toxics. The CAA authorizes EPA to establish, among other things, the gasoline formulation, fuel efficiency, and emissions inspection requirements with which we are all so familiar. The phase-out of lead additives in gasoline must be accounted one of EPA's great and unqualified successes, as it has dramatically reduced average blood lead levels in most Americans. Mobile sources are managed separately by the CAA, however, and we will not focus on them.

[77] Accounts of the origins and passage of the 1970 and 1977 toxics provisions can be found in John P. Dwyer, *The Pathology of Symbolic Legislation*, 17 ECOLOGY L.Q. 233 (1990); John D. Graham, *The Failure of Agency-Forcing: The Regulation of Airborne Carcinogens Under Section 112 of the Clean Air Act*, 1985 DUKE L.J. 100; and David Schoenbrod, *Goals Statutes or Rules Statutes: The Case of the Clean Air Act*, 30 UCLA L. REV. 740 (1983).

not a hazardous air pollutant. The Administrator shall establish any such standard at the level which in his judgment provides an ample margin of safety to protect the public health from such hazardous air pollutant.

Parse the statute. What steps was EPA to take in promulgating NESHAPs? What are the legal standards that apply to each step? Where does EPA have discretion, and where are its actions mandatory?

For a variety of reasons that are discussed below, EPA accumulated an impressive record of inaction under the 1970/1977 version of section 112.[78] Between 1970 and 1990, EPA managed to list and regulate only seven hazardous air pollutants: arsenic, asbestos, benzene, beryllium, mercury, radionuclides, and vinyl chloride. Not only is this a low level of regulatory production (by comparison, Congress identified 189 toxic air pollutants in the 1990 Amendments), but the chemicals in question are hardly tough calls.[79] Vinyl chloride, for example, the chemical at issue in the following case, is a known (not probable, not possible) human carcinogen. The *Vinyl Chloride* case is followed by EPA's less-then-enthusiastic response to the court's holding.

NATURAL RESOURCES DEFENSE COUNCIL V. EPA
(THE *VINYL CHLORIDE* CASE)

824 F.2d 1146 (D.C. Cir. 1987) (*en banc*)

BORK, Circuit Judge:

Current scientific knowledge does not permit a finding that there is a completely safe level of human exposure to carcinogenic agents. The Administrator of the Environmental Protection Agency, however, is charged with regulating hazardous pollutants, including carcinogens, under section 112 of the Clean Air Act by setting emission standards "at the level which in his judgment provides an ample margin of safety to protect the public health." We address here the question of the extent of the Administrator's authority under this delegation in setting emission standards for carcinogenic pollutants.

Petitioner Natural Resources Defense Council ("NRDC") contends that the Administrator must base a decision under section 112 exclusively on health-related factors and, therefore, that the uncertainty about the effects of carcinogenic agents requires the Administrator to prohibit all emissions. The

---

[78] EPA listed asbestos, beryllium, and mercury shortly after the act was passed, but then delayed action on proposed standards. EDF was able to obtain an injunction forcing the promulgation of final regulations. EDF v. Ruckelshaus, 3 ENVTL. L. REP. (ENVTL. L. INST.) 20173 (D.D.C. 1973).

[79] For an influential discussion of toxic substances regulation based on the pre-judicial phase of the vinyl chloride NESHAP, *see* David Doniger, *Federal Regulation of Vinyl Chloride: A Short Course on the Law and Policy of Toxic Substances Control*, 7 ECOLOGY L.Q. 497 (1978).

Administrator argues that in the face of this uncertainty he is authorized to set standards that require emission reduction to the lowest level attainable by best available control technology whenever that level is below that at which harm to humans has been demonstrated. We find no support for either position in the language or legislative history of the Clean Air Act. We therefore grant the petition for review and remand to the Administrator for reconsideration in light of this opinion.

I.

* * *

This case concerns vinyl chloride regulations. Vinyl chloride is a gaseous synthetic chemical used in the manufacture of plastics and is a strong carcinogen.[80] In late 1975, the Administrator issued a notice of proposed rulemaking to establish an emission standard for vinyl chloride. In the notice, the EPA asserted that available data linked vinyl chloride to carcinogenic, as well as some noncarcinogenic, disorders and that "[r]easonable extrapolations" from this data suggested "that present ambient levels of vinyl chloride may cause or contribute to . . . [such] disorders." The EPA also noted that vinyl chloride is "an apparent non-threshold pollutant," which means that it appears to create a risk to health at all non-zero levels of emission. Scientific uncertainty, due to the unavailability of dose-response data and the twenty-year latency period between initial exposure to vinyl chloride and the occurrence of disease, makes it impossible to establish any definite threshold level below which there are no adverse effects to human health. The notice also stated the "EPA's position that for a carcinogen it should be assumed, in the absence of strong evidence to the contrary, that there is no atmospheric concentration that poses absolutely no public health risk."

Because of this assumption, the EPA concluded that it was faced with two alternative interpretations of its duty under section 112. First, the EPA determined that section 112 might require a complete prohibition of emissions of non-threshold pollutants because a "zero emission limitation would be the only emission standard which would offer absolute safety from ambient exposure." The EPA found this alternative "neither desirable nor necessary" because "[c]omplete prohibition of all emissions could require closure of an entire industry," a cost the EPA found "extremely high for elimination of a risk to health that is of unknown dimensions."

The EPA stated the second alternative as follows:

---

[80] Animal and epidemiological evidence have linked it with lung, brain, and liver cancers (liver angiosarcoma is a signature disease for vinyl chloride), as well as leukemia and lymphoma and numerous other chronic and acute effects. Its primary use is as an ingredient in polyvinyl resin, which is the raw material from which polyvinyl chloride (PVC) plastic is manufactured. Nearly 15 *billion* pounds of vinyl chloride were produced in the United States in 1995, and production volumes are growing at about 7% per year. HHS/ATSDR, Toxicological Profile for Vinyl Chloride (Update) (1997).—EDS.

An alternative interpretation of section 112 is that it authorizes setting emission standards that require emission reduction to the lowest level achievable by use of the best available control technology in cases involving apparent non-threshold pollutants, where complete emission prohibition would result in widespread industry closure and EPA has determined that the cost of such closure would be grossly disproportionate to the benefits of removing the risk that would remain after imposition of the best available control technology.

The EPA adopted this alternative on the belief that it would "produce the most stringent regulation of hazardous air pollutants short of requiring a complete prohibition in all cases."

On October 21, 1976, the EPA promulgated final emission standards for vinyl chloride which were based solely on the level attainable by the best available control technology. The EPA determined that this standard would reduce unregulated emissions by 95 percent. With respect to the effect of the standard on health, the EPA stated that it had assessed the risk to health at ambient levels of exposure by extrapolating from dose-response data at higher levels of exposure and then made the following findings:

EPA found that the rate of initiation of liver angiosarcoma among [the 4.6 million] people living around uncontrolled plants is expected to range from less than one to ten cases of liver angiosarcoma per year of exposure to vinyl chloride .... Vinyl chloride is also estimated to produce an equal number of primary cancers at other sites, for a total of somewhere between less than one and twenty cases of cancer per year of exposure among residents around plants. The number of these effects is expected to be reduced at least in proportion to the reduction in the ambient annual average vinyl chloride concentration, which is expected to be 5 percent of the uncontrolled levels after the standard is implemented.

The EPA did not state whether this risk to health is significant or not. Nor did the EPA explain the relationship between this risk to health and its duty to set an emission standard which will provide an "ample margin of safety."

* * *

III.

The NRDC's challenge to the EPA's [vinyl chloride standard] is simple: because the statute adopts an exclusive focus on considerations of health, the Administrator must set a zero level of emissions when he cannot determine that there is a level below which no harm will occur.

* * * We find no support in the text or legislative history for the proposition that Congress intended to require a complete prohibition of emissions whenever the EPA cannot determine a threshold level for a

hazardous pollutant. Instead, there is strong evidence that Congress considered such a requirement and rejected it.

Section 112 commands the Administrator to set an "emission standard" for a particular "hazardous air pollutant" which in his "judgment" will provide an "ample margin of safety." Congress' use of the term "ample margin of safety" is inconsistent with the NRDC's position that the Administrator has no discretion in the face of uncertainty. The statute nowhere defines "ample margin of safety." The Senate Report, however, in discussing a similar requirement in the context of setting ambient air standards under section 109 of the Act, explained the purpose of the "margin of safety" standard as one of affording "a reasonable degree of protection . . . against hazards which research has not yet identified." (emphasis added). This view comports with the historical use of the term in engineering as "a safety factor . . . meant to compensate for uncertainties and variabilities." *See* Hall, *The Control of Toxic Pollutants Under the Federal Water Pollution Control Act Amendments of 1972*, 63 Iowa L.Rev. 609, 629 (1978). Furthermore, in a discussion of the use of identical language in the Federal Water Pollution Control Act, this court has recognized that, in discharging the responsibility to assure "an ample margin of safety," the Administrator faces "a difficult task, indeed, a veritable paradox—calling as it does for knowledge of that which is unknown—[but] . . . the term 'margin of safety' is Congress's directive that means be found to carry out the task and to reconcile the paradox." *Environmental Defense Fund v. EPA*, 598 F.2d 62, 81 (D.C.Cir.1978) [the PCBs case, *supra*]. And while Congress used the modifier "ample" to exhort the Administrator not to allow "the public [or] the environment . . . to be exposed to anything resembling the maximum risk" and, therefore, to set a margin "greater than 'normal' or 'adequate,'" Congress still left the EPA "great latitude in meeting its responsibility."

Congress' use of the word "safety," moreover, is significant evidence that it did not intend to require the Administrator to prohibit all emissions of non-threshold pollutants. As the Supreme Court has recently held, "safe" does not mean "risk-free." *Industrial Union Dep't, AFL-CIO v. American Petroleum Inst.*, 448 U.S. 607, 642 (1980). Instead, something is "unsafe" only when it threatens humans with "a significant risk of harm." *Id.*

Thus, the terms of section 112 provide little support for the NRDC's position. The uncertainty about the effects of a particular carcinogenic pollutant invokes the Administrator's discretion under section 112. In contrast, the NRDC's position would eliminate any discretion and would render the standard "ample margin of safety" meaningless as applied to carcinogenic pollutants.[81] Whenever *any* scientific uncertainty existed about the ill effects of a nonzero level of hazardous air pollutants—and we think it

---

[81] With the exception of mercury, every pollutant the Administrator has listed or intends to list under § 112 is a non-threshold carcinogen. * * *

unlikely that science will ever yield *absolute* certainty of safety in an area so complicated and rife with problems of measurement, modeling, long latency, and the like—the Administrator would have no discretion but would be required to prohibit all emissions. Had Congress intended that result, it could very easily have said so by writing a statute that states that no level of emissions shall be allowed as to which there is any uncertainty. But Congress chose instead to deal with the pervasive nature of scientific uncertainty and the inherent limitations of scientific knowledge by vesting in the Administrator the discretion to deal with uncertainty in each case.

The NRDC also argues that the legislative history supports its position. To the contrary, that history strongly suggests that Congress did not require the Administrator to prohibit emissions of all non-threshold pollutants; Congress considered and rejected the option of requiring the Administrator to prohibit all emissions.

* * *

IV.

We turn now to the question whether the Administrator's chosen method for setting emission levels above zero is consistent with congressional intent. The Administrator's position is that he may set an emission level for non-threshold pollutants at the lowest level achievable by best available control technology when that level is anywhere below the level of demonstrated harm and the cost of setting a lower level is grossly disproportionate to the benefits of removing the remaining risk. The NRDC argues that this standard is arbitrary and capricious because the EPA is never permitted to consider cost and technological feasibility under section 112 but instead is limited to consideration of health-based factors. Thus, before addressing the Administrator's method of using cost and technological feasibility in this case, we must determine whether he may consider cost and technological feasibility at all.

A.

On its face, section 112 does not indicate that Congress intended to preclude consideration of any factor. Though the phrase "to protect the public health" evinces an intent to make health the primary consideration, there is no indication of the factors the Administrator may or may not consider in determining, in his "judgment," what level of emissions will provide "an ample margin of safety." Instead, the language used, and the absence of any specific limitation, gives the clear impression that the Administrator has some discretion in determining what, if any, additional factors he will consider in setting an emission standard.

B.

The petitioner argues that the legislative history makes clear Congress' intent to foreclose reliance on non-health-based considerations in setting standards under section 112. We find, however, that the legislative history can be characterized only as ambiguous.

* * *

C.

The petitioner argues next that a finding that section 112 does not preclude consideration of cost and technological feasibility would render the Clean Air Act structurally incoherent and would be inconsistent with the Supreme Court's interpretation of section 110 of the Act as precluding consideration of these factors. We do not believe that our decision here is inconsistent with either the holding or the statutory interpretation in either case.

* * *

The substantive standard imposed under the hazardous air pollutants provisions of section 112, by contrast with sections 109 [NSPS] and 110 [NAAQS], is not based on criteria that enumerate specific factors to consider and pointedly exclude feasibility. Section 112(b)(1)'s command "to provide an ample margin of safety to protect the public health" is self-contained, and the absence of enumerated criteria may well evince a congressional intent for the Administrator to supply reasonable ones. * * *

* * *

V.

Since we cannot discern clear congressional intent to preclude consideration of cost and technological feasibility in setting emission standards under section 112, we necessarily find that the Administrator may consider these factors. * * * [Nevertheless, d]espite a deferential standard [of review], we find that the Administrator has ventured into a zone of impermissible action. The Administrator has not exercised his expertise to determine an acceptable risk to health. To the contrary, in the face of uncertainty about risks to health, he has simply substituted technological feasibility for health as the primary consideration under Section 112. Because this action is contrary to clearly discernible congressional intent, we grant the petition for review.

Given the foregoing analysis of the language and legislative history of section 112, it seems to us beyond dispute that Congress was primarily concerned with health in promulgating section 112. Every action by the Administrator in setting an emission standard is to be taken "to protect the public health." In setting an emission standard for vinyl chloride, however, the Administrator has made no finding with respect to the effect of the chosen level of emissions on health. Nor has the Administrator stated that a certain level of emissions is "safe" or that the chosen level will provide an "ample margin of safety." Instead, the Administrator has substituted "best available technology" for a finding of the risk to health.

* * *

Thus, in setting emission standards for carcinogenic pollutants, the Administrator has decided to determine first the level of emissions attainable by best available control technology. He will then determine the costs of setting the standard below that level and balance those costs against the risk to health below the level of feasibility. If the costs are greater than the reduction in risk, then he will set the standard at the level of feasibility. This exercise, in the Administrator's view, will always produce an "ample margin of safety."

* * *

We find that the congressional mandate to provide "an ample margin of safety" "to protect the public health" requires the Administrator to make an initial determination of what is "safe." This determination must be based exclusively upon the Administrator's determination of the risk to health at a particular emission level. Because the Administrator in this case did not make any finding of the risk to health, the question of how that determination is to be made is not before us. We do wish to note, however, that the Administrator's decision does not require a finding that "safe" means "risk-free," *see Industrial Union Dep't*, or a finding that the determination is free from uncertainty. Instead, we find only that the Administrator's decision must be based upon an expert judgment with regard to the level of emission that will result in an "acceptable" risk to health. *Environmental Defense Fund*, 598 F.2d at 83-84. In this regard, the Administrator must determine what inferences should be drawn from available scientific data and decide what risks are acceptable in the world in which we live. *See Industrial Union Dep't*, ("There are many activities that we engage in every day—such as driving a car or even breathing city air—that entail some risk of accident or material health impairment; nevertheless, few people would consider those activities 'unsafe.'"). This determination must be based solely upon the risk to health. The Administrator cannot under any circumstances consider cost and technological feasibility at this stage of the analysis. The latter factors have no relevance to the preliminary determination of what is safe. Of course, if the Administrator cannot find that there is an acceptable risk at any level, then the Administrator must set the level at zero.

Congress, however, recognized in section 112 that the determination of what is "safe" will always be marked by scientific uncertainty and thus exhorted the Administrator to set emission standards that will provide an "ample margin" of safety. This language permits the Administrator to take into account scientific uncertainty and to use expert discretion to determine what action should be taken in light of that uncertainty. *See Environmental Defense Fund*, ("by requiring EPA to set standards providing an 'ample margin of safety,' Congress authorized and, indeed, required EPA to protect against dangers before their extent is conclusively ascertained"); *Hercules*, 598 F.2d at 104 ("Under the 'ample margin of safety' directive, EPA's standards must protect against incompletely understood dangers to public health and the environment, in addition to well-known risks."). In determining what is an "ample margin" the Administrator may, and perhaps must, take into account the inherent limitations of risk assessment and the limited scientific knowledge of the effects of exposure to carcinogens at various levels, and may therefore decide to set the level below that previously determined to be "safe." This is especially true when a straight line extrapolation from known risks is used to estimate risks to health at levels of exposure for which no data is available. This method, which is based upon the results of exposure at fairly high levels of the hazardous pollutants, will show some risk at every level because of the rules of arithmetic rather than because of any knowledge. In fact the risk at a certain point on the extrapolated line may have no relationship to reality; there is no particular reason to think that the actual line of the incidence of harm is represented by a straight line. Thus, by its nature the finding of risk is uncertain and the Administrator must use his discretion to meet the statutory mandate. It is only at this point of the regulatory process that the Administrator may set the emission standard at the lowest level that is technologically feasible. In fact, this is, we believe, precisely the type of policy choice that Congress envisioned when it directed the Administrator to provide an "ample margin of safety." Once "safety" is assured, the Administrator should be free to diminish as much of the statistically determined risk as possible by setting the standard at the lowest feasible level. Because consideration of these factors at this stage is clearly intended "to protect the public health," it is fully consistent with the Administrator's mandate under section 112.

We wish to reiterate the limited nature of our holding in this case because it is not the court's intention to bind the Administrator to any specific method of determining what is "safe" or what constitutes an "ample margin." We hold only that the Administrator cannot consider cost and technological feasibility in determining what is "safe." This determination must be based solely upon the risk to health. The issues of whether the Administrator can proceed on a case-by-case basis, what support the Administrator must provide for the determination of what is "safe," or what other factors may be considered, are issues that must be resolved after the Administrator has reached a decision upon reconsideration of the decision withdrawing the proposed 1977 amendments.

PROPOSED RULE
NATIONAL EMISSION STANDARDS FOR HAZARDOUS AIR POLLUTANTS: BENZENE EMISSIONS

Environmental Protection Agency
53 Fed. Reg. 28496 (1988)

Legal Framework Under Vinyl Chloride

The EPA considers the *Vinyl Chloride* decision to further define the legal framework for setting NESHAP under section 112 of the CAA. * * *

Uniqueness of Decision

The effect of the *Vinyl Chloride* decision is to require a unique decisionmaking process for public health protection decisions, unlike any other regulatory decision faced by the Agency. This is the result of the court's prescription of two separate steps for decisionmaking, the first in which only health factors can be considered in setting an acceptable risk level, and the second in which additional factors including cost, technological feasibility, and other relevant factors may be considered in providing an ample margin of safety. This scheme is unlike any other under the CAA itself, or any of the other statutes administered by EPA because the acceptable risk that EPA adopts in the first step cannot be exceeded by the standard EPA adopts in the second step.

In contrast, other EPA statutes have very different structures and legal requirements for decisionmaking on public health standards. For example, while the Safe Drinking Water Act provides for two separate decisions, the first is a purely health-based goal toward which to work, but not necessarily meet; the second is an enforceable standard that is based on cost and feasibility considerations. Under both the Toxic Substances Control Act (TSCA) and the Federal Insecticide, Fungicide, and Rodenticide Act (FIFRA), the balancing of health concerns and benefits of continued chemical use, and control costs are explicitly provided for in decisionmaking. The Resource Conservation and Recovery Act and the Comprehensive Environmental Response, Compensation, and Liability Act both require statutory decisionmaking very different from the bifurcated process mandated by the court for section 112.

Although not reflected in the *Vinyl Chloride* decision reviewed by the D.C. Circuit, the EPA's recent judgments under section 112 were made in integrated approaches that considered a range of health and risk factors, as well as cost and feasibility in certain cases. These approaches were followed in NESHAP for the source categories of radionuclides, arsenic, and the prior decisions on benzene source categories. However, the *Vinyl Chloride* decision eliminates those approaches to section 112, since the integrated approaches did not partition consideration of health factors into a first step separate from consideration of the other relevant factors.

Thus, the *Vinyl Chloride* decision forces EPA to consider whether a risk is acceptable without at the same time considering benefits of the activity causing risk, feasibility of control, or other factors that EPA (or anyone) would normally consider in deciding whether a risk was "acceptable." This problem is particularly acute in the case of many carcinogens, for which the Agency has stated that it is unable to identify a threshold no-effect level.

The very examples cited by the court bring home the unusual nature of the court's "acceptable risk" decision step. The court (quoting the Supreme Court's decision in the OSHA *Benzene* Case) cited "driving a car or even breathing city air" as activities that "few people would consider * * * 'unsafe.'" But driving a car entails risks that most people would consider high; the annual incidence approximates 50,000 fatal accidents, and the average individual risk (not the maximum, but the actuarial average risk) approximates a 1 in 100 chance of automobile-related death over a 70-year lifetime. Yet the court was correct to say that our society accepts (or tolerates) risk from driving cars. As a society we continue to try to reduce the level of risk, but we value the benefits in increased mobility that the automobile affords. The same is true of "breathing city air"—leaving aside the circularity (city air may contain some of the contaminants that EPA is considering regulating), individuals live in cities to be close to the workplace, for the recreational and cultural advantages associated with cities, and for a variety of reasons extrinsic to the risk itself.

If decisions on the acceptability of risks are inherently balancing judgments, how is EPA to make those judgments on acceptability? Later in this section, EPA sets forth four approaches that deal with this issue in differing ways. The approaches cover a range of possible risk levels and they give prominence to different measures of risk, *e.g.*, individual versus population risk. The purpose is to elicit comment that will contribute to the EPA's resolution of the decisionmaking problems presented by *Vinyl Chloride*.

Survey of Societal Risk

After assessing the health risks for emissions of a specific hazardous air pollutant, the Administrator, in following the *Vinyl Chloride* decision, is next faced with the question of how to determine an acceptable risk for a particular source category emitting that pollutant. This question cannot be answered in a vacuum, but requires him to determine "what risks are acceptable in the world in which we live." [Emphasis added]. Such a determination requires some context within which to evaluate and compare risks and other health factors bearing on that question.

In approaching the question of what level of risk is "acceptable or "safe," EPA surveyed a range of health risks that our society faces. The objective of this survey was to develop information to place the benzene risk estimates in perspective. Thus, the survey included risks encountered in everyday life, such as driving a car and breathing city air, which were cited in the *Vinyl Chloride* decision, as well as a range of regulatory judgments or risks. The EPA surveyed both the individual risk and the incidence in the population exposed to risk associated with the activities. Considering incidence comports with the purpose of section 112 to protect "public health" when incidence is viewed as a measure of health of the population as a whole.

The risks surveyed ranged from individual risks of 1 in 10 (10^{-1}) to less than 1 in 10,000,000 (10^{-7}). Everyday risks include risks from natural background radiation as well as risks from home accidents. Natural background radiation at sea level creates individual lifetime cancer risks in the range of 3 in 1,000 (10^{-3}) and an estimated 10,000 cancer cases per year. Naturally occurring radon in homes poses an additional source of radiation risk, and these risks can be as high as 1 in 100 to 1 in 10 (10^{-2} to 10^{-1}) and cause an estimated 5,000 to 20,000 cancer cases/yr. In the U.S., accidents, natural disasters, and rare diseases pose individual risks of death from 1 in 10,000 (10^{-4}) (*e.g.*, tripping and falling which cause approximately 470 deaths per year) to 1 in 10,000,000 (10^{-7}) (*e.g.*, rabies which causes an average of 1.5 deaths per year).

Judgments on risks have also spanned a broad range of risk levels[, from 3 (10^{-3} at NRC to 10^{-5} and 10^{-6} in various FDA and EPA programs].

* * *

No fixed risk level could be identified as acceptable in all cases and under all regulatory programs for two main reasons. First, as discussed above, in most cases the calculation of risks depends on different data, assumptions, and uncertainties. For example, the risk associated with motor vehicle and other common accidents can be calculated directly from accident records and therefore reflect actual risk; whereas environmental risks are based on estimating procedures and assumptions and therefore are more uncertain. Thus, actuarial and environmental risk estimates cannot be directly compared so as to draw precise judgments as to whether one risk is larger, or less acceptable, than another. Second, acceptability of risk is a relative concept and involves consideration of different factors. Considerations in these judgments may include: The certainty and severity of the risk; the reversibility of the health effect; the knowledge or familiarity of the risk; whether the risk is voluntarily accepted or involuntarily imposed; whether individuals are compensated for their exposure to the risk; the advantages of the activity; and the risks and advantages for any alternatives. Thus, different judgments on acceptability can be made for similar numerical risks. In addition, the uses of individual risk and incidence as comparative factors face limitations since the relative size of the risks associated with an activity are sensitive to how the activity is defined. For example, the individual risk and incidence associated with a single leaking pipe at a plant within a particular industry could be quite small, but the cumulative risks associated with all plants within the industry could be significant. This limitation can be ameliorated by careful selection of the appropriate category of sources.

NOTES

1. *The* Vinyl Chloride *two-step*. What is the analytical procedure that the *Vinyl Chloride* case imposes? How does it compare to the two-step process set out in the statute? Do you detect the influence of the *Benzene* decision here?

2. How does section 112 use the term "margin of safety"? How does the court use it-both as an element of its argument and as part of the required analysis? Are section 112 and the opinion consistent? Is the opinion internally consistent on this point?

3. *Acceptable risk.* What does the court say about the level of risk that is "acceptable"? How is EPA to go about setting that level?

How does EPA use "societal risk" as an argument? How might EPA use societal risk to set risk levels?

In the more recent *Michigan v. EPA*, ___ F.3d ___, 2000 WL 180650 *11 (D.C. Cir. 2000), the D.C. Circuit commented on the difficulty of setting a "significant" level of risk without reference to costs, and it asserted that agencies are regularly allowed to consider cost in determining "significant" or "acceptable" levels of risk, citing *Vinyl Chloride*. Is this a fair reading of *Vinyl Chloride*, or does it represent a *post hoc* recognition by the court of the difficulty of the task it set for EPA?

4. EPA's response to the *Vinyl Chloride* decision is remarkable for its clear dislike for the task assigned to it by the court. Much of the elaboration of the risk issues, in fact, can be read as a message to the D.C. Circuit: "Did you have any idea what you were talking about?" Alternatively, EPA's response could be interpreted as bureaucratic pique at being required to make explicit, transparent statements on issues that it prefers to keep murky. Which analysis of *Vinyl Chloride* is more accurate?

What are the "integrated" standards that EPA refers to? Why does EPA so clearly prefer them to any of the other approaches it laid out? Do they really eliminate the difficulties created by *Vinyl Chloride*, or just some of them?

2. Critiques of the 1970/1977 Section 112

By the late 1980s, section 112 had become the poster child for ineffective, poorly crafted toxics legislation. The following are four commentators' explanations (in extremely summary form-the full articles are well worth reading) for its ineffectiveness. As you read them, consider what kinds of reforms of section 112 that each commentator would support.

THE PATHOLOGY OF SYMBOLIC LEGISLATION

John P. Dwyer
17 ECOLOGY L.Q. 233, 233-34, 250 (1990)

The programs mandated by such legislation are more symbolic than functional. Frequently, the legislature has failed to address the administrative and political constraints that will block implementation of the statute. By enacting this type of statute, legislators reap the political benefits of voting for "health and the environment" and against "trading lives for dollars," and successfully sidestep the difficult policy choices that must be made in regulating public health and the environment. Thus, while the statute, literally read, promises a risk-free environment, the hard issues involved in defining acceptable risk are passed on to the regulatory agency or to the courts. The actual regulatory program takes shape only after additional legislative, administrative, or judicial developments that transform symbolic guarantees into enforceable standards.

The enactment of symbolic legislation reflects a breakdown of the legislative policymaking machinery, a system that all too frequently addresses real social problems in an unrealistic fashion. It also creates a dilemma for regulators and judges. While they generally are reluctant to usurp the legislature's policymaking prerogatives by substituting their own version of appropriate public policy, they also are loath to implement and enforce a statute whose costs are grossly disproportionate to its benefits. The critical issue, then, is whether and how the agency or court should take the initiative to transform symbolic legislation into a functional regulatory program.

Believing that it would be irresponsible and politically mad to interpret and implement symbolic statutory provisions literally, the agency's usual response is to resist implementation. Although an agency may experiment with interpretations that moderate the stringent statutory standard-setting criteria, it will implement its reformulation slowly in order to delay judicial review. As a result, the agency adopts very few standards. [Dwyer explains later: "This creates not only greater health risks than are permissible under the statutory health-based standards, but higher risks than would be allowed under the more lenient cost-sensitive standards that EPA prefers."]

The most significant problem with symbolic legislation, however, is not delay; it is the resulting distortions in the regulatory process. Symbolic legislation hobbles the regulatory process by polarizing public discussion in agency proceedings and legislative hearings. Environmental groups take the legislation's promise of a risk-free environment at face value and tend to refuse to compromise the "rights" inherent in such promises. Industry fears that regulators will implement the statute literally and, consequently, vigorously opposes the regulatory process at every stage. By making promises that cannot be kept, and by leaving no middle ground for accommodation, the legislature makes it more difficult to reach a political compromise (either in the agency or the legislature) that would produce a functional regulatory program.

[Dwyer adds: "A statute requiring EPA to do the impossible also undermines the integrity of the rulemaking process and forces the Agency to misrepresent its decisionmaking process to the public and to the courts. When decisionmaking is driven underground, rationality and genuine public participation are sacrificed and public confidence in government is eroded."]

* * *

Section 112 is symbolic legislation because few legislators contemplated (either at the time of enactment or since then) that its commands would be taken literally. Although it is not physically impossible to implement health-based standards, it is inconceivable that an agency would set standards without regard for other social consequences. Unlike most regulatory statutes, section 112 is addressed not to the regulatory agency, but to interest groups and the public at large. Moreover, the message was not intended to be taken literally. The absurdly short deadlines and excessively strict emission criteria communicate a more general message that the legislature recognizes hazardous air pollutants as a frightening and potentially serious public health problem and that EPA should make special efforts to control these hazards.

GOALS STATUTES OR RULES STATUTES: THE CASE OF THE CLEAN AIR ACT

David Schoenbrod
30 UCLA L. REV. 740, 742, 751-54, 786-87 (1983)

The Act ordains that its environmental goals must be achieved. It purports to realize those goals not by stating rules of conduct for polluters but by mandating a process under which entities other than Congress must promulgate controls to achieve the goals. The 1970 Act is, in the first instance, a law that regulates government rather than sources of pollution. It requires government-both federal and state-to take certain actions by certain dates. * * *

* * *

Some statutes, to be called "goals statutes," announce goals and authorize delegates to promulgate controls on conduct in furtherance of those goals. "Rules statutes," on the other hand, state rules of conduct. Pre-1970 air pollution legislation, as well as the 1970 Act (except to the extent that it limited emissions from new cars), were goals statutes because Congress left the choice of permissible conduct to others. * * *

* * *

The Act's abstract level nonetheless left untouched issues which would have necessarily been resolved in generating concrete rules of conduct. First, Congress provided no guidance as to how the costs of achieving the statutory goal should be allocated. Thus, the difficult job of imposing costs to realize the benefit is given to a body with less power than Congress. Under a goals statute, the statutory delegate, such as EPA, is caught between those who inevitably will resist the imposition of costly regulatory burdens and a statutory mandate. Second, when EPA or some other delegate looks for justification in its mandate to achieve the legislated goal, it usually finds that the statute provides insufficient guidance as to the meaning of the goal. Because the legislation was written on the relatively abstract level of social priorities rather than conduct, it is likely to be either spuriously absolute (*e.g.*, protect health regardless of cost), or vacuous (*e.g.*, balance health and cost).

Goals statutes, even those with the supposedly specific action-forcing procedures of the 1970 Act, thus speak in abstractions that generate contention among experts and mask the disparate expectations of lay persons. The problem with the goals statutes that broadly delegate decision-making authority is that they leave key value choices to low visibility decisionmakers fearful of making controversial choices. This is all the more true of the 1970 Act, which makes decisions invisible by overlooking the need to make them. In a goals statute, the legislature does half of a job: it promises benefits without allocating costs, and it broadcasts rights without assigning duties. The unrealistic goals of the 1970 Act are not the fundamental cause of its difficulties but the result of a statutory structure-the goals structure-that facilitates wishful thinking in public opinion and legislation. The Clean Air Act's incantation of goals and procedures concealed a refusal to make choices about the present.

* * *

Rules statutes, in defining permissible versus impermissible conduct, set priorities between goals, such as health protection and the cost of reducing emissions; they also allocate the costs or benefits of reducing emissions between groups. [Schoenbrod offers limits on the emissions from cars per mile traveled or the emissions from power plants per BTU of energy produced, or a tax the quantity of emissions from particular sources as examples of rules.] While goals statutes may purport to make these choices, they do not define conduct, and they thus speak at a more abstract level than rules statutes, which must state their choices in extrinsically meaningful terms. This relative concreteness of rules statutes makes them better able to deal with air pollution * * *.

SCIENCE, POLITICS, AND THE MANAGEMENT OF TOXIC RISKS THROUGH LAW

Sanford E. Gaines
30 Jurimetrics 271, 273, 782-83, 286, 292-93 (1990)

If the scientific or the legal uncertainties were independent of each other, the paralysis would be difficult to explain. The agencies have proven relatively adept, and the courts relatively cooperative, in overcoming scientific uncertainty under clear legal mandates, or in interpreting ambiguous statutes where the scientific information is not in dispute. Therefore, this article takes the view that the paralysis of toxics regulation has a more complex etiology that begins with a synergy between the scientific and legal uncertainties. When the science cannot provide a conclusive description of the problem (or the proposed solution), it becomes philosophically impossible to formulate a definitive statement of the legal objective. The dual uncertainty leaves the agencies without any reliable guidance for their decisions.

* * *

Given the paucity, the softness, and the incompleteness of the scientific data in the context of public administrative decision making-in which the legal system demands, at minimum, a "rational basis" for an affirmative choice to regulate-it should be no surprise that administrators perpetually study, debate, and reanalyze their information, and then call for more study, and rarely propose concrete decisions.

* * *

The uncertainty of the science also imparts a vagueness to the statutory mandate that its drafters may not have expected. If science does not know the health consequences of low level chronic exposures to carcinogens, how can EPA possibly know if its rules will "protect the public health?" Even if a rule satisfies some nebulous notion of health protection, how can the agency define a "margin of safety" for such a tentative scientific conclusion? The critical question thus becomes just what Congress meant-or should mean-by the mandate of section 112.

Without any apparent consideration of the indefinite meaning of "public health," advocates and commentators have tended to equate protection of the public health with the elimination of health hazards to any individual. Even EPA, which insisted that the protection of public health under section 112 does not legally require zero health effects, on occasion expressed the view that only a zero level of exposure "would appear to be absolutely protective of health."

* * *

The preceding caveat leads to another uncertainty of even greater perplexity than the meaning of public health. If the law grants EPA the discretion to regulate hazardous air pollutants in a manner that allows some emissions, and thus some risk to health, what level of risk can be tolerated within the statutory mandate?

* * *

[EPA's response to the uncertainties in section 112 is not wholly satisfactory, either.] Despite its intuitive appeal to appointed agency administrators, the technical feasibility approach to the regulation of hazardous air pollutants had two fatal flaws. First, its tendency to submerge, if not subvert, health protection goals clashed with the moral rights-based conception of toxic pollution held by many who bear the burden of the risk it creates. Second, the agency's approach clearly lacked any basis in the statute, and thus depended for its legal survival on an extreme judicial deference to the agency's interpretation of its mandate. Thus, the constituency naturally opposed to EPA's policy had strong legal weapons with which to wage its struggle.

THE FAILURE OF AGENCY-FORCING: THE REGULATION OF AIRBORNE CARCINOGENS UNDER SECTION 112 OF THE CLEAN AIR ACT

John D. Graham
1985 DUKE L.J. 100, 101, 116-17, 121-22, 130-32

The 'agency-forcing' nature of the Clean Air Act Amendments of 1970 reflects this repudiation of the New Deal model. Under the agency-forcing approach, blind faith in administrative discretion was replaced by strict procedural and substantive demands on bureaucratic policymaking. Activists in Congress, spurred by their allies in consumer and environmental groups, used statutory language and legislative history to specify the ends/means relationships that would be expected to govern administrative decisions. The federal judiciary was recruited as an institutional ally in this aggressive bid to force implementation of health, safety, and environmental programs.

* * *

A. The Cumbersome Listing Process.

Section 112 is designed so that profound regulatory implications flow from the initial decision to list a pollutant as hazardous. Once a pollutant is listed, the EPA has a nondiscretionary duty to promulgate national emission standards within a period of one year. That duty may require, as we shall see, that zero-emission standards be set for all sources of a nonthreshold pollutant, regardless of technological feasibility and the size or affordability of compliance costs. The nondiscretionary duty is enforceable in the courts by citizen suits, which provide environmental organizations a powerful enforcement tool. The regulatory significance of the initial listing decision is enhanced by the difficulty of delisting a pollutant-for delisting requires a showing that a pollutant is 'clearly' not hazardous. Indeed, because it is practically impossible to prove the negative-to show that a pollutant is 'clearly' not hazardous-it is doubtful that the EPA could ever delist a pollutant.

In light of the regulatory implications of the listing decision, the EPA has been extremely careful to study a pollutant extensively before listing it. Unfortunately, the statute and its legislative history provide no guidance concerning what types of scientific data are required to support a decision to list[, and qualitative evaluation of carcinogenicity data raises complex and controversial issues]. * * *

* * *

The plain language and legislative history of section 112 indicate that Congress was particularly concerned about the failure to list a truly hazardous pollutant. The definition of hazardousness-applying to what 'may reasonably be anticipated to result' in increased illness or mortality-is highly precautionary and the 1977 Clean Air Act Amendments emphasize the precautionary and preventive purposes of section 112 and of the Act as a whole. While Congress did not intend to transfer the burden of proof from the EPA to industrial polluters, the legislative history of the 1977 Amendments reveals a conviction that standards of health protection should not be delayed due to the absence of conclusive scientific indications of adverse health effects from pollution. A special concern with false-negative errors is particularly justified in the context of section 112, where the pollutants addressed may cause severe health damage, including various forms of cancer.

* * *

D. Fear of Zero-Emission Standards.

A[nother] basic problem with section 112 is the unworkable statutory test for setting emission standards for nonthreshold pollutants, such as airborne carcinogens. * * *

* * * Even if the EPA lists a pollutant, the fear of excessively stringent emission requirements may paralyze or delay the process of setting standards. For example, the delay between the proposed and final vinyl chloride standards has been attributed in part to legal uncertainty about the degree of reduction of emissions that was intended by Congress. Difficulty in interpreting the 'ample margin of safety' language was apparently a major impediment to implementation of section 112 during the Carter Administration.

NOTES

1. Which explanation(s) do you find most convincing? Why?

2. Is one of the problems with the old section 112 that its listing-regulation structure invited resistance, as Graham argues? Another way of thinking about this problem is that Congress conflated two objects of legislation that should remain separate:

> * * * A statutory design that accomplishes this separation of predicate and target can be found in the hazardous air pollutant control process of the pre-1990 Clean Air Act. That process required EPA first to list chemicals under a low threshold of risk (the predicate), and then required the automatic imposition of very stringent controls (the target). Separating predicate and target allows the agency the greatest flexibility to identify problems, and then to deal with them appropriately. The pre-1990 Clean Air Act failed, however, because it nullified the distinction between predicate and target by requiring that extremely rigorous controls follow automatically from listing. Since EPA could avoid unduly burdensome targets only by exercising discretion not to list in the first place, in most cases it took no action at all.

John S. Applegate, *Worst Things First: Risk, Information, and Regulatory Structure in Toxic Substances Control*, 9 YALE J. ON REG. 277, 309 (1992). Or is the structure simply a symptom rather than a cause? Why did Congress adopt this structure in the first place?

3. *Remedies.* What kinds of remedies do the authors' imply for amendment of the statute? Are they consistent with each other? Is there a consensus on any point? As you turn to Congress' reaction to EPA's inaction, consider whether its solution addresses the real problems with section 112.

3. The 1990 Amendments

Frustrated by the glacial pace of regulation under the original section 112, having received little assistance from the judiciary in moving the program along, and reacting to the first Toxic Release Inventory data (which revealed releases of over 2.7 billion pounds of hazardous air pollutants per year, to which EPA attributed 1000-3000 deaths), Congress devoted much of its effort to air toxics in the wide-ranging revision of the CAA in 1990. The 1990 Amendments as a whole constituted a massive piece of legislation, making significant changes to nearly every part of the original regulatory scheme and addressing several entirely new concerns. The new section 112 was in keeping with the rest of the legislation: it is very long (practically its own, free-standing regulatory structure), very detailed, and very different from the old provision.

Read the current section 112. Start with the table of contents of section 112 to get a sense of what it contains and how it is organized. There has been an avalanche of rulemaking under the 1990 Amendments (which, of course, is what Congress wanted to see); however, there has been almost no reported litigation under the 1990 Amendments and none on its main substantive provisions, so the statutory text is your best guide. There follows an outline of the core elements of section 112, together with questions that are intended to help you work through the details.

Listing

EPA's first step, as before, is identifying and listing HAPs. §112(b). How does the new statute differ from the old? Why did Congress draft its own list? Are any of the definitions (§ 112(a)) important to understanding what is a HAP?

Source Categories

As you might expect in a technology-based system, EPA's next step is to define source categories. §112(c). Why is this step important? How does it differentiate the old and new sections 112? Note the specific inclusion and exclusion of certain sources (§ 112(c)(6)-(9))-what are the rationales for these provisions?

Why did Congress adopt a statutory list of pollutants, and yet order regulation to proceed by industry categories? Don't these approaches suggest different results, chemical-based regulation being more closely related to risk, and industrial process-based regulation to technology? How did Congress create "crosswalks" between the chemical-based and process-based regulation (§ 112(c)(3) is one-there are several others throughout the section)? Why are these crosswalks important?

EPA now has to contend both with a list of 189 pollutants (in the statute) and a list of source categories which currently stands at 179 categories and subcategories (63 Fed. Reg. 7155 (1998)). How does this *streamline* promulgation of NESHAPs?[82]

Maximum Achievable Control Technology (MACT)

How is MACT determined? *See* § 112(d),(e). This determination is not only informed by various listed considerations-what are they? (don't forget (d)(4))-but also by the specification of separate "floors" for existing and new sources. How are the floors determined? Congress expected MACT to achieve 75-90% reductions in HAPs. Note also the range of options given to EPA for structuring its standards-what are the pros and cons of relying on using work practices?

How does the new standard differ from the *Vinyl Chloride/Benzene* analysis? How does it compare with the Clean Water Act BAT approach? Why did Congress (and industry, environmentalists, and EPA) think that it is a better, or at least faster, approach? Are they right?

The voluntary reduction program set out in section 112(i) allows polluters who reduce HAPs by 90% to defer compliance with their MACT obligations by six years.[83] Why might an early reductions program be attractive to polluters? To regulators? Does the following chart, taken from the proposed early reductions rule, explain why the program is acceptable to environmental groups?

---

[82] It is perhaps a measure of the pressure created by the workload of all these categories and lists that EPA pursued and the Department of Justice defended the use of a generic air dispersion model on a chemical that was known to be a *solid* at the model's assumed temperature. EPA's use of the generic model was tartly rejected by the D.C. Circuit. Chemical Mnfrs. Assn. v. EPA, 28 F.3d 1259 (D.C. Cir. 1994).

[83] For a helpful guide to the early emissions program, *see* David P. Novello & Robert J. Martineau, Jr., *Better Earlier than Later: EPA's Air Toxics "Early Reduction" Program*, 24 Envt. Rep. (BNA) 401 (1993).

Emissions Under Early Reductions vs. MACT[84]

Time from proposal to promulgation (years)	MACT scenario	Early reduction scenario
Year 1	100	10
Year 2	100	10
Year 3	100	10
Year 4	100	10
Year 5	2	10
Year 6	2	10
Year 7	2	10
Year 8	2	10
Year 9	2	10
Year 10	2	10
Totals	***412**	***100**

Assumptions: 100 ton/yr source (uncontrolled); MACT achieves 98% control; MACT is effective 3 yrs after promulgation; 9 yrs after MACT promulgation MACT applies to source which received a compliance extension.

* Discounting the implicit valuation of these emissions totals at a 3 percent social discount rate leads to present values of 380 tons/year under the MACT scenario and 85 tons/year under the early reduction scenario.

Is this program consistent with the overall two-step (MACT plus residual risk) policy?

Residual Risk

What is the relationship, in terms of schedule and stringency, between the "standard to protect health and the environment" and the MACT standards? Section 112(f) creates a multi-stage process: EPA reports to Congress; if Congress fails to act by a certain time, then EPA must decide whether to impose new standards; finally, EPA must promulgate such standards. Trace this process through subsection (f).

The subsection goes to some length to preserve the "ample margin of safety" language from the pre-1990 statute, with the important difference that *Vinyl Chloride* is overruled (in what respect?). Subsection (f) also states a 1 in 1,000,000 risk standard. How are the margin of safety and 1 in 1,000,000 related to each other? At what point in the multi-step process do they apply-do they state a predicate for regulatory action, or a target level of stringency? With respect to the target, is EPA required to achieve a 1 in 1,000,000 residual risk for all HAPs? For any? Who has the burden of proof?

By adopting a backstop risk standard for HAPs, the 1990 Amendments necessarily waded into the highly controverted area of risk assessment methodology. Their reliance on risk assessment was made all the greater by the use, in addition to the familiar "ample margin of safety" language, of the

---

[84] 56 Fed. Reg. 27339 (table 1) (1991).

the use, in addition to the familiar "ample margin of safety" language, of the quantitative standard of 1 in 1,000,000 excess lifetime risk for carcinogens. (Where else does section 112 require risk analysis?) Recognizing the difficulties before it, Congress commissioned studies of risk assessment by EPA and outside experts to resolve the thorny issues of how the quantitative standard was to be measured.[85]

The 1990 Clean Air Act Amendments are extremely unusual among federal environmental statutes in using a quantitative risk standard in legislation, instead of solely a narrative standard. What advantages might such "bright-line" standards have? The following challenges the conventional wisdom that numerical standards would improve regulatory certainty and production:

> Our analysis suggests that the recent push for mandating numerical levels of acceptable risk in environmental legislation is misguided. Mandated risk levels per se would do little to constrain the discretion of regulators. While EPA cancer risk estimates may appear precise, the final numbers conceal profound scientific uncertainties about chemical carcinogenesis and patterns of human exposure. Slight modifications in modeling assumptions and subtly different interpretations of data, all plausible, can change risk estimates by factors of a thousand or more. However, bright-line statutes would not prevent agencies from making the same regulatory decisions they make under narrative statutes. Regulators could simply bury these decisions in their calculation of cancer risks.
>
> * * *
>
> Even if highly stringent, simple bright lines were faithfully implemented as Congress intended, they would create additional inefficiencies in public policy. Public health efficiency would be compromised because agencies would squander their scarce resources defending expensive regulations from a deluge of industrial opposition. Economic efficiency would be compromised since any uniform bright line will cause undercontrol of some pollution sources and overcontrol of others.
>
> The bright lines thus far proposed would not advance popular understanding of the regulation of cancer risk, an understanding that has already been compromised by certain forms of symbolic legislation. In a modern industrialized society, regulatory decisions demand balancing, implicitly or explicitly, of competing risks, costs, and benefits. By enacting a statute that allows regulators to consider

---

[85] These include the National Academy of Sciences report *Science and Judgment in Risk Assessment* and the Presidential/Congressional Commission on Risk Assessment and Risk Management both of which figured prominently in Chapter 2 (Toxicology and Risk Assessment), *supra*.

only whether a certain risk level has been achieved, Congress would encourage regulators to conceal the array of considerations that affect public policy decisions. By driving debate about competing interests inside the agency, bright lines would further mislead the courts, Congress, the media, and the public about how environmental policy is made.

If legislators are determined to mandate risk levels, * * * a range of acceptable risk levels such as that used in Superfund cleanups, the so-called fuzzy bright line, is preferable to the tyranny of a single risk number. The range-of-risk approach can assure a minimum level of health protection while allowing regulators to consider key factors such as qualitative scientific evidence and biological judgments about a carcinogen's mechanism of action.

Legislators should also give more thought to incorporating population risk, individual risk, risk-risk tradeoffs, and cost-effectiveness into legislated definitions of acceptable risk. A bright line that takes into account only one policy dimension, such as the risk to the maximally exposed individual, will produce poor policy outcomes by causing regulators to neglect other policy dimensions, such as population risk, competing risks, and cost-effectiveness. A complex bright line that incorporates multiple policy dimensions is more intellectually defensible than a simplistic bright line, and could also promote civic education regarding regulatory dilemmas.

Alon Rosenthal *et al.*, *Legislating Acceptable Cancer Risk from Exposure to Toxic Chemicals*, 19 ECOLOGY L.Q. 269, 339, 360-61 (1992). Why do Rosenthal and his co-authors recommend the avoidance of brightline standards? Why do such standards fail the questions at the beginning of the excerpt?

What are other consequences of identifying a numerical bright line? Does it solve EPA's "acceptable risk" problem, or simply introduce new problems? Does it place too much pressure on quantitative risk assessment? Would a risk *range*-as, for example, EPA has adopted for CERCLA (40 C.F.R. § 300.430 (e)(2)(i)(A)(2))-be preferable?

There was, in fact, a strong push in early CAA amendment bills to make quantitative standards more prominent. For example, the original Senate bill would have required closure of plants that posed a 10^{-4} risk to highly exposed individuals, with that threshold lowering to 10^{-6} over time. This proposal received a number of modifications in the Senate-notably, measuring risk according to the "maximally exposed actual person" instead of the hypothetical "maximally exposed individual"-and was not part of the House bill. The Conference compromise was to abandon quantitative standards as a primary measure, but to keep it as a screening tool (§ 112(c)(9)(B)(i)), as a priority-setting device (§ 112(f)(2)(A)), and as a fallback risk standard

(§ 112(f)(2)(A)).[86] Rosenthal *et al.* argue that these latter are appropriate uses of bright-line standards-why?

THE PEDIGREE OF ONE IN A MILLION

Where did one in a million come from? Why not one in a thousand, or one in a billion? The answer, it appears, is that one in a million is a nice round number that strikes most people intuitively as describing an extremely rare event. It had its origins with FDA (as did risk assessment, not coincidentally):

> During the 1970s, the FDA recognized that some procedure would be necessary to quantify low-dose cancer, risks from meat additives and to determine a degree of risk that could be regarded as "essentially zero." FDA rejected detectability as a standard for safety because serious health risks might exist below chemical detection limits and detection technologies were improving rapidly.
>
> FDA's earliest proposal was to use animal data and a probit [dose-response] model to define a "virtually safe dose" that was associated with an incremental lifetime cancer risk of 1 in 100,000,000. Later, FDA replaced the probit model with a linear dose-response model, which was considered more protective than the probit model. When switching to the more protective dose-response model, FDA determined that a risk level of 1 in 1,000,000 would be adequate to protect public health. FDA considered but rejected 1 in 10,000 as an "essentially zero" level of excess cancer risk. Note that if 200 million Americans were each exposed to a meat additive that posed an 1-in-10,000 lifetime risk, 20,000 excess cases of cancer would be predicted over a lifetime. This example illustrates that the size of the exposed population, as well as the level of individual risk, need to be considered by public officials.

John D. Graham, *The Legacy One in a Million*, 1 RISK IN PERSPECTIVE [Harvard Center for Risk Analysis] 1 (1993). EPA borrowed FDA's number as a convenient benchmark, splitting the difference between certain transportation risk levels and a then-current 10^{-7} proposal. *See* Roy E. Albert, Carcinogen Risk Assessment in the Environmental Protection Agency, 24:1 CRITICAL REV. IN TOXICOLOGY 75, 85 (1994). Should this level be more firmly grounded? If so, grounded in what? Or is any number unavoidably arbitrary, so it makes little difference what its origins are?

Some Special Provisions

Emissions averaging. One of the most important of EPA's tasks was the NESHAP for the emissions of the huge synthetic organic chemical

---

[86] For further analysis of the legislative history, *see* Rosenthal, *supra*, 323-27.

manufacturing industry. The hazardous organic NESHAP (HON) covered 112 of the 189 pollutants that Congress listed. 59 Fed. Reg. 19402 (1994). It covers emissions from process vents, storage vessels, transfer operations (plant to truck or train), wastewater operations, and equipment leaks. Each source type includes numerous mechanisms, each of which EPA must study. Equipment leaks, for example, include "valves, pumps, connectors, compressors, pressure relief devices, open-ended valves or lines, sampling connection systems, instrumentation systems, surge control vessels, bottoms receivers, and agitators * * * and control devices used to control emissions from any of the listed equipment." 59 Fed. Reg. 19402, 19409 (1994) (final rule).

The HON permits emissions averaging, a provision much sought by industry, which traces back to the "bubble" concept in the *Chevron* case that we read in Chapter 4. Congress had implied, without explicitly saying so, that averaging is permitted. *See* § 112(a)(1), (i)(5).

What are the limitations and qualifications imposed on emissions averaging? What is the justification for the limitations?

Accidents. As with most of the statutes we study, the CAA primarily targets normal industrial operations, as opposed to upsets.[87] The deadly release of methyl isocyanate from a Union Carbide plant in Bhopal, India, in 1984, and the subsequent non-lethal release of the same chemical at Carbide's plant in Institute, West Virginia, led to the passage of the Emergency Planning and Community Right-to-Know Act in 1986 and the inclusion of section 112(r) in the 1990 CAA Amendments. Like section 112 as a whole, subsection (r) is almost a statute in itself. It requires EPA to list 100 "extremely hazardous" chemicals that could cause serious acute harm, it places on the managers of plants producing such chemicals the obligation to design their plants to prevent and contain accidental releases and to develop emergency plans, and it establishes a safety board to review all such accidents.

Schedule

Section 112(e) established a schedule for publication of the MACT-based standards. In general, it seems more realistic than the old section 112 in recognizing the enormity of the task before EPA, but Congress also wanted results-there is a "hammer" provision in subsection (j)(2). What triggers the hammer? What happens when it falls? The hammer takes advantage of one of the other innovations of the 1990 Amendments, a comprehensive, state-managed permit system covering all types of air emissions.

EPA has, in fact, made reasonably good progress toward its obligations to set MACT standards. promulgating final standards for about forty source categories. It expects to complete two or three times that number by 2000.

---

[87] The important exceptions are the oil and hazardous substance spill provisions of the Clean Water Act, 33 U.S.C. § 1321, the precursor of CERCLA, and CERLCA itself.

EPA has, to this extent, vindicated the promise of the technology-based revisions to section 112.

The Office of Air and Radiation maintains an extremely user-friendly website, the Unified Air Toxics Website http://www.epa.gov/ttn/uatw/, from which one can easily obtain information about the status of all aspects of the program, as well as key documents.

Judicial review

The new section 112(e)(4) contains a single reference to judicial review. Are section 112 emissions standards reviewable? When and where?

PROBLEM
AREA SOURCES AND URBAN AIR POLLUTION

What are "area sources"? The legislative history indicates that Congress had in mind dry cleaners, wood stoves, service stations, and the like. Why are they separately provided for? What emissions standard applies to area sources? Can EPA tighten the first-stage standard to address residual risks (consider both § 112(f) and (k))?[88]

G. A Summary and a Look Ahead

1. Patterns in Traditional Toxics Regulation

As was suggested earlier, perhaps the most important aspect of this chapter is the comparison of the numerous approaches to toxics regulation that the traditional public health and pollution control statutes and their judicial interpretations represent. In making a comparative evaluation of the various approaches, the first step is to try to find some patterns in them-can they be grouped into a workable number of regulatory strategies? The following excerpt attempts such a categorization. The second step is to decide for yourself which strategies seem most and least successful. This will provide a solid basis for comparison with the "unreasonable risk" strategy pursued in the major toxics statutes (FIFRA, TSCA, RCRA, and CERCLA) that comprise most of the rest of the book.

---

[88] Congress' concern with urban air pollution actually prefigures a growing interest in cumulative exposures in risk assessment methodology and in the fairness of the distribution of environmental harms (environmental justice). An excellent discussion of these issues can be found in Robert B. Kuehn, *The Environmental Justice Implications of Quantitative Risk Assessment*, 1996 U. ILL. L. REV. 103. Under the terms of a consent decree with the Sierra Club, EPA has issued a draft Urban Air Toxics Strategy, including *mobile* source controls. 63 Fed. Reg. 49240 (1998).

RISK REGULATION AT RISK: RESTORING A PRAGMATIC APPROACH

Sidney A. Shapiro & Robert L. Glicksman
ch. 1 (forthcoming)

The Regulatory Structure

Once Congress decided to address the "risks" of technology, it filled up thousands and thousands of pages in the United States Code with dense, turgid text that only a lawyer could love. Despite this level of detail, these laws have two common features that give them a similar and relatively simple structure. Risk regulation legislation can be characterized according to Congress' choice of a "regulatory trigger" and "regulatory standard." Table [6.1] organizes some of the prominent examples of risk legislation according to these two aspects. * * *

Regulatory Triggers

The "regulatory trigger" establishes the evidence burden that an agency has to meet in order to regulate a toxic substance or other hazard. Agencies operate under one of four triggers: no threshold, a threshold based on the existence of a "risk" or "significant risk," or a cost-benefit balancing threshold.

* * *

Regulatory Standards

The second structural element consists of the "regulatory standard" or the standard that specifies the level or stringency of regulation. The standards vary in terms of what factors an agency is to take into account in setting the level of regulation. In the first two categories, absolute prohibition (or phase-out) and risk or ambient quality-based standards, agencies regulate (at least in theory) without consideration of economic factors. Under each of the last three regulatory standards, cost is a factor the regulatory agency must consider in determining the level of regulation, although the three standards vary concerning the degree to which cast and the economic impact of regulation constrain the agency's discretion in determining the appropriate method of regulation. The last standard, cost-benefit balancing, is the most cost-sensitive form of regulation.

* * *

Regulatory Triggers	Regulatory Standards				
	Prohibition or Phase-Out	*Risk or Ambient Quality-Based*	*Constrained Balancing*	*Open-Ended Balancing*	*Cost-Benefit Balancing*
No Threshold	FDCA Delaney Clause (1958)	FDCA Pesticide Residues (1996)	CWA Existing Sources (1972, 1977) New Sources (1972)	CWA Ambient Quality Standards (1972)	
Risk Threshold	CAA Ozone Depletion (1990) TSCA PCBs (1976)		CAA Nonattainment (1977, 1990) PSD (1977) NESHAPs (1990) Mobile Sources (1970) New Sources (1970, 1990)	CAA NAAQS/SIPs (1970)	
Significant Risk Threshold			OSH Act (1970) SDWA (1996) RCRA LDRs (1984)	CERCLA (1980, 1986)	
Cost-Benefit Threshold			NTMVSA[89] (1966, 1994) TSCA (1976)	FIFRA (1972)	CPSA (1972, 1981) APSPA[90] (1994, 1996)

Table 6.1—The Structure of Risk Regulation

The Regulatory Pattern

Table [6.1] indicates the way in which Congress has matched regulatory triggers and standards. The results indicate that Congress generally prefers a regulatory trigger requiring evidence of risk or significant risk and a regulatory standard that involves constrained or open-ended balancing.

NOTES

1. *Toxics two-steps.* To a remarkable extent the legal standards in the statutes in this chapter (before and after judicial interpretation) resolve into two-step tests, for example, the *Benzene* plurality's interpretation of the OSH Act. Can you pick out the two-step tests in the various interpretations of the statutes in this chapter?

Why two steps? It may help in answering this question to consider the distinction that Shapiro and Glicksman make between trigger and standard, and between risk assessment and management. How are the trigger-standard

---

[89] National Transportation and Motor Vehicle Safety Act
[90] Comsumer Product Safety Act

and assessment-management distinctions related? Do they track the two-step analysis?

2. Perhaps the most striking feature of the Shapiro and Glicksman chart is the rejection of cost-benefit analysis and the embrace of what they call "constrained balancing," which typically involves reliance on technology-based standards. Moreover, there is a consistent trend to abandon other strategies in favor of technology, as we saw, for example, with the 1977 Clean Water Act Amendments and the 1990 Clean Air Act Amendments.[91] This is particularly remarkable because, at least among academic commentators, technology-based standards have few adherents. Recall the reasons for and against technology-(or feasibility-) based standards above and in Chapter 3.B.4. Why would Congress so frequently resort to this regulatory strategy?[92]

3. *What do you think?* Which strategy is best suited to regulating toxic substances? Does it depend on the context, such as air *versus* water, or occupational *versus* ambient exposures? Suppose that Congress decided to reexamine the toxics provisions of the Clean Water Act-should it stay with its current standards, or should it make changes?

2. The "Unreasonable Risk" Paradigm

We now turn to the four major statutes whose principal concern is toxic substances and hazardous wastes: the Federal Insecticide, Fungicide, and Rodenticide Act (FIFRA), the Toxic Substances Control Act (TSCA), the Resource Conservation and Recovery Amendments (RCRA) to the Solid Waste Disposal Act, and the Comprehensive Environmental Response, Compensation, and Liability Act (CERCLA, or Superfund). Collectively these statutes empower EPA to regulate the "life cycle" of toxic chemicals-from production to use, disposal, and finally to clean-up of failed disposal-and they all deploy a similar substantive standard for regulatory action.

- FIFRA requires the registration and approval by EPA of all pesticides and their intended uses, based on an evaluation of their benefits and the risks they pose to human health and the environment. The lodestar of approval and cancellation decisions is whether the pesticide will have "unreasonable adverse effects on the environment," a standard that is defined as an "unreasonable risk . . . taking into account the economic, social, and environmental costs and benefits of [the pesticide's] use." 7 U.S.C. §§ 136(bb), 136a(c)(5).

---

[91] The phenomenon is analyzed in Oliver A. Houck, *Of Bats, Birds and B-A-T: The Convergent Evolution of Environmental Law*, 63 MISS. L.J. 403 (1994).

[92] For one set of answers, *see* Howard A. Latin, *Regulatory Failure, Administrative Incentives, and the New Clean Air Act*, 21 ENVTL. L. 1647, 1661-69 (1991).

- TSCA focuses on the production and use of industrial and commercial chemicals, though its potential range is much greater. EPA may take regulatory action against a chemical if it finds "an unreasonable risk of injury to [human] health or the environment." 15 U.S.C. § 2605(a). Congress chose not to define "unreasonable risk," but the legislative history makes it clear that it involves on a case-by-case consideration of the severity and likelihood of harm as against the benefits of the chemical.

- RCRA requires EPA to identify and to regulate the disposal methods for "hazardous waste." Listing is a prerequisite for substantive regulation of waste generation, transportation, storage, and disposal under the standard "as may be necessary to protect human health and the environment." 42 U.S.C. § 6922(a). Again, the legislative history clearly contemplates a greater-than-zero level of post-regulation risk.

- Under CERCLA, EPA or private parties may identify locations contaminated with hazardous chemicals, clean them up, and be compensated for their efforts by the generators of the waste and/or the owner of the site. In selecting the method and stringency of clean-up, EPA is to "select a remedial action that is protective of human health and the environment, that is cost effective, and that utilizes permanent solutions * * * to the maximum extent practicable." 42 U.S.C. § 9621(b), (d). EPA interprets this language to indicate a *range* of potential post-regulation risk levels, the final decision being based on many factors including cost and public acceptance. 40 C.F.R. § 300.430(e)-(f).

The substantive standard chosen by Congress in each of these statutes, although phrased in different ways, can generically be called the *unreasonable risk* paradigm. The unreasonable risk standard exhibits four characteristics whose importance to risk regulation will become apparent as we examine each statute in detail: regulation of risk of harm instead of actually realized harm; a quantitatively undefined regulatory goal of a greater-than-zero risk (*i.e.*, less than complete safety); facilitation, and indeed a requirement, of cost-risk-benefit balancing, to include both health considerations and non-health concerns such as technology, feasibility, and cost; and implementation of this balancing through *ad hoc* or case-by-case determinations. These characteristics directly respond to the scientific, economic, and political difficulties of regulating toxic substances, which have been developed in the foregoing chapters; they also determine to a great extent the shape of the resulting regulatory actions.

Despite the similarity of standard, it is also the case that the four unreasonable risk statutes address widely divergent environmental problems. The arrangement of them according to life cycle is intended to highlight these differences. Indeed, the similarity of the underlying standard underscores the many and complex sources of toxic contamination of the environment. Taken as a group, FIFRA, TSCA, RCRA, and CERCLA can be contrasted to the menu of regulatory strategies in the previous chapter. Individually, they offer a wealth of contrasts as they cope with a wide array of physical, economic, policy, and political conditions.

Chapter 7

Pesticides: The Federal Insecticide, Fungicide, and Rodenticide Act

A. Economic Poisons

Pesticides are valuable poisons. For centuries, humans have used various chemical agents to protect themselves, their buildings, and their crops from the enormous number of biological hazards that threaten, respectively, disease, damage, and blight. The federal government has actively regulated pesticides since 1947, when the Federal Insecticide, Fungicide, and Rodenticide Act (FIFRA) was enacted. FIFRA has received numerous updates and overhauls since 1947. The most important were the 1972 amendments, which gave the statute its current structure.[1]

---

[1] An excellent overview of the requirements of FIFRA, from which the following excerpt is taken, is Linda J. Fisher *et al.*, *A Practitioner's Guide to the Federal Insecticide, Fungicide and Rodenticide Act: Part I*, 24 ENVTL. L. REP. (ENVTL. L. INST.) 10449 (1994); *Part II*, 24 ENVTL. L. REP. (ENVTL. L. INST.) 10507 (1994); *Part III*, 24 ENVTL. L. REP. (ENVTL. L. INST.) 10629 (1994). The 1996 Food Quality Protection Act has superseded only a few aspects of the series.

A PRACTITIONER'S GUIDE TO THE FEDERAL INSECTICIDE, FUNGICIDE AND RODENTICIDE ACT: PART I

Linda J. Fisher *et al.*
24 ENVTL. L. REP. 10449, 10451-52 (1994)

First enacted in 1947, FIFRA has been amended numerous times and revised dramatically over the past 45 years. The principal milestones in FIFRA's history are briefly summarized below.

1. Insecticide Act of 1910

The federal government stepped into the field of pesticide regulation with the Insecticide Act of 1910. The Act was not particularly ambitious, doing little more than prohibiting the sale of fraudulently labeled pesticides. It did not establish specific standards for pesticides nor did it require their registration with the government.

2. 1947 Act

Congress enacted FIFRA in 1947, superseding the Insecticide Act of 1910. The statute had two main features. First, it focused on disclosure to pesticide users by establishing product labeling requirements and providing for seizure of products that did not comply with those requirements (so-called misbranded pesticides). Second, the Act mandated that pesticides sold or distributed in interstate or foreign commerce (but not those sold only in intrastate commerce) be registered with the U.S. Department of Agriculture (USDA). Although a registration requirement remains in force, the 1947 statute's provisions bore little resemblance to those in place today. The Secretary of Agriculture had no mandate to evaluate the environmental effects of the pesticides for which registrations were sought or issued and lacked authority to reject an application or to cancel an existing registration. Indeed, an applicant who was informed by the Secretary that its product did not comply with requirements of the statute could nevertheless obtain a so-called registration under protest.

3. Pre-1972 Developments

There were only two significant developments in the first 25 years after FIFRA's enactment. First, in 1964 Congress amended the Act to strengthen the Secretary of Agriculture's enforcement authority. In particular, for the first time the law empowered the Secretary to refuse to register a new product or to cancel an existing registration, as well as to suspend a registration where necessary to address an imminent hazard to the public. Second, when EPA was created in 1970, it was assigned the functions of the USDA's Pesticide Division and other responsibilities for pesticide matters.

4. Federal Environmental Pesticide Control Act of 1972

The most sweeping amendment in FIFRA's history occurred when Congress enacted the Federal Environmental Pesticide Control Act of 1972 (FEPCA). The most significant change was that the Act directed EPA not to register pesticides that caused unreasonable adverse effects to the environment. To buttress this mandate, FEPCA broadened EPA's jurisdiction and powers. For example, the Act extended the registration requirement to intrastate distribution of pesticides; it required establishments that produced pesticides to be registered; it authorized EPA to regulate the use of pesticides, such as by registering certain pesticides only for restricted use as opposed to general use; it established broad new data submission and record keeping requirements; it directed EPA to review the registration of pesticides in use (reregistration); and it strengthened EPA's enforcement powers.

FEPCA also amended FIFRA in ways intended to benefit pesticide registrants. The statute provided that EPA would pay compensation to registrants and applicators who became unable to sell or use existing stocks of pesticides that were canceled or suspended. In addition, the statute specified that an applicant could not rely on data submitted by another unless the applicant paid reasonable compensation for the data, and created a mechanism for protecting submitted data that qualified as trade secrets.

5. 1975 Amendments

In 1975, Congress again amended FIFRA in several respects. Responding to concern that EPA did not give agricultural need sufficient weight in its decision making, Congress required EPA to give the Secretary of Agriculture advance notice of proposed regulations, registration cancellations, and other actions, and created a Scientific Advisory Panel to review such proposed actions. The 1975 amendments also provided that in deciding whether to issue a notice of intent to cancel a pesticide, EPA must take account of the impact of such a cancellation on agriculture.

6. Federal Pesticide Act of 1978

Another major modification of FIFRA occurred when Congress enacted the Federal Pesticide Act of 1978. These amendments effected many significant changes, including provisions that empowered EPA to issue conditional registrations where all of the necessary data to support the registration were not yet available; that revamped the Special Review process for assessing whether already registered pesticides caused unreasonable adverse effects; and that substantially overhauled the provisions concerning data rights and data compensation.

7. 1988 Amendments

The most significant aspect of the FIFRA Amendments of 1988 was their creation of a comprehensive preregistration program. In 1972, FEPCA had required EPA to reregister all then-registered pesticides within four years under the Administration's new regulations promulgated under FEPCA. In 1978, Congress changed that unmet requirement by instructing EPA simply to undertake preregistration in the most expeditious manner practicable. Because EPA had made little progress, the 1988 Amendments enacted a detailed preregistration program, encompassing all active ingredients first registered before November 1, 1984. The initial time frame for reviewing all active ingredients was nine years, and the program was to be funded by increased fees.

The 1988 Amendments also made several other important changes to FIFRA, such as largely eliminating EPA's responsibility to reimburse holders of canceled or suspended pesticides; addressing the storage and disposal of pesticides (including canceled and suspended pesticides); establishing a fast track procedure for registering "me-too" products; and strengthening EPA's enforcement powers.

—

Congress made minor amendments to FIFRA in 1990 and 1991, but did not address the festering controversy of the so-called Delaney Paradox until 1996. Pesticide residues that concentrated in processed foods were treated as food additives and regulated by FDA under the zero-risk standard of the Delaney Clause (§ 409 of the FFDCA, 21 U.S.C. § 348) of the Federal Food, Drug, and Cosmetic Act, while residues found in raw food or that do not concentrate when processed were subject to a more forgiving "tolerances" procedure (§ 408, 7 U.S.C. § 136a) administered by EPA. This often-arbitrary distinction was finally abolished in the Food Quality Protection Act of 1996 (FQPA). It established a new risk-based standard for pesticide residues,[2] which is stricter than the previous tolerances standard; it forbids consideration of countervailing benefits (where have you seen that before?) of the pesticide in setting the standard; and it requires special consideration of the effects on infants and children. Other, less politically visible provisions of the FQPA modified the registration and preregistration requirements for pesticides to encourage minor but valuable uses of pesticides, to expedite registration of safer pesticides, to replace the automatic five-year cancellation of registrations with a fifteen-year review process, and to increase outside review of EPA decisions. It is a masterpiece of balancing concessions to both sides, though perhaps at the cost of a coherent overall approach to pesticide regulation.

KEY PROVISIONS OF FIFRA

§ 2   *Definitions*—"misbranded"; "pest"; "pesticide"; "unreasonable adverse effects;" "public health pesticide."

§ 3   *Registration*—procedures and criteria for obtaining permission to distribute or sell a pesticide for particular uses; data call-in requirement.

§ 4   *Reregistration*—special procedures for renewing the registration of previously registered pesticides; data compensation.

§ 6   *Suspension*—procedures and criteria for suspending or canceling the registration of a pesticide.

§ 12   *Unlawful acts*—specific prohibitions, including prohibitions on the distribution or sale of adulterated or misbranded products.

§ 16   *Administrative procedure and judicial review*—procedures and standards

---

[2] 21 U.S.C. §346a. Recall that other food additives remain subject to the Delaney standard. *See* Chapter 6(A), *supra.*

> for judicial review.
> § 24   *Authority of states*—preemption of state regulation, relation to state tort law.

1. The Pesticides Dilemma

Earlier versions of FIFRA called pesticides "economic poisons" (7 U.S.C. § 135(a) (repealed)). As the term suggests, pesticides are both hazardous and essential. In reading the following materials, focus on the arguments for and against their use. Do the arguments make sense? Do they fairly respond to each other? Is there common ground?

First, however, read section 2 of the statute. The definitions of "pest" and "pesticide," in particular, give some idea of the range of targets and functions of pesticides, and of the range of persons and environments which come into contact with them. There are many "-cides," but the most common are insecticides, herbicides, and fungicides. The following excerpt provides more detail.

TOXICS A TO Z: A GUIDE TO EVERYDAY POLLUTION HAZARDS

John Harte *et al.*
pp. 112-19 (1991)

A. Overview

Each year about 2.6 billion pounds of pesticides are consumed in the United States. Although the amount of pesticides produced and used is a relatively small percentage of all synthetic organic chemicals, pesticides are of particular concern because they are by definition toxic chemicals (the word "pesticide" literally means "pest killer"). They are specifically intended to kill insects (insecticides), plants (herbicides), molds and mildews (fungicides), rats and mice (rodenticides), mites and ticks (acaricides), bacteria (bactericides), birds (avicides), roundworms (nematicides), and even coyotes—whatever people have deemed to be pests. Moreover, they are intentionally introduced into the environment.

In the United States, agriculture accounts for more than 90% of our domestic pesticide consumption. The remaining fraction—a hefty 260 million pounds or so annually—is used to control fungi and other pests in a great variety of products including paints, dentures, shampoos, disposable diapers, mattresses, paper, flea powders, hair wigs, carpets, and contact lenses. Pesticides are used to control algae in lakes and swimming pools and to prevent damage from termites and fungi (dry rot) in wooden structures; they are sprayed on golf courses, lawns, playing fields, and pastures. Because of their extensive use and the manner in which they are applied, pesticides are found everywhere—in our drinking water, our food, our air, and our soils. In short, pesticides are a part of our everyday life.

Plants are the basic food source for the world's rapidly growing human population. Today more than five billion people world-wide compete for food with many thousands of major plant pests, including as many as 100,000 species of plant pathogens (disease-causing agents), more than 10,000 species of voracious insects, 1000 species of crop-destroying roundworms, and 1800 species of economically important weeds. Many more thousands of species are minor agricultural pests that have the potential to become serious pests. Consequently, agriculture may be hard-pressed to keep pace with the demands of an exploding and hungry human population.

* * *

Following World War II, there was a burgeoning of the synthetic organic chemical industry. An entirely new array of apparently superior, inexpensive pesticides, suitable for application over vast acreages, became readily and widely available. Chemically unlike traditional pesticides, the synthetic organic pesticides have largely replaced the inorganic and botanical or naturally occurring compounds. These so-called miracle chemicals promised to eliminate hunger and disease and improve the quality of life for the world's population. Indeed, over a short period of time, these pesticides have changed the nature of the association between people and pests.

* * *

As the scale of operations has vastly expanded in terms of more crops, more acreage, and more frequent applications, the volume of pesticides used has increased dramatically. Just since 1960, the total amount of pesticides produced has doubled (with peak usage in 1975 and 1980). * * * In the late 1940s, about 50 million pounds of pesticides were used annually in the United States. Now about 50 times as much is being used. During just the last 25 years, there has been roughly a doubling in pesticide consumption in the United States alone. Pesticides are applied so routinely and extensively that, to many, pest control is now synonymous with chemical control.

* * *

B. Classification and Patterns of Use

Pesticides are chemically and functionally very diverse. There are more than 600 different active ingredients (the actual substance that kills) registered for use in the United States. These are combined with various other ingredients, such as other pesticides, synergists, and inert ingredients, into about 40,000 pesticide products. These range from widely available moth crystals, snail baits, and flea and tick collars for pets to highly restricted pesticides for use only by trained and properly equipped personnel. Some pesticides are toxic to a wide variety of species and kinds of organisms; these are called broad spectrum agents. A broad spectrum herbicide might be used, for example, to kill all of the shrubs, weeds, and grasses at a construction site. In contrast, other pesticides are highly specific or selective, effective against a narrowly defined group of organisms such as moths and butterflies.

Insecticides, herbicides, fungicides, and so on are available in various usable forms such as liquid sprays, wettable powders, dusts, and granules.

The products are designed for specific application methods: aerial or ground spraying onto the plant leaves, spraying or dusting onto the soil surface, or injecting directly into the plant or soil around the roots.

In theory, the method of application is designed to deliver the pesticide in the most effective or readily usable form for its mode of action. Some pesticides act on contact with the intended victim or target organism, as it is called. Contact (or knockdown) pesticides are rapidly effective, capable, for instance, of killing houseflies on the wing. In contrast, the slower acting systemic insecticides and herbicides are applied to plants, which are themselves either the target pest or serve as food for a pest insect species. The systemics are absorbed by the roots (when applied to the soil) or leaves (when applied to the foliage) of the plant and moved to other tissues. Systemic herbicides interfere with normal plant functions. Systemic insecticides, in contrast, poison plant-eating insects after being absorbed from the stomach following ingestion of the food plant. While systemic insecticides generally do not harm the plant, their effectiveness depends on system-wide transport and accumulation in those parts of the plant—the fruits, nuts, seeds, and leaves—that not only insects but, ultimately people eat * * *.

———

With the new efficacy and utility of pesticides in the years following World War II came concerns over the enormous toxic potency of these chemicals and the scale on which were being applied. These concerns were crystalized in Rachel Carson's *Silent Spring*. In this classic work, she documented the consequences of the pesticide revolution. (Carson focused on DDT, now banned in the United States, but its hazards are shared by many pesticides.) The excerpt from *Silent Spring* is followed by a very different perspective on pesticide use.

SILENT SPRING

Rachel Carson
pp. 15-23, 105-08 (1962)

Elixirs of Death

For the first time in the history of the world, every human being is now subjected to contact with dangerous chemicals, from the moment of conception until death. In the less than two decades of their use, the synthetic pesticides have been so thoroughly distributed throughout the animate and inanimate world that they occur virtually everywhere. They have been recovered from most of the major river systems and even from streams of groundwater flowing unseen through the earth. Residues of these chemicals linger in soil to which they may have been applied a dozen years before. They have entered and lodged in the bodies of fish, birds, reptiles, and domestic and wild animals so universally that scientists carrying on animal experiments find it almost impossible to locate subjects free from such contamination. They have been found in fish in remote mountain lakes, in earthworms burrowing in soil, in the eggs of birds—and in man himself. For these chemicals are now stored in the bodies of the vast majority of human beings, regardless of age. They occur in the mother's milk, and probably in the tissues of the unborn child.

All this has come about because of the sudden rise and prodigious growth of an industry for the production of man-made or synthetic chemicals with insecticidal properties. This industry is a child of the Second World War. In the course of developing agents of chemical warfare, some of the chemicals created in the laboratory were found to be lethal to insects. The discovery did not come by chance: insects were widely used to test chemicals as agents of death for man.

The result has been a seemingly endless stream of synthetic insecticides. In being man-made—by ingenious laboratory manipulation of the molecules, substituting atoms, altering their arrangement—they differ sharply from the simpler inorganic insecticides of prewar days. These were derived from naturally occurring minerals and plant products—compounds of arsenic, copper, lead, manganese, zinc, and other minerals, pyrethrum from the dried flowers of chrysanthemums, nicotine sulphate from some of the relatives of tobacco, and rotenone from leguminous plants of the East Indies.

What sets the new synthetic insecticides apart is their enormous biological potency. They have immense power not merely to poison but to enter into the most vital processes of the body and change them in sinister and often deadly ways. Thus, as we shall see, they destroy the very enzymes whose function is to protect the body from harm, they block the oxidation processes from which the body receives its energy, they prevent the normal functioning of various organs, and they may initiate in certain cells the slow and irreversible change that leads to malignancy.

Yet new and more deadly chemicals are added to the list each year and new uses are devised so that contact with these materials has become practically worldwide. * * *

* * *

Modern insecticides are still more deadly. The vast majority fall into one of two large groups of chemicals. One, represented by DDT, is known as the "chlorinated hydrocarbons." The other group consists of the organic phosphorus insecticides, and is represented by the reasonably familiar malathion and parathion. All have one thing in common. As mentioned above, they are built on a basis of carbon atoms, which are also the indispensable building blocks of the living world, and thus classed as "organic." To understand them, we must see of what they are made, and how, although linked with the basic chemistry of all life, they lend themselves to the modifications which make them agents of death.

* * *

DDT (short for dichloro-diphenyl-trichloro-ethane) was first synthesized by a German chemist in 1874, but its properties as an insecticide were not discovered until 1939. Almost immediately DDT was hailed as a means of stamping out insect-borne disease and winning the farmers' war against crop destroyers overnight. The discoverer, Paul Müller of Switzerland, won the Nobel Prize.

DDT is now so universally used that in most minds the product takes on the harmless aspect of the familiar. Perhaps the myth of the harmlessness of DDT rests on the fact that one of its first uses was the wartime dusting of many thousands of soldiers, refugees, and prisoners, to combat lice. It is widely believed that since so many people came into extremely intimate contact with DDT and suffered no immediate ill effects the chemical must certainly be innocent of harm. This understandable misconception arises from the fact that—unlike other chlorinated hydrocarbons—DDT in powder form is not readily absorbed through the skin. Dissolved in oil, as it usually is, DDT is definitely toxic. If swallowed, it is absorbed slowly through the digestive tract; it may also be absorbed through the lungs. Once it has entered the body it is stored largely in organs rich in fatty substances (because DDT itself is fat-soluble) such as the adrenals, testes, or thyroid. Relatively large amounts are deposited in the liver, kidneys, and the fat of the large, protective mesenteries that enfold the intestines.

This storage of DDT begins with the smallest conceivable intake of the chemical (which is present as residues on most food-stuffs) and continues until quite high levels are reached. The fatty storage depots act as biological magnifiers, so that an intake of as little of 1/10 of 1 part per million in the diet results in storage of about 10 to 15 parts per million, an increase of one hundredfold or more.[3] These terms of reference, so common-place to the chemist or the pharmacologist, are unfamiliar to most of us. One part in a million sounds like a very small amount—and so it is. But such substances are so potent that a minute quantity can bring about vast changes in the body. In animal experiments, 3 parts per million has been found to inhibit an essential enzyme in heart muscle; only 5 parts per million has brought about necrosis or disintegration of liver cells; only 2.5 parts per million of the closely related chemicals dieldrin and chlordane did the same.

This is really not surprising. In the normal chemistry of the human body there is just such a disparity between cause and effect. For example, a quantity of iodine as small as two ten-thousandths of a gram spells the difference between health and disease. Because these small amounts of pesticides are cumulatively stored and only slowly excreted, the threat of chronic poisoning and degenerative changes of the liver and other organs is very real.

---

[3] For a more recent discussion of this issue, *see* Richard L. Williamson *et al.*, *Gathering Danger: The Urgent Need to Regulate Toxic Substances That Can Bioaccumulate*, 20 ECOLOGY L. Q. 605 (1993)—EDS.

Scientists do not agree upon how much DDT can be stored in the human body. Dr. Arnold Lehman, who is the chief pharmacologist of the Food and Drug Administration, says there is neither a floor below which DDT is not absorbed nor a ceiling beyond which absorption and storage ceases. On the other hand, Dr. Wayland Hayes of the United States Public Health Service contends that in every individual a point of equilibrium is reached, and that DDT in excess of this amount is excreted. For practical purposes it is not particularly important which of these men is right. Storage in human beings has been well investigated, and we know that the average person is storing potentially harmful amounts. According to various studies, individuals with no known exposure (except the inevitable dietary one) store an average of 5.3 parts per million to 7.4 parts per million; agricultural workers 17.1 parts per million; and workers in insecticide plants as high as 648 parts per million! So the range of proven storage is quite wide and, what is even more to the point, the minimum figures are above the level at which damage to the liver and other organs or tissues may begin.

One of the most sinister features of DDT and related chemicals is the way they are passed on from one organism to another through all the links of the food chains. For example, fields of alfalfa are dusted with DDT; meal is later prepared from the alfalfa and fed to hens; the hens lay eggs which contain DDT. Or the hay, containing residues of 7 to 8 parts per million, may be fed to cows. The DDT will turn up in the mild in the amount of about 3 parts per million, but in butter made from this milk the concentration may run to 65 parts per million. Through such a process of transfer, what started out as a very small amount of DDT may end as a heavy concentration. Farmers nowadays find it difficult to obtain uncontaminated fodder for their mild cows, though the Food and Drug Administration forbids the presence of insecticide residues in milk shipped in interstate commerce.

The poison may also be passed on from mother to offspring. Insecticide residues have been recovered from human milk in samples tested by Food and Drug Administration scientists. This means that the breast-fed human infant is receiving small but regular additions to the load of toxic chemicals building up in his body. It is by no means his first exposure, however: there is good reason to believe this begins while he is still in the womb. In experimental animals the chlorinated hydrocarbon insecticides freely cross the barrier of the placenta, the traditional protective shield between the embryo and harmful substances in the mother's body. While the quantities so received by human infants would normally be small, they are not unimportant because children are more susceptible to poisoning than adults. This situation also means that today the average individual almost certainly starts life with the first deposit of the growing load of chemicals his body will be required to carry thenceforth.

All these facts—storage at even low levels, subsequent accumulation, and occurrence of liver damage at levels that may easily occur in normal diets, caused Food and Drug Administration scientists to declare as early as 1950 that it is "extremely likely the potential hazard of DDT has been underestimated." There has been no such parallel situation in medical history. No one yet knows what the ultimate consequences may be.

* * *

And No Birds Sing

The survival of the robin, and indeed of many other species as well, seems fatefully linked with the American elm * * *.

The so-called Dutch elm disease entered the United States from Europe about 1930 in elm burl logs imported for the veneer industry. It is a fungus disease * * *. The disease is spread from diseased to healthy trees by elm bark beetles. * * * Efforts to control the fungus disease of the elms have been directed largely toward control of the carrier insect. In community after community, especially throughout the strongholds of the American elm, the Midwest and New England, intensive spraying has become a routine procedure.

* * *

* * * The trees are sprayed in the spring (usually at the rate of 2 to 5 pounds of DDT per 50-foot tree, which may be the equivalent of as much as 23 pounds per acre where elms are numerous) and often again in July, at about half this concentration. Powerful sprayers direct a stream of poison to all parts of the tallest trees, killing directly not only the target organism, the bark beetle, but other insects, including pollinating species and predatory spiders and beetles. The poison forms a tenacious film over the leaves and bark. Rains do not wash it away. In the autumn the leaves fall to the ground, accumulate in sodden layers, and begin the slow process of becoming one with the soil. In this they are aided by the toil of the earthworms, who feed in the leaf litter, for elm leaves are among their favorite foods. In feeding on the leaves the worms also swallow the insecticide, accumulating and concentrating it in their bodies. Dr. Barker found deposits of DDT throughout the digestive tracts of the worms, their blood vessels, nerves, and body wall. Undoubtedly some of the earthworms themselves succumb, but others survive to become "biological magnifiers" of the poison. In the spring the robins return to provide another link in the cycle. As few as 11 large earthworms can transfer a lethal dose of DDT to a robin. And 11 worms form a small part of a day's rations to a bird that eats 10 to 12 earthworms in as many minutes.

Not all robins receive a lethal dose, but another consequence may lead to the extinction of their kind as surely as fatal poisoning. The shadow of sterility lies over all the bird studies and indeed lengthens to include all living things within its potential range. * * *

Figure 7.1–DDT Spraying at Jones Beach, NY, 1945[4]

A REPORTER AT LARGE: HEART OF THE DELTA

Donovan Webster

The New Yorker, July 8, 1991, p. 46

To understand just why crop dusting is necessary to agriculture in the Mississippi River Delta, it helps to have planted a bean there. On July 4, 1989, I planted a single scarlet-runner-bean seed at the edge of a farm road outside Clarksdale, Mississippi. Seventeen days later, without my ever watering or fertilizing that seed, it had produced a bright-green vine eight feet nine inches long. Then, on the twentieth day, tragedy struck: bugs discovered my vine. The insects (they were aphids, I later learned) were tiny, the size of pencil dots on a sheet of paper, and there were thousands of them. By the evening of that day, July 24th, the vine was so covered with little bugs that it had become a pulsing, gray-white strand running along the ground. Two days after that–only three weeks after I planted my seed–the vine was dead: a brown, wizened strand that no longer attracted any bugs. My vine, as impressive as its sweet youth had been, had died before producing a single bean.

Were it not for crop dusting, the story of agriculture in the Delta would mirror the sad, speedy history of my bean. There is so much farmland there, and so much of it is swampy or (in the case of the rice fields) totally

---

submerged, that the only way to tend it is from the air. If agricultural aviation should suddenly disappear from the Delta, here's what would happen: Most of the United States rice crop would be destroyed by insects and fungi. Forty per cent of our national cotton harvest would be ruined by bollworm and boll weevil. Roughly a quarter of our national soybean yield would never make it to the silo. The cotton gins would stop, the area's grain elevators would empty, and the farmers of the Delta would have almost no new produce to sell. Rice would have to be imported, the price of domestic cotton would skyrocket, and the spiraling cost of soybeans (used in everything from Hamburger Helper to automobile tires and pharmaceuticals) would make the price of being an everyday American rise appreciably.

* * *

[Melvin Hayes began crop dusting in 1951.] "I sprayed a lot of cotton. We used sulfur dust mixed with DDT and benzene hexachloride. Those old cockpits weren't sealed too good, and that stuff would come back and burn you like crazy. It would get caked on your face. Your gullet would get full of it, and tears would start running out your eyes. And the more the tears ran down, the more that stuff burned. But I managed to survive it."

Hayes shakes his head. He lifts his right hand from the chair arm and points a finger my way. "Then Miss Rachel Carson came along, and in 1962 she wrote a little book called 'Silent Spring,'" he says. "And because of it they outlawed DDT. Said DDT was bad for the planet. That was the beginning of the end—that was when Congress got involved in crop dusting. I laid out tons of DDT, and I don't know that it ever hurt me any. I've eaten more DDT than about anybody, and my son was born fine. He came to earth bald and naked. I've never been sick a day in my life. I've never been to a doctor, except when I had my Army physicals. Never had a cold, or anything.

* * *

"I got into rice growing—fertilizing and seeding fields from the air. Then we started spraying hormonal herbicides. The original one was something called 2,4-D, and it worked well. It killed weeds and some of the bugs. Then, at just about that same time, this really fine herbicide came along. It was called 2,4,5-T, and it was what that Agent Orange stuff they used in Vietnam was. Hormonal herbicides make weeds grow themselves to death. When those weeds get sprayed, their growth speeds up considerably, and they don't have reserve food, so they start eating themselves to keep growing. It kills 'em.

"I sprayed those supposedly bad chemicals for most of my adult life, and the only health effect they ever gave me was that one day I spilled some DDT on my boot and it cured my athlete's foot. I'd had athlete's foot real bad, and two days later it was gone. So I spilled some onto my other boot, and I ain't never had athlete's foot from that day forward. And, far as I know, that's the only thing it'll do to a human being. Here I am, sixty-nine years old and still moving. * * *"

* * *

[Gus Rogers still flies.] "The EPA—they're not bad," he says. "They're pretty realistic about our work. They know that we're necessary to the economy here, and that we're careful with our chemicals. They know we're not screwing up the environment—killing fish, and things. There's this EPA lady who came down here awhile back to look us over. I was loading certain chemicals into Jimmy's plane, and she told me to wear an India-rubber suit when I'm doing that. But she knows I won't wear that suit. It's ninety-seven degrees out, and I'm working in the sun on a black asphalt loading area. I ain't gonna wear no heavy rubber suit. Not ever. I won't even wear those elbow-length rubber gloves. But she had to say her warnings, because that's her job, and the EPA laws say that I have to hear her. The EPA's like that. They're not bad. They test all the new chemicals coming out. Not only for what they'll do to the environment but for what they'll do to the people who work with them. The EPA—they're looking out for people as much as for the environment. They're realistic. It's the damned environmentalists, they're who'll drive you crazy.

"You ever see an environmentalist on the TV?" Rogers goes on. "While he's standing there saying don't use chemicals on cotton, what's he wearing? Is he wearing blue jeans and a shirt? Is he wearing a suit? Aren't all those things made of cotton? Where the hell does Mr. Environmental Protection think that cotton comes from?"

Rogers stares out into the rain. "Then Mr. Environmental Protection starts talking about how we need to use cotton diapers, because the plastic ones are bad for the environment," he says. "In his next breath, he's arguing with himself. So what's he want? Plastic? Cotton? I'll tell you what he wants—he wants it all. * * * And those chemicals Mr. Environmentalist wants nixed, they're always the most effective ones—and they're usually the *least expensive* ones. The newer, synthetic chemicals, they're much more expensive, which only makes the price of blue jeans higher. So sooner or later Mr. Environmentalist will start bawling about the high price of blue jeans, too. He'll go complaining that folks less fortunate than him can't buy blue jeans anymore."

* * *

Despite all the claims of age people that "it's never hurt me," the application of agricultural chemicals remains a potentially dangerous matter. * * *

* * * "The denial that the aerial applicators use about how personally and environmentally dangerous these substances are is a self-defense mechanism," says Janet Hathaway, a senior attorney for the Natural Resources Defense Council. * * * "We now have verifiable human data indicating that many herbicides, including 2,4-D, are carcinogenic. Years of tests have proved that to be true. The danger is no longer speculative. The *degree* of hazard arising from use of these chemicals—that remains debatable. But the hazard to human lives is established. * * *"

NOTES

1. *Pros and cons.* What makes pesticides so dangerous? Why are they so useful? Do their dangers overlap with their benefits? What problems does that create for regulating pesticides?

2. How do humans come into contact with pesticides? What are the routes of exposure, and who is exposed? What are the characteristics of pesticides that make exposure more or less likely?

3. Webster's article presents the case for the use of pesticides, as made by their users. What are the sources of resistance to pesticide regulation? What does Gus Rogers mean by "screwing up the environment"? Would Carson regard that as complete? Is Rogers correct that EPA tests all pesticides to assure their safety?

4. The most recent publicly available EPA data shows that in 1995 about 2.2 billion pounds (excluding disinfectants, which alone account for 2.3 billion pounds) of chemicals were used as pesticides in the U.S., which is about 20 per cent of world-wide usage. Annual expenditures on these chemicals was over $11 billion, 70 per cent of which was spent on agriculture. This is one third of pesticide expenditures in the world. *See EPA, Pesticides Industry Sales and Usage: 1994 and 1995 Market Estimates* (available at http://www.epa.gov/ oppbead1/95pestsales/Intro.html).

5. *Global pesticide use.* The United States is not the only consumer of pesticides. Other countries, especially developing countries, have a far more pressing need for high agricultural yields than the U.S. does (the U.S. government still pays farmers *not* to grow certain crops, and agricultural prices are chronically too low due to oversupply). Moreover, the developing world's needs are only likely to grow more acute in the future. The president of the American Crop Protection Association ("crop protection," it must be said, is a euphemism for pesticides), an organization comprising virtually all of the manufacturers, formulators, and distributors of pesticides in the U.S., warns:

> Our world is already adding enough people every month to populate another New York City, added Mexico every year, and population the size of China every 10 years. Experts estimate that by the year 2050, our world's population may well top 11 billion. It is estimated that the world's farmers will have to triple food productions—virtually as much food as the world has produced, in total, since man first began to cultivate the land for food.

> Denis Avery, director of the Hudson Institute Center for Global Food Issues, points out that world farmers farm about 6 million square miles of cropland today. If we neglect our high yield agriculture and its technology, and move toward organic farming or other low-yield, high-cost methods, nearly six times that amount will be needed by mid-century. That amount of land is equal to North and South America, Europe, and much of Asia combined.

Even by destroying valued rain forests and plowing up environmentally fragile wetlands and erodible areas, we could not gain that much needed farmland. * * * Methods of yesteryear cannot meet that challenge.

Jay J. Vroom, *Technology and Agriculture: "A Bounty of Food and Fiber,"* available at the ACPA website http://www.acpa.org/public/educ/teachers/index_hightech.html. You may, of course, want to consider the source in evaluating Vroom's assertions—just as you should have done in all of the principal readings—but he makes some very important points in favor of continued, and perhaps even expanding, pesticide use. Studies by researchers at Texas A&M University and at Auburn University found that "a 50 percent reduction in pesticide use on crops of nine fruits and vegetables (apples, grapes, lettuce, onions, oranges, peaches, potatoes, sweet corn, and tomatoes) would reduce average yields by 37 percent. A 1995 study by Robert C. Taylor of Auburn University estimated that eliminating the application of pesticides to U.S. fruits and vegetables would increase production costs 75 percent, wholesale prices 45 percent, and retail prices 27 percent." Stephen Huebner and Kenneth Chilton, *Environmental Alarmism: The Children's Crusade*, 15:2 ISSUES IN SCIENCE & TECHNOLOGY 35, 37 (Winter 1998-99). These kinds of claims are a powerful counterweight to calls for the elimination of pesticides.

2. A Labeling Statute

FIFRA presents a unusual environmental policy dilemma because the dangerous qualities of the regulated chemicals are precisely what make them useful. This both necessitates and considerably complicates the balancing of the risks, costs, and benefits of each pesticide. Another peculiarity of pesticide regulation is that it must contend with consumers who are not sophisticated industrial or commercial enterprises. Consumers need to be protected both medically and economically: pesticides should be safe to use, and they should perform as promised. The environmental protection and consumer protection functions are not necessarily inconsistent; however, before 1970, the U.S. Department of Agriculture (USDA) both promoted and regulated pesticides. (Where else have you seen this?) The latter two *are* different goals and their conflict led to FIFRA's move to EPA's jurisdiction when the agency was created in 1970.

The Supreme Court has described the evolution of FIFRA as a consumer protection and health regulation statute:

As first enacted, FIFRA was primarily a licensing and labeling statute. It required that all pesticides be registered with the Secretary of Agriculture prior to their sale in interstate or foreign commerce. The 1947 legislation also contained general standards setting forth the types of information necessary for proper labeling of a registered pesticide, including directions for use; warnings to prevent harm to people, animals, and plants; and claims made about the efficacy of the product.

* * *

In 1970, the Department of Agriculture's FIFRA responsibilities were transferred to the then newly created Environmental Protection Agency, whose Administrator is the appellant in this case.

Because of mounting public concern about the safety of pesticides and their effect on the environment and because of a growing perception that the existing legislation was not equal to the task of safeguarding the public interest, Congress undertook a comprehensive revision of FIFRA through the adoption of the Federal Environmental Pesticide Control Act of 1972. The amendments transformed FIFRA from a labeling law into a comprehensive regulatory statute. As amended, FIFRA regulated the use, as well as the sale and labeling, of pesticides; regulated pesticides produced and sold in both intrastate and interstate commerce; provided for review, cancellation, and suspension of registration; and gave EPA greater enforcement authority. Congress also added a new criterion for registration: that EPA determine that the pesticide will not cause "unreasonable adverse effects on the environment." §§ 3(c)(5)(c) and (D).

Ruckelshaus v. Monsanto Co., 467 U.S. 986, 990-92 (1984). In the Environmental Decade, in sum, FIFRA developed into an environmental safety and health statute. FIFRA's structure, however, reflects its early consumer protection aims and U.S. agricultural policy and food supply issues. It explicitly weighs costs and risks in evaluating regulatory policy for pesticides.

In this sense, FIFRA is a microcosm of the development of environmental law generally.[5] Consistent with its consumer protection origins, FIFRA originally required a showing of safety *and* effectiveness. As environmental concerns came to dominate the statute, the latter issue became optional. On the other hand, EPA may not consider whether the particular pesticide is needed and must register both environmentally inferior and superior pesticides where both meet the licensing criteria.

---

[5] FIFRA, like virtually all of the other environmental statutes, makes special provision for substances or activities that Congress particularly wants to attack or protect. One of these is "public health" pesticides, § 2(nn), which receive special treatment in a number of ways, including the definition of "unreasonable adverse effects." § 2(bb). What is the justification for such treatment? Why did Congress worry that such pesticides would not survive the ordinary cost-benefit balancing of FIFRA?

PROBLEM
THE PRESCRIPTION DRUG ANALOGY

As the Supreme Court recounts, FIFRA originated as a consumer protection statute. As such, it was modeled on the Federal Food, Drug, and Cosmetic Act (FFDCA), and it was designed to ensure that pesticides are, like prescription drugs, both safe and effective when properly used. The FFDCA prohibits the sale of drugs that are "adulterated" or "misbranded." Adulteration covers a variety of sins, but its main thrust is what you would expect: products that contain unwholesome contaminants or that have been prepared under substandard conditions. 21 U.S.C. § 351(a). This is largely a matter of inspections and manufacturing practices. The substantive core of the statute is misbranding, and misbranding focuses attention on the drug's labeling.[6] A drug is misbranded if, among other things, its labeling is false or misleading or it has inadequate directions or warnings. § 352(a), (f).

While misbranding is a general statutory prohibition, in fact the principal arbiter of accuracy and adequacy in labeling is the Food and Drug Administration (FDA). A drug must obtain FDA's approval before it can be sold, § 355(a), and the statute creates an elaborate application and approval process. § 355(b)-(d). The manufacturer's application must include samples of all proposed labeling (most importantly, directions and warnings), § 355(b)(1)(F), and FDA must disapprove the application if there is insufficient information to support the claims of safety and effectiveness, or if FDA concludes that the labeling is inadequate. § 355(d)(4), (5), (7). As a practical matter, assuming that a drug can be shown to be effective for some uses and can be reasonably safely prescribed for those uses, much of the approval process involves negotiation over the contents of the warnings and directions on the label. Manufacturers tend to want to expand the number of uses for which a drug is approved and limit the nature and severity of the warnings; FDA officials tend to approach the label from the opposite direction. The label, then, becomes the principal way for the agency to mediate between the medicinal and harmful effects of prescription drugs.

FIFRA is, to a remarkable extent, still structured in the same way. Examine sections 2, 3, and 12 of FIFRA. Section 12 prohibits misbranding and adulteration. What is "adulteration" under FIFRA? How does it protect the public? What is "misbranding?" What is the substantive standard for determining adequacy of labeling, directions, and warnings? Where is it found? What is the process by which EPA makes these determinations? Conversely, criminal penalties are provided for the use of pesticides contrary to their labeling,[7] as they are for prescription drugs. Is that an effective means of control?

---

[6] "Label" and "labeling" are terms of art in the FFDCA and include both packaging and informational and promotional material provided by the manufacturer. Directions and warnings are part of the labeling. 21 U.S.C. §321(k),(m).

[7] *See, e.g.*, U.S. v. Saul, 955 F. Supp. 1073 (E.D. Ark. 1996) (prosecuting a registered private applicator for using a pesticide to render minnows poison bait for blackbirds and white egrets,

> Procedurally, you will notice in both sections 3 and 6 that approval occurs on a case-by-case basis. Is this a necessary corollary to the FFDCA-based regulatory scheme? This is known as a screening or licensing strategy, and we will return to its structure and implications for FIFRA.
>
> Substantively, what is the basis for the drug-pesticide analogy? What assumptions about pesticides does it imply? Are those assumptions correct? Is it as wise, for example, to rely on labeling to assure safety with pesticides, as it is with drugs?

3. Preemption of State and Local Regulation

Because much of FIFRA's effect is to designate the uses, directions, and warnings to be included on the labels of pesticide products, the advantages and disadvantages of relying on labeling to protect public health and the environment have been worked out in cases involving the preemption of state and local pesticide regulation. Under the Supremacy Clause, of course, Congress is empowered to preempt state and local regulation in any area of authorized federal activity. In most environmental regulation, however, Congress reserves an important state role as part of the enforcement system, the allocation of controls, or even standard setting. In this respect, FIFRA is typical. The states are recruited to participate in the enforcement of federal regulation, and they are permitted to impose sale and use restrictions that are equally or more protective than federal requirements. § 24(a). In *Wisconsin Public Intervenor v. Mortier*, 498 U.S. 804 (1991), for example, the Supreme Court sustained the validity of local permit requirements for aerial application of pesticides and for application to public or quasi-public lands.

However, FIFRA (unlike the FFDCA) forbids the imposition of any labeling or packaging requirements in addition to or different from those imposed by EPA. § 24(b). "The states have joint control with the federal government in regulating the use of pesticides, for the safety of its citizens and their environment, with the exception of EPA's exclusive supervision of labeling." *New York State Pesticide Coalition, Inc. v. Jorling*, 874 F.2d 115, 118 (2d Cir. 1989). This arrangement has given rise to a substantial body of case law on preemption.

NEW YORK STATE PESTICIDE COALITION, INC. v. JORLING

874 F.2d 115 (2d Cir. 1989)

IRVING R. KAUFMAN, Circuit Judge:

During the last two decades, America has recognized the imminent threat to the environment presented by continued pollution of our natural resources. Effective regulation of hazardous chemicals, including pesticides, has

---

a use which is not authorized; he killed a possum, raccoons, a great horned owl, in addition to blackbirds).

emerged as basic to our national environmental policy. Increasingly, many state governments have also taken up the cause. New York is the first state to enact a comprehensive Pesticide Notification Program and as such has become the target of various pesticide trade representatives from across the nation who assert that the new provisions conflict with federal law.

We are urged to conclude that the New York law, designed to assure public awareness that poisonous chemicals are being utilized, is preempted by the Federal Insecticide, Fungicide & Rodenticide Act (FIFRA). Because the program constitutes lawful state regulation of the sale and use of pesticides, rather than impermissible "labeling," we hold that it is not.

The facts are not in dispute. Recently, the New York legislature added Title 10, "Special Requirements for Commercial Lawn Applications," to Article 33 of the New York Environmental Conservation Law (ECL). Title 10, and regulations promulgated by appellee, New York Department of Environmental Conservation, to implement it, set forth various notification requirements intended to alert the public to the impending use of poisonous chemicals and to disseminate information to those who may be exposed.

Specifically, the New York regulations demand that all commercial pesticide applicators follow several steps. They must enter into a written contract with the owner of the premises where extermination is to occur, and provide a list of the chemicals to be applied along with any warnings which appear on the pesticide's Environmental Protection Agency (EPA) approved label. Moreover, they are required to give the prospective purchaser a notification "cover sheet" which provides further warnings and safety information. In addition, signs must be posted on the perimeter of the affected property, instructing persons not to enter the area for a 24-hour period. And, in some instances, vendors must notify the public in newspapers of prospective use over large tracts.

Appellants New York State Pesticide Coalition *et al.* ("Pesticide Applicators") are lobbyists for those involved in the business of selling and using pesticides. They argue that Title 10 and § 325 are facially preempted by § 24(b) of FIFRA, and contend that irreparable injury will result from the cost of both compliance and potential liability under the new law. Moreover, they are concerned that other states will create notification schemes similar to New York's.

FIFRA placed the "labeling" of pesticides within the singular province of the EPA. However, it expressly permitted states to impose regulations on the "sale and use" of these substances in addition to federal statutory requirements, so long as there was no conflict.

On cross-motions for summary judgment, the parties agreed that there were no disputed issues of material fact. Judge McCurn granted appellee's motion, holding that the new legislation was not "labeling," but rather a permissible sale and use regulation and thus not preempted by FIFRA. We agree.

* * *

The federal preemption doctrine is a basic principle of our legal system. The Supremacy Clause of the Constitution provides that the law of the United States "shall be the supreme Law of the Land." U.S. Const. art. VI, cl. 2. In determining whether a state statute is preempted by federal law, and thus invalid under the Supremacy Clause, our task is to ascertain the intent of Congress.

Congress may supersede state law in three ways. A federal statute may expressly state that it displaces state law. The principal claim advanced by appellants is whether Congress's express preemption of "labeling" reaches the activities regulated by New York's statute.

Alternatively, congressional intent to occupy the field may be inferred where a scheme of federal regulation is sufficiently comprehensive to "leave no room" for supplementary state regulation. But this rationale is not pertinent in this case since Congress explicitly preserved the states' right to regulate the "sale and use" of pesticides while reserving "labeling" to federal control. *See* FIFRA § 24(a), 7 U.S.C. § 136v(a).

But, where Congress and the states occupy the same field, federal law will preempt state law to the extent the two actually conflict. Such a clash does not occur unless "compliance with both federal and state regulations is a physical impossibility," *Florida Lime & Avocado Growers, Inc. v. Paul*, 373 U.S. 132, 142-43 (1963), or the state law stands "as an obstacle to the accomplishment and execution of the full purposes and objectives of Congress." *Hines v. Davidowitz*, 312 U.S. 52, 67 (1941).

With this discussion of the pertinent law, we approach the present controversy. The meaning of the word "labeling" as used in the statute is decisive. Appellants argue that the New York notification requirements constitute "labeling" within the meaning of that term as set forth in FIFRA and are therefore preempted by § 24(b). Judge McCurn first concluded that the requirements of the ECL were not "labeling" within the meaning of the federal statute, and then considered whether compliance with the ECL and its regulations and FIFRA is a "physical impossibility" or if the New York laws impede "the full purposes and objectives of Congress" in enacting FIFRA. He found no conflict.

The task of statutory construction begins with the language of the statute. Where the meaning is clear, "'the sole function of the courts is to enforce it according to its terms.'" *United States v. Ron Pair Enterprises, Inc.*, 489 U.S. 235 (1989) (quoting *Caminetti v. United States*, 242 U.S. 470 (1917)).

FIFRA defines "label" and "labeling" as follows:

(1) Label.—The term "label" means the written, printed, or graphic matter on, or attached to, the pesticide or device or any of its containers or wrappers.

(2) Labeling.—The term "labeling" means all labels and all other written, printed, or graphic matter—

(A) *accompanying the pesticide or device at any time;* or

(B) to which reference is made on the label or in literature accompanying the pesticide or device . . . .

FIFRA § 2(p), 7 U.S.C. § 136(p) (emphasis added).

The appellants claim that New York's notification provisions constitute "labeling" since those provisions require additional "written, printed, or graphic matter" which "accompan[ies] the pesticide or device at any time."[8] Because the notification materials are present in some spatial and temporal proximity to the applied pesticide, it is asserted they "accompany" it. But this definition is rather strained. "Labeling" is better understood by its relationship, rather than its proximity, to the product.

Clearly, since the key function of the scheme is to identify and describe the poisonous chemicals, statutory "labeling" may include a warning. But this does not bar all other similar statements. FIFRA "labeling" is designed to be read and followed by the end user. Generally, it is conceived as being attached to the immediate container of the product in such a way that it can be expected to remain affixed during the period of use. *See* EPA Labeling Requirements for Pesticides and Devices, 40 C.F.R. § 156.10(a)(4) (July 1, 1988).

By contrast, the target audience of the New York notification program is those innocent members of the general public who may unwittingly happen upon an area where strong poisons are present as well as those who contract to have pesticides applied. The mere proximity of the warning, for example, notices posted around an enclosed field or copies of the EPA's labeling information provided to the contracting parties, does not transform the admonition into "labeling" within the meaning of FIFRA § 2(p).

To support their construction of the statute, appellants principally rely upon *Kordel v. United States*, 335 U.S. 345, 348 (1948), and *United States v. Diapulse Mfg. Corp.*, 389 F.2d 612 (2d Cir.), *cert. denied*, 392 U.S. 907 (1968). In *Kordel*, literature provided by a drug manufacturer constituted labeling under the Federal Food, Drug and Cosmetic Act because the material advised how end purchasers were to use the drugs. Similarly, the *Diapulse* case involved a medical device whose instruction booklet included false claims of effectiveness against specific diseases. The written matter in these cases was aimed at users [*i.e.*, primarily physicians] of the product, not the general public. The New York regulations, on the other hand, essentially ensure minimum warnings to the public at large and a greater degree of disclosure to those contracting to have pesticides applied. We discern no conflict between them and § 24(b).

Identifying congressional purpose is the "ultimate touchstone" of a preemption inquiry. In enacting § 24(b), Congress clearly sought to set minimum standards for pesticide labeling, not to prevent states from

---

[8] Appellants conceded at oral argument that written contracts between applicators and owners of the properties where extermination is to take place do not amount to "labeling" and therefore are not preempted by federal law.

regulating the "sale and use" of the poisonous chemical substances through mandatory written, printed, or graphic materials revealing the ingredients.

Judge McCurn properly noted that FIFRA's prohibition of state labeling "in addition to or different from" that approved by the EPA has as "its main focus . . . preserving the force of the information contained in the FIFRA label." Notification requirements such as cover sheets, signs, and newspaper advertisements do not impair the integrity of the FIFRA label. Rather, they serve to further the purpose of the statute by enlisting state aid to prevent "unreasonable adverse effects [of pesticide use] on the environment." 7 U.S.C. § 136a(c)(5).

To hold otherwise would preempt a wide range of state activities which Congress did not subject to the jurisdiction of the EPA. Indeed, the General Counsel of the EPA has advised that the New York regulations do not contravene § 24(b): "[I]nterpreting 'accompanies' strictly in terms of physical presence would result in clearly extraneous material such as the logo on the applicator's hat and the license plate on the vehicle in which the pesticide is transported being considered labeling." Letter from James C. Nelson, Acting Assoc. Gen. Counsel, Pesticides and Toxic Substances Div., EPA, to Marc S. Gerstman, Deputy Comm'r and Gen. Counsel, N.Y. Dep't of Environ. Conserv. (Jan. 17, 1989). While we do not rest our decision on a deferral to the EPA's interpretation of the statute, we note that our holding is consistent with the EPA's position that "labeling" comprises those materials designed to accompany the product through the stream of commerce to the end user, but not those designed to notify purchasers of services or the general public.

In sum, Congress intended to moderate the behavior of people who sell and apply pesticides. Because the New York provisions are designed to warn the public at large, they do not constitute preempted "labeling" under FIFRA.

Affirmed.

FEREBEE v. CHEVRON CHEMICAL CO.

736 F.2d 1529 (D.C. Cir. 1984),
cert. denied, 469 U.S. 1062 (1984)

MIKVA, Circuit Judge:

This is an appeal by Chevron Chemical Company from a judgment rendered against it after a jury trial in a suit brought by the minor children and the estate of Richard Ferebee. Ferebee, an agricultural worker at the Beltsville Agricultural Research Center (BARC), an installation of the United States Department of Agriculture located in Beltsville, Maryland, allegedly contracted pulmonary fibrosis as a result of long-term skin exposure to dilute solutions of paraquat, a herbicide distributed in the United States solely by Chevron. * * *

* * *

Paraquat is an important agricultural herbicide that has been sold in the United States since 1966. Paraquat is known to be toxic and to cause acute injury if directly absorbed into the body. For this reason, the sale and labeling of paraquat has been extensively regulated since 1966 by the federal government, first by the Department of Agriculture and currently by the Environmental Protection Agency (EPA).

[Ferebee claimed that under Maryland law Chevron had failed to provide adequate warnings of the dangers of paraquat. On appeal, Chevron attacked the adequacy of the evidence connecting Ferebee's disease to paraquat and argued that in any event a state failure-to-warn products liability claim is preempted by section 24(b). The court addressed the causation argument first, holding that the evidence was sufficient to support a verdict. That portion of the opinion is reprinted in Chapter 5 (Toxic Torts), *supra*. The court then turned to the preemption argument.]

* * *

Chevron contends that, because paraquat is sold in the United States only when accompanied by a label approved by the federal EPA, a state jury is not allowed in a tort suit to find that label inadequate. Chevron's contention on this point appears to be twofold: first, that EPA approval of the label requires a jury to find that label adequate, and second, that federal law preempts state common law actions against Chevron which are based on the theory that paraquat was inadequately labeled. We reject both of these contentions.

Under [FIFRA], EPA extensively regulates the sale and labeling of paraquat. The statute precludes EPA from authorizing the sale of paraquat unless the product, as labeled, will not cause "unreasonable adverse effects on the environment." 7 U.S.C. § 136a(c)(5)(c). Such effects are in turn defined as

> any unreasonable risk to man or the environment, taking into account the economic, social, and environmental costs and benefits of the use of [the] pesticide.

7 U.S.C. § 136(bb). The Act further requires that the label be "adequate to protect health and the environment" and that it be "likely to be read and understood . . . ." 7 U.S.C. § 136(q)(1)(E).

After extensive scientific testimony, EPA approved the sale of paraquat with the label which is at issue in this case. According to Chevron, this approval constitutes an expert, federal determination that paraquat as labeled does not pose an unreasonable risk to the normal user—a determination that a jury is not authorized to question. Because the trial court, applying state law, instructed the jury that it could impose liability only if paraquat was "unreasonably dangerous" and the label "inadequate," Chevron concludes that the verdict must be reversed.

Chevron's argument misunderstands the nature of the determination made by EPA and misconceives the relation between federal and state law. The fact that EPA has determined that Chevron's label is adequate *for purposes of FIFRA* does not compel a jury to find that the label is also adequate *for purposes of state tort law* as well. The purposes of FIFRA and those of state tort law may be quite distinct. FIFRA aims at ensuring that, from a cost-benefit point of view, paraquat as labeled does not produce "unreasonable adverse effects on the environment." State tort law, in contrast, may have broader compensatory goals; conceivably, a label may be inadequate under state law if that label, while sufficient under a cost-benefit standard, nonetheless fails to warn against any significant risk. In addition, even if the ultimate purposes of federal and state law in this area are the same, a state (acting through its jurors) may assign distinct weight to the elements which go into determining whether a substance as labeled is of sufficient net benefit as to warrant its use. To approve use and sale of paraquat, for example, EPA was required to assess *inter alia* the health risks from use of paraquat, to assign a cost value to those risks, and to estimate the benefit to society at large from use of the chemical. Unless Congress intended to preempt states from considering these issues, a question we address below, there is no reason a state need strike the same balance on these difficult questions as EPA. Assignment of values to such "soft" variables as human health is among the most difficult tasks faced in a regulatory society, *see* NATIONAL ACADEMY OF SCIENCES, DECISION MAKING FOR REGULATING CHEMICALS IN THE ENVIRONMENT 41 (1975), and a state may choose to tip the scales more heavily in favor of the health of its citizens than EPA is permitted to by FIFRA. Similarly, a state heavily dependent on agriculture may consider use of paraquat more of a benefit than a state whose economy is primarily industrial, and both states may therefore reach a conclusion different from EPA's regarding the net benefit of paraquat use. Unless FIFRA preempts a state from making these choices, a state jury may find a product inadequately labeled despite EPA's determination that, for purposes of FIFRA, the label is adequate. EPA's determination may be taken into account by the jury, and the jury was instructed in this case that it was permitted to do so, but absent preemption the jury need not give that determination conclusive weight.

That brings us to the heart of Chevron's preemption claim: that FIFRA *does* preempt states from reconsidering such questions and that state tort suits of the sort at issue here are completely preempted by the Act. Chevron's position is grounded upon a section of FIFRA which provides that a state "shall not impose or continue in effect any requirements for labeling . . . in addition to or different from those required under this subchapter." 7 U.S.C. § 136v(b). Chevron argues that a damage action based on the inadequacy of a label has a regulatory aim—to assure that adequate labels are used—and that it is precisely this regulatory aim that FIFRA explicitly preempts.

Damage actions typically, however, can have *both* regulatory and compensatory aims. Moreover, these aims can be distinct; it need not be the case, as Chevron apparently assumes, that the company can be held liable for failure to warn only if the company could actually have altered its warning. (In any event, as we discuss below, Chevron *can* take steps to alter its label).

In this case, a Maryland jury found that the EPA-approved label did not sufficiently guard against certain injuries. Even if Chevron could not alter the label, Maryland could decide that, as between a manufacturer and an injured party, the manufacturer ought to bear the cost of compensating for those injuries that could have been prevented with a more detailed label than that approved by the EPA. That is, Maryland can be conceived of as having decided that, if it must abide by EPA's determination that a label is adequate, Maryland will nonetheless require manufacturers to bear the risk of any injuries that could have been prevented had Maryland been allowed to require a more detailed label or had Chevron persuaded EPA that a more comprehensive label was needed. The verdict itself does not command Chevron to alter its label—the verdict merely tells Chevron that, if it chooses to continue selling paraquat in Maryland, it may have to compensate for some of the resulting injuries. That may in some sense impose a burden on the sale of paraquat in Maryland, but it is not equivalent to a direct regulatory command that Chevron change its label. Chevron can comply with both federal and state law by continuing to use the EPA-approved label and by simultaneously paying damages to successful tort plaintiffs such as Mr. Ferebee.

Imposition of such a dual obligation upon a manufacturer is permissible under the Act. While FIFRA does not allow states directly to impose additional labeling requirements, the Act clearly allows states to impose more stringent constraints on the *use* of EPA-approved pesticides than those imposed by the EPA: "A State may regulate the sale or use of any federally registered pesticide or device in the State, but only if and to the extent the regulation does not permit any sale or use prohibited by this subchapter." 7 U.S.C. § 136v(a). Given this provision, Maryland might well have the power to ban paraquat entirely. We need not decide that issue, however, to hold that, if a state chooses to restrict pesticide use by requiring that the manufacturer compensate for all injuries or for some of these injuries resulting from *use* of a pesticide, federal law stands as no barrier. The fact that Congress has authorized this form of state action also disposes of any argument that such _.te tort remedies impose undue burdens on interstate commerce. As a result, Maryland is entitled to control the use of paraquat for compensatory aims by holding Chevron liable for injuries that could have been prevented by a more adequate label.

Moreover, tort recovery in a case such as this one may also promote legitimate regulatory aims. By encouraging plaintiffs to bring suit for injuries not previously recognized as traceable to pesticides such as paraquat, a state tort action of the kind under review may aid in the exposure of new dangers associated with pesticides. Successful actions of this sort may lead manufacturers to petition EPA to allow more detailed labeling of their products; alternatively, EPA itself may decide that revised labels are required in light of the new information that has been brought to its attention through common law suits. In addition, the specter of damage actions may provide manufacturers with added dynamic incentives to continue to keep abreast of all possible injuries stemming from use of their product so as to forestall such actions through product improvement. That Maryland cannot directly order a change in the way in which paraquat is labeled thus does not deprive the state of legitimate aims which it is entitled to further through the imposition of traditional tort liability.

* * *

[The court then reviewed the grounds for finding preemption:] * * * First, Congress has not *explicitly* preempted state *damage* actions; it has merely precluded states from directly ordering changes in the EPA-approved labels. As many state courts have recognized, in general the "mere compliance with [federal or state] regulatory labeling requirements does not preclude a [jury from] finding that additional warnings should have been given." *Burch v. Amsterdam Corp.,* 366 A.2d 1079, 1086 (D.C.1976) (compliance with labeling requirements of Federal Hazardous Substances Act does not immunize manufacturer from liability for defective warning). Given this general background of interpretative decisions against which Congress acted, and given the clear authority of states to regulate the "use" of paraquat, the Act cannot be said to express with the requisite clarity an intent to bar damage actions based on the inadequacy of an EPA-approved label.

Second, compliance with both federal and state law cannot be said to be impossible: Chevron can continue to use the EPA-approved label and can at the same time pay damages to successful tort plaintiffs such as Mr. Ferebee; alternatively, Chevron can petition the EPA to allow the label to be made more comprehensive.

Third, state damages actions of the sort at issue here do not stand as an obstacle to the accomplishment of FIFRA's purposes. Such a conflict would exist only if FIFRA were viewed not as a regulatory statute aimed at protecting citizens from the hazards of modern pesticides, but rather as an affirmative subsidization of the pesticide industry that commanded states to accept the use of EPA-registered pesticides. That interpretation of FIFRA, however, is precluded by both the explicit savings clause at 7 U.S.C. § 136v(b) and by the entire legislative history of the Act. Of equal importance, federal legislation has traditionally occupied a limited role as the *floor* of safe conduct; before transforming such legislation into a *ceiling* on the ability of states to protect their citizens, and thereby radically adjusting the historic federal-state balance * * *. In response, Chevron perhaps will choose not to send paraquat into Maryland; perhaps the company will distribute additional information on paraquat to Maryland users; or Chevron may petition the EPA to be allowed to use a more detailed label. What Chevron cannot do, however, is to force states, under the purported aegis of a statute aimed at protecting against the hazards of modern pesticides, to accept the use of paraquat and to tolerate uncompensated injuries to that state's citizens. Congress has not expressed a "clear and manifest purpose" to achieve such a result; on the contrary, protection of pesticide users and victims by *both* federal and state law lies at the center of the Act's design. Accordingly, we affirm the decision of the district court and allow the jury's verdict to stand.

—

The federal courts' analysis of *implied* preemption claims was recently clarified by the Supreme Court in *Cipollone v. Liggett Group, Inc.*, 505 U.S. 504 (1992). The following case analyzes FIFRA under the *Cipollone* standards.

PAPAS V. UPJOHN CO. [*PAPAS II*]

985 F.2d 516 (11th Cir. 1993),
cert. denied, 510 U.S. 913 (1993)

PER CURIAM:

* * *

Appellants Minas and Ollie Papas brought a diversity action against Zoecon Corporation seeking compensation for injuries Mr. Papas allegedly sustained due to exposure to pesticides manufactured by Zoecon. The Papases' complaint asserted liability based on negligence, strict liability, and breach of an implied warranty of merchantability. Each of these claims was, in whole or in part, a claim of inadequate labeling for alleged dangers arising from exposure to the pesticides. *Papas I,* 926 F.2d [1019, 1020 (11th Cir. 1991)].

In *Papas I*, we reviewed the district court's partial grant of summary judgment in favor of defendants on the labeling claims. We affirmed, holding that "FIFRA impliedly preempts state common law tort suits against manufacturers of EPA-registered pesticides *to the extent that* such actions are based on claims of inadequate labeling." We confined our analysis in *Papas I* to the doctrine of implied preemption. Later, the Supreme Court vacated the judgment in Papas I and remanded this case to us for further consideration in the light of *Cipollone v. Liggett Group, Inc.*, 505 U.S. 504 (1992). Having looked at *Cipollone*, we conclude that FIFRA expressly preempts the Papases' claims to the extent they are based on inadequate labeling or packaging.

I.

In *Cipollone*, the Supreme Court analyzed, for the claims in that case, the preemptive effect of the Federal Cigarette Labeling and Advertising Act, enacted in 1965 ("the 1965 Act"), and its successor, the Public Health Cigarette Smoking Act of 1969 ("the 1969 Act"). The Court found no cause to look beyond the express pre-emption provisions contained in section 5 of the 1965 and 1969 Acts.

When Congress has considered the issue of pre-emption and has included in the enacted legislation a provision explicitly addressing that issue, and when that provision provides a 'reliable indicium of congressional intent with respect to state authority,' [citations omitted] 'there is no need to infer congressional intent to pre-empt state laws from the substantive provisions' of the legislation . . . . Congress' enactment of a provision defining the pre-emptive reach of a statute implies that matters beyond that reach are not pre-empted.

505 U.S. at [517]. The Court then analyzed the pre-emption provisions of the 1965 and 1969 Acts to decide if the provisions expressly preempted the plaintiff's various claims.

* * *

II.

Section 136v(b) pre-empts those of the Papases' state law claims which constitute "requirements for labeling or packaging in addition to or different from" the labeling and packaging requirements imposed under FIFRA. *Cipollone* convinces us that the term "requirements" in section 136v(b) "sweeps broadly and suggests no distinction between positive enactments and the common law." Common law damages awards are one form of state regulation and, as such, are "requirements" within the meaning of section 136v. To the extent that state law actions for damages depend upon a showing that a pesticide manufacturer's "labeling or packaging" failed to meet a standard "in addition to or different from" FIFRA requirements, section 136v pre-empts the claims.

The Papases' concede that each of their negligence, strict liability, and breach of implied warranty counts alleges in part that Zoecon failed to warn users that its product contained certain harmful chemicals and failed to inform users to take appropriate precautionary measures. Those allegations, like the failure to warn claims in *Cipollone*, require the finder of fact to determine whether, under state law, Zoecon adequately labeled and packaged its product. This inquiry is precisely what section 136v forbids. FIFRA denies states the authority to require that pesticide manufacturers conform to a state law standard of care in their labeling and packaging practices. Thus, to the extent that the Papases' claims require a showing that Zoecon's labeling or packaging "should have included additional, or more clearly stated, warnings, those claims are pre-empted." *See Cipollone*, 505 U.S. at [524]. Thus the *Cipollone* opinion dictates, under an express pre-emption analysis, the same result we reached earlier under the implied pre-emption doctrine.

III.

The Papases say that they seek to prove Zoecon failed to disclose to the Environmental Protection Agency ("EPA"), the agency which administers FIFRA, that Zoecon's product contained benzene. The Papases contend that this alleged omission subjects Zoecon to an agency enforcement action for "misbranding," and they urge that common law damages awarded on this omission theory would not constitute a "requirement . . . in addition to or different from" FIFRA requirements. We reject this argument. As we noted in *Papas I*, it is for the EPA Administrator, not a jury, to determine whether labeling and packaging information is incomplete or inaccurate, and if so what label changes, if any, should be made. States may not interfere with the methods designed by Congress to achieve FIFRA's goals. We think FIFRA leaves states with no authority to police manufacturers' compliance with the federal procedures.

IV.

Appellants urge us to hold that their warning claims "unrelated to labeling and packaging" are not pre-empted by section 136v. They contend that because the language of 136v refers only to "labeling or packaging," the section does not pre-empt failure to warn claims based on point-of-sale signs, consumer notices, or other informational materials that are "unrelated" to labeling and packaging. But any claims that point-of-sale signs, consumer notices, or other informational materials failed adequately to warn the plaintiff necessarily challenge the adequacy of the warnings provided on the product's labeling or packaging. If a pesticide manufacturer places EPA-approved warnings on the label and packaging of its product, its duty to warn is satisfied, and the adequate warning issue ends. Plaintiffs may not interfere with the FIFRA scheme by bringing a common law action alleging the inadequacy of, for example, point-of-sale signs. Because claims challenging the adequacy of warnings on materials other than the label or package of a product necessarily imply that the labeling and packaging failed to warn the user, we conclude that these claims are also pre-empted by FIFRA.

* * *

VI.

We conclude that FIFRA expressly pre-empts state common law actions against manufacturers of EPA-registered pesticides to the extent that such actions are predicated on claims of inadequate labeling or packaging. To the extent that appellants' negligence, strict liability, and breach of implied warranty claims require a showing that Zoecon's labeling and packaging caused the alleged injury, those claims are preempted by FIFRA. Claims that do not challenge Zoecon's labeling and packaging practices are not pre-empted.

NOTES

1. Why does section 24 distinguish between use and labeling? Does this distinction make sense?

2. *Preemption of state regulation.* What was at issue in *Jorling*? Are you persuaded that the New York requirements did not constitute labeling?

The *Jorling* approach was followed in *Chemical Specialties Manufacturers Association v. Allenby*, 958 F.2d 941 (9th Cir. 1992), *cert.*

denied, 506 U.S. 825 (1992), which held that the right-to-know provisions of California's Proposition 65 did not conflict with FIFRA, because the Proposition 65 notification requirements could be met in ways that did not constitute labeling. Note, from this perspective, the important difference between the meaning of labeling in FIFRA and the FFDCA—why is the FFDCA more expansive? Would the FFDCA definition have changed the result in *Jorling*?

3. *Preemption of state tort law.* Even before *Cipollone*, the *Ferebee* rationale had not been faring well in the federal courts of appeals (state courts, not surprisingly, had been more receptive). In *Papas I*, as the above excerpt from *Papas II* points out, the Eleventh Circuit ruled against the plaintiffs on implied preemption grounds. Can you construct persuasive arguments *for* implied preemption and effective counter-arguments to *Ferebee*, putting aside *Cipollone*?

4. *Papas II* has been followed by at least seven other circuits. *See Kuiper v. American Cyanamid Co.*, 131 F.3d 656, 662 (7th Cir. 1997). However, even courts that follow *Papas II* recognize the continuing validity of claims based on defective manufacture or design, such as toxic impurities in the pesticide. *See National Bank of Commerce of El Dorado, Arkansas v. Dow Chemical Co.*, 165 F. 3d 602 (8th Cir. 1999).

5. Would *Cipollone* reverse *Jorling* (and *Allenby*, decided three months before *Cipollone*, but as to which cert. was denied afterwards)? Are *Jorling* and *Papas II* consistent (notice the scope of the preemption)?

6. What do the state efforts to regulate pesticides tell us about the limitations of a label-based regulatory strategy? What are the concerns that the New York statute and Maryland and Florida tort law sought to address? Is concurrent state involvement with pesticide safety a strength or weakness of FIFRA?

B. Environmental Regulation

1. Burden of Proof

As we have seen, the modern structure of FIFRA was set in 1972 and 1978, moving from a consumer protection statute to a more familiar environmental statute. Examine sections 3 and 6 of FIFRA. How do they reflect this change? Note, in particular, section 3(c)(5), which permits the waiver of the efficacy requirement. The FFDCA still makes effectiveness a fundamental part of the approval process. What is the significance of FIFRA's change?

FIFRA is nevertheless unique among the toxics statutes in being based on a licensing system. It requires that all pesticides be registered and have their labeling approved. In addition, regulatory restrictions are most often imposed through the cancellation or suspension (or modification) of existing registrations. The cases that follow explore the relationship between FIFRA's licensing strategy and its substantive regulatory standards. They also consider the balance among the many conflicting interests in pesticide manufacture and use that EPA is expected to achieve. As you will see, the cases adopt very different approaches.

ENVIRONMENTAL DEFENSE FUND V. EPA
(THE *HEPTACHLOR/CHLORDANE* CASE)

548 F.2d 998 (D.C. Cir. 1976)

LEVENTHAL, Circuit Judge:

This case involves the pesticides heptachlor and chlordane. Consolidated petitions seek review of an order of the Environmental Protection Agency (EPA) suspending the registration of those pesticides under the Federal Insecticide, Fungicide and Rodenticide Act (FIFRA) for certain uses. The Administrator of EPA issued an order on December 24, 1975. The order prohibited further production of these pesticides for the suspended uses, but permitted the pesticides' continued production and sale for limited minor uses. Even as to the suspended uses, the Order tempered its impact in certain respects: It delayed until August 1, 1976, the effective date of the prohibition of production for use on corn pests; and it permitted the continued sale and use of existing stocks of registered products formulated prior to July 29, 1975.

One petition to review was filed by Earl L. Butz, Secretary of Agriculture of the United States (U.S.D.A.). Secretary Butz and intervenor Velsicol Chemical Corporation, the sole manufacturer of heptachlor and chlordane, urge that the EPA order as to chlordane be set aside on both substantive and procedural grounds.[9] They contend that substantial evidence does not support the Administrator's conclusion that continued use of chlordane poses an "imminent hazard" to human health, and that the Administrator made critical errors in assessing the burden of proof and in weighing the benefits against the risks of continued use of chlordane.

The other petition, filed by Environmental Defense Fund, urges that the Order did not go far enough to protect against the hazards of heptachlor and chlordane use. EDF sought an injunction against the provisions permitting continued production and use of the pesticides on corn pests until August 1, 1976. EDF also challenges the Administrator's decision to allow continued use of the stocks of the two pesticides existing as of July 29, contending that EPA should have provided for retrieval and controlled disposal of such stocks. EDF also contends that the Administrator erred in failing to suspend certain "minor uses" of chlordane and heptachlor.

* * *

---

[9] Velsicol has voluntarily ceased production of heptachlor for the uses suspended by the Administrator, and has not really attacked the Administrator's decision suspending those uses.
* * *

I. STATUTORY FRAMEWORK AND STANDARD OF REVIEW

The issues posed by administrative action pursuant to FIFRA are not new to this court, and we have previously extensively described the statutory framework for such actions. What is involved here is a suspension of registration of two pesticides during the pendency of the more elaborate cancellation of registration proceeding, initiated in this case by a November 18, 1974, notice of intent to cancel. This 1974 notice stated that there existed "substantial questions of safety amounting to an unreasonable risk to man and the environment" from continued use of heptachlor and chlordane. Public cancellation hearings pursuant to that notice were not expected to commence for some time. On July 29, 1975, the Administrator issued a Notice of Intent to Suspend the registrations of most uses of the two pesticides. The Administrator then commented on that expected delay in completing the cancellation hearings, and cited "new evidence * * * which confirms and heightens the human cancer hazard posed by these pesticides." On August 4, 1975, registrant Velsicol Chemical Corporation requested an expedited adversary hearing on the suspension question pursuant to § 6 of FIFRA. Administrative Law Judge Herbert L. Perlman presided over the cancellation hearings beginning August 12. Evidence was limited to human health issues and the benefits of continued use of heptachlor and chlordane. The record was closed December 4, 1975, and on December 12, the ALJ recommended against suspension, stating that he was unable to find that "heptachlor and chlordane are conclusively carcinogens in laboratory animals." The Administrator reversed that decision on December 24, 1975, and suspended most uses of chlordane and heptachlor.

The Administrator is authorized to suspend the registration of a pesticide where he determines that an "imminent hazard" is posed by continued use during the time required for cancellation. Section 6(c) of FIFRA. An "imminent hazard" exists where continued use during the time required for the cancellation proceeding would be likely to result in "unreasonable adverse effects on the environment." Section 2(l) of FIFRA. The term "unreasonable adverse effects on the environment" is, in turn, defined as "any unreasonable risk to man or the environment, taking into account the economic, social, and environmental costs and benefits of the use of any pesticide." Section 2(bb) of FIFRA.

As in our previous suspension case involving aldrin/dieldrin, the primary challenge raised by Velsicol and USDA goes to the adequacy of the evidentiary basis of EPA's finding that the suspended pesticides present an imminent hazard during the time required for cancellation. The standard against which we test that challenge is defined in Section 16(b) of FIFRA:

> The court shall consider all evidence of record. The order of the Administrator shall be sustained if it is supported by substantial evidence when considered on the record as a whole.

The standard of substantial evidence has been defined as:

something less than the weight of the evidence * * * (T)he possibility of drawing two inconsistent conclusions from the evidence does not prevent an administrative agency's finding from being supported by substantial evidence.

In applying this principle of review[10] in the specific context of a suspension of pesticides, this court has reiterated that "the function of the suspension decision is to make a preliminary assessment of evidence, and probabilities, not an ultimate resolution of difficult issues. We cannot accept the proposition * * * that the Administrator's findings * * * (are) insufficient because controverted by respectable scientific authority. It (is) enough at this stage that the administrative record contain(s) respectable scientific authority supporting the Administrator."

These decisions of our court also point out that the Administrator is not required to establish that the product is unsafe in order to suspend registration, since FIFRA places "(t)he burden of establishing the safety of a product requisite for compliance with the labeling requirements * * * at all times on the applicant and registrant." Velsicol and USDA urge that this allocation of burden of proof relied on by the Administrator is inconsistent with the explicit terms of FIFRA. They rely on FIFRA's specific incorporation of subchapter II of the Administrative Procedure Act, which provides in relevant part that "Except as otherwise provided by statute, the proponent of a rule or order shall have the burden of proof." 5 U.S.C. § 556(d).

The EPA regulation governing the burden of proof in suspension proceedings provides:

> At the hearing, the proponent of suspension shall have the burden of going forward to present an affirmative case for the suspension. However, the ultimate burden of persuasion shall rest with the proponent of the registration.

Assuming that the Administrator is the "proponent" of a suspension order and is governed by § 556(d), the [1946] legislative history of that provision indicates that it allocates the burden of going forward rather than the burden of ultimate persuasion and is consistent with the EPA's apportionment of burden:

> That the proponent of a rule or order has the burden of proof means not only that the party initiating the proceeding has the general burden of coming forward with a prima facie case but that other parties, who are proponents of some different result, also for that purpose have a burden to maintain.

---

[10] The problem of applying the substantial evidence standard to decisions made at the frontiers of scientific knowledge was commented on in *Industrial Union v. Hodgson*, 499 F.2d 467 (1974) [discussed, *supra*, in Chapter 4 (Judicial Role)]. Similar problems are presented in review under the arbitrary and capricious standard.

This allocation of the burden of going forward structures evaluation of the factual evidence adduced for both the Administrator and the reviewing court, and is consistent with the traditional approach that this burden normally falls on the party having knowledge of the facts involved.

In urging that the ultimate burden of proof in a suspension proceeding rests on the Administrator, Velsicol and USDA assert that the suspension decision is a drastic step differing fundamentally from both the registration and cancellation decisions made under FIFRA. But we have already cautioned that the "imminent hazard" requisite for suspension is not limited to a concept of crisis: "It is enough if there is *substantial likelihood* that serious harm will be experienced during the year or two required in any realistic projection of the administrative process." "FIFRA confers broad discretion" on the Administrator to find facts and "to set policy in the public interest." *Wellford v. Ruckelshaus*, 439 F.2d 598, 601 (1971). This broad discretion was conferred on the implicit assumption that interim action may be necessary to protect against the risk of harm to the environment and public health while a fuller factual record is developed in the cancellation proceeding. This avenue of protective relief would be effectively foreclosed if we accepted Velsicol's argument that the Administrator must prove imminent hazard apparently in some sense of weight of the evidence, going beyond substantial likelihood. But as we have already pointed out, the basic statutory directive requires affirmation of the Administrator's decision if supported by substantial evidence, and this requires "something less than the weight of the evidence." We reject that renewed invitation to exercise increased substantive control over the agency decision process, and turn to a consideration of whether the Administrator's decision to suspend most uses of heptachlor and chlordane is supported by substantial evidence.

II. SUBSTANTIAL EVIDENCE SUPPORT FOR THE ADMINISTRATOR'S DECISION

To evaluate whether use of a pesticide poses an "unreasonable risk to man or the environment," the Administrator engages in a cost-benefit analysis that takes "into account the economic, social, and environmental costs and benefits of the use of any pesticide." 7 U.S.C. § 136(bb). We have previously recognized that in the "preliminary assessment of probabilities" involved in a suspension proceeding, "it is not necessary to have evidence on * * * a specific use or area in order to be able to conclude on the basis of substantial evidence that the use of (a pesticide) in general is hazardous." *EDF v. EPA*, 489 F.2d at 1254, *quoted in EDF v. EPA (Shell Chemical Co.)*, 510 F.2d at 1301. "Reliance on general data, consideration of laboratory experiments on animals, etc." has been held a sufficient basis for an order canceling or suspending the registration of a pesticide. Once risk is shown, the responsibility to demonstrate that the benefits outweigh the risks is upon the proponents of continued registration. Conversely, the statute places a "heavy burden" of explanation on an Administrator who decides to permit the continued use of a chemical known to produce cancer in experimental animals. Applying these principles to the evidence adduced in this case, we conclude that the Administrator's decision to suspend most uses of heptachlor and chlordane and not to suspend others is supported by substantial evidence and is a rational exercise of his authority under FIFRA.

A. Risk Analysis of Carcinogenicity of Heptachlor and Chlordane

Velsicol and USDA contend that the laboratory tests on mice and rats do not "conclusively" demonstrate that chlordane is carcinogenic to those animals; that mice are too prone to tumors to be used in carcinogenicity testing in any case; and that human exposure to chlordane is insufficient to create a cancer risk. They place strong reliance on the Administrative Law Judge's refusal to recommend suspension because he was "*hesitantly unwilling at this time* to find that heptachlor and chlordane are conclusively carcinogens in laboratory animals." (emphasis in original). The ALJ recognized however, that on the basis of the record made the Administrator "could determine that the pesticides involved pose potential or possible carcinogenic risk to man" and that he could "find that heptachlor and chlordane are conclusively carcinogenic in laboratory animals." While adopting the ALJ's factual findings, the Administrator concluded that the ALJ had applied an erroneous legal standard in requiring a conclusive rather than probable showing that the pesticides were animal carcinogens, and concluded in any case that the evidence showed heptachlor and chlordane to be animal carcinogens. We affirm.

1. Mice and Rat Studies

An ultimate finding in a suspension proceeding that continued use of challenged pesticides poses a "substantial likelihood of serious harm" must be supported by substantial, but not conclusive, evidence. In evaluating laboratory animal studies on heptachlor and chlordane there was sufficient "respectable scientific authority" upon which the Administrator could rely in determining that heptachlor and chlordane were carcinogenic in laboratory animals.

We start by rejecting Velsicol's argument that the "cancer principles" EPA relied on in structuring its analysis of the mice and rat studies improperly biased the agency's open-minded consideration of the evidence. In brief form, the principles accept the use of animal test data to evaluate human cancer risks; consider a positive oncogenic effect in test animals as sufficient to characterize a pesticide as posing a cancer risk to man; recognize that negative results may be explained by the limited number and sensitivity of the test animals as compared to the general human population; note that there is no scientific basis for establishing a no-effect level for carcinogens; and view the finding of benign and malignant tumors as equally significant in determining cancer hazard to man given the increasing evidence that many "benign" tumors can develop into cancers. The Agency's reliance on these principles did not come as a surprise to Velsicol; they were included in the Administrator's Notice of Intent to Suspend; and * * * form part of the

Agency's "scientific expertise." Velsicol was properly given an opportunity to put in evidence contesting those principles, but failed to demonstrate anything more than some scientific disagreement with respect to them. Velsicol's principal complaint that mice are inappropriate test animals was specifically rejected by the Administrator * * *.

* * *

2. Extrapolation of Animal Data to Man

Human epidemiology studies so far attempted on chlordane and heptachlor gave no basis for concluding that the two pesticides are safe with respect to the issue of cancer. To conclude that they pose a carcinogenic risk to humans on the basis of such a finding of risk to laboratory animals, the Administrator must show a causal connection between the uses of the pesticides challenged and resultant exposure of humans to those pesticides. He made that link by showing that widespread residues of heptachlor and chlordane are present in the human diet and in human tissues. Their widespread occurrence in the environment and accumulation in the food chain is explained by their chemical properties of persistence, mobility and high solubility in lipids (the fats contained in all organic substances). Residues of chlordane and heptachlor remain in soils and in air and aquatic ecosystems for long periods of time. They are readily transported by means of vaporization, aerial drift, and runoff of eroding soil particles. The residues have been consistently found in meat, fish, poultry and dairy products monitored in the FDA Market Basket Survey and are also frequent in components of animal feeds. This evidence supports a finding that a major route of human exposure is ingestion of contaminated foodstuffs. EPA's National Human Monitoring Survey data shows that heptachlor epoxide and oxychlordane, the principal metabolites of heptachlor and chlordane respectively, are present in the adipose tissue of over 90% of the U.S. population.

* * *

Velsicol urges that the dietary exposure resulting from agricultural uses of the pesticides is insignificant, and that current exposure is well below "safe" dose levels as calculated by the Mantel-Bryan formula, or by the World Health Organization's Acceptable Daily Intake figures. Mantel himself criticized the use of the formula for a persistent pesticide, and the Administrator rejected the concept of a "safe" dose level defined by mathematical modeling because of "the incomplete assumptions made by the registrant's witnesses about the sources of human exposure in the environment, the natural variation in human susceptibility to cancer, the lack of any evidence relating the level of human susceptibility to cancer from heptachlor and chlordane as opposed to that of the mouse, and the absence of precise knowledge as to the minimum exposure to a carcinogen necessary to cause cancer." That explanation is within the reasonable bounds of the agency's expertise in evaluating evidence. And it is confirmed by the common sense recognition that reliance on average "safe" dietary levels fail to protect people with dietary patterns based on high proportional consumption of residue-contaminated foods (*e.g.*, children who ingest greater quantities of milk than the general population).

There are several non-agricultural uses which involve a large volume of heptachlor and chlordane as well as significant human exposures. For example, the record shows that approximately six million pounds of chlordane are used annually on home lawns and gardens. The Administrator found that these uses involve high risks of human intake "due to the many avenues which exist for direct exposure, through improper handling and misuse, inhalation, and absorption through the skin from direct contact." Velsicol asserts that the mice studies showing carcinogenic effects after ingestion of chlordane do not warrant an inference about the carcinogenic effects of inhaling it or absorbing it through the skin, and that consequently nonagricultural routes of exposure cannot be considered to present a cancer risk. They rely on *Reserve Mining Co v. EPA*, 514 F.2d 492 (8th Cir. 1975) (en banc). That reliance is misplaced. In that case, the court was concerned with the propriety of the district court's granting the immediate relief of shutting down a plant discharging asbestos fibers into the City of Duluth's drinking water source. It instead ordered cessation of dumping within a "reasonable time" pursuant to the unstructured equitable discretion given the court under the Federal Water Pollution Control Act, even though it had concluded that continued discharge posed a hazard to health. By contrast, the FIFRA statutory scheme mandates explicit relief the suspension of registration when an unreasonable risk to health is made out. We have previously held that it is not necessary to have evidence on a specific use to be able to conclude that the use of a pesticide in general is hazardous. Once the initial showing of hazard is made for one mode of exposure in a suspension proceeding, and the pesticide is shown to be present in human tissues, the burden shifts to the registrant to rebut the inference that other modes of exposure may also pose a carcinogenic hazard for humans. Velsicol has totally failed to meet that burden here. * * *

B. Benefits

Velsicol and USDA challenge the Administrator's finding that the benefits derived from the suspended uses of chlordane do not outweigh the harms done. EDF urges that the Administrator's decision to continue some uses was not justified by evidence that the risk of harm was outweighed by benefits from the continued uses.

1. Use on Corn

Heptachlor and chlordane were used on an estimated 3.5% of the total corn acreage in the United States in 1975, largely in an effort to control black cutworm. Cutworms sporadically infest 2 to 8% of total U.S. corn farms, and occur most often in lowland, river bottom areas. Chlordane and heptachlor are used as preplant treatments to insure against possible infestations. The Administrator found, with record support, that no macro-economic impact will occur as a result of suspending those pesticides. He also found that crop surveillance or "scouting" for infestations during the early weeks of plant growth, together with application of post-emergence baits or sprays where necessary, provide an effective alternative to the more indiscriminate prophylactic use of chlordane and heptachlor. Velsicol urges that this approach is not as effective as the persistent protection provided by chlordane. Especially in the absence of proof of a serious threat to the nation's corn, there is no requirement that a pesticide can be suspended only if alternatives to its use are absolutely equivalent in effectiveness. * * *

* * *

3. Non-Agricultural Uses Suspended by the Administrator

Chlordane is a common household, lawn, garden, and ornamental turf insecticide, with over 7.5 million pounds (36% of total use) so employed in 1974. The ALJ and Administrator found on the basis of substantial evidence that the "efficaciousness of the substitutes for control of household and lawn insects is not really at issue" and that when lack of evidence of substantial benefits from continued use is weighed against the special hazards of exposure presented by the possibilities of inhalation, dermal absorption, and the increased dangers associated with improper handling, suspension of those uses was justified. Similarly, on the basis of evidence in the record, the Administrator could reasonably find that the residual capacity of chlordane was not necessary to control either structural pests or ticks and chiggers, given the existence of effective alternatives to each of those uses.

4. The Administrator's Refusal to Suspend Certain Uses

EDF challenges the Administrator's refusal to suspend use of chlordane or heptachlor on strawberries, for seed treatment, pineapples, the white fringed beetle, Florida citrus, white grubs in Michigan, narcissi bulbs, harvester ants, imported fire ant, Japanese beetle quarantine, and black vine weevil quarantine in Michigan. Following the recommendations of the ALJ, the Administrator found that for each use the benefits outweighed the risks for the limited time under consideration, effective alternatives were generally not available, and that the exposure risk arising from the use was minimal. EDF counters that the total exposure resulting from these "minor" uses is in fact significant, and that the Administrator continued these uses whenever a "colorable" case of benefits had been made out.

Once the Administrator has found that a risk inheres in the use of a pesticide, he has an obligation to explain how the benefits of continued use outweigh that risk. We are satisfied that he has met that obligation here, and that substantial evidence supports his decision. We note, however, that we come to this conclusion in the context of a suspension proceeding where perforce the Administrator is engaged in making a "preliminary assessment" of the evidence; a more careful exploration of economic impact and available alternatives would be required to support continued registration in a cancellation proceeding.

C. Continued Sale and Use of Existing Stocks of Chlordane and Heptachlor for Suspended Uses

Although we have no doubt that the Administrator has the power under FIFRA to exempt from a suspension order the use of existing stocks (in this case stocks existing as of July 29, 1975), the Administrator acted arbitrarily when he failed to even inquire into the amount of stocks left, and the problem of returning and disposing of them. Some evidence must be adduced before an exemption decision is made, and it is the responsibility of the registrant to provide it. It may be that the lapse of time has lessened the current significance of this issue but we are in no position to do other than remand for further consideration.

We affirm the Agency's suspension order of December 24, 1975, as clarified by the order of January 19, 1976, except for the exemption of the sale and use of existing stocks. The record is remanded for further consideration of that issue.

SUPPLEMENTAL OPINION ON PETITION FOR REHEARING

Velsicol argues in its petition for rehearing that in upholding the Administrator's allocation of the burden of proof to the registrant this Court misinterpreted § 7(c) of the Administrative Procedure Act. Velsicol points out that the interpretation adopted by this Court was not advanced by any of the parties and that, in fact, the problem of interpreting the APA as opposed to section 6(c)(2) of FIFRA was not briefed or argued in this proceeding.

* * *

This court has repeatedly held that the 1964 amendments to FIFRA were specifically intended to shift the burden of proof from the Secretary (now the Administrator) to the registrant. In *EDF v. Ruckelshaus, supra,* the court explained:

> Prior to 1964, the FIFRA required the Secretary to register "under protest" any pesticide or other item that failed to meet the statutory requirements. The product remained on the market, and the Secretary reported the violation to the United States Attorney for possible prosecution. In 1964 the statute was amended to eliminate the system of protest registration, and substitute the present administrative mechanism for canceling registrations. The stated purpose of the amendment was to protect the public by removing from the market any product whose safety or effectiveness was doubted by the Secretary.

The House Committee Report accompanying the bill specifically stated:

> The principal effect of registration under protest is to shift the burden of proof from the registrant to the Government. If the product is not registered, the penalty or seizure provisions can be applied on that ground. If it is registered under protest, the Government has the burden of proving that the product does not comply with the act.

Thus, at present, the Secretary can be required to register a product even though he is convinced that it is ineffective and dangerous to human life. He can proceed against it in such case only after it has moved in interstate commerce, and he then has the burden of proving that it violates the law. The bill would correct this situation and afford greater protection to the public by repealing the authority for registration under protest. In its place the bill provides that applicants dissatisfied with the Secretary's action in refusing or canceling registration may have recourse to advisory committee proceedings, public hearings, and eventually judicial review. Thus the bill affords adequate protection to the public, and protects applicants for registration from arbitrary or ill-advised action by the Department.

Thus, we found that "(t)he legislative history supports the conclusion that Congress intended any substantial question of safety to trigger the issuance of cancellation notices, shifting to the manufacturer the burden of proving the safety of his product."

Subsequent decisions reaffirmed this interpretation. * * *

* * *

Lastly, we do not discern in the statute an allocation of burden of proof that is different for suspension hearings than for registration or cancellation proceedings. While the suspension proceeding is in progress, the public is subject to the same risks of injury that are present in the cancellation context, the very risks which caused Congress to shift the burden of proof to the registrant in the original registration. Information relevant to the safety issues is or should be in the possession of the manufacturer. * * *

NATIONAL COALITION AGAINST THE MISUSE OF PESTICIDES V. EPA

867 F.2d 636 (D.C. Cir. 1989)

SILBERMAN, Circuit Judge:

The Administrator of the Environmental Protection Agency appeals from an order of the district court permanently enjoining EPA from permitting "sales, commercial use and commercial application of existing stocks" of the termiticides chlordane and heptachlor pursuant to a settlement agreement under which the producers of the chemicals agreed to voluntary cancellation of the chemicals' registrations under the Federal Insecticide, Fungicide and Rodenticide Act ("FIFRA"). We think the district court misconstrued the relevant provisions of FIFRA by holding unlawful EPA's determination to permit continued sale and use of existing stocks of the canceled termiticides. Accordingly, we reverse the district court and remand with instructions to vacate the injunction and thereby allow EPA to fulfill its commitments under the original settlements.

I.

FIFRA provides a comprehensive framework for regulating the sale and distribution of pesticides within the United States. Under the statute, EPA may not approve a pesticide's introduction into commerce unless the Administrator finds that the pesticide "will not generally cause unreasonable adverse effects on the environment" when used in accordance with any EPA-imposed restrictions and "with widespread and commonly recognized practice." 7 U.S.C. § 136a(c)(5)(D) (1982). "Unreasonable adverse effects on the environment" are defined to include "any unreasonable risk to man or the environment, taking into account the economic, social, and environmental costs and benefits of the use of any pesticide." § 136(bb). With few exceptions, FIFRA prohibits the sale, distribution, and professional use of unregistered pesticides. §§ 136a(a) & 136j(a)(1).

Once registered, pesticides are still subject to continuing scrutiny by EPA. Indeed, section 6 of FIFRA requires EPA to cancel a pesticide's registration after the first five years in which the registration has been effective (and at the conclusion of subsequent five year periods if the registration is renewed) "unless the registrant, or other interested person with the concurrence of the registrant, . . . requests . . . that the registration be continued in effect." § 136d(a). And at any time, EPA may propose cancellation of a registration and initiate elaborate cancellation proceedings if "it appears to the Administrator that a pesticide . . . does not comply with [FIFRA] or . . . generally causes unreasonable adverse effects on the environment . . . ." § 136d(b).

During the pendency of cancellation proceedings, the registration remains in effect unless the Administrator "suspend[s] the registration of the pesticide immediately." § 136d(c). But before suspending, the Administrator must determine that an "imminent hazard" exists—that "continued use of the pesticide during the time required for cancellation proceeding[s] would be likely to result in unreasonable adverse effects on the environment . . . ." § 136(*l*). Even then, FIFRA guarantees registrants the right to an expedited administrative hearing on that issue, and the pesticide's registration remains effective during this latter proceeding. § 136d(c)(2). Only if "the Administrator determines that an emergency exists that does not permit him to hold a hearing before suspending" may he prohibit commerce in the pesticide in advance of administrative proceedings. § 136d(c)(3).

While commerce in unregistered pesticides is generally prohibited, the Administrator may permit continued sale and use of existing stocks of pesticides whose registrations have been canceled provided "he determines that such sale or use is not inconsistent with the purposes of this subchapter and will not have unreasonable adverse effects on the environment." § 136d(a)(1). It is this last provision—section 6(a)(1), concerning the disposition of existing stocks—that we are called upon to interpret today.

Chlordane and heptachlor (to which we refer simply as "chlordane") are part of a class of chlorinated hydrocarbon insecticides known generally as "cyclodienes," introduced into the marketplace for general use in the late 1940s and early 1950s. In recent years, the chemical has been sold and distributed both by chlordane's sole manufacturer, Velsicol Chemical Company, and a number of so-called "reformulator" companies who acquire chlordane from Velsicol and manufacture derivative products. Until 1987, Velsicol and the reformulators maintained various registrations for these products with EPA.

The regulatory action challenged here—concerning the termiticide uses of chlordane—follows an earlier, fiercely disputed controversy regarding the more general uses of the chemical. * * *

The termiticide uses of chlordane were not subject to the 1978 settlement, but the risks and benefits of such uses have been under more or less continuous study by EPA since the late 1970s. * * *

* * * [By 1987, EPA was prepared to conclude] that "the risks of continued use [of chlordane] outweigh the benefits"[, and it] prepared a draft notice of intent to cancel the termiticide registrations of chlordane.

In the meantime, NCAMP and the other plaintiffs brought this action in district court seeking cancellation and emergency suspension. Unbeknownst to them, at some point either shortly before or after the institution of litigation, EPA became engaged in settlement discussions with Velsicol concerning Velsicol's termiticide registrations. These negotiations led to an agreement whereby Velsicol consented to cancellation of certain registered termiticide uses, to suspension of certain others pending the completion of outstanding "data call-ins," and to a cessation of all manufacture, distribution, and sale of chlordane. In exchange, EPA agreed to permit indefinitely the sale and use of existing stocks of chlordane outside the control of Velsicol, which EPA estimated to amount to a two-months' supply at normal application rates.[11]

Upon publication of the settlement terms, plaintiffs amended their complaint and moved to restrain EPA from permitting any use of the existing stocks exempted from the EPA-Velsicol agreement, claiming that EPA had arbitrarily and capriciously failed to make the required FIFRA section 6(a)(1) determination that "continued sale and use of [those] existing stocks . . . [would] not have unreasonable adverse effects on the environment." 7 U.S.C. § 136d(a)(1) (1982). * * *

The Assistant Administrator's statement [in support of EPA's position] began by asserting that the evidentiary standards for a cancellation, suspension, and emergency suspension of a pesticide are different, with the latter two of the three being especially rigorous. He then recounted the

---

[11] Contemporaneously, EPA apparently executed similar voluntary cancellation agreements with certain of the reformulator registrants of chlordane. These settlements were not made public until the fall of 1987. Other reformulators had their product registrations suspended for failure to respond to EPA's December 1986 "data call-in," see 7 U.S.C. § 136a(c)(2)(B)(iv) (1982); the existing stocks outside the control of this latter group were subject to no restrictions as well. * * *

scientific evidence (which he claimed was both disputed and incomplete) concerning the health risks of chlordane exposure, and, as required by the statute, weighed those risks against the "substantial" economic benefits of continued use of chlordane. In view of this risk-benefit analysis, and in light of EPA's conclusion that such analysis did not "warrant [ ] an emergency suspension, or even an ordinary suspension," Dr. Moore stated that EPA had preliminarily decided to issue only a notice of intent to cancel chlordane's termiticide registrations. Under these circumstances, according to Dr. Moore, the subsequent settlement with Velsicol, and its existing stocks provision:

> effected a dramatic reduction in the amount of chlordane compared to what would have been sold and used if there had been no settlement. Of course, if the cancellation proceeding did not result in cancellation, substantially greater amounts of chlordane would continue to have been used. Even if there had been a suspension hearing . . . , the six months of hearings would have produced substantially more chlordane than is currently in the hands of applicators and distributors. Thus, the existing stocks provision in the settlement agreement did not constitute a true concession on the Agency's part; it did not permit any additional use that would not have occurred had the Agency declined to adopt the settlement.

Thus, EPA's section 6(a)(1) determination in support of the existing stocks settlement provision rested principally on the notion that formal cancellation (and suspension) proceedings would allow much larger quantities of chlordane to be introduced into the environment.

On cross motions for summary judgment, the district court found EPA's final section 6(a)(1) determination inadequate. * * * The district court thus construed section 6(a)(1) of FIFRA, in the context of cancellation settlements, to require that the Administrator focus his analysis solely on the risks and benefits of continued use of the quantity of *then*-existing stocks, without consideration of what quantities of product might be *added* to pesticide stocks during agency proceedings *sans* a settlement agreement.[12] Accordingly, the district court held that EPA had failed to comply with section 6(a)(1) and issued an order requiring EPA to prohibit by April 15, 1988, "sales, commercial use and commercial application of existing stocks of chlordane . . . which have been the subject of voluntary cancellations . . . ."

II.

The district court implicitly interpreted section 6(a)(1) to require the Administrator, when he negotiates a voluntary cancellation agreement, to assume hypothetically that he has already issued a cancellation order before he considers the existing stocks question. If a cancellation order formally

---

[12] The court therefore found it unnecessary to inquire into the reasonableness of EPA's determination that suspension or emergency suspension of chlordane's registrations was inappropriate.

issued—if cancellation proceedings had concluded—then the Administrator, when he turned to the issue of existing stocks, would have no reason to consider stock sales made during the pendency of litigation. Those sales or uses would have been accomplished and therefore beyond the regulatory power of the Administrator. So, according to appellees and the district court, it is illegitimate for the Administrator to take into account sales or uses that would otherwise be made during the period of litigation when negotiating an agreed-upon cancellation. In other words, the phrase "such sale or use" in section 6(a)(1) refers only to sales or uses separately contemplated after a registration is actually canceled, and therefore the Administrator's interpretation of section 6(a)(1) allowing consideration of sales or uses that would take place absent the settlement is impermissible.

* * *

Keeping in mind that it is common ground that the statute contemplates settlements, * * * the Administrator's interpretation facilitates such voluntary cancellations and the district court and appellees' interpretation does not. If the Administrator were not authorized to enter into settlement agreements containing existing stocks exemptions, registrants would have every incentive to contest cancellation proceedings, both for the prospect of prevailing and to use litigation time to dispose, at minimum, of existing stocks. In construing statutes that authorize enforcement proceedings, we look with disfavor upon interpretations offered by parties, in opposition to the administering agency, that induce litigation by making settlement impracticable.

Appellees contend that this litigation risk, which the Administrator avoids through settlement, is illusory. They emphasize that the proponent of continued registration bears the burden of persuasion as to whether a given chemical "generally causes unreasonable adverse effects on the environment." *See, e.g.*, 40 C.F.R. §§ 164.121(g), 164.80(b) (1987). But this procedural rule—as important as it may be—hardly eliminates the litigation risk for the Administrator, when acting in his prosecutorial role. Nor do our cases holding that the Administrator satisfies his burden of production by proffering "substantial evidence" of harm from respected scientific sources, *see Environmental Defense Fund, Inc. v. EPA*, 548 F.2d 998, 1005 (D.C.Cir.1976). *Environmental Defense Fund, Inc. v. EPA*, 510 F.2d 1292, 1297 (D.C.Cir.1975); *Environmental Defense Fund, Inc. v. EPA*, 465 F.2d 528, 537 (D.C.Cir.1972), mean that the Administrator is guaranteed victory if the proceedings are contested by the registrant and the ultimate order challenged subsequently in federal court. In any event, the Administrator *himself*, wearing his adjudicatory hat, might determine after an administrative hearing (involving the expenditure of substantial administrative resources) that scientific uncertainty as to the danger of a particular pesticide (combined perhaps with the economic impact of cancellation on "agricultural commodities, retail food prices and [ ] the agricultural economy," 7 U.S.C. § 136d(b) (1982)), indicates that the registration should not be canceled.

We cannot see how the statutory purpose is enhanced by interpreting FIFRA's ambiguous language to force the Administrator to litigate aggressively, even where a settlement might avoid administrative costs, litigation imponderables and, perhaps most important, continued sales of the product during administrative proceedings. After all, the Administrator's charge under section 6(a)(1) is to determine whether permission to continue to sell or use existing stocks will have an "*unreasonable* adverse effect" on the environment. § 136d(a)(1) (emphasis added). If entering into a settlement provides for less use than would be the case if the Administrator initiated formal cancellation proceedings, it seems rather obvious that the settlement, at minimum, meets the statutory test of reasonableness.

Appellees argue that the Administrator's primary rationale for agreeing to the settlement terms—that more chlordane would have been sold and used during litigation than the small amount that the Administrator allowed to be disposed of as part of the settlement—is a red herring. The Administrator, it is contended, could have issued a notice of intent to cancel *and* proceeded immediately to a suspension order or an emergency order, either of which would have avoided the existing stocks problem. One obvious difficulty with the appellees' argument in this case, however, is that even a suspension order could not have been issued before a hearing was conducted (assuming one was requested), which we are told would likely have lasted six months. Only by use of a draconian emergency order would the Administrator have avoided a hearing delay. This argument, moreover, is a good deal broader than simply a challenge to the Administrator's settlement policy. Appellees assert that a determination on the part of the Administrator to issue a notice of intent to cancel a pesticide necessarily implies a determination—except in rare cases— that the basis for seeking a suspension or emergency order has been acknowledged. So, goes the argument, it is a violation of the statute—in the normal case[13] —for the Administrator not to seek interim expedited relief when he issues his notice of intent to cancel.

In this case, it will be recalled, the Administrator had not yet issued a notice of intent to cancel. A draft notice had been prepared, but settlement discussions commenced and concluded before the Administrator decided to issue the notice. This is not without significance, for FIFRA generally requires the Administrator to consult with the Secretary of Agriculture (on economic questions) and a seven-member Scientific Advisory Panel (on environmental health questions) prior to making public any notice of intent to cancel. We are informed that the Administrator had not yet engaged in the required consultation by the time the instant litigation began. Nevertheless,

---

[13] Under appellees narrow construction of the statute, the Administrator could refuse to seek suspension or emergency suspension upon noticing a cancellation only if he demonstrated either that short-term exposure to the pesticide does not present the same environmental hazards as long-term exposure, or that economic gains from certain immediate pesticide applications (for which alternative chemicals are not reasonably available) augment the benefit side of the short-term equation.

we do not think this point is decisive. Had the notice issued, we do not believe the case would require different analysis. Appellees' logic fails on this account: the EPA reasonably reads the statute to provide different evidentiary thresholds for the three procedures the Administrator is authorized to pursue in defeating an existing registration. Accordingly, we think appellees incorrect in assuming that grounds which may support a cancellation notice automatically warrant the Administrator's recourse to FIFRA's summary procedures.

The language of the statute and the case law amply demonstrate that EPA's reading, even if arguably not compelled by the legislative text, is at least consistent with it. A notice of intent to cancel is called for if it *"appears to the Administrator that a pesticide . . . generally causes unreasonable adverse effects on the environment."* 7 U.S.C. § 136d(b) (1982) (emphasis added). We have interpreted this standard as obliging the Administrator to issue such a notice "and thereby initiate the administrative process whenever there is a substantial question about the safety of a registered pesticide." *Environmental Defense Fund, Inc. v. Ruckelshaus*, 439 F.2d 584, 594 (D.C.Cir.1971). That standard is perhaps even less rigorous than the typical "reason to believe" with which many agencies begin enforcement proceedings. Analytically, a notice of intent to cancel is little more than "a determination . . . that adjudicatory proceedings will commence."

By comparison, the Administrator may issue a notice of suspension only if he determines it "is necessary to prevent an imminent hazard" to human health or the environment. 7 U.S.C. § 136d(c)(1) (1982). If the notice is contested, the Administrator must conduct an "expedited" hearing before the suspension can take effect. § 136d(c)(2). We have described that standard as calling for more than a mere "substantial question of safety"; it requires an appraisal that harm to humans or the environment "would be likely to result" during the period required for interagency consultation and cancellation hearings. § 136(l); *see also Environmental Defense Fund, Inc.*, 548 F.2d at 1005 ("It is enough [to justify suspension] if there is substantial likelihood that serious harm will be experienced during the . . . administrative process." (*quoting Environmental Defense Fund, Inc.*, 465 F.2d at 540)). The extraordinary step of emergency suspension is available only if the requisite unreasonable harm would be likely to materialize during the pendency of ordinary suspension proceedings. The Administrator therefore reasonably requires a showing of even more immediate harm before he may halt commerce in a pesticide prior to conducting often lengthy administrative proceedings.

From these different statutory standards it follows that the quality and quantity of evidence of harm to the environment that the Administrator properly requires before choosing one of these three procedural routes will vary along a continuum. The statute authorizes the Administrator to reserve expedited procedures for cases in which the available data reliably demonstrate some sort of immediate threat or where the information before him suggests greater certainty concerning the pesticide's danger to humans than would warrant merely initiating cancellation proceedings. It is true that we have held that the Administrator bears a heavy burden of explaining his decision not to seek suspension when he has issued a notice of cancellation under circumstances where there are "no offsetting claim[s] of any benefit to the public" in using the pesticide. However, our prior decisions in no way purport to conflate the varying standards for issuing a cancellation notice, noticing a suspension, and imposing an emergency suspension.

Under EPA's reasonable reading of the statute, then, the facts placed before the Administrator that might justify issuing a notice of intent to cancel may not necessarily justify suspension or emergency suspension procedures. Perhaps the most important variable in the Administrator's decision, one discounted by appellees, is the degree of certainty the scientific data provide as to the pesticide's danger. In cases such as ours, where the scientific data are uncertain and scientific opinion divided, we do not think Congress intended FIFRA to compel the Administrator to initiate expedited procedures. With that understanding we think appellees' argument concerning the proper construction of section 6(a)(1) fails. It is not necessary for us to decide whether, if the Administrator had sought an interim prohibition of commerce in chlordane in this case and been challenged in court, we would have sustained his action. Suffice it for us to recognize that EPA reasonably distinguishes the standards for initiating these procedures. Given the difference in these discrete standards, it follows that there is no statutory bar to the Administrator's permitting sale or use of existing stocks in return for a registrant's consent to cancel an active pesticide registration.

III.

The district court did not reach the question—which it had no need to do given its statutory construction—whether EPA's decision in this case not to pursue interim relief in favor of settling for a voluntary cancellation was arbitrary and capricious. We do so, rather than remand, since the issue is one of law and the record is complete. We believe the Administrator's determination was within the bounds of reasonableness. Assistant Administrator Moore's declaration explained that "many scientists do not think that chlordane poses a major risk to humans" and that "this divergence of viewpoints is one of the reasons [he] believed it important to have the Scientific Advisory Panel review and comment on the cancer issue." Nor did the agency, according to Moore, have reliable data as to the precise impact on fish and wildlife of termiticide uses of chlordane. Appellees do not dispute these contentions, although they do advance the premise that chlordane's risk to humans—whatever the degree of scientific certainty—obliged the Administrator to use expedited procedures in this case. We do not agree. We think the fundamental scientific question concerning the environmental effects of chlordane's termiticide uses was sufficiently unsettled to justify the

Administrator's putative determination to seek only an ordinary cancellation. Under these circumstances, we believe it was reasonable for the Administrator to conclude that the settlement he reached, providing as it did for continued sale and use of existing stocks of chlordane, would involve the introduction of more moderate quantities of the chemical into the environment than would have been so if contested proceedings had ensued. Only an emergency suspension order would have resulted in less distribution than the settlement; the Administrator's determination that no emergency existed seems unassailable.

* * *

For the reasons stated, we reverse and remand with instructions to the district court to vacate its injunction so that EPA may fulfill the obligations it undertook in eliciting the cancellation settlements.

NOTES

1. *Process.* Trace the procedures that EPA followed to cancel these registrations. Using the cases and section 6 (*et al.*) of FIFRA, can you construct a basic "flow chart" of pesticide regulation? What is the range of actions that EPA is authorized to take? What are the substantive standards to be applied to each?

2. *Burden of proof.* The *Heptachlor/Chlordane* case centers on the allocation of the burden of proof, which it divides into a burden of going forward and a burden of persuasion. What is the difference between the two burdens, and how are they allocated by the court?

What is the legal source of the burden of proof holding of the court? Note that it is customary to place the burden of pleading on the party with the best access to information. Cleary, *Presuming and Pleading*, 12 STAN. L. REV. 5, 11-14 (1959). The allocation of the burden of proof can be outcome-determinative in many kinds of cases, and that is surely the case for toxic substances. Why? How did EPA meet its burden in *Heptachlor/Chlordane*?

3. In the early 1970s, as the *Heptachlor/Chlordane* case suggests, EPA had developed a litigation strategy that worked very well. It instituted cancellation proceedings that emphasized animal testing showing carcinogenicity, documented human exposure, and evidence of increasing pesticide resistance (which suggested limited benefits). An environmentally activist D.C. Circuit cooperated and produced a remarkable line of cases which almost seem to outdo each other in finding stringency in the statute. The foundation of these cases, detailed in *Heptachlor/Chlordane*, is the insistence that pesticide registrants prove that their products are reasonably safe, rather than the usual requirement that EPA prove unreasonable risk. *See Environmental Defense Fund v. Ruckelshaus*, 439 F.2d 584, 593-94 (D.C. Cir. 1971) (DDT) ("any substantial question of safety * * * trigger[s] the issuance of cancellation notices, shifting to the manufacturer the burden of proving the safety of his product"). In subsequent cases, the court held that

this burden of proof forced the *agency* to justify its decision *not* to impose its most powerful controls: once it had issued a notice of intent to cancel, the court suggested, the presumption was that suspension ought to follow, *Environmental Defense Fund v. EPA (Aldrin/Dieldrin)*, 465 F.2d 528 (D.C. Cir. 1972), and that sale of the product would be stopped in the interim. *Environmental Defense Fund v. EPA (Aldrin/Dieldrin)*, 510 F.2d 1292 (D.C. Cir. 1975). *Heptachlor/ Chlordane* was the culmination of this line of cases.

4. *Recent history.* The procedural setting of the *NCAMP* case is complex and so the importance of the legal issue is a bit difficult to see. What, precisely, is the question before the court, and why is it important?

The *NCAMP* case was decided by a very different Court of Appeals than *Heptachlor/Chlordane*. Nine years of Reagan appointees to the D.C. Circuit had fundamentally altered its ideological point of view. Where do the two cases differ? Are they legally inconsistent, or simply inconsistent in approach or "mood"?

NCAMP is similar in tone to a decision a year earlier in the Ninth Circuit, which challenged EPA's suspension of the pesticide dinoseb, at least as it applied to farmers in the Pacific Northwest. *Love v. Thomas*, 838 F.2d 1059 (9th Cir. 1988). The court remanded for reconsideration of the suspension because EPA had based its suspension on "only a cursory evaluation of the availability of alternative pesticides and the consequent economic impact of suspension" and because "EPA was aware that the Pacific Northwest was subject to unusual conditions that made reliance on national [benefits] figures tenuous, if not completely arbitrary." *Id.* at 1071-72. This can only be characterized as a striking departure from the D.C. Circuit's approach in the 1970s.

Read section 6(a)(1) of FIFRA, which was added in 1996. Does it confirm or overrule *NCAMP*?

5. *Pesticide uses.* Both *Heptachlor/Chlordane* and *NCAMP* refer to specific "uses" of pesticides, some of which were canceled, some left alone or modified, and some voluntarily abandoned. Why does EPA regulate particular uses separately, instead of a single standard for all uses of a pesticide? Where in FIFRA is EPA's authority to regulate different uses differently? Is the differentiation among uses related to the FIFRA's use of an "unreasonable risk" approach for pesticides?

6. *USDA.* Note also the alignment of Velsicol and USDA in *Heptachlor/Chlordane*—what is going on here? USDA, which had championed chemical-based agriculture, was largely cut out of pesticide regulation when its pesticide responsibilities were transferred to EPA in 1970. In 1975, Congress brought USDA back into the process by requiring EPA to consult with the Secretary of Agriculture, among others,[14] before taking most serious regulatory actions. § 6(b), (d).

---

[14] The 1996 amendments to FIFRA in the FQPA go even further in requiring EPA to consult with outside organizations. *See* § 25(d)(2).

Although these changes are repeatedly described in the legislative history merely as securing good science and balanced consideration of risks and benefits, one observer of FIFRA has concluded that the 1975 Amendments "gave back to the agriculture lobby a little of the ground it lost when pesticide regulation was removed from the U.S. Department of Agriculture and placed within the newly established EPA." Another commentor has stated more bluntly, "[t]he 1975 amendments . . . were the result of agribusiness dissatisfaction with EPA's attempts to take effective, forceful action to protect public health and the environment."

Donald T. Hornstein, *Lessons from Federal Pesticide Regulation on the Paradigms and Politics of Environmental Law Reform*, 10 YALE J. ON REG. 369, 434-35 (1993). Does the "good science" argument sound familiar?

2. Three Problems for Pesticide Regulation

a. The Delaney Paradox and the Food Quality Protection Act of 1996

For many years, a major source of contention in pesticide regulation was the so-called Delaney Paradox. As explained above, the intersection of the Delaney Clause with FIFRA for pesticide residues on food had resulted in a double standard. For pesticide residues on raw agricultural products or in processed food products in which the processing did not cause the pesticide to concentrate, a pesticide tolerance could be issued on the basis of a cost-benefit balancing. For pesticides which concentrated during processing, the Delaney zero-risk standard applied, meaning that no detectable residues were permitted. This arrangement was confirmed in *Les v. Reilly*, 968 F.2d 985 (9th Cir. 1992), a case similar to *Young v. Community Nutrition, supra*, in that it reaffirmed the zero-risk interpretation of the Delaney Clause. Subsequently, the settlement of a California case obliged EPA to begin to set zero tolerances for several pesticides that it had avoided acting upon under the Delaney standard. *California v. EPA*, No. 89-0752 (E.D. Cal., Oct. 12, 1994).

As we saw in the discussion of the Delaney Clause, Congress is extremely reluctant to permit or to appear to permit carcinogens to be added to food. On the other hand, there was general agreement that the differential treatment of residues was logically indefensible. The Food Quality Protection Act of 1996 amends the pesticide tolerance provision of the Food, Drug, and Cosmetic Act (§ 408) to apply a single standard to pesticide residues: "a reasonable certainty of no harm." 21 U.S.C. §§ 321(s), (q), 346a(b)(2). In making this determination, EPA is required to consider all non-occupational sources of exposure in its determination (including drinking water and exposure to other pesticides with similar toxic mechanisms) and it must make an explicit determination that the tolerances are safe for children, using an additional safety factor of ten where necessary to account for uncertainty. Moreover, EPA may consider the benefits of the pesticide only as against cancer risks; benefits may not be used to override reproductive or threshold risks (why does the distinction cut this way?), risks to children, or annual and lifetime risks.

This and other compromises assured overwhelming passage by a Republican Congress and approval by a Democratic president, but the new analyses have been criticized as impractical and still too stringent.[15] EPA is still struggling with the elaborate analytical tasks it must perform to make the findings required by the statute. A very different perspective is offered by John Wargo, an advocate of strict regulation to protect children from pesticide residues.

The new law focuses EPA's attention on risk assessment to forecast the potential for future health loss from pesticide exposure. Yet pesticide manufacturers hold most of the resources for collecting and interpreting data and much of the legal talent to argue that evidence is too uncertain or risks too insignificant to justify regulatory action.

The Delaney Clause contained a decision standard that avoided exposure assessment. It relied instead on toxicity texts to determine if cancer was "induced" in animals and on food processing tests to find if residues concentrated. Unless both of these conditions were met, no action was required. Now agency scientists must not only conduct these tests but also combine the results with estimates of pesticide exposure in diverse environments to judge the scale of risk. An enormous window of uncertainty has thus been added to the risk calculation.

Congress deliberately avoided controlling methods of risk analysis. Scientists and economists regularly state the foolishness of legislating scientific process. Statutory neglect of methods confers extraordinary advantage to industry, however, increasing its capacity to control the image of chemical risk that is presented to government and the public. EPA retains the discretion to choose appropriate data and methods, and subtle changes in either may push and estimate above or beneath a threshold of significance.

The reform package also constrains the circumstances under which benefits may be considered when EPA sets tolerances. For example, claims that the absence of a pesticide would result in "a significant disruption in domestic production of an adequate, wholesome, and economical food supply" may be used to justify a

---

[15] See Frank B. Cross, *The Consequences of Consensus: Dangerous Compromises of the Food Quality Protection Act*, 75 WASH. U.L.Q. 1155 (1997); Dominic P. Madigan, *Note, Setting an Anti-Cancer Policy: Risk, Politics, and the Food Quality Protection Act of 1996*, 17 VA. ENVTL. L.J. 187 (1998); James S. Turner, *Delaney Lives! Reports of Delaney's Death Are Greatly Exaggerated*, 28 ENVTL. L. REP. (ENVTL. L. INST.) 10003 (1998).

doubling of the cancer risk allowed for individual pesticides. In contrast, benefits may not be considered when setting tolerances for chemicals the agency deems to have threshold effects" such as reproductive damage or acute neurotoxicity. The logic of Congress in making this distinction is not clear. Not only does the new law permit continued use of pesticides that are declared by EPA to be carcinogens, it also permits the agency to consider benefits when setting contamination limits for these chemicals in food. FQPA also requires EPA to publish a pamphlet containing information on the risks and benefits of pesticides, any tolerances that EPA has set based on benefits consideration (nearly 9,000 as of 1998), and consumer guidelines for minimizing exposure to pesticides while maintaining a nutritious diet. The pamphlet will serve an educational purpose, but it will not empower consumers to avoid pesticides. In contrast, labeling of food and other products that are treated with pesticides–or purposely containing them–would give purchasers more direct control over their accumulation of risk.

JOHN WARGO, OUR CHILDREN'S TOXIC LEGACY: HOW SCIENCE AND LAW FAIL TO PROTECT US FROM PESTICIDES 303 (2d ed. 1998).

The new FQPA standard is particularly interesting from the perspective of risk assessment, as it implicitly adopts many of the methods of 1990s quantitative risk assessment—including, through the dubious mechanism of legislative history, the one-in-a-million risk level[16]—and tries to give something to everyone in that context. Read 21 U.S.C. § 346a(b)(2). How did Congress accommodate the agriculture industry? the environmentalists? other identifiable groups? Does section 346a(b)(2) make sense as risk assessment policy?

b. Farmworkers

We have already noted that pesticides put several different groups of people (and nature) at risk, and several of those are occupational groups. People who manufacture pesticides, like all workers with toxic substances, are likely to have much higher exposures to the chemicals than the general population. The Kepone pollution of the James River in Virginia, which was largely responsible for the strengthening of the toxics provisions of the Clean Water Act, was the public manifestation of a problem that was already evidenced by serious neurological harm ("the shakes") to the manufacturer's employees. *See* HARTE *ET AL.*, *supra*, at 120.

The Webster article at the beginning of this chapter demonstrates that the individuals who apply pesticides, either professionally or as a farming chore, can be exposed to large amounts of pesticides in many ways. Mixing concentrates, applying them, and then working in treated fields are all major

---

[16] *See* H.R. REP. NO. 104-669, pt. 2, at 41 (1996).

sources of exposure. Similarly, handlers of agricultural products to which pesticides have been applied can be at risk. Grain elevator workers, for example, were exposed to high levels of the fumigant ethylene dibromide (EDB), and those exposures led in part to EPA's decision to forbid its use as a fumigant.[17]

But the most poorly protected occupational group is farmworkers, especially migrant workers, who cultivate and harvest crops in fields that have been treated with pesticides, often immediately prior to their entering the area.

The data concerning the effects of pesticides on migrant workers [are] not fully inclusive. As was previously stated, many migrant farm workers do not report cases of illness and injury. However, of those that are reported, the data is staggering. Studies reveal that migrant farm workers face alarming health hazards. It is estimated that 300,000 farm workers are poisoned annually. These workers face a risk 24.76 times higher than that of the general population of developing pesticide related illnesses.

Other studies disturbingly reveal that infant and maternal mortality rates among farm workers are 125% higher than those found in the general population. Mortality rates from influenza and pneumonia are 200% higher. While farm workers represent less than four percent of the American labor force, they account for nearly fifteen percent of the deaths and seven percent of the disabling injuries.

The plight of the migrant farm worker is personified in Felipe Franco who was born with no legs and no arms. His mother, Ramona Franco, had been working in pesticide treated farms during the early stages of her pregnancy. Their plight is also personified in Esmaralda Sanchez who developed a brain tumor when she was five. She spends her days strapped to a wheel chair, barely able to move and unable to remember. She is beginning to open and shut her mouth, but still she can not cry.

Migrant workers often share these risks with others who live in areas surrounding "treated" crops. The cancer cases among children in two California counties has sparked the biggest outcry to date. In three townships, twenty-one children have been diagnosed with cancer (four times the expected rate), and four children have been diagnosed with leukemia (thirty-five times the expected rate). There

---

[17] EPA, Decision and Emergency Order Suspending Registrations for Pesticide Products Containing EDB, 49 Fed. Reg. 4452 (1984). EDB and its residues have been regulated under almost the complete alphabet soup of environmental statutes: FIFRA, FFDCA (food tolerances), SDWA, RCRA, CERCLA, and OSHA. EDB also presents an interesting example of risk trade-offs, since it is used to suppress the highly carcinogenic aflatoxin mold on corn, peanuts, and other crops. Aflatoxin mold is not only dangerous to ultimate consumers of the products, but dust containing the mold can be hazardous to grain workers. Moreover, some of the alternatives to EDB may be even more toxic.

is, however, a striking difference between the avenues of recourse available to American citizens and those avenues available to migrant farm workers. Because migrant workers are less likely to report cases of injury or illness, they are less likely ro receive compensation for their unjust suffering.

As illegal aliens, the majority of migrant farm workers, are without voting power. Faced with hostility by the powerful agribusiness unions, they lack the power to demand reforms. Because migrant workers often lack educational skills, they cannot be effective in communicating their needs to any available legal or political agency. As a result, the injuries and the deaths remain untold and unrestrained.

Carlo V. Di Florio & Matthew McLees, *Pesticide Regulation: The Plight of Migrant Farmworkers v. The Politics of Agribusiness*, 1 DICK. J. ENVTL. L. & POLICY 148, 149 (1992). What is worse, the protective policies of environmental statutes may in fact systematically (though not intentionally) *transfer* risk from the general public to farmworkers.

The "reasonable certainty of no harm" standard [in the FQPA of 1996] applies to food pesticide residues, but does not consider risks to farmworkers. These risks remain regulated under a looser "unreasonable risk" standard in FIFRA. The differential decision standards parallel the source of the Delaney Paradox and create similar perversities. Under the FQPA and FIFRA, regulation of pesticides will transfer risk from consumers to farmworkers and will probably increase overall pesticide danger in the process.

The risk transference to workers is common throughout environmental law. The choice to regulate a particular environmental problem may not eliminate a risk but instead transfer that risk to another group of people. There is an innate tendency of regulation to shift risks from more influential groups to those with less political sway. Quite often, reducing public risk often means creating occupational risk. Thus, regulating pesticide residues on food can increase pesticide risks to farmworkers, a particularly disempowered group.[18] The differential standards in the law make such a transfer legally acceptable, even if greater overall risk results. The history of pesticide regulation, notably the developments surrounding

---

[18] *See* GEORGE M. GRAY & JOHN D. GRAHAM, REGULATING PESTICIDES, *in* RISK VERSUS RISK: TRADEOFFS IN PROTECTING HEALTH AND THE ENVIRONMENT 173, 189 (John D. Graham & Jonathan Baert Weiner eds., 1995) (observing that "the beneficiaries of reduced residue and persistence—consumers and wildlife—may be enjoying the benefits of a risk transfer to farm workers" who "may be particularly vulnerable when they are migrant, low-income, minority workers who lack a political voice or the English skills to read labels").

regulation of DDT and ethylene dibromicide demonstrates the reality of this concern.[19]

The ban on DDT transferred material risks to innocent farmworkers. DDT was of particular concern to environmentalists, inspired by Rachel Carson, in part because it was environmentally long-lived. DDT was banned, and its applications were replaced by a series of pesticides from a group known as organophosphates. Unfortunately, the organophosphates were much more acutely toxic, so the use of these substances "caused incidents of serious poisoning among unsuspecting workers and farmers who had been accustomed to handling the relatively nontoxic DDT." The failure to consider the risk of replacement to farmworkers is estimated to have "cost several hundred lives." The President of the NAS announced that the "predicted death or blinding by parathion of dozens of Americans last summer must rest on the consciences of every car owner whose bumper sticker urged a total ban on DDT." The undue public and regulatory cathexis on a tiny risk of pesticide residues resulted in a transfer of greater risks to a less politically-prominent group, migrant farmworkers.

Ethylene dibromide ("EDB") cancellation likewise transferred and increased risks from pesticides. EDB was a fumigant employed to control extremely hazardous molds, such as aflatoxin. The need for treatment was such that producers employed a substitute fumigant, but this alternative presented greater risks to workers.

Traditionally, government has blithely ignored the consequences of risk transference to farmworkers. In practice, "risks to applicators and consumers are predicated on the assumption that no other active ingredient will be substituted for one banned in a particular use." Of course, assuming does not make it so. In reality, "such substitutions are the rule rather than the exception[.]"

Nothing in the FQPA eliminates the risk from substitutes, and the projected added regulation could readily exacerbate the risk. Even when the risks from substitutes to farmworkers are acknowledged in regulation, risks will shift and increase. Given the legal language and political realities, "the EPA tolerates higher risks for exposures to pesticides incurred by workers who manufacture, distribute, or apply pesticides than they do for the general population."[20]

---

[19] *See* DONALD T. HORNSTEIN, PARADIGMS, PROCESS, AND POLITICS: RISK AND REGULATORY DESIGN, *in* WORST THINGS FIRST? THE DEBATE OVER RISK-BASED NATIONAL ENVIRONMENTAL PRIORITIES 147, 160 n.7 (Adam M. Finkel & Dominic Golding eds., 1994)(observing that until recently "EPA's risk assessments of pesticides focused predominantly on carcinogenicity among consumers due to residues and all but ignored the workplace exposure to pesticides among the nation's two million hired farmworkers).

[20] JOSEPH V. RODRICKS, CALCULATED RISKS 213 (1992).

Of course, an across-the-board reduction in all pesticide usage would have some health benefit for farmworkers as well. But the effect of FQPA will not be a complete reduction, but will involve a shift in applications and categories of pesticides. As experience with DDT and EDB show, in the past a shift in pesticide categories has been toward greater risks for applicators of pesticides, even while risks to consumers have been reduced. Therefore, overall reduction in the total quantity of pesticides used could increase the cumulative risk from pesticides.

Frank B. Cross, *The Consequences of Consensus: Dangerous Compromises of the Food Quality Protection Act*, 75 WASH. U.L.Q. 1155, 1179-81 (1997).

EPA's efforts on behalf of farmworkers and other agricultural workers[21] have been generally slow in coming and have met a great deal of resistance from agricultural interests.[22] The Worker Protection Standards were promulgated in their current form in 1992,[23] with a few subsequent revisions. Congress delayed the effective date of the regulations until 1995. The regulations prohibit pesticide handlers from applying pesticides while agricultural workers are in the area being treated (and from applying them in such a way that the workers are exposed elsewhere) and from allowing agricultural workers to re-enter a treated area within specified periods after a pesticide has been applied. These are obviously essential to the protection of farmworkers, but they are also costly in terms of reduced productivity, and EPA has been under considerable pressure to shorten re-entry times and to permit exemptions to them. In addition, the regulations require personal protective equipment for handlers and early-entry workers, marking or other notification of treated areas, disclosure of label information, decontamination equipment, training, and emergency assistance. Based on what you have read in this chapter and previously in the book, what are the strengths and weaknesses of the regulatory strategies deployed in the Worker Protection Standards? Are there better ways to protect farmworkers?

How are the problems of pesticide residues in foods and farmworker health interrelated? To the extent that the two safety goals conflict, how should we decide between them?

---

[21] FIFRA has been held to oust jurisdiction over farmworkers' exposure to pesticides from OSHA. Organized Migrants in Community Action, Inc. v. Brennan, 520 F.2d 1161 (D.C. Cir. 1975) (rejecting petition to force OSHA to address the issue).

[22] For an interesting case study of the roles of Congress, USDA, the Office of Management and Budget, and the large and small agriculture lobbies in EPA's pesticide rulemaking, *see* LOUIS P. TRUE, JR., AGRICULTURAL PESTICIDES AND WORKER PROTECTION, *in* ECONOMIC ANALYSIS AT EPA: ASSESSING REGULATORY IMPACT, pp. 303-32 (RICHARD D. MORGENSTERN, ED.; RESOURCES FOR THE FUTURE 1997).

[23] 57 Fed. Reg. 38102 (1992), codified at 40 C.F.R. part 170.

c. International Regulation of Pesticides

The United States exports enormous quantities of pesticides—including pesticides whose use is banned or tightly restricted by EPA—to other countries, including less developed (or Third World) countries. For the latter, pesticides pose a similar, but far more intense, dilemma: they are at once more urgently needed and more dangerous than in industrialized countries like the United States. The international regulatory system, however, is far looser for pesticides exported to less developed countries than are the internal regulatory structures of industrialized countries.

POISONING THE DEVELOPING WORLD: THE EXPORTATION OF UNREGISTERED AND SEVERELY RESTRICTED PESTICIDES FROM THE UNITED STATES

James H. Colopy
13 UCLA J. ENVTL. L. & POL'Y 167, 169-73, 185-87, 196-200
(1994/95)

Over the last fifty years, the pesticide industry has dramatically expanded into a world-wide market. Pesticides first came into use following World War II, when the research and development into rubber and other polymers led to the development of the chemical industry. The production and sale of insecticides, herbicides, and commercial fertilizers quickly exploded, as DDT and other synthetic chemicals appeared to be easy solutions to perpetual pest control problems.

There is no sign that the pesticide market is slowing down. Global pesticide use has doubled in every decade between 1945 and 1985. Approximately four billion pounds of pesticides are currently produced in the world each year, three-fourths of which are used for agricultural purposes. Pesticide demand is unlikely to lessen in the near future. Roughly 37% of all crop production annually is lost to insects and other pests, and despite a ten-fold increase in pesticide amounts and toxicity over the last forty years, the share of crop yields lost to insects has nearly doubled over that same time span.

The United States is a leading manufacturer and exporter of pesticides, exporting between 400 and 600 million pounds of pesticides each year. However, ten to twenty-five percent of these pesticides are not registered for use in the United States. Twenty-seven of the unregistered pesticides are destined for food uses in other countries. Forty-three pesticides have been banned by the EPA and ten have severely restricted uses.

* * *

Historically, the fastest growing market for pesticides has been developing countries. Between 1980 and 1984, for example, pesticide sales in Africa increased 180 percent. Banned or severely restricted pesticides are often exported to those nations because of the available market and limited regulation. In 1989, a survey found "very toxic pesticides" to be "widely available" in over eighty-five developing countries.

* * *

III. U.S. LAWS AND LEGISLATION

A. Federal Insecticide, Fungicide, and Rodenticide Act (FIFRA)

* * *

1. Regulating the Export of Unregistered or Severely Restricted Pesticides

The EPA cannot prohibit the export of unregistered pesticides. As a matter of policy, the agency opposes the institution of a general ban on the exports of unregistered pesticides. First, the EPA believes that banning exports will not solve the pesticide problems of developing nations, since most if not all of the banned pesticides would be available from other pesticide-exporting countries. Second, concentrating on controlling the use and management of all pesticides will be more effective than concentrating upon a few. Third, the agency's regulatory decisions are based upon risk-benefit evaluations specific to the United States. The risk-benefit balance in other countries may differ due to different growing conditions, pest control problems, and environmental and public health considerations. Fourth, pesticide manufacturers may choose not to register a pesticide in the United States simply because there is no market for it. Another concern is that a complete ban might violate the open market provisions of the General Agreement on Trade and Tariffs (GATT).

FIFRA sets out certain requirements for pesticide exports. Section 17(a)(1) mandates that exported pesticides comply with labeling requirements. An exported pesticide would be mislabeled if it were imitating another pesticide, lacking a registration number of the production site and the name of producer or registrant, lacking adequate warning and caution statements, or missing the pesticide's ingredient statement, net weight, and use classification or restriction. All items on the label must be written in English and in the language of the importing country. Labels for unregistered pesticides must prominently bear the statement "Not Registered for Use in the United States of America."

Foreign purchasers of unregistered or severely restricted pesticides must sign statements indicating that the purchaser understands that the pesticide is not registered and cannot be sold in the United States. Within seven days of receiving the statement from the purchaser and before shipping the pesticide, the American exporter must submit this statement to the EPA who in turn sends it to the appropriate government official in the importing country. This statement must be submitted annually for the first shipment of each unregistered product to a particular purchaser for each importing country.

Section 17(b) of FIFRA requires that the EPA also send notices to importing countries and the appropriate international agencies of regulatory actions taken by the EPA, such as cancellation or suspension of the registration of a pesticide. For many years, the EPA never developed a regulation to interpret this part of FIFRA. Instead, the agency issued notices to foreign governments and international agencies regarding those cancellations and suspensions which the EPA considered to be of "national or international significance." The notices explain the action and the health and safety concerns which prompted the action, and the agency provides additional information upon request.

2. EPA Enforcement of FIFRA

The EPA has done a poor job of informing foreign governments of significant registration actions. Starting in the late 1970s, the General Accounting Office (GAO) has studied the EPA's performance three times and each time concluded that the agency failed to properly implement and execute an effective system of notification.

* * *

IV. INTERNATIONAL AGREEMENTS

* * *

A. Prior Informed Consent

The concept of Prior Informed Consent (PIC) has been hotly debated in recent years. As defined by the FAO, PIC means that "no international shipment of a banned or severely restricted pesticide (or a pesticide which may pose special severe hazards to health and the environment in an importing country) should proceed without the prior consent of the competent national authority in the importing country."

In certain respects, implementing PIC is the ideal solution. Importing countries are consulted before receiving a potentially dangerous import, thus avoiding sovereignty concerns, and the international pesticide industry is still able to export pesticides. Developing countries concerned with the health or environmental effects of a particular pesticide can simply choose not to consent. PIC's major disadvantage, however, is that the system by itself does not develop the regulatory expertise of developing countries. In addition, the bureaucratic inefficiencies and reluctance to take affirmative responsibility for decisions common to many developing countries may make the process of obtaining consent difficult in some countries.

The FAO and UNEP have developed PIC systems for pesticides and industrial chemicals, respectively. * * * The United States has strongly endorsed the PIC system developed by the FAO and UNEP, and the EPA has committed itself to implementing PIC to the extent it is compatible with the provisions of FIFRA.

B. U.N. Food and Agricultural Organization

In 1985, the General Conference of the U.N. Food and Agricultural Organization approved the International Code of Conduct on the Distribution and Use of Pesticides ("Pesticide Code").[24] Though voluntary, the Pesticide Code sought to define and clarify the responsibilities of the respective parties involved in the development, distribution, and use of pesticides. The Pesticide Code establishes basic definitions, outlines regulatory processes, and sets out certain guidelines for the pesticide industry. The Pesticide Code also calls for uniform international standards and contains provisions on packaging, labeling, and advertising.

The biggest disadvantage of international codes of conduct such as the Pesticide Code is that they are entirely voluntary and unenforceable. Reports from several developing countries indicate that the pesticide industry routinely violates the provisions and standards of the Pesticide Code. However, the Code provides useful information to developing nations, acting as a "measuring tape" and an expression of support for measures to regulate pesticide exposure. Unfortunately, the developing countries still require the resources to implement the regulatory mechanism necessary to enforce the Pesticide Code.

The Pesticide Code originally lacked any notification mechanism such as PIC. Developing nations strongly pushed for incorporating PIC into the Pesticide Code, despite resistance from industry and pesticide-exporting countries. The 1987 FAO General Conference agreed to adopt PIC in principle and integrated it into the Pesticide Code by 1989. Under the new guidelines, a pesticide that is banned or severely restricted[25] for health or environmental reasons cannot be exported to countries participating in PIC that have stated their desire to not receive that pesticide. Pesticides banned or severely restricted for health or environmental reasons by five or more governments are subject to PIC, although pesticides which are unregistered or voluntarily withdrawn from registration are not covered.

The FAO initiates the PIC system by developing "PIC decision guidance documents" which summarize the pesticide's chemical and physical properties, its uses, and its toxicity. These documents are circulated to participating governments along with notices of any actions taken to control the pesticide, and the importing countries inform the FAO as to whether they will accept shipments of those pesticides.

---

[24] 23 FAO Conf. Res. 10/85 (1985), *reprinted in* LAKSHMAN D. GURUSWAMY *ET AL.*, SUPPLEMENT OF BASIC DOCUMENTS TO INTERNATIONAL ENVIRONMENTAL LAW AND WORLD ORDER 932 (1994).

[25] "Banned" and "severely restricted" are terms of art in the FAO Guidelines. "Banned" has its ordinary meaning, but "severely restricted means pesticides "for which *virtually all* registered uses have been prohibited." Art. 2 (emphasis added). In other words, "severely restricted" is not a large category (the Rotterdam Convention on the Prior Informed Consent Procedure for Certain Hazardous Chemicals and Pesticides in International Trade, discussed below, lists only 22 such pesticides), and certainly does not include all pesticides whose use EPA restricts to a significant degree.–EDS.

C. United Nations Environment Programme (UNEP)

The U.N. Environmental Programme (UNEP) has actively facilitated nearly thirty binding multilateral international environmental agreements. In May 1989, the UNEP Governing Council adopted the Amended London Guidelines for the Exchange of Information on Chemicals in International Trade.[26] The Guidelines set up a PIC system for dangerous industrial chemicals, defined as banned or severely restricted in any participating country.

* * *

Under the Amended London Guidelines, UNEP creates an "alert list" of chemicals that ten or more countries have banned or severely restricted for health or environmental reasons. The alert list, accompanied with technical guidance documents, is circulated among participating governments. After reviewing the alert list, importing countries register their PIC decisions with UNEP and their decisions are made available to all countries. UNEP also reviews chemicals which five to nine countries have banned and adds those which present health or environmental risks, according to standards outlined in the agreement. The designated national authority in each country has the responsibility to ensure that substances are not exported into countries which have placed that substance on their PIC list. If an importing country fails to declare its PIC decision for a particular chemical, the status quo regarding its importation continues.

NOTES

1. *North and South.* In a few well chosen words, a United Nations commission headed by former German Chancellor Willy Brandt summed up the vast differences between the industrialized world (the North) and the less developed countries (LDCs, the South):

> Few people in the North have any detailed conception of the extent of poverty in the Third World or of the forms it takes. Many hundreds of millions of people in the poorer countries are preoccupied solely with survival and elementary needs. For them work is frequently not available or, when it is, pay is very low and conditions often barely tolerable. Homes are constructed of impermanent materials and have neither piped water nor sanitation. Electricity is a luxury. * * * Permanent insecurity is the condition of the poor. * * * In the North, ordinary men and women face genuine economic problems—uncertainty, inflation, the fear if not the reality of unemployment. But they rarely face anything resembling the total deprivation found in the South. Ordinary people in the South would not find it credible that the societies of the North regard themselves as anything other than wealthy.

---

[26] UNEP/PIC/WG.2/2 at 9, UNEP ELPG No.10, UNEP/GC/DEC/15/30, *reprinted in* Gurswamy, *supra*, at 959.

BRANDT COMMISSION ON INTERNATIONAL DEVELOPMENT ISSUES, NORTH-SOUTH: A PROGRAMME FOR SURVIVAL 49 (1980). The latest evidence suggests that in the twenty years since the Brandt Commission's report the gap between North and South has widened. Barbara Crossette, Most Consuming More, and the Rich Much More, New York Times, Sept. 13, 1998, p. A3 (national ed.)

How do these differences affect the need for and the dangers of pesticides? The needs are obvious: exploding populations; limited, low-quality arable land; susceptibility to drought, flood, and other natural disasters; and near-absolute reliance on agricultural, as opposed to industrial, products for personal and national income. As to dangers, Colopy lists, among others, insufficient regulatory resources; insufficient understanding of pesticide dangers leading to unsafe storage,[27] application, and harvesting practices; and conditions of use for which the pesticides have not been tested. Pesticide consumers in LDCs, frequently suffering from lack of education or literacy (or of literacy in the language on the products), are also more susceptible to false or misleading marketing of products, leading to overuse that is both a danger to health and economically ruinous. For consumers in the industrialized world, pesticide misuse in LDCs creates the so-called Circle of Poison, by which food treated with banned or restricted pesticides makes its way back to the United States. *See* DAVID WEIR & MARK SCHAPIRO, CIRCLE OF POISON: PESTICIDES AND PEOPLE IN A HUNGRY WORLD (1981); CIRCLE OF POISON: IMPACT OF U.S. PESTICIDES ON THIRD WORLD WORKERS, 1991:HEARINGS ON S. 898 BEFORE THE SENATE COMM. ON AGRICULTURE, NUTRITION, AND FORESTRY, 102ND CONG., 1ST SESS. (1991).

2. *U.S. export policy.* Do you accept EPA's arguments, reported by Colopy, for continuing to export banned and restricted pesticides to the Third World? If not, why not? For the current statement of EPA's pesticide policy, *see* EPA, Pesticide Export Policy, 58 Fed. Reg. 9062 (1993).

3. *Prior informed consent (PIC).* The FAO defines prior informed consent as "the principle that international shipment of a pesticide that is banned or severely restricted in order to protect human health or the environment should not proceed without the agreement, where such agreement exists, or contrary to the decision" of the importing country. Art. 2. The procedures for exchanging information and obtaining and recording consent are spelled out in article 9 and described above. Why is PIC appealing to both LDCs *and* the United States? What are its strengths? What are its limitations?

---

[27] The relatively limited issue of proper packaging is very revealing of the challenge that LDCs face. Pesticides that are shipped and distributed in bulk are necessarily repackaged in the LDC, since few farmers can afford large amounts of pesticides. When they are repackaged, the new containers usually lack warning labels or directions for use, in any language. The containers may also be reused for water or food, which brings consumers into direct contact with the pesticide. The FAO Guidelines, art. 5, directs the use of packaging that limit these problems.

4. *General Agreement on Tariffs and Trade (GATT).* A critical limitation on international regulation of pesticides is that it occurs in the hostile environment of trade policies that aggressively discourage any restrictions on international commerce. The GATT is the global agreement under which the vast majority of international trade is conducted. It prohibits the use of "non-tariff trade barriers" like regulations, except for those "relating to the conservation of natural resources" as long as they are applied equally to foreign and domestic products. Art. XX(g). The GATT has been consistently read to overcome environmental restrictions and to subject them to a *trade* panel's view of what is a "necessary" or "proportionate" restriction. *See, e.g.,* Dispute Settlement Panel Report on United States Restrictions on Imports of Tuna, No. DS21/R, 30 I.L.M. 1594 (1991) (rejecting U.S. limits based on the Marine Mammal Protection Act as failing to adopt less restrictive alternatives); World Trade Organization, Appellate Body, United States– Standards for Reformulated and Conventional Gasoline (AB-1996-1), 35 I.L.M. 603 (1996) (emphasizing that legitimate environmental measures must nevertheless not discriminate against other nations or be used as a restriction on trade); *see also* Re Disposable Beer Cans: EC Commission v Denmark (Case 302/86), [1988] ECR 4607, [1989] 1 CMLR 619 (interpreting the similar arts. 30 and 36 of the European Community Treaty to require that environmental restrictions be "necessary and * * * not disproportionate to achieve a legitimate aim").

5. *The Rotterdam Convention.* In 1998, UNEP obtained broad agreement, including that of the United States, on a Rotterdam Convention on the Prior Informed Consent Procedure for Certain Hazardous Chemicals and Pesticides in International Trade. (The text is available at http://www.chem.unep.ch.) An important step forward in the international regulation of chemicals and pesticides, it makes mandatory the PIC provisions that were only voluntary under the FAO Code of Conduct and the London Guidelines. The Rotterdam Convention applies to "banned" and "severely restricted" chemicals, defined as the FAO did, and also to "severely hazardous pesticide formulations," a new category. This does not expand the universe of regulation, however; only twenty-two pesticides are included in the initial list of banned or restricted chemicals. It is also interesting that "severely hazardous" is measured by acute effect ("severe health or environmental effects observable within a short period of time," art. 2(c)), rather than cancer, the principal measure under FIFRA. Why the difference?

C. The Licensing Strategy

The previous section considered the substantive consequences of FIFRA's use of licensing to regulate pesticides. Licensing strategies have both strengths and weaknesses. By requiring safety to be demonstrated before the chemical may be sold, they should generate risk information and prevent exposure to chemicals whose effects are harmful. On the other hand, in administrative law terms, licensing requires agencies to operate through case-by-case adjudication and not general rulemaking.[28] There is a real danger—unfortunately realized in FIFRA—that, faced with the overwhelming task of evaluating thousands of chemicals, the regulatory agency will be able to give proper attention only to a few.

THE PERILS OF UNREASONABLE RISK: INFORMATION, REGULATORY POLICY, AND TOXIC SUBSTANCES CONTROL

John S. Applegate
91 COLUM. L. REV. 261, 308-12 (1991)

Licensing.-Placement of the burden of proof affects both substantive regulatory policy and information development. When the burden is on EPA to demonstrate risk, EPA has an incentive to develop toxicity information, but the regulated entity has a strong disincentive to develop it, especially if it seems likely that further information will prove troublesome. Conversely, if as a general rule manufacturers can develop toxicology information more cheaply than EPA, or if the cost is more efficiently or equitably borne by them and their customers, then it makes sense to assign the burden of proof to the manufacturer. In regulatory systems, shifting the burden of proof from the government to industry is typically accomplished by enacting a licensing or screening system. In the case of toxic substances, chemical producers would have to demonstrate the safety of their products before these products could be introduced into commerce. Licensing, therefore, not only provides an incentive to the development of new information; it also shifts the cost of development away from the government to a group that in theory has the capacity to absorb and spread the cost.

Of the toxics statutes, only FIFRA has a true licensing scheme. Before pesticides can be sold, they must be registered and EPA must determine that they do not present an unreasonable risk. The registrant has the initial and continuing burden of demonstrating safety, though EPA has an initial burden of production in a cancellation proceeding and must ultimately be able to support its conclusions by substantial evidence. By placing the burden on the registrant, EPA is able to obtain whatever information it deems necessary to assess whether the chemical poses an unreasonable risk through the simple expedient of specifying data requirements for registration. EPA needs only the most general justification for these requirements, given the breadth of factors relevant to the unreasonable risk determination. Furthermore, the data requirements apply to all pesticides, eliminating the need to demand data on a chemical-by-chemical basis. This technique obviously brings the full profit motive to bear in developing adequate data in an expeditious manner. It is hardly coincidental that of the chemicals surveyed in the *Toxicity Testing*

---

[28] Indeed, the Administrative Procedure Act specifically defines "adjudication" to include licensing. 5 U.S.C. § 551(6)-(7).

report [the results of which were discussed in Chapter 3, *supra*], the two groups about which the most is known are the two—pesticides and ethical drugs—that require premarket licensing.

* * *

Licensing is not without serious drawbacks. First, it is a very cumbersome—hence expensive—way to regulate because each individual product or activity must be evaluated. As a result, it should be used only when the factual differences among products or activities are sufficiently great to justify individual consideration. This limitation leads to a second problem—timing. The safest time to evaluate a risk is *before* thousands are exposed to it. But extensive premarket investigation inevitably causes serious delays in the introduction of useful products, as there is no reliable way to determine accurately *ex ante* which products are hazardous and require further investigation. Screening may have the opposite and equally undesirable effect on old products: the difficulty of individually deciding to *remove* them from the market permits continued exposure to unsafe products. Furthermore, licensing often depends on the presentation of only existing information, much of which falls well short of current scientific standards and practices. Data quality can be improved by establishing standards for the acceptability of data submitted to the agency, as EPA has done, but this approach increases approval delays.

Another quality issue is the source of the data, especially in the uncertain science of long-latency toxic illnesses in which inference and interpretation are always open to debate. The inevitably conflicting interests between EPA and the industries it regulates invite the withholding or slanting of data submissions. The conflict rarely results in outright concealment, falsification, or deliberate misstatement of results (though this unfortunately is not unknown). Rather, every stage of the investigation process, from experimental design to execution to interpretation of results, is subject to judgment and inference—and to bias. A screening or approval system may magnify the bias problem by casting EPA and industry in more obviously adversarial roles. A National Academy of Sciences study of EPA decision making warned about dependence on regulated industries for data and analysis and suggested a number of remedial measures, including reduced use of consulting firms that also work for industry, peer review, review by other agencies, stringent guidelines and protocols, certification of laboratories, and a strong in-house research capacity. * * *

Finally, licensing used alone has limited coverage in two senses. First, the premarket phase of product development is the time when the least information is known about a chemical's long-term effects. Without indications of chronic toxicity, it is hard to justify lengthy, expensive bioassays. Second, a licensing scheme intercepts only new or prospective risks. Since older chemicals are likely to be less well-tested relative to more recently licensed chemicals, the lack of data on existing chemicals constitutes a major gap in an information generation system. This problem can be resolved by a retroactive licensing arrangement like FIFRA's preregistration process. However, preregistration presents EPA with a huge backlog of chemicals to be licensed, which EPA must work through slowly or approve with little investigation; that is, it can either accept delay or risk poor decisions.

LESSONS FROM FEDERAL PESTICIDE REGULATION ON THE PARADIGMS AND POLITICS OF ENVIRONMENTAL LAW REFORM

Donald T. Hornstein
10 YALE J. ON REG. 369, 433-38 (1993)[29]

As EPA successfully began to ban pesticides [in the 1970s], however, it only highlighted the immensity of the Agency's regulatory task: the enormous effort required by the handful of cancellation proceedings hardly made a dent in the Agency's statutory duty to reregister the entire inventory of 50,000 existing products, containing hundreds of active ingredients. The 1972 Amendments had required EPA to promulgate implementing regulations within two years and to complete preregistration of all existing pesticides within four years. Although this task belonged to the Agency's scientists in the Office of Pesticide Programs (OPP) rather than to the OGC [*i.e.*, Office of General Counsel] attorneys, OPP staff borrowed the streamlined analytical approach pioneered by OGC in the cancellation proceedings and crafted an innovative regulatory device, the "rebuttable presumption against registration" (RPAR) for use in the Agency's registration and preregistration programs. If a pesticide ingredient was found to be oncogenic in test animals, it automatically triggered a RPAR process under which the burden of proof formally shifted to manufacturers to submit data rebutting the presumption to avoid Agency issuance of notices of intent to cancel. If further data were not required, products were eligible for full preregistration. The RPAR was viewed as a promising regulatory initiative that "proferred a substantial reduction of [the preregistration] caseload by providing a screening device which would rapidly isolate, and focus available evaluation capacity on, the worst chemicals while the safer ones underwent pro forma preregistration."

* * *

By 1975, the core elements of contemporary pesticide regulation were in place. The ease with which EPA could cancel a registration had been tempered by the new procedural requirements of consultation with [EPA's Science Advisory Panel for pesticides] and USDA and by the substantive requirement of weighting more heavily the agricultural benefits of pesticides. At the same time, EPA's primary regulatory program had shifted from cancellation to preregistration, and from the lawyers at OGC to the scientists at OPP.

---

[29] © Copyright 1993 by the YALE JOURNAL ON REGULATION, P.O. Box 208215, New Haven, CT 06520-8215. Reprinted from Vol. 10:369 by permission. All rights reserved.

This basic structure, of pesticide regulation as a regularized, scientific endeavor, has been reinforced in all subsequent FIFRA amendments. In 1978, FIFRA was amended to expand the role of the SAP and to allow for "Special Reviews" (a new term given to RPARs) only on the basis of a "validated test or other significant evidence of unreasonable adverse risk." EPA shifted its preregistration focus from the 50,000 end products to the more manageable 600 active ingredients of these products, and was given "data call-in" authority in the 1978 Amendments by which the Agency could require registrants to provide data to support a pesticide's continued registration. In 1980, FIFRA was again amended to increase the role of "science" and the SAP, with EPA now required to obtain peer review of its scientific findings and to consult with the SAP on suspension as well as cancellation decisions. In 1988, FIFRA was amended yet again, to accelerate preregistration through a newly created five-step process designed to complete, by 1997, the development of "registration standards" for all active ingredients and the preregistration under those standards of all active ingredients.

Although the growing centrality of risk assessments under FIFRA is often taken to underscore the "scientific" nature of EPA's regulation of pesticides, risk analysis also serves as a procedural device that favors pesticide-using political constituencies in three ways. First, because EPA has no independent method of developing data, risk analysis makes EPA dependent on the data generated by pesticide manufacturers—raising opportunities for various types of bias. Informational bias is not limited to cases of outright data falsification, although certainly it is important to note that falsification scandals have more than once rocked OPP's registration programs. The more intractable problems are foot-dragging in submitting data to OPP and the ability of industry to shade the way data is presented (without falsification) simply by emphasizing the subtle but genuinely contestable "inference options" on which risk assessments depend. In the mid-70s, an internal EPA audit on the data underlying twenty-three randomly selected pesticides found that "all but one of the tests reviewed were unreliable and inadequate to demonstrate safety"— a level of unreliability that, by 1992, continued for at least some pesticides. Not only has OPP proven incapable of policing for such subtle manipulations of data, but the quantity of data is so voluminous that EPA has repeatedly acceded to pressures merely to "satisfice" in its data management: in the mid-1970s EPA sought to create the illusion of regulatory progress by reregistering pesticides simply by determining whether safety data was "on file" rather than accurate; in the late 1980s EPA was crediting itself for the "completion" of interim pesticide registration standards when in fact the standards had only identified missing data. By mid-1992, the Agency openly worried that the rate at which it rejected industry studies was "too high" because it would prevent preregistration by the new target date of 1997, or even beyond an extended target of 2002. In short, the risk assessment enterprise is so information intensive that it creates strategic incentives to avoid a serious scientific examination of "true" levels of public health and environmental risk.

Second, despite the burden of proof ostensibly shouldered by pesticide manufacturers under FIFRA, the informational demands of risk analysis doom the regulatory process to a perpetual state of slow motion. The General Accounting Office (GAO) reported in March 1992 that, "[a]fter some 20 years collecting data to reevaluate the health and environmental effects of 19,000 older pesticides, EPA . . . had reregistered only 2 products." Despite a congressional deadline of 1997 recently set for preregistration, GAO confirms EPA's own projections that the preregistration effort will extend "until early in the next century." Even when EPA chooses to act, the risk analyses required for Special Reviews or cancellation proceedings effectively innoculate pesticide manufacturers against timely action. Special Reviews, which were introduced in the mid-1970s to accelerate the cancellation process which then took an average of two years, now themselves average over seven years. To take action against the fungicide Captan, EPA's Special Review required nine years; action against the ethylene bisdithiocarbamates (EBCDs), another fungicide, took twelve years; action against Alar took seventeen years from the date EPA first learned of data suggesting carcinogenicity. As a practical matter, the burdensomeness of risk analysis has tempered FIFRA's success in shifting the burden of proof to manufacturers.

NOTES

1. *Age discrimination.* A licensing statute can skew substantive policy by setting a higher bar for new products than for old ones. Often this is deliberate and rational—we ought to expect better pollution control from new factories than from old ones, for example, and controls can be more cheaply installed in new facilities—but it also can have perverse results.

> * * * A policy of rigidly screening new technology while merely setting standards for the old locks society into the hazardous present and excludes a possibly safer future. * * * The failure to appreciate these possibilities fuels much of the most cutting criticism of the existing regulatory structure.
>
> Examples of the limits of the present system abound. Saccharin ban opponents charged that consumers would turn to a more hazardous substitute—sugar. Others asserted, without refutation, that cyclamates, banned by the FDA seven years earlier, are safer artificial sweeteners than saccharin. Soft drink bottles made of carcinogenic acrylonitrile were recently banned because of the slight risk that the plastic would leach into the soft drink, yet exploding glass bottles cause 100,000 hospital emergency room entries each year in the United States alone. In addition, the bottle glass adsorbs traces of toxic metals that are then desorbed into the soft drink. The "drug lag" provides an acid test of a regulator's convictions. Lengthy

regulatory review that ultimately removes unacceptable hazards is desirable, but delays in the approval of desirable, life-saving products is very costly. Most anticancer drugs, for example, are themselves carcinogenic. The FDA's real and unenviable task is to weigh the cancer you've got against the one you might get. * * * These criticisms sound a common theme: unwise regulation may promote the more hazardous at the expense of the merely hazardous.

This illustrates the major weakness of a regulatory system divided along the old-new line. Though the bias in favor of the old is generally justified, it is foolish to regulate strictly a hazardous new product that competes with another product that is more hazardous and less strictly regulated. Thus, banning a new, hazardous food additive is senseless if the additive will serve primarily as a substitute for an accepted, more dangerous one. * * * [However,] under a system of comparative risk regulation, once an agency deems a product acceptable for reasons wise or unwise, it regulates more stringently another product competing in the same market only if the new product is less safe.[30]

Peter Huber, *The Old-New Division in Risk Regulation*, 69 VA. L. REV. 1025, 1073-75 (1983). *See also* Richard B. Stewart, *Regulation, Innovation, and Administrative Law: A Conceptual Framework*, 69 CALIF. L. REV. 1256, 1296-97, 1314-15 (1981) (arguing that the old-new division stifles innovation in environmentally preferable products and processes, though finding only weak evidence of this effect under FIFRA).

How does licensing distinguish between old and new? Is Huber right? Doesn't he assume that new products will usually be safer? Even if that is a fair assumption in general (and it may be), don't the environmental, safety, and health laws have something to do with that trend? How do we weed out the exceptional cases in which the new product is *more* dangerous?

And what does "safer" mean, anyway? In what sense is sugar "more hazardous" than saccharine? The discussion of farmworkers suggests that defining safety is itself a complex question. Huber recommends a thorough study of comparative risks to combat the perverse effects of the old-new division.[31] While this remedy follows logically from Huber's diagnosis, do the materials in Chapters 2 and 3 raise some concerns with this idea?

---

[30] This type of comparison is, in effect, a limited form of cost-benefit balancing, but one that avoids the controversial elements of conventional cost-benefit analysis by performing the balance entirely in units of risk. Because comparative risk regulation evaluates costs and benefits in the same units—risks of a certain type—an agency can make a comparative risk decision without placing a price on human life or monetizing other benefits that are equally difficult to value.

[31] Perhaps Congress was implicitly responding to this concern by developing special, more lenient standards for "public health pesticides" that is "used predominantly in public health programs for . . . the prevention or mitigation of viruses, bacteria, or other microorganisms . . . that pose a threat to public health." *See* §§ 2(nn), 6(b), 25(a)(1).

2. Since procedural hurdles alone can doom some useful and acceptably safe products that are only marginally profitable, Congress created special rules for the registration and preregistration of "minor use" pesticides. *See, e.g.*, §§ 2(*ll*), 3(c)(2)(A), (E), 4(d)(6). Why should pesticides so described receive special treatment? If they are so useful, then why won't they command the higher price needed to support development and testing? (Congress has made similar provision for so-called "orphan drugs." *See* 21 U.S.C. § 360aa-360ee.)

3. *Data demands.* FIFRA authorizes EPA to demand additional information to support a registration whenever the agency believes it is necessary. This procedure, found in section 3(c)(2)(B), is known as a "data call-in," and its sweep is remarkably broad.

Recognizing that licensing fails to generate any information for existing chemicals or post-license information for new ones, * * * [in] 1978 Congress added FIFRA's requirement to test, known as a "data call-in," to clarify EPA's power to seek information to facilitate review of previously approved pesticides. The data call-in is a logical extension of a licensing statute that places the burden of proving safety on the registrant. It allows EPA to demand additional data concerning any pesticide whenever the agency "determines that additional data are required" to support the registration. The data call-in provision gives EPA the authority to require the creation of new information, and it empowers EPA to seek any information relevant to the broad range of considerations relevant to determining unreasonable risk under FIFRA. The provision is potentially draconian in application because FIFRA does not limit the occasions for using data call-ins, and EPA has developed neither formal nor informal guidelines for their use. Moreover, registrants have no real choice but to comply because they have no right to challenge the request—the only question on judicial review is whether the registrant did in fact comply with the call-in, not whether it *should* comply.

Data call-ins have not been used to their full potential to generate large amounts of information. Consistent with their role in support of post-licensing review of pesticides, they have rarely been used outside of ongoing preregistration and cancellation proceedings. And because they can impose an enormous financial burden on affected registrants, EPA considers the extent of use and human exposure, as well as the cost impact of data generation, in establishing data call-ins. EPA adopts, in effect, a form of quantitative risk assessment. In addition, some legislative history suggests that the data call-in should be used only in extremely unusual circumstances. As a result, EPA has not used the data call-in as a general source of toxic substances information.

John S. Applegate, *The Perils of Unreasonable Risk: Information, Regulatory Policy, and Toxic Substances Control*, 91 COLUM. L. REV. 261, 313-14 (1991). Look back at the *NCAMP* case: how was the data call-in used there? How did it fit into the cancellation proceeding and settlement? EPA sometimes uses data call-ins to encourage the voluntary cancellation of outdated or marginally useful pesticides. Is this appropriate?

Even without special demand, pesticide registrants must submit adverse health effects data under section 6(a)(2). Not surprisingly, EPA interprets this provision broadly, requiring registrants to develop effective internal and external reporting systems. *See* 40 C.F.R. part 159.[32]

4. *Data compensation*. Many new pesticide formulations are based on already-registered active ingredients. To minimize the burden of "follow-on" registrations and to avoid duplication of effort, FIFRA permits applicants for registration to rely on data previously submitted by others. § 3(c)(1)(F). To address the perceived unfairness of allowing subsequent registrants to profit from prior registrants' investment in research, Congress developed a process in which subsequent data users compensate the original data producers for part of the development costs. *Id.* The Supreme Court upheld the data compensation system against a taking challenge in *Ruckelshaus v. Monsanto*, 467 U.S. 986 (1984). A year later, in *Thomas v. Union Carbide*, 473 U.S. 568 (1985), the Court rejected a constitutional challenge to FIFRA's use of binding arbitration to determine the amount of compensation.

5. *Special Review*. The "unreasonable risk" balancing required by FIFRA demands that EPA consider a wide range of information in evaluating pesticides. Special Review, codified at 40 C.F.R. part 154, sought to avoid formal adjudication by creating an initial informal procedure triggered by the risk characteristics of a particular pesticide, especially toxicity, without considering its benefits—thus simplifying both the process for cancellation and the substantive standard. Even though it *added* a new step to the cancellation process, the expectation was that a settlement would be worked out during the review, making the subsequent formal adjudication a mere formality. Congress adopted the Special Review process in 1978, but also sought to limit it by requiring a "validated test or other significant evidence raising prudent concerns" to trigger reviews. § 3(c)(8). Congress needn't have worried. The Special Review process itself became a highly formal, procedurally complex exercise—in part for the very good reason that as originally envisioned it was to lead to an informal settlement that minimized public participation.[33] Special Reviews began to take longer than cancellation proceedings did, and EPA has effectively abandoned the procedure.

---

[32] For an analysis of the current regulations and their antecedents, *see* Amanda L. Korowsky, Note, *Clarifying FIFRA Section 6(a)(2): The Post-Registration Reporting Obligations of Pesticide Registrants*, 4 THE ENVTL. LAWYER 641 (1998).

[33] *See* John P. Gavior, *Pesticide Safety Regulation under the Federal Insecticide, Fungicide, and Rodenticide Act: Debacle at the EPA*, 1 FORDHAM ENVTL. L. REP. 47 (1989).

6. *Reregistration.* One of Congress' principal concerns in the 1988 and 1996 amendments to FIFRA was the slow pace of *re*registering—*i.e.*, reevaluating but not necessarily canceling—existing pesticides and their uses. The results of Congress' efforts can be seen in the current section 4 (7 U.S.C. § 136a-1), which seeks to give EPA the tools, the incentive, and the money to work through its massive backlog of existing, largely unexamined pesticide registrations. It establishes an elaborately staged process for listing pesticides for consideration, submission of data, and rendering decisions. Priorities were set based on the sensible criteria of presence in food or water, worker safety, and data gaps.

Similar procedures in the 1984 amendments to RCRA (Chapter 9) and the 1990 Clean Air Act Amendments (Chapter 6(F)) have been reasonably successful in forcing agency action. EPA, however, simply did not have the resources to accomplish the preregistration task set for it in 1988, so the FQPA added an "expedited processing fund," streamlined procedures for related registrations, required disclosure of progress (or lack thereof), and judicial enforcement. § 4(k)-(m). It remains to be seen whether EPA will at long last be able to bring the registrations of all pesticides up to date.

D. Pesticide Regulation and Agriculture Policy

Since World War II, the use of pesticides in agriculture has increased many-fold as the result of three interrelated developments. First, the production of new, cheap, extremely potent poisons—exemplified by DDT—made heavy use economically profitable. Second, the development of high-intensity, monocultural farming made pesticide use essential to ensure against catastrophic crop failure. Third,

> [d]espite increasing volume and greater diversity of chemicals, agricultural returns are declining. Although worldwide agricultural yields have doubled since 1950 as a result of new agricultural practices (including use of high-yield grains and massive chemical inputs), we are getting less yield per unit effort. In the period from 1945 to 1984, losses to insects nearly doubled from 7 to 13% and losses to weeds increased from 8 to 12%, all while pesticide inputs soared. Why?
>
> Basically, pesticides have become less effective as a result of several biological consequences of repeated, heavy doses of pesticides. These include resurgence or rebound of the primary pest species following an initial suppression of numbers; secondary outbreaks of other, previously minor pests; the promotion to pest status of previous nonpest species; and the development of pesticide resistance (the ability of a pest to withstand the effects of a pesticide).

HARTE *ET AL.*, *supra,* at 127.[34] Other side effects, such as pesticides in groundwater, have proven to be a troubling development in agricultural areas. In sum, pesticides cannot be regulated, or their use reduced, without taking agriculture policy into account.

LESSONS FROM FEDERAL PESTICIDE REGULATION ON THE PARADIGMS AND POLITICS OF ENVIRONMENTAL LAW REFORM

Donald T. Hornstein
10 YALE J. ON REG. 369, 392-406 (1993)

For all its complexity, however, it is important to underscore what pesticide regulation is not: it is not a body of law that addresses in any strategic way the underlying prevalence of pesticides in American agriculture, nor is it a body of law designed to minimize pesticide use. On reflection, this characteristic is especially striking because the impetus for modern pesticide regulation, if not for the modern environmental movement in general, was the argument made in 1962 by Rachel Carson in *Silent Spring* for developing just such a strategic environmental law. In what she called "the other road," Carson argued for the development of pesticide policies based on the biological understanding of pests as "living organisms . . . [within] the whole fabric of life to which [they] belong." Although EPA still chooses occasionally to boast that the Agency exists as "the extended shadow of *Silent Spring*," in truth the defining features of modern pesticide regulation languish far too much in the "shadow" of Rachel Carson's vision of what an enlightened strategy for crop protection should be—a fact perhaps demonstrated most succinctly by an *increase* in pesticide usage between 1964 and 1982 of 170%. It is to explore the forces which have shaped both pesticide use and pesticide regulation that I now turn.

A. A Cause-Oriented Perspective on Pesticide Use: Prisoners' Dilemmas and Technology Treadmills

It is useful at the outset to question what is perhaps the most direct reason often given for pesticide use in the United States: because it works. The critical issue, of course, is what one means by "works." From the perspective of productivity gains, there is certainly impressive evidence that for many crops, pesticides increase yields and reduce labor costs, at least in the near term; aggregate estimates of productivity gains indicate a 400% rate of return on the pesticide dollar. Yet there is also evidence that these gains are often not sustained over the long run, due to the counterproductive tendency of pesticides to induce genetic "resistance" in target pests and to destroy beneficial insects that previously had helped to check target pest populations. Accordingly, there are aggregate data which reveal that the country lost in 1987 almost precisely the same percentage of its crops to pests as it did in

---

[34] As Colopy reports in the excerpt above, a similar problem exists in the developing world. While U.S. exports to developing countries has increased enormously in the last forty years, loss of crops to pests has in fact increased and yields have decreased.

1900—despite the application in 1987 of some 430 million pounds of pesticides. By yet another measure, which considers the marginal benefits of pesticides over "alternative" pest control measures, there are data showing that pesticide use on some (and perhaps many) crops could be cut in half without significant decreases in yields.

If it is unclear whether the intended effects of pesticides can support the nonqualified claim that pesticides "work," certainly any final judgment on the question must also consider unintended effects. EPA's Science Advisory Board concluded in 1990 that, when compared with dozens of other risks, pesticides presented one of the country's more widespread and severe environmental problems. Apart from accelerating the development of resistant pests, pesticides can cause at least eight other broad types of unintended effects: acute or chronic health effects among workers in the manufacturing process; acute or chronic health effects on third parties due to accidents in manufacturing or transport; acute and chronic health problems among applicators and farmworkers; contamination of groundwater due to leaching; contamination of surface waters from farm run-off; poisoning of wildlife; acute and chronic health problems among consumers due to residues on food; and contamination of the environment due to improper disposal of unused pesticides and their containers. Although there have been few attempts to measure the overall magnitude of these losses (other than the SAB's recent assessment), a sense of scale may be taken from evidence suggesting that pesticides are involved in 15 percent of the wastes at federal Superfund sites imposing extensive remediation costs; there are over 27,000 yearly instances of poisonings by pesticides among applicators and farmworkers; pesticide residues on food are estimated to cause each year hundreds of "excess" chronic health effects, including cancers, among consumers; and pesticides are responsible for significant wildlife losses, including in some instances irreparable losses among populations of threatened or endangered species. From a cost-benefit perspective, the cumulative losses may well outweigh the cumulative benefits of pesticides.

For the purposes of my argument, however, it is unnecessary to conclude dispositively that the aggregate costs of pesticides outweigh the aggregate benefits. In fact, there are insufficient data for such a comprehensive analysis and the precise structure of the calculation would be complex and contestable. But it is enough that there is a plausible case against the simple explanation that pesticides are used in America because, on balance, they "work." For if this most direct justification is questionable, it highlights the possibility that there may well be other factors which account for the pervasive use of pesticides in American agriculture.

There are several economic reasons why individual farmers might use pesticides to a greater extent than might be justified by an aggregate cost-benefit calculation. First, the unintended effects of pesticides might be true economic externalities—losses borne by others without corrective legal mechanisms which can bring back (internalize) the losses to the individual pesticide users. Second, even for those losses that farmers will themselves experience, such as the eventual effects of pesticide-resistant pests, it may still be economically rational for an individual farmer to continue unabated her level of pesticide use. This is because of what Garrett Hardin termed "the tragedy of the commons": the pesticide user will be able to reap the full benefits of high pesticide use in the short term (greater yields on her crops) but will only bear part of the costs of the common problem she will share with all other farmers in the future (resistant pests). Third, there can operate classic prisoners' dilemmas: farmers know they would be better off cooperating to reduce pesticide use; but, fearing "cheating" by other farmers, each decides to maintain the current level of pesticide use even though all will end up the worse for it.

The structure of American agriculture provides ample room for these economic forces to operate. Agriculture remains a keenly competitive enterprise in which individual farmers take large financial risks on their ability to produce a crop. Although there are mechanisms by which farmers can cushion the possibilities of unexpected crop losses or downward market swings, farmers remain classic "price takers"—in most cases unable to influence either the price of inputs (fertilizers, pesticides, labor) or the prices received for their products. As Professor Gerald Torres explains, "[a farmer's] principal control over income is in the number of units he produces for sale."

From an individual farmer's point of view, the importance of crop yield can inflate the attractiveness of pesticides beyond what a purely neutral economic calculation might predict. * * *

The incentive to overspray is further compounded by what is known as the "agricultural treadmill." As crop yields rise, of course, the resulting surpluses drive prices down. Although this prospect might be expected to encourage cooperation to prevent surpluses, the existence of output-enhancing technologies such as fertilizers and pesticides instead trap farmers within a classic prisoners' dilemma: individual farmers are forced to increase productivity lest other farmers increase their yields and create surpluses which drive market prices lower. Moreover, the developing consumer preference for cosmetically "perfect" produce (itself induced by the high level of cosmetic quality achievable with pesticides) reinforces the incentives for individual farmers to use pesticides to avoid being relegated to secondary produce markets at even further reduced prices. The result is a commonly observed pattern in agriculture: farmers who do not adopt improved technologies are "left with shrunken incomes since their unit costs of production remain high while prices received [are] falling." Few rational farmers can afford to step off the agricultural treadmill.

* * *

B. Past Attempts to Develop a Legal Framework to Reduce Pesticide Use
* * *

At the core of any alternative legal framework [for pesticide regulation] must be an appreciation of the strengths and limitations of what is typically described as "alternative" agriculture. To sidestep a sometimes esoteric debate over what measures should qualify as "alternative," there are basically four types of alternative measures most commonly in use, and about which a scientific literature has developed or is developing. First, there are "cultural" methods to control insects, weeds, and diseases, such as crop rotations, altered planting dates, cultivation, and the planting of border crops. Second, there are "biological control" methods such as the release of predatory or parasitic insects. Third, there is the deployment of "biorational" pest control measures such as pheromone-baited traps, the release of microbiological pathogens of insects or weeds, and the use of genetically engineered pest control products. Fourth, and probably most importantly, there is the use of "integrated pest management" (IPM), a decision making system designed to use all "suitable" pest control techniques, including chemical pesticides, to keep pest populations below economically injurious levels while satisfying environmental and production objectives.

It is fairly plain that alternative pest controls can impose on farmers two types of costs that are generally not imposed to the same extent by chemical pesticides. First, there are often significant information costs involved with more finely-tailored alternative forms of crop protection—such as the need to "scout" a crop to discern the optimal timing of pesticide applications (perhaps the most common IPM technique) or the need to familiarize oneself with the relative effectiveness of a wide assortment of nonchemical measures or products—that clearly transcend the information costs involved in the more routine spraying of a chemical pesticide that may be "automatically" effective against a broad range of pests. Second, to the extent that pest-specific products are used, they will by definition cost more than products that work against a broader range of pests because the pest-specific user market will be smaller and the producer must charge proportionately higher prices to recoup her investments in research and development.

Alternative pest control can also pose free rider and collective action problems. For example, the release of predatory insects will rarely be in an individual farmer's economic self-interest because they cannot be confined to the farmer's property and thus will become to that extent a public good whose full value cannot be recouped. Conversely, if farmers seek to join in an area wide organization for the purposes of cooperative pest control, they may face "hold outs" who attempt to free-ride on the cooperating farmers' efforts—or, worse, hold-outs whose recalcitrant activities actually undermine the cooperative efforts (say, by maintaining fields which serve as "reservoirs" for common pests or by continuing the use of chemical pesticides that kill predatory insects released by the alternative farmers).

* * *

C. Probing for Effective Cause-Based Reform

There are, currently, dozens of policy options to encourage low-input agriculture, ranging from mandated reductions in pesticide use by target dates to pesticide risk taxes to expedited registration of "alternative" pest control products. I endorse none of these specific options here. Rather, I want only to underscore two criteria that should guide the merits of the long-overdue development of a true environmental policy for pesticides.

First, Congress should encourage governmental intervention that addresses the underlying reasons for pesticide overuse. Fitting this criteria would be consideration of two obvious problems for any system of low-input agriculture: risk averse farmers may overuse pesticides as a minimax strategy to avoid catastrophic crop losses, and farmers may overuse pesticides because of their relatively low informational costs. Although the issues have their complexities, the arguments appear strong at least in the near term for public subsidization of "IPM" crop insurance premiums and of significant enhancements for existing "extension" programs that have already been developed to train farmers in the new techniques. * * *

Second, Congress should bypass the risk-dominated structures in EPA's pesticide office and legislate direct disincentives to pesticide use. Such an approach would have the benefit of "locking in" structural incentives for low-input agriculture and avoiding the implementation slippage that has inevitably occurred in pesticide regulation. * * * [I]t is here that incremental, rather than comprehensive, decision making would be most appropriate. Congress might consider, for example, fairly limited taxes only on those pesticides posing the greatest risk, ratifying the availability of common-law liability for pesticide use (perhaps with an "IPM" defense), or including farmers among other users of toxic chemicals who must report to the Toxic Release Inventory their discharge of such chemicals into the environment. Mechanisms such as these create market-like incentives, as opposed to rigid command-and-control requirements, that can take account of regional and farm-specific differences and permit growers significant flexibility in deciding how best to avoid the disincentives.

NOTES

1. *Causes.* What are Hornstein's diagnoses of the fundamental problems of pesticide policy? What options does he offer to address them?

Jim Chen, following Aldo Leopold,[35] argues that the roots of the problem are deeper still, in the adoption of an ethic of domination over nature, rather than stewardship. The dominant ethic of agribusiness, like other businesses, is

---

[35] Leopold's *A Sand County Almanac*, like Carson's *Silent Spring*, is one of the seminal works of the environmental movement. "Land, like Odysseus' slave-girls, is still property. The land-relation is still strictly economic, entailing privileges but not obligations," said Leopold. He proposed instead an ethic of cooperation, of seeking community, between human beings and "soils, waters, plants, and animals, or collectively: the land." ALDO LEOPOLD, A SAND COUNTY ALMANAC 238-38 (1949).

short-term profit. The endangered family farm, in whose name much of agriculture policy is formulated, is driven far more strongly by an ethic of survival that offers little incentive to exercise the restraints of long-term stewardship. Jim Chen, *Of Agriculture's First Disobedience and Its Fruit*, 48 VAND. L. REV. 1261 (1995).

2. *Integrated pest management*. One incremental change that is already occurring is the increased use of Integrated Pest Management (IPM) to reduce pesticide use. A form of pollution prevention, reduced pesticide use would ameliorate the negative effects of pesticides. IPM is a comprehensive system for crop and pest management at a given farm, which combines narrowly targeted pesticides with crop rotation, chemical rotation, low-volume spraying, and other techniques to maximize the effect of a minimum amount of added chemicals. This requires careful monitoring of weather, pest populations, and pesticide use. It also requires extensive knowledge of the interrelationships among crops, pests, natural predators, and other elements of the ecosystem, to tailor a system.

> Integrated control is simply rational pest control: the fitting together of information, decision-making criteria, methods, and materials with naturally occurring pest mortality into effective and redeeming pest-management systems.

> Under integrated control, natural enemies, cultural practices, resistant crop and livestock varieties, microbial agents, genetic manipulation, messenger chemicals, and yes, even pesticides become mutually augmentatitive instead of individually operative or even antagonistic, as is the case under prevailing practice (*e.g.*, insecticides versus natural enemies). * * *

> Integrated control systems are dynamic, involving continuous information gathering and evaluation, which in turn permit flexibility in decision-making, alteration of the pathways of action, and variation in the agents used. It is the pest-control advisor who gives integrated control its dynamism. By constantly "reading" the situation and invoking tactics and materials as conditions dictate, he acts as a surrogate insecticide, "killing" insects [and other pests] with knowledge and information as well as pesticides, pathogens, parasites, and predators. * * *

Robert van den Bosch, *quoted in* SHIRLEY A. BRIGGS & RACHEL CARSON COUNCIL, BASIC GUIDE TO PESTICIDES: THEIR CHARACTERISTICS AND HAZARDS 261 (1992). As Hornstein observes, it is very information-intensive. IPM is most frequently used with insect pests, but is beginning to be used for plant disease and weed control. IPM is not organic farming, which eschews the use of synthetic pesticides altogether, but a well planned and executed IPM program can be highly effective in pest control while maintaining high yields of crops. Indeed, the more comprehensive forms of

IPM incorporate many techniques of organic pest control in the farmer's armamentarium.[36]

What challenges face those who want to expand the use of IPM? Read 7 U.S.C. § 136r-1. How does FIFRA encourage the use of IPM? Do you think it will have a major impact? If not, what other steps could Congress take to encourage IPM? Would Hornstein's suggestions be effective?

3. *Pollution prevention.* Pesticides contribute heavily to two forms of conventional pollution: groundwater contamination and surface water run-off. A recent study by two environmental groups reported pesticides in the drinking water supplies of millions of people in the Midwest, due to overuse of pesticides and the inability of conventional water treatment systems to remove them. *Pesticides: Drinking Water of 14 Million People Contaminated with Herbicides, Report Says,* 18 CHEM. REG. REP. (BNA) 937 (1994). Both surface and groundwater pollution raise substantial regulatory difficulties in identifying sources of pollution and imposing controls that do not tread on the traditional state primacy in land use. These problems, especially groundwater contamination, are issues for Congress's next look at FIFRA.

---

[36] Accessible descriptions of IPM can be found in REUVEN REUVENI, ED., NOVEL APPROACHES TO INTEGRATED PEST MANAGEMENT (1995) (especially chapter 1); MIGUEL A. ALTIERI, BIODIVERSITY AND PEST MANAGEMENT IN AGROECOSYSTEMS (1994).

Chapter 8

Manufacture: The Toxic Substances Control Act

A. Toward Comprehensive Regulation

The Toxic Substances Control Act authorizes EPA to investigate and regulate virtually all aspects of the creation, manufacture, distribution, use, and disposal of chemical substances. Its primary focus, however, is economic (*i.e.*, industrial) chemicals rather than waste, and use rather than disposal. From its earliest incarnations, the essential elements of the statute included some form of screening of new chemicals for health risks, information development concerning existing chemicals, and administrative authority to control distribution and use based on the information so obtained. Pressure for enactment of a chemical control law began when the Council on Environmental Quality (CEQ), barely a year old, issued a report, *Toxic Substances*, in support of President Nixon's proposed Toxic Substances Control Act of 1971. These concerns are also reflected in the statute's findings and policy. TSCA § 2.

TOXIC SUBSTANCES

Council on Environmental Quality
pp. 20-21 (1971)[1]

It is clear that current laws are inadequate to control the actual and potential dangers of toxic substances comprehensively or systematically. The controls over manufacture and distribution pertain to only a small percentage of the chemical substances which find their way into the environment. [Many serious environmental harms] relate to substances not covered by present controls over manufacture and distribution.

---

[1] *Reprinted in* House Comm. on Interstate and Foreign Commerce, Committee Print, Legislative History of the Toxic Substances Control Act (1976) at 783-784.

Both controls over production and controls over effluents suffer from the limited focus of their authority. For example, the Food and Drug Administration carefully examines food containers for their effect on food but does not address the environmental and health effects of incinerating the containers. With the exception of radioactive materials, disposal is not a consideration in any program controlling manufacture.

But the problems of focus are broader than specific examples. Setting rational standards for many pollutants under existing legislation is almost impossible. The key factors involved in setting standards are the *total* human exposure to a substance and its *total* effect on the environment. The focus must be on a particular pollutant and all the pathways by which it travels through the ecosystem. Controls over distribution approach this perspective, but most fail to consider important environmental factors adequately.

The obvious limitation of controls over effluents is that they generally deal with a problem only *after* it is manifest. They do not provide for obtaining information on potential pollutants before widespread damage has occurred.

More subtle but more serious limitations of effluent controls arise from their focusing on the media—air or water—in which the pollution occurs. This approach has several consequences: First, it leads to concern with those substances found in air or water in the greatest quantities. For example, the Air Pollution Control Office uses the gross weight of air pollution. Gross weight is a valid indicator, but it disregards the degree of danger of the various pollutants. * * * comparatively small amounts of some substances can cause severe damage, but media-oriented programs tend to overlook the importance of such substances. Another consequence of the media approach is that it cannot deal effectively with the fact that many, perhaps most, toxic substances find their way into the environment through several media. They cannot be characterized strictly as water pollutants or as air pollutants, for they are found in air, in water, and often in soil. The characteristic pervasiveness of toxic substances makes it difficult for the media-oriented programs to engage in adequate and efficient research, monitoring, and control activities for such substances. The need for such a comprehensive approach was a major rationale for the creation of the Environmental Protection Agency (EPA).

The scope of the EPA's authority provides a basis for an integrated approach to toxic substances. However, such an approach cannot be accomplished simply by coordinating the activities of existing media-oriented programs. The activities themselves must be conducted on an integrated basis. Testing to determine the health or environmental effects of a substance must be done in terms of total exposure to the substance, not simply exposure through air or through water. There must exist a capability for integrating the monitoring data from various media and for doing nonmedia analyses, for example, utilizing the materials balance approach. (This approach compares the total amount of a substance produced with the amount of a substance produced with the amount appearing in various end uses. A disparity between the two indicates the approximate amount escaping into the general environment.) Finally, there must exist authority to insure that the effects of a new substance are carefully examined before it enters the air, soil, or water.

The shortcomings of the legal authorities described above, the [health hazards] of toxic substances * * *, their increasing number and amounts * * *, and the inadequate attention paid to such substances all support the need for a new legal and institutional system to deal with toxic substances.

Our awareness of environmental threats, our ability to screen and test substances for adverse effects, and our capabilities for monitoring and predicting, although inadequate, are now sufficiently developed that we need to longer remain in a purely reactive posture with respect to chemical hazards. We need to longer be limited to repairing damage after it has been done; nor should we allow the general population to be used as a laboratory for discovering adverse health effects. There no longer any valid reason for continued failure to develop and exercise reasonable controls over toxic substances in the environment.

—

CEQ offers several reasons for enacting a toxic substances control act. (Can you enumerate them?) However, TSCA is most often described as a gap-filling statute. The existence of such gaps was a concern of CEQ, and TSCA has been amended three times to address gaps with respect to particular chemicals. The original statute specially regulated polychlorinated biphenyls (PCBs); in 1986, Congress added provisions for regulation of asbestos in schools; in 1988, radon gas in homes was added; and in 1992, lead-based paint. Each new title deals with a problem that otherwise fell between the cracks: airborne asbestos exposure of schoolchildren, residential radon gas, and lead paint are not ambient (*i.e.*, outside) air or water problems, nor are the principally affected persons employees under OSHA. And in all of these cases, "gap-filling" also means relying on a prevention, rather than just a control, strategy. Consider the Senate justification for the new statute:

> While air and water laws authorize limitations on discharges and emissions, the Occupational Safety and Health Act authorizes the establishment of ambient air standards for the workplace, and the Consumer Product Safety Act authorizes standards with respect to consumer products, there are no existing statutes which authorize the direct control of industrial chemicals themselves for their health or environmental effects. * * *

> While these other authorities will in many cases be sufficient to adequately protect health and the environment, the alternative of preventing or regulating the use of the chemical in the first instance may be a far more effective way of dealing with the hazards. If expensive sewage treatment facilities can be avoided, for example,

through removing dangerous materials from household and industrial wastes, the authority to do so ought to be provided.

S. REP. NO. 698, 94TH CONG., 2D SESS. 1-2 (1976).[2]

In view of the *extent* of the problems that CEQ had identified, Congress faced highly contentious issues when it turned its attention to toxic substances. As of 1982, the chemical industry comprised 11,500 establishments, employed 1.1 million people, and accounted for more than five percent of the gross national product. CEQ, 13th Ann. Report 115 (1982). Therefore, despite a supportive coalition of consumer, environmental, and labor groups, industry had a major stake in limiting the scope of such legislation.

In 1972 and again in 1973, the bills passed by each House of Congress were so different that no compromise could be reached before adjournment. The main dispute concerned the need for a provision to permit the screening of chemicals prior to entry into the market, the pre-market notification (PMN) that is now section 5 of TSCA. The Senate supported such controls, but the House opposed them. This is a fundamental philosophical issue, because it signals where the "burden of proof" will lie for industrial chemicals. As we saw in the last chapter, FIFRA, which the Senate considered analogous, requires pesticide registrants to demonstrate their products' safety. FIFRA, however, is descended from the Food, Drug, and Cosmetic Act—an old licensing statute—and it is unique among environmental statutes in placing the burden of proving safety on the regulated industry. Screening is also a fundamental practical issue, because the existence *vel non* of pre-market clearance determines in large part the cost of compliance and administration.

Finally, in the closing days of the 94th Congress a compromise, tolerated if not supported by industry, on this and other subjects was agreed to by large margins in each House. Two important elements of the compromise were that EPA's powers were hedged around with numerous procedural and substantive requirements, and that across-the-board regulation was consistently rejected in favor of individualized determinations.[3]

President Ford and Congressional supporters of TSCA hailed it as "one of the most important pieces of environmental legislation that has been enacted by the Congress," and a few chemical companies, equally convinced of the statute's potency, predicted the imminent fall of the Republic. Despite

---

[2] What are the advantages of a preventive approach? In this connection, compare the prevention costs of TSCA with the remediation costs of CERCLA. CERCLA currently gets the lion's share of EPA funding. Does this make sense? *See* Richard A. Ginsburg, *TSCA's Unfulfilled Mandate for Comprehensive Regulation of Toxic Substances—The Potential of TSCA § 21 Citizens' Petitions,* 16 ELR 10330, 10336 (1986) (urging the use of petitions to reverse the trend of EPA ignoring the preventative approach of TSCA in favor of remediation under CERCLA).

[3] The passage and purposes of TSCA are described in detail in Ray M. Druley & Girard L. Ordway, *The Toxic Substances Control Act,* 7 ENVT. REP. (BNA), Monograph No. 24, pp. 6-13 (1977); and Joel Reynolds, Note, *The Toxic Substances Control Act of 1976: An Introductory Background and Analysis,* 4 COL. J. ENVT'L L. 35, 35-60 (1977).

these hyperbolic claims in its support and in opposition, today TSCA is widely conceded to have been on the whole extremely disappointing. Mark Greenwood, an EPA toxic substances official, has been quoted as saying that "TSCA is a statute with powers, but no philosophy."[4] Put another way, TSCA is all technique and no policy. But even as technique, TSCA has run into trouble—when EPA has actually taken action, it has often been stymied by judicial review. As you study the materials in this chapter, you will want to ask yourself both kinds questions. As technique, what are TSCA's strengths and weaknesses? Are there technical remedies that might improve it? As environmental policy, do you agree that TSCA lacks a coherent "philosophy"? If so, can it be reinterpreted today to provide one? These are the crucial issues for TSCA in the coming decade.

KEY PROVISIONS OF TSCA

§ 3.	*Definitions*—"chemical substance"; "mixture"; "unreasonable risk" *not* defined.
§ 4	*Test rules*—procedures and criteria for requiring the testing of chemicals in commerce for toxic effects; priority list of chemicals.
§ 5	*Pre-manufacture notification*—requirement that EPA be notified of new chemicals and new uses of chemicals; submission of existing toxicity data; EPA response to notification and data.
§ 6	*Regulation of hazardous chemicals*—procedures and criteria for restricting chemicals; "unreasonable risk" and "least burdensome requirements; PCB regulation.
§ 7	*Imminent hazards*—authority to take emergency action.
§ 8	*Reporting requirements*—requirements to submit health and safety information; chemical inventory.
§ 9	*Other laws*—coordination with other federal statutes regulating chemicals.
§ 19	*Judicial review*—standard of review; administrative record.
§ 203	*Asbestos in schools*—regulations requiring inspection and removal of asbestos in schools.
§§ 303 - 305	*Radon abatement*—information programs and assistance to state programs for radon abatement in homes.
§§ 402- 406	*Lead-based paint abatement*—information, standards, and assistance to states in abating lead-based paint in homes

---

It is always a good first step when encountering a statute for the first time to scan its table of contents to get an idea of what sorts of things the statute requires, where particular provisions are, and how they are arranged. To begin this process, consider how TSCA ought to function in response to the following situation.

---

[4] *See Special Analysis—Toxic Substances Control Act*, 16 CHEM. REG. RPTR. (BNA) 1896 (1993).

PROBLEM
THE REGULATION OF CHLOROFLUOROCARBONS

At the time of TSCA's passage, there was a growing awareness in the scientific and environmental communities—recognized by Congress—that chlorofluorocarbons (CFCs) pose a risk to the global environment. In an early rulemaking under TSCA, EPA described the problem:

> Ultraviolet radiation is thought to cause or to be a contributory factor to two different types of skin cancer in people. One, nonmelanoma skin cancer, is relatively common, occurring at the rate of about 150 cases per 100,000 population each year in the United States. However, it is very rarely fatal. The other, melanoma skin cancer, is much rarer, occurring at the rate of about four cases per 100,000 population each year in the United States. Melanoma is fatal to about 30 percent of the people who contract it. The incidence of both types of skin cancer is rising rapidly. * * * The association between ultraviolet radiation and melanoma skin cancer is not as well established as the association with nonmelanoma skin cancer but it is still strong enough to warrant serious concern.

> Most of the ultraviolet radiation produced by the sun is absorbed in the atmosphere before reaching the earth's surface. The screening takes place in the stratosphere—the portion of the atmosphere that extends from about five to thirty miles about the earth's surface. The ultraviolet radiation is absorbed by oxygen in two separate reactions. First, an oxygen molecule (O_2) absorbs ultraviolet light and is split into its component oxygen atoms (O). These oxygen atoms then combine with oxygen molecules to form ozone (O_3). Second, the ozone molecules themselves absorb ultraviolet radiation and are broken down again to oxygen molecules and free oxygen atoms.

> * * *

> A more substantial problem for the present involves the introduction of chlorine into the stratosphere from chlorine-containing chemical substances introduced into the atmosphere by man. In the stratosphere, chlorine atoms will enter into a reaction sequence resulting in the destruction of ozone molecules.

> * * *

> * * * No decrease in stratospheric ozone from this source has yet been observed. However, the calculated effect from the amount of these compounds so far released would not be distinguishable from natural variations in ozone levels.

> In all respects in which it has been possible to check the theory described above against real-world observations, the theory has been confirmed. [Chlorofluoro-alkanes, a particularly damaging CFC,] are found in the lower atmosphere and in the stratosphere at levels consistent with the theory. Their ozone destroying potential under

stratospheric conditions has been demonstrated in laboratory experiments.

Accordingly, scientific controversy has increasingly centered not on whether continued use of these compounds will result in a depletion of the ozone layer, but on how much of a depletion would result.

* * *

At present, fully halogenated chlorofluoroalkanes are used in aerosol products, in refrigerators and air conditioners, as foam blowing agents, and as solvents. The major use in the United States, approximately fifty percent, is as aerosol propellants. * * *

Aerosol products release the propellant during normal use. In contrast, except for unintentional leakage, a refrigerator will keep the fully halogenated chlorofluoroalkane sealed within the unit during use. While disposal controls for refrigerators may be possible, this approach is not feasible for aerosols. In addition, substitute propellants or alternatives exist for most aerosol uses, whereas less is known about acceptable alternatives for the other uses. Finally, refrigerant and other nonpropellant uses are more integral to the functioning of society and the economy than aerosol uses, and hence are more difficult to evaluate in considering an appropriate regulatory course.* * *

With respect to aerosol propellant uses, technically feasible and economically acceptable alternatives exist for most uses of fully halogenated chlorofluoroalkane propellants. They fall into two categories: alternative propellants and alternative delivery systems.

EPA, Toxic Substances Control: Fully Halogenated Chlorofluoroalkanes, 42 Fed. Reg. 24542, 24543-44 (1977) (proposed rule, coordinated with FDA and CPSC). (The final rule may be found at 43 Fed. Reg. 11301 (1978).)

1. Suppose that you are the EPA official in charge of TSCA. You have been apprised of the above information by your staff, and you are inclined to take some sort of regulatory action. Assuming no time pressures apart from a general desire to reduce risks promptly, consider how the TSCA process would work.—Are CFCs even covered by the statute? How can you find out more about them? What do you need to find out about them for regulatory purposes? If what you learn concerns you, what authority do you have to take regulatory action? What kind of action can you take and what standards must you meet to take action? Are there procedural hurdles? What kind of judicial review can you expect?

2. Assume instead that you are the general counsel of Acme Chemicals, a major manufacturer of chlorofluoroalkanes. It is Acme's judgment that its products are not the wave of the future, and its scientists have been working on replacements for some time. Their solution, an existing chemical developed in Europe which replaces chlorine with bromine, seems to work as

well as CFCs in most applications. Acme scientists have imported the new substance, and have synthesized small quantities for testing in some of Acme's air conditioning units. Acme has collected all the information it can on the characteristics and effects of the bromine-based chemicals, but EPA has not been notified of this discovery because the company considers it highly secret commercial information.—Has Acme violated TSCA with respect to the bromine-based chemicals? What penalties are available? How can it bring itself into compliance and are there financial risks in doing so?

3. Finally, consider CFCs from the point of view of a staff attorney with the Environmental Defense Fund. EDF believes that EPA should take immediate steps to ban CFCs.—What opportunities do you have to persuade EPA to ban them? To take other regulatory action? Can you *force* EPA to act? Can you recover attorneys' fees for your efforts?

NOTES

1. *Regulation of CFCs*. The final CFC regulations, codified at 40 C.F.R. part 762, have two main parts: the first phases out most aerosol uses of CFCs pursuant to section 6, and the second requires detailed reporting of aerosol uses under section 8. The TSCA regulation does not, however, apply to uses of CFCs as a refrigerant. Those uses were not regulated until the Clean Air Act Amendments of 1990, in response to international treaty commitments under the Montreal Protocol on Substances that Deplete the Ozone Layer, Sept. 16, 1987, 26 I.L.M. 1550 (entered into force Jan. 1, 1989). The Clean Air Act Amendments, in fact, have superseded the TSCA regulations, because they provide comprehensive regulation of CFCs, including the reduction and phase-out of all non-essential uses. 42 U.S.C. §§ 7671-7671p.

2. *CFCs and the purposes of TSCA*. As was noted at the beginning of this chapter, the proponents of the bill identified two basic reasons for enacting TSCA: lack of information concerning toxic substances, and fragmentation and incompleteness in existing legislation. On the gap-filling point, two early commentators observed:

> That there were still loopholes in the law was amply demonstrated by the chlorofluorocarbon controversy. * * * [W]here should the regulation occur? Chlorofluorocarbons are not air pollutants in the usual sense; they are not poisonous; and they pose no hazard in the workplace. Even if regulated as consumer products, under [1977] law there would be no means of regulating them in industrial uses.

Druley & Ordway, *supra*, at 5-6. Were CFCs an appropriate subject of regulation under TSCA on information grounds? Since the 1977 preamble was written, reductions in stratospheric ozone have been confirmed by direct observation. Should EPA have waited for this empirical confirmation? Was it legally required to?

3. *Unreasonable risk*. Look again at the legal standard for applying the various regulatory tools authorized by TSCA. The touchstone of the statute,

clearly, is the term "unreasonable risk." It appears thirty-five or more times in the text. Note that it is used in several different ways—"may present an unreasonable risk" (§ 4(a)), "presents an unreasonable risk" (§ 6(a)), "imminent and unreasonable risk" (§ 7(f))—and for several different purposes—testing, priority-setting, regulating, notification, etc. (Section 4(f), however, uses "significant" risk; how is it different from unreasonable risk?) This was precisely the structural elegance envisioned by Congress. *See* H.R. REP. NO. 1341, 94TH CONG., 2D SESS. 14-15 (1976).

Now see if you can find a definition of unreasonable risk. You can't: Congress very deliberately declined to provide one. *Id.* at 13-15. What are the components of an unreasonable risk determination, based on the statute? The legislative history makes it clear that it is intended to include the full range of risk, cost, and benefit factors.

4. *Comprehensive rationality.* TSCA can be seen as exemplifying an approach to regulation known as "comprehensive rationality," a concept described in more detail in Chapter 3 (Economics and Regulatory Analysis), *supra.*[5] Under this model of administrative action, the agency resolves a problem as a whole, not piecemeal or "incrementally." To do so, it goes through a well-defined process of specifying goals, setting priorities, identifying alternatives, analyzing their consequences, and optimizing choices among the alternatives. Look back at the CFC problem. How did your response to Question 1 reflect comprehensive rationality? How does EPA's actual response?

The comprehensive rationality paradigm has two very important consequences for the way that TSCA functions. First, the broad focus and the analysis of many alternatives make huge information demands. Congress recognized this by making information gathering a centerpiece of the statute and by providing a step-by-step process for obtaining information when needed (automatically under §§ 5 and 8, or on a relatively low showing ("may present") under § 4). Second, a rationalist scheme is ideally quantitative. It will try to measure and compare risks, costs, and benefits. How quantitative was the CFC rulemaking? Compare it to the court's approach in *Corrosion Proof Fittings, infra.*

B. Information Gathering

TSCA's greatest innovation is arguably its recognition of the "data gap" for toxic substances. We saw in Chapter 2 (Toxicology and Risk Assessment) that uncertainty is a fundamental problem in toxic substances regulation and in Chapter 3 (Economics and Regulatory Analysis) that the market and tort systems do not remedy the problem. The government may adopt a number of techniques for obtaining needed information:

---

[5] *See also* WILLIAM H. RODGERS, JR. 3 ENVIRONMENTAL LAW § 6.1 (calling TSCA a "huge law machine" for controlling chemicals).

- *Compilations of existing data,* either for specific purposes or in general libraries, databases, or clearinghouses, allow EPA to acquire, organize, and use the data that do exist.
- *Recordkeeping, monitoring, and inspection* create, as well as simply gather information that EPA can use to spot violations or to detect patterns and trends for regulatory action.
- *Government research* can be either "basic" research—such as fundamental scientific principles, methodologies, and models—or specific research targeted to particular programs or chemicals.
- *Licensing,* the regulatory strategy of FIFRA, not only allows the regulator to screen products or activities in advance of public exposure, but also requires the licensee to provide the information necessary to make this judgment.
- *Requirements to test* allow EPA to obtain information at the manufacturer's expense concerning substances that are not subject to screening or are already through the screen.

How many of these techniques do you find in TSCA?[6] We now turn to the three major data collection provisions of TSCA: premanufacture notification (§ 5), general data collection (§ 8), and test rules (§ 4).Which techniques produce the most data? The best quality data? Which are least expensive? Which most fairly distribute the cost? Which are most appropriate as governmental expenditures?[7]

1. New Chemicals–Pre-Manufacture Notification

Simply put, pre-manufacture notification (PMN) requires that anyone who proposes to manufacture (or to import) a new chemical must notify EPA of its intention to do so ninety days in advance, § 5(a), (d)(2), and must provide EPA with "data which the person submitting the data believes show that * * * the manufacture, processing, distribution in commerce, use, and disposal of the chemical substance will not present an unreasonable risk." § 5(b)(2)(B), (d)(1). *See* 40 C.F.R. parts 720, 721, 723.[8] PMNs must also be

---

[6] Detailed discussions of the information-gathering provisions of TSCA may be found in David J. Hayes, *TSCA: The Sleeping Giant is Stirring,* 4 NAT. RES. & ENVT. 3 (Winter 1990); David J. Hayes, *The Potential for New Life in an "Old" Statute: The Toxic Substances Control Act in its 13th Year,* 13 CHEM. REG. RPTR. (BNA) 57 (1989).

[7] *See generally* John S. Applegate, *The Perils of Unreasonable Risk: Information, Regulatory Policy, and Toxic Substances Control,* 91 COLUM. L. REV. 261, 301-16 (1991); Mary L. Lyndon, *Information Economics and Chemical Toxicity: Designing Laws to Produce and Use Data,* 87 MICH. L. REV. 1795 (1989).

[8] Two good step-by-step guides to the regulatory details, in addition to the Rodgers treatise, are Sanford R. Gaines, *Toxic Substances Control Act,* in A PRACTICAL GUIDE TO ENVIRONMENTAL LAW (D. Sive & F. Friedman, eds. 1987), and DONALD W. STEVER, LAW OF CHEMICAL REGULATION AND HAZARDOUS WASTE (1986 and updated) (3 vols.).

filed before manufacturing or processing existing chemicals for "significant new uses." § 5(a)(2).[9]

The purpose of the PMN submissions, of course, is to give EPA an opportunity to screen the chemical for health and environmental risks. But it is an *opportunity* only—EPA may do nothing, in which case the production may go forward; or it may seek to delay production if it finds that additional data are needed to evaluate the chemical's risks, § 5(e); or, if the PMN information reveals an unreasonable risk, EPA may issue a "proposed rule under section 6" which becomes effective immediately. § 5(f). EPA must go to court to prevent production if it finds that the chemical "may present" an unreasonable risk, § 5(e)(1)(A), but may act on its own if it "presents or will present" an unreasonable risk. § 5(f). Finally, EPA is authorized to grant exemptions from PMN reporting for categories of chemicals that it finds generally do not present an unreasonable risk and for small-volume chemicals for experimentation or test marketing. § 5(h).

The usefulness in practice of PMNs for screening and collecting information is unclear. In FY 1988 EPA received about 3000 PMNs, in FY 1995 about 2300, and in FY 1997 about 1500. Even as the numbers decrease, they are far more than EPA can carefully scrutinize. In its report to Congress for FY 1987 and 1988, EPA stated that it takes no action on 90% of PMNs. In FY 1995, it took no action on 98% of PMN filings. In 1983, the Office of Technology Assessment reported that about half of PMNs contained no toxicity information at all, and less than 20% contained data on long-term toxicity.[10]

NOTES

1. *Screening.* Obviously, the PMN process is a kind of screening device.[11] How is it different from FIFRA? Are the data gathering (and resulting agency judgments) under FIFRA and the PMN equally reliable? How effective, in other words, is the PMN screen? If you conclude that it has gaps, why (apart from simple legislative compromise) did Congress settle for a partial screen under TSCA?

Where is the burden of proof? Notice the conflicting signals in TSCA on burden of proof, reflecting the fact that section 5 was the principal bone of

---

[9] One of the most difficult issues under § 5 has been to develop significant new use rules (SNURs) based on the statutory criteria of projected volume, changes in exposure, increases magnitude or duration of exposure, different manner of manufacture, use, or disposal. § 5(a)(2). Since designation of uses is to be *before the fact*, EPA's tactic in SNURs has been to find a significant new use wherever workplace exposure increases and is not at the same time remediated by worker protection and information. 40 C.F.R. part 721. EPA would like to institute "generic" SNURs to avoid case-by-case decisions on what must be reported. 54 Fed. Reg. 31298 (1989), codified at 40 C.F.R. §§ 721.50–721.185.

[10] OTA, The Information Content of Pre-Manufacture Notices 6-7, 49-54 (1983).

[11] For a detailed description of screening techniques, *see* STEPHEN BREYER, REGULATION AND ITS REFORM 131-55 (1982).

contention between the House and Senate and hence was the most elaborately compromised.

2. *Unreasonable risk*. The basic standard for regulatory action is again unreasonable risk, "a balancing of risks and benefits." S. REP. NO. 698, *supra*, at 12. Is cost-risk-benefit balancing appropriate at this stage? Is it even feasible?

3. *Screening and innovation*. One of the constant themes of the opponents of TSCA was that it would stifle innovation in the chemical industry. Two scholars who reviewed the evidence reached these conclusions:

> The adverse effects [of pre-market approval] appear to be felt most by the small and newer firms, particularly those that produce specialty chemicals for limited, dynamic markets. These effects derive principally from the following factors: the ability of large firms to monitor or influence the political and legal climate; the economies of scale in compliance that large firms may enjoy; and the disproportionate emphasis these regulations place on new as opposed to existing products. * * * The situation under TSCA is exacerbated by the disproportionate emphasis regulatory action has placed on new chemical substances, [which tend to be produced by new, small, and specialty firms,] as opposed to problems associated with existing products. Were strong regulatory actions under TSCA directed at existing products, this would create an incentive for the introduction of new, safer substitutes. * * *

> At the same time, the regulatory premarket approval process may be benefitting many companies by increasing the likelihood that their new products will be successful in the marketplace. Studies from both the pharmaceutical and TSCA areas indicate that the testing and analysis which is now routinely undertaken in the development of the application for government approval often also yields a much better idea of the characteristics of the product under development. In addition, a variety of studies have shown that regulation-related R&D often suggests new uses for products and sometimes new product lines. It appears that these benefits are most likely to occur among companies with significant research establishments where these costs can be absorbed relatively easily. * * *

Ashford & Heaton, *Regulation and Technological Innovation in the Chemical Industry*, 46 L. & CONTEMP. PROBS. 109, 146-57 (Summer 1983). For other aspects of the problem of disparate treatment of old and new substances, *see* Chapter 7 (FIFRA), *supra*.

2. Existing Chemicals–Reporting and Recordkeeping

"TSCA's great strength as a data-gathering statute resides in Section 8,"[12] which requires the compilation of a Chemical Substances Inventory of all chemicals in commerce (§ 8(b)), general reporting and recordkeeping under EPA rules (§ 8(a)), and the special reporting of certain kinds of information (§ 8(c)-(e)). EPA's first step in implementing TSCA was to develop the inventory of chemicals in commerce required by section 8(b), since defining the universe of concern is the first step in a comprehensive approach to regulation. Moreover, the Inventory is the trigger for PMN (a chemical not in the Inventory is "new") and other requirements. The Inventory currently contains about 70,000 entries, of which 3000-4000 are produced in large volumes.[13]

Section 8(a) is TSCA's broadest and most general information provision. It allows EPA by rule to require that a regulated entity maintain and report a wide range of information relevant to the "unreasonable risk" determination, including chemical identity, uses, amounts manufactured or processed (including projections), byproducts from manufacturing or use, existing health and environmental effects data, human exposure, and manner of disposal. § 8(a)(2). EPA can use section 8(a) for general information gathering or for specific projects, as it did in creating the Inventory. The most significant regulatory development under section 8(a) was to be the comprehensive assessment information rule (CAIR), which would have required reporting of an extensive, uniform set of information for subject chemicals.[14] EPA believed that burdensomeness to industry was balanced by the great utility of uniform data collection to both TSCA and non-TSCA programs. CAIR, however, was challenged in court in 1989, and EPA agreed to make substantial modifications to the rule. This has never occurred, and EPA has essentially abandoned the program.[15]

Three other subsections require reporting and recordkeeping of particular types of information. Manufacturers and processors must maintain records of "significant adverse reactions to health or the environment * * * alleged to have been caused by the substance or mixture," § 8(c), and must *immediately* report "information which reasonably supports the conclusion that such substances or mixture presents a substantial risk of injury to health or the

---

[12] David J. Hayes, *The Potential for New Life in and "Old" Statute: The Toxic Substances Control Act in its 13th Year*, 13 CHEM. REG. REP. (BNA) 57, 68 (1989).

[13] EPA, ANNUAL REPORT OF THE OFFICE OF POLLUTION PREVENTION AND TOXICS, FY 1995.

[14] CAIR required detailed information about the reporter; quantities of manufacture, import, use, and storage; substance identification; physical and chemical properties; environmental fate; economic and financial aspects; technical details of manufacturing and processing; treatment and disposal; worker exposure; and environmental release.

[15] *See* EPA, Chemical Substances; Deletion of Certain Chemical Regulations, 60 Fed. Reg. 31917, 31918 (1995) (deleting temporary regulations pending revival of the program sometime in the future).

environment." § 8(e). Both subsections seem to require the reporter to decide in the first place whether a health effect was caused by a chemical and whether the effect is "significant" or "unreasonable." On the causal connection between the effect and the chemical, EPA takes the position that "[s]uch evidence will generally not be conclusive as to the substantiality of the risk; it should, however, reliably ascribe the effect to the chemical."[16] Does this solve the problem? What about the "significance" determination?

Subsection 8(d), by far the broadest of the three, requires the submission of a list or copies of "health and safety studies" conducted by—or simply known to—the manufacturers or processors of specified chemicals. *Dow Chemical Co. v. EPA*, 605 F.2d 673 (3d Cir. 1979), upheld EPA's broad powers to reach information under TSCA. The court first held that EPA is authorized to require reporting of health and safety studies even as to chemicals produced in small amounts solely for research and development. Based on statutory language, the court rejected Dow's argument that the term "for commercial purposes" was limited to public distribution. Second, the court considered whether EPA's power to require the submission of copies of studies under section 8(d)(2) is limited to those required to be listed under section 8(d)(1). The significance of the issue is that, whereas EPA had by rule limited 8(d)(1) to a particular list of chemicals, it read 8(d)(2) to require submission of *any* study "otherwise known to" the manufacturer. The court again upheld EPA's broad interpretation, emphasizing Congress' clear intent to be inclusive.[17]

A threshold problem with section 8(d) is defining what constitutes a "study." Is a preliminary report covered? How much analysis of data is required before it becomes a "study"? EPA's regulations call monitoring data a study "when they have been aggregated and analyzed to measure the exposure of humans." 40 C.F.R. § 716.3. However, in an administrative proceeding, EPA took the position that a short-term collection of air monitoring data for industrial hygiene purposes was a study. EPA subsequently withdrew its complaint when confronted with evidence that it had previously advised the company differently, and it has not yet clarified its meaning through "interpretive guidance."[18]

NOTES

1. *Existing data.* The National Academy of Sciences *Toxicity Testing* report, cited above, was as unimpressed by the quantity as with the quality of existing data. What, then, are the inherent limitations of all of the section 8 authorities in terms of their ability to resolve the general information gap? Do they outweigh the burdensomeness of the requirements?

---

[16] 43 Fed. Reg. 11110, *reprinted in* 21 ELR 35377 (1991).

[17] For an analysis of the *Dow* case raising this and other questions, *see* Comment, *TSCA and Trade Secrets: Third Circuit Upholds EPA's Broad Authority to Obtain Health Studies Under § 8(d)*, 9 ENVT'L L. REP. (ELI) 10163 (1979).

[18] *In re Lonza Inc.*, No. TSCA 87-H-03 (1987); 12 CHEM. REG. REP. (BNA) 116 (1988).

2. *Finality of information.* The definition of "study" in section 8(d) and the implied causal relationship between chemical and effect in sections 8(c) and (d) pose the problem of when to report information that becomes available. Are there good arguments for waiting for relatively well analyzed, complete, or "final" information? What are the dangers?

3. *Innovation and reporting requirements.* The *Dow* court was very concerned that required reporting would "chill" innovation in the chemical industry, and it went to some length in dicta to distance itself from the effects of its decision on innovation. What is the basis for the concern that reporting obligations will reduce innovation? Are they justified? Does industry have independent reasons to conduct its own health effects testing?

How does TSCA try to counteract the disincentives to product development posed by reporting requirements? Does confidentiality limit the usefulness of section 8?

4. *Self-monitoring.* Much American regulation depends on self-enforcement by the regulated entity (think of the I.R.S.), and TSCA is no different. The Third Circuit addressed this issue in *ALM Corporation v. EPA*, 974 F.2d 380 (3d Cir. 1992), *cert. denied,* 507 U.S. 972 (1993). ALM appealed a $19,500 civil penalty assessed by EPA for failure to report the importation of plastic pellets for injection molding. ALM had failed to accompany each of seven shipments with a certification that the shipment either complied with TSCA or was not covered by TSCA. Two later certificates inaccurately stated that TSCA did not apply to the shipments. In fact, all nine shipments were covered by TSCA, and all substantively complied with TSCA. The court held that substantive compliance with TSCA was immaterial to the failure-to-report violation, because the purpose of the reporting requirements is self-monitoring:

> ALM failed to monitor itself. It therefore violated TSCA's reporting requirements, even if it did not violate any restrictions on importing the substances themselves. * * * The penalty is not imposed to redress a particular injury but to ensure self-monitoring among importers. * * *
>
> [Nor does ALM have a right to cure its violations subsequently, because] such a right to rectify would defeat the self-enforcement purpose of the certification requirement by allowing importers to ignore the certification requirements and, if discovered, belatedly submit certification without penalty for their initial violation. This would be likely to encourage non-compliance.

ALM Corp., 974 F.2d at 386.

5. *Third-party reporting obligations.* Both sections 8(d) and (c) clearly encompass the submission of information that the manufacturers or processors did not themselves create, but only know of. Why is this breadth important? Does the logic of this extend to reporting obligations by third parties, such as competitors or university researchers? (The regulations at

present do not reach them. 40 C.F.R. § 716.5.) Professor Rodgers likens third-party reporting to the informants of "totalitarian" regimes. Hyperbole aside, is this a fair criticism?

6. *Voluntary compliance programs.* Notwithstanding the toughness of its position in *ALM Corporation*, EPA has also taken the opposite tack. Its Compliance Audit Program (CAP) for section 8(e) and a similar program for section 5 specifically allow violators to review their files for materials that should have been reported and to turn them in with pre-set maximum penalties or reduced penalties. Congress has urged EPA to adopt a similar program under the Clean Air Act Amendments of 1990. These programs are controversial and their success disputed. Two commentators have urged the extension of such programs under the general rubric of encouraging comprehensive environmental self-audits, noting that they improve compliance and that the purpose of administrative enforcement should be compliance, not punishment.[19]

PROBLEM
RADON IN THE HOME

Clearly, the gathering of information can play a critical supporting role in developing traditional regulatory restrictions. But can *dissemination* of information be itself a valuable form of regulation?

Radon is a colorless, odorless, radioactive gas emitted from naturally decaying uranium in the earth's crust, and it is a serious environmental health problem.[20] When radon is discharged into the atmosphere, it dissipates rapidly and poses little health threat. Under certain conditions, however, it seeps into homes and buildings and accumulates to potentially dangerous levels. When it does, it enters as a gas and then decays into radioactive products. In the decay process, the radioactive products attach to air particles, such as dust or smoke, which, if inhaled, become trapped in the lungs. The decay products continue to break down further in the lungs, releasing radiation which damages the lung tissue and increases the risk of lung cancer. EPA estimates that as many as 20,000 people die from lung cancer each year as the result of long-term radon exposure. It has ranked indoor radon as the number one "environmental problem area" based on population cancer risk. EPA also

---

[19] William N. Farran III & Thomas L. Adams, Jr., *Environmental Regulatory Objective: Auditing and Compliance or Crime and Punishment*, 21 ENVT'L L. REP. (ENVTL. L. INST.) 10239 (1991). On compliance problems generally, *see* WILLIAM DRAYTON, AMERICA'S TOXIC PROTECTION GAP: THE COLLAPSE OF COMPLIANCE WITH THE NATION'S TOXICS LAWS (1984).

[20] *See generally* Dodge and McCarthy, *Radon: Congressional and Federal Concerns,* Cong. Research Service Order Code IB86144 (Aug. 3, 1987); EPA & HHS, A Citizen's Guide to Radon: What It Is and What To Do About It (1986); Paul A. Locke, *Promoting Radon Testing, Disclosure, and Remediation: Practicing Public Health Through the Home Mortgage Market*, 20 ENVTL. L. REP. (ENVTL. L. INST.) 10479 (1990); Deborah A. Bannworth, Note, *Radon in New Jersey: Is it Time for Mandatory Testing?*, 15 SETON HALL LEGIS. J. 171 (1991); MICHAEL LAFAVORE, RADON, THE INVISIBLE THREAT (1987); Kindt, *Radioactive Wastes*, 24 NAT. RESOURCES J. 967 (1984).

estimates that as many as one million homes nationally could be affected by unsafe levels of radon.

Radon presents a special challenge to environmental regulation, which is traditionally based on uniformly applicable restrictions on industrial and commercial activities. First, radon is not a risk created by humans or technology, so there is no obvious entity to target for blame or correction. Second, most people's experience with radon is apparently benign, having lived with it in their homes for a long time without adverse effects, or even being aware of its existence. In fact, radon-induced lung cancer has all of the characteristics of toxic injury identified in Chapter 2: it is the result of chronic, low-dose exposure, has a long latency period, displays no early warning signs, and is indistinguishable from other lung cancers. Third, people who choose their homes in some sense voluntarily expose themselves to radon. Finally, radon exposure varies enormously—and unpredictably—from house to house, depending on soil type, house structure, and behavior of occupants.

Clearly, the place to deal with the serious health threat posed by radon is the home, as there is no significant industrial or other source of the risk. Since indoor air is excluded from the bulk of the Clean Air Act (42 U.S.C. § 7602(g) (limiting "air pollutant" to contaminants of the "ambient air")), the utility-player TSCA would appear to be a good candidate. Indeed, in 1988 Congress amended TSCA to cover indoor radon abatement. However, the new Title III (§§ 301-311) does not authorize direct regulation. Instead, it seeks to provide information to homeowners to enable them to assess risks and to protect themselves against radon.[21] It sets a national goal for radon in buildings, requires EPA to update and republish a *Citizen's Guide*,[22] orders EPA to develop model construction techniques and standards for controlling radon, and authorizes grant assistance for state radon programs. Pursuant to Title III, EPA recently proposed voluntary guidelines for builders to install protective measures in new homes.[23] EPA also urged buyers to require sellers to test for radon before the sale is completed. EPA hopes that national code development organizations, states, and local jurisdictions will adopt its model construction standards and techniques into their requirements.

Do these informational measures adequately protect against unreasonable risks? Is radon abatement an appropriate extension of federal regulation?

---

[21] S. REP. No. 91, 100TH CONG., 1ST SESS. 1 (1987).

[22] EPA publishes a whole range of radon guides for homeowners, tenants, builders, house buyers and sellers, etc. They are available at http://www.epa.gov\iaq\radon\ pubs\index.htm. (The TSCA office publishes similar materials on the other major home hazards, asbestos and lead. They are available at http://www.epa.gov/ opptintr/pubcitizen.htm.)

[23] EPA, Proposed Model Standards and Techniques for Control of Radon in New Buildings, 58 Fed. Reg. 19097 (April 12, 1993).

[24] Paul A. Locke, *Promoting Radon Testing, Disclosure, and Remediation: Practicing Public Health Through the Home Mortgage Market*, 20 ENVTL. L. REP. (ENVTL. L. INST.) 10479 (1990).

TSCA has already developed a significant role in the purchase and sale of residences by providing buyers and sellers with information about the hazards and remediation of lead and asbestos, which are often found in older construction, and radon, which is found in newer, more air-tight and energy-efficient construction. While the requirement to disclose or the right to inspect for these toxic substances is usually a matter of state law, EPA has developed pamphlets for consumers.

Going a step further, should EPA be authorized to *require* radon testing and disclosure as an integral part of residential sales by providing radon information to the primary and secondary mortgage markets, as one commentator has suggested?[24] Should EPA be authorized to require radon abatement measures in homes when houses are sold (there being a stronger federal interest when commerce is involved)?

3. Test Rules

Section 4 of TSCA permits EPA to require that manufacturers and processors of chemical substances generate data on any of the health or environmental issues relating to the underlying "unreasonable risk" determination, including toxicity, chemical characteristics, and exposure. Unlike section 5, test rules are not a screening device; unlike section 8, they generate truly new data. A test rule may be predicated on information obtained under sections 5 or 8, and it is designed to provide the basis for further action under sections 6 or 7. EPA is specifically required to initiate "appropriate action" under section 5, 6, or 7 if it receives information that "indicates to the Administrator that there may be a reasonable basis to conclude that a chemical substance or mixture presents or will present a significant risk of serious or widespread harm to human beings from cancer, gene mutation, or birth defects." § 4(f).

The expense of testing can be high: EPA recently estimated that the cost of compliance with a proposed test rule on glycidols, a category containing 66 different substances, would cost $18,000,000.[25] Congress in enacting section 4 expressed "one of the basic policy objectives of the bill: to require manufacturers and processors to bear the responsibility for adequately testing potentially dangerous chemical substances."[26] Are there sound economic reasons for requiring chemical users to bear ("internalize") testing costs?

Promulgation of test rules is an involved process. First, the test rule process commences, not with EPA itself, but with a list of chemicals produced by an Interagency Testing Committee (ITC) made up of representatives from most federal health agencies. The ITC, based on standard risk assessment criteria, periodically lists chemicals for testing on a priority basis. The list may not exceed fifty chemicals at one time, and EPA

---

[25] 16 CHEM. REG. REP. (BNA) 1878 (1993). *See also* Ausimont U.S.A. Inc. v. EPA, 838 F.2d 93, 95 (3d Cir. 1988) (reporting estimates for fluoroalkanes testing from $4.8 to $9 million).
[26] H.R. REP. NO. 1341, *supra*, at 17; *accord*, § 2(b)(1).

may revise the reports, but it must respond to ITC recommendations either by issuing a test rule or by publicly deciding within one year not to do so. Second, the proposed rule is subject to the elaborate "hybrid rulemaking" procedures specified by section 19(a). Third, it must be based on three express findings: (i) that either the chemical "may present an unreasonable risk of injury to health or the environment," or that the chemical is manufactured in "substantial quantities" to which "significant or substantial human exposure" is likely; (ii) that there exists "insufficient data and experience upon which the effects of [the chemical] can reasonably be determined or predicted"; and (iii) that "testing * * * is necessary to develop such data." Fourth, it is subject to the special judicial review provisions of section 19(c).

NOTES

1. *Relationship to FIFRA*. How does section 4 compare to the FIFRA "data call-in" discussed in Chapter 7? Look particularly at procedures, criteria, and burden of proof. Are these differences consistent with the overall regulatory strategies of the two statutes? The legislative history of TSCA makes the distinction between a selective and a broad testing program. In which category is FIFRA? TSCA? Why did Congress make those choices?

2. *The findings*. What is the purpose of requiring predicate findings at all? Why did Congress choose these particular prerequisites? Do you anticipate that EPA will have difficulty meeting them?

3. *Interagency Testing Committee*. What is the rationale for the ITC's role and composition? Does this function have other uses? EPA regulations have used ITC listing, like inclusion on the Inventory, as a trigger for recordkeeping and reporting requirements under section 8(a) and (d).

4. *Voluntary testing*. The initial litigation under section 4 involved EPA's strategy of entering into voluntary testing agreements with manufacturers. *Natural Resources Defense Council v. EPA*, 595 F. Supp. 1255 (S.D.N.Y. 1984), arose out of NRDC's efforts to force some movement in the stalled section 4 testing program. Instead of initiating formal rulemaking on ITC substances, EPA accepted voluntary testing programs that it had negotiated with industry. The court found that voluntary testing violated the express rulemaking process of the statute. Under section 4, the only way that EPA can decline to initiate rulemaking on an ITC chemical is formally to find that testing is *not* necessary. The court also noted the interlocking nature of TSCA's provisions: a section 4 rule triggers public notice, reporting, recordkeeping, exportation, penalty, and judicial review requirements. Voluntary test rules circumvented all of these—which of course was one reason that industry was willing voluntarily to undertake expensive testing. The court suggested, however, that "negotiation to determine appropriate test protocols as well as other relevant criteria certainly is not only permissible but indeed preferable to blind, often impractical, bureaucratic bumbling." EPA

responded by promulgating regulations for negotiating enforceable test rules, or "testing consent agreements." *See* 40 C.F.R. part 790. Why would industry be willing to negotiate *mandatory* test rules? What is there to negotiate? Are some aspects of test rules more suitable for negotiation than others?

The Chemical Manufacturers Association, whose members include the industries most directly affected by TSCA, recently announced a multi-year, $67-million program to undertake high quality basic research on the potential carcinogenic, endocrine disruption, and respiratory effects of industrial chemicals. Government agencies, including EPA, welcomed the initiative, citing the desperate need for more funding for such research.[27] Why would CMA undertake this project? Is it a vindication of EPA's practice of pursuing only negotiated test rules?

CHEMICAL MANUFACTURERS ASSOCIATION v. EPA [CMA I]

859 F.2d 977 (D.C. Cir. 1988)

Opinion for the Court filed by Chief Judge WALD.

Petitioners, Chemical Manufacturers Association and four companies that manufacture chemicals (collectively, "CMA"), seek to set aside a rule promulgated by the Environmental Protection Agency ("EPA" or "the Agency"). This Final Test Rule was promulgated under section 4 of the Toxic Substances Control Act ("TSCA" or "the Act"), 15 U.S.C. §§ 2601-2629. The Final Test Rule required toxicological testing to determine the health effects of the chemical 2-ethylhexanoic acid ("EHA") * * *.

* * *

Facts and Prior Proceedings

EHA is a colorless liquid with a mild odor. It is used exclusively as a chemical intermediate or reactant in the production of metal soaps, peroxy esters and other products used in industrial settings. EHA itself is totally consumed during the manufacture of these products; as a result, no products offered for sale to industry or to consumers contain EHA.

The Interagency Testing Committee first designated EHA for priority consideration for health effects tests on May 29, 1984. * * *

* * *

EPA issued a proposed test rule on May 17, 1985. The rule proposed a series of tests to ascertain the health of risks of EHA, and it set out proposed standards for the conduct of those tests. EPA based the Proposed Test Rule on a finding that EHA "may present an unreasonable risk" of subchronic toxicity (harm to bodily organs from repeated exposure over a limited period of time), oncogenicity (tumor formation) and development toxicity (harm to the fetus). As to subchronic toxicity, EPA cited studies suggesting that both EHA and chemicals structurally similar to it cause harm to the livers of test animals. As

---

[27] 29 ENVT. REP. (BNA) 2058 (1999).

to oncogenicity, EPA cited studies suggesting that chemicals structurally analogous to EHA cause cancer in laboratory animals. As to developmental toxicity, EPA cited studies indicating that both EHA and its chemical analogues have produced fetal malformations in test animals.

The Proposed Test Rule also addressed the question of whether humans are exposed to EHA, a question of critical importance to this case. The Agency acknowledged that, since no finished products contain EHA, consumer exposure is not a concern. It likewise discounted the dangers of worker exposure to EHA vapors. The Agency based its Proposed Test Rule solely on the potential danger that EHA will come in contact with the skin of workers. As evidence of potential dermal exposure, the Agency noted that approximately 400 workers are engaged in the manufacture, transfer, storage and processing of 20 to 25 million pounds of EHA per year. Further, rebutting claims by industry representatives that gloves are routinely worn during these activities, EPA noted that worker hygiene procedures "can vary widely throughout the industry," that workers are not required by existing federal regulations to wear gloves, and that the industry had not monitored work sites for worker exposure to EHA.

* * *

CMA criticized the toxicology studies cited by EPA and sought to show that the use of gloves by employees of companies working with EHA prevented human exposure to the chemical, thus rendering any test rule invalid. Before publication of the final rule, CMA retained an independent consultant to conduct a survey of glove use by the employees of companies working with EHA (the "Glove Use Survey"). The results of the survey were submitted to EPA. CMA also submitted the results of an Eastman Kodak Co. study of the permeability of nitrile and neoprene gloves (the "Glove Permeability Study").

EPA published the Final Test Rule for EHA on November 6, 1986. The rule required a 90-day subchronic toxicity test, a developmental toxicity test, and a pharmacokinetics test. In the preamble to the Final Test Rule also addressed the industry critique of the prior toxicology studies on EHA. Acknowledging some weaknesses in the studies, EPA nonetheless asserted that they "add to the weight of evidence" supporting findings of potential toxicity and thus helped to justify further testing.

* * *

III. Statutory Interpretation

The Toxic Substances Control Act requires EPA to promulgate a test rule under section 4 if a chemical substance, *inter alia*, "may present an unreasonable risk of injury to health or the environment." 15 U.S.C. § 2603(a)(1)(A)(i). The parties both accept the proposition that the degree to which a particular substance presents a risk to health is a function of two factors: (a) human exposure to the substance, and (b) the toxicity of the substance. *See Ausimont U.S.A., Inc. v. EPA*, 838 F.2d 93, 94 (3d Cir. 1988).

They also agree that EPA must make some sort of threshold findings as to the existence of an "unreasonable risk of injury to health." The parties differ, however, as to the manner in which this finding must be made.

* * *

A. Required Finding of "Unreasonable Risk"

As to the first issue in this case, the standard of probability of an unreasonable risk to health, we find that Congress did not address the precise question in issue. Examining the EPA interpretation under the second prong of *Chevron*, we find it to be reasonable and consistent with the statutory scheme and legislative history. Consequently, we uphold the Agency's construction of TSCA as authorizing a test rule where EPA's basis for suspecting the existence of an "unreasonable risk of injury to health" is substantial—*i.e.*, when there is a more-than-theoretical basis for suspecting that some amount of exposure takes place and that the substance is sufficiently toxic at that level of exposure to present an "unreasonable risk of injury to health."

1. Text and Structure of the Statute

Both the wording and structure of TSCA reveal that Congress did not expect that EPA would have to document to a certainty the existence of an "unreasonable risk" before it could require testing. This is evidence from the two-tier structure of the Act. In order for EPA to be empowered to *regulate* a chemical substance, the Agency must find that the substance "presents or will present an unreasonable risk of injury to health or the environment." TSCA § 6, 15 U.S.C. § 2605(a). The *testing* provision at issue here, by contrast, empowers EPA to act at a lower threshold of certainty than that required for regulation. Specifically, testing is warranted if the substance "*may* present an unreasonable risk of injury to health or the environment." TSCA § 4, 15 U.S.C. § 2603(a)(1)(A)(i) (emphasis added). Thus, the language of section 4 signals that EPA is to make a probabilistic determination of the presence of "unreasonable risk."

2. Legislative History

The legislative history of TSCA compels a further conclusion. It not only shows that "unreasonable risk" need not be a matter of absolute certainty; it shows the reasonableness of EPA's conclusion that "unreasonable risk" need not be established to a more-probable-than-not degree.

A House Report on the version of the bill that eventually became TSCA underscores the distinction between the section 6 standard and the section 4 standard. To issue a test rule, EPA need not find that a substance actually does cause or present an "unreasonable risk."

> Such a finding requirement would defeat the purpose of the section, for if the Administrator is able to make such a determination, regulatory action to protect against the risk, not additional testing, is called for.

H.R.REP. NO. 1341, 94TH CONG., 2D SESS. 17-18 (1976).

* * *

Of course, it is also evident from the legislative history that Congress did not intend to authorize EPA to issue test rules on the basis of mere hunches. The House Report states:

> [T]he term "may" * * * does not permit the Administrator to make a finding respecting probability of a risk on the basis of mere conjecture or speculation, *i.e.*, it may or may not cause a risk.

H.R.REP. NO. 1341, *supra*, at 18. Congress obviously intended section 4 to empower EPA to issue a test rule only after it had found a solid "basis for concern" by accumulating enough information to demonstrate a more-than-theoretical basis for suspecting that an "unreasonable risk" was involved in the use of the chemical.

* * *

3. Interpretation in Other Circuits

We note that EPA's interpretation of section 4 is consistent with the views of the only other two courts of appeals that have examined its "may present" language. *See Ausimont U.S.A., Inc. v. EPA*, 838 F.2d 93 (3d Cir. 1988); *Shell Chemical Co. v. EPA*, 826 F.2d 295 (5th Cir. 1987).

In *Ausimont*, the Third Circuit held that EPA could not require testing "based on little more than scientific curiosity." A test rule could not be sustained, the court stated, if the existence of exposure were "merely a remote possibility founded on theoretical factual situations." * * *

* * *

B. Uses of Inference Versus Direct Evidence of Exposure

The second issue in the case is whether EPA must produce direct evidence documenting human exposure in order to rebut industry-submitted evidence casting doubt on the existence of exposure. * * *

CMA does not contest the proposition that the use of inferences to establish exposure is reasonable as a general matter. CMA challenges only the Agency's reliance on inferences in the face of industry evidence attacking its initial exposure finding. In light of our preceding decision on the quantum of proof necessary for a test rule, however, we see no reason to require EPA to come up with additional evidence of exposure when the industry challenges its initial finding unless the industry evidence effectively reduces the basis for an exposure finding to the realm of theory, speculation and conjecture. We conclude that it is reasonable for EPA to rely on inferences in issuing a section 4 test rule, so long as all the evidence—including the industry evidence—indicates a more-than-theoretical probability of exposure. Whether the Agency's ultimate finding of exposure is supported by sufficient evidence depends on a *weighing* of all the evidence, not on whether the *type* of evidence produced by EPA is direct as opposed to circumstantial.

Even if EPA were required under CMA's scenario to establish exposure as more probable than not, there would be no reason to limit its proof to direct evidence. * * *

* * *

IV. Standard of Review for Agency Findings

The Final Test Rule was promulgated under section 4 of TSCA, 15 U.S.C. § 2603(a). Judicial review of the rule must proceed according to 15 U.S.C. § 2618(c)(1)(B)(i), which specifically states that the Administrative Procedure Act ("APA") standard customarily applied in agency cases, 5 U.S.C. § 706, is inapposite[. Instead,] "the court shall hold unlawful and set aside such rule if the court finds that the rule is not supported by substantial evidence in the rulemaking record * * * taken as a whole. * * * 15 U.S.C. § 2618(c)(1)(B)(i).

* * *

The legislative history of TSCA further indicates that Congress perceived some difference between the standard it chose for TSCA and the APA's arbitrary-and-capricious standard. The House Report explained:

> [I]t is the intent that the traditional presumption of validity of an agency rule would remain in effect, [but] * * * [t]he Committee has chosen to adopt the "substantial evidence test," for the Committee intends that the reviewing court engage in a *searching review* of the Administrator's reasons and explanations for the Administrator's conclusions.

* * *

This fairly rigorous standard of record review should not, however, be confused with the substantive statutory standard previously discussed at length. EPA's permissible interpretation of "may present an unreasonable risk" works in tandem with the "substantial evidence" standard of record review to effectuate a statutory scheme that empowers the Agency to require testing where the existence of an "unreasonable risk of injury to health" is not yet more-probable-than-not, but at the same time the Agency is required to identify the facts that underlie its determination that there is a more-than-theoretical basis to suspect the presence of such a risk. * * *

[The court concluded that EPA had presented "substantial evidence"—both affirmative evidence and rebuttal of CMA's evidence and arguments—to support its conclusions on exposure and toxicity.]

NOTES

1. *Unreasonable risk.* What evidence did EPA offer to support its conclusion that EHA "may present an unreasonable risk"? How did CMA choose to oppose it? Notice that the parties and the court steered clear of the problem of defining what *level* of risk is unreasonable. Given the preliminary nature of the testing decision, this may well be justified. What, then, does the court say about the components of "unreasonable risk"? EPA announced in its

first test rule that it would approach the unreasonable risk analysis by first examining hazard (toxicity), then risk (toxicity × exposure), then unreasonableness (nonzero risk and cost). Chloromethane Test Rule, 45 Fed. Reg. 48524, 48528-29 (1980). Is this policy required by TSCA? Does it commit the Agency to a virtual quantitative risk assessment before issuing a test rule? Are the feasibility and cost issues appropriate for this stage of the regulatory process?

What litigation opportunities does the unreasonable risk standard present to industry? In *CMA I* and in the two other section 4 cases it cites (*Ausimont U.S.A. Inc. v. EPA*, 838 F.2d 93 (3d Cir. 1988), and *Shell Chemical Co. v. EPA*, 826 F.2d 295 (5th Cir. 1987)), industry vigorously challenged EPA's exposure findings. Industry argued that the limited human exposure to the chemicals proposed for testing meant that, no matter what their toxicity, an "unreasonable risk" would never exist. *Ausimont* rejected industry arguments. It accepted as sufficient EPA's assumption that "brief episodes of relatively high exposure followed by extended periods of little or no exposure" (which the industry's own study found), coupled with evidence that there was "no indication of diminished use or of a reduced number of persons potentially affected." *Shell*, however, remanded the matter to the agency on the basis of post-promulgation exposure data, noting that the original exposure case— very limited exposure of about 100 workers—was "a close one." Environmentalists have argued that the multifaceted unreasonable risk analysis is a major reason for the ineffectiveness of section 4.[28]

2. *May present*. The addition of the term "may present" to unreasonable risk was obviously designed to distinguish section 4 from the "presents or will present" standard for regulation in section 6, and hence to relieve the agency of the burden of proving the actual existence of an unreasonable risk at the testing stage. But what does it mean? The legislative history speaks of "basis for concern," but rejects "speculation," "hunches," a purely "theoretical basis," and "mere conjecture." The problem is to apply these verbal formulas to actual evidence in an actual proceeding.

> Much of the confusion results from the proliferation of probabilistic criteria under section 4. * * * EPA must promulgate a test rule when it finds a probability (substantial evidence) or a probability (may present) of a probability (risk). Moreover, each probability is a very different type of calculation: risk is a statement of frequency of effect; 'may present' is a statement of the confidence of the induction from known data to frequency; and substantial evidence is a statement of the overall certainty with which the foregoing statements are made.

---

[28] *See also* GAO, Toxic Substances: Effectiveness of Unreasonable Risk Standards Unclear 4-6 (1990) (criticizing TSCA § 6).

Applegate, *The Perils of Unreasonable Risk, supra,* at 322. Did the *CMA I* court recognize the differences between these types of uncertainty?

Are there good alternatives to the "may present an unreasonable risk standard"? Should TSCA adopt the unadorned "Administrator's judgment" standard from FIFRA data call-ins? If more guidance is desirable, should EPA be able to go forward on the basis of a finding of *any* level of risk? Should it be able to proceed on the basis of exposure or toxicity alone?

3. *Exposure-based testing and the "B-Policy."* TSCA does, in fact, allow testing on the alternative basis of exposure alone where the chemical will be "produced in substantial quantities" *and* will either enter the environment in "substantial quantities" or result in "significant or substantial human exposure." § 4(a)(1)(B). (The other prerequisites remain the same.) This prong of TSCA was considered in *Chemical Manufacturers Association v. EPA*, 899 F.2d 344 (5th Cir. 1990) (*CMA II*). EPA ordered testing of the chemical cumene on the basis of occupational exposure of 700-800 workers and environmental exposure of 3 million pounds per year of air emissions, concentrated in a few major metropolitan areas. Despite a challenge from CMA, the court found that EPA's findings were supported by substantial evidence, noting that the statutory term "substantial" "suggests that rough approximation suffices." The court rejected a series of elaborate textual challenges to EPA's interpretation of the statute, all of which would have required the agency to come forward with very specific evidence of risk (not just exposure) posed by the chemical. Nevertheless, the judges remanded the cumene test rule because "EPA has not articulated any understandable basis—either in the form of a general definition of or a set of criteria respecting the statutory term 'substantial' or in its analysis of the specific evidence respecting cumene—for its ultimate determinations" that the exposure was substantial. EPA was directed to develop such explanation or criteria.[29] In response, EPA developed a formal B-Policy which sets numerical thresholds for "substantial" production, environmental release, and human exposure. TSCA § 4(a)(1)(b) Final Statement of Policy, 58 Fed. Reg. 28736, 28746 (1993). EPA declined to consider toxicity in this analysis. It has relied on the new B-Policy in a number of subsequent test rules.[30]

4. *Substantial evidence.* The *CMA I* court clearly recognized that the substantial evidence standard of judicial review is intended to be a searching one.[31] But what does it mean to produce "substantial evidence to demonstrate not fact, but doubt and uncertainty"? *Ausimont*, 838 F.2d at 96. If a manufacturer opposes a test rule on the ground that the evidence is clear that

---

[29] EPA's announced approach to exposure-only cases did not meet the court's requirements. *See* Dichloromethane Test Rule, 46 Fed. Reg. 30300, 30302 (1981).

[30] *E.g.,* EPA Endocrine Disrupter Screening Program; Proposed Statement of Policy, 63 Fed. Reg. 71542 (1998); EPA, Proposed Test Rules for Hazardous Air Pollutants, 61 Fed. Reg. 33178 (1996).

[31] The differences between arbitrary, capricious and substantial evidence review were discussed in Chapter 4 (Judicial Role), *supra.*

an unreasonable risk does not exist—that EPA will never be able ultimately to impose restrictions—is EPA forced to litigate the merits of actual regulation to counter the manufacturer?

The substantial evidence standard has invited aggressive challenges to test rules. Each of the test rule cases required a large investment of agency time to produce a record to support its action and then to defend its actions. Moreover, EPA's record on appeal is at best mixed. As a result, today EPA's information-gathering activities are limited by the threat of litigation. Is this the proper stage for judicial involvement?

Professor Flournoy traces the problem to the "binary" nature of the administrative and judicial process in protective regulation, in which the only proper reaction to uncertainty is inaction. This is, she argues, wholly inappropriate to the complex and highly uncertain science of toxic substances.

> [In section 4 cases, t]he very fact that these challenges were pursued illustrates the importance attached to the adequacy of the evidence. Even in what would seem to be straightforward cases for agency action—those under section 4, with its obviously reduced threshold of proof, and those in which the Agency has significant documentation (albeit not conclusive proof) of health effects—the question of whether the proof suffices is contentious.

Alyson C. Flournoy, *Legislating Inaction: Asking the Wrong Questions in Protective Environmental Decisionmaking*, 15 HARV. ENVTL. L. REV. 327, 372 (1991).

5. *The interaction of substance and procedure.* The oddity of using substantial evidence here—as well as for the rest of the statute—can be explained as a political compromise. Congress was willing to cede broad substantive powers to control industrial chemicals to EPA, but it wished to constrain EPA's actions within strict procedural limits.

> [TSCA] was a statute that had been debated for five years before passage, as the opposing forces around the bill had produced a legislative stalemate. The bill contains potentially powerful regulatory tools, but they have never been vigorously employed by the EPA, in large part because the statute is so procedurally complex. These procedural sections were drafted strategically, so that once the substantive and procedural provisions are read together, the net result is a bill that does not tilt strongly either in the direction of environmental protection or in the direction of permissively sanctioning industrial manufacture of toxic substances. Instead, it mirrors the closely divided political environment present when the statute was enacted, in which environmental sentiment was substantially offset by the opposition to new regulations on business of President Ford and his supporters in Congress.

James T. Hamilton & Christopher H. Schroeder, *Strategic Regulators and the Choice of Rulemaking Procedures: The Selection of Formal vs. Informal Rules in Regulating Hazardous Waste,* 57(2) L. & CONTEMP. PROBS. 111, 122 n. 33 (1994). The result is that EPA is given considerable authority but industry is given strong grounds for opposing or delaying its exercise. Is this a principled compromise or pusillanimous lawmaking?

6. *Reform.* Since TSCA was passed, the ITC has issued many reports of testing priorities. EPA, however, has been considerably less prolific:

Type of Requirement	Number	Most Recent
Chemical-specific rules in effect	12	1989
Multi-chemical rules in effect	2*	1993
Testing consent agreements in effect		1996**
Expired rules and agreements	18	1989

* EPA proposed a third multi-chemical rule, for 21 hazardous air pollutants, in 1996.
** These are ongoing, and more have been reached since 1996.
SOURCE: 40 C.F.R. part 799 (1998)

EPA has issued only one contested test rule since 1989. GAO has repeatedly expressed dissatisfaction with the productivity of the TSCA testing program.[32] Looking at TSCA's information-generation programs as a whole, the picture is the same, or worse:

> "Unlike pesticides and drugs," explains Donald J. Lisk of Cornell University, "industrial chemicals were not intended to be ingested." Thus studying them is not a priority. Adequate toxicology exists for only 2 to 3 percent of the more than 70,000 substances used to create about five million products, observes Joseph LaDou of the University of California at San Francisco. For 75 percent, there is no toxicology at all.
>
> In the U.S. the Toxic Substances Control Act was designed to fill this gap, but the task proved too enormous. Consequently, more than 60,000 existing chemicals were "grandfathered in," with the Environmental Protection Agency requiring scattered tests on no more than about 100. Of the chemicals introduced since 1979, the EPA restricts the use of 7 percent. But older substances make up about 99.9 percent of the six-trillion-pound total.

Madhusree Mukerjee, *Toxins Abounding,* SCIENTIFIC AMERICAN, July 1995, p. 22. What improvements might be made? EPA plans to make chemical testing, especially screening tests and high production volume chemicals, the focus of its toxics program. The agency will have to continue to rely heavily on voluntary testing, however, as its resources for these activities are shrinking rather than expanding.[33]

---

[32] *See* GAO, Toxic Substances Control Act: Legislative Changes Could Make the Act More Effective 44-53 (1994); GAO, Toxic Substances: EPA's Chemical Testing Program Has Made Little Progress (1990).

[33] 29 ENVT. REP. (BNA) S-21 (1999).

Some legislative changes to the test rule process have been suggested, for example, replacing "unreasonable risk" and "substantial evidence." Others are possible. Bills were introduced in the 98th Congress to shift the burden of demonstrating the absence of a need to test to the manufacturer once a chemical is listed by the ITC. Another possibility would be to use "surrogate" legislative standards to trigger testing: production over a stated amount (as opposed to release or exposure, which are much harder to measure), a positive result on simple toxicity tests, or structural similarity to chemicals already known to be toxic. Congress apparently thought that the "selective" approach in section 4 would be feasible because it expected EPA to be able to use quick and inexpensive tests, such as the Ames salmonella mutagenicity test,[34] to make initial decisions for both PMN purposes and test rules. Certainly, one interpretation of "may present" is that mutagenicity would trigger the need to test further.[35] Would an Ames test result be sufficient under *CMA I*? Under *Shell* and *CMA II*? Should the Ames test or structural similarities be sufficient to justify further testing under section 5(e)?[36]

C. The "Unreasonable Risk" and "Least Burdensome" Standards

Section 6 of TSCA authorizes EPA to prohibit the manufacture, processing, or distribution of a chemical; to limit production to certain amounts, uses, or concentrations; or to require warnings or directions, record retention, tests, or quality control procedures. § 6(a),(b). The exercise of this power must be predicated on:

- a "reasonable basis" for concluding that the chemical presents or will present "an unreasonable risk of injury to health or the environment";
- any regulation must "protect adequately against such risk using the least burdensome requirements"; and
- consideration of not only the health and environmental effects of the substance, but also the benefits associated with it, the availability of substitutes for it, the alternatives to a ban, the costs of any proposal action, and "the reasonably ascertainable economic consequences" of regulation.

---

[34] The Ames test (*see* Chapter 2 Toxicology) is based on the observation that human carcinogenesis is often preceded by mutation of certain genetic material in cells. The Ames test measures the potential for causing such mutations by observing its effect on genetic material in the cells of *salmonella* bacteria.

[35] *See* Comment, *From Microbes to Men: The New Toxic Substances Control Act and Bacterial Mutagenicity/ Carcinogenicity Test*, 6 ELR 10248 (1976).

[36] These and other suggestions for improvement are considered in Applegate, *The Perils of Unreasonable Risk, supra,* at 318-30; GAO, Legislative Changes, *supra*, at 18-21 (emphasizing the substantial evidence hurdle).

TSCA § 6(a), (c)(1). TSCA, in other words, does not mandate regulation without "comparing risks, costs, and benefits." S. REP. NO. 698, 94TH CONG., 2D SESS. 13 (1976). Congress sought to reflect scientific understandings of risk; therefore, EPA must thoroughly study the risks posed by a chemical before it may act. The information-gathering techniques above were intended to make that possible. In addition, the Conference Report described as "key considerations which must be addressed" the following:

> the effects of the substance or mixture on health and the magnitude of human exposure to such substance or mixture; the effects of the substance or mixture on the environment and the magnitude of environmental exposure to such substance or mixture; the benefits of such substance or mixture for various uses and the availability of substitutes for such uses; and the reasonably ascertainable economic consequences of the rule, after consideration of the effects on the national economy, small business, innovation, the environment, and the public health.

H.R. REP. NO. 1679, *supra*, at 75-76. The House Report added: "The Committee has limited the Administrator to taking action only against unreasonable risks because to do otherwise assumes that a risk-free society is attainable, an assumption that the Committee does not make." H.R. REP. NO. 1341, *supra,* at 15.

As originally enacted, TSCA singled out polychlorinated biphenyls (PCBs) for special attention. PCBs had been manufactured and used commercially throughout the 20th century. Because of their stability and fire and electrical resistance, they were widely used in electrical transformers and capacitors. Epidemiological data and experiments on laboratory animals revealed that exposure to PCBs poses serious carcinogenic risks to humans. PCBs were also found to affect wildlife. Concentrations as low as one part per billion seemed to impair the reproductive capacity of aquatic invertebrates and fish. Since PCBs were often discharged to waterways where they bioaccumulate in fish, animals and humans who eat those fish run a risk of ingesting relatively high concentrations of PCBs. By the time TSCA was enacted in 1976, Congress had been made aware of the dangers associated with PCBs and of the large quantity of PCBs that had already entered the environment. Section 6(e) of TSCA specifically addresses the control of PCBs.

ENVIRONMENTAL DEFENSE FUND V. EPA

636 F.2d 1267 (D.C. Cir. 1980)

EDWARDS, Circuit Judge.

* * *

As enacted, section 6(e) of the Act sets forth a detailed scheme to dispose of PCBs, to phase out the manufacture, processing, and distribution of PCBs, and to limit the use of PCBs. Specifically, section 6(e) provides that, within six months of the effective date of the Act (January 1, 1977), EPA must prescribe methods to dispose of PCBs and to require that PCB containers be marked with appropriate warnings. One year later, all manufacture of PCBs is prohibited. Six months after that (*i.e.*, two and one-half years after the effective date of the Act), all processing and distribution of PCBs in commerce is prohibited. Thus, today, except for the specified authorizations and exemptions described below, the Act permits PCBs to be used only in a totally enclosed manner, and it completely prohibits the manufacture, processing, and distribution of PCBs.

The statute sets forth only limited exceptions to these broad prohibitions. * * *

* * *

Criteria for the "Unreasonable Risk" Determination

The Act permits the Administrator to authorize "by rule" non-totally enclosed uses of PCBs if he finds that such uses "will not present an unreasonable risk of injury to health or the environment." § 6(e)(2)(B). Using the criteria set forth in subsection 6(c)(1), the Administrator found that eleven non-totally enclosed uses did not present an unreasonable risk. On the basis of these findings, EPA authorized the continued use of the eleven non-totally enclosed uses here in dispute.

In attacking these use authorizations, EDF claims that the Administrator employed the wrong criteria in making his determinations concerning "unreasonable risk." In particular, EDF argues that Congress intended to preclude the Administrator from using the subsection 6(c)(1) criteria in promulgating the PCB use authorization rules.

* * *

[B]ecause the expression "unreasonable risk of injury to health or the environment" is left undefined in section 6(e), the Administrator was required to give some meaning to it. Since the 6(c)(1) criteria obviously pertain to factors of "unreasonable risk," it was entirely appropriate for EPA to consider such criteria in ascribing a meaning to the use authorization provision in 6(e)(2)(B). EDF has shown nothing to indicate otherwise. In fact, EDF does not really contest use of the first three criteria in 6(c)(1)—*i.e.*, the effects on health and on the environment, and the availability of substitutes. Rather, EDF's primary focus is on the fourth criterion in 6(c)(1), relating to the economic consequences of the authorization. Yet EDF's objections to the "economic consequences" criterion cannot stand in the face of section 2(c) of the Act, which expressly requires the Administrator to consider such factors.

Furthermore, the particular economic factors that EPA took into account were plainly reasonable. The Administrator did not simply propose to consider the effect of the ban on industry, but also the effects on "the national economy, small business, technological innovation, the environment, and public health." This formulation, which considers a broad range of benefits and costs of the ban and use authorization, is entirely consistent with the section 2(c) requirement that the Administrator consider the economic and social impact on his actions.

Because the 6(c)(1) criteria fulfill an express mandate of the statute and reflect a reasonable interpretation of an ambiguous phrase, we conclude that the Administrator did not err in choosing those criteria to make the unreasonable risk determinations under 6(e)(2)(B).

* * *

The Fifty PPM Regulatory Cutoff

As a part of the regulatory scheme for PCBs under section 6(e), EPA limited application of the Disposal and Ban Regulations to materials containing concentrations of at least fifty ppm of PCBs. With one exception, materials with lower concentrations remain unregulated under the TSCA regulations. EDF contends that this limitation contravenes the statutory command in subsections 6(e)(2)(A) and 6(e)(3)(A) to regulate "any polychlorinated biphenyl." While we do not adopt all of EDF's reasoning, we find that, under the application standard of judicial review, there is not substantial evidence in the record to support the Administrator's decision to establish a regulatory cutoff at fifty ppm.

* * *

In the Final Ban Regulations, EPA adopted the proposed fifty ppm regulation cutoff. Although industry favored a cutoff of 500 ppm in order to reduce the costs of complying with the regulations, EPA found that industry could comply with a more stringent standard. Furthermore, lowering the cutoff from 500 to fifty-ppm would "result in substantially increased health and environmental protection."

A cutoff below fifty ppm, on the other hand, would "provide an additional degree of environmental protection but would have a grossly disproportionate effect on the economic impact and would have a serious technological impact on the organic chemicals industry." While it did not have firm data, EPA believed that for some chemical processes, it was technically impossible to eliminate the inadvertent production of PCBs. EPA also feared that because of limited disposal facilities, a lower cutoff would increase disposal requirements and interfere with the disposal of high concentration wastes. In short, EPA believed that the fifty ppm cutoff "provides adequate protection for human health and the environment while defining a program that EPA can effectively implement."

Both EPA and EDF claim that the statutory language and legislative history support their positions on the regulatory cutoff. The statutory language is simple: "no person may * * * use any polychlorinated biphenyl in any manner other than in a totally enclosed manner." § 6(e)(2)(A). Similarly, the prohibitions on manufacture, processing, and distribution refer to "any polychlorinated biphenyl." Taken literally, this language might require EPA to regulate every molecule of PCB. We are reluctant, however to impose such an extreme interpretation absent support in the legislative history.

* * *

[T]he Administrator chose a regulatory cutoff at a level that he felt would exclude the ambient sources from regulation. We are troubled by this regulation, however, since the purpose of section 6(e) is to prevent the "introduction of additional PCBs into the environment." The selection of a cutoff undermines the congressional intent to regulate non-ambient sources of PCBs if non-ambient sources of contamination remain unregulated. It is equally troubling that the Administrator apparently is not aware of the amount of PCBs excluded from regulation by the fifty ppm or other possible cutoffs. Particularly because the Administrator's flat exclusion of some industrial sources of contamination must undergo careful scrutiny. While some cutoff may be appropriate, we note that the Administrator did not explain why the regulation could not be designed expressly to exclude ambient sources, thus directly fulfilling congressional intent, rather than achieve that goal indirectly with a cutoff, thereby partly contravening congressional intent. Thus, a desire to exclude ambient sources of contamination, without more, cannot support the regulatory cutoff.

EPA also seeks to justify the regulatory cutoff on the basis of the serious impact a lower cutoff would have on industries that inadvertently produce PCBs during the manufacturing process. As EPA readily concedes, however, the inadvertent commercial production of PCBs is to be regulated under the Act. By providing a blanket exemption for concentration below fifty ppm, the Administrator has circumvented the authorizations and exemptions requirements provided in the statute. EPA made no finding that the cutoff would involve no unreasonable risk to health or the environment. * * *

* * *

Considerations such as the availability of enforcement resources are relevant to the administrative necessity exemption. It appears, however, that EPA is not even aware of the amount of PCBs left unregulated by the cutoff. Having made no showing that it cannot carry out the statutory commands for concentrations of PCBs below fifty ppm. EPA fails to meet its heavy burden. Thus, administrative need, on this record, provides no basis for the fifty ppm cutoff.

* * *

* * * EPA's *ad hoc* consideration of economic impact and disposal requirements, leading to a conclusion that the fifty ppm cutoff "provides adequate protection for human health and the environment," is neither as rigorous nor as strict as the statutorily required unreasonable risk determination based on subsection 6(c)(1) criteria. Thus, we remand this part of the record to EPA for further proceedings.

NOTES

1. *Burden of proof.* Section 6(e) omits a definition of PCBs. EPA's final regulation under section 6(e) included the following definition: "any chemical substance that is limited to the biphenyl molecule that has been chlorinated to

varying degrees . * * *" In 1991, an entrepreneur petitioned EPA under section 21 of TSCA seeking a rule change that would amend this regulatory definition to exclude from it "less chlorinated biphenyls" (LCBs). The amended definition would have permitted the petitioner to market a solvent using LCBs that would enable high-sulfur coal to be used in power plants without creating high-sulfur pollution. The EPA denied the petition, in part because the entrepreneur had failed to establish that the amended definition would not create an unreasonable risk of injury. The EPA denial was upheld in *Walker v. EPA*, 802 F. Supp. 1568, 1580 (S.D. Tex. 1992). Is it consistent with the overall burden of proof in TSCA to place this burden on private parties seeking a rule change? The petitioner had to prove the negative, that is, he had to show that the requested new definition would *not* create unreasonable risk. How can one ever prove that a proposed rule change does not produce unreasonable risks?

2. *Ambiguous statutory language.* Many cases involving challenges to EPA decisions require statutory interpretation. The question is usually whether EPA has correctly construed an ambiguous provision of a statute. In *EDF v. EPA*, the court had to interpret the phrase "unreasonable risk" found in section 6(e). Since TSCA did not define the phrase in section 6(e), EPA turned to section 6(c) for guidance. Section 6(c) criteria involve a series of cost-benefit balancing exercises. EDF argued in part that the omission of a reference to section 6(c) criteria in section 6(e) evidences a Congressional intent to prevent EPA from considering section 6(c) when defining "unreasonable risk" for rules under section 6(e). Is the absence of affirmative statutory language permitting use of a definition in a parallel statutory provision evidence of intent to preclude the use of the definition in the parallel provision? Conversely, is such an omission evidence of an intent to permit its use?

3. *Implementing zero risk.* Another issue of statutory interpretation in TSCA involves the word "any" in the phrase "no person may * * * use any polychlorinated biphenyl . * * *" The *EDF v. EPA* court rejected the argument that this phrase should be taken literally, which "might require EPA to regulate every molecule of PCB." What is wrong with such a literal construction of the word "any"? Would not a flat prohibition of "every molecule of PCB" produce the result sought by the court (*i.e.*, to exclude ambient sources of PCB), even if, in fact, not every PCB molecule was prevented from invading the ambient environment?

4. *The PCB ban.* After the *EDF* case, EPA set specific cutoff points (in parts per million) below which enclosed and controlled PCBs would be exempt from regulation, and required the phasing out of electrical equipment containing PCBs in food and feed manufacturing facilities. The EPA also issued a rule that set up an inspection and restricted-access program for most electrical equipment containing PCBs, and it banned new installations of transformers containing PCBs after October 1, 1985. EPA in 1988 instituted a

tracking and manifesting system for transformers containing PCBs, similar to that set up under RCRA.[37]

—

TSCA in fact calls for two related kinds of balancing—risk-benefit and cost-benefit—which are intended to reveal the situations in which regulation is "worth it." Both involve a more fine-tuned balancing than feasibility analysis or purely health-based standards. Risk-benefit balancing asks EPA to compare the harms to society that are likely to result from *not* regulating the substance, against the benefits that society receives from the substance producing the risk and that will be foregone or diminished if the substance is regulated. A cost-benefit analysis asks the regulator to compare the costs associated with regulation—usually the economic costs of compliance by regulated firms and the social costs of doing without a banned substance— against the benefits of the regulation—reduced risks to human health and the environment. Both the House and Senate reports emphasized, however, that the balancing should not necessarily entail a formal quantitative comparison of costs and benefits in which monetary values are assigned to risks, costs, and benefits. Such a mathematically precise balancing would be neither "useful" nor "feasible." H.R. REP. NO. 1341, *supra*, at 14.

The agency's decision in 1989 to ban all uses of asbestos provides an excellent example of cost-risk-benefit balancing under TSCA. The decision was preceded by a data collection rule promulgated under section 8(a), ten years of data analysis, 22 days of public hearings, 13,000 pages of comments from more than 250 parties, and a 45,000-page record. (And all of this for a known human carcinogen!) EPA summarized its justification for the ban in the following excerpt. It is followed by the industry challenge to EPA's rule.

ASBESTOS: MANUFACTURE, IMPORTATION, PROCESSING, AND DISTRIBUTION IN COMMERCE PROHIBITIONS

Environmental Protection Agency
54 Fed. Reg. 29460 (1989)

EPA is issuing this final rule under section 6 of the Toxic Substance Control Act (TSCA) to prohibit, at staged intervals, the future manufacture, importation, processing, and distribution in commerce of asbestos in almost all products, as identified in this rule. EPA is issuing this rule to reduce the unreasonable risks presented to human health by exposure to asbestos during activities involving these products. * * *

---

[37] A recent case set aside an EPA penalty under the PCB provisions of section 6 because the regulations were ambiguous and confusing. Rollins Environmental Services (NJ), Inc. v. EPA, 937 F.2d 649 (D.C. Cir. 1991), discussed in Strand, *The "Regulatory Confusion" Defense to Environmental Remedies: Can You Beat the Rap?*, 22 ENVTL. L. REP. (ENVTL. L. INST.) 10330 (1992).

Section 6 of TSCA authorizes EPA to promulgate a rule prohibiting or limiting the amount of a chemical substance that may be manufactured, processed, or distributed in commerce in the U.S. if EPA finds that there is a reasonable basis to conclude that the manufacture, processing, distribution in commerce, use, or disposal of the chemical substance, or any combination of these activities, presents or will present an unreasonable risk of injury to human health or the environment. * * *

To determine whether a risk from activities involving asbestos-containing products presents an unreasonable risk, EPA must balance the probability that harm will occur from the activities against the effects of the proposed regulatory action on the availability to society of the benefits of asbestos. EPA has considered these factors in conjunction with the extensive record gathered in the development of this rule. EPA has concluded that the continued manufacture, importation, processing, and distribution in commerce of most asbestos-containing products poses an unreasonable risk to human health. This conclusion is based on information summarized [below].

EPA has concluded that exposure to asbestos during the life cycles of many asbestos-containing products poses an unreasonable risk of injury to human health. EPA has also concluded that section 6 of TSCA is the ideal statutory authority to regulate the risks posed by asbestos exposure. This rule's pollution prevention actions under TSCA are both the preferable and the least burdensome means of controlling the exposure risks posed throughout the life cycle of asbestos-containing products.

* * *

Evidence supports the conclusion that substitutes already exist or will soon exist for each of the products that are subject to the rule's bans. In scheduling products for the different stages of the bans, EPA has analyzed the probable availability of non-asbestos substitutes. In the rule, it is likely that suitable non-asbestos substitutes will be available. However, the rule also includes an exemption provision to account for instances in which technology might not have advanced sufficiently by the time of a ban to produce substitutes for certain specialized or limited uses of asbestos.

EPA has calculated that the product bans in this rule will result in the avoidance of 202 quantifiable cancer cases, if benefits are not discounted, and 148 cases, if benefits are discounted at 3 percent. The figures decrease to 164 cases, if benefits are not discounted, and 120 cases, if benefits are discounted at 3 percent, if analogous exposures are not included in the analysis. In all likelihood, the rule will result in the avoidance of a large number of other cancer cases that cannot be quantified, as well as many cases of asbestos-related diseases. Estimates of benefits resulting from the action taken in this rule are limited to mesothelioma and lung and gastrointestinal cancer cases avoided, and do not include cases of asbestosis and other diseases avoided and avoided costs from treating asbestos diseases, lost productivity, or other factors.

EPA has estimated that the cost of this rule, for the 13-year period of the analyses performed, will be approximately $456.89 million, or $806.51 million if a 1 percent annual decline in the price of substitutes is not assumed. This cost will be spread over time and a large population so that the cost to any person is likely to be negligible. In addition, the rule's exemption provision is a qualitative factor that supports the actions taken in this rule. EPA has concluded that the quantifiable and unquantifiable benefits of the rule's staged-ban of the identified asbestos-containing products will outweigh the resultant economic consequences to consumers, producers, and users of the products.

EPA has determined that, within the findings required by section 6 of TSCA, only the staged-ban approach employed in this final rule will adequately control the asbestos exposure risk posed by the product categories affected by this rule. Other options either fail to address significant portions of the life cycle risk posed by products subject to the rule or are unreasonably burdensome. EPA has, therefore, concluded that the actions taken in this rule represent the least burdensome means of reducing the risks posed by exposure to asbestos during the life cycles of the products that are subject to the bans.

Based on the reasons summarized in this preamble, this rule bans most asbestos-containing products in the U.S. because they pose an unreasonable risk to human health. These banned products account for approximately 94 percent of U.S. asbestos consumption, based on 1985 consumption figures. The actions taken will result in a substantial reduction in the unreasonable risk caused by asbestos exposure in the U.S.

CORROSION PROOF FITTINGS V. EPA

947 F.2d 1201 (5th Cir. 1991)

SMITH, Circuit Judge.

* * *

Asbestos is a naturally occurring fibrous material that resists fire and most solvents. Its major uses include heat-resistant insulators, cements, building materials, fireproof gloves and clothing, and motor vehicle brake linings. Asbestos is a toxic material, and occupational exposure to asbestos dust can result in mesothelioma, asbestosis, and lung cancer.

* * *

An EPA-appointed panel reviewed over one hundred studies of asbestos and conducted several public meetings. Based upon its studies and the public comments, the EPA concluded that asbestos is a potential carcinogen at all levels of exposure, regardless of the type of asbestos or the size of the fiber.

* * *

* * * In 1989, the EPA issued a final rule prohibiting the manufacture, importation, processing, and distribution in commerce of most asbestos-containing products. Finding that asbestos constituted an unreasonable risk to health and the environment, the EPA promulgated a staged ban of most commercial uses of asbestos. The EPA estimates that this rule will save either 202 or 148 lives, depending upon whether the benefits are discounted, at a cost of approximately $450-800 million, depending upon the price of substitutes.

* * *

The EPA's Burden Under TSCA

TSCA provides, in pertinent part, as follows:

> (a) Scope of regulation.—If the Administrator finds that there is a *reasonable basis* to conclude that the manufacture, processing, distribution in commerce, use, or disposal of a chemical substance or mixture, or that any combination of such activities, presents or will present *an unreasonable risk of injury* to health or the environment, the Administrator shall by rule apply one or more of the following requirements to such substance or mixture to the extent necessary to *protect adequately* against such risk using the *least burdensome* requirements. 15 U.S.C. § 2605(c). [Emphasis added.]

As the highlighted language shows, Congress did not enact TSCA as a zero-risk statute. The EPA, rather, was required to consider both alternatives to a ban and the costs of any proposed actions and to "carry out this chapter in a reasonable and prudent manner [after considering] the environmental, economic, and social impact of any action." 15 U.S.C. § 2601(c).

We conclude that the EPA has presented insufficient evidence to justify its asbestos ban. We base this conclusion upon two grounds: the failure of the EPA to consider all necessary evidence and its failure to give adequate weight to statutory language requiring it to promulgate the least burdensome, reasonable regulation required to protect the environment adequately. Because the EPA failed to address these concerns, and because the EPA is required to articulate a "reasoned basis" for its rules, we are compelled to return the regulation to the agency for reconsideration.

1. Least Burdensome and Reasonable

TSCA requires that the EPA use the least burdensome regulation to achieve its goals of minimum reasonable risk. This statutory requirement can create problems in evaluating just what is a "reasonable risk." Congress's rejection of a no-risk policy, however, also means that in certain cases, the least burdensome yet still adequate solution may entail somewhat more risk than other, known regulations that are far more burdensome on the industry and the economy. The very language of TSCA requires that the EPA, once it has determined what an acceptable level of non-zero risk is, choose the least burdensome method of reaching that level.

In this case, the EPA banned, for all practical purposes, all present and future uses of asbestos—a position the petitioners characterize as the "death penalty alternative," as this is the *most* burdensome of all possible alternatives listed as open to the EPA under TSCA. TSCA not only provides the EPA with a list of alternative actions, but also provides those alternatives in order of how burdensome they are. The regulations thus provide for EPA regulation ranging from labeling the least toxic chemicals to limiting the total amount of chemicals an industry may use. Total bans head the list as the most burdensome regulatory option.

By choosing the *harshest remedy* given to it under TSCA, the EPA assigned to itself the toughest burden in satisfying TSCA's requirement that its alternative be the least burdensome of all those offered to it. Since both by definition and by the terms of TSCA the complete ban of manufacturing is the most burdensome alternative—for even stringent regulation at least allows a manufacturer the chance to invest and meet the new, higher standard—the EPA's regulation cannot stand if there is any other regulation that would achieve an acceptable level of risk as mandated by TSCA.

* * *

* * * What concerns us, however, is the manner in which the EPA conducted some of its analysis. TSCA requires the EPA to consider, along with the effects of toxic substances on human health and the environment, "the benefits of such substances or mixtures for various uses and the availability of substitutes for such uses," as well as "the reasonably ascertainable economic consequences of the rule, after consideration for the effect on the national economy, small business, technological innovation, the environment, and public health." § 2605(c)(1)(C-D).

The EPA presented two comparisons in the record: a world with no further regulation under TSCA, and a world in which no manufacture of asbestos takes place. The EPA rejected calculating how many lives a less burdensome regulation would save, and at what cost. Furthermore the EPA, when calculating the benefits of its ban, explicitly refused to compare it to an improved workplace in which currently available control technology is utilized. This decision artificially inflated the purported benefits of the rule by using a baseline comparison substantially lower than what currently available technology could yield.

Under TSCA, the EPA was required to evaluate, rather than ignore, less burdensome regulatory alternatives. TSCA imposes a least-to-most-burdensome hierarchy. In order to impose a regulation at the top of the hierarchy—a total ban of asbestos—the EPA must show not only that its proposed action reduces the risk of the product to an adequate level, but also that the actions Congress identified as less burdensome would not do the job. The failure of the EPA to do this constitutes a failure to meet its burden of showing that it sections not only reduce the risk but do so in the Congressionally-mandated *least burdensome* fashion.

Thus, it was not enough for the EPA to show, as it did in this case, that banning some asbestos products might reduce the harm that could occur from the use of these products. If that were the standard, it would be no standard at all, for few indeed are the products that are so safe that a complete ban of them would not make the world still safer.

This comparison of two static worlds is insufficient to satisfy the dictates of TSCA. While the EPA may have shown that a world with a complete ban of asbestos might be preferable to one in which there is only the current amount of regulation, the EPA has failed to show that there is not some intermediate state of regulation that would be superior to both the currently-regulated and the completely-banned world. Without showing that asbestos regulation would be ineffective, the EPA cannot discharge its TSCA burden of showing that its regulation is the least burdensome available to it.

Upon an initial showing of product danger, the proper course for the EPA to follow is to consider each regulatory option, in the order mandated by Congress, and the costs and benefits of regulation under each option. The EPA cannot simply skip several rungs, as it did in this case, for in doing so, it may skip a less burdensome alternative mandated by TSCA. Here, although the EPA mentions the problems posed by intermediate levels of regulation, it takes no steps to calculate the costs and benefits of these intermediate levels. Without doing this it is impossible, both for the EPA and for this court on review, to know that none of these alternatives was less burdensome than the ban in fact chosen by the agency.

* * *

Furthermore, we are concerned about some of the methodology employed by the EPA in making various of the calculations that it did perform. * * *

* * *

Of * * * concern to us is the failure of the EPA to compute the costs and benefits of its proposed rule past the year 2000, and its double-counting of the costs of asbestos use. In performing its calculus, the EPA only included the number of lives saved over the next thirteen years, and counted any additional lives saved as simply "unquantified benefits." The EPA and intervenors now seek to use these unquantified lives saved to justify calculations as to which benefits seem far outweighed by the astronomical costs. For example, the EPA plans to save about three lives with its ban of asbestos pipe, at a cost of $128-227 million (*i.e.*, approximately $43-76 million per life saved). Although the EPA admits that the price tag is high, it claims that the lives saved past the year 2000 justify the price.

Such calculations not only lessen the value of the EPA's cost analysis, but also make any meaningful judicial review impossible. While TSCA contemplates a useful place for unquantified benefits beyond the EPA's calculation, unquantified benefits never were intended as a trump card allowing the EPA to justify any cost calculus, no matter how high.

The concept of unquantified benefits, rather, is intended to allow the EPA to provide a rightful place for any remaining benefits that are impossible to quantify after the EPA's best attempt, but which still are of some concern. But the allowance for unquantified costs is not intended to allow the EPA to perform its calculations over an arbitrarily short period so as to preserve a large unquantified portion.

Unquantified benefits can, at times, permissibly tip the balance in close cases. They cannot, however, be used to effect a wholesale shift on the balance beam. Such a use makes mockery of the requirements of TSCA that the EPA weigh the costs of its actions before it chooses the least burdensome alternative.

We do not today determine what an appropriate period for the EPA's calculations would be, as this is a matter better left for agency discretion. We do note, however, that the choice of a thirteen-year period is so short as to make the unquantified period so unreasonably large that any EPA reliance upon it must be displaced.

Under the EPA's calculations, a twenty-year-old worker entering employment today still would be at a risk from workplace dangers for more than thirty years after the EPA's analysis period has ended. The true benefits of regulating asbestos under such calculations remain unknown. The EPA cannot choose to leave these benefits high and then use the high unknown benefits as a major factor justifying the EPA action.

We also note that the EPA appears to place too great a reliance upon the concept of population exposure. While a high population exposure certainly is a factor that the EPA must consider in making its calculations, the agency cannot count such problems more than once. For example, in the case of asbestos brake products, the EPA used factors such as risk and exposure to calculate the probable harm of the brakes, and then used, as an *additional* reason to ban the products, the fact that the exposure levels were high. Considering that calculations of the probable harm level, when reduced to basics, simply are a calculation of population risk multiplied by population exposure, the EPA's redundant use of population exposure to justify its actions cannot stand.

Reasonable Basis

In addition to showing that its regulation is the least burdensome one necessary to protect the environment adequately, the EPA also must show that it has a reasonable basis for the regulation. 15 U.S.C. § 2605(a). To some extent, our inquiry in this area mirrors that used above, for many of the methodological problems we have noted also indicate that the EPA did not have a reasonable basis. * * *

Most problematical to us is the EPA's ban of products for which no substitutes presently are available. In these cases, the EPA bears a tough burden indeed to show that under TSCA a ban is the least burdensome alternative, as TSCA explicitly instructs the EPA to consider "the benefits of such substance or mixture for various uses and the availability of substitutes for such uses." § 2605(c)(1)(c). These words are particularly appropriate where the EPA actually has decided to ban a product, rather than simply restrict its use, for it is in these cases that the lack of an adequate substitute is most troubling under TSCA.

As the EPA itself states, "when no information is available for a product indicating that cost-effective substitutes exist, the estimated cost of a product ban is very high." 54 Fed. Reg. at 29,468. Because of this, the EPA did not ban certain uses of asbestos, such as its use in rocket engines and battery separators. The EPA, however, in several other instances, ignores its own arguments and attempts to justify its ban by stating that the ban itself will cause the development of low-cost, adequate substitute products.

As a general matter, we agree with the EPA that a product ban can lead to great innovation, and it is true that an agency under TSCA, as under other regulatory statutes, "is empowered to issue safety standards which require improvements in existing technology or which require the development of new technology." As even the EPA acknowledges, however, when no adequate substitutes currently exist, the EPA cannot fail to consider this lack when formulating its own guidelines. Under TSCA, therefore, the EPA must present a stronger case to justify the ban, as opposed to regulation, of products with no substitutes.

We note that the EPA does provide a waiver provision for industries where the hoped-for substitutes fail to materialize in time. Under this provision, if no adequate substitutes develop, the EPA temporarily may extend the planned phase-out.

The EPA uses this provision to argue that it can ban any product, regardless of whether it has an adequate substitute, because inventive companies soon will develop good substitutes. The EPA contends that if they do not, the waiver provision will allow the continued use of asbestos in these areas, just as if the ban had not occurred at all.

The EPA errs, however, in asserting that the waiver provision will allow a continuation of the status quo in those cases in which no substitutes materialize. By its own terms, the exemption shifts the burden onto the waiver proponent to convince the EPA that the waiver is justified. As even the EPA acknowledges, the waiver only "may be granted by EPA in very limited circumstances."

The EPA thus cannot use the waiver provision to lessen its burden when justifying banning products without existing substitutes. While TSCA gives the EPA the power to ban such products, the EPA must bear its heavier burden of justifying its total ban in the face of inadequate substitutes. Thus, the agency cannot use its waiver provision to argue that the ban of products with no substitutes should be treated the same as the ban of those for which adequate substitutes are available now.

We also are concerned with the EPA's evaluation of substitutes even in those instances in which the record shows that they are available. The EPA explicitly rejects considering the harm that may flow from the increased use of products designed to substitute for asbestos, even where the probable substitutes themselves are known carcinogens. The EPA justifies this by stating that it has "more concern about the continued use and exposure to asbestos than it has for the future replacement of asbestos in the products subject to this rule with other fibrous substitutes." The agency thus concludes that any "regulatory decisions about asbestos which pose well-recognized, serious risks should not be delayed until the risk of all replacement materials are fully quantified."

This presents two problems. First, TSCA instructs the EPA to consider the relative merits of its ban, as compared to the economic effects of its actions. The EPA cannot make this calculation if it fails to consider the effects that alternate substitutes will pose after a ban.

Second, the EPA cannot say with any assurance that its regulation will increase workplace safety when it refuses to evaluate the harm that will result from the increased use of substitute products. While the EPA may be correct in its conclusion that the alternate materials pose less risk than asbestos, we cannot say with any more assurance than that flowing from an educated guess that this conclusion is true.

Considering that many of the substitutes that the EPA itself concedes will be used in the place of asbestos have known carcinogenic effects, the EPA not only cannot assure this court that it has taken the least burdensome alternative, but cannot even prove that its regulations will increase workplace safety. Eager to douse the dangers of asbestos, the agency inadvertently actually may increase the risk of injury Americans face. The EPA's explicit failure to consider the toxicity of likely substitutes thus deprives its order of a reasonable basis.

* * *

Unreasonable Risk of Injury

The final requirement the EPA must satisfy before engaging in any TSCA rulemaking is that it only take steps designed to prevent "unreasonable" risks. In evaluating what is "unreasonable," the EPA is required to consider the costs of any proposed actions and to "carry out this chapter in a reasonable and prudent manner [after considering] the environmental, economic, and social impact of any action." 15 U.S.C. § 2601(c).

* * *

That the EPA must balance the costs of its regulations against their benefits further is reinforced by the requirement that it seek the least burdensome regulation. While Congress did not dictate that the EPA engage in an exhaustive, full-scale cost-benefit analysis, it did require the EPA to consider both sides of the regulatory equation, and it rejected the notion that the EPA should pursue the reduction of workplace risk at any cost. * * *

Even taking all of the EPA's figures as true, and evaluating them in the light most favorable to the agency's decision (non-discounted benefits, discounted costs, analogous exposure estimated included), the agency's analysis results in figures as high as $74 million per life saved. For example, the EPA states that its ban of asbestos pipe will save three lives over the next thirteen years, at a cost of $128-227 million ($43-76 million per life saved), depending upon the price of substitutes; that its ban of asbestos shingles will cost $23-34 million to save 0.32 statistical lives ($72-106 million per life saved); that its ban of asbestos coatings will cost $46-181 million to save 3.33 lives ($14-54 million per life saved); and that its ban of asbestos paper products will save 0.60 lives at a cost of $4-5 million ($7-8 million per life saved). * * *

While we do not sit as a regulatory agency that must make the difficult decision as to what an appropriate expenditure is to prevent someone from incurring the risk of an asbestos-related death, we do note that the EPA, in its zeal to ban any and all asbestos products, basically ignored the cost side of the TSCA equation. The EPA would have this court believe that Congress, when it enacted its requirement that the EPA consider the economic impacts of its regulations, thought that spending $200-300 million to save approximately seven lives (approximately $30-40 million per life) over thirteen years is reasonable.

* * *

Conclusion

In summary, of most concern to us is that the EPA has failed to implement the dictates of TSCA and the prior decisions of this and other courts that, before it impose a ban on a product, it first evaluate and then reject the less burdensome alternatives laid out for it by Congress. While the EPA spent much time and care crafting its asbestos regulation, its explicit failure to consider the alternatives required of it by Congress deprived its final rule of the reasonable basis it needed to survive judicial scrutiny.

NOTES

1. *"Least burdensome" regulation.* There is little question that asbestos is a very serious health hazard. How would it fare under a health-only risk standard? A feasibility standard? Under TSCA, regulation of this concededly dangerous material came to grief. Why?

The court states that the principal reason was EPA's failure to make a convincing case that the manner of regulation chosen was the "least burdensome." TSCA § 6(a). This requires EPA to choose from an array of regulatory alternatives, ranging from a complete ban (most burdensome) to no regulation at all (no burden).[38] Did the court in the *Corrosion Proof Fittings* case decide that, in order to satisfy the "least burdensome" regulation requirement, EPA had to consider the entire range of regulatory options and to calculate the costs and benefits of regulation for each option? Is there a less burdensome way of interpreting "least burdensome"?

---

[38] A similar requirement is imposed on the Consumer Product Safety Commission, 15 U.S.C. § 2058(f)(3), and CPSC has similarly struggled with judicial review. *See, e.g.*, Gulf S. Insulation v. CPSC, 701 F.2d 1137 (5th Cir. 1983). *See generally* Richard A. Merrill, *CPSC Regulation of Cancer Risks in Consumer Products: 1972-1981*, 67 VA. L. REV. 1261 (1981).

2. *Unquantified benefits*. Clearly the main benefit of the asbestos ban is that it will save lives. In a quantitative cost-benefit analysis, this raises three problems. First, the analysis must attempt to place some value, usually economic, on a human life. Assessing the dollar value of a human life is exceedingly difficult, though the Fifth Circuit obviously had some views on the subject. Second, even if a value can be assigned to human life, that value will vary over the lifetime of any individual—the remaining life of an infant is presumably worth more than a centenarian. A cost-benefit analysis must determine at what age the value of a life is to be calculated. Third, the number of lives saved will increase the longer the regulation is in effect. If one is comparing costs to benefits, during what period of time are the benefits (in lives saved) to be counted? EPA included the number of lives saved over 13 years, and then counted all additional lives saved past the year 2000 as "unquantified benefits." The court thought that this was cheating, because it permitted the benefits side of the balance to weigh too heavily. In light of the many difficulties accompanying a measurement of benefits counted as human lives saved, was EPA justified in relying on the notion of unquantified benefits? Or is the court correct in its belief that such benefits should be used only "to tip the balance in close cases"?

3. *Substitutes*. TSCA also requires EPA to consider "the benefits of such substance or mixture for various uses and the availability of substitutes for such uses." TSCA § 6(c)(1)(c). Whenever EPA is contemplating a substance ban, the issue of substitutes demands that EPA determine whether a cost-effective substitute exists, and if it does, whether new risks may flow from the increased use of substitute products.[39] When substitutes are not readily available, EPA must present a stronger case to justify a ban, because the cost of such a ban is high. On the other hand, banning a substance without substitutes may act to force technological progress toward the development of a safer substitute.

When substitutes are available, *Corrosion Proof Fittings* requires EPA to consider the health effects that alternate substitutes will pose after a ban. Must EPA perform a cost-benefit analysis for substitutes that is as extensive as the cost-benefit analysis for the about-to-be-banned substance?

4. When the court discusses the meaning of TSCA's "unreasonable risk" requirement, does it use a risk-benefit or cost-benefit analysis? In EPA's justification for the asbestos ban, EPA calculated that the ban would result in the avoidance of 202 quantifiable cancer cases, and 148 cases if benefits are discounted at three percent (a discount rate is often used in cost-benefit analysis so that estimates of future costs and benefits are figured at their present value; the higher the discount rate, the smaller the significance of

---

[39] For example, to prevent burning deaths, children's sleepwear was treated with TRIS, a flame retardant. It was later discovered that TRIS is a potent carcinogen whose risks outweighed the fire risk. This misadventure in regulation is chronicled in Merrill, *supra*.

costs and benefits that accrue in the future).[40] Using EPA's numbers, the ban would cost between $2 and $3 million per death avoided. The court, on the other hand, assumes that EPA's figures would result in an expense as high as $74 million per death avoided. Why is there such a large difference in these two numbers?

5. *Hard look.* Why did EPA's PCB regulations receive a far more gentle treatment in *EDF v. EPA* than its asbestos regulations received in *Corrosion Proof Fittings*? Reasons might include the court—the Fifth Circuit has a history of rejecting environmental regulations—or the date—*all* courts have become more exacting in the last decade, as described in Chapter 4. Is it also because EDF wanted to make the regulations *more* stringent, the industry wanted them less stringent, and EPA's position looked like a compromise? Because PCBs are specifically identified by Congress? *See Dow Chemical v. Costle*, 484 F. Supp. 101, 102 n.1 (D. Del. 1980) (noting that in § 6(e) Congress made the statutory finding that under most circumstances PCBs pose an unreasonable risk of injury to health and the environment).

In any event, the court's handling of the agency's decision in *Corrosion Proof Fittings* has received mixed reviews, ranging from high praise to outrage. In the former category are the lawyers who represented industry in the litigation:

> Confronted with this record, the Fifth Circuit reversed EPA's asbestos product bans without the usual delving into technical and scientific issues that is common under hard look judicial review. Instead, the court primarily focused on whether "a reasonable mind" would accept EPA's result. While nominally anchored in TSCA's "substantial evidence" test, the Fifth Circuit's approach effectively turned on whether specific choices made by EPA would accomplish more good than harm.

* * *

> [The] shortcomings in EPA's decision were compounded by the Agency's failure to weigh the health and safety risks posed by substitute products. While acknowledging that EPA does not have "an affirmative duty to seek out and test every workplace substitute," the court nonetheless held that such a duty does arise "once interested parties introduce credible studies and evidence" of the risks from probable substitute products. The likelihood that EPA's regulation might do more harm than good was an important basis for overturning EPA's friction product and A/C pipe product bans. * * *

Just as important as what the court did do is what it did not do. The court overturned EPA's ban because many elements of the

---

[40] For detailed discussion of the propriety of using discounting and of appropriate rates, *see* PAUL R. PORTNEY & JOHN P. WEYANT, EDS., DISCOUNTING AND INTERGENERATIONAL EQUITY (1999); Lisa Heinzerling, *Discounting Life*, 108 YALE L.J. 1911 (1999); Richard L. Revesz, *Environmental Regulation, Cost-Benefit Analysis, and the Discounting of Human Lives*, 99 COLUM. L. REV. 941 (1999).

Agency's action might do more harm than good. In so doing, however, the court expressly eschewed the usual hard look review of the Agency's technical or scientific findings or of the Agency's reasoning process on these issues. For example, the court rejected technical challenges to EPA's cost and benefit calculations and to its decision to treat all types of asbestos the same, stating that "[d]ecisions such as these are better left to the agency's expertise." In declining to scrutinize EPA's reasoning on such technical issues, the court summarized its reviewing role as follows: "On these, and many similar points, the petitioners merely seek to have us reevaluate the EPA's initial evaluation of the evidence. * * * Decisions such as the EPA's decision to treat various types of asbestos as presenting similar health risks properly are better left for agency determination . * * * " In short, instead of focusing on the agency's decisionmaking process, the Fifth Circuit looked directly at the "Medusa" of EPA's decision, not its reflection, in order to determine whether the Agency had acted reasonably.

    * * * The court thus refused to accept lopsided relationships between costs and benefits that a "reasonable mind" would consider unacceptable. It would not sanction product bans when "less burdensome" alternatives appeared more cost-effective. The court also required EPA to target acceptable risk levels above zero and to confront the risk-risk tradeoffs of its actions. Each of these holdings suggests a rule that follows logically from the core principle that agencies act reasonably or rationally only if their actions overall, and at the margin, do more good than harm.

Edward W. Warren & Gary E. Marchant, *"More Good than Harm": A First Principle for Environmental Agencies and Reviewing Courts*, 20 ECOLOGY L.Q. 379, 415-18 (1993). Professor McGarity, in contrast, has argued that the Fifth Circuit overstepped the proper bounds of the judicial role:

> Just as the courts do not explore in detail the ins and outs of every alternative theory when they resolve a question of law, EPA did not feel that it had to go to such extraordinary analytical lengths to justify banning a substance for which human health risks were extremely well-documented. The court, however, set aside the rule because of the agency's failure to "calculate the costs and benefits" of each of the possible intermediate levels of regulation. Otherwise, the court feared that it could not "know that none of these alternatives was less burdensome than the ban in fact chosen by the agency."

>   The *Corrosion Proof Fittings* opinion lays out the conclusions of three intelligent lawyers who had been exposed to a complex statute in a complicated rulemaking context for a very limited period of time. The three judges on the panel had no experience with the difficulties encountered in administering a technically complex

regulatory program, and they lacked any expertise in the scientific and other analytical methodologies necessary to perform the function that Congress had delegated to EPA. The judges, in short, lacked the breadth and depth of experience and expertise necessary to support such confident assertions about how the agency should go about its assigned business. And they almost certainly got it wrong.

The opinion writer, however, did not stop with his highly questionable analysis of the agency's statute. Noting a dispute over how EPA had compared future costs with future benefits, the court gratuitously offered its wisdom on how the job should be done. Despite very substantial arguments in the relevant economic, legal, and ethical literature that future health benefits should not be discounted to present value, the court made short work of the issue with the extraordinarily simplistic observation that failing to discount benefits would make comparisons difficult. To ease the misguided agency's misgivings, the court offered a single article from *The Economist* "explaining [the] use of discount rates for non-monetary goods." The court followed this arrogant bolt-from-the-blue with an embarrassingly ill-informed critique of EPA's reliance upon the onset of exposure as the time to begin discounting, rather than the time of injury. The court was either unaware of or simply ignored the fact that the time of exposure might be estimated with some degree of accuracy with the aid of employment records and such, whereas the time of injury would have been impossible to predict, given the uncertainties in assessing carcinogenic risks and the long latency period of some carcinogens.

Without any apparent awareness of (or serious interest in) the enormous uncertainties encountered in assessing the risks posed by the agency's adoption of one or more of seven alternative approaches to regulating asbestos, the court sent EPA on a potentially endless analytical crusade in search of the holy grail of the least burdensome alternative that still protected adequately against unreasonable risk. Deferring not one whit to EPA's interpretation of its statute or to its exercise of rulemaking expertise, the court wrote its view of the "proper course for the EPA to follow" into the law governing standard setting under section 6 of TSCA. The agency could, of course, avoid the analytical nightmare either by adopting options that were sufficiently inoffensive to the regulated industry to avoid legal challenge or by giving up the quest altogether. The agency has apparently adopted the latter option. In the six years that have passed since the *Corrosion Proof Fittings* opinion, EPA has not initiated a single action under section 6 of TSCA, and it is not likely to use section 6 to impose requirements that regulatees oppose until it is amended to overrule the court's opinion.

In the broader scheme of things, the problem illustrated by the *Corrosion Proof Fittings* opinion is not so much one of judicial incompetence as it is one of judicial overreaching. Many judges would like to see the government play a less intrusive role in private markets, and they have the flexibility under the hard look doctrine to affect regulatory programs radically without being held accountable for the consequences of their actions. Congress can always change the statute to overturn the court, but * * *it is very difficult to get protective legislation enacted. To advocate hard look review in the context of the courts' prescriptive substantive review function is really to advocate greater discretion on the part of judges to substitute their views of appropriate statutory policies and analytical methodologies for those of the agency. In the hands of unsympathetic judges like the author of the *Corrosion Proof Fittings* opinion, this is a license to destroy regulatory programs. Even in the hands of neutral judges, it is an invitation to ossification, because the synoptic paradigm is nearly always more attractive from the perspective of the disinterested outsider than techno-bureaucratic rationality.

Thomas O. McGarity, The Courts and the Ossification of Rulemaking: A Response to Professor Seidenfeld, 75 Tex. L. Rev. 525, 547-49 (1997).

Whose characterization of the case do you find most persuasive? EPA action under TSCA received similarly rough handling in *Flue-Cured Tobacco Cooperative Stabilization Corp. v. EPA*, 4 F. Supp. 2d 435 (M.D.N.C. 1998), in which its risk assessment for second-hand tobacco smoke was remanded for substantive and procedural deficiencies.

PROBLEM
ASBESTOS IN SCHOOLS

An irony of the result in *Corrosion Proof Fittings* is that Congress had previously singled out asbestos for special treatment under TSCA, as it had with PCBs. In the early 1980s, EPA issued a rule requiring the inspection of public and private school buildings as a way to determine whether students were being exposed to airborne asbestos fibers. When this rule proved to be only partly successful, EPA in 1984 began fining school districts for non-compliance. Congress then stepped in to address the asbestos problem in schools by passing the Asbestos School Hazard Abatement Act of 1984, 20 U.S.C. § 4011, followed by title II of TSCA in 1986. TSCA §§ 201-215. Title II envisions regulating asbestos through building inspections, asbestos management plans, emergency response actions when asbestos in a school building presents an "imminent and substantial endangerment," warning labels, and a training-accreditation program for asbestos contractors. EPA must adopt "the least burdensome methods which protect human health and the environment," taking into account "local circumstances, including occupancy and use patterns * * * and short-and long-term costs." § 203(d)(1). EPA's guidelines for minimum standards of allowable asbestos were upheld in *Safe Buildings Alliance v. EPA*, 846 F. 2d 79 (D.C. Cir. 1988). The court gave EPA much deference in light of scientific uncertainties about what constitutes dangerous levels of asbestos, and the court acknowledged that the sheer number of asbestos-containing schools (over 30,000) made local circumstances difficult to reflect in a national rule. Is *Corrosion Proof Fittings* distinguishable?

Ironically, it now appears that the asbestos legislation is quite wrong-headed. The current consensus—embodied *inter alia* in EPA's guidance to homeowners—is that asbestos is usually best left in place and encapsulated. Removal inevitably releases asbestos into the atmosphere, and may well (in the case of schools) place children at greater risk than undisturbed asbestos. Using *Corrosion Proof Fittings*, could a court overrule an EPA removal order for this reason?

D. TSCA's Potential

In many, if not most respects, TSCA has been a conspicuous underachiever among environmental statutes. A 1994 GAO report faulted the TSCA program for failing to place controls on more than a few existing and new chemicals, for failing to assess fully health and environmental risks in its chemical review (PMN) process, for failing to conduct any review of most existing chemicals, and for allowing important and useful data to be sequestered as confidential business information.[41] The report and the foregoing materials suggest some reasons for this disappointing outcome. If

---

[41] GAO, Legislative Changes, *supra*.

TSCA were a glass of water, one would certainly be justified in considering it half empty.

TSCA provides EPA with authorities to ban or to restrict chemical manufacturing, but the burden of going forward is almost always on EPA. For example, TSCA requires chemical manufacturers to notify EPA 90 days before manufacturing a new chemical or an existing chemical for a significant new use. If EPA does not act, the manufacturer can make and market the chemical; an EPA license or "permission" is not needed.

If EPA wants to require a manufacturer to test its chemicals for harmful side effects, it cannot administratively order the manufacturer to do so. EPA must go through the cumbersome notice-and-comment process of rulemaking, which generally takes at least 18 months and often longer. If EPA wants to regulate the chemical's uses while testing is ongoing, EPA is authorized to write a "proposed order" doing so. But if the manufacturer objects to the regulation, EPA's order does not take effect. To press its case, EPA must go to federal court to ask a judge to approve its regulation of the chemical.

TSCA has an "escape valve" to deal with emergencies. Section 7, titled Imminent Hazards, picks up when the normal TSCA scheme is too time-consuming. But even here, EPA cannot order relief, as it could under almost every other pollution abatement statute. Instead, EPA is empowered only to go to federal court and ask a judge to order relief.

In short, TSCA promises more than it delivers. EPA has trouble acting proactively. In a federal bureaucracy, a reason can usually be found not to act: information is rarely as complete as it might be, and somebody would usually benefit from postponement. Unless decisions are compelled, inertia toward the status quo reigns. TSCA plays to this institutional weakness; it gives EPA a paper authority that it could theoretically press to advantage but surrounds the authority with so many procedural hurdles that it is hard to invoke. EPA officials concede that without deadlines for action, TSCA decisions have become more drawn out and difficult to resolve.[42] Little wonder that congressional watchdogs criticize TSCA's performance.[43]

Congress gave EPA little policy guidance when it enacted TSCA. TSCA orders EPA to regulate to remove "unreasonable risk," but it never defines that term. It is as if the most crucial issue—how to balance the benefits against the dangers of modern technology—is

---

[42] EPA officials' statements are summarized in U.S. General Accounting Office, Effectiveness of Unreasonable Risk Standard Unclear 5 (No. GAO/RCED-90-189, July 1990).

[43] U.S. General Accounting Office, EPA's Chemical Testing Program Has Made Little Progress (No. GAO/RCED-90-112, Apr. 1990) [published 14 years after TSCA's enactment].

too sensitive for Congress, so Congress would rather let EPA muddle through. Congress can say it passed a law without having to take the heat for making the hard decisions. And the result, particularly in a federal bureaucracy like EPA's, is that the hard decisions are often not made at all, leaving hazardous chemicals on the market.

Barry Breen, *Environmental Law From Resource To Recovery,* in SUSTAINABLE ENVIRONMENTAL LAW (CAMPBELL-MOHN ET AL., EDS. 1993) at 79-80.

But the glass may also be half full. Congress passed most environmental laws in response to specific crises of environmental degradation (air pollution, water pollution) or threats to human health (pesticides, hazardous wastes). By responding to crises and adopting medium-specific regulations, Congress created a patchwork of laws, each designed to address different problems, but with no overall design or direction. TSCA can provide the basis for comprehensive, integrated regulation.

Congress passed TSCA to fill some of the gaps in regulating chemicals, that is, to reach where other pollution abatement statutes cannot. TSCA does not rely on a particular medium like the other pollution abatement statutes; rather its gap-filling function allows it to cut across traditional boundaries in environmental law. From this perspective, the supporting arguments for TSCA have a distinctly modern ring to them. The excerpt from CEQ's *Toxic Substances* spoke of the need for examining the total risks of a chemical and for integrated management. The Senate Report was even more explicit:

> While individual agencies may be authorized to regulate occupational, environmental, or direct consumer hazards with respect to a chemical substance, there is no agency which has the authority to look comprehensively at the hazards associated with the chemical. Existing authority allows the agency to only look at the hazards within their jurisdiction in isolation from other hazards associated with the same chemical. The bill would grant the Environmental Protection Agency the authority to look at the hazards in total.

S. REP. NO. 698, *supra, at* 2.

Congress specifically mandated coordination with other statutory regimes. Section 9 requires EPA to consult with other agencies, to recommend action under laws other than TSCA, and to avoid redundant or duplicative regulations.[44]

> TSCA has institutionalized an integrated approach to the control of chemicals. It embraces the entire environment, together with total human exposure, and is not confined to the usual divisions between air, land and water, or to particular routes of exposure. Integration is

---

[44] However, one commentator has charged that EPA has used section 9 to *avoid* taking regulatory action. Cynthia Ruggerio, *Referral of Toxic Chemical Regulation Under the Toxic Substances Control Act: EPA's Administrative Dumping Ground*, 17 B.C. ENVTL. AFF. L. REV. 75 (1989).

crystallized by section 9 of TSCA, dealing with the act's relationship to other laws. * * * [Section 9] commands the administrator to coordinate an integrated approach to pollution control established by TSCA with the segmented approaches of the other legislation. * * * In sum, TSCA institutionalizes a countervailing norm of integration. Many of the provisions of apparently single medium statutes can now be interpreted from a different perspective. In the light of TSCA's provisions, it would be very difficult to ignore the applicability of an integrated approach to pollution control in the administration of other legislation.

Lakshman D. Guruswamy, *Integrating Thoughtways: Re-Opening of the Environmental Mind?,* 1989 WIS. L. REV. 463. When TSCA is similar to other federal environmental statutes, section 9 permits EPA to take regulatory action under TSCA and such other federal laws. For example, TSCA is similar to FIFRA in that both regulate toxic chemicals that are useful to society, and which are not injurious waste products. FIFRA is different from TSCA in that it regulates through a licensing and registration system, while TSCA relies on data arising through testing, premanufacture notice, and reporting to determine whether regulation is called for. Both require a risk-benefit balancing analysis to ensure that unreasonable risks are abated without excessive societal or private market cost. Thus, FIFRA and TSCA together served as statutory authority for the EPA to regulate the deliberate release of genetically engineered commercial microorganisms.

PROBLEM
BIOTECHNOLOGY

Given Congress' expansive vision for TSCA, a recurring question is how far its regulatory arms can extend. TSCA might be used to regulate this new—and frightening to many—development in the chemical industry. The following excerpt is taken from a work of fiction, but its description of the perils of biotechnology is compelling.

The late twentieth century has witnessed a scientific gold rush of astonishing proportions: the headlong and furious haste to commercialize genetic engineering. This enterprise has proceeded so rapidly—with so little outside commentary—that its dimensions and implications are hardly understood at all.

Biotechnology promises the greatest revolution in human history. By the end of this decade, it will have outdistanced atomic power and computers in its effect on our everyday lives. In the words of one observer, "Biotechnology is going to transform every aspect of human life: our medical care, our food, our health, our entertainment, our very bodies. Nothing will ever be the same again. It's literally going to change the face of the planet."

But the biotechnology revolution differs in three important respects from past scientific transformations.

First, it is broad-based. America entered the atomic age through the work of a single research institution, at Los Alamos. It entered the computer age through the efforts of about a dozen companies. But biotechnology research is now carried out in more than two thousand laboratories in America alone. Five hundred corporations spend five billion dollars a year on this technology.

Second, much of the research is thoughtless or frivolous. Efforts to engineer paler trout for better visibility in the stream, square trees for easier lumbering, and injectable scent cells so you'll always smell like your favorite perfume may seem like a joke, but they are not. Indeed, the fact that biotechnology can be applied to the industries traditionally subject to the vagaries of fashion, such as cosmetics and leisure activities, heightens concern about the whimsical use of this powerful new technology.

Third, the work is uncontrolled. No one supervises it. No federal laws regulate it. There is no coherent government policy, in America or anywhere else in the world. And because the products of biotechnology range from drugs to farm crops to artificial snow, an intelligent policy is difficult.

But most disturbing is the fact that no watchdogs are found among scientists themselves. It is remarkable that nearly every scientist in genetics research is also engaged in the commerce of biotechnology. There are no detached observers. Everybody has a stake.

MICHAEL CRICHTON, JURASSIC PARK (1990).

Notwithstanding Crichton's assertion that no federal laws regulate biotechnology, TSCA's broad authority to regulate new chemical substances does allow EPA to review the proposed manufacture and use of genetic products.[45] While TSCA's drafters presumably had nonliving chemicals in mind when they defined "chemical substance" (TSCA § 3(2)(A)),[46] EPA has taken the position that bioengineered living organisms fall within the definition of chemical substances and has established an active biotechnology program.[47] Moreover, some naturally occurring microbes appear in the Chemical Substances Inventory. Nevertheless, the reach of the definition of chemical substance remains to be interpreted by the courts, and EPA has not yet taken substantive regulatory action in the biotechnology area.

How should EPA proceed in deciding whether to regulate the biotechnology industry? Does the statutory structure discussed at the beginning of this chapter provide an answer? Once EPA has gathered the information it can, should it attempt comprehensive regulation or proceed incrementally (one case at a time)?

EPA has taken a number of concrete actions under TSCA toward integrated environmental regulation. Most significantly, it has made a practice of using its information-generating capabilities under TSCA on behalf of other statutes. The section 8(a) CAIR program—described above, but now abandoned—was explicitly so designed. The ITC regularly uses (and is structured to be able to use) other programs' needs to establish section 4 testing priorities. For example, after the 11th Circuit had rejected OSHA regulation of 400 air contaminants, the ITC recommended many of them for testing.[48] EPA takes the position that TSCA's gap-filling mandate justifies

---

[45] *See generally* Mellon *et al.*, *Biotechnology*, in Law of Environmental Protection (Novick *et al.* eds. 1993); Shapiro, *Biotechnology and the Design of Regulation*, 17 ECOLOGY L.Q. 1 (1990); Ruth Harlow, Note, *The EPA and Biotechnology Regulation: Coping with Scientific Uncertainty*, 95 YALE L.J. 553 (1986); Shapiro & Bayer, *Federal Regulation of Emerging Genetic Technologies*, 36 VAND. L. REV. 461 (1983).

[46] This is not a problem for the regulation of biologically engineered pesticides, because FIFRA defines chemicals as pesticides in terms of their uses and actions, not their chemistry or provenance. 7 U.S.C. §136(u).

[47] EPA, Statement of Policy: Microbial Products Subject to FIFRA and TSCA, 51 Fed. Reg. 23313 (1986). EPA announced this position in connection with the so-called Coordinated Framework for the Regulation of Biotechnology, 51 Fed. Reg. 23302 (1986), the product of an interagency Biotechnology Science Coordinating Committee organized by OSTP.

[48] 16 CHEM. REG. REP. (BNA) 1302 (1992) & 1876 (1993).

this policy.[49] EPA is currently considering a test rule for twenty-one hazardous air pollutants that are regulated under the Clean Air Act.[50]

Similarly, in a Clean Water Act case, *EPA v. Alyeska Pipeline Service Company*, 836 F.2d 443 (9th Cir. 1988), EPA relied on TSCA to subpoena sworn testimony because the Clean Water Act contains no such power. Alyeska contended that EPA was circumventing the law by using TSCA to attain testimony not otherwise attainable under the CWA. Specifically, Alyeska argued that EPA only had authority to regulate PCBs and imminently hazardous chemicals under TSCA and that the subpoena fell outside the scope of EPA's authority. Alyeska also contended that because Congress intended TSCA only to fill gaps in the statutory scheme, EPA must resort to other statutes *before* invoking TSCA. The Ninth Circuit rejected these arguments and upheld the TSCA subpoena.

Finally, TSCA's integrative capacity can be used to address cumulative risk, an important emerging environmental justice issue in risk assessment methodology:

> [EPA] takes part in a cooperative effort to address cumulative exposure, hazard, and risk issues affecting residents of Cook County, Illinois and Lake County, Indiana. The effort, called the Chicago Cumulative Risk Initiative (CCRI), has its origins in a 1996 petition from 11 community advocacy groups requesting that EPA regulate air deposits of dioxins, furans, mercury, cadmium, and lead from incinerators in the two counties. The petition was denied but OPPT felt that the environmental justice issues raised called for a more comprehensive, cooperative investigation and response. Members of CCRI include EPA Region 5, the Office of Research and Development; the Office of Air and Radiation; the Office of Environmental Justice; Indiana and Illinois officials; and 11 Chicago-area advocacy groups. CCRI has organized its work into four phases.

> *Phase I* of CCRI involves the development of a cumulative "environmental loading profile" to catalog the source and nature of toxic emissions in the study area. The profile will be finalized during the first two quarters of FY 1998. Phase I also involves the development of a user-friendly, PC-based program that enables users to statistically and graphically analyze emissions and ambient data from the study area. Work is underway to make a nationally applicable program available by the end of FY 1998.

> *Phase II* will bring together interested parties in a workshop (scheduled for third quarter of FY 1998) to discuss and reach accords on the environmental loading profile, the cumulative risk assessment, and customer service issues

---

[49] *See* EPA, Office of Solid Waste Chemicals; Final Test Rule, 53 Fed. Reg. 22300, 22301-02 (1988) (rejecting objections that a section 4 rule issued "in support of EPA's hazardous waste regulatory program under [RCRA]").

[50] EPA, Proposed Test Rule for Hazardous Air Pollutants, 61 Fed. Reg. 33178 (1996).

Phase III will involve a cumulative risk analysis that addresses the most significant environmental hazards; their sources and exposure pathways; risks of various health effects from multiple exposure sources and pathways; and locations and other characteristics defining sensitive populations. * * *

FY 1997 Annual Report, *supra*, at 37.

PROBLEM
A SINGLE TOXICS STATUTE

Can TSCA be made into a comprehensive regulatory statute or should Congress draft a new statute? If the latter, what areas would a comprehensive toxics statute address? Should any be excluded? What regulatory tools would such a statute use?

PART 3:

THE DISPOSAL AND CLEAN-UP OF HAZARDOUS WASTES

Chapter 9

Disposal: The Resource Conservation and Recovery Act

A. Introduction

Dumps and landfills have always been an obvious environmental problem in themselves, a source of other environmental problems, like groundwater contamination, air- and waterborne diseases, and aesthetically offensive. Congress first addressed this problem in the Solid Waste Disposal Act of

1965 (SWDA), which concentrated on conventional dumps and landfills[1] and did nothing to displace the traditionally local control over such facilities. In its concern with aesthetic effects and familiar, acute diseases, the 1965 legislation embodied the earlier phases of the environmental movement. The Resource Conservation and Recovery Act (RCRA), enacted in 1976 and technically an amendment to the Solid Waste Disposal Act, represented the changing focus of environmentalism by concentrating federal efforts on hazardous waste and leaving traditional facilities largely to local control. Initially regarded as much less significant than the Toxic Substances Control Act (TSCA), which also passed in 1976, it has become one of the most complex and burdensome—and necessary—elements of toxics regulation. The movement away from aesthetic and infectious disease concern was completed by the Hazardous and Solid Waste Amendments of 1984 (HSWA). It imposed stringent disposal standards and prohibitions, as well as strict deadlines on EPA's regulation of hazardous wastes, and it established the current regulatory structure for these materials.

RCRA is important in itself, since it regulates the deliberate introduction of toxic material into the environment (albeit in a controlled manner), and it introduces us to a new and difficult technical problem in toxics regulation. By differentiating between hazardous and solid wastes—that is, between toxic and conventional pollutants—and focusing federal attention on the hazardous ones, Congress was not only following the trend of emphasizing toxic risks to human health, it was also setting a difficult and fundamental definitional problem for itself.

The problem has two components. First, you will recall that our discussion of toxicology began with Paracelsus' famous dictum, "All substances are poisons; there is none which is not a poison. The right dose differentiates a poison and a remedy." The sliding scale implied by this axiom of toxicology, made even more slippery by the probabilistic nature of the effects of carcinogens, resists the simple categorization of waste materials into "solid" and "hazardous." Yet, this categorization, or something like it, seems a practical necessity in creating a workable regulatory regime for toxic wastes. Otherwise, we would have to define everything as hazardous. Second, as RCRA's name suggests, Congress wanted to encourage reuse and recycling of wastes as an alternative to disposal. The advantages of reuse and recycling should be obvious, but they also raise the problem of either sham or fraudulent reuse, or of reuse that exposes the public to toxic materials. EPA therefore also needs to find a way to distinguish between waste and non-waste.

The resulting statutory provisions and regulations were memorably described by Donald R. Clay, EPA's assistant administrator responsible for the hazardous waste program: "RCRA is a regulatory cuckoo-land of

---

[1] These "sanitary" landfills are often used and/or operated by municipalities, and contain mostly garbage.

definition . . . . It is very complex. We believe that we have five people in the agency who understand what 'hazardous waste' is."[2]

RCRA may be a "cuckoo-land," but is also essential terrain to conquer to gain a complete understanding to toxics regulation. Consequently, we will spend much of our time in this chapter with the threshold definitional question whether a particular material is a waste, and if so, whether it is a hazardous waste. After that, we will turn to the important substantive restrictions that RCRA places on the actual disposal of hazardous waste, restrictions that possess their own ambiguities and difficulties.

EPA Journal, January-February 1990.

1. Love Canal: A Case Study

Before turning to statutory and regulatory detail, it will be helpful to consider the case of *un*regulated dumping of hazardous waste that set the tone for much federal and state regulation. While Love Canal gained its notoriety after the 1976 RCRA, its memory was fresh in the minds of the legislators who passed the 1980 amendments and more importantly the 1984 HWSA. Whatever positive or negative lessons can be drawn from the Love Canal episode,[3] it surely represents a cautionary tale of uncontrolled disposal of hazardous waste.

---

[2] Donald R. Clay, Interviewed in Center For Investigative Reporting & BILL MOYERS, GLOBAL DUMPING GROUND (1990).

[3] Some regard it as emblematic of corporate environmental irresponsibility, *see, e.g.,* Russell Mokhiber & Leonard Shen, *Love Canal, in* WHO'S POISONING AMERICA: CORPORATE POLLUTERS AND THEIR VICTIMS IN THE CHEMICAL AGE 268-310 (Ralph Nader et al. eds., 1981); ADELINE GORDON LEVINE, LOVE CANAL: SCIENCE, POLITICS AND PEOPLE (1982), and others regard it as typical of unjustified public and media overreaction to alleged cancer

UNITED STATES V. HOOKER CHEMICALS & PLASTICS CORPORATION

850 F. Supp. 993 (W.D.N.Y. 1994)

CURTIN, District Judge.

* * *

Background

In 1979, plaintiffs State of New York ("State") and the United States of America ("United States") brought suit against defendant Hooker Chemicals & Plastics Corporation ("Hooker," "OCC," or "the Company") to recover the costs of cleaning up and insuring the safety of the Love Canal area pursuant to Section 107(a) of the Comprehensive Environmental Response, Compensation, and Liability Act, 42 U.S.C. § 9607(a) ("CERCLA"), and New York common law of public nuisance. Between 1942 and 1954, the site was used by Hooker as a landfill for toxic chemical wastes from its Niagara Falls plant. In 1953, the Company transferred the site to the City of Niagara Falls School Board ("School Board" or "Board"), and an elementary school was built in the central section the next year. A State Health Emergency was declared in 1978 when a noticeable quantity of the chemical residues began surfacing and seeping into neighboring homes.

* * *

The State's claim for punitive damages . . . is based upon OCC's creation of a public nuisance at Love Canal in allegedly reckless disregard of the health, safety, and property of the local residents . . . .

* * *

Hooker's Early Growth

Hooker was formed in 1905, and its Niagara Falls plant began operating the following year. By 1910, the Niagara Falls plant was producing 20 tons of caustic soda and 42 tons of bleach per day . . . .

* * *

The Company grew substantially during World War II because of the demands of the United States government and defense contractors. From 1940 until 1953, its sales grew from $7.1 million to $38.7 million. This dramatic growth continued, and by 1970 its annual sales reached $450 million.

Until Hooker began its wartime production, it was able to sewer and dispose of chemicals on-site. Increased volume of chemical waste, combined with growing opposition to open dumping in streams, forced Hooker to consider alternative means of waste disposal. Incineration could not handle the anticipated heavy waste disposal demands. In-ground disposal developed as a viable alternative.

Hooker became interested in the nearby Love Canal site as a landfill for wastes from its Niagara Falls plant in 1941 and obtained permission from the

threats, *see, e.g.,* Timur Kuran & Cass R. Sunstein, *Availability Cascades and Risk Regulation*, 51 STAN. L. REV. 683, 691-98 (1999).

owner, the Niagara Power Development Corporation, to use the site without the expense of an outright purchase . . . . [T]he site posed several obvious advantages. Its proximity to the Niagara Falls plant reduced transport costs and avoided the difficulty of moving odorous chemicals long distances by truck. There was a general perception, held by Hooker executives and residents in the Niagara Falls area, that the soils at Love Canal were composed largely of clay. Lastly, there were no zoning restrictions on the Canal's use, although the Company realized that the operation of a landfill would require measures to keep people and animals from coming in contact with the wastes.

Description Of The Site

* * *

The Love Canal site is a roughly rectangular, 16-acre parcel of land located in the City of Niagara Falls, New York . . . . At the time it was acquired by Hooker, Love Canal was situated on the outskirts of the City, close to the eastern border at 102nd Street . . . .

The Canal was developed in the 1890s by an entrepreneur named William Love, who hoped to create an industrial community which would use the Canal as a source of electric power and as a means of transportation. Love planned to connect the upper and lower Niagara River, bypassing Niagara Falls. He began excavating the Canal in 1894, but abandoned the project when he lost financial backing. Thereafter, the site remained unused, except for informal recreation by people living in the area. Evidently without objection by the owner, it was used for swimming, fishing, trapping, and ice-skating.

The unfinished Canal, located near the center of the parcel, was approximately 3,000 feet long and varied from 8 to 16 feet deep and from 60 to 80 feet wide over most of its length. In 1941, there were mounds of excavated earthen material located along most of the east and west banks of the Canal. The size of mounds varied in height from 10 to 20 feet, and in width from 30 to 40 feet. They were comprised of a mix of clay and silty sand and were covered and surrounded by various forms of vegetation, brush, and grass.

* * *

By 1928, the land immediately west and east of the Canal had been subdivided into building lots; by 1939, the City had planned the installation of Reed and Wheatfield Avenues across the Love Canal site. Before 1940, the population of Niagara Falls had been gradually spreading eastward toward and past Love Canal. This development is apparent from the aerial photographs. Still, by 1954, over 75 percent of the houses were on the east side of 99th Street. Only a few homes had been built adjacent to the site when Hooker began its operations, and new street development did not materialize until much later.

The area to the east of Love Canal began to develop after 1950, when the City rezoned the east side of 99th Street (the side furthest from the Canal) from an "unclassified" to a "second residence" district. Only one house was built on the west side of 99th Street during the time of Hooker's disposal operations. By 1954, 33 of the 40 homes under construction were on the rezoned east side of the Canal.

On the west side of the Canal, the Griffin Manor Housing Project was under construction by 1942, but there were no houses or streets built between the housing project and Love Canal during the period when Hooker was dumping in the northern sector. By World War II, Griffin Manor had about 750 apartments. When disposal operations began in the northern section, the nearest house was approximately 400 feet away.

* * *

Charles Adams, who began trapping in the area in the 1930s, summed up the local knowledge of the soil at the Canal. He said there was a natural well in the middle which provided a continuous flow of water. The topsoil was eight to ten inches deep, underlain by soil which was half clay and half dirt, below which was what he called Tonawanda clay, identifiable by its bluish cast. The clay was very hard and good for brick-making, but it was difficult to dig through below the surface. Generally, the soil was very poor for farming, with very little topsoil and with clay underneath.

* * *

Disposal Operations

* * *

In April 1942, Hooker obtained an operating license from the Niagara Power Development Corporation to begin waste disposal operations. Shortly thereafter, the Company acquired title of the property. Hooker continued to send waste materials from its Niagara Falls plant to the Canal until 1954. At trial, most of the evidence about disposal practices was given by Hooker employees, with some reference to Hooker records. No one lived near the northern section of the Canal while Hooker was using it as a dump site, and only six to ten houses had been built close to the southern section prior to 1954, when building on 97th and 99th Streets began. For this reason, the non-Hooker witnesses who testified about the disposal operation were primarily individuals who had played at the site as children.

The evidence supports a finding that, except for the erection of a fence, the [Hooker] Engineering Department's plan was carried out with only slight modification. The plan provided for construction of at least two earthen dams across the northern part of the Canal before disposal operations began. The purpose of the dams was to prevent contaminated liquids from flowing from disposal areas into the rest of the Canal and nearby creeks and the swale. At the same time, dams prevented water from adjoining areas of the Canal from entering disposal areas. In addition, the dams allowed water to be pumped out of a disposal cell, if appropriate, immediately prior to waste burial. The dams, which were constructed from the surrounding soil, were wide enough to accommodate vehicle traffic. They thus created disposal cells up to 60 feet wide, several hundred feet long, and 10 feet deep.

* * *

Chemical Composition Of The Waste Material

The parties agree that about 25,000 tons of chemical wastes, plus fly ash and general refuse from the plant, were deposited at Love Canal from the time Hooker began to use the site in the early 1940s until it ceased operations in 1954. The available records made it difficult to determine the types and quantities of the wastes sent to Love Canal. Thus, estimates of the amount and concentration of the individual chemicals buried at the landfill differed widely.

* * *

Toxicity And Disposal Methods For Specific Chemicals

Many of the chemicals used by Hooker during the production process were highly toxic and hazardous. The State's accusation of reckless disregard for public safety is premised on the danger posed by chemical wastes both during and after disposal. Several specific chemicals and their waste products were the subject of special attention during the trial because potentially hazardous disposal methods were employed, there were recurring incidents of exposure, or the substances continued to cause problems during or after the disposal operations.

* * *

Chemical Exposure At The Landfill

* * *

Some of the chemicals buried at Love Canal were flammable, and others had flash points of less than 100 degrees Fahrenheit. As a result, there were frequent fires. The danger of fires was enhanced by the presence of chlorobenzenes and hexachlorocyclopentadiene ("C-56"), which form phosgene [a poison gas used in World War I] if burned. In addition, deposits of sulfides and acids had the potential of forming hydrogen sulfide gas when mixed together. Moreover, the flammable character of some of the chemical residues sent by Hooker to Love Canal was such that it was impossible for workers at the site to compact the wastes once they were dumped, which contributed to the subsidence of the cover.

* * *

There were also explosions at the site. Dine Bouley, a former resident who lived on 100th Street, stated that explosions sometimes launched burning debris into the road in front of her house, and sometimes sent debris as far as 102nd Street. Children would sometimes play with the cooled material. Other witnesses recalled explosions, but none supported her recollection that burning pellets from the Canal were hurled that far.

When fires and subsurface explosions occurred, the covered soil was displaced, exposing previously buried drums and wastes. Gerald Craig recalled that when he was a teenager in the 1950s, the ground around buried drums subsided allowing him and his friends to play on the exposed tops. June Craig Wirth, his sister, recalled that once when she touched a black liquid in the pit, it caused a burning sensation.

After a rainstorm, the surface area would become very muddy and swampy and would emit strong, noxious odors which pervaded the neighborhood. Timothy Moriarty recalled that once while walking across the Canal, he sank into the ground to his knees and had to pull his feet from his boots to escape. Dust, powder, and flyash flew from the dumpsite and from trucks into the neighborhood, soiling and sometimes damaging the paint on nearby properties.

In spite of these reportedly foul conditions, the residents, especially children, continued to swim and fish in the unfilled part of the Canal. Two witnesses remembered developing a rash or burning skin sensation after swimming. However, there is no evidence that any serious or permanent injury resulted.

Throughout the disposal period, Hooker personnel and contractors observed that previously filled and covered areas of the landfill were settling and subsiding. The subsidence began to occur as early as 1942, exposing the tops of drums and waste material and increasing chemical odors and puddling.

* * *

The Transfer Of The Love Canal Site To The Niagara Falls Board Of Education

* * *

A March 27, 1952, memorandum from Klaussen to Vice President Young discussed the requests to sell Love Canal and explained the Company's refusal to consider transferring even a portion of the property:

> About a month ago Architect Russell Larke said that a certain party was interested in purchasing Love Canal for the purpose of building low-cost houses and asked if we were interested in selling it, which I told him we were not.
>
> Just a few days ago, Superintendent of Schools Bill Small called at this office and explained that the school board is planning to erect a large school in the general locality of the Love Canal and he asked if we would be willing to sell our property.
>
> Wilcox [the Company's attorney] and I discussed this with Small for some time and we pointed out that we used the Love Canal for plant refuse containing some chemicals which were buried approximately six feet underground and covered. We informed Mr. Small that we were not in a position to sell the property and that the property was not suitable for the erection of school buildings.
>
> At a later date Mr. Small asked if we might sell part of the property for a school ground and I again gave a negative answer.
>
> It is rather clear that the territory on each side of the Love Canal will be used rapidly to provide buildings or a school and it may be advisable for us to discontinue using the Love Canal property for a dumping ground. It is also rather clear to me that we should not sell the property in order to avoid any risks.

Klaussen went on to state that the purpose of the letter was to suggest that Young look for another site suitable for dumping, to ask Operations to prepare a map of the Canal dump, and "suggest ways and means and costs to prepare the property in such a way that it will not create a nuisance." He also suggested filling in the property and creating gardens for the employees, "possibly with a lease which would protect us from any damage."

Within a month, however, at least some members of Hooker management had changed their minds. An April 25, 1952, memorandum written by Klaussen to Hooker's President, R.L. Murray, told Murray that he and Ansley Wilcox, the Company's attorney, had talked several times with Superintendent Small and a representative of the City Planning Board for Niagara Falls about the Board's desire to build a school on or near the Love Canal property. After noting that he and Wilcox had initially opposed the idea, Klaussen wrote: "The more we thought about it, the more interested Wilcox and I became in the proposition and finally came to the conclusion that the Love Canal property is rapidly becoming a liability because of housing projects in the near vicinity of our property."

Klaussen and Wilcox eventually "became convinced that it would be a wise move to turn the property over to the schools provided we would not be held responsible for future claims or damages resulting from underground storage of chemicals." Klaussen suggested that a school could be built on a portion of the central section that had not been filled, and that areas to the north and south that had been filled with chemicals could be used for school grounds and athletic fields. Klaussen added that Hooker would feel free to continue dumping chemicals at Love Canal, but indicated that only fly ash would be dumped in the area contemplated for the school.

* * *

Relying upon its agreement with the Board, Hooker continued to dump chemical wastes and flyash at the site during the initial phase of construction of the school through February, 1954. When Hooker discontinued use of the site, it did not place topsoil, seed, or vegetation on the cover.

Post-Transfer Events

Between the time Hooker transferred the Love Canal site to the School Board in 1953 and the governmental intervention in 1978, several problems arose. Waste exposure during excavation for the school in 1953 forced relocation of the foundations. There was a series of complaints about subsidence, the eruption of potholes, and chemical wastes and drums rising to the surface. There were also some reports of minor injuries from chemical burns. Approximately 15 of these incidents were called to Hooker's attention at the time they occurred,[4] but there is no evidence that the Company was informed of many others which were related at trial.

---

[4] These included, between 1953 and 1976, chemicals found at the school construction site, odor complaints, a crater in the playground, children playing with chemical substances found in the area, explosions of old drums, sludge in construction trenches, acid in holes in the area, and complaints of eye irritation.–EDS.

* * *

Problems During Road Construction: 1958

In 1958, Hooker learned of complaints about subsidence and children being burned by exposed chemicals. In June of 1958, Wilkenfeld wrote to R.F. Schultz, then Hooker's Works Manager, that three or four children had been burned by material at the Canal. Wilkenfeld noted that R. Fadel, Inspector for the City Engineering Department, reported he "had been down there inspecting a new road that was being constructed near the 99th Street School and gave Mr. Arch the impression that these children were burned while playing on earth excavated in the construction of this new road." Despite the warnings Hooker had given earlier to the Board about the dangers of digging into the ground, the contractor was either not informed about the nature of the chemicals underground or, if warned, took no steps to prevent spreading the waste material in the surrounding area.

Wilkenfeld told Schultz that Beck and Johnson had subsequently visited the area and noticed that just south of the road construction, where dumping had occurred, "the ground had subsided and the ends of some drums which may have been thionyl residue drums were exposed and south of the school there is an area where benzene hexaxhloride [sic] spent cake was exposed." Beck and Johnson told Wilkenfeld that "if children had been burned it was probably by getting in contact with this material." They reported that "the entire area is being used by children as a playground even though it is not officially designated for that purpose," and suggested that these areas be recovered to avoid any further contact.

Mr. Beck said he saw as many as a dozen small pieces of spent cake [chemical residue] . . . . Hooker was fully aware that the spent cake that Mr. Beck found lying on the ground posed a great danger to these children. Ingestion of this material could be fatal. Although the spent cake only contained small amounts of lindane [a powerful pesticide], the most acutely toxic form of BHC, the beta isomer and the most chronically toxic form of BHC, was present in much greater quantities. It could be absorbed through the skin, stored, and accumulated in the body, eventually damaging the liver and other organs.

Mr. Beck also found thionyl chloride residue drums exposed to the surface. While the methods Hooker used in disposing of the thionyl residue dissipated most of the toxic liquid, occasionally a barrel which had not been punctured or still contained rework residue with traces of thionyl chloride would continue to react slowly with water and eventually burst, releasing hydrochloric acid (HCL) and sulfur dioxide (SO2) and whatever traces of thionyl chloride or purifiers like toluene were left. The vapors of these chemicals could be irritating to the skin, eyes, nose, throat, and respiratory system.

* * *

[T]hose who were most affected by the exposure were the children who lived, played, and went to school at the Canal site. Once Hooker was notified that children were playing with the spent cake and had access to thionyl chloride residues from the drums exposed to the surface, they had at least some responsibility to these children or their parents to make known to them the extent of the danger and the measures which needed to be taken should a child, despite warnings, touch, inhale, or ingest any of these toxic substances. There is no evidence on record that any such effort was considered or carried out.

Problems During Construction Of Lasalle Highway: 1968

In 1968, the State began construction of the LaSalle Arterial Highway. As part of the project, the State acquired an approximately 55-foot-wide strip of the southern tip of the Love Canal property in order to relocate Frontier Avenue as requested by the City rather than close the road as originally planned. During the course of the planning for the project, Hooker expressed opposition to certain proposed ramp locations but did not warn the State of any potential dangers associated with excavating on or near its former landfill. Yet, the State never explained why their planning failed to take into account the obvious presence of the landfill.

On March 15 of that year, State contractors encountered chemical residues during excavation for a storm sewer trench being dug as part of the relocation of Frontier Avenue . . . .

After analyzing the material, Hooker prepared an internal report dated March 21 which described the sample as "an 'oily' like residue that burned like a 4th of July 'sparkler.'"

It is important to mention that during construction of the highway, the State's performance was equal to or worse than anything for which it upbraids Hooker. Contractors left many truckloads of excavated wastes unattended at the site for some time. Removal did not happen until after nearby residents and the County DOH complained about the strong odors. Hooker agreed to take the residue at its Hyde Park landfill, but most of these wastes were ultimately dumped at the Nash Road landfill in the Town of Wheatfield. After moving about 1,000 cubic yards of material, the contractor used permeable material such as broken stone, gravel, excavated street asphalt, and broken concrete mixed with clay to backfill.

The State and County DOH inspected the Nash Road landfill before using it and determined the site was "acceptable" because its soils were "impervious." The soils at the Nash Road site were similar to those at Love Canal. The landfill was never fenced. Many years later, it was discovered that the wastes in the Nash Road landfill were leaking, contaminating the groundwater and threatening residents because of poor cover maintenance. Ironically, the State criticizes Hooker severely for placing waste in what the Company believed was a secure site in 1942; and 25 years later the State itself is caught up in a similar predicament. At the time of trial, the Nash Road site was on the State's list of hazardous waste disposal sites.

*   *   *

Complaints Of Eye Irritation: 1971-72

In July 1971, Hooker learned that a child's eyes had been burned by exposed BHC wastes on the surface of the northern section near the back lot lines of 97th Street. Hooker employee Fred Olotka talked to the child's mother and went to the area where the incident had occurred. He observed lumps of white powder about the size of a fist on the ground and an exposed fiber drum about two feet in diameter and four feet tall. Olotka was told that the children were touching or throwing the lumps and had received irritation burns. He had several pictures taken which showed exposed chemical residue and the fiber drum, and reported that a landscaper had been working in the area and it appeared that some of the topsoil had been scraped away. Hooker's attorney notified the Board, and the City suggested that additional soil be placed in the area.

In May 1972, Debra Gallo, 11 years old, while playing near swings at the school, found some stone-like material which crumbled into powder. She rubbed her eyes and was taken to the emergency room for treatment. Upon investigation Hooker learned that several young girls had burned their eyes and faces after using dry chunks of exposed residues from Love Canal as chalk to write on a sidewalk. When informed of the Gallo incident by the Fire Department, Mr. Brierly, Hooker's safety supervisor, went to the site and identified wastes found near the south side of the school as benzene hexachloride ("BHC"). He also learned that two young boys had been treated for burns to their face caused by contact with chemicals. All recovered. The Fire Department hosed the area down.

* * *

Governmental Intervention & Off-Site Migration

Complaints about surface exposure to chemical wastes increased during the mid-1970s, eventually accompanied by reports from neighboring residents of chemicals seeping into their homes. These reports led a series of governmental agencies to investigate the site, establish an Interagency Task Force, and decide on a course of remedial action.

* * *

[New York Health] Commissioner Whalen's declaration of a health emergency followed his visit to the site in April 1978. Shortly before their visit, a rainfall left the area quite muddy. In the southern sector a heavy chemical odor pervaded, and pools of water containing a black, oily substance rested on the surface. Boards were placed across some of these puddles to permit walking in the area. There was very little vegetation. The surface area around the school "was relatively intact except for a number of drums that appeared to be surfacing through the underlying vegetation." In the center was a baseball diamond.

North of the school was a play area and a shortcut used by the children to get to school. This area had the most vegetation. However, the Commissioner found a white powdery substance on the surface which he suspected was lindane. Dr. Axelrod [another Health Department official] described some cartons which had surfaced containing "large chunks of the yellowish material [which] were breaking off . . . . [T]he road immediately adjacent to these cartons was stained with the same color as the materials . . . ." He expressed disbelief that the area was being used as a playground with the extent of surface material present.

Commissioner Whalen testified that he observed a total of about 50 pounds of lindane in the area. While he felt this was not an extensive amount, he determined that even this much exposure was intolerable . . . .

Investigation did not reveal any chemicals leaching into the bedding surrounding school property or onto the surface of the schoolyard. Moreover, there was nothing unusual about absenteeism at the school which might have suggested that the children were being affected by the chemical release. However, Commissioner Whalen adopted a cautious approach and asked the Board not to open the school in September 1978, without intending to make it a permanent order. The building became the headquarters for the Love Canal Task Force.

Commissioner Whalen stated that he believed that there was danger of possible carcinogenic effect and liver damage when he declared a health emergency on August 2. Finding that there was a risk to pregnant women and children under the age of two, he suggested that these individuals be relocated temporarily from Ring I homes. Governor Carey's order creating a special Love Canal Agency Task Force followed on August 7. The Love Canal Study Group was disbanded, but much of the CRA remedy plan was later adopted by the State and the EPA.

* * *

Off-Site Migration

The State offered extensive evidence of off-site chemical migration and argues that Hooker knew or should have known when it began its disposal operation at Love Canal in the 1940s that chemicals would migrate to the surrounding area. As previously noted, Hooker maintains it comported with the best industry practice to determine that the site was secure and could not have foreseen the consequences. To test these arguments, it is necessary to set forth briefly a history of off-site migration, a review of the investigations conducted to determine the cause and impact of the migration, and an analysis of the competing arguments.

* * *

Industry Practice

* * *

The overwhelming weight of evidence given by experts in the field of solid waste disposal during the relevant time period shows that Hooker comported with and often exceeded the standards demanded by statute, proposed by health and other government officials, or followed by others in the industry. The concept of sanitary landfilling by periodic covering of buried wastes was still in a formative stage in Western New York in the 1940s. Many companies were still discharging industrial wastes into lakes and streams. Others used open dumps, many located off-site, without any attempt to dig, bury, and cover. Although knowledge of chemical toxicity and the dangers of exposure was growing rapidly, virtually nothing was known about the ability of these chemicals to migrate, nor their hazardous potential after burial of residues. When Hooker's activities are regarded in the light of contemporaneous industry practice of solid waste disposal, the existing regulations and recommendations made by governmental agencies, and the state of knowledge of the dangers of chemical landfills, they do not appear reckless.

* * *

Conclusion

Upon detailed consideration of the entire record, the court finds that while the State documented many specific instances of Hooker's negligence, it has failed to prove by a preponderance of the evidence that Hooker's actions and omissions in operating the Love Canal landfill or transferring it to the City of Niagara Falls School Board for use as school and park grounds displayed a reckless disregard for the safety of others. Hooker's decision to landfill its chemical wastes, its choice and maintenance of the site, and its method of disposal operation all comported with the available knowledge and industry practice of the time. While the Company should have made greater efforts to keep local residents off the property, it violated no ordinance or legal obligation in failing to do so. It responded to complaints about odors, fires, and exposures to chemicals whenever notified, and there was no evidence of injury during the disposal operations that would have signaled a compelling need to provide more protection.

Hooker agreed to transfer the property to the School Board, despite the misgivings of some of its managers, when it became convinced that the rapid population growth in the surrounding area both created the need for a school and ended the site's usefulness as a landfill. The Company disclosed to the Board that many dangerous chemicals were buried at the site, and the ground would have to be maintained properly and not excavated. Hooker did not disclose the composition and amounts of chemical residues buried. While it is likely that this type of disclosure would have given the Board a better understanding of the responsibility they accepted, there is no indication that this information was either sought or deliberately withheld. The sparse record of the negotiations which led up to the transfer makes it difficult for the court to fix blame at this juncture.

Although Hooker's activities after the transfer were clearly unacceptable by present standards and at times violative of common sense, in general, given the state of scientific knowledge and the legal principles of that time, they did not exhibit the degree of recklessness which would warrant a punitive damages award. The Company's failure to respond adequately to the likelihood of serious harm once it learned that children were playing with and being injured by the waste materials argues strongly that Hooker disregarded a threat to public safety. The Company was clearly negligent in failing to warn the Board that chemicals had been dumped in the central section at the proposed site of the school and to inform the Board that many of the chemical-laden barrels were so shallowly buried that subsidence would inevitably expose them and their contents. However, after the transfer, the Company responded to calls for assistance in dealing with incidents of exposure and no immediate, serious injury or damage was reported. By contemporaneous property law precepts, Hooker's legal duties as a seller were very limited. The Company asserted clearly and consistently that the transfer removed its legal responsibility for the site.

Nevertheless, Hooker had superior knowledge about the health hazards of exposure to such substances as lindane wastes which it never disclosed to either the Board or the community. Even though there was a general awareness that dangerous chemicals were buried in the ground, the threat to the children's health was at least partially latent, because the current users of the property did not know what the residues were nor the type of ill effects they could cause. Incidents of exposure should have put the Company on notice that exposure would most likely continue and result in serious illness. At that point, Hooker should have provided more detailed information and sounded an alarm. The history of Hooker's failure to come forward makes for a strong argument that it showed a wanton disregard for the health and safety of others.

However, it is necessary to consider the many factors which have been previously discussed. [A]ctual awards of punitive damage are rare in the absence of conclusive evidence of serious injury or deliberate flaunting of regulatory standards. There is no evidence of either in this record. Additional evidence of damage and wrongdoing may yet be produced in Phase II [of the trial], but the court must make a decision on the present record, which the passage of time left woefully incomplete for many of the crucial events by which intent could be inferred.

Considering all of these circumstances, the court finds that the State has failed to prove by a preponderance of the evidence that Hooker's conduct at Love Canal met the . . . standard necessary for an award of punitive damages. The court emphasizes that this verdict does not signify approval of Hooker's conduct. Hooker was negligent on a number of occasions as the court has already noted. But a finding of outrageous conduct and reckless or wanton disregard of the safety of others requires more. And the conduct must be judged by the law in force at the time of action or inaction. There are further proceedings in this case. Hooker's conduct as set forth in this decision will be considered a part of that future record, if appropriate.

So ordered.

—

To orient you, below is a schematic of the waste site and a map of the affected area.

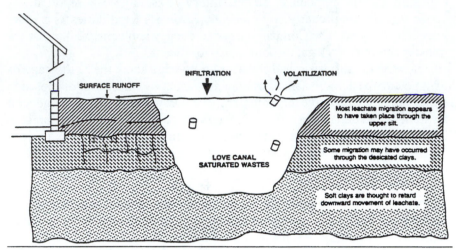

Figure 9.1–Schematic of chemical escape from the Love Canal[5]

[5] Source: State Dep't of Health, New York, Love Canal Emergency Declaration area: Proposed Habitability Criteria 12, app. 6 (1986).

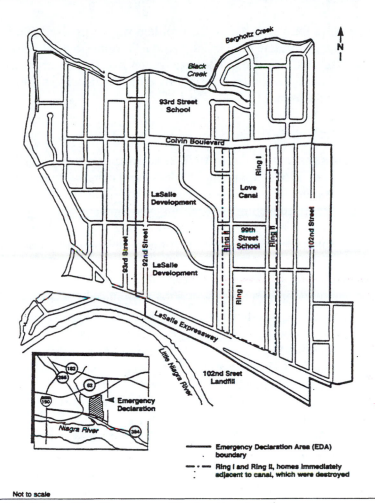

Figure 9.2–Map of the Emergency Declaration Area[6]

NOTES

1. The federal government ultimately obtained a judgment for $68 million from Hooker and $50 million from its parent, Occidental Chemical Co.

2. In what ways does Love Canal represent an example of the need for regulation of hazardous waste disposal practices?

3. By the time RCRA was passed, examples of improper hazardous waste disposal had multiplied. The BEST company in Lathrop, California, contaminated both the soil and the water around the unlined dump where residues were deposited.[7] In Michigan, a fire retardant chemical (PBB) was accidentally mixed with cattle feed, and farmers ate and sold contaminated

---

[6] Source: Region II, U.S. EPA, Love Canal Habitability Study, Introduction and Decision-Making Document, vol. I, 1-2 and 1-4 (1998).

[7] CHRISTOPHER HARRIS ET AL., HAZARDOUS WASTE: CONFRONTING THE CHALLENGE 16-18 (1987).

milk and cows for a year before the problem was recognized. Twenty-five thousand dairy cows had to be killed.[8] And in Virginia, a pesticide company that manufactured Kepone (a chemical much like DDT with neurological effects) contaminated the James River by dumping its wastes into the town sewage treatment plant.[9]

2. An Overview of RCRA

Congress enacted RCRA in 1976 as an amendment to the Solid Waste Disposal Act of 1965, expanding its focus from disposal to manufacturing and transportation. RCRA encouraged states to establish solid waste control plans, encouraged recycling research and development, and set up a cradle-to-grave tracking system for hazardous wastes, known as "Subtitle C,"[10] to be implemented by the federal government unless states developed an "equivalent" system.

Subtitle C controls hazardous wastes by:

- requiring EPA to identify and list hazardous wastes
- establishing a system for tracking hazardous wastes from cradle-to-grave
- setting standards for generators; transporters; and treatment, storage, and disposal facilities (TSDFs)
- establishing a permitting program for TSDFs
- providing authority for states to implement "equivalent" programs
- providing for enforcement

RCRA encourages states to establish their own hazardous waste programs. It also indirectly influences the costs and liabilities of waste management as stricter regulations increase the attractiveness of recycling and recovery. Its tight controls on waste disposal facilities raise the costs and difficulties associated with disposal, providing an incentive to avoid the production of those wastes in the first place.

Despite this grand design, it was not until the early eighties that the EPA began to fulfill its Subtitle C responsibilities in earnest. The Carter Administration gave insufficient priority to RCRA in an effort to complete the promulgation of rules under the Clean Water Act (CWA) and Clean Air Act (CAA), and the Reagan Administration had no enthusiasm for environmental regulation generally. EPA eventually introduced many of the necessary provisions in three phases during 1980 and 1982, in response to a court order,[11] pressure from Congress, and the public.

In 1984, Congress, frustrated by what it perceived as EPA's attempts to undermine RCRA, passed the Hazardous and Solid Waste Amendments

---

[8] *See* Ellen E. Grzeck, *PBB, in* WHO'S POISONING AMERICA: CORPORATE POLLUTERS AND THEIR VICTIMS 60-62 (Ralph Nader, ed., 1981).

[9] *See* C. Brian Kelly, *Kepone, id.* at 86-89.

[10] RCRA §§ 3001-3004, 42 U.S.C. §§ 6921-6924 (1994).

[11] *See* Illinois v. Costle, 9 E.L.R. 20243 (D.D.C. 1979).

(HSWA).[12] The HSWA contained specific guidelines for the development and enforcement of detailed regulatory standards. Congress sought to ensure their timely implementation through the imposition of statutory "hammers," that is, the imposition of extremely strict standards upon EPA's failure to act within a stated period of time.

The HSWA also limited the 1976 exemption for small generators of hazardous wastes from 1000 kilograms per month to 100 kilograms per month. The 1984 amendments also authorized the regulation of underground storage tanks (USTs) and the clean-up of contaminated sites. Most important, the HSWA imposed the so-called "land-ban," enforced by the aforementioned hammers. The present, post-HSWA form of RCRA, therefore, represents an unusually detailed legislative mandate to EPA, matched in specificity only by the 1990 Clean Air Act Amendments.

Control of waste disposal practices was historically an issue of local control and concern, and so, as with air and water pollution, the initial federal forays into regulation were designed to strengthen, yet maintain the primacy of, state authority. RCRA, like the Clean Air Act and Clean Water Act of the early 1970's, marked a shift away from state control. Under RCRA, EPA sets detailed guidelines for state regulation, using its technical expertise to develop the applicable standards and programs. Nevertheless, there remains plenty of room for state action. States are given the opportunity (and funding) to implement the federal programs once the state program is approved by EPA on an interim, then final, basis. EPA must grant final authorization once the state program is determined to be "equivalent" to the EPA's. However, the states are given authority under RCRA to write regulations which are more stringent than the federal standards, as long as they are not otherwise in conflict with the federal regulations. Once authorized, the state program acts in lieu of the federal program, though EPA has the authority to revoke its authorization if the state no longer adheres to the federal standards.

KEY PROVISIONS OF RCRA

Subtitle A: General Provisions
    § 1004Definitions

Subtitle C: Hazardous Waste
    § 3001 Identification and Listing
    § 3002 Generator Standards
    § 3003 Transporter Standards
    § 3004 Treatment, Storage, and Disposal Standards; Land-Ban;
        Corrective Action

---

[12] Pub. L. No. 98-616, 98 Stat. 3221 (codified as amended at 42 U.S.C §§ 6941-6949a). Congress had made several relatively minor changes to RCRA in 1980 in the Used Oil and Recycling Act (which covered issues relating to recycled oil) and the Solid Waste Disposal Amendments. Of greater significance was the passage in late 1980 of CERCLA, explained in Chapter 11, which addresses *past* waste disposal attitudes.

§ 3005 Permit System
§ 3006 State Programs

Subtitle D: Solid Waste

For further reading on the origins and overall structure of RCRA, *see* THE RCRA PRACTICE MANUAL (Theodore L. Garrett, ed., 1994); CHRISTOPHER HARRIS ET AL., HAZARDOUS WASTE: CONFRONTING THE CHALLENGE (1987); THE LAW OF ENVIRONMENTAL PROTECTION, (Sheldon M. Novick ed., 1987); BEYOND DUMPING: NEW STRATEGIES FOR CONTROLLING TOXIC CONTAMINATION, (Bruce Piasecki ed., 1984); EPA, RESOURCE CONSERVATION AND RECOVERY, ACT COMPLIANCE/ ENFORCEMENT MANUAL (1984).

B. A Closer Look at the Subtitle C Regulatory Program

manifest paperwork

Commonly referred to as a "cradle-to-grave" system of hazardous waste regulation, Subtitle C was part of the original hazardous waste legislation passed in 1976 and regulates the hazardous waste stream from the point of generation to the point of disposal. Most generators, transporters, and facilities, that produce, treat, and/or dispose of hazardous waste become subject to Subtitle C regulation. However, there are important exceptions and wide variations in the extent of regulation. We begin with the most important source of exceptions, the definition of hazardous (as opposed to solid) waste. As we suggested earlier, the Definitions section of the statute delimits the universe of the stringent Subtitle C regulation of hazardous waste. Therefore, it is critical both to our understanding of the statute, and to an environmental lawyer's efforts to determine the extent of a client's responsibilities.

RCRA is a stringent and relatively inflexible regulatory regime for those whose activities or waste materials fall within its structure. To a large extent, it is an all-or-nothing statute. If your waste falls within the definition, then you are fully regulated, no matter how low the relative risk. If your waste falls outside the definition, you are unregulated under Subtitle C, no matter how high the risk. Subtitle C has been referred to as "an inch wide and a mile deep." Even in the waste universe, the ratio of unregulated "solid waste" to regulated "hazardous waste" is 40 to 1, or 10 billion metric tons to 250 million metric tons.

As Barry Breen, in *Sustainable Environmental Law*, has observed:

RCRA is one of the important laws governing the manufacturing process, but it also helps control intentional disposal of products after people are finished with them. It tightly regulates hazardous waste. Many products are hazardous by design, and when they are thrown away they become hazardous waste. Paint thinner and other solvents, weed killers and bug killers, and many household cleaning agents, such as bleach and ammonia, rely on hazardous chemicals for their active ingredients. When they are discarded, they become hazardous waste.

In the industrial context, hazardous waste can be the by-product of a chemical reaction needed to make the company's product. If the by-product cannot be sold to someone with a use for it, the company is left with barrels of useless chemical mixtures on its hands, and this is hazardous waste.

RCRA governs the way this waste is reintroduced into the environment. And it matters tremendously whether the hazardous waste comes from a large factory or from small businesses and individual homes. Hazardous waste from a large factory has the full panoply of regulation: starting with time limits on how long it can be stored and the way it can be stored, all the way to expensive safeguards on how it can be buried in the ground. One EPA official estimates that under RCRA it costs $250 to $300 per ton to dispose of hazardous waste in the United States.

But RCRA is odd: it regulates industrial hazardous waste with a vengeance, but some equally dangerous chemicals that come from family households are practically unregulated. For example, paint thinner from the factory must be incinerated or buried in a specially designed landfill; under federal law, paint thinner from your basement can be thrown out with your trash. In addition, while RCRA regulates the 250 million metric tons of hazardous waste produced each year, it leaves to what are essentially voluntary state controls the 10 billion tons of waste that are not hazardous. Two former managers of EPA's RCRA program conclude that "waste currently classified as nonhazardous may look toxicologically identical to hazardous waste," and "the degree of control at the state level varies significantly, but in certain areas, such as industrial wastes, it is uniformly lax."

Another RCRA quirk: it regulates only hazardous waste, not hazardous products that cause just as much damage. For example, some pesticides can legally be applied to fields at high concentrations because the pesticides are products, but the same pesticides cannot be thrown away even in state-of-the-art landfills without first being chemically pretreated. The theory, is that FIFRA has screened these pesticides before they are applied to fields at high concentrations, so that the benefits of more food that are reaped on these fields as a result outweigh the costs of more pesticides in the environment. So the safety of the hazardous products sprayed on food depends on the FIFRA screen.

What theme is running through all this? RCRA regulates how resources are reintegrated into the environment, but only in special cases: chemicals that are "hazardous," that are no longer products and are now wastes, and that are from generators large enough to come within the regulatory system. All three criteria must be met for RCRA to apply. While RCRA regulates stringently within its borders, most returns of resources to the environment escape RCRA's safeguards.

Federal law regulates the way resources return to the environment essentially in exceptional cases only. RCRA is an example.[13]

As a consequence of this regulatory paradox, the definition of "hazardous waste" under RCRA has become the statute's key point of contention.

1. The Regulatory Definition of Solid Waste

Nothing can be a hazardous waste unless it is a solid waste,[14] that is, under both the statute and regulations, a material must first be established as a solid waste before it can be found a hazardous waste that triggers Subtitle C regulation. Moreover, the most difficult definitional problems that EPA and regulated entities encounter is the definition of solid waste, rather than the further narrowing of solid wastes to hazardous ones. This is in part because the hazard determination, as we shall see, can be reduced to a number of fairly straightforward physical tests. The difficulty in defining solid waste versus the relative ease of defining hazardous waste is also due to the broad—and by now familiar—definition of hazard in the statute.

Read § 1003(5). Now read § 1003(27), the definition of solid waste. You will notice first that "solid" includes both liquid and containerized gaseous waste. Indeed, as we will see in RCRA's land disposal restrictions, liquid "solid waste" is one of Congress' and EPA's biggest environmental concerns. You will also notice that there are several explicit exclusions from the scope of solid waste, the most important of which are domestic sewage, industrial point source wastewater subject to the Clean Water Act, irrigation return flows, and radioactive materials regulated by the Nuclear Regulatory Commission. Apart from these, however, the statutory definition is so sweeping that, as noted above, it requires some narrowing if RCRA is to achieve its other goals, most notably that of encouraging recycling.[15] Consequently, EPA's waste identification regulations take on a special degree of importance in understanding RCRA. It is simply impossible to

---

[13] Barry Breen, *Environmental Law from Resource to Recovery in* SUSTAINABLE ENVIRONMENTAL LAW 85-86 (Celia Campbell-Mohn et al., eds., 1993).

[14] For a through treatment of the hazardous waste identification problem, *see* John-Mark Stensvaag, *Hazardous Wastes: Statutory Definition and Regulatory Criteria, in* 1 HAZARDOUS WASTE LAW AND PRACTICE (1993).

[15] EPA's regulatory exclusions from hazardous or solid waste in 40 C.F.R. § 261.4—reclaimed secondary materials returned to the original process, for example—are related to recycling.

determine whether a material is a solid waste without the regulations; the statute alone provides almost no clue.[16]

NOTES

1. As you read this chapter, ask yourself whether Subtitle C (and RCRA generally) is a cradle-to-grave system, or, in Professor's Jeffrey Gaba's apt phrase, a "deathbed-to-grave" system. For example, compare the bulk of §§ 3002 through 3003 (generators and transporters) with 3001 and 3004 (hazardous waste identification and TSDFs). Where and how are waste minimization and pollution prevention addressed? Is it possible to influence waste generation through restrictions on disposal? How? Is it an efficient way to influence generation?

2. RCRA's definitional scheme cannot be understood without access to and direct reference to the applicable regulations. There are several simple ways to obtain them. One is to photocopy the relevant sections, 40 C.F.R. §§ 261.1-261.4, 261.10-261.24, from the Code of Federal Regulations in your library. Another is to download them from EPA's website, http://www.epa.gov/epacfr40/chapt-I.info. Still another is to print them from Westlaw or Lexis. However you obtain them, it is essential that you familiarize yourself with the actual text of the identification regulations.

The difficulties of defining "solid waste" are best understood in the context of recycling. EPA wants to encourage recycling, and clearly one way to do that is to exempt recycled material from the stringent hazardous waste restrictions. On the other hand, the high cost of hazardous waste disposal puts pressure on generators to create sham recycling techniques, such as road filling, burning, or backfilling, that are really disposal methods. Another fairly obviously inappropriate circumvention is the so-called speculative accumulation of materials, which is often really long-term storage on-site. At the other end of the spectrum is the reuse of materials inside a closed-loop production process. Unquestionably, it is far better for a potential waste generator to recover end-of-process residual materials and return them to the front of the process, than for them to be discarded as waste, no matter what precautions are taken with them.

The difficulties arise, as always, in between the extremes. One such difficulty involves end-of-process residues that are not fed directly back into the manufacturing process (as in a closed-loop system), but that require additional processing before they can be reintroduced into the process which originally produced them or into another industrial process. This description covers many activities that most of us would consider worthwhile recycling.

---

[16] *See* John-Mark Stensvaag, *Hazardous Wastes: Statutory Definition and Regulatory Criteria*, in 1 HAZARDOUS WASTE LAW AND PRACTICE § 5.1 (1993) ("The statutory language set forth *in* the 1976 enactment provided only the barest outline of a hazardous waste definition. Congress recognized that the definition task was incomplete and accordingly, established a two-step administrative process for fleshing out the meaning of hazardous waste.").

At the core of this debate is the issue of whether waste management controls, designed to protect health and the environment, should apply to the management of recycled "secondary materials," such as industrial by-products, "post-consumer materials," used electronic equipment, and spent materials that are amenable to beneficial use or reuse. If materials recovered or diverted from the solid waste stream are considered "waste" during collection, transport, storage, and recycling, such activities will be stigmatized. Interstate and international transport of such materials may become difficult. Citizens may object to the siting of recovery activities, and recyclable materials may be subject to storage and other regulations that will increase the costs of recycling. Companies may find it difficult to carry out programs of "product stewardship," taking back and recycling used products. Thus, calling recyclable materials "waste" may impede beneficial recycling activities, increasing rather than diminishing the so-called waste crisis.

J.T. Smith II, *The Solid Waste Definitional Dilemma*, 9 NAT. RESOURCES & ENV'T. 3, 3 (Fall 1994).

This issue arose in the case below. EPA had excluded from the definition of solid waste "secondary materials that are reclaimed and returned to the original process or processes in which they were generated." 40 C.F.R. § 261.4(a)(8). "Secondary materials" are identified as spent materials, sludges, by-products, commercial products, and scrap metal. These materials are considered "solid waste" when they are disposed of, burned for energy recovery or used to produce a fuel, reclaimed, or accumulated speculatively. If a material constitutes a "solid waste" it is subject to RCRA regulation *unless* it is directly used as an ingredient or an effective substitute for a commercial product, or is returned as a raw material substitute to its original manufacturing process.[17]

AMERICAN MINING CONGRESS v. EPA

907 F.2d 1179 (D.C. Cir. 1990)

HARRY T. EDWARDS, Circuit Judge:

Petitioners in these consolidated cases seek review of a final rule, *see* 53 Fed. Reg. 35,412 (1988) (codified at 40 C.F.R. pts. 261 and 302 (1989)) (the "1988 Rule"), promulgated by the Environmental Protection Agency ("EPA" or "agency"). In the 1988 Rule, EPA decided to relist as "hazardous" six wastes generated from metal smelting operations. Petitioners argue . . . in several respects the agency failed to offer an adequate reasoned explanation for its decision . . . .

* * *

As for petitioners' contentions regarding the adequacy of the agency's justifications for the 1988 Rule, we find merit in certain of the claims that

---

[17] *See* American Mining Congress v. EPA, 824 F.2d 1177 (D.C. Cir. 1987).

have been advanced. Accordingly, we are constrained to remand for further consideration and explanation by the agency with respect to the bases for the relistings of certain of the smelting wastes.

I. BACKGROUND

A. Statutory and Regulatory Framework

Subtitle C of RCRA requires EPA to create a comprehensive regulatory scheme for the treatment, storage, and disposal of hazardous wastes. Under RCRA, EPA must "develop and promulgate criteria for identifying the characteristics of" those "solid" wastes that are also "hazardous" wastes.

Pursuant to this statutory mandate, the agency has adopted a scheme under which it deems a solid waste hazardous if the waste meets either of two conditions. One condition is that the agency has, after a rulemaking proceeding, specifically listed the waste as hazardous.[18] The other condition is that the waste satisfies one or more of the following criteria that the agency has, by regulation, identified for hazardous waste: ignitability, corrosivity, reactivity, and extraction procedure toxicity.

Either of these two conditions is sufficient for the agency to deem a "solid" waste "hazardous." When the agency lists or identifies a waste as hazardous, the waste's treatment, storage, and disposal is usually regulated by permit.

B. Procedural Background

Both this court and the agency have fully rehearsed the complex procedural history of this case. *See* Environmental Defense Fund v. EPA, 852 F.2d 1316, 1318-24 (D.C.Cir.1988), *cert. denied*, 489 U.S. 1011 (1989); 1988 Rule, 53 Fed. Reg. at 35,412-13. We therefore need reconstruct here only a skeletal portion of the history.

In 1980, after a rulemaking, the agency listed as "hazardous" six wastes ("six wastes") generated from primary metal smelters. *See* 45 Fed. Reg. 33,066, 33,124, 47,832-34 (1980) ("1980 Rule"). EPA listed the wastes pursuant to 40 C.F.R. § 261.11(a)(3), because they contained one or more of the hazardous constituents listed in 40 C.F.R. pt. 261, App. VIII. The six wastes are as follows:

(1) Waste from Primary Copper Smelting and Refining, EPA Hazardous Waste No. K064 ("K064");

(2) Waste from Primary Lead Smelting, EPA Hazardous Waste No. K065 ("K065");

(3) Waste from Primary Zinc Smelting and Refining, EPA Hazardous Waste No. K066 ("K066");

(4) Waste from Primary Aluminum Reduction (spent potliner), EPA Hazardous Waste No. K088 ("K088");

---

[18] The agency has, in turn, established three grounds upon which to list a waste as hazardous, including a finding that the waste contains any of the toxic constituents appearing in 40 C.F.R. pt. 261, App. VIII. *See* 40 C.F.R. § 261.11(a)(3)—EDS.

(5) Waste from Ferrochromiumsilicon Production, EPA Hazardous Waste No. K090 ("K090"); and

(6) Waste from Ferrochromium Production, EPA Hazardous Waste No. K091 ("K091").

In October of 1980, in response to congressional enactment of the so-called "Bevill Amendment," EPA suspended its listing of the six wastes.

* * *

[A subsequent court order required EPA to repromulgate the listing of the six wastes, because the Bevill Amendment did not apply to them. In repromulgating the listings in 1988,] EPA stated that its "decision to list these wastes today is based on its evaluation of the listing criteria (*i.e.*, these wastes are hazardous) as well as the court finding that these wastes are not Bevill wastes," 1988 Rule, 53 Fed. Reg. at 35,413 n. 3, and that its "determination that these wastes are hazardous is based on its evaluation of the hazardousness of these wastes in 1980," *id.* at 35,417.

* * *

II. ANALYSIS

A. Introduction

Petitioners offer three arguments to show that the agency's listing of the six wastes as "hazardous" in the 1988 Rule is unlawful. First, they challenge the agency's interpretation of the term "discarded" in RCRA, *see* 42 U.S.C. § 6903(27). Relying principally on the decision of this court in *American Mining Congress v. EPA,* 824 F.2d 1177, 1179 (D.C.Cir.1987) ("AMC "), petitioners argue that three of the six wastes are not "discarded," and therefore are not "solid wastes," and therefore cannot be "hazardous" wastes within the meaning of RCRA . . . .

* * *

C. EPA's Interpretation of the Term "Discarded"

As we have noted in a prior decision, EPA's regulatory authority under RCRA Subtitle C "extends only to the regulation of 'hazardous waste.' Because 'hazardous waste' is defined as a subset of 'solid waste,' . . . the scope of EPA's jurisdiction is limited to those materials that constitute 'solid waste.'" AMC, 824 F.2d at 1179 (footnote omitted). Petitioners argue that three of the six wastes at issue in this case (K064, K065, and K066) are not "solid" wastes, because they are not "discarded" within meaning of RCRA, but are instead "beneficially reused in mineral processing operations."

The primary smelting operations that generate these three wastes produce large volumes of wastewater that the smelting company must treat before discharging [ ]. Many smelting operations use surface impoundments to collect, treat, and dispose of the wastewater. These impoundments continuously produce sludges, which precipitate from the wastewater. *See* 42 U.S.C. § 6903(26A) (defining "sludge" to cover "any solid, semisolid or liquid waste generated from a municipal, commercial, or industrial wastewater treatment plant").

Petitioners' basic claim is that sludges from wastewater that are stored in surface impoundments and that may at some time in the future be reclaimed are not "discarded." The agency, however, exercising its expert judgment, has concluded that, because these sludges are the product of wastewater and are stored in impoundments that threaten harm to the health and environs of those living nearby, these materials are "discarded."

Chevron, U.S.A., Inc. v. Natural Resources Defense Council, Inc., 467 U.S. 837 (1984),[19] guides our review of the agency's interpretation of RCRA. Under *Chevron's* well-settled two-step test, we begin by considering "whether Congress has directly spoken to the precise question at issue"; if it has, then we "must give effect to the unambiguously expressed intent of Congress." If Congress has not directly spoken to the precise issue, then we will defer to the agency's reading of the statute as long as it is "permissible," that is, "so long as it is reasonable and consistent with the statutory purpose." *Ohio v. Department of the Interior*, 880 F.2d 432, 441 (D.C.Cir.1989).

This court has recently had occasion to consider the meaning of the term "discarded" in RCRA under the first step of *Chevron* analysis. In *American Petroleum Inst. v. EPA*, 906 F.2d 729 (D.C.Cir.1990) ("*API*"), we concluded that the term "discarded" was marked by the kind of ambiguity demanding resolution by the agency's delegated lawmaking powers. Petitioners direct us to nothing whatsoever in the language, overall structure, or legislative history of the statute, nor do we know of anything therein, that shows the term "discarded" to be any less ambiguous regarding sludges stored in surface impoundments than it was regarding the materials at issue in *API*.

To support their claim that RCRA forecloses EPA regulation of these sludges, petitioners invoke this court's decision in *AMC*. At issue in *AMC* was whether EPA could, under RCRA, treat as "solid wastes" "materials that are recycled and reused in an *ongoing* manufacturing or industrial process" (emphasis in original). We held that the agency could not treat such materials as solid wastes, because they "have not yet become part of the waste disposal problem; rather, *they are destined for beneficial reuse or recycling in a continuous process by the generating industry itself*." (emphasis in original). Because such materials were never "disposed of, abandoned, or thrown away," we concluded, they were not "discarded" within the meaning of RCRA. *Id.* at 1193.

Petitioners read *AMC* too broadly. *AMC's* holding concerned only materials that are "destined for *immediate reuse* in another phase of the industry's ongoing production process," (emphasis added), and that "have not yet become part of the waste disposal problem." Nothing in *AMC* prevents the agency from treating as "discarded" the wastes at issue in this case, which are managed in land disposal units that are part of wastewater treatment systems, which have therefore become "part of the waste disposal problem," and which are not part of ongoing industrial processes. Indeed, *API* explicitly rejected the very claim that petitioners assert in this case,

---

[19] *Chevron* is excerpted in Chapter 4, Judicial Role, *supra*.

namely, that under RCRA, potential reuse of a material prevents the agency from classifying it as "discarded."

Because Congress has not directly spoken to the precise question at issue, we must consider whether the agency's interpretation of the term "discarded" was "permissible," that is, "reasonable and consistent with the statutory purpose." In this case, the agency determined that material placed in wastewater treatment surface impoundments where it is "capable of posing a substantial present or potential hazard to human health or the environment when improperly treated, stored, transported or disposed of, or otherwise managed," 40 C.F.R. § 261.11(a)(3), by leaching into the ground, is "discarded material," and hence a "solid waste." As the agency notes, because of their propensity to leak hazardous materials into the environment, surface impoundments are a central focus of RCRA's regime. See, *e.g.*, 42 U.S.C. §§ 6901(b)(7),[20] 6924(k),[21] and (o), 6925(j). In addition, Congress made clear in the legislative history of RCRA its concern to regulate hazardous materials in surface impoundments. See, *e.g.*, H.R. REP. NO. 1491, 94TH CONG., 2D SESS. 2-3 (1976); S. REP. NO. 284, 98TH CONG., 1ST SESS. 13-16 (1983). In light of this evidence, we conclude that the agency's interpretation of "discarded" is both reasonable and consistent with the statutory purposes of RCRA.

* * *

III. CONCLUSION

The agency did not exceed its statutory authority in treating the six wastes as "discarded," and thus subject to RCRA Subtitle C regulation . . . . However, EPA failed in the 1988 Rule to articulate a rational connection between the data on which it purportedly relied and its decision to reject the petitioners' admittedly significant challenges. Therefore, we remand to the agency for fuller explanation of its decision to list K064, K065, K066, and, in some respects, K090 and K091.

So ordered.

———

The following case defines what is legitimate and what is sham recycling, with dramatic results for the defendant.

---

[20] [C]ertain classes of land disposal facilities are not capable of assuring long-term containment of certain hazardous wastes, and to avoid substantial risk to human health and the environment, reliance on land disposal should be minimized or eliminated, and land disposal, particularly landfill and surface impoundment, should be the least favored method for managing hazardous wastes.

[21] For the purposes of this section, the term "land disposal", when used with respect to a specified hazardous waste, shall be deemed to include, but not be limited to, any placement of such hazardous waste in a landfill, surface impoundment, waste pile, injection well, land treatment facility, salt dome formation, salt bed formation, or underground mine or cave.

UNITED STATES V. SELF

2 F.3d 1071 (10th Cir. 1993)

BALDOCK, Circuit Judge.

Defendant Steven M. Self appeals his convictions on four counts of violating the Resource Conservation and Recovery Act ("RCRA"), 42 U.S.C. § 6928(d), one count of mail fraud, 18 U.S.C. § 1341, and one count of conspiracy to violate RCRA, the Clean Air Act ("CAA"), and the Clean Water Act ("CWA"). 18 U.S.C. § 371. Three of the four substantive RCRA counts (counts 2, 3 and 4) and the mail fraud count (count 7) relate to the diversion of a shipment of natural gas condensate destined for a hazardous waste treatment, storage and disposal facility to a gas station, blending it with gasoline and selling it to the public as automotive fuel. The remaining substantive RCRA count (count 8) relates to the storage of twenty-nine drums of waste material in violation of a RCRA permit. The conspiracy count (count 1) relates to the activity supporting the other counts as well as unpermitted burning of waste and unpermitted dumping of waste water. Defendant raises a number of issues on appeal, and we have jurisdiction under 28 U.S.C. § 1291.

I.

The record reveals the following facts. In 1981, Defendant and Steven Miller formed EkoTek, Inc. Defendant provided most of the capital and became an 85% shareholder and EkoTek's President. Miller held the remaining 15% of the stock and became Vice-President. EkoTek purchased an industrial facility in Salt Lake City, Utah. Using Miller's technical expertise, EkoTek began re-refining used oil into marketable products. Defendant and Miller managed EkoTek on a day-to-day basis with Defendant primarily responsible for the financial aspects of the business, and Miller primarily responsible for the technical aspects.

The facility purchased by EkoTek was an authorized RCRA interim status treatment, storage and disposal facility. *See* 42 U.S.C. § 6925(e)(1). In 1981 and again in 1982, Defendant signed and submitted an updated part A RCRA permit application. *See* 40 C.F.R. § 270.13 (1992). In 1983, Defendant signed and submitted a part B RCRA permit application. *See id.* § 270.14. By submitting the permit applications, EkoTek could continue operating as a treatment, storage and disposal facility under RCRA interim status, pending its RCRA permit approval. *See* 42 U.S.C. § 6925(e)(1). In November 1986, EkoTek began marketing itself as a hazardous waste recycling facility. Defendant and Miller prepared a letter and sent it to hazardous waste brokers and generators which indicated that EkoTek was licensed and prepared to accept a variety of hazardous wastes for recycling at its facility.

In April 1987, a representative of Southern California Gas Company ("SCGC"), met with Miller at EkoTek and discussed EkoTek disposing of SCGC's natural gas pipeline condensate. The parties agreed that the condensate was hazardous waste and should, therefore, be transported and handled under a RCRA manifest. Miller indicated that EkoTek could dispose of the natural gas condensate by burning it as fuel in EkoTek's onsite process heaters or boilers. SCGC subsequently contracted with and agreed to pay EkoTek "to transport, burn, and/or dispose of" natural gas condensate for $2.50 per gallon.

Shortly thereafter, an EkoTek tanker truck driver picked up a shipment of natural gas condensate from a SCGC facility in Los Angeles, California. The driver had been instructed by his supervisor to pick up the shipment and bring it back to EkoTek. As was his routine practice, the driver stopped at a gas station in Barstow, California, which was owned by Defendant, and telephoned his supervisor. On instructions from Defendant, the supervisor told the driver to leave the trailers containing the natural gas condensate at the gas station and return to Los Angeles to pick up an unrelated shipment. Defendant telephoned the gas station manager and instructed him to blend the natural gas condensate with gasoline in a 5-10% mixture and add an octane booster. The gasoline and condensate mixture was then sold to the public as automotive fuel. On Defendant's instructions, Miller told EkoTek's Refinery Operations Manager to sign the manifest to indicate that the natural gas condensate shipment had been received at EkoTek and to falsify EkoTek's operating log accordingly. A copy of the manifest was mailed to SCGC.

In early 1987, EkoTek began receiving fifty-five gallon drums of waste material from different sources. Defendant instructed an employee to store the drums in the south warehouse. When the south warehouse filled up, Defendant instructed the employee to store the drums in the east warehouse. The employee was also instructed by his immediate supervisor to scrape the "hazardous waste" label off of each drum, paint a number on the drum, and list it on an inventory sheet. In July 1987, the State of Utah, pursuant to its delegated RCRA authority, see 42 U.S.C. § 6926(b), granted EkoTek a RCRA permit which prohibited EkoTek from storing hazardous waste in the east warehouse. Defendant discussed this illegal storage practice with Miller. Defendant's office at EkoTek had a view of the doors to the east warehouse which were usually left open and through which stored fifty-five gallon drums were visible. On several occasions, Defendant ordered the doors to the east warehouse closed after being informed that inspectors would be at the facility.

Among the drums stored in the east warehouse were seventeen drums of waste from Avery Label and twelve drums of waste from Reynolds Metals both of which were shipped to EkoTek under RCRA manifests identifying the materials as hazardous wastes. Avery Label's manager of safety and environmental affairs testified that the waste sent to EkoTek was a mixture of ultraviolet curer ink waste, solvent ink waste, and cleaning solvent. Ultraviolet curer ink has a flash point exceeding 200°F and is, therefore, not considered hazardous due to ignitability. See 40 C.F.R. § 261.21(a) (1992). Solvent ink, on the other hand, has a flash point well below 140°F and is, therefore, considered hazardous due to ignitability. *See id.* The Material Safety Data Sheets ("MSDS") for the type of solvent inks that Avery Label used in 1987 indicated that the solvent inks had a flash point of between 16°F and 116°F. According to the Avery Label representative, mixing solvent ink waste with ultraviolet curer ink waste does not raise the flash point because the vapors of the solvent ink waste, which determine its ignitability, rise to the top. In his opinion, the waste sent to EkoTek had a flash point of between 70°F to 100°F. The hazardous waste broker who had arranged for the disposal of the Avery Label waste personally observed the waste sent to EkoTek and recognized it as a solvent-based ink due to its smell.

The RCRA manifest which accompanied the shipment of the Reynolds Metals waste to EkoTek indicated that the material was a mixture of "MEK" (methyl ethyl ketone) and a spray residue. MEK is a listed hazardous waste, *see* 40 C.F.R. § 261.33(f) (1992), and it has a flash point of 23°F. The spray residue has a flash point of 100°F.

In April 1988, the hazardous waste broker responsible for shipping both the Avery Label and Reynolds Metals wastes to EkoTek visited the EkoTek facility after having been informed that drums of waste which he brokered had never been processed and were being illegally stored at the facility. By this time, EkoTek was no longer in business, and Petro Chemical Recycling, with which Defendant had no affiliation, had taken over operation of the facility. The broker observed "a lot of drums" being stored in the east warehouse, none of which were labeled but were crudely marked with a number. Using EkoTek's inventory sheet and recognizing the drums by their distinctive color, the broker identified the seventeen drums of Avery Label waste and the twelve drums of Reynolds Metals waste. He subsequently arranged for Marine Shale Processors to dispose of these as well as several other drums of waste. On documentation submitted to Marine Shale Processors, the broker indicated that the materials were from four types of waste streams, and he identified the material in twenty-four of the 128 barrels as "UV ink waste." Marine Shale Processors tested a sample from each of the four types of waste streams and determined that each type of identified waste had a flash point below 70°F.

II.

With regard to the substantive RCRA counts and the mail fraud count relating to the diversion of the natural gas condensate to the Barstow gas station (counts 2, 3, 4 and 7), Defendant argues that natural gas condensate, when burned for energy recovery, is not a hazardous waste subject to regulation under RCRA. Therefore, Defendant claims the district court erred by denying Defendant's pretrial motion to dismiss, by denying Defendant's motion for a judgment of acquittal, and in its instruction to the jury defining hazardous waste. Because this issue is a question of law, our review is de novo.

A.

RCRA defines "hazardous waste," in relevant part as "a solid waste, or combination of solid wastes, which because of its quantity, concentration, or physical, chemical, or infectious characteristics may ... pose a substantial present or potential hazard to human health or the environment when improperly treated, stored, transported, or disposed of, or otherwise managed." 42 U.S.C. § 6903(5)(B). Natural gas condensate is a relatively volatile substance, having a flash point of less than 140°F and, therefore, is "hazardous" as contemplated by RCRA. *See* 40 C.F.R. §§ 261.3(a)(2)(i), 261.21(a)(1) (1992). Nonetheless, "for a waste to be classified as hazardous, it must first qualify as a solid waste under RCRA."

RCRA defines "solid waste" to include "any ... discarded material, including ... liquid ... material resulting from industrial, commercial, mining, and agricultural operations, and from community activities...."[22] 42 U.S.C. § 6903(27). RCRA regulations narrow the definition of "solid waste" to "any discarded material that is not excluded by § 261.4(a) or that is not excluded by a variance granted under §§ 260.30 and 260.31." 40 C.F.R. § 261.2(a)(1) (1992). As there is no contention that natural gas condensate is subject to the § 261.4(a) exclusion, or that it has been granted a variance under § 260.30 and 260.31, whether natural gas condensate is a solid waste turns on whether it is a discarded material.

RCRA regulations define "discarded material" to include material which is "[a]bandoned" or "[r]ecycled."[23] *Id.* § 261.2(a)(2). A material is abandoned, *inter alia*, by being "[b]urned or incinerated."[24] *Id.* § 261.2(b)(2). A material is recycled, inter alia, by being "[b]urn[ed] for energy recovery" or "[u]sed to produce a fuel or are otherwise contained in fuels."[25] *Id.*

---

[22] RCRA also defines "solid waste" to include "any garbage, refuse, [and] sludge from a waste treatment plant, water supply treatment plant, or air pollution control facility . . . ." 42 U.S.C. § 6903(27). There is no contention that natural gas condensate is any of these types of materials.

[23] The regulations also define "discarded material" to include "any material which is . . . [c]onsidered inherently wastelike." 40 C.F.R. § 261.2(a)(2)(iii) (1992). It is undisputed that natural gas condensate is not an inherently wastelike material.

[24] A material is also abandoned if it is "[d]isposed of," 40 C.F.R. § 261.2(b)(1) (1992), or "[a]ccumulated, stored, or treated (but not recycled) before or in lieu of being abandoned by being disposed of, burned or incinerated." *Id.* § 261.2(b)(3). The determination of whether a material is a solid waste by virtue of being disposed of leads us in circles in that the statutory and regulatory definitions of "disposal" depend in part on whether the material is a solid waste. *See* 42 U.S.C. § 6903(3); 40 C.F.R. § 260.10 (1992) [internal citations omitted]. Nevertheless, it is undisputed that Defendant did not cause the natural gas condensate to be "discharge[d], deposit[ed], inject[ed], dump[ed], spill[ed], leak[ed], or plac[ed] . . . into or on any land or water." *See* 42 U.S.C. § 6903(3); 40 C.F.R. § 260.10 (1992). Therefore, Defendant did not dispose of the natural gas condensate. Similarly, there is no contention that the natural gas condensate was "[a]ccumulated, stored, or treated (but not recycled) before or in lieu of being abandoned by being disposed of, burned or incinerated." *Id.* § 261.2(b)(3).

[25] The regulations also consider certain materials recycled when the material is "[u]sed in a manner constituting disposal," 40 C.F.R. § 261.2(c)(1) (1992), "[r]eclaimed," *id.* § 261.2(c)(3), or "[a]ccumulated speculatively." *Id.* § 261.2(c)(4). It is undisputed that the

§ 261.2(c)(2). Any material that is abandoned by being burned or incinerated is considered a solid waste. *See id.* § 261.2(b). However, we note only certain types of materials that are recycled by being burned for energy recovery are considered solid wastes. *See id.* § 261.2(c).

The only type of material which is considered solid waste when it is recycled by being burned for energy recovery and which might encompass natural gas condensate is a "[b]y-product exhibiting a characteristic of hazardous waste."[26] *See* 40 C.F.R. § 261.2 (Table 1) (1992). As noted earlier, natural gas condensate exhibits the ignitability characteristic of hazardous waste; thus, the issue turns on whether natural gas condensate is a "by-product" as defined by RCRA regulations. RCRA regulations define "by-product" as "a material that is not one of the primary products of a production process and is not solely or separately produced by the production process" exclusive of "co-product[s]." 40 C.F.R. § 261.1(c)(3) (1992). While RCRA's definition of "by-product" is certainly subject to reasonable interpretation, the EPA directly addressed the issue of whether natural gas condensate is a by-product in its 1985 comment to its current regulatory definition of "solid waste":

> Off-specification fuels burned for energy recovery . . . are not by-products, and so would not be considered to be wastes under this provision. An example [is] natural gas pipeline condensate. The condensate contains many of the same hydrocarbons found in liquefied natural gas, and certain higher hydrocarbons that also have energy value. It is generated in the pipeline transmission of natural gas. This condensate is not considered to be waste when burned for energy recovery.[27]

---

natural gas condensate was not used in a manner constituting disposal, *see supra* reclaimed, *see* 40 C.F.R. § 261.1(c)(4) (1992), or accumulated speculatively, *see Id.* § 261.1(c)(8).

[26] The remaining types of materials which, when they are recycled by being burned for energy recovery, are considered solid wastes are "[s]pent materials," listed or characteristic "[s]ludges," listed "[b]y-products," listed "[c]ommercial chemical products," and "[s]crap metal." 40 C.F.R. § 261.2 (Table 1) (1992). Natural gas condensate is clearly not a spent material, sludge, or scrap metal as defined by the regulations. *See id.* § 261.1(c)(1) (defining "spent material" as "any material that has been used and as a result of contamination can no longer serve the purpose for which it was produced without processing"); *id.* § 260.10 (defining "sludge" as "any solid, semi-solid, or liquid waste generated from a municipal, commercial, or industrial wastewater treatment plant, or air pollution control facility exclusive of the treated effluent from a wastewater treatment plant"); *id.* § 261.1(c)(6) (defining "scrap metal" as "bits and pieces of metal parts . . . which when worn or superfluous can be recycled"). Moreover, the government, in this case, has never relied on, nor does it direct us to, anything in the regulations indicating that natural gas condensate is either a listed commercial chemical product, *see id.* § 261.33, or a listed by-product, *see id.* §§ 261.31, 261.32.

[27] In its 1983 proposed rule defining "solid waste," only listed by-products were considered solid wastes when recycled. *See* 48 Fed. Reg. 14,481 (Figure 4) (Apr. 4, 1983); *see also* 50 Fed. Reg. 629 (Jan. 4, 1985). However, the 1985 final rule "determined that all by-products . . . are solid wastes when burned as fuels or used to produce a fuel." 50 Fed. Reg. 629 (Jan. 4, 1985). In adopting this final rule, the EPA stated that by-products are "unlike commercial fuels" and are "significantly different in composition from fossil fuels." *Id.* Distinguishing

50 Fed. Reg. 630 n. 18 (Jan. 4, 1985). Relying on this EPA statement, Defendant argues that so long as natural gas condensate is burned for energy recovery, it is not a by-product and, therefore, not a discarded material by virtue of being recycled, and, therefore, not a solid waste, and, therefore, not a hazardous waste under RCRA.

The government argued below and continues to argue on appeal that natural gas condensate is hazardous waste if it is used in a manner which was not the original intended manner or normal intended use for that material within the industry. In support of this argument, the government first directs us to the EPA's long-standing distinction between legitimate and sham burning for energy recovery. *See* 50 Fed. Reg. 630 (Jan. 4, 1985); 48 Fed. Reg. 14,482 (Apr. 4, 1983); 48 Fed. Reg. 11,157-58 (Mar. 16, 1983); 45 Fed. Reg. 33,093 (May 19, 1980). The government then points to an EPA comment stating that commercial chemical products when burned for energy recovery are considered solid wastes because this is a manner of recycling which differs from their normal manner of use. *See* 50 Fed. Reg. 618 (Jan. 4, 1985). Next, the government relies on an EPA statement that the status of "non-listed commercial chemical products . . . would be the same as those listed in § 261.33—[t]hat is, they are not considered solid wastes when recycled except when they are recycled in ways that differ from their normal manner of use." 50 Fed. Reg. 14,216, 14,219 (Apr. 11, 1985).

By focusing on the EPA distinction between legitimate and sham burning for energy recovery, the government appears to be arguing that the natural gas condensate was not recycled within the meaning of the regulations and, therefore, was abandoned by being burned or incinerated. This distinction would undermine Defendant's argument because any abandoned material is considered solid waste. *See* 40 C.F.R. § 261.2(b) (1992). On the other hand, by focusing on the EPA's rationale for classifying commercial chemical products which are burned for energy recovery as solid waste, the government's argument also suggests that natural gas condensate is a non-listed commercial chemical product, *see generally supra* note 5, and, therefore, must be recycled in a normal manner in order to not be considered a hazardous waste. This argument would also undermine Defendant's argument because recycling commercial chemical products by burning them for energy recovery is not a normal manner of use and, therefore, the natural gas condensate, to the extent it is a commercial chemical product, is a solid waste. The government does not distinguish between these two alternative arguments but rather collapses the EPA's distinction between legitimate and sham burning for energy recovery with the EPA's rationale for classifying commercial chemical products which are burned for energy recovery as solid wastes. In doing so, the government combines otherwise unrelated EPA comments concerning distinct provisions within the regulatory definition of

---

between by-products and fossil fuels, the EPA noted that by-products "are waste-like because they are residual materials containing toxic constituents not ordinarily found in fossil fuels." *Id*. It was in this context that the EPA singled out natural gas condensate as an example of an off-specification fuel that is not a by-product. *Id*. at 630 n. 18.

"solid waste" and misapplies these EPA comments to the facts of this case, as we discuss below.

1.

The legitimate versus sham distinction first arose in 1980 when the EPA defined "solid waste" to include "materials which have served their original intended purpose and are sometimes discarded." 45 Fed. Reg. 33,093 (May 19, 1980). *See also* 48 Fed. Reg. 14,475 (Apr. 4, 1983). Under this definition, "virtually all . . . secondary materials" were considered solid wastes. 50 Fed. Reg. 618 (Jan. 4, 1985). However, the EPA exempted from regulation all recycling activity and the transportation and storage of non-sludges and non-listed hazardous waste which were recycled, *see* 48 Fed. Reg. 11,157 (Mar. 16, 1983); 45 Fed. Reg. 33,105 (May 19, 1980), and recognized that "burning of hazardous wastes as fuels can be a type of recycling activity exempted from regulation." 48 Fed. Reg. 11, 157-58 (Mar. 16, 1983). Expressing concern about, inter alia, the "burning of organic wastes that have little or no heat value in industrial boilers under the guise of energy recovery," 45 Fed. Reg. 33,093 (May 19, 1980), the EPA adopted a policy that in order to fall within the exemption, the burning must "constitute legitimate, and not sham, recycling." 48 Fed. Reg. 11,158 (Mar. 16, 1983); *see also* 45 Fed. Reg. 33,093 (May 19, 1980) (recognizing exemption as "temporary deferral" and noting that it "is confined to bona fide 'legitimate' and 'beneficial' uses and recycling of hazardous wastes").

In 1985, the EPA amended its regulatory definition of "solid waste" to substantially its present form which asks "both what a material is and how it is being recycled before knowing whether it is a solid waste." 50 Fed. Reg. 616 (Jan. 4, 1985). Following the 1985 amendment, the EPA's distinction between legitimate and sham burning became significant, not only by continuing to determine the applicability of the recycling exemption, but also by determining whether a material is being burned or incinerated—*i.e.* burned for destruction—and, therefore, abandoned, or is being burned for energy recovery and, therefore, recycled. *See id.* at 630.

Contrary to the government's argument, the EPA has never distinguished legitimate from sham burning for energy recovery based on whether the burning was the original intended use or normal manner of use of the material within the industry. The "primary" factor in distinguishing legitimate from sham burning for energy recovery is "the energy value of the hazardous waste being . . . burned." 48 Fed. Reg. 11,158 (Mar. 16, 1983); *see also* 56 Fed. Reg. 7183 (Feb. 21, 1991) ("5,000 BTU/lb limit generally considered heretofore to be the minimum for a legitimate hazardous waste fuel"); 50 Fed. Reg. 630 (Jan. 4, 1985) ("burning of low energy hazardous wastes as alleged fuels is not considered to be burning for legitimate energy recovery"). As the EPA stated, "[i]f the wastes being burned have only *de minimis* energy value, the burning cannot recover sufficient energy to characterize the practice as legitimate recycling . . . . [T]he wastes, for practical purposes are being burned to be destroyed." 48 Fed. Reg. 11,158

(Mar. 10, 1983). Natural gas condensate has a relatively high energy value, and the government conceded at oral argument that the natural gas condensate could have been burned for legitimate energy recovery in the boiler or industrial furnace at EkoTek.[28]

The government's reliance on the EPA statement that commercial chemical products, when burned for energy recovery, are solid wastes because this manner of recycling differs from their normal manner of use is completely misplaced. In this statement, the EPA was not distinguishing legitimate from sham recycling methods. Rather, the EPA was explaining its rationale for classifying commercial chemical products as solid waste when they are recycled by being burned for energy recovery. Specifically, the EPA stated that:

> Although [commercial chemical products] . . . ordinarily are not wastes when recycled . . . we are including them as wastes when they are recycled in ways that differ from their normal manner of use, namely, when they are used in a manner constituting disposal, or when they are burned for energy recovery (assuming these materials are neither a pesticide nor a commercial fuel).

50 Fed. Reg. 618 (Jan. 4, 1985) (internal citation omitted). This EPA comment merely explains why the EPA considers commercial chemical products which are legitimately recycled by being burned for energy recovery to be solid wastes even though commercial chemical products which are recycled by other methods, namely reclamation and speculative

---

[28] The EPA has recognized that the "nature of the device in which the wastes are being burned . . . could be significant" to whether "particular burning operations are within the scope of the recycling exemption." *Id.* However, the question here is not whether the natural gas condensate was exempted from regulation as a "recyclable material," *see* 40 C.F.R. § 261.6(a)(2)(ii) (1992), but whether the natural gas condensate was a solid waste as defined under 40 C.F.R. § 261.2 (1992) and, therefore, subject to regulation in the first place. Section 261.6(a)(2)(ii), setting forth the recycling exemption, specifically limits the exemption to "[h]azardous wastes burned for energy recovery in boilers and industrial furnaces that are not regulated under subpart O of part 264 or 265 of this chapter . . . ." *Id.* § 261.6(a)(2)(ii). Notably, § 261.2, which defines solid waste, does not require that material be burned in a boiler or industrial furnace to be burned for energy recovery and, therefore, recycled. Moreover, when the EPA noted that its 1983 sham recycling policy would control the question of whether a material was burned or incinerated and, therefore, abandoned or burned for energy recovery and, therefore, recycled, the EPA specifically characterized the policy as being based on the energy level of the waste being burned. *See* 50 Fed. Reg. 630 (Jan. 4, 1985). This is not to say that the nature of the device in which the material is burned is completely irrelevant to whether the material is recycled by being burned for energy recovery or abandoned by being burned or incinerated. High energy materials burned in an incinerator may not be considered to be recycled because an incinerator's capacity to retrieve the energy from the material is limited. Alternatively, low-energy materials burned in a boiler or industrial furnace may not be considered to be recycled due to their limited energy value. In either case, the EPA considers such materials to be burned for destruction. In this case however, we have a high energy material—natural gas condensate—burned in the internal combustion engines of automobiles. While some internal combustion engines are better than others at retrieving the energy value from fuel to power vehicles, no one can seriously argue that an internal combustion engine does not have the capacity to recover energy from fuel.

accumulation, are not considered solid wastes. *See* 40 C.F.R. § 261.2 (1992); *see also id.* § 261.33 (listed commercial chemical products are "hazardous wastes if and when . . . in lieu of their original intended use, they are produced for use as (or as a component of) a fuel, distributed for use as a fuel, or burned as a fuel"). Indeed, it is implicit in this EPA statement of why commercial chemical products are solid wastes when burned for energy recovery that the commercial chemical product has been legitimately recycled. Contrary to the government's argument, this EPA comment has nothing to do with whether a particular manner of burning for energy recovery is legitimate or sham.

2.

* * *

[The court also held that the natural gas condensate is not a commercial chemical product which is a solid waste even if it is legitimately burned for energy recovery.]

In short, . . . the government's argument that natural gas condensate is a solid waste if it is "used in a manner which was not the original intended manner or normal intended use for that material within the industry" has no support in the statutory or regulatory scheme. On the other hand, Defendant's argument is consistent with the statutory and regulatory scheme, and is clearly supported by the EPA's statement that natural gas condensate when burned for energy recovery is not a solid waste. In light of this construction of the regulatory scheme by the EPA, we agree with Defendant that, under the EPA's interpretation of the regulations in effect as of 1987, natural gas condensate is not a hazardous waste subject to RCRA regulation when it is burned for energy recovery, which includes burning it as automotive fuel.

[The government had also charged Ekotek with transporting, making false statements, and failing to keep proper records concerning the natural gas condensate. These are all important elements of Subtitle C and EkoTek had not met them; however, since the condensate was not a hazardous waste in the first place, EkoTek was not required to comply with them.]

* * *

III.

Count 8 stems from the storage of the seventeen drums of Avery Label waste and the twelve drums of Reynolds Metals waste in the EkoTek's east warehouse. This count charged a violation of 42 U.S.C. § 6928(d)(2)(B) which prohibits "knowingly . . . stor[ing] . . . hazardous waste . . . in knowing violation of any material condition or requirement of [a RCRA] permit." 42 U.S.C. § 6928(d)(2)(B). This count was also charged and the jury was instructed under an aiding and abetting theory. 18 U.S.C. § 2. On appeal, Defendant contends that the evidence was insufficient to prove that the material in the twenty-nine drums was hazardous waste and that he possessed the requisite knowledge.[29] Defendant also contends that the jury instruction concerning knowledge was erroneous.

* * *

1.

Count 8 required the government to prove that the material was hazardous waste identified or listed under [Subtitle C] of RCRA. RCRA regulations define "hazardous waste" as solid waste which either exhibits a characteristic of hazardous waste or is listed in the regulations.[30] The government's theory at trial was that the Avery Label waste was characteristic waste because it had a flash point of less than 140° F, and that the Reynolds Metals waste was both characteristic waste due to its ignitability, and listed waste—*i.e.* MEK.

Defendant's primary contention is that the government failed to present any reliable test data concerning the Avery Label or Reynolds Metals waste. . . . [EPA's test data were questioned.]

While an EPA-approved test of the material would have been persuasive evidence as to whether the material was hazardous waste, the government was not required to prove this element through test data. . . . . Regardless of the flash point of the Reynolds Metals waste, there was evidence that it contained MEK which is a listed hazardous waste.[31] *See* United States v. MacDonald & Watson Waste Oil Co., 933 F.2d 35, 41 (1st Cir. 1991) (fact that soil was contaminated with non-hazardous chemicals in addition to listed hazardous waste would not render soil non-hazardous waste).

The government proved that the material was hazardous waste through the testimony of the Avery Label and Reynolds Metals representatives and the hazardous waste broker. Both representatives identified the manifests which indicated that the materials were hazardous wastes. The Reynolds Metals representative testified that the waste included MEK which is a hazardous waste regardless of its ignitability when combined with other materials. The Avery Label representative identified the specific composition of the waste as solvent ink, ultraviolet curer ink and cleaning solvent. The Material Data Safety Sheets for solvent inks used by Avery Labels in 1987 indicated a flash point of well below 140° F. Moreover, the Avery Label representative testified that the fact that it was mixed with the relatively involatile ultraviolet curer ink would have little effect on the waste material's ignitability. The broker testified that he recognized the Avery Label waste as solvent ink due to its smell. This evidence is sufficient for a reasonable jury to find that the material at issue in count 8 was RCRA hazardous waste. The fact that there may have been other conflicting evidence does not render the

---

[29] It is undisputed that EkoTek's RCRA permit did not authorize it to store hazardous waste in the east warehouse and that this is a material condition of the permit.

[30] Unlike Defendant's argument with respect to the natural gas condensate, there is no dispute that these substances were solid wastes as defined under 40 C.F.R. § 261.2 (1992).

[31] Defendant's own witness who performed the test on the spray material admitted that, if it were mixed with MEK, it would have a "very low flash point."

evidence insufficient as the jury's very function is to resolve conflicting evidence.

* * *

V.

Defendant's convictions on counts 1, 2, 3 and 7 are REVERSED. Defendant's convictions on counts 4 and 8 are AFFIRMED. The case is REMANDED to the district court for proceedings consistent with this opinion.

NOTES

1. Describe the waste materials at issue in *American Mining Congress*. How did the generators of this material propose to recycle them?

The court does not suggest that there is any reason to believe that the smelter operators did not in good faith plan to reuse the sludges in question. That being so, shouldn't EPA have encouraged this reuse by exempting the sludges from treatment as hazardous waste? What other goals was EPA seeking to vindicate?

Is "discarded" a question of the generator's intent, or of environmental impact, or both? How does EPA resolve this question? What is the argument for the contrary position? Why does the court affirm EPA's view?

2. The *Self* defendants' "recycling" technique? What was the legal basis for EPA's objection to it? What were [the defendants] ultimately convicted of?

What was EPA's basic environmental (as opposed to legal) concern with the natural gas condensate? What was environmentally wrong with this alleged recycling?

3. Can you follow the *Self* court's trail through the waste identification rules, identifying each step of the analysis? How does the court know whether the condensate is hazardous, a solid, discarded, recycled, or a by-product?

Why doesn't the fact that this is a form of recycling end the debate in the government's favor, since the regulations appear to take the position that recycling is a form of discarding. *Hint*: it would appear from the structure of the waste identification rules that recycled material is a subset of solid waste (by analogy to hazardous waste being a subset of solid waste), but in fact some recycled material is solid waste and some is not.

Were EkoTek's practices nevertheless sham recycling, in your view?

Note the role of the footnote in the preamble to EPA's regulations in deciding that the condensate was by-product material. For one thing, it points up the potentially great importance of the "legislative history" of regulations. But is it also troubling that one must go to that level of detail to answer the waste/non-waste question, or is it inevitable given the vast number of activities and practices that EPA must regulate under RCRA?

4. The RCRA regulations, § 261.2 (Table 1), identify four types of recycling that normally constitute disposal: "use constituting disposal" (which sounds circular, but actually denotes uses that involve the placement of waste in or on land), energy recovery (*i.e.*, use as fuel), reclamation (this is defined in § 261.1), and speculative accumulation. Is there a common characteristic of these recycling methods?

5. In drafting its RCRA definitions, EPA had many structural and policy choices. Perhaps the most fundamental problem arises from trying to maximize RCRA's dual aims of controlling hazardous waste while encouraging recycling. Why does RCRA care about recycling?

Next, EPA choose an all-or-nothing strategy that imposes heavy burdens on materials determined to be hazardous waste, very light burdens on solid waste, and none on non-waste. Why did EPA adopt that strategy in the first place? What are its advantages?

What are its disadvantages? Put another way, does it make sense for so much to ride on the definition, instead of a more flexible set of substantive requirements?

Finally, why is recycling dealt with in the definition of *solid*, as opposed to *hazardous*? Even if recycling is to be dealt with at the definitional stage, wouldn't it be better to have various levels of "hazardous"?

6. In *Assoc. of Battery Recyclers, Inc. v. EPA*, 208 F.3d 1047 (D.C. Cir. April 21, 2000), the court struck down EPA's classification of residual or secondary materials generated in mining and mineral processing operations as "solid waste." EPA argued that secondary materials are not discarded if and only if reclamation is continuous unless storage for later recycling complies with EPA's regulations. Citing *American Mining Congress v. EPA (I)*, 842 F.2d 1177 (D.C. Cir. 1987), the court held that material stored for recycling is not discarded with RCRA's definition of "solid waste." The court distinguishes, *American Mining Congress v. EPA (II)*, 907 F.2d 1179 (D.C. Cir. 1990) from this case by stating that *AMC II* involved the byproduct of a solid waste. The rule at issue in *Assoc. of Battery Recyclers, Inc. v. EPA* involved regulation of a byproduct of industrial processes.

PROBLEM

One observer describes EPA's regulatory strategy and one alternative to it, as follows:

EPA decided that "discarded material" includes any secondary material used "in a manner constituting disposal" or to make a product such as fertilizer that is used in a "manner constituting disposal." 40 C.F.R. § 261.2(c)(1). Similarly, EPA determined that secondary materials burned for energy recovery or to manufacture a fuel are "discarded." *Id.* § 261.2(c)(2). Certain hazardous secondary materials destined for reclamation are not deemed "discarded," but others are. *Id.* § 261.2(c)(3). Secondary materials accumulated without a clearly discernible pattern of reuse (speculative accumulation) are also deemed "discarded." *Id.* § 261.2(c)(4). Secondary materials that can serve as an ingredient in an industrial process or as a substitute for a commercial product (other than as fuel or to make products used in a manner constituting disposal) are excluded from the definition of waste. *Id.* § 261.2(e).

The agency has thus tried to give a "functional" rather than literal reading to the term "discarded material" so as to balance the statutory objectives of protecting human health and the environment with encouraging resource conservation and recovery. Although well intentioned, EPA's 1985 definition of solid waste is exceedingly complex. As such, it has given rise to compliance disputes and tens of thousands of regulatory inquiries to the agency and to state regulators annually. It also has confused courts.

* * *

In its fifteen-year effort to define "solid waste," EPA has consistently rejected a criterion of market value. Under this approach, a recycled material would be a solid waste if its producer had to pay for its disposition. Conversely, if a recycler would pay the producer for the material, it would not be a waste. While acknowledging the "intuitive appeal" of this approach, EPA has determined that it would not be enforceable given complicated and diverse means of financing materials transfers and frequent shifts in market prices. 48 Fed. Reg. 14,472, 14,481 (1983); 50 Fed. Reg. 614, 617 (1985). Accordingly, under EPA's regulations a secondary material may be sold for substantial consideration and still be deemed a "discarded material" and hence a "solid waste."

Smith, *supra*, at 3-5.

What is a "functional" approach to recycling? Why did EPA adopt it?

Would an economic definition be better? Do you agree with EPA's reluctance to adopt it?

Can you think of other alternatives?

Fertilizer: A Deliberate Exception.

One of the gaps in our environmental statutes that regulate hazardous and toxic substances is that substances defined as hazardous can be used as fertilizers. The following excerpt discusses this deliberate exception to hazardous waste disposal requirements and its implications.

FEAR IN THE FIELDS: HOW HAZARDOUS WASTES BECOME FERTILIZER

Duff Wilson
Seattle Times, July 4, 1997

When a trucker picks up a load of gray, toxic ash from a metal-processing plant in California, he hangs a "hazardous waste" sign on his rig. On crossing the border into Nevada, he takes the sign down. In that state, what he's carrying is no longer considered hazardous waste, but fertilizer ingredients. The waste will be delivered to a factory in Reno, treated to remove part of the heavy metals, blended with other materials and sold as fertilizer to farmers in, among other places, California.

Such is the fractured regulation of the fertilizer industry. Fertilizer—unlike food, animal feed, pesticides, herbicides and sewage sludge—is not controlled by federal law. To the degree it's regulated at all, it's on a state-by-state basis.

A Seattle Times investigation found that, across the nation, industrial wastes laden with heavy metals and other dangerous materials are being used in fertilizers and spread over farmland. The process, which is legal, saves dirty industries the high costs of disposing of hazardous wastes. The lack of national regulation and of labeling requirements means most farmers have no idea exactly what they're putting on their crops when they apply fertilizers.

There's a limit on the amount of lead in a can of paint, but not in fertilizer. There's a limit on the amount of dioxin in a concrete highway barrier, but not in fertilizer.

If that same trucker tried to wheel that ash up Interstate 5, he could take off hazardous-waste sign through Oregon and Washington, which both have less regulation than California.

But when he got to British Columbia, he'd be turned away at the border.

Canada and many European countries have stringent limits on toxic metals found in industrial byproducts. They refuse to buy products that, on American farms, routinely are sprinkled on the ground.

Some U.S. experts say those nations are less interested in science than in trade protectionism. These experts, working for government agencies and the fertilizer companies, say the products are safe and the process of recycling hazardous waste into fertilizer is good for America and Americans.

"It is irresponsible to create unnecessary limits that cost a hell of a lot of money," says Rufus Chaney of the Department of Agriculture's Research Service.

Canada's limit for heavy metals such as lead and cadmium in fertilizer is 10 to 90 times lower than the U.S. limit for metals in sewage sludge. The United States has no limit for metals in fertilizer.

Canada requires tests every six months for metals in recycled-waste fertilizer; the U.S., none.

"In the U.S., I hear them say, OK, how much can we apply until we get to the maximum people can stand?" said Canada's top fertilizer regulator, Darlene Blair. "They're congratulating people for recycling things without understanding what the problems are with the recycled material."

In Canada, Blair said, "We're a little beyond the point where we wait till something is proved bad before we fix it. Sorry, but we won't compromise our health."

Some health and environmental experts are pushing for similar regulation in this country. But from Washington state to Washington, D.C., the fertilizer industry is waging a successful campaign against it.

The $15 billion-a-year business cultivates clout.

In Congress three years ago, lobbyists for The Fertilizer Institute won removal of a section of the proposed Lead Exposure Reduction Act that would have banned fertilizers with more than 0.1 percent lead.

Internal minutes of the institute, the industry's main lobbying group, show it wants to streamline hazardous-material laws and "manage the issue of regulation of heavy metals in fertilizers."

The industry also lobbies its own members to oppose fertilizer regulation.

In Colorado, a manufacturer whose product does not include recycled hazardous waste was told by the director of the Far West Fertilizer Association to "stop adding fuel to the fire" by talking about the risks of heavy metals.

"I told him there are things going on that are bogus and I won't be quiet because I think this is unsafe," replied Kipp Smallwood, sales manager for Cozinco.

"I'm crying for national regulation, or at least truth in labeling," Smallwood said. There is no requirement that toxic substances be listed on fertilizer labels.

The primary argument against labeling or regulating fertilizers with toxic wastes is that it would raise costs, both of waste disposal and food production.

"Agriculture is being used as a dumping ground," Smallwood said. "They get away with it because there's nobody watching, nobody testing. It's the lure of the dollar."

While all the substances in question occur in nature, science is finding there is no safe level for many of them. History has taught that many substances initially believed to be safe were not.

In recent years, doctors and scientists learned that trace amounts of lead can cause developmental problems in children and high blood pressure in adults. Lead is prohibited in gasoline, paint and food-can solder, but not in fertilizer.

In fact, lead is in many fertilizers. It is never disclosed on the label, though, even when it is as high as 3 percent of the product.

As a result, farmers and orchardists are spreading up to one-third of a cup of lead per acre when they follow the manufacturer's recommendations. The farmers and orchardists aren't told about the lead, which has no nutrient value for plants.

Hazardous-waste recyclers say they could remove lead, but it would cost more and make it harder to compete on price unless everybody had to do it.

Bill Liebhardt, chairman of the Sustainable Agriculture Department at the University of California-Davis, previously worked for fertilizer companies but says the industry is wrong to oppose regulation.

"When I heard of people mixing this toxic waste in fertilizer, I was astounded," he said. "And it seems to be a legal practice. I'd never heard of something like that— getting cadmium or lead when you think you are only getting zinc."

"Even if it's legal, to me it's just morally and ethically bankrupt that you would take this toxic material and mix it into something that is beneficial and then sell that to unsuspecting people. To me it is just outrageous."

Janet Phoenix, a physician with the National Lead Information Center, said she had no idea industries were recycling lead into fertilizer.

"I, personally, was under the impression that, at least in this country, lead was no longer allowed to be an ingredient in fertilizer," Phoenix said. "Clearly, it seems to me that a process recycling industrial waste into fertilizer that contains lead would be at odds to efforts to reduce lead in soil. There is no safe level."

Nobody really knows how much risk exists in waste-recycling programs that have sprouted since Congress passed the Resource Conservation and Recovery Act in 1976. The law raised the cost of disposing of hazardous substances five-fold in 12 years.

Soils specialist Charlie Mitchell, an Auburn University professor, says he gets 10 times as many calls as he used to get about recycling industrial byproducts into agricultural products. "Every industry is looking at it," Mitchell said.

"People were scrambling," said John Salmonson, president of Monterey Chemical of Fresno, Calif. "What happened was they were trying to shove the waste onto agriculture."

At least 26 states, including Washington, have created programs to match generators of hazardous waste with recyclers, like blind dates. A brochure from the King County Hazardous Waste Management Program tells companies: "TURN YOUR DISPOSAL COSTS INTO PROFITS."

"Recycle and reuse, that's our national strategy," said the Department of Agriculture's Chaney. "It costs so much more to put it in a landfill. And if the recycling program avoids any chance of risk, then it's a responsible program."

That's the tricky part. While the sewage sludge has been studied exhaustively for 25 years, there is little science on long-term effects of heavy metals in recycled fertilizer.

Shiou Kuo, a Washington State University professor and a consultant to the state, says sewage sludge is a very different material from industrial waste. While he's not particularly worried, he said, "this is something that troubles my mind."

"Deep down in my heart, I think the less amount a toxic substance like cadmium is in the soil, the better," Kuo said. "But, in reality, the question is really how much input can be tolerated. Until we know what the critical level is, this kind of question cannot be answered."

Every state has a fertilizer regulator. But they don't check for heavy metals even when they know the metals are included in the product. They only check for nutrients listed on the label.

"We really don't have any rules or regulations addressing that," said Dale Dubberly, Florida's fertilizer chief. "There's a lot of materials out there that have plant nutrient values, but nobody knows what else is in them."

Testing for heavy metals would cost $50,000 to $150,000 in capital investment for the typical state lab, plus additional staff, plus $10 to $60 per sample, said Dr. Joel Padmore, director of North Carolina's lab and an officer of the American Association of Plant Food Control Officials.

Instead of making that investment, some states—most of them in the Northeast—are cutting back their labs and their regulation of fertilizers. New York doesn't even test for nutrients anymore, he said.

"Once a state has dropped its regulatory apparatus, then essentially anything can be registered because nobody is checking," Padmore said.

The EPA, meanwhile, is focusing not on testing or regulating but on promoting waste recycling.

"We feel the direction they're going is not always in the interest of agriculture," said Maryam Khosravifard, staff scientist for the California Department of Food and Agriculture. "EPA is in charge of getting rid of these materials. They do reuse and recycling. But we do agriculture; we're the stewards of the land."

Edward Kleppinger, a chemist, wrote hazardous-waste rules for EPA in the 1970s and is now a consultant for industry, environmental and health groups. He, too, dislikes EPA's posture on this issue.

"The heavy metals don't disappear," Kleppinger says. "They're not biodegradable. They just use this as an alternate way to get rid of hazardous waste, this whole recycling loophole that EPA has left in place these last 20 years.

"The last refuge of the hazardous-waste scoundrel is to call it a fertilizer or soil amendment and dump it on farmland."

If change is to come, it probably will come slowly.

"It feels like it's the very beginning of this debate," said Ken Cook, president of the Environmental Working Group, a nonprofit research agency.

"Right now, it appears there's an economic use of this waste material. But it may just mean that we haven't looked at it yet," he said. "Sometimes it's a bonanza if it can be recycled, and sometimes it's just a shell game where we're transferring the risk back to the land.

"Even if it gets flushed out, if 80 percent gets flushed out, it just takes longer to build up to the threshold effect," Cook says. "And maybe there is no threshold. Maybe there is no safe level."

The bottom line, Cook says, and many others echo: "We really don't know."

2. The Regulatory Definition of Hazardous Waste

The following schematic is useful in piecing through the definition of a solid waste.

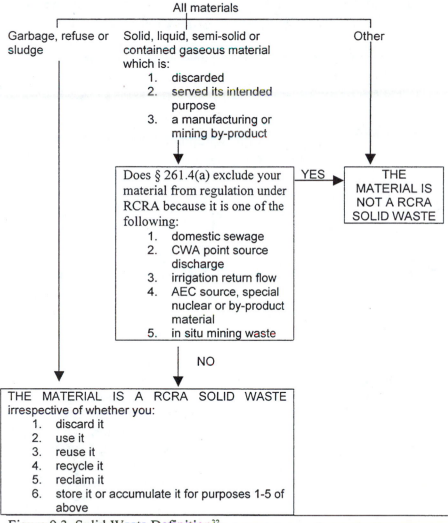

Figure 9.3–Solid Waste Definition[32]

RCRA requires EPA to establish criteria "for identifying the characteristics of hazardous waste, *and* for listing hazardous waste . . ." 42 U.S.C. § 6921(a) (emphasis added). In setting these criteria, EPA was

---

[32] Environment Reporter 151:2116.

directed to take into account "toxicity, persistence, and degradability in nature, potential for accumulation in tissue, and other related factors such as flammability, corrosiveness, and other hazardous characteristics." *Id.* The *American Mining Congress* case, *supra*, described the analysis EPA uses to determine whether a solid waste is hazardous. Go back and review that part of the opinion. Basically, a solid waste is hazardous if it is either *listed* as a hazardous waste or if testing demonstrates that the waste has a hazardous *characteristic*.

Jeffrey M. Gaba sets out the nuances of this terminology this way:

Since both the mixture and derived-from rules distinguish listed from characteristic wastes, to understand the rules it is important to understand the basis for designating a waste as hazardous.

Characteristic Waste. Characteristic wastes are classified as hazardous if, based on tests performed by the generator, they exhibit one of four hazard "characteristics" promulgated by EPA: (1) ignitability, (2) corrosivity, (3) reactivity, and (4) toxicity or TC ("toxicity characteristic").[33] EPA recently adopted the new "TC" rule, which revises the earlier "extraction procedure" or "EP" toxicity characteristic. The new TC rule now provides that a waste is hazardous if an extract of the waste contains certain designated metals or toxic organic constituents above a defined threshold level.

Listed Waste. Listed wastes are hazardous wastes that have been designated by EPA as hazardous on a generic, nationwide basis. A waste is hazardous simply if it falls within the listing description.[34] The lists are broken down into categories of wastes from nonspecific sources (such as certain spent solvents), wastes from specific sources (such as slop oil emulsions in the petroleum refining industry), or wastes from "discarded commercial chemical products."

Although EPA may list a waste because it exhibits one of the four hazard characteristics, it may also list a waste based on the Agency's determination that the waste meets certain "toxicity" or "acute toxicity" criteria. In general, a waste may be listed based on toxicity if it contains any one of a large number of specified toxic chemicals unless the Agency determines that it will not present a substantial risk to human health or to the environment if mismanaged.[35] A waste may be listed based on "acute toxicity" if it

---

[33] 40 C.F.R. §§ 261.20-.24 (2000).

[34] In the past, a generator was not required to test its listed waste to determine if it is hazardous; if listed, the generator could simply declare the waste as hazardous. Pursuant to the new RCRA land ban rules, a generator will be required to determine whether the listed waste also exhibits a hazard characteristic to determine necessary treatment for land disposal. *See* 55 Fed. Reg. 22530 (1990).

[35] 40 C.F.R. § 261.11(a)(2). The list of toxic constituents is found in Appendix VIII of Part 261 (2000).

has been found to be fatal to humans in low doses or fails certain animal toxicity tests.

Unlike the hazard characteristics, there is no simple numerical standard for listing wastes, and application of the criteria generally involves an exercise in judgment. The toxicity listing, for example, involves determinations about various factors, including the concentration and bioaccumulation potential of the toxic constituents, their fate and possible chemical alteration in the environment, and likelihood and consequences of possible mismanagement. The bases for listing wastes-toxicity and acute toxicity-are quite different from the basis for classifying wastes based on the hazard characteristics; a waste may be a listed waste even if it does not exhibit a characteristic.

Jeffrey M. Gaba, *The Mixture and Derived-From Rules Under RCRA: Once a Hazardous Waste Always a Hazardous Waste?*, 21 ENVTL. L. REP. 10033 (1991).

CRITERIA FOR IDENTIFYING HAZARDOUS WASTES

Characteristic Waste
   Ignitability
   Corrosivity
   Reactivity
   Toxicity
Listed Waste
   Mixture Rule
   Derived-From Rule
   Contained-In Policy

The "characteristic" determination is relatively straightforward. As one would expect, generators of solid waste must test the waste to determine whether it exhibits any of the EPA-defined characteristics, as defined at 40 C.F.R. § 261.21-.22:

- *Ignitability.* A solid waste that has a low flash point, burns very vigorously, is ignitable by friction, is an ignitable compressed gas, or is an oxidizer is ignitable.
- *Corrosivity.* Both acids and bases can be corrosive, and EPA makes this judgment based on the pH or the ability of the waste in a liquid form to corrode steel.
- *Reactivity.* A reactive waste is one that readily undergoes violent changes, reacts violently with water, generates toxic or explosive gases when mixed with water, or is readily capable of detonation.
- *Toxicity.* Unlike the other characteristics, toxicity is not an inherent quality of the waste itself but of the solution created when the waste is dissolved in mildly acidic water. EPA uses the Toxicity

Characteristic Leaching Procedure (TCLP) to simulate the leachate from the waste material and it tests the leachate for the presence and concentration of certain toxic constituents.

Likewise, it is a relatively simple matter to examine the lists in Part 261 to determine whether a waste has been listed. The legal complexity in determining whether a solid waste is hazardous arises, instead, from the rules designed to assure that the restrictions on hazardous waste management are not circumvented. These are the so-called mixture rule, derived-from rule, and contained-in policy.

The following excerpt delineates the definitional dilemma—how to capture all hazardous waste without writing regulations that are impossible to decipher.

THE MIXTURE AND DERIVED–FROM RULES UNDER RCRA: ONCE A HAZARDOUS WASTE ALWAYS A HAZARDOUS WASTE?

Jeffrey M. Gaba
21 ENVTL. L. REP. (ENVTL. L. INST) 10033 (1991)

The Presumption of Hazardousness

As a general rule, EPA takes the position that once wastes are listed as hazardous they are presumed to remain hazardous.[36] As one court has stated, EPA has consistently adhered to the general principle "that a hazardous waste does not lose its hazardous character simply because it changes form or is combined with other substances."[37] The mixture and derived-from rules are an outgrowth of this principle.

The need for some form of regulation of mixed and derived-from wastes is obvious. If wastes could become nonhazardous simply by being mixed with other wastes, there would be a tremendous incentive simply to dilute hazardous wastes to avoid regulation. Potentially large quantities of hazardous waste could escape regulation.

Similarly, exempting wastes derived from the treatment or disposal of hazardous wastes would also create a regulatory loophole. Wastes generated from listed hazardous wastes may contain the hazardous constituents that caused the original waste to be listed. Additionally, the treatment or disposal process may alter the chemical characteristics of the waste and generate new toxic constituents.

In developing a response to these problems, EPA was faced with the dilemma of avoiding both overbreadth and underbreadth. A rule that treated all mixtures or derived-from wastes as hazardous would bring an enormous amount of material into the hazardous waste system even though it contained only small amounts of hazardous constituents or had been rendered nonhazardous by the mixing or treatment (*e.g.*, neutralization). A rule

---

[36] *See* 45 Fed. Reg. 33,095, 33,096 (1980); *see also* Chemical Waste Management, Inc. v. EPA, 869 F.2d 1526, 1538-40 (D.C. Cir. 1989).

[37] 869 F.2d at 1539.

requiring that the resulting mixture or derived-from waste itself exhibit a hazard characteristic, on the other hand, would exclude materials that were listed for reasons other than the four Subpart C hazard characteristics and would encourage dilution of wastes through mixing. Claiming reluctance, EPA's response was to presume the continued hazardousness of wastes mixed with or derived from listed, but not characteristic, waste.

[W]astes subject to the mixture and derived-from rules are hazardous regardless of the concentration of hazardous constituents. Wastes containing minute or even no amounts of hazardous constituents can still be classified as hazardous wastes under these rules. Although EPA has repeatedly acknowledged that this approach creates "inequities," EPA's basic response has been to rely on the slow, case-by-case "delisting" process to exclude wastes that may not, in fact, be hazardous.

* * *

Wastes Mixed With Wastes: *The Mixture Rule*

EPA's current mixture rule is deceptively simple. In essence, the mixture rule provides that (1) mixtures of characteristic wastes and nonhazardous wastes are hazardous only if the mixture exhibits a characteristic and (2) mixtures of listed wastes and nonhazardous wastes are hazardous regardless of the amount of listed waste in the mixture. It was originally adopted in 1980 as part of EPA's first regulation defining hazardous wastes. Although the mixture rule was never expressly proposed, EPA claimed that it "intended" waste mixtures containing hazardous waste to be hazardous and managed accordingly. The absence of a mixture rule, EPA stated, would allow generators to simply commingle hazardous and nonhazardous waste and would create "a major loophole in the Subtitle C management system."[38] [The mixture rule can be found at 40 C.F.R. § 261.3(a)(2)(iii)-(iv).]

* * *

It is important to note that the mixture rule by its own terms applies solely to listed wastes. Unlisted, characteristic wastes are handled through the general provision for termination of status as hazardous waste. Under that provision, unlisted hazardous wastes cease being hazardous wastes when they no longer exhibit a hazard characteristic.[39] Thus, a mixture of an unlisted hazardous waste and a solid waste is not hazardous if it does not exhibit a hazard characteristic.

Some of the listed wastes have been listed, however, simply because they exhibit one of the hazard characteristics.[40] As originally promulgated, the mixture rule would have classified mixtures of these wastes as hazardous, although unlisted wastes exhibiting the same characteristic were not regulated. In 1981, EPA amended the mixture rule to treat wastes that were listed because they exhibit a hazard characteristic the same as characteristic waste. Under the current mixture rule, mixtures of solid waste and listed

---

[38] 45 Fed. Reg. 33,095-96 (1980).
[39] 40 C.F.R. § 261.4(d)(1) (1995).
[40] Why *else* would a waste be listed?–EDS.

wastes that were listed solely because they exhibit one of the four hazard characteristics will not be considered hazardous if the resulting mixture does not display a characteristic. This exclusion is self-executing without requiring the filing of a delisting petition.

Consequently, to apply the mixture rule properly it is necessary to identify the criteria used to list the waste. The Subpart D lists contain codes that identify the criteria used. If a waste was listed solely on the basis of one of the four hazard characteristics, the mixture rule does not apply.

A second important point to note about the mixture rule is that it applies only to mixtures of wastes. Products that are produced using hazardous wastes as ingredients may not, as discussed below, themselves be classified as hazardous wastes. Additionally, wastes resulting from the mixture of hazardous substances within an industrial process may not be hazardous. The mixture rule applies only if materials are mixed after they have already become wastes. Thus, it is important to determine at what point in the process materials become both solid wastes and hazardous wastes for purposes of applying the mixture rule.

* * *

Wastes Derived From Wastes: The Derived-From Rule

Under the derived-from rule, solid waste that is the product of the treatment, storage, or disposal of a hazardous waste is itself classified as a hazardous waste. Thus, sludges from waste treatment or leachate from a hazardous waste disposal facility is classified as hazardous simply because it was generated from a hazardous waste.

The derived-from rule was adopted in 1980.[41] EPA explained that it was "reasonable to assume" that wastes that are derived from hazardous wastes are themselves hazardous and asserted that leachate, treatment residues, sludges, and incineration ash typically contain hazardous constituents. The rule, however, operates regardless of the actual concentration of toxic constituents in the resulting wastes, and EPA has stated that the derived-from rule applies even if the resulting waste does not display the toxicity characteristic. The delisting process remains the primary method for excluding derived-from wastes from classification as hazardous wastes.

In 1980, EPA claimed that the derived-from rule was "the best regulatory approach we can devise at this time." The rule has apparently stood the test of time, since it continues, essentially unmodified, since first promulgated.

The derived-from rule is found at 40 C.F.R. § 261.3(c)(2)(i).

* * *

By the terms of § 261.3(c)(2)(i), any solid waste derived from treatment of a hazardous waste is itself a hazardous waste. At first, it appears that wastes derived from the treatment of unlisted, characteristic waste are hazardous waste even if they do not exhibit a characteristic. The regulations

---

[41] *See* 45 Fed. Reg. 33,096 (1980).

do, however, exempt such derived wastes. Under the terms of § 261.3(c), the derived-from rule applies "unless and until" the waste satisfies the general criteria for cessation of status as hazardous waste. These general criteria are (1) in the case of any solid waste that is not listed, it does not exhibit a characteristic or (2) in the case of a listed waste or a waste derived from a listed waste, it is excluded through the delisting process.[42] Thus, wastes that do not exhibit a characteristic that are derived from unlisted, characteristic wastes are not subject to the derived-from rule.

* * *

The derived-from rule acts to classify 'solid wastes' generated from the treatment, storage, or disposal of hazardous waste as hazardous wastes. [P]roducts that are 'derived from' hazardous wastes may not themselves be hazardous wastes. Thus, materials, such as metal reclaimed from the treatment of hazardous waste, will not be hazardous. [This determination is made under the definition of solid waste.]

In most cases it will be clear that the residue of treatment, such as sludges or ash, is itself a waste. If, however, the residue was used in such a way to be excluded from the definition of solid waste, it would presumably not be subject to the derived-from rule. For example, the regulations exclude from classification as solid waste materials that are part of an ongoing commercial process or are used directly as ingredients.[43] Such materials, even if they were derived from the treatment of hazardous waste, might not themselves be hazardous waste.

* * *

Contaminated Soil and Groundwater: The Contained-in Interpretation

One interesting application of EPA's 'presumption of hazardous' involves the status of environmental media, such as soil or groundwater, contaminated by the spill or other release of hazardous waste. Unless the contaminated media is itself a listed waste (such as residue or contaminated soil from spills of a commercial chemical product or manufacturing chemical intermediate) or unless the contaminated media exhibit a hazard characteristic, it is not obvious on what basis it would be classified as a hazardous waste.

Although the Agency has generally taken the position that contaminated media can be hazardous waste, the basis for this position is not completely clear.

In *Chemical Waste Management, Inc. v. EPA*,[44] the D.C. Circuit considered industry claims that contaminated 'environmental media' (*i.e.*, soil and groundwater) were not hazardous waste subject to the RCRA land ban. The court recognized the difficulty of applying either the mixture rule or derived-from rule to sustain the classification of contaminated soil as hazardous waste. The court wrote: "For either of these rules to apply directly,

---

[42] *See* 40 C.F.R. § 261.3(d) (1995).
[43] *See* 40 C.F.R. § 261.2(e) (1995).
[44] 869 F.2d 1526 (D.C. Cir. 1989).

soil or groundwater would have to be considered a 'solid waste.' This does not match the statutory definition: 'The term 'solid waste' means any garbage, refuse, sludge . . . and other discarded material.'[45] Nonetheless, the court upheld EPA's conclusion that contaminated media could be hazardous waste. The court considered this an application of the general principle, embodied in both the mixture and derived-from rules, that 'a hazardous waste does not lose its hazardous character simply because it changes form or is contained within other substances.'[46] The court also noted that EPA had consistently held this position and had ruled on delisting petitions to exclude contaminated media from classification as hazardous waste.[47] Finally, the court noted that provisions of RCRA, added in 1984, implied that some soils contaminated with hazardous waste were themselves hazardous waste.[48]

* * *

As we already have seen several times in the definitions of solid and hazardous waste, EPA must balance its desire to make its rules inclusive (*i.e.*, to encompass all of the materials and activities that pose an environmental risk) with the need to avoid creating an unmanageably large and complex regulatory machine. The mixture, derived-from, and contained-in policies clearly respond to the former concern. In revising the waste identification rules, EPA is turning its attention more to the latter problem. Specifically, it is looking for ways to permit wastes that have been swept up in the regulation's broad net to *exit* the hazardous waste restrictions with a minimum of administrative expense and delay. The present system does not achieve that goal.

EPA's basic position on termination of a material's status as a hazardous waste is simple. Once a waste has been classified as a hazardous waste it generally remains a hazardous waste.[49] There are only two explicit bases for termination of this status. First, an unlisted, characteristic waste ceases to be a hazardous waste if it no longer exhibits a hazardous waste characteristic. Second, a listed waste, a waste containing a listed waste, or a waste derived from a listed waste ceases to be a hazardous waste only if it is has been "delisted" from classification. Although a characteristic waste can lose its status as a hazardous waste without action by EPA, in most cases a listed waste will remain hazardous until EPA affirmatively grants a petition to reclassify the material as nonhazardous.

The delisting process is normally undertaken on a case-by-case basis; generators submit delisting petitions requesting that the specific waste at their facility be removed from classification as hazardous.[50] In general, delisting requires a demonstration that the specific facility's waste does not meet the criteria under what the waste was listed and that there are no other

---

[45] *Id.* at 1538, n. 14.

[46] *See id.* at 1539.

[47] *See id.* at 1540.

[48] *See id.* at 1539.

[49] *See* 40 C.F.R. § 261.3(c)(1) (1995).

[50] These provisions are contained at 40 C.F.R. §§ 260.20 and .22.

factors which would warrant classifying the waste as hazardous.[51] Although the delisting process is intended as an escape hatch for overly stringent listing decisions, the process has been criticized for its slowness, difficulty, and expense.[52]

NOTES

1. *Exit options*. EPA's 1995 Hazardous Waste Identification Rule (HWIR) proposal would establish constituent-specific exit levels for low-risk solid wastes that were designated "hazardous" only because they were listed or had been mixed with, derived from, or contained listed hazardous wastes.[53] This approach, however, requires complex risk assessments to be conducted—not a speedy or inexpensive undertaking, as we saw in Chapter 2—and EPA is still at work on finding ways of making this process feasible. As we have also seen before, EPA must balance its desire for administratively manageable standards with its desire to regulate risk as accurately as possible.

Current System
> *characteristic waste–self-determination*
> *listed waste–only through delisting*
> *treatment under Subtitle C treatment standards*

HWIR Proposal
> *risk-based exit levels*
> *treatment standards capped at exit levels*

---

2. Reread Part III of the *Self* case, *supra*. It is a challenge to the scope of hazardous, rather than solid, waste. What are the defendants' arguments that the wastes were not hazardous? Why did the "characteristic" argument fail? If MEK were not a listed waste, would the defendants have prevailed? Look up MEK in the waste identification regulations—do the defendants have an argument that the ink wastes were not hazardous even though they are listed? If not, why not?

3. There are four categories of listed waste: F-Series wastes (hazardous waste from a non-specific sources, such as spent solvents and sludges), K-Series wastes (hazardous waste from a specific source, such as wood preserving processes, pigment manufacture, and pesticide production), U-Series wastes (discarded commercial products considered hazardous waste,

---

[51] *See* 40 C.F.R. § 260.22(a) (1999). Additionally, the petitioner must demonstrate that the waste does not demonstrate a hazard characteristic. §§ 260.22(d)(3) and .22(e)(2). In the 1984 RCRA amendments, Congress specifically required that EPA, in assessing a delisting petition, consider factors in addition to its original basis for listing. RCRA § 3001(f), 42 U.S.C. § 6921(f).

[52] *See* Jeffrey M. Gaba, *The Mixture and Derived-From Rules Under RCRA: Once a Hazardous Waste Always a Hazardous Waste?*, 21 ENVTL. L. REP. 10033 (Jan. 1991).

[53] *See* 60 Fed. Reg. 66,344 (1995).

such as discarded chemicals and off-specification materials), and P-Series wastes (discarded commercial chemical products that are considered acute hazardous waste). Each listed hazardous waste is assigned an EPA Hazardous Waste Number which precedes the name of the waste.

4. The mixture rule is primarily intended to prevent waste generators from diluting their wastes to the point that they no longer meet the characteristic or listing criteria, a technique that EPA characterized as a major loophole. EPA consistently takes the position that, as the cliché has it, dilution is not the solution to pollution. Why not?

5. The derived-from rule addresses a different aspect of unauthorized waste management—its by-products, ash or leachate, which may pose the same or worse (because it is more concentrated) hazards as the original waste. As we will see, RCRA regulates waste treatment very closely, so the derived-from rule is a way to avoid the circumvention of those rules.

6. The target of the contained-in rule is the consequence of the failure to manage hazardous waste: environmental media that are contaminated (usually accidentally) with waste materials. Why is it important to include these materials in the RCRA regulatory scheme? Why not rely on CERCLA to handle the clean-up of contaminated soil and groundwater?

7. The mixture and derived-from rules were dealt a serious blow in 1990 when the D.C. Circuit overturned them on procedural grounds (inadequate notice and comment) in *Shell Oil Co. v. EPA*, 950 F.2d 741 (D.C. Cir. 1990). In recognition of the enormous impact that the elimination of these rules would have on the hazardous waste program, EPA issued an emergency rule reinstating the mixture and derived-from rules pending full notice and comment, and Congress has forbidden EPA from withdrawing the interim rules until a new waste identification regulatory regime replaces it. The current plan, reached after several rounds of litigation, is that EPA was to propose a new Hazardous Waste Identification Rule (HWIR) by October 31, 1999, and finalize the rule by April 30, 2001. The proposed rule was published on November 19, 1999 at 64 Fed. Reg. 63,382. The comment period ended on February 17, 2000. The edited text of the rule is at the end of this section.

The *Shell Oil* case did not, however, affect the status of the contained-in policy, because it was an EPA interpretation and therefore not subject to notice-and-comment requirements. Additionally, the interpretation was specifically approved by the D.C. Circuit in *Chemical Waste Management, Inc. v. EPA, supra*.

7. *Exemptions*. Section 261.4(b) exempts several solid wastes that would otherwise meet the criteria for being hazardous. These include household waste, solid waste generated from agricultural operations, animal manure, mining "overburden" returned to the mine site, fly ash waste generated from coal combustion, and solid waste from the extraction, beneficiation, and processing of ores and minerals. What are the common themes in this list?

Exclusions. Excluded from the definition of hazardous waste are: lawfully-applied products; household wastes; wastes produced by conditionally-exempt generators; certain mining wastes; industrial wastewater discharges subject to NPDES permits; contaminated soils and groundwater from regulated underground storage tanks; and PCBs. [54]

The following schematics are helpful in piecing through the definitions of a hazardous waste.

DEFINITION OF A HAZARDOUS WASTE

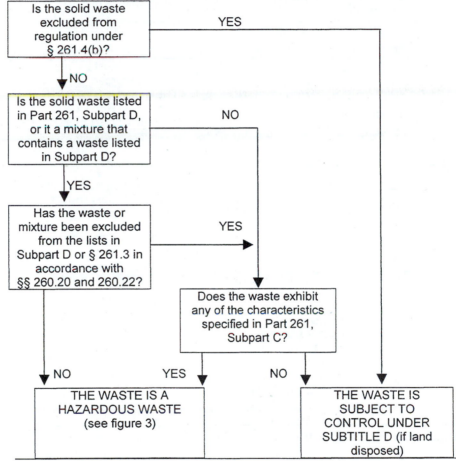

Figure 9.4–Sorting Out the Definition of Hazardous Waste.[55]

---

[54] PCBs are excluded because their use and disposal is regulated primarily by the Toxic Substances Control Act. *See* 15 U.S.C. §§ 2601-2692 (2000); *see also* 40 C.F.R. pt. 761 (2000).

[55] ENVIRONMENTAL REPORTER 151:2117. 40 C.F.R. pt. 260-261.

SPECIAL PROVISIONS FOR CERTAIN HAZARDOUS WASTE

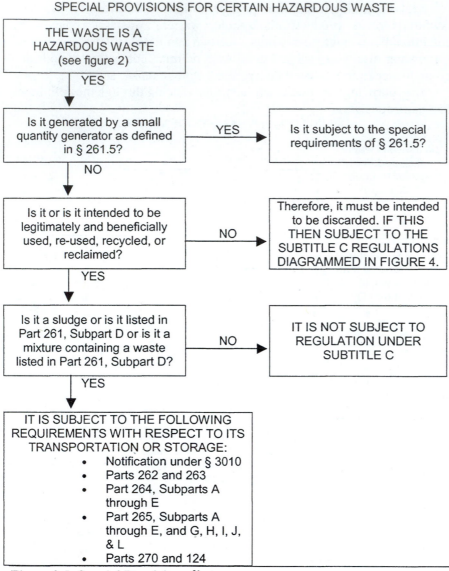

Figure 9.5–Special Provisions.[56]

---

[56] ENVIRONMENTAL REPORTER 151:2118. 40 C.F.R. pt. 260-261.

REGULATIONS FOR HAZARDOUS WASTE NOT COVERED IN FIGURES 9.4
AND 9.5

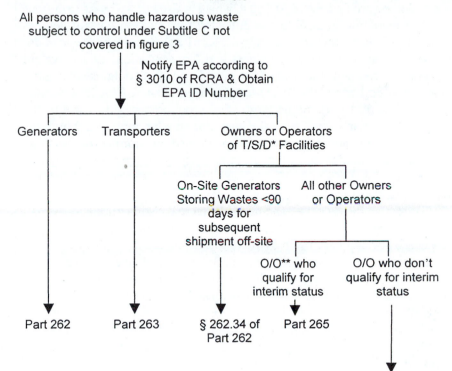

* T/S/D stands for Treatment, Storage, or Disposal
** O/O stands for Owners or Operators

Figure 9.6–Regulating Remaining Hazardous Wastes[57]

---

[57] ENVIRONMENTAL REPORTER 151:2119. 40 C.F.R. pt. 260-261.

PROBLEM

"Electric arc furnace [EAF] dust, which is also known by its hazardous waste designation code K061, is collected by emission control devices when steel is manufactured. EPA listed K061 as a hazardous waste under RCRA primarily because it contains high concentrations of hexavalent chromium, lead, and cadmium. However, K061 also contains substantial quantities of other metals" *Steel Manufacturers Assn. v. EPA*, 27 F.3d 642, 645 (D.C. Cir. 1994). Some large steel producers seek to reclaim the metals, particularly zinc, from the dust. For smaller concerns, which the case does *not* address, reclamation is not economically feasible. Accordingly, smaller steel producers must dispose of the material in more conventional ways, which are extremely expensive because EAF dust is a listed hazardous waste.

To reduce these costs—and maybe even make some money—a small steel producer called Sam's Specialty Steel (S) began to sell its EAF dust to a nearby brickmaker, Beth's Bricks (B). Bricks are made from a mixture of clay and other materials, which is placed in molds that are baked at very high temperatures. B added the EAF dust to the clay mixture from which bricks are made, because it added density and a unique color to the bricks, both of which are highly desirable qualities for B's customers. In addition, some of the other ingredients of EAF dust—iron, calcium, and silica—are routinely added in other ways to increase the strength and brightness of the bricks. B sells thousands of its bricks containing EAF dust, and the bricks are used for all kinds of building purposes.

S and B recently received letters from the local U.S. Attorney informing them that they were about to be indicted for disposing of a hazardous waste—*i.e.*, the bricks made with EAF dust—without a permit. The letter invited S and B to come down to the U.S. Courthouse the next week to offer their reasons why they should not be indicted. You have been retained by S and B to represent them in this matter. Three additional facts are undisputed: neither S nor B has a permit for their management of EAF dust; their management of EAF dust does not meet RCRA's land disposal restrictions; and their management of the EAF dust is perfectly legal if the bricks are not a hazardous waste.

    1. Is the dust a hazardous waste?

    2. Are the resulting bricks a hazardous waste?

The following excerpt is EPA's proposed hazardous waste identification rule. The excerpt explains the purpose and need for the new rule.

HAZARDOUS WASTE IDENTIFICATION RULE (HWIR): IDENTIFICATION AND LISTING OF HAZARDOUS WASTE

Environmental Protection Agency
64 Fed. Reg. 63,382, 63,388 – 89
November 19, 1999

III. Why Is EPA Proposing To Retain the Mixture and Derived-From Rules?

A. What Are the Mixture and Derived-From Rules?

The mixture and derived-from rules are a part of the RCRA regulations that define which wastes are considered to be hazardous and therefore subject to RCRA Subtitle C regulations. The mixture rule discussed in today's notice refer specifically to 40 CFR 261.3(a)(2)(iii) and (iv). Under the mixture rule, a solid waste becomes regulated as a hazardous waste if it is mixed with one or more listed hazardous wastes The derived-from rule discussed in today's notice refers specifically to 40 CFR 261.3(c)(2)(i). Under the derived-from rule, any solid waste generated from the treatment, storage, or disposal of a hazardous waste remains regulated as a hazardous waste. These derived-from wastes include wastes such as sludges, spill residues, ash, emission control dust, and leachate.

B. What Is the Legal History of the Mixture and Derived-From Rules?

EPA promulgated the mixture and derived-from rules in 1980 as part of the comprehensive "cradle to grave" requirements for managing hazardous waste. 45 FR 33066 (May 19, 1980). Numerous industries that generate hazardous wastes challenged the 1980 mixture and derived-from rules in Shell Oil Co. v. EPA, 950 F. 2d 741 (D.C. Cir. 1991). In December 1991 the D.C. Circuit Court of Appeals vacated the rules because they had been promulgated without adequate notice and opportunity to comment. The court, however, suggested that EPA might want to consider reinstating the rules pending full notice and comment in order to ensure continued protection of human health and the environment.

In response to this decision, we promulgated an emergency rule reinstating the mixture and derived-from rules as interim final rules without providing notice and opportunity to comment. 57 FR 7628 (March 3, 1992). We also promulgated a "sunset provision" which provided that the mixture and derived-from rules would remain in effect only until April 28, 1993. Shortly after, we published a proposal containing several options for revising the mixture and derived-from rules. *See* 57 FR 21450 (May 20, 1992). The May 1992 proposal and the time pressure created by the "sunset provision" generated significant controversy. In response, Congress included in EPA's FY1993 appropriation several provisions addressing the mixture and derived-from rules. Pub. L. No. 102-389, 106 Stat. 1571. First, Congress nullified the sunset provision by providing that EPA could not promulgate any revisions to the rules before October 1, 1993, and by providing that the reinstated regulations could not be "terminated or withdrawn" until revisions took effect. However, to ensure that we could not postpone the issue of revisions indefinitely, Congress also established a deadline of October 1, 1994 for the promulgation of revisions to the mixture and derived-from rules. Congress made this deadline enforceable under RCRA's citizen suit provision, section 7002.

On October 30, 1992, we published two notices, one removing the sunset provision, and the other withdrawing the May 1992 proposal. (See 57 FR 49278, 49280). We had received many comments criticizing the May 1992 proposal. The criticisms were due, in a large part, to the very short schedule imposed on the regulation development process itself. Commenters also feared that the proposal would result in a "patchwork" of differing State programs because some states might not adopt the revisions. This fear was based on the belief that States would react in a negative manner to the proposal and refuse to incorporate it into their programs if finalized. Finally, many commenters also argued that the risk assessment used to support the proposed exemption levels failed to provide adequate protection of human health and the environment because it evaluated only the risks of human consumption of contaminated groundwater and ignored other pathways that could pose greater risks. Based on these concerns, and based on EPA's desire to work through the individual elements of the proposal more carefully, we withdrew the proposal. Subsequently, a group of waste generating industries challenged the March 1992 action that reinstated the mixture and derived-from rules without change. Mobil Oil Corp. v. EPA, 35 F.3d 579 (D.C. Cir. 1994). The court rejected this challenge, adopting our argument that the appropriations act made the challenge moot because it prevented both us and the courts from terminating or withdrawing the interim rules before we revised them, even if we failed to meet the statutory deadline for the revisions.

We did not meet Congress' October 1, 1994 deadline for revising the mixture and derived-from rules. In early October 1994 several groups of waste generating and waste managing industries filed citizen suits to enforce the October 1, 1994 deadline for revising the mixture and derived-from rules. The U.S. District Court for the District of Columbia entered a consent decree resolving the consolidated cases on May 3, 1993. Environmental Technology Council v. Browner, C.A. No. 94-2119 (TFH) (D.D.C. 1994). The consent decree originally required the Administrator to sign a proposal to amend the mixture and derived-from rules by November 13, 1995 and a notice of final rulemaking by December 15, 1996, and specified that the deadlines in the appropriations act do not apply to any rule revising the separate regulations that establish jurisdiction over media contaminated with hazardous wastes. On November 13, 1995, the Administrator signed the proposed Hazardous Waste Identification Rule to revise the mixture and derived-from rules, which was published in the Federal Register on December 21, 1995. (60 FR 66344). We received extensive comments, many critical, on the 1995 proposal, particularly with respect to the scientific risk assessment supporting the proposed revisions to the mixture and derived-from rules. As a result of the comments, we concluded that considerable work needed to be done to resolve complex scientific and technical issues raised by the risk assessment and the comments received. On April 11, 1997, the District Court entered an order amending the consent decree in Environmental Technology Council v. Browner. The amended decree provided us with additional time to perform further scientific risk assessment work and requires us to address specific issues and options for revising the mixture and derived-from rules. The amended decree calls for a notice of proposed rulemaking to revise the mixture and derived-from rules, with an October 31, 1999 deadline for the Administrator to sign a proposal, and an April 30, 2001 deadline to sign a notice of final rulemaking. Until this rule is promulgated, the mixture and derived-from rules are considered to remain in effect on an "emergency basis."

The following excerpt is EPA's new Hazardous Waste Identification Rule.

PART 261—IDENTIFICATION AND LISTING OF HAZARDOUS WASTE

Sec. 261.1 Purpose and scope.

(a) This part identifies those solid wastes which are subject to regulation as hazardous wastes under Parts 262 through 265, 268 and Parts 270, 271, and 124 of this chapter and which are subject to the notification requirements of section 3010 of RCRA. In this part:

(1) Subpart A defines the terms "solid waste" and "hazardous waste".

* * *

(2) Subpart B sets forth the criteria used by EPA to identify characteristics of hazardous waste and to list particular hazardous wastes.

(3) Subpart C identifies characteristics of hazardous waste.

(4) Subpart D lists particular hazardous wastes.

(b)(1) The definition of solid waste contained in this Part applies only to wastes that also are hazardous for purposes of the regulations implementing Subtitle C of RCRA.

* * *

(c) For the purposes of Sections 261.2 and 261.6:

(1) A "spent material" is any material that has been used and as a result of contamination can no longer serve the purpose for which it was produced without processing;

(2) "Sludge" has the same meaning used in § 260.10 of this Chapter;

(3) A "by-product" is a material that is not one of the primary products of a production process and is not solely or separately produced by the production process. Examples are process residues such as slags or distillation column bottoms. . . .

(4) A material is "reclaimed" if it is processed to recover a usable product, or if it is regenerated. Examples are recovery of lead values from spent batteries and regeneration of spent solvents.

(5) A material is "used or reused" if it is either:

(i) Employed as an ingredient (including use as an intermediate) in an industrial process to make a product (for example, distillation bottoms from one process used as feedstock in another process). However, a material will not satisfy this condition if distinct components of the material are recovered as separate end products (as when metals are recovered from metal-containing secondary materials); or

(ii) Employed in a particular function or application as an effective substitute for a commercial product (for example, spent pickle liquor used as phosphorous precipitant and sludge conditioner in wastewater treatment).

(6) "Scrap metal" is bits and pieces of metal parts (*e.g.*,) bars, turnings, rods, sheets, wire) or metal pieces that may be combined together with bolts or soldering (*e.g.*, radiators, scrap automobiles, railroad box cars), which when worn or superfluous can be recycled.

(7) A material is "recycled" if it is used, reused, or reclaimed.

(8) A material is "accumulated speculatively" if it is accumulated before being recycled. A material is not accumulated speculatively, however, if the person accumulating it can show that the material is potentially recyclable and has a feasible means of being recycled; and that—during the calendar year (commencing on January 1)--the amount of material that is recycled, or transferred to a different site for recycling, equals at least 75 percent by weight or volume of the amount of that material accumulated at the beginning of the period. In calculating the percentage of turnover, the 75 percent requirement is to be applied to each material of the same type (*e.g.*, slags from a single smelting process) that is recycled in the same way (*i.e.*, from which the same material is recovered or that is used in the same way). Materials accumulating in units that would be exempt from regulation under § 261.4(c) are not be included in making the calculation. (Materials that are already defined as solid wastes also are not to be included in making the calculation.) Materials are no longer in this category once they are removed from accumulation for recycling, however.

* * *

§ 261.2 Definition of solid waste.

(a)(1) A *solid waste* is any discarded material that is not excluded by § 261.4(a) or that is not excluded by variance granted under §§ 260.30 and 260.31.

(2) A *discarded material* is any material which is:

(i) *Abandoned*, as explained in paragraph (b) of this section; or

(ii) *Recycled*, as explained in paragraph (c) of this section; or

(iii) Considered *inherently waste-like*, as explained in paragraph (d) of this section; or

(iv) A *military munition* identified as a solid waste in 40 CFR 266.202.

(b) Materials are solid waste if they are *abandoned* by being:

(1) Disposed of; or

(2) Burned or incinerated; or

(3) Accumulated, stored, or treated (but not recycled) before or in lieu of being abandoned by being disposed of, burned, or incinerated.

(c) Materials are solid wastes if they are *recycled*—or accumulated, stored, or treated before recycling—as specified in paragraphs (c)(1) through (c)(4) of this section.

(1) *Used in a manner constituting disposal.*

(i) Materials noted with a "*" in Column 1 of Table I are solid wastes when they are:

(A) Applied to or placed on the land in a manner that constitutes disposal; or

(B) Used to produce products that are applied to or placed on the land or are otherwise contained in products that are applied to or placed on the land (in which cases the product itself remains a solid waste).

(ii) However, commercial chemical products listed in § 261.33 are not solid wastes if they are applied to the land and that is their ordinary manner of use.

(2) *Burning for energy recovery.*

(i) Materials noted with a "*" in column 2 of Table 1 are solid wastes when they are:

(A) Burned to recover energy;

(B) Used to produce a fuel or are otherwise contained in fuels (in which cases the fuel itself remains a solid waste).

(ii) However, commercial chemical products listed in § 261.33 are not solid wastes if they are themselves fuels.

(3) *Reclaimed.* Materials noted with a "*" in column 3 of Table 1 are solid wastes when reclaimed (except as provided under 40 CFR 261.4(a)(17)). Materials noted with a "---" in column 3 of Table 1 are not solid wastes when reclaimed (except as provided under 40 CFR 261.4(a)(17)).

(4) *Accumulated speculatively.* Materials noted with a "*" in column 4 of Table 1 are solid wastes when accumulated speculatively.

Table 1

	Use constituting disposal (§261.2(c) (1))	Energy recovery/ fuel (§261.2(c) (2))	Reclamation (Sec. 261.2(c)(3)) (except as provided in 261.4(a)(17) for mineral processing secondary materials)	Speculative accumulation (§261.2(c) (4))
	1	2	3	4
Spent Materials	(*)	(*)	(*)	(*)
Sludges (listed in 40 CFR Part 261.31 or 261.32	(*)	(*)	(*)	(*)
Sludges exhibiting a characteristic of hazardous waste	(*)	(*)	---	(*)
By-products (listed in 40 CFR 261.31 or 261.32)	(*)	(*)	(*)	(*)
By-products exhibiting a characteristic of hazardous waste	(*)	(*)	---	(*)
Commercial chemical products listed in 40 CFR 261.33	(*)	(*)	---	---
Scrap metal other than excluded scrap metal (see 261.1(c)(9))	(*)	(*)	(*)	(*)

Note: The terms "spent materials," "sludges," "by-products," and "scrap metal" and "processed scrap metal" are defined in Sec. 261.1.

* * *

(3) The Administrator will use the following criteria to add wastes to that list:

(i)(A) The materials are ordinarily disposed of, burned, or incinerated; or

(B) The materials contain toxic constituent listed in Appendix VIII of Part 261 and these constituents are not ordinarily found in raw materials or products for which the materials substitute (or are found in raw materials or products in smaller concentrations) and are not used or reused during the recycling process; and

(ii) The material may pose a substantial hazard to human health and the environment when recycled.

(e) *Materials that are not solid waste when recycled.*

(1) Materials are not solid wastes when they can be shown to be recycled by being:

(i) Used or reused as ingredients in an industrial process to make a product, provided the materials are not being reclaimed; or

(ii) Used or reused as effective substitutes for commercial products; or

(iii) Returned to the original process from which they are generated, without first being reclaimed or land disposed. The material must be returned as a substitute for feedstock materials. In cases where the original process to which the material is returned is a secondary process, the materials must be managed such that there is no placement on the land. In cases where the materials are generated and reclaimed within the primary mineral processing industry, the conditions of the exclusion found at § 261.4(a)(17) apply rather than this paragraph.

(2) The following materials are solid wastes, even if the recycling involves use, reuse, or return to the original process (described in paragraphs (e)(1) (i)-(iii) of this section):

(i) Materials used in a manner constituting disposal, or used to produce products that are applied to the land; or

(ii) Materials burned for energy recovery, used to produce a fuel, or contained in fuels; or

(iii) Materials accumulated speculatively; or

(iv) Materials listed in paragraphs (d)(1) and (d)(2) of this section.

* * *

§ 261.3 Definition of hazardous waste.

(a) A solid waste, as defined in § 261.2, is a hazardous waste if:

(1) It is not excluded from regulation as a hazardous waste under § 261.4(b); and

(2) It meets any of the following criteria:

(i) It exhibits any of the characteristics of hazardous waste identified in subpart C of this part. However, any mixture of a waste from the extraction, beneficiation, and processing of ores and minerals excluded under § 261.4(b)(7) and any other solid waste exhibiting a characteristic of hazardous waste under subpart C is a hazardous waste only if it exhibits a characteristic that would not have been exhibited by the excluded waste alone if such mixture had not occurred, or if it continues to exhibit any of the characteristics exhibited by the non-excluded wastes prior to mixture. Further, for the purposes of applying the Toxicity Characteristic to such mixtures, the mixture is also a hazardous waste if it exceeds the maximum concentration for any contaminant listed in table I to § 261.24 that would not have been exceeded by the excluded waste alone if the mixture had not occurred or if it continues to exceed the maximum concentration for any contaminant exceeded by the nonexempt waste prior to mixture.

(ii) It is listed in subpart D of this part and has not been excluded from the lists in subpart D of this part under §§ 260.20 and 260.22 of this chapter.

(iii) It is a mixture of a solid waste and a hazardous waste that is listed in subpart D of this part solely because it exhibits one or more of the characteristics of hazardous waste identified in subpart C of this part, unless the resultant mixture no longer exhibits any characteristic of hazardous waste identified in subpart C of this part, or unless the solid waste is excluded from regulation under § 261.4(b)(7) and the resultant mixture no longer exhibits any characteristic of hazardous waste identified in subpart C of this part for which the hazardous waste listed in subpart D of this part was listed. (However, nonwastewater mixtures are still subject to the requirements of part 268 of this chapter, even if they no longer exhibit a characteristic at the point of land disposal).

(iv) It is a mixture of solid waste and one or more hazardous wastes listed in subpart D of this part and has not been excluded from paragraph (a)(2) of this section under §§ 260.20 and 260.22 of this chapter; however, the following mixtures of solid wastes and hazardous wastes listed in subpart D of this part are not hazardous wastes (except by application of paragraph (a)(2)(i) or (ii) of this section) if the generator can demonstrate that the mixture consists of wastewater the discharge of which is subject to regulation under either section 402 or section 307(b) of the Clean Water Act (including wastewater at facilities which have eliminated the discharge of wastewater).

* * *

§ 261.4 Exclusions.

(a) *Materials which are not solid wastes*. The following materials are not solid wastes for the purpose of this Part:

(1)(i) Domestic sewage; and

(ii) Any mixture of domestic sewage and other wastes that passes through a sewer system to a publicly-owned treatment works for treatment. "Domestic sewage" means untreated sanitary wastes that pass through a sewer system.

(2) Industrial wastewater discharges that are point source discharges subject to regulation under Section 402 of the Clean Water Act, as amended.

[*Comment*: This exclusion applies only to the actual point source discharge. It does not exclude industrial wastewaters while they are being collected, stored or treated before discharge, nor does it exclude sludges that are generated by industrial wastewater treatment.]

(3) Irrigation return flows.

(4) Source, special nuclear or by-product material as defined by the Atomic Energy Act of 1954, as amended, 42 U.S.C. 2011 *et seq*.

(5) Materials subjected to in-situ mining techniques which are not removed from the ground as part of the extraction process.

(6) Pulping liquors (*i.e.*, black liquor) that are reclaimed in a pulping liquor recovery furnace and then reused in the pulping process, unless it is accumulated speculatively as defined in § 261.1(c) of this chapter.

(7) Spent sulfuric acid used to produce virgin sulfuric acid, unless it is accumulated speculatively as defined in § 261.1(c) of this Chapter.

(8) Secondary materials that are reclaimed and returned to the original process or processes in which they were generated where they are reused in the production process provided:

(i) Only tank storage is involved, and the entire process through completion of reclamation is closed by being entirely connected with pipes or other comparable enclosed means of conveyance;

(ii) Reclamation does not involve controlled flame combustion (such as occurs in boilers, industrial furnaces, or incinerators);

(iii) The secondary materials are never accumulated in such tanks for over twelve months without being reclaimed; and

(iv) The reclaimed material is not used to produce a fuel, or used to produce products that are used in a manner constituting disposal.

* * *

(b) *Solid wastes which are not hazardous wastes.* The following solid wastes are not hazardous wastes:

(1) Household waste, including household waste that has been collected, transported, stored, treated, disposed, recovered (e.g., refuse-derived fuel) or reused. "Household waste" means any material (including garbage, trash and sanitary wastes in septic tanks) derived from households (including single and multiple residences, hotels and motels, bunkhouses, ranger stations, crew quarters, campgrounds, picnic grounds and day-use recreation areas). A resource recovery facility managing municipal solid waste shall not be deemed to be treating, storing, disposing of, or otherwise managing hazardous wastes for the purposes of regulation under this subtitle, if such facility:

(i) Receives and burns only

(A) Household waste (from single and multiple dwellings, hotels, motels, and other residential sources) and

(B) Solid waste from commercial or industrial sources that does not contain hazardous waste; and

(ii) Such facility does not accept hazardous wastes and the owner or operator of such facility has established contractual requirements or other appropriate notification or inspection procedures to assure that hazardous wastes are not received at or burned in such facility.

(2) Solid wastes generated by any of the following and which are returned to the soils as fertilizers:

(i) The growing and harvesting of agricultural crops.

(ii) The raising of animals, including animal manures.

(3) Mining overburden returned to the mine site.

(4) Fly ash waste, bottom ash waste, slag waste, and flue gas emission control waste, generated primarily from the combustion of coal or other fossil fuels, except as provided by § 266.112 of this chapter for facilities that burn or process hazardous waste.

(5) Drilling fluids, produced waters, and other wastes associated with the exploration, development, or production of crude oil, natural gas or geothermal energy.

* * *

(g) *Dredged material that is not a hazardous waste.* Dredged material that is subject to the requirements of a permit that has been issued under 404 of the Federal Water Pollution Control Act (33 U.S.C.1344) or section 103 of the Marine Protection, Research, and Sanctuaries Act of 1972 (33 U.S.C. 1413) is not a hazardous waste. For this paragraph (g), the following definitions apply:

(1) The term *dredged material* has the same meaning as defined in 40 CFR 232.2;

(2) The term *permit* means:

(i) A permit issued by the U.S. Army Corps of Engineers (Corps) or an approved State under section 404 of the Federal Water Pollution Control Act (33 U.S.C. 1344);

(ii) A permit issued by the Corps under section 103 of the Marine Protection, Research, and Sanctuaries Act of 1972 (33 U.S.C. 1413); or

(iii) In the case of Corps civil works projects, the administrative equivalent of the permits referred to in paragraphs (g)(2)(i) and (ii) of this section, as provided for in Corps regulations (for example, see 33 CFR 336.1, 336.2, and 337.6).

C. Regulation of Generators, Transporters, and Exporters of Hazardous Waste

Once a substance is deemed a hazardous waste, then Subtitle C's cradle-to-grave system applies. Subtitle C's cradle-to-grave system regulates generators, transporters, and owners/operators of treatment, storage or disposal facilities (TSDFs). Regulations governing generators and transporters can be characterized as more procedural or information gathering in nature. Subtitle C not only requires TSDFs to meet similar standards to generators and transporters, but also regulates the design of facilities, and treatment and disposal methods. Congress felt it was necessary to subject TSDFs to more burdensome standards because the facilities represent the final stage of waste disposal back into the environment. This more expansive regulation of TSDFs even led one federal judge to comment that Subtitle C regulates hazardous waste "well beyond the grave" since it continues to regulate long after they close.[58]

1. Generators

The standards applicable to generators of hazardous waste may be found under RCRA § 3002. This section instructs EPA to develop regulations applicable to generators "as may be necessary to protect human health and the environment."[59] The Code of Federal Regulations defines a generator as "any person, by site, whose act or process produces hazardous waste identified or listed in part 261 of this chapter or whose act first causes a hazardous waste to become subject to regulation."[60] A generator may be considered any one of three different classifications depending on the levels of waste generated. These classifications are:

1. *Fully regulated generators,* which produce greater than 1,000 kg of hazardous waste per calendar month;

2. *Small Quantity Generators* (SQG) which produce less than 1,000 kg but greater than 100 kg per calendar month; and

3. *Conditionally Exempt Generators* (CEGs) which produce not more than 100 kg per calendar month.[61]

Although a generator's status may vary from month to month, qualification as a generator allows for no flexibility unless specifically provided for. The many requirements of generators under this section represent the beginning of the cradle-to-grave tracking system.

Part 262 applies to those who generate hazardous waste and those who import hazardous waste into the United States.[62] Moving wastes around (*e.g.,* during clean-up activities) can constitute the generation of hazardous wastes and thus bring otherwise unregulated materials into the regulatory net.[63] The following diagram illustrates the relative quantities of hazardous wastes produced by industrial category.

---

[58] *See* Randolph Hill, *An Overview of RCRA: The "Mind-Numbing" Provisions of the Most Complicated Environmental Statute.* 21 ENVTL. L. REP. 10,254, 10,271 (May, 1991) (quoting Judge Williams from *American Iron & Steel Inst. v. EPA,* 886 F.2d 390, 393 (D.C. Cir. 1989), *cert. denied,* 110 S.Ct. 3237 (1990).

[59] 42 U.S.C. § 6922(a) (1999).

[60] 40 C.F.R. § 260.10 (1999).

[61] *See* 40 C.F.R. §§ 260.10 and 261.5 (1999).

[62] *See* 40 C.F.R. § 262.10 (a) and (d) (1999).

[63] *See* Chemical Waste Mgt., Inc. v. EPA, 869 F.2d 1526, 1535-40 (D.C.Cir. 1989)

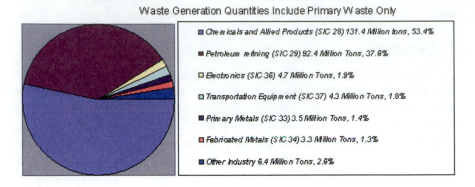

Figure 9.7–Quantities of Primary Hazardous Waste Generated in 1991, by SIC Code[64]

In 1995, 20,873 large quantity generators (LQGs) produced 214 million tons of hazardous waste regulated by RCRA. Section 3002 requires record keeping and information management. Each generator must:

- keep records on the quantity of hazardous waste generated;
- meet labeling and container standards for the storage, transport, or disposal of hazardous wastes;
- furnish information concerning the chemical composition of the waste to transporters and TSDFs;
- use a manifest to assure proper tracking of the transportation, treatment and disposal of the waste; and
- submit biennial reports concerning the quantities, nature, and disposal of hazardous wastes, and describing efforts to reduce the volume and toxicity generated.

Amendments to RCRA in 1984 introduced additional requirements concerning preparation of the manifest. Since September 1, 1985 generators must certify on each shipment of hazardous waste that (1) the generator has a program in place to reduce the volume of waste to the degree determined by the facility to be economically practicable, and (2) the proposed method of treatment, storage, or disposal is that practicable method which minimizes threats to human health and the environment.[65]

Note that § 3002 contains *no* requirements for waste management, to say nothing of waste minimization. Rather, Congress sought through recordkeeping, to achieve a full accounting of the waste management process. So complete are Congress' directives for EPA in its regulation of

---

[64] 1991 Primary Hazardous Waste Quantity = 246 Million Tons. EPA, 1991 BIENNIAL RCRA HAZARDOUS WASTE REPORT (1991).

[65] 42 U.S.C. § 6922(b)(1) and (2) (1994). These two additions were introduced in recognition of the growing practice by generators that would subcontract out the transportation of the waste. *See* S. REP NO. 96-172 H.R. CONF. REP. NO. 96-1444; *see also* 1980 U.S.C.C.A.N. 5019.

generators that the EPA's actual rules provided in the *Code of Federal Regulations* show little variation from the actual statutory language.[66]

Once a fully regulated generator determines it produced a hazardous waste, EPA requires that the generator obtain a hazardous waste identification number.[67] Next, the generator must follow the necessary procedures for off-site transport of the waste including the preparation of a manifest.[68] On the manifest the generator *must* designate a facility that is permitted by the EPA to handle the waste to be treated.[69] Both the designated facility and the transporter must have EPA identification numbers.[70] This enables the waste to be more easily tracked from generation to disposal. The generator signs the manifest describing the waste and those designated to handle its transportation and disposal, retains one copy, and gives the remaining copies to the transporter.[71] The total number of copies with the transporter must be enough to account for the waste's entire disposal or treatment so there is a final copy available to come full circle from the TSDF and be returned to the generator.[72] Depending on the method of transportation of the waste, there may be different rules as to which parties retain copies and how many.[73] In addition, prior to transporting hazardous waste to a designated TSDF, the generator must comply with certain rules concerning the packaging and labeling of the waste as determined by the Department of Transportation (DOT).[74] If a generator chooses to export or import hazardous waste, RCRA accounts for this also.[75]

The following is an example of an EPA manifest.[76]

---

[66] *See* 40 C.F.R. pt. 262.

[67] *See id.* § 262.12 (1995).

[68] *See id.* § 262.20-.23 (1995).

[69] *See id.* § 262.20(b) (1995). A generator *may* also designate an alternate facility in case the original facility designated cannot receive the hazardous waste due to emergency. If such an emergency or any other event takes place which prohibits the transporter from delivering the waste to the designated facility then the transporter must either take it to the alternate facility if designated, or return it to the generator. *See id.* § 262.20(c) and (d).

[70] *See id.* § 262.12(c) (1995)

[71] *See id.* § 262.23 (1995).

[72] *See id.* § 262.22 (1995).

[73] *See id.* § 262.23(c)-.23(d) (1995).

[74] *See id.* §§ 262.30-33. (1995).

[75] *See id.* §§ 262.50-58 (1995) (concerns exporting hazardous waste) *see also id.* § 262.60 (1995) (concerns importing of hazardous waste).

[76] EPA, UNIFORM HAZARDOUS WASTE MANIFEST, FORM NO. 8700-22 (1991).

77

Please print or type   (Form designed for use on elite (12 pitch) typewriter)   Form Approved. OMB No 2050 0039 Expires 9 - 30 91

UNIFORM HAZARDOUS WASTE MANIFEST	1 Generator's US EPA ID No	Manifest Document No.	2. Page 1 of	Information in the shaded areas is not required by Federal law
3. Generator's Name and Mailing Address			A State Manifest Document Number	
			B State Generator's ID	
4. Generator's Phone ( )				
5. Transporter 1 Company Name	6 US EPA ID Number		C. State Transporter's ID	
			D. Transporter's Phone	
7 Transporter 2 Company Name	8 US EPA ID Number		E. State Transporter's ID	
			F. Transporter's Phone	
9 Designated Facility Name and Site Address	10 US EPA ID Number		G State Facility's ID	
			H. Facility's Phone	

11 US DOT Description (Including Proper Shipping Name, Hazard Class, and ID Number)	12 Containers No.	Type	13. Total Quantity	14. Unit Wt/Vol	I. Waste No.
G E N E R A T O R	a					
	b					
	c					
	d.					

J. Additional Descriptions for Materials Listed Above   K. Handling Codes for Wastes Listed Above

15 Special Handling Instructions and Additional Information

16 GENERATOR'S CERTIFICATION: I hereby declare that the contents of this consignment are fully and accurately described above by proper shipping name and are classified, packed, marked, and labeled, and are in all respects in proper condition for transport by highway according to applicable international and national government regulations

If I am a large quantity generator, I certify that I have a program in place to reduce the volume and toxicity of waste generated to the degree I have determined to be economically practicable and that I have selected the practicable method of treatment, storage, or disposal currently available to me which minimizes the present and future threat to human health and the environment; OR, If I am a small quantity generator, I have made a good faith effort to minimize my waste generation and select the best waste management method that is available to me and that I can afford.

Printed/Typed Name	Signature	Month	Day	Year

T R A N S P O R T E R

17. Transporter 1 Acknowledgement of Receipt of Materials

Printed/Typed Name	Signature	Month	Day	Year

18 Transporter 2 Acknowledgement of Receipt of Materials

Printed/Typed Name	Signature	Month	Day	Year

F A C I L I T Y

19 Discrepancy Indication Space

20. Facility Owner or Operator: Certification of receipt of hazardous materials covered by this manifest except as noted in item 19.

Printed/Typed Name	Signature	Month	Day	Year

EPA Form 8700 - 22 (Rev. 9 - 88) Previous editions are obsolete.

---

[77] *See id.*, FORM NO. 8700-22a.

Environmental Protection Agency **Pt. 262, App.**

Please print or type (Form designed for use on elite (12-pitch) typewriter.) Form Approved OMB No. 2050-0039 Expires 9-30-91

UNIFORM HAZARDOUS WASTE MANIFEST *(Continuation Sheet)*	21 Generator's US EPA ID No	Manifest Document No	22 Page	Information in the shaded areas is not required by Federal law

23 Generator's Name

L. State Manifest Document Number

M. State Generator's ID

24 Transporter ____ Company Name 25 US EPA ID Number

N. State Transporter's ID

O. Transporter's Phone

26 Transporter ____ Company Name 27 US EPA ID Number

P. State Transporter's ID

Q. Transporter's Phone

28. US DOT Description *(Including Proper Shipping Name, Hazard Class, and ID Number)*	29 Containers No.	29 Containers Type	30 Total Quantity	31 Unit Wt/Vol	R Waste No.
a					
b					
c.					
d					
e.					
f					
g					
h.					
i.					

GENERATOR

S. Additional Descriptions for Materials Listed Above

T. Handling Codes for Wastes Listed Above

32. Special Handling Instructions and Additional Information

TRANSPORTER

33. Transporter ____ Acknowledgement of Receipt of Materials — Date

Printed/Typed Name | Signature | Month Day Year

34. Transporter ____ Acknowledgement of Receipt of Materials — Date

Printed/Typed Name | Signature | Month Day Year

FACILITY

35. Discrepancy Indication Space

EPA Form 8700-22A (Rev. 9-88) Previous edition is obsolete

Figure 9.8

GENERATOR'S DUTIES

- Determine whether material is a hazardous waste
- Notify proper authorities
- Obtain unique identification number
- Proper marking, storage, training, and contingency plans at generator's facility
- Not accumulate on-site beyond 90 days

By holding the generator responsible for the paper trail of the waste, the generator is held accountable for improper disposal should the waste not be sent to an EPA designated facility. The following case represents the liability that may be attached to a generator should it be shown that the receiving disposal facility was not properly managing the waste or was not an EPA-designated facility.

UNITED STATES V. HAYES INTERNATIONAL CORPORATION

786 F.2d 1499 (11th Cir. 1986)

KRAVITCH, Circuit Judge:

The degree of knowledge necessary for a conviction under 42 U.S.C. § 6928(d)(1), unlawful transportation of hazardous waste, is the principal issue in this appeal. The district court granted judgments of acquittal notwithstanding the jury verdicts . . . . [W]e reverse.

I. BACKGROUND

Hayes International Corp. (Hayes) operates an airplane refurbishing plant in Birmingham, Alabama. In the course of its business, Hayes generates certain waste products, two of which are relevant to this case. First, Hayes must drain fuel tanks of the planes on which it works. Second, Hayes paints the aircraft with spray guns and uses solvents to clean the paint guns and lines, thereby generating a mix of paint and solvents.

L.H. Beasley [Hayes' co-defendant] was the employee of Hayes responsible for disposal of hazardous wastes. In early 1981, Beasley orally agreed with Jack Hurt, an employee of Performance Advantage, Inc., to dispose of certain wastes. Under the agreement, Performance Advantage would obtain from Hayes the valuable jet fuel drained from the planes; Performance Advantage would pay twenty cents per gallon for the jet fuel, and, at no charge, would remove other wastes from the Hayes plant including the mixture of paint and solvents. Performance Advantage was a recycler, and used the jet fuel to make marketable fuel. Wastes were transported from Hayes to Performance Advantage on eight occasions between January 1981 and March 1982.

Beginning in August 1982, government officials discovered drums of waste generated by Hayes and illegally disposed of by Performance Advantage. Approximately six hundred drums of waste were found, deposited among seven illegal disposal sites in Georgia and Alabama. The waste was the paint and solvent which Performance Advantage had removed from Hayes. Some of the drums were simply dumped in yards, while others were buried.

The prosecutions in this case were brought under the Resource Conservation and Recovery Act. 42 U.S.C. §§ 6901-6987. The Act creates a cradle to grave regulatory scheme to ensure that hazardous wastes are properly disposed of. Generators of waste are required to identify hazardous wastes, 42 U.S.C. § 6922(1), and use a manifest system to ensure that wastes are disposed of only in facilities possessing a permit. 42 U.S.C. § 6922(5).

The mixture of paint waste and solvent involved in this case was a characteristic waste based on its ignitability. 40 C.F.R. § 261.21.

Beasley and Hayes each were convicted of eight counts of violating 42 U.S.C. § 6928(d)(1), which provides criminal sanctions for

Any person who (1) knowingly transports any hazardous waste identified or listed under this subchapter to a facility which does not have a permit under § 6925 of this title.[78]

Hayes' liability is based on the actions of Beasley. It is undisputed that Performance Advantage did not have a permit.

*   *   *

II. THE ELEMENTS OF A § 6928(d) OFFENSE

Congress did not provide any guidance, either in the statute or the legislative history, concerning the meaning of "knowing" in § 6928(d). Indeed, Congress stated that it had "not sought to define 'knowing' for offenses under subsection (d); that process has been left to the courts under general principles." S. REP. NO. 172, 96TH CONG., 2D SESS. 39 (1980), U.S. CODE CONG. & ADMIN. NEWS 1980, pp. 5019, 5038. In discerning the relevant general principles, we turn to a few examples from a long line of Supreme Court cases discussing the necessary elements of regulatory offenses.

Whether Knowledge of the Regulations is Required

* * *

[Defendants] argue that a violation of § 6928(d)(1) . . . requires knowledge of transportation, knowledge that the waste is a waste within the meaning of the statute, knowledge that disposal sites must have a permit, and knowledge that the site in question does not have a permit. In short, they contend that the defendants must have known that their actions violated the statute.

* * *

As the Supreme Court has explained, it is completely fair and reasonable to charge those who choose to operate in such areas with knowledge of the regulatory provisions. Indeed, the reasonableness is borne out in this case, for the evidence at trial belied the appellees' profession of ignorance. Accordingly, in a prosecution under 42 U.S.C. § 6928(d)(1) it would be no defense to claim no knowledge that the paint waste was a hazardous waste within the meaning of the regulations; nor would it be a defense to argue ignorance of the permit requirement.

Whether Knowledge of the Permit Status is Required

The government argues that the statute does not require knowledge of the permit status of the facility to which the wastes are transported.

---

[78] The current version of the statute applies to anyone who "transports or causes to be transported." 42 U.S.C.A. § 6928(d)(1) (Supp.1985).

* * *

In this case, the congressional purpose indicates knowledge of the permit status is required. The precise wrong Congress intended to combat through § 6928(d) was transportation to an unlicensed facility. Removing the knowing requirement from this element would criminalize innocent conduct; for example, if the defendant reasonably believed that the site had a permit, but in fact had been misled by the people at the site. If Congress intended such a strict statute, it could have dropped the "knowingly" requirement.

The government does not face an unacceptable burden of proof in proving that the defendant acted with knowledge of the permit status. Knowledge does not require certainty .... Moreover, in this regulatory context a defendant acts knowingly if he willfully fails to determine the permit status of the facility.

Moreover, the government may prove guilty knowledge with circumstantial evidence. In the context of the hazardous waste statutes, proving knowledge should not be difficult. The statute at issue here sets forth certain procedures transporters must follow to ensure that wastes are sent only to permit facilities. Transporters of waste presumedly are aware of these procedures, and if a transporter does not follow the procedures, a juror may draw certain inferences. Where there is no evidence that those who took the waste asserted that they were properly licensed, the jurors may draw additional inferences. Jurors may also consider the circumstances and terms of the transaction. It is common knowledge that properly disposing of wastes is an expensive task, and if someone is willing to take away wastes at an unusual price or under unusual circumstances, then a juror can infer that the transporter knows the wastes are not being taken to a permit facility.

In sum, to convict under § 6928(d)(1), the jurors must find that the defendant knew what the waste was (here, a mixture of paint and solvent), and that the defendant knew the disposal site had no permit. Knowledge does not require certainty, and the jurors may draw inferences from all of the circumstances, including the existence of the regulatory scheme.

III. ANALYSIS

* * *

B.

The appellees' second defense is that the evidence was insufficient to show they knew that Performance Advantage did not have a permit. In considering the evidence, we view it in the light most favorable to the government, with all reasonable inferences drawn in favor of the jury's verdict. The evidence shows that Hayes was not following the regulatory procedure for manifesting waste sent to a permit site, from which the jury could have inferred that the appellees did not believe Performance Advantage had a permit. This inference is strengthened by Hayes' own documents, which set forth this requirement. Performance Advantage also was not charging to haul away the waste (although obviously they found the overall deal advantageous), and Beasley thought he had made a good deal; accordingly the terms were such as to raise suspicion.

The appellees rely on Hurt's testimony that he had had an EPA "number," and that he could not recall whether he had given it to Beasley. Drawing all reasonable inferences in favor of the government, the jury could have found that Hurt did not give the EPA "number" to Beasley. In addition, the "number" was not a permit, and the jury could have inferred that Beasley did not believe the number evidenced an actual permit.[79] Accordingly, the jury could have found that there was no evidence that Performance Advantage professed to be a permit facility. Based on all the above, the jury could have found beyond a reasonable doubt that appellees knew Performance Advantage did not have a permit.

C.

Appellees' third defense is that they believed that Performance Advantage was recycling the waste. At the outset, we accept the theory of this mistake of fact defense . . . . In this case, had the wastes been recycled, then no violation of the statute would have occurred[, because, under the rules in force at the time, they would not have been a hazardous waste].

* * *

We believe, however, that there is sufficient evidence for the jury to have rejected the defense of mistake of fact.

* * *

NOTES

1. Which elements of § 6928(d) required knowledge and which did not? Does this distinction make sense? Which is easier for a generator to determine, the hazard status of the waste, or the permit status of the transporter?

2. How does generator liability of the kind described in *Hayes* promote the proper management of hazardous waste?

3. More generally, will full, cradle-to-grave *accounting* promote proper waste management? Will it promote waste minimization? How?

4. The following is a breakdown of hazardous waste produced by state. How does your home state compare? Does this information affect decisions your might make about your life?

---

[79] Indeed no permit actually existed.

STATE	HAZARDOUS WASTE QUANTITY			LARGE QUANTITY GENERATORS		
	RANK	TONS GENERATED	PERCENTAGE	RANK	NUMBER	PERCENTAGE
ALABAMA	16	12,886,262	0.5	23	278	1.4
ALASKA	51	3,438	0.0	42	65	0.3
ARIZONA	40	66,865	0.0	27	199	1.0
ARKANSAS	33	274,158	0.1	26	204	1.0
CALIFORNIA	3	17,029,474	6.1	2	1,635	8.2
COLORADO	36	169,554	0.1	31	156	0.8
CONNECTICUT	30	310,825	0.1	18	395	2.0
DELAWARE	41	66,021	0.0	43	64	0.3
DISTRICT OF COLUMBIA	54	764	0.0	49	18	0.1
FLORIDA	22	558,122	0.2	17	414	2.1
GEORGIA	25	459,543	0.2	16	430	2.2
GUAM	55	299	0.0	53	13	0.1
HAWAII	21	592,900	0.2	45	53	0.3
IDAHO	17	1,209,841	0.4	46	52	0.3
ILLINOIS	5	13,892,416	5	5	1,151	5.8
INDIANA	12	1,733,196	0.6	40	606	3.0
IOWA	48	11,507	0.0	37	108	0.5
KANSAS	13	1,722,483	0.6	25	212	1.1
KENTUCKY	18	1,149,881	0.4	14	440	2.2
LOUISIANA	4	15,469,654	5.5	21	359	1.8
MAINE	45	19,459	0.0	33	144	0.7
MARYLAND	26	442,826	0.2	27	189	0.9
MASSACHUSETTS	20	606,282	0.2	12	472	2.4
MICHIGAN	6	12,459,834	4.5	9	707	3.6
MINNESOTA	31	293,489	0.1	22	285	1.4
MISSISSIPPI	14	1,579,260	0.6	32	153	0.8
MISSOURI	42	62,070	0.0	2	181	0.9
MONTANA	50	7,640	0.0	47	51	0.3
NAVAJO NATION	56	195	0.0	54	11	0.1
NEBRASKA	38	89,878	0.0	43	64	0.3
NEVADA	49	8,348	0.0	39	78	0.4
NEW HAMPSHIRE	43	26,009	0.0	34	130	0.7
NEW JERSEY	27	437,202	0.2	7	1,049	5.3
NEW MEXICO	35	204,494	0.1	48	44	0.2
NEW YORK	9	2,557,088	0.9	1	1,878	9.4
NORTH CAROLINA	32	286,339	0.1	11	587	2.9
NORTH DAKOTA	23	520,226	0.2	51	16	0.1
OHIO	11	1,774,939	0.6	3	1,354	6.8
OKLAHOMA	24	511,918	0.2	30	168	0.8
OREGON	39	58,187	0.0	24	220	1.1
PENNSYLVANIA	15	1,523,362	0.5	6	1,110	5.6
PUERTO RICO	19	893,006	0.3	41	68	0.3
RHODE ISLAND	44	25,428	0.0	36	112	0.6
SOUTH CAROLINA	34	261,015	0.1	19	371	1.9
SOUTH DAKOTA	53	780	0.0	51	16	0.1
TENNESSEE	2	38,686,622	13.9	13	467	2.3
TEXAS	1	145,073,442	52.0	4	1,397	6.5
TRUST TERRITORIES	46	12,154	0.0	55	3	0.0
UTAH	28	418,523	0.1	38	68	0.5
VERMONT	47	11,811	0.0	40	75	0.4
VIRGIN ISLANDS	52	3,329	0.0	56	1	0.0
VIRGINIA	37	98,678	0.0	19	371	1.9
WASHINGTON	8	3,250,971	1.2	8	721	3.6
WEST VIRGINIA	7	8,489,828	3.0	35	117	0.6
WISCONSIN	29	404,659	0.1	15	432	2.2
WYOMING	10	1,972,177	0.7	50	17	0.1
Total		279,088,670	100		19,908	100.2

Exhibit 1 Quantity of RCRA Hazardous Waste Generated and Number of Waste Generators, by State 1995

Note: Columns may not sum due to rounding

Table 9.1–Quantities of Hazardous Waste Generated[80]

---

[80] EPA, EXECUTIVE SUMMARY, exh. 1, ES-9 (1995).

Small quantity and conditionally exempt generators. Small quantity generators (SQGs) receive somewhat different treatment from that of large quantity generators (LQGs). Originally, EPA's 1980 regulations fully exempted all SQGs from RCRA regulations.[81] Congress' introduction of the 1984 amendments, however, narrowed the full exemption class to those generators that produce no more than 1000kg/month of hazardous waste,[82] and required that SQGs meet the manifest system requirements.[83] EPA's response to the 1984 amendments resulted in SQGs becoming subject to the bulk of the large quantity standards with specified exceptions.[84] The main differences between LQGs and SQGs are in the areas of recordkeeping and reporting obligations. Also, while a LQG is only allowed to accumulate waste for 90 days before receiving TSDF status, a SQG can accumulate hazardous waste for up to 180 days.[85]

The third class of generators are conditionally exempt generators (CEGs) which, because they produce less than 100 kg/month, remain largely exempt from RCRA[86] but for the requirement that they must determine whether the waste produced is hazardous.[87] CEGs are not required to send their waste to RCRA-regulated TSDFs but rather may send their waste to (a) permitted municipal facilities, (b) permitted industrial solid waste facilities, or (c) facilities that will use, reuse, or effectively recycle the wastes or process them for such purposes.[88]

Farmers are also not held to the same obligations of other generators in the application or disposal of pesticides through various agricultural practices. Although required to take certain steps in rinsing chemical containers in accordance with the container label, there is little else that presents any real form of Subtitle C regulation.[89]

2. Transporters

Transporters of hazardous waste are responsible for the delivery of the waste from the generator to the TSDFs. In 1995, 20,497 shippers reported transporting a total of 10.7 million tons of hazardous waste. RCRA § 3003 compels EPA to develop applicable standards that are similar to those demanded of generators concerning recordkeeping, labeling of hazardous waste, compliance with the manifest system, and transfer to EPA designated

---

[81] *See* 40 C.F.R. § 261.5(f) (1984) (superseded).

[82] *See* 42 U.S.C. § 6921(d) (1995).

[83] *See id.* § 6921(d)(3) (1995).

[84] *See* 40 C.F.R. § 262.44 (1995). *See also id.* § 262.20 (1995) (for recycling exemption from manifest requirement).

[85] *See id.* § 262.34(d) (1989).

[86] *See id.* § 261.5(b) (1995).

[87] *See id.* § 261.5(g) (1995).

[88] *See id.* § 261.5 (1995).

[89] *See id.* § 262.70 (1995).

facilities. RCRA also requires EPA to coordinate with DOT in developing such regulations.

EPA in codifying these mandates, requires transporters to obtain an identification number and comply with manifesting, recordkeeping, and labeling requirements. The transporter must deliver the entire amount of the waste to the designated transporter or TSDF. Should the transporter be prevented from delivering the waste in accordance with the designation on the manifest, then the transporter must contact the generator for further instructions and revise the manifest accordingly. In addition, should the transporter have to temporarily "store" the waste, any such period requiring storage for more than ten days requires a permit. Transporters must take immediate action in the event of a discharge to notify appropriate authorities and assist in the clean-up. If a transporter imports waste into the United States or mixes wastes of different codes in the same container, she may be considered a generator.

PROBLEM
TRENDS[90]

The latest publicly available data on waste generation, transport, and management shows decreases in amounts of hazardous waste, despite some increases in coverage.

	1993	*1995*	*Difference*
Generated (LQGs / million tons)	24362 / 258	20873 / 214	-14% / -17%
Transported (shippers / million tons)	23964 / 17.4	20497 / 10.7	-14% / -63%
Management in TSDFs (TSDFs / million tons)	2584 / 235	1983 / 208	-23% / -11%

What do you make of these decreases? Do they represent a successful waste minimization program (assuming that the trend continues)? What do you make of the decreases in numbers of waste handlers? And what might the huge decrease in the amount of waste transported mean?

---

3. The Exportation of Hazardous Waste

The stringency of RCRA's regulation of hazardous waste creates a strong incentive for generators to find alternatives to disposal. This can be a good thing, as when it encourages waste minimization practices and reuse or recycling. But it also creates an incentive to find disposal sites where

---

[90] EPA, THE NATIONAL BIENNIAL RCRA HAZARDOUS WASTE REPORT (Based on 1995 Data) E-3 to E-7 (Aug. 1997).

recycling. But it also creates an incentive to find disposal sites where regulation is less strict and less expensive. And that points to countries where the regulatory infrastructure is limited and where the desperate need for currency is an invitation to official and illegal dumping in an environmentally unsound manner. Even considering transportation costs, disposal in some other countries costs a small fraction of disposal in the U.S. The notorious wandering barge *Khian Sea*—which wandered the globe from port to port looking for a place to dump its toxic cargo—is believed to be just the visible tip of an enormous commerce in hazardous waste from North to South, that is, from industrialized countries in Europe and North America to less developed countries (LDCs) in the Caribbean, Africa, and Asia.

RCRA only minimally regulates the export of hazardous waste: the only substantive requirement of § 3017, 42 U.S.C. § 6938, (which you should now read) is that the exporter must obtain in advance the written consent of the importing country to the shipment. By way of procedure, § 3017 requires the exporter first to notify EPA of any proposed shipment; then EPA (through the Department of State) notifies the recipient nation, informing the country of its right to refuse consent and of the restrictions on the substance in the U.S.; and finally the consent or refusal is transmitted back to the exporter. EPA gathers information about the shipment as part of the notification process, but it has no authority—nor does it seek to exercise any such authority—to evaluate the environmental adequacy of the disposal arrangements in the receiving country.

To combat the growing problem of unregulated export of hazardous waste to LDCs, 116 countries and the European Union adopted the Basel Convention on the Control of Transboundary Movements of Hazardous Wastes and Their Disposal,[91] Most of it is strikingly similar to (albeit more elaborate than) RCRA, that is, it relies primarily on notification, prior informed consent (PIC),[92] and a manifest system to control exports.[93] Several new provisions give added teeth, though:

- by prohibiting exports and imports from non-party nations, the Convention creates in effect a cartel of countries that adopt the PIC principle and procedures, or their equivalent;[94]
- transit nations also have the right to prior informed consent and refusal of consent;[95]
- the importing *and exporting* countries must prevent "the import of hazardous wastes and other wastes if it has reason to believe that the wastes in question will not be managed in an environmentally sound manner";[96]

---

[91] Convention on the Control of Transboundary Movements of Hazardous Wastes and Their Disposal, Mar. 22, 1989, 28 I.L.M. 649 [hereinafter Basel Convention].

[92] *See id.,* art IV, para. 1, 28 I.L.M. at 661.

[93] *See id.,* art IV, para. 7, 28 I.L.M. at 663.

[94] *See id.,* art IV, para. 6, 28 I.L.M. at 661.

[95] *See id.*

[96] *See id.,* art IV, para. 2(g), 28 I.L.M. at 662.

- when management of the wastes in the importing country does not or will not comport with environmentally sound practice, then the exporting country has the duty to ensure that the wastes are *reimported* to it.[97]

The Basel Convention also states as principles that the generation of hazardous waste is to be minimized and it is to be disposed as close as possible to the place of generation. It also declares that illegal traffic in hazardous waste is criminal.

The United States signed and ratified the Basel Convention, but has not yet enacted conforming amendments to RCRA. Consequently, the U.S. is not yet part of the Basel framework, and there seems little immediate prospect of that occurring. Subsequent meetings of the Conference of the Parties established to govern the implementation of the Convention have adopted a complete ban on shipments from industrialized to developing countries, but the U.S. has strongly opposed such actions and is not yet bound by them, in any event.

Of the African nations, however, only Nigeria signed the Basel Convention. The others believed that it did not go far enough in restricting exports of hazardous waste from North to South.[98] As an alternative, therefore, in 1991 the Organization of African Unity sponsored a regional agreement, the African Convention on the Ban on the Import of All Forms of Hazardous Wastes into Africa and the Control of Transboundary Movements of Such Wastes Generated in Africa known as the Bamako Convention.[99] For wastes—broadly defined to include recyclables—generated outside of Africa, the Convention requires that all parties "prohibit the import of all hazardous wastes, for any reason, into Africa from noncontracting Parties."[100] Wastes generated within Africa, by contrast, may move across international boundaries, but under tight controls. Source states must require generators of hazardous waste to submit sufficient information to allow for waste audits by the international Secretariat (called "Dumpwatch");[101] establish strict, joint, and several liability for harm from hazardous waste;[102] and ensure the existence of sufficient facilities within its borders to manage its hazardous wastes in an "environmentally sound" manner.[103] There is an absolute prohibition on exporting in violation of the laws of importing or transit

---

[97] *See id.,* art VIII, 28 I.L.M. at 666.

[98] To some extent they have been proven correct: the recycling exception in Basel has become a large loophole for continued shipments. *See* B. John Ovink, *Transboundary Shipments of Toxic Waste: The Basel and Bamako Conventions: Do Third World Countries Have a Choice?,* 13 DICK. J. INTL. L. 281, 281 (1995).

[99] Convention on the Ban of the Import into Africa and the Control of Transboundary Movement and Management of Hazardous Wastes within Africa, Jan. 29, 1991, 30 I.L.M. 773. For a succinct comparison of the Basel and Bamako conventions, *see* Ovink, *supra.*

[100] *See id.,* art IV, para. 1, 30 I.L.M. at 780.

[101] *See id.,* art V., 30 I.L.M. at 784.

[102] *See id.,* art IV, para. 3(b), at 781.

[103] *See id.,* art IV, para. 3(d).

states, exporting to a country that lacks facilities for the environmentally sound management of hazardous wastes, or exporting from a country in which such facilities are available.

Running through the Convention, in addition to the procedures and prohibitions for movement of hazardous waste, are several basic principles of sound environmental management. Waste minimization is stressed in a number of places, most notably in the obligations of generating states. The Convention adopts the so-called precautionary principle, that environmental regulation should anticipate harm and avoid potential risk:

> Each Party shall strive to adopt and implement the preventive, precautionary approach to pollution problems which entails, *inter alia*, preventing the release into the environment of substances which may cause harm to humans or the environment without waiting for scientific proof regarding such harm.[104]

The Convention also adopts the "polluter pays" principle in its statement of obligations of generators and the establishment of a protocol for liability and compensation for harms resulting from the transboundary movement of hazardous waste.

NOTES

1. Some have argued that Basel is more appropriately viewed as ratifying existing practices with respect to exports than as imposing new controls on them. Do you see the basis for this argument? Is it correct or overstated?

2. Management in "an environmentally sound manner" is undefined in the treaty, which nearly everyone agrees is a major loophole. Why? How should the loophole be plugged? Should industrialized states use their own standards to evaluate disposal elsewhere—or is this unwanted paternalism? If the U.S. seriously imposed its own standards, it would probably permit little if any exportation—is that good or bad?

3. Some have argued that the need for the United States to join the Basel Convention has declined, since states party to the Convention may not accept hazardous waste from the U.S. in the absence of a bilateral treaty, and developing countries not parties can simply refuse to accept U.S. waste (and are bound to do so if they have signed the Bamako Convention). Are these non-Basel safeguards adequate? Does RCRA help?

D. Regulation of Treatment, Storage, and Disposal Facilities

EPA takes it as axiomatic that it is physically impossible *permanently* to prevent leakage of hazardous waste from land disposal facilities; therefore, unless the waste is not generated in the first place, EPA's regulatory options

---

[104] *See id.*, art V, para. 3(f).

are either to detoxify, reduce the mobility of, or isolate the waste for as long as possible.[105] Since many wastes cannot be detoxified, EPA must focus on isolating the wastes.[106] RCRA's approach to TSDFs is divided into four strategies: minimize toxicity through treatment standards (land disposal restrictions); minimize migration through performance standards for design, siting, and closure; corrective action; and, post-closure plans and financial responsibility. EPA uses a technology-based approach for disposal restrictions and TSDF construction, and health-based standards for corrective action clean-up requirements.

[107]

The EPA regulates all TSDFs of hazardous waste pursuant to § 3004 of RCRA. The owner or operator of a TSDF must obtain a TSDF permit or be an operating interim facility under § 3005. The standards for TSDFs are complex and lengthy; the regulations contain 22 subparts that delineate the conduct and operating standards TSDFs must meet.[108]

There are six basic types of TSDFs:

"Incinerators" burn hazardous wastes.

"Surface impoundments" are depressions, excavations, or diked areas that can hold liquid wastes or wastes with free liquids.

---

[105] *See* Standards Applicable to Owners and Operators of Hazardous Waste Treatment, Storage, and Disposal Facilities; Consolidated Permit Regulations, Preamble 46 Fed Reg. 2802 (1981).

[106] *See* John S. Applegate & Stephen Dycus, *Institutional Controls or Emperor's Clothes? Long-Term Stewardship of the Nuclear Weapons Complex*, 28 ENVTL. L. REP. 10631, 10634-36, 10642-44 (Nov. 1998).

[107] EPA JOURNAL, July/August 1991.

[108] *See* 40 C.F.R. pt. 264 (1999).

Common examples are wastewater lagoons, settling ponds, and storage ponds.

"Land treatment facilities" are places where hazardous wastes are either applied onto or incorporated into the soil by spraying, spreading or injection. There are commonly used for petroleum wastes.

"Underground injection wells" deposit hazardous wastes deep beneath the earth's surface in geologically stable, impermeable rock formations. They are the principal exception to the ban on land disposal of hazardous wastes.

"Containers, tanks, and waste piles" permit the temporary collection and storage of hazardous wastes.

"Landfills" belong in a catchall category. They include all placements of hazardous wastes in or on the land under circumstances that do not fit under the other categories.[109]

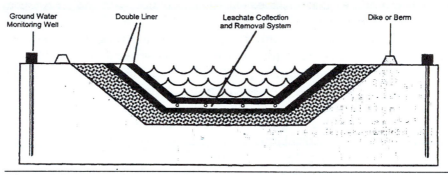

Figure 9.9–Cross-Section of a Surface Impoundment[110]

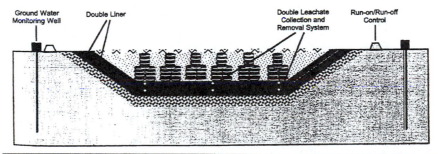

Figure 9.10–Cross-Section of a Landfill[111]

---

[109] John G. Sprankling & Gregory S. Weber, THE LAW OF HAZARDOUS WASTES AND TOXIC SUBSTANCES 206-07 (1997).
[110] Source: RCRA ORIENTATION MANUAL, US EPA at III-76
[111] Source: RCRA ORIENTATION MANUAL, US EPA at III-73

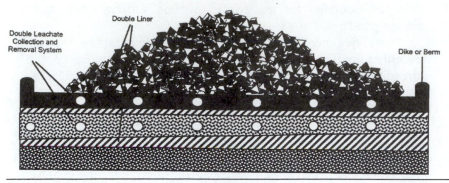

Figure 9.11–Cross-Section of a Wastepile[112]

Requirements for TSDFs vary little from the statutory language in § 3004. Section 3004 requires that the EPA develop and enforce standards for every owner/operator of a TSDF. Owner/operators of TSDFs must follow certain procedures that include: (1) filing a notice with the EPA once managing hazardous waste at a TSDF, (2) obtaining an EPA identification number, (3) maintaining a manifest waste system that tracks the hazardous waste, (4) following standards for location, design, and construction of TSDFs, (5) writing contingency plans for any possible emergencies at the TSDF, and (6) demonstrating financial responsibility.

Although recordkeeping and initial notification requirements are similar for generators and transporters, the EPA requires significantly different manifest system responsibilities for TSDFs. The EPA considers the operational nature of a TSDF worthy of an increased regulatory burden because the "life" of the waste effectively ends at the TSDF. The owner/operator puts the hazardous waste to its "grave" and the hazardous waste could, if not properly regulated, present a continuing risk to human health and the environment.

1. Permitting

The EPA requires owner/operators of TSDFs to comply with an extensive series of regulations. One can find the regulations that govern TSDFs in 40 C.F.R. Parts 264, 265, and 270. The EPA cannot regulate a TSDF under EPA regulations unless the owner/operator of the TSDF stores, treats, or disposes of a hazardous waste at the TSDF.

RCRA defines "disposal" broadly to include the intentional and unintentional placement of hazardous waste at a facility.[113] If an owner/operator of a facility places a solid or hazardous waste into or on any land or water so that hazardous constituents may enter the environment, RCRA regulations are attached to the facility. The EPA defines "disposal

---

[112] Source: RCRA ORIENTATION MANUAL, US EPA at III-81
[113] *See* 42 U.S.C. § 6903(10) (1994).

facility" to mean a facility at which one intentionally places hazardous waste that will remain after the owner/operator closes the facility.[114]

RCRA defines "storage" as the temporary or extended containment of a hazardous or solid waste that does not constitute "disposal."[115] The EPA defines storage to mean "the holding of a hazardous waste for a temporary period at the end of which the hazardous waste is treated, disposed of, or stored elsewhere."[116] According to the EPA, some action must follow "storage" of a hazardous waste for the EPA to believe that a facility disposes of the waste. Although EPA should promulgate a regulation that states when long-term storage becomes *de facto* disposal, the EPA has not promulgated such a regulation.

RCRA defines "treatment" as "any method, technique, or process, including neutralization, designed to change the physical, chemical, or biological character or composition of any hazardous waste so as to neutralize such waste or so as to render such waste non-hazardous, safer for transport, amenable for recovery, amenable for storage, or reduced in volume."[117] The definition covers any activity by TSDF personnel to change the physical or chemical form of a hazardous waste to make the waste non-hazardous.[118]

RCRA requires that all TSDFs of hazardous waste obtain a permit from the EPA.[119] The EPA issues permits to TSDFs that satisfy TSDF performance standards in EPA regulations. When the EPA issues a TSDF a permit and the TSDF follows the permit provisions, the permit generally shields the owner/operator of the TSDF from enforcement proceedings for requirements not stated in the permit.[120] Because the permit can act like a shield from enforcement, the EPA tends to write the permit provisions specifically and conservatively.[121]

Although most TSDFs must obtain RCRA permits, the EPA promulgated regulations exempting certain types of facilities from permitting requirements.

---

[114] *See* 40 C.F.R. § 260.10 (1995). The EPA defines "facilities that dispose of hazardous waste in landfills" with language that may cover intentional and unintentional disposal of hazardous waste. 40 C.F.R. § 264.300 (1995).

[115] *See* 42 U.S.C. § 6903(33) (1994).

[116] 40 C.F.R. § 260.10 (1995).

[117] 42 U.S.C. § 6903(34) (1994).

[118] The EPA also defines other forms of "treatment" in the regulations ("thermal treatment," "land treatment," "totally enclosed treatment," "wastewater treatment unit," "chemical physical and biological treatment facility," and "elementary treatment"). *See generally* 40 C.F.R. Pt. 265 (1995) The EPA standards may differ for each different type of treatment facility.

[119] *See* 42 U.S.C. § 6925 (1994). The EPA can delegate to the states the power to issue a TSDF permit.

[120] *See* 40 C.F.R. § 270.4 (1995).

[121] *See* ABA, THE RCRA PRACTICE MANUAL 71 (Theodore L. Garrett, ed., 1994).

For an owner/operator of a TSDF to obtain a permit, the owner/operator must complete a two-part application.[122] The general standardized form, otherwise known as Part A, is the easier form to complete.

Part B of the application is longer and requires the applicant to spend considerable time providing the EPA with specific information. Part B requires the owner/operator to delineate how she will have the facility follow all the EPA TSDF performance standards. The EPA requires the applicant to send drawings of the facility, descriptions of what type of security will be at the facility, and other descriptions pursuant to procedures in 40 C.F.R. Part 264. Often the owner/operator of the proposed facility will hire a consultant with experience in completing Part B applications.

---

[122] The requirements are found in part 270.–EDS.

The following flow chart illustrates the permitting process.

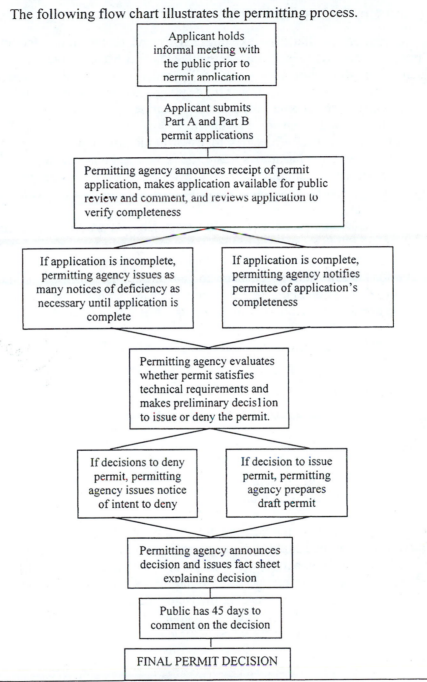

Figure 9.12–The Permitting Process[123]

[123] EPA, RCRA ORIENTATION MANUAL III-125 (1990).

2. Interim Status Facilities

Congress grandfathered existing TSDFs and termed those facilities "interim status" TSDFs.[124] Today, the TSDFs that became interim status facilities in 1980 should have received permits from the EPA or ceased operations. November 8, 1992 was the deadline for 1980 interim facilities to decide whether to become fully permitted facilities.[125]

Two ways still exist for a facility to obtain interim status under EPA regulations. If the EPA decides to list and identify a previously non-hazardous waste as a hazardous waste, the facility receiving the waste must make one of two decisions. First, the facility can choose to stop receiving the waste, or the facility can obtain interim status until the facility decides to obtain a TSDF permit.[126]

To obtain interim status a facility must submit Part A of the permit application within six months of the EPA publishing the regulatory change. Additionally, for interim status a facility must file a Notification of Hazardous Waste Activity pursuant to § 3010(a).[127] The notification must contain a description of the hazardous wastes being handled at the TSDF and the location and description of the hazardous waste activity at the TSDF.

VINELAND CHEMICAL CO., INC. V. EPA
810 F.2d 402 (3d Cir. 1987)

STAPLETON, Circuit Judge

Vineland Chemical Company (ViChem) petitions this court to review the determination made by the U.S. Environmental Protection Agency (EPA or Agency) that ViChem had not satisfied the relevant certification requirements under the Resource Conservation and Recovery Act (RCRA), 42 U.S.C. § 6925(e)(2) (Supp. II 1984), and thus could no longer operate its hazardous waste disposal facility under "interim status."

* * *

On the merits of the petition for review, we hold that the EPA's interpretation of the statute to require certification by November 8, 1985 is reasonable and is compatible with both the statutory language and the intent of Congress, and therefore we defer to the EPA's construction. Given the EPA's interpretation of the statute, the factual determination that ViChem had failed to satisfy the certification requirements was supported by the record and was neither arbitrary nor capricious.

---

[124] 42 U.S.C. § 6925 (1994).

[125] *See* 40 C.F.R. § 270.73 (1995).

[126] *See* 40 C.F.R. § 270.10(e)(i) (1995); *See also id.* § 270.10(e)(ii) for facilities that fall under interim status because of operational changes at the facility.

[127] *See* 42 U.S.C. § 6930 (1994).

I.

Vineland Chemical Company operates two surface impoundments which are classified as land disposal facilities for hazardous wastes. RCRA forbids operation of a hazardous waste disposal facility without a permit. 42 U.S.C. § 6925(a) (Supp. II 1984). Prior to final administrative action on a permit application, however, qualified facilities are allowed to operate without a permit under a grandfather clause. Such permission to operate without a RCRA permit is termed "interim status." 42 U.S.C. § 6925(e) (Supp. II 1984).

Since 1980, ViChem has operated its surface impoundments under interim status, having satisfied the statutory requirements of 42 U.S.C. § 6925(e)(1). Interim status facilities must comply with operating requirements established by regulation. 40 C.F.R. § 265 (1985). Among the interim status operating requirements are the financial responsibility requirements at issue in this case. These regulations require operators to acquire liability insurance and provide financial assurances that there will be sufficient resources available for closure and post-closure costs.[128]

In 1984, Congress amended RCRA to provide for termination of interim status for land disposal facilities, a classification which includes surface impoundments such as ViChem's, 50 Fed. Reg. 38,946, 38,947 (Sept. 25, 1985), if certain conditions were not satisfied. The 1984 amendment stated:

> In the case of each land disposal facility which has been granted interim status under this subsection before November 8, 1984, interim status shall terminate on the date twelve months after November 8, 1984, unless the owner or operator of such facility—
>
> (A) applies for a determination regarding the issuance of a permit under subsection (c) of this section for such facility before the date twelve months after November 8, 1984; and
>
> (B) certifies that such facility is in compliance with all applicable groundwater monitoring and financial responsibility requirements.

statute

Pub.L. No. 98-616, § 213(a)(3), 98 Stat. 3221, 3241 (1984) (codified at 42 U.S.C. § 6925(e)(2) (Supp. II 1984)).

In accordance with § 6925(e)(2)(A), ViChem has submitted a Part B permit application to the New Jersey Department of Environmental Protection (DEP). The EPA has delegated responsibility for administering

---

[128] The purpose of the financial responsibility regulations is to ensure that hazardous waste facility operators (1) are adequately indemnified against both sudden (*e.g.,* an explosion) and non-sudden (*e.g.,* leakage into a ground water aquifer) accidents that may occur during the period of operation, and (2) have sufficient resources to properly close the facility and to provide post-closure care, monitoring and security as required. *See* 40 C.F.R. §§ 265.140-265.150 (interim status standards concerning financial responsibility) (1985). The regulations allow operators to establish financial assurance of closure and post-closure care by establishing a dedicated trust fund, obtaining a surety bond or a letter of credit, procuring insurance, self-insuring, or combining these measures. 40 C.F.R. §§ 265.143, 265.145 (1985).

the RCRA permit program to the DEP as authorized by 42 U.S.C. § 6926. No final action has yet been taken on the ViChem permit application.

On November 8, 1985, ViChem submitted to the EPA a document certifying compliance with groundwater monitoring and liability insurance requirements. The certification did not make any reference to financial assurances to cover closure and post-closure costs. On December 2nd, the EPA notified ViChem by letter that its interim status was terminated as of November 8, 1985 for failure to comply with the certification requirement of § 6925(e)(2)(B). The letter notified ViChem that it could not continue to operate, that it was required to submit a closure plan, and that continued operation could subject ViChem to both civil and criminal penalties. In a letter to the EPA dated December 27, 1985, ViChem attempted to correct the omission by certifying that it had been in compliance with all of the financial responsibility requirements as of November 8. The EPA's reply, dated January 30, 1986, reaffirmed its position that interim status had terminated as of November 8, 1985.

II.

* * *

A.

ViChem first argues that interim status is itself a permit, and thus termination of interim status is a revocation of a "permit under § 6925" reviewable by this court under § 6976(b). We reject this reading. The structure of § 6925 indicates that Congress was quite careful in distinguishing between permits and interim status. For example, the requirements for issuance of RCRA permits are prescribed in §§ 6925(a), (b), (c) and 6974(b), while the less stringent qualifications for interim status are contained in § 6925(e)(1).

ViChem relies on language in § 6925(e)(1) providing that any person who qualifies for interim status "shall be treated as having been issued [a RCRA] permit until such time as final administrative disposition of such application is made." 42 U.S.C. § 6925(e)(1) (Supp. II 1984). However, there would be no need for Congress to state that an interim status holder should be treated as if it were permitted if indeed it was permitted. Thus, we conclude that the statute does not reflect any Congressional intent to include interim status within the meaning of "permit."

In *Hempstead County and Nevada County v. EPA*, 700 F.2d 459 (8th Cir.1983), involving review of an EPA determination that a hazardous waste disposal facility did not qualify for interim status, the Eighth Circuit held that interim status was not a permit within the meaning of § 6925 and thus that there was no appellate jurisdiction conferred by § 6976(b). The Seventh Circuit recently relied on Hempstead in reaching the same conclusion. *Northside Sanitary Landfill, Inc. v. Thomas*, 804 F.2d 371, 384 (7th Cir.1986). We are in agreement with the Seventh and Eighth Circuits to the extent that we find interim status termination is not a permit revocation and thus does not fall within the literal language of § 6976(b). However . . . . we shall not limit our jurisdictional analysis to a literal reading of the § 6976(b) language. Instead, we pursue a common sense analysis of the intent of Congress with respect to judicial review of interim status terminations.

B.

The first step is to determine what intent Congress had with respect to interim status terminations when it enacted § 6976(b) in 1980.

The purpose of this section is, of course, to authorize continued operation of facilities existing on November 19, 1980 until permit proceedings were completed. Prior to final administrative disposition, the authority conferred by § 6925(e) was "functionally similar" to the authority provided by a permit as indicated by the mandate that one having interim status must "be treated as having been issued such permit" during that period. When proceedings on a permit application terminate, so does interim status and operating authority. Such a termination can occur in three ways: (1) by the issuance of a permit, (2) by the denial of a permit, or (3) by a determination that the applicant has failed to provide sufficient information to allow either issuance or denial of a permit. Each of these three decisions is made by the EPA by applying the statutory and regulatory criteria for a permit to a record compiled in a permit application proceeding. Under the regulations, proceedings to terminate interim status for failure to provide sufficient information involves a hearing directed specifically to the issue of the sufficiency of the available information and thus the record is as well developed on the relevant issue as in the other two situations. 40 C.F.R. §§ 270.10(e)(5), 124.71-124.91 (1986). Finally, termination of interim status for failure to provide sufficient information is the functional equivalent of a denial of a permit application on the merits. Both result in the termination of the Agency's proceedings and require the facility to cease operations.

* * *

III.

ViChem asks this court to invalidate the EPA's termination of interim status for its two surface impoundments on the grounds that: 1) the EPA adopted an impermissible interpretation of § 6925(e)(2), and 2) the Agency's refusal to consider ViChem's submissions made after November 8 was arbitrary and capricious.

A.

ViChem argues that the EPA erred in interpreting § 6925(e)(2) to require submission of certification of compliance with the financial responsibility requirements by November 8, 1985. ViChem contends that the law should be construed to require facility operators to certify that they were in compliance by November 8, 1985, with no submission deadline specified.

The statute itself is most reasonably read to require that certification must be submitted by November 8. The statutory provision at issue states that "interim status shall terminate on the date twelve months after November 8, 1984, unless the owner or operator of such facility—

> (A) applies for . . . a permit . . . before the date twelve months after November 8, 1984; and (B) certifies that such facility is in compliance with all applicable groundwater monitoring and financial responsibility requirements." 42 U.S.C. § 6925(e)(2) (Supp. II 1984) . . . . Interim status thus terminates on November 8 unless the certification is made, strongly suggesting that Congress intended that certification be due by that date.

In addition to requiring a strained reading of the provision's language, ViChem's construction would leave the EPA in the woeful position of being unable to distinguish those facilities that no longer qualified for interim status from those which simply had not yet certified that they were in compliance as of November 8. Such a construction runs contrary to the clear Congressional intent to accelerate the EPA's enforcement activities. *See* H.R.REP. NO. 198, 98TH CONG., 2ND SESS., PT. I, at 44, reprinted in 1984 U.S. CODE CONG. & ADMIN. NEWS 5576, 5603 (one purpose of 1984 amendments was "to expedite the final permit review of major land disposal . . . facilities and close those facilities that cannot or will not meet the final standards at the earliest possible date").

* * *

IV.

We hold that this court has jurisdiction to entertain ViChem's petition for review. However, in accordance with the concept of judicial deference to an agency's reasonable interpretation of a statute it administers, the petition for review is denied.

NOTES

1. What is the function of permits?
2. What is the function of interim status? How does interim status work?
3. Why the certification rule instead of *nunc pro tunc* evidence of financial responsibility?
4. What can ViChem do now?

3. Permit Requirements

The EPA sets the minimum requirements for most TSDFs in 40 C.F.R. part 264. A TSDF permit often has two parts. The first part covers the requirements that the state is authorized to administer and implement. The second part covers the requirements in RCRA that the state is not authorized to implement. The effect of having two parts to the permit is that an applicant will often need to deal with two agencies to comply with the permit: the state agency and the federal agency.[129]

KEY PROVISIONS

Subpart B: General Facility Standards

    This section summarizes notification requirements, sampling, security procedures, inspections, personnel training, TSDF siting, and construction quality assurance.[130]

Subpart C: Equipment and Emergency Training at a TSDF

    This section deals with alarm systems, communications in emergencies, and relations with local emergency response personnel.[131]

Subpart D: Contingency Plan

    One section of a Part B permit application requires a TSDF to have a contingency plan approved by the EPA.[132] The owner/operator of a TSDF must hire an emergency response coordinator in case an emergency occurs at the TSDF.[133]

Subpart E: Manifest System Requirements

    The manifest system comes full circle at the TSDF. The TSDF sends the generator a copy to ensure proper disposal.[134]

Subpart F: Groundwater Monitoring

    TSDFs that contain surface impoundments, landfills, and/or land treatment units need to comply with subpart F requirements to monitor groundwater.[135]

Subpart G: Closure and Post-Closure Requirements

    The idea behind closure and post-closure requirements is to prevent the need for future maintenance or corrective action at the TSDF once the TSDF closes. A TSDF must have a closure plan completed six months after receiving the first hazardous waste subject to regulation.[136]

Subpart H: Financial Responsibility

    RCRA requires the EPA to develop financial responsibility standards for TSDFs.[137] The EPA requires owner/operators to provide liability insurance for the life of the TSDF and to provide a financial mechanism to ensure that the owner/operators will meet the cost of the closure and post-closure requirements.[138]

    Query: Does it make sense to have the owner/operator be financially responsible for long-term monitoring or should it be a government responsibility?

Subparts I–O: Specific Facilities

    Congress required landfill and surface impoundments to meet certain minimum technological requirements (MTRs).[139] EPA promulgated specific regulations to implement those requirements, as well as performance requirements for tank systems, incinerators, containers, boilers, and furnaces.[140]

Subpart S: Corrective Action

    If a TSDF leaks, RCRA requires the owner/operator to take corrective actions, similar to Superfund clean-up, to mitigate the harm from a release of hazardous waste.

---

[129] *See* ABA, THE RCRA PRACTICE MANUAL 76 (Theodore L. Garrett ed., 1994).

All RCRA permits have certain boilerplate provisions that cover the conditions the TSDF must follow. The permit states that the TSDF has the duty to:

1. comply with the conditions in the permit;
2. reapply for a permit when the TSDF permit expires;
3. permit EPA officials to inspect the TSDF;
4. monitor the wastes received at the TSDF;
5. properly maintain and operate the facility;
6. provide information to the EPA about anticipated noncompliance with the permit; and
7. notify the EPA if any information on the permit application was incorrect or omitted.[141]

Along with the boilerplate conditions in every TSDF permit, the EPA often includes specific conditions for each TSDF. For example, the EPA might require a TSDF, because of the TSDF's location, to have more groundwater monitoring stations than other TSDFs. Because of the case-by-case provisions, a TSDF permit can be a hundred pages or longer.

The EPA issues special permits for facilities that do not need to obtain a standard TSDF permit. The idea behind special permits is to allow a facility to avoid the complicated process of following a standard TSDF permit.

Sometimes a facility may inadvertently trigger TSDF status and be subject to RCRA and EPA requirements. A facility can trigger TSDF status when the facility accumulates hazardous wastes beyond the time limit set for accumulation, or fails to identify newly regulated hazardous waste that the facility has been receiving.[142] The EPA will usually take the position that the facility operates an unpermitted TSDF and seek injunctive relief and penalties from the facility for receiving the wastes. The facility has two options: either relocate the wastes received at the facility at the facility's cost, or seek to obtain interim status using the procedures discussed above.[143]

---

[130] *See* 40 C.F.R. §§ 264.11-264.19 (1995).
[131] *See id.* §§ 264.32 and 264.37 (1995).
[132] *See id.* §§ 264.51-.52 (1995).
[133] *See id.* § 264.55 (1995).
[134] *See id.* §§ 264.71, 264.72, 264.75 (1995).
[135] *See id.* § 264.90 (1995).
[136] *See id.* § 264.112 (1995).
[137] *See* 42 U.S.C. § 6924(a)(6) (1994).
[138] *See* 40 C.F.R. §§ 264.143-.150 (1995).
[139] *See* 42 U.S.C. § 6942(o) (1995). Basically, the installation of two liners and ground water monitoring.
[140] The EPA has standards for specific types of units in 40 C.F.R. pt. 264.
[141] *See* 40 C.F.R. §§ 270.30-270.31 (1995).
[142] *Supra* note 129 at 81 (1994).
[143] *See* 40 C.F.R. § 270.10(e).

Finally there's the question of what happens when the TSDF is full. The following case explains the closure requirements through a challenge to EPA's closure regulations.

CHEMICAL MANUFACTURERS ASSOCIATION V. EPA

919 F.2d 158 (D.C. Cir. 1990)

WALD, Chief Judge.

Petitioner Union Carbide Chemicals and Plastics Company, Inc. ("Union Carbide") challenges certain aspects of two sets of regulations governing the time for closure of hazardous waste facilities promulgated by the Environmental Protection Agency ("EPA") pursuant to its authority under § 3004(a) of the Resource Conservation and Recovery Act of 1976 ("RCRA"), 42 U.S.C. § 6924(a). Union Carbide asserts that the regulations are "arbitrary, capricious, an abuse of discretion, or otherwise not in accordance with law" in violation of the Administrative Procedure Act ("APA"). 5 U.S.C. § 706(2)(A). More specifically, Union Carbide alleges that: (1) the EPA violated the express intent of Congress in promulgating the contested regulations; and (2) the EPA failed to justify adequately the regulatory choices it made, acted irrationally and inconsistently in adopting the regulations, and applied the wrong legal standard in assessing the need for the regulations. We conclude that the challenged regulations are consistent with congressional intent and that the EPA did not act arbitrarily or capriciously in promulgating them. Accordingly, we deny the petitions for review.

* * *

II. ANALYSIS

A. Did the EPA Exceed Its Statutory Authority?

Union Carbide's first challenge to the 1986 and 1989 closure regulations is that they contradict Congress' express intent in enacting the 1984 Amendments. The EPA responds that the 1984 Amendments left untouched its pre-existing authority under § 3004(a) of the RCRA to promulgate regulations establishing standards for hazardous waste facilities that it finds necessary to protect human health and the environment. The EPA therefore concludes that it had ample statutory authority to issue both sets of regulations.[144]

In evaluating the parties' arguments, we must follow the rules laid down in Chevron U.S.A., Inc. v. NRDC, 467 U.S. 837, 104 S.Ct. 2778, 81 L.Ed.2d 694 (1984). First, we inquire "whether Congress has directly spoken to the precise question at issue." *Id.* at 842, 104 S.Ct. at 2781. In determining whether Congress has so spoken, we must look to "the particular statutory

---

[144] Contrary to Union Carbide's assertion, *see* Petitioner's Brief at 31-32, the EPA did explicitly address in both the 1986 and 1989 regulations in 1984 Amendments' effect on its pre-existing authority under § 3004(a). In fact, it did so in direct response to Union Carbide's arguments. *See* 51 Fed. Reg. 16,432 (May 2, 1986); 54 Fed. Reg. 33,382 (Aug. 14, 1989).

language at issue, as well as the language and design of the statute as a whole," K Mart Corp. v. Cartier, Inc., 486 U.S. 281, 291, 108 S.Ct. 1811, 1817, 100 L.Ed.2d 313 (1988), and we must employ the traditional tools of statutory construction, including, where appropriate, legislative history. Ohio v. United States Dept. of the Interior, 880 F.2d 432, 441 (D.C.Cir.1989). If the intent of Congress is clear, we must give it effect. Chevron, 467 U.S. at 842-43, 104 S.Ct. at 2781-82. If, however, the statute is silent or ambiguous on a particular issue, we must defer to the agency's interpretation of the statute if it is reasonable and consistent with the statute's purpose. *Id.* at 844-45, 104 S.Ct. at 2782-83.

The relevant statutory provision in the 1984 Amendments requires interim status surface impoundments to cease receiving, storing, or treating hazardous waste after November 8, 1988, unless they are retrofitted to meet the minimum technological requirements imposed on permitted facilities. RCRA § 3005(j), 42 U.S.C. § 6925(j). On its face, this provision certainly does not support Union Carbide's claim that Congress intended to deprive the EPA of authority to require unretrofitted surface impoundments to close once they cease receiving hazardous wastes.[145]

statute

* * *

We believe that Congress' intent on this issue was not entirely clear, but conclude under the second prong of Chevron that the EPA's interpretation is a reasonable one and is consistent with the purposes of the RCRA and the 1984 Amendments.[146]

* * *

For all these reasons we defer to the EPA's interpretation of its authority under § 3004(a) as permitting it to continue to regulate the receipt by unretrofitted surface impoundments of non-hazardous wastes "to protect human health and the environment" even after the 1984 Amendments as a "permissible construction" of the statute. See Chevron, 467 U.S. at 843, 104 S.Ct. at 2781.

B. Are the Regulations Arbitrary and Capricious?

Union Carbide also attacks the 1986 and 1989 closure regulations as arbitrary and capricious. We reject these challenges as well. Initially, we note that Union Carbide challenges these regulations only as they apply to unretrofitted surface impoundments; moreover, some of Union Carbide's

---

[145] In fact, § 3005(j) is most naturally read to require the "close or empty" policy adopted by the EPA in the 1989 regulations insofar as it states that unretrofitted surface impoundments "shall not receive, store, or treat" hazardous wastes after November 8, 1988 (emphasis added). The EPA, however, explicitly eschewed reliance on this phrase as a basis for its closure policy, concluding that the legislative history signified only an intent to bar receipt of hazardous wastes for storage after that date. See 54 Fed. Reg. 33,382 (Aug. 14, 1989).

[146] Even if we agreed with Union Carbide's interpretation of the colloquy, we would be reluctant to give controlling weight to an isolated exchange of this type. See, e.g., United Mine Workers v. Federal Mine Safety & Health Review Comm'n, 671 F.2d 615, 620-23 (D.C.Cir. 1982) (surveying the dangers of allowing isolated floor comments, unsupported by other elements of legislative history or statutory language, decisive effect).

arguments apply only to the 1986 closure regulations and not to the 1989 revised closure regulations.[147]

1. Did EPA Fail to Consider the Useful Capacity of Unretrofitted Surface Impoundments for Continued Disposal of Non-hazardous Wastes?

Union Carbide charges that the EPA failed to consider the continued usefulness of unretrofitted surface impoundments that cease to receive hazardous wastes but retain capacity to receive non-hazardous wastes. Curiously, this argument ignores the fact that the principal if not the entire purpose of the EPA's 1989 revision of the closure regulations was to accommodate CMA's and Union Carbide's objections to the stark retrofit-or-close rule embodied in the 1986 regulations. Under the 1989 closure regulations, unretrofitted surface impoundments may remain open to receive non-hazardous wastes so long as they are emptied of accumulated hazardous wastes. The preamble to the 1989 regulations as initially proposed in 1988 clearly indicates that the EPA undertook the process of revision because it now agreed that there were "a number of sound policy reasons why it is desirable to allow units to delay closure to continue to receive non-hazardous waste, provided that it does not jeopardize protection of human health and the environment." 53 Fed. Reg. 20,739 (June 6, 1988). Among these policy reasons were avoiding disincentives to waste minimization in certain situations, preventing unnecessary disruption of operations at facilities with remaining capacity, and avoiding the imposition of unnecessary economic burdens on facility operators. *Id.* Similar statements can be found in the EPA's responses to comments by those objecting to the proposed revisions and in the preamble to the final rule. *See* EPA's Response to Comments to June 6, 1988 Proposed Rule at 62-63, J.A. 312-13; 54 Fed. Reg. 33,382 (Aug. 14, 1989). There is, then, simply no support in the record for Union Carbide's assertion that the EPA adopted the 1989 closure regulations without taking account of remaining capacity or utility of facilities for receiving non-hazardous wastes.

2. Did EPA Fail to Justify Adequately the Requirement that Unretrofitted Surface Impoundments Be Emptied of Hazardous Wastes in Order to Remain Open?

Union Carbide's next line of attack against the closure regulations is that the EPA failed to justify adequately the requirement in the 1989 regulations that unretrofitted surface impoundments be emptied of hazardous wastes if they wish to remain open to receive non-hazardous wastes. More specifically, Union Carbide asserts that the record (1) reveals no analysis of the actual likelihood of leaks from facilities that are not emptied of hazardous wastes, and (2) contains no indication that the EPA considered

---

[147] To the extent that the 1986 closure regulations were superseded by the 1989 regulations, we need look only to the latter. There is no indication in the record that Union Carbide or any other operator of a hazardous waste surface impoundment suffered injury, or in any way altered its operations, due to reliance on a provision of the 1986 closure regulations later revised in the 1989 regulations.

alternatives such as groundwater monitoring, corrective action, and financial assurance requirements that could provide adequate protection of human health and the environment. As a result, it charges that the EPA has failed to meet the requirement of reasoned decisionmaking imposed by the APA and judicial precedent. *See, e.g., International Ladies' Garment Workers' Union v. Donovan*, 722 F.2d 795, 815-18 (D.C.Cir.1983).

The record, however, paints a different picture. As to the specific alternatives Union Carbide mentions, the EPA discussed and rejected each one as inadequate to protect human health and the environment. *See* 54 Fed. Reg. 33,382-83 (Aug. 14, 1989); EPA's Response to Comments to June 6, 1988 Proposed Rule at 7-10, J.A. 257-60. The reason given by the EPA for rejecting these alternatives also refutes Union Carbide's allegation that the EPA failed to analyze the likelihood of leaks from unretrofitted surface impoundments that continue to store hazardous wastes. At several points in the record, the EPA explained that the accumulation of additional quantities of non-hazardous wastes on top of hazardous wastes significantly increases the risk of leaks because wastes in surface impoundments typically take the form of liquids or partial solids surrounded by liquids. Leachate is most likely to emanate from liquid or semiliquid wastes, and the continued accumulation of liquids in a surface impoundment tends to form a "pressure head" that forces downward dispersion of the leachate at the bottom. If an impoundment is unlined or inadequately lined, containment in such situations often is not possible. *See* Closure/Post-closure and Financial Responsibility Requirements (EPA 1986 Background Information Document) at 91-93, J.A. 111-13; 51 Fed. Reg. 16,432 (May 2, 1986); 54 Fed. Reg. 33,382 (Aug. 14, 1989). Thus, the EPA concluded in 1989, surface impoundments must either meet the minimum technological requirements of RCRA § 3004(o), which are designed to reduce significantly the risk of leaks, or remove accumulated hazardous wastes before continuing to receive non-hazardous wastes.[148] *See* 54 Fed. Reg. 33,382 (Aug. 14, 1989). The EPA's analysis of the "pressure head" syndrome was obviously based on research described in greater detail in an earlier set of hazardous waste regulations under the RCRA. *See* 48 Fed. Reg. 14,486 (April 4, 1983).[149]

---

[148] Union Carbide asserts that it does not challenge the need for eventual closure and capping of unretrofitted facilities, but only the need for immediate closing of unretrofitted facilities that are not emptied of accumulated hazardous wastes. The EPA's rationale, however, addresses this question directly: Immediate closure or emptying is required because the accumulation of non-hazardous wastes on top of hazardous wastes creates a significant risk that a pressure head will form and cause a rupture of the impoundment and consequent release of hazardous wastes.

[149] The EPA summarized its research and conclusions on that occasion as follows: Surface impoundments containing hazardous waste pose a particular threat of contaminating ground water and have always been one of the chief concerns of the hazardous waste management program. (*See generally,* the Background Document [to] Subpart K Interim Status Standards, April 28, 1980.) Not only is containment without a liner system usually impossible, but wastes are present as liquids or are constantly in the presence of liquids. This creates the situation most conducive to forming leachate. In addition, the collected liquids in an impoundment will

It is not the role of courts to "second-guess the scientific judgments of the EPA," State of New York v. EPA, 852 F.2d 574, 580 (D.C.Cir.1988), cert. denied, 489 U.S. 1065, 109 S.Ct. 1338, 103 L.Ed.2d 809 (1989), and we give considerable latitude to the EPA in drawing conclusions from scientific and technological research, even where it is "imperfect" or "preliminary." Ethyl Corp. v. EPA, 541 F.2d 1, 28 (D.C.Cir.1976), cert. denied, 426 U.S. 941, 96 S.Ct. 2663, 49 L.Ed.2d 394 (1976). Union Carbide neither refers to the research conducted by the EPA nor provides any reason why this court should not credit the EPA's scientific conclusions based thereon. Further, the EPA's conclusions are consistent with Congress' own finding that surface impoundments "are not capable of assuring long-term containment of certain hazardous wastes," RCRA § 1002(b)(7), 42 U.S.C. § 6901(b)(7), and the EPA's action here fully accords with Congress' determination that preventive measures should be preferred over corrective action in the area of hazardous waste management. One of the RCRA's explicit objectives is "requiring that hazardous waste be properly managed in the first instance [,] thereby reducing the need for corrective action at a future date," RCRA § 1003(a)(5), 42 U.S.C. § 6902(a)(5), for "if hazardous waste management is improperly performed in the first instance, corrective action is likely to be expensive, complex, and time consuming . . . ." RCRA § 1002(b)(6), 42 U.S.C. § 6901(b)(6).

In light of all this, we believe the EPA has demonstrated that it "examine[d] the relevant data and articulate[d] a satisfactory explanation for its action including a 'rational connection between the facts found and the choice made.'" Motor Vehicles Mfrs. Ass'n v. State Farm Mut. Auto. Ins. Co., 463 U.S. 29, 43, 103 S.Ct. 2856, 2866, 77 L.Ed.2d 443 (1983) (quoting Burlington Truck Lines, Inc. v. United States, 371 U.S. 156, 168, 83 S.Ct. 239, 245, 9 L.Ed.2d 207 (1962)).

3. Is the Requirement that Unretrofitted Surface Impoundments Close or Be Emptied Irrational and Inconsistent with Other EPA Regulations?

Union Carbide also asserts that the EPA's justifications for the closure regulations, even if taken at face value, cut too wide a swath because they apply equally to all surface impoundments, including those that are built or retrofitted to meet the minimum technological requirements imposed in 1984 and that are not required to close or be emptied of hazardous wastes. Union

---

form a pressure head, causing downward dispersion of the leached contaminants. Since most impoundments are unlined, and because many are underlain by permeable soils, the potential for downward seepage of contaminated fluids into ground water is high. In fact, incidents of ground water contamination from impoundments have been reported in nearly all states. Thirty-eight of the first 160 Superfund interim priority list sites involve leaching from unsecured surface impoundments.

Surface impoundments also can contaminate surrounding soil and surface water by directly releasing the contaminated liquid via washout, overtopping, or dike breakage. Volatilization of organic contaminants also can pollute air in areas surrounding the impoundment.

In addition to referencing the Background Document, the EPA also footnoted in this passage several studies and reports supporting this analysis.

Carbide places special emphasis on the EPA's statement in the preamble to the final 1986 closure regulations (not repeated in the 1989 regulations) that "all liners will eventually leak" and that closure and capping thus is "critical for the long term control of the unit." 51 Fed. Reg. 16,432 (May 2, 1986). Be that as it may, the EPA's principal justification for regulating the continued delivery of non-hazardous wastes to unretrofitted surface impoundments has always stressed the special incremental risk of leaks from such units. *See id.;* 54 Fed. Reg. 33,382 (Aug. 14, 1989). It comes down to a judgment that all land disposal of hazardous wastes is risky, but some forms are riskier than others. We think the EPA has authority under the RCRA to differentiate between degrees of risk in regulating hazardous waste facilities.

The special danger posed by hazardous waste surface impoundments, combined with the RCRA's obvious preference for prevention over correction, also helps to explain the seemingly anomalous result that surface impoundments that comply with the minimum technological requirements are allowed to continue operating even when they leak, while unretrofitted impoundments are required to either close or be emptied of accumulated hazardous wastes even when they do not leak. The different results are dictated by the different levels of ex ante risks involved in the two situations. It was thus not irrational for the EPA to conclude that the goal of prevention is best served in the first situation by mandating that all surface impoundments intending to continue receiving hazardous wastes meet stringent technological requirements, with correction of any leaks that occur despite the precautions as a secondary safety valve, while prevention is best served in the second situation by requiring either closure or emptying of unretrofitted facilities even when they are not presently leaking.

Finally, Union Carbide claims that the EPA acted irrationally in failing to require the closure or emptying of landfills that do not meet the RCRA's minimum technological requirements while imposing such a requirement on surface impoundments. Again, however, the pressure head scenario provides the explanation. Liquids, whether or not they contain or are classified as hazardous wastes, generally are banned from placement or disposal in landfills, *see* RCRA § 3004(c), 42 U.S.C. § 6924(c), and landfills are therefore significantly less likely than surface impoundments to form pressure heads and to suffer the leachate problems associated with pressure heads. *See* EPA's Response to Comments to June 6, 1988 Proposed Rule at 14, J.A. 264. Further, Congress itself recognized that more stringent regulation of surface impoundments was needed when it decided, in enacting the 1984 Amendments, to require existing surface impoundments, but not existing landfills, either to meet the technological requirements of § 3004(o) or to stop receiving hazardous wastes. *See* RCRA § 3005(j), 42 U.S.C. § 6925(j); 54 Fed. Reg. 33,383 (Aug. 14, 1989).

We therefore conclude that the EPA acted rationally in imposing more stringent closure requirements on unretrofitted surface impoundments than on landfills or on surface impoundments that meet the minimum technological requirements mandated by the 1984 Amendments.

4. Did EPA Use the Wrong Legal Standard in Promulgating the 1989 Regulations?

Union Carbide next asserts that the EPA relied on a standard of "significantly improve[d] protection" of human health and the environment in promulgating the closure regulations rather than on the statutorily-mandated standard of "necessary to protect" human health and the environment. *See* RCRA § 3004(a), 42 U.S.C. § 6924(a). The EPA agrees that the latter standard is the one it is required to apply under the RCRA, but rejects the contention that it failed to apply it.

Although it is true that the EPA changed its tune in 1989 to the extent of permitting unretrofitted surface impoundments to remain open so long as they removed accumulated hazardous wastes, this does not indicate that it was applying the wrong legal standard in 1986.

* * *

III. CONCLUSION

The EPA's interpretation of § 3004(a) of the RCRA as permitting it, subsequent to the 1984 Amendments, to prohibit the continued receipt of non-hazardous wastes by unretrofitted surface impoundments that are not emptied of accumulated hazardous wastes is a permissible one. In addition, the EPA has adequately justified its decision to impose such a ban generally. The petitions for review are accordingly

Denied.

NOTES

1. Is it appropriate for the court to be so deferential to EPA? What is the proper role of the court in reviewing agency decisions?

2. Does EPA's rationale make sense?

3. If you were the Administrator of EPA, how would you change EPA's regulation of TSDFs?

4. Corrective Action Requirements

If a TSDF leaks, RCRA requires the owner/operator to take corrective actions. RCRA contains three corrective action provisions to mitigate the damage a release of hazardous waste can have on human health. Sections 3004(u) and 3008(h), predicate jurisdiction on a release of hazardous waste.[150] Section 3008(v) expands the area under which the EPA can require corrective action.[151]

---

[150] *See* 42 U.S.C. §§ 6924(u), 6928(h) (1994).
[151] *See* 42 U.S.C. § 6924(v) (1994).

The EPA's corrective action process begins when the EPA conducts a RCRA facility assessment (RFA). The RFA describes what the facility[152] does, and whether the EPA needs to conduct a later investigation to determine if corrective action measures are required.[153] If a release of a hazardous waste or constituent is occurring at a facility the EPA will order: a RCRA facility investigation (RFI), a corrective measures study (CMS), and a corrective measures implementation.[154] The inspection and measures done by the EPA delineate the corrective action measures a facility must implement. The EPA can also implement corrective action procedures on facilities that already have a permit. When "the standards and regulations on which the permit was based have been changed" the EPA can impose corrective action on the permitee.[155] The EPA can also impose corrective action requirements when the EPA renews a permit.[156]

The following illustrations explain the corrective action process.

Program Inception Through FY 1994

Assessments	Investigations	Controlling Contaminant Releases
		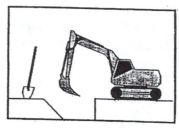
2,864 Facilities of a Total 3,853 Facilities Have Been Assessed (74%)	43% of Facilities Assessed (32% of the Total) Have Begun or Completed Investigation (1,235 Facilities)	19% of Facilities Assessed (14% of the Total) Are Controlling Contaminant Releases (539 Facilities)

Facilities include only Subtitle C treatment, storage, and disposal facilities (TSDFs).

Figure 9.13–Status of Subtitle C Facilities In the Corrective Action Program[157]

Section 3004(u) states that the EPA must require corrective action for "all releases of hazardous waste or constituents" from any TSDF seeking a permit under RCRA after 1985.[158] Additionally, the section requires that a company seeking a permit provide "assurances of financial responsibility" to

---

[152] Corrective action requirements apply to any facility or "solid waste management unit." EPA defines a solid waste management unit as "Any discernible unit at which solid wastes have been placed at any time . . . ." 55 Fed. Reg. 30,798.

[153] See ABA, RCRA PRACTICE MANUAL at 177 (Theodore L. Garrett ed., 1994).

[154] See id. at 178.

[155] 40 C.F.R. § 270.41(a)(3) (1995).

[156] See supra note 153, at 178.

[157] Resource Conversation and Recovery Information System (RCRIS), National Oversight Database, September 19, 1995.

[158] 42 U.S.C. § 6924(u) (1994).

complete the clean-up.[159] Although § 3004(u) applies only to "releases," the EPA argues that they have the authority to require corrective action when a potential release exists.[160]

The EPA states that because there is not a definition of "release" in RCRA, the EPA will use the definition of "release" in CERCLA.[161] A release under CERCLA extends to an abandonment of a closed receptacle containing hazardous substances.[162] The EPA believes that an actual release does not have to be shown to order a facility to take corrective action.

Under § 3004(u) there are two ways the EPA can force a company to take corrective action. First, the EPA can deny a facility a permit if the facility refuses to complete corrective action.[163] Since every facility that handles over a certain amount of hazardous waste needs a permit this would prevent the facility from operating. Second, if the facility agrees to complete the corrective action then later reneges, the government can seek compliance through a civil action in federal court.[164]

Section 3004(u) differs from the other two corrective action sections by mentioning corrective action for release of hazardous "constituents."[165] It is clear from the Senate Report that hazardous constituents are different from hazardous waste.[166] The EPA issued regulations of what wastes it considers to be hazardous constituents. Additionally, a court attempted to delineate the difference between hazardous waste and hazardous constituent.[167] In *National Resources Defense Council, Inc. v. EPA,* the court held that hazardous constituents "are defined by molecular formulae[;] . . . a single molecule."[168] A hazardous waste, by contrast, contains various factors, including the concentration of hazardous constituents which make the waste hazardous to human health or the environment.[169]

Under § 3004(u) the EPA can require corrective action "from any solid waste management unit at a . . . facility."[170] The EPA has interpreted "facility" to include all continuous property owned by the TSDF owner. The EPA considers land owned by the TSDF owner that is separated by roads to be continuous. In the EPA's view, the EPA can inspect and make corrective action assessments from "fence line to fence line" on the TSDF owner's property.[171]

---

[159] *Id.*

[160] Corrective action requirements apply to interim status facilities receiving wastes after July 26, 1982. *See* 42 U.S.C. § 6925(I) (1994).

[161] *See* 61 Fed. Reg. 19,432, 19,442 (1996).

[162] *See* ABA, RCRA PRACTICE MANUAL at 177 (Theodore L. Garrett ed., 1994).

[163] *See* 42 U.S.C. § 6924(u) (1994).

[164] *See id.*

[165] *Id.*

[166] S. REP. NO. 284, at 32 (1983).

[167] *See* 40 C.F.R. § 274.93 (1995).

[168] National Resources Defense Council, Inc. v. EPA, 907 F.2d 1146, 1159 (D.C. Cir. 1990).

[169] *See id.*

[170] 42 U.S.C. § 6924(u) (1994).

[171] 40 C.F.R. § 260.10 (1995).

The following schematic illustrates how a potential corrective action for groundwater contamination may work.

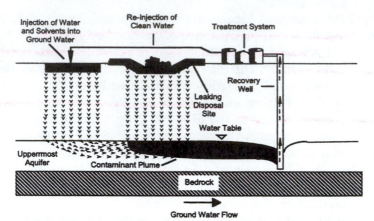

An example of ground water corrective action is a ground water pump and treat system. In order to remediate contamination that has leaked from a disposal site into the uppermost aquifer, the owner and operator injects water and solvents into the ground. The groundwater flow carries the water and solvents to the contaminant plume, flushes the plume of the contamination, and carries the contaminants to a recovery well where the contaminated water is pumped to the surface and treated. Clean water is then re-injected into the ground water for reuse in the pump and treat process.

Figure 9.14–Ground Water Corrective Action[172]

Section 3008(h) permits the EPA to order corrective action to an interim status facility that has released hazardous waste into the environment.[173] The government can seek to impose corrective action requirements on the facility by seeking equitable relief or civil action in a federal court.[174]

Although § 3008(h) does not cover releases of hazardous constituents, the EPA argues that any kind of waste under the statutory definition of hazardous waste is subject to corrective action.[175] Therefore, the EPA considers hazardous wastes under § 3008(h) to cover a broader area than the term suggests. By arguing for broadening the corrective action authority under § 3008(h), the EPA seeks to make the scope of hazardous materials subject to corrective action under § 3008(h), similar to § 3004(u).

Section 3008(h) applies to interim status facilities that never obtained interim status. In *United States v. Environmental Waste Control* the court held that a facility complies to the corrective action order under § 3008(h) even though the facilities interim status expired.[176] In *United States v. Indian Woodtreating* the court held that a facility that never obtained interim status was subject to suit under § 3008(h).[177] The court stated that otherwise a facility could gain exemption from performing corrective action by not

---

[172] EPA, RCRA ORIENTATION MANUAL, III-96 (1990).

[173] *See* 42 U.S.C. § 6928(h) (1994).

[174] *See id.*

[175] *See* 42 U.S.C. § 6903(5) (1994); *see also* 55 Fed. Reg. 30,798, 30,809 (1990).

[176] *See* United States v. Environmental Waste Control, Inc., 710 F. Supp. 1172 (N.D. Ind. 1989), *aff'd,* 917 F.2d 327 (7th Cir. 1990), *cert. denied,* 499 U.S. 975 (1991).

[177] *See* United States v. Indiana Woodtreating Corp., 686 F. Supp. 218 (S.D. Ind. 1988).

submitting forms to obtain interim status. The court felt that this would undermine RCRAís purpose to protect human health and the environment from exposure to hazardous waste.[178]

The following graphic illustrates the status of corrective actions.

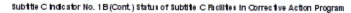

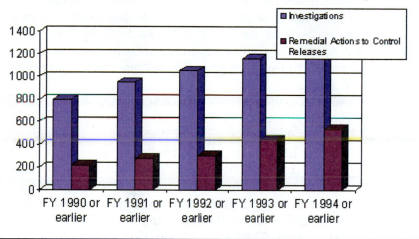

Figure 9.15–Status of Subtitle C Facilities in Corrective Action[179]

Considerable controversy has also arisen whether § 3008(h) assesses liability or is just a jurisdictional statute. Some argue that § 3008(h) is similar to § 106 of CERCLA, which only grants the EPA Administrator the right to issue an administrative or civil action against unspecified parties to abate the release or threatened releases of hazardous substances.[180] If § 3008(h) is only a jurisdictional statute then the persons the EPA can order to take corrective action is limited.[181] The government would have to find the means to assess liability in another provision of RCRA. If § 3008(h) is a statute that assesses liability, the EPA can impose liability on any party that disposed hazardous waste to the site.[182]

Section 3008(h) does seem, at the minimum, to grant the EPA power to order the present owner of a facility to conduct corrective action.[183] Legislative history also suggests that Congress intended present site owners to be responsible for past disposal acts.[184] In the final codification rule the EPA provided present owners with the option of recovering corrective action

---

[178] See id. at 223.
[179] Resource Conservation and Recovery Information System (RCRIS), September 19, 1995.
[180] See United States v. Outboard Marine Corp., 556 F. Supp. 54 (N.D. Ill. 1982).
[181] See Joseph F. Guida, Corrective Action Under the Resource Conservation and Recovery Act, 44 Sw. L. J. 1331, 1345 (1991).
[182] See id.
[183] See id.
[184] See H.R. CONF. REP. NO. 98-1133 (1983).

costs from past owners.[185] However, the scope of liability assessed under § 3008(h) remains unclear.

Section 3004(v) gives the EPA power to require a facility to pay for corrective action outside the facility's premises. The EPA can order such action if it determines that the facility needs to perform corrective action measures to protect human health and the environment.[186] This section allows the owner an opportunity to demonstrate that despite his best efforts, he cannot take action because the owner of the land off-site refuses.[187] The regulation implemented by the EPA requires that the present owner conduct corrective action measures off-site, even if a previous owner was responsible for the waste contamination.[188]

In 1990 the EPA issued a proposed corrective action rule. The EPA renewed the proposed rule in 1996.[189] Although the proposed rule is not binding, the EPA uses the rule to guide the EPA in making corrective action decisions.[190] Once the EPA enacts the rule it will: clarify the applicability of § 3004(u) to facilities, establish the timing of corrective action responses at a facility, and establish a method for choosing a corrective action remedy.[191]

An important issue under RCRA corrective action provisions is: How clean does the site need to be? RCRA leaves the question to the EPA, who borrows standards from CERCLA and the Safe Drinking Water Act (SDWA). The "how clean is clean" issue will be addressed in the chapter on CERCLA.

PROBLEM

Assume that all facts in this modified real-life scenario take place in the 1990's. The Alpha Fuels Company, a wholly-owned subsidiary of Beta Corporation, owns 35 acres on the edge of Boomtown, South Dakota, a growing city in what was formerly a semi-rural, semi-industrial area. Alpha leases out 25 of the 35 acres to Eli Parkins, a beet farmer, and uses the remaining ten acres to operate a uranium processing plant that processes uranium into fuel for nuclear reactors. (Do not assume that any of the wastes at issue in this question are exempt from RCRA under § 1004(27) as "source, special nuclear, or byproduct material as defined by the Atomic Energy Act of 1954, as amended." This exemption is not relevant to your answer.)

Alpha's largest customer is South Dakota Mining and Power Co. (SDMP), which owns several uranium mines as well as a commercial nuclear power plant in South Dakota. Under its contract with SDMP, Alpha

---

[185] *See* 50 Fed. Reg. 28,702, 28,716 (1990).

[186] *See* 42 U.S.C. § 6928(v) (1994).

[187] *See id.*

[188] *See* 40 C.F.R. § 264.101(c) (1995).

[189] 61 Fed. Reg. 19,432 (1996).

[190] *See* ABA, RCRA PRACTICE MANUAL at 179 (Theodore L. Garrett ed., 1994).

[191] *See id.*

processes SDMP's mined uranium and returns the processed uranium to SDMP for use in their commercial reactor. Throughout the transaction, SDMP retains title to the uranium. For a time, another of Alpha's customers was the United States government, which purchased Alpha's uranium pellets for military purposes. In fact, several years ago the federal government requested that Alpha increase its production (which Alpha did) in order to meet the government's demand.

As part of its primary production process, Alpha produces 900 kilograms per month of wastes in several distinct waste streams. The first waste stream (500 kg per month) is know as "raffinate" and contains zinc cyanide (Zn(CN)2) and other CERCLA hazardous substances. The raffinate is also reactive according to 40 C.F.R. Part 261. Alpha adds a liquid solution to the raffinate to eliminate its reactive quality and subsequently ships the raffinate to a municipal landfill.

The second waste stream (100 kg per month) consists of sludge which is also reactive under 40 C.F.R. Part 261. Alpha recovers the zinc from the sludge, sells the zinc to a metals broker, and dumps the remaining sludge (which is no longer reactive) down the drain where it eventually ends up at a publicly owned treatment works (POTW).

Finally, one of Alpha's processes creates a byproduct which EPA has listed as a RCRA hazardous waste. Alpha creates 300 kg per month of this byproduct. After collecting the byproduct in open vats, Alpha eventually returns the byproduct to the original process (the process which produces the byproduct) in place of the mined uranium normally used.

Not a SW
(no disposal)

You are an attorney for Alpha. Write a legal memorandum explaining whether Alpha is in violation of RCRA. As Alpha's lawyer, explain any necessary compliance activities you would recommend.

Due to financial difficulties, Alpha recently implemented staff cuts. Not long after the staff cuts were made, a worker's negligence triggered an explosion in the open tanks that collect the raffinate from the production process. The raffinate coalesced into a stream which ran from the plant and crossed over into Eli Parkins' 25-acre beet field. Left alone, the raffinate stream would have hit a ditch where it could have been easily contained by the Boomtown city firefighters. It just so happened, however, that Eli's gigantic, automatic soil-tiller was barreling down the beet field at the very moment the raffinate "soup" was heading toward the ditch. The soil-tiller hit the raffinate stream and sent it flying about Eli's field, contaminating most of the 25 acres and even spreading some of the raffinate into the State park adjoining Alpha's property, a popular recreational fishing spot.

If Alpha obtains a RCRA permit, what, if any, are the company's responsibilities with regard to the above contamination?[192]

---

[192] Information taken from Professor Kristen H. Engel, Tulane Law School, Hazardous Waste Law Exam, May 8, 1995.

NOTES

1. During the automobile boom of the 1950s and 1960s, hundreds of thousands of underground storage tanks (USTs) were installed in communities throughout the United States. By 1984, 75,000 to 100,000 of the 2,000,000 USTs that existed in the United States already leaked petroleum and other hazardous materials and thousands more were expected to do so in the near future.[193] In response, the 1984 HSWA included provisions for regulating USTs, and the 1986 amendments to CERCLA allowed EPA to impose financial responsibility requirements on all UST owners and operators and established a fund to pay for corrective action at sites where no responsible party could be found.[194] The UST program, as a result, operates as a kind of microcosm of the RCRA program as a whole—from design specifications for new tanks to clean-up standards for old and leaking ones. Also like RCRA as a whole, the states are allowed to operate equivalent programs that replace the federal program.

2. The burden of the UST program falls most heavily on tank's owners and operators, broadly inclusive terms that include, most importantly, lessee-managers of service stations. All owners or operators must notify EPA or the relevant state agency of the existence of UST. Since 1998, all USTs, new and old, must meet federal standards for leak detection, prevention, and clean-up. All USTs installed after 1998 must meet federal design standards for spill, overfill, and corrosion protection. Finally, owners and operators must report and clean spills.

3. The sheer number of USTs (an estimated 1.2 million) threatens to overwhelm the resources of federal and state regulatory authorities, so EPA and the states have begun to consider ways to target the leaking tanks that pose the most serious threats and pay little attention to low-risk leaks.[195] How should EPA or a state go about setting such priorities? What criteria should be employed? Which criteria are most important?

4. Is the need to set priorities an indication that Congress should not have tried to regulate USTs in the first place, leaving it to the states?

5. The following illustration shows how underground storage tanks may be monitored.

---

[193] See Notification Requirements for Owners of Underground Storage Tanks, 50 Fed. Reg. 21,772 (1985). Also see HEARING BEFORE THE SENATE SUBCOMMITTEE ON TOXIC SUBSTANCES AND ENVIRONMENT OVERSIGHT, H.R. REP. NO. 721, 98th CONG. 2D SESS. 73 (1984), and 130 CONG. REC. S9164 (July 25, 1984) (Sen. Durenberger predicts that up to seventy-five percent of existing USTs will leak over the next ten years).

[194] See 42 U.S.C. §§ 6991-6991(i) (1994); see also 40 C.F.R. pt. 280 (1995).

[195] See Christine L. Seidel, EPA Announces Risk-Based Approach to UST Cleanups, WEST'S LEGAL NEWS (Mar. 15, 1996); Brian Louis, States Rethinking Leaking UST Regulations, WEST'S LEGAL NEWS (Apr. 1, 1996).

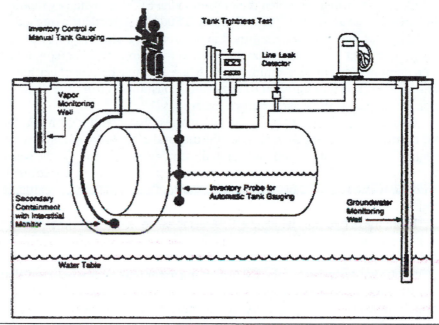

Figure 9.16–Some Leak Detection Methods[196]

E. Land Disposal Restrictions

In the Hazardous and Solid Waste Amendments (HSWA) of 1984 Congress stated that land disposal of hazardous waste should be the least favored method of land disposal.[197] Section 3004(d)(1) of RCRA prohibited land disposal of all hazardous wastes unless the EPA Administrator determined that the "prohibition of one or more methods of land disposal of such waste is not required in order to protect human health and the environment for as long as the waste remains hazardous."[198]

Congress stated that the EPA must look at three areas when determining whether to allow the disposal of untreated hazardous wastes on land. The EPA Administrator must look at:

    1. the characteristic of the waste;

    2. the long term uncertainties associated with land disposal; and

    3. the importance of encouraging proper management of hazardous waste in the first instance.

---

[196] Musts for USTs, US EPA 9

[197] 42 U.S.C. § 6901(b)(7) reads: "certain classes of land disposal facilities are not capable of assuring long-term containment of certain hazardous wastes, and to avoid substantial risk to human health and the environment, reliance on land disposal should be minimized or eliminated, and land disposal, particularly landfill and surface impoundment, should be the least favored method for managing hazardous wastes."

[198] 42 U.S.C. § 6924(d)(1) (1994).

Congress further restricted the discretion the EPA had when evaluating the three factors above in § 3004(d). Section 3004(d) states that "a method of land disposal may not be determined to be protective of human health and the environment . . . unless, upon application by an interested person, it has been demonstrated to the Administrator, to a reasonable degree of certainty, that there will be no migration of hazardous constituents from the disposal unit for as long as the wastes remain hazardous."[199]

Congress did not entirely ban all wastes that could not meet the requirements of § 3004(d). It allowed the disposal of hazardous wastes when treatment of the waste would "substantially diminish the toxicity of the waste or substantially reduce the likelihood of migration of hazardous constituents from the waste so that short-term and long-term threats to human health are minimized."[200]

From these two provisions the EPA established the two policies that lie at the heart of the land disposal provisions; the no migration or prohibition standard, and the treatment standard. The EPA can allow the disposal of a hazardous waste on land if the EPA Administrator reasonably believes that no migration of hazardous constituents will occur for as long as the waste remains hazardous.[201] Or the EPA Administrator can allow the land disposal for hazardous waste if one treats the hazardous waste to a level where the threat of the waste to human health and the environment is minimal.[202] Since EPA believes that no migration is not a realistic standard, these provisions become treatment standards.

---

[199] 42 U.S.C. § 6924(d)(1)(A)(B)&(C) (1994).
[200] 42 U.S.C. § 6924(m) (1994).
[201] See 42 U.S.C. § 6924(d) (1994).
[202] See 42 U.S.C. § 6924(m) (1994).

The following chart explains when LDR's are applicable.

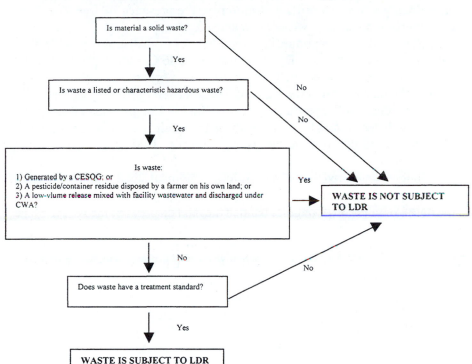

Figure 9.17–Land Disposal Restrictions Applicability[203]

1. Land Disposal and the "Hammer" Provisions

In the HSWA, Congress required that the treatment and prohibition standards for hazardous wastes be phased in on a date-mandated schedule. First, Congress banned the placement of any hazardous waste in salt bed formations, salt domes, mines, or caves after November 8, 1984, unless the EPA finds that such disposal is protective of human health and the environment.[204] The first type of hazardous waste Congress banned was liquid hazardous wastes. By May 8, 1985, Congress banned the land disposal of all non-containerized liquid hazardous wastes.[205] By November 8, 1985, Congress banned the placement of non-hazardous wastes in hazardous waste facilities except in limited circumstances.[206] Congress also directed the EPA

---

[203] EPA, RCRA ORIENTATION MANUAL III-102 (1990).

[204] *See* 42 U.S.C. § 6924(b)(1) (1994).

[205] *See* 42 U.S.C. § 6924(c)(1) (1994).

[206] *See* 42 U.S.C. § 6924(c)(3) (1994). A generator or treatment facility can place non-hazardous waste in a hazardous treatment facility if placement in the facility is the only reasonable alternative to the placement of the waste in an unlined surface impoundment facility. The owner or operator of the facility must demonstrate that placement of the waste in

to promulgate regulations to minimize the disposal of containerized hazardous waste in landfills and minimize the presence of free liquids in containerized hazardous waste from land disposal.[207]

Along with banning liquid hazardous wastes from disposal, Congress set dates to ban other wastes. By November 8, 1986 Congress prohibited the disposal (except by deep well injection) of solvent and dioxin-containing wastes.[208] Congress banned the disposal of so-called California list wastes,[209] (except by deep well injection) by July 8, 1987.[210] Congress also banned the remaining listed wastes by dividing the list into thirds and banning disposal for each successive third on the list by August 8, 1988, June 8, 1989, and May 8, 1990.[211]

Congress required the EPA to develop treatment standards for the listed wastes by a certain date. If the EPA did not develop treatment standards by the date Congress set, Congress banned the land disposal of the waste.[212] The decision to require a ban on disposal of certain hazardous wastes if the EPA did not meet a time limit caused great debate in the Congress. The idea to have certain dates listed for the EPA to act by was the result of the frustration congressional members had with the EPA's slow response to enact regulations banning the disposal of hazardous wastes before 1984. Prior to the passage of HSWA, Senator George Mitchell said: "It has become evident that a strong congressional expression of disapproval of EPA's slow and timid implementation of the existing law is necessary . . . [The] EPA has not implemented the Resource Conservation and Recovery Act aggressively. The Agency has missed deadlines, proposed inadequate regulations, and even exacerbated the hazardous waste problem by superseding certain regulations."[213]

Broad congressional agreement with Senator Mitchell's statement resulted in a provision in HSWA that stated: "[I]f the EPA Administrator failed to promulgate regulations or make a determination . . . for any hazardous waste within 66 months after the date of enactment of the Hazardous Waste and Solid Waste Amendments of 1984, such hazardous waste shall be prohibited from land disposal."[214]

Members of small industries protested the provision. Joe Gerard of the American Furniture Manufacture's Association stated the provision "would

---

the facility will not present a risk of contamination of any underground source of drinking water.

[207] See 42 U.S.C. § 6924(c)(2) (1994).

[208] See 42 U.S.C. § 6924(e) (1994).

[209] California list wastes are wastes that the state of California banned from land disposal in 1982. Included in "California wastes" are liquid wastes and sludges that contain concentrations of heavy metals, arsenic, acidic liquids, organic liquids containing 50 or more ppm PCBs, and halogenated compounds in concentrations of 1000 mg/kg or more.

[210] See 42 U.S.C. § 6924(d)(2) (1994).

[211] See 42 U.S.C. § 6924(g) (1994).

[212] See 42 U.S.C. § 6924(g)(C) (1994).

[213] 130 CONG. REC. S13816 (daily ed., Oct. 5, 1984).

[214] 42 U.S.C. § 6924(g)(C) (1994).

hit them [small businesses] like a hammer."[215] Gerard's reference of the time provisions in HSWA as "hammers" became the popular term for the time provisions.[216]

Congress imposed "soft hammers" and "hard hammers" if the EPA did not promulgate treatment standards for listed wastes under § 3004(g).[217] If Congress did not develop treatment standards for the first-third waste by November 8, 1986, a "soft hammer" would take effect.[218] The "soft hammer" would allow the disposal of first-third wastes on land but any land disposal must occur at a facility that complied with § 3004(o).[219]

Similarly, if treatment standards were not in effect for the second-third wastes by November 8, 1988, the "soft hammer" would take effect on second-third wastes.[220] If the EPA did not promulgate treatment standards for any of the listed thirds by May 8, 1990 (when the third-third prohibition applied) a "hard hammer" would come down.[221] The "hard hammer" prohibited any land disposal of the listed waste without a treatment standard.

Congress also required the EPA to establish prohibition or treatment standards for wastes identified as hazardous after 1984 within six months after the EPA identifies or lists the waste.[222] However, if the EPA does not act within six months the waste will not be banned from land disposal. Congress chose not to apply a "hammer" provision to newly identified hazardous wastes.[223]

2. Technology vs. Risk-Based Standards for Treating Hazardous Wastes

Faced with Congressional "hammers" the EPA promulgated treatment standards for most of the listed wastes. Initially, a major issue was whether the EPA should promulgate treatment standards using a risk-based or a technology-based analysis. EPA chose Best Demonstrated Available Technology (BDAT), and numerous industry groups challenged EPA's choice in *Hazardous Waste Treatment Council v. EPA.*

HAZARDOUS WASTE TREATMENT COUNCIL V. EPA *[HWTC III]*
886 F.2d 355 (D.C. Cir. 1989)

PER CURIAM.

---

[215] CHRISTOPHER HARRIS *ET AL.*, HAZARDOUS WASTE: CONFRONTING THE CHALLENGE 86 (1987).

[216] *See id.*

[217] 42 U.S.C. § 6924(g) (1994).

[218] *Id.*

[219] Basically, § 3004(o) requires the facility to have double liners, leachate collection systems, and ground water monitoring.)

[220] *See* 42 U.S.C. § 6924(g) (1994).

[221] *See id.*

[222] *See id.*

[223] *See id.*

In 1984, Congress amended the Resource Conservation and Recovery Act ("RCRA"), 42 U.S.C. § 6921-6991 (1982 & Supp. IV 1986), to prohibit land disposal of certain hazardous solvents and wastes containing dioxins except in narrow circumstances to be defined by Environmental Protection Agency ("EPA") regulations. *See* Hazardous and Solid Waste Amendments, § 201(a), 42 U.S.C. § 6924(e) (Supp. IV 1986). In these consolidated cases, petitioners seek review of EPA's final "solvents and dioxins" rule published pursuant to Congress' 1984 mandate. We conclude that the rule under review is consistent with RCRA, but remand one aspect of the rulemaking to the agency for further explanation.

I.

A. Statutory Scheme.

The Hazardous and Solid Waste Amendments of 1984 ("HSWA"), Pub. L. No. 98-616, 98 Stat. 3221 (1984), inter alia, substantially strengthened EPA's control over the land disposal of hazardous wastes regulated under RCRA's "cradle to grave" statutory scheme. In preambular language to the HSWA, Congress, believing that "land disposal facilities were not capable of assuring long-term containment of certain hazardous wastes," expressed the policy that "reliance on land disposal should be minimized or eliminated." 42 U.S.C. § 6901(b)(7). In order to effectuate this policy, HSWA amended § 3004 of RCRA to prohibit land disposal of hazardous waste unless the waste is "pretreated" in a manner that minimizes "short-term and long-term threats to human health and the environment," *Id.* § 6924(m), or unless EPA can determine that the waste is to be disposed of in such a fashion as to ensure that "there will be no-migration of hazardous constituents from the disposal [facility]. . . ." *Id.* § 6924(d)(1), (e)(1), & (g)(5).

As amended, RCRA requires EPA to implement the land disposal prohibition in three phases, addressing the most hazardous "listed" wastes first. *See id.* § 6924(g).[224] In accordance with strict statutory deadlines, the Administrator is obligated to specify those methods of land disposal of each listed hazardous waste which "will be protective of human health and the environment." *Id.* In addition, "[s]imultaneously with the promulgation of regulations * * * prohibiting * * * land disposal of a particular hazardous waste, the Administrator" is required to promulgate regulations specifying those levels or methods of treatment, if any, which substantially diminish the toxicity of the waste or substantially reduce the likelihood of migration of

---

[224] EPA was given the task of dividing the wastes presently "listed" as hazardous under RCRA into thirds according to their "intrinsic hazard," 42 U.S.C. § 6924(g)(2) (Supp. IV 1986). In keeping with RCRA's deadline, the resulting schedule, promulgated in 1986, *see* 51 Fed. Reg. 19,300 (1986), required EPA to implement the land disposal prohibition and promulgate treatment standards for each third by dates no later than 45, 55, and 66 months after enactment of the HSWA, respectively. *See* 42 U.S.C. § 6924(g)(4). One aspect of EPA's regulations governing the "first third" of these wastes was recently upheld on review in Chemical-Waste Management, Inc. v. EPA, 869 F.2d 1526 (D.C.Cir.1989).

hazardous constituents from the waste so that short-term and long-term threats to human health and the environment are minimized. *Id.* § 6924(m).

Respecting two categories of hazardous wastes, including the solvents and dioxins at issue here.[225] Congress, however, declined to wait for phased EPA implementation of the land disposal prohibition. For these wastes, Congress imposed earlier restrictions, prohibiting land disposal after dates specified in the HSWA except in accordance with pretreatment standards or pursuant to regulations specifying "protective" methods of disposal. *Id.* § 6924(e)(1). These prohibitions, as applied to the solvents and dioxins listed in the HSWA, were to take effect November 8, 1986. *Id.*

In order to further RCRA's basic purpose of mandating treatment of hazardous wastes in lieu of land disposal, Congress further provided that storage of wastes falling within the land disposal prohibition would be "prohibited unless such storage is solely for the purpose of the accumulation of such quantities of hazardous waste as are necessary to facilitate proper recovery, treatment or disposal." *Id.* § 6924(j). Congress believed that permitting storage of large quantities of waste as a means of forestalling required treatment would involve health threats equally serious to those posed by land disposal, and therefore opted in large part for a "treat as you go" regulatory regime.

B. The Rulemaking Under Review.

In January 1986, EPA issued a notice of proposed rule-making announcing its draft implementation of the land disposal prohibition for solvents and dioxins. *See* 51 Fed. Reg. 1602 (1986) (hereinafter "Proposed Rule"). Approximately ten months later, after receiving extensive public commentary on the draft blueprint, EPA published a final solvents and dioxins rule differing in some respects from its draft approach. *See* 51 Fed. Reg. 40,572 (1986) (hereinafter "Final Rule"). These differences were especially striking in EPA's implementation of § 3004(j) and § 3004(m) of RCRA, governing the storage prohibition and treatment standards, respectively, for solvents and dioxins. These portions of the rule, together with other discrete portions of the rulemaking faulted by petitioners, are summarized below.

1. Section 3004(m) Treatment Standards.

In the Proposed Rule, EPA announced its tentative support for a treatment regime embodying both risk-based and technology-based standards. The technology-based standards would be founded upon what EPA determined to be the Best Demonstrated Available Technology ("BDAT"); parallel risk-based or "screening" levels were to reflect "the maximum concentration [of a hazardous constituent] below which the Agency believes there is no regulatory concern for the land disposal program and which is protective of human health and the environment." Proposed

---

[225] The other category is the so-called "California List" wastes, the rule for which is the subject of Hazardous Waste Treatment Council v. Thomas, 885 F.2d 918 (D.C. Cir. 1989).

Rule at 1611. The Proposed Rule provided that these two sets of standards would be melded in the following manner:

First, if BDAT standards were more rigorous than the relevant health-screening levels, the latter would be used to "cap the reductions in toxicity and/or mobility that otherwise would result from the application of BDAT treatment [.]" *Id.* Thus, "treatment for treatment's sake" would be avoided. Second, if BDAT standards were less rigorous than health-screening levels, BDAT standards would govern and the screening level would be used as "a goal for future changes to the treatment standards as new and more efficient treatment technologies become available." *Id.* at 1612. Finally, when EPA determined that the use of BDAT would pose a greater risk to human health and the environment than land disposal, or would provide insufficient safeguards against the threats produced by land disposal, the screening level would actually become the 3004(m) treatment standard. *Id.*

EPA invited public comment on alternative approaches as well. The first alternative identified in the Proposed Rule (and the one ultimately selected by EPA) was based purely on the capabilities of the "best demonstrated available technology." *Id.* at 1613. Capping treatment levels to avoid treatment for treatment's sake, according to EPA, could be accomplished under this technology-based scheme by "the petition process":

> Under this approach, if a prescribed level or method of treatment under § 3004(m) resulted in concentration levels that an owner/operator believed to be overly protective, the owner/operator could petition the Agency to allow the use of an alternative treatment level or method or no treatment at all by demonstrating that less treatment would still meet the petition standard of protecting human health and environment.

Id. at 1613. And the function served by health-screening levels of providing a default standard when the application of BDAT technology would itself pose a threat to human health and the environment could likewise be fulfilled by the petition process: "an owner operator could [ ] petition the Agency . . . to allow continued land disposal of the waste upon a demonstration that land disposal of the waste would not result in harm to human health and the environment." *Id.*

The Agency received comments supporting both approaches, but ultimately settled on the pure-technology alternative. Of particular importance to EPA's decision were the comments filed by eleven members of Congress, all of whom served as conferees on the 1984 RCRA amendments. As EPA recorded in the preamble to the Final Rule:

> [these] members of Congress argued strongly that [the health screening] approach did not fulfill the intent of the law. They asserted that because of the scientific uncertainty inherent in risk-based decisions, Congress expressly directed the Agency to set treatment standards based on the capabilities of existing technology.

The Agency believes that the technology-based approach adopted in [the] final rule, although not the only approach allowable under the law, best responds to the above stated comments.

Final Rule at 40,578.

EPA also relied on passages in the legislative history supporting an approach under which owners and operator of hazardous waste facilities would be required to use "the best [technology] that has been demonstrated to be achievable." *Id.* (quoting 103 CONG. REC. S9178 (daily ed. July 25, 1984) (statement of Senator Chaffee). And the agency reiterated that the chief advantage offered by the health-screening approach—avoiding "treatment for treatment's sake"—could "be better addressed through changes in other aspects of its regulatory program." *Id.* As an example of what parts of the program might be altered, EPA announced that it was "considering the use of its risk-based methodologies to characterize wastes as hazardous pursuant to § 3001 [of RCRA]." *Id.*; *see* 42 U.S.C. § 6921 (1982 & Supp. IV 1986).[226]

Petitioner CMA challenges this aspect of the rule as an unreasonable construction of § 3004(m)'s mandate to ensure that "short-term and long-term threats to human health and the environment are minimized." 42 U.S.C. § 6924(m) (1982 & Supp. IV 1986). In the alternative, CMA argues that EPA has failed to explain the basis—in terms of relevant human health and environmental considerations—for its BDAT regime, which allegedly requires treatment in some circumstances to levels far below the standards for human exposure under other statutes administered by EPA. Thus, CMA claims that EPA's action in promulgating a technology-based rule is arbitrary and capricious.

2. Section 3004(j) Storage Prohibition.

Section 3004(j) of RCRA, as noted above, prohibits the storage of wastes falling within a land disposal prohibition "unless such storage is solely for the purpose of the accumulation of such quantities of hazardous waste as are necessary to facilitate proper recovery, treatment, or disposal," 42 U.S.C. § 6924(j) (1982 & Supp. IV 1986). In the Proposed Rule, EPA tentatively implemented this provision to allow generators to accumulate hazardous wastes on-site for up to 90 days, no questions asked. EPA selected this period in the belief "that it would allow a reasonable period for accumulation prior to further management without interfering with a generator's production process [.]" Proposed Rule at 1709. It observed that as a matter of prevailing industrial practice "most wastes were removed from the site of generation within 90 days." *Id.* Nevertheless, out of concern that "a longer

---

[226] Under section 3001, the Administrator is empowered to list particular wastes as hazardous, and thus within RCRA's ambit, "taking into account toxicity, persistence, [ ] degradability in nature, potential for accumulation in tissue, and other related factors such as flammability, corrosiveness, and other hazardous characteristics." 42 U.S.C. § 6921(a) (1982). The statute provides that the Administrator "shall [ ] revise[ ] [these lists] from time to time as may be appropriate." *Id.* EPA's current list is set forth at 40 C.F.R. pt. 261, Subparts C and D.

time may, in some cases, be necessary to accumulate sufficient quantities to facilitate proper recovery, treatment, or disposal," *Id.*, the agency solicited comments on alternative storage periods that might be appropriate.

The comments received by the Agency ranged far and wide, but all found the 90-day period inadequate. A majority of the commentors favored a one-year storage period in order to accommodate small-quantity generators and others whose waste streams "accumulate[ ] more slowly than others." Final Rule at 40,582. On the basis of these remarks, EPA agreed that 90 days was an insufficient period for the adequate accumulation of wastes to facilitate recovery, treatment or disposal.

EPA ultimately settled on a one-year storage period, but the implementing regulation differed significantly in character from the 90-day proposal. The Final Rule provides:

> An owner/operator of a treatment facility may store [ ] wastes for up to one year unless the Agency can demonstrate that such storage was not solely for the purpose of accumulation of such quantities of hazardous waste as are necessary to facilitate proper recovery, treatment, or disposal.

Id. at 40,643 (codified at 40 C.F.R. § 268.50(b) (1988)). A companion provision requires owners and operators to bear the burden of proving that storage for over a one-year period was for proper purposes under RCRA. *See id.* (codified at 40 C.F.R. § 268.50(c) (1988)).

Characterizing the final storage rule, in effect, as a "shifting of the statutory burden of proof" which "effectively allows a one year override of the statutory prohibition" against storage, petitioners Hazardous Waste Treatment Council ("HWTC") and the Natural Resources Defense Council ("NRDC") challenge the rule as inconsistent with § 3004(j) of RCRA.

3. Responsibility for Testing Wastes Prior to Disposal.

A determination as to whether and to what degree treatment of a waste is required prior to land disposal depends upon the concentration of hazardous constituents in the waste. To facilitate these determinations and to ensure compliance with the land disposal prohibitions and applicable treatment standards, EPA proposed to implement requirements for mandatory testing in some circumstances. Proposed Rule at 1691.

The Agency was immediately confronted with the question of who, among generators, treatment facilities and land disposal facilities, should shoulder the responsibility of testing the waste prior to disposal. While several alternatives were available, EPA initially proposed that the land disposal facility alone be responsible for such testing. Proposed Rule at 1692.

> Under this approach, the disposal facility must either conduct an analysis of the waste or obtain an analysis of the waste from the generator or treater. Similarly, the owner or operator of a land disposal facility could arrange for the generator or treatment facility to supply all or part of the required testing data. However, if the

generator or treater did not supply the testing data and the land disposal facility owner or operator chose to accept the waste, the owner or operator would be responsible for conducting the required testing.

Id. at 1691. The agency cautioned that this approach did not leave the generator without responsibility altogether. The generator was still obliged to determine "whether he must treat his waste prior to disposal." *Id.* "[R]ather than specifically requiring the generator to conduct testing, [however], the Agency [proposed to] allow determination of whether wastes meet the regulatory thresholds to be based on either testing or knowledge of the characteristics of the waste." *Id.* The Agency found this proposal desirable because "[i]t is flexible, does not require redundant testing, fits into the current regulatory scheme for the waste analysis plan and requires the testing to take place where the liability for disposal exists—at the land disposal facility." *Id.* at 1691.

The Final Rule bears substantial resemblance to that initially proposed by EPA, with one principal exception. As the agency explained, "[b]ecause the [treatment] approach promulgated [in the Final Rule] does not cap BDAT with screening levels, more wastes will require treatment to meet the specified treatment standards." Final Rule at 40,597. Given this expanded role for the treatment industry, EPA decided in the Final Rule to impose testing requirements on both treatment facilities and land disposal facilities. But, the agency followed the proposed rule insofar as it did not require testing by generators. *See id.* Thus, when sending waste to either a treatment facility for pretreatment or directly to a land disposal facility, the Final Rule permits generators to base their determinations as to the concentration of hazardous constituents in the waste on "waste analysis data, knowledge of the waste, or both." *Id.* No matter what the basis for their determinations, generators forwarding wastes directly to land disposal facilities must certify their conclusions to the facilities' operators. False certifications, under the Final Rule, may result in criminal penalties. *See* 40 C.F.R. § 268.7 (1988); *see also* 42 U.S.C. § 6928(d)(3) (Supp. IV 1986).

Petitioners HWTC and NRDC contend that it is arbitrary and capricious for EPA to require operators of treatment and land disposal facilities, but not generators, to test wastes within the land disposal prohibition.

II. SECTION 3004(m) TREATMENT STANDARDS

CMA challenges EPA's adoption of BDAT treatment standards in preference to the approach it proposed initially primarily on the ground that the regulation is not a reasonable interpretation of the statute. CMA obliquely, and Intervenors Edison Electric and the American Petroleum Institute explicitly, argues in the alternative that the agency did not adequately explain its decision to take the course that it did. We conclude, as to CMA's primary challenge, that EPA's decision to reject the use of screening levels is a reasonable interpretation of the statute. We also find, however, that EPA's justification of its choice is so fatally flawed that we cannot, in conscience, affirm it. We therefore grant the petitions for review to the extent of remanding this issue to the agency for a fuller explanation.

A. The Consistency of EPA's Interpretation with RCRA.

Our role in evaluating an agency's interpretation of its enabling statute is as strictly circumscribed as it is simply stated: We first examine the statute to ascertain whether it clearly forecloses the course that the agency has taken; if it is ambiguous with respect to that question, we go on to determine whether the agency's interpretation is a reasonable resolution of the ambiguity. *Chevron v. Natural Resources Defense Council*, 467 U.S. 837, 842-45.

1. Chevron Step I: Is the Statute Clear?

We repeat the mandate of § 3004(m)(1): the Administrator is required to promulgate "regulations specifying those levels or methods of treatment, if any, which substantially diminish the toxicity of the waste or substantially reduce the likelihood of migration of hazardous constituents from the waste so that short-term and long-term threats to human health and the environment are minimized." 42 U.S.C. § 6924(m)(1).

CMA reads the statute as requiring EPA to determine the levels of concentration in waste at which the various solvents here at issue are "safe" and to use those "screening levels" as floors below which treatment would not be required. CMA supports its interpretation with the observation that the statute directs EPA to set standards only to the extent that "threats to human health and the environment are minimized." We are unpersuaded, however, that Congress intended to compel EPA to rely upon screening levels in preference to the levels achievable by BDAT.

* * *

2. Chevron Step II: Is EPA's Interpretation Reasonable?

The screening levels that EPA initially proposed were not those at which the wastes were thought to be entirely safe. Rather, EPA set the levels to reduce risks from the solvents to an "acceptable" level, and it explored, at great length, the manifest (and manifold) uncertainties inherent in any attempt to specify "safe" concentration levels. The agency discussed, for example, the lack of any safe level of exposure to carcinogenic solvents, 51 Fed. Reg. at 1,628; the extent to which reference dose levels (from which it derived its screening levels) understate the dangers that hazardous solvents pose to particularly sensitive members of the population, *id.* at 1,627; the necessarily artificial assumptions that accompany any attempt to model the migration of hazardous wastes from a disposal site, *id.* at 1,642-53; and the lack of dependable data on the effects that solvents have on the liners that bound disposal facilities for the purpose of ensuring that the wastes disposed in a facility stay there, *id.* at 1,714-15. Indeed, several parties made voluminous comments on the Proposed Rule to the effect that EPA's estimates of the various probabilities were far more problematic than even EPA recognized. *See, e.g.*, Comments of Natural Resources Defense Council, Record at 29,000-62.

CMA suggests, despite these uncertainties, that the adoption of a BDAT treatment regime would result in treatment to "below established levels of hazard." It relies for this proposition almost entirely upon a chart in which it contrasts the BDAT levels with (1) levels EPA has defined as "Maximum Contaminant Levels" (MCLs) under the Safe Drinking Water Act; (2) EPA's proposed "Organic Toxicity Characteristics," threshold levels below which EPA will not list a waste as hazardous by reason of its having in it a particular toxin; and (3) levels at which EPA has recently granted petitions by waste generators to "delist" a particular waste, that is, to remove it from the list of wastes that are deemed hazardous. CMA points out that the BDAT standards would require treatment to levels that are, in many cases, significantly below these "established levels of hazard."

If indeed EPA had determined that wastes at any of the three levels pointed to by CMA posed no threat to human health or the environment, we would have little hesitation in concluding that it was unreasonable for EPA to mandate treatment to substantially lower levels. In fact, however, none of the levels to which CMA compares the BDAT standards purports to establish a level at which safety is assured or "threats to human health and the environment are minimized." Each is a level established for a different purpose and under a different set of statutory criteria than concern us here; each is therefore irrelevant to the inquiry we undertake today.

* * *

B. Was EPA's Explanation Adequate?

The Supreme Court has made it abundantly clear that a reviewing court is not to supplement an agency's reasons for proceeding as it did, nor to paper over its plainly defective rationale: "The reviewing court should not attempt itself to make up for such deficiencies [in the agency's explanation]; we may not supply a reasoned basis for the agency's action that the agency itself has not given." *Motor Vehicles Manufacturers Ass'n v. State Farm Mut. Auto Ins. Co.*, 463 U.S. 29, 43 (1983) (citing *SEC v. Chenery Corp.*, 332 U.S. 194, 196 (1947)). "We will, however, 'uphold a decision of less than ideal clarity if the agency's path may reasonably be discerned.'" *Id.* (quoting *Bowman Transportation, Inc. v. Arkansas-Best Freight System, Inc.*, 419 U.S. 281, 286 (1974)). Accordingly, in order to determine whether we can affirm EPA's action here, we must parse the language of the Final Rule to see whether it can be interpreted to make a sensible argument for the approach EPA adopted. We find that it cannot.

As we have said, EPA, in its Proposed Rule, expressed a tentative preference for an approach that combined screening levels and BDAT. It indicated that it thought either that approach or BDAT alone was consistent with the statute, and recognized that there were myriad uncertainties inherent in any attempt to model the health and environmental effects of the land disposal of hazardous wastes. It initially concluded, however, that despite those uncertainties, the better approach was to adopt the combination of screening levels and BDAT. Nevertheless, in the Final Rule, it rejected its earlier approach, and adopted a regime of treatment levels defined by BDAT alone.

In order fully to convey the inadequacy of EPA's explanation, we quote the relevant portion of the Final Rule at length:

> Although a number of comments on the proposed rule favored the first approach; that is, the use of screening levels to "cap" treatment that can be achieved under BDAT, several commenters, including eleven members of Congress, argued strongly that this approach did not fulfill the intent of the law. They asserted that because of the scientific uncertainty inherent in risk-based decisions, Congress expressly directed the Agency to set treatment standards based on the capabilities of existing technology.

> The Agency believes that the technology-based approach adopted in today's final rule, although not the only approach allowable under the law, best responds to the above-stated comments. Accordingly, the final rule establishes treatment standards under RCRA § 3004(m) based exclusively on levels achievable by BDAT. The Agency believes that the treatment standards will generally be protective of human health and the environment. Levels less stringent than BDAT may also be protective.

> The plain language of the statute does not compel the Agency to set treatment standards based exclusively on the capabilities of existing technology. * * * By calling for standards that minimize threats to human health and the environment, the statute clearly allows for the kind of risk-based standard originally proposed by the Agency. However, the plain language of the statute does not preclude a technology-based approach. This is made clear by the legislative history accompanying the introduction of the final § 3004(m) language. The legislative history provides that "[T]he requisite levels of [sic] methods of treatment established by the Agency should be the best that has been demonstrated to be achievable" and that "[T]he intent here is to require utilization of available technology in lieu of continued land disposal without prior treatment." (Vol. 130, CONG. REC. 9178, (daily ed., July 25, 1984)). Thus, EPA is acting within the authority vested by the statute in selecting [sic] to promulgate a final regulation using its proposed alternative approach of setting treatment standards based on BDAT.

> The Agency believes that its major purpose in adopting the risk-based approach of the proposal (*i.e.*, to allow different standards for relatively low-risk, low-hazard wastes) may be better addressed through changes in other aspects of its regulatory program. For example, EPA is considering the use of its risk-based methodologies to characterize wastes as hazardous pursuant to § 3001.

51 Fed. Reg. at 40,578.

To summarize: after EPA issued the Proposed Rule, some commenters, including eleven members of Congress, chastised the agency on the ground that the use of screening levels was inconsistent with the intent of the statute. They stated that because of the uncertainties involved, Congress had mandated that BDAT alone be used to set treatment standards. EPA determined that the "best respon[se]" to those comments was to adopt a BDAT standard. It emphasized, however, that either course was consistent with the statute (and that it was therefore not required to use BDAT alone). Finally, it asserted, without explanation, that its major purpose in initially proposing screening levels "may be better addressed through changes in other aspects of its regulatory program," and gave an example of one such aspect that might be changed.

This explanation is inadequate. It should go without saying that members of Congress have no power, once a statute has been passed, to alter its interpretation by post-hoc "explanations" of what it means; there may be societies where "history" belongs to those in power, but ours is not among them. In our scheme of things, we consider legislative history because it is just that: history. It forms the background against which Congress adopted the relevant statute. Post-enactment statements are a different matter, and they are not to be considered by an agency or by a court as legislative history. An agency has an obligation to consider the comments of legislators, of course, but on the same footing as it would those of other commenters; such comments may have, as Justice Frankfurter said in a different context, "power to persuade, if lacking power to control." *Skidmore v. Swift & Co.*, 323 U.S. 134, 140 (1944).

* * *

Accordingly, we grant the petitions for review in this respect.

III. SECTION 3004(j) STORAGE PROHIBITION

HWTC and NRDC contend that the Administrator's regulation allowing generators to store wastes on-site for periods of up to one year unless EPA "can demonstrate that such storage was not solely for the purpose of accumulati[ng]" quantities of waste suitable for treatment, 40 C.F.R. § 268.50(b) (1988), violates Congress' "plain intent" in enacting § 3004(j) of RCRA. According to these petitioners, this provision's flat prohibition against storage of wastes "unless such storage is solely for [proper purposes]," 42 U.S.C. § 6924(j) (Supp. V 1987), requires generators—and not EPA—to bear the burden of proving that their motives in storing prohibited wastes are consistent with § 3004(j), no matter what the circumstances. "By shifting the statutory burden of proof of EPA . . .", we are told, "the rule effectively allows a one year override of the statutory prohibition."

* * *

At bottom, what petitioners quarrel with is the precise point at which the Administrator can satisfy his initial burden of production in proceedings charging a § 3004(j) violation solely by introducing evidence of the duration of the generator's storage. Indeed, petitioners conceded at oral argument that they in all likelihood would not have challenged the Administrator's proposed rule—providing a 90-day storage window—had it been carried forward. But petitioners offer no basis to question the Administrator's professional judgment on this score. The record amply supports the Administrator's conclusion that aggregation of wastes for proper treatment may require accumulation for periods of up to one year. It was eminently reasonable, under these circumstances, for the Administrator to determine that he would have to come forward with more than the mere duration of storage for less than one year to make out a prima facie case under § 3004(j). Accordingly, we hold that 40 C.F.R. § 268.50(b) is reasonable and consistent with RCRA.

IV. TESTING RESPONSIBILITY

As part of its implementation of the Hazardous and Solid Waste Amendments of 1984 ("HSWA"), Pub.L. No. 98-616, 98 Stat. 3221, the EPA developed an enforcement plan to assure that wastes that are prohibited from land disposal will not make their way into the ground. Under the EPA's scheme, restricted wastes will follow one of two paths. First, if the generator of the waste determines that he is managing a restricted waste and the waste does not meet the applicable treatment standards, he must notify the treatment facility of the appropriate treatment standards, *see* 40 C.F.R. § 268.7(a)(1); the treatment facility is then required, pursuant to 40 C.F.R. § 268.7(b), to test the treatment residue to assure that the waste, once treated, meets those standards before forwarding the waste to a land disposal facility,[227] which is also required to test the waste, 40 C.F.R. § 268.7(c). Alternatively, if a generator determines that he is managing a restricted waste, but that the waste can be land disposed without further treatment, he may ship the waste directly to landfill operators, the final handlers of the waste who, under the EPA scheme, bear ultimate responsibility for testing and determining that land disposed wastes meet the applicable treatment standards. *See* 51 Fed. Reg. 40,597 (November 7, 1986).

Although earlier handlers of wastes—both waste generators and treatment facilities—are also required by the regulations to certify that waste leaving their control and marked for land disposal meets the appropriate treatment standards, only the latter are expressly required to test the waste in order to certify compliance. *See* 40 C.F.R. § 268.7(b). Generators of waste are "recommend[ed]" to conduct "a comprehensive analysis of each waste stream . . . at least annually," 51 Fed. Reg. at 40,598, but in the end the agency's regulations leave generators the option of certifying that their wastes comply with treatment standards on the basis of, *inter alia,* their "knowledge" of the waste:

---

[227] As the EPA announced in the preamble to its final rules, "These testing requirements for treatment residuals apply to generators who treat, store, and dispose onsite." 51 Fed. Reg. at 40,598.

If a generator determines that he is managing a restricted waste under this part, and determines that the waste can be land disposed without further treatment, with each shipment of waste he must submit, to the land disposal facility, a notice and a certification stating that the waste meets the applicable treatment standards. . . .

(ii) The certification must be signed by an authorized representative and must state the following:

I certify under penalty of law that I personally have examined and am familiar with the waste through analysis and testing or through knowledge of the waste to support this certification that the waste complies with the treatment standards specified in 40 C.F.R. Part 268 Subpart D and all applicable prohibitions set forth in 40 C.F.R. 268.32 or RCRA § 3004(d). I believe that the information I submitted is true, accurate and complete. I am aware that there are significant penalties for submitting a false certification, including the possibility of a fine and imprisonment.

40 C.F.R. § 268.7(a)(2).

HWTC and NRDC challenge the agency's decision to allow generators to rely on their knowledge to certify that wastes are within treatment standards. Petitioners note that wastes requiring treatment must be tested before being sent to land disposal facilities, and they therefore argue that it is arbitrary and capricious for the agency to fail to require generators of waste to test their waste streams in order to certify that admittedly restricted wastes conform to the applicable treatment standards. They charge that since the applicable treatment standards are stated in terms of specific and minute concentrations of hazardous constituents, without actual test data, "generators cannot possibly determine whether their wastes are generated meet these treatment standards and can be land disposed." Brief for Petitioners HWTC and NRDC at 14. They urge this court to replace the agency's rule with a requirement of their own: "[W]astes, which a generator has determined (by whatever means) to be: 1) hazardous and 2) subject to a land disposal restriction (*e.g.*, they are a listed solvent or dioxin waste), must be tested by the generator if the generator is to certify that the wastes meet treatment standards and can be transported directly to a land disposal facility." HWTC/NDRC Reply Br. at 12 (emphasis in original). This is a requirement we are unwilling to impose.

* * *

V. CONCLUSION

We conclude that the solvents and dioxins rule is not arbitrary, capricious, or contrary to RCRA in any of the respects argued by petitioners, but remand the matter for the EPA to clarify its reasons for adopting the Final Rule in preference to the Proposed Rule. In order to avoid disrupting EPA's regulatory program, we will withhold issuance of our mandate for 90 days, during which the agency may either withdraw the Final Rule or publish an adequate statement of basis and purpose.

Judgment Accordingly.

NOTES

1. Why did EPA chose a technology-based standard? Why BDAT in particular?

2. What was industry's objection to the BDAT system?

3. Where does the court find authority for BDAT in the statute? Why is substitution of a technology-based standard for a health-based standard permissible? What if the BDAT were higher than the "acceptable risk"? Is there an analogy to *Vinyl Chloride* here?

4. Was the court right to allow EPA to apply different risk levels in different contexts?

5. Could the EPA now adopt a risk-based cap on treatment requirements? Is that a reasonable "third way" (EPA is considering it in HWIR)?

6. On remand, the EPA issued new regulations that still applied the BDAT. The EPA explained that although the EPA would like to issue risk-based treatment standards, the EPA could not issue a risk-based standard because the EPA did not know what level provided the minimal threat to human health and the environment.[228] Therefore, the EPA determined that treatment must occur to the full extent technologically possible until EPA can set minimal levels for the wastes.

EPA has recently stated that state-of-the-art quantitative determination in calculating risk will allow EPA to issue risk-based treatment standards that minimize the threat to human health and the environment.[229]

7. Once the EPA established that BDAT applied to treatment levels for hazardous waste, the American Petroleum Institute sued the EPA. In *API v. EPA*,[230] API argued that land treatment (in conjunction with some pretreatment) was the BDAT for petroleum wastes. The EPA disagreed with API and stated that in HSWA Congress prohibited land treatment as a form of treatment for hazardous waste. The EPA's position was that a land disposal facility must fully treat the hazardous waste before disposing the waste on land. The Court agreed with the EPA stating that "RCRA clearly specifies . . . that hazardous wastes must be treated before being land disposed. Unless [a generator or treatment facility disposes a waste in a unit demonstrated to meet the 'no migration' test . . . the waste] may not be land disposed unless the waste "has complied with the pretreatment regulations under" § 3004(m)."[231] The court concluded that BDAT must substantially

---

[228] 55 Fed. Reg. 6,640 (1990).

[229] *See* 60 Fed. Reg. 66,344, 66,380 (1995).

[230] American Petroleum Institute v. EPA, 906 F.2d 729 (D.C. Cir. 1990).

[231] *Id.* at 735.

diminish the toxicity of the waste or reduce the likelihood of that waste's hazardous constituents before land disposal.

3. Regulatory Treatment Standards

40 C.F.R. part 268 contains many of the treatment standards that apply to hazardous wastes. The EPA divided the treatment standards into: (1) a numerical standard that a waste must reach before a waste is land disposed, or (2) a type of treatment standard that a generator or treatment facility must apply to the waste before disposal.[232] If a numerical standard applies to a waste, the treatment facility can measure the standard by extracting a sample from the waste or by testing the waste itself.[233]

The EPA also maintained that the land ban provisions for a waste attached at any time the waste exhibited a hazardous characteristic. Therefore, if at the point of generation a waste exhibited a hazardous characteristic, the treatment levels would still apply to the waste even if the characteristic no longer existed in the waste before land disposal.[234]

Industry groups challenged the EPA's rule stating that EPA could not apply the land ban provision to a waste if the waste was no longer hazardous. In *Chemical Waste Management v. EPA*[235] the court upheld the EPA's rule. The court stated that the language in § 3004(m)(1) "to minimize" the threat to human health and the environment goes beyond the levels of the characteristic that makes the waste hazardous.[236] The court concluded that the EPA's jurisdiction to regulate the waste begins at the "point of generation" and continues even if the characteristic that was present when the waste was generated is later removed.[237]

Dilution is not a permissible form of treatment of restricted wastes or residuals from the restricted wastes.[238] The court in *Chemical Waste Management* stated that the EPA can use dilution as a form of treatment for characteristic wastes if dilution meets the "minimized threat" treatment levels under § 3004(m). The court held that the EPA failed to prove that dilution can meet the § 3004(m) treatment levels and vacated a proposal by the EPA to use dilution as a permissible treatment for ignitable, corrosive, or reactive characteristic wastes.[239]

Variances to the treatment standards. To ease the harsh consequences the "hammer" provisions would have on some generators and treatment facilities of hazardous waste, Congress allowed the EPA to issue variances from the time restrictions or "hammers" established by Congress. Consider

---

[232] *See* 40 C.F.R §§ 268.41-.43 (1995).

[233] *See id.*

[234] 54 Fed. Reg. 48,372, 48,419 (1989).

[235] Chemical Waste Management v. EPA, 976 F.2d 2 (D.C.Cir. 1992).

[236] *Id.* at 13.

[237] *Id.*

[238] *See* 40 C.F.R. § 268.3 (1996).

[239] *See* 976 F.2d at 22. the EPA adopted a "Phase II" land disposal restriction rule that set treatment levels for characteristic wastes. *See* 59 Fed. Reg. 47,982 (1994).

the implications of this variance. What are the pros and cons of allowing variances?

Under § 3004(h), Congress allowed the EPA to issue a variance for the waste for up to four years. Section 3004(h)(2) permits the EPA to issue a national capacity variance when a later date than established by Congress is the "earliest date on which adequate alternative treatment, recovery, or disposal capacity that protects public health and the environment will be available."[240] Congress specified that the latest date to extend the variance can be no longer than two years from when Congress set the latest date for the EPA to issue a treatment standard.[241] The EPA has used the national capacity variance standards often. For example, the EPA allowed many third-third characteristic wastes to have an additional two years to develop adequate treatment standards.[242] If the EPA applies a national capacity variance to a waste, a generator or a treatment facility does not need to treat the waste before land disposal. However, a generator or treatment facility must dispose the waste in a minimum technological land disposal facility pursuant to § 3004(o).[243]

The EPA can also issue a case-by-case variance under § 3004(h)(3). Under § 3004(h)(2) the EPA can issue a variance for any hazardous waste where "the applicant demonstrates that there is a binding contractual commitment to contract or otherwise provide such alternative capacity but due to circumstances beyond the control of such applicant such alternative capacity cannot reasonably be made available by such effective date."[244] The EPA can issue the variance for one year and renew the variance for only one additional year. Any waste under a case-by-case variance must be land disposed in a § 3004(o) facility.[245]

The EPA allows an applicant to obtain a variance in treatability standards if a waste cannot meet the treatabilty standards the EPA has promulgated. To obtain a variance in a treatment standard the applicant must demonstrate to the EPA that the treatment standard the EPA requires under the regulations is legitimately unachievable or the treatment technology required by the EPA is inappropriate.[246] The EPA often issues a treatability variance by using a site-specific administrative action but can promulgate a rule to specify an alternative treatment standard. The applicant must follow the treatment variance that the EPA issues.

Alternative to treatment: no-migration units. The main alternative to treating a hazardous waste before land disposal is for the applicant to demonstrate to the EPA that the hazardous waste will not migrate from a unit for as long as the wastes remain hazardous. Section 3004(d)(1) describes no

---

[240] 42 U.S.C. § 6924(h)(2) (1994).
[241] *See id.*
[242] *See* 40 C.F.R. § 268.35 (1996).
[243] *See* 40 C.F.R. § 268.5(h) (1995).
[244] 42 U.S.C. § 6924(h)(2) (1994).
[245] *See* 40 C.F.R. § 268.5(h) (1995).
[246] *See* 40 C.F.R. § 268.44 (1995).

migration units as units that an applicant has demonstrated "to a reasonable degree of certainty, that there will be no migration of hazardous constituents from the disposal unit or injection zone for as long as the wastes remain hazardous."[247] Congress expected that the test of "no migration" be satisfied and based on natural occurring conditions. An applicant cannot demonstrate that no migration will occur from a unit by placing liners or artificial barriers around a unit.[248]

The EPA requires applicants who want to dispose waste in a no migration unit to provide a large amount of specific information. The EPA can use the information to determine, with the greatest certainty, whether no migration of the hazardous waste will occur from the disposal unit.[249]

The EPA also issued regulations interpreting "no migration of hazardous constituents" as meaning no migration of a concentration of hazardous constituents that would meet or surpass the minimal health-base levels the EPA promulgated. The NRDC challenged the EPA's interpretation in *NRDC v. EPA*.[250] The NRDC contended that the EPA interpretation of the statute violated its plain language. The NRDC claimed that no migration of hazardous constituents means no migration of even one hazardous constituent, even if the migration was not above the minimal health-based threshold.[251] The court narrowly upheld the EPA's interpretation. The court conceded that "read literally," the 'no migration' standard would" seem to prohibit the migration of even a single molecule (or perhaps an appropriate *de minimis* amount) for the statutory time period, even though the migrating waste is itself not hazardous at all."[252] However, the court noted an ambiguity in the no migration provisions of RCRA. The court focused on no migration of hazardous *constituents for "as long as the wastes remain hazardous"*[253] "To which 'wastes,'" the court asked, "did the clause refer?"[254] The EPA interpreted the wastes to refer to the wastes containing the hazardous constituents that are leaving the injection zone.[255] The EPA contended that hazardous constituents may migrate so long as the wastes immediately surrounding them at the border are no longer in high enough concentrations to be hazardous wastes. The court said that although NRDC's argument was persuasive, the statutory provision contained enough ambiguity that under *Chevron*, the court must defer to the EPA's interpretation of the statute.[256]

The LDR provisions and CERCLA. At any time the EPA identifies a waste as hazardous, that waste becomes a RCRA hazardous waste, even if

---

[247] 42 U.S.C. § 6924(d)(1) (1994).

[248] *See* 40 C.F.R. § 268.6 (1995).

[249] *See id.* To demonstrate no migration, a party must show that no migration will occur for as long as the waste remains hazardous or for 10,000 years, whichever period is shorter.

[250] NRDC v. EPA, 907 F.2d 1146 (D.C. Cir. 1990).

[251] *See* 907 F.2d at 1152.

[252] *Id.* at 1159.

[253] *Id.*

[254] *Id.*

[255] *See id.*

[256] *See id.* at 1160.

one disposed the waste before Congress enacted RCRA.[257] However, a waste does not come under RCRA regulation if one does not actively manage the waste after the EPA Administrator identifies or lists the waste as hazardous.[258] Often a waste becomes actively managed during a corrective action proceeding under CERCLA or RCRA. The main issue then becomes what to do with the contaminated soil or debris after one removes the waste.

Congress permitted the land ban provisions to apply to soil or debris that were handled during remedial activity under RCRA or CERCLA.[259] The EPA has attempted to limit the scope of the land ban provisions on remedial activity by stating that contaminated soil or debris within an existing land disposal unit is not subject to the land ban provisions because the waste never crosses the facility boundary.[260] The EPA also allows the Regional Administrator of the EPA to delineate a corrective action management unit (CAMU) at a remediation site. If one handled, treated, or disposed of the waste within the unit, the waste does not fall under the land ban provisions.[261]

The EPA promulgated special provisions for contaminated debris recovered as part of remediation work. Under the regulations, debris applies to any solid material larger than 60 mm that is a manufactured object, plant, animal matter, or natural geological material.[262] One must treat the contaminated debris to remove, destroy, or immobilize hazardous constituents. Once one treats the debris, one can dispose of it in a non-Subtitle C facility, but one must manage the residue from the treatment as a hazardous waste.[263]

NOTES

1. In reviewing the LDR standards, ask yourself whether the EPA is using technology, health-based, or media-based standards, and which standards would make the most sense.

2. An analysis of the assumptions behind Subtitle C also reveals an implicit assumption that Congress accepts some exposure to risk in exchange for the benefits of toxic and hazardous chemicals. The basic problems are that hazardous wastes remain hazardous for long periods. There is a likelihood of migration because of the physical impossibility of permanently preventing leakage, and the need for perpetual monitoring and

---

[257] See 53 Fed Reg. 31,148 (1988). See also Chemical Waste Management Inc. v. EPA, 869 F.2d 1526 (D.C. Cir. 1989).

[258] See 53 Fed. Reg. 31,148, 31,149 (1988).

[259] See 42 U.S.C. § 6924 (d)(3) & (e)(3) (1994).

[260] See 55 Fed Reg. 8,666, 8,790 (1990).

[261] See 58 Fed. Reg. 8,658 (1993).

[262] See 57 Fed. Reg. 37,194 (1992). An "object" can include crushed metal drums, or bricks. "Plant" or "animal matter" can include tree stumps, etc. "natural geological material" can include rocks, etc.

[263] See id.

maintenance.[264] The answer would seem to be to restrict creation of the waste. To what extent does RCRA require waste minimization. To what extent does RCRA rely on technological fixes through regulation of TSDFs? Also, does Subtitle C contain technology-forcing provisions, like many of the environmental statutes (*e.g.*, the CAA and CWA) or does it rely on EPA to develop the technology?

3. The 1984 Amendments represent Congressional distrust of EPA at its height. Is highly prescriptive regulation such as RCRA (land bans, hammers, lists of chemicals, etc.) a good idea?

F. Enforcement

RCRA provides EPA with a menu of enforcement procedures to compel compliance with RCRA provisions. EPA can seek administrative, civil, criminal or corrective action against any person who violates a RCRA provision.[265] EPA uses RCRA enforcement provisions to prevent people who handle hazardous waste from avoiding RCRA regulations. Although compliance with the hazardous waste regulations may be timely and expensive, failure to comply with the regulations can be much more costly.

Most RCRA enforcement actions begin at an EPA regional office. There are ten regional offices that monitor facilities subject to compliance with RCRA. Besides the regional offices, the Office of Enforcement and Compliance Assurance (OECA) at EPA headquarters has a major role in enforcing RCRA provisions. Although RCRA gives EPA authority to seek remedies in a federal court, EPA cannot institute litigation. It refers all litigation to the Department of Justice (DOJ). Within DOJ, the Environmental and Natural Resources Division (ENRD) decides whether to pursue enforcement of a RCRA violation referred by EPA.[266]

The states also play an important part in enforcing RCRA. Almost all the states have EPA-authorized RCRA programs.[267] However, states that have their programs are still subject to EPA enforcement. EPA will enforce a state program if EPA feels that a state is "unwilling or unable" to "timely" enforce the state's RCRA provisions.[268] Therefore, most states have RCRA programs; but, EPA oversees the state program to make sure they are enforcing RCRA provisions properly.

---

[264] *See* Standards Applicable to Owners and Operators of Hazardous Waste Treatment, Storage, and Disposal Facilities; Consolidated Permit Regulations, Preamble, 46 Fed Reg 2,802 (1981).

[265] 42 U.S.C. § 6928 (1994).

[266] *See* ABA, THE RCRA PRACTICE MANUAL 224 (Theodore L. Garrett, ed., 1994).

[267] *See id.*

[268] *Id.*

1. Information-Gathering Provisions

RCRA is a complicated statute that requires EPA to have thorough data on persons that generate and handle hazardous waste. To insure that all information on hazardous waste would be available to EPA, Congress enacted §§ 3007 and 3013.[269] These sections give EPA power to inspect a facility that handles hazardous waste, require a facility that handles hazardous waste to produce documents and other information on such wastes, and force certain handlers of hazardous waste to conduct testing and produce new information to EPA.[270]

Section 3007(a) enables EPA officials to have access to information and copy records from "any person who generates, stores, treats, transports, disposes, handles or has handled hazardous wastes."[271] EPA can also enter "at reasonable times" any establishment regulated under Subtitle C of RCRA to inspect and obtain samples from the establishment.[272] If EPA takes samples from the facility, EPA must give the person in charge of the facility a receipt describing the sample obtained. Once EPA analyzes the sample EPA must give the owner a copy of the results.[273]

Section 3007(e) of RCRA permits EPA to conduct mandatory inspections.[274] EPA inspects privately owned TSDFs twice a year and publicly owned facilities once a year.[275] Ten or more federal and state inspectors conduct the inspections that can last more than a week. The inspections focus on how the facility handles hazardous waste and how sufficiently the TSDF is keeping proper records.[276] EPA may also obtain and test samples of soils, waters, and wastes.

NATIONAL-STANDARD COMPANY V. ADAMKUS

881 F.2d 352 (7th Cir. 1989)

RIPPLE, Circuit Judge.

This case involves Environmental Protection Agency (EPA) inspections of two facilities owned by National-Standard Company (National-Standard) in Niles, Michigan. In its original declaratory judgment action, the appellant challenged whether the Resource Conservation and Recovery Act (RCRA), as amended by the Hazardous and Solid Waste Amendments of 1984 (HSWA), 42 U.S.C. §§ 6901 et seq., authorizes EPA to inspect the National-Standard facilities. The district court upheld EPA's inspection authority, and

---

[269] 42 U.S.C. §§ 6927 and 6934 (1994).

[270] See id.

[271] 42 U.S.C. § 6927 (1994).

[272] Id.

[273] See id.

[274] See 42 U.S.C. § 6927(e) (1994).

[275] ENVIRONMENTAL LAW PRACTICE GUIDE: STATE AND FEDERAL LAW, § 29.10[2][b] (Michael B. Gerrard, ed., 1992).

[276] See id.

granted the agency summary judgment. It also denied National-Standard's discovery motion. We now affirm.

I. BACKGROUND

National-Standard is a Delaware corporation that manufactures wire products at its Lake Street and City Complex facilities located in Niles, Michigan. National-Standard's manufacturing process generates, and the company stores, materials such as hydrochloric acid, sulfuric acid, and alkaline wastes. These by-products are within the RCRA definition of "hazardous waste." . . . As required by § 6925(a), National-Standard applied to EPA for a permit for the treatment, storage, and disposal of the hazardous wastes it generated. At present, its application remains pending, so that National-Standard's facilities currently are operating under "interim status." Interim status facilities are required to handle hazardous wastes as if operating under a permit. As part of the process of obtaining a permit, corrective action must be taken with regard to any releases of hazardous wastes. Interim status facilities that experience hazardous waste releases are also subject to corrective action.

On March 24 and 25, 1987, EPA officials visited the facilities and performed visual site inspections. During that tour, the officials determined that there were several "solid waste management units" (SWMUs) at each facility and that corrective action would be necessary. On April 3, EPA formally notified National-Standard that it was planning a sampling visit at National-Standard's facilities as the next stage of the corrective action program required under § 6924(u) and 6927. In the Notification Letters, EPA stated that it wanted to conduct a hazardous waste inspection and collect samples to determine the nature of any corrective action required at National-Standard's facilities before granting the company a permit to store hazardous wastes. The Notification Letters also stated that EPA contractors (defendants-appellees Harding-Lawson Associates and K.W. Brown & Associates, Inc.) were to assist with the sampling, and that representatives of the Michigan Department of Natural Resources would observe the inspection. Finally, the Letters identified thirty SWMUs at the Lake Street and City Complex facilities that would be targeted by the inspection team.

National-Standard refused to consent to the inspection. It protested the breadth of EPA's intended sampling, and stated that § 6924(u) did not authorize the "fishing expedition" proposed by EPA. It also alleged that many of the proposed sampling sites were not SWMUs. Soon afterwards, National-Standard filed a declaratory judgment action in the district court for the Northern District of Illinois. The complaint sought declaratory relief on the ground that EPA lacked authority under § 6924(u) to inspect the National-Standard facilities and that any inspections allowed under § 6924(u) and 6927(a) were limited to hazardous wastes specifically listed in the Code of Federal Regulations. Venue was grounded on the location in Chicago of the EPA Regional Administrator charged with overseeing RCRA enforcement at the facilities.

Three days after the filing of the complaint, EPA applied for and obtained ex parte an administrative search warrant to inspect the National-Standard facilities from the United States magistrate in the district court for the Western District of Michigan (the district that encompasses Niles). Attached to the warrant application was the affidavit of Ms. Carol Witt, an EPA geologist. Ms. Witt had been part of the EPA visual site inspection team that visited the National-Standard facilities on March 24th and 25th; as a result of this inspection, she had determined that there were several SWMUs at each facility. She further stated that, based on her observations of discolored soil, surface water body sediments, discontinuities in vegetation, and odors, there had been releases of what may be hazardous wastes or constituents from some of the SWMUs. She believed the releases may have been hazardous wastes because they were near known SWMUs containing ignitable solid wastes, copper cyanide, lead, or waste water treatment sludges from electroplating operations. Ms. Witt proposed taking no more than sixty solid waste, water, and air samples, including background samples, at the facilities. On July [June?] 15, 1987, three days after obtaining the warrant, EPA commenced execution.

On June 16, 1987, National-Standard responded, filing in the district court for the Western District of Michigan: (1) a complaint seeking preliminary and permanent injunctive relief barring EPA from continuing the inspection and from using the inspection results; and (2) an emergency motion to quash the administrative search warrant and to transfer venue of all Michigan proceedings to the district court for the Northern District of Illinois. After conferring with the district judge presiding over the pending declaratory judgment action in the Northern District of Illinois, the chief judge of the Western District of Michigan ordered all proceedings transferred to Illinois.

Eventually, all matters were consolidated in the Northern District of Illinois. Upon making a finding of relatedness, the district court joined the Michigan-initiated proceedings with the original declaratory judgment action. The court also entered an agreed order whereby EPA could continue its inspection and take samples from the National-Standard facilities, but could not obtain the results of the analyses from EPA's contract laboratories. National-Standard then filed an amended complaint seeking declaratory relief, an order quashing the administrative search warrant, and preliminary and permanent injunctive relief as to the results of the first inspection. This complaint, when read in its totality, requests a broad adjudication as to the inspection powers of EPA with respect to a facility such as National-Standard's.

The district court later granted EPA's motion to deny National-Standard's discovery requests and granted summary judgment in favor of EPA and its contractor codefendants. *National-Standard Co. v. Adamkus*, 685 F. Supp. 1040 (N. D. Ill.1988) (memorandum opinion and order). The court also vacated the agreed order—releasing the sampling results to EPA.

However, on the basis of the record before us, it appears that no EPA corrective action has been ordered since it received the sampling results.

* * *

III. WARRANT ANALYSIS

A. EPA's Statutory Authority

The primary issue raised by the appellant before this court is whether RCRA authorizes EPA to inspect the National-Standard facilities. National-Standard submits that § 6924(u) and 6927(a) bar these EPA inspections. EPA responds that RCRA clearly authorizes inspection searches like the ones conducted here, and alternatively submits that EPA's interpretation of § 6927 is reasonable and thus merits deference by this court. . . . We hold that the RCRA inspection provision relied upon by the magistrate—§ 6927(a)—authorizes EPA's entry and inspection of National-Standard's facilities, and thus we affirm the judgment of the district court.

The starting point of statutory interpretation is the now-familiar two-part test delineated in *Chevron U.S.A., Inc. v. Natural Resources Defense Council, Inc.* . . . We turn, then, to the first step and examine the language employed by Congress.

Section 6927(a) provides:

(a) Access entry

For purposes of developing or assisting in the development of any regulation or enforcing the provisions of this chapter, any person who generates, stores, treats, transports, disposes of, or otherwise handles or has handled hazardous wastes shall, upon request of any officer, employee or representative of the Environmental Protection Agency, duly designated by the Administrator, or upon request of any duly designated officer, employee or representative of a State having an authorized hazardous waste program, furnish information relating to such wastes and permit such person at all reasonable times to have access to, and to copy all records relating to such wastes. For the purposes of developing or assisting in the development of any regulation or enforcing the provisions of this chapter, such officers, employees or representatives are authorized—

(1) to enter at reasonable times any establishment or other place where hazardous wastes are or have been generated, stored, treated, disposed of, or transported from;

(2) to inspect and obtain samples from any person of any such wastes and samples of any containers or labeling for such wastes.

Each such inspection shall be commenced and completed with reasonable promptness. If the officer, employee or representative obtains any samples, prior to leaving the premises, he shall give to the owner, operator, or agent in charge a receipt describing the sample obtained and if requested a portion of each such sample equal in volume or weight to the portion retained. If any analysis is

made of such samples, a copy of the results of such analysis shall be
furnished promptly to the owner, operator, or agent in charge.

42 U.S.C. § 6927(a).

National-Standard submits that the plain language of this provision
explicitly limits any authorized inspections solely to "inspect and obtain
samples from any person of any such wastes and samples of any containers
or labeling for such wastes." EPA thus exceeded its authority in broadening
its search to the collection of samples that, according to National-Standard,
"relate to" hazardous wastes. In National-Standard's view, § 6927(a) permits
EPA inspections only when a given facility identifies itself as possessing
hazardous wastes, at which point EPA may sample from any SWMU those
wastes, or their containers, or container labels only. Furthermore, those
hazardous wastes which may be sampled are to be defined by the hazardous
waste facility, not EPA.

We cannot accept such an interpretation of § 6927(a). We agree with the
district court that this interpretation would "emasculate EPA's ability to
pursue the broad remedial goals of RCRA." Like the district court, we
believe that "[t]he main purpose of an inspection and sampling visit is to
detect the presence of hazardous wastes. If EPA could not inspect an area
unless it knew hazardous wastes were stored there, EPA would be rendered
effectively powerless." EPA's broad inspection authority is tempered by its
need to show probable cause and obtain an administrative search warrant,
discussed infra, when a hazardous waste facility owner, such as National-
Standard, does not consent to the inspection.

Section 6927(a) inspections are authorized "[f]or the purposes . . . of
enforcing the provisions of this chapter." Chapter 82 of Title 42 of the
United States Code, 42 U.S.C. §§ 6901-6991i, provides EPA with a broad
mandate for enforcing the national policy of treating, storing, and disposing
of hazardous wastes "so as to minimize the present and future threat to
human health and the environment." 42 U.S.C. § 6902(b). The Notification
Letters' reference to a particular provision that authorizes corrective action
orders for hazardous waste releases from SWMUs—§ 6924(u)—does not
limit EPA's ability to inspect and sample from areas other than SWMUs.
EPA's inspection and sampling authority derives from the broad language in
§ 6927(a), which empowers the agency to enforce the entire RCRA scheme,
not just a particular provision. In determining the material that EPA may
sample under § 6927(a), Congress significantly chose the broad, general term
"hazardous waste" defined in § 6903(5) (set out in Part I) rather than
"hazardous waste identified or listed under this subchapter," employed in
other provisions. See, *e.g.*, 42 U.S.C. §§ 6924(a), 6925(a). This broad range
of materials Congress intended to subject to sampling under § 6927(a) was
demonstrated in the HSWA legislative history:

EPA's authority under these provisions [RCRA § 3007 and 7003] is not
limited to wastes that are 'identified or listed' as hazardous, but rather
includes all wastes that meet the statutory definition of hazardous wastes.

H. REP. 198, 98TH CONG., 1ST SESS. 47 (1983), 1984 U.S.CODE CONG. & ADMIN. NEWS 5606.

Finally, National-Standard's interpretation of § 6927(a) as being limited to situations of proven actual releases is also incorrect. A similarly narrow interpretation of the Clean Water Act was rejected by this court in *Mobil Oil Corp. v. EPA*, 716 F.2d 1187 (7th Cir.1983), *cert. denied*, 466 U.S. 980 (1984). In *Mobil*, this court refused to quash an administrative search warrant for the sampling of untreated waste water. The court interpreted the Clean Water Act and held that:

These provisions of [the Clean Water Act inspection provision] leave no doubt that the Congress that enacted that Section was firmly convinced that the interest of permit holders such as Mobil in keeping secret information about the pollutants in its waste water is not entitled to protection.

716 F.2d at 1190. Likewise, § 6927(a) clearly vests broad authority in EPA to inspect and sample any facility at which the agency has probable cause to believe that violations of the statute are occurring.

* * *

——

When a facility refuses to allow EPA to enter, EPA must obtain an administrative search warrant.[277] EPA will go before a district court and seek an *ex parte* administrative search warrant. To obtain the search warrant EPA must prove that they have "probable cause" to enter the facility.[278] A facility that denies access to EPA officials can be liable to civil penalties up to $25,000 a day.[279]

Section 3013 is the other RCRA section EPA uses to monitor the presence of hazardous waste.[280] Congress enacted § 3013 in 1980 to permit EPA to order a facility or site to conduct testing, monitoring, or analysis at the facility. EPA can issue a § 3013 order once EPA makes a formal finding that the presence of the waste at the facility may present a substantial hazard to human health and the environment.[281] If the party disputes EPA's determination, the party can ask a district court to review EPA's decision.[282]

Like § 3007, challenges to limit the scope of § 3013 has largely failed. In *Wyckoff v. EPA*, the defendant asserted that since Washington State had a federally approved plan, § 3013 did not apply to businesses in Washington.[283] The court rejected the defendant's argument. The court held that they could discern nothing in RCRA that would prohibit EPA from issuing orders under § 3013 while a state operated a RCRA approved program. The court noted

---

[277] *See* Marshall v. Barlows, Inc., 436 U.S. 307 (1978); *but cf.* Dow Chem. Co. v. U.S., 476 U.S. 227 (a warrant is not needed when the EPA flies over a facility).

[278] *See* National Standard, 881 F.2d at 361.

[279] *See* 42 U.S.C. § 6928(g) (1994).

[280] 42 U.S.C. § 6934 (1994).

[281] *See id.*

[282] *See* DuPont v. Daggett, 610 F. Supp. 260 (W.D.N.Y. 1985).

[283] *See* Wyckoff v. EPA, 796 F.2d 1197 (9th Cir. 1986).

that EPA does not abdicate responsibility to monitor facilities under RCRA once EPA approves a state program. The court held that EPA's position that EPA had the power to issue the order was reasonable.

Enforcement of a § 3013 order is similar to that of a § 3007 order. Once the facility or site has not returned a plan in 30 days to conduct the testing required by EPA, EPA can seek to enforce the order. Section 3013(e) also gives EPA the option to go to district court to order the facility or site to conduct the testing. EPA can order the facility to conduct testing "deemed reasonable" to gather information. on the extent of the hazard. EPA can seek an administrative search warrant to enter the premises and conduct the testing themselves. If EPA conducts the testing, EPA can seek reimbursement from the facility. If EPA needs to conduct testing at an inactive site EPA may do so. EPA can later seek to have the previous owner of the site to pay for the testing done. The district court can assess a penalty of not more than $5,000 for each day the facility violates the EPA order.

The following chart compares 1988-89 versus 1990-91 number of class one violations EPA found at it last inspection.

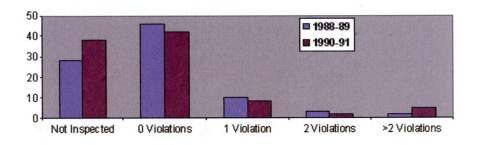

Figure 9.18–Comparison of Class I Violations Found at the Last Inspection During 1988-1989 and 1990-1991, By Percent of Facilities[284]

2. Administrative Action

Most of the enforcement actions pursued by EPA under RCRA are administrative rather than judicial. EPA considers about seventy percent of all enforcement actions "informal." Informal proceedings include warning letters and violation notices to bring a RCRA violator into compliance. Of the remaining enforcement possibilities, EPA prefers an administrative "formal" action to a court action. Part of the reason EPA prefers administrative actions is that enforcement through administrative means moves more quickly than going to a federal court. Additionally, EPA likes to keep control over the enforcement action. When EPA decides to seek action in a district court the Department of Justice (DOJ) takes control of the case.

---

[284]EPA, NATIONAL BIENNIAL REPORTING SYSTEM (1994).

Section 3008(a) and (c) gives EPA the power to enforce a RCRA violation by issuing a compliance order or eliminating a permit. EPA usually issues a compliance order with an assessed penalty attached to the order. EPA may assess a penalty of $25,000 a day for each day a violation is alleged. EPA can issue a compliance order to any generator, transporter, or TSDF that has violated a RCRA section.

The following chart compares class one violations by number of facilities and volume of waste.

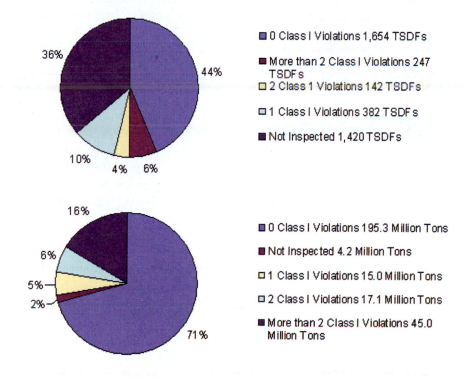

Figure 9.19–Comparison of Class I Violations Found at the Last Inspection During 1990-1991, By Number of Facilities and Volume of Waste[285]

3. Civil Enforcement through the Courts

The EPA will seek civil action through the courts if (1) the company or person is a chronic violator of RCRA policy and is not expected to adhere to a compliance order, (2) the company or person violated a compliance order or consent agreement, or (3) the company or person willfully violated RCRA policy and EPA did not seek criminal penalties from that willful violation. Note that although the government brought civil judicial actions three times

---

[285] Source: 1991 Biennial Reporting System–Resource Conservation and Recovery Information System (RCRIS), 1994.

less than administrative actions, the penalties EPA received from the civil actions are higher.

Once EPA decides to bring a RCRA violator before a civil court, EPA must refer the case to the DOJ. EPA derives its power to seek a civil remedy or an injunction in a civil court through § 3008(a). Section 3008(a) gives EPA administrative power to "begin a civil action in a U.S. district in the district where the violation occurred, for appropriate relief, including a temporary or permanent injunction."

Section 3008(g) gives EPA authority to seek up to $25,000 a day for each violation. Section 3008(g) allows a civil penalty for "any person who violates any requirement" of Subtitle C of RCRA. Therefore, § 3008(g) imposes strict liability on a violator of a RCRA provision. Good faith to comply with a RCRA provision will not excuse a violator from liability. Although good faith could affect the penalty amount assessed.

The 1990 Civil Penalty Policy guides EPA penalty assessment to a violator. The federal judge has the option of accepting EPA's penalty assessment or using other factors to determine the penalty assessed. Courts have noted that a penalty amount brought before the court is at the sole "discretion of the court." In *United States. v. Ecko Housewares*,[286] the court used the same factors as EPA in assessing the penalty but added the government's conduct and the clarity of the obligation involved as additional factors.[287] In using these two additional factors the court slightly reduced the penalty imposed on the defendant.

In reaching settlements under RCRA, EPA may sometimes choose to reduce the penalty assessment in exchange for a Supplemental Environmental Project (SEP). EPA defines SEP's as "environmentally beneficial projects which a defendant/respondent agrees to undertake in settlement of an enforcement action, but which the defendant/respondent is not otherwise legally required to perform." For 1996, EPA estimated that the value of SEP's in RCRA cases was $14.2 million.

EPA's most important civil enforcement power is that of abating imminent hazards. Under § 7003, EPA can order or bring a suit for injunctive relief to contain any hazardous waste contamination that may present "an imminent and substantial endangerment to human health and the environment." EPA can obtain relief under this section if the government proves: (1) conditions at a site present an imminent or substantial endangerment, (2) the endangerment is caused or was caused by the handling of hazardous waste, (3) the defendant has contributed or is contributing to the hazardous waste that poses the threat.

To satisfy the first requirement the government does not have to prove the hazardous waste is causing current harm or exposure. Courts have construed the word "endangerment" in the section to mean "something less

---

[286] United States v. Ecko Housewares, Inc., 62 F.3d 806 (6th Cir. 1995).

[287] *See id.* at 814.

than actual harm. When one is endangered, harm is threatened."[288] The court measures the harm threatened by the risk of danger involved. Standards one court used to assess risk were "suspected relationships between facts, from trends among facts, from theoretical, but not completely substantiated, projections from imperfect data, [or] from probative preliminary data."[289] Therefore, if the government uses data that suggests, but does not prove there is a risk to human health and the environment, that still is enough to show that a substantial or imminent endangerment exists.

The government will often bring an equitable action seeking an injunction against the defendant to enforce a § 7003 order. The government usually asks the court to order the defendant to take certain steps (including closure of the facility in some cases) to abate any danger posed by the hazardous waste. In those cases the court imposes a balancing test to determine whether to grant the government's request. In *United States v. Vertac Chemical Corp.*[290] the court balanced the benefits conferred and the hazards created by the facility to determine the action the court should take.[291] Among the factors considered by the court in balancing the two interests were: (1) the type of possible future harm, (2) the burden imposed on the company and their employees from granting the injunction, (3) the financial ability of the company to convert to other methods of waste disposal, and (4) the margin of safety for the public.[292] Although the court found the facility should take certain steps (like capping certain waste sites and drilling monitoring wells), the court thought closing the facility would be too harsh an action to take.

For a defendant to be liable under § 7003, the defendant had to contribute to the hazardous waste posing the threat. Therefore, under § 7003 the government must prove that the defendant "contributed to" the hazardous waste at the site. Courts have liberally interpreted "contributed to" to mean "to have a share in any act or effect."[293] All the government needs to show is that the defendant has a "share in" disposing the waste at the site. For instance, one generator who arranged for waste to be disposed at a TSDF had a "share in" disposing waste at the site. Once the government proves the defendant "contributed to" the hazardous waste at the site, the company is strictly liable for the harm the waste presents. Any effort by the defendant to claim good faith or ignorance of how to dispose the waste does not relieve the defendant of liability.

Courts have loosened the traditional requirements of issuing injunctions because in RCRA "Congress sought to invoke the broad and flexible equity powers of the federal courts . . . where hazardous waste threatened human

---

[288] Ethyl Corp. v. EPA, 541 F.2d 1 (D.C. Cir. 1976), *cert. denied*, 96 S Ct 2662 (1996).

[289] *Id.* at 28.

[290] United States v. Vertac Chemical Corp., 489 F. Supp 870 (E.D. Ark. 1980).

[291] *See id.* at 886.

[292] *See id.*

[293] *See id.* at 887.

health."[294] Traditionally, courts do not issue injunctions unless the party seeking the injunction can prove that he will suffer irreparable injury if the court does not act. The court in *United States v. Price*,[295] however, stated that under RCRA the irreparable harm standard does not apply because Congress specifically authorized injunctions where there is a risk of harm. In cases where the public health is at issue courts have generally focused on what was in the public interest.[296]

UNITED STATES V. PRICE

688 F.2d 204 (3d Cir. 1982)

RE, Chief Judge of the Court of International Trade [sitting by designation].

In this action, brought under section 7003 of the Resource Conservation and Recovery Act (RCRA), 42 U.S.C. § 6973, and section 1431 of the Safe Drinking Water Act (SDWA), 42 U.S.C. § 300i, plaintiff United States, on behalf of the Administrator of the Environmental Protection Agency (EPA), appeals from the denial of its application for a preliminary injunction. The requested injunction would have required defendants to (1) fund a diagnostic study of the threat to Atlantic City's public water supply posed by toxic substances emanating from Price's Landfill, a former commercial landfill, and (2) provide an alternate water supply to homeowners whose private wells have been contaminated by substances leaching from the landfill.

The question presented on this appeal, whether the district court abused its discretion in denying plaintiff's request for preliminary relief, is answered in the negative. Therefore, we affirm and direct the district court to proceed as expeditiously as possible with a trial on the merits of this action. In view of certain findings and conclusions of the district court, we deem it necessary to comment on the availability of equitable relief in actions brought under these provisions.

Background

Section 7003 of RCRA provides that whenever the United States receives evidence that the handling, storage, treatment, transportation or disposal of hazardous waste may present an "imminent and substantial endangerment to health or the environment," it may bring suit immediately to restrain any person contributing to such activity or "to take such other action as may be necessary." Section 1431 of SDWA authorizes the Federal Government to commence "a civil action for appropriate relief, including a restraining order or permanent or temporary injunction" whenever it receives information that "a contaminant which is present in or is likely to enter a public water system may present an imminent and substantial endangerment to the health of persons."

---

[294] United States v. Aceto Agric. Chem. Corp., 872 F.2d 1373, 1384 (8th Cir. 1989).
[295] United States v. Price, 688 F.2d 204 (3d Cir. 1982).
[296] *See id.* at 211.

Pursuant to the authority conferred by these provisions, the United States, on December 22, 1980, filed this action against the present owners and the former owners and operators of Price's Landfill. A hearing, which was held on plaintiff's application for preliminary relief, resulted in extensive and detailed findings of fact by the district court. These findings may be summarized as follows:

Price's Landfill is a twenty-two acre lot situated on the border of the City of Pleasantville and the Township of Egg Harbor in New Jersey. It was owned by Charles and Virginia Price from 1960 until 1979 when they sold it to the present owners, A. G. A. Partnership.

In 1970, on his initial application for a license to conduct a sanitary landfill operation, Charles Price listed the materials he intended to accept for disposal at Price's Landfill. He specifically excluded "Chemicals (Liquid or Solid)." In his proposed landfill design, submitted on September 29, 1971, he made no provision for the disposal of chemical wastes, despite the fact that earlier that year he had begun accepting chemical wastes for disposal at the landfill.

When Charles Price applied to renew his permit in February 1972, for the first time he sought permission to accept and dispose of chemical wastes. His permit was renewed, however, only on the condition that no soluble or liquid industrial wastes, petrochemicals, waste oils, sewage sludge or septic tank wastes be disposed at the site. Nevertheless, Price's Landfill continued to accept chemical and industrial wastes for disposal in direct contravention of the conditions of the license.

During 1971 and 1972, Price's Landfill accepted for disposal approximately 9 million gallons of assorted industrial and chemical wastes. These wastes were disposed of with minimal precautions. Frequently, they would be poured into the refuse from an open spigot on a tank truck; at other times, drums of chemicals would simply be buried under the refuse. The dumping of chemical wastes at Price's Landfill ended in November of 1972, and, in 1976, the operation of the site as a commercial landfill ceased.

Upon purchasing the property in 1979, A. G. A. Partnership acknowledged in writing that the site had been used as a landfill. Although two of the three members of the A. G. A. Partnership, including the member who negotiated the purchase, were licensed real estate brokers, no one inquired whether hazardous wastes had been deposited there. Neither did anyone from or on behalf of A. G. A. inspect the property or take steps to determine if the landfill had been properly closed.

As a result of the chemical dumping which occurred during 1971 and 1972, water samples drawn from the area in and around Price's Landfill during the years 1979-81 were found to contain numerous contaminants in quantities likely to create grave hazards to human health. Among the contaminants were: arsenic, a highly toxic metal and an established human carcinogen; lead, a toxic metal and a suspected human carcinogen and teratogen; benzene, a highly toxic petroleum derivative and a potent carcinogen and teratogen; vinyl chloride, a toxic halogenated hydrocarbon and a suspected carcinogen and mutagen; and 1, 2 dichloroethane, a toxic chlorinated hydrocarbon, and a suspected carcinogen and teratogen.

Geohydrological evidence presented to the district court revealed that contaminants leaching down through the groundwater and away from Price's Landfill are forming a plume or region of contamination emanating into the Cohansey Aquifer, a saturated geologic deposit supplying water to approximately 35 private wells, and to 10 of the Atlantic City Municipal Utility Authority's 12 operating public wells. Many of the private wells are already contaminated beyond use, and 4 of the municipal wells are in imminent danger of serious contamination. Atlantic City has no readily accessible alternative source of water should these wells become contaminated.

These facts led the district court to conclude that Atlantic City's public water supply is in imminent and substantial danger of serious contamination by substances leaching from Price's Landfill. The court found that an extensive geohydrological study of the area around the landfill was "essential in devising a strategy to contain and mitigate the pollution and to protect Atlantic City's water supply," and that it was "imperative that such a study be done immediately." In ruling on various motions for summary judgment, the district court expressed its belief that the defendants could ultimately be held liable for the cost of abating this toxic hazard.

Despite these findings, stating that the remedies requested by plaintiff were inappropriate forms of preliminary relief, the district court denied plaintiff's application for a preliminary injunction. The court indicated that the issue of who should bear the costs of studying the toxic hazard, and obtaining an alternate water supply, should not be resolved on an application for a preliminary injunction.

Post-Hearing Action

* * *

During the pendency of this appeal, the state of New Jersey extended public water mains into the area where private wells have been contaminated. Additionally, the EPA authorized funding of an initial study of the toxic hazard emanating from Price's Landfill.

Plaintiff contends that the funding of a diagnostic study and the provision of an alternate water supply are permissible forms of preliminary equitable relief both at common law and under the endangerment provisions of RCRA and SDWA. Consequently, it maintains that, having found an imminent and substantial endangerment to a public water supply and to human health for which the defendants were probably liable, the district court should have granted the requested relief. Plaintiff submits that the district court rejected its application merely because the proposed injunction would have required payments and expenditures of money.

Defendants urge us to dismiss this appeal for two reasons. First, they state that plaintiff failed to file a timely notice of appeal. Second, they argue that the appeal is moot because the relief requested has been provided by parties other than defendants. Alternatively, defendants contend that the district court did not abuse its discretion in denying plaintiff's request for preliminary equitable relief.

* * *

Equitable Relief

It is not questioned that the decision to grant or deny a preliminary injunction is committed to the sound discretion of the district court. Its decision must be affirmed unless it has abused its discretion, committed an obvious error in applying the law, or made a serious mistake in considering the proof.

* * *

Judicial precedents indicate that the preliminary relief requested by plaintiff in this action was not inappropriate. Furthermore, it seems clear that it falls within the range of remedies contemplated and specifically authorized by Congress when it enacted the endangerment provisions of RCRA and SDWA.

Statutory Equitable Relief

Section 7003 of RCRA authorizes the federal government to bring suit "to immediately restrain" certain activities "or to take such action as may be necessary" when the handling, storage, treatment, transportation or disposal of hazardous waste "may present an imminent and substantial endangerment to health or the environment." The expansive language of this provision was intended to confer "overriding authority to respond to situations involving a substantial endangerment to health or the environment." H.R. COMMITTEE PRINT NO. 96-IFC 31, 96TH CONG., 1ST SESS. at 32 (1979) (the Eckhardt Report). As stated in the Eckhardt Report:

> The section's broad authority to "take such other actions as may be necessary" includes both short-and long-term injunctive relief, ranging from the construction of dikes to the adoption of certain treatment technologies, upgrading of disposal facilities, and removal and incineration.
>
> Imminence in this section applies to the nature of the threat rather than identification of the time when the endangerment initially arose. The section, therefore, may be used for events which took place at some time in the past but which continue to present a threat to the public health or the environment.
>
> The unequivocal statutory language and this legislative history make it clear that Congress, by enacting section 7003, intended to confer upon the courts the authority to grant affirmative equitable relief to the extent necessary to eliminate any risks posed by toxic wastes. Under section 7003, a court could not order the cleanup of a waste disposal site which posed no threat to health or the environment. There is no doubt, however, that it authorizes the cleanup of a site, even a dormant one, if that action is necessary to

abate a present threat to the public health or the environment. It is also clear that if a threat to human health can be averted only by providing individuals with an alternate water supply, that remedy, in an appropriate case, may be granted under the authority of section 7003.

The district court correctly observed that section 1431 of SDWA may not be invoked to protect private water supplies. Nevertheless, in terms of the types of relief which may be employed to protect public water supplies, the authority conferred on the courts by section 1431 of SDWA is quite as broad as that conferred by RCRA. Section 1431 of SDWA authorizes the United States to protect public water supplies from contamination by "commencing a civil action for appropriate relief, including a restraining order or permanent or temporary injunction." The forms of relief which are "appropriate" must be determined on a case by case basis in order to achieve the remedial purposes contemplated by the act.

In the words of the House Report:

Section 1431 reflects the Committee's determination to confer completely adequate authority to deal promptly and effectively with emergency situations which jeopardize the health of persons.

* * * (T)he section authorizes the Administrator to issue such orders as may be necessary . . . to protect the health of persons, as well as to commence civil actions for injunctive relief for the same purpose. H. R. REP. NO. 93-1185, 93D CONG., 2D SESS., REPRINTED IN (1974) U.S.CODE CONG. & AD. NEWS 6454, 6487.

Both the specific statutory language and the House Report's concomitant expression of legislative intent are broad enough to authorize the diagnostic study requested in this action. Indeed, the House Report explicitly mentions the authority to issue orders "to obtain relevant information about impending or actual emergencies, * * * to treat or reduce hazardous situations once they have arisen, or to provide alternative safe water supply sources in the event any drinking water source which is relied upon becomes hazardous or unuseable."

Congress, in the endangerment provisions of RCRA and SDWA sought to invoke nothing less than the full equity powers of the federal courts in the effort to protect public health, the environment, and public water supplies from the pernicious effects of toxic wastes. Courts should not undermine the will of Congress by either withholding relief or granting it grudgingly.

Although it was within the power of the district court to grant the requested preliminary relief, the procedural posture of this litigation militates against granting it on this appeal. It would bind only a few of more than 35 defendants, and to require these few to bear the entire cost of the requested relief might prove impractical and unfair.

The district court found that an imminent danger existed at the time of the hearing. Nevertheless, it may well be that the public interest counseled against the grant of the requested preliminary relief. Very large sums of money were required to pay for the diagnostic study, and there may have been some question about the original defendants' financial ability to fund it. In those circumstances, the most practical and effective solution may well have been to refuse the government's request for a preliminary injunction thereby necessitating the study be undertaken by EPA without delay. Prompt preventive action was the most important consideration. Reimbursement could thereafter be directed against those parties ultimately found to be liable.

* * *

—

Additionally, courts have rejected arguments from defendants that the government cannot order a defendant to pay for action the government took because injunctions do not traditionally apply to monetary remedies. When seeking to impose an equitable remedy the courts have balanced the interests of the public against the private needs. If a court finds that the public interest outweighs the private interest "payments of money . . . may be an appropriate form of preliminary relief." Cases deciding the scope of § 7003 demonstrate that courts have the flexibility to issue equitable remedies to the government when public health is at issue.

The following charts illustrate the number of civil judicial penalties under RCRA versus other EPA statutes and the total civil penalties respectively.

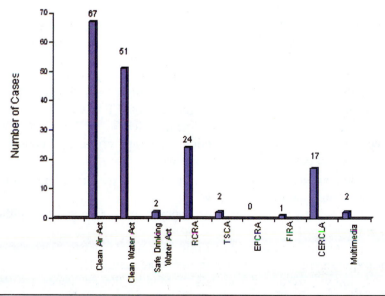

Figure 9.20–Number of Civil Judicial Penalties by Statute/Program Area[297]

---

[297] Source: FY 1994 Enforcement and Compliance Assurance Accomplishments Report– EPA.

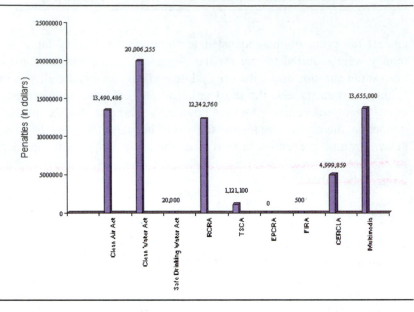

Figure 9.21–Total Amount of Civil Judicial Penalties by Statute/Program Area[298]

4. Criminal Enforcement

Section 3008(d) gives EPA authority to seek criminal actions against knowing violations of some RCRA provision. Over the last few years EPA has become more aggressive in seeking criminal prosecutions. In 1990 EPA initiated 112 criminal cases but, in 1994 EPA initiated 525 cases. In 1994 EPA opened 173 criminal investigations and gave the DOJ 173 criminal referrals under RCRA.

One commentator suggested two reasons for EPA's aggressive approach. First, the broader use of prosecuting all areas of white-collar crimes. Second, the established existence of the hazardous waste program that leads EPA to be less sympathetic to persons who are ignorant of hazardous waste policy. Another reason criminal referrals increased is that EPA expanded the staff of criminal agents from 42 to 123 in a 5-year period.

Section 3008(d) delineates actions that are criminal. Section 3008 applies criminal penalties to any person who:

1) knowingly transports or causes to be transported any hazardous waste to an unpermitted facility

2) knowingly treats, stores, or disposes of hazardous waste without a permit

3) knowingly omits material information or makes a false statement or requirement in any document maintained under RCRA

4) knowingly alters, conceals or fails to file the necessary RCRA documents

---

[298] *Id.*

5) knowingly transports or causes hazardous waste to be transported without a manifest

6) knowingly transports hazardous waste to another country without that country's permission or in violation of an agreement between the United States and that country

7) knowingly treats, stores, or disposes of any used oil.

Conviction under § 3008 (d) exposes a person to a fine of up to $50,000 a day for each criminal count. Additionally, a person found liable under § 3008(d) can receive a prison term between 2 and 5 years. A second conviction under § 3008(d) doubles the maximum monetary penalty and prison term.

Much of the discussion in the courts over § 3008 has been about Subsections 3008(d)(1) and (d)(2). Section 3008(d)(1) forbids transportation of hazardous waste to a facility without a permit and § (d)(2) forbids a person from knowingly treating, disposing, and storing a hazardous waste without a permit.

Under both §§ 3008(d)(1) and (d)(2), courts have rejected the argument by defendants that to be criminally liable the defendant must have known the hazardous waste was regulated under RCRA. In several cases courts have held that RCRA is a public welfare statute designed to protect the public from dangers posed by hazardous waste. Because the handling of hazardous waste materials poses a great risk "the probability of regulation is so great that anyone who is aware that he is in possession of them or dealing with them must be presumed to be aware of the regulations." Ignorance of the law is not a sufficient defense when the public interest is at issue. Based on jury instructions that have been upheld on appeal, it seems all the defendant has to know was that the waste is potentially harmful, in other words, not an innocuous substance like water.

As we saw in *U.S. v. Hayes, supra,* under § 3008 (d)(1) the courts have reached a consensus that a person needs to have knowledge that the facility did not have a permit to be criminally libel.[299] Courts require the transporter to have actual knowledge of the facility's permit status for fear that innocent conduct might be punished. Otherwise, one court noted, the facility manager could lie to the transporter about the facility's permit status and then the transporter could be criminal prosecuted because he believed the statement by the facility manager.[300] Although the wording of Subsection (d)(1) is ambiguous, courts do not believe that Congress intended courts to presume that transporters know about a facility's permit status.[301] Courts have also noted that if Congress wished to impose a knowledge requirement on

---

[299] *See* United States v. Laughlin, 768 F.Supp. 957, 966 (N.D.N.Y. 1991); Hayes, 786 F.2d at 1504.

[300] *See* Hayes, 786 F.2d at 1504.

[301] *See id.*

transporters, Congress would not have included the word "knowingly" at the beginning of § 3008(d)(1).[302]

While courts have come to a consensus on the "knowledge" requirement for a facility's permit status in § 3008(d)(1), courts have split on that issue as it applies to Subsection (d)(2). Courts differ over whether the omission of the word "knowing" in Subsection (d)(2)(A) means that Congress intended a defendant who handles, stores, disposes, or treats hazardous waste is presumed to know that he had to have a permit.

UNITED STATES v. JOHNSON & TOWERS, INC.

741 F.2d 662 (3d Cir. 1984)

SLOVITER, Circuit Judge.

Before us is the government's appeal from the dismissal of three counts of an indictment charging unlawful disposal of hazardous wastes under the Resource Conservation and Recovery Act. In a question of first impression regarding the statutory definition of "person," the district court concluded that the Act's criminal penalty provision imposing fines and imprisonment could not apply to the individual defendants. We will reverse.

I.

The criminal prosecution in this case arose from the disposal of chemicals at a plant owned by Johnson & Towers in Mount Laurel, New Jersey. In its operations the company, which repairs and overhauls large motor vehicles, uses degreasers and other industrial chemicals that contain chemicals such as methylene chloride and trichlorethylene, classified as "hazardous wastes" under the Resource Conservation and Recovery Act (RCRA), 42 U.S.C. §§ 6901-6987 (1982), and "pollutants" under the Clean Water Act, 33 U.S.C. §§ 1251-1376 (1982). During the period relevant here, the waste chemicals from cleaning operations were drained into a holding tank and, when the tank was full, pumped into a trench. The trench flowed from the plant property into Parker's Creek, a tributary of the Delaware River. Under RCRA, generators of such wastes must obtain a permit for disposal from the Environmental Protection Agency (EPA). The EPA had neither issued nor received an application for a permit for Johnson & Towers' operations.

The indictment named as defendants Johnson & Towers and two of its employees, Jack Hopkins, a foreman, and Peter Angel, the service manager in the trucking department. According to the indictment, over a three-day period federal agents saw workers pump waste from the tank into the trench, and on the third day observed toxic chemicals flowing into the creek.

* * *

The counts under RCRA charged that the defendants "did knowingly treat, store, and dispose of, and did cause to be treated, stored and disposed

---

[302] *See* Laughlin, 768 F.Supp. at 966.

of hazardous wastes without having obtained a permit * * * in that the defendants discharged, deposited, injected, dumped, spilled, leaked and placed degreasers . . . into the trench . . . ." The indictment alleged that both Angel and Hopkins "managed, supervised and directed a substantial portion of Johnson & Towers' operations . . . including those related to the treatment, storage and disposal of the hazardous wastes and pollutants" and that the chemicals were discharged by "the defendants and others at their direction." The indictment did not otherwise detail Hopkins' and Angel's activities or responsibilities.

Johnson & Towers pled guilty to the RCRA counts. Hopkins and Angel pled not guilty, and then moved to dismiss counts 2, 3, and 4. The court concluded that the RCRA criminal provision applies only to "owners and operators," *i.e.*, those obligated under the statute to obtain a permit. Since neither Hopkins nor Angel was an "owner" or "operator," the district court granted the motion as to the RCRA charges but held that the individuals could be liable on these three counts under 18 U.S.C. § 2 for aiding and abetting. The court denied the government's motion for reconsideration, and the government appealed to this court under 18 U.S.C. § 3731 (1982).

We hold that section 6928(d)(2)(A) covers employees as well as owners and operators of the facility who knowingly treat, store, or dispose of any hazardous waste, but that the employees can be subject to criminal prosecution only if they knew or should have known that there had been no compliance with the permit requirement of section 6925.

II.

The single issue in this appeal is whether the individual defendants are subject to prosecution under RCRA's criminal provision, which applies to:

[a]ny person who—

* * *

(2) knowingly treats, stores, or disposes of any hazardous waste identified or listed under this subchapter either—
(A) without having obtained a permit under section 6925 of this title . . . or
(B) in knowing violation of any material condition or requirement of such permit.

42 U.S.C. § 6928(d). The permit provision in section 6925, referred to in section 6928(d), requires "each person owning or operating a facility for the treatment, storage, or disposal of hazardous waste identified or listed under this subchapter to have a permit" from EPA

The parties offer contrary interpretations of section 6928(d)(2)(A). Defendants consider it an administrative enforcement mechanism, applying only to those who come within section 6925 and fail to comply; the government reads it as penalizing anyone who handles hazardous waste without a permit or in violation of a permit. Neither party has cited another case, nor have we found one, considering the application of this criminal provision to an individual other than an owner or operator.

A.

As in any statutory analysis, we are obliged first to look to the language and then, if needed, attempt to divine Congress' specific intent with respect to the issue. The language of the particular section under consideration does not readily support either interpretation proffered by the opposing parties. Had Congress merely intended an administrative enforcement measure, as defendants contend, it could have specified that any person required under section 6925 to obtain a permit would be liable for acting without one. On the other hand, if Congress had meant to subject to prosecution anyone who did not have a permit, as the government argues, it could have phrased subsection (A) of section 6928(d)(2) to provide that any treatment, storage or disposal in the absence of a permit or outside the terms of such a permit is illegal. It did not so state explicitly.

However, if we view the statutory language in its totality, the congressional plan becomes more apparent. First, "person" is defined in the statute as "an individual, trust, firm, joint stock company, corporation (including a government corporation), partnership, association, State, municipality, commission, political subdivision of a State, or any interstate body." 42 U.S.C. § 6903(15) (1982). Had Congress meant in section 6928(d)(2)(A) to take aim more narrowly, it could have used more narrow language. Since it did not, we attribute to "any person" the definition given the term in section 6903(15).

Second, under the plain language of the statute the only explicit basis for exoneration is the existence of a permit covering the action. Nothing in the language of the statute suggests that we should infer another provision exonerating persons who knowingly treat, store or dispose of hazardous waste but are not owners or operators.

Finally, though the result may appear harsh, it is well established that criminal penalties attached to regulatory statutes intended to protect public health, in contrast to statutes based on common law crimes, are to be construed to effectuate the regulatory purpose.

The statutory construction issue here, whether the criminal provision may be applied to the individual defendants who were not in the position to secure a permit, is similar to that presented to the Supreme Court in *United States v. Dotterweich*[, 320 U.S. 277 (1943)]. There the defendant, a jobber, had been convicted of violating the Food and Drugs Act, providing a criminal penalty for "any person" shipping adulterated or misbranded drugs. Under the statute, there was no violation if a guaranty had been issued with the goods stating that they were not contaminated or misbranded. The drugs in question originated with the manufacturer and the jobber had undertaken only to label and ship them. The Court of Appeals overturned the conviction, concluding that the guaranty provision could apply only to principals and that the penalty provision must be correspondingly limited. The court found it "difficult to believe that Congress expected anyone except the principal to get such a guaranty, or to make the guilt of an agent depend upon whether his employer had gotten one." *United States v. Buffalo Pharmacal Co.*, 131 F.2d 500, 503 (2d Cir.1942).

The Supreme Court reinstated the conviction. In construing the term "any person," it rejected the Second Circuit's restrictive view, and said:

> The Food and Drugs Act of 1906 was an exertion by Congress of its power to keep impure and adulterated food and drugs out of the channels of commerce. By the Act of 1938, Congress extended the range of its control over illicit and noxious articles and stiffened the penalties for disobedience. The purposes of this legislation thus touch phases of the lives and health of people which, in the circumstances of modern industrialism, are largely beyond self-protection. Regard for these purposes should infuse construction of the legislation if it is to be treated as a working instrument of government and not merely as a collection of English words.

Dotterweich, 320 U.S. at 280.

Thus, we must inquire into the congressional intent to determine whether RCRA should be construed in the same manner as was the Food and Drugs Act in *Dotterweich*.

B.

Congress enacted RCRA in 1976 as a "cradle-to-grave" regulatory scheme for toxic materials, providing "nationwide protection against the dangers of improper hazardous waste disposal." H.R. REP. NO. 1491, 94TH CONG., 2D SESS. 11 [(1976)]. RCRA was enacted to provide "a multifaceted approach towards solving the problems associated with the 3-4 billion tons of discarded materials generated each year, and the problems resulting from the anticipated 8% annual increase in the volume of such waste." *Id*. at 2. The committee reports accompanying legislative consideration of RCRA contain numerous statements evincing the Congressional view that improper disposal of toxic materials was a serious national problem.

The original statute made knowing disposal (but not treatment or storage) of such waste without a permit a misdemeanor. [RCRA § 3008(d).] Amendments in 1978 and 1980 expanded the criminal provision to cover treatment and storage and made violation of section 6928 a felony. The fact that Congress amended the statute twice to broaden the scope of its substantive provisions and enhance the penalty is a strong indication of Congress' increasing concern about the seriousness of the prohibited conduct.

Although Congress' concern may have been directed primarily at owners and operators of generating facilities, since it imposed upon them in section 6925 the obligation to secure the necessary permit, Congress did not explicitly limit criminal liability for impermissible treatment, storage, or disposal to owners and operators. The House Committee's discussion of enforcement contains several references relevant only to owners and operators, but it says, in addition: "This section also provides for criminal penalties for the person who . . . disposes of any hazardous waste without a permit under this title . . . ." H.R. REP. NO. 1491, *supra* at 31. The "also" demonstrates that the reach of section 6928(d)(2) is broader than that of the rest of the statute, particularly the administrative enforcement remedies. The acts that were made the subject of the criminal provision were distinguished in the House Report from the other conduct subject to administrative regulation because they were viewed as more serious offenses. As the Report explained, "[the] justification for the penalties section is to permit a broad variety of mechanisms so as to stop the illegal disposal of hazardous wastes."

We conclude that in RCRA, no less than in the Food and Drugs Act, Congress endeavored to control hazards that, "in the circumstances of modern industrialism, are largely beyond self-protection." *United States v. Dotterweich*, 320 U.S. at 280. It would undercut the purposes of the legislation to limit the class of potential defendants to owners and operators when others also bear responsibility for handling regulated materials. The phrase "without having obtained a permit under section 6925" merely references the section under which the permit is required and exempts from prosecution under section 6928(d)(2)(A) anyone who has obtained a permit; we conclude that it has no other limiting effect. Therefore we reject the district court's construction limiting the substantive criminal provision by confining "any person" in section 6928(d)(2)(A) to owners and operators of facilities that store, treat or dispose of hazardous waste, as an unduly narrow view of both the statutory language and the congressional intent.

III.

A.

Since we must remand this case to the district court because the individual defendants are indeed covered by section 6928(d)(2)(A), it is incumbent on us to reach the question of the requisite proof as to individual defendants under that section. The government argues that "knowingly" applies only to "treats, stores, or disposes" of any hazardous waste, and that it does not have to show that the defendant knew either that the waste was hazardous or that there was no permit. Letter brief for Appellant at 2. Thus, the government argues, it need prove only that (1) the defendant is a "person"; (2) the defendant handled hazardous material, and (3) there was no permit for such disposal or treatment. We conclude that this interpretation is overly literal.

We focus again on the statutory language:

[a]ny person who—
(2) knowingly treats, stores, or disposes of any hazardous waste identified or listed under this subchapter either—

(A) without having obtained a permit under section 6925 of this title * * * or

(B) in knowing violation of any material condition or requirement of such permit.

42 U.S.C. § 6928(d) (1982).

If the word "knowingly" in section 6928(d)(2) referred exclusively to the acts of treating, storing or disposing, as the government contends, it would be an almost meaningless addition since it is not likely that one would treat, store or dispose of waste without knowledge of that action. At a minimum, the word "knowingly", which introduces subsection (A), must also encompass knowledge that the waste material is hazardous. Certainly, "[a] person thinking in good faith that he was [disposing of] distilled water when in fact he was [disposing of] some dangerous acid would not be covered." *United States v. International Minerals & Chemical Corp.*, 402 U.S. 558, 563-64 (1971).

Whether "knowingly" also modifies subsection (A) presents a somewhat different question. The district court concluded that it is not necessary to show that individual defendants prosecuted under section 6928(d)(2)(A) knew that they were acting without a permit or in violation of the law. Since we have already concluded that this is a regulatory statute which can be classified as a "public welfare statute," there would be a reasonable basis for reading the statute without any *mens rea* requirement, as the [Supreme Court has done.] However, whatever policy justification might warrant applying such a construction as a matter of general principle, such a reading would be arbitrary and nonsensical when applied to this statute.

Treatment, storage or disposal of hazardous waste in violation of any material condition or requirement of a permit must be "knowing," since the statute explicitly so states in subsection (B). It is unlikely that Congress could have intended to subject to criminal prosecution those persons who acted when no permit had been obtained irrespective of their knowledge (under subsection (A)), but not those persons who acted in violation of the terms of a permit unless that action was knowing (subsection (B)). Thus we are led to conclude either that the omission of the word "knowing" in (A) was inadvertent or that "knowingly" which introduces subsection (2) applies to subsection (A).

As a matter of syntax we find it no more awkward to read "knowingly" as applying to the entire sentence than to read it as modifying only "treats, stores or disposes." The Eighth Circuit recently addressed a similar linguistic problem in a statute penalizing any person who "knowingly uses, transfers, acquires . . . or possesses [food] coupons . . . in any manner not authorized by this chapter . . . ." 7 U.S.C. § 2024(b). That court observed:

[P]urely as a verbal matter, the word "knowingly" in subsection (b) may naturally be read to modify the entire remainder of the clause in which it appears, including the phrase, "in any manner not authorized," etc. To read "knowingly" as having nothing to do with the phrase "in any manner not authorized" is, we suppose, verbally tenable, but it is not the only meaning the words will bear, nor even, we think, the more natural one.

United States v. Marvin, 687 F.2d 1221, 1226 (8th Cir.1982), *cert. denied*, 460 U.S. 1081 (1983). We believe that analysis to be appropriate here.

B.

However, our conclusion that "knowingly" applies to all elements of the offense in section 6298(d)(2)(A) does not impose on the government as difficult a burden as it fears. On this issue, we are guided by the Court's holding in *United States v. International Minerals & Chemical Corp.*, 402 U.S. at 563, that under certain regulatory statutes requiring "knowing" conduct the government need prove only knowledge of the actions taken and not of the statute forbidding them. As the Court stated in *International Minerals*,

> The principle that ignorance of the law is no defense applies whether the law be a statute or a duly promulgated and published regulation. In the context of these proposed 1960 amendments we decline to attribute to Congress the inaccurate view that that Act requires proof of knowledge of the law, as well as the facts, and that it intended to endorse that interpretation by retaining the word "knowingly."

402 U.S. at 563.

The Court recognized that under certain statutes, such as the income tax law, the government must show a purpose by defendant to bring about the forbidden result. However, the Court in *International Minerals*, construing a statute and regulations which proscribed knowing failure to record shipment of chemicals, stated,

> [W]here, as here and as in *Balint* and *Freed*, dangerous or deleterious devices or products or obnoxious waste materials are involved, the probability of regulation is so great that anyone who is aware that he is in possession of them or dealing with them must be presumed to be aware of the regulation.

402 U.S. at 565.

Even the dissenting Justices, viewing the highly regulated shipping industry, agreed that the officers, agents, and employees are under a species of absolute liability for violation of the regulations despite the "knowingly" requirement. This, no doubt, is as Congress intended it to be. Likewise, prosecution of regular shippers for violations of the regulations could hardly be impeded by the "knowingly" requirement for triers of fact would have no difficulty whatever in inferring knowledge on the part of those whose business it is to know, despite their protestations to the contrary. 402 U.S. at 569.

The indictment in this case specified the crime in the language of the statute. Thus it did not include language spelling out the knowledge requirements of the statute discussed in text. Nevertheless, in light of our interpretation of section 6928(d)(2)(A), it is evident that the district court will be required to instruct the jury, inter alia, that in order to convict each defendant the jury must find that each knew that Johnson & Towers was required to have a permit, and knew that Johnson & Towers did not have a permit. Depending on the evidence, the district court may also instruct the jury that such knowledge may be inferred.

The indictment charged that both individual defendants "managed, supervised, and directed a substantial portion of Johnson & Towers' operations at the Mount Laurel plant, including those related to . . . disposal of hazardous wastes and pollutants." This case reaches us without any evidence or findings of the defendants' actual knowledge of the facts at issue, and with inconsistent descriptions of defendants' responsibilities. As the Supreme Court said in *Dotterweich,* the question of responsibility can be left to "the good sense of prosecutors, the wise guidance of trial judges, and the ultimate judgment of juries." 320 U.S. at 285.

IV.

In summary, we conclude that the individual defendants are "persons" within section 6928(d)(2)(A), that all the elements of that offense must be shown to have been knowing, but that such knowledge, including that of the permit requirement, may be inferred by the jury as to those individuals who hold the requisite responsible positions with the corporate defendant. For the foregoing reasons, we will reverse the district court's order dismissing portions of counts 2, 3 and 4 of the indictment, and we will remand for further proceedings consistent with this opinion.

NOTES

1. The majority view of the courts has held that the omission of "knowing" in subsection (d)(2)(A) was intended by Congress to "not require as elements of the offense knowledge that the absence of a permit violates the law."[303] Courts holding this view have pointed to section 3008(d)(B)&(C) where Congress included the word "knowing" for specific violations of a permit.[304] Courts have used the word "knowing" at the beginning of subsection (d)(2)(B) and (C) to reject any argument that "knowingly" at the beginning of subsection (d)(2) applies the knowledge requirement to subsection (d)(2)(A).[305]

2. EPA has also argued that in certain situations a person should be criminally liable under section 3008(d) even when the government cannot prove the defendant knew the facts constituting the criminal conduct. EPA argues that under the "responsible corporate officer" doctrine EPA can hold criminally liable any corporate officer that should have known of the

---

[303] Laughlin, 768 F.Supp. at 965.

[304] *See* Hayes, 786 F.2d at 1504; Laughlin, 768 F.Supp. at 966.

[305] *See* Laughlin, 768 F.Supp. at 966.

violation.[306] The only case that has heard the government argue this doctrine rejected it stating "a mere showing of official responsibility . . . is not an adequate substitute for direct or circumstantial proof of knowledge."[307] However, EPA will likely continue to argue this position in future cases.

———

In 1984, as part of the HSWA, Congress added § 3008(e)—the knowing endangerment provision.[308] Section 3008(e) provides that "any person who knowingly treats, disposes, transports, disposes of, or exports any hazardous waste [and] knows then that he thereby places another person in imminent danger of death or serious bodily injury" will be liable under RCRA.[309] A court can fine a person found guilty under this section up to $250,000 and imprison a person for up to 15 years. A court can fine a corporation for up to $1,000,000.[310]

For conviction under § 3008(e) the government must prove the defendant is aware of the violation. A person "knows" of a circumstance that causes endangerment if "he is aware or believes that a circumstance exists" and "knows" that danger of death or bodily injury will result from his actions if he is "substantially certain" that danger of death or serious bodily injury will occur.[311] Additionally, the defendant cannot have knowledge of the danger to others attributed to him.[312] Section 3008(f) also strictly defines "serious bodily injury" and lists defenses a defendant can use if charged with "knowing endangerment."[313] Congress construed the statute to apply to the most egregious cases. That is why more than ten years after enactment only two convictions have occurred under this section.

In *United States v. Protex* a company and its CEO were found guilty of knowing endangerment under § 3008(e).[314] In *Protex* the court found the company did not provide its employees with adequate protection to handle hazardous waste. As a result, several employees became ill with various ailments, including memory loss. The court held that the company knew of the dangers posed by the hazardous waste but chose to ignore the risks.[315]

UNITED STATES V. PROTEX INDUSTRIES, INC.

874 F.2d 740 (10th Cir. 1989)

SAFFELS, District Judge.

---

[306] ENVIRONMENTAL LAW PRACTICE GUIDE: STATE AND FEDERAL LAW, at § 29.10[5] (Michael B. Gerrard ed., 1992).

[307] United States v. MacDonald and Watson Oil Co., 933 F.2d 35 (1st Cir. 1991).

[308] *See* 42 U.S.C. § 6928(e) (1994).

[309] *Id.*

[310] *See id.*

[311] 42 U.S.C. § 6928(f) (1994).

[312] *See id.*

[313] *Id.*

[314] United States v. Protex Indus., Inc., 874 F.2d 740 (10th Cir. 1989).

[315] *See id.* at 742.

This appeal was taken from the first criminal conviction under the "knowing endangerment" provision of the federal Resource Conservation and Recovery Act ("RCRA"), 42 U.S.C. § 6928(e), recently enacted by Congress. Appellant Protex Industries, Inc. ("Protex") appeals from its criminal conviction under that provision as well as from its other convictions under the RCRA.

Protex operated a drum recycling facility. It purchased used 55 gallon drums, many of which previously contained toxic chemicals. It cleaned and repainted the drums and used them to store and ship other products it manufactured.

The Environmental Protection Agency ("EPA") inspected Protex's facilities annually. One of these inspections was conducted on July 24, 1984, by a representative of the Colorado Department of Health under contract with the EPA. The Department of Health conducted the inspection pursuant to section 3012 of the RCRA, 42 U.S.C. § 6933, which requires each state to compile an inventory of sites at which hazardous waste has at any time been disposed of, treated or stored. The inspector took soil samples while at the site, but results of the laboratory analysis of those samples were never provided to Protex.

Another inspection was conducted in August of 1985. Again samples were taken, but results were not provided to Protex.

On March 10 and 11, 1986, investigators from the EPA and the Federal Bureau of Investigation executed a search warrant at Protex's drum recycling facility. A federal grand jury later returned a nineteen count indictment against Protex, and Protex was convicted of sixteen of those nineteen counts.

Counts 17 through 19 of that indictment charged Protex with knowingly placing three of its employees in imminent danger of death or serious bodily injury as a result of its other alleged violations of the RCRA. The evidence showed that safety provisions for the employees in the drum recycling facility were woefully inadequate to protect the employees against the dangers of the toxic chemicals. Government experts testified that without these proper safety precautions, the employees were at an increased risk of suffering solvent poisoning. Solvent poisoning may cause psychoorganic syndrome, of which there are three types. Symptoms of Type 1 psychoorganic syndrome are disturbances in thinking, behavior and personality, and sleeping disorders. Type 1 is reversible quickly and goes away when exposure ends. Type 2 psychoorganic syndrome is divided into two categories, A and B. An individual suffering from Type 2-A suffers changes in personality and has difficulty controlling impulses; the individual engages in unplanned and unexpected behavior, lacks motivation, and usually experiences severe mood swings. If exposure to the toxic chemicals ends, an individual suffering from Type 2 A will eventually recover. An individual suffering from Type 2-B psychoorganic syndrome, however, will have additional, nonreversible symptoms, such as concentration problems, short and remote memory problems, decreased learning ability, and cognitive impairment. Finally, an individual suffering from Type 3 psychoorganic syndrome suffers a severe loss of learning capabilities, severe memory loss, severe psychiatric abnormalities and gross tremor. The government experts also testified that in addition to being at risk for psychoorganic syndrome, the employees suffered an increased risk of contracting cancer as a result of their extended exposure to the toxic chemicals.

The testimony of government experts further showed that two of the employees certainly had Type 2-A psychoorganic syndrome and may have had Type 2-B. The government expert testified that he could not demonstrate that the third employee was suffering from psychoorganic syndrome at the time he was examined, but pointed out that he might still have suffered from the syndrome and since recovered from its symptoms. Finally, the expert testified that all three individuals had an increased permanent and irreversible risk of developing cancer due to their prolonged exposure to the toxic chemicals.

Protex states three grounds for its appeal. It contends that the trial court rendered 42 U.S.C. § 6928(e) unconstitutionally vague as applied in two regards. First, it argues that the trial court erred in allowing the "knowing endangerment" counts to go to the jury, despite the alleged absence of any evidence showing the employees were placed in imminent danger of serious bodily injury as specifically defined by 42 U.S.C. § 6928(f)(6). Secondly, it contends the trial court rendered the section unconstitutionally vague as applied because it improperly instructed the jury that an individual was placed in "imminent danger" if it "could reasonably be expected" that the set of conditions would cause death or serious bodily injury. Defendant contends this language did not track the language of the statute and it unconstitutionally expanded it beyond the intent of Congress. Finally, appellant contends the trial court erred in refusing to give a requested instruction on Protex's defense that the government failed to meet its duty to provide results of any on-site inspections to Protex, as required by 42 U.S.C. § 6927(a).

I.

The question of whether a statute has been rendered unconstitutionally vague as applied is a question involving issues of law and our standard of review is therefore *de novo*.

* * *

Title 42, United States Code, Section 6928(e) provides that: "Any person who knowingly transports, treats, stores, disposes of, or exports any hazardous waste identified or listed under [the RCRA] in violation of [the criminal provisions of the RCRA] who knows at that time that he thereby places another person in imminent danger of death or serious bodily injury, shall [be guilty of an offense against the United States.]" Title 42, United States Code, Section 6928(f)(6) defines "serious bodily injury" as: (A) bodily injury which involves a substantial risk of death; (B) unconsciousness; (C) extreme physical pain; (D) protracted and obvious disfigurement; or (E) protracted loss or impairment of the function of a bodily member, organ, or mental faculty. Protex contends that the trial court rendered section 6928(e) unconstitutionally vague by expanding the definition of "serious bodily injury" beyond that set out in section 6928(f)(6). Protex states that if the employees were placed in any "danger" at all, it was a danger of developing Type 2-A psychoorganic syndrome, a condition which does not come within the scope of subparagraphs (A)-(E) of section 6928(f)(6). Protex also argues that the enhanced "risk" of contracting some indeterminate type of cancer at some unspecified time in the future is not sufficient to constitute "serious bodily injury."

Appellant's position demonstrates a callousness toward the severe physical effect the prolonged exposure to toxic chemicals may cause or has caused to the three former employees. There was evidence presented at trial to show that the three individuals not only had been in danger of serious bodily injury, but had in fact suffered serious bodily injury: Type 2-A and Type 2-B psychoorganic syndrome may cause an impairment of mental faculties.

II.

Protex contends secondly that the statute was rendered unconstitutionally vague because in instructing the jury, the district court defined "imminent danger" as "the existence of a condition or combination of conditions which could reasonably be expected to cause death or serious bodily injury unless the condition is remedied." Protex contends this definition was in error, because in 42 U.S.C. § 6928(f)(1)(c), Congress referred to a "substantial certain[ty]" to cause death or serious bodily injury. Protex contends the use of the term "reasonable expectation," rather than the statutory term "substantial certainty," rendered the statute unconstitutionally vague as applied. Our standard of review is again *de novo*.

In asserting its position on this point, Protex ignores the fact that the court indeed did instruct the jury in language directly derived from the statute. 42 U.S.C. § 6928(f)(1)(c) provides that "a person's state of mind is knowing with respect to * * * a result of his conduct, if he is aware or believes that his conduct is substantially certain to cause danger of death or serious bodily injury." Thus, the "substantially certain" standard appears to define the mens rea necessary for commission of the crime, rather than the degree to which defendant's conduct must be likely to cause death or serious bodily injury. And the court did quote directly from section 6928(f)(1)(c) in instructing the jury. Protex's contention that the term "substantial certainty," rather than the term "reasonable expectation," should have been used in defining "imminent danger" has no basis in the statutory language.

* * *

III.

Finally, Protex takes the position that the district court erred in failing to instruct the jury of the government's duty to report test results as required under 42 U.S.C. § 6927(a). Since we are presented with a question of law, our standard of review is again *de novo*.

Section 6927(a) provides that if any laboratory analysis is made of samples taken at the site in question, "the results of such analysis shall be furnished promptly to the owner, operator, or agent in charge." The parties agree that the Colorado Department of Health, acting under contract with the EPA, failed to promptly provide to Protex the results of the 1984 and 1985 tests.

The court must first address whether this defense was properly raised below. The subject of the government's duty under section 6927(a) arose twice in the course of the trial below. It arose first in a motion to suppress the evidence obtained from the searches. That motion was denied. Then in the instruction conference, the defendant's attorney proposed an instruction which recited the language of 42 U.S.C. § 6927(a). The motion to suppress was again discussed and the court adopted its previous ruling. Defense counsel went on to state: "[T]he instruction of the proper statement of the law that should have been followed by these officials during the 1984 and 1985 inspections[,] they did not follow this law and there has [sic] been a lot of questions asked in the evidence about their duty to notify Protex. And so it's in the context of the trial and the evidence at trial that we are requesting this particular instruction."

It is not at all clear from this discussion that defendant did in fact tell the court that the government's failure to notify it of the test results was an essential part of its defense, or that the 1984 and 1985 searches were relevant to any matter other than the motion to suppress. Thus, the matter may not have been properly raised in the court below, and the issue may not have been preserved. *See* Fed. R.Civ.P. 51.

Any confusion regarding whether the issue was raised below is certainly understandable, since even at this stage, the parties and the court are not at all clear as to why section 6927(a) should provide a defense to a RCRA criminal action.[316] In an abundance of caution, the court will give the benefit of the doubt to the defendant and treat the issue as if it had been raised properly below. If the issue was properly raised, defendant was entitled to a specific jury instruction on that defense if the instruction was at all supported by the evidence and the law. Protex vehemently argues that its requested instruction had a basis in the law, and it is correct in arguing so; the proposed instruction correctly set out the statutory mandate. Further, Protex's argument was supported by the facts, because the government concedes it

---

[316] Protex does admit it is not arguing that the government's duty to provide test results is a condition precedent to criminal prosecution under section 6928. It further concedes that its theory is not that because the government failed to provide test results, Protex did not know that it was violating the RCRA and it therefore was not liable. Rather, Protex seems to argue that since the government failed to provide it with test results, it reasonably assumed that nothing adverse showed up in those results and further assumed that it was in compliance with the RCRA. It also seems to contend that had it been informed that it was in violation, it would have promptly corrected the problem.

did not comply with its duty under section 6927(a) and promptly provide Protex with the results of the analyses. However, these undisputed facts and law only mandate that the court instruct the jury accordingly if that evidence and law establish a valid defense to a criminal action. The government, concededly, acted improperly in this instance; Protex did not receive the results of the 1984 and 1985 inspections. But this is a proceeding against Protex, not against the EPA. There is no authority in the RCRA or in its legislative history which would make an abrogation of the government's duty a mitigating factor in a criminal prosecution. Protex had an independent duty under RCRA to ensure that it was in compliance with the criminal and civil provisions of that Act. *See United States v. Hayes Int'l Corp.*, 786 F.2d 1499, 1503 (11th Cir.1986) (defendant's ignorance that it was in violation of RCRA is not sufficient to absolve it from criminal liability); *see also* 40 C.F.R. Parts 262-65 (setting out detailed, self-policing duties of handlers of hazardous wastes). Any information the government might provide pursuant to its duty under section 6927 to Protex was simply surplusage for purposes of Protex's potential criminal liability. Further, even if the government had notified Protex of the violations discovered after the 1984 and 1985 inspections, Protex's subsequent remedial activity would not have abrogated its criminal liability for those violations. Instead, it would only help to prevent further criminal violations.

Since section 6927(a) provides no defense to criminal charges under the RCRA, the district court was not in error in refusing to instruct the jury in the language of that statute.

Finding no error in the proceedings below, the judgment of the district court is AFFIRMED.

—

Both subsections (a)(1)(A) and (a)(1)(B) actions are further restricted if the Administrator is "diligently prosecuting" the violation. Courts have considered any legal action occurring in the federal or state courts to be diligent prosecution.[317] Additional restrictions apply to citizen suits if a citizen brings an imminent and substantial endangerment suit. If EPA is already cleaning the site or has obtained a judicial or administrative order that the party is following by removing hazardous waste, conducting an investigation or feasibility study, or proceeding with remedial action, no citizen can file suit under the imminent and substantial provision.[318] The purpose of the restrictions is to avoid complicating the corrective action process by having additional parties involved. However, courts have held that EPA compliance orders, state administrative actions, negotiations, and

---

[317] *See* McGregor v. Industrial Excess Landfill, Inc., 856 F.2d 39 (6th Cir. 1988); *see also* ENVIRONMENTAL LAW PRACTICE GUIDE at § 29.10[8] (Michael B. Gerrard ed., 1992).
[318] *See* 42 U.S.C. § 6972(2)(B) (1994).

other administrative action are not considered "diligent prosecution."[319] Courts have noted that the plain language of the statute forbids citizen action when the government "has commenced . . . a civil or criminal action" in state or federal court.[320] Additionally, if EPA prosecuted a violator and the government is not ensuring timely compliance with the judicial order, the courts preclude a citizen from instituting suit.[321] Citizens cannot argue that the government is not "diligently prosecuting" the case if the government did not use the theories or sue the persons the plaintiff prefers.[322] RCRA does allow a follow-up citizen suit only if the government loses the suit and the citizens show the government did not try the suit adequately. But if the government wins the suit, the courts preclude a citizen from further action.[323]

Finally, a citizen can initiate suit against any person including the federal government. But, a citizen can sue only against continuing violations.[324] Citizen suits also can not be applied retroactively for violations before 1976. Courts interpret section 7002 to forbid "wholly past" based on the phrase "to be in violation" in the section. Since that phrase is written in the present tense, courts have interpreted that phrase to mean that the Section covers only present violations.[325]

An action brought by a citizen can expose a defendant to penalties of up to $25,000 a day.[326] The penalty amount is at the court's discretion. The citizen can also seek an order to force the defendant to comply with an order, permit, or regulatory violation.[327] A citizen can enjoin any action by the defendant that is contributing to the imminent and substantial endangerment. A citizen suit under section 7002(a)(1)(B) can be brought to force section 7003 corrective measures on a facility. If the citizen prevails a court can order the defendant who violated RCRA revisions to pay the citizen reasonable attorney fees.[328]

5. Citizen Suits

Section 7002 provides citizens with the opportunity to sue to enforce the provisions in RCRA.[329] Section 7002 (a)(1)(A) authorizes citizens to sue any person, including the federal government, for a violation of "any permit, standard, regulation, condition, requirement, prohibition or order" under

---

[319] Coalition for Health Concern v. LWD, Inc., 834 F.Supp. 953 (W.D. Ky. 1993); Lykins v. Westinghouse Elec. Corp., 715 F.Supp. 1357 (W.D. Ky. 1989).

[320] LWD, 834 F.Supp. at 956.

[321] See id.

[322] See Supporters to Oppose Pollution v. Heritage Group, 973 F.2d 1320, 1325 (7th Cir. 1992).

[323] See id.

[324] See Ascon Properties, Inc. v. Mobile Oil Co., 866 F.2d 1149 (9th Cir. 1989).

[325] See id.; see also Lutz v. Chromatex, Inc., 718 F.Supp. 413 (M.D. Pa. 1989).

[326] See 42 U.S.C. § 6972(a) (1994).

[327] See id.

[328] See id.

[329] See 42 U.S.C. § 6972 (1994).

RCRA.[330] Section 7002(a)(1)(B) permits action against past and present handlers of hazardous waste whose action "may present an imminent and substantial endangerment, to human health and the environment."[331] Most importantly, section 7002(a)(1)(B) permits a citizen to bring a § 7003 action when the government is unwilling to do so.

Although subsections (a)(1)(A) and (a)(1)(B) give citizens broad powers to sue, § 7002(b) restricts this power.[332] Section 7002(b) contains many restrictions on a citizen's power to sue under RCRA. Among these are: to sue under (a)(1)(A) the citizen must give 60 days notice to EPA Administrator (90 days under (a)(1)(B)) notice must be given to the State where the violation occurs; and, notice must be given to the facility accused of violating a provision of RCRA.[333] In *Hallstrom v. Tallimook County* the Supreme Court held that the 60 day notice provision under Subsection (a)(1)(A) is absolute and jurisdictional.[334]

MEGHRIG V. KFC WESTERN, INC.

516 U.S. 479 (1996)

Justice O'CONNOR delivered the opinion of the Court.

We consider whether § 7002 of the Resource Conservation and Recovery Act of 1976 (RCRA), 42 U.S.C. § 6972, authorizes a private cause of action to recover the prior cost of cleaning up toxic waste that does not, at the time of suit, continue to pose an endangerment to health or the environment. We conclude that it does not.

I

Respondent KFC Western, Inc. (KFC), owns and operates a "Kentucky Fried Chicken" restaurant on a parcel of property in Los Angeles. In 1988, KFC discovered during the course of a construction project that the property was contaminated with petroleum. The County of Los Angeles Department of Health Services ordered KFC to attend to the problem, and KFC spent $211,000 removing and disposing of the oil-tainted soil.

Three years later, KFC brought this suit under the citizen suit provision of RCRA, 42 U.S.C. § 6972(a), seeking to recover these cleanup costs from petitioners Alan and Margaret Meghrig.

KFC claimed that the contaminated soil was a "solid waste" covered by RCRA, *see* 42 U.S.C. § 6903(27), that it had previously posed an "imminent and substantial endangerment to health or the environment," *see* section 6972(a)(1)(B), and that the Meghrigs were responsible for "equitable restitution" of KFC's cleanup costs under § 6972(a) because, as

---

[330] *Id.* § 6942 (a)(1) (1994).

[331] *Id.* § 6972 (a)(1)(B) (1994).

[332] *See id.* § 6972(b) (1994).

[333] *See id.*

[334] Hallstrom v. Tillamook County, 493 U.S. 20 (1989).

prior owners of the property, they had contributed to the waste's "past or present handling, storage, treatment, transportation, or disposal."

The District Court held that § 6972(a) does not permit recovery of past cleanup costs and that § 6972(a)(1)(B) does not authorize a cause of action for the remediation of toxic waste that does not pose an "imminent and substantial endangerment to health or the environment" at the time suit is filed, and dismissed KFC's complaint. The Court of Appeals for the Ninth Circuit reversed, over a dissent, 49 F.3d 518, 524-528 (1995) (Brunetti, J.), finding that a district court had authority under § 6972(a) to award restitution of past cleanup costs,, and that a private party can proceed with a suit under § 6972(a)(1)(B) upon an allegation that the waste at issue presented an "imminent and substantial endangerment" at the time it was cleaned up.

The Ninth Circuit's conclusion regarding the remedies available under RCRA conflicts with the decision of the Court of Appeals for the Eighth Circuit in *Furrer v. Brown*, 62 F.3d 1092, 1100-1101 (1995), and its interpretation of the "imminent endangerment" requirement represents a novel application of federal statutory law. We granted certiorari to address the conflict between the Circuits and to consider the correctness of the Ninth Circuit's interpretation of RCRA, and now reverse.

II

RCRA is a comprehensive environmental statute that governs the treatment, storage, and disposal of solid and hazardous waste. Unlike the Comprehensive Environmental Response, Compensation, and Liability Act of 1980 (CERCLA). RCRA is not principally designed to effectuate the cleanup of toxic waste sites or to compensate those who have attended to the remediation of environmental hazards. RCRA's primary purpose, rather, is to reduce the generation of hazardous waste and to ensure the proper treatment, storage, and disposal of that waste which is nonetheless generated, "so as to minimize the present and future threat to human health and the environment." 42 U.S.C. § 6902(b).

Chief responsibility for the implementation and enforcement of RCRA rests with the Administrator of the Environmental Protection Agency (EPA), *see* §§ 6928, 6973, but like other environmental laws, RCRA contains a citizen suit provision, § 6972, which permits private citizens to enforce its provisions in some circumstances.

Two requirements of § 6972(a) defeat KFC's suit against the Meghrigs. The first concerns the necessary timing of a citizen suit brought under § 6972(a)(1)(B): That section permits a private party to bring suit against certain responsible persons, including former owners, "who ha[ve] contributed or who [are] contributing to the past or present handling, storage, treatment, transportation, or disposal of any solid or hazardous waste which may present an imminent and substantial endangerment to health or the environment." The second defines the remedies a district court can award in a suit brought under § 6972(a)(1)(B): Section 6972(a) authorizes district courts "to restrain any person who has contributed or who is contributing to the past or present handling, storage, treatment, transportation, or disposal of any solid or hazardous waste . . ., to order such person to take such other action as may be necessary, or both."

It is apparent from the two remedies described in § 6972(a) that RCRA's citizen suit provision is not directed at providing compensation for past cleanup efforts. Under a plain reading of this remedial scheme, a private citizen suing under § 6972(a)(1)(B) could seek a mandatory injunction, *i.e.*, one that orders a responsible party to "take action" by attending to the cleanup and proper disposal of toxic waste, or a prohibitory injunction, *i.e.*, one that "restrains" a responsible party from further violating RCRA. Neither remedy, however, is susceptible of the interpretation adopted by the Ninth Circuit, as neither contemplates the award of past cleanup costs, whether these are denominated "damages" or "equitable restitution."

In this regard, a comparison between the relief available under RCRA's citizen suit provision and that which Congress has provided in the analogous, but not parallel, provisions of CERCLA is telling. CERCLA was passed several years after RCRA went into effect, and it is designed to address many of the same toxic waste problems that inspired the passage of RCRA. Compare 42 U.S.C. § 6903(5). (RCRA definition of "hazardous waste") and § 6903(27) (RCRA definition of "solid waste") with § 9601(14) (CERCLA provision incorporating certain "hazardous substance[s]," but specifically excluding petroleum). CERCLA differs markedly from RCRA, however, in the remedies it provides. CERCLA's citizen suit provision mimics § 6972(a) in providing district courts with the authority "to order such action as may be necessary to correct the violation" of any

CERCLA standard or regulation. 42 U.S.C. § 9659(c). But CERCLA expressly permits the Government to recover "all costs of removal or remedial action," § 9607(a)(4)(A), and it expressly permits the recovery of any "necessary costs of response, incurred by any . . . person consistent with the national contingency plan," § 9607(a)(4)(B). CERCLA also provides that "[a]ny person may seek contribution from any other person who is liable or potentially liable" for these response costs. *See* § 9613(f)(1). Congress thus demonstrated in CERCLA that it knew how to provide for the recovery of cleanup costs, and that the language used to define the remedies under RCRA does not provide that remedy.

That RCRA's citizen suit provision was not intended to provide a remedy for past cleanup costs is further apparent from the harm at which it is directed. Section 6972(a)(1)(B) permits a private party to bring suit only upon a showing that the solid or hazardous waste at issue "may present an imminent and substantial endangerment to health or the environment." The meaning of this timing restriction is plain: An endangerment can only be "imminent" if it "threaten[s] to occur immediately," Webster's New International Dictionary of English Language 1245 (2d ed.1934), and the reference to waste which "may present" imminent harm quite clearly excludes waste that no longer presents such a danger. As the Ninth Circuit itself intimated in *Price v. United States Navy,* 39 F.3d 1011, 1019 (1994), this language "implies that there must be a threat which is present now, although the impact of the threat may not be felt until later." It follows that § 6972(a) was designed to provide a remedy that ameliorates present or obviates the risk of future "imminent" harms, not a remedy that compensates for past cleanup efforts. Cf. § 6902(b) (national policy behind RCRA is "to minimize the present and future threat to human health and the environment").

Other aspects of RCRA's enforcement scheme strongly support this conclusion. Unlike CERCLA, RCRA contains no statute of limitations, compare § 9613(g)(2) (limitations period in suits under CERCLA § 9607), and it does not require a showing that the response costs being sought are reasonable, compare §§ 9607(a)(4)(A) and (B) (costs recovered under CERCLA must be "consistent with the national contingency plan"). If Congress had intended § 6972(a) to function as a cost-recovery mechanism, the absence of these provisions would be striking. Moreover, with one limited exception, *see Hallstrom v. Tillamook County,* 493 U.S. 20, 26-27 (1989) (noting exception to notice requirement "when there is a danger that hazardous waste will be discharged"), a private party may not bring suit under § 6972(a)(1)(B) without first giving 90 days' notice to the Administrator of the EPA, to "the State in which the alleged endangerment may occur," and to potential defendants, *see* §§ 6972(b)(2)(A)(i)-(iii). And no citizen suit can proceed if either the EPA or the State has commenced, and is diligently prosecuting, a separate enforcement action, *see* §§ 6972(b)(2)(B) and (C). Therefore, if RCRA were designed to compensate private parties for their past cleanup efforts, it would be a wholly irrational mechanism for doing so. Those parties with insubstantial problems, problems that neither the State nor the Federal Government feel compelled to address, could recover their response costs, whereas those parties whose waste problems were sufficiently severe as to attract the attention of Government officials would be left without a recovery.

Though it agrees that KFC's complaint is defective for failing properly to allege an "imminent and substantial endangerment," the Government (as amicus) nonetheless joins KFC in arguing that § 6972(a) does not in all circumstances preclude an award of past cleanup costs. The Government posits a situation in which suit is properly brought while the waste at issue continues to pose an imminent endangerment, and suggests that the plaintiff in such a case could seek equitable restitution of money previously spent on cleanup efforts. Echoing a similar argument made by KFC, the Government does not rely on the remedies expressly provided in § 6972(a), but rather cites a line of cases holding that district courts retain inherent authority to award any equitable remedy that is not expressly taken away from them by Congress.

RCRA does not prevent a private party from recovering its cleanup costs under other federal or state laws, *see* § 6972(f) (preserving remedies under statutory and common law), but the limited remedies described in § 6972(a), along with the stark differences between the language of that section and the cost recovery provisions of CERCLA, amply demonstrate that Congress did not intend for a private citizen to be able to undertake a cleanup and then proceed to recover its costs under RCRA. As we explained in *Middlesex County Sewerage Authority v. National Sea Clammers Assn.*, 453 U.S. 1, 14 (1981), where Congress has provided "elaborate enforcement provisions" for remedying the violation of a federal statute, as Congress has done with RCRA and CERCLA, "it cannot be assumed that Congress intended to authorize by implication additional judicial remedies for private citizens suing under" the statute. "'[I]t is an elemental canon of statutory construction that where a statute expressly provides a particular remedy or remedies, a court must be chary of reading others into it.'"

Without considering whether a private party could seek to obtain an injunction requiring another party to pay cleanup costs which arise after a RCRA citizen suit has been properly commenced, cf. *United States v. Price*, 688 F.2d 204, 211-213 (C.A.3 1982) (requiring funding of a diagnostic study is an appropriate form of relief in a suit brought by the Administrator under § 6973), or otherwise recover cleanup costs paid out after the invocation of RCRA's statutory process, we agree with the Meghrigs that a private party cannot recover the cost of a past cleanup effort under RCRA, and that KFC's complaint is defective for the reasons stated by the District Court. Section 6972(a) does not contemplate the award of past cleanup costs, and § 6972(a)(1)(B) permits a private party to bring suit only upon an allegation that the contaminated site presently poses an "imminent and substantial endangerment to health or the environment," and not upon an allegation that it posed such an endangerment at some time in the past. The judgment of the Ninth Circuit is reversed.

PROBLEM
CONGRESSIONAL MICROMANAGEMENT

RCRA was passed at a time when Congress did not trust the EPA to fulfill its intent. Therefore, Congress tried to be very specific in RCRA and to create new tools, like "hammers," to force EPA to act. Now that you have an intimate knowledge of the statute, what are the advantages and disadvantages of Congress' writing very specific environmental legislation? What are the implications for the balance of power among the branches of government?

Chapter 10

The Siting of Waste Treatment and Disposal Facilities: A RCRA Case Study

A. The Siting Dilemma in the United States

The United States has generated, and continues to do so, enormous quantities of hazardous waste. A substantial portion of that waste has been mismanaged–that is, disposed without any formal effort to determine the suitability of the location or disposal method–the result of which is the need for the Superfund program. RCRA attempts to address the disposal problem prospectively by requiring formal decisions regarding the methods and location of disposal. Unfortunately, the record in the United States of siting and opening new facilities to handle hazardous and radioactive waste has largely been one of failure. State after state has been unable to site new hazardous waste facilities; the situation with low-level radioactive waste is so bad that the entire interstate compact system created by the Low-Level Radioactive Waste Policy Act of 1985 is on the brink of disintegration.

This failure is typically blamed on the NIMBY or "Not In My Back Yard" reaction of citizens to the suggestion that they accept an environmental facility in their vicinity. The NIMBY reaction is widespread and has been successful in stopping most major efforts to site waste facilities. In fact, it can be described as among the most successful organizational efforts of grassroots politics in the last twenty years.[1] The

---

[1] *See* BRUCE WILLIAMS & ALBERT MATHENY, DEMOCRACY, DIALOGUE, AND EVIRONMENTAL DISPUTES: THE CONTESTED LANGUAGE OF SOCIAL REGULATION (1995); DIMENSIONS OF HAZARDOUS WASTE POLITICS AND POLICY (Charles E. Davis & James P. Lester, eds., 1988); DANIEL MAZMANIAN & DAVID MORELL, BEYOND SUPERFAILURE: AMERICA'S TOXIC POLICY FOR THE 1990s (1992); DAVID MORELL & CHRISTOPHER MAGORIAN, SITING HAZARDOUS WASTE FACILITIES: LOCAL OPPOSITION AND THE MYTH OF PREEMPTION (1982); KENT E. PORTNEY, SITING HAZARDOUS WASTE TREATMENT FACILITIES: THE NIMBY SYNDROME (1991); MICHAEL R. GREENBERG AND RICHARD F. ANDERSON, HAZARDOUS WASTE SITES: THE CREDIBILITY GAP (Center for Urban Policy

following excerpt offers the intriguing suggestion that the instinct of territoriality is a reason for the failure of hazardous waste siting in the United States.

TERRITORIALITY, RISK PERCEPTION, AND COUNTERPRODUCTIVE LEGAL STRUCTURES: THE CASE OF WASTE FACILITY SITING

Michael B. Gerrard
27 ENVTL. L. 1017, 1017-1030 (1997)

I. Introduction

Law is a civilizing influence, but it has limits. When law attempts to run against a fundamental human instinct or a deep prejudice, immense conflict is inevitable. This is well known in such areas as the regulation of conduct and racial integration. However, it does not seem to have been observed how territoriality, an innate human trait, has rendered certain important structures in environmental law wholly ineffective.

For more than twenty years, Congress has been passing and periodically fine-tuning laws designed to find sites for the disposal of hazardous and radioactive waste. Several billion dollars have been spent in this quest. For all this effort, in the last twenty years only two landfills for hazardous and radioactive waste have been built on new sites anywhere in the United States. Scores of other efforts have floundered.

This Article argues that a major reason for this failure is that the current system of environmental law unwittingly runs counter to the territorial instinct. This is an instinct that takes several forms, all revolving around the importance of borders. Outsiders–those on the other side of the border–should not be sending their trash into your territory, or telling you what to do. If they try, the natural, deep-seated reaction is to fight back.

* * *

II. Territoriality and the Urge for Self-Determination

Territoriality has been defined as "a behavioral phenomenon associated with the organization of space into spheres of influence or clearly demarcated territories which are made distinctive and considered at least partially exclusive by their occupants or definers."[2] Essential to the concept is that territories are defended from encroachment, by violence if necessary.

This phenomenon did not begin with human beings. Indeed, the biologist Edward O. Wilson has written that "nearly all vertebrates and a large number of the behaviorally most advanced invertebrates, conduct

---

Research 1984); THE POLITICS OF HAZARDOUS WASTE MANAGEMENT (James P. Lester & Ann O'M. Bowman 1983).

[2] EDWARD SOJA, THE POLITICAL ORGANIZATION OF SPACE 19 (1971)(quoted in DAVID SEAMON, A GEOGRAPHY OF THE LIFEWORLD 70-71 (1979)).

their lives according to precise rules of land tenure, spacing, and dominance. These rules mediate the struggle for competitive superiority."[3]

* * *

Mary Douglas, a cultural anthropologist who has spent many years studying risk perception, also writes of the importance of being inside or outside of a society. She tells us that some primitive cultures blame outsiders for what we see as natural disasters and that this blaming mechanism enhances internal loyalty.

* * *

III. Effect of Territoriality on Risk Perception

Since territoriality is lodged so deeply within the human psyche, it is not surprising that it affects (among many other things) the perception of risks. This has frequently been seen in the context of the siting of unwanted facilities. Many governments have tried to impose landfills, incinerators, and the like on lower units of government. Localities see these attempts as an invasion of local territory by a hostile outside force. As such, they are swiftly, and often effectively, repulsed. Efforts to override local authority usually backfire and increase local opposition, in part because these efforts increase the local perception of the facility's danger. Some studies have shown that people will accept voluntary risks approximately a thousand times more dangerous than risks they perceive as involuntarily imposed. An externally-imposed risk is an involuntary one, and thus much more feared (and fought).

This sense of hostile invasion amplifies the perception of risk in numerous contexts. People are more likely to oppose the siting of a social service facility (such as a homeless shelter or a group home) in their neighborhood if it will serve people from outside the community. If toxic substances are seen as entering someone's home, they violate the most sacred territory and evoke an exceptionally strong response.

* * *

Noted researchers Paul Slovic and others have used psychometric techniques involving detailed interviews, focus groups, and polls to measure the factors that go into the perception of risks from various hazards, especially proposed facilities. These studies have identified numerous such factors, and consistently among them are several that relate to territoriality (though not using that term), including the circumstances of the hazard's origin, whether the hazard is controlled by the respondent or by an outside force, and whether the hazard is equitably distributed.[4]

The point about equitable distribution is especially important. People react adversely to risks that they see as being unfairly imposed, especially if the beneficiaries of the activity do not share in the risk. Likewise, there

---

[3] EDWARD O. WILSON, SOCIOBIOLOGY 256 (1975).

[4] Some of Slovic's conclusions were presented in Chapter 2 (Toxicology and Risk Assessment), *supra.*—EDS.

is great resistance to paying the costs of cleaning up someone else's mess. This sense of unfairness is one of the major motivators of the environmental justice movement, many of whose leading voices favor local control under the banner of "empowerment" which connotes "enabling those who will have to live with the results of environmental decisions to be those who actually make the decisions."[5] It is no coincidence that individuals with egalitarian viewpoints and anti-hierarchical personalities have been shown to be especially adverse to technological risks.

IV. Law's Counterproductive Disregard for Territoriality

In the face of this compelling psychological evidence, much of it not only backed by solid information but much of it also intuitive, one would expect the legal system to try to accomplish its objectives with a minimum of unnecessary intrusion and other anti-territorial tactics. In the realm of waste facility siting, this would mean seeking disposal sites in communities that have volunteered for them, not compelling localities to take outsiders' waste, and seeking alternatives that do not involve siting new facilities at all.

Unfortunately, this is not what has happened. At least four aspects of our legal system for siting new facilities collide head-on with our deepest psychological impulses of territoriality. These four aspects are, the Commerce Clause, the use of the preemption doctrine, the framing of the issue as a locational problem, and the consideration of one waste stream at a time.

A. Commerce Clause

Hazardous waste is generated everywhere and it is constantly crossing state borders on its way to the cheapest or most suitable disposal spot. All fifty states export some hazardous waste to out-of-state treatment or disposal facilities and forty-eight states (all but Alaska and Montana) import hazardous waste.

Many states are very resentful about the importation of wastes into their borders. However, there is little they can do about it. The United States Supreme Court has consistently held that waste (whether solid or hazardous) is an item in interstate commerce and that, under the Commerce Clause of the U.S. Constitution, the states may not ban or tax either its export or its import.[6] Several bills have been introduced into

---

[5] Luke W. Cole, *Empowerment as the Key to Environmental Protection: The Need for Environmental Poverty Law*, 19 ECOLOGY L. Q. 619, 661 (1992). *See also* NICHOLAS FREUDENBERG, NOT IN OUR BACKYARDS!, COMMUNITY ACTION FOR HEALTH AND THE ENVIRONMENT 40 (1984). For a discussion of the role of geography in this context, *see* John J. Fahsbender, *An Analytical Approach to Defining the Affected Neighborhood in the Environmental Justice Context*, 5 N.Y.U. ENVTL. L.J. 120 (1996).

[6] *See generally* C & A Carbone, Inc. v. Town of Clarkstown, 511 U.S. 383 (1994) (holding that the town's flow control ordinance, which required all solid waste to be processed at a designated transfer station before leaving the municipality, violated the Commerce Clause because it deprives out-of-state competitors of access to the local market); Chemical

Congress to give states a limited right to regulate the interstate flow of municipal solid waste, but so far none have been enacted into law.

B. Preemption

The Supremacy Clause of the federal Constitution gives Congress the power to supersede state laws, though there are some limits on this authority. States have even greater control over municipalities. Local governments are not sovereigns and are traditionally seen as creatures of the states, with as much or as little autonomy as the states care to give them.

These preemptive powers are broadly exercised in the facility siting context. The federal government is (in legal theory) the sole decision maker in the siting of nuclear facilities. With respect to hazardous wastes, the principal federal statute, the Resource Conservation and Recovery Act (RCRA) cedes some authority to the states,[7] but this is significantly limited. At the state level, at least twenty-four states have laws that specifically override local zoning authority in the siting of hazardous waste facilities. Predictably, this external control over the placement of a much feared facility in a locality has often aroused tremendous resentment.

C. Locational Focus

The federal and state statutes and regulations governing the management of hazardous waste focus on where and how the waste should be disposed. They go into great detail on whether certain material falls within the hazardous waste regulatory scheme; if it does, it must be handled, treated, and disposed of in tightly defined ways.

There is very little regulatory attention paid to the creation of the waste, however. Though the Clean Air Act[8] and the Clean Water Act[9] impose elaborate regulatory control over the generation of air and water pollution, RCRA and other hazardous waste laws all but ignore this issue at the front end of the process and focus almost exclusively at the back end-disposal.[10] A great deal of discussion is now taking place concerning pollution prevention, but in the hazardous waste area, the programs have almost no regulatory teeth.

Waste Management, Inc. v. Hunt, 504 U.S. 334 (1992) (finding that an additional disposal fee imposed on out of state hazardous waste was an impermissible barrier on interstate commerce); Fort Gratiot Sanitary Landfill, Inc. v. Michigan Dep't of Natural Resources, 504 U.S. 353 (1992) (holding that a Michigan statute which prohibited private landfill owners from accepting solid waste that originated outside the county in which the facility is located unless authorized by the county's solid waste management plan, violated the provisions of the Commerce Clause); City of Philadelphia v. New Jersey, 437 U.S. 617 (1978) (finding outright bans on the importation of solid or liquid waste are constitutionally impermissible).

[7] See 42 U.S.C. § 6929.

[8] 42 U.S.C. §§ 7401-7671 (1994).

[9] 33 U.S.C. §§ 1251-1387 (1994).

[10] See, e.g., Resource Conservation and Recovery Act, 42 U.S.C. §§ 6901-6992k (1994).

If hazardous waste is created, it does indeed have to go somewhere. By implicitly assuming current levels of hazardous waste creation as a given, RCRA makes inevitable the focus on localities as the final resting place for this waste. This point has been strongly made by Robert W. Lake and L. Disch:

> By assuming private generation of toxic wastes and public jurisdiction for waste treatment and disposal, state hazardous waste policy inevitably leads to the necessity of finding sites for hazardous waste facilities. The basic assumptions of hazardous waste regulation define the hazardous waste problem as a locational problem for the state rather than a production problem for industry. This transformation enforces the externalization of wastes from the production process, translates an economic problem for capital into a political problem for the state, and insulates capital from the negative consequences of accumulation.[11]

The derogatory term "NIMBY" (not in my backyard) is an expression of this basic assumption that hazardous waste is inevitable, that it must go somewhere, and that those who resist its importation into their communities are selfish and irresponsible.

D. Focus on Individual Waste Types

There are dozens of types of waste streams. Each is regulated separately, with its own siting program (or non-program). Among non-radioactive materials, the different waste streams include 1) hazardous waste regulated under RCRA, 2) remedial waste from cleanup of civilian inactive hazardous waste sites, such as Superfund sites, 3) remedial waste from the cleanup of RCRA corrective action sites, 4) wastes from the removal or upgrading of underground storage tanks, 5) cleanup wastes from old military facilities, 6) obsolete chemical weapons requiring destruction, 7) asbestos, lead, PCBs, and other wastes from demolition of buildings and structures, 8) industrial, special and orphan wastes (often meeting some of the RCRA hazardous waste characteristics, but legally exempt), 9) mining wastes, 10) oil and gas extraction wastes, 11) sewage sludge 12) residue from air pollution control devices, 13) ash from incinerators, and 14) medical waste.

The radioactive wastes include 1) high-level waste and transuranic waste from nuclear weapons production, 2) spent fuel from nuclear reactors, 3) low-level radioactive waste from power plants and from medical, industrial, and scientific uses, 4) remedial waste from nuclear weapons production sites, 5) nuclear warheads facing retirement, 6) decommissioned nuclear power plants and nuclear fuel production facilities, 7) uranium mill tailings, 8) naturally-occurring radioactive materials, and 9) mixed radioactive/hazardous waste.

---

[11] R.W. Lake & L. Disch, *Structural Constraints and Pluralist Contradictions in Hazardous Waste Regulation,* 24 ENV'T & PLANNING 663, 671 (1992).

With this profusion of different waste types, it is easy for one state to feel that it handles an unfair share of the nation's RCRA hazardous waste disposal burden. For instance, if one state happens to have a large RCRA disposal facility, the state may feel that it is shouldering an unfair proportion of the nation's hazardous waste, while forgetting that other states are taking its radioactive waste, medical waste, sewage sludge, and all manner of other waste streams. The compartmentalization of disposal programs and laws fosters a sense of geographic inequity and leads to state rejection of offers from communities that have volunteered for certain facilities. Each state is sensitive to the few kinds of wastes that it takes in, but ignores the many more types of wastes that it exports.

V. Failed Efforts to Respect Territoriality

In the recent history of waste management in the United States, there have been several efforts to provide geographic equity and to reduce the forced importation of waste from one area into another. Most of these efforts have failed.

One such effort was the Superfund Amendments and Reauthorization Act of 1986 (SARA). Congress was concerned that most states were making little progress in siting new hazardous waste disposal facilities and that "Superfund money should not be spent in States that are taking insufficient steps to avoid the creation of future Superfund sites." In an effort "to solve the 'NIMBY' . . . problems that arose because of political pressure and public opposition," Congress therefore provided that, after October 17, 1989, no state would be eligible for Superfund assistance for remedial actions at hazardous waste sites unless it provided satisfactory assurances of "the availability of hazardous waste treatment or disposal facilities which . . . have adequate capacity for the destruction, treatment, or secure disposition of all hazardous wastes that are reasonably expected to be generated within the State" during the next twenty years.[12] These facilities could be within the state or outside it if there was an interstate agreement for its use.

Acting under this authority, the United States Environmental Protection Agency (EPA) required every state to submit a "capacity assurance plan" detailing the sources, quantities, and characteristics of the hazardous wastes generated within its borders and explaining how those wastes would be handled. Every state submitted a plan and EPA approved almost all of them, even where states relied on new facilities that were later rejected or on facilities in other states that opposed importation. There is no evidence, however, that the capacity assurance requirement has led to the initiation or approval of any new hazardous waste facilities, and EPA has all but abandoned the effort.

---

[12] Comprehensive Environmental Response, Compensation, and Liability Act of 1980 (CERCLA), 42 U.S.C. § 9604(c)(9)(A) (1994).

A second effort came in the Low-Level Radioactive Waste Policy Act of 1980 (LLRWPA).[13] This statute declared that the states, acting alone or in compacts with other states, were responsible for disposing of their own low-level radioactive waste (LLRW). The LLRWPA gave South Carolina, Nevada, and Washington, the only states then with operating LLRW disposal facilities, the power to exclude other states' waste after 1986. By 1985, little progress had been made in siting new LLRW facilities and Congress again stepped in with the Low-Level Radioactive Waste Policy Amendments Act of 1985. This new enactment extended the deadlines, provided interim milestones, and allowed the three sited states to exclude waste from states that missed the deadlines. It also provided that, in 1993, states that had not made provisions for the disposal of LLRW generated in their borders would have to "take title" to this waste, thereby assuming liability for damage that it causes.

In 1990, New York State, struggling to site a LLRW facility and acting under pressure of two counties tentatively designated as the location for a potential LLRW facility, challenged the constitutionality of the 1985 amendments. In 1992, the U.S. Supreme Court invalidated the "take title" provision as a violation of the state's rights under the Tenth Amendment, but upheld the balance of the statute.[14] The federal requirement that states site LLRW facilities has sparked enormous controversy all over the country and, to date, no facility sited under this process is anywhere near licensing, much less opening.

The third effort came in the Nuclear Waste Policy Act of 1982 (NWPA), which required the Department of Energy (DOE) to establish a system of "long term" or "permanent" deep geologic disposal facilities for both kinds of high-level radioactive waste (HLW)-waste from bomb production and spent fuel rods. The Act instructed DOE to recommend to the President three sites to be studied in depth. DOE eventually recommended Yucca Mountain, Nevada, Deaf Smith County, Texas, and Hanford, Washington. In 1986 President Reagan approved these three sites.

Just as the studies were about to begin, however, Congress stepped in. In a rider to a budget bill, Congress ordered DOE to halt any investigations of the Texas and Washington sites, to bypass the preliminary studies, and to put the HLW facility at Yucca Mountain.[15] In response, Nevada began a long campaign of litigation against the site. This campaign has not resulted in cancellation of the project, but it has disclosed many technical problems with the site and has considerably

---

[13] Low-Level Radioactive Waste Policy Act of 1980 (LLRWPA), 42 U.S.C. §§2011-2023 (1994).

[14] See New York v. United States, 505 U.S. 114 (1992) (holding that the Act's monetary and access incentive provisions are constitutionally permissible but that its "take title" provision transcends the scope of Congress's enumerated powers and therefore violates the 10th Amendment).

[15] See 42 U.S.C. § 10172(a) (1994).

delayed the project. Today that opening is not projected for another fifteen to twenty years at the earliest. The sense of procedural fairness that DOE so wanted to cultivate has utterly evaporated, and residents call the statute designating Yucca Mountain the "Screw Nevada Bill."

Why did all three of these efforts to achieve geographic equity in waste facility siting-the hazardous waste, LLRW, and HLW programs-fail? I believe a primary reason is that each of them dealt with only one type of waste stream, so that facilities would be needed in only a few states. This created a scramble for states to be excluded from this select group. The results of successful siting efforts would inevitably have been inequitable, with a few losing states and a lot of free riders.

The failure of these and other efforts to site new facilities has led to the extensive use of on-site treatment and disposal. This is arguably the most equitable method of all, because the waste ends up where it was generated. However, the locations may be very poor from an environmental and public health standpoint. Many factories and other waste generating facilities are located in population centers, near their labor force and markets, thus increasing human exposure to any harmful emissions from the disposal facility. Many factories were also sited years ago with little attention paid to whether the site was one which would minimize adverse environmental impacts.

VI. Toward a Reconciliation

* * *

A national program for allocating waste disposal facilities would have several advantages. If every state had at least one facility, and the larger states had the larger facilities, the states would have much less of a sense of regional unfairness. The larger states might have centralized facilities, taking a variety of waste streams and subjecting them to several different kinds of processes. Each kind of waste would be more likely to find its ideal treatment process. Such a comprehensive approach would also afford considerable economies of scale. Along these lines, several European nations-Denmark, Sweden, Finland, and the German states of Bavaria and Hessen-have successfully established centralized hazardous waste disposal facilities, as have the Canadian provinces of Alberta and Manitoba.

NOTES

1. Gerrard's theory is certainly intriguing, but is he "right"? That is, do you find this a convincing explanation for the extreme difficulty that the United States has had in siting chemical and radioactive waste facilities?

2. If territoriality is the problem, what is the solution? How should governments approach siting choices?

3. What other explanations are available instead of or in addition to territoriality? Do they suggest different approaches to siting?

4. In what sense is siting in the U.S. a *dilemma,* rather than, say, a failure of political will? What are the conflicting policies at work here?

B. The Canadian Experience[16]

As Gerrard points out, Canada has been more successful in siting hazardous waste facilities (although Canadians presumably share the instinct of territoriality). NIMBY problems have stopped hazardous waste facilities in Ontario, British Columbia, and in the Maritimes, but our neighbors are presently in the process of siting a low-level radioactive waste facility in Ontario, and they have already sited three major hazardous waste facilities in Quebec, Alberta, and Manitoba. Why have the Canadians succeeded where we have failed? The following excerpt suggests that the answer is an "assurance" approach.

PUBLIC CHOICE, ASSURANCE, AND ENVIRONMENTAL RISK

John Martin Gillroy
(unpublished monograph, 1993)

Hazardous waste and its disposal, as well as the resultant NIMBY reactions, are examples of individuals facing environmental risk within institutional political structures. Both the United States and Canada have federal democracies where central government shares power with sub-national units (states or provinces). In addition, the central governments of both nations are characterized by combinations of executive, legislative, and judicial branches, each with their respective duties in the political-legal environment.

In Canada, however, the "balance" of power is different.[17] First, Canadian federalism is unlike its counterpart in the United States in that the provincial governments have more jurisdiction and are equal partners with, or sometimes superior powers to, the federal government, especially in environmental matters. It is therefore more appropriate to understand Canadian federalism as twelve equal governmental units (eleven

---

[16] *See also* Barry G. Rabe *et al., NIMBY and Maybe: Conflict and Cooperation in Siting of Low-level Radioactive Waste Disposal Facilities in the United States and Canada,* 24 ENVTL. L. 67 (1994); John Martin Gillroy & Barry G. Rabe, *Environmental Risk And The Politics of Assurance: NIMBY Solutions in Canada,* (forthcoming). For more work in the theory and practice of assurance games and just facility siting, *see* John Martin Gillroy, *Moral Considerations and Public Policy Choice: Individual Autonomy and the NIMBY Problem,* 5 PUBLIC AFFAIRS QUARTERLY 319-31 (1991); Barry G. Rabe & John Martin Gillroy, *Intrinsic Value and Public Policy Choice: The Alberta Case,* in ENVIRONMENTAL RISK, ENVIRONMENTAL VALUES AND POLITICAL CHOICES, 150-70 (John Martin Gillroy ed., 1993); Barry G. Rabe, *Beyond NIMBY: Hazardous Waste Siting in Canada and the United States* (1994); and John Martin Gillroy, JUSTICE FROM AUTONOMY: ENVIRONMENTAL RISK AND A KANTIAN PARADIGM FOR ECOSYSTEM LAW & POLICY, 10 (forthcoming).

[17] *See generally* RAND DYCK, CANADIAN POLITICS: CRITICAL APPROACHES (1993); POLITICS: CANADA (Paul Fox & Graham White eds., 7th ed. 1991); STEPHEN BROOKS, PUBLIC POLICY IN CANADA: AN INTRODUCTION (2nd ed. 1993).

provincial and one federal) than as a system with a dominant federal government and less powerful sub-national units, as we have in the United States. Second, within the structure of both federal and provincial governments, the internal balance of power between legislative, executive, and judicial functions is more unitary in the Canadian system. The executive and legislative power is always in the hands of a single party and the judicial decisions have a tendency to increase executive authority in environmental matters. This streamlined governmental structure and the reality of equal federalism have combined to allow the executive in each province the freedom to design policy so that it both anticipates problems and responds to the specific demands of its constituents.

* * *

Canada, like the United States, grants considerable authority over hazardous waste facility siting to sub-national units of government. Prior to the late 1970s, most Canadian provinces had little or no policy that addressed hazardous waste management, much less siting. This changed rapidly during the 1980s, as provinces began to erect a wide variety of laws on hazardous waste and establish distinct approaches to the siting process. The unitary executive power in these provinces and the courts support of their discretion in environmental matters did not *guarantee* successful siting, however. Failed approaches ranged from near-complete control by provincial officials over every dimension of the siting process, to near-complete delegation over siting, to private corporations that attempted to entice local communities to accept new facilities. So perhaps it was not the institutional power relationships but the more consensual, less adversarial political culture of Canada[18] that is responsible for the siting success. But, if this were the case, siting would be more uniformly successful across provinces. In provinces such as British Columbia, Ontario, and Saskatchewan, highly adversarial politics continue, transcending any capacity of a more consensual political culture to dampen conflict when an issue as volatile as hazardous waste facility siting is under consideration. If anything, Canadian politics is generally moving in the more litigious, adversarial direction of American politics, thereby dampening any overriding impact of its distinctive socio-cultural attributes.

---

[18] George Holberg, *Governing the Commons: Environmental Policy in* CANADA AND THE UNITED STATES *in,* CANADA AND THE UNITED STATES IN A CHANGING WORLD (Richard Simeon & Keith Banting, eds., forthcoming). CHRISTOPHER LEMAN, THE COLLAPSE OF WELFARE REFORM: POLITICAL INSTITUTIONS, POLICY AND THE POOR IN CANADA AND THE UNITED STATES (1980); *See, e.g.,* SEYMOUR MARTIN LIPSET, NATIONAL PLANNING ASSOCIATION, CONTINENTAL DIVIDE: THE VALUES AND INSTITUTIONS OF THE UNITED STATES AND CANADA (1989); Alastair R. Lucas, *The New Environmental Law in* CANADA: THE STATE OF THE FEDERATION (Ronald L. Watts & Douglas M. Brown. eds.) (1989); RICHARD M. MERELMAN, PARTIAL VISIONS: CULTURE AND POLITICS IN BRITAIN, CANADA AND THE UNITED STATES (1991).

The cases of Canadian siting conflict suggest that the prevailing approaches to siting, utilized in both Canada and the United States, are unlikely to work not because of culture but because of a failure to design processes that mitigate conflict and encourage cooperation. Earlier analyses that advocated either greater sub-national controls over local opposition or near-exclusive reliance on economic incentives to entice local assent proved overly simplistic when attempted in various provinces during the 1980s. As a result, Ontario floundered in its efforts to use strong bureaucratic pressure to impose a comprehensive disposal facility on various communities, and became increasingly dependent on exporting waste to Quebec. In turn, periodic efforts by private corporations in British Columbia to approach potential host communities were quickly thwarted, making illegal dumping and the search for export markets its primary waste disposal strategy. Other provinces, such as Saskatchewan, suffered reactions similar to those of British Columbia and largely abandoned hope for siting agreements although private corporations remain free to approach and attempt to entice individual communities into an agreement.

In contrast, the experiences of the three provinces that attained major siting pacts in the past decade suggests that use of a combination of centralized executive/legislative power with decentralized citizen involvement allows them to synthesize a new combination of anticipatory and responsive policy that can be called the "politics of assurance."

Quebec and Alberta opened new hazardous waste facilities in the 1980s and Manitoba opened a site in 1994. These facilities are Canada's initial movement toward a waste management system that will handle their hazardous waste well into the next century. These facilities use the best new technology available and replace the mix of open dumps, landfills, and incineration stations that characterize Canadian and the United States' hazardous waste disposal. Although many of these old-type facilities continue in use, at least three Canadian provinces [will] move into a new era when the modern sites come on line.[19]

Quebec

The first successful siting involves the Stablex Canada Inc. facility in Blainville, Quebec. Local residents endorsed this hazardous waste facility in 1981 and it opened for business in early 1983. It was designed to become the central facility for handling the entire province's hazardous waste and has since become the dominant actor in this arena.

In the late 1970s, upon revelation of haphazard waste disposal procedures and extensive contamination of provincial water supplies, the provincial government moved to site a new and larger central hazardous waste facility. Provincial officials applied various siting criteria to narrow consideration to a list of 13 potentially acceptable sites. Officials

---

[19] DOUG MACDONALD, THE POLITICS OF POLLUTION: WHY CANADIANS ARE FAILING THEIR ENVIRONMENT (1991).

designated the Montreal-area communities of Blainville, Laval, and Mascouche as particularly promising. Laval and Mascouche responded with strong local opposition that led the province to drop them from further consideration. However, the Blainville City Council expressed interest in the proposal and passed a resolution in September 1980 that invited the province to explore the matter further. After numerous public meetings and the formation of a variety of local committees to study the matter, strong local support for the project was evident in the community of 12,000 residents located 46 kilometers northwest of Montreal.

The province selected Stablex to construct and operate a facility for inorganic waste, employing the Sealosafe technology that the firm uses in numerous sites in Western Europe. This approach converts inorganic hazardous liquids, sludges, and solid wastes into a solid, stable product that resembles concrete and is placed in a landfill. The Stablex facility lacks the capacity of the Alberta facility (considered next) to incinerate wastes, conduct certain treatment functions, or handle organic wastes such as polychlorinated biphenyls (PCBs), but it has the capacity to solidify and landfill more than 70,000 metric tons of inorganic hazardous wastes each year.

Alberta

Following a radical transformation of the provincial siting process, Alberta opened the Swan Hills Special Waste Treatment Center in September 1987. Site proposals advanced by private corporations in the late 1970s met outraged local resistance in the communities of Fort Saskatchewan and Two Hills, making the prospects for any future agreement seem limited at best. In response, the Alberta environmental ministry declared a moratorium on future siting and established a committee to review the provincial siting process and propose reforms.

This resulted in a siting process that involved the province in extensive new ways, contrary to earlier policy whereby private corporations dominated the process. Alberta established a crown corporation (a publicly-held enterprise, quite common in Canada) to manage any major waste facility jointly with a private corporation that would be selected by the province.[20] It also developed a comprehensive program for educating the public and considered siting only in communities that volunteered as site candidates and then met provincial environmental standards. After a multi-layered process of consultation with varying local governmental jurisdictions, 5 communities came forward as potential site hosts. A community of 2,500 residents located 209 kilometers northwest of Edmonton, Swan Hills was selected in 1984 after a plebiscite in which 79% of its voters supported the facility proposal.

---

[20] *See* JEANNE KIRK LAUX & MAUREEN APPEL MOLOT,. STATE CAPITALISM: PUBLIC ENTERPRISE IN CANADA (1988).

The Swan Hills Waste Treatment Center is the most comprehensive waste disposal facility in North America, with [the] capacity to incinerate organic liquids and solids, treat inorganic liquids and solids, and landfill contaminated bulk solids. It has a potential capacity of more than 100,000 metric tons of hazardous waste annually, adequate to cover the vast majority of hazardous wastes generated in Alberta each year. It is designed as part of a comprehensive waste management program which includes regional transfer stations and an extensive program that promotes waste recycling and on-site waste reduction. This effort to reduce the total volume of waste requiring treatment at the Center is the most far-reaching of any Canadian province, making prevention a central part of the provincial waste management strategy. The Center enjoys wide support among local residents and proposes a major expansion of its capacity to dispose of organic wastes.

Manitoba

The successful Alberta approach served as a model for Manitoba's comprehensive efforts to design a siting process that will gain public support and meet long-term provincial needs in hazardous waste management. Manitoba's relatively smaller population and manufacturing base generate lesser volumes and diversity in the types of wastes that require treatment and disposal, leading the province to seek a somewhat more modest version of the facility in operation at Swan Hills.

The Manitoba siting approach involved extensive public consultation and emphasizes that only communities that actively seek consideration as site hosts will be considered. It established a three-phase process beginning with public involvement to discuss facility-types and requirements, develop siting criteria, and screen out areas inappropriate for site location. This was followed by extensive public education and outreach efforts that were even broader than those used in Alberta. They were intended to build support for the facility and encourage eligible communities to explore the possibility of accepting a site.

Five communities expressed strong initial interest in hosting the facility but two of these withdrew from contention after referenda were narrowly defeated. In September 1991, 67% of the voters in a referendum held in the town of Montcalm approved construction of a major waste disposal facility for the province. Organizers completed the licensing procedures and began construction in the Fall of 1993. The facility opened in 1994.

The host community consists of approximately 1,700 residents and 75 percent of the eligible voters participated in the referendum. The proposed facility has also received "visible and vocal" support from all surrounding communities. The facility will be located in the center of the second most industrial area of the province. As in Alberta, a crown corporation will play an active role in site construction and long-term management, while the province will hold title to all land upon which the facility will be built.

C. New Approaches in the United States

In contrast to Canada, the siting of new hazardous and radioactive waste facilities is not successful in the United States. The distinctions between the two approaches will be highlighted in the next section. Here we analyze the siting approach in the United States, using the proposed site in Ward Valley, California as a case study.

The United States government's main source of statutory authority over the siting of hazardous waste disposal and treatment facilities is RCRA,[21] and RCRA grants to states the authority to site toxic and hazardous waste facilities. Congress incorporated only two specific siting standards-the seismic zone standard[22] and the floodplains standard[23]-both of which are designed to protect ground water. Thus, they merely establish criteria for siting a hazardous waste disposal facility, rather than deciding where a facility should be located.

States handle all other aspects of siting facilities as part of their delegated authority to implement a waste management program, as explained in Chapter 9, *supra*, and many states have legislation that addresses the siting of hazardous waste disposal and treatment facilities. Most state statutes governing the site selection process provide for: establishment of a state siting board or commission, procedures to designate areas suitable for siting, guidelines for public participation, and a determination of the level of local authority. While the state siting board designates the suitability of sites, the local community is most affected by the decision. Therefore, the level of authority afforded to the local governments is critical to the success of siting.[24]

Maryland expressly preempts local authority in its siting statute.[25] It provides for the issuance of a "certificate of public necessity" which

---

[21] Although RCRA is the main source of statutory authority governing the siting of hazardous waste facilities, the issuance of a permit for a new facility is also influenced by other environmental protection statutes. For example, the EPA Administrator is required to insure that the proposed facility will not conflict with or jeopardize the statutory purposes of the National Historic Preservation Act, the Endangered Species Act, or the Coastal Zone Management Act. The EPA Regional Administrator must also consult with the state agency with jurisdiction over wildlife resources in compliance with the Fish and Wildlife Coordination Act.

[22] *See* 40 C.F.R. § 264.18(a)(1).

[23] *See* 40 C.F.R. § 270.14(b)(11)(iii).

[24] *See* Township of Cascade v. Cascade Resource Recovery, Inc., 325 N.W.2d 500, 504 (Mich.1982).

[25] *See* MD. CODE ANN., NAT. RES. §§ 3-705, 3-795 (1989) (transferred to MD. CODE ANN., ENV'T §§ 7-41 through 7-413 (1999). *Accord* UTAH CODE ANN. § 19-6-206 (1985). There is rarely any question that states have this authority over their municipalities. In Clermont Environmental Reclamation Co. v. Wiederhold, 442 N.E.2d 1278, 1281 (Ohio 1982), the Ohio Supreme Court reasoned that the management of hazardous wastes was a matter of "statewide concern" which necessitated the preemption of local authority. The Supreme Court of North Carolina, in Granville County Bd of Comm'rs v. N.C. Hazardous Waste Management Comm'n, 407 S.E.2d 785, 790 (N.C. 1991), also recognized that the management of hazardous wastes was an "extremely urgent problem" and therefore the

outlines the description of the site, location of all facilities, and describes buffer and security areas. Once issued, the certificate of public necessity "exempts the site, the design, construction, and operation of the facilities on the site, and the transportation of hazardous [wastes] . . . from any regulation, policy, law, or ordinance, including zoning, . . . and from any other State law or regulation that requires approval of any political subdivision of [the] state."[26]

In contrast, Florida's siting act allows the political subdivisions of the state to review the proposed site to determine whether the proposed facility will comply with local ordinances.[27] The potential permittee may seek a variance (if necessary) from the local regulations. If the variance is denied by local authorities, the Governor may grant the variance of local regulations if she finds that the facility "will not have a significant adverse impact on the environment" or the "economy of the region."[28]

Another group of states increases local involvement in the siting process by incorporating negotiation between the community and the developer in their siting statutes. The Massachusetts siting statute adopts a process of negotiated compensation between the developer and concerned communities.[29] The state legislature was concerned over increased out of state transportation costs associated with out of state disposal and over illegal dumping. It also hoped the statute would avoid the impasse with local governments and communities that had doomed past siting attempts. The Statute creates a local assessment committee that represents the "interests of the host community" in the negotiation with the developers of the proposed facility.[30] The committee is empowered to negotiate terms of a siting agreement that protect the health and economy of the community and to enter into a binding contract with the developer.[31] The committee negotiates technical operational issues as well as political and economic concerns. A Hazardous Waste Facility Site Safety Council (Council) is responsible for overseeing the negotiation process, assists in the exchange of information between the parties, and determines whether an impasse in negotiation exists, requiring binding arbitration.

The Massachusetts act has been criticized for its failure to site any hazardous waste disposal facilities since it was enacted in 1980. Approximately nineteen other states have adopted negotiation statutes

---

court "should be reluctant to interfere until the administration's decision has been finalized."

[26] MD. CODE ANN., ENV'T § 7-405(d)(1) (1999).

[27] FLA. STAT. ANN. § 403.723. (1993).

[28] *Id.* § 403.723(7)(a)&(b).

[29] *See* MASS. GEN. LAWS ANN. Ch. 21D, §§ 1-19 (1999) and WIS. STAT.§§ 289.33 (1999). *See specifically* MASS. GEN. LAWS ANN. CH. 21D § 5 & 13.

[30] MASS. GEN. LAWS ANN. Ch. 21D, § 5 (1999).

[31] *Id.* § 12.

with similar results.[32] What do you think accounts for the striking lack of success of these well-intentioned and often highly sophisticated plans?

One explanation is that reliance on compensation as a means of assuaging public concern over safety and health is misplaced. The Massachusetts and Wisconsin statutes assumed that the local community will agree to a facility if the monetary compensation is great enough. Charges could be applied to the developer to mitigate any impacts of the facility to the community and to compensate the host community for risks associated with the facility. In fact, however, compensation does little to *resolve* public health concerns and may in fact heighten concerns because it is perceived as a bribe by the developer. Compensation is only productive if the community is convinced that the facility will not pose a hazard to the health of the public, or at least can be designed in such a way. These and other issues were raised in the attempt to locate a low-level radioactive waste facility in Ward Valley, California.[33]

Ward Valley, California, lies in the Mojave Desert, in the southeastern corner of California, just north of the Colorado River. At first glance, it appears to be a wasteland, but in fact the Mojave is a thriving ecosystem that is prime habitat for the endangered desert tortoise, the kit fox, jack-rabbits, rattlesnakes, and lizards. Ward Valley itself is a gently sloping area of relatively virgin desert covered by cactus, yucca, creosote, and burrosush. It is bisected by Interstate 40, providing easy access to the site. The area has been seismically stable, the depth to the water table is nearly seven hundred feet, and the valley receives between four and six inches of rainfall per year. In short, Ward Valley seemed an ideal location for a low-level radioactive waste site.

The Low-Level Radioactive Waste Policy Act of 1980,[34] required all states to develop their own low-level waste disposal facilities and imposed time constraints for compliance. In 1985, Congress revised the legislation when it became apparent that the original act lacked sufficient incentive

---

[32] *See* Michael B. Gerrard, WHOSE BACKYARD, WHOSE RISK: FEAR AND FAIRNESS IN TOXICS AND NUCLEAR WASTE SITING 129 (1994).

[33] Sources for this case study include California Radioactive Materials Mgt. Forum v. Dep't of Health Services, 19 Cal. Rptr.2d 357 (Cal. Ct. App. 1993); Todd Woody, *Critics of the Ward Valley Dump Have Reopened the Fight by Exposing the Hazards of Burying Radioactive Waste in the Desert*, THE RECORDER, Feb. 21, 1996, at 1; Barry G. Rabe, *et. al.*, *NIMBY and Maybe: Conflict Facilities in the United States and Canada*, 24 ENVTL. L. 67, 83 (1994); GUIDANCE TO THE UNITED STATES ECOLOGY ON DISPOSAL TECHNOLOGY, DEP'T OF HEALTH SERVICES, WESTLAW, BUSINESS WIRE, Dec. 5, 1988, *Groups Object to Califonria Disposal Site; Proposed Operator Says Safeguards Adequate*; 21 ENVTL. RPTR, No. 32, 1528, Dec. 7, 1990; *Three Candicate Sites Selected for Low-Level Radioactive Waste Disposal,* WESTLAW, BUSINESS WIRE, Feb. 19, 1987; *Low-Level Radioactifve Waste Disposal Site to be Near Needles,* WESTLAW, BUSINESS WIRE, MAR. 16, 1988, *Three Candidate Sites Selected for Low-Level Radioactive Waste Disposal,* WESTLAW, BUSINESS WIRE, Feb. 18, 1987; Ron Roach, § 3 DESERT SITES SELECTED FOR NUCLEAR WASTE DUMP, SAN DIEGO TRIBUNE, Feb. 19, 1987, at A3.

[34] Low-Level Hazardous Waste Policy Act of 1980, Pub. L. No. 96-573, 94 Stat. 3347 (repealed 1986).

for states to develop disposal sites. The Low-Level Radioactive Waste Policy Act Amendments of 1985 (LLRWPAA)[35] permitted the few states with operating facilities to charge high fees to other states wishing to use them. It also encouraged states to join compacts to share responsibility for disposal. Any state or compact failing to develop a new facility before a specified date could be excluded from the existing repositories and would be forced by the act to take title to all waste generated within their borders.[36]

California attempted to comply with the Low-Level Radioactive Waste Policy Act. In 1982, the California Legislature approved a bill which required the state to establish its own permanent low-level radioactive waste disposal facility.[37] The legislation placed the responsibility for developing such a facility in the Department of Health Services (DHS). DHS was required to promulgate regulations for the licensing and operation of the proposed facility and to plan for the interim storage of low-level waste material until the facility could be opened.

The DHS solicited bids from contractors interested in developing and operating California's proposed disposal facility. Although four companies submitted bids, three dropped out because of substantial pre-construction investments required by the state. Despite some official recommendations against them, the only remaining firm, US Ecology, was selected by DHS in 1985. US Ecology operates two of the three commercial low-level repositories still in operation in the U.S. US Ecology's job would be to guide the new facility through the state licensing process, design and build the actual repository, operate it over its projected thirty-year life span, oversee its closure, and monitor the area following closure to check for leaks and migration of contaminants. First, however, US Ecology would have to select a site and navigate the political obstacles to construction.

The LLRWPAA offers no guidance for selecting a site appropriate for radioactive waste disposal. California chose a rationalistic method whereby the state would pick potential locations, inform the selected communities that one of them would become the home of low-level radioactive waste for the next several thousand years, and eventually select the disposal site.

US Ecology's most important criterion for siting a facility was remoteness, both to reduce risk and to avoid opposition. Remoteness, however, creates its own problems. Easy access to the site by transporters is very important to minimize costs and to reduce the amount of overland

---

[35] Low-Level Radioactive Waste Policy Act Amendments of 1985, 42 U.S.C. §§ 2021b-2021j (1988).

[36] The constitutionality of this take title provision would later be challenged and overturned in New York v. United States, 505 U.S. 144 (1992), setting the stage for lengthy nationwide delays in the siting and development of new low-level disposal facilities.

[37] Calif. A.B. 1513 (1982).

travel required to reach the facility. Nearby transportation conduits, such as major highways and railroads, are thus valuable assets. Remoteness also presents staffing problems. Any facility requires people to run it, so the ideal location requires a balance between having neighbors too close and having employees too far away. Urban and suburban areas would have populations that were too large to provide this balance, so the search came down to choosing the right rural location.

US Ecology's experience at the Richland and Beatty facilities-and common sense-suggested that arid sites are preferable to moist ones. Water is the main way that radioactivity could be carried offsite, and surface and groundwater are principal objects of the protective measures to prevent release from the facility. Moisture in the soil itself is detrimental to radioactive waste storage. Both Maxey Flats and West Valley experienced serious problems because of the high moisture content in the soils at those sites. US Ecology sought to find locations with coarse, dry soils which would shed moisture quickly and prevent rainwater and runoff from collecting around the waste. By contrast, the Beatty facility, located in the desert on the western side of Nevada, was believed to be a nearly ideal location from the standpoint of annual rainfall. Finding a similar dry area in California would be relatively easy, given the vast amounts of desert in the eastern half of the state.

Although migration of radioactivity can be minimized with good engineering, it cannot be eliminated completely over the long term. Therefore, the depth to the water table became an important site selection criterion. US Ecology wanted to find the deepest possible water table that was covered by stable geology. This stability was almost as important as the depth to the water table because a dense layer of impervious rock would help prevent contaminated water from ever reaching the table below. Finding stable geology in California's fractured landscape can be a real challenge, however, so US Ecology sought areas with a history of the least and mildest seismic activity.

Physical criteria were not the only considerations. Community support, even in remote areas, would be essential for ultimate success. DHS and US Ecology, assisted by Hill & Knowlton, a national public relations company with local offices in San Francisco, devised a Citizen's Advisory Committee to help choose a site. They publicized the project and distributed a guidebook that provided information about the selection process, as well as current practices in low-level radioactive waste disposal practices.

This process led to the creation of eighteen locations that fit the initial siting criteria. In 1987, two years after being hired, US Ecology announced that they had narrowed the list to three finalists. Ward Valley, a section of the Mojave Desert located between the Turtle and Old Woman mountain ranges, just over twenty miles west of the town of Needles, was the first choice. Also selected were the Silurian Valley, fifteen miles north of Baker, and Panamint Valley, thirty miles north of

Trona, all in the desert southeast of California. The selection of Ward Valley as the final choice followed further analysis of technical considerations and recommendations from local advisory committees established in each community.

Because the process had been covered thoroughly in the media, the initial reaction to Ward Valley was favorable. US Ecology had spent a great deal of time in the finalist community providing awareness of safety and of economic development resulting from the facility. Local residents in Needles welcomed the project because it represented a substantial boost to their economy from new jobs. Other California communities were happy that the new site was "not in their backyards." The NIMBY syndrome seemed to have been averted at Ward Valley because the site was located in a relatively uninhabited area of the desert and because US Ecology had done the essential preparatory work to encourage acceptance.

During the site selection process the governor of California was actively involved in negotiations with other states to join a regional waste disposal compact. According to the LLRWPAA, states belonging to compacts would be permitted to exclude non-member states from their facility.[38] In addition, the system of rotating host states would prevent any one member from being saddled with all the waste forever. California's progress in finding a site and working towards licensing made it a very attractive partner for other states. Eventually Arizona, North Dakota and South Dakota joined California to become the Southwest Regional Compact. The California Legislature approved the union and pursuant to the LLRWPAA, Congress quickly ratified the compact.

The proposed site for the repository covers nearly seventy acres of public land controlled by the Bureau of Land Management (BLM). Transfer of the Ward Valley site could be accomplished by the swipe of the pen from the Secretary of the Interior and the California State Land Commission. The federal government and the State of California were cooperating in a long standing land swap, and Ward Valley could have been transferred without cost by simple agreement between the two parties. This simple transfer, however, has been the source of most of the delays surrounding the Ward Valley controversy. Although other licensing and development activities have occurred, the land transfer still has not been completed.

Initially, few groups came forward to oppose the Ward Valley facility. As US Ecology prepared its license application, DHS sponsored hearings in Needles, Los Angeles, and in Sacramento to hear public comment and to answer questions about the development. The license application consisted of complying with the California Environmental Quality Act (CEQA), the state equivalent of the National Environmental Protection Act (NEPA). CEQA required US Ecology to prepare an Environmental Impact Report, which would be submitted along with the

---

[38] *See* 42 U.S.C. § 2021e(f)(1)(B)(ii).

license application and reviewed by DHS. In December 1989, DHS deemed US Ecology's application complete. The department reviewed the application in detail and published it for public review and comment. At this point hopes were high that the license application would be quickly approved and that construction of the facility would begin. The repository would be operating by 1992 if everything went according to schedule. It didn't.

In 1990, Secretary of the Interior Manuel Lujan designated the desert tortoise a threatened species under the Endangered Species Act (ESA). The Secretary did not, however, designate a critical habitat. In January 1993, just before leaving office, Secretary Lujan attempted to transfer the Ward Valley land from the BLM to the State of California. His efforts were blocked by a coalition of nuclear activists who filed suit in the United States District Court for the Northern District of California.[39] The plaintiffs obtained a temporary restraining order blocking the land transfer and an injunction from subsequent transactions until the Secretary designated a critical habitat. Shortly thereafter, incoming Secretary Bruce Babbitt agreed to designate the tortoise habitat and the plaintiffs agreed to dismiss the suit without prejudice. The final rule declaring the habitat was issued in February 1994, and it included Ward Valley.

As the comment period for US Ecology's application continued, opposition from environmental groups started to grow. Although the earlier Citizen's Advisory Committee meetings were attended by groups such as the Sierra Club, Native American Heritage Foundation, and League of Women Voters (all of whom contributed significantly to the selection of the most appropriate site) other environmental groups began to challenge the process. The hearings became heated debates concerning the safety of the proposed facility, US Ecology's blemished safety record at their other facilities, the suitability of the location, and technical specifications of the site.

As the issues gathered greater media coverage they became highly politicized. Following the 1992 state senatorial elections, the California Senate was Democratically controlled. This majority was blocking Republican Governor Pete Wilson's candidate for Secretary of DHS. As a compromise to speed along confirmation, Wilson's candidate agreed to hold adjudicatory hearings over the licensing of the Ward Valley site. Following this agreement, US Ecology and the California Radioactive Materials Forum filed suit in State Court against DHS and the Senate Rules Committee, alleging that the formal review was unnecessary for the license agreement and that the deal between the Rules Committee and DHS was an unconstitutional abuse of power without legislative authorization. The state court of appeals agreed, voiding the agreement and allowing DHS to review the license application without formal

---

[39] *See* Bay Area Nuclear Waste Coalition v. Lujan, 42 F.3d 1398 (9th Cir. 1994)(unpublished).

administrative hearings.[40] Several months later, in September 1993, DHS granted US Ecology its license to develop Ward Valley.

The land transfer from BLM was forthcoming, however. Following the license approval, several scientists from the United States Geological Survey (USGS) reported that the Beatty, Nevada disposal facility run by US Ecology had leaked radioactive material to within several feet of the water table. The report noted that the geological and meteorological conditions at Beatty, including the depth to the water table, were nearly identical to Ward Valley. US Ecology's early studies indicated that migration of radioactive materials below the surface of both facilities would be only a few inches or feet every thousand years, so by the time any material could make it to the water table it would have radiologically decayed below harmful levels. The USGS scientists were asking how the US Ecology predictions could have been so wrong.

Consequently, in February 1996, Secretary Babbitt announced that he would not transfer the Ward Valley land until more testing of the site could be accomplished. Nearly identical bills in both the House and Senate sought to bypass the Secretary's requirements and force the transfer of over 1000 acres to the State of California. In addition, in 1995 the Fort Mojave Indian Tribe had sought to revoke the DHS license because DHS violated the CEQA.[41] While the trial court denied the petition on all substantive grounds, the judge set the approvals aside and required that US Ecology's application be reconsidered in light of the USGS report. Both parties immediately appealed. In October the Court of Appeals reversed the trial court's decision and directed that the petition be denied.[42] The California Supreme Court refused to hear the case, clearing the way, it was believed, to finally transferring the Ward Valley land from BLM to the State of California.

Babbitt, however, has consistently declined to make the transfer and halted work on the transfer until its legality, challenged by opponents in the California legislature, has been resolved. In March 1999, a federal court ruled that facility proponents could not force Babbitt to transfer the land.[43] This may or may not be the death knell of the Ward Valley site, as some have suggested,[44] but it certainly means that approval is still a long way off, if ever. "The future of Ward Valley now lies in the hands of California's new governor, Gray Davis, a past critic of the facility."[45]

---

[40] *See* California Radioactive Materials Mgt. Forum v. Dep't. of Health Services, 15 Cal. App. 4th 841, 19 Cal. Rptr. 2d 357 (Cal Ct. App. 1993).

[41] *See* Fort Mojave Indian Tribe v. California Dep't. of Health Services, 45 Cal. Rptr. 2d 822, 826 (Cal. Ct. App. 1995).

[42] Fort Mojave Indian Tribe v. California Dep't. of Health Services, 45 Cal. Rptr. 2d 822, 826 (Cal. Ct. App. 1995).

[43] California Dep't. of Health Services v. Babbitt, 46 F.Supp. 2d 13 (D.D.C. 1999).

[44] *See* Carolyn Whetzel, *Radioactive Waste: No Federal Duty to Release Ward Valley Land to California, U.S. District Court Rules*, 29 ENVT. REP. (BNA) 2414 (1999).

[45] *Id.*

It has been nearly two *decades* since California first set out to comply with the Low-Level Radioactive Waste Policy Act of 1980. Since then repeated deadlines for opening low-level radioactive waste disposal facilities have come and gone and not a single state or regional compact has opened a site. After all this time not a single piece of waste has been placed in a new permanent disposal facility. In California and other states, waste generation continues at its normal pace, and generators of low-level radioactive waste continue to stockpile it in temporary facilities like warehouses and parking lots. Whether or not Ward Valley is a good site or not-what do *you* think?-it should not take twenty years of unpredictable administrative, legislative, judicial, and political activity to reach a conclusion. What went wrong at Ward Valley, and by extension in all of the other unsuccessful siting attempts?

D. The Assurance vs. the Prisoners' Dilemma Approach

The Canadian and U.S. approaches to siting differ in their success rates, and in several other respects as well. Before you turn to the next reading, you might ask yourself whether you have reached any tentative explanations of the differences between the siting success in our two neighboring, industrialized, culturally similar countries.

The following excerpt continues Professor Gillroy's study of the Canadian and U.S. approaches to facility siting. He characterizes the former as an "assurance" approach and the latter as a "prisoners' dilemma" approach.

PUBLIC CHOICE, ASSURANCE, AND ENVIRONMENTAL RISK

John Martin Gillroy
(unpublished monograph, 1993)

[46]

The Prisoners' Dilemma Process

Both of the traditional approaches to siting in the U.S.-run by the state in a centralized and authority-driven manner, and the use of decentralized market incentives to provide facilities-fail because both frame the issue as a prisoner's dilemma. That is, it becomes a private confrontation between welfare-maximizing consumers, and it is assumed that each agent is an egoistic welfare maximizer preferring to exploit the cooperation of the others so that they might enjoy any collective goods produced by the society without having to pay for them. This characterization of the strategic situation leads to the four-step siting process that has generated intense NIMBY reactions and has therefore shown little siting success.

1. *Feasibility Study*: The first task of those wanting to site a facility in a prisoner's dilemma atmosphere, is to employ experts (engineers, bureaucrats, and scientists) to decide what type of facility is necessary and what type of geography is best suited for its construction.

2. *Siting Short List*: The next step is to survey the communities within one's jurisdiction in order to pick three to five that have a compatible geography for site construction.

3. *Public Participation*: Once the short list is compiled, then an announcement of its contents is made to the public and general meetings are arranged by the experts to provide information to these communities on the details of the site they are being asked to host.

---

[46] Gary Oliver, *Vermont Sierran,* VT. SIERRA CLUB, Sep. 1999, at 5.

4. *Economic Compensation*: The experts will provide a package of economic benefits which will become the centerpiece to "sell" the site to one of the short list communities.

Taken as a whole, the assumption in this process is that no one will want the site, so large economic compensation packages must be offered to elevate the welfare benefits of the site over and above the potential cost (or risk). This further assumes we are dealing with consumers and not citizens, with individuals who have no other ends but their own material welfare and who want nothing other than to move the site to someone else's back yard unless they are suitably compensated.[47]

THE PRISONERS' DILEMMA

The prisoners' dilemma is a set of incentives based on the following hypothetical: Two prisoners, who are suspected to have collaborated in the same crime, are arrested. The prosecutor tells each that he will receive the lightest sentence if he confesses and implicates his friend, the heaviest if he does not confess and his friend confesses, and intermediate sentences if neither confesses or if both confess, as in the following matrix (A's sentence, B's sentence):

	A confesses	*A does not confess*
B confesses	(5, 5)	(10, 1)
B does not confess	(1, 10)	(2, 2)

The essence of the prisoners' dilemma is that they can maximize their *joint* utility (*i.e.*, minimize their collective jail time) by both not confessing, but can maximize their individual utility by confessing. What are the incentives for each prisoner? What difference, if any, does it make if the prisoners can communicate with each other or if they are held incommunicado?–EDS.

Under these conditions it is not surprising that siting is almost completely carried on behind closed doors. It is not until the publication of the community short list that the public is brought fully into the information loop of the siting process. With secrecy and public participation only after announcement of the short list, it is assumed that at the very least the decision-makers can focus and limit the opposition to only those communities that will be potentially affected; that is, to those

---

[47] You will recall that Mark Sagoff made a similar distinction in relation to cost-benefit analysis in Chapter 3, *supra*. Do the two contexts shed light on each other? – EDS.

who can be directly approached with the economic compensation package.

Distinguished from the prisoner's dilemma approach to siting, the assurance approach in some of the Canadian examples makes a series of distinctions in framing the dilemma faced by those who want the facility and those who will eventually accept it into their backyard. It employs a different series of steps to facility siting, and these emphasize an interaction, not as within a market of consumers over private goods, but as a political bargaining process between citizens and a government that anticipates and regulates environmental risk in the provision and disposition of, not private, but collective or public goods. In the case of assurance politics, it must be assumed that citizens have the protection and empowerment of their moral autonomy as their highest priority. For the first time the citizen or policy-maker must consider that the ethical consideration informing his or her deliberations is not the instrumental value of efficiency but the intrinsic value of individual moral integrity.

Put another way, the prisoners' dilemma provides a continuing incentive for one party to exploit the other, thus undermining an optimal cooperative arrangement. Instead, the only really stable cooperative outcome is distinctly suboptimal. On the other hand, this stable suboptimal outcome does not require either information or trust between the parties: it looks solely to individual optimization. The assurance approach, by contrast, requires a commitment to broad dissemination of accurate information, open communication, and central regulatory involvement that credibly assures all players that they will not be exploited in the decision to cooperate.

With the government in place as the collective representative of each citizen, working to anticipate and protect each person from risk that would otherwise be imposed upon them, each individual has the capacity to appreciate her obligation to shoulder her "share" of collective burdens and each also has the predisposition to cooperate, if given the "assurance" that they will not be exploited in this cooperative action. The assurance, given by the state, is that if I cooperate, others will also cooperate toward the collective end or be sanctioned by government.

Elements of an Assurance Approach

Fieldwork indicates that five characteristics are integral to the successful Canadian siting cases and to the politics of assurance. Each played an important role in gaining the public support necessary for successful facility siting.

Early and Extensive Public Involvement. It is critical that decision-makers start from the assumption that citizens have a predisposition to cooperate if assured that they will not be exploited. However, many Canadian provinces approach the question of public participation in various stages of the siting process with pause. They delay public involvement until the latter stages of the process, once a specific site has been announced by either a governmental agency (as in Ontario) or a private corporation (as in British Columbia). Although consistent with a prisoner's dilemma rationality, this is far too late to attain meaningful public input or build trust between site proponent and proposed host, much less mount "the systematic and sustained effort necessary to create true democratic dialogue among citizens" in environmental policy.[48]

Early public involvement, however, has been unusually extensive and successful in the Quebec, Alberta, and Manitoba cases, particularly the latter two.

* * *

These participatory efforts were also time-consuming and involved extensive provincial commitment of staff to travel and visit various community groups. "I wore out one and a half cars going from town to town . . . I learned what the concerns were," explained one former senior provincial official. Alberta Environmental officials hosted more than 120 meetings in every county, municipal district, and special area in the province. They responded to citizen inquiries, provided briefings on the hazardous waste situation in the province, and offered information on the procedures to be followed in the siting process. "I was against the proposal, but agreed to go to all the meetings," recalled one prominent community leader. "I had no idea that so much hazardous waste was being generated and that it came from so many sources. I got to the point where I really wanted to know where it was going. And the officials from the province answered all my questions and put it into language that I understood."

Fifty-two communities expressed interest in potential participation and continued to have far-reaching access to provincial officials and hazardous waste data. They also received a detailed provisional analysis of their area, which would prove useful to them in considering the viability of a hazardous waste site as well as potential landfill sites or other land uses. Fourteen of these communities sought further consideration by the province, although nine were subsequently eliminated on either environmental grounds or in response to vocal public opposition. The five remaining communities held plebiscites in 1982 that drew heavy voter turnout and support for the idea of hosting a hazardous waste facility. This gave provincial officials a choice among possible sites, leading to the selection of Swan Hills in March 1984.

Substantial public participation continues since the opening of the facility, through a number of formal and informal mechanisms that maintain communication between Swan Hills residents, provincial authorities, and representatives of the crown and private corporations that manage the facility. Many citizens take great pride in the fact that they are partners in the waste management process and that they have made it possible for their province to move beyond the haphazard disposal

---

[48] BRUCE WILLIAMS & ALBERT MATHENY, DEMOCRACY, DIALOGUE AND SOCIAL REGULATION: BEING FAIR VERSUS BEING RIGHT (forthcoming).

practices so common in many other parts of Canada. "We are becoming the environmental capital of Canada, with new technology and training," noted one local elected official. "We're in the middle of the new industrial revolution, trying to clean up what others have screwed up."

* * *

Compensation. If individual citizens are assumed to have their moral autonomy as the critical matter of concern and not their welfare preferences, then while compensation packages are not rendered immaterial, but can only be entertained after assurance has been given and it is understood that they are not being exploited. Otherwise, the compensation package can be seen as nothing other than a bribe. In playing out a modified prisoner's dilemma logic, siting policies in British Columbia, Saskatchewan, and the Maritime provinces were premised on the assumption that a community might well accept a hazardous waste facility if various economic incentives were dangled before its eyes. The practice of placing primary reliance on compensation to resolve siting conflicts has failed dismally in Canada, as it has in the United States. However, compensation can play an important role in promoting siting agreements when it follows assurance by the public authority, acceptance by the community that their moral capacities are not at stake, and packaging as part of a larger, more comprehensive process.[49]

The extensive participatory processes in Alberta assured the citizens of the province, *ex ante*, and therefore made possible prolonged political bargaining between provincial, private corporate, and local officials concerning the compensation benefits that would be accorded Swan Hills in the event the community accepted a comprehensive hazardous waste facility.

* * *

Government as citizen-advocate in public/private partnership. If individuals are to see the acceptance of a site as part of their public responsibility, they must be assured that the public authorities have protection of citizen-autonomy as their central priority. Therefore government must take the lead in the public-private partnership as citizen advocates. In these cases, the governments, while not dominating the process, took the lead in coordinating and monitoring the role of private

---

[49] The anticipated compensatory benefits were significant contributors to the agreements reached in Alberta and Quebec, and may well play a similar role in Manitoba. Swan Hills was clearly in dire economic straits in the late 1970s and early 1980s after the collapse of the oil and gas extraction industries, as were many Western Canadian towns of the period (Williams, 1978; McParland, 1981). Blainville was a working-class suburb with an unemployment rate of more than 15 percent at the time of the Stablex agreement. By contrast, none of the three Manitoba communities that remain active candidates for hosting a site can be characterized as economically depressed or desperate for any source of development available. It should also be noted that dozens of other communities in both the United States and Canada have been approached with facility proposals and rigorously rejected them, indicating the limits of any siting strategy that focuses on economic criteria alone.

corporations and the market, as the trustee for its citizens, charged with the *ex ante* regulation of environmental risk. They avoided the extremes of government authority-driven siting approaches (such as in Ontario and the United States) and market-driven approaches (such as in British Columbia, Saskatchewan, and the United States) that tend to draw considerable public distrust. In the former, the role of government is seen as too heavy-handed and not specifically concerned with citizen safety. In the latter, the role of private corporations is seen as overly extensive, often independent of serious provincial involvement and oversight and concerned not with respecting citizens, but with immediate profit and self-interested wealth maximization.

Alberta responded to this dilemma by creating a crown corporation to share in all aspects of facility construction and management with Bow Valley Resource Services. The crown corporation gives the province an enduring presence in the facility, one that is distinctive from the continuing enforcement role played by Alberta Environment. This proved particularly attractive to Swan Hills officials and residents, who were painfully familiar with earlier private developers who pulled up stakes when the oil and gas industries went bust, often leaving behind major economic dislocations and serious environmental problems. At the same time, the inclusion of a private corporation reduces potential public expenditures and also provides for use of various waste disposal technologies and personnel that may not be readily available from provincial agencies. Manitoba has found this blend of public and private functions attractive, having developed its own crown corporation with somewhat greater responsibilities than its counterpart in Alberta while being far less intrusive than government has been in Ontario. "We had a relatively small project team with about 20 professionals and we were given freedom to experiment, to fail, and to finally settle on the best way to do this," explained one senior official of the Manitoba crown corporation.

* * *

Siting as part of a comprehensive hazardous waste strategy. The politics of assurance cannot work without the citizen's trust that she will not have her basic moral capacities exploited by environmental risk, or be expected to bear all of the related costs. This trust involves the coordination of a comprehensive environmental plan where the particular siting is only a single component part. In this way, each citizen can see that she will have to take responsibility for some facet of the problem, if not the site itself. She will cooperate therefore to preserve joint cooperation toward the provision of the collective good of environmental quality given the assurance that no one will free-ride on her cooperation, but will bear their fair share of sacrifice for a quality environment.

Hazardous waste facility siting is frequently presented as a take-it-or-leave-it proposition from a private firm or a governmental agency to an individual community. In many cases, both in Canada and the United

States, it has not been treated as part of a broader strategy to protect the environment and safeguard public health, which might involve multiple communities or regions simultaneously and define the problem in collective rather than private terms. This pattern has been especially evident in provinces such as British Columbia, in which siting proposals from private corporations are not linked in any manner to other aspects of provincial waste management. Ontario has been somewhat more successful in devising a broader strategy, but its primary focus has remained on siting rather than its integration with other aspects of waste management. The prospects for cooperation in Alberta, Quebec, and now Manitoba may have been enhanced by taking a larger perspective.

* * *

[Alberta] also devised ambitious programs to promote waste reduction and recycling, providing incentives and requirements to reduce the volumes of wastes that would be sent to Swan Hills. "It's absolutely essential that waste recycling and minimization be part of our process, rather than focus solely on siting," noted one provincial official. "At the same time, we realize we have vast storage of wastes that can't be ignored and that there will always be residues from our industries and communities that require safe disposal. This all needs to be pulled together rather than put into separate compartments." It created a waste exchange system whereby one firm's wastes might be re-used in the production process of another. The province has also placed special emphasis on environmental education in the public schools.

* * *

Control of exports and imports. Implementing a politics of assurance must not only include the understanding that the problem is the responsibility of the community itself but that this obligation does not extend to waste from elsewhere. Provincial officials attempted to build support for new facilities by portraying them as a linchpin in provincial plans to begin to take greater responsibility for wastes generated within provincial boundaries. Officials lamented the reliance on exporting substantial amounts of hazardous waste to other provinces, states, and nations as both morally offensive and economically risky given the uncertain future availability of disposal facilities elsewhere. Consistent with the statements of others, a senior provincial environmental official expressed disapproval of the Albertan reliance on Oregon facilities to dispose of about one thousand cubic feet of PCBs per month.

* * *

At the same time, Alberta officials vowed to confine use of new waste disposal facilities, if accepted, to those wastes generated in the province. "We had no intention of becoming some sort of host for other provinces or states," explained one former local official. "You might find support for taking some wastes from areas such as the Yukon and Northwest Territories, which are poor and don't generate much waste," noted a community leader. "But it's up to the provinces like BC to take care of their own wastes. The same goes for Eastern Canada. Let them do what we've already done." In this way the government defines the provincial role up-front and also assures citizens that they will have to take responsibility for only that waste they themselves have generated. Alberta officials vigorously resisted efforts in 1981 to explore regional disposal plans that called for housing a main multi-provincial facility in their province. They frequently stated their intent to prohibit waste trading with other states and provinces. Many local officials and residents of Swan Hills emphasize that provincial prohibition on waste exports and imports was a vital component in gaining-and maintaining-public support.[50]

* * *

By contrast, other provinces have failed to articulate such controls on imports and exports as an *ex ante* condition of their respective siting processes. In Ontario, for example, the absence of proposed provincial curbs on accepting imports at any new facility led to widespread concern that out-of-province wastes would be readily accepted. In fact, the search for a site near the southern border of the province fed fears that such a provincially-funded facility would serve as a magnet for wastes from American states unable to open their own facilities, as has occurred in recent years in Quebec.

The Assurance Process

The foregoing elements, which define the assurance approach to siting, also suggest that a different sequence of events in the siting process may render success.

Public participation. Instead of public participation being the third step, as it was within the traditional prisoner's dilemma approach, it is now the first step. Before any facility is chosen or a short list of communities is compiled, the public must be involved in all dimensions of the problem.

Feasibility study. The feasibility study now has a completely different connotation, for it is not a secret study undertaken by experts, but a report of public meetings and input with the conclusions drawn by the combination of expert and civilian arguments. Now that conclusions of the research are the results of a community effort, the feasibility study does not appear to be a *fait accompli.* Instead it is the best recommendations of a community to take care of a jointly generated problem.

Short-list. The short-list is now the process of a community interested in the facility voting to place themselves in competition for the site. No longer will communities awaken to find that a predetermined risk-generating facility is going to be placed in their back yard without their consent. Instead, they have consented to a facility that they had input in defining. Both the type and placement of the facility has been forged

---

[50] You will see that a similar ban on "imports" was essential to siting a waste disposal facility at the Fernald site in Ohio, described in Chapter 12 (Federal Facilities), *infra*-EDS.

through months of debate and is being accepted by the community as its part in the cooperative effort to provide the collective good of a quality environment. Siting is now a choice made by all through the ballot box with prior and complete information, before any geological or engineering study of their particular community is undertaken. Once a community volunteers for the short list, environmental engineers will begin the process of determining whether their particular geography is fit for the facility under consideration. In this way the experts go in only after assurance, from the state to the citizens, has been given and the citizens themselves have spoken through an organized grassroots information and participation campaign.

Compensation. The fourth and final step in the siting process remains economic compensation but, unlike the prisoner's dilemma approach to siting that perceives this package as the core of the siting, it is now a reward for the 'public spirit' of a community. The compensation package becomes a catalyst for long-term bargaining and a contract between the qualified community and the authorities that makes the licensing, construction, and running of the site as smooth and safe as possible.

NOTES

1. *The prisoners' dilemma.* How do the approaches taken in the U.S. and in the eastern Canadian provinces resemble the prisoners' dilemma? What is the stable but suboptimal outcome that these approaches have achieved?

2. *Success.* What is a "successful" siting policy? Is there an argument that *not* siting is a good thing? What are the counter-arguments?

Public opinion strongly recognizes the need to site new facilities and yet strongly supports the refusal to host.[51] How does this affect your evaluation of what should be considered success in siting?

3. How different are the prisoners' dilemma and assurance approaches? Are the differences fundamental, or do they have more to do with the siting authority's attitude toward the problem? Conversely, might there be differences between U.S. and Canadian citizens' attitudes toward their respective governments that make a difference?

4. Although RCRA is the main source of statutory authority governing the siting of hazardous waste facilities, the issuance of a permit for a new facility is also influenced by other environmental protection statutes.[52] For example, the EPA Administrator is required to insure that the proposed facility will not conflict with or jeopardize the statutory purposes of the National Historic Preservation Act, Endangered Species Act, or Coastal Zone Management Act. The EPA Regional Administrator must also consult with the state agency with jurisdiction over wildlife

---

[51] John M. Gillroy & Robert Y. Shapiro. *The Polls: Environmental Policy.* 50 PUBLIC OPINION Q. 270-79 1986.

[52] *See* 40 C.F.R. § 270.3.

resources in compliance with the Fish and Wildlife Coordination Act. How should policy-makers deal with the strategic use of the above statutes by groups whose aim it is to stop all facility siting, thereby forcing the reduction of waste generation?

5. If you had the opportunity to revise, as completely as you want, the policies and processes for siting hazardous and radioactive waste, how would you change them?

Chapter 11

Clean-Up: The Comprehensive Environmental Response, Compensation, and Liability Act

Of all the statutes that have been passed to address the problem of toxic substances and hazardous wastes, the Comprehensive Environmental Response, Compensation, and Liability Act (CERCLA) has had perhaps the most profound effect on the environmental law landscape. It authorizes and funds the remediation of inactive, leaking hazardous waste sites, and it defines the nature and scope of liability for past environmental harms. Since potential CERCLA liability is huge and the statute itself is no model of legislative draftsmanship, it has spawned thousands of lawsuits, and hundreds of judicial decisions attempting to interpret its terms. From this body of case law one can derive the "law of CERCLA," which is the topic of this chapter.

    The chapter begins with a summary of CERCLA, so that we can have a broad conception of what CERCLA and the Superfund are, before delving into details. Then the chapter addresses all the key component parts of CERCLA. We start with the CERCLA cornerstones—its blueprint for action (the National Contingency Plan and National Priorities List), actions that may be taken to clean up contaminated sites (removal and remedial actions), and the availability *vel non* of judicial review of these actions. Next, the chapter explains CERCLA's unique liability scheme, which ensures that when private parties linked to the site can be identified, the costs of clean-up are borne by those parties responsible for the contaminated waste site, and its imminent or potential harm to the environment. If such parties cannot be found, the Superfund is used, and that is the focus of the next section of the chapter. Finally, we review the various kinds of costs for which parties may find themselves liable, and the procedures for assigning and allocating liability.

A. Overview

Before one embarks on an analysis of the many provisions that constitute CERCLA, it might be helpful to begin with a brief overview of the statute. The next section provides a brief discussion of what CERCLA does, how it does it, and why it was passed. This overview also explains what the Superfund is, what a Superfund site is, and how such sites are cleaned up. Additionally, the structure and organization of CERCLA's interlocking parts will be discussed.

1. What Is CERCLA?

CERCLA's current regulatory scheme is the result of two major enactments. The original *Comprehensive Environmental Response, Compensation and Liability Act*, Pub. L. No. 96-510, 94 Stat. 2767, was enacted in 1980. In 1986, Congress reauthorized and revised CERCLA in the Superfund Amendments and Reauthorization Act (SARA), Pub. L. 99-499, 160 Stat. 1615. Known collectively as CERCLA, 42 U.S.C. §§9601-9675, the statutes address two main issues: the identification, investigation, and remediation of contaminated sites; and the allocation of financial responsibility for clean-up activities.

The passage of CERCLA represents the final piece of Congress's mosaic of environmental legislation. The National Environmental Policy Act of 1969 (NEPA) required federal agencies to consider, in advance of making decisions, the environmental impacts of these decisions. The 1970 Clean Air Act (CAA) regulated air pollution. The 1972 Clean Water Act (CWA) sought to control polluted discharges in rivers and lakes. The Resource Conservation and Recovery Act of 1976 (RCRA) regulated toxic and hazardous discharges to land and groundwater. But no statute addressed pre-existing environmental harms, especially those caused by the threat from hazardous waste disposal sites. The purpose of CERCLA was to address acts occurring in the past, in order to prevent environmental disasters in the future. It is not a traditional regulatory statute, like the CAA, CWA, or RCRA. It is a remediation statute that imposes liability for past conduct with present effects.

There are numerous interactions between the remediation and liability aspects of CERCLA, but they are conceptually and statutorily quite separate. The remediation aspect of CERCLA identifies the kinds of sites ("facilities") that require attention, sets priorities among them, provides for their analysis, and finally specifies in some detail the nature and degree of clean-up activities. These parts of CERCLA look very much like the regulatory regimes we have already examined, and you will find many familiar issues.

The liability aspect of CERCLA is new and unique in toxics regulation. In essence, CERCLA is a retrospective statute that uses tort-like liability to reach a range of private parties to pay the costs of cleaning up hazardous waste sites. CERCLA is not primarily regulatory or preventive, like RCRA which provides for cradle-to-grave control of current activities regarding hazardous waste. Instead, CERCLA is *remedial*. It is designed to repair past waste disposal practices. If parties responsible for hazardous waste sites can be identified and located, they will be liable for both past and future clean-up costs of these sites, as well as the cost of preventing spills and releases of toxic and hazardous waste into the environment. *O'Neil v. Picillo*, 823 F.2d 176 (1st Cir. 1989). If such parties cannot be found (*e.g.*, when hazardous waste sites have been abandoned by their original owners), or if the owners of the site have become bankrupt, the Superfund created by CERCLA serves as a monetary source from which the government may finance clean-up of these "orphan" sites.

Although the text of CERCLA is ambiguous about the liability it imposes, subsequent court interpretations have established that the nature of the liability is *strict*; the scope of the liability is *joint and several*; and the effect of the liability is *retroactive*. Consequently, fault and causation are largely irrelevant; a person responsible for a small percentage of the site's waste could be liable for 100% of the clean-up costs; and a party may be liable for extensive clean-up costs for disposal practices occurring pre-CERCLA that were legal at the time the disposal took place.[1] Not only is the liability scheme in CERCLA strict, broad, and backwards looking, it is also subject to only a few statutory defenses: acts of God; acts of war; acts or omissions of a third party not in contractual privity with the person asserting the defense; innocent landowners (or innocent purchasers) who can demonstrate causation by a third party and adequate precautions by the buyer; and lenders who did not participate in the management of the waste site.

---

[1] United States v. Northeastern Pharmaceutical Chem. Corp., 810 F.2d 726, 734 (8th Cir. 1986) (Congress intended for CERCLA to apply to pre-CERCLA acts, and such retroactivity does not violate due process).

If a party's actions with respect to a waste site satisfy CERCLA's liability triggers (*i.e.*, there is a threatened release of a hazardous substance from a "facility"—a site or area where a

CERCLA LIABILITY
Nature ⇒ STRICT
Scope ⇒ JOINT& SEVERAL
Effect ⇒ RETROACTIVE

hazardous substance has been deposited), and if the party becomes a "PRP"— a Potentially Responsible Party (*i.e.*, an owner, operator, etc.), then CERCLA provides that this unfortunate soul is liable for "all costs of removal or remedial action incurred by the United States Government or a State or an Indian tribe not inconsistent with the [NCP]." §107(a)(4)(A).[2] Courts have interpreted the "all costs" phrase quite literally, so that where the government takes action to investigate or monitor a release, or pays a contractor to perform work under agency direction, all these costs can be reimbursed. Most courts also allow the government to recover enforcement-related costs, indirect costs, such as rent and clerical supplies, and overhead, such as travel and legal expenses. Attorneys' fees are expressly authorized for government response actions, but are not in private cost recovery actions. In *Key Tronic Corp. v. United States*, 511 U.S. 809 (1994), the Supreme Court ruled that attorney's fees incurred in prosecuting a CERCLA liability action are not a "necessary cost of response," but did allow recovery of fees incurred by an attorney in tracking down other PRPs.

Another provision of CERCLA, §107(a)(4)(c), imposes on PRPs the duty to pay for injury to, destruction of, or loss of natural resources . * * *" The federal government, the states and local governments, and Indian tribal governments are designated as trustees empowered to sue for natural resource damages. Although cost recovery claims have dominated actions involving CERCLA, liabilities associated with natural resource damage claims may eventually exceed the billions of dollars spent on cleaning up waste sites. This is because (1) the term "natural resources" is given an extremely broad definition in the statute's definition section, (2) unlike recovery of response costs, the government need not expend money to recover natural resource damages, and (3) the appropriate measure of damages is not just the diminution of use values, but rather the cost of restoration and replacement of the damaged land and ecosystem. The potential cost to private parties found liable for this kind of clean-up and restoration action could be crippling. *See, e.g., Kennecott Utah Copper Corp. v. U.S. Dept. of Interior*, 88 F.3d 1191, 1217 (D.C. Cir. 1996).

---

[2] CERCLA §107(a)(4)(B) creates a similar right in any private party, with the additional requirement that private parties bear the responsibility of demonstrating that costs incurred were consistent with the NCP. The government's costs are presumably recoverable unless a private defendant proves inconsistency with the NCP.

CERCLA pursues three objectives: (1) It prevents further contamination and release of toxic substances by requiring prompt clean-up of existing hazardous waste sites; (2) it ensures that the costs of cleaning up these sites are borne by "responsible" parties; and (3) its sweeping liability provisions help to deter future environmental releases by imposing high costs on careless waste management and disposal practices. *B.F. Goodrich Co. v. Murtha*, 958 F.2d 1192 (2d Cir. 1992). On

THREE OBJECTIVES OF CERCLA
1) Prevents contamination and releases of toxic substances
2) Ensures costs for cleanup are borne by responsible parties
3) Deters future environmental releases

the other hand, CERCLA does *not* provide a cause of action, like a new toxic tort, to compensate for personal or economic injuries resulting from hazardous waste contamination. *Exxon Corp. v. Hunt*, 475 U.S. 355, 375 (1986). Nor does it provide clear and explicit guidance about how its provisions should be interpreted. Congress left much of CERCLA ambiguous, so the judiciary has created a kind of federal common law of CERCLA.

Within CERCLA's vague and ambiguously drafted framework, the U.S. Congress created a two-pronged approach to meeting its twin objectives—cleaning up hazardous waste sites and recovering costs. On the one hand, the *federal government* (through the EPA) was given authority to respond to hazardous releases at abandoned and inactive waste disposal sites. The federal government may rely on the Superfund to clean up a site and then seek reimbursement from any

STEPS THAT CAN BE TAKEN BY THE FEDERAL GOVERNMENT
1) initiate clean up itself
2) require that responsible parties take the appropriate action
3) encourage responsible parties to engage in the appropriate clean up

responsible parties, or it may proceed directly against responsible parties, or it may encourage "voluntary" clean-up by threatening responsible parties with court action and sanctions if they do not agree to the EPA's chosen action. On the other hand, *private parties* may spend their own money to clean-up, then sue those responsible to recover those clean-up costs. Even if private parties are partially responsible themselves, they may sue other responsible parties for their share of clean-up costs. *See* Susan R. Poulter, *Clean-up and Restoration: Who Should Pay?,* 18 J. LAND RESOURCES & ENVTL. L. 77 (1998).

If either the government or a private party can identify and locate a party responsible for the hazardous waste site, that responsible party is subject to a particularly stringent form of liability. Under CERCLA, liability is *not* determined by traditional tort principles, which require some degree of causative link between the defendant's conduct and the actual harm to another person. It was thought that this principle would obstruct clean-up of sites where multiple parties disposed of toxic substances years or decades before anyone became aware of the hazardous nature of the site. By the time the site's threat to the public and the environment becomes known, it may be impossible to identify the persons who actually contaminated it (or their relative share of the contamination). Even when parties who were responsible for the contamination are located, they may be incapable of shouldering the costs due to bankruptcy or insolvency.

As a result, CERCLA imposes liability when there is a causal link between certain classes of defendants—generally site owners and waste generators—the release of a hazardous substance, and the *incurrence of clean-up costs*. Neither harm (other than incurring clean-up costs) nor carelessness or illegality of the defendant's conduct need be proven. Defendants are also jointly and severally liable, so that, in theory at least, a person responsible for only a tiny percentage of the waste at a site can be liable for the total cost of cleaning it up if no other PRPs can be located.[3] Moreover, the courts have interpreted CERCLA as imposing retroactive liability, which means that potentially responsible parties (PRPs) are liable for conduct occurring before CERCLA's 1980 enactment. *United States v. Olin Corp.*, 107 F.3d 1506 (11th Cir. 1997). This result is consistent with CERCLA's purpose of cleaning up all hazardous sites, regardless of when they were created.

2. What Is the Superfund?

The other distinguishing feature of CERCLA, besides its unique liability scheme, is its revolving trust fund, the "Superfund." As originally envisioned, the Superfund exists to finance government-directed clean-up efforts, to pay claims arising from clean-up activities of private parties who are not liable as PRPs under CERCLA, and to compensate federal and state governments for damages to natural resources caused by a hazardous waste site. The Superfund receives its money from excise taxes on companies such as the petroleum and chemical industries.

To determine which sites are worthy of Superfund dollars, CERCLA authorizes the EPA to create a list of the worst hazardous waste sites in the country, the National Priorities List (NPL). To determine which sites should be placed on the NPL, EPA employs a Hazard Ranking System (HRS) which assigns a score to each site, based on a few salient risk assessment criteria (*e.g.*, potential for contaminating drinking water, for producing public health hazard, or for destroying sensitive ecosystems). Once a site is placed on the

---

[3] Some courts have decided that clean-up costs may be apportioned among PRPs if (1) the defendant satisfies the burden of proving that responsibility and/or harm is divisible, (2) responsibility for the contamination and/or harm from the site is in fact divisible, and (3) the other PRPs contributing to the site may be found. United States v. Alcan Aluminum Corp., 964 F.2d 252 (3d Cir. 1992). Other courts have suggested that if a current site owner were able to prove that none of the hazardous substances found at the site were fairly attributable to it, such an owner's apportioned share of the clean-up costs could be zero. United States v. Rohm & Haas Co., 2 F.3d 1265 (3d Cir. 1993).

NPL, the National Contingency Plan (NCP) establishes the procedures and standards for responding to releases of hazardous substances from the site. CERCLA authorizes two kinds of responses: (1) short-term "removal" actions designed to alleviate immediate dangers, and (2) long-term "remedial" actions meant to provide a more permanent remedy.

Together, the NPL and NCP determine the *kinds of actions* that may be taken at hazardous waste sites and the ability of government and private parties to *recover costs* for cleaning up such sites. Placement of a site on the NPL is a prerequisite only to use of Superfund monies for clean-up; a non-federal party can always use its own money to clean up a facility and then, if possible, recover from responsible parties. However, a federal, state, or tribal government's costs of cleaning up a waste site are recoverable from other responsible parties *unless* the defendant in a cost-recovery action shows an inconsistency with the NCP, *United States v. Northeastern Pharmaceutical & Chemical Co., Inc.*, 810 F.2d 726, 747 (8th Cir. 1986), while a private party can only recover costs for their clean-up actions if such actions are demonstrated to be in substantial compliance with the NCP.

The following recounts how the failed Summitville mine in Colorado came to be listed on the NPL.

THE SUMMITVILLE STORY: A SUPERFUND SITE IS BORN

Luke J. Danielson, Laura Alms, and Alix McNamara
24 ENVTL. L. REP. 10388 (1994)

From the top of the Summitville mine's defunct heap leach, a mass of leached-out gold ore hundreds of feet high, the signs of environmental disaster are visible everywhere. The leach pad, a pond-like structure covering 46 acres, contains over nine million tons of ore. Murky green water collects in pools along the heap's border, and milky water drains from old tunnels. Long coils of black pipe, once used to pump cyanide solution onto the heap, are now used to percolate water through the cyanide- and metal-laden ore as part of a detoxification process that will take years and millions of tax dollars to complete. Trailers filled with portable water treatment systems dot the site, and the scar of the open pit is visible for miles. The contrast with the surrounding landscape, where the austere, rugged peaks of Colorado's San Juan Mountains slope into miles of pristine wilderness, is dramatic.

In just eight years, the Summitville mine has progressed from initial permitting [as an ongoing mining operation] to an U.S. Environmental Protection Agency (EPA) emergency response site. Soon, it will land on the Comprehensive Environmental Response, Compensation, and Liability Act (CERCLA) national priorities list.

* * *

Summitville began construction of the heap leach pad and liner in the fall of 1985 and continued construction throughout the winter of 1985-86. Many of the problems that would later plague the mine during its operating life resulted directly from the company's decision to complete construction of the liner during the winter. Critical to the success of a heap leaching operation is an impermeable liner under the crushed ore material. This liner has two functions. First, it collects the "pregnant" cyanide solution that has percolated through the heap in order to convey it to the processing plant where the gold is ultimately removed from the solution.

Second, it prevents the solution from entering the environment.

Despite the importance of the liner for environmental control, the permit did not restrict winter installation. Liner construction occurred through the depth of the 1985 winter. This ill-advised winter construction, compounded by frequent snow slides, led to liner rips and tears and inadequately sealed seams that culminated in cyanide leaks soon after the company began initial operations in June 1986. A recent Canadian Broadcasting Corporation report describes the severe problems experienced during winter construction:

> *The pad* was built under nightmarish conditions—sub-zero temperatures, 35 feet of snow, and avalanches that crashed into the construction site. In the words of one report, the pad liner froze, buckled, cracked, and eventually leaked.

* * *

The regulators' optimism that the company had committed itself to a program that would remedy some of the site's worst problems was dashed in December 1992, when the company declared bankruptcy without warning, terminating its commitment to pay for continuing operation of the water treatment plant and the complex system of pumps and pipes that was keeping massive active discharges of contaminants from overflowing the heap. The company's withdrawal from its agreements with 11 days' notice was a supreme act of corporate irresponsibility. The bankrupt mining operation left both state and federal regulators, without any advance warning, heirs to an abandoned mine at the beginning of one of the most severe winters in recent history. The timing of the bankruptcy was extremely unfortunate and has been the subject of much deserved criticism.

* * *

Since assuming control of the site, EPA has spent over $10.8 million on monitoring. During the winter, EPA was spending an average of $30,000 a day to prevent heap overflow. Overall costs during the winter totaled $3.5 million dollars. It is estimated that clean-up could cost up to $120 million. The immediate project of moving the six million-ton waste pile to an acceptable location is in itself an enormous engineering task.

The expected Superfund listing of Summitville is triggering a rash of litigation. Galactic [the parent of the mining company], its officers, other mining companies whose only involvement in Summitville may have been a little core drilling or sampling, landowners, engineering consultants, and others are girding for battle over their relative responsibilities for on-site conditions. For EPA, state regulators, lawyers, potential criminal defendants, and the various mining companies who will be PRPs at this site, Summitville will go on for a long time.

Without a Superfund, the Summitville mine site could never have been cleaned up. The State of Colorado did not have the necessary funds to pay the costs of preventing the cyanide from killing everything downstream; state regulators had failed to secure an adequate performance bond; the principal PRP itself, the Summitville Mining Company, was bankrupt. The Superfund is therefore essential to the eventual success of CERCLA. Although more solvent mining companies, such as Galactic, may also become PRPs at the Summitville site, protracted litigation among these companies with respect to their relative "contribution" shares will delay the United States recovering its costs paid out of the Superfund.

But has Superfund been a success? When Congress succeeded in passing the only major amendments to CERCLA in 1986, the Superfund Amendments and Reauthorization Act (SARA), the size of the Superfund was expanded to $8.5 billion. Most of this was to be raised by a so-called

"Superfund tax" on certain industries (*e.g.*, petroleum and chemical) whose products were judged to create most of the clean-up problem. At the end of 1995, Congress failed to reach agreement on CERCLA reauthorization, and the Superfund tax expired. Between 1996 and 2000, Congress continued to consider CERCLA reauthorization bills, but was unable to achieve consensus. CERCLA remains a statute in need of reauthorization. The EPA's efforts under CERCLA, as well as the Superfund, have been able to continue only because of a continuing resolution originally enacted in 1996. Technically, the Superfund has always been something of an accounting charade; however, since the Superfund tax expired, the EPA's CERCLA operations have been funded at only 75 percent of prior levels, curtailing clean-up activities at hundreds of NPL sites and forcing a dramatic reduction in remediation activities.

In addition to suffering from inadequate funding and a failure by Congress to reauthorize CERCLA, the Superfund clean-up process can be criticized because of the long period of time that can elapse between the time a site comes to the EPA's attention, and the time when remedial work is completed. Nearly four years can pass from the time a citizen or a state notifies the EPA of a possible CERCLA site, before that site is assessed and then receives a sufficiently high score on the HRS to be placed on the NPL for Superfund clean-up. After listing, there must be a remedial investigation and feasibility study completed before the EPA issues a Record of Decision (ROD) detailing the clean-up action that will be taken. This can take five years or more. The clean-up of the site can then begin, but it is not complete until a remedial "design" is finished and subsequent remedial "action" has physically removed (or halted) the contamination from the site. This clean-up work can last four or more years. What is the total elapsed time between discovery of site and its clean-up? On average, that elapsed time is between 13 to 15 years.[4] The major steps in the Superfund process are illustrated below.

AVERAGE TIME TO COMPLETE STEPS IN SUPERFUND CLEANUP PROCESS

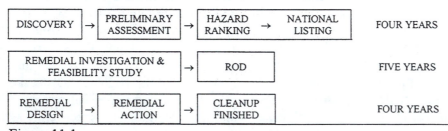

Figure 11.1

---

[4] Further delays can occur if administrative and judicial challenges are brought by PRPs while the EPA is engaged in the clean-up process.

CERCLA has also been criticized because of its high administrative costs. The Rand Corporation concluded that of $2.6 billion paid out of the Superfund by the EPA through 1988, only $1.6 billion were devoted to remedial investigations and response actions at waste sites. J. Acton, Understanding Superfund: A Progress Report (1989). The remainder ($1 billion) had been spent on transaction costs—administration, management, laboratory, and litigation expenses. Of this $2.6 billion paid out of Superfund, EPA had recovered $230 million of its costs through settlements at 328 sites.

Both the Congress and EPA have tried to accelerate the clean-up process and reduce transaction costs. To speed up clean-ups, SARA imposed timetables and statutory deadlines for EPA to complete preliminary assessments and site inspections; it also directed EPA to begin 275 remedial investigation and feasibility studies, 175 remedial clean-up actions within three years of enactment, and an additional 200 in the next two years. To lower administrative costs, EPA has established presumptive remedies and other administrative improvements, encouraged settlements among private parties, and ratified allocations of costs initiated by PRPs. EPA has also been experimenting with non-judicial solutions in which neutral mediators negotiate allocations of responsibility.

SPIRIT OF COOPERATION SOUGHT AT CLEAN-UP SITE

Steve Lipsher
The Denver Post, March 30 (1998)

BRECKENRIDGE—Like many other mining sites in Colorado, French Gulch just west of this Victorian resort village claims a glorious history—and a toxic legacy.

But then, this is a story of contradictions.

For while the lower stretches of French Gulch are so contaminated that they support no aquatic life, the upper portions host a healthy population of an endangered trout isolated from competition.

While a few local residents known as "gulch rats" have been forced to move because of health concerns, a developer aspires to build affordable housing on the hard-rock rubble nearby.

And while the U.S. Environmental Protection Agency could declare French Gulch a Superfund site—meaning a costly clean-up and years of legal tangles—the agency is trying a new approach of conciliation toward the mine owners and full community involvement in hopes of greater cooperation and less expense.

"You hear the horror stories—millions of dollars in legal expenses, years and years on-site," said Paul Rogers, the EPA's chief negotiator in French Gulch. "Hopefully, it will become clear that cooperation is much more beneficial to everyone. This is a very exciting project."

In a spectacular alpine valley overlooking the Breckenridge ski area, the rust-toned tailings piles and the husk of a four-story, weathered-wood mill remain visible reminders of the legendary Wellington-Oro Mine.

Carried invisibly in the clear trickle of French Creek are enough heavy metals—manganese, iron, lead and arsenic—that it is sterile for a 2-mile stretch down to the Blue River.

The gulch is so contaminated that it could qualify for the National Priorities List under the federal Superfund law.

"The site is of sufficient concern that it is what I call an NPL-caliber site," Rogers said.

Beside the well-traveled dirt road up the drainage are small piles of "roaster fines," highly contaminated burnt red rock and spongy soil left over from the chemical-smeltering process.

More insidious is the water that floods the 16 miles of tunnels underground and carries heavy metals with it into the French Creek.

"It's pretty nasty stuff," said Bill McKee of the state health department's water-quality control division. "If it's ever going to be used, * * * they would probably have to clean up the site to some extent."

But stinging from public criticism over the other Superfund sites—notably in nearby Leadville, where local politicians have threatened to hang EPA officials from light poles in the wake of a multimillion dollar clean-up that has lasted more than a decade—the agency has tried to avoid putting the site on the Superfund list.

"The EPA on a couple of other sites * * * experienced a significant amount of community resistance," said Robert Ray, the water-quality program director for the Northwest Colorado Council of Governments. "They felt there might be a better approach."

Enter the French Gulch Remediation Opportunities Group, or FROG, established by the EPA to bring residents, local officials, the mining company and a professional mediator to the table to determine the course of clean-up.

"Everyone recognizes and has concerns about how the Superfund tool is used," Rogers said. "Rather than just charging directly into a full-blown Superfund process, we decided what we really needed to do was get a lot of the stakeholders involved in the process . * * * Hopefully, there is less fear and more understanding."

The agency hired the local Keystone Center, a nonprofit mediation group with an international reputation, to open discussions with the mine owner, B&B Mining Co., and keep the process out of court.

"Typical (legal) costs of Superfund sites are about 40-60 percent of the costs, which is all litigation. It doesn't go toward any clean-up," said mediator Kristi Parker.

Negotiating with B&B, the group is fast approaching an agreement on sharing the costs and could begin cleaning up the site as soon as this summer.

"We're doing our very best to help the project along and try to keep it as friendly as possible," said B&B attorney Greg Penkowski. "We're trying to come up with something cost-effective that makes sense and deals with whatever problem there may be."

That includes figuring out how to clean up the water, either by preventing it from entering the mine in the first place or keeping it from leaving, as well as the easier task of removing the surface waste.

"The state submitted a proposal to do an encapsulation of the surface wastes," Ray said. "The proposal was to dig a hole on the site, line it with a geosynthetic membrane that doesn't allow water to go through it, and put the roaster fine and some of the mill tailings in it. We called it the 'burrito project' because we were wrapping up the nasty stuff."

While such proposals seem fanciful, it's the type of creativity all sides are encouraging to stem costs. And if all else fails to effectively clean the site, the EPA can resort to putting it on the Superfund list.

"It is a big hammer, no doubt about it," Penkowski said. "We've kind of got a tiger by the tail, and we're hanging on. Hopefully we'll come up with a workable solution."

Since instituting several administrative reforms, the pace of clean-up has picked up considerably. *See* SUPERFUND: Half the Sites Have All Cleanup Remedies in Place or Completed, GAO/RCED-99-245 (July, 1999).

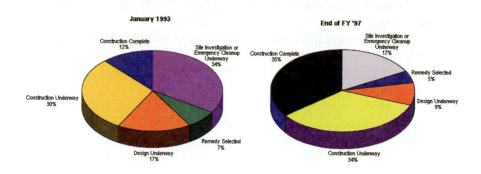

Figure 11.2–NPL Site Cleanup Status[5]

3. How to Clean up a Contaminated Site

CERCLA and the Superfund are meant to accomplish one central goal, which is the prevention of "releases" of hazardous substances from specific sites where soil or groundwater is, or may be, contaminated. A PRP or the EPA has several options available to it when contemplating how to remove the threat posed by a contaminated waste site. Each carries with it certain dangers that must be factored into the eventual clean-up decision. The most logical option is to remove the source of the threat, treat it, and then dispose of it, either on-site or at an off-site commercial facility. The removal option has the advantage of controlling the source of the environmental threat; but it has disadvantages. Sometimes the site is so large, and the contamination so pervasive, that removal of all contamination is virtually impossible; removal is usually extremely expensive; and the mere act of removing and/or transporting large amounts of hazardous substances can itself harm the environment or the public.

The standard techniques for managing the hazards of Superfund sites are described in the following excerpt, which also emphasizes the hazards inherent in clean-up activities:

> * * * the clearest way to understand the sources of the physical effects of remediation is to see a clean-up project for what it is–a construction site and industrial operation. Construction and trans portation risks account for the great majority of the fatalities suffered by remediation workers. Cleaning up Superfund sites also requires some or all of the following kinds of operations:
>
> 1) restricting site access and imposing institutional controls to limit post-remediation land use;
> 2) decontaminating, decommissioning (shutting down), and demolishing buildings and other structures;

---

[5]Source: http://www.epa.gov/superfund/shasissf/mgmtrpt.htm.

3) handling hazardous materials in tanks, ponds, pits, drums, and other containers;

4) managing contaminated media such as soil, sediment, surface water, and groundwater;

5) treating wastes or contaminated media to stabilize, compact, or neutralize it; and

6) transporting hazardous materials away from a site and transporting construction and treatment equipment and materials to it.

* * *

[R]emediation risks consist of both (i) the toxic and unfamiliar risks associated with the hazard that triggered the clean-up in the first place, and (ii) the mechanical or accident-related risks associated with the physical demands of construction and transportation work. * * *

[Finally, there are several] different receptors of risks. * * * The primary receptors of remedial risks are (i) project workers, including both those regularly employed at the site and transportation workers; (ii) the general public, including immediate neighbors, affected area population, and residents of transportation corridors; and (iii) the natural world, especially sensitive ecosystems like wetlands in and around the site. * * *

John S. Applegate & Steven M. Wesloh, *Short Changing Short-Term Risk: A Study of Superfund Remedy Selection*, 15 YALE J. ON REG. 269, 277-79 (1998).

To avoid some of the problems inherent in clean up activities, *in situ* treatment methods are now being tried. If the site is capable of being enclosed and surrounded, it may be "impounded," often by wrapping it with several impermeable layers of some plastic product. Impoundments work only if the site can in fact be encased, and if the encasement is truly impermeable and capable of resisting the most toxic of volatile substances. Impoundments are usually surrounded by monitoring wells, so that any leakage into groundwater can be detected.

A more sophisticated and experimental clean-up option entails the on-site treatment of hazardous wastes to alter their chemical and toxic nature. This can occur in a number of ways, ranging from adding chemicals or bacteria to alter the molecular structure of the wastes, to circulating gas through soil in order to remove harmful chemicals when they react with the gas, to sending electrical charges into contaminated soil. When a Superfund site is an enormous mile-deep pit filled with lethal water, some of these *in situ* options seem very appropriate.

Figure 11.3–Berkeley Pit, Butte, Montana

BUTTE BREAKS NEW GROUND TO MOP UP A WORLD-CLASS MESS

Jim Robbins
New York Times, July 21, 1998

So much copper was dug from the mountain this city in the Rockies was built on, it was dubbed the Richest Hill on Earth.

Now the copper is largely gone, and the bill for a century's worth of mining has come due. The mountains and waterways around Butte are so contaminated they make up the largest Superfund complex in the country. The contamination is so widespread and difficult to deal with that company scientists have been forced to look for new solutions. Butte has, in essence, become a giant test laboratory for clean-up technologies.

The heart of the problem is in the city of Butte itself, which is next to one of the largest open-pit mines in the world. The mine was abandoned in 1979 and the Atlantic Richfield Co. stopped pumping water out of the pit in 1981. As maroon-colored water pours into the pit through mining tunnels that honeycomb the remains of the mountain, and more washes in from the surface, the water carries large amounts of sulfuric acid and a variety of heavy metals, including zinc, nickel, cadmium and arsenic, and especially high levels of copper.

In 1995, 342 snow geese landed on the water and never took off again. Burns in the esophagus indicated they died from drinking the water. "It's basically acid," said Michael Tuck, president of MSE Technology Applications, a company owned by the Montana university system and funded by grants from the Department of Energy, the National Aeronautics and Space Administration and other Federal agencies. "And it has the potential to contaminate wells and creeks."

* * *

Any solution will be less than perfect. Berkeley Pit's poisonous brew is expected to pollute the surrounding aquifer by 2022 if nothing is done. Atlantic Richfield plans to spend $48 million to build two plants to treat the water indefinitely at a cost of $14 million a year. The plan is to add lime to the water and neutralize the sulfuric acid, allowing the metal to precipitate out. But the process creates 1,000 tons of lime sludge each day, which would be dumped backed into the pit or stored in a lagoon.

MSE Technology Applications is studying other ways to treat the water, and to remove copper and other metals in order to help offset treatment costs. MSE looked at some 150 proposals and was evaluating 15 that seemed most promising.

One idea that works, at least chemically, is another precipitation scheme, in which sulfides are added to the brew. This makes the metal ions heavier, which means the most valuable metals, copper and zinc, precipitate out and could be sold. It would reduce the sludge to 300 tons a day, from 1,000. "Chemistry is straightforward, but the economics of building a treatment plant are another matter," said Mary Ann Harrington-Baker, manager of MSE's Heavy Metals Program.

*　*　*

Down the valley from the pit, is Silver Bow Creek, the small meandering stream where gold was originally found. Seven smelters lined the creek at one time. Thousands of tons of tailing laden with heavy metals were dumped along its banks. This stream was so polluted that 26 of its 30 miles had no fish.

Atlantic Richfield moved and buried the tailings, and planned to build a plant to treat the water with lime. Instead, engineers designed and built a two to three-acre artificial wetland, complete with cattails. Contaminated water from the creek is pumped into a reservoir behind the wetland and seeps through the mud at the rate of three to five feet per day.

Bacteria in the mud consume carbon and oxygen from decaying plants. Once they deplete the oxygen, the bacteria begin to eat the sulfur from the acid mine drainage and make it more alkaline. As the water becomes more alkaline, the zinc and copper precipitate out. The water flows through another artificial swamp, where it is reoxygenated, forcing out the methane and hydrogen sulfide gases.

"Contrasted with a system with a lot of lime, it's cost effective," said Sandy Stash, who directs the clean-up operation for Atlantic Richfield in Montana, "but it's not cheap."

After a Superfund site is cleaned up, and the levels of contamination are brought down so that neither human health nor the environment is threatened, the next question is what to do with the site in its post-Superfund state. If humans are to live on the site, then additional remediation work might be necessary. If the site is to return to a natural condition, human intervention may be needed to jump start nature. For example, at the former Bunker Hill smelter site in Idaho, logging and sulphur dioxide emissions had denuded the nearby hillsides. To minimize erosion of lead-contaminated soil and to restore the forest, EPA has ordered a massive revegetation program that will take three years and cost about $8 million.

MASSIVE REVEGETATION

The Associated Press, September 27, 1998

Big helicopters will dust Kellog, Idaho's former Bunker Hill smelter site, with fertilizer and grass seed in what managers call the largest revegetation contract in the United States.

The project at the massive federal Superfund site will continue each fall and spring for the next three years.

"It's the largest revegetation contract in the United States, and it could be the biggest in the world," said project manager Rich Fink of the U.S. Army Corps of

Engineers. Tri-State Hydro-Seeding of Kingston won the $8 million contract.

The hillsides were denuded over the past century by logging, fires and sulfur dioxide that spewed from the stacks of Bunker Hill's zinc refinery. The emissions combined with water to make sulfuric acid. The barren slopes are also contaminated with lead.

The best way to stop erosion is to get something to grow.

As you study the law of CERCLA, it is important to remember that it all comes down to moving, incinerating, treating, or encapsulating chemicals, soil, and water. The physical demands of these activities drive the risks and costs which in turn drive the regulatory system.

B. CERCLA in Context

CERCLA was the last of the major environmental statutes enacted during the "Environmental Decade," 1969-1980. At the beginning of that period, between 1969 and 1972, Congress required that certain procedures be followed to assess the environmental impacts of major governmental actions. It also established programs for regulating air and water pollution, and for protecting drinking water. By the mid-1970s, scientific and medical knowledge had grown considerably. It was now possible to detect chemicals in the environment at levels one part per billion and lower. This was unheard of 20 years before. The medical community was beginning to establish links between numerous chemical substances and negative health effects, especially cancer. Soon policymakers began to suspect that very low levels of many toxic chemicals in the environment could pose a threat to public health. As we have seen, one statutory response to that discovery was the enactment of federal laws to regulate the sale and production of toxic substances, in order to control market access to products that might contain chemicals harmful to humans. Among the prime examples of this kind of statute are the Federal Insecticide, Fungicide, and Rodenticide Act of 1947 (FIFRA), and the Toxics Substances Control Act of 1976 (TSCA), discussed above in Chapters 7 and 8, respectively. The Resource Conservation and Recovery Act of 1976 (RCRA), covered in Chapter 9, was designed to prevent the active disposal of toxic wastes onto the soil and into groundwater. However, RCRA, like FIFRA and TSCA, did not address the threat posed to humans and the environment from *past* waste disposal practices.

1. Love Canal and the Statute's History

The problem of inadequate hazardous waste disposal was dramatically brought home to America by the Love Canal disaster. As the case study in Chapter 9 explains, the Love Canal site was a classic abandoned waste dump. Standard disposal practice for factories, refineries, and mines was simply to place hazardous wastes in barrels, drums, or open pits and then to bury and abandon them. Consistent with this tradition, for ten years the Hooker

Chemical Company had dumped tens of thousands of tons of chemical waste into an old canal, covered it, and had given the site to the local board of education. The new owners built a school on the land and sold the remainder to homebuilders. After a series of illnesses began to plague the area, investigators discovered that toxic chemicals migrating from the canal had contaminated the subsoil and groundwater, and had even seeped into residential basements. Panic set in, the Love Canal story made national headlines, the area's residents were hastily evacuated, and the problem of non-active waste sites was placed at the doorstep of Congress.

Three questions had to be addressed. First, how grave was the problem of hazardous waste dumps? Before CERCLA was enacted, both the EPA and congressional subcommittees estimated (based on surveys of the largest chemical manufacturers) that there could be between 1,500 and 2,000 dump sites across the United States that contained wastes so hazardous that they threatened human health.[6] The EPA concluded that virtually all of the hazardous wastes generated in this country were being disposed of improperly, and that there were over 3,000 new spills of toxic chemicals each year. Second, who should pay for the clean-up of hazardous waste sites? There were two choices—(1) the federal government could bear the cost, perhaps by creating a clean-up fund through the imposition of a tax on classes of industries that tended to dispose of hazardous waste; or (2) the private parties responsible for the waste dumps could be liable for clean-up costs, if a formula could be devised for determining who exactly was responsible.[7] Third, if a waste site was not an "orphan site" (one whose owners had disappeared), what mechanism should be established for reaching a range of liable private parties to pay clean-up costs that often run into the tens of millions of dollars per site?

With respect to the first question, the fact that CERCLA was passed at all reflected congressional concern that the problem of environmental contamination from hazardous waste sites was indeed national in scope, and was both grave and threatening. As we saw at the beginning of this chapter, the second question was answered by establishing a program that combined the ideas of federal responses to locations containing hazardous substances, as well as private party liability for past and ongoing releases of such substances. We also saw that the third question was answered by imposing strict, joint and several, and retroactive liability on parties deemed "responsible" for the contaminated sites.

---

[6] After CERCLA's enactment, EPA compiled an inventory of over 35,000 sites contaminated by past dumping of hazardous wastes. Of these, over 10,000 sites still require further federal investigation to determine if they should be placed on the National Priority List. By 1999, there were nearly 1400 on the NPL. The remainder of the sites are subject to clean-up by private parties or clean-up under state law.

[7] In the case of the Love Canal, the federal government paid for relocating its residents, while the Occidental Petroleum Company, owner of the Hooker Chemical Company, paid for the remediation work.

CERCLA's structure was modeled on section 311 of the Clean Water Act, which establishes a revolving fund for use by the Coast Guard and EPA to respond to oil spills (and, after 1978, hazardous substance spills) into navigable waters. It applies the principle of strict liability to persons responsible for releases of "harmful quantities" of oil.[8] Within §311 are the seeds of CERCLA. Section 311(b)(5) requires any person "in charge" of a vessel or facility discharging harmful quantities of oil to report the discharge to the EPA or Coast Guard.[9] Section 103 of CERCLA requires reporting of releases of hazardous substances to the National Response Center. Under §311(c), the federal government may respond to the discharge or threatened discharge of oil or other hazardous substances into navigable waters, so long as the action is consistent with the National Contingency Plan (NCP). The initial costs of clean-up may be paid out of the Oil Spill Liability Trust Fund. In a similar fashion, section 104 of CERCLA authorizes response action consistent with the NCP. Section 111 of CERCLA creates a Superfund which can be used to finance governmental response actions, and to reimburse private parties for costs incurred in carrying out the NCP. Section 311(f) imposes liability for clean-up costs and natural resources damages on owners or operators of vessels or facilities from which spills have occurred or are threatened. Section 107 of CERCLA imposes liability on current and past owners and operators of facilities where hazardous substances are released, or threatened to be released.[10]

---

[8] The term National *Contingency* Plan, is a vestige of CERCLA's origins. The original NCP dealt exclusively with oil spills; oil and hazardous substance spills on water are now a small part of the NCP. *See* 40 C.F.R. §§ 300, 300-335.

[9] What is a harmful quantity of oil? *See* United States v. Chotin Transp., Inc., 649 F. Supp. 356 (S.D. Ohio 1986) (20 gallons spilled into the Ohio River may be harmful).

[10] Like CERCLA's liability scheme, §311(f) of the CWA incorporates principles of strict liability, Stevant Transp. Co. v. Allied Towing Corp., 596 F.2d 609, 613 (4th Cir. 1979), as well as joint and several liability where the harm is indivisible. United States v. M/V Big Sam, 681 F.2d 432, 439 (5th Cir. 1982).

KEY PROVISIONS OF CERCLA

§101   *Definitions*–"facility"; "release"; "disposal"; "hazardous substance."

§104   *Removals* and *remedial action* authorized if consistent with the National Contingency Plan (NCP).

§105   National Contingency Plan requires establishment of hazard ranking system and a National Priorities List (NPL).

§106   *Abatement* orders may be issued if actual or potential releases create imminent and substantial endangerment.

§107   *Liability* is imposed on potentially responsible parties (PRPs), defined as owners, operators, arrangers, and transporters of hazardous waste, for all costs of removal or remedial action incurred by the federal government not inconsistent with the NCP, for other response costs incurred by any person consistent with the NCP, or for damages to natural resources.

§111   Creates a *Superfund* to finance governmental response actions, and to reimburse private parties for costs incurred in carrying out the NCP.

§113   Prevents pre-enforcement *judicial review* of response actions; permits private *contribution* actions against PRPs.

§116   Sets out *schedules* for listing sites on the NPL, for undertaking remedial investigation and feasibility studies, and for taking remedial clean-up action at sites.

§121   Fixes standards for CERCLA clean-ups. There is a preference for permanent solutions where the site must be cleaned up to a level meeting a "legally applicable or relevant and appropriate standard, requirement, criteria or limitation" (*ARARs*) found in federal environmental law, or state law if it is more restrictive than federal law.

§122   Articulates standards for government-initiated *settlements* with PRPs.

The Clean Water Act also contains an "imminent hazard" provision authorizing EPA to seek administrative and judicial action against those causing these hazards. 33 U.S.C. §1364 (a). The CWA's provisions regarding spills do not extend to spills or discharges of contaminated materials onto land,[11] however. Therefore, CERCLA was a huge expansion of the oil spill provisions, but its passage in 1980 was nevertheless extremely hurried. The actual language was the product of a last-minute compromise by a small bipartisan group of influential senators. With virtually no debate, the statute passed in a lame-duck session by the Senate, and the House then agreed to accept the Senate version without even holding a conference committee. The result was unclear draftsmanship and very little legislative history. Many judges have in fact assumed that Congress left much of CERCLA vague so that the courts would, by their decisions construing its language, develop a federal common law to supplement the statute. Whether intended or not, this is in fact what happened on the liability side of CERCLA, which is managed

---

[11] The Oil Pollution Act of 1990, PUB. L. 101-380, parallels §311 of the CWA. Both assume that the party responsible for the oil spill should be the one who should pay for the costs of cleaning it up, and that the government should be able to recover any public monies that had to be spent.

by the courts through litigation. The preclusion of most judicial review of
remedy selection has, by contrast, resulted in very little judicial guidance on
the regulatory side, which is managed administratively.

The two amendments to CERCLA since 1980 have not significantly
altered its original structure though they have clarified (often by ratifying
judicial or administrative practice) some major provisions. The Superfund
Amendments and Reauthorization Act of 1986 (SARA) sorted out several
liability issues, established a methodology for deciding the nature and degree
of clean-up, and increased the Superfund amount to $8.5 billion. It also made
a number of procedural changes designed to accelerate the clean-up process.
Chief among these were provisions facilitating contribution among
responsible parties and encouraging settlements. An obscure amendment
enacted in 1996 (as part of the Asset Conservation, Lender Liability, and
Deposit Insurance Protection Act, Pub. L. No. 104-208) clarified the scope of
lender liability and provided additional protections for fiduciaries.

2. CERCLA and RCRA

As noted above, RCRA was passed to provide a comprehensive structure
for managing hazardous and non-hazardous solid wastes, primarily at active
waste disposal sites. CERCLA, on the other hand, was intended to address
ongoing problems associated with past improper waste disposal activities.

> Unlike [CERCLA], RCRA is not principally designed to
> effectuate the clean-up of toxic waste sites or to compensate those
> who have attended to the remediation of environmental hazards. *Cf.*
> *General Electric Co. v. Litton Industrial Automation Systems, Inc.*,
> 920 F.2d 1415, 1422 (C.A.8 1990) (the "two * * * main purposes of
> CERCLA" are "prompt clean-up of hazardous waste sites and
> imposition of all clean-up costs on the responsible party"). RCRA's
> primary purpose, rather, is to reduce the generation of hazardous
> waste and to ensure the proper treatment, storage, and disposal of
> that waste which is nonetheless generated, "so as to minimize the
> present and future threat to human health and the environment." 42
> U.S.C. § 6902(b).

Meghrig v. KFC Western, Inc., 516 U.S. 479, 783 (1996). Despite this
difference in focus, there are still similarities and overlap between CERCLA
and RCRA. Jurisdictionally, there is a great deal of potential overlap, since
CERCLA incorporates RCRA's list of hazardous wastes, and RCRA includes
corrective action provisions for cleaning up RCRA-permitted facilities. This
provides EPA with remedial choices when the contaminated site is also a
"treatment, storage, and disposal facility" (TSDF) regulated under RCRA.
TSDFs are subject to strict RCRA requirements, including the need to obtain
a permit before wastes can be received, and the need to take corrective actions
to clean up uncontrolled wastes that may be hazardous. EPA may choose to

rely on either CERCLA or RCRA to bring about a clean-up at a TSDF.[12] If EPA proceeds under CERCLA, the owner/operator may object, because CERCLA actions are often more public and less flexible, and because the owner/operator then becomes a PRP from whom response costs may be recovered. Despite these concerns, the rule is that RCRA does not limit CERCLA, and CERCLA may have applicability to a RCRA TSDF. *Apache Powder Co. v. United States*, 968 F.2d 66 (D.C. Cir. 1992) (EPA may include a TSDF subject to RCRA on the CERCLA National Priorities List). *See also Chemical Waste Management, Inc. v. Armstrong World Industries, Inc.*, 669 F. Supp. 1285 (E.D. Pa. 1987) (a TSDF allegedly in violation of RCRA may nonetheless seek cost recovery under CERCLA).

There is also a striking similarity between RCRA §7003, which empowers EPA to clean up hazardous waste sites that pose an "imminent and substantial endangerment to health or the environment," and CERCLA §106(a), which empowers EPA to issue a responsible party an abatement order when an actual or threatened release of hazardous substances presents an "imminent and substantial endangerment" to health or the environment. Initially, RCRA §7003 was understood to apply only to active hazardous waste sites. In 1984, Congress amended RCRA so that §7003 was applicable to both "past and present handling, storage, treatment, or disposal" of hazardous wastes.[13] As a result, EPA sometimes uses RCRA §7003 and CERCLA §106(a) in tandem when it confronts a particularly dangerous waste disposal site.[14] If EPA can identify a PRP at such a site, it might also proceed under the cost-recovery provisions of CERCLA §107 (setting out liability standards when cost recovery actions are initiated for clean-up expenses).

CERCLA §106 is available only to the federal government; states and private parties seeking abatement must use RCRA's citizen suit provision, §7002(a)(1)(B) in conjunction with § 7003. *See Sealy Connecticut, Inc. v. Litton Industries*, 989 F. Supp. 120, 123 (D. Conn. 1997) (present owner could bring RCRA §7002 action against prior owner, even though present owner was a CERCLA PRP). Private parties may not obtain compensatory relief for personal injury or property under §7003 or §7002, since these

---

[12] EPA usually declines to address waste problems at RCRA TSDFs under CERCLA, in large part because a non-CERCLA response conserves the Superfund. *See, e.g.,* 54 Fed. Reg. 41,004 (1989).

[13] Some earlier RCRA cases assumed that §7003 applied just to inactive sites, because a contrary interpretation would have limited the government's ability to respond to "disasters precipitated by earlier poor planning." United States v. Waste Industries, Inc., 734 F.2d 159 (4th Cir. 1984).

[14] That RCRA is primarily intended to correct present hazardous waste practices, while CERCLA is more focused on past disposal actions, still has relevance in two contexts: (1) when parties bring an action under both RCRA and a *state* waste management statute, where the state statute is a prospective regulatory regime, Acme Printing Ink Co. v. Menard, Inc., 870 F. Supp. 1465 (E.D. Wis. 1994); and (2) when an RCRA remedy might interfere with a CERCLA clean-up. McClellan Ecological Seepage Situation v. Perry, 47 F.3d 325 (9th Cir. 1995).

RCRA provisions are equitable. CERCLA §107 is the preferred statutory provision for recovery of clean-up costs. RCRA §7003 may also be broader than CERCLA, since it includes within its reach those who "contribute" to the practices that create the endangerment; RCRA's provisions also extend to non-hazardous "solid waste"; and RCRA is not subject to CERCLA's petroleum exclusion (CERCLA §§101(14) and 101(33)). Moreover, CERCLA has been interpreted to require that the "hazardous substances" exist in sufficient concentrations to subject a party to response costs. *Amoco Oil Co. v. Borden, Inc.*, 889 F.2d 664 (5th Cir. 1989). On the other hand, the "hazardous substances" subject to CERCLA cover a broader range of materials than RCRA's "hazardous wastes." The CERCLA term includes RCRA hazardous wastes as well as substances regulated under the Clean Air Act (CAA), the Clean Water Act (CWA), and the Toxic Substances Control Act. §101(14); *State of California v. Summer Del Caribe, Inc.*, 821 F. Supp. 574 (N.D. Cal. 1993).

3. CERCLA and State Law

CERCLA has something of a love-hate relationship with state law. On the one hand, CERCLA liability is a logical statutory extension of state common law tort doctrine. Moreover, it contains a broad savings clause, which provides that nothing in the statute "shall affect * * * the obligations or liabilities of any person under * * * State law, including common law, with respect to releases of hazardous substances or other pollutants or contaminants." §302(d). This savings clause is to prevent the creation of an inference that CERCLA is intended to be the exclusive remedy for harms that also violate the statute. CERCLA was not intended to wipe out the common law of toxic torts. *See PMC, Inc. v. Sherwin-Williams Co.*, 151 F.3d 610, 618 (7th Cir. 1998); *Gordon v. United Van Lines, Inc.*, 130 F.3d 282, 288-89 (7th Cir. 1997). Nor does CERCLA preempt state statutes that do not conflict with federal cleanup objectives. *Fireman's Fund Ins. Co. v. City of Lodi*, 41 F. Supp. 1100 (E.D. Cal. 1999) (CERCLA does not preempt California Hazardous Substance Account Act). It is therefore common for actions against parties responsible for contaminating a waste site to be grounded both in CERCLA and state statutory and common law.

On the other hand, CERCLA does preempt state laws and actions arising under state common law that would have the effect of preventing the accomplishment of federal statutory clean-up goals. *See, e.g.,* Gregory Romano, *"Shovel First and Lawyers Later": A Collision Course for CERCLA Clean-ups and Environmental Tort Claims*, 21 WM & MARY ENVTL. L. & POLICY REV. 421 (1997); *Arrest the Incinerator Remediation, Inc. v. Ohm Remediation Services, Corp.*, 5 F. Supp. 291 (M.D. Pa. 1998) (CERCLA preempts private state law nuisance action seeking to block ongoing clean-up of Superfund site); *In re Pfohl Bros. Landfill Litigation*, 68

F. Supp. 2nd 236, 249 (W.D.N.Y. 1999)(CERCLA preempts state statute of limitations that would otherwise have removed liability from those who Congress intended to be responsible for clean-up costs); *BASF Corp. v. Central Transport, Inc.*, 830 F. Supp. 1011 (E.D. Mich. 1993) (CERCLA preempts state law which otherwise would have limited the liability of a dissolved corporation under §107).

Even though CERCLA builds upon, and is a direct extension of, common law principles of strict liability for abnormally dangerous activities, it alters traditional common law tort doctrine in several ways. It often goes farther than traditional tort law, allowing the government and private plaintiffs to do things that would be quite difficult for the common law to do.

Similarities To The Common Law

1. Under CERCLA, an "owner" PRP is liable for clean-up costs irrespective of negligence or fault. Liability may also be imposed on an owner PRP regardless of whether the government has been able to prove actual harm (as opposed to threatened harm or risk) stemming from the site. Some jurisdictions have likewise deemed property owners subject to strict liability notwithstanding that they had not disposed of any waste during their tenure on the now contaminated property. *See, e.g., State of New York v. Shore Realty Corp.*, 759 F.2d 1050, 1051 (2d Cir. 1985); RESTATEMENT (SECOND) OF TORTS §839.

2. CERCLA provides that companies that arrange for the disposal of hazardous waste may be PRPs and be liable for clean-up costs. Similarly, some courts have decided that a company's decision to generate wastes, and to dispose of these wastes, either by itself or through an independent contractor, may be an "abnormally dangerous activity" giving rise to common law strict liability. *See, e.g., United States v. Hooker Chemicals and Plastics Corp.*, 722 F. Supp. 960 (N.D. N.Y. 1989) (generate and dispose of wastes on company's own property); *Sterling v. Velsicol Chemical Corp.*, 647 F. Supp. 303 (N.D. Tenn. 1986) (same); *Kenney v. Scientific, Inc.*, 497 A.2d 1710 (N.J.Super.,1985) (through independent contractor).

3. CERCLA provides for recovery, by the government, for natural resource damages, which encompass environmental harms to "public" natural resources not owned by private parties. The common law also recognizes that a nuisance can be "public," when there is an "unreasonable interference with a right common to the general public." RESTATEMENT (SECOND) OF TORTS §821B. As with CERCLA natural resources damages claims, such public rights are usually protected by a public body. *State of New York v. Schenectady Chemicals, Inc.*, 479 N.Y.S.2d 1010 (N.Y.A.D. 3 Dept. 1984).

Extensions Of The Common Law

1. As any first-year law student knows, the common law of torts usually requires a proximate causal linkage between the plaintiff's injury and the defendant. It was noted in Chapter 5 (Toxic Torts), that one of the chief

difficulties in bringing a tort action against an entity that has discharged some hazardous substance into the environment is demonstrating that (1) the substance under control of the defendant eventually wound up inside, or somehow made contact with, the plaintiff, and (2) once there, it caused some harm, such as cancer. The drafters of CERCLA rightly saw that individuals injured by the release of hazardous wastes faced substantial barriers to recovery under the common law, since proving the above two causation elements would be an especially high barrier to overcome. In response, CERCLA establishes a dramatically relaxed standard of proof of causation.

To establish CERCLA §107 liability, only two conditions must be met: (1) a release of a hazardous substance must cause the incurrence of response costs; and (2) the defendant must fall within one of four categories of responsible parties based on relationship to the waste or to the site, rather than on the quality of the defendant's conduct. The first condition does not require proof that the defendant's hazardous waste actually migrated to the plaintiff's property; it is sufficient that legitimate response costs were incurred by the defendant. *Dedham Water Co., Inc., v. Cumberland Farm Dairy, Inc.*, 972 F.2d 453 (1st Cir. 1992). The second condition assumes that CERCLA's strict liability standard is satisfied regardless of the ignorance, action, or inaction of the defendant; all that is relevant is the defendant's status with respect to the waste.

2. Another problem facing plaintiffs who wish to bring a common law toxic tort action is that there is usually a long latency period between the time of initial exposure to the harmful substance and the manifestation of the physical harm or illness. This is especially true of cancer. Since many cancers can occur years or decades after the plaintiff's contact with the cancer-causing substances, the relevant statute of limitations may have run before the plaintiff is aware of any injury. To address this long-latency issue, CERCLA §309 provides that for injuries caused by exposure to hazardous substances, state statutes of limitations for *state law* causes of action do not begin to run until the plaintiff has reason to know that the injury was caused by exposure to a hazardous substance.[15]

---

[15] Section 113 (g) sets out the period of time in which various CERCLA actions must be brought–(1) natural resources damages (within 3 years from the date of the discovery of the loss); (2)(A) cost recovery for removal action (within 3 years after completion of the action); (2)(B) cost recovery for remedial action (within 6 years after initiation of physical on-site construction); (3) contribution (within 3 years of date of judgment for a cost recovery action).

While §113(g)(2)(B) provides that "initial action" to recover costs must be commenced within 6 years for remedial action, any "subsequent action . . . for further response costs may be maintained at any time during the response action . . . ." "Sometimes it is difficult to determine whether an action is "initial" or "subsequent" to an initial action. *See* U.S. v. Navistar Intern. Transp. Corp., 152 F.3d 702 (7th Cir. 1998) (government action to recover oversight costs was "initial action," notwithstanding the government's earlier action to establish liability of third party, because government never previously asserted any claim against a PRP).

3. Under the common law, it is quite difficult for a property owner to pursue a strict liability claim against a former owner who has contaminated the property with hazardous waste. This is because of the caveat emptor doctrine, which holds that a vendee is required to make inspection of the property prior to purchase, so that the vendor is not responsible to the vendee for the property's "defective" condition existing at the time of transfer. *See, e.g., Philadelphia Electric Co. v. Hercules, Inc.*, 762 F.2d 303 (3d Cir. 1985); RESTATEMENT (SECOND) OF TORTS §352. CERCLA deals with the *caveat emptor* problem in two ways. First, contracting parties may allocate environmental risks between themselves by contract. §107(e)(1); *Olin Corp. v. Yeargen, Inc.*, 146 F.3d 398, 407-08 (6th Cir. 1998). Second, CERCLA permits one of the "responsible parties" (*i.e.*, the current owner) to sue other responsible parties (*e.g.*, the prior owner) for reimbursement of costs of clean-up in a contribution action. §113(f)(1).

4. In a common law tort action, the winning plaintiff's damages are typically determined by calculating the plaintiff's loss. The damage assessment under CERCLA §107(a)(4)(A) is not this traditional measure of damages; instead, it is based on the actual total costs of environmental remediation. Moreover, damage awards under the common law rarely include corrective action that will ultimately benefit society, or nature (not parties to the typical lawsuit). CERCLA §107(c) permits damages for injury to natural resources, while §107(d) includes as damages the total costs of health assessments to members of the public who may have been adversely affected by the waste site.

C. The Clean-Up Cornerstones

CERCLA is built on four cornerstones of remedial action. On one side of the CERCLA structure are the two basic components of the statute's blueprint for action—the *National Contingency Plan* (NCP) and the *National Priorities List* (NPL). These establish the procedures and standards for responding to releases of hazardous substances (the NCP) and for determining priorities among releases and threatened releases (the NPL). On the other side of the foundation are the two kinds of clean-up or response actions that may be taken once a release or threatened release has been confirmed. These are "removal" and "remedial" actions. "Removal" and "remedial" actions are defined in sections 101(23) and (24) of CERCLA. Removal actions prevent or minimize immediate threats posed by a release; remedial actions concern the final, long-term management of the site.

1. The National Contingency Plan (NCP)

CERCLA §105 states that clean-ups of hazardous waste sites are to be governed by a master plan, called the National Contingency Plan (NCP). *Redwing Carriers, Inc. v. Saraland Apartments*, 94 F.3d 1489 (11th Cir.

1996). The purpose of the NCP is to "establish procedures and standards for responding to releases of hazardous substances, pollutants, and contaminants," §105(a), including methodologies for identifying sites most in need of remediation, analyses for determining the risks to human health and the environment posed by waste sites, requirements for state and community involvement in decision-making, systems for selecting cost-effective remedies, guidance for remedial actions that use Superfund money, and standards for judging the extent and scope of a clean-up. The NCP also allocates authority among federal, state, and local governments for implementing the plan's clean-up provisions.

To ensure that the NCP has teeth, CERCLA provides that response costs cannot be recovered if the response actions violate the NCP. Governmental parties (the EPA, states, or Indian tribes) can only recover "costs of removal or remedial action" which are "not inconsistent with the [NCP]." §107(a)(4)(A). Private plaintiffs can recover only response costs which are "consistent with the [NCP]." §107(a)(4)(B); *ABB Indus. Systems, Inc. v. Prime Technology, Inc.*, 32 F. Supp. 2d 38 (D.Conn. 1998). What might this distinction in language mean? For present purposes, it means that the NCP is to be followed in any clean-up action. Later, when we consider liability and cost recovery, we will explore the distinction in more detail.

a. Evolution of the NCP

The original 1980 version of CERCLA called for revision of the existing NCP for oil spills to create a "national hazardous substance response plan." This plan was to detail a step-by-step process for dealing with a contaminated waste site, and to establish standards for determining the remediation measures to be deployed. The 1986 SARA amendments called for additional revision of the NCP, particularly in the area of remedy selection. The post-1986 NCP was also to give preference to remedial actions that "permanently and significantly" reduced the volume, mobility, and toxicity of the contaminants from a site. SARA also ordered the development of a Hazard Ranking System to be used to determine which sites may be added to the NPL. The new ranking system incorporates a risk assessment methodology that requires the EPA to accurately assess the relative "degree of risk to human health and the environment posed by sites and facilities subject to review." §105(c)(1).

The current product of these statutory commands is the 1990 National Contingency Plan.[16] *See* 40 C.F.R. part 300. The 1990 NCP has several important components:

National Response System—The discharge of oil, or the release of hazardous substances in reportable quantities, triggers a regulatory and

---

[16] Numerous challenges to the 1990 NCP were rejected in State of Ohio v. U.S. EPA, 997 F.2d 1520 (D.C. Cir. 1993).

statutory duty to notify the National Response Center. The reporting requirements, set forth in CERCLA §103(a), require that any person who knows of a release of a "reportable quantity" of a hazardous substance must notify the National Response Center. The reportable quantity varies, depending on the nature of the contaminant involved.[17] A lead agency is assigned, which then designates an On-Scene Coordinator (OSC) and Regional Project Manager (RPM) to direct response efforts. Together the OSC and RPM coordinate clean-up activities at the site, manage costs paid out of the Superfund, and ensure compliance with the NCP. State and local participation in response planning is provided by commissions and committees created under the Emergency Planning and Community Right-to-Know Act of 1986, 42 U.S.C.§11001 et seq.

Removals and remedial actions–The NCP articulates three steps that must be taken in order to clean up a hazardous waste site. First, those sites deemed worthy of some kind of clean-up job must be identified. This step is accomplished through the site identification and preliminary inspection assessment process (which entails listing on the Comprehensive Environmental Response Compensation and Liability Information System— the CERCLIS list of over 30,000 sites), and then listing on the NPL (over 1400 sites). Second, a decision must be made as to whether the CERCLA "response" should be an emergency "removal" or long-term "remedial" action. If the latter, a "remedial investigation/feasibility study" must be conducted to determine how best to clean up the site. Third, for remedial actions, the NCP requires that the remedy eventually chosen be cost-effective, a permanent solution, protective of human health and environment, and compatible with "applicable or relevant and appropriate" legal standards. *See* § 121.

Enforcement–The NCP provides guidance to the parties who may enforce various CERCLA provisions. If the EPA wishes to proceed under §106 administrative abatement authority when there is a threat that a release presents an "imminent and substantial endangerment," the NCP lays out what must appear in the administrative record. When private parties undertake response costs, the NCP spells out when such private actions are "consistent with the NCP" for purposes of cost recovery lawsuits under §107. When natural resources damages are claimed, CERCLA authorizes that officials may "act on behalf of the public as trustees for natural resources." §107(f)(2). The NCP identifies who these trustees are and sets out their responsibilities.

---

[17] Only an actual release of a hazardous substance into the environment triggers the reporting requirement; §103 does not apply to threats of a release. *See* The Fertilizer Institute v. EPA, 935 F.2d 1303 (D.C. Cir. 1991). The release reporting requirement ensures "that the government, once timely informed, will be able to move quickly to check the spread of a hazardous release." United States v. Carr, 880 F.2d 1550 (2d Cir. 1989). There are penalties for failing to report. §109; United States v. Freter, 31 F.3d 783 (9th Cir. 1994). CERCLA reporting requirements have nothing to do with whether a polluter is liable for clean-up costs. United States v. Alcan Aluminum Corp., 990 F.2d 711 (2d Cir. 1993).

Even though the NCP seems quite detailed—and it is far more detailed than the statute—the myriad subissues that arise in individual clean-up actions are resolved by reference to hundreds of CERCLA "guidance documents." Guidance, which need not be subjected to the rulemaking requirements of the Administrative Procedure Act, is issued at both the national and regional levels, and the result is an enormous body of "law" and practice that must be consulted in choosing response actions.

b. NCP Procedures

The NCP establishes procedures which the EPA and other government agencies must follow when responding to a contaminated waste site through either a removal or remedial action. This lengthy step-by-step process lays out what must be done, and who should do it, from the time a site is initially discovered to when the clean-up commences. The key stages in the process are as follows:

Preliminary assessment and site investigation—The first step leading to implementation of NCP procedures is, of course, the initial identification of a site that possibly contains hazardous waste. A site can be identified by neighbors, employees, site owners, interested passers by, environmental organizations, local, state, or federal officials. After identification of the suspect site, the OSC and lead agency (often EPA, but sometimes a state agency) then go through a series of steps to determine if the site poses an immediate threat to the public health, or if instead it warrants a long-term federal response, or if no action is needed. More specifically, these steps are:

- *Removal site evaluation*—a quick assessment to see if the problem at the site requires an immediate clean-up, that is, a "removal" action;
- *Preliminary assessment*—an assessment that either eliminates the site from further investigation if it poses no threat, or if there is a threat, a determination whether permanent remedial action is needed;
- *Site investigation*—a more thorough on-site and off-site field investigation of the release or threatened release to decide whether the site should be placed on the NPL for remedial action.[18] If EPA determines that no further response action is needed no additional federal action will be taken absent new developments or the discovery of new information.

Removal actions—Where a rapid response is necessary, the NCP imposes few procedural barriers. Removal actions are addressed more fully below.

---

[18] CERCLA allows the EPA to order any person to furnish information relating to the hazardous substances at the site (§104(e)). EPA personnel may also enter such sites and collect soil and groundwater samples. §104(e)(5)(B); United States v. Long, 607 F. Supp. 343 (S.D. Ohio 1987). Is it a "taking" if EPA has access to private property to monitor contaminated groundwater by wells drilled on private land? Hendler v. United States, 38 Fed. Cl. 611 (1997) (no); Juliano v. MUSSWMA, 983 F. Supp. 319 (N.D. N.Y. 1997) (yes).

Remedial investigation and feasibility study—If remedial action appears to be required at a site (regardless of whether removal action is taken), a remedy must be selected. The remedial investigation and feasibility study (RI/FS) is the pre-decision assessment that permits selection of an appropriate remedy. The remedial investigation and feasibility study take place concurrently, although they deal with separate evaluations. The remedial investigation is, in essence, a data acquisition exercise about the conditions at the site. In EPA jargon, the RI is used to "characterize" the site. It considers the nature of the hazardous substances there, and their threat to "human and environmental receptors," based on estimates of actual or potential exposure.[19]

The feasibility study analyzes remedial alternatives for a response that will satisfy CERCLA's clean-up criteria. Like an environmental impact statement, it typically proposes a few alternative remedies (including no action) and evaluates them according to the substantive requirements of the NCP. The RI/FS does not choose the remedy, but it does permit a remedy to be selected that will be protective of human health and the environment, and conform to applicable federal and environmental standards.[20]

Proposed plan—SARA added a final pre-decision step to enhance public participation in the remedy selection process. The proposed plan (PP) announces EPA's initial conclusions from the RI/FS process; that is, it announces EPA's preferred remedy. This is then made available for public commentary before a final decision is made[21] and state concurrence.[22]

Record of decision—The record of decision (ROD) memorializes EPA's final remedy selection. It is, in fact, the PP as modified in response to public comments, and it *includes* a response to all significant comments. The ROD describes the site and its risks; alternative remedial actions available; why the final remedy was chosen; how the action complies with the NCP; the remediation goals for the site; the extent to which hazardous substances will remain after the clean-up is done; and how community involvement affected the final plan.[23]

---

[19] The remedial investigation is intended to be a risk assessment, which considers "potential threats to human health and the environment" and establishes "acceptable exposure levels for use in developing remedial alternatives." 40 C.F.R. §300.430(d)(4).

[20] While the risk assessment portion of the RI/FS is done by the EPA, much of investigation and site assessment is done by the PRPs (when they can be found) and their contractors. The public also plays a role in the RI/FS process. The NCP requires the lead agency conduct interviews in the community, and prepare a community relations plan which ensures opportunities for public involvement in site-related decisions.

[21] *See* §117(a); VME Americas, Inc. v. Hein-Werner Corp., 946 F. Supp. 683 (E.D. Wis. 1996) (property owners allege that state agency did not comply with NCP requirement for public notice, and that therefore recovery of response costs was precluded).

[22] Section 104(c)(3) prevents EPA from taking remedial action if the relevant state has not agreed that it will play a role with respect to future maintenance of the remedial action; §121(f) requires that states have "meaningful" involvement in the selection of remedies.

[23] RODs are not planning documents; they provide an after-the-fact rationale for the remedy selected. As we will soon see, CERCLA prevents judicial challenges to remedy selection before implementation. §113(h). As a result, courts rarely decide cases where the plaintiffs

Remedial design and remedial action–The final stage prior to a construction and clean-up contract being awarded to a private contractor to implement the remedy is the "remedial design/remedial action" (RD/RA) step. This sets out the actual design of the remedy, and the construction that will take place to achieve the remedy's clean-up goal. After the RD/RA step, construction begins and eventually is completed. Compare EPA's progress between 1993 and 1997.

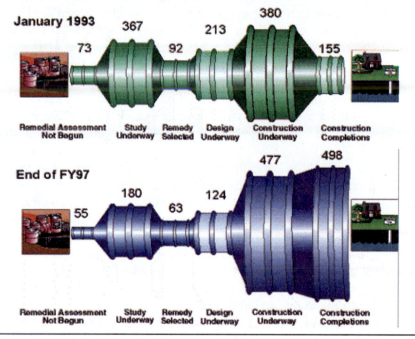

Figure 11.4–**Measuring the Progress of Site Mediation at NPL Sites**[24]

c. NCP Substantive Standards

There are two substantive aspects of determining the appropriate remedial action at a Superfund site–the method of clean-up (the actual remedy, so to speak–excavation, incineration, capping, liners, etc.), and the degree of clean up (sometimes called the "how clean is clean" question). These two standards must comply with the mandate set out in § 121. The two are interlinked, as the remedy is selected in large part on the basis that it will satisfy applicable clean-up goals, and clean-up goals are often chosen on the basis of available remedies. In drafting the NCP, the EPA combined the two sets of statutory factors into nine criteria, each of which was assigned a particular weight in remedy selection. Interestingly, detailed remedy selection criteria are relative newcomers to the statute. The 1980 CERCLA offered

argue that the remedy goes too far (when the plaintiff is a PRP) or not far enough (when the plaintiff is a citizen group), despite he centrality of these issues to CERCLA.
[24]Source–http://www.epa.gov/superfund/whatissf/mgmtrpt.htm

little guidance on remedy selection, so the 1986 SARA added section 121 to clarify the standards that EPA is to apply. The criteria themselves are discussed below when we address the cleanup, which is called a "response." There are two kinds of response actions contemplated by the NCP: "removal" actions and "remedial" measures. §104(a).

2. The National Priorities List

CERCLA may be used to clean up any contaminated site, but Congress also wanted to identify and clean up the most dangerous sites in the United States. This goal is accomplished by §105(a)(8)(B), which requires that a National Priorities List (NPL) be established. By the close of the 20th century, there were over 1,400 sites on the NPL, including those on private and public (usually federal) property. Both the United States Congressional Budget Office and the General Accounting Office estimate that there could be as many as 3,000 new non-federal sites eventually added to the NPL from the large inventory of sites listed in the CERCLA Information System (CERCLIS).

The road to the NPL generally begins with the Preliminary Assessment and Site Identification (PA/SI) phase of the NCP. One of the purposes of the PA/SI is to determine if a site is such a potential hazard that it warrants an NPL listing. The most commonly used mechanism for placing a site on the NPL is through a modeling system known as the Hazard Ranking System (HRS). The HRS assigns a numerical "score" to each site based on (1) various risk assessment criteria (*e.g.,* the likelihood of release, the nature of the hazardous substance, the probability of dilution, the distance from the site to the threatened target, and the nature of the endangerment to human population or environment); and (2) the potential exposure "pathways" to threatened humans and the environment (*e.g.,* soil, surface water, groundwater, and air). The resulting HRS score represents an estimate of "the probability and magnitude of harm * * * from exposure to hazardous substances as a result of contamination of groundwater, surface water, [soil], or air." *Eagle-Picher Industries v. U.S. EPA*, 759 F.2d 905 (D.C. Cir. 1985). Sites compiling a score of 28.50 or greater are eligible for the NPL list.[25]

a. Consequences of an NPL Listing

In theory, inclusion of a site or facility on the NPL list entails no liability, no fault, and no necessary legal consequences. The EPA could therefore assume a rather casual attitude about NPL listing, since it is only the first step in a process that requires further studies, investigation, public comment, and

---

[25] Under §105(a)(8)(B), states may designate sites or facilities that pose the greatest danger to "public health or welfare or the environment," regardless of their HRS score. If the Agency for Toxic Substances and Disease Registry issues a health advisory recommending "disassociation" of individuals from the site, that site may be listed on the NPL even if its HRS score is below 28.50. 40 C.F.R. §300.425(c)(3).

remedial evaluation under the NCP. The listing itself does not even definitively set the borders of the site, since the full extent of the contamination will usually be revealed only after more rigorous assessment of the pollution problem. Indeed, it is not uncommon for the EPA to enlarge the area of the site if, after exploration, the area of contamination is more widespread than originally assumed. *Washington State Dept. of Transp. v. EPA*, 917 F.2d 1309 (D.C. Cir. 1990).

While an NPL listing is necessary for the EPA to use Superfund money for remedial action, the NPL is not a pre-condition to a number of other clean-up options available under CERCLA. Among the more important non-NPL actions are:

- EPA may perform short term *removal* actions with Superfund money. State of New York v. Shore Realty Corp., 759 F.2d 1032, 1045-47 (2nd Cir. 1985).
- EPA may order parties to undertake short and long-term clean-up measures pursuant to its abatement authority under §106. See 40 C.F.R. §300.425(b)(4).
- State governments, local governments, or private parties may clean up a site and then bring a §107 action to recover their response costs. New York v. General Elec. Co., 592 F. Supp. 291 (N.D.N.Y. 1984);
- Settlement through consent decrees can take place under §122.

In other words, the NPL is an important element of CERCLA, but it is by no means a prerequisite or threshold for CERCLA-based action.

To the site owner, however, listing on the NPL is *very* significant.[26] To be on the NPL means that the EPA has determined that from nearly 40,000 sites on the CERCLA Information System list, this site poses a sufficient degree of concern about threats to health or the environment to warrant a full federal investigation and possible response. The NPL-listing is a prerequisite to EPA's use of Superfund money to pay for the cost of long-term, permanent remedial actions. 40 C.F.R. §300.425(b). Since these Superfund-subsidized remedial actions are reserved for only the gravest and most dangerous sites, an owner finding the site on the NPL is left with the sinking feeling that it will almost certainly be the focus of a major EPA CERCLA clean-up action. Whether or not that actually comes to pass, it is usually very different to sell or borrow against NPL-listed property, for obvious reasons.

b. Delistings and Deletions

For site owners and for PRPs, NPL listing is extremely bad news. Moreover, there is no administrative procedure in place for bringing about a "delisting" of an area that is not in fact contaminated and therefore

---

[26] The consequences of NPL listing and the resulting incentive to litigate the listing decision are discussed in John S. Applegate, *How to Save the National Priorities List from the D.C. Circuit—and Itself*, 9 J. OF NATURAL RES. & ENVTL. LAW 211 (1994).

improperly listed *ab initio*. The only way to delist a site that has been added to the NPL is to overturn EPA's listing decision in court.[27] Since NPL-listing is done by rulemaking, affected parties can obtain pre-enforcement judicial review. Hence, NPL listing decisions have engendered a surprisingly large amount of litigation.[28] While challengers have enjoyed some success in this litigation, EPA's decision to put a site on the list may be judicially changed only if proven to be arbitrary and capricious. Under this standard, most courts defer to the EPA.[29] An EPA decision to list a site on the NPL will usually only be reversed if the agency makes a listing call based either on (1) criteria other than those specified by statute,[30] or (2) assumptions about the nature and extent of contamination that are not supported by the record.[31]

Sites can be *deleted* from the NPL for a number of reasons, such as completion of all necessary response actions. But even when a site has been deleted, EPA can restore the NPL listing if it is discovered that the threat of dangerous releases remains due to a flawed clean-up. The EPA's goal for the year 2000 is the deletion of 650 sites from the NPL.

3. Removal Actions

Relatively simple, short-term clean-ups at sites posing an immediate "threat to the public health or welfare" (40 C.F.R. §300.415(b)) are called removal actions. *ABB Indus. Systems, Inc. v. Prime Technology*, 32 F. Supp. 2d 38, 42 (D. Conn. 1998). In theory, none of these responses are intended to be effective in the long term; rather, they are expected to be superseded by a permanent remedy. They include actions like installation of fences and warning signs; removal of drums, barrels, or tanks that may leak or spill; excavation or removal of highly contaminated soils that could migrate; stabilizing dikes or impoundments; and evacuating individuals threatened by a release.

An important part of EPA's initial investigation of a site is to ascertain whether the immediacy of the threat requires removal action, or whether there is a long-term risk sufficient for an NPL-listing and remedial action.[32] As noted above, this threshold determination is important since the NCP prevents the EPA from undertaking remedial actions unless the site qualifies for an NPL-listing. The EPA may spend Superfund dollars on removal actions for

---

[27] Specifically, in the D.C. Circuit Court of Appeals—*see* §113(a); United States v. M. Genzale Plating, Inc., 723 F. Supp. 877, 884 (E.D.N.Y. 1989)

[28] *See* Applegate, *National Priorities List, supra.*

[29] *See, e.g.,* Board of Regents of Univ. of Washington v. EPA, 86 F.3d 1214 (D.C. Cir. 1996); 957 F.2d 882 (D.C. Cir. 1992).

[30] Mead Corp. v. Browne, 100 F.3d 152, 153-55 (D.C. Cir. 1996).

[31] National Gypsum v. EPA, 968 F.2d 40 (D.C. Cir. 1992)

[32] In 1993, EPA adopted the Superfund Accelerated Clean-up Model which places sites into three categories—(1) non-NPL-sites which need time-critical action; (2) NPL-caliber sites deserving of non-emergency early action; and (3) NPL sites where remedial responses are justified.

sites that are not on the NPL. So a site must be labeled as worthy of either removal or remedial action as an initial step. But how does EPA make that call?

The language of CERCLA provides some guidance. CERCLA §101(23) defines "removal" to include clean-up actions necessary to deal with a threatened release. These essential measures designed to "dispose of removal material" and "prevent or mitigate damage to the public health or welfare or to the environment." This statutory definition blurs the line between temporary fixes (removals) and permanent ones (remedial action). Case law is equally unhelpful in separating the two response actions. *Compare General Electric Co. v. Litton Industrial Automation Services, Inc.*, 920 F.2d 1415, 1418-19 (8th Cir. 1990) (excavation work was removal action), *with Channel Master Satellite Systems, Inc. v. JFD Electronics Corp.*, 748 F. Supp. 373, 384-86 (E.D.N.C. 1990) (excavation was remedial action).

The NCP compounds the definitional confusion between the two concepts. Removal action may be undertaken whenever there is a "threat," based on potential exposure to hazardous substances, contamination of drinking water supplies or ecosystems, or high levels of hazardous substances in soils that may migrate. 40 C.F.R. §300.415(b)(2). The same conditions trigger the need for more permanent remedial measures. The NCP defines the term "removal" extremely broadly as well, encompassing any response actions that might be taken when there is a release or a threatened release from a contaminated site. 40 C.F.R. §300.5. Neither the NCP definition nor the implementing regulations require that removals be limited to short-term, emergency threats. Indeed, pursuant to §104(a)(2), the EPA must undertake removal actions that are also consistent with "the efficient performance of long-term remedial action."

Because there is so much overlap between removal and remedial action, EPA may be tempted to perform full and permanent "remedial" clean-ups at a non-NPL site under its removal authority. There are two incentives for this approach: (1) the Superfund may be used to finance removal actions at sites not listed on the NPL; and (2) the procedures for removal actions allow the EPA to act more quickly than it may under its remedial action authority. However, courts have tried to keep the types of actions separate and have discouraged remedial clean-ups labeled as removals. Several cases seem to establish that early sampling, surveillance, and assessment studies are removal actions, especially when they are interim actions undertaken in emergency settings to address an immediate threat. *Hanford Downwinders Coalition, Inc. v. Dowdle*, 71 F.3d 1469 (9th Cir. 1990); *State of California v. Alton Chemical Corp.*, 901 F. Supp. 1481 (N.D. Cal. 1995). Responses to non-urgent situations are considered remedial actions. *Yellow Freight System, Inc. v. AFC Industries, Inc.*, 909 F. Supp. 1291 (E.D. Mo. 1995). One non-judicial limit on EPA's removal authority is found in §104(c)(1). This section provides that removal action at a site cannot continue after $2 million has been spent for response work, or one year has elapsed from the date of the initial agency response.[33]

If it is determined that removal action is needed, activity proceeds as follows. First, the action must "begin as soon as possible to * * * prevent * * * mitigate, or eliminate the threat . * * *" 40 C.F.R. §300.415(b)(3). Second, the public should be informed of the action, and be allowed to provide a certain amount of input to the decision makers. 40 C.F.R. §300.415(m). Third, when the removal action is being planned, the NCP provides that all Superfund-financed removal actions are, to the extent practicable, to meet the "applicable or relevant and appropriate requirements" (ARAR's) that determine the clean-up standard. ARAR compliance is only necessary for those actions that are directly part of the removal action, but not for other clean-up steps that are not encompassed by the removal plan. Fourth, when the response action is removal in nature, the party seeking cost recovery must prove that its actions were in "substantial compliance" with those portions of the NCP pertaining to removal actions. Morrison Enterp. McShares, Inc., 13 F. Supp. 2d 1095, 1115 (D. Kan. 1998). Fifth, the owner, operator, or PRP must provide EPA with relevant information about the site and the nature of the hazardous substances there and with physical access to the site. §104(e); *United States v. Omega Chemical Corp.*, 156 F.3d 994, 999-1000 (9th Cir. 1998).

If the removal action is completed by EPA, it will file suit to recover its costs if a PRP is available. Section 107 provides that a PRP "shall be liable for all costs of removal * * * incurred by the United States Government . * * *" A frequently litigated question, which will be taken up again later in this chapter, is whether a PRP should be required to repay the EPA for costs that are not directly connected to the actual clean-up. For example, should a PRP be liable for the government's "oversight costs"—the costs incurred by the EPA in monitoring private parties' compliance with their legal obligations during a removal action?

UNITED STATES V. ROHM AND HAAS CO.

2 F.3d 1265 (3d Cir. 1993)

STAPLETON, Circuit Judge.

* * *

Nowhere in the definition of removal is there an explicit reference to oversight of activities conducted and paid for by a private party. Nowhere is there an explicit statement that Congress considers administrative and regulatory costs incurred overseeing the removal and remedial actions of a private party to be removal costs in and of themselves. Nevertheless, EPA

---

[33] However, two statutory exceptions swallow the limitation. The §104(c)(1) limits are not applicable if EPA finds that additional response action is required, or that continuation of the removal action is consistent with the subsequent remedial action.

contends that the requisite clear statement of congressional intent as to the recoverability of oversight costs may be found in the third of the five categories in the definition of "removal," *i.e.*, "such actions as may be necessary to monitor, assess, and evaluate the release or threat of release of hazardous substances." [§ 101(23).]

Examined in a vacuum, this language could be understood to encompass at least some oversight of the activities of a private party, particularly private activities focusing on assessment of the risk. On the other hand, it is at least as plausible to read this language as referring only to actual monitoring of a release or threat of release rather than oversight of the monitoring and assessment activities of others. This latter reading would be consistent with an understanding of the definition that distinguishes at all stages—assessment, response formulation, and execution—between actions taken to define the scope of the risk created by a release or threatened release and actions taken to evaluate the performance of others to determine whether they are meeting their legal obligations. We believe a reading of the statutory definition that embraces this distinction is linguistically the more plausible one.

* * *

Turning from that which Congress omitted to that which it saw fit to include, various statutory provisions, as well as the general structure of CERCLA, suggest to us that Congress did not intend to include necessary removal and remedial actions so long as EPA finds that "such action will be done properly and promptly." However, the section also provides that:

> No remedial investigation or feasibility study (RI/FS) [by a responsible party] shall be authorized except on a determination by the President that the party is qualified to conduct the RI/FS and only if the President contracts with or arranges for a qualified person to assist the President in overseeing and reviewing the conduct of such RI/FS and if the responsible party agrees to reimburse the Fund for any cost incurred by the President under, or in connection with, the oversight contract or arrangement. [§ 104(a)(1).]

An RI/FS is an "investigation" of the type contemplated in § 104(b) and is clearly a removal action. If Congress considered government oversight of a private removal action to be a removal action in itself, the provision of § 104(a) requiring reimbursement of costs incurred by the government overseeing the private RI/FS would be unnecessary as § 107(a) would authorize the recovery of such oversight costs. Even more significant is the fact that although § 104(a) authorizes EPA to permit private parties to undertake all kinds of removal and remedial actions, it only discusses government oversight, and reimbursement for such oversight, with regard to RI/FS's. Had Congress intended the government's cost of overseeing private party removal and remedial activity other than RI/FS's to be recoverable, surely it would have added something to § 104(a) to manifest that intent.

* * *

The government's role in overseeing a private clean-up effort is far removed from any sort of literal government "removal" or activity peripherally connected to such removal. CERCLA § 107 appears to have been drafted primarily with CERCLA § 104 in mind; its cost recovery provisions allow recovery of all costs of government removal and remedial activity (*i.e.* the activity explicitly authorized by § 104(a)) as well as the costs of investigatory activity of the type authorized by § 104(b). On the other hand, there is no clear indication in § 107, § 104, [or] the definition of removal, * * * that government oversight actions were intended to be recoverable removal costs.

RECOVERABLE COSTS

The question of whether oversight costs are recoverable is a subset of the larger problem of whether indirect and administrative costs should be recoverable for either removal or remedial actions. For example, should the government's indirect overhead costs for a removal action be recoverable? The language of CERCLA is completely silent on this issue. *See National Cable Television Ass'n, Inc. v. United States*, 415 U.S. 336, 342 (1974), interpreted by *Skinner v. Mid-America Pipeline Co.*, 490 U.S. 212, 224 (1989) (before the federal government may impose financial burdens on private parties, "Congress must indicate clearly its intention to delegate to the Executive the discretionary authority to recover administrative costs not inuring directly to the benefit of regulated parties").

---

4. Remedial Actions

The other response action contemplated by CERCLA is remedial action, generally encompassing more extensive, long-term, permanent clean-ups of contaminated sites. *See Public Service Co. of Colorado v. Gates Rubber Co.*, 175 F.3d 1177 (10th Cir. 1999) (cleanup was remedial where landowner engaged in lengthy study of the site, expended $9 million, took four years to complete cleanup, and intended a permanent remedy); *State of Minnesota v. Kalman W. Abrams Metals, Inc.*, 155 F.3d 1019, 1025 (8th Cir. 1998) (permanent nature of remedy and the "leisurely manner" in which the clean-up problem was addressed made it a remedial action). CERCLA §101(24) defines "remedial action" as actions that are "consistent with permanent remedy," taken "instead of or in addition to removal actions" so as to "prevent or minimize the release of hazardous substances . * * *" Remedial actions may include removing contaminated groundwater, excavating contaminated soil, disposing of hazardous materials offsite, constructing barriers above, below, or around sites to prevent migration, and relocating residents. The NCP forbids the EPA from undertaking such clean-up measures unless the site subject to remediation is listed on the NPL. Remediation is therefore the mandated response action at the approximately 1,400 NPL sites. For these sites, deemed the most dangerous in the United States, clean-up will be slow (10-20 years from discovery to completion) and costly ($25-$30 million per site on average).

For remedial actions, the EPA must take care to comply with all the procedural and substantive requirements of the NCP.[34] As is the case with removal actions, EPA is authorized under §107 to sue any of the parties responsible for the contamination to recover EPA's costs of performing remediation activities.

PROBLEM

Read sections 121(a), (b) and (d) of CERCLA that call for the promulgation of cleanup criteria. Now take a look at how EPA implemented the criteria in the NCP:

Nine criteria for evaluation. The analysis of alternatives under review shall reflect the scope and complexity of site problems and alternatives being evaluated and consider the relative significance of the factors within each criteria. The nine evaluation criteria are as follows:

(A) *Overall protection of human health and the environment.* Alternatives shall be assessed to determine whether they can adequately protect human health and the environment, in both the short-and long-term, from unacceptable risks posed by hazardous substances, pollutants, or contaminants present at the site by eliminating, reducing, or controlling exposures to levels established during development of remediation goals * * *. * * *

(B) *Compliance with ARARs.* The alternatives shall be assessed to determine whether they attain applicable or relevant and appropriate requirements under federal environmental laws and state environmental or facility siting laws or provide grounds for invoking one of the waivers * * *.

(C) *Long-term effectiveness and permanence.* Alternatives shall be assessed for the long-term effectiveness and permanence they afford, along with the degree of certainty that the alternative will prove successful. * * *

(D) *Reduction of toxicity, mobility, or volume through treatment.* The degree to which alternatives employ recycling or treatment that reduces toxicity, mobility, or volume shall be

---

[34] Section 104(c) provides that EPA may not implement remedial action unless the state in which the site is located—

- agrees to pay 10 percent of clean-up costs;
- assures maintenance of the site upon completion of remedial action;
- demonstrates a 20-year capacity for the treatment and destruction of all resulting wastes.

assessed, including how treatment is used to address the principal threats posed by the site. * * *

(E) *Short-term effectiveness*. The short-term impacts of alternatives shall be assessed considering the following:

(1) Short-term risks that might be posed to the community during implementation of an alternative;

(2) Potential impacts on workers during remedial action and the effectiveness and reliability of protective measures;

(3) Potential environmental impacts of the remedial action and the effectiveness and reliability of mitigative measures during implementation; and

(4) Time until protection is achieved.

(F) *Implementability*. The ease or difficulty of implementing the alternatives shall be assessed by considering the [(1) technical feasibility, (2) administrative feasibility, and (3) availability of services and materials, including adequate off-site treatment].

(G) *Cost*. The types of costs that shall be assessed include [(1) capital costs, (2) annual operation and maintenance costs; and (3) present value of future costs].

(H) State [government] acceptance. * * *

(I) *Community acceptance*. This assessment includes determining which components of the alternatives interested persons in the community support, have reservations about, or oppose. * * *

40 C.F.R. § 300.430(e)(9)(iii), (f)(1)(i). These are the nine criteria used to select a remedy. How does the EPA's statement of NCP criteria differ from § 121 in form? In substance? Is it an improvement over the statute? Does it emphasize the same policies as the statute? The NCP has been held to be consistent with the statute. *Ohio v. EPA*, 997 F.2d 1520 (D.C. Cir. 1993).

Under the NCP, the most important considerations in selecting a remedy are the "protection of human health and the environment," the "applicable or relevant and appropriate" federal and state standards, permanence of remedies (including the preference for treatment), and cost effectiveness. Others have a lesser role—"state and community acceptance" because it is regarded as a modifying factor that only comes into play when a remedy has been tentatively selected, and "short-term effectiveness" because, as two commentators have suggested, the criterion is poorly understood and significantly complicates the analysis.[35] "Implementability" is in effect a catch-all for various practical, common sense considerations in selecting a remedy. Only the four most important remedy-selection considerations warrant extended discussion.

---

[35] John S. Applegate & Steven M. Wesloh, *Short Changing Short-Term Risk: A Study of Superfund Remedy Selection*, 15 YALE J. OF REG. 269 (1998).

a. Protectiveness

The protection of human health and the environment, the first of the NCP threshold criteria, must be met before a remedial alternative is acceptable. §121(b)(1); 40 C.F.R. §300.430(f)(1)(i)(A). Protectiveness means the acceptable exposure level representing concentrations to which humans (including sensitive ones) may be exposed without adverse effect. 40 C.F.R. §300.430(e)(2)(i)(A)(1).

To make this determination, EPA performs a two-part risk assessment analysis. For known or suspected carcinogens, the appropriate level for CERCLA sites is defined in the NCP as a range between 10^{-4} to 10^{-6} individual lifetime excess cancer risk. *See United States v. Burlington Northern Railroad Co.* 200 F.3d 679 (10th Cir. 1999)(a risk level of 1 in 100,000 does not mean that 100,00 people need to be exposed for one person to contract cancer; it means that for every person exposed there is a .00001% chance the person will get cancer). The toxicity portion of the equation is based, of course, on the contaminants of concern. The exposure portion is based on a "reasonable maximum exposure" (RME) scenario which calculates the amount of exposure to the harm-producing substances that may still remain after remediation is completed, and the likelihood that it still poses a risk to human health. This calculation of exposure is based on the cumulative effect of multiple contaminants, the potential for human exposure to toxic pathways from the site in light of exposure frequency and duration, the sensitivities of the population that may be in contact with the site, as well as some uncertainty factors.[36] The "protectiveness" goal is met when there would be a less than 1 in 500 chance that an individual exposed to a cleaned up Superfund site would receive exposure greater than the RME.[37]

b. ARARs

One of the most difficult questions under CERCLA is how clean the waste site should be once the remedial action is finished. The most specific guidance in section 121(d)(2) is that any "legally applicable" or "relevant and appropriate" rule under federal or state law (ARAR) must be achieved for on-site clean-ups or explicitly waived for specific reasons. The ARAR concept is an extremely important element of CERCLA because it does not judge the suitability of a clean-up according to some ad hoc, case-by-case measure, but according to either existing federal standards, such as those arising under RCRA, the Safe Drinking Water Act (SDWA), the Clean Water Act, and the

---

[36] One of the most important current issues in remedy selection is the choice of scenarios based on the anticipated future use of a site. This issue is explored in detail in Chapter 12 (C) (Federal Facilities), *infra*.

[37] Although §121(b)(1) requires protection of both human health and the environment, EPA's risk assessment analysis has largely ignored the risks to the environment. The rationale here is probably that humans are either more sensitive than ecosystems, or more important.

Toxic Substance Control Act, or their state counterparts (if more stringent than federal standards).[38] The ARAR requirement is also an extremely complex element of CERCLA, because it often involves adapting standards that were not originally developed for clean-up purposes, an exercise akin to fitting a square peg in a round hole.

The NCP makes a distinction between "applicable" and "relevant and appropriate" requirements. An "applicable" requirement includes "those clean-up standards, standards of control, and other substantive requirements * * *under federal environmental or state * * *laws that specifically address a hazardous substance . * * *" This language means that if a law would be legally enforceable at the site, regardless of CERCLA remediation, it must be attained unless grounds for a waiver exist.[39] "Relevant and appropriate" requirements are "clean-up standards * * * that, while not 'applicable,' * * * address problems sufficiently similar to those encountered at the CERCLA site that they use is well suited to the particular site." 400 C.F.R. §300.5. Unlike "applicable" requirements, which are largely objective, "relevant and appropriate" requirements are discretionary, and assume that "best professional judgment" will be used to decide if a given clean-up requirement addresses problems at the site (*i.e.*, is relevant), and is suited to the particular characteristics of the site (*i.e.*, is appropriate). EPA also uses a third category, "to be considered," for standards that are neither applicable nor suitable for direct adoption, but which may provide useful guidance.

An ARAR, particularly one based on an "applicable" requirement, can come from any number of federal or state laws. Most commonly, an ARAR is pegged to a health or risk-based numerical value, such as the maximum contaminant levels set under the Safe Drinking Water Act, (SDWA) that establish limits on contaminants in the water of a public water system. 42 U.S.C. §300(f) et seq. An ARAR can be a technology or activity-based requirement, such as RCRA's land disposal restrictions for RCRA "hazardous wastes" (which may have been disposed of at a CERCLA site). If a RCRA waste has been dumped at a CERCLA site, the RCRA requirement is the applicable requirement even if the wastes were disposed of at the site prior to the statutory date that they were deemed hazardous. *Chemical Waste Management, Inc. v. United States EPA*, 869 F.2d 1526, 1535-7 (D.C. Cir. 1989). Location-specific ARARs are also possible, if a legal restriction is triggered solely because the hazardous substance is in a specified location,

---

[38] *See, e.g.,* State of Missouri v. Independent Petrochemical Corp., 104 F.3d 159 (8th Cir. 1997) (a post-ROD county ordinance imposing stricter standards than federal law could not be an ARAR, since ARARs are frozen on the date of the ROD); United States v. City and County of Denver, 100 F.3d 1509, 1513 (10th Cir. 1996) (local zoning law in conflict with a CERCLA remedial order cannot be an ARAR).

[39] Section 121(d)(4) permits waiver of an ARAR if one of a number of conditions are present, such as—compliance with the ARAR will result in greater risk than alternative options; compliance with an ARAR is technically impractical; the ARAR derives from state law, but the state has not consistently applied it.

such as a wetland, a protected wildlife habitat, or a water body subject to an anti-degradation law under state law. *United States v. Akzo Coatings of America, Inc.*, 949 F.2d 1409, 1439-50 (6th Cir. 1991).

PROBLEM
THE SAFE DRINKING WATER ACT

CERCLA §121(d)(2)(a)(I) designates as an ARAR "any standard, requirement, criteria, or limitation" under the SDWA. The SDWA establishes two potential ARAR standards: maximum contaminant levels (MCLs), which represent the maximum permissible levels of contaminants that can be in the public water system; and maximum contaminant level goals (MCLGs), which are health-based goals, set without regard to their achievability or cost. EPA has determined that MCLGs of zero are not "appropriate" and therefore may not be ARARs. Instead, MCLs will become the applicable ARARs, even though the MCL ARAR would permit a site with contaminated groundwater to be declared clean when its groundwater still contained some detectable levels of the contaminant. In *State of Ohio v. EPA*, 997 F.2d 1520 (D.C.G. 1993), the court upheld EPA's decision to exclude zero-based MCLGs as ARARs.

- If an MCL is the ARAR, and not a MCLG of zero, some risk remains because MCLs may tolerate pollutants in groundwater at very low levels. Is this result consistent with CERCLA's goals?
- If MCLs are ARARs for groundwater, should the standard be met anywhere in the groundwater, or just at the drinking water tap?
- Should MCLs be an ARAR when the contaminated groundwater is otherwise unsuitable as drinking water (*e.g.*, if it is naturally saline)?

---

c. Case Study: ARARs and PCBs

EPA is often called upon to remediate hazardous substances found at abandoned, or sometimes operational, municipal dumps. These dumpsites are characterized by large volumes of extremely heterogeneous, mostly non-hazardous waste material. However, some hazardous wastes are frequently present, sometimes in high concentrations. For example, if electrical equipment manufacturer had disposed of PCB-containing articles and waste materials at the dump, there are typically some areas of the landfill with very high levels of PCB contamination and many areas with some contamination.

PCB-contaminated landfills present difficult practical and legal clean-up problems. The practical problem begins with characterization: the large volume of waste means that sampling the entire site is extremely expensive and may well be impractical. Moreover, the excavation and treatment of such volumes of waste is even more expensive. Alternatively, transportation to a licensed hazardous waste facility is not only expensive, but it involves transportation risks associated with moving thousands of truckloads of waste over highways—and there is a great deal of resistance to the idea that moving landfill risk from one neighborhood to another. Consequently, EPA's policy is to attempt to locate the worst of the contamination ("hot spots," in EPA jargon), treat and/or transport it elsewhere, and to place a weatherproof cap on the remainder of the landfill to limit further migration of water though the landfill.

The principal legal difficulty lies in determining the appropriate ARARs. The NCP requires ARARs to be identified, as follows:

(1) The lead and support agencies shall identify requirements applicable to the release or remedial action contemplated based upon an objective determination of whether the requirement specifically addresses a hazardous substance, pollutant, contaminant, remedial action, location, or other circumstance found at a CERCLA site.

(2) If, based upon paragraph (g)(1) of this section, it is determined that a requirement is not applicable to a specific release, the requirement may still be relevant and appropriate to the circumstances of the release. In evaluating relevance and appropriateness, the factors in paragraphs (g)(2)(i) through (viii) of this section shall be examined, where pertinent, to determine whether a requirement addresses problems or situations sufficiently similar to the circumstances of the release or remedial action contemplated, and whether the requirement is well-suited to the site, and therefore is both relevant and appropriate. The pertinence of each of the following factors will depend, in part, on whether a requirement addresses a chemical, location, or action [*i.e.*, the three types of ARARs]. The following comparisons shall be made, where pertinent, to determine relevance and appropriateness:

(i) The purpose of the requirement and the purpose of the CERCLA action;

(ii) The medium regulated or affected by the requirement and the medium contaminated or affected at the CERCLA site;

(iii) The substances regulated by the requirement and the substances found at the CERCLA site;

(iv) The actions or activities regulated by the requirement and the remedial action contemplated at the CERCLA site;

(v) Any variances, waivers, or exemptions of the requirement and their availability for the circumstances at the CERCLA site;

(vi) The type of place regulated and the type of place affected by the release or CERCLA action;

(vii) The type and size of structure or facility regulated and the type and size of structure or facility affected by the release or contemplated by the CERCLA action;

(viii) Any consideration of use or potential use of affected resources in the requirement and the use or potential use of the affected resource at the CERCLA site.

(3) In addition to applicable or relevant and appropriate requirements, the lead and support agencies may, as appropriate, identify other advisories, criteria, or guidance to be considered for a particular release. The "to be considered" (TBC) category consists of advisories, criteria, or guidance that were developed by EPA, other federal agencies, or states that may be useful in developing CERCLA remedies. * * *

40 C.F.R. § 300.400(g)(2); *see also* 40 C.F.R. § 300.5 (defining "relevant and appropriate requirements"). One of the very few judicial decisions on the meaning of "relevant and appropriate" construed it broadly:

> Even if Michigan's anti-degradation law were not applicable to this site, its consideration would certainly be "relevant and appropriate." Among possible factors to be considered, the environmental media ("groundwater"), the type of substance ("injurious") and the objective of the potential ARAR ("protecting aquifers from actual or potential degradation)," are all "relevant" in this case because they pertain to the conditions of the Rose Site. Moreover, considering the aforementioned factors, the use of Michigan's anti-degradation law is well-suited to the site at issue and therefore "appropriate" in this case.

U.S. v. Akzo Coatings of America, 949 F.2d 1409, 1445 (6th Cir. 1991).

At first blush, one would think that the appropriate analogy is other hazardous waste landfills. The relevant TSCA (why TSCA?) and RCRA regulations require that PCB landfills have not just a cap, but also a bottom liner, leachate collection system, relatively impermeable bedrock. They also limit the concentrations of PCBs in the landfill; concentrations higher than 100 ppm must be incinerated. 40 C.F.R. part 761. The cap-in-place remedy obviously does not meet these standards.

Consider the following arguments that may be used by EPA to justify not following the PCB regulations:

(a) The regulations in question were designed for new, as opposed to existing, landfills. Therefore, by their own terms, they are not "applicable" and need not be followed.

(b) New and existing landfills are fundamentally different; therefore, regulations the apply to new landfills are not even "relevant and appropriate" to existing ones? (In considering this argument, you will need to think about *why* new and existing landfills are different, and whether those distinctions should or should not make a *legal* difference.)

(c) PCB disposal regulations need not be literally followed because they are only "relevant and appropriate," not "applicable." EPA treats potentially relevant requirements on a sliding scale from "applicable," which must be followed absolutely; to "relevant and appropriate, which EPA tries to follow; to "to be considered," which EPA can freely choose to follow or not.

(d) Capping in place is the equivalent of on-site disposal of remediation waste; therefore, EPA need not meet the requirements of other hazardous waste disposal laws. (Hint: *see* 42 U.S.C. § 9621(e).)

(e) Even if the PCB disposal regulations are an ARAR, EPA can waive them. (The NCP's waiver requirements can be found at 40 C.F.R. § 300.430(f)(1)(ii)(c).)

d. Permanence

While protectiveness and compliance with ARARs clean-up goal are "threshold" criteria, long-term effectiveness and "permanence" constitute one of the "primary balancing criteria" which may be used to decide among different clean-up strategies. A closely related balancing criteria is "reduction of toxicity, mobility, or volume through treatment." Both are designed to assure that remedial action will in fact be final, that the problem will not reappear several years in the future. Thus, the statute states a distinct preference that "treatment" or other "permanent" solutions are a "principal part" of any remedy.

EPA endorses a guideline that achieves between 90 to 99 percent reductions in toxicity or mobility. Such a strict standard is driven by the realization that over 26% of the NPL are expected to become residential, while 80% will likely have residents surrounding the site. 60 Fed. Reg. 29595, 29596 (June 5, 1995). On the other hand, the NCP assumes that some residual hazardous waste will still exist after clean-up is completed. It presumes the permanence standard is satisfied if the "threat posed by the hazardous substances remaining can be adequately managed by "engineering or institutional controls." These are seemingly contradictory impulses: treatment because people are likely to come into contact with the contamination in the future, and yet acceptance of significant amounts of residual contamination. Reliance on the exposure scenarios of a limited future use adds to the conundrum—how can the preference for treatment and permanence be reconciled with remedies that deliberately leave waste in place?

e. Cost

CERCLA §121(a), (b)(1) requires that a remedy be "cost effective." This is an especially slippery term that can have multiple meanings. The NCP and EPA have seized upon two alternative interpretations that are mirror images of each other. On the one hand, a cost-effective remedy is simply a means of achieving a predetermined clean-up goal. EPA decides what level of environmental and health protection is appropriate (*i.e.*, a level that is protective and permanent), and then it may select the remedy that is the cheapest effective way of obtaining that level. Alternative comparable technologies that are more costly than others will be rejected.[40] On the other hand, cost can help decide the appropriate level of environmental clean-up (the goal) by being weighed against the benefits conferred by that level. If the costs are disproportionate to the benefits, the clean-up standard itself can be ratcheted down. In this way, "cost-effectiveness" becomes a surrogate for a cost-benefit analysis.

NOTES

1. Are health and environmental returns justified in terms of their expense?[41] You will recall the different cost-benefit standards discussed in Chapter 3. Which is the better interpretation of the statute?

2. How are permanence and cost to be reconciled? In fact, cost, not permanence, is the most important factor for three critical parties: PRPs, who must pay for the clean-up; states, which must provide 10 percent of the cost that PRPs do not pay; and EPA, which has limited available funding and wishes to conserve the Superfund. J.H. HIRD, SUPERFUND: THE POLITICAL ECONOMY OF ENVIRONMENTAL RISK 144 (1994). This covers just about all of the interested parties (who is excepted?), so although permanence is a variable that is equally weighed along with cost, cost-effectiveness has come to dominate the legal preferences for treatment of CERCLA sites. Is this a betrayal of the goals of CERCLA—or does it simply bring CERCLA into line with the other statutes we have studied?

Come run the hidden pine trails of the forest
Come taste the sunsweet berries of the earth
Come revel in all the riches all around you
And for once never wonder what they're worth.

Color of the Wind, Walt Disney Co.

---

3. When the EPA is determining costs and cost-effectiveness of a proposed remedy, should any of the following be considered?

- The cost of no clean-up at all (the contaminated sited becomes a "scorched earth" no-use zone, isolated from all human contact and most pathways to the natural environment).

---

[40] "[T]he decisionmaker should both compare the cost and effectiveness of each alternative individually and compare the cost and effectiveness of alternatives in relation to one another." 55 Fed. Reg. 8728 (Mar. 8, 1990).

[41] "A remedy shall be cost-effective if its costs are proportional to its overall effectiveness." 40 C.F.R. §300.430(f)(1)(ii)(1). *But see* Northwest Resource Information Center, Inc. v. Northwest Power Planning Council, 35 F.3d 1371, 1394 (9th Cir. 1994) (achievement of biological objectives in a least-cost manner does not require a cost-benefit analysis).

- The opportunity cost of an expenditure on the site (the environmental clean-up opportunities foregone by spending money on one waste site and not on other sites).

- The cost of alternative remedies that do not require site clean-up (the cost of providing bottled water to a community whose well water supplies have been contaminated).

- The cost of the remedy compared to the value of the cleaned up property (should a site be cleaned up if the remedial costs will be hundreds of times the ultimate economic worth of the remediated site?).

- Long-term of costs of operating water treatment or waste disposal facilities, or of restricting access to sites at which contamination remains.

5. Judicial Review

There are several reasons why a private party might wish to bring a lawsuit challenging a decision under CERCLA. The general public, including environmental organizations, may believe that an EPA regulation is too lax or may be concerned that a specific clean-up operation will be inadequate. By contrast, a PRP may wish to attack a rule or a particular clean-up decision for being too harsh. In such cases, two CERCLA provisions are key. Section 310(a) "giveth"—it permits suits against (1) any person alleged to be in violation of any CERCLA rule, or (2) any federal official who has failed to perform a non-discretionary act under CERCLA. Section 113(h) "taketh away"—it restricts federal court jurisdiction to entertain challenges to EPA decisions with respect to the clean-ups of a hazardous waste site. It bars most pre-implementation review, and possibly even pre-enforcement review.

In addition to the critical restrictions found in section 113(h), if a citizen suit alleges a violation of CERCLA, notice of the alleged violation must be given to the EPA, to the relevant state, and the perpetrator of the violation. Section 310(d)(1). Moreover, the cause of action may not be based upon past violations; the defendant must be in violation at the time of the litigation, or the violation must be likely to recur. *Lutz v. Chromatex, Inc.*, 718 F. Supp. 413 (M.D. Pa. 1989). The notice provision, therefore, gives governmental defendants an opportunity to take the demanded action, and private defendants the opportunity to sin no more without facing litigation.

CERCLA section 113(h) provides that "[n]o Federal court shall have jurisdiction under Federal law * * * to review any challenges to removal or remedial action selected" by the EPA under sections 104 or 106(a) except in cost-recovery or enforcement lawsuits in which money or response actions are actually demanded. *Gopher Oil Co. v. Bunker*, 84 F.3d 1047, 1051 (8th Cir. 1996); *Arkansas Peace Ctr. v. Arkansas Department of Pollution Control & Ecology*, 999 F.2d 1212, 1216 (8th Cir. 1993). Federal courts have interpreted section 113(h) to mean that they have no jurisdiction to review challenges to removal or remedial actions *until those actions have been completed. Clinton County Comm'rs v. EPA*, 116 F.3d 1018 (3d Cir. 1997) (en banc) (overruling a prior case permitting preemptive challenges in special circumstances), *cert. denied sub nom. Arrest the Incinerator Remediation Inc. v. EPA*, 118 S. Ct. 687 (1998); *Schalk v. Reilly*, 900 F.2d 1091, 1095 (7th Cir. 1990) ("The obvious meaning of this statute is that when a remedy has been selected, no challenge to the clean-up may occur prior to the completion of the remedy."). In other words, pre-implementation review is forbidden. *Alabama v. EPA*, 871 F.2d 1548 (11th Cir. 1989); *Oil, Chemical & Atomic Workers Int'l Union v. Peña*, 18 F. Supp. 6, 21 (D.D.C. 1998). *See generally* Michael P. Healy, *The Effectiveness and Fairness of Superfund's Judicial Review Preclusion Provision*, 15 VA. ENVTL. L. J. 271 (1995-1996); Michael P. Healy, *Judicial Review and CERCLA Response Actions: Interpretive Strategies in the Face of Plain Meaning*, 17 HARV. ENVTL. L. REV. 1 (1993).

Why would Congress have imposed such a barrier to lawsuits that wish to limit EPA's clean-up expenditures in advance? After all, pre-implementation review might prevent excessive, and possibly *ultra vires*, expenditures. It also might prevent the implementation of remedies which themselves posed serious dangers to the community.[42] The answer is that, in enacting section 113(h), "Congress intended to prevent time-consuming litigation which might interfere with CERCLA's overall goal of effecting the prompt clean-up of hazardous waste sites." *United States v. City and County of Denver*, 100 F.3d 1509, 1514 (10th Cir. 1996); *Clinton County Comm'rs v. U.S. EPA*, 116 F.3d 1018, 1022-25 (3d Cir. 1997). Therefore, once an activity has been classified as a section 104 removal or remedial action, section 113(h) "amounts to a blunt withdrawal of federal jurisdiction." *Hanford Downwinders Coalition, Inc. v. Doudle*, 71 F.3d 1469, 1474 (9th Cir. 1995). The rule apparently is to clean up first and ask questions later.

Some courts have taken this philosophy to its logical extreme. In *Voluntary Purchasing Groups, Inc. v. Reilly*, 889 F.2d 1380 (5th Cir. 1989), the court barred pre-enforcement review. According to the court, the PRPs at the site could not challenge a fully implemented clean-up decision until EPA had filed a cost recovery action against them. Despite the fact that a post-implementation, pre-enforcement lawsuit could not halt the already completed remedy, the court concluded there was "no indication [that section 113(h)] only applies when a delay in clean-up would ensue." 889 F.2d at 1388-89.

Section 113(h) also precludes "any challenges" to CERCLA removal and remedial actions, not simply those brought under the provisions of CERCLA itself. *McClellan Ecological Seepage Situation v. Perry*, 47 F.3d 325, 329 (9th Cir. 1995) ("Section 113 withholds federal jurisdiction to review any of

---

[42] A panel of the Third Circuit permitted pre-implementation review for this reason, U.S. v. Princeton Gamma-Tech, Inc., 31 F.3d 138 (3d Cir. 1994), but it was overruled by the *Clinton County* case, *supra*.

[plaintiff's] claims, including those made in citizen suits under non-CERCLA statutes, that are found to constitute 'challenges' to ongoing CERCLA clean-up actions"); *United States v. State of Colorado*, 990 F.2d 1565, 1577 (10th Cir. 1993).

While the courts have been under considerable pressure to find (or permit) exceptions to section 113(h), they have by and large held the line on broad preclusion. In *United States ex. rel. Costner v. URS Consultants, Inc.*, 153 F.3d 667 (8th Cir. 1998), the court permitted a False Claims Act suit alleging that EPA's clean-up contractors had submitted fraudulent bills for services to the government. However, it made the limitations of its ruling clear:

> In *Arkansas Peace* [999 F.2d 1212 (8th Cir. 1993)], we determined that plaintiffs' claims, "although couched in terms of a RCRA violation," constituted a challenge to the EPA removal action so as to invoke the section 113(h) bar. In that case, however, plaintiffs sought and had been granted a preliminary injunction against incineration activity at the Vertac site. *Here, relators seek neither review of nor injunction against any remedial activity on the site.* Instead, they allege fraud and seek civil penalties on behalf of the United States. Resolution of this suit in relators' favor "would not involve altering the terms of the clean-up order," but would result only in financial penalties for alleged fraud regarding payments sought and received for past completed work. Thus, the complaint does not seek to interfere with the remediation process ongoing at the site, nor is the suit "directly related to the goals of the clean-up itself." *McClellan*, [47 F.3d 325 (9th Cir. 1995)]. Accordingly, we hold that relators' FCA suit does not constitute a section 113(h)-barred challenge to remedial action at the Vertac site. 153 F.3d at 675 (emphasis added).

NOTES

1. Several other circuits have addressed the issue of what constitutes a challenge under section 113(h). None have identified a particular test to be used in making this determination. *Compare United States v. Colorado*, 990 F.2d 1565, 1575 (10th Cir. 1993) (action by the state to enforce a compliance order under its state waste management act, issued pursuant to its EPA-delegated authority to enforce state hazardous waste laws under RCRA was not a challenge to a CERCLA response action under section 113(h)), *with McClellan Ecological Seepage Situation v. Perry*, 47 F.3d 325 (9th Cir. 1995) (section 113(h) barred an environmental group's challenges based on both RCRA and the Clean Water Act); *Boarhead Corp. v. Erickson*, 923 F.2d 1011, 1021-22 (3d Cir. 1991) (section 113(h) barred an action under the National Historic Preservation Act seeking to stay a CERCLA response action pending determination of whether the property at issue qualified for historic

site status); *Schalk v. Reilly*, 900 F.2d 1091, 1095 (7th Cir. 1990) (section 113(h) barred private citizens from bringing a CERCLA citizens suit challenging a consent decree between the EPA and the PRP alleging violation of the National Environmental Policy Act for failure to prepare an environmental impact statement).[43]

2. In two other situations courts have been willing to carve out exceptions to the ban on pre-implementation review. In *United States v. Akzo Coatings of America*, 949 F.2d 1409, 1424 (6th Cir. 1991), the court allowed non-settling PRPs to attack remedies incorporated into negotiated consent decrees under section 106. This holding is based upon one of the exceptions to section 113(h), which permits judicial review where EPA moves to compel remedial action under section 106. The *Akzo* court reasoned that in light of this exception, courts should be able to inquire into the acceptability of remedies in the consent decree that is about to be entered in court under section 106. *See,* 949 F.2d at 1424 n.11.

3. In *United States v. Princeton Gamma-Tech, Inc.*, 31 F.3d 138 (3d Cir. 1994), the court concluded that "when irreparable harm to public health or the environment is threatened [by portions of an EPA cleanup strategy], an injunction may be issued under the citizens' suit exception of [section 113(h) even though the cleanup may not yet be completed." The court's thinking was that delay in preventing such threatened injury because of the ban on judicial review would be contrary to the objectives of CERCLA.

4. Does section 113(h) also preclude state court challenges to CERCLA cleanup? *See Fort Ord Toxics Project, Inc. v. California EPA*, 189 F.3d 828 (9th Cir. 1999) (no state court determination allowed as only federal courts have jurisdiction to adjudicate challenges to CERCLA cleanup).

D. Liability

The first purpose of CERCLA is to protect the public and the environment by responding to hazardous spills and releases of contaminated waste and by bringing about a prompt clean-up of hazardous waste sites. The foregoing section discussed how the four clean-up cornerstones of CERCLA (the NCP, NPL, and remedial and removal actions) accomplish this task. But Congress was not content with simply decontaminating waste sites, especially when the costs of the clean-up would be borne by EPA (*i.e.*, the American taxpayer) and the Superfund (*i.e.*, companies taxed to finance the Fund). Accordingly, CERCLA's second purpose is to ensure that the costs of clean-up efforts are borne by responsible parties. The Act accomplishes this goal by providing mechanisms for reaching a range of liable parties. CERCLA, in

---

[43] Does the §113(h) ban extend to constitutional challenges to remedial action taken under CERCLA? *Compare* Reardon v. EPA, 947 F.2d 1509, 1514-17 (1st Cir. 1991) (facial challenges allowed), *with* Barmet v. Aluminum Corp. v. Reilly, 927 F.2d 289, 293 (8th Cir. 1991) (§113(h) precludes even constitutional challenges).

short, creates a new cause of action, so it must set out (or at least imply) the nature of the liability, the identity of who may be liable, the triggers for liability, remedy, and the defenses to liability. If the conditions to liability are met, and the defenses are unavailable, the consequence, according to section 107(a)(4), is that the responsible party is liable for three types of costs incurred as a result of a release or threatened release of hazardous waste: (1) governmental response costs (incurred by the federal government, Indian tribes, or states); private party response costs (incurred by private parties if consistent with the NCP); and damages to natural resources. We now discuss how persons may find themselves liable under CERCLA, as well as the elements of damages for which PRPs may be liable.

PROBLEM
INTERPRETING SECTION 107

1. Read section 107(a) and (b) to identify the sources of the elements of a CERCLA cause of action (nature of liability, persons liable, triggers, remedy, and defenses). Were you able to find them all?

2. Does the organization of section 107 confuse matters?

3. Now, relying on the statutory language, see if you can state succinctly the elements of a CERCLA cause of action.

4. Finally, identify the key terms in section 107(a) and (b) and refer to section 101, the definitions. Which terms are statutorily defined? What are the effects of the definitions? Do they expand or restrict liability? Both?

---

1. The Standard of Liability

Although section 107(a) merely states that certain "person[s]" meeting CERCLA's test for responsible parties "shall be liable," this phrase has been interpreted by the courts to impose (1) strict, (2) joint and several, and (3) retroactive liability. All of these elements were established in judicial decisions shortly after CERCLA was enacted. *See, e.g., United States v. Chem-Dyne Corp.*, 572 F. Supp. 802 (S.D. Ohio 1983). Since Congress had the opportunity to modify these results in the 1986 SARA, its failure to do so must be considered an affirmance of these interpretations.

a. Strict Liability

The standard of liability under section 107(a) is strict liability, even though the statute nowhere expressly demands this result. Section 101(32) merely states that the term "liability" is to be the same as "the standard of liability which obtains under [§311 of the Clean Water Act]." Since most pre-CERCLA courts had interpreted §311 as imposing strict liability, the same was imposed under CERCLA. This means that a plaintiff, governmental or private, need not prove that the release of hazardous substances was due to the defendant's negligent conduct, nor that the defendant's conduct was intentional or unreasonable. Under a CERCLA strict liability theory, proof of only four central elements is needed to establish the defendant's responsibility for response costs: the site is a "facility"; the defendant is a responsible "person"; release or threatened release of a "hazardous substance" has occurred; and the release has caused the plaintiff to "incur response costs." *Westfarm Assoc. v. Washington Suburban Sanitation Com'n*, 66 F.3d 669 (4th Cir. 1995); *Akzo Coatings, Inc. v. Ainger Corp.*, 909 F. Supp. 1154 (N.D. Ind. 1995).

Another important consequence of strict liability is that causation, normally a central component to a common law toxic tort action, is relevant in a completely new way. Current and prior owners and operators of hazardous waste sites, as well as generators of hazardous wastes, may be liable irrespective of whether they in fact caused the presence or release of hazardous waste. Instead, the required linkage is whether the *release* (or threat of release) caused response costs to be incurred. *New York v. Shore Realty Corp.*, 759 F.2d 1032 (2d Cir. 1985); *United States v. Monsanto*, 858 F.2d 160, 167-69 (4th Cir. 1988); *United States v. Alcan Aluminum Corp.*, 964 F.2d 252, 264-66 (3d Cir. 1992); *Textron, Inc. by and through Homelite v. Barber*, 903 F. Supp. 1508 (W.D. N.C. 1995). This very weak causation requirement has several benefits: (1) companies are given a powerful incentive to internalize their waste clean-up costs; (2) clean-up costs will usually be borne by the businesses that generate and dispose of the wastes, not by affected neighbors or taxpayers; (3) the Superfund (*i.e.,* taxpayer money*)* is conserved. The cost is that a generator of wastes or owner of a facility can be liable even if it was not at fault or if it took "every precaution in the disposal of its wastes," *O'Neil v. Picillo*, 682 F. Supp. 706, 720-21 (D.R.I. 1988), *aff'd*, 883 F.2d 176 (1st Cir. 1989), since due care is not a defense to strict liability. This has struck some observers—notably PRPs—as unfair. Moreover, the strict liability standard stands in the way of some good faith cleanup efforts.

MINE CLEANUP PROVES DIRTY JOB

By Steve Lipsher
The Denver Post, February 27 (1999)

Everyone wants to clean up the water draining from the Pennsylvania Mine into Peru Creek, but no one is willing to wade in for fear of legal liability.

"It strikes me that you have the same sort of problem if you get a permit or not. Somehow you need to go forward and set the liability concerns aside," said Connie Lewis, a mediator with the Meridian Institute, addressing a group of state and federal government officials, ski-resort operators and water-quality monitors gathered Friday at the Dillon Ranger District Office.

High in the mountains just west of the Continental Divide, the Pennsylvania Mine has been a hot potato in recent years, inherited by its current owner, who doesn't have the deep pockets or moral obligation to clean the water gushing from its workings and posing a political dilemma for environmental health officials.

But now, with increasing pressure to divert water from the Snake River drainage for ski-area snowmaking and development, officials are grappling with ways to clean up the tainted site without getting their hands dirty, financially.

"Is there a way we can put together a group that could, in two or three or five years, get it cleaned up?" asked Bill McKee of the water-quality control division of the state Department of Public Health and Environment.

The answer is a resounding maybe.

The biggest problems, it seems, are the very environmental laws intended to cleanse such polluted sites, which brand landowners as "responsible parties" liable for cleanup costs.

The state once experimented with a lime-based cleanup project at the mine but was scared off when a California federal court case established that "good Samaritans"–including state agencies–could be held liable for the cleanup costs in perpetuity.

"No one * * * is going to stick their neck out for this when they can run into millions of dollars of expenses, not just in legal fees, but to operate a treatment plant in perpetuity," Bruce Stover of the state Division of Minerals and Geology said in a telephone interview.

And because the mine runoff pollutes the relatively clean Snake River downstream, ski areas and developers have been hamstrung from diverting water for their projects.

b. Joint and Several Liability

Apart from imposing strict liability, CERCLA §107(a) has been universally interpreted as allowing joint and several liability among potentially responsible parties. *United States v. Chem-Dyne Corp.*, 572 F. Supp. 802 (S.D. Ohio 1983). As every first year torts student knows, liability that is joint and several means that the entire burden can be shifted to any contributor to the harm, even one that has only a tiny role, leaving to that party the task of seeking contribution from other defendants, if possible. Because CERCLA is silent on the issue, early CERCLA cases assumed that Congress intended the courts to exercise their discretion in deciding whether to impose joint and several liability. The central question became whether, in light of general tort principles apportioning liability among multiple defendants,[44] the harm can be said to be sufficiently divisible or severable. Early cases like *Chem-Dyne*, with leaking landfills in mind, expected that divisibility could be shown only in rare cases.

---

[44] RESTATEMENT (SECOND) OF TORTS §433A is the most influential tort principle.

UNITED STATES V. MONSANTO
858 F.2d 160 (4th Cir. 1998)

"Under common law rules, when two or more persons act independently to cause a single harm for which there is a reasonable basis of apportionment according to the contribution of each, each is held liable only for the portion of harm that he causes. When such persons cause a single and indivisible harm, however, they are held liable jointly and severally for the entire harm. We think these principles * * * represent the correct and uniform federal rule applicable to CERCLA cases."

Nevertheless, the potentially high cost of remediation gave defendants in a §107(a) CERCLA liability suit a continuing incentive to try to show that the harm is divisible, and conversely, rebut the plaintiff's argument that it is indivisible. *See In re Bell Petroleum Services, Inc.,* 3 F.3d 889, 902-03 (5th Cir. 1993) (it is the defendant's burden to establish a reasonable basis by which to apportion liability, or to establish that distinct harms exist). This considerable burden can be met only at the atypical hazardous waste site, where the defendant's waste has produced a separate, identifiable harm which is distinct from all other harms, or where it is possible to determine the defendant's separate contribution to the single harm, for example, where many generators of the same kind of toxic waste in a non-leaking site can calculate the exact percentage of the total quantity of waste for which they were responsible.[45]

CERCLA defendants have discovered that it is quite difficult to meet the burden of proving divisibility. *O'Neil v. Picillo,* 883 F.2d 176 (1st Cir. 1989); *U.S. v. Dico,* 979 F. Supp. 1255, 1259-61 (S.D. Iowa 1997); *Cooper Industries, Inc. v. Agway, Inc.,* 956 F. Supp. 240 (N.D. N.Y. 1997). *But see Dent v. Beazer Materials & Services, Inc.,* 993 F. Supp. 923, 946 (D.S.C. 1995) (burden met for showing reasonable basis for division of liability when one party was "the only cause of the harm inflicted on the environment") *aff'd* 156 F.3d. Divisibility is almost impossible to show in the usual abandoned waste site, which has been contaminated by numerous, commingled hazardous substances, often by multiple parties. *United States v. Vertac Chemical Corp.,* 966 F. Supp. 1491 (E.D. Ark. 1997); *United States v. Wallace,* 961 F. Supp. 969 (N.D. Tex. 1996). When a defendant fails to establish a reasonable basis as a matter of fact for apportioning liability among potentially responsible parties, a court may find any given defendant jointly and severally liable for *any* hazardous substance that is found at the site, whatever its source, and regardless of that defendant's percentage

---

[45] If there are many migration paths from the waste site, it is not possible to know what generator is responsible for the waste leaking into one or more of these pathways.

contribution to the over-all waste problem at the site. *United States v. Township of Brighton*, 153 F.3d 307, 317 (6th Cir. 1998); *Town of Windsor v. Tesa Truck, Inc.*, 919 F. Supp. 662 (S.D. N.Y. 1996). And when §107(a) liability is joint and several, no equitable defenses apply. *Aluminum Co. of America v. Beazer East, Inc.*, 124 F. 3d 551, 562-3 (3d Cir. 1997).

In *PMC, Inc. v. Sherwin-Williams Co.*, 151 F.3d 610 (7th Cir. 1998), the court decided that, as between a purchaser and seller who both concededly dumped toxic wastes at a site, the seller was liable for 100 percent of the total clean-up cost. Although the seller argued that this result was unfair (after all, the purchaser had admitted dumping wastes at the site on a number of occasions after the sale), the appeals court was unimpressed:

> [The purchaser's] spills may have been too inconsequential to affect the cost of cleaning up significantly, and in that event a zero allocation to [the purchaser] would be appropriate . * * * Granted, it might seem an invitation to purchasers of polluted sites to do a little polluting deliberately, in the hope of not having to pay anything to clean it up; but in the first place, this is a risky strategy, since it might induce the judge to exercise his equitable discretion against the wise guy; and in the second place, the deliberate disposal of wastes without a permit is forbidden by RCRA. 42 U.S.C. §6928(d)(2).

151 F.3d at 616.

While *strict liability* has the advantage of transferring the costs of environmental damage to those in the best position to reduce risks (by higher insurance premiums or safer disposal practices), *joint and several* liability may have several disadvantages. Karl Tilleman & Shane Swindle, *Closing the Book on CERCLA Section 107 "Joint and Several" Claims by Liable Private Parties*, 18 VA. ENVT'L L. REV. 159 (1999). It may be very unfair to make one party responsible for the cost of an entire clean-up when it can be demonstrated that there are several parties who caused the problem. *See* J. Hyson, *"Fairness" and Joint and Several Liability in Government Cost Recovery Actions Under CERCLA*, 21 HARV. ENVTL. L. REV. 137 (1997). A party liable for the lion's share of the clean-up cost may be, at one end of the spectrum, a deep pocket responsible party who contributed a tiny fraction of the hazardous waste. Or, at the other end of the spectrum, 100 percent liability can fall on a small-fry generator of wastes, a naïve purchaser of the contaminated property, or a former lessee with only fleeting contact with the waste site, each of whom had little to do with dumping significant waste quantities there. Moreover, joint and several liability may actually act as a disincentive for those involved with hazardous waste to take precautions. If one dumping wastes can escape liability altogether if a co-dumper is saddled with 100 percent responsibility for the ultimate clean-up, then there is little reason to prevent releases, and even less reason to settle with other responsible parties. *See* Richard Epstein, *Two Fallacies in the Law of Joint Torts*, 73 GEO. L. J. 1377 (1985).

The potential harshness of joint and several liability did not escape the attention of Congress. In SARA in 1986, Congress chose to leave the case law alone, thereby permitting courts to resolve the liability issue on the basis of the predominant "divisibility" rule discussed above; however, it added two important provisions designed to mitigate the sometimes unfair consequences of joint and several liability. First, EPA is directed to offer early settlements to defendants who are responsible for only a small portion of the harm, so-called *de minimis* settlements. §122(g). Second, there is now a statutory cause of action in *contribution*, which permits courts to "allocate response costs among liable parties using such equitable factors as the court determines are appropriate." §113(f)(1). The latter provision, which will be discussed more fully later in this chapter, has become the main tool for softening the blow for defendants who fail to satisfy the divisibility test. *See The Pinal Creek Group v. Newmont Mining Corp.*, 118 F.3d 1298 (9th Cir. 1997) (CERCLA's claim for contribution provisions create several-only liability, which means that each responsible party is liable only for the amount of hazardous waste it contributed to the site); *Gould, Inc. v. A&M Battery and Tire Service*, 901 F. Supp. 906 (M.D. Pa. 1995).

In addition some courts have tried to moderate the impact of joint and several liability in appropriate cases. Both the Second and Third Circuits inject causation into the liability question (although the burden of proof remains on the defendant) by permitting an otherwise responsible party to avoid §107(a) liability if it can prove that its wastes, when mixed with other hazardous wastes, "did not [or could not] contribute to the release and the resultant response costs [or contributed at most to only a divisible portion of the harm]." *United States v. Alcan Aluminum Corp.*, 990 F.2d 711, 722 (2d Cir. 1993); *United States v. Alcan Aluminum Corp.*, 964 F.2d 252, 270-1 (3d Cir. 1992).[46] Other cases have attempted to shield certain parties from joint and several liability by suggesting that "passive owners" (*e.g.*, ones who purchased a site without adequate pre-purchase investigation, but who did not contribute any wastes to it) may escape liability if they "were able to prove that none of the hazardous substances found at the site were fairly attributable to it . * * * [If this were shown] we might well conclude that apportionment was appropriate and [the passive owners'] apportioned share would be zero."

---

[46] Unfortunately, this so-called *Alcan* defense will likely only benefit financially well-off, technically sophisticated defendants. *See* Harris and Milan, *Avoiding Joint and Several Liability Under CERCLA*, 23 ENV. REP. 1726, 1728 (1992):

"If *Alcan's* holding becomes widely followed, EPA response actions will become more like private contribution actions. Potentially responsible parties will need to retain toxicologists, environmental chemists, and clean-up cost specialists to aid in proving the harm caused by a particular waste."

United States v. Rohm and Haas Co., 2 F.3d 1265, 1280 (3d Cir. 1993).[47] Still others have stretched joint and several liability doctrine to find the harm to be divisible and the resulting liability capable of apportionment. The leading case is *In the Matter of Bell Petroleum Services, Inc.*, 3 F.3d 889 (5th Cir. 1993). In *Bell Petroleum*, three parties had successively operated a business that discharged one contaminant (chromium) into groundwater. The Fifth Circuit decided it could apportion damages based on circumstantial evidence of the volumes of chromium-contaminated water discharged by each party. Other lower courts, more cautiously, have found that harms were divisible for purposes of a §107(a) action where in no chemicals similar to those found at the site were released during the party's prior ownership of the site, *Dent v. Beazer Materials and Services, Inc.*, 156 F.3d 523, 530-1 (4th Cir. 1998), and where the facility involved "distinct pollutants" that were "geographically separated." *Memphis Zane May Assocs. v. IBC Mfg. Co.*, 952 F. Supp. 541 (W.D. Tenn. 1996); *see also United States v. Rohm & Haas Co.*, 2 F.3d 1265, 1280 (3d Cir. 1993) (recognizing that upon proof that a hazardous substance found at a site could not be "fairly attributable" to a party sued under §107(a), that party's "apportioned share would be zero"); *United States v. Broderick Investment Co.*, 862 F. Supp. 272 (D. Colo. 1994) (harm divisible based on geographic considerations).

c. Retroactive Liability

As if strict and joint and several liability were not enough, CERCLA has also been consistently interpreted to impose retroactive liability, that is, the statute's liability standards apply to hazardous wastes deposited years (or decades) before its enactment. Private parties responsible for dumping such wastes prior to 1980 have found themselves subject to CERCLA's tough clean-up rules and cost recovery actions even though at the time of the dumping activity it may have been perfectly legal to discard wastes at a site now listed on the NPL.[48] Not surprisingly, defendants fighting CERCLA's liability provisions have frequently attacked the Act's sweeping retroactive effect on constitutional grounds. To date, all these constitutional challenges have been unsuccessful. *See, e.g., United States v. Monsanto*, 858 F.2d 160, 173-74 (4th Cir. 1988); *United States v. Northeastern Pharmaceutical & Chemical Co.*, 810 F.2d 726, 732-34 (8th Cir. 1986); *United States v. Shell Oil Co.*, 605 F. Supp. 1064, 1069 (D. Colo. 1985).

These cases conclude that CERCLA did not create retroactive liability at all, because it simply imposed post-enactment prospective obligations for past, pre-enactment private actions. Alternatively, since one of the triggers of

---

[47] In part because this *dicta* flies in the face of CERCLA's strict liability premise, it has not been followed elsewhere—and did not even permit the defendant in the *Rohm and Haas* case to avoid liability, since it failed to meet its burden of providing a reasonable basis for determining its relative contribution to the harm.

[48] In fact, however, most major Superfund sites involve disposal practices that were irresponsible by any standard.

CERCLA liability is a present or threatened *release*, CERCLA can be understood to apply prospectively to remedy current problems, not punish past conduct. *See, e.g., Usery v. Turner Elkhorn Mining Co.*, 428 U.S. 1 (1976); *Concrete Pipe & Products of California, Inc. v. Construction Laborers Pension Trust for Southern California*, 508 U.S. 602 (1993). Following two recent Supreme Court cases on retroactivity in other settings, *Landgraf v. USI Film Products*, 511 U.S. 244 (1994) and *Eastern Enterprises v. Apfel*, 118 S. Ct. 2131 (1998) (plurality), some have seen an opening for a renewed attack on CERCLA. Bruce Howard, *Environmental Law: CERCLA Retroactivity*, THE NATIONAL LAW JOURNAL at B7 (Jan. 4, 1999); T. Waugh, *CERCLA's Retroactivity: Has the Door Been Opened for a Reevaluation of whether CERCLA Applies to Preenactment Activities?* 14 J. OF NATURAL RESOURCES AND ENVT'L LAW 31 (1999). So far, however, the lower courts have continued to uphold CERCLA's constitutionality. *Combined Properties/Greenbriar Ltd. Partnership v. Morrow*, 58 F. Supp. 2d 675 (E.D. Va. 1999); *United States v. Alcan Aluminum Corp.*, 49 F. Supp. 2d 96 (N.D.N.Y. 1999).

2. Potentially Responsible Parties

We now consider the potential defendants in CERCLA actions. CERCLA liability applies to four classes of parties:

(1) the "owner and operator" of a hazardous waste site or "facility";

(2) "any person who at the time of disposal of any hazardous substance owned or operated" a site or facility where "hazardous substances were disposed of";

(3) "any person who by contract, agreement, or otherwise arranged for disposal or treatment, or who arranged with a transporter for transport for disposal or treatment" of hazardous substances; or

(4) "any person who accepts or accepted any hazardous substances for transport" to "facilities * * * or sites" for disposal or treatment.

§ 107(a). These "potentially responsible parties," or PRPs, may be liable for all of the costs specified by the statute, under the standards of liability just described. Note especially that these categories are not exclusive. There is no reason that a PRP cannot be liable cumulatively or alternatively under any category that fits.

The actual task of determining who fits into these categories has been arduous, spawning hundreds of lawsuits. Some of the questions have arisen from the vague contours of the four statutory categories of PRPs, and we will address them first. We then address other questions that have arisen in the context of particular *types* of defendants—corporations, secured lenders, and others—whose characteristics fit awkwardly with the statutory categories. For example,

- should a truly innocent purchaser of a contaminated site become an "owner" and thereby a liable PRP?
- May a purchaser of such a site avoid liability by selling it to some unsuspecting buyer?
- Is the parent corporation of a subsidiary that owns a hazardous waste site also an "owner"?
- Is a successor corporation responsible for the liabilities that took it over?
- May a company be an "operator" if it does not actively manage the day-to-day activities of the waste disposal site?
- Is a lender who makes loans to a waste-disposal business an "operator"?
- Is the sale of a not-yet contaminated product an act that constitutes "arrang[ing] for disposal"?

Like the standards of liability, early PRP decisions tended to read the PRP provisions quite expansively in order to accomplish the statute's broad remedial design, but later decisions have retreated somewhat. Unlike the standards of liability, in regard to PRP provisions, Congress has decisively stepped in to resolve some of the more glaring problems with the original statute.

a. Current Owner/Operator

Section 107(a)(1) imposes liability on the "owner and operator" of a facility. Although the presence of the word "and" indicates that this is a conjunctive test (the owner must also operate the facility or site), the courts have read it to be disjunctive in context, that is, *either* present owners *or* operators may be liable. *Redwing Carriers, Inc. v. Saraland Apartments*, 94 F.3d 1489, 1498 (11th Cir. 1996). If one wishes to receive guidance on the question of who is an "owner," and who is an "operator," the statute's basic definition is spectacularly unhelpful in its circularity. Section 101(20)(A) defines "owner or operator" as "any person owning or operating." One is left with the commonsense notion that Congress must have intended to hold strictly liable those parties whose status put them in a position to do something about the waste at the site—the present owner has most immediate control over how the land is used, and the operator in some way manages the activity that resulted in the release of hazardous substances. For these two parties, it should be immaterial that they might not have caused the problem, or that they could have been ignorant of it. The more troubling issue is, of course, that a present owner/operator may still be liable even though that party neither owned nor operated the site or facility at the time of the disposal or release of the hazardous substance there. *State of New York v. Shore Realty Corp.*, 759 F.2d 1032, 1043-44 (2d Cir. 1985); *City of Phoenix v. Garbage Services Co.*, 816 F. Supp. 564 (D. Ariz. 1993).

i. Owners

A current owner is liable under §107(a)(1) so long as that owner holds title in fee simple. In that case, it is irrelevant that the waste disposal was done by someone other than the owner, such as a lessee. *United States v. Monsanto Co.*, 858 F.2d 160, 168 (4th Cir. 1988); Anthony Fejfar, *Landowner-Lessor Liability Under CERCLA*, 53 MD. L. REV. 157 (1994). The hard cases with respect to ownership involve lesser property interests. Easement holders are usually not owners if they exercise little control over the waste site. *Long Beach Unified School Dist. v. Dorothy B. Goodwin California Living Trust*, 32 F.3d 1364 (9th Cir. 1994); *Comment, Extending Liability Under CERCLA: Easement Holders and the Scope of Controls* 87 NW. U. L. REV. 992 (1993). Lessees may be liable as an owner if they maintain substantial "site control." *United States v. A&N Cleaners & Launderers, Inc.*, 788 F. Supp. 1317, 1330-34 (S.D. N.Y. 1992). Corporate owners and shareholders may likewise find themselves liable as §107(a) "owners" if they influence or control waste disposal decisions. *Lansford-Coaldale Joint Water Auth. v. Tonolli Corp.*, 4 F.3d 1209, 1225 (3d Cir. 1993) (partial owner of a corporation may be liable under CERCLA); *State of Idaho v. Bunker Hill Co.*, 635 F. Supp. 665-670-72 (D. Idaho 1986) (parent corporation liable for actions of subsidiary); *Donahey v. Bogle*, 987 F.2d 1250 (6th Cir. 1993) (sole shareholder with sufficient authority to prevent contamination may be an "owner"). *See generally* E.C. Birg, *Redefining "Owner or Operator" Under CERCLA to Preserve Traditional Notions of Corporate Law*, 43 EMORY L.J. 771 (1994).[49]

WHEN DOES A PERSON BECOME AN "OWNER?"

A contaminated site might be bought and sold multiple times after it poses a threat due to the hazardous substances that have been dumped there. Sometimes ownership is fleeting—a party could own the site only for a few months before it is sold. When the waste site is subject to many changes of ownership in a short period of time, the question arises as to when an owner becomes a current owner for purposes of §107(a)(1). Current ownership

---

[49] *See also* Fishbein Family Partnership v. PPG Indus., Inc., 871 F. Supp. 764 (D.N.J. 1994) (stock ownership alone does not establish "owner" status).

Similarly, limited partners have been found not to be "owners" under applicable state law, and therefore not "owners" under §107(e). Redwing Carriers, Inc. v. Saraland Apartments, 94 F.3d 1489 (11th Cir. 1996). Some fiduciaries holding title for another may be an "owner," such as a trustee of a testamentary trust. Briggs & Stratton Corp. v. Concrete Sales & Services, 20 F. Supp. 2d 1356, 1367 (M.D. Ga 1998); City of Phoenix v. Garbage Services Co., 816 F. Supp. 564 (D. Ariz. 1993); W.C. Santos, *Trustee Liability in CERCLA: Confronting the Problems and Proposing Solutions*, 19 WM. & MARY ENVTL. LAW AND POLICY REV. 69 (1994). Other fiduciaries, such as executors or conservators, have far less power and control than trustees, and they are not "owners." Castlerock Estates, Inc. v. Estate of Walter S. Markham, 871 F. Supp. 360, 366 (N.D. Cal. 1994).

> could be based on who the owner was at the time the site first became contaminated, the time the site was identified as a threat, the time the site was NPL-listed, or the time a CERCLA liability lawsuit was filed. *United States v. Fleet Factors Corp.*, 901 F.2d 1550, 1554 (11th Cir. 1990) (time complaint is filed).

Three common relationships to property have given rise to much CERCLA litigation:

Secured creditors—One class of passive owners who have tried to resist CERCLA liability are lenders and secured creditors. There is an explicit statutory exclusion from the "owner or operator" category of a person "who, without participating in * * * management * * * holds indicia of ownership primarily to protect his security interest in the * * * facility."[50] Nonetheless, one important case found liable a secured creditor whose "involvement with the management of the facility is sufficiently broad to support the inference that it could affect hazardous waste disposal decisions if it so chose." *United States v. Fleet Factors Corp.*, 901 F.2d 1550, 1558 (11th Cir. 1990). Subsequent cases, as well as the EPA, have backed off the *Fleet Factors* result by immunizing secured creditors who do not actually participate in the management of the contaminated site. *United States v. McLamb*, 5 F.3d 69 (4th Cir. 1993); *Lansford-Coaldale Water Auth. v. Tonolli Corp.*, 4 F.3d 1209; (3d Cir. 1993); *Organic Chemical Site PRP Group v. Total Petroleum*, 58 F. Supp. 2d 755 (W.D. Mich. 1999); J.S. Flood, *The EPA's Interpretative Rule on CERCLA §101(20)(A): Does it Create a Safe Harbor for Secured Lenders?*, 24 RUTGERS L.J. 511 (1993).

Lessor/Lessee Liability—As an owner of the site, a lessor may be liable for contamination caused by the lessee. *United States v. Monsanto*, 858 F.2d 160, 168-69 (4th Cir. 1989). A lessee may also qualify as an "owner" for purposes of §107(a). *United States v. A&N Cleaners and Launderers, Inc.*, 788 F. Supp. 1317 (S.D. N.Y. 1992). Lessees may therefore be liable under CERCLA, particularly if they could control decisions regarding disposal of waste at the site. *Nurad, Inc. v. Hooper & Sons Co.*, 966 F.2d 837, 842 (4th Cir. 1991) (lessee was an "operator"). A lessee might be able to escape liability if the contamination was entirely caused by the lessor, and preceded the lessee's tenancy. *Cf. Westwood Pharmaceuticals, Inc. v. National Fuel Gas Dist. Corp.*, 964 F.2d 85, 89 (2d Cir. 1992).

Innocent Purchaser Liability—If a buyer of contaminated land becomes the "owner" of the waste site, that purchaser may become liable under §107(a). To prevent this result in the case of truly innocent purchasers, the SARA amendments clarified that such buyers can be relieved of liability if they did not have knowledge of the hazardous substances when the land was

---

[50] CERCLA §101(20)(A)(iii). This section has been subject to a 1992 EPA interpretative rule, and a clarifying CERCLA amendment, both of which will be addressed later in the chapter under "lender liability."

acquired, and if at acquisition the buyer conducted "all appropriate inquiry into the previous ownership and uses of the property." §101(35)(B). This provision requires environmental assessments prior to purchase. Inadequate preacquisition inquiry voids the innocent purchaser defense. *See, e.g., In re Hemingway Transport, Inc.*, 993 F.2d 915, 933 (1st Cir. 1993). Purchasers should also be advised to consult relevant insurance policies prior to acquisition. *See* David M. Smith, *Sudden Exposure: Accessing Historic Insurance Policies for the Environmental Liabilities Associated With Newly Acquired Properties or Acquisitions*, 25 ECOLOGY L. Q. 439 (1998).

Is there a common element in the resolution of these questions about who is an "owner?" What is the "touchstone" for determining whether someone is an owner? Does the touchstone make sense?

ii. Operators

Non-owners can be liable if they are termed "operators." An operator is one who has the legal authority to control the activities at the site, and who actually exercises that control. Most cases do not find individuals or entities liable under §107(a)(1) unless they had "substantial control" or "authority" over the activities of another party who produced the pollution, and in fact exercised that authority, either by personally performing the tasks necessary to dispose of the hazardous wastes, or by directing others to perform those tasks. *United States v. Gurley*, 43 F.3d 1188, 1193 (8th Cir. 1994); *FMC Corp. v. United States Dept. of Commerce*, 29 F.3d 833 (3d Cir. 1994); *Lansford-Coaldale Joint Water Authority v. Tonolli Corp.*, 4 F.3d 1209, 1221 (3d Cir. 1993). If there is not "active involvement" in the activity that produces the contamination, "operator" liability will not attach. *Geraghty and Miller, Inc. v. Conoco, Inc.*, 27 F. Supp. 2d 918, 924-925 (S.D. Tex. 1998) (environmental contractor not an operator who was employed merely to investigate and assist in construction of a facility for remedying contamination in the soils); *Washington v. United States*, 930 F. Supp. 474, 483 (W.D. Wash. 1996) (no liability if party had only contractual relationship to entity engaged in waste disposal, where the contractual relationship was limited to managing costs, not instructing the polluting entity whether, or how, to dispose of its wastes).

If the necessary control is present, then a wide range of parties can be held liable as a §107(a)(1) operator:

- *Tenants*—*Clear Lake Properties v. Rockwell Intern. Corp.*, 959 F. Supp. 763 (S.D. Tex. 1997) (as current operator, tenant was liable under CERCLA even absent showing that tenant had ability to control facility at time of release of hazardous substance); *Pierson Sand & Gravel, Inc. v. Pierson Township*, 851 F. Supp. 850, 854 (W.D. Mich. 1994) (lessee's control over the operation makes it liable).

- Contractors–*Ganton Technologies, Inc. v. Quadion Corp.*, 834 F. Supp. 1018, 1021-22 (N.D. Ill. 1993) (contractors hired to clean up hazardous wastes can be operators if they make the contamination worse).

- *Trust Fund Beneficiaries–State of North Carolina ex rel. Howes v. W.R. Peele, Sr. Trust*, 876 F. Supp. 733 (F.D. N.C. 1995) (if an individual is an "operator" PRP, the trust fund beneficiary of that PRP can be liable as well).

- *Estates–United States v. Martell, 887 F. Supp.* 1183, 1188 (N.D. Ind. 1995) (estate of deceased operator may be liable).

- *Agents–Redwing Carriers, Inc. v. Saraland Apartments*, 94 F.3d 1489 (11th Cir. 1996) (property management agent that prepares budgets, inspects, and performs repair work is an operator).

- *Transporters–Browning-Ferris Ind. of Ill. v. Ter Maat*, 13 F. Supp. 2d 756, 765 (N.D. Ill. 1998) (transporter may also be liable as operator where transporter was joint-operator of the contaminated waste site).

- *Corporate Officers and Directors–United States v. Lowe*, 29 F.3d 1005 (5th Cir. 1994) (a corporate official is liable as an operator, because the official created the harmful condition, and might receive indemnification under corporate bylaws).

- *Corporations–Sidney S. Arst. Co. v. Pipefitters Welfare Educ. Fund*, 25 F.3d 417, 421-22 (7th Cir. 1994) (corporation "operates" hazardous waste site, not an individual within the corporation, when the individual did not directly and personally engage in the conduct that led to the environmental damage).[51]

Governmental entities can also be liable as operators. One leading case, *FMC Corp. v. U.S. Department of Commerce*, 29 F.3d 833 (3d Cir. 1994) (*en banc*) found that the United States qualified as an operator of the plaintiff's facility where it required a company to manufacture a product that yielded a hazardous waste product and maintained a significant degree of control over the production process through regulations and on-site inspectors. The court also concluded that the federal government could be liable when it "engaged in regulatory activities extensive enough to make it an operator * * * even though no private party could engage in the regulatory activities at issue." *Id.* at 840. Although the *FMC Corp.* case hinted that the government could be liable under CERCLA merely for its regulatory activities, subsequent cases have tended to reject such arguments. *See United States v. Town of Brighton*, 153 F.3d 307, 315-16 (6th Cir. 1998) (mere regulation does not suffice to

---

[51] The direct liability provided by CERCLA for corporations is distinct from the *derivative liability* that results from piercing the corporate veil. The United States Supreme Court has concluded that if a subsidiary that operates, but does not own, a waste site is so pervasively controlled by its parent for a sufficiently improper purpose to warrant veil piercing, the parent may be held derivatively liable for the subsidiary's acts as an operator. United States v. Bestfoods, 118 S. Ct. 1876, 1886 n.10 (1998).

make a government entity liable, but actual operation and "macromanagement" does); *Washington v. United States*, 970 F. Supp. 474, 483 (W.D. Wash. 1996) (government's contractual relationship with company that caused hazardous waste problem insufficient for operator liability where there was no "[a]ctive involvement in the activity that produce[d] the contamination"); *Delaney v. Town of Carmel*, 55 F. Supp. 2d 237 (S.D.N.Y. 1999) (government entities liable as operators only upon a showing of actual and substantial control); *United States v. American Color & Chemical Corp.*, 858 F. Supp. 445 (M.D. Pa. 1994) (United States not an "operator" when it is acting in a regulatory capacity to bring about a clean-up).

Courts that have differed in finding operator liability have often differed on the test of control. Some courts hold that a party may be an operator simply because that party had the legal authority to control and make decisions about the site in which case it is irrelevant that control may not have been exercised. They have "decline[d] to absolve from CERCLA liability a hypothetical party who possessed the authority to abate the damage * * * but who declined to actually exercise that authority by undertaking efforts at a clean-up." *Nurad Inc. v. William E. Hooper & Sons Co.*, 966 F.2d 837, 842 (4th Cir. 1992). *See also Pierson Sand & Gravel, Inc. v. Pierson Township*, 851 F. Supp. 850, 855 (W.D. Mich. 1994), *aff'd* 89 F.3D 835 (6th Cir. 1996) (applying "authority" test in concluding that township was operator in leasing property and contracting with the owner to operate a landfill); *Nutrasweet Co. v. X-L Engineering Corp.*, 933 F. Supp. 1409 (N.D. Ill. 1996) (corporate official is operator who has knowledge of the waste disposal activity, and authority to prevent it, but acquiesces); *State of California v. Celtor Chemical Corp.*, 901 F. Supp. 1481 (N.D. Cal. 1995) (same). This line of authority stands in contrast to courts that have adopted an "actual control" test. Under this test, two conditions must be met before operator liability attaches: (1) the defendant had the authority to determine whether and how there would be a disposal of hazardous wastes, and (2) that defendant actually exercised the authority, either by personally performing the tasks necessary to dispose of the wastes, or by directing others to perform the tasks. *United States v. Gurley*, 43 F.3d 1188, 1193 (8th Cir. 1994); *Lansford-Coaldale Joint Water Auth. v. Tonolli Corp.*, 4 F.3d 1209, 1220-24 (3d Cir. 1993); K.C. 1986 *Ltd. Partnership v. Reade Manufacturing*, 33 F. Supp. 2d 1143 (W.D. No. 1998); *Maxus Energy Corp. v. United States*, 898 F. Supp. 399 (N.D. Tex. 1995). Without some level of involvement in day-to-day operations, entities are not operators even though they may have had the power to control the waste disposal practices of another party. *United States v. Consolidated Rail Corp.*, 729 F. Supp. 1461 (D. Del. 1990) (no operator liability even though defendant initially set up the operations at the waste site and pre-approved shipments of hazardous wastes there). Conversely, one who is "in charge" or who supervises the operations at a site is an "operator." *United States v. Northeastern Pharmaceutical & Chemical Co.*, 810 F.2d 726, 743-44 (8th

Cir. 1986). One of the central components of the "actual control" test is that CERCLA "operator" liability cannot be triggered simply by being in a position to prevent contamination. *Long Beach Unified School Dist. v. Godwin California Living Trust*, 32 F.3d 1364 (9th Cir. 1994). *See also Z & Z Leasing, Inc. v. Graying Reel, Inc.*, 873 F. Supp. 51, 54-55 (E.D. Mich. 1995) (mere capacity to influence hazardous waste decisions does not suffice to establish operator status). An important corollary of the actual control test is that the rationale affirmative acts are a prerequisite to liability; omissions will not suffice. *United States v. Township of Brighton*, 153 F.3d 307, 315 (6th Cir. 1998).[52]

In 1998, the United States Supreme Court had occasion to take up the meaning of "operator" under CERCLA in *United States v. Bestfoods*, 524 U.S. 51 (1998).

> [W]e * * * again rue the uselessness of CERCLA's definition of a facility's "operator" as "any person * * * operating" the facility, 42 U.S.C. §9601(20)(A)(ii), which leaves us to do the best we can to give the term its "ordinary or natural meaning." In a mechanical sense, to "operate" ordinarily means "[t]o control the functioning of; run: *operate a sewing machine*." American Heritage Dictionary 1268 (3d ed. 1992); *see also* Webster's New International dictionary 1707 (2d ed. 1958) ("to work; as, to *operate* a machine"). And in the organizational sense more obviously intended by CERCLA, the word ordinarily means "[t]o conduct the affairs of; manage: *operate a business*." American Heritage dictionary, *supra*, at 1268; *see also* Webster's New International Dictionary, *supra*, at 1707 ("to manage"). So, under CERCLA, an operator is simply someone who directs the workings of, manages, or conducts the affairs of a facility. To sharpen the definition for purposes of CERCLA's concern with environmental contamination, an operator must manage, direct, or conduct operations specifically related to pollution, that is, operations having to do with the leakage or disposal of hazardous waste, or decisions about compliance with environmental regulations.
>
> * * *
>
> In our enquiry into the meaning Congress presumably had in mind when it used the verb "to operate," we recognized that the statute obviously meant something more than mere mechanical activation of pumps and valves, and must be read to contemplate

---

[52] The actual control test also means that those who supply materials to a hazardous waste facility, or design and build such a facility, are likely not "operators." *See* Edward Hines Lumber Co. v. Vulcan Materials Co., 861 F.2d 155 (7th Cir. 1988);

"The statute does not fix liability on slipshod architects, clumsy engineers, poor construction contractors, or negligent suppliers of on-the-job training . . . . The liability falls on owners and operators; architects, engineers, construction contractors, and instructors must chip in only to the extent they have agreed to do so by contract." *Id* at 157.

"operation" as including the exercise of direction over the facility's activities.

524 U.S. at 66-71.

NOTES

1. Why *not* hold the government liable as an operator for regulating a facility? Even if such a rule were considered too broad, could certain *types* of regulation give rise to liability? What about failure to regulate?[53]

2. What test does the *Bestfoods* case seem to adopt: "authority to control" or "actual control"? Which test is the better one? It depends, presumably on the purposes of CERCLA—what are the relevant purposes of CERCLA, and which test best serves them? Which test is best coordinated with the meaning of "owner"—should the tests for the two terms be parallel or complimentary?

3. Suppose that your client has her eye on a piece of property, which she strongly suspects is contaminated, which she would like to use for future expansion of her chain of sports equipment stores. The client would ordinarily purchase the property now, but she does not want to incur the risks of CERCLA liability until she knows that her business is expanding. Can you think of ways that she might prevent the sale of the property to another business, without becoming an owner or operator? Would an option contract work?

b. Past Owners/Operators "At the Time of Disposal"

Section 107(a)(2) states that a PRP may be "any person who at the time of disposal of any hazardous substance owned or operated any facility at which such hazardous substances were disposed of." Under this provision, *past* owners and operators may be liable. CERCLA therefore creates two categories of PRPs—those that currently own or operate the waste site/facility, and those that did so in the past. This latter, "past owner/operator" category, in turn can be divided into two further classes. In the first class, the easy case, a person owned the land at the time a "disposal of any hazardous substance" took place. Section 101(29) of CERCLA defines "disposal" by borrowing RCRA's broad definition, which includes "the discharge, deposit, injection, dumping, spilling, leaking, or placing of * * * hazardous waste into or on any land or water . * * * " RCRA §1004(3). So, if a party owned land on which wastes were "deposited" or "dumped" or "discharged" that party would be a past owner PRP under § 107(a)(2). *See*

---

[53] *Compare* United States v. Dart Indus., 847 F.2d 144, 146 (4th Cir. 1988) (declining to classify local government as operator merely for failing to regulate adequately), with CPC International, Inc. v. Aerojet-General Corp., 731 F. Supp. 783, 788-89 (W.D. Mich. 1989) (government may be an operator if it assumes clean-up responsibilities, but fails to finish the job, thereby increasing remediation costs).

National Acceptance Co. v. Regal Products, Inc., 838 F. Supp. 1315, 1319-20 (E.D. Wis. 1993).

Note that the RCRA definition includes both active (dumping, placing) and passive (leaking, spilling) means of entry into the environment. Thus, the second class of past owner/operator, the more difficult case, involves persons who owned or operated the waste site *after* the time the initial disposal took place but *before* the time the CERCLA liability lawsuit is filed. The question facing courts considering this second class is whether such past owners/operators may also be liable under §107(a)(2) if the wastes may have, without human intervention, migrated further into the soil or groundwater during the alleged PRP's ownership or operation of the site. Courts have split on this issue. If CERCLA intended that term to apply only during a one-time occurrence deposit of hazardous wastes, then passive past owners are immunized from liability. If "disposal" includes any migration or movement of the wastes after they have been dumped at the site, then passive owners/operators may be liable. The RCRA definition (§1004(3)) uses words like "deposit" and "injection" and "dumping," which suggest a single occurrence. However, the definition also uses the word "leaking," and assumes that there may be disposal when the hazardous waste "enter[s] the environment." These phrases presume that a "disposal" is present as a result of a process that may occur over a lengthy period of time.

The leading case opting for an interpretation of "disposal" sufficiently broad to include passive owners is *Nurad, Inc. v. William E. Hooper & Sons Co.*, 966 F.2d 837 (4th Cir. 1992). The court there believed that the "disposal" definition contemplates action that has a passive component, encompassing the leakage or spillage of hazardous waste without any active human participation. *See also Redwing Carriers, Inc. v. Saraland Apartments*, 94 F.3d 1489, 1508 (11th Cir. 1996); *State ex rel. Howes v. W.R. Peele, Sr. Trust*, 876 F. Supp. 733, 747 (E.D. N.C. 1995). One rationale for these decisions is that absent liability for passive disposal, there would be no disincentive for past owners who did nothing while hazardous wastes slowly contaminated the surrounding environment.

Other courts refuse to follow the *Nurad* rationale. These define "disposal" more narrowly to require that a person introduce ("place") formerly controlled or contained hazardous substances into the environment. Under this interpretation, only prior owners or operators who had a relationship with the site at the time the hazardous substances were actively added may be liable. *ABB Industrial Systems, Inc. v. Prime Technology, Inc.* 120 F.3d 351 (2d Cir. 1997) (CERCLA definition of "disposal" does not mention leaching); *United States v. CDMG Realty Co.*, 96 F.3d 706 (3d Cir. 1996) (since definitional terms "discharge" and "deposit" and "dumping" require some human action, courts should similarly construe terms "spilling" and "leaking," which then negates a definition of "disposal" encompassing gradual passive migration of contaminants); *Jolyn Manufacturing Co. v. Kuppers Co., Inc.*, 40 F.3d 750

(5th Cir. 1994) (no active disposal occurred during defendant's ownership of the site).

Several rationales support the "active disposal" cases. Since CERCLA's primary policy is to enforce a "polluter pays" principle, prior owners and operators should not be liable for mere passive migration since these parties are not true polluters. Also, the two terms that arguably justify liability for passive owners/operators—"leak" and "spill"—both seem to assume something other than slow passive migration of wastes. *See Idylwoods Assocs. v. Mader Capital, Inc.*, 915 F. Supp. 1290 (W.D. N.Y. 1996). A "leak" usually requires a discharge from some measurable opening, not a diffuse movement of a substance. A "spill" also suggests a rapid torrent, not a passive migration over the course of several years. *In re Tutu Wells Contamination Litigation*, 994 F. Supp. 638, 668 (D. Virgin Islands 1998). Moreover, an interpretation of "disposal" that includes passive disposal might gut the so-called "innocent landowner" defense found in §101(35)(A). This defense protects purchasers who acquire land "after disposal" of a hazardous substance and who have no knowledge of the contamination. If otherwise innocent buyers could not assert the §101(35)(A) because they are liable as passive owners, then the innocent purchaser defense would largely become a nullity. *United States v. CDMG Realty Co.*, 96 F.3d 706, 716 (3d Cir. 1996); *United States v. Petersen Sand & Gravel, Inc.*, 806 F. Supp. 1346 (N.D. Ill. 1992). *See generally* Craig May, Note, *Taking Action—Rejecting the Passive Disposal Theory of Prior Owner Liability Under CERCLA*, 17 VA. ENVTL. L. J. 385 (1998); Andrew R. Klein, *Hazardous Waste Clean-up and Intermediate Landowners: Reexamining the Liability-Based Approach*, 21 HARV. ENVTL. L. REV. 337 (1997).

Figure 11.5–Is this a "spill?"[54]

NOTES

1. Can you think of other reasons for adopting the active or passive disposal theory? Can you make anything of the difference between "disposal"and "release," another term in the statute? (You will first need to figure out what "release" means and how it is used.)

2. Can you develop an argument based on the language of section 107(a)(2)? Why is past ownership qualified by "at the time of disposal," while present ownership is not? Who was Congress trying to protect? Does that suggest an answer to the passive-active question?

c. Generators of Waste–Persons Who "Arranged for Disposal or Treatment"

A third PRP category is set out in §107(a)(3): persons who "by contract, agreement, or otherwise arranged for disposal or treatment, or arranged with a transporter for disposal or treatment, of hazardous substances" which they

---

[54]Photo by Greg Lief (photos@gregleif.com, http://www.gregleif.com).

"owned or possessed." Arrangers—typically, the generators of the waste—are the first cause of the contaminated site that will be subject to a CERCLA clean-up. Prior to CERCLA, generators could rid themselves of hazardous waste simply by hiring a waste hauler who would take care of it: out of sight, out of mind. With the advent of arranger liability, a generator of wastes cannot ignore how the wastes will eventually be treated or discarded; if a hazardous substance generated by a private party is sent to a site where a release occurs (or threatens), that party is subject to CERCLA liability.

The language of §107(a)(3) has become one of the most frequently litigated provisions of CERCLA, in part because it is unclear in several important respects (a trait is shares with other parts of CERCLA), and in part because it is the provision that creates by far the largest universe of PRPs.[55]

The language of §107(a)(3) makes a person liable where there has been an arrangement for "disposal" of hazardous substances "at any [site] * * * containing such hazardous substances." The word "such," in referring to the "hazardous substances" contained at the dump site, could be read to require either that the site contain the waste generated by the defendant, or that hazardous substances like those found in the defendant's waste must be found there. Most courts have rejected the "proof of ownership" requirement, and have adopted instead a four-element test for generator liability:

(1) the generator in some fashion disposed of its hazardous substances at the site in question;

(2) the site now contains hazardous substances *like* those disposed by the generator

(3) there has been a release (or threat of release) of some hazardous substance (not necessarily the generator's or wastes like the generator's);

(4) which has caused the incurrence of response costs.

United States v. Monsanto Co., 858 F.2d 160, 169 (4th Cir. 1988); *United States v. Mottolo*, 695 F. Supp. 615, 625 (D.N.H. 1988); *United States v. Wade*, 577 F. Supp. 1326 (E.D. Pa. 1983).

A few core issues predominate the analysis of generator liability:

Is it relevant that the generator was not at fault and acted with due care?–The general rule of strict liability applies with respect to generators who took every precaution in the disposal of their wastes. They are liable if the transporter of the wastes, or some subsequent entity who disposed of the wastes, left behind a contaminated waste site. *See Pierson Sand & Gravel, Inc. v. Pierson Township*, 851 F. Supp. 850, 855 (W.D. Mich. 1994), *aff'd* 89 F.3d 835 (6th Cir. 1996) (arranger liability may attach even though defendant did not know the substances would be deposited at a particular site); *Acme Printing Ink Co. v. Menard, Inc.*, 881 F. Supp. 1237, 1249 (E.D. Wis. 1995)

---

[55] There are about 1400 NPL sites, so the number of present and even past owners is relatively circumscribed. But many of those sites had dozens or even hundreds of waste contributors.

(defendant subject to generator liability even though it did not choose the destination of the waste); *United States v. Parsons*, 723 F. Supp. 757, 761-62 (N.D. Ga. 1989) (generator liable although it had insisted that proper disposal practices be followed).

What does it mean to require that the hazardous substances be "owned or possessed" by the arranger?–To be found liable as an arranger-generator, the party must have had actual or constructive "ownership" or "possession" of the hazardous wastes. While the ownership prong is satisfied if the generator retains formal title to the product throughout its journey to the site, *United States v. Aceto Agr. Chemicals Corp.*, 872 F.2d 1373, 1375 (8th Cir. 1989); *United States v. Vertac Chemical Corp.*, 966 F. Supp. 1491, 1501 (E.D. Ark. 1997), proof of continuing ownership is not a prerequisite to liability. *Cadillac Fairview/California, Inc. v. United States*, 41 F.3d 562, 565 (9th Cir. 1994). Since the "owned or possessed" requirement is written in the disjunctive, possession alone can satisfy §107(a)(3), where constructive possession suffices. *United States v. Northeastern Pharmaceutical & Chemical Co., Inc.*, 810 F.2d 726, 743 (8th Cir. 1986). Constructive possession is present if the generator had the authority or duty to exercise control of the hazardous substance, *Briggs & Stratton Corp. v. Concrete Sales & Service, Inc.*, 990 F. Supp. 1473, 1479 (M.D. Ga. 1998), or was actively involved in the decision to dispose of waste. *General Electric Co. v. AAMCO Transmissions, Inc.*, 962 F.2d 281, 286 (2d Cir. 1992). While the "authority to control" test usually demands that the authority be exercised by affirmative act, in some cases it may be satisfied by authority and failure to act. *Redwing Carriers, Inc. v. Saraland Apartments*, 94 F.3d 1489, 1506 (11th Cir. 1996).

Are some parties excused from arranger liability?—Most courts agree that it is consistent with CERCLA's remedial purpose to interpret the loose language of §107(a)(3) broadly and to extend liability beyond the typical manufacturer who hired a contractor or arranged with a transporter to dispose of its wastes at a dump site. Thus, while generators are the principal target of section 107(a)(3), a party need not have generated the waste to be found liable. *See, e.g., United States v. Mottolo*, 629 F. Supp. 56, 60 (D.N.H. 1984); *United States v. Parsons*, 723 F. Supp. 757, 762 (N.D. Ga. 1989) (liability attaches to one who simply possessed drums of waste and arranged with another company to transport them elsewhere); *United States v. Bliss*, 667 F. Supp. 1298, 1303 (E.D. Mo. 1987) (party who actively participated as a broker in the disposal of its customer's waste is liable). The question arises whether the large number of persons or entities who may have some control or relationship with the waste between its generation and ultimate disposal are also be liable. The cases tend to require some decisional nexus with the disposal of the hazardous materials, or some affirmative action influencing or profiting from the transactions leading to the disposal. *See, e.g., South Florida Water Management Dist. v. Montalvo*, 84 F.3d 402, 406-09 (11th Cir. 1996) (factors such as intent, ownership, and actual knowledge are relevant in deciding "arranger" liability); *United States v. Vertac Chemical*

Corp., 46 F.3d 803, 810-812 (8th Cir. 1995) (United States was not an arranger when it did not control the production of a hazardous substance, but merely contracted for its production); *Chatham Steel Corp. v. Brown*, 858 F. Supp. 1130, 1144 (N.D. Fla. 1994) (if a party does not have some control over the location and method of disposal, it should not be liable). Other courts have ruled that the mere ability or opportunity to control the disposal of hazardous substances does not make an entity an arranger; it is the *obligation* to exercise such control that is critical. *General Electric Co. v. AAMCO Transmissions, Inc.*, 962 F.2d 281, 286 (2d Cir. 1992); *United States v. Davis*, 1 F. Supp. 2d 125, 130-1 (D.R.I. 1998). The rationale behind these decisions has permitted courts to reject arranger liability for a number of parties who have been only indirectly connected with the disposal decision. *See, e.g., Redwing Carriers, Inc. v. Saraland Apartments*, 94 F.3d 1489 (11th Cir. 1996) (limited partners who promised to clean up); *United States v. TIC Investment Corp.*, 68 F.3d 1082, 1091 (8th Cir. 1995) (parent corporation did not incur arranger liability for a subsidiary's off-site disposal practices); *City of North Miami v. Berger*, 828 F. Supp. 401, 414 (E.D. Va. 1993) (attorneys who provided advice to owner of contaminated site not arrangers). Nor are parties liable as arrangers when unanticipated events produce contamination. *Amcart Indust. Corp. v. Detrex Corp.*, 2 F.3d 746, 751 (7th Cir. 1993) ("No one arranges for an accident."); *RSR Corp. v. Avanti Development, Inc.*, 68 68 F. Supp. 2d 1037 (S.D. Ind. 1999)(no arranger liability where event causing the release was an unanticipated fire).

Do sales of a product give rise to liability?—One recurring question is whether the sale of a product that might later be dumped or discarded is tantamount to arranging the disposal of a hazardous substance. Courts have wrestled with articulating a test for determining when a party is engaged in the sale of a product (that has some use to the buyer) and the disposal of waste. Some jurisdictions simply ask whether the ultimate disposal of the product was intended or caused by its sale, or whether its disposal was a transaction, or event, that was independent of the sale. This "intent-causation" test seems most appropriate with respect to products, such as asbestos materials or PCB-contaminated transformers, that were sold not because the seller wanted or intended to rid itself of a hazardous substance, but because the seller intended for the product to satisfy some market demand. *Prudential Ins. Co. v. United States Gypsum Co.*, 711 F. Supp. 1244, 1254 (D.N. J. 1989) (asbestos); *Florida Power & Light Co. v. Allis Chalmers Corp.*, 893 F.2d 1313 (11th Cir. 1990) (PCBs).

Most courts have adopted the "useful product" test. The purpose of the test is to protect potentially responsible parties who were engaged in the sale of a useful product, as opposed to parties who were merely trying to get rid of something because it had, in effect, become waste. *See Carter-Jones Lumber Co. v. Dixie Distribution Co.*, 166 F.3d 840 (6th Cir. 1999) (buyer of transformers was "arranger" when evidence showed transformers were being scrapped rather than reused); *AM Int'l, Inc. v. International Forging Equip. Corp.*, 982 F.2d 989, 998-99 (6th Cir. 1993). The idea behind the test is to sort out a legitimate sales transaction from a disguised arrangement for disposal. *Compare Freeman v. Glaxo Wellcome, Inc.*, 189 F.3d 160 (2d Cir. 1999) (if a party merely sells a "virgin" product, without additional evidence that the transaction includes an arrangement for the ultimate disposal of a hazardous substance, CERCLA liability will not be imposed); *RSR Corp. v. Avanti Development, Inc.*, 68 F. Supp. 2d 1037 (S.D. Ind. 1999) (selling a useful marketable product that will not necessarily enter the environment as waste is not a disposal by an arranger), *with* EPA by and through *U.S. v. TMG Enterprises*, 979 F. Supp. 1110, 1123-4 (W.D. Ky. 1997) (arranger liability attaches when company no longer had any use for its product, and then sold it to another party, thereby creating a threat that hazardous substances contained in the product would be released during disposal); *Pneumo Abex Corp. v. Bessemer and Lake Erie Railroad Co.*, 921 F. Supp. 336 (E.D. Va. 1996) (sale of worn bearings was disposal when seller made decision to send bearings to facility that processed hazardous wastes); *New York v. General Electric Co.*, 592 F. Supp. 291, 297 (N.D. N.Y. 1984) (sale of contaminated waste oil to a drag strip for use as a dust control agent was simply an arrangement to relieve the buyer of the waste).

The Ninth Circuit has employed a third test, which asks whether the material being arranged for disposal would qualify as a "solid waste" under RCRA. In *Catellus Development Corp. v. United States*, 34 F.3d 748 (9th Cir. 1994), it was found that the seller of spent automotive batteries to a lead reclamation plant could be liable for arranging for a disposal, primarily because spent batteries would be considered solid waste under RCRA. *See also Cadillac Fairview/California, Inc. v. United States*, 41 F.3d 562 (9th Cir. 1994) (rubber companies who sold contaminated styrene back to chemical company for reprocessing were "arrangers" because reprocessing called for removal/release of hazardous substances).

Who are arrangers by "contract, agreement, or otherwise"?—In what has to be one of the most sweeping interpretations of arranger liability, the court in *United States v. Aceto Agricultural Chemicals Corp.*, 872 F.2d 1373, 1379 (8th Cir. 1989), found that producers who contracted with another company to formulate commercial grade pesticides had "arranged for" the releases that occurred at the formulator's factory site. This conclusion was based on the assumption that the escape of contaminated waste products was "inherent" in what the formulator did. (The mixing of pesticides for commercial use is not necessarily a precision activity.) The formulators had caused the wastes to be released as a result of the contract with the producers, while the producers had retained title to the pesticide at all times. Moreover, the final product had been shipped back to the producer or to the producer's customers. *In accord Jones-Hamilton Co. v. Beazer Materials & Services*, 973 F.2d 688 (9th Cir. 1992); *United States v. Vertac Chemical Corp.*, 966 F. Supp. 1491, 1501 (E.D. Ark. 1997). The prevailing view, however, is that the

Aceto rule is too extreme. *See South Florida Water Management Dist. v. Montalvo*, 84 F.3d 402, 406-09 (11th Cir. 1996) (landowners who contracted with crop dusting company to have their fields sprayed with pesticides had not arranged for the company to spill pesticide wastes). Most courts demand that the alleged arranger have some direct participation in the waste disposal action. The nature of the connection between the alleged arranger and the disposal varies by jurisdiction:

- Exercised direct control over disposal–*United States v. Vertac Chemical Corp.*, 46 F.3d 803, 811 (8th Cir. 1995); *General Electric Co. v. AAMCO Transmissions, Inc.*, 962 F.2d 281 (2d Cir. 1992).
- Made decision to dispose of the hazardous substance–*Edward Hines Lumber Co. v. Vulcan Materials Co.*, 685 F. Supp. 651, 654-6 (N.D. Ill. 1987).
- Had knowledge that disposal would occur–*United States v. North Landing Line Construction Co.*, 3 F. Supp. 2d 694, 701 (E.D. Va. 1998).
- Evidence of actual intent to dispose of the wastes–*United States v. Cello-Foil Prods., Inc.*, 100 F.3d 1227 (6th Cir. 1996); *Struhan v. City of Cleveland*, 7 F. Supp. 2d 948, 952 (N.D. Ohio 1998). *But see Mathews v. Dow Chemical Co.*, 947 F. Supp. 1517, 1524 (D. Colo. 1996) (rejecting test that focuses exclusively on the intent of the arranger).

NOTES

1 What strikes you as unusual about the four elements of generator liability? What elements make it so broad?

Why such a broad test for liability? Wouldn't a more narrowly tailored provision meet the needs of a polluter pays statute? What would a more narrowly tailored provision look like?

Is there any way for generators to avoid liability if plaintiffs need not trace the contaminants in the site to the generator? Consider four arguments:

(i) The generator can try to prove that its wastes are not at all similar to the wastes released at the site.

(ii) The generator can try to prove that there was at the site no release of hazardous substances that are similar to its hazardous substances.

(iii) The generator can demonstrate that its wastes do not contain hazardous substances. *B.F. Goodrich Co. v. Murtha*, 840 F. Supp. 180 (D. Conn. 1993).

(iv) The generator can try to prove that its particular wastes never in fact arrived at the contaminated site. *But see United States v. Bliss*, 667 F. Supp. 1298 (E.D. Mo. 1987) (generators liable if "trace" amounts of their waste were in mixtures that were deposited at a site).

2. You have by now seen several instances in which the test for liability turns on the ability or obligation to control or make decisions regarding the hazardous waste in question. Why is control or decisionmaking authority so important? If CERCLA's purpose is simply to find a deep pocket for clean-up, why complicate matters with questions of control and authority?

3 Which test would you adopt for distinguishing between wastes and products? Wouldn't it make most sense to adopt the RCRA test as a way of reconciling the two statutes and simplifying administration?

With RCRA still in mind, how should CERCLA handle the problem—central to RCRA's definitional provisions—of sham recycling? Should intent govern, or should it be irrelevant?

4. Section 107(a)(3) makes liable as a PRP a person who "arranged for * * * treatment" of hazardous substances. Does this language make liable parties who arrange for the treatment of hazardous substances, whether or not such substances are waste? Or does it encompass only those parties who arrange for the treatment of hazardous substances which are also waste? Section 101(29) of CERCLA incorporates by reference RCRA's definition of "treatment": "The term 'treatment,' when used in connection with hazardous waste, means any method, technique or process * * * designed to change the * * * character or composition of any hazardous waste so as to neutralize such waste or so as to render such waste nonhazardous . * * *" RCRA §1004. Does this definition refer to a party arranging for the processing of *discarded* hazardous substances, or processing resulting in the discard of hazardous substances? *See Pneumo Abex v. High Point Thomasville & Denton*, 142 F.3d 769, 774 (4th Cir. 1998).[56]

d. Transporters Involved in Site Selection

The fourth PRP category imposes liability on those who accept hazardous substances for transport "to disposal * * * sites selected by such person."§107(a)(4). Like past owners, the category is qualified. The "selected by" language excuses transporters or shippers for releases during transportation resulting from circumstances beyond their control. *United States v. M/V Santa Clara I*, 887 F. Supp. 825 (D.S. C. 1995). Here, Congress wanted to include as PRP only transporters who helped cause the pollution problem by picking up the hazardous substance and then dumping it at locations of their choice. *See, e.g., United States v. Bliss*, 667 F. Supp. 1298, 1303 (E.D. Mo. 1987). This category includes both legitimate "full service" waste disposal companies who transport and dispose of their customers' hazardous waste, and so-called midnight dumpers who dispose of wastes illegally. However, transporter liability is not so far-reaching that

---

[56] In Shell Oil Co. v. United States, 950 F.2d 741 (D.C. Cir. 1991), the court found that a resource recovery process was not a "treatment" as that term is defined in RCRA.

anyone who has ever transported waste material to a site becomes a PRP, even if the material was wholly innocuous. To impose liability, a CERCLA plaintiff must prove that a defendant transported material containing a hazardous substance to the site. *Prisco v. A&D Carting Co.*, 168 F.3d 593, 605 (2d Cir. 1999).

Although CERCLA §107(a) specifies four distinct classes of PRPs, the lines blur with respect to the "owner" and "transporter" categories. *See, e.g., Atlantic Richfield Co. v. Blosenski*, 847 F. Supp. 1261 (E.D. Pa. 1994) (owner of site may be liable as transporter). On the other hand, there are distinctions between arrangers and transporters. An arranger-generator may be several transactions away from a decision to dump wastes, particularly in a sales context, but the transporter usually has direct control with, and influence over, the decision to dump at a waste site. Nonetheless, despite the transporter's closer ties to the dump site, the liability of transporters is not as extensive as that of arrangers. *United States v. Hardage*, 750 F. Supp. 1444, 1458 (W.D. Okl. 1990). Indeed, some courts have suggested that transporters may not be liable as arrangers under §107(a)(3). *United States v. Western Processing Co.*, 756 F. Supp. 1416 (W.D. Wash. 1991). Of course, one key difference between arranger and transporter liability is that CERCLA limits PRP status to those who transport to "[disposal] sites selected by such person." The "selected by" language excuses transporters or shippers for releases during transportation resulting from circumstances beyond their control. *United States v. M/V Santa Clara I*, 887 F. Supp. 825 (D.S.C. 1995).

Two interpretative issues have arisen regarding transporter liability. First, because CERCLA §101(26) defines "transport" to include "the movement of a hazardous substance by any mode," does CERCLA liability attach to a person who does not move the hazardous substances over some distance, but who merely spreads it further after it has already been dumped? *See Kaiser Aluminum & Chemical Corp. v. Catellus Development Corp.*, 976 F.2d 1338 (9th Cir. 1992) (building contractor who excavated a development site and spread contaminated soil was engaged in the transportation of hazardous materials). Second, how much role must a transporter play in the actual "selection" of the dump site? *See B.F. Goodrich v. Betkoski*, 99 F.3d 505, 520 (2d Cir. 1996) (a transporter is only liable if it has substantial input into the choice of the site); *United States v. USX Corp.*, 68 F.3d 811, 825 (3d Cir. 1995) (transporter liability may not be imposed "solely on the basis of an officer's or shareholder's active involvement in the corporation's day to day affairs [but instead this corporate personnel must] actually participate in the liability-creating conduct"); *Tippers, Inc. v. USX Corp.*, 37 F.3d 87, 94 (1994) (transporter liable who has substantial input into which site is ultimately chosen).

e. Corporations

i. Officers, Directors, and Employees

In some cases it appears that CERCLA's remedial purposes would be better served if liability were imposed not only on the company that was an owner, operator, arranger, or transporter, but also on personnel within that company (officers, directors, and employees), or on corporate entities that have some relationship to that company, such as parent corporations (for subsidiaries), successor corporations (for businesses subsequently acquired), and dissolved corporations (dissolved prior to the filing of the CERCLA claim). Under traditional corporate law, owners of a corporation may be held personally liable only if a court believes it proper to "pierce the corporate veil" because the corporation is something less than a bona fide independent entity.

Rather than resort to "veil piercing" theories in CERCLA cases, courts have ruled that individuals owning or working for a corporation may be personally liable as "operators" or "arrang[ers] for disposal" under §107(a), if certain conditions are met. *See Sidney S. Arst Co. v. Pipefitters Welfare Educ. Fund*, 25 F.3d 417, 420 (7th Cir. 1994) ("the direct, personal liability provided by CERCLA is distinct from the derivative liability that results from piercing the corporate veil"). The theory is that the term "person" in CERCLA includes both corporations and individuals, and does not exclude corporate officers or employees. Since individuals within a corporation may be liable for torts they personally commit, individuals may likewise be liable under §107 if they personally participated in the conduct that violated CERCLA. *See, e.g., Riverside Market Dev. Corp. v. International Bldg. Prods., Inc.*, 931 F.2d 327, 330 (5th Cir. 1991) ("CERCLA prevents individuals from hiding behind the corporate shield when, as 'operators,' they themselves actually participate in the wrongful conduct prohibited by the Act"); *United States v. Kayser-Roth Corp.*, 910 F.2d 24, 26 (1st Cir. 1990); *United States v. Northeastern Pharmaceutical & Chemical Co., Inc.*, 810 F.2d 726, 743-4 (8th Cir. 1986).

When operator liability is alleged, courts have had some difficulty with the correct standard to apply to corporate officers or employees. At the one extreme is the view that the only issue is whether the individual had the authority to control the hazardous substances that were ultimately released into the environment. If such capacity existed, then the individual within the corporation is liable, regardless of whether control was in fact never exercised. *See, e.g., United States v. Carolina Transformer Co.*, 978 F.2d 832 (4th Cir. 1992) (if president was in charge of company and responsible for its operations, he was an "operator" under CERCLA because he had the power to prevent the release of hazardous waste); *Nurad, Inc. v. Hooper & Sons Co.*, 966 F.2d 837, 844 (4th Cir. 1992). At the other extreme are cases concluding that an individual qualifies as an operator only if she had *both* the authority to control the activity that resulted in the release and exercised that authority. *See, e.g., Riverside Market Development Corp. v. International Building Products, Inc.*, 931 F.2d 327 (5th Cir. 1991) (majority shareholder not an "operator" if not actually involved with the handling of hazardous substances). A middle ground approach considers several criteria:

> (1) the individual's degree of authority with respect to hazardous waste disposal;
>
> (2) the individual's position in the corporate hierarchy;
>
> (3) actual responsibility undertaken for waste disposal practices; and
>
> (4) evidence of responsibility undertaken and neglected, as well as affirmative attempts to prevent hazardous waste disposal.

See Kelley v. Thomas Solvent Co., 727 F. Supp. 1532 (W. D. Mich. 1989).

Corporate officers, directors, or employees may also become PRPs if they are deemed to be "arrangers." Courts may impose arranger liability if the individual either "owned or possessed" the wastes at issue. Ownership may stem from that party's ownership rights to the corporation that conducted the disposal operation. Possession follows if the individual alleged to be an arranger had actual control over the wastes, approved an arrangement for their transportation, and was directly responsible for deciding how and where they would be discarded. *United States v. Northeastern Pharmaceutical & Chemical Co.*, 810 F.2d 726 (8th Cir. 1986).

ii. Parent-Subsidiary

For many years, the courts split on the circumstances under which a parent corporation could be held responsible for its subsidiary's CERCLA liability without piercing the corporate veil. Finally, in 1998 the United States Supreme Court stepped in and resolved the conflict in the circuits among three competing theories of liability.

UNITED STATES V. BESTFOODS

524 U.S. 51 (1998)

JUSTICE SOUTER delivered the Opinion of the Court.

In 1957, Ott Chemical Co. (Ott I) began manufacturing chemicals at a plant near Muskegon, Michigan, and its intentional and unintentional dumping of hazardous substances significantly polluted the soil and ground water at the site. In 1965, respondent CPC International Inc. incorporated a wholly owned subsidiary to buy Ott I's assets in exchange for CPC stock. The new company, also dubbed Ott Chemical Co. (Ott II), continued chemical manufacturing at the site, and continued to pollute its surroundings. CPC kept the managers of Ott I, including its founder, president, and principal shareholder, Arnold Ott, on board as officers of Ott II. Arnold Ott and several other Ott II officers and directors were also given positions at CPC, and they performed duties for both corporations.

* * *

It is a general principle of corporate law deeply "ingrained in our economic and legal systems" that a parent corporation (so-called because of control through ownership of another corporation's stock) is not liable for the acts of its subsidiaries . * * * Thus it is hornbook law that the exercise of the "control" which stock ownership gives to the stockholders * * * will not create liability beyond the assets of the subsidiary. That "control" includes the election of directors, the making of by-laws * * * and the doing of all other acts incident to the legal status of stockholders. Nor will a duplication of some or all of the directors or executive officers be fatal . * * * Although this respect for corporate distinctions when the subsidiary is a polluter has been severely criticized in the literature, * * * nothing in CERCLA purports to reject this bedrock principle, and against this venerable common-law backdrop, the congressional silence is audible * * * The Government has indeed made no claim that a corporate parent is liable as an owner or an operator under §107 simply because its subsidiary is subject to liability for owning or operating a polluting facility.

But there is an equally fundamental principle of corporate law, applicable to the parent-subsidiary relationship as well as generally, that the corporate veil may be pierced and the shareholder held liable for the corporation's conduct when, *inter alia*, the corporate form would otherwise be misused to accomplish certain wrongful purposes, most notably fraud, on the shareholder's behalf . * * * Nothing in CERCLA purports to rewrite this well-settled rule, either. CERCLA is thus like many another congressional enactment in giving no indication "that the entire corpus of state corporation law is to be replaced simply because a plaintiff's cause of action is based upon a federal statute," *Burks v. Lasker*, 441 U.S. 471, 478 (1979), and the failure of the statute to speak to a matter as fundamental as the liability implications of corporate ownership demands application of the rule that "[i]n order to abrogate a common-law principle, the statute must speak directly to the question addressed by the common law," *United States v. Texas*, 507 U.S. 529, 534 (1993) (internal quotation marks omitted). The Court of Appeals was accordingly correct in holding that when (but only when) the corporate veil may be pierced, may a parent corporation be charged with derivative CERCLA liability for its subsidiary's actions.

If the act rested liability entirely on ownership of a polluting facility, this opinion might end here; but CERCLA liability may turn on operation as well as ownership, and nothing in the statute's terms bars a parent corporation from direct liability for its own actions in operating a facility owned by its subsidiary. As Justice (then-Professor) Douglas noted almost 70 years ago, derivative liability cases are to be distinguished from those in which "the alleged wrong can seemingly be traced to the parent through the conduit of its own personnel and management" and "the parent is directly a participant in the wrong complained of." Douglas & Shanks, *Insulation from Liability Through Subsidiary Corporations*, 39 YALE L.J. 193, 207, 208 (1929). In such instances, the parent is directly liable for its own actions . * * * The fact that a corporate subsidiary happens to own a polluting facility operated by its parent does nothing, then, to displace the rule that the parent "corporation is [itself] responsible for the wrongs committed by its agents in the course of its business," *Mine Workers v. Coronado Coal Co.*, 259 U.S. 344, 395, 42 S.Ct. 570, 577, 66 L.Ed. 975 (1922), and whereas the rules of veil-piercing limit derivative liability for the actions of another corporation, CERCLA's "operator" provision is concerned primarily with direct liability for one's own actions. *See, e.g., Sidney S. Arst Co. v. Pipefitters Welfare Ed. Fund*, 25 F.3d 417, 420 (C.A.7 1994) ("the direct, personal liability provided by CERCLA is distinct from the derivative liability that results from piercing the corporate veil") (internal quotation marks omitted). It is this direct liability that is properly seen as being at issue here.

Under the plain language of the statute, any person who operates a polluting facility is directly liable for the costs of cleaning up the pollution. *See* 42 U.S.C. § 9607(a)(2). This is so regardless of whether that person is the facility's owner, the owner's parent corporation or business partner, or even a saboteur who sneaks into the facility at night to discharge its poisons out of malice. If any such act of operating a corporate subsidiary's facility is done on behalf of a parent corporation, the existence of the parent-subsidiary relationship under state corporate law is simply irrelevant to the issue of direct liability.

* * *

[We] * * * think that the appeals court erred in limiting direct liability under the statute to a parent's sole or joint venture operation, so as to eliminate any possible finding that CPC is liable as an operator on the facts of this case.

By emphasizing that "CPC is directly liable under section 107(a)(2) as an operator because CPC actively participated in and exerted significant control over Ott II's business and decision-making," 777 F. Supp., at 574, the District Court applied the "actual control" test of whether the parent "actually operated the business of its subsidiary," *id.*, at 573, as several Circuits have employed it.

* * *

The well-taken objection to the actual control test, however, is its fusion of direct and indirect liability; the test is administered by asking a question about the relationship between the two corporations (an issue going to indirect liability) instead of a question about the parent's interaction with the subsidiary's facility (the source of any direct liability). If, however, direct liability for the parent's operation of the facility is to be kept distinct from derivative liability for the subsidiary's own operation, the focus of the enquiry must necessarily be different under the two tests. "The question is not whether the parent operates the subsidiary, but rather whether it operates the facility, and that operation is evidenced by participation in the activities of the facility, not the subsidiary. Control of the subsidiary, if extensive enough, gives rise to indirect liability under piercing doctrine, not direct liability under the statutory language." Oswald, Bifurcation of the Owner and Operator Analysis under CERCLA, 72 Wash. U.L.Q. 223, 269 (1994). The District Court was therefore mistaken to rest its analysis on CPC's relationship with Ott II, premising liability on little more than "CPC's 100-percent ownership of Ott II" and "CPC's active participation in, and at times majority control over, Ott II's board of directors." 777 F. Supp., at 575. The analysis should instead have rested on the relationship between CPC and the Muskegon facility itself.

In addition to (and perhaps as a reflection of) the erroneous focus on the relationship between CPC and Ott II, even those findings of the District Court that might be taken to speak to the extent of CPC's activity at the facility itself are flawed, for the District Court wrongly assumed that the actions of the joint officers and directors are necessarily attributable to CPC. The District Court emphasized the facts that CPC placed its own high-level officials on Ott II's board of directors and in key management positions at Ott II, and that those individuals made major policy decisions and conducted day-to-day operations at the facility: "Although Ott II corporate officers set the day-to day operating policies for the company without any need to obtain formal approval from CPC, CPC actively participated in this decision-making because high-ranking CPC officers served in Ott II management positions." *Id.*, at 559.)

* * *

In imposing direct liability on these grounds, the District Court failed to recognize that it is entirely appropriate for directors of a parent corporation to serve as directors of its subsidiary, and that fact alone may not serve to expose the parent corporation to liability for its subsidiary's acts.

* * *

This recognition that the corporate personalities remain distinct has its corollary in the well established principle [of corporate law] that directors and officers holding positions with a parent and its subsidiary can and do 'change hats' to represent the two corporations separately, despite their common ownership . * * * Since courts generally presume that the directors are wearing their 'subsidiary hats' and not their 'parent hats' when acting for the subsidiary, it cannot be enough to establish liability here that dual officers and directors made policy decisions and supervised activities at the facility. The Government would have to show that, despite the general presumption to the contrary, the officers and directors were acting in their capacities as CPC officers and directors, and not as Ott II officers and directors, when they committed those acts. The District Court made no such enquiry here, however, disregarding entirely this time-honored common law rule.

In sum, the District Court's focus on the relationship between parent and subsidiary (rather than parent and facility), combined with its automatic attribution of the actions of dual officers and directors to the corporate parent, erroneously even if unintentionally, treated CERCLA as though it displaced or fundamentally altered common law standards of limited liability. Indeed, if the evidence of common corporate personnel acting at management and directorial levels were enough to support a finding of a parent corporation's direct operator liability under CERCLA, then the possibility of resort to veil piercing to establish indirect, derivative liability for the subsidiary's violations would be academic. There would in essence be a relaxed CERCLA-specific rule of derivative liability that would banish traditional standards and expectations from the law of CERCLA liability. But, as we have said, such a rule does not arise from congressional silence, and CERCLA's silence is dispositive.

[The Court then remanded the case to the trial court to make further factual findings about the CPC agent's role in Ott II's environmental affairs. The critical fact that needed to be resolved on remand is whether the CPC agent made CPC liable as a parent corporation, since the agent's actions show that CPC managed, directed, and conducted Ott II's operations that are specifically related to waste disposal.]

NOTES

1. Does federal common law or state law govern parent or subsidiary liability, according to the Court? Which, in your view, is the better rule? Why?

2. The *Bestfood's* decision turned on whether a parent could be liable as an "operator" for the acts of its subsidiary. CERCLA imposes a different liability test regarding parent corporations in the context of being an "arranger for disposal." Consider the following explanation set forth in *United States v. TIC Investment Co.*, 68 F.3d 1082, 1091-92 (8th Cir.1995):

> "[S]ubsection (a)(2) requires only that the person operate the facility where disposal occurs * * *; by contrast, subsection (a)(3) requires that the person arrange for the disposal.
>
> Therefore while a parent corporation need only have the authority to control, and exercise actual or substantial control, over the operations of its subsidiary in order to incur direct [operator] liability, we believe that, in order for a parent corporation to incur direct arranger liability for a subsidiary's off-site disposal practices, there must be some causal connection or nexus between the parent corporation's conduct and the subsidiary's arrangement for disposal, or the off-site disposal itself."

The *United States v. TIC Investment Co.* case deals with direct liability, not derivative liability. Direct, personal liability provided by CERCLA is distinct from the derivative liability that results from piercing the corporate veil. *SidneyS. Arst Co. v. Pipefitters Welfare Educ. Fund*, 25 F.3d 417 (7th Cir. 1994). Some courts have concluded that it is within the intent of CERCLA, and consistent with *Bestfoods*, to impute derivative arranger liability upon a parent corporation if their corporate veil can be pierced, and if their subsidiary can be adjudged an arranger. *AT&T Global Information v. Union Tank Car Co.*, 29 F. Supp. 2d 857, 863 (S.D. Ohio 1998). *See also United States v. Wallace*, 961 F. Supp. 969 (N.D. Tex. 1996) (derivative liability does not require actual participation in wrongful conduct).

3. Does *Bestfoods* cast doubt on the current understanding that corporate officers may be reached as "operators," considered above in section (i)? In other words, must CERCLA plaintiffs use state veil-piercing law instead of the federal definition of "operator"? What difference would it make? *See Donahey v. Bogle*, 129 F.3d 838 (6th Cir. 1997) (holding that when a single individual owns 100 percent of a corporation's stock, that person could not be liable under CERCLA unless the elements necessary to pierce the corporate veil were present).

iii. Successor Corporations

If one corporate entity purchases or "takes over" another corporate entity, two CERCLA liability questions arise. First, can the corporation that has been acquired by another avoid liability as a result of the transaction? The answer is a clear no. CERCLA has a prohibition on transferring liability (in the absence of an indemnification agreement) in order to prevent companies from divesting themselves of direct liability by shifting responsibility for their waste problem to another corporation. §107(e); *Harley-Davidson, Inc. v. Mirstar, Inc.*, 41 F3d 341, 342-4 (7th Cir.1994).

Second, is a successor corporation responsible for the waste disposal practices of the corporate entity it has acquired? While the issue is not resolved by the plain language of CERCLA, *Smith Land and Improvement Corp. v. Celotex Corp.*, 851 F2d 86, 91 (3d Cir.1988), courts agree that Congress intended successor liability to apply. *B.F. Goodrich v. Betkoski*, 99 F3d 505 (2d Cir.1996); *United States v. Carolina Transformer Co.*, 978 F.2d 832 (4th Cir. 1992). CERCLA's definition of "person" is broadly written to include a "firm, corporation, association * * * [or] commercial entity." §101(21). Congress itself has directed the judiciary to apply a rule of construction to the United States Code that requires, when the word "association" is used "in reference to a corporation, [it] shall be deemed to embrace the words 'successors and assigns.'" 1 U.S.C.A. §5. Moreover, they have ample opportunity to examine the potential liabilities of the target corporation.

Where the successor only buys the assets of its predecessor, the question is more complicated. The general common law rule is that an asset purchaser does not acquire the liabilities (*e.g.,* PRP liabilities under CERCLA) of the seller. *See, e.g., City Management Corp. v. U.S. Chemical Co.*, 43 F. 3d 244,

256 (6th Cir. 1994). In the CERCLA context, however, there are four exceptions to this general rule:

1. *The purchaser expressly or impliedly agrees to assume liabilities.*–To fall within this exception, courts are interested in whether the purchase agreement contains language transferring "all liabilities." This phrase is usually construed to include environmental liability under CERCLA. *Philadelphia Electric Co. v. Hercules, Inc.,* 762 F 2d 303, 309-10 (3d Cir 1985). Another factor indicating that a successor intends to assume the predecessor's environmental liability is the successor's knowledge of the pollution problems at the site it has acquired. *United States v. Iron Mountain Mines, Inc.,* 987 F. Supp 1233, 1243 (E.D. Cal. 1997).

2. *The transaction is a "de facto" merger or consolidation.*–Courts consider several factors in deciding whether to characterize a purported sale of assets as a *de facto* merger.

- Is there continuity of management, personnel, physical location, assets, and general business operations?
- Is there a continuity of shareholders resulting from the successor corporation paying for the acquired assets with shares of its own stock?
- Has the purchasing corporation assumed the obligations of the seller necessary for uninterrupted continuation of business operations?

See North Shore Gas Co., v. Solomon Inc., 152 F. 3d 642 (7th Cir. 1998). *Louisiana-Pacific Corp v. Asarco, Inc.,* 909 F2d 1260, 1264 (9th Cir.1990).

3. *The purchaser is a mere "continuation of the seller.*–The mere continuation exception to successor non-liability applies when a corporation otherwise liable under a law like CERCLA transfers its assets to another corporation, so that post-transfer there is only one corporation with stock, stockholders, and directors identical to the acquired corporation. Since this exception is easily avoided by either continuing the predecessor corporation in some form, or altering the stock, shareholders, or directors between the two entities, successors can often escape CERCLA liability by invoking the normal rule that purchasers are not responsible for the liabilities of acquired corporations. *See, e.g., United States v. Vermont American Corp.,* 871 F. Supp. 318 (W.D. Mich, 1994); *Blackstone Valley Elec. Co. v. Stone & Webster, Inc.,* 867 F. Supp.73 (D. Mass.1994).

In order to make more flexible and fact-specific the scope of successor liability, some courts have broadened the "mere continuation" exception with a "substantial continuation" (or "continuity of enterprise") standard. This exception requires the plaintiff to establish that the predecessor and successor share continuity of employees, supervisory personnel, location, product, company name, and assets, as well as holding itself out as a continuation of the seller. In the absence of such a continuity of the seller's enterprise, successor liability does not attach. *See Oner II, Inc. v. United States EPA,* 597

F2d 184 (9th Cir. 1979); *United States v. Carolina Transformer Co.*, 978 F.2d 832 (4th Cir. 1982); *Andritz Sprout-Bauer, Inc. v. Beazer East. Inc.*, 12 F Supp. 2d 391, 405-406 (M.D. Pa.1998). Some courts adopting the "substantial continuation" exception also require the acquiring company to have actual notice of its potential liabilities. *Louisiana-Pacific Corp. v. Asarco, Inc.*, 909 F 2d 1260 (9th Cir. 1990; *Hunt's Generator Committee v. Babcock & Wilcox Co.*, 863 F. Supp. 879, 883 (E.D.Wis. 1994).

4. *The transaction is an effort to fraudulently escape liability.*–Many jurisdictions reject the broader "substantial continuation" exception on the basis that when it has been applied to hold an asset purchaser liable, there has almost always been some fraudulent intent or collusion, in which case the purchaser would have been liable under the fraudulently-entered transaction exception. *Atchison, Topeka & Santa Fe Ry. v. Brown & Bryant, Inc.*, 132 F. 3d 1295, 1301-02 (9th Cir. 1997). For example, in the leading "substantial continuation" case, *United States v. Carolina Transformer Co.*, 978 F.2d 832 (4th Cir. 1992), the children of the seller's owner were the sole shareholders of the successor, giving the "unmistakable impression that the transfer * * * was part of an effort to continue the business in all material respects yet avoid the environmental liability." 978 F2d at 339-41.

Consider why establishing successor liability is important to the effectiveness of CERCLA. Is it fair to hold the successor liable? *See* Fox, Corporate Successors Under Strict Liability: A General Economic Theory and the Case of CERCLA, 26 Wake Forest L. Rev. 183 (1991).

iv. Dissolved Corporations

CERCLA makes "persons" liable as PRPs, but does not explicitly include dissolved corporations within the statute's definition of "persons." The question that emerges is whether dissolution under state law, coupled with the typical state law prohibition against corporations being sued within two years of their dissolution, defeats a CERCLA §107(a) claim against a former owner.

Does CERCLA preempt state laws that prevent dissolved corporations from being sued? On the one hand, Federal Rule of Civil Procedure 17(b) states that a corporation's capacity to be sued must be determined by the state law where it was organized. If a dissolved corporation is no longer a legal entity pursuant to state law and Rule 17 (b), then it follows that a §107(a) lawsuit must fail. On the other hand, if such state law stands as an obstacle to the accomplishment of CERCLA, then the state rule is preempted. The courts are divided on the preemption issue. Some say that since Rule 17(b) is a "procedural" rule, it is not superseded by CERCLA's substantive imposition of liability. *See, e.g., Levin Metals corp. v. Parr-Richmond Terminal Co.*, 817 F.2d 1448, 1451 (9th Cir. 1987); *Citizens Elec. Corp. v. Bituminous Fire & Marine Ins. Co.*, 68 F. 3d 1016 (7th Cir. 1995). Other courts hold that CERCLA preempts state laws, which could limit liability under CERCLA.

They argue that the difference between statutes defining substantive liability (CERCLA) and those defining capacity to be sued (Rule 17(b) and state law) is a distinction without a difference. Why? *See United States v. Sharon Steel Corp.*, 681 F. Supp. 1492, 1497 (D. Utah 1987); *Town of Oyster Bay v. Occidental Chem. Corp.*, 987 F Supp. 182 (E.D. N.Y 1997). Is it relevant that although Congress did not include dissolved corporations within its statutory scheme of liability, it did provide that PRPs should be held liable for clean-up costs "[n]otwithstanding any other provision or rule of law" (§107(a))?

If CERCLA does preempt state law, then to what extent may dissolved corporations be subject to §107(a) liability? In addressing this issue, the courts have differentiated between "dead" corporations (dissolved entities) and those that are "dead and buried" (dissolved and all assets distributed). Most courts have held that only dead corporations can be amenable to suit. *Idylwoods Assocs. v. Maden Capital, Inc.*, 915 F. Supp. 1290, 1304 (N.D. N.Y. 1996). The rationale here is that dead and buried corporations are no longer entities that can be sued or defend themselves against suit, and therefore should be excused from CERCLA liability. *Burlington Northern and Santa Fe Ry Co. v. Consolidated Fibers, Inc.* 7 F. Supp. 2d 822, 828 (N.D. Tex. 1998). Other courts have refused to recognize any distinction between the CERCLA liability of dead, and dead and buried, corporations. These courts emphasize that the language of CERCLA places no limitation on the term "corporation " as used in the statute. *United States v. SCA Services of Indiana, Inc.*, 837 F. Supp. 946, 953(N.D. Ind. 1993). Which approach is more persuasive? How do you think the problem of dissolved corporations should be handled?

f. Lenders

Lender liability under CERCLA has had a convoluted history. Lenders initially escaped liability due to an exclusion in the definition of "owner or operator." *See* §101(20) (excluding as "owners" or "operator" a person who held "indicia of ownership" in a facility in order to protect a "security interest," without "participating in the management" of the facility). However, the case law of the early 1990s expansively held the lender's "capacity to influence" the borrower's operational decisions could create liability. *See e.g. United States v. Fleet Factors Corp.*, 901 F.2d 1550, 1557 (11th Cir. 1990) (a secured creditor could be liable if its involvement with the waste site leads to the inference that it could affect hazardous waste disposal decisions if it so chose). Some cases even suggested that liability could attach if the lender acquired the property through foreclosure. *See e.g., Guidice v. BFG Electroplating and Manufacturing Co.*, 732 F. Supp. 556 (W.D. Pa. 1989).

The pendulum swung the other way when in 1992 the EPA issued an interpretative rule rejecting the test that the lender's *capacity* to influence waste disposal decisions was sufficient, without the lender's active participation, to hold a lender liable under CERCLA. 40 C.F.R. §300.1100(c).(d). This rule also allowed lenders to escape liability for both foreclosure and repurchase at a foreclosure sale, so long as (1) these were simply mechanisms for protecting security interests, and (2) the foreclosing lender acted quickly to divest itself of the property. In 1994, lenders again faced CERCLA liability when a D.C. Circuit panel struck down the EPA interpretative rule because CERCLA did not delegate to EPA authority to define through regulation the scope of §107 liability. *Kelley v. EPA*, 15 F.3d 1100 (D.C. Cir. 1994). Once again, lenders' rights to control borrowers' waste sites could, in some jurisdictions, create owner/operator liability under CERCLA.

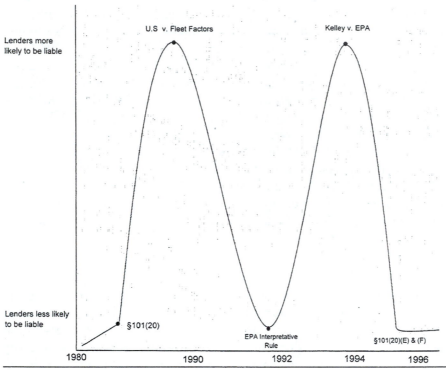

Figure 11.6–Shifts in Lender Liability

Finally, in 1996 Congress altered the extent of lender exposure to liability when it statutorily amended CERCLA. The Asset Conservation, Lender Liability, and Deposit Insurance Protection Act of 1996 rejects the capacity-to-influence test. Now, the lender must be "actually participating in the management or operational affairs" of the borrower. §101(20)(F)(i)(I-II). Moreover, a lender will not become an owner/operator simply by acquiring contaminated property by foreclosure, or by undertaking related post-foreclosure activities. Similar to the EPA interpretative rule, the lender must try to resell or transfer the contaminated facility or waste site "at the earliest practicable, commercially reasonable time . * * *" §101(20)(E)(ii). For now, the ups and downs of lender liability appear to have stabilized, though the application of this rule in particular cases continues to be litigated. More important, lenders continue to insist on inquiry into the environmental condition of mortgaged property or property pledged as collateral, not so much to protect themselves from liability, but mainly to assure that their security does not become worthless because contamination is found.[57]

g. Fiduciaries, Estates, and Beneficiaries

A "fiduciary" is defined by CERCLA to include trustees, executors, administrators, custodians, guardians, conservators, or personal representatives. §107(n)(5)(A). A fiduciary may be liable as a PRP. *Canadyne-Georgia Corp. v. Nationsbank, N.A.*, 183 F.3d 1269 (11th Cir. 1999) (trustee who held legal title to pesticide manufacturing business is an owner of plant site for CERCLA purposes). CERCLA does provide some protection since the liability cannot exceed the sum of the assets held in a fiduciary capacity. *Briggs & Stratton Corp. v. Concrete Sales & Services*, 20 F. Supp. 2d 1356, 1368 (M.D. Ga. 1998). Moreover, a fiduciary may conduct response actions at the contaminated site, and administer an already-contaminated facility, without incurring personal liability under CERCLA.[58] There is no private right of action against a fiduciary. 107(n)(5)(A)(i), (n)(5)(B).

CERCLA does not expressly impose liability on the estates of those found to be PRPs. The definitions section fails to include as a "person" a beneficiary of an inheritance. §101(21). Instead, Congress endorsed traditional rules of property descent by creating an exception to §107 liability within the "innocent landowner defense." §107(b)(3). Under this defense, which is discussed in detail below, a person who inherits contaminated property, thereby becoming an "owner" and a PRP, is entitled to assert the innocent landowner defense and escape liability. *Witco Corp. v. Beekhuis*, 38 F.3d 682, 689 (3d Cir. 1994). Thus, beneficiaries do not become PRPs under CERCLA simply because they inherited a hazardous waste site from someone who was a PRP. *Norfolk Southern Ry. Co. v. Shulimson Bros. Co.*, 1 F. Supp. 2d 553, 557-8 (W.D. N.C. 1998).

h. Federal, State, and Local Governments

In addition to individuals and businesses, a "person" under section 107(a) may also be the "United States Government, [a] State, municipality, commission, political subdivision of a state, or any interstate body." §101(21). In the case of the federal government, CERCLA waives sovereign immunity for facilities owned and operated by the federal government, such

---

[57] *See* William Buzbee, *CERCLA's New Safe Harbors for Banks, Lenders, and Fiduciaries*, 26 ENVTL. L. RPTR. 10656 (1996).

[58] These protections are not applicable if the fiduciary's negligence contributes to the release of a hazardous substance. §107(n)(1)-(4).

as military facilities, which are considered in Chapter 12, *infra*. Section 120(a)(1) also provides that the United States is subject to CERCLA to the same extent as any private, nongovernmental entity. Should the federal government be able to impose joint and several liability on private PRPs, even when federal agencies are themselves PRPs? *See United States v. Hunter*, 70 F. Supp. 2d 1100 (C.D. Cal. 1999)(yes). The waiver of sovereign immunity is, however, inapplicable when the United States acts in a regulatory capacity (*e.g.,* when EPA performs §104 remedial work). *See In re Paoli Railroad Yard PCB Litigation*, 790 F. Supp. 94 (E.D. Pa 1992) *aff'd* 980 F. 2d 724 (3d Cir. 1992).

Although states are expressly included within the definition of "person" subject to CERCLA liability, several doctrines reduce their risk. When a private PRP sues a state for "contribution" under §113(f), such a suit runs up against the case of *Seminole Tribe of Florida v. Florida*, 517 U.S. 44 (1996). *Seminole Tribe* holds that Congress cannot abrogate, by statutes passed under the commerce power, the states' Eleventh Amendment immunity from private suits. This case seems to prevent private parties from suing states for contribution under §113(f).[59] Apart from constitutional limitations on certain private litigation, states may avoid CERCLA liability by demonstrating that the waste site was only regulated, but not owned, by the state. *United States v. Dart Industries*, 847 F.2d 144 (4th Cir. 1988). On the other hand, a state may be liable if it selected a site for hazardous waste disposal and controlled operations at the site. *United States v. Stringfellow*, 31 E.R.C. 1315 (C.D. Cal. 1990). Municipalities can be liable under §107(a)(3) for having arranged to dispose of municipal solid waste at sites where CERCLA response actions take place. *B.F. Goodrich v. Murtha*, 958 F.2d 1192, 1205-06 (2d Cir. 1992) (industrial PRPs can bring a contribution action against towns that sent municipal waste to a landfill subject to a CERCLA response action); *New Jersey v. Gloucester Env. Mgt. Serv.*, 821 F. Supp. 999 (D. N.J. 1993) (PRPs can bring contribution claim against municipalities that arranged for dumping of municipal and household waste at landfills).

3. Triggers For Liability

As we have seen, to make a prima facie case of liability under §107, the plaintiff must prove that (1) a "hazardous substance," (2) has been "release[d]" or there is a "threat" that it may be released, (3) from a "facility", and that the release (4) causes the plaintiff (the government or some "other person") to incur "response costs" which are "not inconsistent with" (or "consistent with") the NCP. These four conditions are sometimes considered

---

[59] The Supreme Court's decision in Florida Prepaid Postsecondary Education Expense Board v. College Savings Bank [Florida Prepaid I], 119 S. Ct. 2219 (1999), would seem to confirm this interpretation. *See also* Burnette v. Carothers, 192 F.3d 52 (2d Cir. 1999)(state's Eleventh Amendment immunity barred homeowners' CERCLA claim against state officers for response costs).

jurisdictional in nature, and they have been the topic of numerous interpretative battles in court. Each of the four liability triggers is now considered.

a. Hazardous Substances

A CERCLA "hazardous substance" includes a broad range of pollutants, contaminants, and wastes. Since the statute uses the term "substance," CERCLA liability can even be triggered when there is no "waste." *Uniroyal Chemical Co., Inc. v. Deltech Corp*., 160 F.3d 238, 245 (5th Cir. 1998). But since hazardous substances are commonly found in hazardous wastes, and since hazardous wastes are so ubiquitous, as a practical matter CERCLA has primary applicability to wastes. *See, e.g., Transportation Leasing Co. v. State of California*, 861 F. Supp. 931 (C.D. Cal. 1993) (wastes from governmental, commercial, and residential activities can be hazardous substances). To the extent municipal wastes contain a hazardous substance, and there is a release or threatened release, such wastes fall within the CERCLA liability framework. To the consternation of local governments, CERCLA may even impose liability on municipalities disposing of household waste that contains hazardous substances. *B.F. Goodrich v. Murtha*, 958 F.2 d 1192 (2d Cir. 1992).

Chemicals are designated as "hazardous substances" in three ways. First, §101(14) incorporates lists of substances regulated under other federal environmental statutes, such as RCRA, the Clean Water Act, the Clean Air Act, and TSCA. Second, §102(a) permits EPA to designate any substance that "may present substantial danger" as hazardous.[60] Mixtures of hazardous and non-hazardous substances qualify as "hazardous" under CERCLA if somewhere within it there is a CERCLA hazardous substance. *B.F. Goodrich v. Betoski*, 99 F. 3d 505, 515 (2d Cir. 1996) ("It is enough that a mixture of waste solution contains a hazardous substance for that mixture to be deemed hazardous under CERCLA.").

Does it follow from this "mixture" rule that if copper is a listed hazardous substance, a person who drops a copper penny at a waste site can therefore be responsible for cleaning up the site? *See United States v. Wade*, 577 F. Supp.1326, 1339-41 (E.D. Pa. 1983). (Yes, but not for much of it.) In other words, is there is some minimum level of concentration or quantity which must exist before CERCLA liability can be triggered? This question becomes important when PRPs face staggering clean-up costs for wastes that contain hazardous substances in such minute amounts that they cannot be considered dangerous. Courts that have addressed this question universally agree that CERCLA's definition of hazardous substance has no minimum level requirement. *See United States v. Alcan Aluminum Corp*., 990 F. 2d 711,720

---

[60] The resulting EPA list contains close to 2,000 hazardous substances. 40 C.F.R. §302.4, Table 302.4.

(2d Cir. 1993); *United States v. Alcan Aluminum Corp.*, 964 F.2d 252, 260-63 (3d Cir. 1992); *B.F. Goodrich Co. v. Murtha*, 958 F.2d 1192, 1199-1201 (2d Cir. 1992). The primary rationale for this conclusion is that the CERCLA definition refers simply to "any substance," §101(14), and the accompanying EPA regulations give no minimum levels.

PROBLEM

1. Is there any argument available to a PRP that finds itself liable for clean-up costs when the actual quantity of hazardous substance in a waste mixture is so small that there could be no risk to human health and the environment? Consider §107(a)(4), discussed later in this chapter, which defines a liable person as one responsible for a release "which causes the incurrence of response costs." When there is very little hazardous substance in a waste deposit, but EPA orders a clean-up anyway, what is the "cause" of the incurrence of the response costs? Does the release of the wastes pose a serious enough threat to justify the response, in which case the PRP's wastes have caused the need to incur response costs? Or is the response caused by the agency's overzealousness? If the latter is true, can the PRP then argue that the "release" has not caused the incurrence of response costs? *Compare Amoco Oil Co. v. Borden, Inc.*, 889 F.2d 664, 669 (5th Cir. 1989) (possibly a good argument), *with A&W Smelter and Refiners, Inc. v. Clinton*, 146 F.3d 1107, 1110-1111 (9th Cir. 1998) (the argument reads too much into the word "causes" in §107(a)(4)).

2. Should courts be more receptive to this argument, or would it unduly undermine CERCLA's liability scheme?

The petroleum exclusion. Petroleum products are expressly exempted from the definition of "hazardous substance" in §101(14). Although petroleum-based wastes may contain other toxic constituents, they were exempted because petroleum product spills into navigable waters were already covered by §311 of the Clean Water Act and because at the time Congress was considering CERCLA, it was also debating a parallel land-based oil-spill bill (which never passed). As a result, much petroleum contamination on land would be outside the scope of CERCLA liability, except that courts have tended to interpret the petroleum exclusion quite narrowly.

A defendant bears the burden of proving that it is not liable based on the petroleum exclusion. *Organic Chemicals Site PRP Group v. Total Petroleum, Inc.*, 6 F. Supp. 2d 660, 663 (W.D. Mich. 1998). The easiest way to meet this burden is to show that an otherwise hazardous substance is inherent (that is, occurs naturally) in petroleum. *Wilshire Westwood Assoc. v. Atlantic Richfield Corp.*, 881 F.2d 801 (9th Cir. 1989); *United States v. Poly-Carb, Inc.*, 951 F. Supp. 1518, 1526 (D. Nev. 1996); *Niecko v. Emro Mktg. Co.*, 769 F. Supp. 973, 981-82 (E.D. Mich. 1991). The petroleum exclusion also applies if the hazardous substance is added during the refining or production process, *United States v. Gurley*, 43 F.3d 1188, 1199 (8th Cir. 1994), if there is no indication that the petroleum products were used waste oil or that they were contaminated with hazardous substances, *Foster v. United States*, 926 F. Supp. 199, 205-06 (D. D.C.), or if petroleum products are mixed with soil that itself is nonhazardous. *Southern Pacific Trans. Co. v. Caltrans.*, 790 F. Supp. 983, 985-6 (C.D. Cal. 1991).

Because the judiciary has sought to limit the scope of the petroleum exclusion (in order to extend CERCLA's reach to some petroleum-based wastes), several theories may now be employed if one wishes to affix liability despite the presence of petroleum at the waste site or facility.[61] Among these are:

- No petroleum exclusion for waste oil contaminated with hazardous substances other than those which are constituents of petroleum in greater than normal concentrations—*ACME Printing Inc. Co. v. Menard*, 881 F. Supp. 1237, 1251 (E.D. Wis. 1995).

- While useful petroleum products fall within the exclusion, petroleum that has been contaminated by a waste product, or that has been commingled with other hazardous substances, is not within the exclusion—*Cose v. Getty Oil Co.*, 4 F.3d 700 (9th Cir. 1993) (subsurface crude oil tank bottom waste not covered by the exclusion); *Diversified Services, Inc. v. Simkins Inds.*, 974 F. Supp. 1448, 1454 (S.D. Fla. 1997)(petroleum commingled with other sources of contamination not within the exclusion); *Mid Valley Bank v. North Valley Bank*, 764 F. Supp. 1377, 1382-84 (E.D. Cal 1991) (non-useful waste oil combined with hazardous substances is adulterated waste oil not protected by the exclusion).

- The exclusion does not apply to petroleum products that have been contaminated by hazardous substances after refining, during the manufacturing process—*City of New York v. Exxon Corp.*, 766 F. Supp. 177 (S.D. N.Y. 1991)

- While the exclusion applies to petroleum containing indigenous hazardous substances in its natural or refined state, it does not apply to petroleum to which hazardous substances have been added through use—*United States v. Alcan Aluminum Corp.* 964 F. 2d 252 (3d Cir.1992); *Ekotek Site PRP Cmte. v. Self*, 932 F. Supp. 1319 (D. Utah 1996); *United States v. Amtreco, Inc.*, 846 F. Supp. 1578, 1584 (M.D. Ga. 1992).

- The exclusion does not apply to waste oil sludges that have become contaminated with hazardous substances generated through chemical

---

[61] Petroleum is not excluded from RCRA, however. Therefore, if one of the foregoing rationales does not apply, EPA can often use RCRA's corrective action authority (*see* Chapter 9, *supra*) for the petroleum component of a waste site.

reactions between the waste oil and the tanks in which they were stored—United States v. Western Processing Co., Inc., 761 F. Supp. 713 (W.D. Wash. 1991).

b. Release or Threatened Release

The term "release" is broadly defined to include "any spilling, leaking, * * *emitting, * * * discharging, * * * escaping, leaching, dumping, or disposing into the environment. * * *" §101(22). Courts have interpreted this language to cover virtually all avenues by which pollutants can escape and do damage to human health or the environment. All that seems needed is some kind of *movement* of hazardous substances into the general environment. *See, e.g., Westfarm Assocs. Ltd. Partnership v. Washington Suburban Sanitary Comm.*, 66 F 3d 669, 600-81 (4th Cir. 1995) (PCE leaking from sewers is a release); *United States v. M/V Santa Clara I*, 887 F. Supp. 825 (D. S. Ct. 1995) (the loss overboard a ship of arsenic trioxide is a release); *EIF Atochem North America, Inc. v. United States*, 868 F. Supp. 707-711-13 (E.D. Pa 1994) (waste entering pipes that lead to outdoor waste pit has been released); *HRW Systems, Inc. v. Washington Gas Light Co.*, 823 F. Supp. 318 (D. Md. 1993) (hazardous substances found in soil have *ipso facto* been released); *State of Vermont v. Stano, Inc.*, 684 F. Supp. 822, 832-33 (D. Vt. 1988) (the escape of mercury from a plant used to make thermometers in the clothing of workers is a release). Despite the breadth of the term, however, there are some exceptions in CERCLA and in the case law:

- The statutory definition in §101(22) excludes releases in the workplace, emissions from motor vehicles, nuclear material from a processing site, and "the normal application of a fertilizer."
- CERCLA §104(a)(3) instructs federal authorities not to initiate removal or remedial actions in response to a release of a "naturally occurring substance in its unaltered form," from "products which are part of the structure of, and result in exposure within, residential * * * business or community structures," or into "public or private drinking water supplies due to deterioration of the system through ordinary use."
- Parties who previously controlled property are not liable for a release if there has been passive migration of hazardous chemicals spilled by their predecessor. *ABB Ind. Systems, Inc. v. Prime Technology*, 120 F. 3d 351 (2d Cir. 1997); *Foster v. United States*, 922 F. Supp. 642 (D. D.C. 1996)(defendant must have some control over the disposal to be liable).
- Although "abandonment" is a form of release (*e.g.,* discarding barrels or closed receptacles), it is not a release if the defendant merely transfers possession of the closed receptacle to some other entity. *A&W Smelter and Refiners, Inc. v. Clinton*, 146 F. 3d 1107, 1111-1112 (9th Cir. 1998).

Can you see any common themes, or is it just a collection of special cases?

Section 107 also reaches parties whose action creates a "threatened release." *See also* §§104(a)(1), 106(a). Most courts require that two conditions be met before such potential future releases trigger liability: (1) there must be evidence of the *presence* of a hazardous substance at a facility, and (2) there should be evidence of unwillingness of a party to assert control over the substances. *G.J. Leasing Co. v. Union Elec. Co.*, 854 F. Supp. 539, 561 (S.D. Ill. 1994), *aff'd* 54 F3d 379 (7th Cir. 1995); *Amland Properties Corp. v. ALCOA*, 711 F. Supp. 784, 793 (D. N.J.1989). Why the second requirement?

Should there be some quantitative level that must be reached before a release of a hazardous substance triggers CERCLA liability? After all, some hazardous substances, like radionuclides, are used and produced in thousands of locations throughout the United States. The courts are split on this issue. *Compare Nutrasweet Co. v. X-L Engineering Corp.*, 933 F. Supp. 1409 (N.D. Ill. 1996) (there is no minimum quantitative requirement for a release); *Priscol v. State of New York*, 902 F. Supp. 374 (S.D. N.Y 1995) (very low levels of concentration of hazardous waste can be a release), *with United States v. Ottati & Goss, Inc.*, 900 F. 2d 429, 438 (1st Cir. 1990) (release must exceed naturally occurring levels); *Amoco Oil Co. v. Borden, Inc.*, 889 F. 2d 664, 670 (5th Cir. 1989) (only quantitative levels in a release that correspond to CERCLA "ARAR" clean-up standards may give rise to §107 liability). Recall that the courts have uniformly found that there is no quantitative limit on "hazardous substance"—why not adopt the same policy here?

THE PROBLEM OF ASBESTOS I

Although asbestos has been EPA-listed as a hazardous substance under CERCLA (40 C.F.R. table 302.4), should a past construction project using asbestos subject the builder to §107(a) liability for including within the structure a "hazardous substance"? Some courts have concluded that a release of a hazardous substance within a building is not a release "into the environment" under §107(a)(4) (holding liable parties who cause a release) and §101(22)(defining "release"). *See Covalt v. Carey Canada, Inc.*, 860 F.2d 1434, 1436-37 (7th Cir. 1988). Other courts hold that one who constructs a building with asbestos does not "dispose of" asbestos under §107(a)(2). *See 3550 Stevens Creek Assoc. v. Barclays Bank*, 915 F.2d 1355, 1361 (9th Cir. 1990). Also, §104(a)(3)(B) withholds Superfund expenditures when there is a "release" of asbestos from residential, business or community buildings. If someone undertakes asbestos removal from a structure, does CERCLA apply?

c. Facility

Section 101(9) defines "facility" to include "any site or area where a hazardous substance has been deposited, stored, disposed of, or placed, or otherwise come to be located." Thanks to the catch-all language "come to be located," rather than serve as any kind of substantive limitation, the term "facility" includes "every conceivable area where hazardous substances may be found." *State of New York v. General Elec. Co.*, 592 F. Supp. 291, 296 (N.D. N.Y. 1984). Thus, it has been interpreted to cover sewer pipes, manufacturing equipment, 220 miles of highway, a dragstrip, mine tailings at the base of a dam, and mines. Most attempts to limit the term "facility" have failed. Moreover, it is irrelevant that the facility is an ongoing disposal site and so could be regulated under RCRA. *See, e.g., Mardan Corp. v. C.G.C. Music, Ltd.*, 600 F. Supp. 1049, 1053-54 (D. Ariz. 1984), *aff'd* 804 F.2d 1454 (9th Cir. 1986).

The real issue in defining "facility," therefore, is the *scope* of the site to be cleaned up. At one extreme, a large geographic area (*e.g.,* all property under the control of a PRP) could be defined as a facility based on the presence of a hazardous substance in one portion of it. At the other extreme, the facility could be defined with such precision to include only those specific cubic meters of a PRP's property where hazardous substances were deposited or eventually found. The words of the statute suggest that the bounds of a facility should be defined at least in part by the bounds of the contamination. *See* §101(9) (defining a facility where the hazardous substances were "deposited, stored, disposed of. * * *"). *See also e.g., Northwestern Mut. Life Ins. Co. v. Atlantic Research Corp.*, 847 F. Supp. 389, 395-96 (E.D. Va. 1994) ("What matters for purposes of defining the scope of the facility is where hazardous substances * * * [have] otherwise come to be located."); *ACC Chemical Co. v. Halliburton Co.*, 932 F. Supp. 233 (Iowa 1995) (where PCE had been pumped from a truck into a landfill at a manufacturing site, the relevant facility was the manufacturing site, not the truck); *Nurad, Inc. v. Hooper & Sons Co.*, 966 F.2d 837, 842-43 (4th Cir. 1992) (facility limited to portion of property that had been contaminated). However, an area that cannot reasonably or naturally be divided into multiple parts or functional units should be defined as a single "facility," even if it contains parts that are non-contaminated. *United States v. 150 Acres of Land*, 204 F.3d 698 (6th Cir. 2000)(parcels not separated when they were transferred on the same deed, and all were in the same undeveloped state; irrelevant that parcels were separate on land records); *United States v. Township of Brighton*, 153 F. Supp. 307, 313 (6th Cir. 1998) (even though most dumping was in southwest corner of property, entire property is a facility where some hazardous material was moved throughout the property); *Clear Lake Props. v. Rockwell Int'l Corp.*, 959 F. Supp. 763, 767-68 (S.D. Tex. 1997) (rejecting argument that surface structures constitute separate facility from subsurface soil and groundwater).

THE PROBLEM OF ASBESTOS II

One important limitation on the reach of "facility" is the CERCLA definitional exclusion for a "consumer product in consumer use." This language has been consistently interpreted as excluding from CERCLA liability the costs of removal of asbestos-containing materials from the structure of buildings. *Kane v. United States*, 15 F.3d 87 (8th Cir. 1994); *Dayton Independent School Dist. v. United States Mineral Products*, 906 F.2d 1059, 1065-66 (5th Cir. 1990). The exclusion does not, however, apply to a housing subdivision where asbestos was found in the soil and air, *United States v. Metate Asbestos Corp.*, 584 F. Supp. 1143, 1148 (D. Ariz. 1994), or to a site contaminated with asbestos. *CP Holdings, Inc. v. Goldberg-Zoino & Assoc., Inc.*, 769 F. Supp. 432 (D. N.H. 1991).

Courts have relied upon several commonsense principles to declare a large area to be a single facility:

- The entire parcel is a facility if contamination extended throughout property, and property was never subdivided or leased to different tenants. *Alex Johnson, Inc. v. Caroll Carolina Oil Co.*, 191 F.3d 409 (4th Cir. 1999)

- The entire parcel is facility when there is no way of telling exactly where on the parcel the hazardous substances are located–*In re Approximately Forty Acres in Tallmadge Township*, 566 N.W. 2d 652, 656 (1997).

- The entire area is facility where each of its quadrants are contaminated–*Northwestern Mut. Life Ins. Co. v. Atlantic Research Corp.*, 847 F. Supp. 389, 399 (E.D. Va. 1994).

- If hazardous substances came to be located in several locations at a site, divided into five distinct geographical areas, the relevant facility was entire site and therefore defendants who asserted contribution claim were not required to establish liability for contribution with respect to each area within the site–*Akzo Coatings, Inc. v. Aigner Corp.*, 960 F. Supp. 1354 (N.D. Ind. 1996).

- If the federal government incurs response costs in cleaning up certain parcels on a site that housed hazardous materials, and wishes to place a lien upon all of the site under §107(1) of CERCLA, the defendant's property should be treated as a single unit, in order not to limit the strength of the lien provision as a CERCLA cost recovery tool–*United States v. Glidden Co.*, 3 F. Supp. 823, 831 (N.D. Ohio 1997).[62]

---

[62] *But see* Union Carbide Corp. v. Thiokol Corp., 890 F. Supp. 1035, 1042-43 (S.D. Ga. 1994) (where solid waste management units are geographically distinct from the landfill, contain a variety of wastes not present in the landfill, and may require different clean-up actions than the landfill, then they should be considered separate facilities from the landfill).

The definition of the site has regulatory as well as financial consequences. The most important is that on-site disposal of remediation waste (*e.g.,* contaminated soils) need not go through state or federal licensing processes (*e.g.,* under RCRA) for waste disposal. § 121(e).

THE PROBLEM OF ASBESTOS III

Although asbestos has been EPA-listed as a hazardous substance under CERCLA (40 C.F.R. table 302.4), should a past construction project using asbestos subject the builder to §107(a) liability for including within the structure a "hazardous substance"? Some courts have concluded that a release of a hazardous substance within a building is not a release "into the environment" under §107(a)(4) (holding liable parties who cause a release) and §101(22)(defining "release"). *See Covalt v. Carey Canada, Inc.,* 860 F.2d 1434, 1436-37 (7th Cir. 1988). Other courts hold that one who constructs a building with asbestos does not "dispose of" asbestos under §107(a)(2). *See 3550 Stevens Creek Assoc. v. Barclays Bank,* 915 F.2d 1355, 1361 (9th Cir. 1990). *Also,* §104(a)(3)(B) withholds Superfund expenditures when there is a "release" of asbestos from residential, business or community buildings.

Another problem regarding asbestos the term "facility." One important limitation on the reach of "facility" is the definitional exclusion for a "consumer product in consumer use." This language has been consistently interpreted as excluding from CERCLA liability the costs of removal of asbestos-containing materials from the structure of buildings. *Kane v. United States,* 15 F.3d 87 (8th Cir. 1994); *Dayton Independent School Dist. v. United States Mineral Products,* 906 F.2d 1059, 1065-66 (5th Cir. 1990). The exclusion does not, however, apply to a housing subdivision where asbestos was found in the soil and air, *United States v. Metate Asbestos Corp.,* 584 F. Supp. 1143, 1148 (D. Ariz. 1994), or to a site contaminated with asbestos. *CP Holdings, Inc. v. Goldberg-Zoino & Assoc., Inc.,* 769 F. Supp. 432 (D. N.H. 1991).

---

d. Causes the Incurrence of Response Costs

If there is a "release or threatened release" of a "hazardous substance" at a "facility," liability cannot attach unless the above conditions "cause" the "incurrence of response costs." This final liability trigger is comprised of three elements: (1) the actions of the PRP must have brought about (however indirectly) the release or threatened release; (2) the release or threatened release must have caused response costs to be

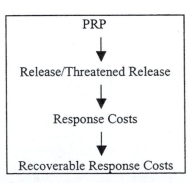

incurred; and (3) the costs incurred must be within the scope of recoverable response costs. Element (3) is discussed in the section that follows. Elements (1) and (2), however, warrant closer examination, because their idea of causation seems to require linkages between the PRP and the release or threatened release, and between the release or threatened release and incurred response costs.[63]

Connection between a PRP and a release—As noted above in the discussion of CERCLA's strict liability scheme (particularly with respect to arranger-generator liability), courts typically need only one connection between the PRP and the release or threatened release: the PRP delivered hazardous substances to the site where there is now, or may be, a release. There need be no specific linkage established between the delivery and the threat of release, or between the release and environmental damage. *See, e.g., United States v. Wade*, 577 F. Supp. 1326, 1333 (E.D. Pa. 1983). Plaintiffs do not need to "trace ownership of" or "fingerprint" the wastes, or prove conclusively that the hazardous substances at the site originated with the PRP-defendant. Courts are justifiably concerned about the difficulties in requiring such connections at sites where there are multiple contributors of waste. *See, e.g., United States v. Alcan Aluminum Corp.*, 990 F.2d 711, 720 (2d Cir. 1993); *State of New York v. Shore Realty Corp.*, 759 F.2d 1032, 1044 (2d Cir. 1985); *Town of Oyster Bay v. Occidental Chemical Corp.*, 987 F. Supp. 182, 195 (E.D. N.Y. 1997) ("causation is not required to establish liability under CERCLA").

Since a defendant normally cannot disprove the presumed causal link between the defendant's conduct and the release or threat of release, the next best defense is to argue, in the case of more than one defendant, that the harm is divisible, and that each defendant should be liable just for the harm attributable to that defendant's wastes. As noted above in the discussion of joint and several liability, most courts have interpreted CERCLA to impose such liability when the environmental harm is indivisible, but to allow for apportionment when two or more persons independently are responsible for a single harm that is divisible. *In re Bell Petroleum Servs., Inc.*, 3 F.3d 889, 895 (5th Cir. 1993); *United States v. R.W. Meyers, Inc.*, 889 F.2d 1497, 1507 (6th Cir. 1989). Such divisibility analysis, however, is different from the fairness-or equity-based analysis used for contribution and apportionment of liability. The court bases its decision on fact-based considerations, such as the ability to divide clean-up responsibilities geographically, *United States v. Broderick Investment Co.*, 862 F. Supp. 272, 275-77 (D. Colo. 1994), or on a volumetric basis (*In the Matter of Bell Petroleum Services, Inc. v. Sequa Corp.*, 3 F.3d 889 (5th Cir. 1993), *appeal after remand*, 64 F.3d 202 (5th Cir.

---

[63] *See generally* John Nagle, *CERCLA, Causation, and Responsibility*, 78 MINN. L. REV. 1493 (1994).

1995)), rather than on equitable allocation principles. *United States v. Township of Brighton*, 153 F.3d 307, 318-19 (6th Cir. 1998).

Connection between a release and incurred response costs—In order to establish CERCLA liability, a plaintiff must show that the defendant falls within one of the four categories of PRPs, that the site is a "facility," and that there is a "release or a threatened release of hazardous substances at the facility." The final element that must be proven is that the plaintiff must have incurred costs in responding to the release or threatened release. *B.F. Goodrich v. Betkoski*, 99 F.3d 504, 514 (2d Cir. 1996). It is not a defense that the particular hazardous substance attributable to a *specific defendant* is not linked to the plaintiff's response costs. *Prisco v. A&D Carting Corp.*, 168 F.3d 593, 603 (2d Cir. 1999). But the plaintiff must establish that the release/threatened release caused *the plaintiff* to incur response costs. *Kalamazoo River Study Group v. Rockwell Intern.*, 171 F.3d 1065 (6th Cir. 1999).

Especially when the release is merely threatened, the question arises whether there is a sufficient causal link between the defendant's conduct that gives rise to the threat and the incurrence of response costs. Since most courts do not require the plaintiff to show that the defendant's wastes caused the threat, the plaintiff instead must demonstrate that response costs were incurred *because of* the threat of release. This causation standard is met if the plaintiff can show a good faith belief that clean-up actions were necessary in light of the threat, and a clean-up response that is objectively reasonable. *Lansford-Coaldale Joint Water Auth. v. Tonolli Corp.*, 4 F.3d 1209, 1216-20 (3d Cir. 1993); *Dedham Water Co., Inc. v. Cumberland Farms Dairy, Inc.*, 972 F.2d 453 (1st Cir. 1992). As one leading decision states: "[W]e believe that the question of whether a release has caused incurrence of response costs should rest on a factual inquiry into the circumstances of the case [where the relevant inquiry is] whether the particular hazard justified any response action." *Amoco Oil Co. v. Borden, Inc.*, 889 F.2d 664, 670 (5th Cir. 1989).

The difficult next question, of course, is determining whether response costs incurred are "justified." The *Amoco* case states that the liability requirement is met if it is shown that "any release violates * * * any applicable [ARAR], including the most stringent." *But see United States v. Western Processing Co., 734 F. Supp. 930, 942* (W.D. Wash. 1990) (government need not show particular defendant's waste caused ARAR to be violated).

The courts are somewhat split on the issue of which party has the burden of proving or disproving the causal nexus between the release and the incurrence of response costs. On the one hand, some jurisdictions assume that after the plaintiff makes a prima facie case of defendant's-conduct-causing-a-release (typically met by showing that defendant dumped waste at the site and hazardous substances in that waste are also at the site), then "the burden of proof falls on the defendant to disprove causation." *Westfarm Assocs. Ltd. Partnership v. Washington Suburban Sanitary Com'n*, 66 F.3d 669, 681 (4th

Cir. 1995); *Town of New Windsor v. Tesa Tuck, Inc.*, 919 F. Supp. 662, 669 (S.D. N.Y. 1996). On the other hand, several jurisdictions not only hold that the plaintiff must establish causation between a release and incurrence of response costs; these cases have also concluded that such causation is *not* shown if response costs are incurred merely because of a finding of hazardous substances above background levels. *United States v. DICO, Inc.*, 136 F.3d 572, 577-79 (8th Cir. 1998); *Licciardi v. Murphy Oil U.S.A. Inc.*, 111 F.3d 396, 398 (5th Cir. 1997)

Some observers are concerned that the causal link between release and costs will become a back-door way of introducing a threshold test based on the quantity, concentration, or risk of release of hazardous substances. The *Licciardi* case, in particular, may be headed in that direction. Would such a threshold test be a bad thing? If one is introduced, should it be based on quantity, concentration, or risk—or all of them, or something else? And, where should the threshold test be located in the statutory structure—here, or elsewhere?

4. Recoverable Costs

Section 107 provides that once a PRP has been found liable, it is responsible for "all costs of removal or remediation action," by the government. § 107(a)(4)(A).[64] These costs can be in the tens of millions of dollars. Moreover, where applicable, a PRP may also be liable for "damages * * * to * * * natural resources." §107(a)(4)(C),[65] which may total hundreds of millions of dollars. The two questions we now address are: (1) What does "all costs" mean? (2) What are, and how does one measure, "damages to natural resources"?

a. "All Costs"

The operative words in §107(a)(4)(A) and (B) are "all," and "any." Read literally, the government is authorized to recover for all and any expenditures incurred as part of a clean-up operation. These costs include expenses for investigating, monitoring, and assessing a release, as well as the government's payments reimbursing contractors who actually do the §104 remediation work. *Johnson County Airport Com'n v. Parsonitt Co., Inc.*, 916 F. Supp.

---

[64] Section 107(a)(4)(A) also provides that such costs shall be "not inconsistent" with the NCP.

The costs recoverable for response actions by private parties are governed by § 107(a)(4)(B) and they are slightly more restricted in two ways: First, only "necessary costs" may be recovered; second, the costs must be "consistent with" the NCP (as opposed to "not inconsistent" in paragraph (A)). These differences are examined in detail in connection with private party cost-recovery actions in section E(3).

[65] Section 107(a)(4)(D) also makes PRPs liable for health effects studies carried out by the Agency for Toxic Substances and Disease Registry, part of the Centers for Disease Control, pursuant to § 107(i).

1090 (D. Kan. 1996). Recoverable costs may entail "indirect" costs, such as planning, overhead, and oversight costs. *See, e.g., United States v. Chromalloy American Corp.*, 158 F.3d 345, 351-52 (5th Cir. 1998); *United States v. Lowe*, 118 F.3d 399 (5th Cir. 1997); *United States v. R.W. Meyer, Inc.*, 889 F.2d 1497, 1503 (6th Cir. 1989); *Browning-Ferris Ind., Inc. v. Ter Maat*, 13 F. Supp. 2d 756, 769 (N.D. Ill. 1998).

Some courts have rejected medical monitoring and evacuation costs as outside the scope of CERCLA, on the theory that recoverable costs should be limited to remediation efforts, not victims' relief. *In re Burbank Envir. Litigation*, 42 F. Supp. 976 (C.D. Cal. 1998) (private medical monitoring costs not recoverable); *Price v. United States Navy*, 39 F.3d 1011 (9th Cir. 1994); *Daigle v. Shell Oil Co.*, 972 F.2d 1527 (10th Cir. 1992); *Romeo v. General Chemical Corp.*, 922 F. Supp. 287 (N.D. Cal. 1994). *But see Pnemo Abex Corp. v. Bessemer and Lake Erie R.R. Co.*, 936 F. Supp. 1250 (E.D. Va. 1996) (medical monitoring costs recoverable). Other courts have permitted recovery for monitoring of a release, but not the oversight of the monitoring of others. *United States v., Rohm and Haas Co.*, 2 F.3d 1265 (3d Cir. 1993). While some courts have left open the question of whether unreasonable, unnecessary, or excessive costs can be recovered, *Matter of Bell Petroleum*, 3 F.3d 889, 907 n.26 (5th Cir. 1993), others have simply assumed that the modifier "all" permits recovery of even apparently unreasonable costs. *United States v. Hardage*, 982 F.2d 1436 (10th Cir. 1992).[66]

Future costs are another important issue. While CERCLA does not contemplate awards of future monetary damages, §113(g)(2) permits courts to enter a declaratory judgment on liability for "further response costs or damages." *United States v. Hughes, Hubbard & Reed*, 68 F.3d 811 (3d Cir. 1995); *Kelley v. E.I. DuPont de Nemours & Co.*, 17 F.3d 836 (6th Cir. 1994); *United States v. Davis*, 20 F. Supp. 2d 326, 332 (D.R.I. 1998). When there is such a judgment, PRPs may be liable to CERCLA plaintiffs for future costs not inconsistent with the NCP. *Laidlaw Waste System, Inc. v. Mallinckrodt, Inc.*, 925 F. Supp. 624 (E.D. Mo. 1996).

CERCLA LIENS

Section 107(l)(1) provides that "[a]ll costs and damages for which a person is liable to the United States * * * shall constitute a lien in favor of the United States" upon all real property owned by the PRP which is subject to a removal or remedial action. Since the lien is imposed without normal procedural safeguards (prior notice or pre-deprivation hearing), one leading case has found that the section violates procedural due process. *Reardon v. United States*, 947 F.2d 1509 (1st Cir. 1991).

---

[66] The government is entitled to recover its attorneys' fees and other costs of litigation. United States v. Bell Petroleum Services, Inc., 734 F. Supp. 771 (W.D. Tex. 1990), *rev'd on* other grounds, 3 F.3d 889 (5th Cir. 1993).

b. "Not Inconsistent with the National Contingency Plan"

CERCLA also requires that the governmental party's[67] actions giving rise to the costs to be recovered be "not inconsistent with" the NCP. § 107(a)(4)(A). This double-negative construction has been read to mean that the *challenger* of the costs of a removal or remedial action has the burden of proving that costs incurred were inconsistent with the NCP. This is generally a difficult task. PRPs may succeed only if they can show that the NCP's substantive or procedural requirements were not followed, making the government's clean-up orders arbitrary and capricious. Moreover, pre-enforcement suits are generally forbidden by CERCLA §113(h), *Lone Pine Steering Committee v. United States EPA*, 600 F. Supp. 1407, 1493 (D.N.J. 1985), so a challenger is in the position of asking EPA to redo the remedy and asking taxpayers to foot more of the bill. Most courts are extremely reluctant to second guess the EPA's choice of remedy. *United States v. Northeastern Pharmaceutical & Chemical Co., Inc.*, 80 F.2d 726 (8th Cir. 1986) (choice of a particular clean-up method is within discretion of government). For PRPs, this presumption means that so long as response costs are in accord with the NCP, (1) there is no obligation on the United States to minimize its response costs to benefit PRPs liable for the costs, *United States v. Akzo Nobel Coatings, Inc.*, 990 F. Supp. 892 (E.D. Mich. 1998), and (2) all costs expended on these NCP-consistent remedies are recoverable. *United States v. Hardage*, 982 F.2d 1436, 1443 (10th Cir. 1992).

Although the deck is certainly stacked against PRPs wishing to assert that certain costs are inconsistent with NCP, it is still possible for PRPs to avoid paying unreasonable costs. *See, e.g., State of Minnesota v. Kalman W. Abrams Metals, Inc.*, 155 F. 3d 1019, 1024-5 (8th Cir. 1998) (state clean-up was arbitrary and capricious and inconsistent with NCP for failure to do feasibility study before selecting remedy). The leading case is *In re Bell Petroleum Services, Inc.*, 3 F.3d 889 (5th Cir. 1993). The NCP provides for an alternate water supply when there was a "substantial danger to public health or the environment," but the otherwise liable PRP successfully argued that the administrative record failed to demonstrate any "substantial danger." The court was unpersuaded by EPA's position that costs incurred during remediation should be accepted by courts, since EPA had in place internal agency audits and other self-regulating systems:

Acceptance of the EPA's position would effectively prohibit judicial review of the EPA's expenditures. In short, we would give the EPA a blank check in conducting response actions. We seriously doubt that Congress intended to give the EPA such unrestrained spending discretion. Moreover, such unbridled discretion removes any restraint upon the conduct of the EPA

---

[67] Private parties' costs must be "consistent with" the NCP. § 107(a)(4)(B). The meaning of this difference in language is addressed below in connection with private cost recovery actions.

in exercising its awesome powers; if the EPA knows there are no economic consequences to it, its decisions and conduct are likely to be less responsible. 3 F.3d at 906-07.

Inconsistency may also be present if there is a government violation of the NCP's procedural standards. Failure to comply with the NCP requirement for public notice and comment can be grounds for precluding recovery of response costs. *VME American, Inc. v. Hein-Werner Corp.*, 946 F. Supp. 683 (E.D. Wis. 1996). If the government incurs response costs for remedial work without conducting an adequate remedial investigation (the RI/FS) or evaluating alternative remedies, there is inconsistency with the NCP. Such costs are non-recoverable for being arbitrary and capricious. *Washington State Dept. of Transp. v. Washington Natural Gas Co.*, Pacificorp., 59 F.3d 793 (9th Cir. 1995).

c. Natural Resource Damages

Apart from "all costs of removal and remedial action," a PRP may also discover that it is liable for "damages for injury to, destruction of, or loss of natural resources." §107(a)(4)(C). Such natural resource damage (NRD) claims can be staggering—sometimes twice to three times the amounts involved in a cost-recovery claim. There are four immediate differences between cost-recovery and natural resource damage actions. First, the government need not spend any money first in order to seek natural resource damages. Second, any monetary recovery received for such damages may only be used to "restore, replace, or acquire the equivalent of such natural resources." §107(f)(1). Third, there is an exception to the normal rule of unlimited retroactive CERCLA liability, in that §107(f)(1) precludes recovery where the release, and damages from the release, occurred prior to CERCLA's enactment. Fourth, §113(g) sets out special statutes of limitations for natural resource damage claims.[68]

What does the statutory terminology mean? The following sections explore each of §107(a)(4)(C)'s terms in detail.

i. "Natural Resources"

The words "natural resources" are broadly defined in §101(16) to include "land, fish, wildlife, biota, air, water, ground water, drinking water supplies, and other such resources" that "belong * * * to, [are] managed by, held in trust by, * * * or otherwise controlled by the United States [,] * * * any State or local government, any foreign government, [or] Indian tribe . * * *" This language encompasses virtually all effects a hazardous substance can have on

---

[68] For federal facilities, facilities on the NPL, and those subject to remedial action, the statute of limitations does not begin to run until three years after completion of remedial work. For all other sites, the statute runs three years after the discovery of the loss, or the date on which regulations are promulgated for assessing natural resource damages, whichever is later. *See* 43 C.F.R. §11.91(e).

nature, so long as that which is affected is somehow owned or controlled or held in trust by a government entity.

ii. Injuries Caused by a Release

Section 107(a)(C) of CERCLA requires that natural resources damages "result[] from [a] release." In order to satisfy this statutory standard of causation, the Department of Interior—which was given authority to issue NRD regulations—has established criteria that must be proven by the party bringing the natural resource damage claim. The party must show that the injury alleged to have occurred is a "commonly documented" response to releases of such hazardous substances; that the hazardous substances are known to cause such injury in field studies or controlled experiments; and that the injury can be measured by practical techniques and has been "adequately documented in scientific literature." 43 C.F.R. §11.62(f)(2). Natural resources damages are limited by the boundaries of the NPL site described in the original NPL listing, and may not be expanded to a surrounding area, despite the presence of hazardous substances in a larger area. *United States v. Asarco, Inc.*, 28 F. Supp. 2d 1170 (D. Idaho 1998).

Although these criteria have been sustained, *State of Ohio v. U.S. Dept. of Interior*, 880 F.2d 432 472 (D.C. Cir. 1989) (*Ohio II*), questions persist about the standard of proof required to demonstrate that natural resources injuries "result[] from" a particular release. Specifically, should the causation-of-injury standard be less demanding than that of the common law? And should CERCLA §301(c)(2)'s requirement that "best available procedures" be used to determine natural resources damages permit speculative assessments of causation? In 1998, the United States Court of Appeals for the District of Columbia considered both questions.

* * * Regarding causation, this court has repeatedly held that CERCLA is ambiguous on the precise question of what standard of proof is required to demonstrate that natural resource injuries were caused by, or "result[] from," a particular release. *See Ohio II*, 880 F.2d at 472 ("[W]hile we agree with petitioners that Congress expressed dissatisfaction with the common law as a norm in several areas of damage assessment, we conclude that CERCLA is at best ambiguous on the question of whether the causation-of-injury standard under § 107(a)(4)(C) must be less demanding than that of the common law."); Kennecott, 88 F.3d at 1224 ("CERCLA left it to Interior to define the measure of damages in natural resources damage assessment cases. * * * While the statutory language requires some causal connection between the element of damages and the injury—the damages must be 'for' an injury 'resulting from a release of oil or a hazardous substance'—Congress has not specified precisely what that causal relationship should be.") (citation omitted).

Similarly, we find nothing in the "resulting from" language of subsections 107(a)(4)(C) and 301(c)(1), or other provisions of CERCLA, to indicate that the Congress unambiguously intended a particular kind or quantity of causation and injury proof as a prerequisite to recovery of natural resources damages. While we have noted that the "best available procedures" language of subsection 301(c)(2) indicates that it would be inconsistent with CERCLA to permit "unduly speculative assessments," *Ohio II*, 880 F.2d at 462, we have never held that simply because assessments procedures are in some measure "speculative" or "predictive" they are contrary to CERCLA's "best available procedures" admonition. Rather, predictive submodels that represent rational scientific judgments about the probability that a particular release will cause a specific type and amount of injury are consistent with the Congress's intent to develop a "standardized system for assessing such damage which is efficient as to both time and cost." S.REP. NO. 96-848, at 85 (1980); cf. Ohio II, 880 F.2d at 455 ("[S]upport for the proposition that Congress adopted common-law damage standards wholesale into CERCLA is slim to nonexistent.").

Natural Ass'n of Manufacterers v. Dep't of the Interior, 134 F.3d 1095, 1105 (D.C. Cir. 1998).

PROBLEM

1. What is the law of National Resources Damage causation after the *National Association of Manufacturers* case?

2. Can you apply the *National Association of Manufacturers* test to the following facts, where the question is whether a party's "release" has caused a "specific type * * * of injury"?

Outside of Denver is a 40 square mile area once called the most polluted spot in the world. This is the Rocky Mountain Arsenal, where for several decades both the Shell Oil Company (which was making pesticides) and the United States Army (which was making nerve gas) discharged toxic and dangerous wastes into unlined lagoons. When birds or mammals (*e.g.,* chipmunks and prairie dogs) drank from the lagoons, they became sick, and usually died. When the Army and Shell stopped their operations, the poisoned waters in the lagoons eventually seeped into the ground water, where they remain to this day. The surface waters in the lagoons on the site have been replaced by water from rain and snowfall. A thriving animal population has emerged on the now abandoned Arsenal grounds. Bald eagles find this 40 square miles is perfect habitat to nest and raise their young. Mule deer have invaded the site. The Arsenal grounds have become a part of the National Wildlife Refuge System.

3. What are the "natural resources damages" at the Arsenal, and who, or what, is the cause?

iii. Who may bring suit

Unlike the rest of section 107, which permits any responder to sue, only certain public "trustees" may sue for natural resources damages—the United States, the states, and Indian tribes (and local governments if specifically authorized by state law). § 107(F)(1); *Artesian Water Co. v. Government of New Castle County*, 851 F.2d 643, 649 (3d Cir. 1988). Conversely, public trustees recover for damages to private property or other "purely private" interests. *Ohio II*, 880 F.2d at 460; *Exxon Corp. v. Hunt*, 475 U.S. 355, 375 (1986) (compensation to "third parties for damage resulting from hazardous substance discharges * * * [is] clearly beyond the scope of CERCLA").

It is not always easy to determine whether a particular loss of natural resources is "private" or "public." Consider the case of a release of hazardous substances in the Great Lakes, or marine environments within the jurisdiction of a coastal state, that kill game or fish. CERCLA defines "natural resources" to encompass "fish" and "wildlife." §101(16). Case law assumes that a state has a sovereign interest in natural resources within its boundaries. *Alaska Sport Fishing Assoc. v. Exxon Corp.*, 34 F.3d 769, 773 (9th Cir. 1994). If the release kills so much fish or game in the Great Lakes or coastal marine environments that they are no longer usable for commercial purposes, is the adverse effect of the release on harvesting activities a "purely private" loss for which the public trustee may not recover? Does it make any difference that commercial hunting and fishing operations there may not pay anything to the state for the privilege of exploiting public fish and game stocks? *See National Assoc. of Manufacturers v. U.S. Dept. of Interior*, 134 F.3d 1095, 1114 (D.C. Cir. 1998).

iv. "Damages"

Section 107(a)(4)(C) provides that public trustees may recover "damages for injury to, destruction of, or loss of natural resources . * * *," while §107(f)(1) cautions that these damages "shall not be limited by the sums which can be used to restore or replace such resources." Furthermore, CERCLA §301(c) directs the Department of Interior to promulgate two kinds of assessment methodologies for measuring natural resources damages: Type A rules "for simplified assessments requiring minimal field observation;" and Type B rules "for conducting [more complex] assessments in individual cases to determine the type and extent of short-and long-term injury, destruction or loss."[69]

When the Interior Department was prescribing methods for estimating the amount of money to be sought for natural resources damages that would comply with §§301(c) and 107(f)(1), several questions arose.

---

[69] Damage assessments made pursuant to these regulations enjoy a rebuttable presumption of validity. §107(F)(2)(c).

- Should natural resources damages be based on restoration/replacement costs, or the diminution-of-use value?
- If use values are relevant, as of when should these be calculated?
- Should use values be limited to market prices, or may measurement techniques be employed, such as "contingent valuation," which sets up hypothetical markets to elicit an individual's economic valuation of a natural resource?[70]
- May "non-use" values be used to calculate natural resource damages, for example, "option" and "existence" value, which measure an individual's willingness to pay to avoid an injury to a natural resources site, even if the individual will never visit (use) the site?[71]

The Interior Department's initial "Type B" regulations for assessing natural resources damages provided that the dollar amounts recoverable would be either restoration/replacement costs, or diminution of use values, whichever was less. These regulations chose to measure "use" values in large part according to market values. Only when it or a similar resource is not traded in a market would contingent valuation be acceptable. The regulations also largely excluded non-use values in the damages calculation. The case that follows, *Ohio II*, analyzes whether these regulations comport with CERCLA and with sound economic methodology.[72]

OHIO V. DEPT. OF THE INTERIOR [*OHIO II*]

880 F.2d 432 (D.C. Cir. 1989)

WALD, Chief Judge, and SPOTTSWOOD W. ROBINSON III and MIKVA, Circuit Judges.

* * *

III. The "Lesser-Of" Rule

The most significant issue in this case concerns the validity of the regulation providing that damages for despoilment of natural resources shall be "the *lesser of*: restoration or replacement costs; or diminution of use values." 43 C.F.R. § 11.35(b)(2) (1987) (emphasis added).

State and Environmental Petitioners challenge Interior's "lesser of" rule, insisting that CERCLA requires damages to be at least sufficient to pay the cost in every case of restoring, replacing or acquiring the equivalent of the damaged resource (hereinafter referred to shorthandedly as "restoration").

---

[70] *See* B. Binger, R. Coppole, & Elizabeth Hoffman, *The Use of Contingent Valuation Methodology in Natural Resource Damage Assessments: Legal Fact and Economic Fiction*, 89 NORTHWESTERN U.L. REV. 1029 (1995).

[71] Option value is the dollar amount an individual is willing to pay, although the individual is not using a resource, but wishes to reserve the option to use that resource in the future. Existence value is the dollar amount an individual is willing to pay although that individual does not ever plan to use the resource.

[72] *See generally* Douglas Williams, *Valuing Natural Environments: Compensation, Market Norms, and the Idea of Public Goods*, 27 CONN. L. REV. 365 (1995).

Because in some—probably a majority of—cases lost-use-value will be lower than the cost of restoration, Interior's rule will result in damages award too small to pay for the costs or restoration.

* * *

Although our resolution of the dispute submerges us in the minutiae of CERCLA text and legislative materials, we initially stress the enormous practical significance of the "lesser of" rule. A hypothetical example will illustrate the point: imagine a hazardous substance spill that kills a rookery of fur seals and destroys a habitat for seabirds at a sealife reserve. The lost use value of the seals and seabird habitat would be measured by the market value of the fur seals' pelts (which would be approximately $15 each) plus the selling price per acre of land comparable in value to that on which the spoiled bird habitat was located. Even if, as likely, that use value turns out to be far less than the cost of restoring the rookery and seabird habitat, it would nonetheless be the only measure of damages eligible for the presumption of recoverability under the Interior rule.

* * *

Interior's "lesser of" rule operates on the premise that, as the cost of a restoration project goes up relative to the value of the injured resource, at some point it becomes wasteful to require responsible parties to pay the full cost of restoration. The logic behind the rule is the same logic that prevents an individual from paying $8,000 to repair a collision-damaged car that was worth only $5,000 before the collision. Just as a prudent individual would sell the damaged car for scrap and then spend $5,000 on a used car in similar condition, DOI's rule requires a polluter to pay a sum equal to the diminution in the use value of a resource whenever that sum is less than restoration cost. What is significant about Interior's rule is the point at which it deems restoration "inefficient." Interior chose to draw the line not at the point where restoration becomes practically impossible, nor at the point where the cost of restoration becomes grossly disproportionate to the use value of the resource, but rather at the point where restoration cost exceeds—by any amount, however small—the use value of the resource. Thus, while we agree with DOI that CERCLA permits it to establish a rule exempting responsible parties *in some cases* from having to pay the full cost of restoration of natural resources, we also agree with Petitioners that it does not permit Interior to draw the line on an automatic "which costs less" basis.

Interior's "lesser of" rule squarely rejects the concept of any clearly expressed congressional preference for recovering the full cost of restoration from responsible parties. The challenged regulation treats the two alternative measures of damages, restoration cost and use value, as though the choice between them were a matter of complete indifference from the statutory point of view: thus, in any given case, the rule makes damages turn solely on whichever standard is less expensive. * * *

Based on the discussion that follows, we conclude that CERCLA unambiguously mandates a distinct preference for using restoration cost as the measure of damages, and so precludes a "lesser of" rule which totally ignores that preference.

The strongest linguistic evidence of Congress' intent to establish a distinct preference for restoration costs as the measure of damages is contained in § 107(f)(1) of CERCLA. That section states that natural resource damages recovered by a government trustee are "for use only to restore, replace, or acquire the equivalent of such natural resources." It goes on to state: "The measure of damages in any action under [§ 107(a)(C)] shall not be limited by the sums which can be used to restore or replace such resources."

By mandating the use of all damages to restore the injured resources, Congress underscored in § 107(f)(1) its paramount restorative purpose for imposing damages at all. It would be odd indeed for a Congress so insistent that all damages be spent on restoration to allow a "lesser" measure of damages than the cost of restoration in the majority of cases. * * *

In this connection, it should be noted that Interior makes no claim that a "use value" measure will provide enough money to pay for *any* of the three uses to which all damages must be assigned: restoration, replacement, *or acquisition of an equivalent resource*. Nor could Interior make such a claim, because its "lesser of" rule not only calculates use value quite differently from restoration or replacement cost but it also fails to link measurement of use value in any way to the cost of acquiring an equivalent resource. For example, Interior could not possibly maintain that recovering $15 per pelt for the fur seals killed by a * * * release would enable the purchase of an "equivalent" number of fur seals.

The same section of CERCLA that mandates the expenditures of all damages on restoration * * * provides that the measure of damages "shall not be limited by" restoration costs. § 107(f)(1). This provision obviously reflects Congress' apparent concern that its restorative purpose for imposing damages not be construed as making restoration cost a damages ceiling. But the explicit command that damages "shall not be limited by" restoration costs also carries in it an implicit assumption that restoration cost will serve as the basic measure of damages in many if not most CERCLA cases. It would be markedly inconsistent with the restorative thrust of the whole section to limit restoration-based damages, as Interior's rule does, to a minuscule number of cases where restoration is cheaper than paying for lost use.

* * *

The legislative history of CERCLA confirms that restoration costs were intended to be the presumptive measure of recovery. Senate proponents of the legislation, in the committee report and on the Senate floor, repeatedly emphasized that their primary objective in assessing damages for public resources was to achieve restoration.

Interior justifies the "lesser of" rule as being economically efficient. Under DOI's economic efficiency view, making restoration cost the measure of damages would be a waste of money whenever restoration would cost more than the use value of the resource. Its explanation of the proposed rules included the following statement:

> [I]f use value is higher than the cost of restoration or replacement, then it would be more rational for society to be compensated for the cost to restore or replace the lost resource than to be compensated for the lost use. Conversely, if restoration or replacement costs are higher than the value of uses foregone, it is rational for society to compensate individuals for their lost uses rather than the cost to restore or replace the injured natural resource.

50 Fed.Reg. at 52,141. *See also* 51 Fed. Reg. at 27,704 ("lesser of" rule "promotes a rational allocation of society's assets").

This is nothing more or less than cost-benefit analysis: Interior's rule attempts to optimize social welfare by restoring an injured resource only when the diminution in the resource's value to society is greater in magnitude than the cost of restoring it. * * *

The fatal flaw of Interior's approach, however, is that it assumes that natural resources are fungible goods, just like any other, and that the value to society generated by a particular resource can be accurately measured in every case—assumptions that Congress apparently rejected. As the foregoing examination of CERCLA's text, structure and legislative history illustrates, Congress saw restoration as the presumptively correct remedy for injury to natural resources. To say that Congress placed a thumb on the scales in favor of restoration is not to say that it forswore the goal of efficiency. "Efficiency," standing alone, simply means that the chosen policy will dictate the result that achieves the greatest value to society. Whether a particular choice is efficient depends on *how the various alternatives are valued*. Our reading of CERCLA does not attribute to Congress an irrational dislike of "efficiency"; rather, it suggests that Congress was skeptical of the ability of human beings to measure the true "value" of a natural resource. Indeed, even the common law recognizes that restoration is the proper remedy for injury to property where measurement of damages by some other method will fail to compensate fully for the injury. Congress' refusal to view use value and restoration cost as having equal presumptive legitimacy merely recognizes that natural resources have value that is not readily measured by traditional means. Congress delegated to Interior the job of deciding at what point the presumption of restoration falls away, but its repeated emphasis on the primacy of restoration rejected the underlying premise of Interior's rule, which is that restoration is wasteful if its cost exceeds—by even the slightest amount—the diminution in use value of the injured resource.

* * *

vi. The Hierarchy of Assessment Methods

The regulations establish a rigid hierarchy of permissible methods for determining "use values," limiting recovery to the price commanded by the resource on the open market, unless the trustee finds that "the market for the resource is not reasonably competitive." 43 C.F.R. § 11.83(c)(1). If the trustee makes such a finding, it may "appraise" the market value in accordance with the relevant sections of the "Uniform Appraisal Standards for Federal Land Acquisition," *see* 43 C.F.R. § 11.83(c)(2). Only when neither the market value nor the appraisal method is "appropriate" can other methods of determining use value be employed, *see* 43 C.F.R. § 11.83(d).

* * * While it is not irrational to look to market price as one factor in determining the use value of a resource, it is unreasonable to view market price as the exclusive factor, or even the predominant one. From the bald eagle to the blue whale and snail darter, natural resources have values that are not fully captured by the market system. DOI's own CERCLA 301 Project Team recognized that "most government resources, particularly resources for which natural resource damages would be sought[,] may often have no market." DOI has failed to explain its departure from this view. Indeed, many of the materials in the record on which DOI relied in developing its rules regarding contingent valuation expressed the same idea; it is the incompleteness of market processes that gives rise to the need for contingent valuation [CV] techniques. * * *

* * *

Neither the statute nor its legislative history evinces any congressional intent to limit use values to market prices. On the contrary, Congress intended the damage assessment regulations to capture fully all aspects of loss. CERCLA section 301(c)(2) commands Interior to "identify the best available procedures to determine [natural resource] damages, including both direct and indirect injury, destruction or loss." 42 U.S.C. § 9651(c)(2). The Senate CERCLA report stated that assessment procedures should provide trustees "a choice of acceptable damage assessment methodologies to be employed [and should] select the most accurate and credible damage assessment methodologies available." S.REP. NO. 848, 96TH CONG., 2D SESS. 85-86 (1980). The current rules defeat this intent by arbitrarily limiting use values to market prices.

On remand, DOI should consider a rule that would permit trustees to derive use values for natural resources by summing up all reliably calculated use values, however measured, so long as the trustee does not double count. Market valuation can of course serve as one factor to be considered, but by itself it will necessarily be incomplete. In this vein, we instruct DOI that its decision to limit the role of non-consumptive values, such as option and existence values, in the calculation of use values rests on an erroneous construction of the statute.

* * * First, section 301(c)(2) requires Interior to "take into consideration factors including, *but not limited to* * * * use value." 42 U.S.C. §9651(c)(2) (emphasis added). The statute's command is expressly not limited to use value; if anything, the language implies that DOI is to include in its regulations other factors in addition to use value. Second, even under its

reading of section 301(c), DOI has failed to explain why option and existence values should be excluded from the category of recognized use values. Indeed, the CERCLA 301 Project Team draft referred to option and existence values as "non-consumptive use values" (emphasis added). Option and existence values may represent "passive" use, but they nonetheless reflect utility derived by humans from a resource, and thus, prima facie, ought to be included in a damage assessment. DOI is entitled to rank methodologies according to its view of their reliability, but it cannot base its complete exclusion of option and existence values on an incorrect reading of the statute.

* * *

XIII. Contingent Valuation

* * *

The CV process "includes all techniques that set up hypothetical markets to elicit an individual's economic valuation of a natural resource." CV involves a series of interviews with individuals for the purpose of ascertaining the values they respectively attach to particular changes in particular resources. Among the several formats available to an interviewer in developing the hypothetical scenario embodied in a CV survey are direct questioning, by which the interviewer learns how much the interviewee is willing to pay for the resource; bidding formats, for example, the interviewee is asked whether he or she would pay a given amount for a resource and, depending upon the response, the bid is set higher or lower until a final price is derived; and a "take or leave it" format, in which the interviewee decides whether or not he or she is willing to pay a designated amount of money for the resource. CV methodology thus enables ascertainment of individually-expressed values for different levels of quality of resources, and dollar values of individuals' changes in well-being. The regulations also sanction resort to CV methodology in determining "option" and "existence" values.

Industry Petitioners' complaint is limited to DOI's inclusion of CV in its assessment methodology. They claim fatal departures from CERCLA on grounds that CV methodology is inharmonious with common law damage assessment principles, and is considerably less than a "best available procedure." * * *

* * *

The primary argument of Industry Petitioners is that the possibility of bias is inherent in CV methodology, and disqualifies it as a "best available procedure." In evaluating the utility of CV methodology in assessing damages for impairment of natural resources, DOI surveyed a number of studies which analyzed the methodology, addressed the shortcomings of various questionnaires, and recommended steps needed to fashion reliable CV assessments. For example, an early study by the Water Resources Council advised that questions in CV surveys be "carefully designed and pretested," a warning DOI was quick to heed.

Industry Petitioners urge, however, that even assuming that questions are artfully drafted and carefully circumscribed, there is such a high degree of variation in size of the groups surveyed, and such a concomitant fluctuation in aggregations of damages, that CV methodology cannot be considered a "best available procedure." We think this attack on CV methodology is insufficient in a facial challenge to invalidate CV as an available assessment technique. The extent of damage to natural resources from releases of oil and hazardous substances varies greatly, and though the impact may be widespread and severe, it is in the mission of CERCLA to assess the public loss. Certainly nothing in CV methodology itself shapes the injury inflicted by an environmental disaster, or influences identification of the population affected thereby. The argument of Industry Petitioners strikes at CERCLA, not CV's implementation, and can appropriately be considered only by Congress.

Similarly, we find wanting Industry Petitioners' protest that CV does not rise to the status of a "best available procedure" because willingness-to-pay— a factor prominent in CV methodology—can lead to overestimates by survey respondents. The premise of this argument is that respondents do not actually pay money, and likely will overstate their willingness-to-pay. One study relied upon by Industry Petitioners hypothesizes that respondents may "respond in ways that are more indicative of what they would like to see done than how they would behave in an actual market," and also observes that the converse is possible. The simple and obvious safeguard against overstatement, however, is more sophisticated questioning. Even as matters now stand, the risk of overestimation has not been shown to produce such egregious results as to justify judicial overruling of DOI's careful estimate of the caliber and worth of CV methodology.

NOTES

1. *Ohio II* made short work of Interior's regulations—which was not too surprising because they were promulgated by the Reagan Administration which was extremely hostile to natural resource damages at all. In *Colorado v. U.S. Dept. of Interior*, 880 F.2d 481 (D.C. Cir. 1989), the Interior Department's Type A regulations were invalidated in part for the same reasons that the *Ohio II* case invalidated much of the Type B regulations. The revised Type A regulations were later upheld in *Nat'l Assoc. of Manufacturers v. U.S. Dept. of Interior*, 2. 134 F.3d 1095 (D.C. Cir. 1998).

2. Do you agree with the court's resolution of these issues? Was there merit to the effort to introduce efficiency and market valuation into the assessment of damages? Was Congress acting wisely in its emphasis on restoration?

3. Assume that a release of a hazardous substance in Year 0 will require a restoration project costing $10 million in Year 10. CERCLA requires that the PRP pay natural resources damages in Year 0 sufficient to cover those $10 million of costs in Year 10. Because of the inherent time value of money

when invested, as well as inflation, an amount less than $10 million invested in Year 0 will yield CERCLA's required $10 million at the time restoration costs are actively incurred in Year 10. However, it is not possible to know exactly how much should be collected from a liable PRP in Year 0 if one does not know in Year 0 exactly how much restoration costs will be in Year 10 (*i.e.*, if the $10 million figure proves to be wrong). Moreover, even if the Year 10 future restoration costs can be properly estimated in Year 0, the dollars collected from the PRP in Year 0 will not cover the Year 10 costs if the interest rate ("discount rate") applied to the Year 0 dollars is incorrect.

So, two related uncertainties arise as a result of the need to collect and invest natural resources damages judgments in the present, in order to pay for restoration costs in the future. First, one must take into account the reality that the value of a particular natural resource, and the cost of a restoration project, may rise over time. In ascertaining the measure of damages in Year 0, the public trustee must try to predict what the *future* Year 10 cost of restoration will be. An error of estimation in the present, when damages are paid by PRPs, will produce insufficient revenue to pay the cost of restoration in the future. Second, a mistake made in predicting the discount rate over time will also produce insufficient funds when the time arrives to restore the damaged natural resources. The higher the discount rate selected in Year 0, the smaller the present value of the funds that must be collected from the PRP in Year 0 to pay for restoration costs in Year 10. If the discount rate between Year 0 and Year 10 proves to be less than the rate selected in Year 0, there will not be enough funds to pay for the restoration in Year 10. The situation is compounded when the cost of future Year 10 restoration is underestimated in Year 0.

5. Defenses

CERCLA is extremely unsympathetic to traditional defenses to liability. Instead of using defenses applicable to common law tort actions, parties facing CERCLA liability must (1) negate the elements of the plaintiff's case described above; (2) assert one of the four statutory defenses to CERCLA liability set out in §107(b); or (3) rely on one of the few non-§107(b) defenses that are available.

We have already considered the numerous elements of the CERCLA plaintiff's case (consistency with the NCP, PRP status of defendant, causation, etc.) and defendants' potential responses. Negating the plaintiff's case is likely to be extremely difficult. We turn our attention now to the statutory and non-statutory defenses.

a. Section 107(b) Defenses

Reread section 107(b). In order for a defendant successfully to employ a §107(b) defense, there must be proof that the "damages resulting [from a release]" were "caused solely" by some other source—an "act of God," or "an act of war," or "an act or omission of a third party" with whom the defendant does not have a "contractual relationship." The SARA Amendments of 1986 added a definition of "contractual relationship" which was intended to exclude from liability innocent landowners or buyers. CERCLA §101(35)(A). All four of these defenses share the common requirement that the damages be caused *solely* by events having nothing to do with the defendant. *G.J. Leasing Co. v. Union Elec. Co.*, 854 F. Supp. 539, 566-67 (S.D. Ill. 1994). Conversely, if the defendant in any conceivable way contributed to the release or amount of damages incurred, then the §107(b) defense is not available. *See United States v. Mottolo*, 26 F.3d 261 (1st Cir. 1994). The defenses will fail if the PRP had any role, no matter how attenuated, in the hazardous waste problem for which clean-up costs have been incurred. *See State of New York v. Shore Realty Corp.*, 759 F.2d 1032, 1048-49 (2d Cir. 1985).

i. Acts of God and Acts of War

The CERCLA definition of an "act of God" is "an unanticipated natural disaster or other natural phenomenon * * * the effects of which could not have been prevented or avoided by the exercise of due care . * * *" §107(b)(1). The operative words here are "unanticipated" and "could not have been * * * avoided by * * * due care." Courts have construed these terms to defeat act of God claims involving winds, heavy rains or floods when the defendant should have exercised due care in preparing for the catastrophic but foreseeable event. *See United States v. Poly-Carb, Inc.*, 951 F. Supp. 1518 (D. Nev. 1996) (windstorm); *United States v. M/V Santa Clara I*, 882 F. Supp. 825 (D. S.C. 1995) (storm); *State of Colorado v. Idarado Mining Co.*, 707 F. Supp. 1227, 1236 (D. Colo. 1989) (floodwaters). Section 107(b) permits the defense only if the release of hazardous substances has been caused "solely" by the act of God. If other factors causally contribute to the release, such as omissions or lack of "due care" by the defendant, then the defense must fail. *See, e.g., United States v. Barrier Industries, Inc.*, 991 F. Supp. 678, 679-80 (S.D. N.Y. 1998); *United States v. Alcan Aluminum Corp.*, 892 F. Supp. 648, 658 (M.D. Pa. 1995).

As with the act of God defense, courts have narrowed the "act of war" defense of §107(b)(2). The defense has been by companies that contaminated a site because of wartime contracts that required large production of a hazardous substance. Their claim is that spillage and leaks were the inevitable consequences of producing such enormous volumes of a substance. These arguments have been wholly unsuccessful. An "act of war" requires the use of force by one government against another, or the wartime destruction of private property so as to harm the enemy, neither of which is present when there is simply a contractual relationship between the United States and the defendant. *See United States v. Shell Oil*, 841 F. Supp. 962 (C.D. Cal. 1993).

ii. Third Party Defense

Section §107(b)(3) provides that if the release or threatened release was solely caused not by the defendant, but some other party whose "act or omission" did not occur "in connection with a contractual relationship," then the defendant may escape liability if two other conditions are met—the defendant exercised "due care" with respect to the hazardous substance concerned, and "took precautions against foreseeable acts or omissions of any such third party . * * *" This defense is really limited to cases where an unrelated third party or total outsider dumped the contaminant on, or in, the defendant's property. *United States v. Poly-Carb. Inc.*, 951 F. Supp. 1518, 1530 (D. Nev. 1996) (no liability if release by vandals); *United States v. Stringfellow*, 661 F. Supp. 1053, 1061 (C.D. Cal. 1987). The defense can be easily defeated if the defendant has some contractual relationship with the party causing the release, *Chatham Steel Corp. v. Brown*, 858 F. Supp. 1130, 1154-55 (N.D. Fla. 1994), or fails to satisfy the "due care" or "took precautions" requirements of §107(b)(3). *State of North Carolina ex rel. Howes v. W.R. Peele, Sr. Trust*, 876 F. Supp. 733, 745-46 (E.D. N.C. 1995).

In effect, then, there are four elements to the defense. The Defendant must show: (1) that the release was caused *solely* by the third party (which, as we have seen, is a nearly impossible standard to meet); (2) that third party's act or omission did not occur "in connection with a contractual relationship;" (3) that the defendant exercised "due care" with respect to the hazardous substance; and (4) that the defendant "took precautions against foreseeable acts or omissions" of third parties.

Absence of a Contractual Relationship–Much of the litigation surrounding the so-called "third party defense" has focused on the kinds of legal relationships between defendant and dumper that arguably fall within the "in connection with a contractual relationship" language. Many cases extended the notion of a contractual relationship to include not only agreements where the contractor did the dumping according to the defendant's instructions, *Shapiro v. Alexanderson*, 743 F. Supp. 268, 271 (S.D. N.Y. 1990), but also to virtually any legal relationship between defendant and dumper, no matter how casual or disconnected to waste disposal activities. *United States v. Monsanto Co.*, 858 F.2d 160 (4th Cir. 1988) (landlord-tenant); *Chatham Steel Corp. v. Brown*, 858 F. Supp. 1130, 1154-55 (N.D. Fla. 1994) (battery seller-recycler). Other courts have taken a closer look at the text of §107(b)(3) and have concluded that a defendant should be precluded from raising the defense only if the contract between the defendant and dumper-third party is connected with the handling of hazardous substances. This result stems from the "in connection with" language. This phrase seems to require that there be a linkage between the release and the contract. *See, e.g., Shapiro v. Alex Anderson*, 743 F. Supp. 268, 271 (S.D. N.Y. 1990); *Westwood Pharmaceuticals, Inc. v. National Fuel*

Gas Dist. Corp., 964 F.2d 85 (2d Cir. 1992); *American Nat. Bank and Trust Co. v. Harcos Chemicals, Inc.*, 997 F. Supp. 994, 1001 (N.D. Ill. 1998); *Reichhold Chemicals, Inc. v. Textron, Inc.*, 888 F. Supp. 1116 (N.D. Fla. 1995).[73] Thinking back to Congress' apparent intent in creating and limiting this defense, which is the better approach? Would a narrow reading of "contractual relationship" create an unacceptable loophole?

Exercise of Due Care–The "due care" inquiry tends to focus on whether the defendant had knowledge of the contamination and release, and if so, what steps it took to limit harm. If the defendant had no awareness of the potential for release, it may be excused for failure to exercise due care. *United States v. A&N Cleaners and Launderers, Inc.*, 788 F. Supp. 1317 (S.D. N.Y. 1992). But if the property owner has notice of the potential threat, and chooses to take no action, such a party has failed to exercise due care. *Idylwoods Assocs. v. Mader Capital, Inc.*, 915 F. Supp. 1290 (W.D. N.Y. 1996) (defendant failed to take corrective steps after learning of barrels of PCB-contaminated waste on the land); *State of North Carolina ex rel. Howes v. W.R. Peele, Sr. Trust*, 876 F. Supp. 733, 745-46 (E.D. N.C. 1995) (defendant who owned facility remained idle while hazardous waste was leaking). On the other hand, due care is present when a new owner made aware of the problem takes affirmative steps to notify affected parties, monitor, and prevent the condition from worsening. *State of New York v. Lashins Arcade Co.* 91 F.3d 353 (2d Cir. 1996); *Redwing Carriers, Inc. v. Saraland Apts.*, Ltd., 875 F. Supp. 1545, 1566 (S.D. Ala. 1995).

Precautions–As with the "due care" element of a third party defense, the "taking precautions" requirement asks if the defendant knew or should have known of the activity creating the threat of a release. *See, e.g., Lincoln Properties, Inc. v. Higgins*, 823 F. Supp. 1528 (E.D. Cal. 1992) (defendant may use defense when no awareness of dumping, and no further precautions were warranted). In contract to the due care condition, here courts tend to concentrate on whether the defendant should and could have taken precautionary steps before the release (or its discovery) to prevent the discharge of hazardous substances. *United States v. A&N Cleaners & Launderers, Inc.*, 854 F. Supp. 229, 243 (S.D. N.Y. 1994) (failure to make inquiry forecloses third party defense). The critical element is whether the waste disposal acts of third parties were foreseeable. If so, the defendant must take precautions against these acts. *United States v. Rohm and Haas Co.*, 939 F. Supp. 1142 (D. N.J. 1996); *Foster v. United States*, 922 F. Supp. 642 (D. D.C. 1996). Failure to take reasonable precautions against the foreseeable consequence of a pre-existing condition (*e.g.,* cracked sewer pipes) voids the third party defense when a third party actually triggers the release. (*e.g.,* pours

---

[73] *See* M.A. Meehan, *Towards Defining the Contractual Relationship Exception to CERCLA's Third Party Defense*, 5 VILL. ENVTL. L.J. 237 (1994); J.B. Ruhl, *The Third-Party Defense to Hazardous Waste Liability: Narrowing the Contractual Relationships Exception*, 29 S. TEX. L. REV. 291 (1987).

hazardous substances into the pipes). *Westfarm Assocs. v. Washington Suburban Sanitary Com'n*, 66 F.3d 669 (4th Cir. 1995).

iii. The Innocent Purchaser

Prior to 1986, real estate deeds, land contracts, and other instruments transferring title were deemed "contractual relationships" that prevented the use of the third party defense by an unsuspecting buyer of previously contaminated property. SARA changed this result in 1986 by adding §101(35), which provides that such purchasers are not in contractual relationships for purposes of the third party defense when:

(1) the "facility" on which there is a hazardous substance was acquired *after* disposal of the substance. If disposal occurs during ownership, or while the purchase is being consummated, the defense is inapplicable. *United States v. Monsanto Co.*, 858 F.2d 160, 168-69 n.14 (4th Cir. 1988).[74]

(2) at the time of acquisition the defendant "did not know and had no reason to know that any hazardous substance * * * was disposed of on, in, or at" the newly acquired property.[75] Actual knowledge of discharge of hazardous waste on the property defeats the defense. *United States v. Broderick Investment Co.*, 862 F. Supp. 272 (D. Colo. 1994). If a tenant had knowledge of the environmental contamination of a neighboring property when it took possession of a site, the tenant cannot raise the innocent landowner defense. *Clear Lake Properties v. Rockwell Int. Corp.*, 959 F. Supp. 763 (S.D. Tex. 1997). Knowledge at the time of purchase is also equivalent to a failure to exercise the "due care" standard of the third party defense—a buyer cannot remain idle after being informed of the presence of hazardous substances on the property. *Kerr-McGee Chemical Corp. v. Lefton Iron & Metal Co.*, 14 F.3d 321 (7th Cir. 1994); *Idylwoods Assoc. v. Mader Capital, Inc*, 915 F. Supp. 1290, 1302 (W.D. N.Y. 1996).

PROBLEM

In 1996, title to condominium units was acquired by a partnership made up of individual owners. Between 1996 and 1999, the individual owners became aware of mercury of the premises of the condominium. In the year 2000, each owner received title to the individual units in the condominium. What is the appropriate "date of acquisition" for purposes of asserting the innocent owner defense? The date the partnership

---

[74] The innocent owner defense would "hardly ever be available" if "disposal" included passive leaking. *ABB Industrial Systems, Inc. v. Prime Technology, Inc.*, 120 F.3d 351, 358 (2d Cir. 1997).

[75] Section 101(35)(A)(ii-iii) also excepts from the definition of "contractual relationship" situations where (1) the defendant is a government entity which acquired the facility through escheat, involuntary transfer, or eminent domain, or (2) the defendant acquired the facility by inheritance or bequest.

> acquired title to the premises as a whole, or the date ownership transferred from the partnership to each owner? *See Grand Street Artists v. General Electric Co.*, 28 F. Supp. 291 (D.N.J. 1998).

The "innocent buyer" or "innocent landowner" can then avoid liability if the other third party defense requirements, discussed above, are satisfied—

(3) release caused solely by someone other than the buyer,

(4) due care and

(5) adequate precautions taken by the buyer. *See, e.g., Matthews v. Dow Chemical Co.*, 947 F. Supp. 1517 (D. Colo. 1996) (due care satisfied by making reasonable environmental inspection); *Kerr-McGee Chem. Corp. v. Lefton Iron & Metal Co.*, 14 F.3d 321 (7th Cir. 1994) (failure to take precautions to prevent damage from hazardous substances known to be present on site precludes innocent buyer defense). It is, in other words, a narrow defense, but it provides a roadmap for the would-be purchaser to avoid CERCLA liability.

As a practical matter, the essence of the innocent land owner defense—or at least the aspect that a purchaser is in the best position to influence—is that the buyer had no reason to know that any hazardous substance had contaminated the property. To establish "no reason to know," §101(35)(B) requires that "all appropriate inquiry [be made] into the previous ownership and uses of the property consistent with good commercial and customary practice . * * *"[76] These provisions in effect require prudent buyers to undertake some pre-purchase environmental assessment of the property. To engage in such an environmental investigation is to satisfy both the "all appropriate inquiry" standard of the innocent landowner defense, and the "due care" requirement of the third party defense. *American Risk v. City of Centerline,* 69 F. Supp. 2d 944 (E.D. Mich. 1999). Failure to make inquiries or to engage in an investigation of the site (and of the previous owner's activities that could create a hazardous waste problem) usually makes the innocent landowner defense unavailable. *Foster v. United States*, 922 F. Supp. 642 (D. D.C. 1996); *United States v. A&N Cleaners and Launderers, Inc.*, 854 F. Supp. 229, 243 (S.D. N.Y. 1994); *Acme Printing Ink Co. v. Menard, Inc.*, 870 F. Supp. 1465, 1480-81 (E.D. Wis. 1994).

Although CERCLA does not flesh out what exactly constitutes "all appropriate inquiry," both courts and the EPA have provided some guidance. Judicial interpretation of the legislative history of the innocent landowner defense reveals a three tier system: commercial transactions are held to the strictest standard; private transactions for personal or residential use are

---

[76] The statute also requires that certain factors be taken into account in determining whether "all appropriate inquiry" has been made: (1) specialized knowledge by the landowner; (2) the relationship of the purchase price to the value of the uncontaminated property if uncontaminated; (3) commonly known information about the property; and (4) the obviousness of the presence of the contamination and the ability to detect it by inspection.

afforded more leniency; inheritances and bequests are given the most leniency. *In re Hemingway Transport, Inc.*, 993 F.2d 915, 933 (1st Cir. 1993); *United States v. Pacific Hide & Fur Depot, Inc.*, 716 F. Supp. 1341, 1348 (D. Idaho 1989). EPA innocent purchaser guidance states that two other important variables are known prior uses of the property (was it used as a residence or a waste disposal site?), and date of purchase (was it bought in 1950 or 1980?). EPA Guidance on Landowner Liability (June 6, 1989) at 11-12. Much of the pressure to undertake investigations of property comes from lenders, not surprisingly, who don't want their security to become worthless overnight. Consequently, lenders and private industrial standards organizations have reached a general consensus (with EPA acquiescence) on a tiered set of investigations ("Phase I," "Phase II," etc.) depending on the above factors.

NOTES

1. Should the act of God defense be available when a pollution release occurs because of a fire caused by a lightning strike? *See Wagner Seed Co. v. Daggett*, 800 F.2d 310 (2d Cir. 1986).

2. Can you think of a plausible act of war situation in the U.S.? Would a release due to terrorism fall within this defense?

3. How do the "taking precautions" requirements affect the liability of lessors of property to industrial, commercial, or waste management concerns?

4. Suppose you have a client who wants to buy property that is currently occupied by a waste treatment operation. How risky is such a purchase?

5. Purchaser wishes to buy property from seller, but is concerned that it may be contaminated with hazardous substances. Purchaser hires an attorney who suggests that "all appropriate inquiry" be made to ensure an innocent purchaser defense if contamination is later discovered. Purchaser conducts a soil investigation with a bulldozer and backhoe which not only reveals the presence of contamination, but also causes the spread of contaminants. Should the innocent purchaser defense be available? *See United States v. CDMG Realty Co.*, 96 F.3d 706, 711 (3d Cir. 1996).

b. Other Defenses

In addition to §107(b) defenses, a PRP can raise a number of other statutory and non-statutory defenses to avoid or minimize liability. These include: statute of limitations; equitable defenses; and indemnity or hold-harmless agreements.

i. *Statute of Limitations*

Section 113(g) establishes the limitations period for bringing a cost recovery action. A cost recovery action for a removal action must be filed within *three* years after "completion of the removal action," while an "initial action" must be filed within *six* years after "an initiation of physical on-site construction of [a] remedial action." §113(g)(2). *See, e.g., United States v. Ambroid Co.*, 34 F. Supp. 2d 86 (D. Mass. 1999) (closing by EPA of a site subject to a removal action is evidence of completion of action, which starts the running of CERCLA's three-year limitations period for recovery of cleanup costs); *United States v. Findett Corp.*, 75 F. Supp. 2d 982 (E.D. Mo. 1999) (to be an "initial action" for remedial treatment action, the case need not result in the entry of a declaratory judgment).

An important threshold issue is whether the clean-up action is characterized as a removal or remedial action. The general rule is that the investigation and study of clean-ups is "removal" action, even when a party is developing and testing—but not implementing—the contamination source control remedy. *Kelley ex rel. State of Michigan v. E.I. Dupont de Nemours*, 786 F. Supp. 1268 (E.D. Mich. 1992), *aff'd*, 17 F.3d 836, 840 (6th Cir. 1994). "Remedial" actions are response actions conducted in accordance with a Record of Decision over an extended period of time. *Advanced Micro Devices, Inc. v. National Semiconductor Corp.*, 38 F. Supp. 2d 802 (N.D. Cal. 1999); *United States v. Akzo Nobel Coatings, Inc.*, 990 F. Supp. 897, 904 (E.D. Mich. 1998). For remedial actions, the pertinent statute of limitations question is when "physical on-site construction" occurs. An event often must meet several criteria to be considered the initiation of physical on-site construction: (1) there is some "physical" action; (2) that physical action happens on the site; (3) the action is part of the remedial action; (4) the action constitutes "initiation" of the remedial action; and (5) the action plays a critical role in implementation of the permanent remedy. *See State of California v. Hyampsom Lumber Co.*, 903 F. Supp. 1389, 1393-94 (N.D. Cal. 1995).[77]

ii. Equitable Defenses

Most courts read §107(a) literally when it states that CERCLA liability is "subject only to the defenses" of §107(b). This means that while equitable considerations such as estoppel, laches, unclean hands, and caveat emptor may have a role in apportionment of liability in a contribution action, they will not be considered in actions that determine whether a party is liable as a PRP in the first place. *United States v. Rohm and Haas Co.*, 939 F. Supp. 1142 (D. N.J. 1996); *United States v. Martell*, 887 F. Supp. 1183 (N.D. Ind. 1995); *Transportation Leasing Co. v. State of California*, 861 F. Supp. 931, 940-41 (C.D. Cal. 1993). Equitable defenses are particularly unsuccessful when asserted against the government. *O'Neil v. Picillo*, 682 F. Supp. 706, 726-27 (D.R.I. 1988), *aff'd*, 883 F.2d 176 (1st Cir. 1989). There are some

---

[77] When natural resources damages are sought, §113(g)(1) requires that suit be filed within three years of "after the latter of the following: (A) The date of the discovery of the loss . . . . (B) The date on which regulations are promulgated under §301(c)." *See* California v. Montrose Chemical Corp., 104 F.3d 1507 (9th Cir. 1997) (limitations period for §301(c) regulations began on March 20, 1987).

rare decisions that presume equitable defenses are available in private cost recovery actions. *Folino v. Hampden Color & Chemical Co.*, 832 F. Supp. 757 (D.Vt. 1993); *Mardan Corp. v. C.G.C. Music, Ltd.*, 600 F. Supp. 1049, 1057-58 (D. Ariz. 1984). *But see Velsicol Chem. Corp. v. Enenco, Inc.*, 9 F.3d 524, 530 (6th Cir. 1993) (laches not available in private cost recovery action).

iii. Indemnity and Hold Harmless Agreements

If a person or company wishes to minimize the risk of financial liability in connection with a property sale, it is common to enter into an indemnification or hold harmless agreement with the other party to the transaction. Such risk allocation schemes do not constitute a defense in an EPA enforcement action as against a non-party to the agreement, *Smithkline Beecham Corp. v. Rohm & Haas Co.*, 89 F.3d 154 (3d Cir. 1996) (parties to an indemnification or hold harmless contract remain jointly and severally liable to the government), but they do permit the parties to allocate environmental responsibility among themselves. In §107(e), CERCLA specifically recognizes the enforceability of indemnification and hold harmless agreements among responsible parties. *See Joslyn Manufacturing Co. v. Koppers Co., Inc.*, 40 F.3d 750 (5th Cir. 1994); *Olin Corp. v. Consolidated Aluminum Corp.*, 5 F.3d 10 (2d Cir. 1993); *Stearns & Foster Bedding Co. v. Fraklin Holding Corp.*, 947 F. Supp. 790 (D.N.J. 1996).

The two issues that arise with respect to such agreements are whether the language of the agreement is broad enough to cover CERCLA liability, and whether a party may contract to indemnify or hold harmless another for environmental liability even though CERCLA was not in existence at the time of contracting. An "as is" or "all claims" clause, or a narrowly written clause, may not be sufficient to include CERCLA liability. *FINA, Inc. v. ARCO*, 200 F.3d 266 (5th Cir. 2000). But CERCLA liability is encompassed by language that evinces a strong intent to cover all liability arising in connection with occupancy or use of the property (*e.g.*, "Party A should indemnify and hold harmless Party B against all claims, actions, demands, losses, or liabilities arising from the use or operation of the land."). *See Velsicol Chemical Corp. v. Reilly Industries*, 67 F. Supp. 2d 893 (E.D. Tenn. 1999). A party may also contract with another with respect to allocation of environmental liability even if the contract arose pre-CERCLA, so long as the language is sufficiently broad to suggest an intent to cover all possible liability claims. *Kerr-McGee Chem. Corp. v. Lefton Iron & Metal Co.*, 14 F.3d 321, 327 (7th Cir. 1994).

NOTES

1. The EPA brings a §107(a) suit against a PRP seeking reimbursement of response costs already incurred at a Superfund site. Much of these costs

have been from monitoring wells that have been drilled into the site by the EPA to sample the extent of the underground contamination. The PRP files a cross-motion for a preliminary injunction directing the EPA to cease installation of the wells, and to encase existing wells, alleging that the drill holes for the wells have exacerbated existing environmental damage, and will cause further irreparable harm to the environment. Should the PRP's request for equitable relief be granted if the allegations appear to be true? *See United States v. Princeton Gamma-Tech, Inc.*, 31 F.3d 138, 141-46 (3d Cir. 1994).

2. *Bankruptcy*. Claims that arise before the debtor files bankruptcy may sometimes be discharged under federal bankruptcy law. CERCLA is silent on the question of *when* an economic claim under CERCLA (*e.g.,* liability under §107) arises for purposes of bankruptcy. In some jurisdictions, a CERCLA action becomes a claim under bankruptcy law when the release of hazardous materials occurs. *See, e.g., Ekotek Site PRP Comm. v. Self*, 932 F. Supp. 1328 (D. Utah 1996). This result permits discharge of a debtor prior to when the plaintiff may be able to identify the debtor as a PRP. Other courts that have considered the question of when a CERCLA claim arises for discharge purposes have decided that the critical time is when the claimant (usually a purchaser) can "tie the bankruptcy debtor to a known release of a hazardous substance which this potential claimant knows will lead to CERCLA response costs." *In re Chicago, Milwaukee, St. P. & Pac. R.R.*, 974 F.2d 774, 786 (7th Cir. 1992). This standard asks if sufficient information existed, had the claimant-purchaser sought it out, to give the claimant constructive knowledge that it possessed a CERCLA claim during the bankruptcy. *AM Int'l, Inc. v. Datacard Corp., DBS, Inc.*, 106 F.3d 1342, 1347-48 (7th Cir. 1997).

3. Should an EPA administrative order under §106 demanding clean-up action be considered a claim dischargable in bankruptcy?

E. Cost-Recovery Actions and Apportionment of Liability

CERCLA allows both government entities (the Federal Government, the states, and Indian tribes) and private parties to initiate clean-up actions with or without prior EPA approval. We now turn to the features of the actions that the government and private parties may initiate to recover response costs and (in the case of the government) to require PRPs to take response actions themselves. Not only are several types of civil action available to CERCLA plaintiffs, but they raise thorny issues of statutory interpretation, complex case management, and environmental policy.

1. Government Cost-Recovery and Enforcement Actions

When a government (federal, state, or tribal) takes the lead in responding to a release or threatened release of a hazardous substance, it may choose among several courses of action. As described above in subchapter C, the

EPA may investigate and then clean up the contaminated site. In such a case, §104(a) permits EPA to spend Superfund money as long as the response actions are consistent with the NCP. After the EPA has incurred response costs, it may recover those costs from PRPs found liable under §107(a).[78] In several ways (and for obvious reasons) CERCLA requires governments to make only the basic (*i.e.,* the easiest) case for CERCLA liability. It can take advantage of the low standard of liability, the range of PRPs, the relaxed thresholds for liability, the full range of recoverable costs, and the extremely limited defenses to liability. Therefore, with the Superfund at its back and a ready ability to impose liability on others, it is not surprising that most Superfund litigation is initiated by the EPA. Indeed, the EPA and PRPs will often resolve liability issues by settlement *in advance* of using Superfund money, because the PRPs' liability is all but assured.

In addition to cost recovery under section 107, section 106 authorizes the United States (but not states, tribes, or private parties) to "secure such relief as may be necessary" from a court "as the public interest and equities of a case may require," or to "take other action * * * including * * * issuing such [administrative] orders as may be necessary to protect public health and welfare and the environment" when (a) there may be an imminent and substantial endangerment, (b) because of an actual or threatened release of a hazardous substance. In other words, when the situation warrants, the EPA can proceed directly against a responsible party by court injunction or administrative order.

a. Judicial Relief

Section 106 adds considerably to EPA's bargaining power in cost-recovery actions or threatened cost-recovery actions. While actions under §107 and §106 are similar in many ways, there are also important differences:

ACTIONS UNDER §106 AND §107 COMPARED	
DIFFERENCES	
Authority to bring §106 action	A §106 action may be initiated only by the federal government, not states, *New York v. Shore Realty Corp.,* 759 F.2d 1032, 1049-50 (2d Cir. 1985), not cities, *Mayor and Council v. Klokner & Klockner,* 811 F. Supp. 1039 (D.N.J. 1993), and not private parties. *Cadillac Fairview/California, Inc. v. Dow Chemical Co.,* 840 F.2d 691, 697 (9th Cir. 1988). A §107 action is available to federal and state governments, Indian tribes, and certain

---

[78] The elements of governments' cause of action for response costs were, in essence, the subject of subchapter D.

	private parties.
Who pays?	Under §106, "responsible" parties pay directly for the clean up.
Speed of clean-up	Section 106 can bring about a clean-up much more quickly, because it avoids the procedural hurdles of §104.
National Priorities List	A site subject to §106 need not be on the NPL; remedial action under §104 is limited to sites on the NPL.
Triggers	Section 107 becomes relevant when there is a release/threatened release that causes the incurrence of response costs; §106 is triggered when there is also an imminent and substantial endangerment because of a release/threatened release.
Defenses	While equitable defenses are generally unavailable in a §107 context, they are available under §106(a), which provides that courts should grant such relief "as the public interest and the equities of the case" require.
SIMILARITIES	
Liable parties	Both §§106 and 107 apply to persons qualifying as PRPs under §107(a).
Standard of Liability	Most courts interpret §106(a) as imposing the same standard of liability as is applicable for §107(a), *i.e.,* strict liability. *United States v. Price*, 577 F. Supp. 1103, 1113 (D.N.J. 1983); *United States v. Outboard Marine*, 556 F. Supp. 54 (D. Ill. 1982).
Defenses	Although §106 does not acknowledge any defenses, §106(b)(2)(C) & (D) authorize parties who must remediate a site under §106 to seek reimbursement from the Superfund, provided that they are not otherwise liable for response costs under §107. One can construe this proviso as making available to §106 defendants all the statutory defenses available under §107(b).

The key element of proof in section 106 actions is the requirement of "may be an imminent and substantial endangerment to the public health or welfare or the environment." In the leading case of *United States v. Conservation Chemical Co.*, 619 F. Supp. 162 (W.D. Mo. 1985), virtually every one of the words in that phrase were broadly construed so as to encompass non-emergency situations when there is only the potential threat of harm. According to the court, the word "imminent" does not require proof that harm will occur "tomorrow," only that factors are present now giving rise to future endangerment. "Substantial" does not require quantification of the endangerment, merely reasonable cause for concern that someone or something may be exposed to a risk of harm. "Endangerment" does not require quantitative proof of actual harm, just a threatened or potential harm (the language of §106 is triggered when there "may" be endangerment). Also,

§106 relief is available when *either* "the public health" *or* "welfare" *or* "the environment" is endangered.

Section 106 in some ways parallels RCRA §7003, which authorizes the federal government to act when hazardous waste contamination produces an "imminent and substantial endangerment to health and the environment." But there are important differences. RCRA §7003 has primary applicability to emergencies at active sites; §106 includes emergency and non-emergency situations at both active and inactive sites. RCRA §7003 is triggered when there is endangerment to public health or the environment; §106 also protects "public welfare." RCRA §7003 requires that the endangerment arise from the handling or storage of solid or hazardous waste; §106 requires endangerment from a "release or threatened release of a hazardous substance." On the other hand, RCRA § 7003 covers the petroleum wastes excluded from CERCLA. Moreover, RCRA § 7003 is enforceable by private parties (and states) through RCRA's more generous citizen suit provision (§ 7002).

b. Administrative Orders

Section 106(a) permits the President (through the EPA) to "issue such orders as may be necessary" to clean up a contaminated site. This administrative mechanism has several advantages over the judicial route. A "unilateral" order is much quicker, and it permits EPA to control the nature of the remedy imposed. Preenforcement judicial review of these orders is precluded by §113(h), and if a challenge to the order is mounted after the clean-up is complete, courts must defer to the order unless it is arbitrary or capricious or illegal. §113(j).

An administrative order usually results from one of two scenarios. EPA may notify the responsible party of its decision to require the clean-up of a site where the site is usually under the control of the responsible party (*e.g.*, as owner). The responsible party then contacts the EPA and the two begin to negotiate an order that will be acceptable to both. Based on these negotiations, the EPA issues a §106 consent order that is binding on the responsible party. Alternatively, the responsible party may choose to resist such an order, and not negotiate.[79] In that case, EPA marshals evidence, compiles an administrative record, and then issues a unilateral order directing the responsible party to remediate the site. The recalcitrant party receives no hearing (only notice), and is denied the right to preenforcement judicial review by §113(h). *Solid State Circuits, Inc. v. United States EPA*, 812 F.2d 383 (8th Cir. 1987); *Wagner Seed v. Daggett*, 800 F.2d 310 (2d Cir. 1986).

---

[79] One reason why a responsible party may be inclined to resist an EPA §106 order is that such orders may require the party to clean up all hazardous substances at the site, including those that were not the result of that party's disposal practices. Employers Insurance of Wausau v. Clinton, 848 F. Supp. 1359 (N.D. Ill. 1994).

While judicial review is available when EPA moves to enforce its order, a recalcitrant party who is in fact liable under §107 may be fined up to $25,000 per day of noncompliance. §106(b)(1). If the noncompliance is "without sufficient cause," it may also be subject to punitive damages in an amount up to three times the EPA's clean-up costs. §107(c)(3). "Sufficient cause" has been subject to considerable judicial debate. Some courts assume that sufficient cause exists if the responsible party has an *objectively* reasonable basis for believing the order is invalid. *Solid State Circuits, Inc. v. United States EPA*, 812 F.2d 383, 391 (8th Cir. 1987). Others permit a more *subjective* good faith belief by the responsible party that the order is invalid. *Aminoil, Inc. v. United States*, 646 F. Supp. 294, 299 (C.D. Cal. 1986); *United States v. Reilly Jar & Chemical Corp.*, 606 F. Supp. 412 (D. Minn. 1985).[80] Thus, if a responsible party believes that it should not be liable for clean-up of a site, the more prudent course of action is either to comply with the order and sue to recover the costs from the Superfund (§106(b)(2)),[81] or to bring a private cost recovery action against third parties (§107(a)(4)(B)). Unfortunately, recovery under either option is not guaranteed; moreover, the allegedly "innocent" responsible party will surely have to incur substantial litigation and/or clean-up expenses in order to eventually enjoy vindication.

PROBLEM

Although it is agreed that an EPA decision to seek injunctive relief, and not an administrative order, is subject to the liability standards of §107, there is no consensus about whether the eventual remediation plan (to be carried out by the liable party) should be formulated by the court issuing the injunction or by EPA. Relevant statutory language includes:

- §106(a)–"the * * * court * * * shall * * * grant such relief as the public interest and the equities of the case may require . * * *"
- §121(a)–"Selection of remedial action. The [EPA] shall select appropriate remedial actions determined to be necessary * * * which are in accordance with [§121] and * * * the [NCP]."
- 113(j)(2)–"In considering objections raised in any judicial action * * * the court shall uphold the [EPA's] decision in selecting the response action unless * * * the decision was arbitrary and capricious . * * *"

What argument can be made that courts are to determine the appropriate remedy when EPA opts for injunctive relief under §106? *See United States v. Ottati & Goss, Inc.*, 900 F.2d 429 (1st Cir. 1990). What arguments can be

---

[80] Inability to pay punitive damages does not constitute "sufficient cause." United States v. Parsons, 723 F. Supp. 757, 763-64 (N.D. Ga. 1989).

[81] If the clean-up is unsuccessful (*i.e.*, hazardous substances remain), then it may be alleged that there is noncompliance with an administrative order, and reimbursement from the Superfund will be precluded. Employers Insurance of Wausau v. Clinton, 848 F. Supp. 1359 (N.D. Ill. 1994).

made that the EPA should make the selection of remedies when injunctive relief is sought under §106? *See United States v. Akzo Coatings of America, Inc.,* 949 F.2d 1409, 1425 (6th Cir. 1991).

2. Settlements and Consent Decrees

Although much of this chapter has been devoted to litigation remedies, the reality is that most CERCLA enforcement is accomplished through negotiation and settlement, a practice that was encouraged and regularized by SARA in section 122. Settlements are often memorialized in a consent decree, an order of the court, agreed to by all parties, which sets out in greater or lesser detail the remedy selected and the allocation of liability. There are incentives and disincentives for both the government (EPA) and private parties to avoid litigation. EPA has only a certain amount of congressionally-appropriated enforcement funding, and the Superfund monies are likewise limited. EPA does not have enough personnel to oversee the work of government-hired clean-up contractors at every NPL site. It is preferable for the EPA to shift the costs of CERCLA compliance to the PRPs, and to have responsible parties (and their contractors) do the clean-up work, after these parties have conceded their liability in a settlement. It is in that spirit that §122(a) encourages settlements that are in the public interest and consistent with the NCP.

For their part, PRPs do not want to face the prospect of extended §107 litigation or preemptory §106 orders. Like EPA, private parties wish to reduce their costs, and PRPs who do not settle may be saddled with tens of millions of dollars in litigation expenses and liability costs. CERCLA adds a further, critical incentive to settlement: PRPs who settle are protected against additional, future liability, and they may seek contribution against non-settling PRPs. § 113(f)(2); *United States v. Colorado & Eastern Railroad Co.,* 50 F.3d 1350 (10th Cir. 1995). Moreover, since settling PRPs are themselves free of further contribution responsibility, if the settlement does not recover a percentage of the total clean-up cost attributable to the settling PRPs, those PRPs who did not settle will eventually have to pay more than their fair share of the cost.

The road to settlement often begins when the EPA determines that a site is contaminated with hazardous substances. The next step is to collect data on possible levels and sources of the contamination and to try to identify the individuals or companies who are PRPs. EPA then estimates the cost of remediating the site, and puts together an initial list of PRPs, together with an assessment of their financial wherewithal. CERCLA provides EPA with two sources of authority for collecting pertinent information: section 104(e) permits the EPA to seek information about all environmental matters, as well as about "the ability of a person to pay for or perform a clean-up," and section 122(e)(3)(B) gives EPA the power to issue subpoenas in order to implement the settlement provisions of §122. Indeed, it is often the receipt of a "general notice" or "104(e) letter" that first notifies a PRP of its impending liability. The letter tells the recipients about the site, lists the other PRPs that have been identified, and warns of the potential liability for response costs. It states that EPA prefers to negotiate with all the PRPs as a single entity, so the letter also asks them to form a steering committee, which can begin settlement discussions on behalf of the entire group of PRPs. A number of actions may follow:

- The PRPs create subgroups in order to facilitate negotiations with EPA. There are typically two types at a major site—one or a few "major parties" who contributed most of the hazardous waste and many "de minimis parties" who contributed only a small volume.

- EPA may try to encourage settlement by preparing a "nonbinding preliminary allocation of responsibility" (NBAR) which offers an estimate of the relative liability of each PRP. §122(e)(3).

- The EPA may already have incurred response costs with respect to the site, in which case it may use the threat of future §107 liability to encourage a settlement. EPA can have the PRPs repay the Superfund according to their financial ability to pay. *United States v. Bay Area Battery*, 895 F. Supp. 1524 (N.D. Fla. 1995).

- EPA may employ the "special notice" procedures found in §122(e), which permit PRPs to fast track the settlement process by making a proposal within 60 days to perform or finance a government clean-up. During this negotiation-settlement time period, a moratorium is imposed both on EPA response actions under §104(a) and on unilateral administrative orders under §106.

- A PRP, or a sub-group of PRPs, may decide not to settle (typically because they believe that the proposed settlement imposes a disproportionate burden). When this happens, the non-settlors face lawsuits both from the EPA (§107 liability) and the settling PRPs (§113 contribution). Lawsuits filed by non-settlors challenging the procedural and substantive components of the settlement inevitably fail. *See, e.g., United States v. Cannons Engineering Corp.*, 899 F.2d 79 (1st Cir. 1990).

POST-LITIGATION SETTLEMENT

Settlement can take place *after* litigation, sometimes even after settlement and litigation. Take the case of the Stringfellow Superfund site in California. The Stringfellow Acid Pits industrial waste facility is where 35 million gallons of hazardous substances were dumped into unlined ponds before 1972. It was the first location in California to be identified as a CERCLA Superfund site.

The property was first subject to a cleanup pursuant to a 1992 consent decree, under which the approximately 20 private generators of industrial waste agreed to remediate the site. Since it was a superfund site, the United

States also incurred cleanup costs. The PRPs have spent $90 million there, while the United States has incurred $80 million in costs. In 1993, a federal court found California liable as well for the cleanup at Stringfellow, because of its negligence in investigating, choosing, and designing the facility. In 1998, the federal court found the United States and California to be liable, along with the 20 private defendants. This 1998 order held that California was subject to counterclaims under CERCLA §107(a) for cost recovery, and under §113 for contribution.

In early 1999, after the consent decree and all this extensive litigation, it was announced that there was a proposed settlement between California and some 17 private PRPs that would finally end litigation over the cleanup of Stringfellow. The settlement has two conditions precedent to its execution: (1) the United States must agree to forbear from seeking to execute on a prior judgment regarding its past costs; and (2) California must secure sufficient monies from its insurance carriers to fulfill its financial obligations under CERCLA. After hundreds of millions of dollars spent on cleaning up the site, and after exhaustive CERCLA litigation, a settlement might be at hand that would end the uncertainty and adversarial relationship between the parties.

a. Major Party Settlements and Consent Decrees

Before EPA can begin negotiations with the major contributors to a site, it first must cull those that had only a de minimis role. For those parties, CERCLA encourages specialized and flexible "de minimis settlements" under §122(g). EPA then engages in settlement negotiations with the major parties, in which the ultimate goal is for all of them to sign a consent decree embodying the proposed settlement terms. For those who choose to opt out of a settlement/consent decree, the alternative is to face an EPA unilateral order or an EPA-lead clean-up. Moreover, non-settlors ("recalcitrants") are also subject to contribution claims by settling PRPs. *State of New York v. Solvent Chemical Co.*, 984 F. Supp. 160, 167 (W.D. N.Y. 1997). The proposed consent judgment is filed with the appropriate federal district court, where if approved, it is entered as a final judgment. §122(d)(1).

The settling PRPs typically pay for and/or perform the RI/FS and all remaining remedial activities at the site. Most important, they agree to an allocation of responsibility among themselves. EPA or a professional facilitator may act as a mediator in order to achieve some consensus, often using the NBAR as a starting point. The usual measure of apportioning liability is according to harm, *United States v. Cannons Engineering Corp.*, 899 F.2d 79, 87 (1st Cir. 1990), which is itself often measured primarily by the volume of waste attributable to each PRP. *United States v. Davis*, 11 F. Supp. 183, 190 (D.R.I. 1998); *United States v. Union Elec. Co.*, 934 F. Supp.

324, 329-30 (E.D.M. 1996) (liability should be based on volume rather than toxicity), *aff'd*, 132 F.3d 422 (8th Cir. 1997). If the apportionment of liability seems substantively unfair, a reviewing court will reject a proposed consent decree. *United States v. Allied Signal, Inc.*, 62 F. Supp. 2d 713 (N.D.N.Y. 1999)(proposed consent decree unfair where municipalities were responsible for a majority of waste at site, but their liability would be less than cost of capping one acre of 74 acre site).

When the PRPs and EPA reach agreement CERCLA rewards them with several benefits. EPA signs a "covenant not to sue" settling PRPs for future liability, §122(f)(1), though it is subject to a "reopener" for conditions unknown at the time of remediation completion or that endanger human health or the environment. §122(f)(6). EPA may provide contribution protection to settling PRPs, largely immunizing them from contribution actions filed by non-settling PRPs. §§113(f)(2) & 122(h)(4). Another CERCLA provision, §122(b)(1), permits EPA to agree to pay from the Superfund all remediation costs attributable to "orphan shares," that is, hazardous substances dumped on the site by bankrupt or unknown parties. Otherwise, the settling parties have to pay their pro rata percentage of the clean-up costs of the orphan share.

THE PERIL OF NON-SETTLORS

CERCLA intends that non-settlors have no contribution rights against settlors regarding matters addressed in the settlement. When the government reaches a settlement, it does not bear the risk that it settled for too little with one party, because under the Uniform Contribution Among Tortfeasors Act (UCATA), it may still pursue the non-settling parties for the remainder. *United States v. Cannons Engineering Corp.*, 899 F.2d 79, 92 (1st Cir. 1990) (when a party settles with the government, the non-settling party's liability is reduced only by the amount of the settlements); *State of New York v. Solvent Chemical Co., Inc.*, 984 F. Supp. 160, 168 (W.D. N.Y. 1997). If a settlor brings a contribution action against non-settlors, it may do so, and the claim would be governed not by the UCATA, but by the Uniform Comparative Fault Act, which reduces a non-settlor's liability by the amount of the settlor's equitable share of the obligation, as determined by a trial on liability. *United States v. Gen Corp.*, 935 F. Supp. 928, 932-35 (N.D. Ohio 1996); *United States v. SCA Services of Indiana*, 827 F. Supp. 526, 533-36 (N.D. Ind. 1993). *See* Christopher Man, *The Constitutional Rights of Nonsettling Potentially Responsible Parties in the Allocation of CERCLA Liability*, 27 ENVTL. L. 375 (1997). Moreover, most courts have held that non-settlors should not be entitled to intervene when EPA and the settling parties seek to have a court approve the consent decree. *See, e.g., United States v. ABC Industries*, 153 F.R.D. 603, 608 (W.D. Mich. 1993); *Arizona v. Motorola, Inc.*, 139 F.R.D. 141, 146-47 (D. Ariz. 1991). *Contra United States v. Union Elec. Co.*, 64 F.3d 1152, 1166-67 (8th Cir. 1995) (nonsettlors have protectable interest under §113(i) in ensuring that their contribution claim is not extinguished). *See* J.F. Mahoney, *Allowing Intervention by Non-Settling PRPs: Not the "Environmentally Correct" Decision, but One that is Unavoidable*, 14 PACE ENVTL. L. REV. 733 (1998).

b. De Minimis Settlements

Even before the EPA attempts to negotiate with major parties, it seeks to reach agreement with "de minimis" PRPs, those whose contribution to the site is minimal and for whom joint and several liability would be least fair. Section 122(g) urges the EPA to settle promptly with generators whose actions have produced small amounts of hazardous substances at the site.[82] Although the statute speaks of minimal contribution both with respect to quantity and toxicity, §122(g)(1)(13), the courts have generally permitted volume to be the sole determinant. *United States v. Cannons Engineering Corp.*, 899 F.2d 79, 88 (1st Cir. 1990); *United States v. Wallace*, 893 F. Supp. 627, 633 (N.D. Tex. 1995). The rule-of-thumb is that any PRP who contributed less than 1% of total volume is a de minimis party.

There are several advantages to a de minimis settlement. As with major party settlements, de minimis settlements provide settling parties with government covenants not to sue, §122(f) and (g)(2), and contribution protection from potential suits by other PRPs. §§113(f)(2) and 122(g)(4) and (h)(4). Unlike major party settlements, de minimis settlements do *not* contain "reopeners" allowing EPA to pursue settlors if conditions are discovered that were unknown at the time of settlement,[83] giving them true finality to the matter. De minimis settlements also reduce transaction costs, both for the government and the PRP, because such settlements occur relatively early in the negotiation process and do not need to be entered as a consent decree. In the 1990s, the EPA has reached de minimis settlements with over 10,000 parties.

Since the federal government largely loses its ability to revisit de minimis settlements, it requires that three conditions be met before it agrees to the settlement. First, it demands that PRPs provide it with all information relevant to the site, as well as an assurance that they will be cooperative with respect to all response activities at the site, whether carried out by EPA or the PRPs. Second, EPA will require that the settlors pay an amount equal to their share of the clean-up costs. Third, in exchange for the ability to settle without the normal reopeners, the EPA demands a "premium" payment in addition to the

---

[82] Section 122(g)(1)(B) also authorizes EPA to enter into de minimis settlements with the owners of a contaminated site if the owners are not responsible in any way for the presence of hazardous wastes there.

[83] Reopeners are still available if a PRP should not have been classified as a de minimis party, or if there are serious cost overruns in the clean-up.

pro rata share. The premium, which ranges from 60% to 100% of actual costs, is intended to compensate EPA for the risks associated with possible cost overruns for a not-yet-selected remedy, EPA's potential inability to recover response costs from the Superfund or other responsible parties, and uncertainties about the nature of future response actions.

For PRPs whose contribution to a site is tiny, EPA has decided that it is appropriate to offer "de micromis" settlements so as to resolve their liability with virtually no transaction costs. To qualify for this special type of de minimis settlement, the parties must be responsible for an extraordinarily small percentage of the waste at a site (0.001% by volume). The de micromis settlement is similar to a de minimis settlement except that EPA does not demand a "premium" payment. A de micromis PRP must pay only its percentage share of the clean-up cost, and then it is immunized from both EPA and other PRP litigation.

3. Case Study: Leadville

About 100 miles southwest of Denver lies the city of Leadville. Unfortunately, the city has gained fame for less than ideal reasons. Since 1860, mining has been a major industry in the small Colorado town. In fact, Leadville is where some millionaires got their start. Mining in Leadville resulted in a number of family fortunes, including those of Marshall Field, Charles Dow, James Brown (husband of an unsinkable Molly) and Solomon Guggenheim. Both state and congressional legislatures encouraged the mining of the area through direct funding and legislative promotion. Leadville produced and supported mineral processing of lead, copper, silver, gold, and zinc.

Figure 11.7–Miner's cabin in the California Gulch, 1980's[84]

---

[84]Source: Colorado Historical Society.

Leadville mining was concentrated in the California Gulch area, drained by the Arkansas River. Mine tailings surrounded California Gulch. When the California Gulch Mines shut down in the latter part of the 19th Century, the tailings, along with their high concentrations of heavy metals, remained in place. When the abandoned mines drained excess waters, primarily through the Yak Tunnel in California Gulch, the already polluted waters picked up more contaminants from the tailings piles, and spread toxic substances to the Arkansas River.

Figure 11.8–California Gulch Area[85]

Trouble began in 1982, when dead fish began floating down the Arkansas River. The death of fish was linked to the mines and the mine waters upstream from Leadville. The mines had shut down after 120 years of operation, but had left behind waste, mine tailings and slag that had polluted the surface waters.

---

[85]Source: Colorado Historical Society,

Figure 11.9–Mine Tailings Site

The State of Colorado decided to conduct a blood lead level study for the Leadville area. In order to test the entire town, the state sent out what was labeled the "brown envelope letter." This letter requested that each resident allow the EPA to come to the property and test their soil and water; the letter also stated that failure to permit this sampling would result in the EPA investigating the recipient as a PRP. At this point, local outrage against the EPA began.

The investigations found high concentrations of lead, iron, manganese, cadmium, and zinc in the waters. Concern had mounted regarding immediate cleanup as a result of studies demonstrating that varied levels of lead in the human blood stream could be linked to learning deficits and lead poisoning. One area of particular concern was that the mining slag had been used in the asphalt to pave virtually all of the town's roads. The lead had been spread in thin layers on the streets of Leadville.

About a year later, in 1983, the Colorado Department of Public Health and Environment (CDPHE) initiated an action under CERCLA for "natural resources damage." The PRP Defendants in the case, mining and natural resources companies, denied the claims and filed a counterclaim against the United States and other third parties. CDPHE amended its complaint to include claims for reimbursement of costs already incurred, and those likely to be incurred in response to the release or threat of release of hazardous substances at the Yak Tunnel, California Gulch and for portions of the Arkansas River. CDPHE alleged strict liability and common law negligence claims against various PRPs for cleanup costs and other damages resulting from the contamination discharges.

The EPA joined with the CDPHE in concluding that a cleanup was mandated because of the health risks associated with the polluted runoff and lead deposits throughout Leadville. But the local community resisted. It was an unexpected reaction. Normally, the EPA is summoned by the community to clean up a site, and is praised for doing so. In Leadville, the EPA was hated. The community felt that the lead in the environment was not a problem. After all, many long time residents had lived to a ripe old age in Leadville without any health problems or complications from the lead. The community did not seem to care when the spring thaw came, and the flow of the Arkansas River was a rusty orange-red color instead of the bluish clear it should be. The runoff was being tainted by the iron and lead mine tailings, resulting in the red coloring, but the community was more concerned about federal intermeddling in local matters.

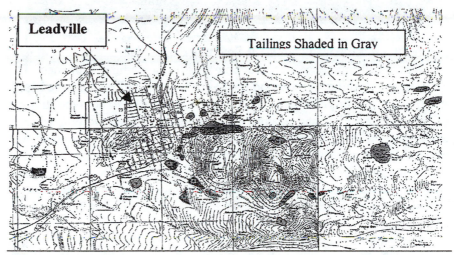

Figure 11.10–Mine Tailings Around Leadville

In 1986, the EPA became the lead agency, when the federal and state proceedings were combined. The EPA prepared to bring a § 107 action against all responsible parties. There were a total of 13 parties listed as defendants in the EPA's August 6, 1986 action. Of them, eight were either orphan shares or resulted in de minimis settlements. The remaining parties were: Resurrection Mining Co.; Asarco; Res-Asarco; Denver & Rio Grande Western Railroad (D&RG); and Hecla Mining Co.

In the beginning, the parties did not cooperate. Each PRP turned the blame onto the others. Each claimed the cause was from a different source, not under the control of that PRP. Some said it was the tailings, others alleged it was the slag, and others even blamed the smelters.

Figure 11.11–American Mining & Smelting Co.[86]

When trial time began approaching rapidly, something happened. The PRPs began working together and themes of "settlement" began to be heard. It is thought that this change of heart was a result of a leak about the strength of the case the EPA had against the defendants. The prevailing wisdom among the PRPs was that the evidence was so strong, that settlement was preferred over an EPA cleanup followed by certain § 107 liability. Prior to trial, consent decrees were reached with D&RG, Hecla, Resurrection, and Asarco. These decrees were somewhat unique because the Record of Decision (ROD), guiding cleanup and apportionment process, had not been completed yet.

The final decree of May 17, 1994 manifests a major party settlement resolving the cleanup responsibilities of Resurrection, Asarco, Res-Asarco, and the United States. The site is in excess of 16 square miles. Of this area, some will be cleaned up by some of the PRPs, another portion will be remediated by the EPA, and the remaining cleanup will be enforced through complaints against specific PRPs.

The EPA determined that each individual defendant's work area would be defined to correspond with the impacts attributable to each defendant's smelting, milling, or mining-related activities at the site. EPA began by settling with Asarco, Resurrection, and Res-Asarco. The PRPs are committed to perform cleanup activities in their work areas, but are released from liability in other areas of the site in which they may have had some contribution. However, the liability they may have avoided by their settlement is off-set by their agreeing to accept responsibility for orphan shares. Because they had minimal involvement in the contamination of the site, Hecla and D&RG will have to satisfy more limited responsibilities, and are protected from contribution claims by other PRPs.

---

[86] Source: Leadville: Colorado's Magic City, Blair.

Some issues are reserved for resolution at a later time, such as water treatment, contamination of the Arkansas River floodplain, and the natural resources damages. The settlements will allow the United States to recover virtually all of its past response costs for the period of time prior to the settlement's allocation of liability at the site.

Despite the settlement, there remained mixed community feelings towards the EPA. New residents of Leadville were concerned for the health of their children and wanted both the cleanup and continued investigations. Locals and long time residents believed the EPA was over-reacting; they were not worried about the lead and assumed that there was no risk. They were also outraged because they felt the studies conducted by the EPA never proved that lead in its natural state (not in paint, water or exhausts) was harmful when ingested. Blood levels seemed to confirm their suspicions. Children's blood levels in Leadville were at acceptable levels, and were even better than the levels at other mining towns.

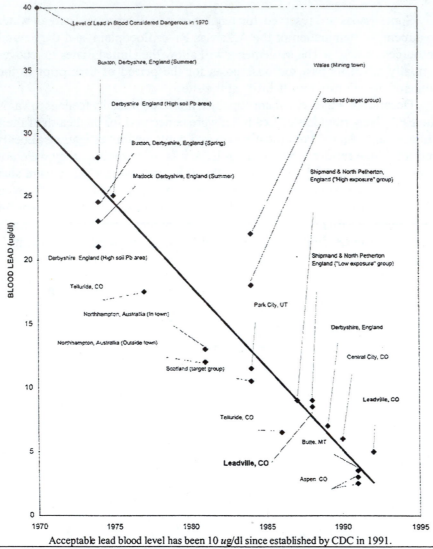

Figure 11.12–Children's Blood Lead Level in Mining Towns

Many in the community interpreted the lack of harm as an indication that the EPA was being stubborn and stupid. Many townspeople became belligerent toward the EPA; some even posted signs on their doors warning EPA investigators to stay away. A Colorado Representative half-jokingly threatened to "string up an EPA administer at each end of town" to keep them out of the community. The Denver Post, Section B1, April 4, 1995.

By 1999, it was the PRPs that had received most community support. One mining company that retains a marginal presence in the town has incorporated community projects into its proposals for cleanup. It has a plan to identify all the sources of lead as a part of its "Kids First" program. The program is designed to monitor children's blood lead levels and to reduce the risk for each resident based on specific site assessments.

Much of the hatred towards the EPA is also a result of the secondary effects this CERCLA action has had on the Leadville community. The land value in the area has plummeted and real estate sales have suffered. There have been industrial plans that have been halted and the amount of tourists visiting the area has decreased. A single mine at one time paid 85% of the taxes in the surrounding county. Its closing resulted in rundown schools. Some area schools are forced to place buckets around classrooms to catch leaks from the roof. Other schools cannot use an overhead projector because the wiring is so bad, and the heating systems are so inefficient that in many schools children sit at their desk in their full coat and gloves while others are sweating. There are even Leadville schools that are so rundown that the windows do not shut all the way, and miniature snowdrifts develop in the classrooms during snowstorms. CERCLA may have produced a settlement and some cleanup, but there are many in Leadville who believe it contributed to the death of a once viable town.

NOTE ON BROWNFIELDS

"Brownfields," as defined by EPA, are "abandoned, idled, or under used industrial and commercial sites where expansion or redevelopment is complicated by real or perceived environmental contamination that can add cost, time or uncertainty to a redevelopment project." There are an estimated 400,000 contaminated brownfield sites in the United States, that could cost as much as $650 billion to clean up. In part because of fear of CERCLA liability, many contaminated sites within urban areas sit idle and undeveloped, although their location might otherwise make them attractive to investors. Instead, developers go to rural suburban sites ("greenfields") where there has been no contamination and no risk of CERCLA liability. To respond to this unintended side-effect of CERCLA, in January 1995, EPA announced reforms designed to loosen the grip of CERCLA and encourage brownfields' redevelopment.[87] This brownfields reform agenda has seven components:

1. *Landowners*–The EPA encourages greater use of "comfort letters," which assure owners that their properties will not be targets of CERCLA enforcement actions if the owners engage in voluntary clean-ups.

2. *Prospective Purchasers*–The EPA uses "prospective purchaser agreements" that provide similar assurances to potential buyers of brownfields if the purchaser agrees to perform a specified portion of the clean-up.

---

[87] *See generally* William Buzbee, *Brownfields, Environmental Federalism, and Institutional Determinism*, 21 WM. & MARY ENVTL. L. & POLICY REV. 1 (1997); Robert Abrams, *Superfund and the Evaluation of Brownfields*, 21 WM. & MARY ENVTL. & POLICY REV. 265 (1997); Stephen Johnson, *The Brownfields Action Agenda: A Model for Future Federal/State Cooperation in the Quest for Environmental Justice?*, 37 SANTA CLARA L. REV. 85 (1996).

3. *Coordination with States*–The brownfields initiative encourages EPA to work with states and localities to clarify liability of prospective purchasers, lenders, and property owners, and to coordinate federal-state-local enforcement priorities so that brownfields redevelopment can take place. Some EPA regions have entered into Memorandums of Agreement (MOAs) with state environmental agencies. Under these MOAs, the EPA promises not to take enforcement action at sites where private parties have conducted clean-ups under the state's direction. In addition, most states have adopted their own programs of liability protection for brownfield redevelopers.

4. *Delisting*–In order to remove the stigma of being listed on the CERCLIS master inventory of potential NPL sites, the EPA has delisted nearly 30,000 brownfields sites. A delisting confirms that no further remedial action is planned at these sites.

5. *Future Land Use*–In order to expedite remedy selection for sites on the NPL, EPA has issued a directive permitting future land uses to be considered when deciding upon appropriate exposure scenarios for the risk assessment of the site.

6. *Grants*–EPA has agreed to fund economic redevelopment projects at brownfield sites. Initially, it provided cities and states with grants of up to $200,000 for brownfields pilot projects. In 1997, the Clinton Administration announced a Brownfields National Partnership program that included $300 million in federal funds for brownfields clean-ups, as well as the involvement of several private organizations and federal agencies to redevelop 5000 brownfield sites.

7. *Tax Incentives*–As part of the Taxpayer Relief Act of 1997, Pub. L. No. 105-34, companies developing brownfields sites can deduct their clean-up costs.

Which elements of CERCLA remedy selection and liability are moderated by these elements of brownfields reform? Do they go too far, or not far enough, in addressing the brownfields problem?

4. Private Cost-Recovery Actions

It is the rare situation that a Superfund site involves just one PRP. Usually, multiple parties were involved with the site over a long period of time. In cases where more than one private party has played a role in the site, and there has been a private expenditure of response costs (voluntarily or as a result of some government action), the party who has expended funds will seek to recover some or all of the costs from other PRPs. CERCLA offers two ways for a private party to initiate a cost recovery action. Section 107(a)(4)(B) provides that a PRP shall be liable for "any other necessary costs of response" that have been "incurred by any other person." This provision is similar (but not identical) to governmental cost recovery under §107(a)(4)(A), discussed above in Subchapter D. Alternatively, CERCLA §113(f)(1) authorizes "any person" who is liable or potentially liable under §107—*i.e.,* a PRP—"seek contribution from any other person who is [similarly] liable or potentially liable under [§107(a)] during or following a civil action under [§§106 or 107(a)]." Private party cost recovery claims do not need prior governmental approval unless EPA has initiated RI/FS activities. *See* §122(e)(6); *Richland-Lexington Airport Dist. v. Atlas Properties, Inc.*, 901 F.2d 1206 (4th Cir. 1990). These private party v. private party cases now comprise the bulk of CERCLA litigation.

A private party who is not a PRP (and thereby limited to a contribution claim) may bring a cost-recovery action under §107(a)(4)(B) if four conditions are met:

(1) plaintiff is a "person,"
(2) defendant caused the plaintiff to incur response costs,
(3) plaintiff incurred necessary costs of response,"
(4) The costs were "consistent with the national contingency plan,"

We treat these requirements in order.

a. "Any Other Person"

Section 107(a)(4)(B) makes a responsible party liable for response costs incurred by "any other person." Since §107(a)(4)(A) already provides a cost recovery action for United States, states, and Indian tribes, a party able to bring a private cost recovery action under §107(a)(4)(B) is anyone other than these three entities. One court has restricted the class of private parties further, by requiring that the plaintiff have a property interest in the contaminated site. *Pennsylvania Urban Development Corp. v. Golen*, 708 F. Supp. 669 (E.D. 1989). This ruling has not been widely followed—can you figure out why not?

b. Causation

As noted previously, under CERCLA a plaintiff need not directly link acts of a PRP to environmental harm. *Dedham Water Co. v. Cumberland Farms Dairy, Inc.*, 889 F.2d 1146, 1154 (1st Cir. 1989). However, CERCLA does require some proof that a defendant caused the plaintiff to incur response costs. *New Jersey Turnpike Authority v. PPG Industries*, 197 F.3d 96, 105 (3d Cir. 1999); *Matter of Chicago, Milwaukee, St. Paul & Pac. R. Co.*, 78 F.3d 285, 289-90 (7th Cir. 1996); *American National Bank and Trust v. Harcos Chem. Inc.*, 997 F. Supp. 994, 1000 (N.D. Ill. 1998). *See also Memphis Zane May Assocs. v. IBC Mfg. Co.*, 952 F. Supp. 541 (W.D. Tenn. 1996).

c. "Necessary Costs of Response"

The costs recoverable by a private party are the same as those by a governmental party excepting natural resources damages. *M.R. v. Caribe*

General Electric Products, Inc., 31 F. Supp. 2d 226 (D.P.R. 1998) (costs for providing alternative drinking water as a result of another's pollution are recoverable response costs); *City of Toledo v. Beazer Materials and Services, Inc.*, 923 F. Supp. 1001 (N.D. Ohio 1996) (recoverable response costs included costs of monitoring, assessment, and evaluation of hazardous substances at the site). The question has arisen, however, whether the qualifier "necessary" operates as a real limitation on recoverable costs. Courts have held that it does. The plaintiff must establish that an actual and real threat exists prior to initiating a response action. *Southfund Partners III v. Sears, Roebuck & Co.*, 57 F. Supp. 2d 1369 (N.D. Ga. 1999) (where no costs were needed to make property safe for its current use as an *industrial* site, response costs incurred to remove low level contamination in order to prepare site for *residential* use were not "necessary"). While costs associated with voluntary remediation efforts are recoverable, the plaintiff bears the burden of proving that the voluntary effort was "necessary" at the time it was undertaken. *South Fund Partners III v. Sears, Roebuck & Co.*, 97-CV-1058-RWS (N.D. Ga., July 30, 1999) (costs were not "necessary" response costs because plaintiff conducted the remediation to improve the land's value, not to address a threat to health or the environment); *Carson Harbor Village, Ltd. v. Unocal Corp.*, 990 F. Supp. 1188, 1193 (C.D. Cal. 1997).[88] Why impose this additional step on private claims? Is there any practical likelihood that a private party would risk serious money on an unnecessary clean-up? *See G.J. Leasing Co. Inc. v. Union Elec. Co.*, 54 F.3d 379, 386 (7th Cir. 1995).

One other important question has been whether attorney's fees are "necessary costs of response." In *KeyTronic Corp. v. United States*, 511 U.S. 809 (1994), the Supreme Court held that CERCLA did not authorize an award of attorney fees associated with bringing a cost recovery action. Nor were non-litigation fees incurred in negotiating a consent decree with EPA recoverable. The court concluded that such expenses did not constitute necessary costs of response because the activities primarily served to protect the plaintiff's interests regarding its own liability for the clean-up. *See also AM International, Inc. v. Datacard Corp.*, 106 F.3d 1342 (7th Cir. 1997); *Ekotek Site PRP Comm. v. Self*, 1 F. Supp. 2d 1282, 1294-95 (D. Utah 1998). The *KeyTronic* Court carved out a narrow exception for lawyers' work performed in identifying other PRPs. *KeyTronic*, 511 U.S. at 819; *Atlantic Richfield Co. v. American Airlines, Inc.*, 98 F.3d 564, 571 (10th Cir. 1996).

d. "Consistent With the National Contingency Plan"

CERCLA makes consistency with the NCP a condition to a private cost recovery action. As we saw above in connection with governmental cost recovery, consistency requires compliance with both procedural rules (*e.g.*,

---

[88] The question of whether a response measure is necessary is usually answered at the damages stage of a case. Cadillac Fairview/California, Inc. v. Dow Chemical Co., 840 F.2d 691, 695 (9th Cir. 1988).

site investigations and public comment opportunities), and substantive requirements (*e.g.*, remedy selection, degree of clean-up). You will also recall that governmental plaintiffs may obtain reimbursement for costs "not inconsistent with" the NCP, § 107(a)(4)(A), while §107(a)(4)(B) permits private cost recovery only if "consistent with the NCP." The semantic difference between the two sections has been construed to mean that the PRP-defendant bears the burden of showing that the government's costs are "not consistent with" the NCP, while the private party seeking cost recovery from a PRP has the burden of showing that its costs are "consistent with" the NCP. *County Line Investment Co. v. Tinney*, 933 F.2d 1508, 1512 (10th Cir. 1991); *Tanglewood East Homeowners v. Charles-Thomas, Inc.*, 849 F.2d 1568, 1574-75 (5th Cir. 1988).

This burden can be substantial. Before the 1990 NCP, private parties were held to a "strict compliance" standard. *Alcan-Toyo America, Inc. v. Northern Illinois Gas Co.*, 904 F. Supp. 833 (N.D. Ill. 1995) (since the bulk of plaintiff's site investigation costs were incurred prior to the effective date of the 1990 NCP, the question of whether these costs were consistent with the NCP would be governed by the 1985 requirement of strict compliance). With the advent of the revised NCP in 1990, EPA began to require only "substantial compliance" with procedural requirements and a "CERCLA-quality clean-up" under the substantive standards. 40 C.F.R. §300(c)(3)(I). Accordingly, private parties must decide whether the benefits of a potential cost recovery are worth (1) the cost of undertaking a RI/FS and going through a public comment process,[89] as well as (2) the burden of showing that the remedy selected is the least costly alternative that is still permissible with the NCP. Although "CERCLA-quality clean-up" assumes that private party remedial action will meet the NCP's substantive requirements (*i.e.*, protective of human health, a permanent, cost-effective solution, and one that attains ARARs), the "substantial compliance" term is meant to soften some of the NCP's procedural demands. *See Anschutz Mining Corp. v. NL Ind., Inc.*, 891 F. Supp. 492 (E.D.Mo. 1995); 55 Fed. Reg. at 8793 (March 8, 1990) (EPA demands only "substantial" compliance because it recognizes that to provide a list of rigid requirements might defeat cost recovery for meritorious clean-up actions that experienced a mere technical failure).

5. Cost-Recovery *vs.* Contribution Actions

The other way for a private party to shift some or all of the costs of a clean-up to other private parties is through a private contribution action. Under §113(f)(1) a SARA addition, "any person may seek contribution from any other person who is liable or potentially liable under §107(a) during or

---

[89] *See* Union Pacific Railroad Co. v. Reilly Industries, Inc., 981 F. Supp. 1229 (D. Minn. 1997) (failure to provide public comment regarding remedial action is substantial departure from NCP, precluding private cost recovery).

following any civil action under §106 or §107(a)." As a result, plaintiffs who already are or may be liable for clean-up costs may, instead, demand contribution under section 113. There are many similarities between a private cost recovery action under §107 and a contribution action under §113. The substantive elements and the defenses are the same. *Uniroyal Chemical Co., Inc. v. Deltech Corp.*, 160 F.3d 238, 242 (5th Cir. 1998) (elements); *United States v. Taylor*, 909 F. Supp. 355 (M.D. N.C. 1995) (defenses). Regardless of whether a plaintiff proceeds under §107 or §113, it may also seek a judicial determination that the defendants are liable in the future for some or all of the clean-up costs; it may obtain this declaration of future liability once it has commenced an investigation at the site, or after it has incurred recoverable response costs. §113(g)(2). Some courts have even integrated cost recovery and contribution actions; they test the merits of the claim for cost recovery against §107, and allocate response costs between plaintiff and defendant according to §113. *See Amoco Oil Co. v. Borden, Inc.*, 889 F.2d 664, 672-73 (5th Cir. 1989).

However, cost recovery and contribution actions are not identical. For several reasons it may be important to establish whether the private party is proceeding under §107 or §113. First, under §107, as we have seen, liability is generally joint and several. By contrast, in actions seeking contribution under §113, liability is several only; the PRP is liable for its equitable *share* of all response costs. *See Kalamazoo River Study Group v. Rockwell Intern.*, 3 F. Supp. 799, 805 (W.D.Mich 1998); *United States v. Conservation Chemical Co.*, 619 F. Supp. 162, 229 (W.D. Mo. 1985). Consequently, in contribution actions the burden is on the *plaintiff* to establish the defendant's equitable share of response costs. *Adhesives Research, Inc. v. American Inks & Coatings Corp.*, 931 F. Supp. 1231, 1244 n.13 (M.D. Pa. 1996). In addition, the 1986 SARA amendments added a new six-year statute of limitations for §107(a), but a three-year period for contribution claims. §113(g)(2)(3). Also, while courts have turned away most non-statutory defenses in cost recovery actions, they are sometimes willing to acknowledge equitable defenses in contribution actions. *See e.g., Shapiro v. Alexanderson*, 741 F. Supp. 472, 478-79 (S.D. N.Y. 1990) (fraudulently obtained indemnification agreement). Thus, PRPs who themselves contributed to the contamination of a Superfund site wanted to seek § 107 cost recovery, as well as § 113 contribution. The following case decided whether this is permissible.

CENTERIOR SERVICE CO. V. ACME SCRAP IRON & METAL CORP.

153 F.3d 344 (6th Cir. 1998)

NATHANIEL R. JONES, Circuit Judge.

Before this court, the plaintiffs argue that the plain language of §107, which authorizes the recovery of "necessary costs by *any other person*," 42 U.S.C. §9607(a)(4)(B) (underline added), allows joint and several cost recovery actions by PRPs because it does not limit persons to "innocent" persons, but simply any other persons regardless of culpability. Plaintiffs argue that the section unequivocally grants standing to any persons who have incurred necessary response costs, and that nothing in CERCLA indicates that only innocent persons fall within the definition of "any other persons." Thus, the plaintiffs assert that the test for determining whether a party may seek joint and several cost recovery under CERCLA does not rest on whether a party is liable or potentially liable, but rather depends only on whether a party has incurred necessary costs of response.

The government responds by asserting that CERCLA does not provide two separate and distinct causes of actions, but that the two sections, §107(a) and §113(f) work in conjunction. It argues that an action for contribution must be brought pursuant to §107(a), but is governed by §113(f). In other words, the government asserts that §113(f) applies to claims asserted under §107(a). The government points out that §107 provides the basis and the elements of a claim for recovery of response costs and lists the parties who are liable, as well as the defenses to liability. Therefore, one must necessarily look to §107 in contribution actions involving §113(f). Under such a reading, if §113(f) is incorporated under §107, then a §113(f) action *is* an action to recover the necessary costs of response by any other person, as referred to in §107. The action only happens to be an action for contribution. We agree.

Section 107(a) clearly establishes the right of parties to seek "necessary costs of responses." It does not specify whether these costs will arise from joint and several liability or sound in contribution. [B]efore the adoption of §113(f), courts found that §107(a) created an implied right of action for both contribution and joint and several recovery. Additionally, as the government asserts, parties seeking contribution under §113(f) must look to §107 to establish the basis and elements of the liability of the defendants, as well as any defenses to that liability. According to the plain language of §113(f) which provides that "any person may seek contribution from any other person who is liable or potentially liable under section [107(a)]," it is §107(a) that establishes the cause of action for contribution. While a party seeking contribution under §113(f) may not recover under joint and several liability, it is clear that under a plain reading of the statute, the party is seeking to recover its "necessary costs of response" as referred to in §107(a).

Thus, the plaintiffs are correct—to a point. Any party may seek response costs regardless of its status as a liable or potentially liable party. Whether that party may seek joint and several cost recovery, or is limited to an action for contribution governed by §113(f), however, depends on the nature of the cause of action pleaded.

Cost recovery actions by parties not responsible for site contaminations are joint and several cost recovery actions governed exclusively by §107(a). Claims by PRPs, however, seeking costs from other PRPs are necessarily actions for contribution, and are therefore governed by the mechanisms set forth in §113(f). To explain our reasoning, we must define contribution in both the common law and under CERCLA.

Black's Law Dictionary defines contribution as the "[r]ight of one who has discharged a common liability to recover of another also liable, the aliquot portion which he ought to pay or bear." Black's Law Dictionary 328 (6th ed. 1990). The RESTATEMENT (SECOND) OF TORTS §886A provides that: "(1) * * * When two or more persons become liable in tort to the same person for the same harm, there is a right of contribution among them, *even though judgment has not been recovered against all or any of them.*"

* * *

Based on the above definitions, and looking to the claim pleaded by the plaintiffs, it is apparent that their claim is by necessity a claim for contribution. The plaintiffs are all PRPs, who have never asserted their innocence or challenged their liability under §107(a). * * * [T]hey had a legal obligation to conduct the site clean-up, which they fulfilled and in so doing, paid more than their fair share of the obligation. Plaintiffs now seek costs for this clean-up from other PRPs who also contributed to the site contamination and are also potentially liable under §107(a) but who did not contribute their pro rata share. As stated by other circuit courts, this is the "quintessential" action for contribution. It is thus governed by the procedures set forth in §113(f) for such actions.

* * *

Additionally, §113(f) codifies this aspect of the common law by providing that "[n]othing in this subsection shall diminish the right of any person to bring an action for contribution in the absence of any civil action under section 9606 of this title or section 9607 of this title." 42 U.S.C. §9613(f)(1). Contribution, then, under both the common law and §113(f) applies in claims such as these where a potentially responsible party has been compelled to pay for response costs for which others are also liable, and who seeks reimbursement for such costs. Indeed, it is disingenuous at best for the plaintiffs, who have not challenged their status as PRPs, to claim their action is not one for contribution simply because the EPA was not forced to take them to court.

At no point have the plaintiffs ever attempted to imply that they are "innocent" parties not responsible for a portion of the site contamination, and not liable under §107. In fact, the plaintiffs have in all respects conceded their liability under CERCLA by failing to assert their innocence and recognizing that if this court were to permit them to seek joint and several cost recovery, the defendants would be able to seek contribution against them.

Moreover, we believe our reading of the statute, finding that §113(f) and §107 work together, is supported by its legislative history.[90] * * * [T]he right

---

[90] Our reading of the statute is further supported by our recognition that any other reading would render §113(f)'s contribution protection provision meaningless. As noted earlier, §113(f)(2) provides that parties who settle with the United States or a State may not be sued for contribution. *See* 42 U.S.C. §9613(f)(2). While the issue is not before us today, were we to

of contribution has always been established pursuant to §107, yet only after the codification of §113(f) was the right made explicit.

Our reading of the statute limiting the PRP plaintiffs to contribution, gives meaning to the language in §107(a) referring to any person, as well as the explicit contribution provisions found in §113(f). Whether the plaintiffs themselves characterize their action as one for cost recovery or contribution, it is clear to us that they are seeking contribution, and are thus governed by §113(f).

NOTES

1. *Centerior* reflects the prevailing view among the federal circuits, which is that PRPs are limited by the provisions of § 113(f) in seeking cost recovery. Nevertheless, the contrary result—allowing PRPs to assert claims for joint and several liability under 107(a)—would arguably be more consistent with the goals of CERCLA. If PRPs could bring §107(a) cost recovery actions, wouldn't more of them come forward and initiate a clean-up, because they would then have a better chance of recovering the costs they incur? One response to this argument is that §113(f) has its own incentives for quick clean-up and cooperation with the government. Section 113(f)(1) expressly authorizes a court to allocate response costs between the parties using any *equitable* factors the court deems appropriate. Among the equitable factors a court may consider is the degree of cooperation of the parties with the government, *Amoco Oil Co. v. Borden, Inc.*, 889 F.2d 664, 672-73 (5th Cir. 1989), and the degree to which the private party has acted to prevent harm to the public or environment, *United States v. Colorado & Eastern Railroad Co.*, 50 F.3d 1530, 1536 n.5 (10th Cir. 1995), and the extent to which a party's share of hazardous waste deposited at a site constitutes no more than "background" amounts of such substances. *Acushnet Co. v. Mohasco Corp.*, 191 F.3d 69 (1st Cir. 1999). Is this response adequate? Are there other reasons for keeping the section 113 limitations?

2. Assume that X, Y, Z, A, and B are potentially responsible parties at a contaminated site. X, a major party, voluntarily begins a clean-up (to avoid the government bringing a §107(a) or § 106 action) and incurs costs far greater than X's equitable share. X cannot bring a pure cost recovery action against Y and Z, so X brings a contribution action against them. As contribution defendants, Y and Z are not liable to X for more than their fair, several share of the clean-up. Can Y and Z bring a contribution actions

---

allow PRPs to seek joint and several cost recovery under §107(a), they could do so against parties who had settled, and against whom they were precluded from seeking contribution. Thus, in effect, while precluded from apportioning liability against settling PRPs, plaintiffs could seek to recover their joint and several response costs under §107(a)'s joint and several liability scheme. Obviously such a result would be absurd, and Congress cannot have intended PRPs to seek joint and several liability or it would have included a provision prohibiting joint and several cost recovery against settling PRPs as well as contribution.

against A and B? *United Technologies Corp. v. Browning-Ferris Industries, Inc.*, 33 F.3d 96, 103 (1st Cir. 1994) (no); *City of Merced v. R.A. Fields*, 997 F. Supp. 1326, 1332 (E.D. Cal. 1998) (no). Can X then bring contribution claims against A and B?

3. The *Centerior* case points out that the plaintiffs there did not argue that they were "innocent" parties not responsible for any portion of the site contamination, and therefore not liable as PRPs under §107. Had they been able to successfully allege that they were innocent PRPs who had not contributed to site contamination, there is precedent that they would have been able to file a §107 cost recovery claim. *Rumpke of Indiana, Inc. v. Cummins Engine Company, Inc.*, 107 F.3d 1235 (7th Cir. 1997); *AM Intern., Inc. v. Datacard Corp.*, 106 F.3d 1342 (7th Cir. 1997). The question then becomes this: Who is an "innocent" PRP, eligible, because of its innocence, to bring a cost recovery action. Consider the following situations. Which, if any, should qualify as innocent PRPs?

1. A landowner forced to clean up hazardous materials that a third party had spilled onto its property. *See Akzo Coatings, Inc. v. Aigner Corp.*, 30 F.3d 761, 764 (7th Cir. 1994).

2. An owner who did not know that its tenants were disposing of hazardous substances on its land. *Soo Line RR Co. v. Tany Ind., Inc.*, 998 F. Supp. 889, 894 (N.D. Ill. 1998).

3. A landowner who did not contribute actively to the contamination, but who had some privity with the polluter. *Bedford Affiliates v. Sills*, 156 F.3d 416, 425 (2d Cir. 1998).

4. An original owner of a site that subsequent owners discovered was contaminated; the original owner denied liability but nonetheless entered into a consent decree with the EPA in which the original owner agreed to remediate the site. *Redwing Carriers, Inc. v. Saraland Apts.*, 94 F.3d 1489, 1494-96 (11th Cir. 1996); *Chem-Nuclear Systems v. Arivec Chemicals*, 978 F. Supp. 1105, 1109-1110 (N.D. Ga. 1997).

5. A purchaser who had no actual knowledge of the presence of hazardous substances on the land, but who did not investigate the possibility of contamination prior to purchase. *Lefebvre v. Central Maine Power Co.*, 7 F. Supp. 64, 70-1 (D. Me. 1998); *M&M Realty Co. v. Eberton Terminal Corp.*, 977 F. Supp. 683, 687 (M.D. Pa. 1997).

6. A purchaser who knew of the contamination on the land, paid less for it because it was contaminated, but did not contact the EPA concerning the contamination, instead attempting self-help clean-up procedures that violated EPA regulations. *Estes v. Scotsman Group, Inc.*, 16 F. Supp. 2d 983, 988-89 (C.D. Ill. 1998).

6. Apportionment of Liability

CERCLA §113(f)(1) provides only very general direction on the crucial issue of apportioning costs among PRPs: "In resolving contribution claims, the court may allocate response costs among liable parties using such equitable factors as the court determines are appropriate." This language gives courts extremely broad latitude in adopting factors, weighting them, and balancing them among PRPs. *See, e.g., Kerr-McGee Chemical Corp. v. Lefton Iron & Metal Co.*, 14 F.3d 321 (7th Cir. 1994). Nevertheless, there are several recognized methods available to courts.

The commentary to The RESTATEMENT (SECOND) OF TORTS §886A suggests a "pro rata" approach in actions for contribution tortfeasors. Under this methodology, it is easy to calculate a PRP's pro rata share in a CERCLA case: the total clean-up costs are simply divided by the number of present and solvent PRPs found to be jointly and severally liable. The pro rata method has the advantage of ease of calculation, but it has the obvious—and fatal— disadvantage of being inequitable if PRPs have different degrees of responsibility for the status of the site.

Many courts have turned to the so-called "Gore Factors," named after a failed amendment to CERCLA proposed by then-Congressman Al Gore:[91]

- the parties' ability to distinguish their contribution
- the quantity of the hazardous substance
- the toxicity of the hazardous substance
- the degree of involvement in generation, transportation, treatment, storage, or disposal of the hazardous substance
- the degree of care exercised by the parties
- the degree of cooperation by the parties with government officials.

See generally Gould, Inc. v. A&M Battery & Tire Service, 987 F. Supp. 353, 370 (M.D. Pa. 1997); *Control Data Corp. v. S.C.S.C. Corp.*, 53 F.3d 930 (8th Cir. 1995); *Kerr-McGee Chemical Corp. v. Lefton Iron & Metal Co.*, 14 F.3d 321, 326 (7th Cir. 1994). Most courts relying on the Gore factors have concluded that the "volume" and "toxicity" of the material shipped to the site is the most useful basis for making an allocation decision. And as between volume and toxicity, volume is by far the easiest to measure. *Boeing Co. v. Cascade Corp.*, 207 F.3d 1177 (9th Cir. 2000); *Bancamerica Commercial Corp. v. Mosher Steel of Kansas, Inc.*, 100 F.3d 792, 802 (10th Cir. 1996); *In re Bell Petroleum Services, Inc.*, 3 F.3d 889 (5th Cir. 1993); *Kamb v. U.S. Coast Guard*, 869 F. Supp. 793, 799 (N.D. Cal. 1994).

Even the Gore factors, however, are only the starting point for allocation methodologies. Most courts have assumed that §113(f)(1) permits

---

[91] It is interesting to consider whether it is appropriate to adopt a legal standard from an amendment that did not pass Congress. Why might this be *in*appropriate? Why do you think courts have adapted it?

consideration of "any factor," including "the state of mind of the parties, their economic status, any contracts between them bearing on the subject, any traditional equitable defenses as mitigating factors and any other factors deemed appropriate to balance the equities in the totality of the circumstances." *United States v. Davis*, 31 F. Supp. 2d 45 (D.R.I. 1998); *see, e.g., Akzo Nobel Coatings, Inc. v. Aigner Corp.*, 197 F.3d 302, 305 (7th Cir. 1999)(expense of doing cleanup work better measure than toxicity). When a court uses such equitable factors, it is properly invoking "its moral as well as legal sense." *Id.; United States v. Shell Oil Co.*, 13 F. Supp. 2d 1018, 1030 (C.D. Cal. 1998).

With such broad discretion granted to the judiciary, courts may choose to ignore both the pro rata method and the Gore factors in allocating responsibility. Consider the following case, which rejects the traditional Gore factors of volume and toxicity, adopts instead a pure fault based methodology.

BROWNING-FERRIS INDUSTRIES OF ILLINOIS V. TER MAAT

195 F.3d 953 (7th Cir. 1999)

POSNER, Chief Judge.

Browning-Ferris and several other companies have brought a suit for contribution under the Comprehensive Environmental Response, Compensation, and Liability Act (CERCLA—the Superfund statute). The suit is against Richard Ter Maat and two corporations of which he is (or was— one of the corporations has been sold) the president and principal shareholder; they are M.I.G. Investments, Inc. and AAA Disposal Systems, Inc.

Back in 1971 the owners of a landfill had leased it to a predecessor of Browning-Ferris, which operated it until the fall of 1975. Between then and 1988 it was operated by M.I.G. and AAA. In June of that year, after AAA was sold and Ter Maat moved to Florida, M.I.G. abandoned the landfill without covering it properly. For tax reasons, M.I.G. had been operated with very little capital, and it lacked funds for a proper cover. Two years after the abandonment, the EPA placed the site on the National Priorities List, the list of the toxic waste sites that the Superfund statute requires be cleaned up, * * * and shortly afterward Browning-Ferris and the other plaintiffs, which shared responsibility for some of the pollution at the site, agreed to clean it up.

Section 113(f)(1) of the Superfund law authorizes any person who incurs costs in cleaning up a toxic-waste site to "seek contribution from any other person who is liable or potentially liable under section 9607(a) of this title. . . . In resolving contribution claims, the court may allocate response costs among liable parties using such equitable factors as the court determines are appropriate." 42 U.S.C. § 9613(f)(1). Section 107(a)(1), 42 U.S.C. § 9607(a)(1), a part of the statutory provision to which section 113(f)(1) refers, includes in the set of potentially liable persons anyone who owned or operated a landfill when a hazardous substance was deposited in it, and this set is conceded to include both M.I.G. and AAA.* * * So far as corporate liability for clean-up costs was concerned, the judge ruled that of the 55 percent of those costs that he deemed allocable to transporters and operators (the other 45 percent he allocated to the owners of the landfill and the generators of the toxic wastes dumped in it), 40 percent was the responsibility of Browning-Ferris and the other 60 percent the responsibility of M.I.G. and AAA. As between those two, the judge allocated responsibility equally, holding that, although the two corporations had operated the landfill jointly, the statute required him to allocate liability severally rather than jointly.

Browning-Ferris and the other companies that have incurred clean-up costs at the site of the former landfill have appealed. All of them join in making the following * * * arguments: * * * [T]he Superfund statute does permit joint liability in a contribution suit and it would be equitable to make AAA pay for the whole amount allocated to the two corporations, since they were jointly liable and M.I.G. is assetless (or may be—it has some insurance). Finally, Browning-Ferris argues that the district court allocated too much of the liability for the pollution at the site to it relative to M.I.G. and AAA.

* * *

[W]e think that CERCLA does not preclude the imposition of joint as distinct from several liability in a suit for contribution. This is, or at least should be considered, a case of first impression at the appellate level. * * *

* * *

In traditional common law, when two or more persons inflict an indivisible injury each is fully liable for the injury. That is, the plaintiff can if he wants sue one of the tortfeasors for the entire damages and let the other go, and the one who is sued has no remedy against the one who got off scot-free. CERCLA modifies the traditional common law rule (as many other statutes do and as many state courts have done by modifying the common law) by allowing one liable party to sue another for contribution. It does not follow that if, as in this case, contribution is sought from more than one party, the defendants cannot be held jointly liable. It is up to the district judge, guided only by equitable considerations—a broad and loose standard, see *Kerr-McGee Chemical Corp. v. Lefton Iron & Metal Co.*, 14 F.3d 321, 326 (7th Cir. 1994); *Environmental Transportation Systems, Inc. v. ENSCO, Inc.*, 969 F.2d 503, 509 (7th Cir. 1992); *United States v. Colorado & Eastern R.R.*, 50 F.3d 1530, 1536 (10th Cir. 1995)—to decide, and it is easy to imagine cases, of which this may be one, where such considerations weigh heavily in favor of joint liability.

Suppose, to alter the facts for simplicity's sake, that Browning-Ferris had been made to clean up the entire site even though it had made only a small (say, 1 percent) contribution to its toxicity. Suppose M.I.G. and AAA were the bad actors jointly responsible for the other 99 percent. Suppose that for tax or other reasons M.I.G. had no assets. Under the view of the district court, even though M.I.G. and AAA had combined to inflict an indivisible injury (the contamination for which they were jointly responsible as joint operators),

AAA would have to pay only 50 percent of the contamination for which it and M.I.G. were jointly liable, or 49.5 percent of the total clean-up cost (remember that we're assuming that the two corporations are jointly responsible for 99 percent of the total contamination), while Browning-Ferris would have to pay 50.5 percent of the total clean-up cost even though it was responsible for only 1 percent of that cost. * * * These are not our facts, but they show that a rule against ever holding contribution defendants jointly liable would be inconsistent with the statutory direction that the district court allocate liability equitably among the liable parties. * * * The judge did not make such an allocation, mistakenly believing himself constrained to allocate liability equally among joint polluters, and so this is [an] issue requiring further consideration on remand.

The next issue is whether the district judge allocated too large a share (40 percent) of responsibility for the cost of the clean up to Browning-Ferris relative to the defendants, who had operated the landfill for a lot longer time and had dumped a much larger quantity of wastes in it. The judge allocated as large a share as he did to Browning-Ferris because he found that it had operated the landfill poorly and had dumped particularly toxic wastes from a nearby Chrysler plant in violation of its operating permit, and the liquid character of the wastes had hastened their absorption into groundwater. Browning-Ferris argues both that these findings are erroneous and that, in any event, there is no evidence that the wastes from the Chrysler plant increased the cost of cleaning up the site and anyway the amount dumped in the landfill was not as great as the district judge found. From evidence that a considerable portion of the Chrysler wastes were dumped elsewhere, Browning-Ferris argues that defendants' expert had exaggerated the amount deposited in the landfill. Browning-Ferris may be correct on all these factual points, but we cannot say that the district court committed any *clear* errors in finding as it did, and that of course is our criterion.

The trickier question, which returns us to the issue of the district court's equitable discretion in allocating liability among polluters, is whether the court must find a causal relation between a party's pollution and the actual cost of cleaning up the site. To answer this question we have to distinguish between a necessary condition (or "but-for cause") and a sufficient condition. If event A is a necessary condition of event B, this means that, without A, B will not occur. If A is a sufficient condition of B, this means that, if A occurs, B will occur. If A is that the murder weapon was loaded and B is the murder, then A is a necessary condition. If A is shooting a person through the heart and B is the death of the shooting victim, then A is a sufficient condition of B but not a necessary condition, because a wound to another part of the victim's body might have been fatal as well.

This distinction may sometimes be important in the pollution context. It is easy to imagine a case in which, had X not polluted a site, no clean-up costs would have been incurred; X's pollution would be a necessary condition of those costs and it would be natural to think that he should pay at least a part of them. But suppose that even if X had not polluted the site, it would have to be cleaned up—and at the same cost—because of the amount of pollution by Y. (That would be a case, perhaps rare, in which the clean-up costs were sensitive neither to the amount of pollution nor to any synergistic interaction between the different pollutants.) Then X's pollution would not be a necessary condition of the clean up, or of any of the costs incurred in the clean up. But that should not necessarily let X off the hook. For suppose that if X had not polluted the site at all, there still would have been enough pollution from Y to require a clean up, but that if Y had not polluted the site X's pollution would have been sufficient to require the clean up. In that case, the conduct of X and the conduct of Y would each be a sufficient but not a necessary condition of the clean up, and it would be entirely arbitrary to let either (or, even worse, both) off the hook on this basis. So far as appears, this is such a case; Browning-Ferris's pollution was serious enough (if indeed it dumped a large quantity of Chrysler's particularly toxic wastes) to require that the site be cleaned up, but the other pollution at the site was also enough. If Browning-Ferris's conduct was thus a sufficient though not a necessary condition of the clean up, it is not inequitable to make it contribute substantially to the cost.

We do not suggest that this is one of the presumably rare cases in which the total costs of clean up are unaffected by the number of polluters or the specific amounts or types of pollution contributed by each. Browning-Ferris's pollution was not, so far as appears, so serious all by itself as to have required the incurring of all the clean-up costs that were incurred. Even so, no principle of law, logic, or common sense required the court to allocate those total costs among the polluters on the basis of the volume of wastes alone. Not only do wastes differ in their toxicity, harm to the environment, and costs of cleaning up, and so relative volume is not a reliable guide to the marginal costs imposed by each polluter; but polluters differ in the blameworthiness of the decisions or omissions that led to the pollution, and blameworthiness is relevant to an equitable allocation of joint costs. (Presumably it would not entitle the judge to make one polluter pay for separable costs wholly imposed by other polluters.) The district judge did not abuse his discretion in deciding that all these factors warranted making BrowningFerris bear more than its proportional volumetric share of the pollution.

NOTES

1. The *Ter Maat* fault-based approach to contribution liability has been used by other courts. *Kerr-McGee Chemical Corp. v. Lefton Iron & Metal Co.*, 14 F.3d 321 (7th Cir. 1994); *Environmental Transportation Systems v. Ensco, Inc.*, 969 F.2d 503 (7th Cir. 1992); *United States v. Shell Oil Co.*, 13 F. Supp. 2d 1018 (C.D. Cal. 1998). Similar reliance on fault can be seen in *United States v. Di Biase*, 45 F.3d 541, 545 (1st Cir. 1995)(when the PRP

was warned of a potentially dangerous condition "he twiddled his thumbs: he failed to safeguard the site"), and *Hatco Corp. v. W.R. Grace & Co.—Conn.*, 849 F. Supp. 987, 993-95 (D.N.J. 1994). ("The contaminated soil * * * was carelessly spread * * * during this particular remediation effort.").

2. Another issue addressed by the Seventh Circuit was whether the president of the corporation could be held personally liable. This issue turns on whether the president personally operated the landfill, rather than merely directing the business of a company that operated the landfill. This is how Judge Posner posed the issue; "If an individual is hit by a negligently operated train, the railroad is liable in tort to him but the president of the railroad is not. Or rather, not usually; had the president been driving the train when it hit the plaintiff, or had been sitting beside the driver and ordered him to exceed the speed limit, he would be jointly liable with the railroad."

3. The district court judge in *Ter Maat* discussed the important role of "allocation experts." This new class of experts, sometimes called waste accountants, appears quite frequently in cases litigating cost allocation issues. Their function is to provide estimates of each PRP's contribution to a Superfund site in terms of volume, form (liquid or solid), toxicity, and effect on the environment. Some firms combine this expertise with a mediation service to facilitate an agreed-upon apportionment of responsibility.

PROBLEM
ORPHAN SHARES

An orphan share describes the share of a responsible party which is insolvent, bankrupt, dissolved, or impossible to find. In the context of a CERCLA private party action under §113(f) or §107(a)(4)(B), an orphan share means that a plaintiff will not be able to assign a measure of responsibility to an otherwise responsible party. In theory, there are two ways to allocate orphan shares. First, the traditional tort law rule is that defendants are liable only for their own share. RESTATEMENT (SECOND) OF TORTS. §886A. Under this approach, the plaintiff in a private cost recovery action bears the risk of loss. Second, under §2(d) of the Uniform Comparative Fault Act (UCFA), a court can apportion orphan shares among the economically viable parties. The UCFA approach permits courts to reallocate any orphan shares among all identifiable and solvent PRPs.

Nothing in CERCLA requires either result; nor does CERCLA prohibit a court from allocating orphan shares to all liable parties. *United States v. Kramer*, 953 F. Supp. 592, 598 (D.N.J. 1997). Which approach is better, especially in light of the purposes of CERCLA? *See Browning-Ferris Ind. of Ill. v. Ter Maat*, 13 F. Supp. 756, 773 (N.D. Ill. 1998); *City of New York v. Exxon*, 697 F. Supp. 677, 683 n.9 (S.D. N.Y. 1988). If orphan shares are to be apportioned to the PRPs, should it be to both plaintiffs and defendants in a private cost recovery or contribution action, or just to defendants? *Charter Township of Oshtemo v. American Cyanamid Co.*, 898 F. Supp. 506, 509

(W.D. Mich. 1995). And if, as the UCFA provides, orphan shares are to be allocated among *all* viable parties, then how should these shares be apportioned among the PRPs? *Allied Corp. v. ACME Solvent Reclaiming, Inc.*, 771 F. Supp. 219, 223 (N.D. Ill. 1990).

F. The Future of CERCLA

The Superfund tax expired in 1995, necessitating that CERCLA be reauthorized by the end of that year. However, Congress failed to reach agreement on reauthorization by 1995, so the tax expired and the Superfund program has depended ever since upon a series of continuing resolutions. *See* Ann Klee & Ernie Rosenberg, The Moribund State of CERCLA Reauthorization, 13 Natural Resources & Environment 451 (Winter 1999). With the future shape of CERCLA uncertain, and the prospects for reauthorization dwindling each year between 1996 and 2000, clean-up activities have slowed, and EPA's Superfund initiatives have been cut back. Reauthorization would provide some certainty and predictability, but fundamental conflicts over the scope of private liability have paralyzed the legislative process. The central conflict is between supporters of industry, who propose to repeal retroactive liability, replace joint and several liability with some proportionate liability system, and relax CERCLA clean-up standards. The Clinton Administration's principles for Superfund legislative reform, on the other hand, have focused on properly assigning liability shares, lowering transaction and clean-up costs, clarifying the kinds of natural resources damages that may be recoverable, and supporting "brownfields" (economic redevelopment of contaminated sites) and other voluntary clean-up programs. When and if reauthorization occurs, reform and amendment is likely to be in four areas.

1. *Polluter pays*. Congress must re-examine the "polluter pays" principle in CERCLA. This principle permits EPA to require parties responsible for contributing to the contamination of a hazardous waste site, to pay the costs of cleaning up the site, either initially, or by reimbursing the EPA for its costs. Two important consequences of the "polluter pays" principle are that federal Superfund costs have been lowered (by minimizing federal clean-ups), but transaction costs associated with litigating assignment of liability have been increasing. In effect, CERCLA has shifted the transaction costs of deciding "who should pay" to private parties, and away from the federal government. This has occurred because under the statute's liability scheme, EPA usually determines which private parties are responsible for the contamination of a hazardous waste site and then requires these parties *in gross* to pay for all clean-up costs. Since CERCLA imposes joint and several liability, responsible parties seek compensation from other parties through contribution litigation, even though a party to such an action may have been only minimally involved in the site's contamination. These parties to a contribution

action will vigorously litigate the liability issue, especially if their role has been minimal and their pockets are deep.

Superfund pits one firm against another. This creates an environmental conflict in which several players invest effort to win a fixed reward—the avoided clean-up costs. The rules of the conflict set the underlying incentives that can either increase or decrease the transaction costs. An economics literature has emerged to better understand what rules make people fight harder, and thus increase the level of transaction costs in Superfund. A few key insights are worth keeping in mind as one considers methods to reduce the level of transaction costs in Superfund. First, conflicts often involve fights between unevenly matched firms—a favorite and an underdog. The literature has shown that if the underdog commits to its effort first, transaction costs are less than if the favorite moves first. The reason is that both players find it profitable when the underdog moves first because he reveals his relative lack of strength, thereby, allowing the favorite to respond efficiently. Since the underdog expects the favorite to react in proportion to his effort, he also reduces his effort. Consequently, overall transaction costs are lower, and both players and society gain from having the underdog move first. For Superfund, this implies that rules that allow smaller firms to move first may result in less transaction costs.

Second, the question of the potential for reimbursement of legal fees in Superfund conflicts may be an issue. Currently, most major federal environmental laws allow for some reimbursement of private enforcement if the enforcer wins its case. The evidence suggests that private enforcement will increase in importance, and, thus, it is important to understand the efficiency impacts of reimbursement. Citizen suits, for example, have increased to 266 in 1986—from fewer than 25 between 1970 and 1978 and only 41 in 1982. Private enforcement actions have a very high probability of success if they reach the settlement stage, and success virtually guarantees recovery of attorney's fees. Transaction costs will be influenced by how the reimbursement rules are defined in a Superfund conflict. If reimbursement is as in the British rule system (loser pays system), then either both parties will generate high transaction costs trying to win the case, or neither party will enter into the conflict for fear of spending more fighting than the prize is worth.

Reforming the current liability system is needed because of the perverse incentives and high transaction costs created by the "polluter pays" principle. The administration, by strongly favoring the principle does not advocate alternative tax or liability structures that could address the incentive and cost problems. One feasible reform is a two-step approach—(1) develop a tax-based system to fund clean-up of existing waste sites, and (2) implement a separate liability-based system to address current and future pollution concerns. A targeted emissions tax would allow existing hazardous waste sites to be cleaned up using revenues generated through a corporate environmental tax, while ignoring the issue of liability altogether. This would eliminate the excessive transaction costs associated with apportioning clean-up costs. Concurrently, a liability-based system would address current and future pollution, providing the incentive to reduce the benefits to private parties from releasing hazardous waste.[92]

Thomas A. Rhoads and Jason F. Shogren, *Current Issues in Superfund Amendment and Reauthorization: How is the Clinton Administration Handling Hazardous Wastes?* 8 DUKE ENVTL L. POL'Y FORUM 245, 254-55 (1998).

There are, of course, some serious downsides to such reforms. A tax scheme would allow genuinely "bad guy" polluters, who caused the hazardous waste problem by recklessness or carelessness, to dilute their share of the financial responsibility for the clean-up, since others—"good guy" firms or taxpayers generally—who had nothing to do with the contamination would also be liable for the tax. An environmental tax seems especially unlikely as a matter of political reality.

2. *Clean-up levels*. Clean-ups under CERCLA traditionally have had to achieve a high degree of decontamination. Remedies that are permanent, and that permit virtually any land use on the site, have in the past been favored by EPA and CERCLA itself certainly suggests this approach. However, this has resulted in some extremely expensive clean-ups, and EPA has been criticized for allocating Superfund money to clean up sites that pose relatively small risks to human health and the environment. Future changes in CERCLA will most likely require the EPA to make a remedy selection based on the likely future land use[93] and to allocate funds and enforcement priorities to high-risk hot spots that pose the most serious and immediate threats.

3. *Natural resources damages*. In addition to clean-up costs, CERCLA authorizes recovery from PRPs of damage to natural resources. The Clinton Administration uses the cost of restoring damaged resources to their original state as the basis for assessing the cost of natural resources damages. In addition, a PRP can be liable for the loss and non-use of the site's natural resources during the interim period between contamination and clean-up. Loss and nonuse values are measured by the contingent valuation method, a technique that asks people how much they would pay to restore a resource to

---

[92] Changing CERCLA's *retroactive* liability scheme may create inequities. If new legislation either releases PRPs from liability for sites where waste disposal operations had ceased prior to CERCLA's enactment, or releases PRPs from liability for sites currently on the NPL, then tax monies would pay for most clean-ups. Such a change in retroactive liability would be unfair to PRPs who have already begun to pay for, or have completed, clean-ups at CERCLA sites.

[93] The "future use" approach is examined in greater detail in Chapter 12(C) (Federal Facilities), *infra*.

its pre-damaged state.[94] Since no limit exists on these values, it is possible that a contingent valuation assessment could calculate natural resources damages at very high levels. CERCLA reform will need to consider whether and how to put bounds on nonuse values.

4. *Brownfields*. Another area of CERCLA reform involves "brownfields"—abandoned, typically urban industrial or commercial properties where redevelopment may be hindered by environmental contamination. Brownfields are often not on the National Priorities List since they are numerous and often not the most hazardous sites. But because of CERCLA's strict, joint and several, and retroactive liability scheme, potential developers of these properties are reluctant to purchase brownfield areas out of fear that they will be subject to liability for clean-up costs. As a result, urban brownfields often sit idle and abandoned, while growth patterns leapfrog over them to the suburbs. To halt the brownfields' effect, any revision of CERCLA must consider equitable ways to limit the extent to which developers would be liable for past contamination. Apart from liability relief, it might also be helpful to provide tax incentives to encourage redevelopment of brownfields. Congress may eliminate EPA's role in dealing with sites not sufficiently contaminated to merit full-fledged Superfund status, but nonetheless require cleaning. The cleanup job at these sites (estimated to be hundreds of thousands in number, compared to the slightly over 200 additional sites that might yet be added to the NPL) would be turned over to the states.

Each of these potential reforms implicates a number of interlocking elements of the CERCLA remediation and liability scheme. As with all environmental statutes, which are subject to revision by Congress, you should evaluate the existing provisions of the law which you have just studied with an eye to improvements or possible changes. Looking back on CERCLA's clean-up and liability scheme as a whole, do you think that retroactive liability is appropriate to the problem of abandoned hazardous waste sites? Are CERCLA's clean-up standards too strict? Should they be loosened generally, or only in specific cases where there are offsetting benefits (*e.g.,* brownfields redevelopment)? Or should they be strengthened to assure long-term protection of human health and the environment?

---

[94] W. Michael Hanemann, *Valuing the Environment Through Contingent Valuation*, 8 J. ECON. PERSP. 19 (1994).

Chapter 12

Federal Facilities: A CERCLA Case Study

The federal government is one of the nation's largest industrialists—specializing in military production—and owns about one third of this nation's land. In the last decade, it has become increasingly apparent that the federal government is also one of the nation's largest polluters, both in volume and in degree of hazard. Over two thousand federal facilities create, store, discharge, and are contaminated with tremendous amounts of highly toxic and highly radioactive waste materials. In addition, federal lands contain former oil, gas, and mining operations; conventional landfills and dumps; electric power plants; maintenance and repair facilities; and other sites where toxic and hazardous wastes may have been dispersed or stored. Any examination of the problem of toxic substances and hazardous wastes in the United States must, accordingly, consider pollution by the federal government.

	DOE	**DOD**	**DOI**	**USDA**	**NASA**
Nature of contamination	Radioactive, hazardous and mixed waste and fissile material	Fuels and solvents, industrial waste and unexploded ordinance	Mining, municipal and industrial wastes	Hazardous, mining and chemical wastes	Fuels and solvents and industrial waste
Number of potentially contaminated sites and major site types	10,000 sites - former weapons production facilities	21,425 sites - underground tanks - landfills -spill areas - storage areas	26,000 sites - abandoned mines ** - oil & gas production - landfills	3,000 sites - abandoned mines ** - landfills	730 sites - underground storage tanks - spill areas
Number of potentially contaminated facilities	137	1,769	NA	NA	NA
Number of active sites	10,000	11,785	26,000	3,000	575
Current estimate to complete clean-up	$200 to $350 billion ***	$30 billion	$3.9-$8.2 billion	$2.5 billion	$1.5-2 billion
Estimate being revised	Released March 1995	Yes	None scheduled	Yes: due FY 1996	Yes: due FY 1995
Estimate of years to finish clean-up	30-75+ yrs	20 yrs	NA	10 yrs–landfills 40 yrs–mines 50 yrs–NRD †	25 yrs
Annual budget: 1994 actual 1995 enacted 1996 request	$6.1 billion *** $5.9 billion *** $6.6 billion ***	$2.5 billion †† $2.0 billion †† $2.1 billion ††	$61 million $65 million $66 million	$16 million $16 million $45 million	$34 million $21 million $37 million
Current funding source	Federal	Federal	Federal	Federal	Federal
Responsibility for contamination	Agency	Agency	Agency, private parties and local governments	Agency, private parties and local governments	Agency

* Adapted from *Improving Facilities Clean-up,* Report of the Federal Facilities Policy group, October 1995.
** The DOI and USDA believe that abandoned and inactive mines on public lands are not generally "federal facilities" under Section 120 of CERLCA.
*** DOE's budget includes waste management, facility standardization, technology development, and associated support costs that include many unique operational, safety, and national security costs in addition to environmental clean-up.
†Natural Resources Damage.
†† DOD includes only Defense environmental security Clean-up budges.

Figure 12.1—Federal Facilities Profile[1]

It is, to be sure, a bitter irony that the nation's chief environmental regulator and guardian of public lands has simultaneously polluted the environment and fouled those lands. It is also a major legal problem. How should the federal government regulate itself? Can one agency, EPA, effectively discipline others, like the Departments of Energy (DOE), Defense (DOD), or the Interior (DOI)? Should the states whose territory and citizens have been put at risk be permitted to regulate the federal polluters? And which (if any) of the regulatory techniques that are used against private polluters are appropriate or effective ways to enforce the law against the federal government?

---

[1] FINAL REPORT OF THE FEDERAL FACILITIES ENVIRONMENTAL RESTORATION DIALOGUE COMMITTEE (April 1996)

This chapter is built around a case study of environmental remediation at a single DOE site. Until it stopped production in 1989, the former Feed Materials Production Center at Fernald, Ohio, manufactured most of DOE's supply of uranium metal for nuclear weapons. The clean-up decisionmaking for Fernald, which is now largely complete (though the clean-up itself is not), offers an opportunity to study the legal regime for remediation of federal facilities in a concrete setting. Fernald also provided the setting for much of the case law concerning federal facilities. The leading case on sovereign immunity,[2] a major decision limiting the government contractor defense,[3] and the first ever interagency fine, all arose out of disputes at Fernald.

Part A addresses the regulatory structure and the challenges of regulating federal facilities. As industrial facilities, federal facilities are capable of violating the requirements of the principal federal environmental statutes that we have already studied and the state statutes enacted pursuant to them. All of the statutes that address the question directly apply to federal facilities. In addition, Executive Order No. 12088, 43 Fed. Reg. 47707 (1978), requires executive agencies to comply with all of the major pollution control and toxics statutes. In other words, the mere fact of being a *defense* agency does not excuse compliance,[4] though the relevant statutes permit explicit exemptions. A federal facility can also be a common law nuisance or otherwise incur tort liability under the Federal Tort Claims Act.

Fernald in particular and the Nuclear Weapons Complex in general also provide an opportunity to examine two specific issues of environmental remediation. Public participation has been discussed occasionally in the risk assessment and the statutory chapters. When the subject of regulation is a publicly owned facility, however, the case for public participation is far stronger. Section B examines the various forms that such participation might take, its strengths, and its limitations. Section C addresses the longevity of the types of waste generated by the production of nuclear weapons. You are undoubtedly familiar with the public debate over proposed long-term repositories at Yucca Mountain, Nevada, and elsewhere. While the difficulties of managing long-lived wastes are by no means limited to nuclear weapons production, to nuclear power, or to federal facilities, DOE facilities offer a particularly striking example of the problem.

A. Cleaning Up Federal Facilities

A "federal facility" can be a building, a structure, an installation, a military base, a laboratory, or simply land. There are nearly 30,000 federal facilities. Under CERCLA, all owners and operators of facilities were

---

[2] Ohio v. Department of Energy, 503 U.S. 607 (1992).

[3] Crawford v. National Lead Co., 784 F. Supp. 439 (S.D. Ohio 1989).

[4] *See* Legal Environmental Assistance Foundation, Inc. [LEAF] v. Hodel, 586 F. Supp. 1163 (E.D. Tenn. 1984); Weinberger v. Catholic Action of Hawaii/Peace Education Project, 454 U.S. 139 (1981).

required by 1981 to notify EPA of the existence of facilities where hazardous wastes were stored. These notification requests applied to the federal government, as well as to its contractors and lessees. Despite this statutory demand, by 1984, only 5 of 16 federal agencies had undertaken any survey of their hazardous waste sites. In an attempt to accelerate federal agencies' response to hazardous waste problems, SARA section 120 clarified CERCLA's application to federal facilities and called for EPA to establish and maintain a docket listing potentially contaminated federal facilities. In February, 1988, EPA published the first docket, consisting of 823 facilities. By 1993, EPA had added to the docket seven times, more than doubling its size to 1946 facilities. Currently, 165 of these sites are on the National Priorities List (NPL), and others are still being evaluated. Federal facilities on the NPL may contain numerous sites requiring registration and clean-up, and may pose more complex clean-up problems than typical non-federal sites. The scope and severity of federal facilities' environmental problems also makes them a kind of canary in the mine—an early warning of issues that private facilities will eventually encounter.

Given the size of the federal land holdings, toxic contamination of the public lands is far more problematic than the attention it receives. The federal government owns approximately 29% or 662 million acres of the land in the United States.[5] The defense facilities are just one category within these vast holdings, comprising just 3% of federal land, but the cost of cleaning them up is staggering. DOD and DOE operate on a grandiose scale, employing literally millions of men and women.[6] The results of these activities are air emissions, water discharges, and production of solid and hazardous wastes, some of which are typical of analogous civilian activities and some of which are unique to military functions. Unexploded and surplus ordnance, millions of gallons of liquid waste that is both extremely corrosive

---

[5] The Departments of the Interior and Agriculture (through the U.S. Forest Service) own thousands of square miles of land polluted by the toxic and hazardous waste residue of mining, timber harvesting, and grazing activities on public lands. These tend to be ignored, because natural resource lawyers focus on management issues such as how much timber to cut, how many cows to graze, and how to protect watersheds on the public lands. Pollution abatement lawyers focus on issues such as air pollution, water pollution, and toxic and hazardous waste contamination on private property. As a result toxic contamination and disposal on federal public lands has fallen through the cracks. Public land managers are just beginning to identify, inventory, and assess the problem of toxic and hazardous waste contamination on public lands. A thorough overview of the problem of managing hazardous materials on federal lands can be found in Robert L. Glicksman, *Pollution on the Federal Lands III: Regulation of Solid and Hazardous Waste Management*, 13 Stan. Envtl. L.J. 3 (1994) and Robert L. Glicksman, *Pollution on the Federal Lands IV: Liability for Hazardous Waste Disposal*, 12 UCLA J. Envtl. L. 233 (1994).

[6] For an excellent treatment of the defense agencies, *see* Stephen Dycus, National Defense and the Environment (1996), and Melissa R. Kassen, *The Inadequacies of Congressional Attempts to Legislate Federal Facility Compliance with Environmental Requirements*, 54 Md. L. Rev. 1475 (1995). Some of this chapter is adapted from John S. Applegate, *National Security and Environmental Protection: The Half-Full Glass*, 26 Ecology L.Q. 350 (1999) (book review of Dycus, *supra*).

and highly radioactive, chemical weapons, excess nuclear warheads and weapons-grade plutonium, and defoliant production residues are just some of the more exotic materials that have to be managed. In the United States, there are approximately 13,000 potentially contaminated sites at 172 DOD installations, with environmental compliance costs reaching $30 billion, and about 14,000 separate contaminated locations at 137 DOE facilities, with estimates of the total cost of cleaning up the entire weapons complex ranging from $146 to $350 billion.

In theory, three classes of plaintiffs can bring actions against environmental harm at federal facilities: EPA, the federal agency normally charged with enforcing federal environmental statutes; a state agency enforcing state environmental statutes that otherwise apply to the federal facility; and, subject to the requirements of standing, a private party or public interest organization under a tort theory or in a citizen suit permitted by the applicable federal environmental law. After describing the Fernald facility, the chapter considers each type of action in turn.

1. The Department of Energy's Fernald Facility

The Departments of Energy and Defense own the federal facilities of greatest environmental concern. While the numerical majority of such facilities are the responsibility of DOD, the DOE facilities are generally larger, contain far more hazardous wastes (toxic and radioactive), and hence are far more expensive to remediate.[7] The former Feed Materials Production Center at Fernald, Ohio—now called the Fernald Environmental Management Project (FEMP) to reflect its clean-up mission—is one part of a much larger industrial infrastructure for designing, building, and testing nuclear weapons. The following excerpt describes DOE's Nuclear Weapons Complex.[8]

---

[7] "For every pound of plutonium produced at the Hanford, Washington, site, approximately 170 gallons of high-level liquid waste and 27,500 gallons of low-level waste were generated. In all, the nuclear weapons complex has generated enough radioactive waste to cover 515 football fields three feet deep." Pamela Murphy, *Coming Clean: The Public's Evolving Role in Nuclear Waste Clean-up*, 43:3 THE NATIONAL VOTER 17 (March/April 1994).

[8] For more information on the Nuclear Weapons Complex and nuclear waste disposal generally, *see* BNA Special Report, *Cleaning Up Federal Facilities: Controversy over an Environmental Peace Dividend*, 23 ENVT. REP. 2659 (Feb. 5, 1993); LEAGUE OF WOMEN VOTERS, THE NUCLEAR WASTE PRIMER (1993). A good description of Hanford, Washington, perhaps the most challenging and certainly the most expensive of DOE's sites, may be found in Glenn Zorpette, *Hanford's Nuclear Wasteland*, SCIENTIFIC AMERICAN, May 1996, pp. 88-97. A thorough overview of the clean-up problems for DOD bases can be found in Richard A. Wegman & Harold G. Bailey, Jr., *The Challenge of Cleaning Up Military Wastes When U.S. Bases Are Closed*, 21 ECOLOGY L.Q. 865 (1994).

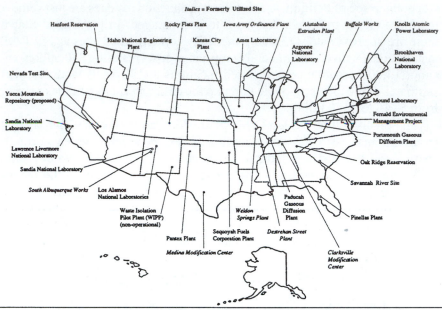

Figure 12.2—U.S. Department of Energy Nuclear Weapons Complex

COMPLEX CLEAN-UP: THE ENVIRONMENTAL LEGACY OF NUCLEAR WEAPONS PRODUCTION

Office of Technology Assessment
(1991)

It is difficult to appreciate the scale of what is now known as the Nuclear Weapons Complex unless one has actually viewed the vast, tumbleweed-tossed plains of the Hanford Reservation; seen the tank farm at Savannah River where more than 50 underground tanks—each as big as the Capitol dome—house the high-level radioactive waste that inevitably results from plutonium production; or visited the area of east Tennessee, known as Site X during World War II, where the equivalent of the annual timber output of Minnesota was used to build what was then the largest roofed structure in the world. It is difficult, without seeing them, to imagine the huge concrete rooms known as "canyons" in which weapons-grade plutonium is chemically separated from other constituents in irradiated fuel elements behind thick protective walls, where the radioactivity is so intense that all work must be done by robotic manipulators.

The Nuclear Weapons Complex is an industrial empire[9]–a collection of enormous factories devoted to metal fabrication, chemical separation processes, and electronic assembly. Like most industrial operations, these

---

[9] In the mid-1950s, the nuclear weapons program accounted for nearly four percent of the *total* industrial production in the United States. Arjun Makhijani, *Energy Enters Guilty Plea*, BULL. OF THE ATOMIC SCIENTISTS 18, 20 (Mar./Apr. 1994).—EDS.

factories have generated waste, much of it toxic. The past 45 years of nuclear weapons production have resulted in the release of vast quantities of hazardous chemicals and radionuclides to the environment. There is evidence that air, groundwater, surface water, sediments, and soil, as well as vegetation and wildlife, have been contaminated at most, if not all, of the Department of Energy (DOE) nuclear weapons sites.

* * *

Contamination of soil, sediments, surface water, and groundwater throughout the Nuclear Weapons Complex is extensive. At every facility the groundwater is contaminated with radionuclides or hazardous chemicals. Most sites in non-arid locations also have surface water contamination. Millions of cubic meters of radioactive and hazardous wastes have been buried throughout the complex, and there are few adequate records of burial site locations and contents. Contaminated soils and sediments of all categories are estimated to total billions of cubic meters.

Descriptions of vast quantities of old buried waste; of contaminants in pits, ponds, and lagoons; and of the migration of contamination into water supplies serve to dramatize the problem. * * *

Many factors have contributed to the current waste and contamination problems at the weapons sites; the nature of manufacturing processes, which are inherently waste producing; a long history of emphasizing the urgency of weapons production in the interest of national security, to the neglect of environmental considerations; a lack of knowledge about, or attention to, the consequences of environmental contamination; and an enterprise that has operated in secrecy for decades, without any independent oversight or meaningful public scrutiny.

* * *

Size and Location

DOE Weapons Complex facilities are spread across the Nation, from South Carolina to Washington State; they vary greatly in both size and proximity to populated regions. Fernald, which has produced uranium metal, and Rocky Flats, which produces plutonium "triggers," are relatively small facilities located near populated areas. The 1,450 acre Fernald site is 20 miles northwest of Cincinnati, OH, in a farming area. Although Rocky Flats covers about 6,550 acres, all major structures are concentrated in fewer than 400 acres. The plant is within 16 miles of downtown Denver, Boulder, and Golden, CO. About 80,000 people live within 3 miles of the facility.

Other sites are much larger. Hanford encompasses approximately 360,000 acres in southeastern Washington State: Richland, Pasco, and Kennewick (the Tri-Cities area, with a population of 140,000) are nearby, downstream on the Columbia River. Portland, OR (population 360,000), is about 230 miles downstream. Hanford's primary mission has been the production of weapons-grade plutonium. The Savannah River Site, which produces tritium and plutonium, consists of 192,000 acres on the north bank of the Savannah River. Built in the early 1950s, the site is approximately 13 miles south of Aiken, SC (population 15,000), and 20 miles southeast of Augusta, GA (population 50,000). The average population density in counties surrounding the site ranges from 23 to 560 people per square mile, with the largest population (more than 250,000) in the Augusta, GA, metropolitan area. Savannah River, which employs more than 20,000 people, is the largest plant (in terms of employment) in the Weapons Complex.

The Oak Ridge Reservation covers approximately 58,000 acres in Tennessee. Oak Ridge, among other activities, produces uranium and ceramic weapons components. The City of Oak Ridge (population 28,000) is adjacent to the Y-12 Plant; Knoxville, TN (population 350,000), is about 20 miles to the east of Oak Ridge. The Idaho National Engineering Laboratory (INEL), which reprocesses naval reactor fuel to recover uranium-235 for reuse as fuel in the Savannah River production reactors, is the largest weapons site in terms of area, covering 570,000 acres in southeastern Idaho and overlapping five counties.

—

The Fernald[10] site is now a major DOE clean-up project. In 1951, to meet the nuclear weapons program's need for large quantities of uranium metal,

---

[10] One of the authors (Applegate) served as chair of the Department of Energy's citizens advisory board at Fernald from 1993 to 1998. The portrait of Fernald presented here is based on personal observation, official documents, news stories, and correspondence or interviews with most of the key figures at Fernald. Only documents with independent significance or explanatory value are cited as sources.

For descriptions of the Fernald site and its contamination, *see* DOE, FEMP, Site Development Plan (Draft, Sept. 1993); DOE, FEMP, 1992 Site Environmental Report (June 1993); DOE, Site-Wide Characterization Report (Site-Wide RI/FS) (March 1993); http://www.fernald.gov; DOE, FMPC, *A Closer Look at Uranium Metal Production: A Technical Overview* (March 1988); Office of Technology Assessment, *Complex Clean-up: The Environmental Legacy of Nuclear Weapons Production* (Feb. 1991); DOE, *Environmental Restoration and Waste Management Five-Year Plan*, FY 1994-1998, Installation Summaries (Jan. 1993); 1992 Site Environmental Report, *supra*; *In re* Feed Materials Production Center, Site No. OH6-890-008-976, Consent Agreement as Amended Under CERCLA Sections 120 and 106(a), EPA Region V Administrative Docket No. V-W-90-C-057 (June 298, 1990); *id.*, Federal Facilities Compliance Agreement (July 18, 1986); *id.*, Amended Consent Agreement (Sept. 20, 1991); DOE, FEMP, Fiscal Year 1994 Roadmap (Draft, Sept. 30, 1993); DOE, FEMP, Site Specific Plan, Fiscal Year 1993 (Final Draft 1992); State of Ohio v. U.S. Department of Energy, Civ. No. C-1-86-0217 (S.D. Ohio), Consent Decree (Dec. 2, 1988), Stipulated Amendment to Consent Decree (Jan. 22, 1993).

Interviews and newspaper articles were particularly significant for the history of Fernald's troubles. Especially useful articles included Laurie Garret, *Uncle Sam's Hot Spot: Troubles at a Vital Federal Nuclear Plant*, WASHINGTON POST MAGAZINE, p. 6, July 28, 1985; Pamela Reynolds, *At Ohio Uranium Plant, A Cloud of Fear and Anger*, BOSTON GLOBE, p.3, Oct. 25, 1988; Barbara Burgower, *A Living Nightmare: Nobody Told the Crawford Family that Their Drinking Water Was Laced with Uranium*, LADIES HOME JOURNAL, p. 74 (March 1989); *Fernald Residents Miss Out on Lobbying Push*, UPI/NEXIS, April 2, 1989; Rochelle Distelheim, *The Betrayal of Fernald, Ohio: Radioactive Contamination*, GOOD HOUSEKEEPING, p. 176 (Sept. 1989); Gregg LaBar, *Fernald: Hazardous Waste and Harbored Fears*, 51 OCCUPATIONAL HAZARDS 95 (Oct. 1989).

For general descriptions of the Task Force process, *see* FERNALD CITIZENS TASK FORCE, RECOMMENDATIONS ON REMEDIATION LEVELS, WASTE DISPOSITION, PRIORITIES, AND FUTURE

the Atomic Energy Commission (predecessor to DOE) selected a rural 1,050-acre site, about a mile and a half square, in southwestern Ohio. The location had ready access to relatively cheap skilled and unskilled labor, a politically supportive populace, and close proximity to a network of major rail and road transportation.

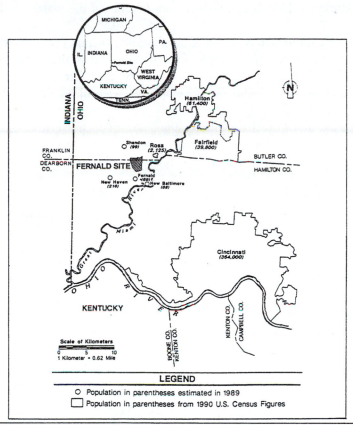

Figure 12.3—Fernald Vicinity

The first metal was produced by a pilot plant on October 11, 1951, and construction of the main facilities was complete by 1954. The plant was operated by National Lead of Ohio (NLO), often with extremely limited DOE oversight.

USE (1995); John S. Applegate, *Beyond the Usual Suspects: The Use of Citizens Advisory Boards in Environmental Decisionmaking*, 73 IND. L.J. 903 (1998); John S. Applegate, *A Beginning and Not and End in Itself: The Role of Risk Assessment in Environmental Decision-Making*, 63 U. CIN. L. REV. 1643,1653-54 (1995); John S. Applegate & Douglas J. Sarno, *Coping with Complex Facts and Multiple Parties in Public Disputes*, CONSENSUS, July 1996, at 1; Jennifer J. Duffield & Stephen P. Depoe, *Lessons from Fernald: Reversing NIMBYism Through Democratic Decision-Making*, INSIDE EPA'S RISK POL'Y REP., Feb. 21, 1997, at 31; http://www.fernald.gov. The Task Force is now called the Fernald Citizens Advisory Board.

The actual production area at Fernald was limited to a 136-acre tract near the center of the site. The production area is surrounded by fields and woods. A stream called Paddys Run flows along the western boundary of the site. Paddys Run soon joins the Great Miami River, which lies about a mile to the east of the site. Directly beneath the site are two sources of groundwater: shallow "perched" lenses of water trapped in the clay, and the deeper Great Miami Buried Valley Aquifer which serves some of the water needs of the region.

The area immediately surrounding Fernald remains primarily rural and dominated by agriculture. People live literally across the street from the plant, and until recently dairy cattle grazed on plant property. Residential, commercial, and light industrial development exists along the nearby Great Miami River and highway corridors. Commercial and public land uses also include sand and gravel operations along the river, nurseries and produce stands, schools, and parks. Downtown Cincinnati is seventeen miles away, and Fernald adjoins the intensive suburban development of a metropolitan area of 1.2 million persons.

The production process. A variety of chemical and metallurgical processes were used at Fernald for the manufacture of high-purity uranium metal from uranium ore and recycled materials. The refining process began with uranium ore. From 1953 to 1955, the Fernald refinery processed "K-65" pitchblende ore left over from the Manhattan Project, which contained substantial amounts of highly radioactive radium. After 1955, the refinery feedstock consisted of less radioactive uranium concentrates from Canada and the United States. In the refinery plants, chemical and heating processes extracted uranium from the ore to produce purified uranium metal ingots.

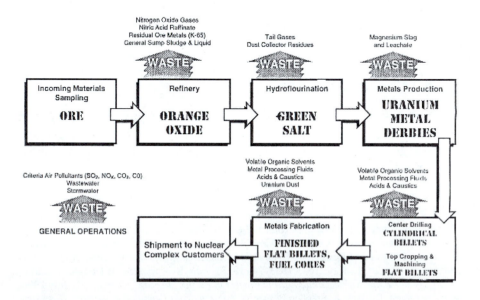

Figure 12.4–Fernald's Production Process and Waste Stream

The ingots (known as "derbies") were either shipped directly to facilities at Oak Ridge and Rocky Flats, or subjected to further metalworking processes on site. The resulting "billets" were used in the cores of DOE's plutonium production reactors at Hanford and Savannah River.

These processes created, among other things, emissions of corrosive hydrogen fluoride, nitrogen oxides (an air pollutant), and large quantities of uranium dust. The site was also served by a coal-burning boiler plant that emitted conventional air pollutants, and a wastewater treatment plant that discharged sanitary sewage, sump water, and storm water drainage into the Great Miami River.

Fernald's production peaked in 1960 at approximately 10,000 metric tons of uranium metal. A production decline beginning in 1964 reached a low in 1975 of about 1400 metric tons. During the 1970s DOE strongly considered closing Fernald, so capital improvements, maintenance, and staffing were minimized. Starting in 1981, however, President Reagan's defense build-up meant increased production requirements for Fernald, despite the lack of modernization. This combination produced an unexpected kind of uncontrolled chain reaction.

Fernald's problems come to light. Severe safety and radiation release problems plagued Fernald virtually from the time the plant began full-scale operations. Blowouts filling the buildings with uranium dust, overexposure of workers to radioactive material, spills of hazardous liquids, and atmospheric releases of uranium were commonplace. The problems came to a head in December 1984, when two accidents a week apart covered workers with hundreds of pounds of uranium dust. The initial response of DOE and NLO was typical of the Cold War production-at-all-costs mentality: while admitting that uranium releases in excess of 300 pounds a year were normal, they insisted that the plant posed absolutely no risk to its employees or neighbors.[11]

In January 1985, however, DOE released a report showing that three local wells contained significantly elevated levels of radioactive (uranium and strontium-90) and toxic (heavy metals) material. This discovery led to the filing of a class action against NLO on behalf of all persons who lived near the Fernald site, alleging increased risk, loss of property value, and emotional distress. It also led to intensified regulatory interest in the site. In the following months and years, radon gas leaks, uranium spills, and airborne releases of uranium further fueled the concern of regulators, workers, and the public. Then, in October 1988, DOE filed a brief in the class action that detailed a regular practice of deliberate violations of environmental laws, resulting in the release of hundreds of thousands of pounds of uranium into the air and the dumping of millions of pounds of waste into leaking pits. In 1989, Ohio began to levy fines on Westinghouse, the new contractor at the site, and EPA placed Fernald on the National Priorities List. In 1990, a large

---

[11] Less than a year later, the same management had to be told by outside consultants that a company picnic for workers' families *inside the plant* would be "an extremely poor idea."

groundwater plume of uranium contamination was discovered *beyond* site boundaries. In 1991, the Feed Materials Production Center was officially closed and its mission became exclusively environmental restoration.

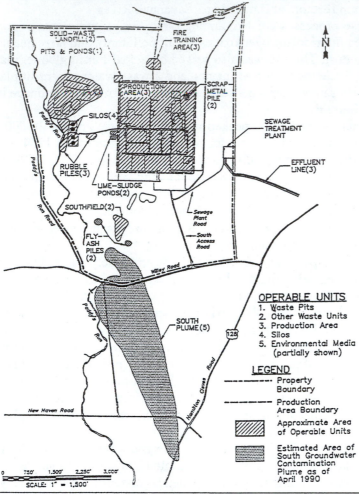

Figure 12.5—Site Map and Operable Units

The sources and nature of contamination. For clean-up purposes, the Fernald site is divided into five areas of roughly similar waste characteristics, called operable units (OUs), as indicated in the site map. Until 1984, solid and slurried production wastes were simply dumped into open pits on site. The six waste pits comprise Operable Unit 1. They range from 15 to 25 feet deep and most are lined only with clay. Waste Pit 4, for example, contains over 6,000,000 pounds of uranium, 136,000 pounds of thorium, traces of plutonium, and other hazardous wastes. These materials were carried to the ambient environment by storm water runoff, leaching into adjacent soils and groundwater, and airborne dust.

Uranium itself is a relatively common element in nature. Uranium-238, while not highly radioactive, is chemically very toxic. However, even its limited radioactivity is a serious hazard when inhaled, as uranium dust remains in direct contact with unprotected lung tissue. Thorium is more dangerous than uranium in the body. It targets the bones, liver, lungs, and lymphatic glands if it penetrates the skin through a cut. Plutonium is "the most radiotoxic of the elements and one of the most toxic substances known; [its] dangerous ionizing radiation persists indefinitely [and it is] a powerful carcinogen. [Plutonium] must be handled by remote control and with adequate shielding."[12] Plutonium was not processed at Fernald, but was returned to it as a contaminant of recycled uranium

Operable Unit 2 includes more conventional wastes—a landfill, building debris, lime sludge ponds from water treatment, and a flyash pile from the coal-fired boiler plant—that are contaminated with uranium to a greater or lesser degree. Some of these conventional waste pits were excavated into the aquifer, so that rainwater dripping through the waste leaches uranium and heavy metals *directly* into the groundwater supply. Other pits are located adjacent to Paddys Run, so that storm water runoff flows into the stream, contaminating the surface water, sediments, and ultimately the Great Miami River.

Operable Unit 3 consists of the buildings and infrastructure of the central production area, most of which is heavily contaminated with uranium. The underlying soils contain hazardous industrial chemicals and metals. The *coup de grâce*, however, is that the buildings are *themselves* hazardous waste: many of the outside walls are made of transite sheeting, a form of asbestos. The buildings, therefore, must be removed, and the resulting debris must be handled with caution for both radioactive and toxic risks. Moreover, the surface decontamination of the structures produces large amounts of uranium-tainted wastewater.

The "hottest" area is Operable Unit 4, which includes two concrete silos containing the used K-65 pitchblende ore. The radioactivity of the ore is high due to its radium content, and it emits extremely dangerous quantities of radon gas. The silos are about 800 feet from a public road, and in the winter when the trees are bare they seem to rise just on the other side of the fence line. In the middle 1960s, earthen berms were built around these silos to support their deteriorating walls and to contain the radiation; more recently, a layer of clay was placed on top of the ore to reduce radon emissions.

Operable Unit 5 covers environmental media, including groundwater, surface water, soils, sediments, air, and vegetation. These are the most direct sources of exposure to the general public, and they represent the largest volume of clean-up material. The soils below the waste pit, production, and surface silo areas are highly contaminated, and surface soils around the site contain varying degrees of uranium dust and other particulate emissions. The south-flowing plume of uranium in the aquifer now reaches over a mile off-

---

[12] W. IRVING SAX & RICHARD J. LEWIS, SR., HAWLEY'S CONDENSED CHEMICAL DICTIONARY 929 (11th ed. 1987); *see also* JOHN HARTE *ET AL.*, TOXICS A TO Z: A GUIDE TO EVERYDAY POLLUTION HAZARDS (1991).

site. Pumping operations have slowed the progress of and will eventually remediate the plume.

Source	Potential Human Exposure
Air emissions and fugitive dust	
Uranium[a]	Ambient air
Radon[b]	Soil
Criteria air pollutants	Grass
Thorium[c]	Produce
Lead	Milk
Hydrogen fluoride	Direct radiation
VOCs (perchlorethylene)	
Soil	
Radon	Direct contact
Uranium	Produce
Lead	Milk
VOCs (perc, tricholethane)	
Asbestos	
PCBs	
Surface water	
Uranium[d]	Effluent
Radionuclides	River water
Metals (chromium)	Fish
Conventional water pollutants	Sediments
Groundwater	
Uranium	Private wells
Metals (barium, chromium)	Monitoring wells
Thorium	(on- & off-site)
Radionuclides (cesium-137, strontium-90, neptunium-237)	

[a]A Centers for Disease Control (CDC) Exposure Reconstruction Study in 1993 estimated that 1,000,000 pounds of uranium were released to the air between 1951 and 1989.
[b]CDC estimates release of 170,000 curies of radon.
[c]DOE estimates that 14,300 pounds of thorium were released into the air.
[d]CDC estimates that 217,800 pounds were discharged to surface waters.

Figure 12.6—Exposure Pathways

Bad as it is, Fernald is not the most severely contaminated site in the Nuclear Weapons Complex. Hanford, Rocky Flats, Oak Ridge, and Savannah River have huge amounts of high-level radioactive waste like spent fuel, enriched (and more highly radioactive) uranium (U_{235}), and plutonium. At Hanford, there are 177 tanks of liquid high-level waste, many of them old and leaking. The management of high-level wastes, and in particular the location of storage facilities for them, is extremely contentious. Congress made an effort to resolve these issues in the Nuclear Waste Policy Act of 1982, 42 U.S.C. §§ 10101-10226, but has had little success.[13] Uranium mill tailings (a byproduct of mining uranium ore) pose the inverse

---

[13] *See* Chapter 10 (Siting of Waste Treatment and Disposal Facilities: A RCRA Case Study).

problem of low radioactivity but immense volume. The are being remediated under the Uranium Mill Tailings Radiation Control Act of 1978 (UMTRCA), 42 U.S.C. §§ 7901-7942, in lieu of CERCLA.[14]

2. EPA and the Problem of the Unitary Executive

Although EPA is charged with enforcing federal environmental statutes against polluters, it cannot sue federal facilities. Under the "unitary executive" doctrine, since all federal executive agencies work for the President, one executive branch agency cannot take judicial action against another executive branch agency because such an action would, in effect, have the President bringing an action against himself. Moreover, the court, which resides in a different branch of government, might well regard the intrabranch dispute as a non-justiciable political question or as failing to meet the judicial branch's own "case or controversy" requirement.[15]

The Federal Facility Compliance Act of 1992 (FFCA), 42 U.S.C. §§ 6903(15), 6961, which clarified the application of RCRA to federal facilities, attempts to minimize the chances of such an occurrence. It requires EPA to first negotiate with the offending agency and then hold high-level consultations between the agencies, prior to permitting the issuance of an enforcement order. This is consistent with Executive Orders No. 12088 and No. 12146, which require submission of all intrabranch policy and legal disputes to, respectively, the Office of Management and Budget and the Attorney General. Ultimately, however, the FFCA authorizes *administrative* actions by EPA against other agencies, though the Justice Department, which represents EPA in court, would undoubtedly decline to pursue the matter judicially. The FFCA simply strengthens EPA's hand in negotiating with other agencies or in "arbitration" by OMB or the Justice Department.[16]

In order to address the serious environmental problem of toxic pollution at and around federal facilities in ways that do not involve EPA enforcement actions, EPA has negotiated many interagency agreements (IAGs) or federal facilities agreements (FFAs) with sister agencies. An IAG or FFA is a promise by a federal agency to the EPA in which the federal facility agrees to meet predetermined standards according to a time schedule contained in the agreement, subject to penalties for noncompliance.

---

[14] For an outline of the regulation of the disposal of defense radioactive waste, *see* John S. Applegate & Stephen Dycus, *Institutional Controls or Emperor's Clothes? Long-Term Stewardship of the Nuclear Weapons Complex*, 28 ENVTL. L. REP. (ENVTL. L. INST.) 10631, 10635-38 (1998); Steven R. Miller, *The Applicability of CERCLA and SARA to Releases of Radioactive Materials*, 17 ENVTL. L. REP. 10071 (1987).

[15] *See* Adam Babich, *Circumventing Laws: Does the Sovereign Have a License to Pollute?*, 6 NAT. RESOURCES & ENV'T 28 (1991).

[16] *See* Stephen J. Darmody, *Hazardous Waste Law for the Federal Employee: An Analysis of the Legal Framework*, 40 FED. BAR NEWS & J. 650 (1993); Andrew Michael Gaydosh, *The Superfund Federal Facility Program: We Have Met the Enemy and It Is Us*, 6(3) NAT. RESOURCES & ENVT. 21 (Winter 1992).

Despite these efforts to address environmental contamination at federal facilities, one financial obstacle may still prevent effective enforcement of federal compliance with environmental rules. The Antideficiency Act, 31 U.S.C. §§ 1341 *et seq.*, in effect criminalizes the Constitutional prohibition (art. I, §9) on spending unappropriated funds. The Act forbids federal officials from creating financial obligations in excess of appropriations; therefore, a federal facility cannot enter into a binding, multi-year compliance or consent decree which is not contingent on future funding. Since Congress usually does not make appropriations for years beyond the next fiscal year, federal officials cannot make meaningful commitments to obey environmental laws in subsequent years, because they do not know if Congress will appropriate the needed funds. More than sovereign immunity, the Antideficiency Act may be the trump card that ultimately exempts the federal government from enforceable federal and state environmental laws.

PROBLEM
INTERAGENCY FINES AT FERNALD

EPA first became seriously interested in Fernald after the *Crawford* litigation was well underway and repeated accidents and discharges had brought Fernald to national attention. Fernald was placed on the National Priorities List in November 1989, and DOE and EPA signed an administrative Consent Agreement on June 19, 1990. This document divided the site into the five operable units and established a complex set of deadlines for dozens of CERCLA decisionmaking documents. DOE repeatedly failed to meet the original schedule, however, and so Fernald holds the dubious distinction of paying the first ever fine from one agency of the United States Government to another. When the fines had reached $400,000, DOE and EPA settled for $100,000 plus $150,000 in extra environmental restoration work—contingent on a special appropriation in the 1993 budget.

DOE and EPA also negotiated an Amended Consent Agreement which provides the current framework for environmental decisions at the site. Each of the elements of National Contingency Plan decisionmaking process is regarded as a "milestone," and each document is submitted to EPA for approval and made public. The Consent Agreement required a number of removal actions to address immediate threats. These included capping the K-65 material in the silos to reduce radon emissions, controlling storm water runoff from the waste pit area, fencing all waste disposal areas to prevent unauthorized access, pumping to slow expansion of the groundwater plume, and early decontamination and demolition of some of the more unsafe buildings. In all, thirty removal actions were required.

Are fines are an effective tool in obtaining federal government compliance? The Fernald fine was specifically appropriated in the 1993 energy appropriations bill. Where did that money come from? If from the overall budget, what deterrence effect will it have on DOE? If from DOE, what programs did it sacrifice—more clean-up? defense programs? nuclear safety regulation? Is that good policy?[17] EPA placed the fine in the Superfund trust fund for use in cleaning up other sites—is this how Congress should allocate funds? Are there better ways of assuring compliance?[18]

Was EPA even penalizing the right thing? DOE incurred the fines by failing to meet numerous "milestones" of decisionmaking, that is, documents that are part of the CERCLA RI/FS process. Actual discharges of uranium or lack of actual clean-up activity are not at issue. Does this make sense? If not, why has it happened that way?

3. The States and the Problem of Sovereign Immunity

When an action based on a federal environmental statute is brought by a state against a federal agency that owns or operates a federal facility, the biggest barrier to the action is the principle of sovereign immunity. Under the Supremacy Clause, the activities of the federal government are free from involuntary regulation by states. Since sovereign immunity bars suits against the United States, analysis begins with the question whether Congress has waived sovereign immunity in the statute that is the basis for the action against the federal facility. Waivers of immunity are construed strictly in favor of the sovereign.[19] When state regulation would be tantamount to prohibiting operation of a federal installation, or would impact the public fisc, the Supreme Court has been particularly narrow in its construction of waivers of sovereign immunity.[20]

---

[17] Can one limb of the executive branch really punish another? If EPA takes money away from DOE as a penalty, what should be done with the money? If it goes to EPA for other environmental activities or to the general Treasury fund, how do we know that the new use of the money is more important than the inadequate federal compliance or clean-up activity that has been penalized? Alternatively, if Congress replaces the penalty funds to ensure continuation of the environmental activities, what has been accomplished? The bottom line is that federal agencies penalizing each other is a zero-sum game. If the target accounts are already devoted to useful activities (at least, activities that Congress has decided are useful, and there is no guarantee that objectively useless activities would be de-funded first), then a fine will reduce the amount of that activity that takes place.

It is said that Katharine Hepburn's father once received a letter from Bryn Mawr College in which the dean expressed serious misgivings about his daughter's continuation at Bryn Mawr in view of her apparent lack of seriousness about her studies. Hepburn's father, a physician, replied that in his profession it was not customary to throw a sick patient out of the hospital. BARBARA LEAMING, KATHARINE HEPBURN 226 (1995).

[18] For an assessment of the limitations of fines as a means of enforcement, *see* Melinda R. Kassen, *The Inadequacies of Congressional Attempts to Legislate Federal Facility Compliance with Environmental Requirements*, 54 MD. L. REV. 1475 (1995); Andrea Gross, Note, *A Critique of the Federal Facilities Compliance Act of 1992*, 12 VA. ENVTL. L.J. 691 (1993).

[19] McMahon v. United States, 342 U.S. 25, 27 (1951); Eastern Transportation Co. v. United States, 272 U.S. 675, 686 (1927); Ruckelshaus v. Sierra Club, 463 U.S. 680, 685-86 (1983).

[20] Library of Congress v. Shaw, 478 U.S. 310 (1986)(interest on attorney's fees could not be recovered by plaintiff in suit brought against federal defendant under Title VII of 1964 Civil Rights Act); Hancock v. Train, 426 U.S. 167 (1976)(the CAA does not subject federal

All of the major federal environment statutes contain sections that to some degree waive sovereign immunity and make federal facilities subject to their provisions.[21] Courts have had no difficulty concluding that substantive standards contained in federal environmental laws apply to federal facilities.[22] Uncertainty arose, however, over the application of state standards by state regulators against federal polluters. For the CWA, CAA and RCRA, the critical term was "requirements," and whether a waiver for state requirements extended to various enforcement options.[23] For CERCLA, the issue was whether the term "enforcement" included all procedural aspects of enforcement. The federal government conceded that declaratory and injunctive relief was available, particularly for violation of court orders. Instead, the scope of the waiver of sovereign immunity was litigated in the context of the ability to assess civil penalties against federal polluters for past statutory violations. It was also somewhat uncertain whether criminal penalties may be imposed directly against federal employees for violations of environmental statutes.[24] Lower federal court decisions construing the scope of the immunity waiver in RCRA and the CWA were divided[25]

In *Ohio v. United States*, 503 U.S. 607 (1992), the state sought to enforce state water and hazardous waste statutes enacted pursuant to FWPCA and RCRA, respectively, at the Fernald site. Ohio sought two kinds of relief: fines for past violations, and prospective injunctive relief backed up by fines to ensure compliance. The Supreme Court interpreted RCRA and the CWA to permit "coercive" penalties to induce compliance with previously issued orders and injunctions, but not to waive federal immunity from "punitive" civil penalties, those designed to punish past violations of environmental laws. This holding also called into question the legality of punitive criminal penalties imposed against federal employees. When a citizen suit was brought against a private polluter, civil penalties were always available. It

---

installations to state permit requirements); EPA v. State Water Resources Control Board, 426 U.S. 200 (1976)(federal facilities not required to pay charges incident to a state permit program under the CWA).

[21] The Clean Water Act, Clean Air Act, and RCRA provide that federal facilities must comply with, *inter alia*, "all federal, state, interstate, and local requirements." 33 U.S.C. §1323(a)(CWA); 42 U.S.C. §7418(a)(CAA); 42 U.S.C. §6961(a)(RCRA). CERCLA provides that federal facilities must comply with "[s]tate laws regarding enforcement." 42 U.S.C. §9620(a)(4).

[22] Hancock v. Train, 426 U.S. 167, 181 (1976); United States v. Washington, 872 F.2d 874, 877 (9th Cir. 1989). *See* Barry Breen, *Federal Supremacy and Sovereign Immunity Waivers in Federal Environmental Law*, 15 Envtl. L. Rep. (Envtl. L. Inst.) 10326 (1985).

[23] *See* United States v. New Mexico, 32 F.3d 494 (10th Cir. 1994)(reading "requirements" broadly).

[24] United States v. Dee, 912 F.2d 741, 743 (4th Cir. 1990)(upholding criminal conviction under RCRA); California v. Walters, 751 F.2d 977, 979 (9th Cir. 1985)(per curiam)(forbidding state prosecution of federal employee for RCRA violations).

[25] *Compare* Mitzenfelt v. Department of Air Force, 903 F. 2d 1293 (10th Cir. 1993); United States v. Washington, 872 F. 2d 874 (9th Cir. 1989) (limited waivers of immunity from a state's assessment of civil penalties), *with* Ohio v. United States Dept. of Energy, 904 F. 2d 1058 (6th Cir. 1990); Maine v. Department of Navy, 702 F. Supp. 322 (D. Me. 1988) (broad waiver).

was less clear whether states could use citizen suits to obtain civil penalties against the United States. In the *Ohio* case, the Supreme Court also held that a state generally could not use a citizen suit provision in a federal environmental statute to obtain civil penalties against the United States.

In response to the *Ohio* decision, Congress passed the Federal Facility Compliance Act of 1992 (FFCA) to provide the unequivocal waiver that the *Ohio* case required. 42 U.S.C. §§ 6903(15), 6961. The FFCA subjects federal agencies to civil penalties, both punitive and coercive, and waives federal employees' immunity from criminal prosecution. States can choose from a number of enforcement mechanisms, including administrative orders, civil penalties, and civil actions. Finally, if a state wishes to pursue its RCRA claims in a citizen's suit, it may do so because the FFCA now defines "person" subject to liability to include the United States. 42 U.S.C. § 6903(15). In addition to permitting EPA and state agencies to impose civil penalties and fines for past violations of RCRA, the FFCA requires DOE to inventory all sites with mixed radioactive and hazardous wastes, and to prepare site plans for treating the mixed waste. The Act also allows EPA to declare emergencies when waste disposal practices at federal facilities threaten human health.

By early 1994, EPA had identified 48 sites in 22 states which are both radioactive and chemically dangerous under RCRA. EPA had also imposed millions of dollars in fines on various federal facilities (primarily military installations) for past RCRA violations. It had even begun to declare emergencies for federal sites (again, usually military bases) where local underground water supplies were discovered to be contaminated by chemicals discarded by the federal owner.[26]

Although the FFCA is a powerful tool for those who wish to take action against polluting federal facilities, it expands only the waiver provision of RCRA, and thereby lets the *Ohio* decision rationale remain in effect for the Clean Water Act.[27] Moreover, it does not address the waiver of sovereign immunity found in either the Clean Air Act or CERCLA. Thus, the CWA waiver is still valid for coercive penalties and for criminal enforcement actions brought against federal employees.[28] Since the Air Act's waiver language[29] is nearly identical to the language of the Water Act, it is also doubtful that courts will construe the Clean Air Act to include a waiver of punitive penalties.

The CERCLA waiver section states that federal facilities are liable for clean-up costs "in the same manner and to the same extent, both procedurally

---

[26] *See* Klaiman, *Base Closure and Reuse: Environmental Issues at Closing Military Bases in California*, 4 FED. FACILITIES ENVTL. J. 265 (1993).

[27] Nelson D. Cary, Note, *A Primer on Federal Facilities Compliance with Environmental Laws: Where Do We Go From Here?* 50 WASH. & LEE L. REV. 801, 820-21. (1993).

[28] United States v. Curtis, 988 F. 2d 946 (9th Cir. 1993).

[29] 42 U.S.C. § 7418(a).

and substantively, as any nongovernmental entity," 42 U.S.C. § 9620(a)(1),[30] and they must comply with "[s]tate laws regarding enforcement. "42 U.S.C. § 9620(a)(4). Is there ambiguity in the CERCLA term "enforcement," as there was in the terms "sanction" and "requirements" found in the RCRA, Air, and Water waivers of sovereign immunity? One court has concluded that, after *Ohio*, "enforcement" means only coercive penalties assessed for violation of court orders, and therefore CERCLA's waiver should not extend to punitive penalties.[31] CERCLA waives sovereign immunity for "state laws concerning removal and remedial action." 42 U.S.C § 9620 (a)(4). Does this phrase waive sovereign immunity only for state laws that are "mini-CERCLA's," which would require specific, predetermined standards for the clean-up of waste? Or is the phrase "removal and remedial action" broad enough to waive immunity to state laws which generally require polluters to assess and clean up contamination at federal sites? *See United States v. Commonwealth of Pennsylvania Dept. of Env. Res.*, 778 F. Supp. 1328 (M.D. Pa. 1991) (the waiver is broad, not narrow or technical).

The following case addresses a difficult CERCLA-RCRA interaction: does the existence of a CERCLA clean-up effort oust state jurisdiction under RCRA? This is crucially important to states, which have only a minor role in CERCLA decisionmaking but the lead role under RCRA.

UNITED STATES V. STATE OF COLORADO

990 F.2d 1565 (10th Cir. 1993),
cert. denied, 510 U.S. 1092 (1994)

BALDOCK, Circuit Judge.

* * *

The Rocky Mountain Arsenal ("Arsenal") is a hazardous waste treatment, storage and disposal facility subject to RCRA regulation, which is located near Commerce City, Colorado, in the Denver metropolitan area. The United States government has owned the Arsenal since 1942, and the Army operated it from that time until the mid-1980's. Without reiterating its environmental history, suffice it to say that the Arsenal is "one of the worst hazardous waste pollution sites in the country." *Daigle v. Shell Oil Co.*, 972 F.2d 1527, 1531 (10th Cir. 1992). The present litigation focuses on Basin F which is a 92.7 acre basin located within the Arsenal where millions of gallons of liquid hazardous waste have been disposed of over the years. [The

---

[30] The D.C. Circuit has held that this waiver of sovereign immunity "is coextensive with the scope of the substantive liability standards of CERCLA." East Bay Municipal Utility Dist. v. Dep't of Commerce, 142 F.3d 479, 481 (D.C. Cir. 1998).

[31] Maine v. Dep't of Navy, 973 F. 2d 1007 (10th Cir 1992). Congress is considering creating a general waiver of sovereign immunity under CERCLA. *See* H.R. 617, 106TH CONG., 1ST SESS. (1999); S. 8, 105TH CONG., 1ST SESS. (1997). DOD and DOE have opposed this measure, arguing that it would make little difference in actual operation of CERCLA, but could be read to expand federal liability enormously. DOD & DOE, Report to Congress: Potential Impacts of the Proposed Amendment to the CERCLA Waiver of Sovereign Immunity (1999).

wastes are primarily pesticides and herbicides, their solvents and constituents.]

* * *

II.

In November 1980, the Army, as the operator of the Arsenal, submitted to the EPA part A of its RCRA permit application which listed Basin F as a hazardous waste surface impoundment. By submitting the part A RCRA application, the Army achieved RCRA interim status. In May 1983, the Army submitted part B of its RCRA permit application to the EPA which included a required closure plan for Basin F, and the following month, the Army submitted a revised closure plan for Basin F. In May 1984, the EPA issued a notice of deficiency to the Army regarding part B of its RCRA permit application and requested a revised part B application within sixty days under threat of termination of the Army's interim status. The Army never submitted a revised part B RCRA permit application to the EPA; rather, in October 1984, the Army commenced a CERCLA remedial investigation/feasibility study ("RI/FS"). [The Army now maintains that its CERCLA response action precludes Colorado from enforcing its EPA-delegated RCRA authority at the Arsenal.]

Effective November 2, 1984, the EPA, acting pursuant to [RCRA] § 6926(b), authorized Colorado to "carry out" the Colorado Hazardous Waste Management Act ("CHWMA"), "in lieu of" RCRA. That same month, the Army submitted its part B RCRA/CHWMA permit application to the Colorado Department of Health ("CDH") which is charged with the administration and enforcement of CHWMA. Notably, the part B application was the same deficient application that the Army submitted to the EPA in June 1983. Not surprisingly, CDH found the application, specifically the closure plan for Basin F, to be unsatisfactory.

Consequently, in May 1986, CDH issued its own draft partial closure plan for Basin F to the Army, and in October 1986, CDH issued a final RCRA/CHWMA modified closure plan for Basin F and requested the Army's cooperation in immediately implementing the plan. The Army responded by questioning CDH's jurisdiction over the Basin F clean-up.

* * *

In September 1989, CDH, acting in accordance with the district court's February 1989 order, issued a final amended compliance order to the Army, pursuant to CDH's authority under CHWMA. The final amended compliance order requires the Army to submit an amended Basin F closure plan, as well as plans and schedules addressing soil contamination, monitoring and mitigation, groundwater contamination, and other identified tasks for each unit containing Basin F hazardous waste as required under CHWMA. The final amended compliance order also requires that CDH shall approve all plans and that the Army shall not implement any closure plan or work plan prior to approval in accordance with CHWMA.

As a result of the final amended compliance order, the United States filed the present declaratory action, invoking the district court's jurisdiction under 28 U.S.C. § 2201. The United States' complaint sought an order from the federal district court declaring that the final amended compliance order is "null and void" and enjoining Colorado and CDH from taking any action to enforce it. * * *

* * *

IV.

The district court focused on CERCLA's provision governing civil proceedings which grants federal courts exclusive jurisdiction over all actions arising under CERCLA. 42 U.S.C. § 9613(b). As the district court recognized, § 9613(h) expressly limits this grant of jurisdiction by providing, with exceptions not relevant here, that "no Federal court shall have jurisdiction under Federal law * * * to review any challenges to removal or remedial action selected under section 9604 of this title . * * *" *Id.* § 9613(h). However, contrary to the district court's reasoning, § 9613(h) does not bar federal courts from reviewing a CERCLA response action prior to its completion; rather, it bars federal courts from reviewing any "challenges" to a CERCLA response actions. This is a critical distinction because an action by Colorado to enforce the final amended compliance order, issued pursuant to its EPA-delegated RCRA authority, is not a "challenge" to the Army's CERCLA response action. To hold otherwise would require us to ignore the plain language and structure of both CERCLA and RCRA, and to find that CERCLA implicitly repealed RCRA's enforcement provisions contrary to Congress' expressed intention.

A.

Congress clearly expressed its intent that CERCLA should work in conjunction with other federal and state hazardous waste laws in order to solve this country's hazardous waste clean-up problem. CERCLA's "savings provision" provides that "nothing in [CERCLA] shall affect or modify in any way the obligations or liabilities of any person under other Federal or State law, including common law, with respect to releases of hazardous substances or other pollutants or contaminants." 42 U.S.C. § 9652(d). Similarly, CERCLA's provision entitled "relationship to other laws" provides that "nothing in [CERCLA] shall be construed or interpreted as preempting any State from imposing any additional liability or requirements with respect to the release of hazardous substances within such State." 42 U.S.C. § 9614(a). By holding that § 9613(h) bars Colorado from enforcing CHWMA, the district court effectively modified the Army's obligations and liabilities under CHWMA contrary to § 9652(d), and preempted Colorado from imposing additional requirements with respect to the release of hazardous substances contrary to 9614(a).

As a federal facility, the Arsenal is subject to regulation under RCRA. More importantly, because the EPA has delegated RCRA authority to

Colorado, the Arsenal is subject to regulation under CHWMA. While the President has authority to exempt federal facilities from complying with RCRA or respective state laws "if he determines it to be in the paramount interest of the United States," 42 U.S.C. § 6961, nothing in this record indicates that the Army has been granted such an exemption with respect to its activities at the Arsenal. Thus, Colorado has authority to enforce CHWMA at the Arsenal, and "any action taken by [Colorado]* * * [has] the same force and effect as action taken by the [EPA] . * * *" § 6926(d).

Notwithstanding Colorado's RCRA authority over the Basin F clean-up, and CERCLA's express preservation of this authority, § 9613(h), which was enacted as part of SARA, limits federal court jurisdiction to review challenges to CERCLA response actions. Congress' expressed purpose in enacting § 9613(h) was "to prevent *private responsible parties* from filing dilatory, interim lawsuits which have the effect of slowing down or preventing the EPA's clean-up activities." H.R. REP. NO. 253(I), 99TH CONG., 2D SESS. 266 (1985)(emphasis added). Nonetheless, the language of § 9613(h) does not differentiate between challenges by private responsible parties and challenges by a state. Thus, to the extent a state seeks to challenge a CERCLA response action, the plain language of § 9613(h) would limit a federal court's jurisdiction to review such a challenge.

Be that as it may, an action by a state to enforce its hazardous waste laws at a site undergoing a CERCLA response action is not necessarily a challenge to the CERCLA action. For example, CDH's final amended compliance order does not seek to halt the Army's Basin F interim response action; rather it merely seeks the Army's compliance with CHWMA during the course of the action, which includes CDH approval of the Basin F closure plan prior to implementation. Thus, Colorado is not seeking to delay the clean-up, but merely seeking to ensure that the clean-up is in accordance with state laws which the EPA has authorized Colorado to enforce under RCRA. In light of §§ 9652(d) and 9614(a), which expressly preserve a state's authority to undertake such action, we cannot say that Colorado's efforts to enforce its EPA-delegated RCRA authority is a challenge to the Army's undergoing CERCLA response action.

* * *

B.

Not only is the district court's construction of § 9613(h) inconsistent with §§ 9652(d) and 9614(a) of CERCLA, it is also inconsistent with RCRA's citizen suit provision. *See* 42 U.S.C. § 6972. While CERCLA citizen suits cannot be brought prior to the completion of a CERCLA remedial action, RCRA citizen suits to enforce its provisions at a site in which a CERCLA response action is underway can be brought prior to the completion of the CERCLA response action.

RCRA's citizen suit provision permits any person to commence a civil action against any other person, including the United States government or its agencies, to enforce "any permit, standard, regulation, condition, requirement, prohibition, or order which has become effective pursuant to" RCRA. 42 U.S.C. § 6972(a)(1)(A). Such suits are prohibited if the EPA or the state has already "commenced and is diligently prosecuting" a RCRA enforcement action. § 6972(b)(1)(B). Federal courts have jurisdiction over such suits and are authorized "to enforce the permit, standard, regulation, condition, requirement, prohibition, or order . * * *" 42 U.S.C. 6972(a).

RCRA's citizen suit provision also permits any person to commence a civil action against any other person, including the United States government or its agencies, to abate an "imminent and substantial endangerment to health or the environment * * *." § 6972(a)(1)(B). These types of RCRA citizen suits are prohibited, not only when the EPA is prosecuting a similar RCRA imminent hazard action pursuant to 42 U.S.C. § 6973, but also when the EPA is prosecuting a CERCLA abatement action pursuant to 42 U.S.C. § 9606; the EPA is engaged in a CERCLA removal action or has incurred costs to initiate a RI/FS and is "diligently proceeding" with a CERCLA remedial action pursuant to 42 U.S.C. § 9604; or the EPA has obtained a court order or issued an administrative order under CERCLA or RCRA pursuant to which a responsible party is conducting a removal action, RI/FS, or remedial action. § 6972(b)(2)(B). Federal courts have jurisdiction over RCRA citizen imminent hazard suits and are authorized "to restrain any person who has contributed or who is contributing to the past or present handling, storage, treatment, transportation, or disposal of any solid or hazardous waste. * * *" § 6972(a).

By prohibiting RCRA citizen imminent hazard suits with respect to hazardous waste sites where a CERCLA response action is underway, while not prohibiting RCRA citizen enforcement suits with respect to such sites, Congress clearly intended that a CERCLA response action would not prohibit a RCRA citizen enforcement suit. * * *

C.

Rather than challenging the Army's CERCLA remedial action, Colorado is attempting to enforce the requirements of its federally authorized hazardous waste laws and regulations, consistent with its ongoing duty to protect the health and environment of its citizens. CERCLA itself recognizes that these requirements are applicable to a facility during the pendency of a CERCLA response action. Further, RCRA contemplates that enforcement actions may be maintained despite an ongoing CERCLA response action, and we cannot say that CERCLA implicitly repealed RCRA's enforcement provision given CERCLA's clear statement to the contrary. While the decision to use CERCLA or RCRA to clean-up a site is normally a "policy question[] appropriate for agency resolution," the plain language of both statutes provides for state enforcement of its RCRA responsibilities despite an ongoing CERCLA response action. Thus, enforcement actions under state hazardous waste laws which have been authorized by the EPA to be enforced by the state in lieu of RCRA do not constitute "challenges" to CERCLA response actions; therefore, § 9613(h) does not jurisdictionally bar Colorado from enforcing the final amended compliance order.

V.

Even if an action by Colorado to enforce the final amended compliance order would be a "challenge" to the Army's CERCLA response action, the plain language of § 9613(h) would only bar a federal court from exercising jurisdiction over Colorado's action. Colorado, however, is not required to invoke federal court jurisdiction to enforce the final amended compliance order. Rather, Colorado can seek enforcement of the final amended compliance order in state court. Therefore, § 9613(h) cannot bar Colorado from taking "any" action to enforce the final compliance order.

* * * As the operator of a federal facility subject to regulation under CHWMA, the Army is subject to "process or sanction" of the Colorado state courts with respect to enforcement of CHWMA. 42 U.S.C. § 6961. Because Colorado may bring an enforcement suit in state court, § 9613(h) does not preclude Colorado from taking "any" action to enforce the final amended compliance order.

* * *

VII.

The United States alternatively contends that CERCLA's provision, which grants the President authority to select the remedy and allow for state input through the ARAR's process, *see* 42 U.S.C. § 9621, bars Colorado from enforcing state law independent of CERCLA. This is a curious argument in light of §§ 9614(a) and 9652(d) which expressly preserve state RCRA authority, and we find it to be without merit.

A.

While the United States does not dispute that Congress intended states to play a role in hazardous waste clean-up, the United States argues that the states' role when a CERCLA response action is underway is confined to CERCLA's ARAR's process. Undoubtedly, CERCLA's ARAR's provision was intended to provide "a mechanism for state involvement in the selection and adoption of remedial actions which are federal in character." Nonetheless, nothing in CERCLA supports the contention that Congress intended the ARAR's provision to be the exclusive means of state involvement in hazardous waste clean-up.

Contrary to the United States' claim, Colorado is not invading the President's authority to select a CERCLA remedial action. Rather, Colorado is merely insuring that the Army comply with CHWMA which §§ 9614(a) and 9652(d) of CERCLA expressly recognize is applicable. Sections 9614(a) and 9652(d) were included within CERCLA when it was originally enacted in 1980. However, the ARAR's provision was not enacted until the 1986 amendments to CERCLA. Certainly, Congress could not have intended the ARAR's provision to be the *exclusive* means of state involvement in hazardous waste clean-up as provided under §§ 9614(a) and 9652(d) when the ARAR's concept did not even come into being until six years after CERCLA was enacted.

Moreover, while the ARAR's provision requires the President to allow a state to participate in remedial planning and to review and comment on remedial plans, 42 U.S.C. § 9621(f)(1), it only allows states to ensure compliance with state law at the completion of the remedial action. However, §§ 9614(a) and 9652(d) expressly contemplate the applicability of other federal and state hazardous waste laws regardless of whether a CERCLA response action is underway. Given that RCRA clearly applies during the closure period of a regulated facility, *see* 40 C.F.R. § 264.228 (1992); *id.* § 265.228, the ARAR's provision cannot be the exclusive means of state involvement in the clean-up of a site subject to both RCRA and CERCLA authority.

Contrary to the United States' claim, permitting state involvement in hazardous waste clean-up outside of CERCLA's ARAR's process, based on independent state authority, does not render the ARAR's process irrelevant. When a state does not have independent authority over the clean-up of a particular hazardous waste site, the ARAR's provision insures that states have a meaningful voice in clean-up. However, when, as here, a state has RCRA authority over a hazardous waste site, §§ 9614(a) and 9652(d) expressly preserve the state's exercise of such authority regardless of whether a CERCLA response action is underway.

NOTES

1. *Fernald.* Historically, the State of Ohio played a more aggressive role than EPA in pursuing clean-up at Fernald. After assuming responsibility for RCRA enforcement, Ohio Environmental Protection Agency (OEPA) inspectors visited Fernald and discovered numerous violations of Ohio's hazardous waste laws. Eventually, OEPA was forced to file suit against DOE and NLO under RCRA and the Clean Water Act (which the state also enforces). The resulting 1988 Consent Decree and its 1993 amendment have become the basis for the state's involvement at Fernald. The civil penalties in the Decree were ultimately appealed to the Supreme Court, which held in 1992 that penalties for past conduct were not available, but that injunctive relief was available. *Ohio v. U.S. Dep't of Energy, supra.*

OEPA currently takes primary responsibility for the handling, storage, and disposal of hazardous waste on site. Since Fernald has a huge inventory of such wastes from past production and from clean-up operations, this is a key role and makes the state integral to the regulation of the site. Thus, while Ohio is not technically a party to the DOE-EPA Consent Agreement under CERCLA, it was heavily involved in the negotiations leading up to it and in CERCLA decisionmaking generally. OEPA has been able to develop a productive *modus vivendi* with EPA and DOE for participation in decisionmaking at Fernald. But what happens when the federal-state relationship is strained, as at the Rocky Mountain Arsenal? According to the Tenth Circuit, what powers does the state have to impose its will on the federal facility?

In the 1988 Fernald Consent Decree, the State of Ohio expressly reserved its RCRA rights, which DOE disputed, to be involved in the CERCLA decisionmaking process *beyond* the specific provisions of CERCLA sections 120 and 121. Does *Colorado* increase Ohio's leverage with EPA and DOE?

2. *State regulation or self-regulation.* Why did DOD fight Colorado tooth and nail? Are there both good and bad reasons? Consider the following:

> Waiver of sovereign immunity *vis à vis* the states is, like abandoning the unitary executive doctrine, problematic, though it too may be the right thing to do. Such waivers would naturally be (and currently are) subject to a requirement of uniform treatment, that is, states must treat federal facilities and activities no more strictly than non-governmental ones. The problem is that, while most federal facilities are cognate to private facilities (for example, housing, fleets of ordinary vehicles, water treatment plants, conventional factories), many are not, and the latter group includes some of the worst environmental problems. Excess plutonium, reprocessing wastes, nerve gas, and unexploded ordnance are, one hopes, unique to defense activities. How is the principle of uniformity to be maintained in such cases?
>
> [For example, the] state standards for the chemical diisopropyl methylphosphonate (DIMP) at Rocky Mountain Arsenal and the ban on the transportation of nuclear materials in quantity through New York City were both facially nondiscriminatory, but in fact they applied only or mainly to a federal defense facility. DIMP is a chemical unique to Rocky Mountain Arsenal, and the ban on transportation of spent nuclear fuel through New York City really only affected DOE's Brookhaven National Laboratories. DOD and DOE could be justifiably concerned that such state rules reflect an effort impose its own version of appropriate national policy, to foist unpopular defense activities onto other states—it is probably not coincidental that the alternative route for spent fuel from Brookhaven involved barging to neighboring Connecticut—or simply a convenient way to be "tough on polluters" without local repercussions. In any event, the defense agencies are entitled to some assurance that military activities will not be governed by idiosyncratic state regulation. * * *

Applegate, *Half-Full Glass, supra*, at 378-79. How should states' interest in environmental protection be balanced against the federal interest in uniform and reasonable standards? How should a statutory balancing be structured? What criteria should be applied to state regulation?

The Tenth Circuit subsequently held that DOE's Los Alamos National Laboratory was subject to state RCRA requirements, including limits on radioactive emissions. *U.S. v. New Mexico*, 32 F.3d 494 (10th Cir. 1994). On the other hand, DOE is not only self-regulated under the AEA, but it also has the option to *decline* to regulate. Thus, one of the most compelling arguments for state regulation is that under the Atomic Energy Act much of DOE's activity is self-regulating in both senses. *See* Michael W. Grainey & Dirk A. Dunning, *Federal Sovereign Immunity: How Self-Regulation Became No Regulation at Hanford and Other Nuclear Weapons Facilities*, 31 GONZAGA L. REV. 83 (1995/96).

3. *The unitary executive revisited.* Elsewhere in the *Colorado* opinion, the court expressed concern that the Department of Justice represented both EPA and DOD in the litigation. What potential conflicts exist between those parties? While the existence of a unitary executive undoubtedly avoids the ethical problem of a Justice Department lawyer representing both parties (*see* ABA Model Code of Professional Responsibility, DR 5-105, EC 5-14 -5-17; ABA Model Rules of Professional Conduct, Rule 1.7), is such representation good policy? Does it make a difference that state and local governments are involved in the decisionmaking? That the general public is not?

How does *Colorado* affect EPA's role in regulating federal facilities? *See* Alana Bissonnette, *Note, Clean Up Your Federal Mess in My State: Colorado has a State RCRA-Voice at the Rocky Mountain Arsenal*, 71 DEN. U.L. REV. 257 (1993)(characterizing EPA as "crippled" by the decision).

4. *The Hanford Tri-Party Agreement.* As *Colorado* illustrates, the relationship between state and federal authorities can be stormy. By contrast, Washington State and federal authorities at Hanford entered into a Hanford Federal Facility Agreement and Consent Order (known as the Tri-Party Agreement) that not only creates an enforceable framework of schedules for compliance with state and federal law, but also establishes a lasting organization that allocates regulatory responsibility and permits change over time through cooperation and negotiation. *Heart of America Northwest v. Westinghouse Hanford Co.*, 820 F. Supp. 1265 (E.D. Wash. 1993) (Tri-Party Agreement supersedes CWA and RCRA claims due to § 113(h) preclusion). One consequence of the Tri-Party Agreement framework was that all interested parties were able to reach consensus on a future use plan for the site. *See* Hanford Future Uses Working Group, The Future for Hanford: Uses and Clean-up (Final Report, Dec. 1992).

4. Private Actions

Individuals can challenge federal environmental actions or decisions in three very different ways. They can use the citizen suit provisions of applicable environmental statutes to challenge regulatory decisions; they can use the Federal Tort Claims Act to recover for injuries to themselves; and they can sue government contractors for violation of the applicable statutes. Since they are designed for this purpose, the citizen suit provisions have seen the most activity, and they have been a major source of the developing law of federal facilities remediation.

a. Citizen Suits

While EPA may be barred by the unitary executive doctrine from acting directly against other agencies, violations of its regulations can in some circumstances be enforced by individual citizens as to whom the representational conflicts do not apply. *See, e.g.*, 42 U.S.C. § 6972 (a)(1)(A) (RCRA). Citizen suits have substantial procedural limitations, *see, e.g. Gwaltney of Smithfield, Ltd. v. Chesapeake Bay Foundation, Inc.*, 484 U.S. 49 (1987) (holding that the Clean Water Act citizen suit provision applied only to ongoing, not past, violations),[32] so they are not equivalent to EPA action. Nevertheless, their potential for federal facilities is illustrated in the *LEAF* case, which is generally thought to have initiated the DOE environmental remediation program. *LEAF* is followed by a very recent CERCLA case which, if followed, could signal a new era in federal facilities clean-up efforts.

LEGAL ENVIRONMENTAL ASSISTANCE FOUNDATION, INC. [LEAF] v. HODEL

586 F. Supp. 1163 (E.D. Tenn. 1984)

ROBERT L. TAYLOR, Chief Judge.

Plaintiffs allege that defendants are in violation of the Resource Conservation and Recovery Act, 42 U.S.C. §§ 6901-6987, and the Clean Water Act, 33 U.S.C. §§ 1251-1376. Plaintiffs seek declaratory and injunctive relief plus the imposition of civil penalties. This case is now before the Court on cross motions for summary judgment.

Defendants are the United States Department of Energy and the Secretary of DOE. Defendants operate the Y-12 Plant in Oak Ridge, Tennessee, pursuant to the Atomic Energy Act [AEA]. 42 U.S.C. §§ 2011-2284. Plaintiffs, Legal Environmental Assistance Foundation and Natural Resources Defense Council, Inc., are non-profit corporations concerned with environmental protection. Several members of these organizations reside in the Oak Ridge, Tennessee, area and the organizations have standing to bring this suit. The State of Tennessee intervened as plaintiff to protect its interest in hazardous waste and water quality regulation.

The Y-12 Plant consists of approximately 260 buildings located on 600 acres. Y-12 is primarily engaged in the fabrication and assembly of nuclear weapons components. It is an essential and unique facility in this country's system of nuclear defense. Y-12 produces a large amount of hazardous wastes containing chromium, mercury, PCBs, cadmium and other pollutants.

---

[32] For a convenient summary of the current status of citizen suit law, *see* Glazer v. American Ecology Envtl. Serv. Corp., 894 F. Supp. 1029 (E.D. Tex. 1995).

Some of these wastes are leaked or discharged into ground water and the tributaries of the Clinch River.

The questions before the Court are: 1) Whether the Y-12 Plant is subject to the provisions of the RCRA, and 2) Whether defendants have violated the CWA by allowing unpermitted discharges of pollution at Y-12.

RESOURCE CONSERVATION AND RECOVERY ACT

One purpose of the RCRA is "to promote the protection of health and the environment . . . by . . . regulating the treatment, storage, transportation, and disposal of hazardous wastes which have adverse effects on health and the environment." 42 U.S.C. § 6902. The RCRA and its accompanying regulations establish a comprehensive program for the handling of hazardous wastes. This comprehensive program is applicable to federal facilities. 42 U.S.C. § 6961. Nothing in the RCRA, however, "shall be construed to apply to (or to authorize any State, interstate, or local authority to regulate) any activity or substance which is subject to the . . . Atomic Energy Act of 1954 except to the extent that such application (or regulation) is not inconsistent with the requirements of such [Act]." 42 U.S.C. § 6905(a).

Defendants oppose application of the RCRA to Y-12. They argue that application of the RCRA to Y-12 is inconsistent with the AEA for three reasons. First, the AEA precludes state regulation of activities of DOE, 42 U.S.C. § 2018, but the RCRA subjects federal facilities to state regulation. 42 U.S.C. § 6961. Second, the RCRA gives the United States Environmental Protection Agency, state and local authorities the authority to set standards for waste disposal, 42 U.S.C. § 6902, yet the AEA places that authority with DOE. 42 U.S.C. § 2201(i)(3). Third, the AEA restricts dissemination of restricted data pertaining to nuclear weapons and materials, 42 U.S.C. §§ 2014(y), 2274, 2277, but the RCRA would subject this information to public disclosure. 42 U.S.C. § 6927.

Section 271 of the AEA, 42 U.S.C. § 2018, provides that:

> Nothing in this chapter shall be construed to affect the authority or regulations of any Federal, State, or local agency with respect to the generation, sale, or transmission of electric power produced through the use of nuclear facilities licensed by the [Atomic Energy] Commission: Provided, That this section shall not be deemed to confer upon any Federal, State, or local agency any authority to regulate, control, or restrict any activities of the Commission.

The parties are in disagreement as to whether this section prohibits any state or local regulation of Y-12 or whether it merely prohibits state and local regulations of electricity. In any event, plaintiffs assert, and defendants do not deny, that Y-12 is currently subject to federal, state and local regulations under several other environmental statutes. *See, e.g.*, [NEPA, SDWA, CAA, CWA, TSCA]. Admittedly, none of these other environmental laws contain a provision limiting its application to consistency with the AEA. The fact that Y-12 is subject to other state and local environmental regulations, however, precludes the argument that state and local environmental regulation of Y-12 is inconsistent with the AEA.

"Federal installations are subject to state regulations only when and to the extent that congressional authorization is clear and unambiguous." Environmental Protection Agency v. California ex rel. State Water Resources Control, 426 U.S. 200, 211 (1976). On the other hand, a court must give full effect to a statute unless it is in "irreconcilable conflict" with another statute. "[W]hen two statutes are capable of co-existence, it is the duty of the courts . . . to regard each as effective." [Radzanower v. Touche Ross & Co., 426 U.S. 148, 155 (1976).] The RCRA and the AEA are certainly not in irreconcilable conflict. Congress must have intended that the RCRA be at least partially applicable to facilities operated pursuant to the AEA. Otherwise 42 U.S.C. § 6905(a) would have simply excluded application of the RCRA to AEA federal facilities. Although defendants have taken the position that Y-12 is totally excluded from RCRA regulations, § 6905(a) precludes RCRA application only to the extent it is inconsistent with the AEA. Defendants' position would render § 6905(a) a nullity.

The RCRA provides a comprehensive program for the handling of most hazardous wastes, but expressly excludes regulation of nuclear wastes. 42 U.S.C. § 6903(27). The AEA regulates nuclear material, regardless of whether it is considered waste. 42 U.S.C. § 2014(e), (z), (aa). The Court concludes that the most reasonable reconciliation of the RCRA and the AEA is that AEA facilities are subject to the RCRA except as to those wastes which are expressly regulated by the AEA: nuclear and radioactive materials. Although it could be said this interpretation renders § 6905(a) redundant with § 6903(27), the Court believes that these two sections support one another and firmly evince Congressional intent as to the application of the RCRA.

Section 161 of the AEA, 42 U.S.C. § 2201, provides that:

In the performance of its functions the [Atomic Energy] Commission is authorized to— . . . .

> (i) prescribe such regulations or orders as it may deem necessary
> . . . .
>
> (3) to govern any activity authorized pursuant to this chapter, including standards and restrictions governing the design, location, and operation of facilities used in the conduct of such activity, in order to protect health and to minimize danger to life or property.

It does not appear that 42 U.S.C. § 2201(i)(3) vests DOE with exclusive authority to regulate health and safety standards in the operation of Y-12. Accordingly, the RCRA is not inconsistent with the AEA in this respect. *Cf. Blaber v. United States*, 212 F.Supp. 95 (E.D.N.Y.1962), *aff'd*, 332 F.2d 629 (2nd Cir.1964) (DOE's authority to prescribe health and safety regulations is discretionary, not mandatory).

If application of the RCRA to Y-12 would require disclosure of restricted nuclear material data protected by 42 U.S.C. §§ 2014(y), 2274, 2277, this would be inconsistent with the AEA. The burden is upon defendants, however, to show that such an inconsistency would result. Nothing the Court says today should be construed to require disclosure of restricted nuclear material data, however, defendants have not shown that application of the RCRA to Y-12 would result in such disclosures. Defendants' conclusory statement that such disclosures would be required is unsupported. The Court can no more assume that the RCRA would require defendants to disclose restricted nuclear material data than it could assume that the RCRA would require private business to disclose trade secrets. If security of nuclear material data would conflict with the RCRA, defendants should apply for a Presidential exemption from the RCRA for Y-12. 42 U.S.C. § 6961. Apparently, defendants have not sought a Presidential exemption. Where DOE has not applied for a Presidential exemption, national security considerations should not be considered by the Court. *See United States v. Puerto Rico*, 721 F.2d 832, 835 n. 4 (1st Cir.1983) (interpreting the Clean Water Act, which has a similar Presidential exemption. 33 U.S.C. § 1333(a)).

The Court concludes that application of the RCRA to Y-12 will not be inconsistent with the AEA. The restriction upon the RCRA found in 42 U.S.C. § 6961 merely clarifies the Congressional intent to exclude nuclear wastes from coverage by the RCRA. The AEA still provides exclusive regulation of nuclear wastes. Defendants acknowledge that they have neither an EPA permit, 42 U.S.C. § 6925, nor a state permit, 42 U.S.C. § 6926, for the treatment, storage or disposal of hazardous waste. Accordingly, summary judgment for plaintiffs is appropriate for their claim under the RCRA.

CLEAN WATER ACT

The goal of the CWA is to eliminate the discharge of pollutants into navigable waters. 33 U.S.C. § 1251. Except as permitted under certain exceptions, "the discharge of any pollutant by any person shall be unlawful." 33 U.S.C. § 1311(a). One exception is granted for discharges allowed by a National Pollutant Discharge Elimination System [NPDES] permit issued pursuant to 33 U.S.C. § 1342. The "discharge of a pollutant" is defined as "any addition of any pollutant to navigable waters from any point source." 33 U.S.C. § 1362(12). "The term 'point source' means any discernible, confined and discrete conveyance, including but not limited to any pipe, ditch, channel, tunnel, conduit, well, discrete fissure, container, rolling stock, concentrated animal feeding operation, or vessel or other floating craft, from which pollutants are or may be discharged." 33 U.S.C. § 1362(14). Every identifiable point that emits pollution is a point source which must be authorized by a NPDES permit. *United States v. Earth Sciences, Inc.*, 599 F.2d 368 (10th Cir.1979); 40 C.F.R. § 122.1(b)(1).

The EPA issued a NPDES permit for Y-12 in 1974 which was to expire on February 15, 1980. Since DOE made application for a renewal of this permit more than 180 days before it was to expire, the 1974 permit is still in effect. 40 C.F.R. § 122.10(b)(2) (1979) (recodified at 40 C.F.R. § 122.21(d)(2) (1983)). This permit authorizes discharges at four points: Kerr Hollow Quarry, Rogers Quarry, New Hope Pond and Bear Creek. The parties acknowledge that at one time it was EPA policy to designate the facility boundary as the point of discharge, but that this is no longer consistent with the requirements of the CWA. Apparently the 1974 permit conforms with EPA's prior policy.

Plaintiffs claim that defendants are violating the CWA because they do not have a NPDES permit covering Y-12 discharges at four other locations: the Oil Landfarm, the S-3 ponds, the Burial Ground Oil Pond and over 200 discharge pipes into Upper East Fork Poplar Creek. It seems clear to the Court, and defendants have offered no evidence to the contrary, that these four locations are point sources that are discharging pollutants into navigable waters. Since this lawsuit was filed, DOE has submitted NPDES permit applications for many of these point sources.

DOE argues that because it has a NPDES permit for Y-12, any discharge of pollution from Y-12 is not in violation of the CWA. DOE says that judicial review of the permit may only be by the appropriate Court of Appeals within ninety days after the permit was issued. 33 U.S.C. § 1369(b)(1). Plaintiffs, on the other hand, claim that they are not challenging the issuance of the 1974 permit. They construe this case as a complaint against the unlawful discharge of pollutants without a permit, which may be challenged in a citizen's suit such as this. 33 U.S.C. § 1365. The Court is inclined to agree with plaintiff's characterization of this suit. The 1974 permit does not purport to allow pollutant discharges at the Oil Landfarm, S-3 ponds, Burial Ground Oil Pond or Upper East Fork Poplar Creek. The permit allows pollutant discharges only in accordance with the limitations and conditions of the permit. Defendants have taken the position that a NPDES permit for one point source of pollution, allows many other point sources of pollution unless someone appeals the issuance of the permit. This position is inconsistent with the remedial purpose of the CWA and the requirement that any point source of pollutant discharge be authorized by permit. 40 C.F.R. § 122.1(b)(1).

* * *

REMEDY

The Court concludes that defendants are in violation of the RCRA and the CWA. At this time, however, the Court will impose neither an injunction nor civil penalties upon defendants for the following reasons:

1. The Y-12 Plant is a unique and essential element of this nation's system of nuclear defense. *See Weinberger v. Romero-Barcelo*, 456 U.S. 305, 310 (1983).

2. Defendants have already taken and have agreed to take steps that will reduce environmental harm caused by violations of the RCRA and the CWA.

FORT ORD TOXICS PROJECT, INC. V. CALIFORNIA EPA

189 F.3d 828 (9th Cir. 1999)

WIGGINS, Circuit Judge.

Plaintiffs, two nonprofit groups and two individuals, sued California and federal government agencies in an effort to force the agencies to comply with a provision of California environmental law prior to conducting a Comprehensive Environmental Response, Compensation, and Liability Act ("CERCLA") cleanup of the military installation at Fort Ord. The district court dismissed the suit, holding that CERCLA § 113(h), 42 U.S.C. § 9613(h), precludes jurisdiction. We reverse.

I.

In February 1990, Fort Ord was placed on the Environmental Protection Agency's ("EPA") National Priorities List, a list of sites that are given priority in cleanup. That summer, the Army, the EPA, the California Department of Toxic Substances Control ("DTSC"), and the California Regional Water Quality Control Board entered into an agreement setting forth the procedures for a CERCLA remedial cleanup of Fort Ord. As part of this cleanup, and with DTSC's approval, the Army placed contaminated soil in a landfill on the base. In response, plaintiffs filed this action in state court against DTSC, the California Environmental Protection Agency, and the Army. Plaintiffs' complaint alleged that DTSC violated the California Environmental Quality Act ("CEQA") in failing to prepare an environmental impact statement prior to granting the Army the authority to deviate from the requirements of California's prohibition against land disposal of hazardous wastes. Plaintiffs requested a preliminary injunction against the Army's cleanup.

The Army removed the case to federal court. Plaintiffs moved to have the case remanded to the state court. The district court granted the motion with respect to the state defendants, but denied it with respect to the Army. The Army then moved to dismiss the lawsuit, invoking CERCLA § 113(h)'s jurisdictional bar. The district court granted the motion and dismissed the case. Plaintiffs timely appealed to this court. We review de novo the district court's dismissal for lack of subject matter jurisdiction.

II.

Plaintiffs argue that the district court erred in dismissing their lawsuit on the basis of § 113(h)'s jurisdictional provision. First, plaintiffs claim that § 113(h) postpones jurisdiction only for claims that challenge CERCLA cleanups on the basis of state law that is "applicable or relevant and appropriate" ("ARAR") to the CERCLA cleanup. There is no dispute that the basis for plaintiffs' claim, CEQA, is not ARAR. Therefore, plaintiffs argue that § 113(h) is inapplicable. [The court decisively rejected this argument.]

* * *

C. The Distinction between § 104 and § 120

Plaintiffs' final argument, like the preceding two, would lead to a rule that is intuitively unappealing. Plaintiffs argue that § 113(h) applies only to cleanups conducted under the authority of § 104, not cleanups, like that at Fort Ord, conducted under the authority of § 120. This argument is troubling because its acceptance would allow plaintiffs to sue to enjoin many cleanups on federal property even though plaintiffs could not sue to enjoin a similar cleanup on private property. But this argument, unlike plaintiffs' other claims, appears to be the most reasonable interpretation of the statutory language, and we reverse the district court on this basis.

CERCLA's jurisdictional bar only removes jurisdiction "to review any challenges to removal or remedial action selected under section 9604 of this title, or to review any order issued under section 9606(a) of this title . . . ." 42 U.S.C. § 9613(h). There is no dispute that the cleanup at Fort Ord was conducted pursuant to the provisions of § 120. Therefore, plaintiffs claim that § 113(h), which fails to mention actions selected under § 120, must not apply to the Fort Ord cleanup. The Army disagrees. In its view, § 120 and § 104 are not separate grants of authority; rather, § 104 is the overarching grant of authority to conduct cleanups on both private and federal property, and § 120 simply sets special standards for cleanups at federal facilities.

We have twice applied § 113(h)'s jurisdictional bar to cleanups at federal facilities. See [McClellan Ecological Seepage Situation (MESS) v. Perry, 47 F.3d 325, 325 (9th Cir. 1995)]; Hanford Downwinders Coalition, Inc. v. Dowdle, 71 F.3d 1469 (9th Cir.1995). But on neither occasion did we specifically address whether § 120 cleanups, by virtue of their independence from § 104 cleanups, fall outside of § 113(h)'s jurisdictional bar. Therefore, our decision here is not controlled by those earlier cases.

In fact, no circuit court has published a decision reaching this question. But the Army's claim that § 120 cleanups do not proceed under a separate grant of authority but, rather, are conducted under the broad authority of § 104 is supported by the decisions of those district courts that have reached this issue. See Werlein v. United States, 746 F.Supp. 887, 981-92 (D.Minn.1990); Heart of America Northwest v. Westinghouse Hanford Co., 820 F.Supp. 1265, 1278 (E.D.Wash.1993); Worldworks I v. U.S. Army, 22 F.Supp.2d 1204, 1207 (D.Colo.1998). In addition, it is seemingly supported by some legislative history. See P.L. 99-499 at 2877 ("This section requires the Administrator to select appropriate cost-effective remedial actions to be carried out under section 104 or secured under section 106.").

The problem is that the Army's position does not seem to be supported by the statutory text. First, § 120 does seem to create a grant of authority separate from §§ 104 and 106. "[N]o authority vested in the Administrator under this section may be transferred, by executive order of the President or otherwise, to any other officer or employee of the United States or to any other person." 42 U.S.C. § 9620(g). Other CERCLA provisions also identify § 120 as a grant of authority separate from § 104. In fact, § 117, which was passed in the same bill as §§ 113 and 120, discusses § 120 cleanups as separate from § 104 cleanups. "Before adoption of any plan for remedial action to be undertaken by the President, by a State, or by any other person, under section 9604, 9606, 9620, or 9622 of this title, the President or State, as appropriate, shall take both of the following actions . . . ." 42 U.S.C. § 9617(a). Even other parts of § 113 seem to imply that some remedial actions are conducted pursuant to § 104 while others are conducted pursuant to § 120. *See* 42 U.S.C. § 9613(g) (". . . if the President is diligently proceeding with a remedial investigation and feasibility study under section 104(b) or section 120 [42 U.S.C.S. § 9604(b) or § 9620] (relating to Federal facilities).").

If § 120 creates a grant of authority separate from § 104, then the plain language of § 113(h) would exempt § 120 cleanups from its jurisdictional bar. Determining which provision governs a particular cleanup requires a close look at the different types of CERCLA cleanups and at the specific grants of authority in § 120. CERCLA distinguishes between two types of cleanups: removal actions and remedial actions. *See* 42 U.S.C. § 9601(23) and (24). In short, removal actions are temporary measures taken to protect against the threat of an immediate release of hazardous substances into the environment, whereas remedial actions are intended as permanent solutions. Under § 120(e)(2), the Administrator of the EPA is granted authority to conduct remedial actions on federal property. See 42 U.S.C. § 9620(e)(2). There is no analogous authority under § 120 for the commencement of removal actions. Thus, removal actions on federal property must fall under the general provisions of § 104. See 42 U.S.C. § 9604(a).

The text of § 113(h), then, would preclude challenges to a CERCLA removal action on federal property, because such actions are conducted under § 104's grant of authority. But § 113(h) would not preclude challenges to a CERCLA remedial action, because such actions are conducted under § 120's grant of authority. Whether the legislators who voted for § 113(h) subjectively intended this distinction is unclear to us. One commentator has argued that there are powerful reasons why Congress did intend such a distinction. *See* Ingrid Brunk Wuerth, *Challenges to Federal Facility Cleanups and CERCLA Section 113(h)*, 8 TUL. ENVTL. L.J. 353, 370 (1995) (noting that "[t]he delay in reviewing challenges to remedial actions is less serious since immediate action is authorized under section 104"). It is also unclear whether the legislators who voted for § 113(h) subjectively intended to allow immediate challenges to remedial actions at federal facilities even while disallowing such challenges at private facilities. Some commentators have argued that this policy choice makes sense as well. But we are not concerned with the wisdom of Congress' policy choice, and we lack the luxury to entertain the subjective intentions of various legislators. Our job is to effectuate Congressional intent as expressed in the statutory text. Thus, despite any misgivings we may have, we adopt this distinction between removal and remedial actions at federal facilities because the statutory language seems to require it.

It is undisputed that the present cleanup at Fort Ord is a remedial action conducted pursuant to § 120. As a result, § 113(h) is inapplicable.

NOTES

1. *Intrabranch disputes.* Why is *LEAF* an important case for the regulation of federal facilities? What principles does it establish? EPA, you will notice, was not a party to the litigation—what does that tell us about the difficulties of applying federal law to federal facilities?

2. *Injunctive relief.* If the purpose of court action against a federal facility is an injunction, the penalty problem is lessened (though not entirely eliminated, since compliance with injunctions costs money). But, as *LEAF* itself suggests, injunctive relief against defense facilities is not easily obtained. The defense establishment is not exempt from any of the major environmental laws, and DOE clearly violated both RCRA and the Clean Water Act. Even though DOE made no effort to obtain the available national security waivers under either statute, the court refused to enjoin further discharges based on the representation that the Y-12 plant was unique and its operation militarily necessary. Stephen Dycus argues that this problem is systemic and that the federal courts have allowed defense agencies to behave *as though* they were exempt from environmental laws by giving extreme deference to claims of defense necessity. DYCUS, *supra*, at 16-19, 43, 60, 72, 154-58.

On the other hand, some deference to the demands of national security is surely applicable. How should the courts draw the line between appropriate and excessive deference? What would a less deferential approach in *LEAF* have looked like? What are the hard questions that the court might have asked DOE?

3. *Reviewing clean-up decisions.* As you know and the *Fort Ord* case emphasizes, judicial review of CERCLA remedy selection is strictly limited. What is at stake in the *Fort Ord* decision? What effect will the case have on the clean-up of federal facilities, if it is followed?

The *Fort Ord* holding creates two apparent inconsistencies. It treats federal and private facilities differently with respect to judicial review, and within federal facilities it treats removal and remedial actions differently. The court acknowledged the awkwardness of both inconsistencies, but found that they were inescapable under the language of CERCLA. Do you agree that the court's interpretation of CERCLA was inevitable? Is the result really awkward—are there good reasons to differentiate federal and private facilities, and removal and remedial actions, in this respect? Should Congress overturn the *Fort Ord* result?

4. *Standing.* If a private party or environmental organization wishes to proceed against a federal facility through a citizen suit provision of a federal environmental law, as opposed to a tort claim, standing is the threshold barrier that must be overcome. A party wishing to bring a citizen suit against a federal facility must meet three elements: (1) the plaintiff must suffer an

actual, non-hypothetical injury in fact; (2) there must be a causal connection between the injury and the conduct complained of (the injury has to be fairly traceable to the challenged action); and (3) it must be likely that the injury will be redressed by a favorable decision. *Lujan v. Defenders of Wildlife*, 504 U.S. 555 (1992); *Valley Forge Christian College v. Americans United for Separation of Church and State*, 454 U.S. 464, 472 (1982). The injury in fact requirement may be met by an allegation that the plaintiff's right to use areas around the federal facility may be adversely affected by exposure to toxic substances. Plaintiffs must be precise in identifying the exact locale of their usage of the affected area. *Lujan v. National Wildlife Federation*, 497 U.S. 871 (1990). The alleged injury should also be supported by concrete plans for the plaintiffs to revisit the area where they would suffer the impacts of the federal facility operation. *Lujan v. Defenders of Wildlife, supra,* 504 U.S. at 562-64; *Japan Whaling Ass'n v. American Cetacean Soc.,* 478 U.S. 221, 230 n. 4 (1986). The Supreme Court has recently upheld a plaintiff's standing in a citizen suit case, rejecting further restrictions on such litigation. *Friends of the Earth v. Laidlaw Environmental Services (TOC), Inc.,* ___ U.S. ___, 120 S.Ct. 693 (2000).

b. Federal Tort Claims Act

If an individual wishes to sue a federal facility in tort, the Federal Tort Claims Act (FTCA) waives the sovereign immunity of the federal government with regard to certain claims for personal injuries. 28 U.S.C. § 1346(b). Thus, damages may be recovered from the federal government for the negligent and wrongful conduct of governmental employees to the same extent a private person would be liable under state law. 28 U.S.C. §2674. However, the FTCA exempts the waiver from all claims that are "based upon the exercise or performance or the failure to exercise or perform a discretionary function or duty on the part of a federal agency or an employee of the Government, whether or not the discretion involved be abused." 28 U.S.C. § 2680(a). This "discretionary function" exception applies either when the act involves an element of judgment or choice (*i.e.*, there is no mandatory regulation, statute, or policy requiring a particular course of action), or when the discretion involved is of a kind that the discretionary function was designed to shield, that is, discretion based on considerations of public policy. It would not, for example, protect discretion exercisable by a government agent in safely driving an automobile.[33]

In tort claims against employees of federal facilities, discretionary function cases have fallen into three broad categories: challenges to alleged negligent design or construction of a facility, challenges to alleged negligent operation or clean-up of the facility, and challenges to alleged negligent failure to warn of a hazardous condition. If the plaintiffs fail to produce evidence showing violations of specific, mandatory directives, the courts

---

[33] United States v. Gaubert, 499 U.S. 315, 323-25 (1991); Berkovitz v. United States, 486 U.S. 531, 536 (1988).

have tended to assume that most decisions involving federal facilities are policy choices shielded from liability by the discretionary function exception. *Aragon v. United States*, 146 F.3d 820 (10th Cir. 1998)("as may be practicable" language in executive order gave rise to duty-created discretion in agency, which precluded FTCA claim). If the action is arguably based on policy considerations, then both a federal employee's own negligent acts and negligence in supervising (or failure to supervise) a contractor are included in decisions protected by the discretionary function exception.[34]

Discretionary function immunity may also be used by private contractor defendants. If a contractor can show that a government official approved the contractor's activities, and if this approval involved the permissible exercise of policy judgment, then a contractor's behavior is not independent of the government, and the actions of both the contractor and the government would fall within the government's discretionary function immunity. *Boyle v. United Technology Corp.*, 487 U.S. 500, 512 (1988)(design of a helicopter door). This "government contractor defense" is unavailable when (1) the government exercises such pervasive control over the work done by the employees of an independent contractor as to transform those employees essentially into government employees for purposes of the FTCA, and (2) the government's control is *not* an exercise of policy judgment (triggering the discretionary function exception), but is pursuant to a federal statute, regulation, policy specifically prescribing a course of action for the employee to follow. In such cases the employees of the independent contractor may be liable under the waiver of immunity found in the FTCA.[35]

c. Government Contractor Liability

It is often suggested that one reason for the environmental degradation of many federal facilities was the nearly complete the delegation of operation and management responsibilities to a private contractors. This was certainly the *modus operandi* of the military-industrial complex. (The current lingo designates these facilities as government-owned, contractor-operated (GOCO) facilities.) Under the standard Management and Operation (M&O) contract, DOE essentially gave its checkbook to its contractors by paying the contractor on the basis of costs plus profit, and indemnifying it for all liabilities. Fernald, for example, was operated from 1951 to 1985 by National Lead Company of Ohio under an M&O contract. Even though NLO regularly employed about 2000 persons, less than 20 DOE employees were on site, and *none* between 1972 and 1985. Lack of supervision and total indemnification were only part of the problem, however. According to the brief that DOE filed in the class action by Fernald residents against NLO, DOE officials knew of and acquiesced in regular and deliberate violations of

---

[34] United States v. S.A. Epresa de Viacao Aerea Rio, 467 U.S. 797, 820 (1984).

[35] Logue v. United States, 412 U.S. 521, 527-28 (1993); Kirchmann v. United States, 8 F. 3d 1273, 1275 (8th Cir. 1993).

environmental laws, despite contractual language mandating compliance. *Crawford v. National Lead Co.*, 784 F. Supp. 439 (S.D. Ohio 1989). GOCO contractors, as a result, had little or no incentive to run environmentally responsible establishments.

The legal situation is changing in three ways. First, the district court in the *Crawford* case firmly rejected NLO's assertion of the government contractor defense.

> Plaintiffs argue that defendants cannot satisfy the threshold requirements [in *Boyle v. United Technologies Corp.*, 487 U.S. 500 (1988) (recognizing the government contractor defense)] for displacement of state [tort] law. Although conceding that operation of [Fernald] involves a uniquely federal interest, that of national defense, plaintiffs contend that there is no significant conflict between federal and state laws or interests. Specifically, they claim that defendants' actions giving rise to the state law tort claims also violated applicable environmental laws, and therefore that "significant conflict between federal interest and state law," required for displacement of state law under *Boyle*, does not exist. Defendants agree that if plaintiff's prove that actions undertaken by defendants which are relevant to plaintiffs' claims also violated applicable environmental laws, the government contractor defense would not apply to shield defendants from tort liability for those actions. We agree with the parties' analysis,[36] and therefore consider the laws pertinent to defendants' operation of [Fernald].
>
> * * *
>
> Because defendants violated pertinent environmental laws [*i.e.,* the Refuse Act of 1899 and regulations of the Atomic Energy Commission and USEPA] by discharging radioactive material into the environment surrounding [Fernald], there is no conflict between state tort law and the federal interests at issue here. Therefore, the government contractor defense does not apply . * * *[37]

Crawford, 784 F.Supp. at 445-47. The subsequent summary jury trial awarded $136 million to the plaintiffs, and the case settled for $78 million.

Some commentators have suggested that, nevertheless, contractors should rely on their relationship to the government as a defense:

---

[36] The Supreme Court defined the parameters of the "significant conflict" requirement by reference to the discretionary function exemption to the Federal Tort Claims Act (FTCA), 28 U.S.C. § 2680(a). Thus, for the government contractor defense to apply, the court must find that the discretionary function exemption to the FTCA would bar any liability on the part of the United States. We agree that the operation of the Fernald plant required an exercise of government discretion in balancing safety concerns against security considerations. However, there is no discretion to violate specific environmental standards, Berkovitz v. United States, 486 U.S. 531 (1988), and if such violations occurred, the defense does not apply.

[37] If the *Boyle* threshold requirements were met, the contractor defense could be defeated on grounds that NLO/NLI did not conform to government approved specificiations for operation of the FMPC.

[Despite *Crawford*,] government contractors can and should use their relationships with the government as a defense in environmental enforcement litigation. They can argue that they must comply with contract specifications that cause the alleged violations; that they are compelled to continue their performance of the contracts because of the Defense Production Act of 1950, 50 U.S.C. app. § 2061-2169 (1982 & Supp. III 1985); that they lack the *authority* to comply with environmental standards without express permission from the government; and that they cannot expend their own funds to bring federal facilities into compliance because this would violate the Anti-Deficiency Act, 31 U.S.C. §§ 1341-42 (1982).

These arguments also may be used by GOCO contractors to bring the government-agency owner into litigation and shift any liability to the United States. In fact, a GOCO contractor recently was successful in doing so. In 1987, the Department of Justice (DOJ) brought suit on behalf of EPA against a contractor for alleged Clean Air Act violations at a GOCO facility. Throughout the action, in which it asserted a counterclaim, the contractor argued that the Air Force, as the owner of the facility, was the liable party for any Clean Air Act violations and that the Air Force was financially responsible for any corrective action as well as any fines and penalties.

After various rulings by the court finding that the United States could sue the contractor, that the contractor was the operator of the facility, that violations of the Clean Air Act occurred at the facility, and that the court had jurisdiction over the contractor's counterclaim, the parties settled the case on the eve of trial. The settlement agreement recognized what the contractor had been arguing throughout the case: ultimate legal and financial responsibility for environmental compliance at a government-owned facility rests with the government. The agreement requires the contractor to pay a fine, but also states that the fine is set off by the government's liability to the contractor under the contractor's counterclaim. Thus, while the contractor could not avoid the suit, the company succeeded in placing the financial and legal responsibility for compliance on the government.

Herbert Fenster *et al., Operating a Federal Facility to Avoid Environmental Law Liabilities*, 6 NAT. RESOURCES & ENV'T 24, 25-26 (Summer 1991).

Second, federal agencies are also developing contracts that share liability between government and contractor. Using private contracting models, these new arrangements recognize the central role of environmental compliance and seek to create incentives for high-quality performance in this area, as well.

Third, EPA is in the process of instituting a policy of pursuing GOCO facility contractors independently of DOE or DOD. If a contractor is in fact operating a facility, then it should be named on the permit for air, water, waste, and clean-up—and should be responsible for violations. EPA's policy is flexible and will impose penalties based on degree of responsibility, fault, cooperation, and the other usual criteria.[38] For EPA, the great advantage of suing the contractor is avoidance of the unitary executive problem.

Query: Should DOE indemnify its contractors? If not, will it be able to retain defense contractors? Is contractor indemnification consistent with the policies of CERCLA on liability and indemnification?

B. Public Participation at Federal Facilities

Federal facilities are public facilities, so their remediation is a matter of special public concern. Moreover, the public is on both sides of the equation, benefiting from clean-up and footing the bill. Federal facilities therefore offer an opportunity to examine the techniques for involving the public in environmental (in particular, clean-up) decisions, and to ask how much public participation is appropriate.

1. Models of Public Participation

How does the government involve the public in environmental decisions? Are existing opportunities to comment on governmental proposals and to seek judicial review sufficient? And who is "the public," anyway? These threshold questions are addressed in the following excerpt.

BEYOND THE USUAL SUSPECTS: THE USE OF CITIZENS ADVISORY BOARDS IN ENVIRONMENTAL DECISIONMAKING

John S. Applegate
73 IND. L.J. 903, 906-26 (1998)

I. Changing Paradigms for Public Participation
* * *

A. Basic Review-and-Comment

The most common mode of public participation in administrative decisionmaking includes, in outline, three steps.

- First, the agency develops a proposal internally. This is typically the most lengthy part of the process, during which the agency seeks to reach a firm understanding of the issues and settle on a basic approach. There is often much back-and-forth within the agency and among agencies, including the Office of Management and Budget. This phase may also involve, on an ad hoc basis, consultation with

---

[38] *GOCO Enforcement Policy Guidance Issued; Greater Responsibility Seen for Contractors,* 23 ENVT. REP. 1692 (1994).

the organized interests with whom the agency has an ongoing relationship. Occasionally, broader input is solicited through an advance notice of a proposed action in the Federal Register. It is otherwise a closed process. These discussions are not typically designed to achieve broad agreement outside the agency.

- Second, the full proposal is presented to the general public and comments of all kinds and from all quarters are solicited. The agency sometimes identifies particularly difficult issues and sometimes not, but there are no limitations on the subject, form, or source of comments.

- Third, the agency revises the proposal in light of the comments, if it is so inclined, and publishes the final version.

This procedure is required by the Administrative Procedure Act (APA) for informal rulemaking, where it has the name "notice-and-comment rulemaking."[39] The term "review-and-comment," taken from a recent National Research Council report, encompasses the similar way that many adjudicatory decisions are managed. Some form of review-and-comment is in fact used in virtually all proceedings that include public participation but do not require trial-like procedures, ranging from the preparation of environmental impact statements to forest management plans to Superfund remedy selection.

The review-and-comment paradigm is clearly capable of providing a quantitatively high degree of public participation in governmental decisions, and it is certainly flexible enough to permit a free-flowing dialogue among citizens and government. Nevertheless, in practice the three steps often amount to "decide, announce, and defend." That is, the agency makes its decision internally, announces it to the public only nominally as a proposal, and then defends its proposal against criticism rather than seriously reexamining it in light of comments. * * *

B. Enhanced Review-and-Comment

Both the courts and Congress reacted to the limitations of review-and-comment by adding to the procedures required in particular situations. * * * In the initial phase of the *Vermont Yankee* litigation,[40] for example, the District of Columbia Circuit addressed the public interest interveners' argument that "the bare minima" of notice-and-comment rulemaking "denied them a meaningful opportunity to participate in the proceedings."

Many procedural devices for creating a *genuine dialogue* on these issues were available to the agency-including informal conferences between interveners and staff, document discovery, interrogatories, technical advisory committees comprised of outside experts with differing perspectives, limited cross-examination, funding independent research by interveners, detailed annotation of

---

[39] 5 U.S.C. §553.
[40] Discussed in Chapter 4 (Judicial Role), *supra.*—EDS.

technical reports, surveys of existing literature, memoranda explaining methodology.[41]

The court did not mandate any particular procedures, but it made it clear that something more than notice-and-comment was required. The Supreme Court, however, reversed in a stinging rebuke that forbade courts from imposing additional procedures beyond those expressly required by Congress.

While *Vermont Yankee* effectively brought judicial development of hybrid procedures to a halt, it could not curtail congressional innovation. Even before the *Vermont Yankee* decision, Congress had begun to provide for procedures beyond the review-and-comment minimum. The Clean Air Act, for example, requires the establishment of a rulemaking docket, detailed information about the agency's factual and scientific basis and reasoning, oral presentation of views, response to public comments, and a host of other requirements-all nominally within the context of informal rulemaking. Whether the additional procedures improve dialogue between the agency and the public is open to question, however. While procedures like public hearings can be a good opportunity for many people to hear presentations, to express their views, and perhaps to engage in question-and-answer sessions, they cannot provide the forum for extensive development of information, a shared baseline of understanding, and the development of a consensus. There is probably an inverse relationship between the size of the hearing and its communicative effectiveness. Well-attended hearings often respond to highly controversial proposals, and "venting" and defensiveness are the order of the day. Smaller hearings, in which genuine dialogue can occur, tend to be routine meetings attended only by "regulars." The pedestrian needs of simply setting an agenda and presenting information within a compressed time give the agency enormous influence over the meeting, and limits those holding opposing views to relatively disorganized presentations.

* * *

C. Regulatory Negotiation

The limitations of review-and-comment spurred the development of regulatory negotiation as an alternative framework that would circumvent procedural rigidity and permit a genuine dialogue among regulators, the regulated, and other interested parties. * * *

Proponents of negotiated rulemaking make a number of claims for it, the primary one being efficiency: it is a way to speed the slow pace of current rulemaking, encrusted as it is with hybrid procedures and the millstone of judicial review. * * *

Better results are also claimed. Procedurally, the negotiation forum is conducive to cooperative, problem-solving behaviors instead of position taking. This environment can also stimulate creative solutions that would not be thought of otherwise or which one side would be reluctant to present

---

[41] Natural Resources Defense Council, Inc. v. U.S. Nuclear Regulatory Comm'n, 547 F.2d 633, 653 (D.C. Cir. 1976)(emphasis added), *rev'd sub nom.* Vermont Yankee [Nuclear Power Corp. v. Natural Resources Defense Council, Inc., 435 U.S. 519 (1978)].

alone. Substantively, dialogue allows the negotiators and agency jointly to identify all of the issues that need to be addressed. The decisions, when made, can be better informed because the parties holding the information are at the table and are available to answer questions. The resulting decision is thus better grounded in reality: it is feasible to comply with it and measure compliance, and truly unnecessary requirements can be jettisoned.

Finally, proponents expect negotiated decisions to meet with better acceptance, not only as measured by the absence of judicial challenge, but also by voluntary compliance and political support. A negotiation can provide the opportunity to understand and accept the trade-offs that must be made between goals. * * *

* * *

As many commentators have emphasized, [however, negotiating] groups are not necessarily representative of, nor are they accountable to, the public generally or to the general public good. Grass-roots, local, or diffuse interests are difficult to identify in the first place, to limit in number, and to engage at a technically sophisticated level. These are also the groups who are disadvantaged by a lack of resources. While this is a weakness in national negotiations, it is fatal to use at a local level where the affected interests are typically unorganized, poorly resourced, and technically unsophisticated. "Negotiation * * * is participation for elites, for people whose job it is to represent interests that have a stake in the outcome of the process." * * *

* * *

Even more fundamentally, a successfully negotiated solution does not necessarily constitute a consensus on what constitutes the public good. * * * Critics of regulatory negotiation see it as little more than horse trading, log rolling, or any of the other metaphors for dickering among negotiators. * * * Under these circumstances, the agency's claim that it is acting in accordance with the general public good, memorialized in its explanation of the decision, is unreliable, * * *. In this sense, in fact, it is a secret or opaque process, since the true reasons for the results reached may never be acknowledged.

Worse, negotiated solutions can really only be counted on to help the participants in the negotiation, the agency having in effect been captured by the negotiating group. * * *

* * *

D. Citizens Advisory Boards

As a generic description, a citizens advisory board is selected by a sponsoring agency (or other entity whose actions are at issue) from among citizens who are interested in or are in some way affected by the agency. The appropriate constituency is most easily defined in decisions with a strongly local or regional impact, and citizens advisory boards are most obviously suited to such controversies. The subject matter is limited to a particular activity or decision, designated at the outset, the outcome of which has not yet been determined. The members must be willing to approach the issues with an open (but not empty) mind. The process is deliberative, meaning that the essential activities are learning about the issues, candidly discussing reasons for and against various alternative solutions, and striving to reach a consensus resolution. This in turn requires active facilitation of the effort, not only in the sense of moderating discussion, but also in developing and presenting relevant information. Ideally, the discussions result in a consensus recommendation to the sponsoring agency. However, even if consensus cannot be reached, a successful citizens advisory board can narrow areas of disagreement, help affected parties recognize others' concerns and their bona fides, bring forward alternatives that had not previously been considered, and (if nothing else) elucidate the issues that remain to be resolved.

* * * The foregoing sketch simply highlights the relationship of the citizens advisory board to its predecessors' limitations: inclusiveness, openness, procedural fairness, and dialogue. Citizens advisory boards can provide the breadth of input that characterizes review-and-comment. Like negotiation, a citizens advisory board consists of a defined and relatively small group, so breadth must be achieved qualitatively in selecting members. Membership is not characterized by representation of an organized group, but by the more generalized idea of an identifiable interest that contributes to achieving a broad range of potentially affected interests.

Unlike the negotiation model, the hallmark of a citizens advisory board is its transparency. All aspects of its operations and decisions must be open to inspection and understood by those not involved directly in the process. In addition, a deliberative process is well suited to issues that implicate conflicting values. It is a truism of regulatory negotiation that it should not be used for disagreements that involve values and principles, as opposed to exchangeable commodities (like money). This, however, severely limits its utility in almost every area of public debate, especially environmental issues. Thus a process that is capable of discussing values is an important addition to agencies' procedural options.

* * *

Since an advisory board is not an extended exchange among sophisticated players, as in negotiated decisionmaking, the participants must be "brought up to speed" on the key issues. The central problem of negotiated decisionmaking is not the idea of consensus-based decisionmaking, but the conflict between broad representation and a knowledgeable membership. For all their other weaknesses in public participation, the 1986 Superfund amendments made an effort to resolve this tension by providing technical assistance to existing community groups to "level the playing field" between decisionmakers and the general public. However, the technical assistance grants program has not been very successful for a variety of reasons, including a daunting application process, restrictions on the amount and use of funds, and often hostile administrators. Thus it has not made any serious inroads into the rather bleak picture of Superfund public participation described above.

Finally, citizens advisory boards can provide the deliberative, influential participation of regulatory negotiation. Unlike review-and-comment, citizens are given the opportunity to understand the technical issues, which is the basis for making informed and confident evaluations of technical issues. Indeed, one basic goal of such boards is to create a forum for lay and technical people to work together with back-and-forth communication, instead of the usual didactic approach. Unlike review-and-comment or a hearing where the public can only listen and react, the process is not a one-time-only exchange, but rather an opportunity for the public to be involved in the decision. It is an opportunity to meet face-to-face with and personally persuade decision makers, which is not available under review-and-comment and that will be attractive to a wider range of stakeholders.

NOTES

1. *Input or participation.* What is the difference between public input and public participation? What does it mean to "participate" in a decision? What are the mechanisms that environmental law currently uses to obtain public input into decisions? Can you think of other techniques? What are their strengths and weaknesses?

2. *Breadth and depth.* Is there a trade-off between the scale of outreach to the public and the intensity of their participation, as is frequently the case when time or resources are limited?

Education may be one element of that balancing: few ordinary citizens have the background and resources to participate effectively in highly technical issues. To what extent does the government have an obligation to educate citizens on such issues? Do private facilities have this obligation? How should such educational efforts be accomplished?

2. The Fernald Experience

Among the unique attributes of the federal facilities clean-up problem is the high degree of secrecy that surrounded the operations and certainly the mishaps of the Nuclear Weapons Complex.[42] At Fernald, most residents either misunderstood the true nature of the site or thought it best not to know exactly. As the Cold War drew to a close and public understanding of the off-site effects grew, it has become increasingly important to involve the public actively in the clean-up process. The defense establishment had for so long been insulated from public and regulatory scrutiny that a high level of distrust had built up between the Complex facilities and federal and state regulators, as well as with the public at large. Moreover, CERCLA is not particularly generous in allowing public involvement in clean-up decisionmaking. *See* CERCLA § 117. The provisions for federal facilities clean-up, which are relatively lavish in soliciting the participation of state and local governments (*see* CERCLA §§ 120(f), (i), 121(d), (f), say nothing about the general public.

---

[42] *See generally Colloquium on the Implications of Secrecy in Environmental Law*, 2 N.Y.U. ENVTL. L.J. 187 (1993).

In an effort to address the situation, EPA established a Federal Facilities Environmental Restoration [FFER] Dialogue Committee in 1992. Composed of representatives of EPA, the major federal facility agencies, state regulators, tribal governments, local citizen groups, national environmental groups, organized labor, and others, the committee sought to identify the sources of mistrust in federal facility clean-up and to suggest some remedies. Its recommendations focused on citizen participation, information sharing, and priority setting.

In response to this concern for a greater role in the decision-making process, various statutory, regulatory, and other mechanisms have been established to help solicit input from affected stakeholders. Historically, however, these opportunities for citizen involvement have been inconsistent and have not necessarily provided for a meaningful dialogue between participants. Among the issues of greatest concern to these stakeholders are:

1) Affected stakeholders have not been substantively consulted in the early stages of decision-making. At sites where FFAs have been negotiated, for example, public comment has typically been solicited only after the signing agencies have agreed to circulate a draft agreement. The perception is that the public is consulted only after the key decisions have been negotiated by the agencies.

2) The laws governing the generation and disposal of wastes did not contemplate problems of the complexity and scale that exist at federal facilities. The public involvement mechanisms in these laws tend to focus on the specific proposal at issue, and do not allow consideration of how that proposal may relate to other proposed or existing activities.

3) Compounding the problem of late public involvement in decision-making is the lack of opportunity for meaningful dialogue in the formal comment and response process used in the regulatory decision-making process. Some perceive there is a strong tendency for this process to serve the needs of agencies to defend decisions rather than incorporate common or insightful concerns into decision-making. Likewise, it does not allow for an interactive and substantive exchange that promotes better understanding and consensus-building.

4) Finally, the burgeoning number of public involvement opportunities—including NEPA, those required by regulators in permitting, FFA processes, and other voluntary and required facility-sponsored events—is in many instances overwhelming and dissipates the public's ability and interest to participate effectively. There is a need to focus, coordinate, and streamline, where possible, the public

involvement process especially at larger sites involving literally dozens of permitted units.

The net result is that many stakeholders consider the current methods for soliciting input to be too late in the process, inefficient due to overlap with other efforts, and ineffective because the result is often a one-way communication instead of a two-way dialogue.

Federal Facilities Environmental Restoration Dialogue Committee, Interim Report 19-20 (1993). The committee recommended the establishment of site-specific advisory boards (SSABs), that is, citizen advisory boards, at major facilities.

EPA embraced the FFER committee report, and DOE announced plans to establish SSABs at its major sites. Fernald was the first to get an SSAB up and running. The members of the Fernald Citizens Task Force, as the SSAB was called, were selected by an independent convener who was hired by DOE to identify potential participants, to recommend a chair, and to provide a charter drafted in consultation with DOE, U.S. EPA, Ohio EPA, and local residents. The charter identified four issues for the Task Force to address: the appropriate future use of the site (*i.e.*, the post-remediation use), residual risk levels, waste disposition (on-site and/or off-site), and clean-up priorities. Together these amounted to a blueprint for the entire remediation project.

The seventeen original members of the Task Force included members of local and national environmental groups, neighbors of the site, township and county government officials, representatives of the major trade union councils at the site, local businesspeople, health professionals, and area educators. Some were chosen primarily for their connection with important constituencies (*e.g.*, environmental activists, labor, local government); others were selected for their experience or expertise on the relevant issues (engineers, health professionals). There was substantial diversity in education, income, occupation, and social background among the members; the common denominator was a connection to the site or area. The senior site officials of DOE, U.S. EPA, and Ohio EPA joined the Task Force as nonvoting members.

The Task Force began its work by establishing a general strategy for approaching the four issues in its mission and then hiring an independent technical consultant to assist in developing and presenting the information it needed. Consensus recommendations were issued in two parts: an interim report on future use and residual risk levels in November 1994, and a full report in July 1995. On all of the issues, the Task Force sought a principled middle ground that ensured protection of human health while recognizing technological and fiscal constraints. The Task Force recommended that only the most intensive future uses of the site (residential and agricultural) be prohibited; that residual risk levels should protect the aquifer from further contamination but also minimize surface disruption and waste generation; that the aquifer be cleaned; that the most dangerous waste be transported off site, while high-volume/low-risk material be deposited in an on-site facility;

and that an accelerated clean-up plan be adopted to reduce overhead costs quickly. DOE has estimated that the recommendations will save the taxpayers more than $2 billion over the lifetime of the project.

All of the recommendations were unanimous except waste disposition, as to which one member dissented from an on-site disposal facility. Another member, while not dissenting from the recommendations, believed that the residual risk estimates were unduly conservative. The decision whether to dispose of some of the waste in an on-site disposal facility was by far the most difficult facing the Task Force, for the reasons that all siting decisions are difficult. The following explains the group's reasoning:

RECOMMENDATIONS ON REMEDIATION LEVELS, WASTE DISPOSITION, PRIORITIES, AND FUTURE USE

Fernald Citizens Task Force
July 1995

The Fernald Citizens Task Force recommends the construction of an on-site disposal facility to accept, from the Fernald site only, materials solely with low levels of contamination meeting the site-specific waste acceptance criteria. However, on-site storage of low-level materials at Fernald is acceptable only in the context of the considerations laid out in the following section and under the following conditions, such considerations and conditions being inseparable from the recommendations:

The Fernald Citizens Task Force recommends the construction of an on-site disposal facility to accept, from the Fernald site only, materials solely with low levels of contamination meeting the site-specific waste acceptance criteria [to be determined by the State of Ohio under its RCRA and siting authorities]. However, on-site storage of low-level materials at Fernald is acceptable only in the context of the considerations laid out in the following section and under the following conditions, such considerations and conditions being inseparable from the recommendations:

- The Fernald Citizens Task Force strongly and unanimously opposes the use of the Fernald site for the permanent disposal or long-term storage of any waste or contaminated materials originating from other locations.
- Any on-site disposal facility will be built for long-term performance using the best design, technology, and engineering available.
- Any on-site disposal facility at Fernald will be designed to make the least possible negative aesthetic impact. The Fernald Citizens Task Force and the public at large shall be explicitly involved in the process for determining the ultimate appearance of the disposal facility.
- Any on-site disposal facility at Fernald will provide an adequate buffer area to minimize negative impacts to neighboring properties and the future use of the Fernald property. The Fernald Citizens

Task Force and the public at large shall be explicitly involved in the planning and design process for the disposal facility.

- The U.S. federal government will retain permanent ownership of any property containing the disposal facility.
- The U.S. federal government will continually monitor the disposal facility and report these findings in a timely manner to residents and interested parties.
- The U.S. federal government will commit to retrieve and treat or redispose of the materials contained in the disposal facility if a new, proven, and economically justified technology to manage these materials should become available.
- The U.S. federal government shall have in place adequate procedures to identify and correct any and all failures in performance of the disposal facility before any increased risk to public health occurs.
- The U.S. Department of Energy commits to the above conditions.
- The U.S. Department of Energy budget adjustments in the short or long term will not adversely impact the substance of this recommendation.

Waste disposition was the most difficult decision faced by the Fernald Citizens Task Force and the only one in which complete consensus could not be achieved. The Task Force spent a great deal of time collecting and evaluating data regarding the ramifications of on-site *vs.* off-site disposal. * * * [It] first became evident how many trucks or trains would be required to haul the millions of cubic yards of materials off-site. It was this realization, combined with the associated short-term risks of transportation, that most members found most compelling in recommending on-site disposal.

Another compelling reason was the desire to get the most hazardous materials off-site as soon as possible. A balanced approach in which DOE, EPA, and OEPA showed willingness to manage at least part of the waste on-site was seen as the most prudent in achieving this goal. It was strongly believed that exhibiting an unwillingness to deal with part of the problem at Fernald would result in political consequences with the states which are to receive Fernald waste, resulting in the inability to get any waste sent off-site. Additionally, most Task Force members were sensitive to the safety concerns of other citizens living along transportation routes and in the vicinity of the receiving facilities.

[Additional reasons included:] All Task Force members live or work in communities impacted by the decisions being made at Fernald, and 8 of 14 live or work in the direct vicinity of the site. No Task Force member wishes to see contaminated materials from Fernald or any other location stored on the Fernald property indefinitely. Because it adjoins residential and agricultural lands and is situated directly above a sole-source aquifer, Fernald is not an ideal location for disposal of contaminated materials.

Nevertheless, the Task Force is aware of the many engineering, political, and financial challenges facing a project the size of the Fernald remediation. The Task Force's primary goals are protecting human health and the Great Miami Aquifer. The Task Force believes that a balanced approach to remediation, in which the most hazardous materials are disposed off the Fernald property and the least hazardous materials are stored safely on the property, will result in prompt, enduring protection for the local communities. The Task Force ultimately arrived at this recommendation in consideration of the following issues, the understanding of which is critical to the entire recommendation:

- The sooner source materials are taken out of the environment, the better the aquifer is protected and the sooner it can be restored. The Fernald Citizens Task Force believes an on-site disposal facility is the quickest way to protect the aquifer and the overall environment.
- The hazard associated with the materials to be placed in the on-site disposal facility is very low. The maximum level of contamination to be allowed in the disposal facility would allow for a land use as a developed park under remediation levels recommended by the Task Force. The materials are to be contained in a disposal facility solely for the purpose of long-term protection of the aquifer. Failure of the disposal facility would not present any immediate or significant threat to human health.
- In the off-site option, the risk of transporting the expected 2.4 million cubic yards of low-level contaminated soil and debris from the Fernald site to Utah and/or Nevada includes a probability of six fatalities within the public along the transportation routes, while relatively little health and safety risk is incurred by the public under the on-site option. Both on-and off-site options require similar levels of work in excavating, loading, unloading, and disposing of materials; therefore, the risk to remediation workers in both options is roughly equivalent. The Fernald Citizens Task Force believes the on-site option is the most responsible with regard to overall safety.
- The cost of off-site disposal is three times that of on-site disposal. The Fernald Citizens Task Force believes that under current and foreseeable budget conditions, an off-site decision would greatly delay remediation and may prevent any progress. An on-site disposal facility is more viable under the current budget and political constraints.
- Both Utah and Nevada have written to Fernald, encouraging a balanced approach to remediation. The Fernald Citizens Task Force is concerned that if the decision were made to send all Fernald waste and contaminated materials off-site, Fernald would face the likelihood of reprisals from other states resulting in its inability to send any waste off-site. The Fernald Citizens Task Force believes it is of paramount importance for off-site shipment of the most hazardous materials to be the first priority of remediation, and it should be carried out expeditiously.

- Because the entire Fernald property is situated over a sole-source aquifer, only the lowest-level materials, as defined by the site-specific waste acceptance criteria, will be allowed into an on-site disposal facility. The waste acceptance criteria for Fernald were established by modeling the proposed disposal facility over a 1,000-year period to prevent any contamination at levels that would exceed the federal maximum levels of contamination for drinking water from reaching the aquifer. This modeling assumed only natural materials would be used in providing protection of the aquifer and excluded consideration of man-made liners that are subject to failure over the 1,000-year period.

- The Fernald Citizens Task Force wants to prevent any waste or contaminated materials from coming to Fernald from other sites for permanent disposal or long-term storage. Under the Federal Facilities Compliance Act of 1992, that potential exists. By managing the Fernald materials fairly and effectively, the Fernald Citizens Task Force believes Fernald will be in a more equitable position to prevent a decision to send outside wastes to Fernald.

NOTES

1. *Waste disposition.* Waste disposition—essentially a siting decision—is a very difficult issue for citizens and government, as Chapter 10 (Siting), *supra*, demonstrates. It is therefore notable that Fernald's neighbors were able to reach consensus on an on-site disposal facility. But at what cost? Does it permit too much residual risk? Does it demand too much in exchange for the on-site facility? Do you think that the decision was sound, based on your understanding of the Fernald site? Are the assurances that the Task Force demanded realistic?

The recommendations were formally accepted by DOE and its regulators after general public comment. Does the process for arriving at the decision and the general governmental acceptance it received make it the "right" decision?

2. *Stakeholders.* Membership is one of the most difficult organizational problems in establishing a CAB or SSAB. Who or what is a "stakeholder"? What perspectives or groups should be represented? How should the members be selected? Should members be representatives of particular constituencies, or "their own persons"? Is it feasible to have an open membership: "if you come to the meetings, you're a member"?

3. *Impact on decisionmaking.* Another problem that the Fernald Citizens Task Force encountered was finding a way to function within the confines of the elaborate CERCLA-based decisionmaking schedule established in the Consent Decree and Consent Agreement. Should SSABs have a special kind of input, as opposed to simply commenting on documents as they are published? Would that be legal? Some Superfund reauthorization proposals

would create "community working groups" for major sites. What formal role do you think they should they be given?

4. *Going national.* Establishment of SSABs was driven in large part by the realization that the scope of the clean-up problem far outstrips the available resources. As the FFER Dialogue Committee recognized, this gives rise to intra-and inter-site allocation issues. Why would public participation be important to these decisions? How can individual site groups help to set priorities *among* sites? Can a citizens advisory board process be expanded to cover national, as opposed to local, issues?[43]

The FFER Report recommends "fair-share" allocation of budget shortfalls among sites, meaning that each site would receive the same percentage cut. In what other ways might DOE set budget-cutting priorities? Is fair-share preferable to risk-based or "worst-first" strategies?

5. *Grassroots activism.* The clean-up effort at Fernald would never have even begun without pressure from a local citizens group, Fernald Residents for Environmental Safety and Health (FRESH). Environmental activism around Fernald had begun around 1980, when a group of students and environmentalists called Citizens Against a Radioactive Environment received, in response to a FOIA request, documents detailing spills and the concerns of DOE and NLO about other hazards. There was little public reaction to these disclosures, however, because the plant enjoyed strong public support. Indeed, when the December 1984 uranium spills occurred, Lisa Crawford, then a 27-year-old secretary who had lived across the road from the plant with her husband and young son since 1979, paid little attention.

Shortly after the New Year, however, the Crawfords' landlord told them that DOE had informed him that their well was contaminated. The well, which the Crawfords used for all of their household water, contained forty times EPA's limit for uranium. Crawford's first reaction was paralyzing fear for herself and her family, but her fear quickly turned to outrage when she learned that the contamination of the wells had been discovered three years earlier. She took two actions that proved to be turning points for Fernald: she contacted a prominent plaintiffs' lawyer in Cincinnati and became a lead class representative in the residents' suit against DOE and NLO, and she joined FRESH.

Crawford soon assumed leadership of FRESH and became an effective spokesperson for the fear and anger that Fernald's neighbors felt. When DOE filed its 1988 brief admitting systematic violation of environmental laws, she was perfectly positioned to capture the attention of the national media, the Governor of Ohio, and Congress. Since that time, FRESH has maintained a high media and political profile, and has heavily influenced clean-up efforts at the site.

---

[43] This question is explored in John S. Applegate & Sharon Lloyd-O'Connor, *Decision Time for DOE: LWVEF Urges National Dialogue on Nuclear Facilities Clean-up*, THE NATIONAL VOTER [League of Women Voters], January 1998, p. 14.

FRESH's success is not attributable to size (the active or "core" group is quite small), but to its clear mission and gifted leadership. Like Crawford, its members are local people who are deeply concerned about their own and their families' well-being. FRESH operates on a shoestring—it has no paid staff, just some office equipment in Crawford's house. Coming from a politically conservative community, none of its members came easily to challenging their government, but they felt a strong sense of betrayal by a government they trusted. Above all, FRESH is always there: the active members know as much about the site as anyone, and they show up at every single public meeting with tough questions and strongly held views. No significant action is taken at Fernald without consulting FRESH.

6. *Women and grassroots environmentalism.* The active membership in FRESH is overwhelmingly, and the leadership group exclusively, female. Many other well known environmental movements are also led by women: Lois Gibbs was the leader of the residents of Love Canal, and Ann Anderson was the lead plaintiff in the Woburn case described in *A Civil Action*.

This kind of activism has a long history. You will recall that the modern environmental movement is often dated to Rachael Carson's publication of *Silent Spring*. Some recent research has shown that women's clubs played an important role in the drive for better environmental quality as early as the turn of this century:

[U]pon close examination, the story of these women's clubs' environmental work is unnervingly contemporary both in process and language. Relegated to the rank of silent partner, thousands of Victorian- and Progressive-era club women across the states and territories nevertheless initiated and doggedly pursued critically needed environmental and public health protection projects in their towns and cities. The problems they addressed were problems that continue to bewilder policy makers today: polluted drinking water, inadequate waste disposal, risks from environmental toxics, and other multimedia quandaries. In essence, it is becoming clear that women's clubs were in great part responsible for laying the foundation of community-based environmental protection.

* * *

Many of these existing laws and nuisance provisions become central components of women's fights against pollution. Clubs used legal process to their advantage, usually by adopting one of three strategies: Often, following [Mrs. E.B.] Turner's [a national leader of women's clubs] advice, they became well-informed about legal matters to indirectly effect change by calling for enforcement of existing law, helping to shape public opinion, and persuading individual municipal officials and other community leaders to fight the good fight and do the right thing. At other times, they deftly made use of their own limited legal rights such as the right to vote on local tax matters to place themselves directly into environmental policy making positions. And in some instances, they directly applied legal process in the form of litigation to seek redress for damages.

* * *

One of the more curious consequences of omitting women's clubs' early environmental work is that typical accounts of the origins of the U.S. environmental movement begin with the conservation movement. Early environmental history has become synonymous with early conservation history. It is almost as if pollution as we know it today did not rear its ugly head until the 1960s, when Rachel Carson warned us of its threat in *Silent Spring*. By giving "community housekeeping" work its proper due as community-based environmental protection, our basic assumptions about the early forces that shaped growth of environmental awareness in this country could be significantly altered.

Elaine Koerner, *Silent Partners*, 14(5) THE ENVTL. FORUM 18 (March/April 1997). What do you think accounts for the prominent role of women in environmental activism?

3. The Value of Public Participation

Much discussion of public participation begs the question why public participation is a good thing. Recall that the materials on risk assessment in Chapter 2 suggested that the public can provide useful information and that lay people tend to have a richer, more multi-dimensional understanding of risk than numerical estimates express. The Presidential/Congressional Commission on Risk Assessment and Risk Management summarized the reasons for public participation:

1. Supports democratic decision-making.
2. Ensures that public values are considered.
3. Develops the understanding needed to make better decisions.
4. Improves the knowledge base for decision-making.
5. Can reduce the overall time and expense involved in decision-making.
6. May improve the credibility of agencies responsible for managing risks.
7. Should generate better accepted, more readily implemented risk management decisions.

The Presidential/Congressional Commission on Risk Assessment and Risk Management, *supra*, at 15-18. In addition, public participation can provide a "reality check":

Outside review of technical decisions by a group that is not expert in the underlying subject matter should not strike lawyers, in particular, as odd or inappropriate. It is a premise of judicial review of agency action as it has developed since about 1970. An outsider, whether a court or a citizens advisory board, can ask basic "why" questions about assumptions and cast a critical eye on the logic of the conclusions drawn. Judge Leventhal argued that the administrative system very much needs generalists who will go to the heart of the issue and help the agency to take a clear, objective view of its work. Judge Wald speaks of "an agency responsibility to convince an educated generalist judge that the agency's rule is the product of intelligent policymaking, not sloppy work or pure political ideology." The quality of an agency's original consideration probably improves when it knows that it will have to explain the basis of and reasons for a decision to people who are not part of its technical circle and who may not be disposed to accept its assertions.

* * *

Citizens advisory boards are similarly situated to see the big picture, to look across organizational or technical boundaries, and to demand a coherent, integrated resolution. The Task Force process provided the forum for looking at the Fernald site as a whole. For regulatory purposes, following standard CERCLA practice, the site was divided into five "operable units" containing roughly similar problems. Useful as it may have been for administration, this arrangement discouraged systematic site-wide consideration of issues that affected two or more operable units, such as an on-site disposal facility (which affected the disposition of the waste in most operable units, future use, and residual risk levels), the final configuration of the site, and the sequencing of remedial activities to reduce carrying costs. The Task Force, on the other hand, was free to address each of these issues in a holistic way. This paved the way for the balanced approach to waste disposition in which the management of one type of waste was predicated on the management of other types. Such balancing is not possible within a single unit. Likewise, the recommendations together constituted a coherent plan for Fernald's future that could be widely understood and attract broad support.

Applegate, *Usual Suspects, supra*, at 949-51. The materials in this chapter and Chapter 2 will surely suggest other reasons to you.

Expanded public participation is not without its drawbacks, however. In the following excerpt, Professor Frank Cross puts the case for a "republican" form of public participation.

THE PUBLIC ROLE IN RISK CONTROL

Frank B. Cross
24 ENVTL. L. 887 (1994)

There is clearly more to risk perception than simple ignorance, but ignorance may indeed form a substantial part of public risk perceptions. While it has become common to refer to public risk perception as "richer" than probabilistic estimates, that conclusion is facile and usually unjustified. The values that appear to give public perceptions such richness may often be the poverty of prejudice or dubitable heuristics [*i.e.*, rules of thumb].

* * *

The most obvious problem with false positive [*i.e.* erring on the side of taking regulatory action] regulation of harmless substances or activities is resource diversion. Assuming that resources for risk reduction are limited, the devotion of resources to a smaller risk would prevent government from addressing a greater risk.

* * *

Because of the resource limits on regulation, private economic costs, and the risk of dangerous errors, government reliance on public perception can actively endanger public health. Indulging the media and public ignorance, heuristics, and values will mean death for some Americans. The appeal of value judgments and other features underlying public perception diminishes when there is a cost in human life.

* * *

A variety of measures could be taken to facilitate the government's use of scientifically accurate measures of risk rather than mistaken public perceptions. Foremost is the reduction in opportunities for public participation in decisionmaking. * * *

* * * Several reasons justify the limitation of public participation in decisionmaking.

First, it is not clear that the public desires government policy to closely reflect their risk perceptions. The individualism prevalent in personal risk decisions need not be translated into the more altruistic and communal province of government decisionmaking. The public might believe that different standards should be employed for individual and public risk decisions. Individuals might also embrace "self-paternalism" in which people might both voluntarily choose to smoke but at the same time desire the government to create obstacles that prevent their smoking. Americans "are too lazy to spend the time to buckle up, or too macho to wear a motorcycle helmet, but they would vote for laws forcing them to wear either one."[44]

The second reason why the public might not desire that its risk opinions be automatically reflected in policy is that the people might recognize the

---

[44] This is an interesting twist on Mark Sagoff's argument in Chapter 3 (Economic Analysis), *supra*, that we have different standards for personal and public decisions.—EDS.

shortcomings of their own perceptions and choose to defer to scientific expertise in government policy. Indeed, this is a highly sensible attitude. Individuals might realize that the considerable time, effort, and ability required to adjust their personal perceptions and actions is not worth the benefits, a concept that Herbert Simon described as "satisficing." The government, however, has greater resources and economies of scale to research, and should therefore seek more scientifically accurate risk measures. These would be the measures taken by the people if they had sufficient time and faculties. In this manner, the public may humbly acknowledge their own limitations.

* * *

Third, a republic such as the United States is not built upon direct democracy. It must not be forgotten that, even in the total absence of direct public participation, government decisions are ultimately made by the elected representatives of the people. Even faceless bureaucrats generally respond to the desires and dictates of higher-level, elected officials. Political theory does not require direct participation for an effective and responsive democracy. For example, the nations of Western Europe are certainly democratic, but generally allow little public participation in environmental decisionmaking.

A fundamental aspect of American republicanism is deliberation. James Madison argued that government should not adopt prevailing public opinion, but the more thoughtful decisions of the people's representatives which would "be more consonant to the public good than if pronounced by the people themselves, convened for the purpose." In our civic-republican state, "deliberative decisionmaking also enriches the polity's choice of values by expanding the impoverished subset of governmental choices made available by pluralistic democracy." This impoverishment of choice is especially clear in environmental policy, where the public may only have the right to say "no" without other options.

Fourth, public participation does not necessarily further true majoritarian democracy. A common belief is that opportunity for participation is central to democracy. However, an EPA official observed that while "the public participation movement promoted substantive democratic values, it did very little to promote the procedural ends of democracy, and may even have corroded them, by reinforcing American tendencies toward adversarialness and confrontation." In practice, participation often degrades into a battle of unrepresentative private interest groups. For example, the participants in environmental regulation are generally affected industries and certain environmental protection organizations. A study of an elaborate North Carolina participation system found that a majority of participants "represented an organized interest group, and the participants as a whole were above average in socioeconomic status." Participation may therefore have a built-in bias which favors the affluent and reduces the democratic influence of ordinary citizens, especially the underprivileged.

* * *

In addition, when public perception drives the regulatory process, the resulting actions may violate the intent of the law. Democracy in the United States recognizes the rule of law, not men, and forbids the compromise of laws for the sole reason that they are unpopular. Most risk regulation statutes, as interpreted by the courts, call for regulation based on science, not public participation. For example, the Supreme Court has decided that the National Environmental Policy Act was meant to identify actual environmental effects and did not extend to public fears of adverse effect. The introduction of public perception may therefore violate legal commands.

NOTES

1. *Pro and con.* Can you think of additional reasons for and against public participation? Are you convinced that the public should have a role in environmental decisionmaking, beyond electing the legislators and executives who write and enforce the statutes? Is expansive public participation more or less "democratic"?

2. *Forms and fora.* To accept the appropriateness of public participation is not necessarily to accept it in all forms and on all subjects. We don't invite non-expert citizens to help engineer bridges—why should risk be different? Cross doesn't dispute the appropriateness of some input from the public, though he is clearly believes that there can be "too much" democracy in this area. Professors Kwan and Sunstein have similarly suggested that "availability cascades"—"a self-reinforcing process of collective belief formation, which can exaggerate small risks into major crises"—require that agencies be insulated from ill-informed public opinion. Timur Kuran & Cass R. Sunstein, *Available Cascades and Risk Regulation*, 51 STAN. L. REV. 683 (1999). How should public participation be channeled to be most useful and least harmful?

Are there systematic biases, however, in emphasizing technically competent participation and limiting participation based on "perception"?

3. *The public.* Doesn't your view on public participation depend a great deal on who you think the public is? Is it ordinary citizens, the regulated industry or organized interest groups, or all three?

C. Remediation, Future Use, and Stewardship

If the Twentieth Century taught us anything, it is that human beings can create things that they cannot completely control. Nuclear weapons exemplify this phenomenon, and their proliferation poses a continuing threat to world peace. Environmentally, the waste products of nuclear technology—with highly toxic and radioactive properties and their extremely long half-lives—pose severe difficulties for clean-up and disposal. Looking over the multitude of seemingly intractable problems that federal facilities raise, one is tempted to suggest, as a frustrated Senator John Glenn once said of Fernald, "Just put a fence around it and walk away."[45] Indeed, some have suggested that the more highly contaminated facilities be designated "national sacrifice zones" that are unfit for any human use. This solution has some obvious attractions, not the least of which is cost; nevertheless, the risks posed by contamination will not be contained by a fence. Groundwater contamination is usually the most important of the off-site risks, but significant airborne, surface water, and soil routes of off-site exposure also exist. In short, we have created places that we cannot entirely or easily control.

The cost of remediating the Nuclear Weapons Complex sites is, as we have seen, enormous. (The same is true of private sites taken as a whole.) "Putting a fence around it" is not only an unattractive solution on environmental grounds, but it also wastes the previous investment in the property and excludes future economic development in communities that depend on the sites. A "future use" approach to clean-up has been advocated to address these problems. The approach is described by one of its early advocates:

> * * * The first step in establishing a good approach to clean-up decision making is to create a strong focus on the end product of clean-up—for what will this property be used? The future use of land and natural resources is, without question, the clearest way to identify the objective of a contaminated site clean-up. It provides an unambiguous representation of what can be expected from clean-up and how that result can be compared to the current condition of the site. If a site is returned to a commercial or industrial use, the health and economic benefits are clear: humans can work on the site safely where once they were at risk, and the site is capable of providing economic benefit where once no use could be permitted.
>
> * * *
>
> The future uses of land and natural resources will be represented by general categories of use that define a class of exposure to contamination. These uses will generally be limited to five categories: residential, open space, commercial, industrial, and restricted. More alternatives would not result in distinctly different clean-up levels. The descriptions of these uses, the limitations and restrictions associated with each, and the associated risk factors should be consistent for the entire facility.
>
> The range of reasonable future uses for a specific site will be determined by surrounding land uses and projections for likely development in the area of the site and will be consistent with the facility's comprehensive plan. * * *

---

[45] He didn't mean it. Glenn was a strong supporter of an environmentally sound clean-up of the site.

* * * Specific clean-up levels can [then] be established for each contaminant of concern under each future use under consideration. * * * In applying risk assessment to develop clean-up levels, it is important to establish a single residual risk target to ensure a consistent level of protection of human health regardless of the land use selected. For example, achieving a 10^{-6} risk level in a residential scenario might require reducing all on-site concentrations of a particular contaminant to 5 ppm. In an industrial setting, 20 ppm may be all that is necessary to achieve the same level of residual risk. Though different *clean-up* levels are used, the same level of residual *risk* is achieved because exposure is controlled. Targeting a single level of risk for calculating clean-up levels base-wide is essential for this process to achieve credible results.

Douglas J. Sarno, *Future Use Considerations in the Clean-up of Federal Facilities*, 6(2) HAZARDOUS MATERIALS CONTROL 20 (1993). As the following excerpt describes, both EPA and DOE have embraced this approach.

But reliance on future use also has drawbacks. DOE does not have a monopoly on long-lived hazardous wastes. NRC regulates clean-up of radionuclides at decommissioned civilian nuclear power generating plants and other licensed facilities. Heavy metals like lead, mercury, and chromium are common constituents of privately owned Superfund and RCRA corrective action sites. Moreover, as the future use approach and brownfields redevelopment increasingly result in less complete clean-ups, the private long-term stewardship problem will far outstrip DOE's. DOE's sites, while vast, are relatively few in number, and most are quite well known. There are, by contrast, nearly one-half million private industrial sites at which some waste or contamination may remain indefinitely. This raises the question of our ability to exercise long-term control over partially remediated sites.

INSTITUTIONAL CONTROLS OR EMPEROR'S CLOTHES? LONG-TERM STEWARDSHIP OF THE NUCLEAR WEAPONS COMPLEX

John S. Applegate & Stephen Dycus
28 ENVTL. L. REP. (ENVTL. L. INST.) 10631 (1998)

The Problem of Long-Lived Wastes

* * *

Many of DOE's wastes are extremely long-lived. They include industrial pollutants commonly found in CERCLA remediations, such as heavy metals, that do not break down over time. Of even greater concern for DOE are the many radionuclides in its wastes. The rule of thumb is that radioactive materials are hazardous for about 10 times their half-lives; thus, strontium-90, with a half-life of a modest 29 years, poses a significant hazard for nearly three centuries. Plutonium-239—a principal product of the nuclear weapons complex, a major item in inventory, a common constituent of TRU waste, and a soil contaminant at Rocky Flats and elsewhere—has a half-life of approximately 24,000 years. Plutonium is one of the most hazardous materials known; inhalation of an almost infinitesimal amount is nearly certain to cause lung cancer. And uranium-238—an alpha-emitting radionuclide, highly dangerous to the lung, and a heavy metal with deleterious effects on the kidney—has a half-life of 4.5 billion years. Moreover, these materials' decay products are often themselves very dangerous. Uranium decays into radon, which is short-lived and poses a significant lung cancer risk in confined spaces.

The treatment and disposal options for all of these materials are extremely limited. Because they are nearly indestructible, such materials cannot be treated to reduce their toxicity. They can be treated to reduce their volume or their mobility in the environment: wet material can be dried or mixed with a solidifying agent; dry material can be enclosed in a matrix of concrete, plastic, or glass. A stabilized material is less likely or will take longer to leak out of a disposal facility and into or through the environment, or it will do so in significantly lower concentrations. Even after a stabilized material is disposed of, however, it must be isolated for the entire time that it remains hazardous.

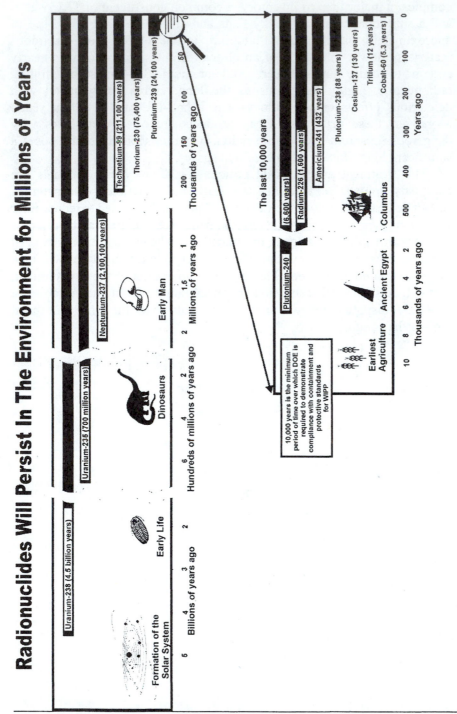

Figure 12.7–Radionuclides Time Line[46]

---

[46] Source: Department of Energy.

Clean-up Versus Remediation: How Dirty Is Clean?

* * * The use of [terms like "clean-up"] * * * may suggest that the hazardous materials can simply be made to disappear. However, even if all the long-lived material is removed from one site, it will continue to exist at a disposal site (ideally but not necessarily in a more stable and isolated configuration), unless it can be treated to render it no longer hazardous. For long-lived wastes, in other words, CERCLA and RCRA [do not "clean up", but] simply establish the terms under which such wastes will remain in the environment.

CERCLA and Its ARARs

* * *

While RCRA contemplates stewardship in the form of continued operations at a disposal site after it has been closed, this requirement is limited to a 30-year horizon. For some purposes, such as the no-migration standard for injection wells, EPA uses the very distant horizon of 10,000 years. Likewise, EPA's regulations governing radioactive waste disposal at the WIPP geologic repository include a 10,000-year standard. Yet, while this time period is beyond the extreme limit of our predictive abilities and technical capabilities, it is well short of even the half lives of many of DOE's radioactive wastes, to say nothing of long-lived nonradioactive hazardous wastes. The NRC, by contrast, adopts a 500-year horizon for low-level waste and a 1,000-year horizon for decommissioned facilities and for uranium mill tailings (both NRC rules are potential ARARs for DOE facilities). The 1,000-year horizon is largely aspirational, however, because it is qualified by the term "to the extent reasonably achievable" and by a mandatory minimum of only 200 years.

CERCLA calls for the review of remediated sites every five years if the remedy "results in any hazardous substances, pollutants, or contaminants remaining at the site." Because of the nature of the wastes that will remain at most DOE sites, such periodic reviews could continue indefinitely. Yet CERCLA neither imposes restrictions on the use of property nor establishes the kinds of institutions that would be required to maintain a surveillance program for the centuries or millennia that some long-lived waste will need to be isolated.

Future Use and Institutional Controls

* * *

[A]ccording to the "future use" * * * approach to clean-up, if the uses of land around the waste can be restricted, then potential exposure and hence the expected residual risk level may both be lowered. If the future use of [a lake with contaminated sediments] is a wildlife refuge, remedial action may not need to be taken if the contamination is contained in stable sediments. At the other end of the land use spectrum, agricultural use of a site involves exposure to the farmer through direct dermal contact with soil and groundwater, extended opportunities to inhale contaminated dust, and occasional ingestion. Residential use has a similar exposure profile, because children play in their yards and adults dig in their gardens. Industrial and commercial uses, however, involve considerably less potential contact, if only because the concrete slab of a building and the asphalt of a parking lot insulate workers from contamination beneath them. The isolation in such situations is not perfect, but, so long as the structure remains in place, it will cut off some routes of exposure. Recreational uses of green space involve even less exposure, because most people spend far less time at recreational sites than at work or home, and their activities (apart from sports) typically involve only limited contact with the soil. Finally, a highly restricted land use, in which only trespassers or occasional monitors visit the site, yields a very low exposure profile, though at the price of permanently underutilized land. The assumption of a particular future land use, therefore, has a profound effect on the calculated exposure and hence the risk at a contaminated site.

Future use developed as an alternative to what had been the usual assumption in Superfund risk assessments that a property will have an intensive post-remediation use like agricultural or residential, which requires a level of clean-up sufficient for all eventualities. Advocates of the future use approach argue that, because many Superfund sites are located in industrial areas that have no foreseeable prospect of a use other than industrial or commercial, clean-up activities can be limited accordingly. Clean-up to make an industrial site safe for farming, the thinking goes, is clean-up for its own sake. It is wasteful of resources, and, in an environment of limited resources, it may result in more serious contamination going unremedied. The difference between clean-up levels is substantial: adoption of commercial instead of residential use in one study of U.S. Air Force facilities showed a tenfold difference in acceptable levels of residual contamination. By lowering clean-up costs, the future use approach benefits potentially liable parties (including federal agencies) and in some cases may encourage industrial redevelopment. Many states, eager for this so-called brownfields redevelopment, encourage reliance on assumed future use. Consideration of future land use is also a feature of CERCLA reform proposals and pending reauthorization legislation.

The future use approach to planning for clean-up and disposal of hazardous wastes can only be justified, however, if the future use of the land can be predicted with confidence. This means that the future use approach must be applied prescriptively, not just predictively. Thus, if future uses of the above-mentioned lake were uncertain, one might attempt to close the lake to development to ensure no disturbance of its sediments. The techniques for prescribing and maintaining future uses are known as institutional controls. They include physical barriers, like fences and guards; information transmission, like warnings and public records; and legal controls, like ownership, zoning, and deed restrictions. Institutional controls are important to ensure that predictions for the foreseeable future actually come to pass. But they are absolutely essential to prescribing land use conditions in the long-term future, as to which accurate prediction is extremely dubious.

Institutional controls, in other words, are the *sine qua non* for reliance on future use, and so the legitimacy of future use depends on the availability and efficacy of appropriate institutional controls. Conversely, if institutional controls are ineffective over the long term, then they must either not be relied on, or systems must be in place to respond when they fail.

EPA has come to embrace future use as part of a broad trend toward exposure-based risk control. A 1995 directive to regional offices from EPA's Office of Solid Waste and Emergency Response (OSWER) declares that "[r]easonably anticipated future use of the land at NPL [national priorities list] sites is an important consideration in determining the appropriate extent of remediation." * * *

Consistent with its future use policy, EPA also recognizes institutional controls as a legitimate part of a remedial plan:

> In appropriate site situations, treatment of the principal threats posed by a site, with priority placed on treating waste that is liquid, highly toxic or highly mobile, will be combined with engineering controls (such as containment) and institutional controls, as appropriate, for treatment of residuals and untreated waste.[47]

Many CERCLA records of decision now rely on institutional controls to achieve the calculated residual risk levels. "Water use and deed restrictions" are specifically mentioned as potential components of a completed remedy. CERCLA § 120 provides that when contaminated federal lands are conveyed or leased to a non-federal owner, the instrument of transfer must include "necessary restrictions on the use of the property to ensure the protection of human health and the environment."

In evaluating alternative remedies, EPA must consider the "adequacy and reliability of controls such as containment systems and institutional controls," the "type and quantity of residuals that will remain following treatment," and cost, including annual operation and maintenance costs. Where an aquifer is contaminated, "[r]apid restoration may also be appropriate where the institutional controls to prevent the utilization of contaminated groundwater for drinking water purposes are not clearly effective or reliable." According to the NCP,

> the use of institutional controls shall not substitute for active response measures (*e.g.*, treatment and/or containment of source material, restoration of groundwaters to their beneficial uses) as the sole remedy unless such active measures are determined not to be practicable, based on the balancing of trade-offs among alternatives that is conducted during the selection of a remedy.[48]

The D.C. Circuit has emphasized that EPA's discretion under this regulation is limited: "[A]ny remedy relying on institutional controls must meet the

---

[47] 40 C.F.R. § 300.430(a)(l)(iii)(C). * * *
[48] 40 C.F.R. § 300.430(a)(l)(iii)(D).

threshold requirement of protectiveness."[49] In sum, CERCLA's threshold criterion of protecting human health and the environment can be satisfied only if genuinely reliable institutional controls are available to ensure that an inappropriate use will not be made of the site.

Future use is of special interest to DOE. It holds the potential for reducing the amounts of contaminated soil and water that the legal standards require to be treated, for permitting on-site disposal or in-situ isolation of waste materials (thus avoiding the economic and political costs of transportation), and for achieving a protective remedy where permanent, total clean-up technologies do not exist. * * *

EPA's 1995 OSWER directive would appear to validate DOE's plans to accomplish its clean-up of the nuclear weapons complex by leaving some contamination in place and some waste on-site, based on a prediction and/or prescription of limited land uses. However, while DOE can undoubtedly control the foreseeable future of sites it owns, its reliance on institutional controls to achieve its long-term stewardship goals may not be justified. The history of such controls is checkered at best. It is frequently observed that Love Canal, which provided the original impetus for the Superfund program, was a case of failed institutional controls. What, then, must be done to protect present and future generations from DOE's residual wastes?

NOTES

1. *How clean is clean?* How does predicted future use affect the degree of clean-up? *Should* the degree of clean-up depend on expected future use? The future use approach is often accused of being a "Trojan Horse" for reduced safety. Is this a fair criticism? Other skeptics have said, "Work on clean-up first, and *then* worry about what the place will look like when it's done." Is there a good answer to that argument?

2. *Is this legal?* What is the statutory basis for considering future use and relying on institutional controls? Are there contrary indications in CERCLA?[50]

3. *Institutional controls—types.* To be serious about future use, one also has to be serious about the use of physical barriers and use restrictions on reclaimed property to keep future risk levels low.[51] Applegate & Dycus list the following types of controls:

---

[49] Ohio v. U.S. EPA, 997 F.2d 1520, 1537 (D.C. Cir. 1993)

[50] Recent proposed amendments to CERCLA addressing land use issues are analyzed in Krista J. Ayers, *The Potential for Future Use Analysis in Superfund Remediation Programs*, 44 EMORY L.J. 1503, 1519-22 (1995); Rena I. Steinzor, *The Reauthorization of Superfund: Can the Deal of the Century Be Saved?* 25 ELR 10016 (Jan. 1995); Anne D. Weber, *Institutional Controls-An Expedited and Cost-Effective Means for Returning a Superfund Site to Beneficial Use*, 9 J. NAT. RESOURCES & ENVTL. L. 461, 470-76 (1994); National Commission on Superfund, Final Consensus Report of the National Commission on Superfund (Keystone Center & Vermont Law School 1994).

[51] A variety of institutional controls are described and analyzed in Mary R. English *et al.*, Institutional Controls at Superfund Sites: A Preliminary Assessment of Their Efficacy and Public Acceptability 21-31 (Joint Institute for Energy & Environment 1997); John

Active: continuing governmental ownership, monitoring and reporting, affirmative easements, direct federal regulation of non-federal lands, records preservation, publicity, research and development, emergency planning, and liability;

Passive: physical barriers, containment structures, markers; deed notices; covenants and equitable servitudes; negative easements; reversionary interests; zoning;

Procedures and institutions: decisionmaking for the long term, stewardship institutions.

Continuing federal ownership is obviously one of the most likely ways to effectuate monitoring, repair, and use restrictions. CERCLA would appear to support this approach by requiring clean-up of federal property before it is transferred out of federal ownership. 42 U.S.C. § 9620(h). However, the "fine print" allows the use of restrictive covenants and leases that avoid the requirement of prior clean-up. 42 U.S.C. § 9620(h)(3); *Conservation Law Foundation v. Busey*, 79 F.3d 1250, 1269-70 (1st Cir. 1996). Are these enough? Do new types need to be invented?

4. *Institutional controls—effectiveness*. The use of institutional controls is controversial. What are the arguments for recognizing such controls in assessing the risks posed by a site? Against? Applegate & Dycus express some skepticism:

As a measure of the "long-term effectiveness and permanence" required by the NCP, these physical barriers and containments must perform for as long as the wastes remain dangerous. Yet, our experience to date raises serious doubts about their reliability. The ancient Egyptians used two forms of isolation to protect their royal tombs and the vast treasures they contained. The pyramids at Giza and Saqqara (c. 2650-2500 B.C.) announced the presence of the tombs prominently (to say the least) and relied on the massiveness of their construction to thwart grave robbers. The tombs of the Valley of the Kings (beginning c. 1550 B.C.), in contrast, were structurally modest and were deliberately hidden in an isolated valley. Both the pyramids and the Valley of the Kings were guarded and attended by religious establishments. Despite the obvious ingenuity of the Egyptian builders, the provision for surveillance, and the survival (in name at least) of the Egyptian monarchy into the Roman era under the Ptolemys, neither technique was at all effective, even in the near term. While it is unlikely (and for good reason) that future generations will search for DOE waste with Howard Carter's persistence in searching for Tutankhamen's tomb, the Egyptians' efforts to isolate the mummies of their deified kings

Pendergrass, *Use of Institutional Controls as Part of a Superfund Remedy: Lessons From Other Programs*, 26 ELR 10109 (Mar. 1996); Susan C. Borinsky, *The Use of Institutional Controls in Superfund and Similar State Laws*, 7 FORDHAM ENVTL. L.J. 1, 14-19 (1995); David F. Coursen, *Institutional Controls at Superfund Sites*, 23 ELR 10279 (May 1993).

and queens is a cautionary tale for us, their descendants. Ultimately, of course, even Tutankhamen's lost tomb yielded to Carter's intrusion, although it had lain undisturbed for only 3,200 years—one tenth of the half-life of plutonium and one hundredth of the period during which it remains hazardous. Modern construction methods and materials might extend the life of structures at DOE sites, but we must expect that those structures will need to be repaired or replaced long before the wastes they enclose cease to pose a threat.

* * *

It is nearly impossible to imagine an institution capable of caring for nuclear wastes for as long as they will remain dangerous, but the experience of two familiar European institutions, the Roman Catholic Church and the British monarchy, may be instructive. They have remained recognizable, distinct organizations for, respectively, nearly two thousand and more than nine hundred years. Over long periods of time, each institution has performed a relatively continuous set of functions, has raised money to perform those functions, has withstood enormous internal and external changes, has successfully called on generations of followers for tangible and intangible support, has transmitted knowledge about itself over generations, and has adapted to new circumstances while maintaining a core identity. This is precisely what a long-term stewardship institution must achieve.

How did church and throne do it? Both institutions established and nurtured a relationship with their followers. Whether based on power, legal status, or religious belief, the relationship is reciprocal: the institution protects and cares for its members (gives value, to put it bluntly), and the membership in return supports it materially and with its confidence. Such a relationship (or expectation of it) is not only essential in the near term to obtain the political will to create a long-lived institution, but it is even more important in the long run to assure the continuing existence and efficacy of the institution.

Applegate & Dycus, *supra*, at 10652.[52] Are these analogies appropriate? How should we address the problem of long-term stewardship? What characteristics should a program of long-term stewardship possess?

5. *On- or off-site disposal.* One future use of many federal facilities, including Fernald, may be the permanent disposal of the wastes generated by the facility. What issues should be considered in choosing on- or off-site disposal? The aquifer beneath Fernald is a "sole-source" aquifer, rendering most of the site unsuitable for hazardous waste disposal under Ohio law. It would be feasible to ship at least some of the Fernald wastes to locations in Utah or Nevada. What risks would you need to evaluate?

---

[52] The difficult (and fascinating) problem of communicating to distant generations the nature and hazards of nuclear waste is addressed in GREGORY BENFORD, DEEP TIME: HOW HUMANITY COMMUNICATES ACROSS MILLENNIA 31-85 (1999).

PART 4:

EMERGING ISSUES

Chapter 13

Environmental Justice

A. Introduction

The following case study poignantly illustrates several environmental justice issues. As you read the article, ask yourself what legal tools could policymakers and affected individuals invoke to redress their situation.

PURSUING THE RIGHT TO BREATHE EASY

Steven Keeva
ABA JOURNAL, Feb. 1999, pp. 48-49

For Zulene Mayfield, doing everything possible to keep polluting facilities out of her hometown is something she describes not as activism but as love.

"I do it because I love my community," says Mayfield, who chairs Chester (Pa.) Residents Concerned for Environmental Quality. "I was born here, and my mother and father are here. I just don't see what I'm doing as activism."

Success in Battle

Whatever you call the work she does, it is clear that Mayfield does it well. Since 1994, she has led the charge in Chester to stop what she sees as the racist practice of permitting far too many unhealthful facilities in the cities. On two occasions, the residents group mounted enough pressure to get permits denied. That had never happened before in Chester.

A poor town of 42,000 people that is roughly 70 percent black, Chester sits on the Delaware River about 20 miles southwest of Philadelphia.

The contours of the pollution problem become clear when you compare Chester to the rest of Delaware County, which has a population of about half a million and is more than 90 percent white.

For example, of seven permits that have been granted in the county for waste facilities, five are in Chester. And while the combined annual permit capacity of waste outside Chester is 1,400 tons, inside the city it is slightly more than 2 million tons.

Put another way: Chester may as well be the city whose picture appears next to a textbook explication of the issues underlying the environmental justice movement, the fight to keep polluting facilities out of poor and minority neighborhoods.

Some have opted for another label to describe the clustering of these facilities in places like Chester: environmental racism.

Last June, Chester made headlines when the U.S. Supreme Court took a case that originated there and raised a question that has long simmered on the burners of the lower federal courts: May private citizens use federal civil rights laws to block state decisions to locate polluters in minority neighborhoods?

The Chester residents group had claimed in the suit that the state's approval of the permits violated U.S. environmental regulations forbidding the use of federal funds for purposes that have a discriminatory effect. The group wanted to use Title VI of the Civil Rights Act of 1964 to enforce the regulations.

The case reached the Court after the 3rd U.S. Circuit Court of Appeals at Philadelphia reversed a District Court holding that such a cause of action did not exist.[1] This brought the 3rd Circuit into step with the majority of federal appeals courts.

Luckily for environmental justice advocates who feared [that] the Court took the case to reverse the 3rd Circuit, something happened on the way to the courthouse.

The company whose permit to build a soil-treatment facility that gave rise to the case abandoned its plans, and the state revoked its permit. The issue was rendered moot.

Still, the EPA slogs along, issuing fairly detailed guidance on how to use Title VI and, in the process, incurring something of an avalanche of criticism, particularly from the state agencies that receive federal money.

A Frontline View

From where she sits, Mayfield isn't overly concerned about what the Supreme Court might have in mind regarding Title VI remedies for the kinds of problems her community faces.

Life has never been easy in Chester and communities like it, and Mayfield knows that such a remedy is at best one weapon in what must, perforce, be a varied arsenal that includes grassroots organizing, political action, and legal combat under various environmental statutes.

---

[1] Chester Residents Concerned for Quality Living v. Seif, 132 F.3d 925 (3d Cir. 1997), *judgement vacated*, 119 S. Ct. 22 (1998). The district court opinion is reported at 944 F. Supp. 413 (E. D. Pa. 1996).-EDS.

What is important to Mayfield is improving the local air and water, and-this is something that most people overlook-stopping the ceaseless rumble of heavy trucks as they lumber to and from the waste facilities through streets on which children play.

Still, lawyers show significant interest in the civil rights remedy when the government allows polluters in minority neighborhoods, according to a survey sponsored jointly by the American Bar Association and the National Bar Association. The amount of support, however, differs considerably by race, with black lawyers being far more likely to favor this use of the law.

Damon Whitehead is a staff attorney at the Environmental Justice Program of the Lawyers Committee on Civil Rights Under Law in Washington, D.C., who litigates environmental justice cases. He acknowledges this racial disparity, at least indirectly, when he talks about what he sees as the inadequate efforts by national environmental organizations to deal with environmental justice problems.

"What needs to be done is that we have to show these groups how this fits in with what they're already doing," he says. "If they don't feel comfortable bringing Title VI claims-if they think it might upset their constituencies-then we have to show them how to make environmental justice fit in with what they are doing. Say they do Clean Air Act work; fine, then include it in urban communities of color. It's a matter of broadening their constituency."

A lot has changed since Mayfield took on the environmental justice case five years ago. At the time, the issue was just beginning to make it on the radar screens of lawyers and civil rights activists.

The year before, the ABA had adopted a resolution on environmental justice, urging governments, private entities and academic institutions to achieve equitable enforcement of environmental laws.

It also urged lawyers to deliver legal services in the area of environmental law to minority and low-income communities.

Going Public

Since then, environmental justice issues have become the regular work of legal services offices and public interest organizations.

Jerome Balter of the Public Interest Law Center of Philadelphia, who represented the Chester citizens group, specializes in environmental law. He is not the aberration he would have been even a few years back. "When the environment is affected by violations of civil rights, then I get involved in civil rights," he says.

Another key change is that in the first half of the decade, equal protection was the preferred ground on which to base legal claims because Title VI of the Civil Rights Act had not yet been tested.

Now, more courts are accepting Title VI along with its easier standard of proof. Under the law, plaintiffs need only show a disparate impact rather than an intent to discriminate.

So Chester can be seen as a key moment in the coming of age of Title VI as a remedy for disparate environmental impact. But-to the relief of activists and advocates for affected communities-it hasn't yet been tested by the nine justices who, many observers say, may very well wish to nullify its usefulness.

For Mayfield, having a lawyer has had a dramatic effect on getting industry and local and state government to take the Chester residents group seriously.

Now a member of the EPA's National Environmental Justice Advisory Council, she feels hopeful that the new forum for her concerns will lead to additional change.

"There's a lot that goes into fighting environmental racism," she says. "There's no recipe. You just keep at it until you find what works. But we've definitely found that we need the extra armament of having legal counsel. When you have that, people show you more respect.

—

Studies show that poor and minority people are more likely than their white counterparts to live near freeways, sewer treatment plants, municipal and hazardous waste landfills, incinerators, and other noxious facilities.[2] This phenomenon is defined by many as "environmental injustice" or "environmental racism." The environmental justice movement claims that such disproportion is due to racism and classism in the siting of locally undesirable land uses (LULUs), in the enforcement of environmental laws and regulations, and in the remediation of hazardous sites.[3]

The call for environmental justice surfaced during the late 1970s with the work of grassroots organizations such as Chicago's People for Community Recovery and Mothers of East Los Angeles. Grassroots organizations formed across the United States to combat specific environmental problems that were impacting their communities. Each of these groups shared one unifying belief: that the poor and minorities are systematically discriminated against in the siting, regulation, and remediation of industrial and waste facilities. These groups became an effective voice for the concerns of inner-city residents as they aggressively challenged local developments that the community considered undesirable. However, in the absence of detailed empirical research, the evidence for the organizations' claims of discrimination remained largely anecdotal. As a result, their influence on policy was limited.[4]

It was not until the release of several studies that appeared to substantiate their assertions did the environmental justice movement gain national

---

[2] *See* Robert D. Bullard, *Environmental Equity: Examining the Evidence of Environmental Racism*, LAND USE FORUM, Winter 1993, at 6.

[3] *See* Vicki Been, *What's Fairness Got to do With It? Environmental Justice and the Siting of Locally Undesirable Land Uses*, 78 CORNELL L. REV. 1001 (1993).

[4] *See* CHRISTOPHER BOERNER & THOMAS LAMBERT, CENTER FOR STUDY OF AMERICAN BUSINESS, EVIRONMENTAL JUSTICE?, POLICY STUDY NO. 121 (1994).

attention. The first major attempt to provide empirical support for the environmental justice claims was conducted by sociologist Robert D. Bullard. In his first study, Dr. Bullard examined population data for communities hosting landfills and incinerators in Houston, Texas. Dr. Bullard found that, while African-Americans made up only twenty-eight percent of the city's population, six of its eight incinerators and fifteen of its seventeen landfills were located in predominantly African-American neighborhoods.[5]

The issue of environmental justice first attracted national media attention in 1982 when 500 protestors were arrested after they threw their bodies in front of trucks carrying polychlorinated biphenyl (PCB)-contaminated soil to a landfill in a poor, predominantly black Warren County, North Carolina. Warren County is one of the poorest communities in North Carolina and has one of the highest percentages of African-American residents in the state.[6] Leaders from national environmental and civil rights groups joined local citizen protests and directed national attention to Warren County. While the Warren County activists were unsuccessful in stopping the landfill, their actions highlighted the need for cooperation between civil rights advocates and environmentalists.

Since 1990, academicians, civil rights leaders, and environmental groups have worked with grassroots organizations to identify and address inequities in the distribution of environmental hazards. They found that distributional inequities exist in areas beyond the siting of hazardous waste facilities. For example, minority and lower-income children retain the highest risk of elevated lead levels in their blood and incur the highest occupational health risks such as exposure to pesticides, solvents, and metals.[7] Other studies have found slower remediation of Superfund sites and lower fines for pollution in poor and minority communities.[8] Still others have, on more theoretical grounds, suggested that the distributional consequences of environmental regulation is regressive, that is, its benefits and burdens are not symmetrical.[9] However, for simplicity in illuminating the environmental justice movement itself, this chapter will focus on the siting of hazardous waste facilities. This is also the area that has received the greatest attention in environmental justice literature and activism.

---

[5] *See* Robert D. Bullard, *Solid Waste Sites and the Black Houston Community,* 53 SOC. INQUIRY 273 (1983). Of the three sites in non-black neighborhoods, one was located in a neighborhood undergoing transition from a white to an African-American community, one was located in a Hispanic neighborhood, and one was adjacent to a predominantly white community. *See id.* at 279-82.

[6] *See* Daniel Suman, Book Review, *Robert Bullard: Dumping in Dixie: Race, Class and Environmental Quality,* 19 ECOLOGY LAW Q. 591, 599 (1992).

[7] *See* Gerald Torres, *Environmental Burdens and Democratic Justice,* 21 FORDHAM URBAN L.J. 431, 435 (1994).

[8] *See* Marianne Lavelle & Marcia Coyle, *Unequal Protection: The Racial Divide in Environmental Law,* NAT'L L.J., Sep. 21, 1992 at s2.

[9] *See* Richard J. Lazarus, *Pursuing "Environmental Justice": The Distributional Effects of Environmental Protection,* 87 NW. U.L. REV. 787 (1993).

The siting of waste facilities is controlled primarily by state and local governments. Historically, land uses have been governed by the state, and attempts by the federal government to control local land uses met with strong opposition. Therefore, the Environmental Protection Agency's (EPA) role in permitting comes only after the site has been chosen, and principally involves technical considerations.[10]

Decisions to site hazardous waste facilities in minority communities may or may not be made with reference to the racial or ethnic composition of the community. A company wishing to locate a hazardous waste facility may unconsciously follow a path of least resistance. This approach would target land of relatively low value and minimal zoning restrictions without considering the composition of the local community. The poor tend to live in areas of lower land values and mixed industrial/residential uses and, as a result, are disproportionately affected by decisions relating to siting hazardous facilities. The evidence strongly suggests, however, that the siting of LULUs in poor minority communities is actually more calculated than planners otherwise claim. A 1984 report prepared for the California Waste Management Board by a consulting firm, Cerrell Associates, Inc., is revealing. It recommended that project planners "select a site that offers the least potential of generating public opposition" and confrontation.[11] The report concluded that opposition is most likely to come from highly educated, middle-and high-income groups in large urban areas, and least likely to come from lower socioeconomic neighborhoods in industrial areas. Whether or not this is racism per se, it is certainly a recipe for siting LULUs in poor and minority communities.

Others suggest that the disproportionate location of sources of toxic pollution in poor minority communities is the result of various development patterns. First, residential communities where poor minorities now live were originally the homes of whites who worked in the facilities that generate toxic emissions. Whites vacated the housing for better shelter as their socioeconomic status improved, and poorer minority individuals who enjoyed much less residential mobility took their place. Second, in other cases, housing for African-Americans and Latinos was built in the vicinity of existing industrial operations because the land was cheap and the people were poor. Third, sources of toxic pollution were placed in existing minority communities.[12] Finally, the siting of new facilities, even hazardous industries, brings the promise of economic prosperity and tax revenues. This forces

---

[10] *See* Chapter 10 (Siting), *supra.*

[11] *See* Suman, *supra* note 6 at 596-97 (citing CERRELL ASSOCIATES, INC., POLITICAL DIFFICULTIES FACING WASTE-TO-ENERGY CONVERSION PLANT SITING (1984)).

[12] For a further discussion on this subject, *see* Regina Austin & Michael Schill, *Black, Brown, Poor & Poisoned: Minority Grassroots Environmentalism and the Quest for Eco-Justice,* KAN. J.L. & PUB. POL'Y, p. 69-70 (1991); Vicki Been, *What's Fairness Got to do With It? Environmental Justice and the Siting of Locally Undesirable Land Uses,* 78 CORNELL L. REV. 1001 (1993); Richard J. Lazarus, *Pursuing "Environmental Justice": The Distributional Effects of Environmental Protection,* 87 NW. U.L. REV. 787 (1993).

communities which often have high unemployment to choose between economic security and environmental degradation. Benefits anticipated from these facilities often do not materialize for the following reasons: hazardous waste facilities provide few jobs for area residents, jobs that are created usually require technical education and are often brought in from outside the community, and the increased tax revenues do not generally go to social services or other community development projects, but toward expanding the infrastructure to better serve the industry being developed.

The siting of hazardous waste facilities, therefore, not only serves as a proxy for the broader range of distributional consequences of environmental regulation, but it also raises difficult and fundamental questions about achieving environmental justice. Is maldistribution racism and classism, or is it the result of a free market economy that inevitably favors the more well-to-do? If racism, then can we adjust traditional civil rights remedies to address this new problem? If the market, then to that extent can and should environmental law consider the distribution of environmental amenities and harms?

B. Statistical Studies Related to the Siting of Hazardous Waste Facilities

Much of the evidence for environmental injustice is anecdotal: there are many examples of minority and low-income communities throughout the United States that are adversely affected by the disproportionate siting of hazardous waste and other polluting facilities in their communities. One of the most well-known communities is the Altgeld Gardens housing project on Chicago's southeast side. Altgeld Gardens is a 6,000-unit housing complex for thousands of low-income African-Americans which was built over 40 years ago on top of an abandoned landfill. The neighborhood is home to 150,000 residents-70% African-American and 11% Latino. The housing complex is surrounded by 11 separate polluting facilities: landfills, incinerators, oil refineries, a paint factory, a steel mill, a sewage treatment plant, a chemical plant, a scrap metal yard, a lagoon, a sludge drying bed, and a freeway.[13] This community has one of the highest concentrations of severe environmental problems and concerns in the country.

South Central Los Angeles is another community which suffers from a disproportionate siting of polluting facilities. The community is comprised of 52% African-Americans and 44% Latinos. The one-square mile area is saturated with abandoned toxic waste sites, freeways, smokestacks, and

---

[13] *See Hearings on Environmental Justice Before the Subcomm. on Civil and Constitutional Rights of the House Comm. on the Judiciary,* 103D CONG., 1ST SESS. (1993) (testimony of Hazel Johnson, Resident of Altgeld Gardens and founder and Executive Director for People for Community Recovery on Environmental Justice).

wastewater pipes from polluting industries.[14] In fact, more than 18 industrial firms in 1989 discharged more than 33 million pounds of waste chemicals in the environment within the boundaries of the zip code area of 90058.[15] *See also* Maryanne Vollers, *Everyone Has Got to Breathe*, 97 Audubon 64 (March/April 1995); Paul Mohai and Bunyan Bryant, *Environmental Injustice: Weighing Race and Class as Factors in the Distribution of Environmental Hazards*, 63 U. Colo. L. Rev. 921 (1992).

A number of studies have sought to demonstrate a *systematic* pattern of hazardous waste sites and other polluting facilities being placed in minority and low-income communities in the United States. Waste facility inequity was identified by the United States General Accounting Office (GAO) as early as 1983, following the Warren County landfill protests. GAO's investigation of hazardous waste facility siting in EPA Region IV found a strong relationship between the location of off-site hazardous waste landfills, race, and the socioeconomic status of the surrounding communities in the system. Specifically, GAO studied the racial and economic characteristics of the zip code areas surrounding the four hazardous waste sites present in Region IV. The GAO found that three out of four landfills in the Southeast were located in predominantly poor and African-American communities.[16] African-Americans comprised fifty-two, sixty-six, and ninety percent of the population in the three communities, whereas they only comprised between twenty-two and thirty percent of the host state populations. In addition, the communities were also relatively poor, with a range of twenty-six to forty percent of the populations living below the poverty threshold. In comparison, in the host states, the portion of the population living below the poverty level was between fourteen and nineteen percent.

The findings of the GAO prompted other studies to be undertaken. The most significant study was conducted by the Commission for Racial Justice, United Church of Christ (UCC) in 1987 and updated in 1994. It's landmark study, *Toxic Wastes and Race*,[17] found race to be the single most important siting factor-more important than income, home ownership rate, and property values-in the location of toxic waste sites. According to the study, non-whites are forty-seven percent more likely than whites to live near a toxic waste site and are three times more likely to live in a community with more than one such site. Through an examination of neighborhoods surrounding commercial hazardous waste TSDFs, the study concluded that a large minority population was the most statistically significant factor those communities had in

---

[14] *See* Robert D. Bullard, *The Threat of Environmental Racism*, 7 NAT. RESOURCES. & ENV. 23, 26 (1993).

[15] The San Francisco Examiner described this zip code area as the "dirtiest" in state. *Id.*

[16] *See* U.S. GEN. ACCT. OFF., SITING OF HAZARDOUS WASTE LANDFILLS AND THEIR CORRELATION WITH RACIAL AND ECONOMIC STATUS OF SURROUNDING COMMUNITIES, June 1, 1983, at 2.

[17] COMMISSION FOR RACIAL JUSTICE, UNITED CHURCH OF CHRIST, TOXIC WASTES AND RACE IN THE UNITED STATES: A NATIONAL REPORT ON THE RACIAL AND SOCIO-ECONOMIC CHARACTERISTICS OF COMMUNITIES WITH HAZARDOUS WASTE SITES (1987).

common. Specifically, the study found that three of the nation's largest hazardous waste landfills representing roughly forty percent of the total estimated landfill capacity in the U.S. are located in areas where the population is predominantly African-American or Hispanic.[18] Furthermore, the UCC study concluded that approximately sixty percent of the nation's Latino and African-American residents live in communities that contain uncontrolled toxic waste sites (*i.e.*, candidates for Superfund remediation).

Greenpeace also conducted a study that reviewed incinerator siting practices.[19] The study concluded that the minority portion of the population in communities with existing incinerators is eighty-nine percent higher than the national average. Furthermore, communities where incinerators are proposed have minority populations sixty percent higher than the national average. The study also looked at the average income and property values of communities with incinerators and found that the average income is fifteen percent less than the national average and property values are thirty-eight percent lower than the national mean.

The GAO, UCC and Greenpeace studies caught the attention of EPA, which launched its own investigation to assess the merits of the earlier studies. EPA's study focused on racial minority and low-income populations and was published as *Environmental Equity: Reducing Risk For All Communities*.[20] In the report, EPA defined "environmental equity" as being concerned with a variety of issues which fall into three general categories: the distribution and effects of environmental problems, the environmental policy making process, and the administration of environmental protection programs. EPA concluded that racial minority and low-income populations experience higher than average exposures to certain air pollutants, hazardous waste facilities, contaminated fish, and agricultural pesticides in the workplace. The reason for the higher exposure rates is because such low-income and minority populations tend to live in areas with high air pollution levels or may be more likely to live near a waste site.[21]

Not only are communities of color differentially impacted by industrial and waste facility siting and the resulting pollution, they can expect different

---

[18] The nation's largest landfill is located in Emelle, Alabama (Sumter County), which is 78.9% African-American. Scotlandville, Louisiana, home of the fourth largest landfill has a population which is 93% African-American. The country's fifth largest site is located in Kettleman City, California, where Hispanics make up 78.4% of the population. *See id.*

[19] PAT COSTNER & JOE THORNTON, PLAYING WITH FIRE: HAZARDOUS WASTE INCINERATION-A GREENPEACE REPORT (1990).

[20] *See* EPA, WORKGROUP REPORT TO THE ADMINISTRATOR, ENVIRONMENTAL EQUITY: REDUCING RISK FOR ALL COMMUNITIES, VOL I (1992). The report was an initial step in the Agency's response to environmental equity concerns. Case studies of EPA Program and regional offices revealed that opportunities existed for addressing environmental equity issues and that there was a need for environmental equity awareness training. A number of EPA regional offices have initiated projects to address high risks in racial-minority and low-income communities.

[21] In addition, EPA found that a significantly higher percentage of African-American children compared to white children have unacceptably high blood lead levels.

enforcement treatment from the government. In 1992, the *National Law Journal* (NLJ) conducted an 8-month investigation that examined the relationship between race and the enforcement of environmental laws by the EPA. NLJ analyzed every EPA environmental lawsuit concluded in the preceding 7 years and every residential toxic waste site (1,777 in all) in the then 12-year old program under CERCLA. The study concluded that EPA had discriminated against minority communities in the cleanup of hazardous waste sites and the prosecution of environmental law violations.[22] In particular, the study found: (1) on average, penalties against violators in minority areas are 54% lower than those in wealthy communities; (2) under the Superfund program, abandoned hazardous waste sites in minority areas take 20% longer to be placed on a national priority list than those in white areas; and (3) racial imbalance occurs whether the community is wealthy or poor. Turning to remedy selection, the NLJ reported that permanent treatment remedies were selected twenty-two percent more frequently than containment technologies at sites surrounded by white communities and that communities of color waited up to four years longer than white communities to get a Superfund site cleaned up. In contrast, at sites surrounded by communities of color, containment technologies were selected more frequently than permanent treatment by an average of seven percent. The findings suggest that unequal environmental protection, a form of environmental injustice, is placing communities of color at special risk.

NOTES

1. *Local studies*. In addition to the above-mentioned studies which demonstrated a disproportionate burden of environmental risks and hazards on minority and low-income communities, many local studies have been undertaken. For example, a Louisiana study of the hazardous waste incineration facilities in the Baton Rouge area found that minority communities had an average of one such site for every 7,349 residents, while white communities had only one site for every 31,110 residents. For further examples of local studies, *see* Vicki Been, *What's Fairness Got to do With It? Environmental Justice and the Siting of Locally Undesirable Land Uses*, 78 CORNELL L. REV. 1001 (1993).

2. *LULUs and the market*. Some critics have noted that the evidence in the above reports is flawed. According to Professor Been, the apparent disparity in siting decisions may be the result of market forces such as residential mobility, that is, the evidence does not establish that siting decisions intentionally discriminated against people of color or the poor. In particular she asserts that most studies leave open the possibility that the LULUs were not disparately sited in poor and minority neighborhoods but that the dynamics of the housing and job markets led people of color and the

---

[22] Marianne Lavelle & Marcia Coyle, *Unequal Protection: The Racial Divide in Environmental Law*, NAT'L L.J. Sep. 21, 1992, at s2.

poor to move to areas surrounding LULUs because those neighborhoods offered the cheapest available housing. *See id.*; Vicki Been, *Locally Undesirable Land Uses in Minority Neighborhoods: Disproportionate Siting or Market Dynamics?*, 103 YALE L.J. 1383 (1994). What is the impact and import of distinguishing whether a community preexisted a siting decision or moved into the area due to low property values?

3. *Evidence of no impact.* A few studies also claim to find no significant and consistent national evidence of commercial hazardous waste facilities being disproportionately located in minority communities. The most significant study was conducted by the University of Massachusetts.[23] It examined census tracts as opposed to the zip code areas as used by the GAO and UCC. They looked at each census tract that had a treatment, storage, and disposal facility and drew a five-mile diameter circle around each of the ten census tracts chosen for the study. What they found to be most consistent and significant was the percentage of industrial employment being highest near the facility and declining steadily as one moves outward. The study thus concluded that the tracts containing hazardous waste facilities are not more likely to be located in minority areas. They are instead, primarily in industrial neighborhoods. The Massachusetts study also illustrates the great difficulty in defining subpopulations or communities defined as a basis for measuring the distribution of the burdens of hazardous waste sites. Results of social and economic data analysis for subpopulations can vary considerably according to the geographic unit chosen for the data, just as they can vary with the subpopulation definition used (as can be seen by the various results reached by the UCC and University of Massachusetts). For a detailed explanation of this issue, *see* Rae Zimmerman, *Issues of Classification in Environmental Equity: How We Manage is How We Measure*, 21 FORDHAM L.J. 633 (1994). How does this conclusion impact environmental justice claims?

4. *A longitudinal study.* Having criticized previous studies for failing to include longitudinal data (*i.e.,* showing changes over time), Professor Been undertook her own study of hazardous waste siting data. Her conclusions follow:

> The study shows that the percentage of African Americans in a tract in 1990 is a significant predictor of whether or not that tract hosts a facility. It provides no significant evidence, however, that the percentage of African Americans in a tract at the beginning of a decade affected the probability that the tract would be selected to host a facility sometime in that decade. Thus, the evidence provides little support for the claim that siting processes follow a PIBBY-Put It in Blacks' Backyards-strategy, at least as to sitings in the last twenty-five years.

* * *

---

[23] Douglas L. Anderton, *et al.*, *Environmental Equity: The Demographics of Dumping*, 31 DEOMOGRAPHY 229 (1994).

With regard to Hispanics, the study reveals that the percentage of Hispanics in a tract in 1990 affects the probability that the tract hosts a facility. It also shows that the percentage of Hispanics at the beginning of a decade increased the probability that the tract would be selected to host a facility in that decade. The study therefore supports the claims of the environmental justice movement that siting processes in the past few decades have had a disproportionate effect upon Hispanics.

* * *

The results indicate that siting processes do not intentionally or unintentionally target neighborhoods with high percentages of people with incomes below the poverty level. Indeed, the study shows that high poverty rates are negatively correlated with the probability that a tract will be selected to host a facility. Again, contrary to the assertion that poor neighborhoods are targeted to host facilities, average or median family income is positively correlated with siting choices. Further, the distributional analyses show that working class and lower middle income neighborhoods, not poor neighborhoods, are at greatest risk of being disproportionately chosen to host facilities.

* * *

The analysis provides little support for the theory that market dynamics following the introduction of a TSDF into a neighborhood might lead it to become poorer and increasingly populated by racial and ethnic minorities.

* * *

This study advances the research on environmental justice in [several] significant ways. It is the first study to lend any support to the claims of the environmental justice movement that is carefully designed to separate the effects race or ethnicity might have on sitings from the effects sitings might have on race or ethnicity. Second, the study reveals that it is Hispanics, rather than African Americans, who are most at risk from the siting processes. Third, the analysis shows that the very poor are not hosting a disproportionate share of facilities, and indeed, that neighborhoods with high levels of poverty appear to repel, rather than attract, facilities. Instead, it is working class or lower middle class neighborhoods that bear a disproportionate share of facilities.

Vicki Been, *Coming to the Nuisance or Going to the Barrios? A Longitudinal Analysis of Environmental Justice Claims*, 24 ECOLOGY L.Q. 1, 33-35 (1997). In view of the conflicting evidence, what are some solutions to toxic distributional issues? Are we creating industrial sacrifice zones? Should we spread out toxic impacts so that the environmental burdens are distributed more evenly across various types of natural systems? Should we site toxic impacts in wilderness areas so humans are less directly impacted?

5. *What do statistics have to do with it?* More fundamentally, does it matter whether disproportionate impact can be statistically documented at a national level? Is the problem one of distribution hazardous waste sites-or is it really about distribution of political and economic power? The following reading addresses this question.

ENVIRONMENTAL JUSTICE: BRIDGING THE GAP BETWEEN ENVIRONMENTAL LAWS AND "JUSTICE"

Alice Kaswan
47 AM. U. L. REV. 221, 230-39 (1977)

Defining "Justice"

The types of justice relevant to environmental justice disputes can be classified into two primary categories. One form of justice is distributive: environmental justice concerns are raised by the disproportionate burden of environmental hazards or undesirable land uses borne by low-income and minority communities. The second form of justice focuses on the political process: environmental justice concerns are raised by the discriminatory manner in which decisions with environmental consequences are made.

The environmental justice literature includes a great many things under the rubric of "justice" with relatively little analysis of the form and nature of the justice being sought. While any given instance of perceived environmental injustice may involve claims of both distributive and political injustice, the two forms of injustice present two different kinds of injuries and may require two different types of solutions.

Environmental Justice as Distributive Justice

Many communities suffer the ill effects of environmental problems or the stigma of socially undesirable land uses. To some extent, all communities must be expected to bear some such burdens as unavoidable by-products of a complex industrial society. But whether these burdens are "equitably" distributed among communities is a central theme of the environmental justice movement. Analysis of this question is fraught with difficulty. Much depends upon how relevant communities are defined and upon what constitutes a "proportional" distribution of desirable or undesirable land uses. There are no easy or absolute answers to either of these questions. However, that it is difficult to define an abstract measure of "community" or "equity" does not mean that unfair disparities do not exist. Nor does it mean that communities are never justified in feeling "put upon" by a disproportionate burden.

The environmental justice literature includes frequent reference to studies suggesting that minority and low-income communities currently endure undesirable land uses to a greater extent than other communities.

* * *

Environmental Justice as Political Justice

Environmental justice implicates not only distributive justice, but also political justice. What I term "political justice" concerns the fairness of the decisionmaking process. Professor Ronald Dworkin captures this conception of justice with his reference to the ideal that all citizens should be treated "with equal concern and respect."[24] For example, if an African-American neighborhood rather than a white neighborhood was selected as the site for a new prison because the decisionmakers valued the interests of the white neighborhood more than the interests of the African-American neighborhood, then the African-American neighborhood was not treated with equal concern and respect. More generally, the familiar term "environmental racism" describes a type of political injustice-namely, the failure to treat minority communities with the same concern and respect as white communities.

Claims for environmental justice often include both distributive and political components. Using the prison-siting example, the African-American community may be concerned about such issues as the impact of the prison on the quality of life, property values, and the like. But the community may be as or more concerned about the decision as symptomatic of the lack of respect the decisionmaking body has for the community. The community may view the decision as indicative of their lack of status in the body politic.

There is some debate regarding the role that claims for political justice—and more particularly claims of racial discrimination—should play in the environmental justice movement. As Professor Gerald Torres has observed, the environmental justice movement arose out of the civil rights movement and is therefore inclined to apply civil rights theories and approaches.[25] Environmental harms suffered by minorities are often presumed to be a result of "environmental racism." Professor Torres wisely cautions against a premature allegation of environmental racism, particularly where the movement presumes (without more) that existing disparities are the result of discriminatory decisions.

He argues that the movement's emphasis on racism "seems designed to begin a relatively fruitless search for a wrong-doer, or in other words, the bad person with evil intent. [T]his is probably the wrong road to follow if real changes for the communities at risk are to be achieved." Professor Torres acknowledges the existence of a "subcategory" of activities that could be characterized as racist, or, in his terms, considered "part of a system of racial subordination." This subcategory, however, is simply a "subset of a more general category of inquiry that has as its object a close examination of the distributional effects of environmental policy." Thus, under Professor Torres' characterization, the pursuit of political justice is generally "the wrong road to follow" and, even where merited, it is a sideline to the more important issue of distributive justice.

---

[24]*See* RONALD DWORKIN, TAKING RIGHTS SERIOUSLY, 272-73 (1977).
[25] Gerald Torres, *Environmental Justice: The Legal Meaning of a Social Movement*, 15 J.L. & COM. 597, 602-05 (1996).

Professor Torres' concerns regarding the danger of "knee-jerk" and unsubstantiated accusations of racism are well taken. That charges of racism should be used cautiously does not, however, mean that the pursuit of political justice should be minimized in comparison with the pursuit of distributive justice. In many local settings, the political justice element of the environmental justice movement is as central as the achievement of improved environmental quality. When a legitimate question of fair process arises, the environmental issue becomes "a single dimension of an overall social condition." As such, local grassroots debates about individual decisions with environmental consequences become steps in a much larger effort to increase the political status of the burdened community.

Questions of political justice arise in a number of different settings, from the typical siting dispute to government policy, enforcement, or remediation decisions. In the siting context, a question of political justice would arise if a community believed that it had been selected for an undesirable use due to the decisionmakers' failure to treat that community with the same concern and respect given to other communities.

* * *

Most siting decisions are not, however, accompanied by the kind of "smoking gun" presented by the Cerrell Associates report [discussed *supra*]. Since government and industry are unlikely to announce intentional discrimination against low-income or minority communities, instances of unfair treatment may be difficult to identify. A decision motivated by discriminatory factors may be justified publicly with reference to allegedly neutral factors. In many cases, the discrimination may be entirely unconscious. Thus, instances of unfair treatment may be more pervasive than is suggested by observing only explicit acts of discrimination.

Questions concerning the fairness of decisionmaking processes also arise when federal, state, or local governments make environmental policy decisions. Environmental policy choices may favor certain groups by providing them with more benefits or burdens than others. For example, if saving open space were to become a governmental priority over slowing pollution in urban areas, that policy choice would be to the benefit of those already living in more remote areas, such as the suburbs. Poorer urban communities would be less likely to receive a benefit from such a policy choice. Thus, to the extent that decisions are made that appear less likely to consider the needs of minority or low-income communities, such communities may not be receiving equal concern and respect in the decisionmaking process.

Environmental enforcement decisions may also favor some at the expense of others. Agencies lack sufficient funds to enforce every violation, and enforcement agencies have considerable discretion in choosing enforcement priorities. Enforcement issues arise in connection with many different types of environmental laws, including national, state, and local pollution control laws, laws establishing agricultural pesticide practices, laws to alleviate lead poisoning, and the like. To the extent governmental decision-makers place less priority on enforcement in communities of color and low-income communities, these communities may not receive "equal concern and respect."

* * *

The Relationship Between Distributive and Political Justice

The correlation-or lack thereof-between distributive and political justice has been a subject of much dispute. Does an unjust process necessarily lead to an unjust distribution? Does a just process necessarily lead to a just distribution? Or, phrased conversely, is an unjust distribution necessarily the result of an unjust process, and a just distribution necessarily the result of a just process? What is clear is that no absolutes can be stated; the extent of the correlation will depend upon the particular facts associated with particular claims and how those facts are interpreted.

* * *

How would you answer the questions in the last paragraph? In particular, does a just process by definition result in a just distribution? If not, how should a just distribution be defined?

PROBLEM
RADIOACTIVE WASTE ON INDIAN LANDS

In its search for a solution to the massive radioactive waste disposal problem, the federal government has approached some Indian tribes to determine whether or not they want to host an interim storage facility. The inducements are substantial: up-front payments for even considering such a proposal and a long-term source of income for tribes where poverty and unemployment are the norm. At the same time, this arrangement would create some level of risk to the members of the tribe (how much is disputed) and would tie up land resources for the foreseeable future.

Advocates of interim storage argue that the managing of radioactive waste is an exemplary form of environmental stewardship and that non-Indian opponents are engaged in the worst form of paternalism. Opponents call it economic blackmail, taking advantage of highly vulnerable populations whose vulnerability was itself caused by the federal government. Native Americans are deeply split on the issue. The Mescalero Apache tribe, for example, has held repeated, close votes on the question, reaching different results.

Should the federal government encourage Indian tribes to accept an interim storage facility? Should it *refuse* to permit tribes to accept such a facility? Who should decide? What kinds of information are relevant to the decision? Is compensation (in cash, in economic development, or in goods and services) an appropriate inducement to accept such a facility?

C. Environmental Justice Claims by Individuals and Citizen Groups

There are several legal approaches to litigating environmental injustices. These include constitutional claims and statutory claims.

1. Constitutional Claims

Reflecting uncertainties in the causes and proof of environmental injustices, legal theories to redress such injustices are still in an early stage of development and have not, in general, proven very helpful to environmental justice plaintiffs. The first place to look for legal relief, not surprisingly, is the Equal Protection Clause of the Constitution. In order to bring a federal equal protection challenge, a plaintiff must show not only that a particular decision (for example, the siting of a particular facility) had a disparate impact on a protected group, but also that the decision was motivated in part by discriminatory intent. Prior to 1976, some federal courts allowed plaintiffs to prevail on equal protection claims if they established that the challenged practice had a statistically discriminatory impact.[26] However, in *Washington v. Davis*, 426 U.S. 229 (1976), the Supreme Court narrowed the applicability of the Equal Protection Clause, ruling that the plaintiff was required to prove discriminatory intent, as well. The Court ruled that "disproportionate impact is not irrelevant, but it is not the sole touchstone of an invidious racial discrimination forbidden by the Constitution."[27] Because no decisionmaking body would ever explicitly state that its siting decision is based on racial grounds, plaintiffs must provide indirect evidence that the decision was motivated by discriminatory purpose.

While *Davis* avoided the issue, *Village of Arlington Heights v. Metropolitan Housing Development Corp.*, 429 U.S. 252 (1977), explored in some detail what types of evidence would lead a court to the conclusion that there had been a discriminatory purpose. The *Arlington Heights* Court stated that whether invidious discriminatory purpose was a motivating factor demands a sensitive inquiry into such circumstantial and direct evidence of intent as may be available. The Court suggested, but did not require, that five factors be taken into account: (1) the impact of the official action that falls more heavily on one race than another and that cannot be explained on any other grounds besides race; (2) the historical background of the decision, especially if it uncovers "a series of official actions taken for invidious purposes;" (3) the sequence of events leading up to the challenged decision; (4) substantive or procedural departure from the normal decision-making

---

[26] *See, e.g.*, Hawkins v. Town of Shaw, 437 F.2d 1286 (5th Cir. 1971), *rev'd in part*, 461 F.2d 1171 (5th Cir. 1972) (*per curiam*) (*en banc*).

[27] 426 U.S. at 242.

process; and (5) the legislative and administrative history.[28] In a closing footnote, the court observed that, even if a racially motivated purpose were established, the government had the opportunity to show that "the same decision would have resulted even had the impermissible purpose not been considered."[29] Thus, not only did the plaintiff have to show that the decision was motivated by intentional discrimination, but that the discrimination was prejudicial.

Arlington Heights was itself a LULU case, involving a plan to site a mixed-income housing development in a prosperous community of single-family homes. It thus has taken on great importance in environmental siting cases. The following cases address the issue of proving discriminatory intent in the siting context. They highlight the difficulty of prevailing under an equal protection theory. It is followed by an important equal protection case.

BEAN V. SOUTHWESTERN WASTE MANAGEMENT CORP.

482 F.Supp. 673 (S.D. Tex. 1979)

McDONALD, District Judge.

* * *

On October 26, 1979, plaintiffs filed their complaint and Motion for Temporary Restraining Order and Preliminary Injunction contesting the decision by the Texas Department of Health to grant Permit No. 1193 to defendant Southwestern Waste Management to operate a Type I solid waste facility in the East Houston-Dyersdale Road area in Harris County. They contend that the decision was, at least in part, motivated by racial discrimination in violation of 42 U.S.C. § 1983 [which implements the Equal Protection Clause] and seek an order revoking the permit. The defendants deny the allegations and have moved to dismiss this case

* * *

VI. THE PRELIMINARY INJUNCTION

There are four prerequisites to the granting of a preliminary injunction. The plaintiffs must establish: (1) a substantial likelihood of success on the merits, (2) a substantial threat of irreparable injury, "(3) that the threatened injury to the plaintiff(s) outweighs the threatened harm the injunction may do to defendant(s), and (4) that granting the preliminary injunction will not disserve the public interest." *Canal Authority of State of Florida v. Callaway*, 489 F.2d 567, 572 (5th Cir. 1974).

The plaintiffs have adequately established that there is a substantial threat of irreparable injury. They complain that they are being deprived of their constitutional rights. That, in itself, may constitute irreparable injury, but more is present here. The opening of the facility will affect the entire nature of the community its land values, its tax base, its aesthetics, the health and

---

[28] 429 U.S. at 266-68.

[29] *Id.* at 270-71 n. 21.

safety of its inhabitants, and the operation of Smiley High School, located only 1700 feet from the site. Damages cannot adequately compensate for these types of injuries. Similarly, if a substantial likelihood of success on the merits were shown, there is no doubt that the threatened injury to the plaintiffs would outweigh that to the defendants and that the public interest would not be disserved by granting the plaintiffs an injunction.

The problem is that the plaintiffs have not established a substantial likelihood of success on the merits. The burden on them is to prove discriminatory purpose. *Washington v. Davis*, 426 U.S. 229 (1976); *Village of Arlington Heights v. Metropolitan Housing Development Corp.*, 429 U.S. 252 (1977). That is, the plaintiffs must show not just that the decision to grant the permit is objectionable or even wrong, but that it is attributable to an intent to discriminate on the basis of race. Statistical proof can rise to the level that it, alone, proves discriminatory intent, as in *Yick Wo v. Hopkins*, 118 U.S. 356 (1886), and *Gomillion v. Lightfoot*, 364 U.S. 339 (1960), or, this Court would conclude, even in situations less extreme than in those two cases, but the data shown here does not rise to that level. Similarly, statistical proof can be sufficiently supplemented by the types of proof outlined in *Arlington Heights*, *supra*, to establish purposeful discrimination, but the supplemental proof offered here is not sufficient to do that.

Two different theories of liability have been advanced in this case. The first is that TDH's [Texas Department of Health] approval of the permit was part of a pattern or practice by it of discriminating in the placement of solid waste sites. In order to test that theory, one must focus on the sites which TDH has approved and determine the minority population of the areas in which the sites were located on the day that the sites opened. The available statistical data, both city-wide and in the target area, fails to establish a pattern or practice of discrimination by TDH. City-wide, data was produced for the seventeen (17) sites operating with TDH permits as of July 1, 1978. That data shows that 58.8% of the sites granted permits by TDH were located in census tracts with 25% or less minority population at the time of their opening and that 82.4% of the sites granted permits by TDH were located in census tracts with 50% or less minority population at the time of their opening. In the target area, an area which roughly conforms to the North Forest Independent School District and the newly-created City Council District B and is 70% minority in population, two (2) sites were approved by TDH. One, the McCarty Road site, was in a census tract with less than 10% minority population at the time of its opening. The other, the site being challenged here, is in a census tract with close to 60% minority population. Even if we also consider the sites approved by TDWR [Texas Department of Water Resources] in the target area, which, as discussed earlier, are not really relevant to TDH's intent to discriminate, no pattern or practice of discrimination is revealed. Of all the solid waste sites opened in the target area, 46.2 to 50% were located in census tracts with less than 25% minority population at the time they opened. It may be that more particularized data would show that even those sites approved in predominantly Anglo census tracts were actually located in minority neighborhoods, but the data available here does not show that. In addition, there was no supplemental evidence, such as that suggested by *Arlington Heights*, *supra*, which established a pattern or practice of discrimination on the part of TDH.

The plaintiffs' second theory of liability is that TDH's approval of the permit, in the context of the historical placement of solid waste sites and the events surrounding the application, constituted discrimination. Three sets of data were offered to support this theory. Each set, at first blush, looks compelling. On further analysis, however, each set breaks down. Each fails to approach the standard established by *Yick Wo*, *supra*, and *Gomillion*, *supra*, and, even when considered with supplementary proof, *Arlington Heights*, *supra*, fails to establish a likelihood of success in proving discriminatory intent.

The first set of data focuses on the two (2) solid waste sites to be used by the City of Houston. Both of these sites are located in the target area. This proves discrimination, the plaintiffs argue, because "the target area has the dubious distinction of containing 100% of the Type I municipal land fills that Houston utilizes or will utilize, although it contains only 6.9% of the entire population of Houston." There are two problems with this argument. First, there are only two sites involved here. That is not a statistically significant number. Second, an examination of the census tracts in the target area in which the sites are located reveals that the East Houston-Dyersdale Road proposed site is in a tract with a 58.4% minority population, but that the McCarty Road site is in a tract with only an 18.4% minority population. Thus, the evidence shows that, of the two sites to be used by the City of Houston, one is in a primarily Anglo census tract and one is in a primarily minority census tract. No inference of discrimination can be made from this data.

The second set of data focuses on the total number of solid waste sites located in the target area.[30] The statistical disparity which the plaintiffs point to is that the target area contains 15% of Houston's solid waste sites, but only 6.9% of its population. Since the target area has a 70% minority population, the plaintiffs argue, this statistical disparity must be attributable to race discrimination. To begin with, in the absence of the data on population by race, the statistical disparity is not all that shocking. One would expect solid waste sites to be placed near each other and away from concentrated population areas. Even considering the 70% minority population of the target area, when one looks at where in the target area these particular sites are located, the inference of racial discrimination dissolves. Half of the solid waste sites in the target area are in census tracts with more than 70% Anglo population. Without some proof that the sites affect an area much larger than

---

[30] It should be noted that there are some problems with the definition of the target area as selected and defined by the plaintiffs. There is some question as to whether the definition of the area was entirely scientific. Even so, the approach is a useful one and the target area data should be examined.

the census tract in which they are in, it is very hard to conclude that the placing of a site in the target area evidences purposeful racial discrimination.

The third set of data offered by the plaintiffs focuses on the city as a whole. This data is the most compelling on its surface. It shows that only 17.1% of the city's solid waste sites are located in the southwest quadrant, where 53.3% of the Anglos live. Only 15.3% of the sites are located in the northwest quadrant, where 20.1% of the Anglos live. Thus, only 32.4% of the sites are located in the western half of the city, where 73.4% of the Anglos live. Furthermore, the plaintiffs argue, 67.6% of the sites are located in the eastern half of the city, where 61.6% of the minority population lives.[31] This, according to the plaintiffs, shows racial discrimination.

The problem is that, once again, these statistics break down under closer scrutiny. To begin with, the inclusion of TDWR's sites skew the data. A large number of TDWR sites are located around Houston's ship channel, which is in the eastern half of the city. But those sites, the Assistant Attorney General argues persuasively, are located in the eastern half of the city because that is where Houston's industry is, not because that is where Houston's minority population is. Furthermore, closer examination of the data shows that the city's solid waste sites are not so disparately located as they first appear. If we focus on census tracts, rather than on halves or quadrants of the city, we can see with more particularity where the solid waste sites are located. Houston's population is 39.3% minority and 60.7% Anglo. The plaintiffs argue, and this Court finds persuasive, a definition of "minority census tracts" as those with more than 39.3% minority population and Anglo census tracts as those with more than 60.7% Anglo population. Using those definitions, Houston consists of 42.5% minority tracts and 57.5% Anglo tracts. Again using those definitions, 42.3% of the solid waste sites in the City of Houston are located in minority tracts and 57.7% are located in Anglo tracts. In addition, if we look at tracts with one or more sites per tract, to account for the fact that some tracts contain more than one solid waste site, 42.2% are minority tracts and 57.8% are Anglo tracts. The difference between the racial composition of census tracts in general and the racial composition of census tracts with solid waste sites is, according to the statistics available to the Court, at best, only 0.3%. That is simply not a statistically significant difference. More surprisingly, from the plaintiffs' point of view, to the extent that it is viewed as significant, it tends to indicate that minority census tracts have a tiny bit smaller percentage of solid waste sites than one would proportionately expect.

In support of the proposition that there is a city-wide discrimination against minorities in the placement of solid waste sites, the plaintiffs also argue that the data reveals that, in 1975, eleven solid waste sites were located in census tracts with 100% minority population and none were located in census tracts with 100% Anglo population. There are problems with this

---

[31] The defendants quarrel with this proposition. They say that the data shows that 64.1% of the solid waste sites are located in the eastern half of the city and that 62.8% of its minority population lives there.

argument, too, however. To begin with, the 1975 data is not entirely reliable. Compared with both the 1970 and the 1979 data, the 1975 data appears to overcount minority population. For example, of the eleven sites mentioned by the plaintiffs, only one had a 100% minority population in 1979. More importantly, there were, in fact, two sites located in 100% Anglo tracts in 1975. In addition, 18 other sites were located in tracts with a 90% or greater Anglo population in 1975. Thus, even according to the 1975 data, a large number of sites were located in census tracts with high Anglo populations.

Arlington Heights, supra, suggested various types of non-statistical proof which can be used to establish purposeful discrimination. The supplementary non-statistical evidence provided by the plaintiffs in the present case raises a number of questions as to why this permit was granted. To begin with, a site proposed for the almost identical location was denied a permit in 1971 by the County Commissioners, who were then responsible for the issuance of such permits. One wonders what happened since that time. The plaintiffs argue that Smiley High School has changed from an Anglo school to one whose student body is predominantly minority. Furthermore, the site is being placed within 1700 feet of Smiley High School, a predominantly black school with no air conditioning, and only somewhat farther from a residential neighborhood. Land use considerations alone would seem to militate against granting this permit. Such evidence seemingly did not dissuade TDH.

If this Court were TDH, it might very well have denied this permit. It simply does not make sense to put a solid waste site so close to a high school, particularly one with no air conditioning. Nor does it make sense to put the land site so close to a residential neighborhood. But I am not TDH and for all I know, TDH may regularly approve of solid waste sites located near schools and residential areas, as illogical as that may seem.

It is not my responsibility to decide whether to grant this site a permit. It is my responsibility to decide whether to grant the plaintiffs a preliminary injunction. From the evidence before me, I can say that the plaintiffs have established that the decision to grant the permit was both unfortunate and insensitive. I cannot say that the plaintiffs have established a substantial likelihood of proving that the decision to grant the permit was motivated by purposeful racial discrimination in violation of 42 U.S.C. § 1983. This Court is obligated, as all Courts are, to follow the precedent of the United States Supreme Court and the evidence adduced thus far does not meet the magnitude required by *Arlington Heights, supra*.

* * *

[The court denied both the plaintiffs' motion for a preliminary injunction and the defendants' motion to dismiss.]

—

The following case illustrates an equal protection claim.

EAST BIBB TWIGGS NEIGHBORHOOD ASSOCIATION V. MACON-BIBB COUNTY PLANNING & ZONING COMMISSION

706 F. Supp. 880 (M. D. Ga. 1989), *aff'd on other grounds*, 896 F.2d 1264 (11th Cir. 1989)

OWENS, Chief Judge.

This case involves allegations that plaintiffs have been deprived of equal protection of the law by the Macon-Bibb County Planning & Zoning Commission ("Commission"). Specifically, plaintiffs allege that the Commission's decision to allow the creation of a private landfill in census tract No. 133.02 was motivated at least in part by considerations of race. Defendants vigorously contest that allegation.

Facts

On or about May 14, 1986, defendants Mullis Tree Service, Inc. and Robert Mullis ("petitioners") applied to the Commission for a conditional use to operate a non-putrescible waste landfill at a site bounded at least in part by Davis and Donnan Davis Roads. The property in question is located in census tract No. 133.02, a tract containing five thousand five hundred twenty-seven (5,527) people, three thousand three hundred sixty-seven (3,367) of whom are black persons and two thousand one hundred forty-nine (2,149) of whom are white persons. The only other private landfill approved by the Commission is situated in the adjacent census tract No. 133.01, a tract having a population of one thousand three hundred sixty-nine (1,369) people, one thousand forty-five (1,045) of whom are white persons and three hundred twenty (320) of whom are black persons. That site was approved as a landfill in 1978. The proposed site for the landfill in census tract No. 133.02 is zoned A-Agricultural, and the parties are in agreement that property so zoned is eligible for the construction of and subsequent operation as a landfill of this type.

* * *

The Commission reconvened on June 23, 1986, to consider petitioners' application. Petitioners were present and were represented by Mr. Charles Adams. Approximately one hundred fifty (150) individuals opposed to the landfill attended the Commission meeting. Numerous statements were made, and various opinions were offered. Included among those reasons offered in opposition to the landfill were the following: (1) threat to the residential character of the neighborhood; (2) devaluation of the residents' property; (3) danger to the ecological balance of the area; (4) concern regarding the possible expansion of the landfill into a public dump; (5) hazards to residents and children from increased truck traffic; and (6) dissatisfaction with the perceived inequitable burden borne by the East Bibb Area in terms of "unpleasant" and "undesirable" land uses.

* * *

When the above-mentioned allegations of unfairness were raised by opponents to the landfill, Commission Chairperson Dr. Cullinan expressed concern regarding that perception. He stated as follows:

I'm interested in your comments about manipulations and information may have been passed *sub rosa* in some way. I'm interested in that because I think government and ultimately democracy functions on the legitimacy of its purpose and if people don't have faith in their institutions, the system won't work. They may not like all of the decisions that government institutions make, but I would feel badly if they thought that there was some sort of conspiracy a foot and I can tell you that I received a number of calls before and after my own meanderings through that land and I received no calls from big corporate people asking me to vote a particular way. Although, I did receive numerous calls from people in the area. Although, I can't speak for the other commissioners, my feeling is that their experiences are similar to mine. I think that the record should show to the best of this chairman's knowledge there is not manipulations or conspiracies a foot and if you have such information I would be interested in having it entered into the record.

Dr. Cullinan further stated that "anything that I have any knowledge of will be in the record. We're not going to let vague charges of conspiracy go unchallenged here. We want this Board to be a legitimate Board and speak to the will of all of the people . . . ." *Id.*

* * *

On November 10, 1986, the Commission approved the final site plan for the landfill. On November 20, 1986, the EPD issued a permit to Mullis Tree Service conditioned upon the permittee complying with the following conditions of operation.

Discussion

* * *

Having considered all of the evidence in light of the [*Arlington Heights*] factors, this court is convinced that the Commission's decision to approve the conditional use in question was not motivated by the intent to discriminate against black persons. Regarding the discriminatory impact of the Commission's decision, the court observes the obvious—a decision to approve a landfill in any particular census tract impacts more heavily upon that census tract than upon any other. Since census tract No. 133.02 contains a majority black population equaling roughly sixty percent (60%) of the total population, the decision to approve the landfill in census tract No. 133.02 of necessity impacts greater upon that majority population.

However, the court notes that the only other Commission-approved landfill is located within census tract No. 133.01, a census tract containing a majority white population of roughly seventy-six percent (76%) of the total population. This decision by the Commission and the existence of the landfill in a predominantly white census tract tend to undermine the development of a "clean pattern, unexplainable on grounds other than race . . . ." *Village of Arlington Heights*, 429 U.S. at 266.

Plaintiffs hasten to point out that both census tracts, Nos. 133.01 and 133.02, are located within County Commission District No. 1, a district whose black residents compose roughly seventy percent (70%) of the total population. Based upon the above facts, the court finds that while the Commission's decision to approve the landfill for location in census tract No. 133.02 does of necessity impact to a somewhat larger degree upon the majority population therein, that decision fails to establish a clear pattern of racially motivated decisions.[32]

Plaintiffs contend that the Commission's decision to locate the landfill in census tract No. 133.02 must be viewed against an historical background of locating undesirable land uses in black neighborhoods. First, the above discussion regarding the two Commission approved landfills rebuts any contention that such activities are always located in direct proximity to majority black areas. Further, the court notes that the Commission did not and indeed may not actively solicit this or any other landfill application. The Commission reacts to applications from private landowners for permission to use their property in a particular manner. The Commissioners observed during the course of these proceedings the necessity for a comprehensive scheme for the management of waste and for the location of landfills. In that such a scheme has yet to be introduced, the Commission is left to consider each request on its individual merits. In such a situation, this court finds it difficult to understand plaintiffs' contentions that this Commission's decision to approve a landowner's application for a private landfill is part of any pattern to place "undesirable uses" in black neighborhoods. Second, a considerable portion of plaintiffs' evidence focused upon governmental decisions made by agencies other than the planning and zoning commission, evidence which sheds little if any light upon the alleged discriminatory intent of the Commission.

Finally, regarding the historical background of the Commission's decision, plaintiffs have submitted numerous exhibits consisting of newspaper articles reflecting various zoning decisions made by the Commission. The court has read each article, and it is unable to discern a series of official actions taken by the Commission for invidious purposes. Of the more recent articles, the court notes that in many instances matters under consideration by the Commission attracted widespread attention and vocal opposition. The Commission oft times was responsive to the opposition and refused to permit the particular development under consideration, while on other occasions the Commission permitted the development to proceed in the face of opposition. Neither the articles nor the evidence presented during trial provides factual support for a determination of the underlying motivations, if any, of the Commission in making the decisions. In short, plaintiffs' evidence does not establish a background of discrimination in the Commission's decisions.

---

[32] The court further finds it clear that the Commissioner's decision to approve petitioners' application is not a "single invidiously discriminatory act" which makes the establishment of a clear pattern unnecessary. *See Village of Arlington Heights*, 429 U.S. at 266 n. 14.

"The specific sequence of events leading up to the challenged decision also may shed some light on the decisionmaker's purpose." *Village of Arlington Heights*, 429 U.S. at 267. Plaintiff identifies as the key piece of evidence in this regard a statement contained in "Action Plan for Housing," a study of the status of housing in the Macon area conducted by the Macon-Bibb County Planning and Zoning Commission. The study states that "[r]acial and low income discrimination still exist in the community."[33] The study was issued in March of 1974, and it constitutes a recognition by the Commission that racial discrimination still existed in the Macon community in 1974. That recognition in no way implies that racial discrimination affected the decision-making process of the Commission itself. Rather, the statement indicates the Commission's awareness that certain individuals and/or groups in society had yet to come to grips with the concept of equality before the law. The Commission's recognition of the situation does not constitute its adoption. Indeed, such recognition probably encourages that Commission to exercise vigilance in guarding against such unprincipled influence. The statements of the various Commissioners during their deliberations indicates a real concern about both the desires of the opposing citizens and the needs of the community in general.

In terms of other specific antecedent events, plaintiffs have not produced evidence of any such events nor has the court discerned any such events from its thorough review of the record. No sudden changes in the zoning classifications have been brought to the court's attention. Plaintiffs have not produced evidence showing a relaxation or other change in the standards applicable to the granting of a conditional use. Thus, this court finds no specific antecedent events which support a determination that race was a motivating factor in the Commission's decision.

Plaintiffs contend that the Commission deviated from its "normal procedures" in several ways. First, plaintiffs point to the Commission's efforts to encourage input from the County and the City. These efforts do not constitute evidence that "improper purposes are playing a role"[34] in the Commission's decision. The statements of the Commissioners make clear that such efforts had their genesis in the Commission's concerns about accountability to the public for certain controversial governmental decisions and about centralized planning for the area's present and future waste disposal problems.

Plaintiffs' contentions regarding other alleged procedural irregularities, including the requirement that the Commission make certain findings of fact and that a rehearing was improperly granted, are without merit. The court has

---

[33] The court believes this evidence is more probative of the "historical background of discrimination" than it is indicative of the specific sequence of events leading up to the challenged decision. Even considered in the historical context, the statement neither admits nor indicates that such discrimination existed in the Commission itself.

[34] *See Village of Arlington Heights*, 429 U.S. at 267.

examined the Comprehensive Land Development Resolution in light of the actions taken and has been unable to identify any procedural flaws.

The final factor identified in Village of Arlington Heights involves the legislative or administrative history, particularly the contemporary statements made by members of the Commission. Plaintiffs focus on the reasons offered by the Commission for the initial denial of petitioners' application, *i.e.*, that the landfill was adjacent to a residential area and that the approval of the landfill in that area would result in increased traffic and noise, and they insist that those reasons are still valid. Thus, plaintiffs reason, some invidious racial purpose must have motivated the Commission to reconsider its decision and to approve that use which was at first denied. This court, having read the comments of the individual commissioners, cannot agree with plaintiffs' arguments.

Mr. Pippinger, who first opposed the approval of the conditional use, changed his position after examining the area in question and reviewing the data. He relied upon the EPD's approval of the site and upon his determination that the impact of the landfill on the area had been exaggerated. Mrs. Kearnes, who also inspected the site, agreed with Mr. Pippinger.

Dr. Cullinan also inspected the site. After such inspection and after hearing all of the evidence, he stated that, based "on the overriding need for us to meet our at large responsibilities to Bibb County I feel that [the site in question] is an adequate site and in my most difficult decision to date I will vote to support the resolution."

Both Dr. Cullinan and Mr. Pippinger were concerned with the problems of providing adequate buffers protecting the residential area from the landfill site and of developing an appropriate access to the site for the dumping vehicles. These concerns were in fact addressed by both the Commission and the EPD.

The voluminous transcript of the hearings before and the deliberations by the Commission portray the Commissioners as concerned citizens and effective public servants. At no time does it appear to this court that the Commission abdicated its responsibility either to the public at large, to the particular concerned citizens or to the petitioners. Rather, it appears to this court that the Commission carefully and thoughtfully addressed a serious problem and that it made a decision based upon the merits and not upon any improper racial animus.

For all the foregoing reasons, this court determines that plaintiffs have not been deprived of equal protection of the law. Judgement, therefore, shall be entered for defendants.

SO ORDERED.

NOTES

1. *Bean v. Southwestern Waste* was the first suit in the country to challenge the siting of an unwanted waste facility. Does it strike you as odd that the court found that the state's decision to grant the permit "both

unfortunate and insensitive," yet held that the evidence did not rise to the level of discriminatory intent? How did the plaintiff's statistical data fail to demonstrate discriminatory intent on the part of state officials? The *Bean* court suggested some types of analysis that future environmental justice advocates should present in order to mount a successful claim. What are they? If the plaintiffs had presented such data, do you think that they would have prevailed?

2. The decision in *East Bibb Twiggs* illustrates how the *Arlington Heights* factors bearing on discriminatory intent are to be applied in siting cases. While rejecting the plaintiff's equal protection claim, this court, too, offers some suggestions for challenging future siting decisions. What kinds of non-statistical evidence should plaintiffs look for?

Environmental laws can be useful sources of information to assist in proving equal protection cases. Can you think of examples? *See* Alice Kaswan, *Environmental Law: Grist for the Equal Protection Mill*, 70 U. COLO. L. REV. 387 (1999); *see also* John S. Applegate, *Risk Assessment, Redevelopment, and Environmental Justice: Candidly Evaluating the Brownfields Bargain*, 13 J. NAT. RESOURCES & ENVTL. L. 243 (1997-98).

3. *Environmental impact-based claims.* Environmental justice advocates have had more success bringing actions under environmental statutes themselves. Traditional environmental laws can be used to challenge the siting of pollution industries, the issuance of construction and operating permits, excessive discharges from existing facilities, and non-enforcement of clean-up provisions. As race is not the central issue in such lawsuits, plaintiffs who bring these claims need not prove that the defendants intended to discriminate on the basis of race or that the defendants' actions had a disparate impact on minorities.

In *El Pueblo para el Aire y Agua Limpio v. County of Kings*, 22 Envtl. L. Rep. 20,357 (1991), residents of Kettleman City challenged a decision of the Kings County Board of Supervisors to grant a conditional permit for the construction and operation of a hazardous waste incinerator in Kettleman City.[35] The residents alleged that the Environmental Impact Statement (EIS) report prepared by the county failed to comply with the California Environmental Quality Act (CEQA), the California cognate of the National Environmental Policy Act (NEPA). The court agreed. The court found that the EIS's analysis of air quality impacts, agricultural impacts, and available alternative sites was flawed. Most significantly, the court held that the county's failure to provide Spanish translations of the EIS, public notices, and public meeting testimony to the community, where nearly forty percent of the residents speak and read only Spanish, violated the public participation requirements of CEQA.

4. *Medicaid.* Another route attempted by plaintiffs is the use of the federal Medicaid statute. Environmental justice advocates have brought

---

[35] Kettleman City was already the home to the largest hazardous waste facility west of the Mississippi River, owned and operated by Chemical Waste Management.

actions against government agencies to comply with mandatory federal Medicaid statutes and guidelines that require the Department of Health Services to detect and treat lead poisoning in poor children. *See New York City Coalition to End Lead Poisoning v. Koch*, 524 N.Y. Supp. 2d 314 (1987); *Matthews v. Kizer*, Case No. C90-3620-EFL (Dist. Ct. N.D. Calif. 1990). In *Matthews v. Kizer*, the plaintiffs presented evidence showing that over 67% of African-American inner-city children and almost 17% of all urban children in the United States have been contaminated by excessive levels of lead. The Federal Medicaid Act imposes a mandatory duty upon the Department of Health Services to ensure that lead levels are measured in poor children and to provide necessary treatment. Specifically, the Act requires the department to include in its Medicaid program early and periodic screening, diagnosis, and treatment for eligible children under age 21. *See* 42 U.S.C. §§ 1396a(a)(43), 1396 d(a)(4)(B), and 1396d(r). The Department of Health Services is also required to provide treatment for the effects of lead poisoning discovered during the screening. 42 U.S.C. § 1396d(r). Plaintiffs alleged that California's program failed to provide for or require lead level assessments and treatment in violation of the Federal Medicaid Act. As a result of the action, the parties entered into a Settlement Agreement in which the Department of Health Services agreed to expand the laboratory-based reporting system and disseminate information regarding childhood lead poisoning.

5. In structuring a lawsuit to challenge a siting decision, there are strong reasons first to consider state law strategies (*e.g.*, state constitutional claims,[36] state statutory claims, and state common-law claims[37]). Considering the fact that the United States Supreme Court has made it difficult for litigants to vindicate individual rights under the equal protection clause of the Fourteenth Amendment, plaintiffs may have more success under state law claims. In fact, some state courts are diverging from federal norms and extending protections to civil rights litigants under state law that are greater than those provided by federal law. Because siting decisions implicate health, safety, and land use concerns, it is appropriate to seek redress first in the state courts. In bringing a state action, a litigant should focus on finding: (1) general statutory language that was ignored in the siting decision, and (2) possible defects in the state's review of the environmental and social impact of the proposed site.

---

[36] To bring a state constitutional law challenge, plaintiffs must first establish disparate treatment in the siting of hazardous waste facilities. It is important to note that some states have interpreted their state constitutional equality provisions more expansively than the federal doctrine. *See* Naikang Tsao, *Ameliorating Environmental Racism: A Citizen's Guide to Combating the Discriminatory Siting of Toxic Waste Dumps*, 67 N.Y. UNIV. L. REV. 366, 398 (1992). Litigants who reside in states which have been willing to interpret their constitutions more broadly than the federal Constitution should seriously consider a state court challenge.

[37] A plaintiff could argue that the cumulative effect of an additional noxious facility in an area already supporting a number of facilities may rise to a level of "nuisance" under state common-law theories.

2. Federal Statutory Claims

Under Title VI of the Civil Rights Act of 1964,[38] which bars discrimination by federally funded programs, plaintiffs may prove discrimination by demonstrating that a federal program (*e.g.*, a siting or permitting program) disproportionately impacts minorities. Plaintiffs need not establish that there was any intent to discriminate, as is required under an equal protection challenge.[39] Because Title VI applies only to federally funded programs, private industries and state-run enterprises that do not receive federal assistance are beyond the reach of Title VI. Therefore, many commercial enterprises such as hazardous waste disposal firms, private lead smelters, or petrochemical production plants are likely to be immune. However, it does cover all federal agencies and federal environmental statutes that provide funding to state programs that carry out federally mandated environmental laws.

The first Title VI environmental justice case to be reported was *Coalition of Concerned Citizens Against I-670 v. Damian*, 608 F.Supp. 110 (S.D. Ohio 1984). The coalition sued under the Department of Transportation's Title VI regulations to enjoin highway construction that threatened their neighborhood. The court found that the plaintiff had made out a *prima facie* case of disparate impact. The court also stated that Title VI prohibits taking action with differential impacts without adequate justification. Although the plaintiff had made out a *prima facie* case of disparate impact, the court concluded that the highway authorities had met their burden of proof by articulating legitimate, non-discriminatory reasons for siting decisions.[40]

D. Government Responses to the Environmental Justice Movement

EPA placed a priority on environmental equity by creating the Workgroup on Environmental Equity to assess evidence indicating that these communities were at a greater risk of exposure to environmental contamination than was the population at large. A final report of the workgroup, *Environmental Equity: Reducing Risks to All Communities*, was released in February 1992. In November 1993, EPA announced the establishment of the 25-member National Environmental Justice Advisory Counsel (NEJAC) to advise the Administrator on environmental justice

---

[38] "No person in the United States shall, on the ground of race, color, or national origin, be excluded from participation in, be denied the benefits of, or be subjected to discrimination under any program or activity receiving Federal financial assistance." 42 U.S.C. § 2000d (1994).

[39] In the absence of a showing of discriminatory intent, however, equitable remedy is the only remedy available to redress a Title VI violation.

[40] *See also* Guardians Ass'n v. Civil Serv. Comm'n of N.Y., 463 U.S. 582 (1983) (holding that a private party could bring a suit for prospective relief to enforce Title VI regulations that prohibited disparate racial impact).

matters, as well as to promote communication concerning environmental justice issues.[41] In the same month, the Assistant Administrator of EPA organized the Office of Solid Waste and Emergency Response (OSWER) Environmental Justice Task Force, composed of 67 employees from OSWER offices and other federal agencies. This task force examined various environmental justice concerns relating to RCRA, Superfund, the clean-up and regulation of underground storage tanks, and other programs.

In February 1994, the Clinton Administration issued an executive order, "Federal Actions to Address Environmental Justice in Minority Populations and Low-Income Populations," for federal agencies to protect minority communities from disproportionate pollution and to determine the extent to which "environmental racism" is a national problem. The Executive Order (1) requires every executive agency to adopt an environmental justice strategy; (2) creates the Interagency Working Group on Environmental Justice; (3) encourages public participation to resolve this issue; and, (4) requires further research into environmental inequities.

EXECUTIVE ORDER NO. 12898

59 Fed. Reg. 7629 (1994)

1-103. *Development of Agency Strategies.* (a) . . . each Federal agency shall develop an agency-wide environmental justice strategy . . . that identifies and addresses disproportionately high and adverse human health or environmental effects of its programs, policies, and activities on minority populations and low-income populations. The environmental justice strategy shall list programs, policies, planning and public participation processes, enforcement, and/or rulemakings related to human health or the environment that should be revised to, at a minimum: (1) promote enforcement of all health and environmental statutes in areas with minority populations and low-income populations; (2) ensure greater public participation; (3) improve research and data collection relating to the health of and environment of minority populations and low-income populations; and (4) identify differential patterns of consumption of natural resources among minority populations and low-income populations. In addition, the environmental justice strategy shall include, where appropriate, a timetable for undertaking identified revisions and consideration of economic and social implications of the revisions.

* * *

Sec. 2-2. *Federal Agency Responsibilities for Federal Programs.* Each Federal agency shall conduct its programs, policies, and activities that substantially affect human health or the environment, in a manner that ensures that such programs, policies, and activities do not have the effect of excluding persons (including populations) from participation in, denying persons

---

[41] EPA's environmental justice website, http://www.epa.gov/oeca/oejbut.htm is a valuable source of information.

(including populations) the benefits of, or subjecting persons (including populations) to discrimination under, such programs, policies, and activities, because of their race, color, or national origin.

* * *

6-608. *General.* Federal agencies shall implement this order consistent with, and to the extent permitted by, existing law.

6-609. *Judicial Review.* This order is intended only to improve the internal management of the executive branch and is not intended to, nor does it create any right, benefit, or trust responsibility, substantive or procedural, enforceable at law or equity by a party against the United States, its agencies, its officers, or any person. This order shall not be construed to create any right to judicial review involving the compliance or noncompliance of the United States, its agencies, its officers, or any other person with this order.

TAKING ENVIRONMENTAL JUSTICE CLAIMS SERIOUSLY

Jeffrey B. Gracer
28 ENVTL. L. REP. (ENVTL. L. INST.) 10373, 10373-10375 (1998)

Environmental justice claims are gaining acceptance in the courts and administrative agencies and recently have created significant impediments to successful project development. As a result, it is becoming essential for developers to anticipate the possibility of such claims at the project planning and permit application stages and to integrate environmental justice concerns into the permitting process.

* * *

Environmental justice concerns typically arise when a predominantly minority community asserts that it is shouldering more than its fair share of the burdens associated with polluting activities. Although there has been considerable political debate about the issue for years, that debate is now having impact on pending projects. To cite just a few examples:

- In April 1997, the New Jersey Department of Environmental Protection withheld approval of an application to convert a solid waste transfer station into a $63 million sludge treatment plant after EPA and Newark residents raised environmental justice concerns.

- In July 1997, community groups in Los Angeles, California, filed a federal civil rights lawsuit against the South Coast Air Quality Management District and the California Air Resources Board challenging approval of a pollution trading program for local refineries. The groups allege that allowing pollution credits to replace stack emission reductions has an adverse impact on minority communities.

- In September 1997, EPA withheld approval of air permits for a proposed $700 million plastics manufacturing plant in Convent, Louisiana, after a coalition of citizen groups alleged the facility would "disproportionately burden the surrounding predominantly

African-American and low-income populations with increased levels of pollution, and increased health and environmental risks."

Companies tend to underestimate the ability of environmental justice concerns to delay or derail projects. EPA's regulations implementing Title VI of the 1964 Civil Rights Act (Title VI) have long required state environmental agencies to avoid "criteria or methods" that "have the effect of subjecting individuals to discrimination because of their race, color, national origin, or sex"[42] President Clinton's 1994 environmental justice Executive Order also directs federal agencies to consider the impacts of their actions on minority and low-income populations. Until recently, however, there were relatively few high-profile cases in which environmental justice claims became material impediments to project development or permit renewal. The issue played out most often in task forces and broad policy formulations, with little practical impact on the regulated community.

That picture has changed for two principal reasons. First, in a case of first impression, the Third Circuit held last December in *Chester Residents Concerned for Quality Living v. Seif*[43] that community groups can bring civil rights actions in federal court to collaterally attack state environmental permit decisions. The Supreme Court accepted this case for review.[44] Second, EPA issued an interim guidance document on environmental justice, which, among other things, would allow community groups to challenge state permit decisions after they are made-including permit renewals and modifications.[45] These twin developments raise important strategic issues for developers and companies seeking governmental approvals for projects located in geographic areas with significant minority or low-income populations.

The *Chester Residents* Decision

In *Chester Residents*, a community group asserted that the Pennsylvania Department of Environmental Protection (PADEP) licensed a disproportionate number of waste facilities in a predominantly minority neighborhood in violation of EPA's Title VI regulations. They relied on data showing that PADEP issued five waste facility permits with a total annual capacity of 2.1 million tons in the city of Chester, a predominantly African American community, but issued only two such permits with a total annual capacity of 1,400 tons in other areas of predominantly white Delaware County. The community group filed suit in the Eastern District of Pennsylvania, alleging that PADEP's permit decision had a discriminatory impact on minorities. The district court dismissed the suit, holding that

---

[42] 40 C.F.R. § 7.35(b).

[43] 132 F.3d 925 (3d. Cir. 1997).

[44] As noted above, the Supreme Court subsequently vacated the judgement without reaching a substantive decision. The issue remains ripe for decision, however, and a new case raising it is only a matter of time.-EDS.

[45] U.S. EPA, INTERIM GUIDANCE FOR INVESTIGATING TITLE VI ADMINISTRATIVE COMPLAINTS CHALLENGING PERMITS (Feb. 5, 1998).

plaintiffs did not have a private right-of-action to enforce EPA's Title VI regulations. The Third Circuit reversed.

In many respects, the Third Circuit's ruling could be viewed as a straightforward application of traditional civil rights law. Although § 601 of Title VI reaches only intentional discrimination, § 602 allows federal agencies to regulate policies or practices that are neutral on their face but have a disparate impact on minorities.[46] The Supreme Court will now decide whether litigants have a private right-of-action to enforce disparate impact regulations, as several federal appellate courts have so held. Accordingly, the Third Circuit's holding was not a significant departure from prior case law.

Of greater practical significance, the Third Circuit also held that citizen groups can bring suit directly in federal court without first exhausting administrative remedies before EPA. While EPA's regulations establish an administrative process for raising environmental justice claims, the Third Circuit's ruling allows private litigants to bypass that process entirely. Indeed, the panel expressly rejected PADEP's argument that EPA is a necessary "gatekeeper to enforcement." This aspect of the court's ruling raises important questions of finality for project developers.

Collateral Attacks on State Permits

The *Chester Residents* decision provides powerful leverage to community groups in siting and permitting matters. Whenever a project can be alleged to result in a disproportionate impact on a minority community, the permit can be challenged immediately and directly in federal court.

* * *

EPA's Environmental Justice Guidance

On February 5, 1998, EPA issued an interim guidance document on environmental justice. The document's stated purpose is to provide a framework for processing administrative complaints regarding environmental permitting activities within EPA's Office of Civil Rights.

* * *

The guidance states that "individuals may file a private right of action in court to enforce the nondiscrimination requirements in Title VI or EPA's implementing regulations without exhausting administrative remedies." It thus adopts the *Chester Residents* decision as nationwide policy.

The guidance also allows environmental justice claims to be raised in connection with permit modifications and renewals. Minor permit modifications generally will not trigger environmental justice concerns. However, permit modifications "that result in a net increase of pollution impacts . . . may provide a basis for an adverse disparate impact finding." Of even greater significance, EPA will review permit renewals as if they were plenary applications for new facility permits, even if the facility is not proposing a net increase in activities. As a result, facilities that have been

---

[46] Alexander v. Choate, 469 U.S. 287 (1985); Guardians Assoc. v. Civil Service Comm'n, 463 U.S. 582 (1983).

operating in a community for years could face environmental justice challenges in connection with permit renewals as well as major permit modifications.

To determine whether a community group has stated a prima facie case of disparate impact, EPA's interim guidance document provides only a broad framework. According to the guidance, EPA will: (1) identify the population affected by the permit; (2) analyze other permitted facilities in the community and their aggregate impacts on racial and ethnic populations; (3) compare the impacts on affected and unaffected populations; and (4) determine whether any observed disparate impacts are significant. The document does not specify how EPA will define the affected and unaffected populations, although it does refer generally to proximity and contamination pathways. It also does not define what methodology EPA will utilize to determine whether a disparity is statistically significant. These issues-the proper unit of measure for disparate impact analysis and statistical significance-lie at the heart of disparate impact analysis and have generated considerable debate in court decisions and professional literature. Although the courts and administrative agencies have acquired substantial experience applying disparate impact theory in the employment discrimination and fair lending contexts over a period of years, extension of that theory to the environmental permitting context is essentially untested. In the absence of more specific guidance regarding what constitutes a disparate impact in this context, environmental justice claims will be decided on a case-by-case basis against a backdrop of substantial uncertainty.

In addition, EPA appears to have shifted the ultimate burden of proof to the permitting agency. Under traditional civil rights jurisprudence, once a plaintiff makes out a prima facie case of disparate impact, the burden shifts to the defending party to demonstrate either that there is no disparate impact or that any impact is justified by legitimate considerations. After that intermediate burden is met, the burden shifts back to the plaintiff to carry its ultimate burden of proving that the business objective can be met in a less discriminatory manner. EPA's guidance appears to place the final burden of proof improperly on the permitting agency. In other words, the state agency not only must establish that the permit is necessary to advance a "substantial, legitimate interest,"[47] but must also prove that there is no less discriminatory alternative. EPA's guidance does not require the project challenger to prove that less discriminatory alternatives would satisfy legitimate business interests. Because disparate impact cases are often won or lost based on which party bears the burden of proof, this departure from established practice could be significant.

The guidance also identifies alternatives and mitigation measures as key concepts, but it does not indicate how these concepts should be applied in the environmental justice context. For example, analysis of project alternative is a

---

[47] INTERIM GUIDANCE, *supra*, at 5.

standard feature of environmental impact analysis. It is unclear in the environmental justice context, however, whether a developer can choose not to pursue an alternate site based on cost, site access or suitability, market factors, availability of infrastructure, or other legitimate business considerations. Similarly, mitigation of environmental impacts is a familiar concept. Mitigation of environmental justice concerns if far less familiar. EPA does not identify categories of mitigation measures that would be acceptable, such as job training for community residents or host community benefit payments, for example. Additional guidance would be helpful in this regard.

In effect, EPA seeks to establish a broad, open-ended administrative process for assessing environmental justice complaints that is separate and apart from the state permitting process and that takes place after the state permit is issued. This raises substantial finality concerns. For example, when a permit is issued under a federally delegated program, EPA's environmental comments are typically addressed by the state *before* the final permit is issued. Under the environmental justice guidance, even after the traditional permitting process has been successfully completed, another unit of EPA could demand additional changes or withdrawal of the permit based on environmental justice concerns.

EPA's proposal has raised substantial concerns. For example, the Environmental Council of the States, an organization of environmental officials from 49 states, the District of Columbia, and two U.S. territories, recently issued a resolution asking EPA to withdraw the interim guidance, noting that it would "clearly disrupt the management of environmental permitting programs."

* * *

NOTES

1. *Executive Order No. 12898.* What are the strengths and weaknesses of the approach in Executive Order No. 12898? What practical effect do you think it will have on agency decisions?

One indication of the impact of the presidential order may be found in a May 1997 licensing decision of the United States Nuclear Regulatory Commission (NRC) in May 1997. *In the Matter of Louisiana Energy Services*, Docket No. 70-3070-ML, the NRC rejected an environmental impact statement submitted by Louisiana Energy Services. NRC's decision denied a permit for the placement of the nation's first private uranium enrichment facility near two predominantly low-income African-American communities. The NRC determined that evidence of racial discrimination existed in the facility siting process and that its staff had failed to consider the environmental, social, and economic impact on the African-American communities, as required by NEPA. The Lawyers' Committee for Civil Rights Under Law, a party to the action, gathered evidence and applied a disparate impact analysis to the facts surrounding the siting process and demonstrated that race rather than legitimate criteria motivated the siting decision. During the selection process, each of the sites under consideration in northern Louisiana had successively higher percentages of African-Americans. The site ultimately selected had a population that is 97.1% African-American. The NRC decision stated that a "thorough staff investigation is needed [of discrimination claims] not only to comply with Executive Order 12898, but to avoid the constitutional ramifications of the agency becoming a participant in any discriminatory conduct through its grant of a license." The NRC further stated that "if the President's directive is to have any meaning in this particular licensing action, the staff must conduct an objective, thorough, and professional investigation that looks beneath the surface."

2. *Environmental Justice Legislation.* Although several bills have been proposed, no legislation specifically addressing environmental justice has been enacted. The Environmental Justice Act of 1992, introduced by then Senator Albert Gore, called for a comprehensive survey of every county in the nation in an attempt to rank the 100 counties most severely contaminated by toxic chemical releases. The bill would have imposed a moratorium on new pollution sources in those counties.[48] The Environmental Justice Act of 1993, which was introduced in the 103rd Congress, differed from its predecessor by prohibiting new industrial activity only in those areas determined to receive toxic discharges in quantities found to adversely impact human health.[49] Another proposed bill, the Environmental Equal Rights Act of 1993 (H.R. 1924), would have allowed citizens to challenge and prohibit the construction of waste facilities in "environmentally disadvantaged communities." Under the bill, a challenge would be granted and the proposed facility's construction and operating permits denied unless the facility proponent demonstrated that there is no alternative location in the state that poses fewer risks and that the proposed facility will neither release contaminants nor increase the impact of present contaminants.[50] If you were on a Senate or House Committee assigned to draft legislation on environmental justice, what would you include in such a bill?

3. The Gracer article identifies both substantive and procedural issues raised by the *Chester Residents* case and EPA's Interim Guidance. Taking the procedural first, what is the "finality" problem that Gracer raises? Why do the states overwhelmingly oppose the approach taken in the guidance?

Substantively, how do the case and guidance (and the EPA regulations on which they are based) change requirements of Arlington Heights? Is this a good idea? Can agencies, industries, and developers assure themselves, in advance, that they are in compliance with Title VI?

4. *State actions.* Because the states are responsible for implementing the RCRA and other EPA regulations, they effectively control the siting of toxic

---

[48] S. 2806, 102d Cong., 2d Sess. (1992).

[49] H.R. 2015, 103d Cong., 1st Sess. (1993).

[50] H.R. 1924, 103d Cong., 1st Sess. (1993).

and hazardous waste landfills. In addition, because siting decisions implicate health, safety and land use concerns, the state and local governments traditionally regulate the siting and development of facilities under their police power (*e.g.*, through the use of zoning).[51]

Some state legislatures actively address the issue of environmental justice. For example, in 1993, the New York State Assembly considered a bill to ensure that minorities were not disproportionately affected by toxic waste sites.[52] New York City adopted an innovative legislative approach that attempts to achieve a greater degree of fairness in the siting of city facilities- he "Fair Share" approach.[53] Under the legislation, the City Planning Commission developed a set of "fair share criteria" in response to the mandate-the goal of which was to add the factor of fair geographical distribution to other more traditional factors used to assess siting proposals.[54]

PROBLEM
CONCLUDING QUESTIONS

How do you think that environmental regulation should address justice or distributional issues? Is it even an appropriate subject for environmental regulation, or (to restate the question from the beginning of the chapter) is it really an issue for civil rights or some other area of the law?

If environmental justice is an appropriate subject of environmental regulation, which of the regulatory tools discussed in Chapter 1-

- standard setting ("command and control")
- research and development
- social funds
- civil penalties
- liability
- planning
- economic incentives
- criminal sanctions
- information gathering and dissemination

---

[51] Many local governments have used exclusionary zoning provisions to bar the siting of waste dumps in their municipalities.

[52] N.Y.A.B. 7140, 215th General Assembly, 2d Reg. Sess. (1993).

[53] NEW YORK CITY CHARTER § 203(A).

[54] *See* Naikang Tsao, *Ameliorating Environmental Racism: A Citizen's Guide to Combating the Discriminatory Siting of Toxic Waste Dumps*, 67 N.Y. U.L. REV. 366, 376 (1992) (discussing the "Fair Share" approach and listing the "fair share criteria").

- property rights
- contracts and negotiation-

is most likely to be effective in addressing environmental justice concerns? How would they work in this setting?

Chapter 14

Alternative Control Strategies

Virtually all of the statutes and regulatory schemes we have studied to this point adopt a fundamentally similar approach to toxic substances. They identify a particular problem, develop standards to control it, and impose those standards on the persons or firms responsible for creating the problem. This basic approach to the control of toxic substances and hazardous wastes relies primarily on (1) government-set standards; (2) *reacting* to existing toxic threats, seeking to minimize rather than eliminate them, and (3) governmental action and firm compliance, rather than individual citizen accommodation, to achieve the goal of environmental protection.

The two alternative control strategies that we consider in this chapter take a significantly different tack: right-to-know and pollution prevention. Right-to-know, which we first encountered in the areas of occupational health and safety (Chapter 6) and pesticide labeling (Chapter 7), treats toxic substances regulation more like, say, commercial or securities transactions, insisting on full disclosure and letting market actors take it from there. Pollution prevention is potentially more far-reaching, as it seeks to eliminate toxic threats entirely, by reengineering the processes that generate them.

As you read these materials, consider first how right-to-know and pollution prevention strategies differ from the usual approaches to toxics regulation. Then ask yourself whether they are in fact worthwhile alternatives to existing regulatory strategies, or whether they abandon important goals or regulatory techniques embodied in existing strategies. Finally, consider how they might be integrated into existing strategies to improve protection of human health and the environment.

A. The Right to Know: The Emergency Planning and Community Right-to-Know Act (EPCRA)

In addition to requiring emergency preparedness, EPCRA uses information to utilize as a tool to promote environmental quality improvement. EPCRA seeks to empower local communities by telling them what chemicals are being stored and released by neighboring industries. The following explains EPCRAís history and legal framework.

1. From Bhopal to EPCRA

In 1969, as part of its global operations, Union Carbide Corporation set up its pesticide formulation unit in the northern end of the city of Bhopal in central India. Initially it mixed and packaged pesticides imported from the U.S. but was gradually expanded. In December 1979 its Methyl Iso Cyanate (MC) plant with an installed capacity of 5000 tons went into production.

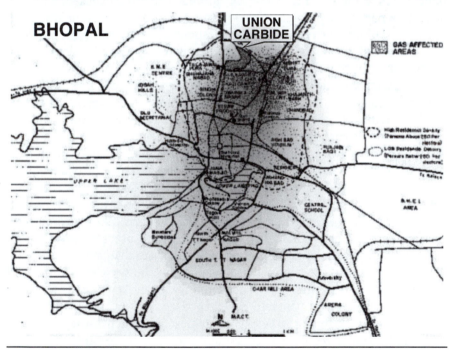

Figure 14.1–Bhopal[1]

On the night of December 2, 1984, during routine maintenance operations in the Methyl Iso Cyanate (MC) plant, at about 9:30 p.m., a large

---

[1]Source: http://www.ucaqld.com.au/community/bhopal/event.html

quantity of water entered storage tank no. 610 containing over 60 tonnes of AEC.

This triggered off a runaway reaction resulting in a tremendous increase of temperature and pressure in the tank and 40 tonnes of MIC along with Hydrogen Cyanide and other reaction products burst past the ruptured disc and into the night air of Bhopal at around 12:30 a.m. Safety systems were grossly under-designed and inoperative. Senior factory officials knew of the lethal build-up in the tank at least one hour before the leakage, yet the siren to warn neighbourhood communities was sounded more than one hour after the leak started.

By then, the poisons had enveloped an area of 40 sq.kms. killing thousands of people in its immediate wake. Over 500 thousand suffered from acute breathlessness, pain in the eyes and vomiting as they ran in panic to get away from the poison clouds that hung close to the ground for more than four hours.[2]

Figure 14.2–Bhopal

The deadly cloud of methyl isocyanate killed over 2000 residents of Bhopal and injured over 200,000 more. As television stations aired images of the devastation, it became apparent that the Indian government was not prepared for a chemical release from the Union Carbide plant. The chemical industry, including Union Carbide, assured the American public that an incident similar to Bhopal occurring in the United States was very unlikely; however, in August 1985 a Union Carbide plant in Institute, West Virginia, released a different pesticide into the air. Nearly 150 people needed medical attention. Investigators determined that plant administrators did not adequately notify emergency response personnel, and that emergency response officials did not know what the substance was, or its characteristics, that had escaped from the facility.

---

[2]*Id.*

BHOPAL DISASTER STILL POISONS LIVES AGONY GOES ON AS EPIDEMICS RAVAGE SURVIVORS

THE PLAIN DEALER (CLEVELAND), *Aug. 23, 1998, p. 25A*

NATIONAL

One Sunday night 14 years ago, a choking white cloud swept through the old quarters of Bhopal from the Union Carbide pesticide plant on the city's outskirts. The methyl isocyanate and hydrogen cyanide gases in the cloud burned and scarred the lungs of all who breathed it.

On Monday morning, more than 2,000 lay dead in the streets. Tens of thousands more were left with wrecked lungs and eyes seared by the gas. And in the 5,000 days since the world's worst industrial disaster, at least another 5,000 have died from their injuries.

An official report on the medical legacy of the Dec. 3, 1984, disaster, drawing on data collected over the 10 years following the accident and due to be published later this year, will reveal that the agony goes on as epidemics of tuberculosis, emphysema, asthma- like symptoms and cataracts ravage the 500,000 people who were caught by the cloud.

Dr. M.P. Dwivedi, director of the report set up by the Indian Council of Medical Research, says that almost one in 14 people in the worst affected zones of the city now suffer from TB, a bacillus that finds a ready home in their damaged lungs. This rate is three times the Indian national average, and it continues to rise.

On the streets around the plant today, the slums seem busy. But enter almost any of the homes in the mostly Muslim quarters near the plant and you find a world where victims rarely go out for want of breath, energy or hope for the future.

Chand Khan worked in Union Carbide's workshop but was at home nearby on the night the cloud escaped. "I woke and smelled what I thought was burning chilies," he recalls, but soon he discovered that his home was filled with a white cloud.

Choking, he grabbed his two children, aged five years and one month, and ran with them into the night. After a third of a mile, still inside the cloud, he collapsed. When he woke, he found his baby was dead. The older child coughed for four years, before he, too, died.

Today, Chand Khan, 43, weighs only 99 pounds. It hurts to eat, his vision is blurred and he can barely breathe. He hasn't worked for eight years. Union Carbide, in a deal reached with the Indian Supreme Court in 1989, agreed to a final settlement of $470 million as compensation for Bhopal's victims, with individual payments ranging from virtually nothing to a maximum of 400,000 rupees (about $9,750).

Chand Khan has spent his compensation (about $1,135) on doctor bills. Now, he says, he has nothing to live for: "I wake at night and ask my wife to give me poison."

His story is typical, says Dwivedi, who this month is finally writing up the results of the study which is set to be unequivocal and damning: "Union Carbide keeps saying that there are no long-term or delayed effects from the gas and that only a few people were seriously injured. My data shows they are wrong."

Today Union Carbide's old pesticides plant is rusting and encroached by weeds. The factory walls are daubed with graffiti: "Bhopal equals Hiroshima," says one. Its poison lingers on underground.

In an alley in the shadow of the plant, the reek of solvent from a pump where a line of women and children fill buckets and kettles with water is unmistakable.

These and some 250 other wells in the area have a small red sign, erected by public health engineers last year, declaring that the water is "unfit for drinking." But it is drunk. There is nothing else.

Since the accident, more than 300,000 people have been awarded compensation for injuries, though 500,000 people were covered by the cloud, says Dwivedi, of whom 95 percent suffered from it. About 50,000 people still suffer, according to the International Medical Commission on Bhopal, an independent volunteer organization of physicians and public health experts set up in response to appeals from community groups in the city.

The only good news from Dwivedi's report is that the predicted plague of blindness has not materialized, though among the over-40s the rate of cataracts is now 10 times the national average.

Nobody knows the total number of people who have died from the effects of the toxic cloud. Union Carbide quotes the state government's figure of 3,800. But 15,000 people made compensation claims for dead loved ones, and awards have been made to just over 5,000 of them. In many cases, there were no loved ones left to make a claim. An entire encampment of gypsies was wiped out.

Three years ago, the local government welfare commissioner listed 8,017 deaths as "exposure related." The toll continues to rise. Dwivedi says the annual death rate in the affected communities of Bhopal is still between 500 and 1,000 times higher than it is in neighboring slums.

The toxic releases in Bhopal and Institute occurred while CERCLA-itself a response to the Love Canal crisis-was up for reauthorization. A separate bill, the Emergency Planning and Community Right-to-Know Act (EPCRA), soon became Title III of the Superfund Amendments and Reauthorization Act (SARA). EPCRA responded to Bhopal and Institute in two ways. First, it requires towns that have certain kinds of businesses to form emergency plans in case a release occurs, and it requires those businesses to notify government bodies if there is an accidental release into the surrounding community. Second, EPCRA forces businesses that store or release toxic chemicals to provide the public with information on quantities and the releases of those chemicals. Congress hoped that these measures would avoid an incident like Bhopal from occurring in the United States.

EPCRA is organized into three subtitles: Subtitle I delineates emergency planning and emergency release notification provisions;[3] Subtitle II outlines reporting requirements that EPCRA-regulated businesses must make for toxic releases;[4] and Subtitle III sets out miscellaneous provisions. The miscellaneous provisions include enforcement, trade secret protection, citizen suits, and preemption.[5]

Emergency Planning Provisions, §§301-303. EPCRA requires the governor of each state to create a State Emergency Response Commission (SERCs) or to choose a state agency to serve as the SERC. The SERC serves as the main conduit between the locality and the EPA. The SERC then divides the state into regions and appoints members to serve on the Local Emergency Planning Commissions (LEPCs).[6] The membership of the LEPCs must include, at a minimum, state and local officials; businesses subject to EPCRA regulations; firefighters; law enforcement, civil defense, and first aid personnel; local environmental, hospital, and transportation personnel; broadcast and print media; and community groups.

EPCRA requires an owner or operator of a facility that uses or stores extremely hazardous substances (EHS)-that is, substances that demonstrate toxicity, reactivity, volatility, dispersibility, combustibility, or flammability-

---

[3] *See* 42 U.S.C. §§ 11001-11005 (1999).
[4] *See* 42 U.S.C. §§ 11021-11023 (1999).
[5] *See* 42 U.S.C. §§ 11041-11050 (1999).
[6] *Id.* §§ 1101-1103.

at or above the threshold planning quantities (TPQs) to meet the emergency planning requirements. EPA lists all substances considered an EHS in EPCRA's regulations, along with the TPQs.[7] All facilities subject to the emergency planning provisions needed to notify the SERC by May 17, 1987 or within 60 days of becoming subject to the emergency planning requirements.[8] They must then submit detailed emergency Planning information to SERCs and LEPCs who, in turn, must process the information and respond to requests for information from the public. The governor of any state can designate additional facilities that are subject to the emergency planning requirements after the facility has an opportunity to comment on the governor's designation.[9] The facility must also designate a representative to work with the locality in emergency planning and response. The LEPC must develop an emergency plan that includes evacuation routes, medical information on the risks of exposure, types and use of warning signals and coordination plans for fire and police departments, the media and emergency medical teams.

Emergency Release Provision, §304. EPCRA requires owners or operators of facilities that use, produce, or store hazardous substances to report immediately to the LEPC or SERC a release if the release that is above reportable quantity (RQ, not TPQ) for an EHS or a CERCLA hazardous substance. EPCRA defines a "release" as "any spilling, leaking, pouring, emitting, discharging injecting, escaping, leaching, dumping, or disposal into the environment."[10] The term "into the environment" has been read restrictively to mean a substance actually moving into the environment and not the mere exposure of a substance to the environment.[11] Although EPCRA exempts on-site releases,[12] the EPA has stated that a release does not need to cause actual exposure to off-site persons to be a reportable release.[13]

The notice to emergency and local officials must include the chemical name or identity of the substance released, whether the substance is also an EHS, the quantity of the release, the medium to which the release occurred, known and anticipated health risks from the substance, precautions to take because of the release, and the numbers and names of individuals to contact for further information.[14] A follow-up emergency notice containing an update on the information provided in the original notice and any procedures taken to contain or ameliorate the effects of the release must be filed as soon as practical after the release.

Community Right-To-Know Provisions, §§ 311-313. Sections 301-304 delineated a system for federal, state, and local officials to prepare for a

---

[7] 40 C.F.R. Pt. 355, Apps. A and B (1996).

[8] *See* 40 C.F.R. § 355.30(b) (1999).

[9] *See* 42 U.S.C § 11002(b)(2).

[10] *See id.* § 11049(8).

[11] *See* Fertilizer Inst. v. EPA, 935 F.2d. 1303, 1310 (D.C. Cir. 1991).

[12] *See* 40 C.F.R.§ 355.40(a)(2)(i) (1999).

[13] *See* 52 Fed. Reg. 13,378, 13,381 (April 22, 1987).

[14] *See* 40 C.F.R. § 355.40(b) (1999).

disaster like the Union Carbide release in Bhopal. The right-to-know sections of EPCRA are the most controversial aspects of EPCRA because they provide the public with information on the chemicals present at and released by covered facilities.

Any facility that produces, uses, or stores a "hazardous chemical" above the required threshold must comply with the reporting requirements of EPCRA. The term "hazardous chemical" is defined in the Occupational Safety and Health Act (OSHA). OSHA defines "hazardous chemical" as either a "physical hazard or a health hazard,"[15] and facilities that have hazardous chemicals on their premises must file a Material Safety Data Sheet (MSDS). OSHA regulations require that an MSDS contain the following information:

- identity of the hazardous chemical;
- its physical and chemical characteristics;
- physical hazards;
- health hazards, including symptoms of exposure;
- routes of entry into the body;
- applicable exposure limits;
- carcinogenicity (if any);
- precautions for use and handling;
- control measures;
- emergency and first aid procedures; and
- name, address, and phone number of preparor of MSDS.[16]

The MSDS is also the basis for reporting under EPCRA.

The following is the MSDS summary on hydrogen cyanide, of the gasses released in Bhopal.[17]

SAFETY DATA FOR HYDROGEN CYANIDE

General

Synonyms: prussic acid, hydrocyanic acid, formonitrile
Molecular formula: H C N
CAS No: 74-90-8
EC No: 200-821-6

Physical data

Appearance: colourless or pale blue liquid, or colourless gas, (depending upon temperature) with a bitter almond odour

---

[15] *See* 29 C.F.R. § 1910.1200(c) (1999). A "physical hazard" is defined as any "Chemical for which there is scientifically valid evidence that it is a combustible liquid, a compressed gas, explosive, flammable, an organic peroxide, an oxidizer, pyrophoric, unstable (reactive or water reactive)." "Health hazard" is defined as "a chemical for which there is statistically significant evidence based on at least one study conducted in accordance with established scientific principles that acute or chronic health effects may occur in exposed employees." *Id.*
[16] 29 C.F.R. § 1910.1200(g) (1999).
[17] Source: http://physchem.ox.ac.uk/MSDS/H/hydrogen_cyanide.html

Melting point: -14° C
Boiling point: 25.6° C
Vapour density:
Vapour pressure:
Specific gravity: 0.6899 g/cm^3 at 18° C
Flash point: -18° C
Explosion limits:
Autoignition temperature:

Stability

Stable. Incompatible with acids, strong oxidizing agents. Reaction with acids releases highly toxic gas. Highly flammable.

Toxicology

Very toxic by inhalation, ingestion and through skin contact. Inhalation, ingestion or skin contact may be fatal. Note low LD50s.
ORL-MUS LD50 3.7 mg/kg.
IHL-MUS LC50 323 ppm.
IV-MUS LD50 1 mg/kg.
IV-RBT LD50 <1 mg/kg.
ORL-MAN LDLO <1 mg/kg.

Transport information

UN Major hazard class
Packing group

Personal protection

Safety glasses, gloves, good ventilation. Only use if no suitable alternative chemical is available. Do not work on your own. Keep a cyanide poisoning kit available at all times, and ensure that fellow workers know how to use it.

EPA requires reporting of hazardous chemicals that are present at a facility for any one time in the amount of ten thousand pounds or more, 500 pounds or the TPQ for EHSs.[18] A facility may choose not to submit copies of MSDS sheets for the public record for a hazardous chemical at the facility; however, it must at least submit a list of the hazardous substances that require an MSDS sheet, and provide the MSDS to the LEPC, SERC, and local fire department.

The annual "Tier I Form" includes an estimate of the maximum amount of hazardous chemicals present at the facility during the previous year, the average amount of hazardous chemicals present during the previous year, and the present approximate placement of the hazardous chemicals at the facility. Tier I information is to be submitted by the owner of the facility to the designated community planning committee, the SERC, and the local fire department.[19] The "Tier II Form," which is voluntary, contains the same

---

[18] 40 C.F.R. § 370.20(b)(1), (b)(4) (1999).
[19] 42 U.S.C. § 11022(1)(a)-(c).

information as a Tier I Form but in more detail. For example, a Tier I Form describes the general location of a hazardous substance in a facility, and a Tier II Form contains specific information. Tier II Forms contain restrictions on public dissemination, in essence requiring a need to know its contents before it can be released.

Section 313 of EPCRA requires that facilities inform the public of all releases of hazardous chemicals that cumulatively exceed threshold quantities. Covered releases are not limited to accidents. They include routine releases into streams and water bodies, fugitive or non-point air emissions, stack or point emissions, and other transfers of waste to public sewers or treatment facilities. Facilities that are subject to § 313 have 10 or more employees, fall within the Standard Industrial Classification (SIC) Codes 30 through 49,[20] and manufacture, process, or otherwise use a toxic chemical in amounts greater than the applicable reporting threshold. EPA has yet another list of covered chemicals and yet another set of threshold quantities for these purposes.

Releases are reported annually on "Form R", the Toxic Chemical Release Form, to the EPA.[21] It includes the name, location, and the type of business of the facility.[22] The Form R must also describe: whether the toxic chemical at the facility is manufactured, processed, or otherwise used; the category of each chemical; the *estimate* of the type of releases that occurred from the facility in the previous year; the methods of disposal for each waste stream and the treatment efficiency for each waste stream; and, the annual quantity of toxic chemicals that enter the environment every year.[23] EPA collects the information acquired from Form Rs and assembles it in a computer database called the Toxic Release Inventory (TRI). TRI data are now available on the Web in both tabular and geographic forms.[24]

Only facilities that manufacture, process or otherwise use a toxic chemical are subject to regulation under § 313.[25] EPCRA defines "manufacture" to mean "produce, prepare, import, or compound a toxic chemical."[26] If a facility coincidentally produces a toxic chemical during the manufacturing process, the EPA considers that chemical "manufactured."[27]

EPCRA defines the word "process" as the preparation of a toxic chemical for distribution into commerce if the chemical is in the same form

---

[20] SIC Codes 30-49 cover manufacturers of goods. Among the industries covered by the code are lumber and wood, tobacco, petroleum refining, and industrial and commercial machinery. *See* 42 U.S.C. §11023(b)(1). In 1993 the President signed an Executive Order requiring federal facilities to comply with EPCRA. More than 190 federal facilities became subject to EPCRA's provisions. Executive Order 12856. *See also*, 58 Fed. Reg. 41,981 (Aug. 3, 1993).

[21] 42 U.S.C. § 11023(a).

[22] 42 U.S.C. § 11023(g).

[23] *See id.*

[24] This information can be accessed through RTK.NET at http://www.ombwatch.org/rtknet/ or http://www.epa.gov/swercepp/crtk.html.

[25] *See* 42 U.S.C. § 11023(b)(1)(a).

[26] *See* 40 C.F.R. § 372.3 (1999).

[27] *Id.*

or physical state as, or in a different form or physical state from, that in which the chemical was received by the person preparing the substance or as part of an article containing the toxic substance.[28] The EPA defines "otherwise use" as any use of a toxic chemical that is not covered by the terms manufacture or process and includes use of a toxic chemical contained in a mixture or other trade name product or waste.[29]

Miscellaneous Provisions, §§ 321-330. None of the provisions in EPCRA preempts a stricter state level emergency planning or right-to-know law; and a facility located in a state with a stricter emergency planning or right-to know statute must follow those provisions along with EPCRA's provisions.[30] EPCRA includes a fairly narrow trade secrets exemption to protect business from competitors who may use the public right-to-know provision to discover proprietary manufacturing processes. Trade secret protection does not permit a facility to avoid the emergency notice provision of § 304.

The enforcement sections of EPCRA contain a patchwork of enforcement options depending on the type of violation. For instance, the EPA can seek criminal penalties for violators of § 304 but not for violators of § 302 and 303. EPA can also seek administrative or judicial penalties against violators of a broader range of EPCRA provisions. These enforcement options, as well as citizen suits, are addressed in the following case. States and localities may initiate certain enforcement actions, as well.

STEEL COMPANY V. CITIZENS FOR A BETTER ENVIRONMENT

523 U.S. 83 (1998)

Justice SCALIA delivered the opinion of the Court.

* * *

Respondent, an association of individuals interested in environmental protection, sued petitioner, a small manufacturing company in Chicago, for past violations of EPCRA. EPCRA establishes a framework of state, regional and local agencies designed to inform the public about the presence of hazardous and toxic chemicals, and to provide for emergency response in the event of health-threatening release. Central to its operation are reporting requirements compelling users of specified toxic and hazardous chemicals to file annual "emergency and hazardous chemical inventory forms" and "toxic chemical release forms," which contain, inter alia, the name and location of the facility, the name and quantity of the chemical on hand, and, in the case of toxic chemicals, the waste-disposal method employed and the annual quantity released into each environmental medium. 42 U.S.C. §§ 11022 and 11023. The hazardous-chemical inventory forms for any given calendar year

---

[28] *Id.*

[29] *Id.*

[30] *See* 42 U.S.C. § 11041(a)(1) & (a)(3).

are due the following March 1st, and the toxic-chemical release forms the following July 1st. §§ 11022(a)(2) and 11023(a).

Enforcement of EPCRA can take place on many fronts. The Environmental Protection Agency (EPA) has the most powerful enforcement arsenal: it may seek criminal, civil, or administrative penalties. § 11045. State and local governments can also seek civil penalties, as well as injunctive relief. §§ 11046(a)(2) and (c). For purposes of this case, however, the crucial enforcement mechanism is the citizen-suit provision, § 11046(a)(1), which likewise authorizes civil penalties and injunctive relief, see § 11046(c). This provides that "any person may commence a civil action on his own behalf against . . . [a]n owner or operator of a facility for failure," among other things, to "[c]omplete and submit an inventory form under § 11022(a) of this title . . . [and] § 11023(a) of this title." § 11046(a)(1). As a prerequisite to bringing such a suit, the plaintiff must, 60 days prior to filing his complaint, give notice to the Administrator of the EPA, the State in which the alleged violation occurs, and the alleged violator. § 11046(d). The citizen suit may not go forward if the Administrator "has commenced and is diligently pursuing an administrative order or civil action to enforce the requirement concerned or to impose a civil penalty." § 11046(e).

In 1995 respondent sent a notice to petitioner, the Administrator, and the relevant Illinois authorities, alleging-accurately, as it turns out-that petitioner had failed since 1988, the first year of EPCRA's filing deadlines, to complete and to submit the requisite hazardous-chemical inventory and toxic-chemical release forms under §§ 11022 and 11023. Upon receiving the notice, petitioner filed all of the overdue forms with the relevant agencies. The EPA chose not to bring an action against petitioner, and when the 60-day waiting period expired, respondent filed suit in Federal District Court. Petitioner promptly filed a motion to dismiss under Federal Rule of Civil Procedure 12(b)(1) and (6), contending that, because its filings were up to date when the complaint was filed, the court had no jurisdiction to entertain a suit for a present violation; and that, because EPCRA does not allow suit for a purely historical violation, respondent's allegation of untimeliness in filing was not a claim upon which relief could be granted.

* * *

The "irreducible constitutional minimum of standing" contains three requirements. First and foremost, there must be alleged (and ultimately proven) an "injury in fact"—a harm suffered by the plaintiff that is "concrete" and "actual or imminent, not 'conjectural' or 'hypothetical.'" Second, there must be causation—a fairly traceable connection between the plaintiff's injury and the complained-of conduct of the defendant. And third, there must be redressability—a likelihood that the requested relief will redress the alleged injury. This triad of injury in fact, causation, and redressability comprises the core of Article III's case-or-controversy requirement, and the party invoking federal jurisdiction bears the burden of establishing its existence.

* * *

The complaint contains claims "on behalf of both [respondent] itself and its members." It describes respondent as an organization that seeks, uses, and acquires data reported under EPCRA. It says that respondent "reports to its members and the public about storage and releases of toxic chemicals into the environment, advocates changes in environmental regulations and statutes, prepares reports for its members and the public, seeks the reduction of toxic chemicals and further seeks to promote the effective enforcement of environmental laws." The complaint asserts that respondent's "right to know about [toxic chemical] releases and its interests in protecting and improving the environment and the health of its members have been, are being, and will be adversely affected by [petitioner's] actions in failing to provide timely and required information under EPCRA." Ibid. The complaint also alleges that respondent's members, who live in or frequent the area near petitioner's facility, use the EPRCA-reported information "to learn about toxic chemical releases, the use of hazardous substances in their communities, to plan emergency preparedness in the event of accidents, and to attempt to reduce the toxic chemicals in areas in which they live, work and visit." The members' "safety, health, recreational, economic, aesthetic and environmental interests" in the information, it is claimed, "have been, are being, and will be adversely affected by [petitioner's] actions in failing to file timely and required reports under EPCRA."

As appears from the above, respondent asserts petitioner's failure to provide EPCRA information in a timely fashion, and the lingering effects of that failure, as the injury in fact to itself and its members. We have not had occasion to decide whether being deprived of information that is supposed to be disclosed under EPCRA—or at least being deprived of it when one has a particular plan for its use—is a concrete injury in fact that satisfies Article III. And we need not reach that question in the present case because, assuming injury in fact, the complaint fails the third test of standing, redressability.

The complaint asks for (1) a declaratory judgment that petitioner violated EPCRA; (2) authorization to inspect periodically petitioner's facility and records (with costs borne by petitioner); (3) an order requiring petitioner to provide respondent copies of all compliance reports submitted to the EPA; (4) an order requiring petitioner to pay civil penalties of $25,000 per day for each violation of §§ 11022 and 11023; (5) an award of all respondent's "costs, in connection with the investigation and prosecution of this matter, including reasonable attorney and expert witness fees, as authorized by § 326(f) of [EPCRA]"; and (6) any such further relief as the court deems appropriate. None of the specific items of relief sought, and none that we can envision as "appropriate" under the general request, would serve to reimburse respondent for losses caused by the late reporting, or to eliminate any effects of that late reporting upon respondent.

The first item, the request for a declaratory judgment that petitioner violated EPCRA, can be disposed of summarily. There being no controversy over whether petitioner failed to file reports, or over whether such a failure constitutes a violation, the declaratory judgment is not only worthless to respondent, it is seemingly worthless to all the world.

Item (4), the civil penalties authorized by the statute, *see* § 11045(c), might be viewed as a sort of compensation or redress to respondent if they were payable to respondent. But they are not. These penalties-the only damages authorized by EPCRA—are payable to the United States Treasury. In requesting them, therefore, respondent seeks not remediation of its own injury—reimbursement for the costs it incurred as a result of the late filing—but vindication of the rule of law—the "undifferentiated public interest" in faithful execution of EPCRA. This does not suffice.

Item (5), the "investigation and prosecution" costs "as authorized by § 326(f)," would assuredly benefit respondent as opposed to the citizenry at large. Obviously, however, a plaintiff cannot achieve standing to litigate a substantive issue by bringing suit for the cost of bringing suit. The litigation must give the plaintiff some other benefit besides reimbursement of costs that are a byproduct of the litigation itself. An "interest in attorney's fees is . . . insufficient to create an Article III case or controversy where none exists on the merits of the underlying claim." Respondent asserts that the "investigation costs" it seeks were incurred prior to the litigation, in digging up the emissions and storage information that petitioner should have filed, and that respondent needed for its own purposes. The recovery of such expenses unrelated to litigation would assuredly support Article III standing, but the problem is that § 326(f), which is the entitlement to monetary relief that the complaint invokes, covers only the "costs of litigation." § 11046(f).

The remaining relief respondent seeks (item (2), giving respondent authority to inspect petitioner's facility and records, and item (3), compelling petitioner to provide respondent copies of EPA compliance reports) is injunctive in nature. It cannot conceivably remedy any past wrong but is aimed at deterring petitioner from violating EPCRA in the future. *See* Brief for Respondent 36. The latter objective can of course be "remedial" for Article III purposes, when threatened injury is one of the gravamens of the complaint. If respondent had alleged a continuing violation or the imminence of a future violation, the injunctive relief requested would remedy that alleged harm. But there is no such allegation here—and on the facts of the case, there seems no basis for it. Nothing supports the requested injunctive relief except respondent's generalized interest in deterrence, which is insufficient for purposes of Article III.

* * *

The judgment is vacated and the case remanded with instructions to direct that the complaint be dismissed. [Justices Stevens, Souter, and Ginsburg concurred in the judgment on the ground that, even though the plaintiffs had Constitutional standing, as a statutory matter EPCRA's citizens suit provision precluded actions for wholly past violations.]

NOTES

1. Congress consistently favors the planning over the right-to-know provisions of EPCRA. Can you see how this is so? Why would Congress regard the planning provisions as more important?

2. The Pollution Prevention Act of 1990 expanded the type of releases a facility must report.[31] How are right-to know and pollution prevention related? How does right-to-know support pollution prevention?

3. EPCRA makes some effort to simplify compliance by incorporating OSHA's MSDS chemicals and information. Otherwise, however, it is a wealth of separate lists and threshold quantities (CERCLA's reportable quantities, 42 U.S.C. §§ 9602(b), for example, are not incorporated). Why so many limits?

4. What is the significance of the difference between the majority's and the concurrence's resolution of the *Steel Co.* case? Is it possible for Congress, if it were so inclined, to amend EPCRA to cure the redressability problem that the Court identifies? Would it make a difference whether the violations were in the past or continuing?

Why, in the Court's view, were plaintiff's injuries not redressable? Can you develop counterarguments?

5. The following analysis of EPCRA emphasizes enforcement issues. Does *Steel Co.* alleviate or exacerbate the commentators' concerns?

> Useful as EPCRA may be to states accident protection programs, it suffers a serious flaw in that its vigorous enforcement provisions are reserved to EPA and unavailable to states, local governments, or the public. The available remedies for anyone other than EPA appear to be limited to "enforcing the requirement concerned." In other words, states, municipalities, and citizens can apply to the courts for an order compelling a facility to supply accident reports or right to know information but cannot obtain penalties for noncompliance. This process is cumbersome and time-consuming, and may encourage some companies to adopt a "wait-and-see" attitude towards compliance. While injunctive relief may be useful to compel compliance in specific instances, it does not have the strong deterrent effect of the civil and criminal penalties available to EPA. In addition, one of the principle concerns about EPCRA is that is will be ineffective due to a lack of funding and lack of EPA commitment to oversight and enforcement. * * *

Robert Abrams & Douglas H. Ward, *Prospects for Safer Communities: Emergency Response, Community Right to Know, and Prevention of Chemical Accidents,* 14 Harv. Envtl. L. Rev. 135, 162-63 (1990).

6. The Court's opinion also casts doubt on the existence of any real injury to these plaintiffs from the defendant's violation of EPCRA. Do you

---

[31] *See* 42 U.S.C. §§13106. The information includes recycling, source reduction and on-site TRI chemical recycling and treatment.

agree? If the Court were to so hold, what effect would it have on citizen enforcement of EPCRA or other right-to-know laws? Are citizen suits an important part of the enforcement of EPCRA?

2. Information As Regulation: The Toxic Release Inventory

Unlike environmental statutes that regulate the disposal of chemicals and wastes at certain point sources, EPCRA attempts to use information to limit production and disposal of toxic chemicals and hazardous waste. One commentator has called the TRI "the citizen's tool" because citizens can use TRI information to embarrass industry into reducing production and releases of hazardous waste:[32]

Both utilitarian and entitlement rationales have been advanced to support these provisions. The Hazard Communication Standard [the OSHA regulation which requires MSDSs,] emphasizes utilitarian reasons: additional information encourages workers to take available precautionary measures and to develop new ones, and also assists them in seeking compensation for toxic injuries through the tort system. EPCRA's main utilitarian aim is local emergency planning. Its data also can be used to establish and revise laws and regulations, to influence lawmakers and regulators, and to negotiate or litigate with emitters. The predominant rhetoric of EPCRA, however, is not utilitarian but, as its name suggests, "a fundamental right to know about what chemicals, toxic chemicals, are being released into [the American people's] environment hour after hour, day after day, year after year."[33]

What the public is to do with the information to which it has a right is less clear. The knowledge of the presence of hazardous substances in the community seldom brings with it the ability to do anything about them.[34] Supporters of EPCRA suggested that it

---

[32] David Abell, Comment, *Emergency Planning and Community Right to Know: The Toxics Release Inventory*, 47 SMU L. REV. 581, 588 (1994).

[33] *Superfund Provisions: Community Right-to-Know and Cleanup of Abandoned Hazardous Wastesites Located at Federal Facilities: Hearings before the subcomm. on Commerce, Transportation, and Tourism of the House Comm. on Energy and Commerce*, 99th Cong., 1st Sess. 8 (1985). The idea of a right to know is addressed by several commentators, and courts. A more subtle version of this argument is that the pervasive scientific uncertainty concerning toxic substances results in risk decisions being not simply factual but highly value-laden. Under these circumstances, citizens have much to contribute to value and policy choices.

[34] An individual can, of course, engage in the lobbying, negotiation, or litigation mentioned above, but the average citizen is unlikely to be able to take meaningful safety precautions. The only remaining response is to move away from the source of danger. *See* N.J. STAT. ANN. § 34:5A-2 (West 1988) ("individuals have an inherent right to know . . . so that they can make reasoned decisions and take informed action concerning their employment and their living conditions"); *see also OSHA, Hazard Communication*, 48 Fed. Reg. 53,280, 53,323, 53,328 (suggesting that workers could change jobs to achieve "better matches between the risk preferences of workers and true job risks"). But encouraging mass emigration from industrial areas seems an unrealistic and extremely undesirable social policy.

provides communities with "the quantitative information necessary to use this data effectively" and would "allow communities to gauge the potential long-term chronic health effects of toxic chemical releases." At least in theory, workers can take precautions, bargain with their employers for safety, suggest safer procedures, refuse certain work, or even change jobs. Citizens generally, on the other hand, are in a much poorer position to reduce risk themselves. Moreover, it is questionable whether consumers or workers are in a position to make intelligent use of the information. Nevertheless, by providing toxicity and exposure information paralleling quantitative risk assessment, the data requirements of the right-to-know laws encourage individuals to undertake their own, informal risk assessments.

Once the public appetite for risk information is whetted by a sense of entitlement to it, and once data gaps are publicly identified, it is hard to see how government and industry can avoid additional demands for more specific information regarding the chemicals. If, as some advocate, risk assessments are routinely to be made available to the public, and if these risk assessments appropriately disclose their data gaps and assumptions, the public would be acutely aware of just how little is known about the chemicals to which it is exposed. Having opened the door to public scrutiny and comment on the risks associated with chemicals, the government will be called upon, with or without the unreasonable risk standard, to develop large amounts of the kind of information used in quantitative risk assessment. And when that happens, the gap between existing and desired information will widen rather than close.

John S. Applegate, *The Perils of Unreasonable Risk: Information, Regulatory Policy, and Toxic Substances Control*, 91 COLUM. L. REV. 261, 295-98 (1991).

The political use of TRI data established itself immediately upon the release of the first TRI report in 1989, which covered releases in 1987. Citizens were shocked by the amounts of waste reported. Even the EPA stated that the volume of releases was "far higher than we thought was going to occur."[35] About 22,000 facilities released 5.7 billion pounds of toxic chemicals into the environment. One hundred twenty-seven facilities produced almost 60% of the releases reported. Monsanto and American Cyanamid released more than 7% of the national total.[36]

---

[35] Sidney M. Wolf, *Fear and Loathing About the Public Right to Know: The Surprising Success of the Emergency Planning and Community Right-to-Know Act*, 11 J. LAND USE & ENVTL. L. 217, 282 (1996).

[36] *See* David J. Abell, Comment, *Emergency Planning and Community Right to Know. The Toxics Release Inventory*, 47 SMU L. REV. 581, 588 (1994). Forty-two percent of the releases were into the air, twenty-one percent were placed in underground injection wells and sixteen percent of the wastes were transferred off-site. *See id.*

The report embarrassed many businesses who did not want the reputation of a polluter. Monsanto and many other businesses promised to reduce releases at their facilities. Many environmental groups produced reports listing the companies that released the largest amount of toxic chemicals. Environmentalists also used the TRI information to galvanize public opposition to the release of toxic chemicals. Following Monsanto's lead, many businesses reduced releases from their facilities. Other facilities substituted toxic chemicals for cleaner chemicals. For example, a Massachusetts citizen group used TRI data to persuade Raytheon to replace a chemical that caused ozone depletion, and in North Carolina a local group used TRI data to convince public officials that the town needed a new water treatment plant.[37]

EPCRA provides hard data to support claims of the extent of the pollution problem in the United States. During debate on the 1990 Amendments to the Clean Air Act supporters effectively used TRI data as support for the need of stricter environmental controls on hazardous air pollutants.[38]

EPA, too, has used TRI data to enforce compliance with other environmental laws—for example, EPA filed suit against pulp and paper manufacturers, metal manufacturers, and other industries when TRI data showed significant toxic releases by those industries—and for permitting and inspection.[39]

PROBLEM

You are president of Local Citizens Concerned About the Chesapeake Bay. What TRI data would you collect? In what ways would you use the data?

One general concern about the TRI data is the reliability of the information on Form R. EPA does not monitor businesses to ensure that the information businesses report are accurate,[40] and unlike, say, the Clean Water Act (CWA), EPCRA does not require direct monitoring of releases. Instead, it permits a facility to use "reasonable estimates" when determining the amounts released from the facility.[41] Some groups argue that the "reasonable estimates" allow businesses too much discretion in reporting.[42] Businesses

---

[37] *See* Wolf, *supra* note 35, at 288.

[38] The first TRI report showed that businesses released nearly 2.7 billion pounds of toxic chemicals into the air. TRI data also showed that air releases for carcinogenic chemicals totaled over three hundred million pounds. The 1990 Amendments directed that the EPA regulate 170 toxic chemicals that had been in the TRI data. *See* Wolf, *supra,* at 300.

[39] *See* Abell, *supra* note 36, at 590.

[40] *See* Eric M. Falkenberry, *The Emergency Planning and Community Right-To-Know Act: A Tool for Toxic Release Reduction in the 90s,* 3 BUFF. ENVTL. L.J. 1, 30 (1995).

[41] 42 U.S.C. §11023(g)(2).

[42] One study found that almost seventy percent of TRI data are based on estimation techniques that are the least reliable. *See* Abell, *supra.*

find that reporting "reasonable estimates" can be difficult because a product often goes through many stages of production. No one has developed a really accurate method of measuring many releases like evaporation, spilling, and burning.[43] Unfortunately, monitoring and more accurate estimates would impose significant costs on businesses and the government, which Congress and the EPA are unwilling to impose.

Another significant limitation of the TRI database is that it contains only the name of the substance, the media to which the substance was released, the location of the release, and the amount of the substance released. This is fairly raw data, which poses the problems discussed in the following excerpts.

PROSPECTS FOR SAFER COMMUNITIES: EMERGENCY RESPONSE, COMMUNITY RIGHT TO KNOW, AND PREVENTION OF CHEMICAL ACCIDENTS

Robert Abrams & Douglas H. Ward
14 HARV. ENVTL. L. REV. 135, 154-63 (1990)

The community right to know provisions of EPCRA have made a wealth of information available to the public and government about chemicals in the community. Useful as the information generated could be, it lacks explanation, context, or regulatory direction. It provides no analysis of the data, and contains no mechanisms to assure that the dangers noted in the hazard information have been minimized or eliminated. EPCRA's community right to know provisions may thus encourage public outcry or litigation as the vehicle to force industry to take protective measures. Fear of the result could encourage industry to be less than forthcoming with information on chemicals or on-site practices. In this way, EPCRA threatens to divide industry from workers and the public despite all parties' pursuit of a common goal-facility and neighborhood safety. As one commentator summarized it:

> *EPCRA is hollow* at the core. Missing from the extensive array of communication duties is any authority for anyone, agency or industry, to do a rigorous, site-specific facility safety analysis . . . . In this light, risk communication . . . depends on potential conflicts in local communities, tort actions in state courts, and the threat of such events as a motivator for firms to voluntarily evaluate and improve safety at their facilities."[44]

* * *

Tier I information is readily available, Tier II information is less accessible. Both the public and government officials cannot obtain the information directly from the [reporting] facility and must

---

[43] *See id.*

[44] Michael Baram, *Risk Communication Law and Implementation Issues in the United States and the European Community*, 6 B.U. INT'L L.J. 21, 37-38 (1988).

request it through the emergency response planning committees. This unnecessary step needlessly burdens underfunded agencies who should be using their limited resources for planning rather than responding to information requests. . . . [T]he public may be unable to obtain Tier II information without showing need.

A perennial question with EPCRA is whether it over informs or under-informs the public. Both the Abrams and Ward article and the following article present problems with the way in which EPCRA data is presented and used.

THE CANCER-CLUSTER MYTH

Atul Gawande, The New Yorker, Feb. 8, 1999, pp. 34-37

No doubt, one reason for the veritable cluster of cancer clusters in recent years is the widespread attention that cases like those in McFarland and Los Alamos received, and the ensuing increase in public awareness and concern. Another reason, though, is the way in which states have responded to that concern: they've made available to the public data on potential toxic sites, along with information from "cancer registries" about local cancer rates. The result has been to make it easier for people to find worrisome patterns, and, more and more, they've done so. In the late eighties, public-health departments were receiving between thirteen hundred and sixteen hundred reports of feared cancer clusters, or "cluster alarms,"each year. Last year, in Massachusetts alone, the state health department responded to between three thousand and four thousand cluster alarms. Under public pressure, state and federal agencies throughout the country are engaging in "cancer mapping" to find clusters that nobody has yet reported.

A community that is afflicted with an unusual number of cancers quite naturally looks for a cause in the environment-in the ground, the water, the air. And correlations are sometimes found: the cluster may arise after, say, contamination of the water supply by a possible carcinogen. The problem is that when scientists have tried to confirm such causes, they haven't been able to. Raymond Richard Neutra, California's chief environmental health investigator and an expert on cancer clusters, points out that among hundreds of exhaustive, published investigations of residential clusters in the United States, not one has convincingly identified an underlying environmental cause.

* * *

When public-health investigators fail to turn up any explanation for the appearance of a cancer cluster, communities can find it frustrating, even suspicious. After all, the investigators are highly efficient in tracking down the causes of other kinds of disease clusters. [This was the technique that identified Legionnaires' disease, H.I.V., DES, and indeed the first recognized environmental carcinogen, Percivall Pott's discovery in 1775 that soot caused scrotal cancer in chimney sweeps.]

* * *

[M]any clusters fall apart simply because they violate basic rules of cancer behavior. * * *

To produce a cancer cluster, a carcinogen has to hit a great many cells in a great many people. A brief, low-level exposure to a carcinogen is unlikely to do the job. Raymond Richard Neutra has calculated that for a carcinogen to produce a sevenfold increase in the occurrence of a cancer (a rate of increase not considered particularly high by epidemiologists) a population would have to be exposed to seventy per cent of the maximum tolerated dose in the course of a full year or the equivalent. "This kind of exposure is credible as part of chemotherapy or in some work settings," he wrote in a 1990 paper, "but it must be vary rare for most neighborhood and school settings." For that reason, investigations of occupational cancer clusters have been vastly more successful that investigations of residential cancer clusters.

* * *

If true neighborhood clusters-that is, local clusters arising from a common environmental cause-are so rare, why do we see so many? In a sense, we're programmed to: nearly all of them are the result of almost irresistible errors in perception. In a pioneering article published in 1971, the cognitive psychologists Daniel Kahneman and Amos Tversky identified a systematic error in human judgement which they called the Belief in the Law of Small Numbers. People assume that the pattern of a large population will be replicated in all its subsets. But clusters will occur simply through chance. After seeing a long sequence of red on the roulette wheel, people find it hard to resist the ideas that black is "due"-or else they start to wonder whether the wheel is rigged. We assume that a sequence of R-R-R-R-R-R is somehow less random than, say, R-R-B-R-B-B. But the two sequences are equally likely. (Casinos make a lot of money from the Belief in the Law of Small Numbers.) Truly random patterns often don't appear random to us.

* * *

In epidemiology, the tendency to isolate clusters from their context is known as the Texas-sharpshooter fallacy. Like a Texas sharpshooter who shoots at the side of a barn and then draws a bull's eye around the bullet holes, we tend to notice cases first-four cancer patients on one street-and then define the population base around them. With rare conditions, such as Haff disease or mercury poisoning, even a small clutch of cases really would represent a dramatic excess, no matter how much Texas sharpshooting we did. But most cancers are

common enough that noticeable residential clusters are bound to occur. Raymond Richard Neutra points out that, given a typical registry of eighty different cancers, you could expect twenty-seven hundred and fifty of California's five thousand census tracts to have statistically significant but perfectly random elevations of cancer. So if you check to see whether your neighborhood has an elevated rate of a specific cancer, chances are better than even that it does-and it almost certainly won't mean a thing. Even when you've established a correlation between a specific cancer and a potential carcinogen, scientists have hardly any way to distinguish the "true" cancer cluster that's worth investigating from the crowd of cluster imposters.

One helpful tip-off is an extraordinarily high cancer rate. In Karain, Turkey, the incidence of mesothelioma was more than *seven thousand times* as high as expected. [The disease was traced to an abundant local mineral.] In even the most serious cluster alarms that public-health departments have received, however, the cancer rate has been nowhere near that high.

The 1986 Chernobyl disaster exposed hundreds of thousands of people to radiation; scientists were able to establish that it caused a more than one hundred-fold increase in thyroid cancer among children years later.

* * *

Public-health departments aren't lavishly funded, and scientists are reluctant to see money spent on something that has proved to be as unproductive as neighborhood cluster alarms or cancer mapping. Still, public confidence is poorly served by officials who respond to inquiries with a scientific brush-off and a layer of bureaucracy.

NOTES

Congress built EPCRA on the idea that knowledge is power. It empowers states and municipalities by providing them with information on the identities, amounts, and characteristics of hazardous substances at EPCRA-covered facilities. States and municipalities can use their new knowledge to create emergency plans, to fight fires, to make appropriate land-use decisions, and so on. EPCRA also empowers citizens by requiring facilities to publish the amounts and types of releases from them. Members of the public can make their own judgements whether that amount is excessive and take appropriate action. What are "appropriate actions" by members of the public?

1. EPCRA's proponents claim that its successes demonstrate the powerful tool EPCRA can be to reduce environmental pollution. Proponents believe that EPCRA represents the future of environmental law where a knowledgeable public demands corporations to be environmentally responsible instead of depending on the "gotcha" game that presently exists between the government and businesses. Are information statutes a substitute for command and control regulation? Can we decrease reliance on centralized agencies and increase reliance on the private market to control pollution through greater reliance on information as a legal tool?

2. Does EPCRA over-inform or under-inform the public? Or both?

Abrams & Ward and Gawande address two different kinds of "raw" data, but they raise complementary concerns. What are they? Similar issues have been raised by industries that report high toxic releases but believe that they pose low risks because, for example, the releases occur in very low concentrations or few people are exposed to them.[45] There are obvious attractions to presenting risk information rather than simply release or injury data, but there are also drawbacks. What are the advantages and disadvantages?

3. Currently, if citizens want to "marry" exposure with toxicity information, they must use a variety of sources, many of which are available on-line. One of the most useful for evaluating toxicity is the HazDat database of the Agency for Toxic Substances and Disease Registry (ATSDR) http://www.atsdr.cdc.gov. ATSDR focuses on Superfund chemicals, but its information is designed for public use.

4. Are there environmental justice implications of reliance on information statutes like EPCRA? *See generally* John S. Applegate, *Risk Assessment, Redevelopment, and Environmental Justice: Candidly Evaluating the Brownfields Bargain*, 13 J. NAT. RESOURCES & ENVTL. L. 243 (1998) (advocating use of risk assessment to inform residents of brownfields redevelopment zones).

PROBLEM
STRUCTURING AN INFORMATION PROGRAM

Are there better ways of disseminating environmental information? At one end of the spectrum is the notification that a product or place contains or emit a carcinogen, which is the approach of California's Proposition 65. CAL. HEALTH & SAFETY CODE §§ 25249.5-25249.13.

  § 25249.6. Required warning before exposure to chemicals known to cause cancer or reproductive toxicity

  No person in the course of doing business shall knowingly and

---

[45] This argument is made for electric utilities in George M. Gray, *Toxic Pollution From Powerplants: Large Emissions, Little Risk*, 7 (2) Risk in Perspective (Harvard Center for Risk Analysis) 1 (April 1999).

intentionally expose any individual to a chemical known to the state
to cause cancer or reproductive toxicity without first giving clear
and reasonable warning to such individual, * * *.

§ 25249.8. List of chemicals known to cause cancer or reproductive
toxicity

(a) On or before March 1, 1987, the Governor shall cause to be
published a list of those chemicals known to the state to cause
cancer or reproductive toxicity within the meaning of this chapter,
and he shall cause such list to be revised and republished in light of
additional knowledge at least once per year thereafter. * * *

(b) A chemical is known to the state to cause cancer or
reproductive toxicity within the meaning of this chapter if in the
opinion of the state's qualified experts it has been clearly shown
through scientifically valid testing according to generally accepted
principles to cause cancer or reproductive toxicity, or if a body
considered to be authoritative by such experts has formally
identified it as causing cancer or reproductive toxicity, or if an
agency of the state or federal government has formally required it to
be labeled or identified as causing cancer or reproductive toxicity.
* * *

The required warning is the statutory language: the contents or discharge is
"known to the state of California to cause cancer."

At the other end of the spectrum is the MSDS, described above, which
contains a wide variety of often technical information. Somewhere in the
middle is detailed consumer information provided, for example, to home
buyers and sellers to inform them of the dangers of and remedies for
asbestos, radon, and lead. You can find EPA's booklets on these hazards on
the web at:

- http://www.epa.gov/iaq/radon/pubs/
- http://www.epa.gov/opptintr/lead/leadpdfe.pdf
- http://www.epa.gov/ARD-R5/

Choose one and read it critically. Do they provide all the information
that home buyers or sellers need? Is it presented in an understandable way?
The books overstate or understate the hazards based on the material you read
in Chapters 8 (TSCA—radon), 2 (Toxicology—lead), or 4 (Judicial Role—
asbestos)? What do they say about remediation? Do they help to understand
the relationship of costs and benefits in remediation?

If you were legislative counsel assigned to write an EPCRA
reauthorization bill, which of these models would you propose? If none, how
would you reform it?

B. Pollution Management and Prevention

Another recent regulatory innovation in addition to using information, is trying to prevent or minimizing pollution rather than regulate it after-the-fact. President George Bush described pollution prevention in 1991:

> Environmental programs that focus on the end of the pipe or the top of the stack, on cleaning up after the damage is done, are no longer adequate. We need new policies, technologies, and processes that prevent or minimize pollution-that stop it from being created in the first place.[46]

This section introduces the concept of pollution management and prevention, describes RCRA's pollution prevention strategies, introduces the Pollution Prevention Act, and describes future initiatives.

1. An Introduction to Pollution Prevention

Traditional command and control media-specific pollution control programs have made great strides in improving environmental quality in the United States. However, in many industries we are reaching the limit of the amount of environmental improvement that can readily be realized from these command and control programs. Pollution prevention has emerged as an alternative to traditional regulatory systems. Simply put, pollution prevention is the idea that it is easier and more efficient to reduce or eliminate wastes through process and production improvements at the source than it is to control them after they are created (at the "end-of-the-pipe"). In the waste management context, pollution prevention is best seen as "a hierarchy of management options in descending order of preference: prevention, environmentally-sound recycling, environment-ally-sound treatment, and environmentally-sound disposal."[47] The key distinction between pollution prevention programs and command and control systems is that the former are largely voluntary, participatory programs whereas the latter impose mandatory obligations on the regulated entity. Pollution prevention is as much a management philosophy as it is a pollution reduction system.[48]

---

[46] President George Bush, *quoted in* 56 Fed. Reg. 7849 (Feb. 26, 1991).

[47] 58 Fed. Reg. 31,114, 31,115 (May 28, 1993).

[48] ". . . if one is to properly understand the true significance of pollution prevention in the remaining years of the twentieth century and the transition to the twenty-first century, one must appreciate pollution prevention's strategic importance in helping American manufacturers and their employees compete effectively with the rest of the world. The overarching resonance and allure of pollution prevention, then, is that it has the potential to appreciably enhance both the environmental protection and economic development potentialities of the United States by focusing our private and public efforts on use, and persistent improvement, of clean technologies to manufacture clean products." Robert F. Blomquist, *Government's Role Regarding Industrial Pollution Prevention in the United States*, 29 GA. L. REV. 349, 352-53 (Winter 1995) (internal citations omitted).

Pollution prevention is gaining acceptance among regulated enterprises for quite a different reason. Many companies have discovered the economic advantages, in terms of increased cost efficiency and competitiveness, that can be gained from preventing pollution at the sources.

CLEANING UP: CHEMICAL FIRMS FIND THAT IT PAYS TO REDUCE POLLUTION AT SOURCE BY ALTERING PROCESSES TO YIELD LESS WASTE, THEY MAKE PRODUCTION MORE EFFICIENT

Scott McMurray, Wall St. J., June 11, 1991, p. A1

The chemical industry's record on the environment has been a sorry one. Despite tougher regulation and pressure from public interest groups, it still accounts for nearly half of all the toxic pollution produced in the U.S.

Yet lately, a new force has been driving the industry to clean up its act: economics.

In a major shift, chemical companies are viewing waste not as an unavoidable result of the manufacturing process, but as a measure of its efficiency. The more unusable byproducts a process creates, the less efficient it is—and the more economic incentive there is for making it better.

That's what Du Pont Co. discovered at its Beaumont, Texas, plant, which makes products for plastics and paint. For years, the facility had been spewing out a staggering 110 million pounds of waste annually. Du Pont engineers argued that reducing the pollution would be too expensive.

But when they took a second look last year, they found just the opposite was true. By adjusting the production process to use less of one raw material, they were able to slash the plant's waste by two-thirds. Yields went up and costs went down. The savings: $1 million a year.

"When I heard about it, I just said: 'That's amazing,'" says Edgar Woolard, Du Pont's chairman and chief executive officer. He says the company now even sees waste reduction as a way to achieve a competitive advantage.

Environmentalists heartily support this view. Slashing toxic waste production "is very similar to energy conservation in the 1970s: There is a potential for massive savings," says David Roe, a lawyer with the Environmental Defense Fund.

* * *

According to the EPA, in 1989 . . . the industry produced nearly half of the 5.7 billion pounds of toxins generated nationwide and tracked by the EPA. Chemical company officials say that, since then, the proportion has stayed roughly the same, though the total amount of toxins released in the country is believed to have declined. Some environmentalists have argued, however, that the EPA significantly understates the total amount of toxins discharged into the environment.

Richard Mahoney, Monsanto Co.'s chairman and chief executive officer, estimates that there is $125 million worth of material that currently isn't recovered from the waste that leaves the company's plants. What's more, other costs associated with waste are rising. They include processing, disposal and cleanup, not to mention lawsuits and government fines when those jobs don't get done right.

Dow Chemical Co., for instance, recently spent $30 million building a waste incinerator and dump to handle toxic materials at its plant site in Midland, Mich. And, earlier this year, Monsanto paid the state of Massachusetts $1 million to settle claims that its Everett, Mass., plant didn't report certain waste-water discharges. It paid another $192,000 to a trust fund that supports the cleanup of Boston harbor. Last year, it forked over $27 million to clean other sites. At year end, it had an accrued liability of $120 million on its balance sheet to cover certain future cleanup costs.

* * *

In the past, chemical companies used to focus merely on complying with federal and state pollution laws for specific chemicals or plants. They didn't pay much attention to the aggregate amount of waste they produced each year, or the future liability it represented. Waste disposal costs were low, and the typical approach to pollution often was the dilution solution: Dilute wastes in massive amounts of air up a smokestack or water out the end of a sewer pipe. More-permanent solutions were unattractive. They almost always involved adding equipment, which meant higher costs, and, thus, intense corporate resistance.

That began to change after the deaths of more than 3,800 people in Bhopal, India, following the release of a cloud of toxic gas at a Union Carbide Corp. subsidiary in 1984. The disaster led to U.S. legislation in 1986 directing the EPA to compile and publicize a survey of toxic emissions, which put pressure on big polluters to do more than just meet minimum government standards.

In the process, companies began to discover economic advantages, as well. Some came from increasing production efficiency, while others came from finding other uses for some of the byproducts. Along the way, companies began to conclude that pollution was a sign of a bad manufacturing system. "When you make a lot of waste you know you don't have control of your operation," says Mr. Woolard, Du Pont's chairman.

* * *

In some cases, the industry is constructing new plants that incorporate the latest waste reduction technology. A new Du Pont herbicide plant, near Dunkirk, France, is expected to produce 90 percent less pollution than an existing facility. Among other things, it will distill and recycle solvents.

In other cases, chemical companies are tying together production processes at different plant sites to cut waste and save on raw material costs. Last fall, a Du Pont plant in Mobile, Ala., that makes herbicides and insecticides began tapping into the waste stream leaving the plant, pulling out solvents and titanium byproduct that it used to incinerate. The solvents get recycled into the plant's own operations, while the titanium is treated and shipped to a Du Pont plant in DeLisle, Miss., where it is used to make paint pigments. By integrating production this way, the Mobile plant cut its annual toxic emissions by about 25 million pounds, nearly 20 percent.

Besides cutting costs, these waste reduction programs help companies earn public good will, as well as meet demands from regulators and environmentalists. * * *

* * *

Even though some of the short-term costs for the new waste reduction programs have been high—more than $200 million a year at the largest chemical companies—Monsanto's Mr. Mahoney says it is money well spent. "Our initiative and commitments to environmental protection will, over the long term, make us more efficient, more cost effective and more competitive," he predicts.

The idea of pollution prevention is not new. In the 1984 Hazardous and Solid Waste Amendments to RCRA, Congress declared the national policy of the United States to be that "wherever feasible, the generation of hazardous waste is to be reduced or eliminated as expeditiously as possible. Waste that is nevertheless generated should be treated, stored, or disposed of so as to minimize the present and future threat to human health and the environment."[49] In 1990, Congress increased its support for this policy by enacting the Pollution Prevention Act (PPA)[50] to further promote pollution prevention as an alternative to traditional regulatory programs:

---

[49] 42 U.S.C. § 6902(b) (1999).
[50] *See* 42 U.S.C. §§ 13101-13109 (1999).

> The Congress hereby declares it to be the national policy of the United States that pollution should be prevented or reduced at the source whenever feasible; pollution that cannot be prevented should be recycled in an environmentally safe manner, whenever feasible; pollution that cannot be prevented or recycled should be treated in an environmentally safe manner whenever feasible; and disposal or other release into the environment should be employed only as a last resort and should be conducted in an environmentally safe manner.[51]

This hierarchy-reduce or reuse, recycle, treat, dispose-is the substantive core of the statute and of Congress' and EPA's waste policy.

As a process, the term "pollution prevention" has no standardized definition. Instead, it is best understood as encompassing all systems used to minimize or eliminate pollution before it is generated.

> The three primary components of pollution prevention are: (1) changes in raw material inputs to industrial systems, especially reducing the use of toxic chemicals and of scarce and nonrenewable natural resources; (2) waste reduction by making industrial systems more efficient in converting raw materials into products and wastes into valuable byproducts; and (3) changes in the design, composition, and packaging of products to create "green," or environmentally preferable, products that minimize harm to public health and the environment over their entire life cycles.[52]

The statutory definition does not, however, include any practice which alters the physical, chemical, or biological characteristics or the volume of a hazardous substance, pollutant, or contaminant through a process or activity which itself is not integral to and necessary for the production of a product or the providing of a service."[53] That is, EPA wants pollution prevention to mean new ways of operating, not simply upgrading and renaming traditional waste disposal techniques.[54]

2. Pollution Prevention Activities Required by RCRA

The pollution prevention requirements in RCRA appear to be an exception to the rule that most pollution prevention activities are voluntary. RCRA § 3002(b) requires that all generators of hazardous waste subject to the manifest requirements of 3002(a) certify that "the generator of the hazardous waste has a program in place to reduce the volume or quantity and toxicity of such waste to the degree determined by the generator to be

---

[51] 42 U.S.C. § 13101(b) (1999).

[52] Joel S. Hirshhorn, *Symposium Address: Pollution Prevention Comes of Age*, 29 GA. L. REV. 325, 326 (1995).

[53] 42 U.S.C. § 13102(5)(B) (1999).

[54] "EPA believes that recycling activities closely resembling conventional waste management activities do not constitute waste minimization . . . [m]ost types of recycling are in fact classified as treatment, and some also meet the definition of disposal." 58 Fed. Reg. at 31,115; *see* 48 Fed. Reg. at 14502-14504 (April 4, 1983).

economically practicable."[55] Section 3005(h), using the same language, requires generators of hazardous wastes whom are also permitted treatment, storage, and disposal facilities (TSDFs) to certify that they have a waste minimization program in place.[56] "These two requirements for certification, taken together, have the effect of insuring that waste minimization programs are put in place for facilities that generate hazardous waste regardless of whether the wastes are managed on-site or off-site."[57] The certification is a prerequisite to any RCRA permit issued.[58]

The following excerpt describes EPA's ideal waste minimization effort under RCRA. It serves as an exploration of what EPA believes waste minimization programs require.

GUIDANCE TO HAZARDOUS WASTE GENERATORS ON THE ELEMENTS OF A WASTE MINIMIZATION PROGRAM

**Environmental Protection Agency
58 Fed. Reg. 31,114 (1993)**

EPA believes that each of the general elements discussed below should be included in a waste minimization program, although the Agency realizes that each element may be implemented in different ways depending on the needs and preferences of individual organizations or facilities.

A. Top management support. Top management should support an organization-wide effort. There are many ways to accomplish this goal. Some of the methods described below may be suitable for some organizations, while not for others. However, some combination of these techniques or similar ones will demonstrate top management support:

- Make waste minimization a part of the organization policy. Put this policy in writing and distribute it to all departments and individuals. Ideally, a waste minimization program should become an integral part of the organization's strategic plan to increase productivity and quality.
- Set explicit goals for reducing the volume and toxicity of waste streams that are achievable within a reasonable time frame.
- Commit to implementing recommendations identified through assessments, evaluations, waste minimization teams, etc.
- Designate a waste minimization coordinator who is responsible for facilitating effective implementation, monitoring and evaluation of the program. It is also useful to set up self-managing waste minimization teams chosen from a broad spectrum of operations: engineering, management, research & development, sales & marketing, accounting, purchasing, maintenance and environmental staff personnel.

---

[55] *See* 42 U.S.C. §§ 6922(b) (1999); *see also* 40 C.F.R. § 262.20(a) (1999).
[56] 42 U.S.C. § 6925(h) (1999).
[57] 58 Fed. Reg. at 31,116.
[58] *See* 40 C.F.R. § 264.73(b)(9) (1999).

- Publicize success stories.
- Recognize individual and collective accomplishments. Reward employees [who] identify cost-effective waste minimization opportunities.
- Train employees on the waste-generating impacts that result from the way they conduct their work procedures.

B. Characterization of waste generation and waste management costs. Maintain a waste accounting system to track the types and amounts of wastes as well as the types and amounts of the hazardous constituents in wastes, including the rates and dates they are generated.

Additionally, a waste generator should determine the true costs associated with waste management and cleanup, including the costs of regulatory oversight compliance, paperwork and reporting requirements, loss of production potential, costs of materials found in the waste stream (perhaps based on the purchase price of those materials), transportation/treatment/storage/disposal costs, employee exposure and health care, liability insurance, and possible future RCRA or Superfund corrective action costs. Both volume and toxicities of generated hazardous waste should be taken into account. Substantial uncertainty in calculating many of these costs, especially future liability, may exist. Therefore, each organization should find the best method to account for the true costs of waste management and cleanup.

C. Periodic waste minimization assessments. Different and equally valid methods exist by which a waste minimization assessment can be performed.

Most successful waste minimization assessments have common elements that identify sources of waste and calculate the true costs of waste generation and management. Each organization should decide the best method to use in performing a waste minimization assessment that addresses these two general elements:

- Identify opportunities at all points in a process where materials can be prevented from becoming a waste (for example, by using less material, recycling materials in the process, finding substitutes that are less toxic and/or more easily biodegraded, or making equipment/process changes). Individual processes or facilities should be reviewed periodically. In some cases, performing complete facility material balances [i.e., measuring how much, in gross, goes in and goes out] can be helpful.
- Analyze waste minimization opportunities based on the true costs associated with waste management and cleanup. Analyzing the cost effectiveness of each option is an important factor to consider, especially when the true costs of treatment, storage and disposal are considered.

D. A cost allocation system. Where practical and implementable, organizations should appropriately allocate the true costs of waste management to the activities responsible for generating the waste in the first place (*e.g.*, identifying specific operations that generate the waste, rather than charging the waste management costs to "overhead"). Cost allocation can properly highlight the parts of the organization where the greatest opportunities for waste minimization exist; without allocating costs, waste minimization opportunities can be obscured by accounting practices that do not clearly identify the activities generating the hazardous wastes.

E. Encourage technology transfer. It is important to seek or exchange technical information on waste minimization from other parts of the organization/facility, from other companies/facilities, trade associations/ affiliates, professional consultants and university or government technical assistance programs.

F. Program implementation and evaluation. Conduct a periodic review of program effectiveness. Use these reviews to provide feedback and identify potential areas for improvement.

The above is guidance; the actual legal requirements imposed by RCRA are rather unobtrusive. Covered facilities must certify only that they have implemented a waste minimization program, and no specific amount of waste reduction is required.[59] Facilities must certify that their waste minimization program will reduce the volume and toxicity of generated wastes "to the degree determined by the generator to be economically practicable."[60] Two aspects of EPA's guidance are worthy of particular note. First, it is extremely general and extremely voluntary. This is certainly in keeping with the general approach to pollution prevention—but if pollution prevention is such a good idea, why doesn't Congress or EPA *require* it? Second, the guidance is directed to areas of business' operations that do not seem very "environmental," like accounting, purchasing, health care, and organization. Why does EPA believe it appropriate to give advice and require planning in these areas? Does the answer to this question help to answer the first one?

3. The Pollution Prevention Act (PPA)

The Pollution Prevention Act of 1990 (PPA) established pollution prevention as the preferred policy for waste reduction in the United States. The PPA directs EPA to consider source reduction in all of its decision-making processes and to coordinate source reduction activities throughout the federal government.[61] To aid industry, the PPA required EPA to collect

---

[59] RCRA § 3002(a)(6) requires that covered facilities submit a biennial report to EPA detailing "the efforts undertaken during the year to reduce the volume and toxicity of waste generated; and . . . the changes in volume and toxicity of waste actually achieved during the year in question in comparison with previous years, to the extent such information is available for years prior to November 8, 1984." 42 U.S.C. § 6922(a)(6)(C)-(D) (1999).

[60] 42 U.S.C. § 6922(b)(1) (1999).

[61] "Source reduction" means:

[A]ny practice which—(i) reduces the amount of any hazardous substance, pollutant, or contaminant entering any waste stream or otherwise released into the environment

and distribute information on voluntary pollution prevention activities, creating a source reduction clearinghouse for pollution prevention information.[62] The Act provided grants to states to help them promote voluntary source reduction activities.[63] The only mandatory provisions in the Act are source reduction and recycling data collection requirements applicable to any company filing a toxic chemical release form under EPCRA § 313.[64]

FROM REACTION TO PROACTION: THE 1990 POLLUTION PREVENTION ACT

Stephen M. Johnson
17 COLUM. J. ENVTL. L. 153, 171-73, 179-203 (1992)

Section 4 [§ 6604] of the Act details EPA's responsibilities, which primarily consist of: (1) publicizing and facilitating voluntary pollution prevention, and (2) collecting and analyzing data to develop and refine a comprehensive pollution prevention program. Under this section, EPA must establish an Office of Pollution Prevention within the Agency. Section 4 also requires the Agency to develop a pollution prevention strategy.

* * *

While the central focus of the Act is on voluntary pollution prevention by industry, the Act does include mandatory source reduction reporting requirements. Building on the structure established by SARA Title III, § 7 [§ 6607] of the Pollution Prevention Act requires each owner or operator of a facility that is required to file a toxic chemical release form under SARA Title III to include, on that form, information regarding the source reduction and recycling activities undertaken at the facility in the previous year for each toxic chemical for which reporting is required. All of that information is then made available to the public to the same extent as information submitted under SARA Title III. Section 7 of the Act also provides that the civil and administrative penalty and citizen suit provisions of SARA Title III are applicable to the reporting requirements of the Pollution Prevention Act to the same extent as they apply to the reporting requirements of SARA Title III.

* * *

The key aspects of the Act are its definitions, focus on voluntary rather than mandatory compliance, lack of a planning requirement, and minimal

---

(including fugitive emissions) prior to recycling, treatment, or disposal; and (ii) reduces the hazards to public health and the environment associated with the release of such substances, pollutants, or contaminants. The term includes equipment or technology modifications, process or procedure modifications, reformulation or redesign of products, substitution of raw materials, and improvements in housekeeping, maintenance, training, or inventory control.
42 U.S.C. § 13102(5)(A) (1999).

[62] *See* 42 U.S.C. § 13105 (1999).

[63] *See* 42 U.S.C. § 13104 (1999).

[64] *See* 42 U.S.C. § 13106 (1999); EPCRA § 313 is found at 42 U.S.C. § 11023 (1999).

reporting requirements. The Act also has many shortcomings, including its failure to: (1) provide adequate funding, (2) provide a specific enforcement role for citizens and employees, (3) establish specific goals, and (4) provide for regulatory incentives whereby EPA could reduce pollution control requirements in exchange for pollution prevention by industry.

* * *

Rather than referring to "waste minimization," the Pollution Prevention Act addresses "source reduction." By specifying that recycling, treatment, and disposal are not source reduction practices and by focusing on pollutants and contaminants in general rather than merely on hazardous waste, the definition of "source reduction" is a clear break with the pollution control focus of the past and a shift toward true pollution prevention.

Some commentators have suggested that legislation mandating both pollution control and pollution prevention requirements sends a mixed signal to industry about the importance of pollution prevention. While this concern is valid, pollution prevention will not eliminate the need for pollution control. No matter how successful pollution prevention measures are, they will never completely eradicate pollution.[65] Therefore, pollution control may be addressed in pollution prevention legislation if the legislation clarifies that pollution control is a last resort. The pollution prevention hierarchy in the Pollution Prevention Act is a good example of the proper way to correlate pollution control with pollution prevention in legislation. This approach is very different from an approach that allows companies to achieve reductions in pollution generation either through pollution control or pollution prevention, in which case the companies can ignore pollution prevention and focus solely on pollution control.

* * *

Central to the Pollution Prevention Act is the principle that voluntary pollution prevention efforts by industry will be adequate to achieve the ambitious reductions in pollution envisioned by the drafters of the Act. Reports from EPA and OTA[66] significantly shaped the Act by indicating that voluntary efforts would be more effective in achieving pollution prevention than mandatory, regulatory efforts. The general conclusion of the EPA and OTA reports, and the basic premise of the Pollution Prevention Act, is that the primary obstacle to pollution prevention is ignorance among industry managers about the benefits of pollution prevention. EPA and OTA argue that increased dissemination of information about pollution prevention opportunities will result in widespread voluntary pollution prevention. To the extent that pollution prevention makes economic sense for companies and firms [sic] are ignorant of the pollution prevention opportunities in existence,

---

[65] Does this contradict the claim made earlier in the chapter that pollution prevention will *complete* the job begun by regulation?—EDS.

[66] *See* U.S. ENVIRONMENTAL PROTECTION AGENCY, REPORT TO CONGRESS: MINIMIZATION OF HAZARDOUS WASTE, EXECUTIVE SUMMARY AND FACT SHEET (Oct. 1986); U.S. CONGRESS, OFFICE OF TECHNOLOGY ASSESSMENT, SERIOUS REDUCTION OF HAZARDOUS WASTE (1986).

the voluntary approach of the Pollution Prevention Act may be a sufficient impetus for successful pollution prevention.

Proponents of the voluntary approach to pollution prevention suggest additional reasons why their approach is preferable to mandatory efforts. First, there are presently no standard methods for measuring or quantifying pollution prevention. Without these methods, it is impossible to mandate specific quantitative reductions in the amount of pollution generated by individual polluters. Second, those who support voluntary pollution prevention argue that since EPA does not generally regulate industrial production processes, it lacks the expertise to prescribe mandatory pollution prevention techniques or measures for those processes. Finally, supporters of the voluntary approach argue that mandatory pollution prevention requirements will stifle innovation and could reduce international competitiveness for some American industries and products. This argument is untenable, though, assuming the validity of Congress' and EPA's assertions that pollution prevention measures and technologies generally increase the efficiency of processes and the economic efficiency of companies that employ them.

For these and perhaps other reasons, the Pollution Prevention Act does not include mandatory pollution prevention requirements. Compared with voluntary requirements, mandatory pollution prevention requirements provide a greater impetus for companies to find and implement pollution prevention practices.

Several different types of mandatory pollution prevention requirements could be implemented on the federal level. One mandatory measure that has been considered by EPA and OTA is the imposition of performance standards or operating procedures for industrial processes. Under this approach, the standards would be based on the best technology or pollution prevention practices available for the process. Closely related to the mandatory performance standards approach is a proposal that would require industrial processes to achieve specific throughput levels established by EPA. Both of these approaches have been criticized on the ground that EPA lacks the resources or expertise to set such standards. The throughput approach has been further criticized on the ground that the lack of standard measuring methods renders it unenforceable. A final type of mandatory pollution prevention measure that has been explored by EPA and OTA is a prohibition or restriction on the use of certain substances or on the generation of certain wastes.

A combination of mandatory and voluntary pollution prevention measures might yield greater pollution prevention results than a program based solely on voluntary efforts. For instance, instead of requiring EPA to establish mandatory pollution prevention performance standards for every industrial process by a certain date, Congress could authorize the Agency to establish mandatory standards for processes when it has sufficient information to establish such standards. To the extent that EPA lacked the expertise or resources to set standards, it would not be required to act.

However, if a segment of industry were to develop technological modifications or management practices that significantly and effectively reduced pollution generation in a specific process, EPA could require other industries to implement those proven technologies or practices.

*   *   *

Although the Pollution Prevention Act focuses on voluntary pollution prevention efforts, the Act does not foreclose future legislative expansion of EPA's authority to mandate pollution prevention measures. In fact, many of the requirements in the Act provide a strong foundation upon which mandatory requirements could be layered. For instance, improved data collection and the development of a uniform system of measuring pollution prevention could allow EPA to mandate measurable reductions in the amount of pollution generated by industry. Similarly, these improvements in data collection, together with expanded reporting of pollution prevention practices, and the development of a national source reduction clearinghouse, could refine EPA's expertise in setting mandatory performance standards for industrial processes and establishing bans. Implementation of the Pollution Prevention Act could therefore pave the way towards future legislative expansion of EPA's authority to mandate pollution prevention.

*   *   *

One of the fundamental deficiencies of the Pollution Prevention Act is its failure to address pollution prevention planning. Unlike the majority of state pollution prevention laws, the federal Act does not require preparation or implementation of pollution prevention plans.

Mandatory pollution prevention planning is an important component of a comprehensive pollution prevention program for several reasons. First and foremost, planning ensures that persons actually explore and consider opportunities to prevent pollution. By imposing specific procedural requirements for the preparation of plans, mandatory planning provisions force persons to take a closer look at pollution prevention opportunities than if they were merely required to certify that they had explored pollution prevention opportunities. Mandatory pollution prevention planning also stimulates interest in pollution prevention opportunities.

*   *   *

Mandatory reporting requirements stimulate pollution prevention in several ways. By detailing the practices and technologies that are being used to prevent pollution, reporting provides EPA with a broad base of information about available pollution prevention opportunities that the Agency can disseminate to other interested parties. Mandatory reporting also ensures that persons remain accountable for implementing pollution prevention practices and technologies and achieving actual reductions in pollution generation. To maximize the impact that mandatory pollution prevention reporting has on gathering information and fostering accountability, reporting provisions should: (1) require the submission of as much information as needed and (2) ensure that it is as accurate and precise as possible.

While the Pollution Prevention Act includes provisions that require persons to report source reduction and recycling activities to EPA, several amendments are necessary to maximize the impact of those reporting requirements. First, reports should be required from a broader spectrum of polluters than persons required to file toxic release information forms under SARA Title III.

* * *

Pollution prevention reports should also address pollution prevention practices on a process-specific rather than on a facility-wide basis. Since facilities often use several different processes, and production levels for particular processes vary significantly over time, facility-wide reporting does not allow EPA or the public to determine whether reductions reported for a facility are due to specific pollution prevention programs that the facility has implemented, or are merely due to cuts in production.

* * *

Finally, mandatory reporting provisions should require persons to report the specific practices and technologies they utilize to achieve reductions in pollution generation. The Pollution Prevention Act merely requires reporting of such practices by category. The more general the pollution prevention information submitted to EPA, the less useful it is.

None of the amendments to the reporting requirements suggested above are likely to draw praise from the regulated community.

* * *

Another aspect of pollution prevention that is not adequately addressed in the Pollution Prevention Act is the role of citizens and employees in implementation and enforcement. Public accountability can be a useful tool to force industry to implement pollution prevention measures. Additionally, since citizens and employees are intimately affected by pollution, they have an interest in forcing industry to reduce potential hazards and risks to their health and the environment by preventing the generation of pollution. Citizens and employees cannot be effectively involved in the implementation and enforcement of federal pollution prevention legislation unless two prerequisites are satisfied. First, citizens and employees must be provided with coherent, meaningful information about the efforts undertaken by industries to meet pollution prevention requirements. The Pollution Prevention Act includes several provisions aimed at improving the quality and clarity of data on pollution prevention and improving the dissemination of that data. Thus, the Act appears to satisfy the first requirement.

Second, legislation must specifically empower citizens and employees to act upon the information that they receive about pollution prevention efforts by industry. Citizens and employees should be authorized to bring citizen suits to ensure that industries and businesses comply with the expanded pollution prevention requirements. Pollution prevention legislation in some states empowers local citizen groups to play a role in preparing pollution prevention plans for industries. The Pollution Prevention Act, on the other hand, does not empower citizens and employees to play a significant role in fostering pollution prevention.

Due to their familiarity with processes and technologies used by industrial facilities, employees are uniquely situated to assist employers in complying with pollution prevention requirements and identifying pollution prevention opportunities.

* * *

Another concept that is gaining favor with EPA and Congress, but was not included in the Pollution Prevention Act, is the concept of "regulatory incentives." To the extent that EPA is authorized to do so under existing statutes, the Agency has begun to modify its administrative practices to encourage pollution prevention. Future legislation could expand EPA's authority to use the administrative process to encourage pollution prevention.

Both EPA and OTA have explored the possibility of authorizing the Agency to waive or modify, by rule or through individual permits, pollution control requirements of the environmental protection statutes in exchange for the implementation of pollution prevention practices or technologies.

NOTES

1. Should pollution prevention remain voluntary or should Congress expand EPA's authority to mandate pollution prevention and source reduction?

2. Johnson urges a combination of reporting and planning that is strongly reminiscent of the EPCRA strategy. Is this just coincidence, or are pollution planning and right-to-know fundamentally similar?

3. Citizen involvement is another parallel with EPCRA. Does citizen involvement go far enough under the Pollution Prevention Act? Should Congress require mandatory pollution prevention with a citizen suit provision? Are there drawbacks to such an arrangement?

4. EPA responded to the mandates of the PPA by developing a pollution prevention strategy which was released in 1991.[67] President Clinton issued Executive Order 12856 on "Federal Compliance With Right-to-Know Laws and Pollution Prevention Requirements,"[68] requiring federal agencies to comply with § 313 of EPCRA (the Toxic Release Inventory or TRI) and § 6607 (data collection) of the PPA. Federal agencies reported releases and transfers of hazardous chemicals for the first time in 1994. The Order also required every federal agency to develop a written pollution prevention strategy to effect a 50 percent reduction in the total amount of toxic chemicals released by the agency by 1999, which are to be achieved, to the maximum extent possible, through source reduction. The Order is significant not only because it will reduce the amount of hazardous wastes generated by

---

[67] *See* 56 Fed. Reg. 7849 (Feb. 26, 1991). For a comprehensive overview of pollution prevention in the federal government, *see* EPA, POLLUTION PREVENTION 1997: A NATIONAL PROGRESS REPORT, No. 742-R-97-00 (June 1997).

[68] Exec. Order No. 12,856, 58 Fed. Reg. 41,981 (1993).

the federal government but because it challenges the federal government to lead by example.

EPA's own efforts to implement pollution prevention are constrained by the command and control approach of its authorizing statutes. EPA has tried to identify pollution prevention approaches that could be used to implement many of the air, water, and solid waste regulations it is developing. The Office of Enforcement and Compliance Assurance (OECA) has created Compliance Assistance Centers where regulated entities may obtain information on pollution prevention and regulatory compliance. OECA has also attempted to integrate pollution prevention into enforcement settlements through Supplemental Environmental Projects in lieu of administrative penalties. In a settlement, a corporation in some cases may substitute pollution prevention activities that go beyond statutory requirements instead of paying fines. These are called Supplemental Environmental Projects. Nevertheless, the heart of pollution prevention activities in the EPA are the agency's voluntary programs. Participants set voluntary goals for pollution reduction which they may meet in the manner of their choice. These programs are intended to reach more cost-effective solutions than traditional regulatory approaches.

Two examples are the "33/50 Program" and the "Waste Minimization National Plan." The 33/50 Program's goal was to reduce the release and transfer of 17 high priority toxic chemicals by 33 percent by 1992 and by 50 percent by 1995, using 1988 TRI data as a baseline.[69] Over 1,300 companies participated in the program. The program met the interim goal and met the final goal a year early. "Releases and transfers of the 17 target chemicals declined at 4 times the rate reported for all other TRI chemicals between 1991 and 1992 (10.4% vs. 2.6%),[70] and accounted for more than half of the total reduction in releases and transfers of all TRI chemicals during that period."[71] These results indicate that voluntary pollution prevention activities *can* play a sizable component in the nation's overall pollution reduction efforts.

The Waste Minimization National Plan (WMNP) is the follow-up to the 33/50 Program.[72] WMNP is a voluntary long-term effort to reduce the generation of hazardous chemicals in wastes regulated by RCRA. Its

---

[69] The chemicals are: benzene, cadmium and compounds, carbon tetrachloride, chloroform, chromium and compounds, cyanides, dichloromethane (also referred to as methylene chloride), lead and compounds, mercury and compounds, methyl ethyl ketone, methyl isobutyl ketone, nickel and compounds, tetrachloroethylene, toluene, 1,1,1-trichloroethane, trichloroethane, trichloroethylene and xylenes. EPA, OFFICE OF POLLUTION PREVENTION AND TOXICS, EPA's 33/50 PROGRAM FIFTH PROGRESS UPDATE, No. 745-R-94-002 (May 1994).

[70] Of course, this does not speak well for the effectiveness of reporting requirements alone, does it?—EDS.

[71] *Fifth Progress Update* at 3.

[72] EPA, OFFICE OF SOLID WASTE AND EMERGENCY RESPONSE, No. 530-F-95-026, WASTE MINIMIZATION NATIONAL PLAN, (Feb. 1996).

emphasis is on source reduction as an alternative to treatment and disposal. The goal of the WMNP is to reduce the generation of the most persistent, bioaccumulative, and toxic (PBT) chemicals in hazardous wastes by 25% by the year 2000 and 50% by 2005. This program is still in its infancy, however. Information can be obtained at http://www.epa.gov/epaoswer/hazwaste/minimize/.

4. The Future of Pollution Prevention

The best indicators of pollution prevention's effectiveness at reducing the amount of toxics released into the environment or transferred to TSDFs are the TRI reporting data. The data for 1995 showed that the amount of production-related wastes generated had increased by 6.8 percent since 1991 to over 35 billion pounds,[73] a trend that has generally continued.[74] The reporting requirements of the PPA have revealed that only 29 percent of all TRI eligible facilities have reported to have undertaken at least one source reduction activity, and of those, the most common activity was "good operating practices." The next most common activities were process modifications and spill/leak prevention.[75] Clearly, pollution prevention has a long way to go before it reaches its theoretical potential.

THE UNFINISHED BUSINESS OF POLLUTION PREVENTION

Kenneth Geiser
29 GA. L. REV. 473, 477-79, 488-91 (1995)

Given that less than a decade has elapsed since the Office of Technology Assessment report first fully clarified pollution prevention as a separate policy approach, there has been substantial progress in the acceptance and implementation of pollution prevention. Yet, this progress has been uneven. While many governments and companies apparently have established pollution prevention programs that, in some cases, have prevented the release of certain pollutants, there has been a surprising lack of attention to certain fundamental aspects that might facilitate more successful pollution prevention programs. These missing elements include: (1) developing effective systems for measuring progress; (2) establishing priorities among pollutants; (3) accounting for the effects of substitutions in implementing pollution prevention; (4) considering products as sources of pollution; and (5) integrating pollution prevention into environmental regulatory regimes.

Measuring Progress

From the first years of the state programs, there appeared a continuous stream of anecdotal stories and case studies of businesses implementing pollution prevention programs and achieving remarkable results in terms of

---

[73] *See supra* note 69, at 48.
[74] EPA, POLLUTION PREVENTION 1997: A NATIONAL PROGRESS REPORT 48-49 (1997).
[75] *See id.*

both environmental and economic improvements. Yet, there has been little systematic effort to present quantitative assessments of the effectiveness of the state and industry programs aimed at reducing pollution.

* * *

At first glance it may appear fairly easy to develop quantitative measures for evaluating the effectiveness of pollution prevention programs. One would simply compare quantities of pollutants released today against quantities released at some base year and correlate that figure against some quantitative measure of pollution prevention program inputs. However, several problems make such accounting difficult.

First, there are problems with the data. Most states do not require businesses to report systematically and comprehensively on all their pollutant discharges. Since 1987 the federal government has required annual reports of all toxic chemical releases from nearly 60,000 facilities covered under the TRI. Because data collected during the first three years of the inventory did not classify chemicals transferred off site for recycling as a release, it was impossible to determine if reductions in releases were a result of source reduction or recycling. Since 1991, companies have been required to report source reduction and recycling activities separately on the annual TRI reporting form. Because the form does not require a reporting on total waste generated prior to source reduction and recycling activities, it is impossible to verify the effects of true source reduction activities.

Second, there is the problem of establishing effective performance indices. Some states focus on reducing hazardous wastes alone, while others focus on reducing all non-product releases from a facility including releases to the air, water, and land.

Third, it is difficult to assess the correlation, if any, between actual decreases in pollution and government pollution prevention programs. Even in states with more sophisticated programs, the reported sharp reductions in the use and release of ozone depleting chemicals (*e.g.*, chlorofluorocarbons, halons, carbon tetrachloride, and 1,1,1-trichloroethane) probably are due to special targeting under the Clean Air Act and the international Montreal Protocol.[76]

Further, there are confounding factors that determine changes in pollution such as the economy itself. Lower production levels are likely to lead to lower levels of pollution, and plant closings certainly are an undesirable contributor to pollution reduction. To be effective, pollution data need to be normalized to some economic measure such as an employment indicator, a sales figure, or an "activity index" as prescribed under the TRI system.

* * *

Integrating Regulations

The commitment to pollution control that marked the conventional government approach to environmental protection for the past twenty years

---

[76] Does this suggest a continuing role for traditional regulation?—EDS.

has left a legacy of federal and state regulations that focus on end-of-pipe discharge and emission permits. While these regulations have done much to curtail large-volume releases of serious contaminants and raised the cost of waste treatment to a point where preventing pollution can be cost effective, they do not readily promote pollution prevention. Indeed, some of these regulations actually impede the introduction of pollution prevention technologies.

For instance, operators of a facility with a relatively simple wastewater discharge permit under the Clean Water Act (CWA) may seek to reduce pollution by installing a closed loop water treatment and reuse system that would reduce, if not eliminate, their wastewater discharge. If they do choose to install such a system, they will be considered a "wastewater treatment facility" under the Resource Conservation and Recovery Act (RCRA), and as such they will be required to apply for a much more complex "Part B" permit.

* * *

Most state compliance and enforcement divisions are organized by medium-air, water, and waste-such that efforts to reduce emissions in one medium may raise concerns of regulators charged with enforcing regulations in other media. In fact, the organization of state agencies into single medium programs with single medium enforcement agents often is mirrored in large corporations by the same medium-specific organizational structure in the environmental divisions. Thus, efforts to develop cross-media or multimedia pollution prevention programs are hindered by an organizational structure that separates professionals into narrow compliance oriented divisions.

Many states have initiated programs designed to integrate pollution prevention into conventional environmental regulations and to better integrate the single medium programs into more coordinated and unified approaches to permitting and compliance assurance.

But state level regulatory integration will not be enough to overcome all the legal barriers to pollution prevention. Some federal regulations, particularly those promulgated under the CWA and RCRA, will need to be modified to encourage pollution prevention, and federal media programs will need to be redesigned to encourage cross-media integration. Recently, the EPA has launched the Common Sense Initiative to focus multi-stakeholder work groups on six industrial sectors to identify opportunities to change inconsistent environmental regulations into comprehensive strategies for environmental protection. While the initial plans for this initiative look promising, the task is enormous.

The Way Forward In Preventing Pollution

Pollution prevention has come a long way in a short time. Like any professional reform movement, it has grown more opportunistically than through a centrally planned strategy. However, the emerging maturity of the various programs and initiatives suggests that there is need for reassessment and identification of missing elements. If pollution prevention is to become fully institutionalized as mainstream policy, public and private policy makers will need to address several issues that until now have emerged more slowly.

* * *

A more comprehensive approach to environmental protection will need to embed the material and technology focus of pollution prevention into the central concerns of industrial management such as efficiency, productivity, and financial return. Thus, the transition from pollution control to pollution prevention could be seen as a historical step in a policy evolution that leads from traditional environmental risk management to a more comprehensive examination of materials use, technology design, product development, and production efficiencies.

Although information and pollution prevention are important alternatives control strategies, the future of toxic substance and hazardous waste law may be in systemic reforms. The following excerpt suggests some such strategies.

SUSTAINABLE ENVIRONMENTAL LAW

Celia Campbell-Mohn *et al.*
pp. 1367-1370 (1993)

The first premise of [comprehensive environmental law reform] is that environmental law must unite natural resource and pollution abatement law. Originally environmental law and natural resource management were a subset of property law. When nuisance suits and zoning ordinances could not protect the environment, the Earth Day generation passed dozens of federal statutes-statutes that divide legal approaches to natural resource management and pollution control. Environmental law became a subset of administrative law, apart from natural resources law and independent of the tort and contract laws of everyday life. [Law reform efforts should reunite] natural resource and pollution management and integrate[] other fields of law with environmental law.

The history of environmental law . . . also shows how environmental laws emerge primarily in response to specific crises, such as an oil spill, industrial accident, or expanding dust bowl. Responding to crises led to a piecemeal approach. Congress, the executive, the judiciary, and the states govern some activities more than others and some parts of one activity more than other parts, without consideration of the whole. This has resulted in a crazy quilt of overlapping regulations where a regulated industry may be affected by a dozen environmental laws with competing goals and inconsistent commands.

While decisionmakers respond to specific crises, ecologists research the complex interrelations within natural systems. The incomplete and often inconsistent pattern of environmental law contrasts with the interconnected ecological patterns of the real world. The divergence between the piecemeal legal approach and the interconnectedness of natural systems impedes effective environmental law. The law regulates individual pieces of a complex system, while the whole deteriorates.

The revision of environmental law should follow the resource to recovery cycle * * *. This cycle consists of three parts: resource extraction, product manufacture, and product and waste disposal.

In the resource extraction phase, existing environmental law focuses on just parts of the natural system-wetlands but not wildlands, endangered species but not biological diversity. The resource to recovery approach focuses on all impacts of human activities on the environment and encourages conservation of resources through their efficient use.

Our current system of environmental law now impacts the middle phase of the cycle-product manufacturing-most heavily. In the manufacturing phase, the law focuses on select pollutants emitted into the environment, but not on all pollutants or on siting the facility emitting the pollutants. [Environmental law reform examine] other phases of the cycle * * * to discover where environmental law can produce better environmental and social results. [Environmental laws should also be] clustered by industry so that gaps and overlaps may be examined and reformed.

In the disposal phase, environmental law now seeks to control pollution but not seriously to prevent it. The law seeks to clean up waste but not seriously to minimize it. The resource to recovery approach would minimize pollution before the resources are extracted from the ecosystem.

No laws currently address all three phases together. In contrast, the resource to recovery approach relies on foresight and planning through all phases of the cycle.

* * * As E. Donald Elliott explains * * *:

> In the [next] stage [if environmental law], which is only now beginning to emerge as a glimmer on the horizon, the goal shifts from efficient amelioration of environmental "problems" to a broader focus on the management of complex systems on a sustainable, global basis . . . . [T]he vision [is] of environmental protection programs as an effective system for managing human activity on a sustainable basis.
> * * *

* * * Organizing environmental law around human activities from extracting to discarding resources can lessen piecemealism. By considering activities from resource to recovery, lawmakers can begin to plan resource use, environmental impacts, and disposal strategies. In addition, organizing environmental law by activity dovetails environmental law with other areas of law, making it more effective.

* * *

The revision of law should proceed natural resource by natural resource, industry sector by industry sector, based on the total cycle of resource to recovery, being careful to avoid capture by the regulated activity. By tailoring law more closely to the patterns of human behavior, administration and enforcement will be more efficient, thus strengthening respect for and effectiveness of the law.

To move from the present piecemeal system to an effective and efficient system of environmental laws first requires analysis of the objectives of environmental law. These objectives include: protection of human health, efficiency, national security, preservation for aesthetics and recreation, sustainability, intergenerational equity, community stability, biocentrism, and pursuit of scientific knowledge and technology. As our understanding of the natural and social world evolves, the objectives of environmental law are changing from perpetuating the health and economic efficiency of the present generation to incorporating sustainability across generations. A comparison of the legal objectives of the past, with an understanding of how ecosystems function and notions of humans' role in the universe, will help to incorporate objectives such as sustainability into the law. Although some resource extraction statutes mention sustainable yields, environmental law as a body of law does not reflect the sustainability objective.

Reforming environmental law requires making the law reflect and choose among objectives. The objectives cannot be realized until Congress sets priorities among them. Such prioritization of objectives is necessary to force decisionmakers to implement concrete results.

Second, effective environmental law requires using all legal tools optimally. Currently, environmental laws rely heavily on command and control regulation backed up by civil penalties and criminal sanctions. Incentives through federal grants and subsidies have fueled many recent environmental programs. The mechanisms of tort, contract, and property are underutilized. New tools, including information and incentives, need to be developed and implemented. Because no single tool is the panacea for the environment, tools must be used to their maximum advantage to achieve an optimal mix of legal methods. We have only just begun to explore the reaches of legal tools as they apply to environmental law.

Once an effective strategy for dealing with each activity is developed, the cumulative and synergistic effects of various groups of activities must be analyzed and regulated. In other words, once each industrial sector has been analyzed, then the analysis must be applied to aggregate sectors of the economy.

Finally, a new system of sustainable environmental law must be implemented on an international scale. The future of a sustainable system of environmental law lies in international efforts such as the United Nations Conference on the Environment and Development.

* * *

—

PROBLEM

What should be the path forward on pollution prevention? Which of the regulatory tools discussed in Chapter 1 —standard-setting; research and development; social funds; civil penalties; liability; planning; economic incentives; criminal sanctions; information gathering/dissemination; property rights; and/or contracts and negotiation—are most likely to be effective in encouraging or requiring pollution prevention activities? How would they work in this setting?

At the beginning of this chapter we argued that the various regulatory schemes for toxics include three common elements: (1) reliance on government-set standards; (2) standards that seek to minimize, rather than eliminate, toxic threats; and (3) standards that rely primarily on government imposition and firm compliance, rather than individual citizen accommodation. How do the right-to-know and pollution prevention strategies differ from these traditional elements? Are they worthwhile alternatives, or do they abandon important goals or regulatory techniques embodied in existing strategies? Are there particular areas of toxic regulation in which these alternative strategies may be particularly useful?

Are there other systemic reforms that we should look to for the future of toxic substance and hazardous waste law? What are the pros and cons of those mentioned here? What are other approaches?

INDEX

References are to pages

_____

1-56662-758-3

90000

9 781566 627580